TEACHER'S WRAPAROUND EDITION

ART
IN FOCUS
FOURTH EDITION

AESTHETICS   CRITICISM   HISTORY   STUDIO

Gene A. Mittler, Ph.D.
Professor Emeritus
Texas Tech University

 **Glencoe**
McGraw-Hill

New York, New York   Columbus, Ohio   Woodland Hills, California   Peoria, Illinois

About the Author

Gene Mittler

Gene Mittler is the author of *Art in Focus*, Glencoe's senior high school art history textbook which uses a chronological approach to art. He is also one of the authors of Glencoe's middle school/junior high art series, *Introducing Art, Exploring Art,* and *Understanding Art,* and *Creating and Understanding Drawings* for high school. He has taught at both the elementary and secondary levels and at Indiana University. He received an M.F.A. in sculpture from Bowling Green State University and a Ph.D. in art education from Ohio State University. He has authored grants and published numerous articles in professional journals and has lectured in the United States and abroad. Dr. Mittler is currently Professor Emeritus at Texas Tech University.

About Artsource®

 The materials provided in the *Performing Arts Handbook* are excerpted from *Artsource®: The Music Center Study Guide to the Performing Arts*, a project of the Music Center Education Division. The Music Center of Los Angeles County, the largest performing arts center in the western United States, established the Music Center Education Division in 1979 to provide opportunities for lifelong learning in the arts, and especially to bring the performing and visual arts into the classroom. The Education Division believes the arts enhance the quality of life for all people, but are crucial to the development of every child.

About the Cover

The image of the Delphian Sibyl on the cover is a detail from Michelangelo's paintings on the ceiling of the Sistine Chapel in the Vatican. Completed in 1512, this immense ceiling was divided into nine main sections. In each section, Michelangelo painted a scene from the biblical story of humanity. Along the edge of the ceiling, prophets and their female counterparts, the sibyls, are depicted. Sibyls were prophetesses in ancient Greek and Roman mythology. The Delphian Sibyl is so named because she resided in the town of Delphi.

Cover Art: Michelangelo Buonarroti. Delphian Sibyl (detail from the ceiling of the Sistine Chapel). 1508–12. Fresco (post-restoration). Vatican, Sistine Chapel, Vatican City, Rome, Italy. Scala/Art Resource, New York.

Glencoe/McGraw-Hill

A Division of The McGraw-Hill Companies

Printed in the United States of America.

Send all inquiries to:
Glencoe/McGraw-Hill
21600 Oxnard Street, Suite 500
Woodland Hills, California 91367

ISBN 0-02-662408-7 (Student Edition)
ISBN 0-02-662409-5 (Teacher's Wraparound Edition)

3 4 5 6 7 8 9   004/043   06 05 04 03 02 01

New Directions in the Visual and Performing Arts

*W*elcome to *Art in Focus*—an exciting, comprehensive art history program written and designed for beginning and advanced level art history classes. You know that a quality, comprehensive art program enriches students' lives and allows for discovery and creative problem solving. It provides students with a broader perception of their environment and a greater understanding of historical and cultural perspectives. In the process, a quality art program cultivates learners who are able to make positive contributions to society.

Art in Focus Addresses the New Directions

Art in Focus answers the new directions in art education by providing this comprehensive program designed specifically for the high school student. This chronologically organized program has been updated and expanded to include more accessible student activities, new visual learning features, curriculum and performing arts connections, technology projects, and over 600 artworks. The artworks selected represent a wide range of cultures, artistic styles, and art media.

Providing a Comprehensive Art Program

Art in Focus is based on several assumptions, which include:
■ In order for students to comprehend art concepts, it is important to provide meaningful, hands-on learning experiences that allow for personal growth and creative expression.
■ A comprehensive art program integrates the areas of aesthetics, art criticism, art history, and studio production.
■ A quality art education program provides students with experiences that are sequentially planned, building on previous concepts, and provides learning opportunities that incorporate a variety of media, artistic styles, and historical periods.
■ An up-to-date art program includes information and practice with the computer and other new technologies.

Integrating the Four Components

■ **Artistic Perception** At the very center of arts instruction is the process of being able to talk about works of art and learning the

basic skills and knowledge necessary to communicate in each art form. By learning the elements and principles of art, working with various media, and evaluating master artists' works, students develop an appreciation for the presence of art both within the classroom and in their everyday experiences.

■ **Creative Expression** Studio projects and activities give students the opportunity to create works of art and use various media and techniques, including computers.

■ **Historical and Cultural Context** Throughout the program, works of art from various periods, styles, and cultural groups, develop a broad base for students to celebrate cultural diversity and understand various global views.

■ **Aesthetic Valuing** As students explore, theorize, and apply the principles of aesthetics and art criticism to their own artworks and the artworks of others, they formulate a lifelong appreciation and satisfying experience in the arts.

Addressing the National Standards for Arts Education

The National Standards for Arts Education provide guidelines that set benchmark standards for grade-appropriate competency in the performing and visual arts. *Art in Focus* is correlated to the National Standards (see Scope and Sequence on page TM 10), and can help teachers design their lessons around these standards.

Linking the Performing Arts

Glencoe's *Art in Focus* program is designed to present the exploration of visual art as it correlates to all the performing arts. Students experience how the foundation of all areas of art are built upon corresponding concepts.

New Developments in Technology

The new *Art in Focus* program provides a range of technology options that encourage exploration of new possibilities both in art education and production.

Engaging the Students

With *Art in Focus*, your students will travel through a chronological time line, experiencing over 600 works of art. Artworks for this edition have been carefully selected from museums and private collections throughout the world. The artists who have been selected represent a variety of historical and cultural contexts, including regional coverage of the Americas, Africa, India, China, and Japan. Teaching captions and credit lines reinforce chapter content and can be used as an effective learning tool in the classroom.

CHAPTER OPENING Each chapter opens with a full-color, motivational reproduction of a work of art related to the chapter's contents. A brief introduction helps students focus on the chapter.

FOCUS ON THE ARTS The visual and performing arts are mutually reinforcing. *Art in Focus* is designed to underscore that unity by correlating the visual arts to music, dance, theatre, and literature in the Focus on the Arts feature.

ART CONNECTIONS A cross-curriculum feature links artworks with other curriculum areas, including Language Arts, Social Studies, and Mathematics.

YOUR PORTFOLIO With the increasing attention given to art portfolios as both a presentation and an assessment tool, each chapter begins with a suggestion of how students can use or adapt the activities within the chapter for their art portfolios. Students are encouraged to keep sketchbooks and to develop a portfolio featuring their selected works of art.

TIME & PLACE Each chronological art history chapter showcases a visually appealing assortment of artifacts from the time period being studied. This provides students with a window into the historical and social context of artists and their works.

Meeting the Needs of All Students

Art in Focus is a visually oriented program incorporating reproductions of master's works and student artworks. Using a chronological approach, *Art in Focus* effectively integrates and interrelates aesthetics, art criticism, art history, and studio production throughout the program.

Believing that art is for all students, *Art in Focus* includes activities and teaching strategies that help teachers adapt the art classroom to the specific needs of students. This inclusive approach reinforces the universal value of art education. Visual-verbal learning features, performing arts links, and curriculum connections give students access to key art concepts in a context that students can understand.

STUDIO LESSONS Within each chapter, Studio Lessons are provided that build on previous narrative lessons. Each one gives students the opportunity to use various media and techniques. The lessons are illustrated with exemplary student artworks.

ASSESSMENT STRATEGIES Frequent self-examination of completed artworks provides ongoing evaluation of each student's progress, fostering a sense of accomplishment and a commitment to high standards of art production, and preparing them for the transition to excellence in the workplace.

THE ARTSOURCE®: PERFORMING ARTS HANDBOOK is an exciting new addition to *Art in Focus*. It features 17 artists or groups from the three fields of performing arts—dance, music, and theatre, correlated to the chapters in the book.

THE CAREERS IN ART HANDBOOK showcases 14 diverse opportunities available to students interested in pursuing an art career. Description of employment situations and educational requirements are presented in an interview format.

Support for the Art Teacher

The Teacher's Wraparound Edition provides complete lesson plans, teaching suggestions, supplemental information, cross-references, and more—all conveniently "wrapped" around every page of the reduced student text. You will discover a variety of teaching strategies to motivate students; to introduce, teach, and reinforce concepts; and alternative teaching strategies for adapting the program to your own teaching style and to the learning styles of your students.

Chapter Planning Guides

For your convenience, a two-page planning guide precedes each chapter. This planning guide outlines Teacher's Classroom Resources, Text Features, and additional Chapter Resources that go with the chapter and lessons. Here you will also find suggestions for ideas Beyond the Classroom and teaching strategies for highlighting the main parts of a lesson or chapter

Organized with the Teacher in Mind

LESSON PLANS The teaching material follows a consistent, easy-to-use pattern. The complete lesson cycle—*Focus, Teach, Assess,* and *Close*—make it easy for you to plan a lesson.

TEACH
- Various activities related to the lesson's content, including Art Criticism, Aesthetics, Art History, and Studio Skills.
- Teaching strategies for each in-text visual-verbal feature.

FOCUS
- A list of student objectives, Vocabulary skill builder, Motivator activity, and Introduction
- Cross-references to supplemental blackline masters in the Teacher's Classroom Resources

ASSESS
- Assessment techniques, including review answers and strategies for reteaching.
- Enrichment and Extension activities.

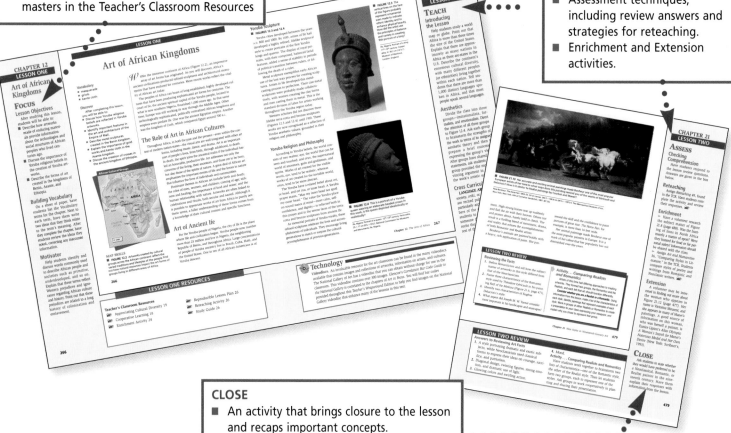

CLOSE
- An activity that brings closure to the lesson and recaps important concepts.

Making Art Accessible for All Students

Teaching strategies in the Meeting Individual Needs and Cultural Diversity boxes incorporate cultural perspectives, strategies for special needs students, and strategies for addressing different learning styles.

ADDITIONAL RESOURCES To enhance the content of each chapter, students and teachers can choose activities from the Performing Arts Handbook, the Careers in Art Handbook, and at Glencoe's Art Online World Wide Web page on the Internet.

STUDIO LESSONS Each studio lesson and activity in the Student Text has a corresponding box in the Teacher's Wraparound Edition that provides alternative ways for students to address the hands-on activity.

STUDENT ART Exemplary student artwork of high school students is displayed with each Studio Lesson in the text to motivate your students.

EXAMINING YOUR WORK This section guides students in applying the process of art criticism to their own works of art.

EXPANDING THE ARTS THROUGH TECHNOLOGY Advances in technology offer exciting opportunities to art teachers and students. Through videodiscs, CD-ROMS, and the Internet, students can sharpen their visual perception. With computer art programs, students push the limits of their creative expression beyond their expectations.

BOTTOM COLUMN ANNOTATIONS Boxes at the bottom of the page give you additional information related to the content of the Student Text. Categories include: About the Artwork, Cultural Diversity, Technology, Meeting Individual Needs, and Assessment.

COOPERATIVE LEARNING

Classroom Art Show. Remind students that the Armory Show of 1913 played a significant part in the which they are pleased. When each student has a piece of art to contribute, have them arrange the artworks in the classroom, giving some thought to the arrangement that best showcases their efforts. Tell students that they should be prepared to answer any questions viewers might have about their particular artworks.

Technology
National Gallery of Art Videodisc Use the following images as examples of more works by artists introduced in this lesson.

Henri Matisse — *Large Composition with Masks*
Edvard Munch — *The Scream*
Pablo Picasso — *Family of Saltimbanques*

Search Frame 2212
Use Glencoe's *Correlation Bar*

MEETING INDIVIDUAL NEEDS

Language Proficiency. Bringing the lessons alive can often aid in students' understanding of a different life style or historical period. If possible, arrange a class visit to a local art museum to view some eighteenth-century decorative arts. Viewing the actual household furnishings of aristocrats of the period and relating these to those pictured in Rococo paintings can help students—especially less capable readers—to gain a more vivid sense of daily life in the eighteenth century. Point out that many Rococo painters also worked in the decorative arts. For example, François Boucher created designs for tapestries and porcelain, the latter a particularly popular medium since the West was being flooded by Chinese goods.

The Teacher's Classroom Resources

A separate *Art in Focus* Teacher's Classroom Resources program provides you with correlated supplemental materials. It contains a wealth of additional handouts, teaching strategies, and resource material designed for more effective teaching. You can choose the materials that complement the skill level, time framework, and interest level of your class. The Teacher's Classroom Resources is organized into individual booklets. These include:

Appreciating Cultural Diversity Activities give students the unique opportunity to see how various cultures use art as a form of personal, social, and creative expression. Worksheets are presented for each chapter to help students celebrate their cultural diversity and understand various global views.

Art and Humanities Activities show students how the visual arts and other forms of art—including literature, music, dance, and theatre, influence each other and how similar historical periods and events influenced all the arts.

Studio Activities correlated with text chapters enable students to further comprehend what is being taught. These field-tested activities encourage students to apply the art criticism operations to their own artworks.

Reproducible Lesson Plans provided for each lesson of *Art in Focus* follow the teaching cycle developed in the Teacher's Wrap-around Edition. The lesson plans include references to all resources available with the *Art in Focus* program.

Advanced Studio Activities have been added to provide studio activities for advanced art students. These activities can assist students in Advanced Placement™ courses in preparing their portfolios.

Application Activities, Cooperative Learning Activities, Enrichment Activities, Reteaching Activities, Study Guides, and **Testing Program** booklets include worksheets to help students review and extend what they have learned.

Assessment All subject areas recognize the importance of measuring individual student performance in attaining specified goals and objectives. A booklet titled *Portfolio and Assessment Techniques* is designed to address basic information used in portfolio assessment for visual art.

Internet Activities Each Internet Activity offers ways for teachers and students to access and make use of Glencoe's new Fine Arts Web site. Additionally, the feature offers strategies for implementing safe, educational Internet exploration in the classroom.

Media and Technology Support

Fine Art Transparency Package

The ready-to-use overhead color transparency package contains 36 full-color Fine Art overhead transparencies. Accompanying the transparencies is an Instructor's Guide with background information and student activity sheets to assist the teacher in guiding discussion, all in a convenient 3-ring binder.

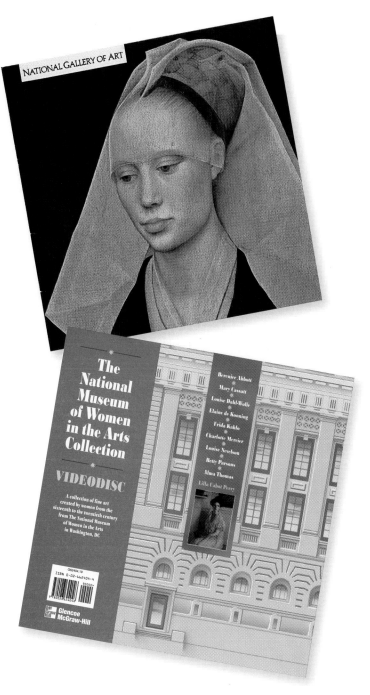

Fine Art Print Package

Twenty-five quality art masterpieces are printed on sturdy self-supporting stock to supplement the artwork appearing in the student text. The laminated prints are resistant to wear and are presented in a durable portfolio for convenient classroom use and storage. This package includes an Instructor's Guide with a page for teaching strategies and a student worksheet for each print.

National Gallery of Art Videodisc

This videodisc features 1,645 artworks from the National Gallery of Art collection, along with a tour of the gallery. Glencoe has published a separate *Correlation Bar Code Guide to the National Gallery of Art* for your convenience, including 300 artworks from the entire videodisc collection. Selected bar codes are reprinted in the Teacher's Wraparound Edition that correlate to lesson contents. The videodisc is available on loan free of charge by contacting:

Department of Education Resources,
Extension Programs Section, Education Division
National Gallery of Art
Washington, D.C. 20565
202-842-6273   www.nga.gov

National Museum of Women in the Arts CD-ROM and Videodisc

This videodisc of 200 artworks from the collection of the National Museum of Women in the Arts includes a video introduction to the museum itself. The videodisc includes a 24-page bar code guide for all images. The CD-ROM provides multi-media access and activities for the 200 works, including an assessment tool to test students' knowledge of artist, time, location, media, and subject.

Artsource®: Performing Arts Package

This new performing arts package provides a multi-media resource for further exploration of artists and groups within the three performing arts areas—dance, music, and theatre. The units within the package supplement the *Performing Arts Handbook* in the Student Text, and include an Instructor's Guide that provides additional information about each artist and group and their performances. The media package includes both video and audiocassettes.

(R) = Chapter Review (H) = Handbook (1), (2), (3), etc. = Lessons	Chapter 1 Art and You	Chapter 2 Developing a Visual Vocabulary	Chapter 3 Creating Art: Media and Processes
NATIONAL STANDARDS FOR THE VISUAL ARTS	1. (a, b) 3. (a, b) 5. (a) 2. (a, b, c) 4. (a, b, c) 6. (a, b)	1. (a, b) 3. (a, b) 5. (a, b) 2. (b, c) 4. (a) 6. (a)	1. (a) 3. (a, b) 5. (a, b) 2. (a, b) 4. (a, b, c) 6. (b)
ARTISTIC PERCEPTION	Recognizing various forms of art (1) Studying art criticism (2) Value of studying art (2)	Identifying elements, principles (1) Recognizing style (1) Discovering design relationships (2) Using design chart (2)	Video, digital media and creativity (2) Using video media to create art (2) Solving problems with digital media (2) Selecting media, tools (3) Expressing humor in art (3)
CREATIVE EXPRESSION	Making decisions/solving problems (1) Activity: Draw a logo (1R) Understanding studio production (2) Creating a sculpture (2R) Design a logo (R)	Expressing mood (1R) Studio: Draw a still life (2) Design basics (R)	Activity: Photograph images (2R) Studio: Relief sculpture (4) Studio: Paint whimsical subject (4) Experiment with media, processes (R)
HISTORICAL/CULTURAL CONTEXT	Understanding why art is created (1) Arts in the community (1) Functions of museums, other resources (1) Studying art history (2) Art history operations (2) Value of art history (2)	History of art principles (2)	Recognizing cultural influences (1) History of printmaking (2) Historical construction processes (4) Modern construction processes (4) Industrial Revolution and architecture (4) Effect of inventions on architecture (4)
AESTHETIC VALUING	Recognizing aesthetic approaches (1, 2) Fine arts/applied arts defined (1) Art criticism operations (2) Uses of art criticism/art history (2)	Examining Your Work (2)	Understanding subject matter (1) Photography as art (1) Evaluating practical functions of art (4) Examining Your Work (4)
ELEMENTS AND PRINCIPLES OF ART	Visual vocabulary defined (2) Thinking Critically: Artistic decisions (R)	Art elements, principles defined (1) Identifying elements, principles (1) Achieving illusion of 3-D space (1) Achieving harmony, unity (2)	Media, processes affect creativity (1) Arranging art elements (1) Line in drawing (1)
ART FORMS			Drawing, painting (1) Printmaking, photo, video, digital (2) Sculpture (3) Architecture (4)
MEDIA, TOOLS, TECHNIQUES AND PROCESSES	Media and processes defined (2)	Recognizing art elements, principles in various media (1)	Media, processes defined (1) Identifying painting media and tools (1) Printmaking, photography, video and digital media defined (2) Identifying types of sculpture, media, tools (3) Materials, processes of architecture (4)
CURRICULUM AND PERFORMING ARTS CONNECTIONS	Art & Music (1) Focus on the Arts (1) Dance (R, H)	Art & Mathematics (1) Focus on the Arts (1) Dance (2)	Art & Language Arts (1) Focus on the Arts (1) Dance (R)
CAREERS/PORTFOLIOS	Portfolio ideas (1) Art and real-world connections (1, R, H)	Portfolio ideas (1) Careers in Art, Art Director (R, H)	Portfolio ideas (1) Careers in Art, Graphic Designer (R, H)

Chapter 4 Art Criticism and Aesthetics	Chapter 5 Art History	Chapter 6 Art of Earliest Times	Chapter 7 The Art of Ancient Egypt
1. (a, b) **3.** (a, b) **5.** (a, b, c) **2.** (a, b, c) **4.** (a, c) **6.** (a)	**1.** (b) **3.** (a, b) **5.** (a, b) **2.** (a, b) **4.** (a, b, c) **6.** (a, b)	**1.** (a, b) **3.** (a, b) **5.** (a, b, c) **2.** (a, b) **4.** (a, b, c) **6.** (a)	**1.** (a, b) **3.** (a, b) **5.** (a, b, c) **2.** (a, b) **4.** (a, b, c) **6.** (a)
Purpose of art criticism (1) Analyzing *Sleeping Gypsy* (1) Identifying emotional vs. reasoned responses (2)	Purpose of art history (1) Style defined (1) Comparing styles (1) Recognize style (R)	Artistic skill of prehistoric people (1) Understanding Sumerian art (2) Examining Neo-Sumerian sculpture (2) Recognizing symbolism (2) Understanding Assyrian reliefs(2) Examining the Ishtar Gate (2) Appreciating Persian art (2)	Interpreting Egyptian painting (2) Hieroglyphs described (2)
Activity: Create, critique a design (1) Studio: Paint a still life (2)	Activity: Create a virtual exhibit (2R) Studio: Paint abstract still life (2) Studio: Create a collage (2)	Activity: Create plaster animal (1R) Activity: Draw imaginary creature (2R) Studio: Contour drawing (2) Studio: Clay modeling (2)	Studio: Paint sarcophagus cover (2)
Nonobjective art defined (2) Research art theories (R)	Art history operations (1) Describing artwork/artist (1) Understanding art styles/ movements (1) Recognizing influence of time/place (1) Value of art history (1) Activity: Examine art history operations (1R) Media, art history (R)	Dating prehistoric artworks (1) Interpreting cave paintings (1) Mesopotamian civilization, cultures (2) Describing law code stele (2) Persian Empire introduced (2) Thinking Critically: Art in context (R) Prehistoric structures (R)	Ancient Egyptian culture (1) Major historical periods (1) Function, structure of pyramids (1) Recognizing influence of religion (1) Interpreting Egyptian sculpture (2) Time & Place Connection (1, 2)
Art criticism and aesthetics defined (1) Steps of art criticism (1) Literal and expressive qualities (1) Theories of aesthetics defined (2) Appreciating nonobjective art (2)	Steps of art history (1) Analyzing, identifying personal style (1) Focus on external clues (1) Using art history and art criticism (2) Examining Your Work (2)	Examining Your Work (2)	Egyptian style (2) Rules of Egyptian art (2) Examining Your Work (2)
Identifying art elements (1) Analyzing design qualities (1) Using design chart (1)	Use of elements and principles in artworks (1)	Describing elements and principles in cave paintings (1) Emphasis (2)	Shape, proportion in pyramids (1)
Art criticism applied to architecture (2)	Determining styles (2)	Painting (1) Architecture (1, 2) Sculpture (2)	Architecture (1) Sculpture (2) Painting (2)
Nonobjective art media, processes (2)	Painting, still life (2) Collage (2)	Cave painting (1) Ziggurat defined (2) Stele defined (2) Looking Closely: Materials, processes (1) Prehistoric tools, media, processes (1)	Mastaba, sarcophagus, obelisk defined (1) Limestone structures (1) Stone carving (2)
Art & Science (1) Focus on the Arts (1) Music (R)	Art & Social Studies (1) Focus on the Arts (1) Dance (R)	Art & Language Arts (1) Focus on the Arts (1) Music, dance, theatre (R)	Art & Social Studies (1) Focus on the Arts (1) Music, dance, theatre (R, H)
Portfolio ideas (1) Careers in Art, Art Critic (R, H)	Portfolio ideas (1) Careers in Art (R)	Portfolio ideas (1) Careers in Art (R)	Portfolio ideas (1) Careers in Art, Architect (R, H)

ART IN FOCUS SCOPE AND SEQUENCE

(R) = Chapter Review (H) = Handbook (1), (2), (3), etc. = Lessons	Chapter 8 Greek Art	Chapter 9 Roman Art	Chapter 10 The Art of India, China, and Japan
NATIONAL STANDARDS FOR THE VISUAL ARTS	**1.** (a, b) **3.** (a, b) **5.** (a, b, c) **2.** (a, b) **4.** (a) **6.** (b)	**1.** (a) **3.** (a, b) **5.** (a, b) **2.** (a, b) **4.** (a, b, c) **6.** (b)	**1.** (a, b) **3.** (a, b) **5.** (c) **2.** (a, b) **4.** (a, b, c) **6.** (a, b)
ARTISTIC PERCEPTION	Recognizing Greek architecture (1) Identifying Greek architectural details (1) Greek artistic accomplishments (2)	Purpose of public structures (2)	Influences of Hinduism, Buddhism (1) Symbolism in Indian art (1) Meditation and Chinese painting (2) Chinese sculpture, painting (2) Chinese influence on Japanese art (3)
CREATIVE EXPRESSION	Studio: Draw features of Greek architecture (2) Studio: Paint with analogous colors (2)	Studio: Create a relief (2)	Studio: Visual symbols (3) Studio: Paint negative shape (3)
HISTORICAL/CULTURAL CONTEXT	Understanding Greek culture (1, 2) Archaic, Classical and Hellenistic periods (2) Influence of Greek artists (2) Time & Place Connection (2)	Understanding Roman culture (1, 2) Greek, Etruscan influences (1) Public buildings past and present (2) Time & Place Connection (1)	Indus Valley civilizations (1) Hinduism, Buddhism defined (1, 3) Describing Buddhist architecture (1) Recognizing Hindu sculpture (1) Understanding Chinese culture (2) Understanding Japanese culture (3) Ukiyo-e, yamato-e defined (3) Time & Place Connection (2)
AESTHETIC VALUING	Decorative orders (defined) (1) Realism, idealism in Greek sculpture (1) Expressive qualities (2) Changing aesthetics of sculpture (2) Examining Your Work (2)	Recognizing aesthetics of realism (1) Examining Your Work (2)	Interpreting Buddhist sculpture (1) Identifying Hindu architecture (1) Chinese landscape painting (2) Cultural sources of aesthetics (3) Examining Your Work (3)
ELEMENTS AND PRINCIPLES OF ART	Color, balance, harmony in architecture (1) Symmetrical balance, harmony in sculpture (2) Line, texture, repetition, movement (2)		Line, value, space, form in scroll painting (2) Vanishing point described (2) Movement, line in painting (3) Proportion in architecture (3)
ART FORMS	Architecture (1) Sculpture (1, 2)	Sculpture (1) Painting (1) Mosaics (1) Architecture (1, 2)	Architecture, sculpture (1, 2, 3) Painting (2, 3) Pottery (2, 3) Printmaking (3)
MEDIA, TOOLS, TECHNIQUES AND PROCESSES	Frieze, colonnade defined (1) Post and lintel construction (1) Stone carving (1) Clay modeling (1) Marble carving (2) Bronze casting (2)	Murals (1) Wax masks (1) Stone, marble carving (1, 2) Innovations in materials, processes (1) Introduction of concrete (1) Arches, vaults, aqueducts defined (1) Architectural techniques defined (2)	Clay pottery (1, 2) Bronze, stone sculpture (1, 2, 3) Weaving, cotton cloth (1) Wood structures (1, 3) Scroll painting (2, 3) Watercolor, pen or brush and ink (2, 3) Woodblock printing (3)
CURRICULUM AND PERFORMING ARTS CONNECTIONS	Art & Mathematics (1) Focus on the Arts (1) Music, dance, theatre (R, H)	Art & Music (1) Focus on the Arts (1) Music, dance, theatre (R, H)	Art & Science (1) Focus on the Arts (1) Dance/Music (R, H)
CAREERS/PORTFOLIOS	Portfolio ideas (1) Careers in Art, Scenic Designer (R, H)	Portfolio ideas (1) Careers in Art, Urban Planner (R, H)	Portfolio ideas (1) Careers in Art, Landscape Architect (R, H)

Chapter 11 The Native Arts of the Americas	Chapter 12 The Arts of Africa	Chapter 13 Early Christian, Byzantine, and Islamic Art	Chapter 14 Gothic Art
1. (a, b) **3.** (a, b) **5.** (c) **2.** (a, b) **4.** (a, b, c) **6.** (a, b)	**1.** (a, b) **3.** (a, b, c) **5.** (a, b, c) **2.** (a, b) **4.** (a, b, c) **6.** (a, b)	**1.** (a, b) **3.** (a) **5.** (a, b) **2.** (a, b, c) **4.** (a, b, c) **6.** (a, b)	**1.** (a, b) **3.** (a) **5.** (b, c) **2.** (a, b, c) **4.** (a, b, c) **6.** (b)
Identifying natural symbols (1) Recognizing cultural influences (1) Spiritual meaning of art (1) Pre-Columbian artistic contributions (2)	Recognizing spiritual meaning of masquerade (1) Interpreting Jenne architecture (1) Variety of African art (2) Understanding purposes of sculpture (1, 2)	Understanding religious symbolism (1) Purpose of Byzantine mosaics (1) Recognizing Byzantine art (1) Stylized designs, motifs in Islamic art (2)	Interpreting church sculpture (2) Recognizing artistic imagination (2) Understanding religious symbols (2)
Studio: Draw abstract design (2)	Activity: African art presentation (1R) Activity: Create a design motif (2R) Studio: Create papier-mâché mask (2)	Studio: Paint Byzantine style self-portrait (2) Studio: Draw a word design (2)	Studio: Woodblock print (2)
Introducing Native American cultures: Arctic, Northwest Coast region, Southwest region, Great Plains, Woodland region (1) Totem pole defined (1) Pre-Columbian defined (2) Understanding Mexican cultures (2) Time & Place Connection (1)	Understanding African cultures (1) Kente cloth tradition (1) Christian Ethiopian religious art (1) African influences on Western art (2) Difficulties art historians encounter (2) Significance of African art (2) Time & Place Connection (2)	Influence of Christian church (1) Identifying Roman influences (1) Influence of Byzantine culture (1) Influence of Islam on art (2) Mosque, minaret, mihrab, alcazar defined (2) Time & Place Connection (1)	European Middle Ages described (1) Identifying medieval periods: Early Medieval, Romanesque, Gothic (1) Understanding role of religion in art (1) Recognizing effects of feudalism, growth of cities (1, 2) Identifying purpose of pilgrimage churches (2) Time & Place Connection (1)
Identifying function of ritual masks (1) Development of Mayan art (2) Appreciating non-representational art (2) Examining Your Work (2)	Abstract sculpture defined (1) Characteristics of figure carving (2) Ceremonial importance of art (2) Interpreting African carvings (2) Examining Your Work (2)	Recognizing purpose of Christian art (1) Interpreting church sculpture (1) Interpreting Islamic architecture (2) Understanding Islamic art (2) Examining Your Work (2)	Purpose of religious buildings (1) Describing castle function, design (2) Romanesque architecture (2) Church art as storytelling (2) Examining Your Work (2)
Color in sculpture, architecture (1, 2) Repetition, color in weaving (1) Ornamentation in sculpture (2) Colors, shapes in Aztec art (2)	Line, shape, repetition, rhythm, movement in African art (1, 2) Harmony, balance in sculpture (2)	Balance, proportion in Byzantine architecture (1) Color in painting, sculpture (1, 2) Art elements in Islamic painting (2)	Principles in architecture (1, 2) Unity in sculpture (2) Line, color, pattern, shape in painting (2)
Sculpture, architecture (1, 2) Crafts (1) Painting (1) Picture writing (2)	Architecture (1) Sculpture (1, 2) Crafts (1)	Painting, architecture (1, 2) Mosaics (1) Calligraphy (2) Sculpture (2)	Architecture (1, 2) Painting (1, 2) Manuscript illumination (1, 2) Sculpture (1, 2)
Ivory carving (1) Assembling, weaving natural fibers (1) Wood, stone carving (1, 2) Pueblo dwellings (1) Painted hide (1) Earthworks (1) Painted books (2)	Weaving natural fibers (1, 2) Wood, iron, gold, bronze jewelry-making (1, 2) Modeling papier-mâché (2) Wood carving (2) Copper, bronze casting (2) Lost-wax process (2) Terra cotta sculpture (2)	Murals (1) Campanile, piers defined (1) Recognizing dome construction (1) Mosaics (1) Pen or brush and ink (2) Stone carving (2) Stucco ornamentation (2)	Transept, cloister defined (1) Pen and ink (1) Stone carving (1) Woven, painted or embroidered cloth; tapestry defined (2) Stone buildings (2) Tympanum, ambulatory defined (2)
Art & Social Studies (1) Focus on the Arts (1) Dance (R, H)	Art & Social Studies (1) Focus on the Arts (1) Dance (R, H)	Art & Social Studies (1) Focus on the Arts (1) Dance/Music (R, H)	Art & Language Arts (1) Focus on the Arts (1) Music (R, H)
Portfolio ideas (1) Careers in Art (R)	Portfolio ideas (1) Careers in Art (R)	Portfolio ideas (1) Careers in Art, Advertising Artist (R, H)	Portfolio idea (1) Careers in Art (R)

(R) = Chapter Review (H) = Handbook (1), (2), (3), etc. = Lessons	Chapter 15 Gothic Art	Chapter 16 The Italian Renaissance	Chapter 17 Fifteenth-Century Art in Northern Europe
NATIONAL STANDARDS FOR THE VISUAL ARTS	1. (a, b) 3. (a) 5. (a) 2. (a, b) 4. (a, b) 6. (b)	1. (a, b) 3. (b) 5. (b, c) 2. (a, b) 4. (b, c) 6. (a, b)	1. (a, b) 3. (a, b) 5. (b) 2. (b) 4. (a, b) 6. (b)
ARTISTIC PERCEPTION	Understanding stained glass art (1) Recognizing role of religion in art (1, 2) Identifying realism, emotionalism in art (2, 3) Understanding symbolism (2) Recognizing artistic imagination (2)	Vanishing point, linear perspective, aerial perspective discovered, defined (1) Illusion of light, space (2, 3) Understanding symbolism (3)	Recognizing symbolism (1, 2) Creating illusion of space (1) Value of emotionalism (1) Representation of commoners (2)
CREATIVE EXPRESSION	Studio: Draw landscape tympanum (3) Studio: Carve tympanum relief (3)	Studio: Paint a cityscape (3)	Studio: Create detail drawing (2) Studio: Design visual symbol (2)
HISTORICAL/CULTURAL CONTEXT	Comparison of Romanesque and Gothic architecture (1) Influence of Gothic architecture (1) Influence of stained glass art (2) International Style defined (2) Influence of Byzantine artists (3) Historical Connection (R) Time & Place Connection (1)	Understanding Italian Renaissance (1) Introduction of printing press (1) Acceptance of Renaissance ideals (2) Description of women's roles (3) da Vinci's artistic contributions (3) Time & Place Connection (1)	Oil paint discovered (1) Influence of Northern Renaissance art (1) Combining realism, emotionalism (2) Influence of van der Weyden (2) Time & Place Connection (1, 2)
AESTHETIC VALUING	Church art as storytelling (2) Interpreting religious art (2) Purpose of illustrated books (2) Fresco technique (3) Examining Your Work (3)	Renaissance, Gothic ideals (1) Cathedral design (2) Analyzing *Alba Madonna* (3) Examining Your Work (3)	Identifying effect of oil painting (1) Detail in van Eyck's work (1) Understanding emotionalism (2) Recognizing uses of distortion (2) Examining Your Work (2)
ELEMENTS AND PRINCIPLES OF ART	Elements in architecture, stained glass (1) Color, space in painting (2, 3) Principles used for dramatic effect (3)	Perspective (1) Hue, value, intensity in painting (1, 3) Perspective in sculpture (2) Proportion in sculpture (3)	Balance, perspective in painting (1) Color, line, texture, shape in painting (1, 2) Design principles (2)
ART FORMS	Architecture (1) Stained glass (1) Sculpture (1, 2) Illumination (2)	Painting (1, 2, 3) Sculpture (1, 2, 3) Architecture (2)	Painting (1, 2)
MEDIA, TOOLS, TECHNIQUES AND PROCESSES	Innovations in architecture (1) Pen and ink (2) Stone carving (2) Painting, wood panels (3) Fresco defined (3) Charcoal (3) Plaster, pigment (3)	Innovations of Masaccio (1) Bronze casting (1) Innovations in sculpture (1) Stone carving (2, 3) Dome construction (2) Fresco (3) Portrait painting (3)	Tempera defined (1) Gesso defined (1) Oil paint discovered, defined (1) Wood, canvas (1)
CURRICULUM AND PERFORMING ARTS CONNECTIONS	Art & Social Studies (1) Focus on the Arts (1) Music (R, H)	Art & Social Studies (1) Focus on the Arts (1) Music (R, H)	Art & Mathematics (1) Focus on the Arts (1) Music (R, H)
CAREERS/PORTFOLIOS	Portfolio idea (1) Careers in Art, Illustrator (R, H)	Portfolio idea (1) Careers, Video Game Designer (R, H)	Portfolio ideas (1) Careers in Art (R)

Chapter 18 Art of Sixteenth-Century Europe	Chapter 19 Baroque Art	Chapter 20 Rococo Art	Chapter 21 New Styles in Nineteenth-Century Art
1. (a, b) **3.** (a) **5.** (a, c) **2.** (a, b) **4.** (a, b, c) **6.** (a, b)	**1.** (a, b) **3.** (a, b) **5.** (a, b, c) **2.** (a, b) **4.** (a, b, c) **6.** (b)	**1.** (a) **3.** (a, b) **5.** (a, b) **2.** (a, b) **4.** (a, b, c) **6.** (b)	**1.** (a) **3.** (a, b) **5.** (a, b) **2.** (a, b) **4.** (a, b, c) **6.** (b)

Value of emotionalism (1, 2)
Purpose of distorted figures (2)
Brutal realism of Grünewald (3)
Religious tension as subject
   matter (3)
	Mood, drama in Baroque art (1)
	Controversial realism in
	   Caravaggio (1)
	Baroque, Renaissance styles (1)
	Expressive work of Rembrandt (2)
	Realism in Spanish religious art (3)
	Effects of church division on art (3)
		Changing subject matter (1)
		Significance of Goya's realistic
		   war scenes (2)
		Recognizing break with artistic
		   tradition (2)
			Influence of French Revolution on art (1)
			Importance of Academy (1)
			Dramatic and exotic expression (2)
			Influence of industrialization on art (2)
			Emergence of realism (2)
			Art as personal expression (2)
			Understanding Impressionism (3)

Studio: Paint imaginary creature (3) Studio: Humorous face (3)	Studio: Shape with movement (3) Studio: Draw charcoal figure (3)	Studio: Draw chalk still life (2) Studio: Create collage (2)	Studio: Paint still life (3)

Venetian culture (1)
Recognizing Byzantine influence (1)
Mannerism defined (2)
Understanding Reformation (2)
Spread of Renaissance to the
   North (3)
Continued influence of Gothic ideas (3)
Time & Place Connection (2)
	Understanding
	   Counter-Reformation (1)
	Baroque defined (1)
	Influence of Caravaggio,
	   Gentileschi (1)
	Recognizing Dutch genre painting (2)
	Discovery of Judith Leyster (2)
	Time & Place Connection (1)
		Understanding French
		   aristocracy (1)
		Paris as center of art world (1)
		Rococo art defined (1)
		English artists emerge (2)
		Time & Place Connection (1)
			Academies, Salons defined (1)
			Neoclassic art defined (1)
			Romantic art, Realism defined (2)
			Impressionism introduced (3)
			Japanese influence (3)
			Influence of photography (3)
			Time & Place Connection (2)

Expressing mood in painting (1)
Recognizing effects of religion,
   politics, culture on art (2)
Describing Holbein's works (3)
Examining Your Work (3)
	Analyzing Rembrandt's work (2)
	Secular painting as storytelling (2)
	Analyzing Velázquez's works (3)
	Examining Your Work (3)
		Expressing mood in painting (1)
		Art as social criticism (2)
		Satire defined (2)
		Interpreting artists' works (2)
		Examining Your Work (2)
			Renewed emphasis on Classical
			   ideas (1)
			Art as social/political criticism (1)
			Effect of light on subject (2, 3)
			Aesthetics of Impressionism (3)
			Examining Your Work (3)

Color, texture in painting (1, 2)
Hue, line create mood (1)
Principles create tension, instability (2)
Unusual perspective,
   proportion (2, 3)
	Elements and principles in archi-
	   tecture, sculpture (1)
	Movement, value, line, space in
	   painting (1, 2, 3)
	Harmony, design in painting (3)
		Design, repetition (1)
		Light, texture in painting (1)
		Color, pattern in painting (1, 2)
		Value, pattern, unity in
		   architecture (2)
			Line, color, balance in painting (1, 2, 3)
			Pattern, color create movement,
			   mood (2)
			Value, intensity in painting (3)
			Texture in sculpture (3)

Painting (1, 2, 3) Drawing (3) Printmaking (3)	Architecture (1) Sculpture (1) Painting (1, 2, 3)	Architecture (1, 2) Painting (1, 2)	Painting (1, 2, 3) Printmaking (3) Sculpture (3)
Portrait painting (1) Oil, canvas (2, 3) Engraving (3) Pen and ink (3)	Façade defined (1) Stone carving (1) Mural (1) Chiaroscuro defined (1) Still life (2) Genre painting defined (2)	Oil, canvas (1) Pastels (1) Portrait painting (2) Wren's design innovations (2)	Portrait painting (1) Oil, canvas (1, 2, 3) Watercolor (2) Woodblock printing (3) Landscape, genre painting (3) Bronze casting (3)
Art & Language Arts(1) Focus on the Arts (1) Theatre (R, H)	Art & Social Studies (1) Focus on the Arts (1) Music (R, H)	Art & Social Studies (1) Focus on the Arts (1) Music, dance, theatre (R, H)	Art & Language Arts (1) Focus on the Arts (1) Music (R, H)
Portfolio ideas (1) Careers in Art, Fashion Designer (R, H)	Portfolio ideas (1) Careers in Art (R)	Portfolio idea (1) Careers in Art (R)	Portfolio idea (1) Careers in Art, Photographer (R, H)

(R) = Chapter Review (H) = Handbook (1), (2), (3), etc. = Lessons	Chapter 22 Art of the Later Nineteenth Century	Chapter 23 Art of the Early Twentieth Century	Chapter 24 Modern Art Movements to the Present
NATIONAL STANDARDS FOR THE VISUAL ARTS	**1.** (a, b) **3.** (a) **5.** (a, b) **2.** (a, b) **4.** (a, c) **6.** (a, b)	**1.** (a, b) **3.** (a) **5.** (a, b) **2.** (a, b) **4.** (b, c) **6.** (a, b)	**1.** (a, b) **3.** (a) **5.** (a, c) **2.** (a, b, c) **4.** (a, b, c) **6.** (a, b)

ARTISTIC PERCEPTION	Value of personal, expressive art (1)
	Declining interest in realism (1)
	Realism in American art (2)
	Lack of sentimentality, Eakin (2)
		Identifying European art
		  movements (1)
		Personal experience as inspiration (1)
		Intellectual approaches to art (1)
		Political and social subject matter (2)
		Emotionalism of Mexican
		  muralists (2)
			Controversy over art movements (1)
			Realism of Regionalists (1)
			Effects of painting on sculpture (2)
			Pei's problem-solving creativity (2)

CREATIVE EXPRESSION	Studio: Aesthetic painting (2) Studio: Create tempera batik (2)	Studio: Create abstract cutout (3) Studio: Paint in Cubist style (3)	Studio: Create Relief (2)

HISTORICAL/CULTURAL
CONTEXT
	Post-Impressionism defined (1)
	Understanding 19th century
	  American culture (2)
	American art introduced (2)
	African-American artistic
	  contributions (2)
	Time & Place Connection (2)
		The Fauves introduced (1)
		Expressionism, Nonobjective,
		  Cubism (1)
		Influence of Mexican muralists (2)
		Ashcan school defined (2)
		Impact of Armory Show of 1913 (2)
		Effects of technology on
		  architecture (3)
		Time & Place Connection (2)
			Dada, Regionalism defined (1)
			Nonobjective American art (1)
			Surrealism, Abstract Expressionism
			  defined (1)
			Pop Art, Op Art, Hard-edge,
			  Photo-Realism defined (1)
			Canadian art introduced (2)
			Time & Place Connection (2)

AESTHETIC VALUING	Emergence, non-representational art (1) Analyzing artists' works (1,2) Recognizing religious themes (2) Examining Your Work (2)	Aesthetics of Expressionism (1) Understanding nonobjective art (1) Art as public property (2) Eclectic style defined (3) Examining Your Work (3)	Recognizing Surrealist aesthetic (1) Interpreting artists' works (1,2) Examining Your Work (2)

ELEMENTS AND
PRINCIPLES OF ART
	Plane defined (1)
	Color, form, balance, variety (1)
	Line in painting (2)
	Organization in painting (2)
		Elements, principles in
		  nonobjective art (1)
		Value, line, shape, texture
		  create mood (1)
		Perspective in Cubism (1)
		Rhythm, repetition in painting (2)
			Form, shape, texture in painting (1)
			Color in painting (1, 2)
			Natural forms (1, 2)
			Shape, line in painting (2)

ART FORMS	Painting (1, 2) Sculpture (2)	Printmaking (1) Collage, defined (1) Painting, sculpture (1,2) Architecture (3)	Painting (1, 2) Sculpture (2) Mobile (2) Architecture (2)
MEDIA, TOOLS, TECHNIQUES AND PROCESSES	Oil, canvas (1, 2) Marble carving (2)	Oil, canvas (1, 2) Lithography (1) Woodcut, etching (1) Mural (2) Enamel, wood (2) Architectural materials, construction (3) Steel frame (3)	Oil, canvas, watercolor (1) Portrait painting (1) Action painting methods (1) Wood, marble carving (2) Bronze casting (2) Innovations in sculptural design (2) Metal, assemblage (2)
CURRICULUM AND PERFORMING ARTS CONNECTIONS	Art & Science (1) Focus on the Arts (1) Music/Dance (R, H)	Art & Social Studies (1) Focus on the Arts (1) Dance (R, H)	Art & Language Arts (1) Focus on the Arts (1) Music (R, H)
CAREERS/PORTFOLIOS	Portfolio idea (1) Careers in Art, Medical Illustrator (R, H)	Portfolio idea (1) Careers in Art, Cinematographer (R, H)	Portfolio idea (1) Careers in Art (R)

ART
IN FOCUS
FOURTH EDITION

AESTHETICS CRITICISM HISTORY STUDIO

Gene A. Mittler, Ph.D.
Professor Emeritus
Texas Tech University

Glencoe
McGraw-Hill

New York, New York   Columbus, Ohio   Woodland Hills, California   Peoria, Illinois

About the Author

Gene Mittler

Gene Mittler is the author of *Art in Focus*, Glencoe's senior high school art history textbook, which uses a chronological approach to art. He is also one of the authors of Glencoe's middle school/junior high art series, *Introducing Art, Exploring Art,* and *Understanding Art,* and *Creating and Understanding Drawings* for high school. He has taught at both the elementary and secondary levels and at Indiana University. He received an M.F.A. in sculpture from Bowling Green State University and a Ph.D. in art education from Ohio State University. He has authored grants and published numerous articles in professional journals and has lectured in the United States and abroad. Dr. Mittler is currently Professor Emeritus at Texas Tech University.

About Artsource®

 The materials provided in the *Performing Arts Handbook* are excerpted from Artsource®: The Music Center Study Guide to the Performing Arts, a project of the Music Center Education Division. The Music Center of Los Angeles County, the largest performing arts center in the western United States, established the Music Center Education Division in 1979 to provide opportunities for lifelong learning in the arts, and especially to bring the performing and visual arts into the classroom. The Education Division believes the arts enhance the quality of life for all people, but are crucial to the development of every child.

About the Cover

The image of the Delphian Sibyl on the cover is a detail from Michelangelo's paintings on the ceiling of the Sistine Chapel in the Vatican. Completed in 1512, this immense ceiling was divided into nine main sections. In each section, Michelangelo painted a scene from the biblical story of humanity. Along the edge of the ceiling, prophets and their female counterparts, the sibyls, are depicted. Sibyls were prophetesses in ancient Greek and Roman mythology. The Delphian Sibyl is so named because she resided in the town of Delphi.

Cover Art: Michelangelo Buonarroti. Delphian Sibyl (detail from the ceiling of the Sistine Chapel). 1508–12. Fresco (post-restoration). Vatican, Sistine Chapel, Vatican City, Rome, Italy. Scala/Art Resource, New York.

Glencoe/McGraw-Hill

A Division of The McGraw·Hill Companies

Send all inquiries to:
Glencoe/McGraw-Hill
21600 Oxnard Street, Suite 500
Woodland Hills, California 91367

ISBN 0-02-662408-7 (Student Edition)
ISBN 0-02-662409-5 (Teacher's Wraparound Edition)

5 6 7 8 9   004/043   06 05 04 03 02 01

Studio Lesson Consultants

Acknowledgements: We wish to express our gratitude to the following art coordinators, teachers, and specialists who participated in the field test of the studio lessons.

Donna Banning, El Modena High School, Orange, CA; Jeanette Burkhart, Red Bank High School, Chattanooga, TN; Barbara Cox, Glencliff Comprehensive High School, Nashville, TN; Anne Dowhie, Central High School, Evansville, IN; Melissa Farrel, Klein Forest High School, Houston, TX; Ed Howland, Shasta High School, Redding, CA; Annette Loy, Jefferson County High School, Dandridge, TN; Quita McClintoc, Hewitt-Trussville High School, Trussville, AL; Susan McEwen, Klein Forest High School, Houston, TX; Karen Nichols, Reseda High School, Reseda, CA; Roberta Sajda, Klein Forest High School, Houston, TX; David Sebring, Dobson High School, Mesa, AZ

Student Art Contributors

The following students contributed exemplary works for Studio Lessons.

Figure 3.52 Eric Sargeant, El Modena High School, Orange, CA; Figure 5.19 Jesse Smith, El Modena High School, Orange, CA; Figure 5.18 Kate Sawyer, Shasta High School, Redding, CA; Figure 6.19 Joanna Lipinski, Reseda High School, Reseda, CA; Figure 6.20 Miranda Meadows, El Modena High School, Orange, CA; Figure 7.15 Edward Robinson, Reseda High School, Reseda, CA; Figure 8.24 Tiffany Ruiz, Klein Forest High School, Houston, TX; Figure 10.36 Jay Jackson, Central High School, Evansville, IN; Figure 10.37 Jessica Farrelli, El Modena High School, Orange, CA; Figure 11.23 Aleta Thomas, Shasta High School, Redding, CA; Figure 12.26 Katherine McClister, Red Bank High School, Chattanooga, TN; Figure 13.26 Angela Krezinski, Klein Forest High School, Houston, TX; Figure 14.29 Michael Ho, Klein Forest High School, Houston, TX; Figure 15.23 Alex Penescu, Reseda High School, Reseda, CA; Figure 15.24 Daniel Rubio, Reseda High School, Reseda, CA; Figure 16.26 Ruben Garcia, Reseda High School, Reseda, CA; Figure 17.10 Natalie Hammer, Jefferson County High School, Dandridge, TN; Figure 18.17 José Ventura, Reseda High School, Reseda, CA; Figure 19.24 Gilberto Carrillo, Reseda High School, Reseda, CA; Figure 19.25 Mario Rivero, Klein Forest High School, Houston, TX; Figure 20.16 Susan Fielden, Jefferson County High School, Dandridge, TN; Figure 21.24 Lyndsey Hagen, Glencliff Comprehensive High School, Nashville, TN; Figure 22.18 Anthony Muñoz, Klein Forest High School, Houston, TX; Figure 22.19 Justin Marion, Jefferson County High School, Dandridge, TN; Figure 23.31 Daniel Rubio, Reseda High School, Reseda, CA; Figure 23.32 Annie Medina, El Modena High School, Orange, CA; Figure 24.38 Komsam Klinudom, Glencliff Comprehensive High School, Nashville, TN

Table of Contents

Credit line on page 22.

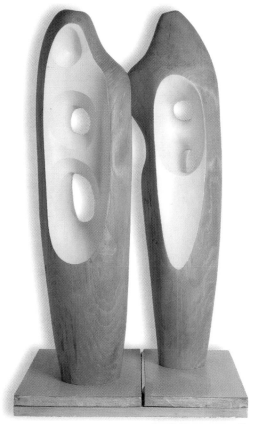

Credit line on page 8.

Credit line on page 146.

Credit line on page 179.

Credit line on page 244.

Credit line on page 327.

UNIT 6 *Art of an Emerging Modern Europe*

Credit line on page 369.

Credit line on page 446.

UNIT 7 *Art of the Modern Era*

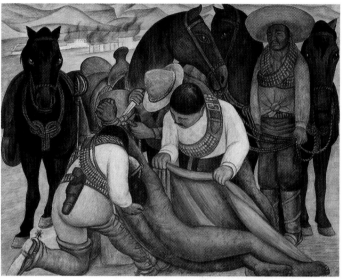

Credit line on page 529.

Handbooks

Credit line on page 561.

Chapter Features

Styles Influencing Styles

LOOKING Closely

Features in Art

Time & Place CONNECTIONS

Creating and Understanding Art

Unit One provides students with an overview of the field of art, providing an operational definition of the term *art* and touching on aspects of art history, art criticism, and aesthetics.

Chapter 1 *Art and You* offers reasons for studying art and why artists create.

Chapter 2 *Developing a Visual Vocabulary* introduces the elements and principles of art.

Chapter 3 *Creating Art: Media and Processes* offers a primer on drawing, painting, printmaking, photography, video, digital media, as well as sculpture and architecture.

Chapter 4 *Art Criticism and Aesthetics* introduces the art criticism operations used by art critics and introduces students to the three aesthetic theories.

Chapter 5 *Art History* introduces students to the art history operations used by art historians when examining artworks, and takes students through the steps to help them understand artworks through art history.

National Museum of Women in the Arts

You may wish to use the National Museum of Women in the Arts videodisc and/or CD-ROM. The videodisc features a bar code guide, and the interactive CD-ROM provides stimulating activities.

More About... **The Wreck of Ole '97.** Tell students that this work by Thomas Hart Benton was probably based upon an actual incident. The artist sought to capture a cross section of American life in his works, and *The Wreck of Ole '97* is very typical of Benton's style and choice of subject matter. The details in this work, including the man and boy shown struggling in the wagon, the other figures participating in the scene, the rutted dirt road, the steam engine, and railroad crossing reveal the artist's desire to capture the event, the time period, and feeling of the region in which it was painted. Discuss with students their reaction to this work. What were their thoughts when first viewing this work? Were they impressed by the style or by the story it tells?

UNIT 1

Creating and Understanding Art

"He never paints the pleasant or the pretty. For all his vitality, there is seldom joy. There is love and sorrow, pity and wit, but no playfulness. He is harassed by what he sees in American life. That is why his canvasses are restless."

Ruth Pickering
Arts and Decoration magazine
(February, 1935)

Thomas Hart Benton. *The Wreck of the Ole '97*. 1943. Egg tempera on gessoed masonite. 72.4 × 113 cm (28$^1/_2$ × 44$^1/_2$"). Hunter Museum of American Art, Chattanooga, Tennessee. Gift of the Ben Wood Foundation.

3

Introducing the Unit

Ask students to brainstorm terms that are synonymous with *artist*, and record their responses on the board in the form of a word web. If students call out "painter," circle the term and ask: What other types of artists can you name? Are there other people apart from artists who are involved in the field of art?

Discussing the Quotation

Instruct students to examine the work closely and ask if the term "restless" is proper when discussing this artist's painting style. Have them explain how love and sorrow, pity and wit are illustrated in this work. Next, turn their attention to the way this painting is organized. Ask them to explain how the artist leads the viewer's eye to the center of interest. Why is it appropriate to refer to the "triangular design" of this painting?

Teacher Notes Remember to leave time for response

Art and You

ADDITIONAL CHAPTER RESOURCES

Activities
- 📁 Advanced Studio Activity 1
- 📁 Application 1
- 🖱 Chapter 1 Internet Activity
- 📁 Studio Activity 1

Fine Art Resources
- 🕹 **Transparencies**

  Art in Focus Transparency 1

      Janet Fish. *Arcanum*

  Art in Focus Transparency 2

      Maria Helena Vieira da Silva. *The City*
- 🖼 **Fine Art Print**

  Focus on World Art Print 1

      Faith Ringold. *Groovin' High*

Assessment
- 📁 Chapter 1 Test
- 📁 Performance Assessment

Multimedia Resources
- 🎭 Artsource® Performing Arts Package
- 💿 National Gallery Laser Disc
- 💿 National Museum of Women in the Arts CD-ROM
- 📼 Arts & Entertainment Videos

NATIONAL STANDARDS FOR ARTS EDUCATION

The National Standards for Arts Education provide guidelines for grade-appropriate competency in the visual arts. The Content Standards for grades 9–12 are:

1. Understanding and applying media, techniques, and processes.
2. Using knowledge of structures and functions.
3. Choosing and evaluating a range of subject matter, symbols, and ideas.
4. Understanding the visual arts in relation to history and cultures.
5. Reflecting upon and assessing the characteristics and merits of their work and the work of others.
6. Making connections between visual arts and other disciplines.

Listed below are the National Standards for the Visual Arts addressed in this chapter. For a breakdown of the categories listed under each content standard, refer to the *Reproducible Lesson Plans* booklet in the TCR.

   1. (a, b)   **2.** (a, b, c)   **3.** (a, b)   **4.** (a, b, c)   **5.** (a)   **6.** (a, b)

🕐 **Out of Time?** If time does not permit teaching this chapter in its entirety, you may wish to preview the artwork and captions with students. Scan the heads in each lesson with students. Discuss the topics in each of the lessons and explain that students will learn more about understanding art as they study this chapter.

HANDBOOK MATERIAL

Chuck Davis
(page 577)

(page 594)

Beyond the Classroom

National, state, and community groups sponsor art education in many ways. They can provide guest speakers, resource information, and exhibitions of professional and student work. For support and resources to encourage the appreciation of art outside the classroom, visit our Web site at *www.glencoe.com/sec/art*.

Art and You

Art and You

INTRODUCE

Chapter Overview

CHAPTER 1 provides students with an overview of an approach to perceiving and understanding works of art. This approach combines aesthetics, art criticism, and art history and enables students to arrive at and explain their own decisions about artworks.

Lesson One explains the various forms art may take, and offers reasons why artists create. This lesson also identifies the decision making and problem solving tasks students must contend with when creating art or studying art.

Lesson Two provides reasons for studying art and defines the tasks of aestheticians, art critics, and art historians.

*Art&*Social Studies

Have students examine Figure 1.1, *Hot Still-Scape for Six Colors—7th Avenue Style* with students. Read the social studies connection with the class. Ask students to identify aspects of the painting that remind them of music, and of jazz music in particular. Have volunteers name other artworks that remind them of different musical styles.

National Standards

This chapter addresses the following National Standards for the Arts.

1. (a,b)	**4.** (a,b,c)
2. (a,b,c)	**5.** (a)
3. (a,b)	**6.** (a,b)

*Art&*Music ■ **FIGURE 1.1** Stuart Davis's painting combines the sights and sounds of a modern American city with the lively rhythms of the jazz music he loved. Using blaring colors, vigorous, twisting lines, and contrasting, angular shapes Davis captured the sounds of a wailing saxophone, a vibrant piano, and a pulsating bass. He created a kind of "visual jazz" that makes viewers feel the excitement of a thrilling moment in front of a red-hot jazz group.

Stuart Davis. *Hot Still-Scape for Six Colors—7th Avenue Style.* 1940. Oil on canvas. 91.4 × 114.3 cm (36 × 45"). Boston Museum of Fine Arts, Boston, Massachusetts. Gift of the William H. Lane Foundation and the M. and M. Karolik Collection, by exchange. © Estate of Stuart Davis/Licensed by VAGA, New York, New York.

4

CHAPTER 1 RESOURCES

Teacher's Classroom Resources

📁 Advanced Studio Activity 1
📁 Application 1
🖱 Chapter 1 Internet Activity
📁 Studio Activity 1

Assessment

📁 Chapter 1 Test
📁 Performance Assessment

Fine Art Resources

 *Art in Focus* Transparencies
   1, Janet Fish. *Arcanum*
   2, Maria Helena Viera da Silva. *The City*
▪ *Focus on World Art* Print 1
   Faith Ringgold. *Groovin' High*

*I*t is virtually impossible to imagine any society
without art of some kind. Indeed, the visual arts, music,
drama, dance, and other forms of art, add a
sense of pleasure to life. The arts are a
vital part of civilization, an essential part of
any culture. They are the universal languages through
which human beings express their dreams,
their aspirations, their ideas, and their feelings.
They make it possible for all of us to communicate, understand,
and appreciate each other. The arts have always been
and always will be the language of civilization.

YOUR Portfolio

Keep your best artworks in your portfolio to maintain a record of your growth and development as an artist. Choose entries for your portfolio that exhibit your strongest works and demonstrate your best skills and use of different media. As you create artworks for the lessons in this text, keep in mind which ones you would like to add to your portfolio. Make sure that each entry includes your name and the date you completed the artwork. Include a summary and self-reflection of your work and the processes used to complete the assignment. Review your portfolio often to evaluate your progress over time.

Focus ON THE ARTS

LITERATURE
The rich oral folk traditions of ancient Africa, which predate the development of writing, are a living testament to the need of peoples throughout the ages to express themselves creatively with words.

MUSIC
Like visual artists, musicians have drawn on a variety of sources for inspiration— sometimes the visual arts themselves. Russian composer Modest Mussorgsky's 1874 piano suite, *Pictures at an Exhibition* was inspired by the paintings he saw at an art exhibit.

THEATRE
The same creative impulses that have driven visual artists are evident in drama. Consider the morality play, a type of drama popularized in the 1400s in which characters symbolized good and evil.

5

Introducing the Chapter

Create a page of exotic-looking nonsense words and sentences (e.g., *FrijnÏ upsum Āglarshkji ʔipmes est*). Distribute copies of the page to students, telling them that the page is an important document for them to read. Explain that any exchange of information is possible only when people share a common language. Explain that in the chapters to follow, students will be learning the language of artists.

A R T
S O U
R C E

Dance Use *Performing Arts Handbook* page 577 to explain how Chuck Davis and his African American Dance Ensemble bring the message of love, peace, and respect.

Focus ON THE ARTS

Point out to students that art—whether it is executed on canvas, on a stage in a darkened auditorium, on a word processor, or on a sheet of music paper—is motivated by the same needs, desires, hopes, and dreams.

To help students further appreciate the universality of the creative experience, divide the class into three groups for an arts "scavenger hunt." One group should focus on literature, one on drama, and one on music. Ask each group to gather examples that attempt to answer the question: "What is art?"

DEVELOPING A PORTFOLIO

Presentation. Inform students that the purpose of a portfolio is to exhibit their competence as an artist. A portfolio is most effective when it showcases strengths and minimizes weaknesses. Students will need to pay close attention to the selection and the order of the pieces they include. Students should keep in mind a portfolio reflects their pride in their work. It should never be incomplete, presented late, or carelessly put together. A student's sincere concern with the formalities of presentation and attention to detail could influence the overall impact their portfolio has on evaluators.

Exploring Art

Focus

Lesson Objectives

After studying this lesson, students will be able to:

■ Provide their own definition for art.

■ Identify and describe the different forms of art.

■ Identify the decisions that must be made when creating art.

■ Identify the decisions that must be made when examining a work created by another artist.

■ Name community resources where art can be viewed and studied.

Building Vocabulary

On the board list the vocabulary terms for the lesson. Point to each term and ask students to raise their hands if they feel confident they could define or paraphrase it. Encourage students to watch for the appearance of these terms in the text and, where necessary, consider how they might revise their definitions.

Motivator

Ask students to name ten famous artists that you write on the chalkboard without referring to the text. Then ask them to discuss what they know about these artists. In addition to artistic skill, what traits do these artists have in common? Were all these artists successful in their lifetimes? Did the lack of success experienced by some deter them in their desire to create art? Read aloud and have students react to the following quote by George Bernard Shaw: "The artist will let his wife starve, his children go barefoot, and his mother drudge for a living at 70 sooner than work at anything but his art."

Exploring Art

Vocabulary
■ visual arts
■ fine arts
■ applied arts

Discover
After completing this lesson, you will be able to:

■ Identify the essential difference between fine arts and applied arts.

■ Discuss why cultures and artists create art.

■ Explain the benefits of studying art.

■ Identify art sources within a community.

*W*hy do people choose to make, perform, and respond to art? After all, it is not necessary to create or experience art in order to ensure physical survival. Art is not needed to maintain life in the way that food, clothing, and shelter are. Yet, humans have persisted in creating every form of art since earliest times (Figure 1.2). The desire to create, perform, and appreciate works of art is universal among humans. Just what is it that has made, and continues to make, art so special in the lives of all people? To answer that question we must first arrive at a definition for art in general and then, more specifically, for the visual arts.

What Is Art?

The arts are a basic form of human communication. The visual arts, music, literature, and poetry may be considered the means by which people, past and present, express themselves in unique sights and sounds that capture the interest, imagination, and appreciation of others.

■ **FIGURE 1.2** The tombs of important Egyptians included painted relief sculptures like this. What signs of the artist's skill can you identify in this ancient work?

Nina de Garis Davies. *Goldsmiths and Joiners.* Copy of an Ancient Egyptian wall painting from a tomb at Thebes. 20th century. Watercolor. The British Museum, London, England.

6

LESSON ONE RESOURCES

Teacher's Classroom Resources

📁 Appreciating Cultural Diversity 1

📁 Cooperative Learning 1

📁 Enrichment Activity 1

📁 Reproducible Lesson Plan 1

📁 Reteaching Activity 1

📁 Study Guide 1

■ **FIGURE 1.3** This American artist has been immensely popular since 1948, when he exhibited his famous painting entitled *Christina's World*. **Do you feel that the artist succeeded in creating a lifelike picture? What features do you find especially realistic?**

Andrew Wyeth. *Soaring.* 1950. Tempera on masonite. 130 × 221 cm (48 × 87″). Shelburne Museum, Shelburne, Vermont.

Arriving at a more specific definition for the visual arts may not sound too difficult at first—until you realize that this task has challenged scholars throughout history. Great philosophers, including the ancient Greeks Plato and Aristotle, have attempted to define the nature of art and understand its unique contribution to human life. In their efforts to define art, scholars have tried to establish the qualities that identify an object as a work of art. You may find that your own ideas about art take into account some of the same qualities noted by scholars:

- Art should mirror reality. It must look like something seen in the real world (Figure 1.3).
- Art must be pleasing to the eye, even if it is not realistic (Figure 1.4).
- Art should express the artist's ideas, beliefs, and feelings so that others can understand them (Figure 1.5, page 8).

Perhaps you feel that *all* these qualities are important, although they need not all be evident in the same work. After all, some works are successful because they do look real.

■ **FIGURE 1.4** This sculpture is composed of colored metal parts that have been welded together. **Does it appear to be heavy or light, strong or fragile? Do you find it visually appealing?**

Nancy Graves. *Zaga.* 1983. Cast bronze with polychrome chemical patination. 182.9 × 124.5 × 81.3 cm (72 × 49 × 32″). The Nelson-Atkins Museum of Art. Kansas City, Missouri (Gift of the Friends of Art). © Nancy Graves Foundation/Licensed by VAGA, New York, New York.

Chapter 1 *Art and You* **7**

Introducing the Lesson

Ask students to examine Figures 1.3, 1.4, and 1.5. Have them identify the ones they find most appealing and least appealing on a slip of paper. Tally the results on the chalkboard. Determine the most appealing work. Have students who responded to the work as most appealing explain why. Have students who judged this same work as least appealing explain their decision. Turn students' attention to the least appealing work and ask those who respond to it in that manner their reasons. Have students who judge this same work as most appealing provide reasons for their answers. Ask students what they learned from this discussion.

TEACH
Art Criticism

Tell students that one of the purposes of art criticism is to describe a work of art *thoroughly*. Divide the class into groups of three or four students, and give each group an illustration of a familiar object cut from a magazine or catalog. Have each group prepare a description of the object and orally present it to the class *without naming it*. After each presentation, ask the students if they can identify the object.

Art History

Select a team of two or three students to conduct a library search of Andrew Wyeth. Instruct them to bring in an illustration of his painting *Christina's World* and explain the circumstances surrounding the creation of this painting. Ask the class why they think this painting became so well known.

Art History

Ask students to imagine they are art historians living several centuries in the future. What might they be able to learn about Western Culture after studying Barbara Hepworth's "newly discovered" *Figure* (Figure 1.6)? Is there a work illustrated in the text that might be more helpful in shedding light on life in the twentieth-century?

Studio Skills

Instruct students to create a work of art in 15 minutes using any medium. Do not give any additional instructions. Tell students to keep a written account of the decisions they made at each step of the creative process. Have them compare their decisions with those identified in this lesson.

Critical Thinking

Have students extend their application of the questions posed in the lesson by asking: *Why study _____?*, (e.g., science, history, or language). Encourage students to think about the rationale behind required classes. The discussion need not be confined solely to subjects included in the high school curriculum. It may be extended to include such areas as medicine, astronomy, and oceanography.

■ **FIGURE 1.5** This artist used his imagination to create figures noted for their humor as well as their seriousness. **Do you think this work succeeds in expressing despair?**

Hugo Robus. *Despair.* 1927. Bronze. 34.9 × 34.9 × 24.8 cm (13³/₄ × 13³/₄ × 9³/₄"). Whitney Museum of American Art, New York, New York. Museum purchase.

■ **FIGURE 1.6** Hepworth was a student of nature and applied what she learned to her work in sculpture. **Can you see how these sculptures may have been influenced by nature? Can you identify some of the features that suggest the human figure?**

Barbara Hepworth. *Two Figures.* 1947–48. Elmwood with white paint. 96.5 × 68.6 × 58.4 cm (38 × 27 × 23"). Frederick R. Weisman Art Museum, University of Minnesota, Minneapolis, Minnesota. Gift of John Rood Sculpture Collection.

8 Unit One *Creating and Understanding Art*

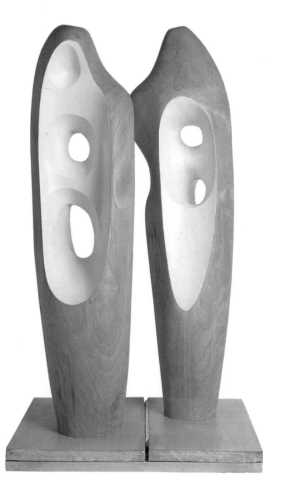

Others do not mirror reality, but are still pleasing to the eye. Still others do not look lifelike and are not visually appealing, but succeed in communicating ideas or feelings. If you take into account all these qualities, you can define **visual arts** as *unique expressions of ideas, beliefs, experiences, and feelings presented in well-designed visual forms.*

Various Forms of Art

Artists use their imaginations, creativity, and skills to express themselves in a tangible, visually appealing way. Whenever you paint a picture, sculpt a figure with clay, or express

CULTURAL DIVERSITY

Sculpture. Point out to students that the sculpture of different cultures has had a major influence on certain European artists such as the founder of Fauvism, Henri Matisse. Have students form research committees and investigate, in art encyclopedias or other library resources, the links between various non-European cultures and Western art. For example, Matisse was also profoundly influenced by Near Eastern art. Committees can place their findings in a classroom file to be used later as a resource for reports and reference.

yourself in a song, a dance, or a poem, you are creating art. However, art can take different forms. Two primary forms are fine arts and applied arts.

Fine Arts

In the visual arts, **fine arts** refers to *painting, sculpture, and architecture, arts which have no practical function and are valued in terms of the visual pleasure they provide or their success in communicating ideas or feelings* (Figure 1.6). The one exception is architecture, which involves designing structures that strive to be *both* attractive and functional. A building's primary purpose, however,

is to provide shelter and service other human needs. Therefore, architecture is also considered a form of applied arts.

Applied Arts

There is no clear dividing line between fine arts and applied arts. The term **applied arts** is most often used to describe *the design or decoration of functional objects to make them pleasing to the eye.* Made either by hand or by machine, works of applied art are intended primarily to serve a useful function (Figure 1.7). Artists who create applied arts or crafts are usually referred to as designers, artisans, or craftspeople.

■ **FIGURE 1.7** The designs created by craftspeople are often highly complex and skillful. What impresses you most about this work, its design or its practical usefulness?

Maria and Julian Martinez. Black-on-black storage jar. 1942. Clay shaped by Maria and design painted by Julian. 47.6 × 56 cm (18³/₄ × 22″). Courtesy of the Museum of New Mexico, Santa Fe, New Mexico. School of American Research Collections.

Aesthetics

Instruct each student to bring an example of applied art to class they consider attractive and functional. (A photograph can be used.) Have students explain *why* they think it is attractive. Ask them to point out how the design enhances the object's function. If they were asked to improve on the appearance or the design of the object, what would they do? Ask them if they think the appearance of the object was a major consideration of the manufacturer. Can students think of any product that failed to sell because the public found it unattractive or poorly designed? Can they think of any product that has remained popular over the years because it is attractive and well designed?

Studio Skills

Have students use pencil and sketch paper to create an attractive new design for a stapler. The stapler must look like no other stapler and yet be capable of performing in the same efficient manner as all other staplers. Exhibit the drawings and have each student explain why his or her stapler is an improvement over existing models. This exercise gives students insights into the task faced by applied artists.

Art History

Point out that the work in Figure 1.7 can be identified as *both* fine art and applied art. Ask them to find other examples of works in the text that fit both categories. Explain that throughout history, the distinction between fine art and applied art has been blurred by works that are beautiful and serve a functional purpose. An excellent example is the instructional medieval stained glass windows seen in Chapter 15.

COOPERATIVE LEARNING

Art Survey. Have students brainstorm a list of questions that might be included in a survey of public attitudes about art and artists. Questions might include: How often do you visit a museum? Have you ever been to an art gallery? Do you have a favorite artist? What is your knowledge of art history? Once a list has been compiled, divide the class into groups of three or four students. Have each group choose a different group of people (i.e., teachers, family and friends, or merchants) and survey that group. Allow time for students to tabulate and compare their findings. In a classroom discussion, encourage them to speculate about their conclusions.

Art History

Review with students some of the sources of inspiration artists have historically turned to (e.g., personal visions, historical events, literature). Ask students what might most motivate or guide works they would create. Next, ask them to consider how their artistic inspiration might be influenced, positively or negatively, by the expectations of a patron.

Cross Curriculum

LANGUAGE ARTS. Point out that the effort to create works that are functional and visually pleasing is not limited to the visual arts. Have students identify examples of writing (e.g., advertisements or newspaper articles) that attempt to meet both goals. Ask if they think art created "for art's sake" is better or more desirable than art produced to serve a particular function.

Art History

Without reference to the text, ask students to name as many women artists as possible. Write their responses on the chalkboard. If they have difficulty naming many artists, ask them why. Ask students to speculate on the reasons why history fails to record the accomplishments of more women artists. Direct them to the text and ask them to identify the period in which the first woman artist is identified. As a written assignment, have each student write a brief biography of a contemporary woman artist.

Why Art Is Created

Art of some kind has been created by cultures throughout the course of history. This prompts the question: Why do cultures create art? Although it would be impossible to list all the reasons, the following warrant consideration:

- **Aesthetics.** Some cultures create art simply for its visual appeal and for the pleasure it brings to those who understand and appreciate the creative efforts of artists. In Chapter 4 you will learn to identify the various aesthetic qualities inherent in works of art. These aesthetic qualities must be taken into account to understand and judge works of art.

- **Morals/Ethics.** In many cultures art is used to depict people and behaviors that are considered noble and good. (See Figure 20.7, page 451.)

■ FIGURE 1.8 This is no ordinary mask. It combines realism and bold abstraction to create a work of mystery and power. The mask was created to bridge the gap between this world and the world of spirits. **How does an understanding of its purpose affect your appreciation of this mask?**

Mask. From Zaire River coastal area, Zaire-Angola. Africa. 20th century. Wood. H: 22.8 cm (9″). Kimbell Art Museum, Fort Worth, Texas.

10 **Unit One** *Creating and Understanding Art*

- **Spirituality.** Works of art are often considered a means of connecting people with supernatural forces. A carved mask from Africa (Figure 1.8), for example, represents the spirit of a dead ancestor called upon to help regulate the political, cultural, and social life of the community. Some cultures also rely on art to tell the stories and lessons associated with their religions.

- **History.** Many artworks provide valuable information about important people, places, and events. (See Figure 10.25, page 234.) Paintings and sculpture often reveal how people looked and dressed, and they even record their behavior and accomplishments. Pictures also illustrate places and significant events and reveal how artists felt about them.

- **Politics.** Art serves as a tool of persuasion or propaganda when it is used to convince people to adopt a certain point of view or to enhance the power of a ruler or political party. (See Figure 21.3, page 468.) The power of art to inspire patriotism or cultural spirit is undeniable. (See Figure 5.2, page 107.)

Knowing *why* an artwork was created can help you gain a better understanding of the artist as an individual and of the culture within which that artist worked.

Why Artists Create

Knowing the various purposes served by art does not explain why individuals create art. Are they motivated by the promise of great wealth? This might seem to be the case with some very successful artists. One of these was the fifteenth-century Italian painter Titian (**tish**-un) (Figure l.9). Titian's fame as a painter to kings and nobles enabled him to earn huge commissions and to live like a prince.

However, not all artists were as fortunate. The Dutch artist Rembrandt (**rem**-brant) spent his last days bankrupt, living as a lonely hideaway. His countryman, Frans Hals (frahns hahls), died in a poorhouse and was buried in a pauper's grave.

Do artists create as a means of gaining recognition and glory? Actually, the quest for

■ **FIGURE 1.9** Titian painted this full-scale oil sketch to serve as a model from which official portraits of the Spanish king could be made. **Why do you think parts of this painting were left unfinished? What hints does this portrait offer about the personality of King Philip II?**

Titian. *Portrait of Philip II.* c. 1549–51. Cincinnati Art Museum, Cincinnati, Ohio. Bequest of Mary M. Emery.

Art History

Tell students the art of different cultures has had an influence on European artists such as Pablo Picasso. Have students form research committees and investigate, using library resources, the links between non-European art forms and Western art. For example, Picasso was greatly influenced by African art. Committees can place their findings in a classroom file to be used later as a resource for reference.

Critical Thinking

Appoint a committee of students to research the history of museums and report their findings to the class. Discuss how the purposes and use of museums have changed over the centuries. In addition to exhibiting important works of art, what do contemporary museums do to inform people about artists and works of art? What more could they do in this regard?

Did You Know?

Direct students' attention to Titian's painting (Figure 1.9). Inform them that in the history of art, Titian's lived the longest and his worldly fame and success were the least interrupted. He was mainly an artist of the nobility. Among his patrons were the infamous Lucrezia Borgia and the powerful Emperor Charles V, who made Titian a knight and a count. He died in a plague that killed one-quarter of the population of Venice, the city in which he lived and worked. While others were loaded into carts at night and carried off to a remote island for burial, Titian was given a lavish burial in a church adorned with his paintings.

personal recognition that we see in Western cultures today is relatively new in art. During the Middle Ages, the names of most artists were unknown. Artists wanted to create art that glorified God, not themselves.

This changed during the Renaissance, when artists hoped to gain fame through their art. Many earned the respect and admiration of society. Not all succeeded, however. For example, Judith Leyster (**lie**-ster) was completely ignored for generations after her death in 1660, because, as a woman, she was considered incapable of producing significant art. Her paintings were attributed to another Dutch artist, Frans Hals, until her signature

was accidentally discovered on a work previously credited to Hals. This prompted scholars to re-examine her paintings. They recognized that paintings like Leyster's *Boy Playing the Flute* (Figure 1.10, page 12) were the work of a very accomplished artist.

The Impulse to Create

It seems unlikely that artists create only out of a desire for either wealth or glory. Regardless of the artist's culture or nationality, all artists seem to have one trait in common: they are driven by the impulse to create. Most would admit that they continue to create art simply because they have to; they are not happy doing anything else.

Chapter 1 *Art and You* **11**

More About… **Artists.** Tell students that while some artists like Titian were famous and successful during their lifetimes, others were not recognized until after their deaths. Vincent van Gogh was such an artist. Have students offer their opinions about the reasons for this change in public opinion over time. Discuss the reasons why Titian enjoyed fame, while van Gogh was ignored, during their lifetimes. Ask students what van Gogh could have done to gain recognition from his contemporaries? Why did he choose not to do this?

Aesthetics

Ask students if they think the sale price of an artwork should be taken into consideration when determining its aesthetic merits. Should Vincent van Gogh be regarded as a great painter and his *Portrait of Dr. Gachet* a masterpiece because it sold for $82.5 million dollars? What other things should be taken into consideration when attempting to determine the importance of an artist and the aesthetic value of his or her work? Are these things more important in judging a work of art than the amount of money paid for it? Inform students that during his lifetime van Gogh sold only one painting—for 400 francs at an exhibition in Brussels. The identity of the painting remains a mystery.

Critical Thinking

Call attention to the claim that art is more popular today than ever before. Ask students why they agree or disagree with that claim. If they agree, to what do they attribute this popularity? Have interested students prepare a panel discussion on this topic. Appoint a moderator and student participants to represent varying opinions. Encourage the rest of the class to ask the panel questions after the discussion.

■ **FIGURE 1.10** This painting is skillfully designed. It also succeeds in expressing a quiet, restful mood. What kind of music do you think the boy is playing? What makes you think so?

Judith Leyster. *Boy Playing the Flute.* c. 1609–60. Oil on canvas. 73 × 62 cm (28³/₄ × 24¹/₂″). National Museum, Stockholm, Sweden.

Examples of this single-minded dedication are found throughout art history. The proud, restless, and irritable Japanese artist Katsushika Hokusai (kah-tsoo-**shee**-kah **ho**-koo-sigh), for example, was so consumed with the need to create that he provided illustrations for novels, poems, calendars, greeting cards, and even popular, inexpensive publications similar to modern comic books. It has been estimated that he illustrated 437 different volumes and enriched the art of Japan with no fewer than 30,000 pictures. (See Figure 4.1, page 84.)

Clearly, for an artist like Hokusai, art is not a means of livelihood or glory. Art is life itself—life dominated by and often complicated by the overpowering impulse to create.

More About... **Judith Leyster.** In 1609, in the Dutch city of Haarlem, at a time when women seeking art careers were often helped by artist fathers, Judith Leyster, a brewer's daughter, had to rely on talent alone. Her choice of subject matter was quite different from other female painters. Instead of delicate still lifes, Leyster did robust genre paintings and portraits. By 17, she had gained a reputation as an artist of great promise. Leyster learned from other major painters of her day. She was influenced by the brush technique of Franz Hals, and the use of light in the work of Caravaggio. However, her works have a look that on careful inspection, is unmistakably hers. Her portraits seem to invite the viewer in, as if subject and viewer were close friends.

Art in Your Life

You might wonder why you should involve yourself in the creation of art. When you create original works of art, you experience the creative process, and you develop your own capabilities for self-expression. Presented with a puzzling visual problem, you learn how to approach the problem and resolve it as an artist might.

Self-Expression

Assume for a moment that you want to express an idea or emotion in a work of art. As you paint, draw, or sculpt, you look for ways to convey this idea or feeling to others. This task involves more than manipulating material with your hands; it also requires that you use your mind and draw upon your emotions. To illustrate this point, suppose that two artists decide to paint the same subject—a landscape that both identify with the same title: *Starry Night*. However, the completed paintings have little in common. Why? Because each artist created a version of the scene that reflected his own personal ideas and feelings.

One artist used his painting to communicate personal emotions in a subtle and poetic manner (Figure 1.11). With limited colors and simplified forms, he pictured a world marked by the melancholy and loneliness he experienced throughout his life.

■ **FIGURE 1.11** Munch sold few paintings during his lifetime. He left nearly all his works to his native city of Oslo, Norway. What color dominates in this painting? How does this color help express the mood of the work?

Edvard Munch. *Starry Night.* 1893. Oil on canvas. 135 × 140 cm (53³/₈ × 55¹/₈″). The J. Paul Getty Museum, Los Angeles, California.

Art Criticism

Tell students to imagine they are art critics reviewing an exhibition in which the works illustrated in Lesson One are on display. Instruct them to pick out one work and write a positive or negative critique of it. Collect these critiques and save them for comparison with critiques to be done after students have learned how to use the art criticism operations (See Chapter 4).

Art History

Write the name of a different artist or artwork identified in the text on note cards, 3 × 5 inches. Pass these out to students. Tell them to visit the school or community library and find out as much as they can about the artist or artwork on their card. Have them record this information in writing. Collect these assignments. Pass them out to the proper student as each artist or artwork is encountered in subsequent discussions. Students can add to the discussion by referring to this collected information.

𝒯eacher 𝒩otes

Classroom Files. Classroom files of various types can be extremely helpful in many ways. A file (such as the one specified in the Art History activity above) containing information on artists and artworks to be discussed later, can supplement information provided in the text. It can also encourage students who may be reluctant to participate in class discussions to speak up by providing them with something relevant to say.

Studio Skills

Tell students artists often encounter and seek solutions to various artistic problems during the course of creating a work of art. Frequently they must "think their way" to these solutions. Tell students to think *their* way to a solution of the following problem:

Use colored pencils and sketch paper to draw an animal that is small, with a long nose, ears, and tail. The tail is hairless and can hold or grab onto limbs in climbing. It has claws resembling those of a bear. The best-known species is about the size of a cat, is gray in color, and has woolly fur. Have students compare their drawings with each other. When they are finished, have students compare their drawings to a photograph of an opossum, the animal described.

Study Guide

Distribute *Study Guide* 1 in the TCR. Assist students in reviewing key concepts. 📁

Art and Humanities

Have students complete *Cooperative Learning* 1, "What Is Art?" in the TCR. In this activity students read a profile of artist Andy Goldsworthy and discuss the philosophical implications of questions such as the following: What is art? Who is an artist? 📁

The other artist used vigorous brush strokes, pure colors, and the distortion of natural forms to illustrate a different emotional reaction to the night sky (Figure 1.12). His painting captures the energy and creative forces of nature—stars spinning and swirling violently above a quiet, unsuspecting village.

Creating art offers you the opportunity to express your own ideas and emotions. Studying the art created by others enables you to share the ideas and emotions expressed by others—and in the process to recognize and appreciate the differences that distinguish us all as unique individuals.

Decision Making and Problem Solving

Whenever you create art or examine the art created by someone else, you engage in two important activities: decision making and problem solving. Creating a work of art involves decision-making tasks for all artists. These are some of the decisions you face:

- What subject should I paint or sculpt?
- Which medium and technique should I use?

- What colors, shapes, lines, and textures should I emphasize?
- How can I arrange those colors, shapes, lines, and textures most effectively?
- How will I recognize that the work is finished and the creative process has ended?

You have already seen how two artists painting the same subject—the night sky—arrived at two different solutions after making these kinds of decisions. Consider all the decisions both artists made before setting aside their paints and brushes. These are the same kinds of decisions you must face every time you become involved in making art.

Creating art also requires problem-solving skills. Artistic creation involves the exploration of an open-ended problem that has no "right" answer. With every drawing, every sculpture, and every work you create, you try to solve the problems involved in clarifying, interpreting, and communicating what is important to you.

Critically examining a work of art involves similar decision-making and problem-solving activities. These are some of the tasks of the serious viewer:

■ **FIGURE 1.12** Like Munch, van Gogh received little public recognition during his lifetime. He sold only one painting. **In what ways is this painting similar to the painting with the same title by Munch? How are the two paintings different?**

Vincent van Gogh. *The Starry Night.* 1889. Oil on canvas. 73.7 × 92.1 cm (29 × 36¼″). The Museum of Modern Art, New York, New York. Acquired through the Lillie P. Bliss Bequest.

More About... **Post-Impressionists.** Vincent van Gogh, Paul Gauguin, and Paul Cézanne belonged to an art movement (a group of artists with similar styles and goals) called Post-Impressionism. The term *Post-Impressionism* was first used in a showing of Post-Impressionist works in 1919, several years after some of the most important artists of the movement were dead. The exhibition was met with laughter and derision by the public and anger and scorn by critics. In spite of this initial response, the artworks and ideals of the Post-Impressionists ultimately paved the way for some of the most important art movements of the twentieth century.

- Identify the subject depicted in the artwork.
- Determine the medium and technique used.
- Identify the colors, shapes, lines, and textures, and note how they are organized.
- Decide whether the work is successful, and be prepared to defend that judgment with good reasons.

Real-World Connections

There is another, more practical reason for creating and critically viewing art—a reason expressed more and more frequently in the workplace. Leaders in business and industry point to a need for creativity in the modern workplace. They note that the arts help build ideas and nurture a place in the mind for original ideas to take hold and grow. Businesses today require knowledgeable and sensitive workers with a wide range of higher-order thinking skills, the kind of thinking skills one gains when creating and viewing art.

An art education helps build a variety of important thinking skills that can be applied to real-world situations. It provides important experience in following each step in the problem-solving process:

- Clarify the problem.
- Identify possible solutions.
- Test each possible solution.
- Select the solution that seems most appropriate.
- Apply the chosen solution.
- Determine whether the solution resolves the problem.

An art education also nourishes an appreciation of differing points of view, flexible thinking, and self-discipline. Further, it helps you recognize the importance of collaboration and teamwork. Art experiences can help you become a decision maker, a problem solver, and an imaginative and creative thinker. These are precisely the kinds of skills that businesses value today. These skills explain why an arts education is now generally regarded as basic and vital.

Arts in Your Community

Art is more popular today than ever. Every day, people visit galleries and museums to see works created by famous—and not-so-famous—artists. Movies and television programs feature the lives of artists, and newspapers regularly record the sale of noteworthy artworks. Many people report that viewing art provides them with a sense of pleasure and adds meaning to their lives.

It is not surprising, then, that almost every community offers opportunities to view and learn about art. These opportunities include museums, exhibits, libraries, and other sites.

Museums

The function of a museum is to encourage the enjoyment of art through direct interaction with original works of art. Museums identify and display artworks that have been judged to be significant by members of the art community (Figure 1.13).

■ FIGURE 1.13 Museums today enable people to become personally involved with actual works of art representing every age and time period. **What are some of the things you can learn during a museum visit?**

J. Paul Getty Museum at the Getty Center, Los Angeles, California.

Chapter 1 *Art and You* **15**

Studio Activities

Have students review the three aesthetic theories presented in the lesson. In particular, call their attention to the emotionalist theory. Then assign *Studio* 1, "Collaging Your Day," in the TCR. This worksheet helps students create an expressive collage representing events of a day in their lives. 📂

ASSESS

Checking Comprehension

Have students complete the lesson review questions. Answers appear in the box below.

Reteaching

➤ Assign *Reteaching* 1, found in the TCR. Have students complete the activity and review their responses. 📂

➤ Provide photographs that show examples of fine art and applied art. Have students work in pairs to identify the category to which each work belongs.

Enrichment

Assign students *Enrichment* 1, "Decoding Credit Lines," in the TCR. Students will learn the important information contained in credit lines accompanying artworks. 📁

Extension

➢ Have students read and complete *Appreciating Cultural Diversity* 1, "Artists as Living National Treasures," in the TCR. In this activity, students learn how Japan honors its artists and craftspeople. It invites students to explore ways to elevate the status of artists in their school and the United States. 📁

➢ Have students select artworks that were originally created as applied art and are now recognized as fine art (e.g., needlepoint, tapestry, ornate Japanese kimonos). Then have students research the circumstances under which these works were created and the factors that explain why they are now viewed differently.

CLOSE

Ask students: If a person wants to become an artist, what important qualities should he or she have, or attempt to develop?

Museums provide visitors with various opportunities to learn about the works on display. Information about artists and their works is available in brief overviews, exhibition catalogues, and other publications found in the museum bookstore. Often, guides lead tours, during which they share information and answer questions about artworks. Museums also invite guest speakers and sponsor special workshops, many of which include studio activities.

In addition to their permanent collections, museums frequently present special exhibits that feature the works of a particular artist or artworks borrowed from other collections. These special exhibits usually include presentations made by artists, art historians, art critics, or other speakers who share information and insights about the works on display.

Exhibits

Many different kinds of art exhibits are provided in almost every community. Local artists may exhibit their works in galleries, shopping malls, schools, libraries, office buildings, and other locations. Visiting these exhibits gives you a chance to see what subjects artists choose to paint and how they work with various media to interpret those subjects.

Libraries and Online Resources

Certainly one of the best sources of information about art and artists is the library. There, encyclopedias and other reference books offer overviews and basic facts about artists' lives and works. For more in-depth information, biographies are also available. Beginning and advanced students can find books that explain various techniques for using art media. History and art history books present different approaches to the study of art, from prehistoric times to the present. Magazines and art periodicals feature articles about artists, art periods, and art styles. Many libraries also maintain collections of films and videotapes that profile famous artists and artworks.

Computers can be used at home or at school to research art-related topics, artists, and artworks. In addition, libraries are often equipped with computers that can be used by patrons. You can use a computer to view CD-ROMs that feature the art collections of the world's most famous museums or to access the Internet. The Internet can be used as a resource to obtain information on artists and artworks. You can visit the Web sites of museums and galleries, as well as artists' personal Web pages. These online resources offer many possibilities for exploring art.

LESSON ONE REVIEW

Reviewing Art Facts

1. Explain how fine arts differ from applied arts.
2. What valuable kinds of activities does one engage in when creating or examining works of art?
3. Why is an arts education valued by today's leaders in business and industry?
4. Identify three places where a person can obtain information about art and artists.

Activity... *Personal Logos*

The work of artists is all around us every day. Think about your home, your clothing, or electronic equipment. Everything we use is touched by an artist at some point. The artist can no longer be defined as a person who just creates beautiful paintings. As an example, products we use every day are identified by symbols called logos that are created by artists called graphic designers.

Create a personal logo as a visual symbol of you and your life. Research logos in newspapers, magazines, the Internet, and other media. Bring examples to share with your class. Using sketch paper and colored pencils, sketch images that have a personal meaning for you and combine them into a logo as a symbol of yourself.

LESSON ONE REVIEW

Answers to Reviewing Art Facts

1. Fine art does not require a practical function. Applied art refers to functional objects.
2. Decision-making and problem-solving.
3. In addition to developing problem-solving and decision-making skills, learning in art nourishes an appreciation of differing points of view, flexible thinking, and self-discipline and stresses the importance of teamwork.
4. Art exhibits, museums, and libraries.

Activity...*Personal Logos*

Have students brainstorm examples of logos in business, advertising, or entertainment. Encourage students who are interested to create their own original logos for this project and save their creations in their portfolios.

Understanding Art

Vocabulary
- aesthetics
- criteria

Discover
After completing this lesson, you will be able to:
- Explain the distinction between art media and art process.
- Explain what art criticism and art history involve.
- Discuss the benefits of including studio experiences in a study of art.

*C*reating a work of art that succeeds in expressing your ideas and feelings can be fulfilling and satisfying. Gaining an understanding and appreciation for a work of art created by another artist can be equally satisfying. However, both kinds of experiences require preparation, the kind of preparation this book is designed to provide.

The Visual Vocabulary of Art

This book will help you acquire the skills necessary to understand, judge, and support your personal decisions about a variety of visual art forms. It will also provide you with opportunities to engage in the decision-making and problem-solving activities associated with creating your own art forms. However, in order to do both, you must first learn the vocabulary of art.

Artists use many different colors, values, lines, textures, shapes, forms, and space relationships to create their artworks. These are called the *elements of art*, and they are used by artists in countless combinations. If you are to fully understand a painting, a sculpture, or a building, you will need to recognize the elements of art within each and discover for yourself how they are being used (Figure 1.14). In Chapter 2 you will learn how to do this. This knowledge will not only add to your understanding of how others create, it will also help you express yourself through art. A visual vocabulary then, is essential when you are trying to do the following:

- Gain insights into the artworks produced by others.
- Create your own artworks with different media and techniques.

Media and Processes

In order to create art, artists use a variety of different materials. Almost any material can function as an art medium, provided artists are able to mark with it, bend it, or shape it to suit their purposes. Art media are usually distinguished by whether they can be used to make marks on a two-dimensional surface, as in drawing or painting, or can be manipulated as a three-dimensional form, as in sculpture. Pencils, charcoal, paint, clay, stone, and metal are all common art media. Recently, this list of media has been expanded to

■ **FIGURE 1.14** This artist successfully combines traditional and contemporary features in her paintings of beautiful women—long a popular subject in Japanese art. **How many art elements can you identify in this painting? Is any one more important than the others?**

Uemura Shoen. *Mother and Child.* 1934. Color on silk. 170 cm × 117 cm (67 × 46"). National Museum of Modern Art, Tokyo, Japan.

17

FOCUS

Lesson Objectives
After studying this lesson, students will be able to:
- Identify the elements of art.
- Explain the difference between art media and art process.
- Point out how art criticism and art history differ.

Building Vocabulary
Tell students the more extensive the vocabulary, the sharper the perception. Ask them to use as many words as possible to describe "the white stuff falling from the sky in the winter." Then tell them that the peoples living near the Arctic Circle have a great many words to describe snow. An extensive vocabulary benefits anyone wishing to see and respond to as much as possible in works of art.

Motivator
Before reading this lesson, write the terms *art criticism* and *art history* on the chalkboard. Ask students to arrive at a definition for each that all can agree to. Leave these definitions on the board until after the lesson is read. Then ask students if their definitions point out that art criticism derives information from a work of art, while art history gathers information about a work of art.

Introducing the Lesson
Tell students to imagine they are creating an artwork of their own. When they are finished with their work, how do they decide if it is successful? This lesson is an introduction to an art criticism approach that will make it easier for them to evaluate their own artwork and the works of other artists.

TEACH

Art Criticism

List the elements of art on the chalkboard. Ask students to identify the various ways each of these elements could be used in a work of art (e.g., colors could be complex, lines could be repeated, shapes could be balanced). Ask students if they know the term used to identify the various ways the elements can be used. Write the term, *principles of art* on the chalkboard. Under it list *balance, emphasis, harmony, variety, gradation, movement and rhythm,* and *proportion.* Tell students they will learn about these principles of art in Chapter 2. In Chapter 4, they will learn how an examination of these principles is important in understanding and judging works of art.

Aesthetics

Write the words *aesthetics* and *aesthetician* on the chalkboard, and review the definitions for each. Then write the words *aesthetic experience* and tell students this describes a person's intelligent and sensitive response to a work of art. Tell students to imagine they are standing in front of a masterpiece by a famous artist. Have them speculate what they must do to ensure pleasure and satisfaction from this experience—in other words, what they must do to have an aesthetic experience.

Studio Skills

Ask students to list the elements of art on a sheet of paper. Have them write an adjective before each of these elements (e.g., *red* color, *angular* shape, *rough* texture). Instruct them to create a composition with torn or cut colored construction in which they use the elements as described on their list.

include the computer. Almost anything can be used by artists to express themselves in visual form (Figure 1.15).

The difference between art media and art process is important. Art media consist of the *materials* the artist uses to create artworks. Art process is the *action* involved in making art. Examples of art processes include drawing, painting, printmaking, modeling, weaving, digitizing, and casting.

■ FIGURE 1.15 This work—one of the largest sculptures in the world— consists of 60 automobiles embedded in concrete. **What do you think the artist was trying to say with this work?**

Arman. *Long-Term Parking.* 1982. Autos in concrete. 18.2 × 6.1 × 6.1 m (60 × 20 × 20′). Le Montcel Park, Jouy-en-Josas, France.

Once you have mastered a vocabulary of art and gained a knowledge of the various art media and processes, you will be prepared to learn how aesthetics, art criticism, and art history can be used to gather information from and about works of art.

Understanding Aesthetics

What is meant by the term *aesthetics?* **Aesthetics** is *a branch of philosophy concerned with identifying the criteria that are used to understand, judge, and defend judgments about works of art.* An *aesthetician* is a scholar who specializes in identifying the criteria to be used in determining the significance of artworks.

Aestheticians share a concern for the study of art with art critics and art historians. However, art critics and art historians operate from two different points of view. Art critics direct their attention to a thorough examination of works of art. They ask and then answer questions that enable them to gain information *from* those works. With this information, they can make intelligent judgments about the success of artworks. Art historians, on the other hand, seek objective facts *about* works of art and the artists who created them. Their efforts include gathering information on major art periods and on styles of different times and places. Historians research the lives and works of leading artists, and chronicle the development of art from the distant past to the present day.

Studying Art Criticism

Have you ever been asked to express your opinion about a work of art? Imagine that, while visiting an art museum with a friend, you stop to look closely at a particular painting. Noticing your interest, your friend asks, "Well, what do you think of it?" In situations like this, when you are asked to provide a judgment about a work of art, you are cast in the role of an art critic. You assume this role whenever you try to learn as much as you can from an artwork in order to determine whether or not it is successful.

 Technology

National Gallery of Art Videodisc Use the following images as examples of more works by artists introduced in this lesson.

Paul Cézanne
Landscape near Paris

Search Frame 1432

Paul Cézanne
Houses in Provence

Search Frame 1436

Paul Cézanne
Still Life with Apples and Peaches

Search Frame 1460

Use Glencoe's *Correlation Bar Code Guide to the National Gallery of Art* to locate more artworks.

The Art Criticism Operations

Many people seem to think that art criticism is very complicated and difficult. This is simply not true. Art criticism can be easily learned and will add a great deal of interest and excitement to your encounters with art. You can think of art criticism as an orderly way of looking at and talking about art. It is a method used to gather information *from* the work of art itself.

To gain information from a work of art, you must know two things: what to look for and how to look for it. In Chapter 4, you will become more familiar with the aesthetic qualities you should be prepared to look for when examining a work. Those qualities represent the **criteria,** or *standards of judgment,* you will need when making and supporting decisions about art. You will also learn to use a search strategy that will make the task of finding those qualities in works of art much easier. The search strategy for art criticism consists of four operations, or steps. These operations will be introduced in Chapter 4.

The Value of Art Criticism

Using the art criticism operations enables you to examine and respond to a variety of visual art forms with a more critical eye. You can discover for yourself the aesthetic qualities that elevate certain artworks above others, and experience the satisfaction and pleasure those artworks can provide. At the same time, you will find yourself less likely to accept passively the judgments of others. Instead, you will make and explain your own judgments.

Studying Art History

Have you ever encountered a work of art that you wanted to know more about? Use your imagination to put yourself in the following scene. While helping clean out an attic, you find a picture hidden from view in a dark corner. Examining it closely, you see that it is an oil painting of a young girl holding a fan (Figure 1.16). A number of questions come to mind: Who painted the picture? Is the artist famous? When and where was the work

■ **FIGURE 1.16** Royo is a well-known Spanish artist who often uses his wife and daughter as models for his paintings. **If you could ask the artist one question about this picture, what would it be?**

Royo. *Girl with Fan.* 1997. Agora 3 Gallery, Sitges, Spain.

painted? Is it an important work? In situations like this, when you seek to learn more about a work of art and the artist who created it, you assume the role of an art historian.

The Art History Operations

Works of art are not created in a vacuum. Your understanding of them cannot be complete unless you determine who made them, as well as when, where, how, and why they were made. A complete understanding of a work requires that you learn as much as

Chapter 1 *Art and You* **19**

Art History

Tell students that Paul Cézanne painted *Mont Sainte-Victoire* (Figure 1.17) more than 60 times. Other artists, such as Claude Monet, are also noted for having painted the same subject over and over again. Ask students to speculate on why these artists chose to do this. Was it simply because they were fascinated with the subject, or are other explanations possible?

Aesthetics

Tell students to look closely at José Clemente Orozco's painting of *Zapatistas* (Figure 1.18.) Have them express their initial impressions of this work. Then tell them to use their imaginations to listen to the sounds in the painting. What do they hear? Are these sounds loud or soft? Ask students to speculate on what might be going through the minds of the people in the picture. Have students describe in a single word the feelings this work arouses in them. List these on the chalkboard. Do the feelings indicated by the words have anything in common? Ask students if their initial responses to this work have changed as a consequence of examining it more closely.

Did You Know?

Cézanne's patience was not limited to painting the same mountain over and over again. He required the well-known art dealer Ambroise Vollard to pose 115 times for a single portrait. When it was finished, Cézanne said that he was pleased—with the way he had painted the front of Vollard's shirt!

19

Art Criticism

Write the word *repetition* on the chalkboard. Ask students if they would use this word in describing José Clemente Orozco's painting of *Zapatistas* (Figure 1.18). Ask them to point out places in the work where repetition has been used. What overall effect is created by this use of repetition?

Studio Skills

Ask the class to examine Orozco's painting (Figure 1.18) with attention directed to the artist's efforts to suggest movement. Instruct students to complete a large charcoal drawing in which repetitions of lines and shapes are used to suggest movement in a particular direction. Students may choose to show figures in motion, as in Orozco's painting, or create an abstract design composed entirely of lines and shapes. Place the finished drawings on display and encourage the class to point out the direction of movement in each.

Art History

José Clemente Orozco's way of painting his subjects prompted many to refer to him as "the Mexican Goya." Direct students' attention to Francisco Goya's painting *The Third of May 1808* (Figure 20.13, page 457). Have them compare and contrast this painting with Orozco's (Figure l.l8) and then ask them if they think Orozco merits the title. Have them provide reasons for their answers.

possible about the artist and the circumstances that caused that artist to paint certain subjects in certain ways.

Most people looking at Mont Sainte-Victoire, a rather ordinary mountain in southern France, would probably turn away after a few moments. The artist Paul Cézanne (say-**zahn**) painted this mountain over and over again (Figure 1.17). Why? Because he saw something in this mountain that others failed to see. Repeated efforts to capture what he saw enabled him to arrive at a new style of painting. If you look closely at his painting, you will see that Cézanne used overlapping patches of color to give the mountain a solid, three-dimensional appearance. This had never been done before.

While most people would attach little importance to a group of marching peasants (Figure 1.18), José Clemente Orozco (hoh-**say** cleh-**men**-tay oh-**ross**-coh) recognized the significance of such a scene taking place in Mexico in the early 1930s. For him, these people symbolized the courageous effort of an oppressed people determined to overcome tyranny.

To fully understand and appreciate these two works—or any other work—you must learn about the circumstances that influenced the sight and the insight of the artists who created them.

A search strategy can be just as useful in gathering art history information as it is in gathering art criticism information. The search strategy for art history also consists of four operations or steps. It is important to keep in mind, however, that when it is applied to art history, this search strategy operates from a different point of view. It is used to gather information *about* a work of art rather than information *from* the work. The four operations used in art history will be fully explained in Chapter 5.

The Value of Art History

Art is often considered a kind of mirror to the past, a way of gaining valuable insights into bygone eras. After all, how could anyone fully understand the civilization of ancient Egypt without studying the pyramids? Similarly, a study of the Renaissance would be, at best,

■ **FIGURE 1.17** Paul Cézanne painted more than 60 versions of this mountain. Why do you think an artist would choose to paint the same subject over and over?

Paul Cézanne. *Mont Sainte-Victoire seen from the Bibemus Quarry.* c. 1897. Oil on canvas. 65.1 × 80 cm. (25¹/₂ × 31¹/₂"). Baltimore Museum of Art, Baltimore, Maryland. The Cone Collection, formed by Dr. Claribel Cone and Miss Etta Cone.

20   Unit One *Creating and Understanding Art*

More About...   **Cézanne.** The American painter Mary Cassatt described Cézanne in the following manner: "He looked like a cut-throat with large red eyeballs standing out from his head in a most ferocious manner, a rather fierce-looking pointed beard, quite gray, and an excited way of talking that positively makes the dishes rattle." Later she said she misjudged his appearance, for "far from being fierce and cut-throat, he has the gentlest nature possible, 'like a child' as he would say."

incomplete without reference to the works of Michelangelo (**my**-kel-**an**-jay-lo), or Leonardo da Vinci (lay-oh-**nar**-doh da **vin**-chee).

If we agree that an understanding of the present can be enhanced by a study of the past, then a chronological examination of art makes good sense. By starting at the beginning and observing the development of art from year to year, decade to decade, century to century, we can see that the origins of today's art are to be found in the art of the past. Every period in history is a blend of the past and the present, and the proportions of past and present within that mixture determine the quality of the world at any given moment in time. Art history offers us one way of measuring those proportions—and gaining a better understanding of our time, our place, and ourselves.

Combining Art Criticism and Art History

In Chapter 5 you will learn how to combine the art criticism operations and the art history operations to create a comprehensive search strategy. When examining a work of art, you will begin by drawing on your knowledge of art criticism to gain information *from* the artwork. Then you will turn to art history to gain information *about* the work and the artist who created it. Combining information from both art criticism and art history will enable you to make a final judgment about the artwork.

Why Study Art?

In addition to the satisfaction and pleasure it affords, a study of art will help you gain a better understanding of yourself and those around you. You can begin by studying works created by artists representing cultures and periods different from your own. By studying the creative expressions of artists from all backgrounds, you can become aware of the beliefs, ideas, and feelings of people of various ethnic origins, religions, or cultures.

It may surprise you to learn that by studying art, you prepare yourself for an active role in keeping your culture alive. Artists, writers, and musicians cannot hope to accomplish this task alone. They require your

■ **FIGURE 1.18** This painting shows determined peasants marching forward to participate in the revolution under the leadership of Zapata. **How did the artist suggest the relentless forward movement of these peasants?**

José Clemente Orozco. *Zapatistas.* 1931. Oil on canvas. 114.3 × 139.7 cm. (45 × 55"). Museum of Modern Art, New York City, New York. Given anonymously. © Estate of José Clemente Orozco/Licensed by VAGA, New York, New York.

support as part of a knowledgeable and appreciative audience.

As you use this book, you will discover that art has the power to enrich, inspire, and enlighten. It has the power to stir the imagination, arouse curiosity, instill wonder and delight—and even incite strong emotional reactions. Can there be any better reason for studying it?

Studio Production

Learning in art is not limited to examining the artworks produced by others. It also involves planning, testing, modifying, and completing your own artworks with a variety of materials and techniques (Figure 1.19, page 22). In this book, you will find studio lessons that provide these kinds of experiences at the end of each chapter. It is hoped that they will serve as a springboard for further exploration. Remember that, if your efforts with these studio experiences are to be successful and satisfying, you must make maximum use of your

Art Criticism

Have students examine Jacob Lawrence's painting of *The Studio* on page 22, and ask them to express their first impressions about it. Have them describe what they see in this work. Ask them to identify the elements of art they considered to be the most important. What is the man doing? Does the work arouse pleasant or unpleasant feelings? Ask students if their opinion of the work has changed following this brief examination. Tell them that the questions they have been answering are art criticism questions that provide the answers needed to render an intelligent judgment about a work of art. Ask students if they thought this process was difficult or confusing.

Art History

Point out that Mexico has produced several fine muralists, one of whom, José Clemente Orozco, is represented on this page. Have a group of volunteers research another of Mexico's notable muralists, Diego Rivera. In a report, students can explain when Rivera lived, how he became interested in mural painting, and what cities, both Mexican and American, have or had his works.

Did You Know ?

Jacob Lawrence admits he never saw an art gallery until he was 18 years old. His general awareness of art came from his teachers, books, local exhibitions, and frequent visits to New York's Metropolitan Museum of Art. In 1941, he became the first black artist to be represented by a major New York gallery.

MEETING INDIVIDUAL NEEDS

Cooperative Groups. Group activities enable a student to learn from others while building his or her own self-confidence. However, it is important that teachers do not randomly assign students to groups. Inadvertently assigning students with leadership qualities to the same group could result in tension, confusion, and conflict as each attempts to assume the leader's role. On the other hand, a group composed of students accustomed to following the lead of others is likely to exhibit little, if any, progress. Effective grouping requires an effort to include leaders and followers in each group.

ASSESS
Checking Comprehension
➤ Have students complete the lesson review questions. Answers appear in the box below.
➤ Have students complete *Application* 1, "Help Wanted," in the TCR. In this worksheet, students imagine themselves employed by the classified department of a newspaper. Their task is to identify art-related job titles and prerequisites for the position based on partial information. 📁

Reteaching
Assign *Reteaching* 2, found in the TCR. Have students complete the activity and review their responses. 📁

Enrichment
Assign students *Enrichment* 3, "Creativity—A Gift to All," in the TCR. This worksheet invites students to explore ways to expand their own creative energies. 📁

Extension
Instruct students to write on a sheet of paper one thing that they learned from this chapter. Collect and list these on the chalkboard. What was mentioned most often? Ask the class if any important information provided in the chapter is not included in the list. Add this information to the list on the board.

CLOSE
Ask students to explain what aesthetics, art critics, and art historians do. Tell them that in subsequent chapters they will be doing the same thing. Ask them to explain how this will help them when creating their own art or examining art created by others.

imagination and enthusiasm. These are as essential to the creative process as paints, brushes, clay, and the skill required in manipulating these and other kinds of art media.

Knowledge and skill in aesthetics, art criticism, and art history will serve you well during efforts to create your own art. Aesthetics and criticism will help you measure the quality of your creations. Each studio exercise includes a series of art criticism questions that will help you evaluate your work.

Knowledge of art history will enable you to identify artists who have faced—and solved—the same kind of problems you will confront when creating art. References to art history will also help you find ideas for subject matter, illustrate how other artists used and organized the elements of art, and point out the different techniques they used to communicate their ideas and feelings.

Careers in Art

If you enjoy studying or creating art, you will want to become familiar with the many career opportunities in the art field. Schools, museums, art galleries, small businesses, and large corporations look for creative people to fill a variety of art and art-related positions. An awareness of some of these opportunities may help you as you think about your own career plans. For this reason, information concerning career opportunities in the visual arts is provided in the *Careers in Art Handbook* at the back of this book.

■ **FIGURE 1.19** This artist received his first art lessons in Harlem during the Depression in a government sponsored workshop. In what way do the shapes of the objects in this painting reflect the overall shape of the work?

Jacob Lawrence. *The Studio*. 1977. Gouache on paper. 76.2 × 55.8 cm (30 × 22"). Seattle Art Museum, Seattle, Washington. Partial gift of Gull Industries, John H. and Ann Hauberg; Links, Seattle; and gift by exchange from the estate of Mark Tobey, 90.27.

LESSON TWO REVIEW

Reviewing Art Facts
1. Explain the difference between art media and art process.
2. Define the term *aesthetics*.
3. What two things must a person know before attempting to gather information from a work of art?
4. How does the approach of an art critic differ from the approach of an art historian?

Activity... *Creating a Sculpture*
In this lesson you learned that almost any material can function as an art medium. With a little imagination you can use a readily available medium such as illustration board to create a work of art.

Create a sculpture that can be combined with those created by classmates to make a class project. With pencil, divide a section of white illustration board measuring 12 × 12" into ten different shapes. Cut out each shape and carefully glue them together to form a unique, visually pleasing sculpture. Try various configurations when combining your sculpture with those of other students to form a large construction.

LESSON TWO REVIEW

Answers to Reviewing Art Facts
1. Art media refers to the materials used; art process is the action of making art.
2. Aesthetics is a branch of philosophy concerned with identifying the criteria within works of art that are used to understand, judge and defend judgments about those works.
3. What to look for and how to look for it.
4. An art critic gains information from an artwork; the art historian gathers information about the artwork and the artist who created it.

Activity...*Creating a Sculpture*
Have students work carefully with scissors or a cutting knife with a sharp blade when cutting the illustration board, and work on a protected surface.

Reviewing the Facts

Lesson One

1. What are visual arts?
2. In your own words, define the word *artist*.
3. Name one trait all artists have in common.
4. What are your reasons for studying art?

Lesson Two

5. What are art media? Give three examples.
6. What are art processes? Give three examples.
7. Who are aestheticians and what do they do?
8. How can a knowledge of art history aid you in efforts to create artworks of your own?

Thinking Critically

1. **EXTEND.** Look at Orozco's *Zapatistas* (Figure 1.18). How might this scene change if a rifle shot was suddenly heard? Do you think this would discourage the forward movement of the peasants? Share your ideas with other members of your class. Then conduct a library search to determine if the followers of Zapata faced opposition in their quest for justice. Determine if they were successful in this quest.
2. **ANALYZE.** Study Lawrence's *The Studio* (Figure 1.19) carefully tracing a finger along the *horizontal and vertical* lines in the picture. Explain how these lines help guide the viewer's eye around the painting.

■ CAREERS IN If you enjoy studying or creating art, read about a fascinating art-related career opportunity in the *Careers in Art Handbook*, page 594.

*inter*NET
CONNECTION Visit Glencoe Art Online at *www.glencoe.com/sec/art*. Explore online museums, learn about the lives of artists, and try challenging activities.

 DANCE. Use the *Performing Arts Handbook*, page 577 to learn about Chuck Davis and the African American Dance Ensemble.

Technology Project

Designing a Personal Logo

Artists of the past frequently used pictorial symbols to express ideas and give meaning to their work. A symbol is a visual representation of an abstract idea or concept. For example, in early Christian art, a dove represents the presence of the Holy Spirit. In the arts of the Near East, all letter forms of the alphabet started out as pictorial symbols that represented conceptual ideas or sounds.

Graphic design artists make use of symbols and logos. Logos might include the use of letter forms as well as simplified or abstract pictorial images. Learning to use symbols and logos can make your artwork more interesting. Research pictorial symbols and logos to determine how artists of all time periods use them to enrich their work.

1. Create a personal logo as a symbol for your identity. Include both letter forms and a visual image.
2. When your logo is complete, scan it into the computer and save it. Use your logo to create a composition to function as a cover design for an autobiography about your life.
3. Use an image manipulation program to select, duplicate, enlarge, reduce, and re-arrange your logo in several ways. Create a composition that includes it as an emphasized motif or repeated design element. You may cut and paste images and combine them with your logo, or you may create your own new images to add to the artwork.
4. Decide whether to create your composition as a realistic or abstract work of art or as a functional work of art such as an advertisement.
5. Print a copy of your work and share it with the class.

Review Answers

Reviewing the Facts

1. The visual arts are unique expressions of ideas, beliefs, experiences, and feelings manifested in well-designed visual form.
2. Answers will vary. Possible answer: An artist is a person whose life is dominated by the overpowering impulse to create.
3. All artists share the same impulse to create.
4. Answers will vary. Some students will cite the desire to learn how to express their ideas and emotions in their own artworks. Some will express an interest in learning how to look at, understand, and appreciate works of art created by others. Others will indicate that they wish to gain more information about different artists and art movements.
5. The materials used to create artworks. Examples: pencils, charcoal, paint, clay, stone, metal.
6. The action involved in making art: drawing, printmaking, modeling, weaving, digitizing, casting.
7. An aesthetician is a scholar who specializes in identifying the criteria used in determining the significance of art works.
8. Art history knowledge will help you find ideas for subjects, and show you other artists' techniques and problem-solving.

Thinking Critically

1. Answers will vary.
2. Students should follow the lines around the shapes in the painting and explain how they are guided in viewing the artwork.

 Teaching the Technology Project

Review the distinction between image manipulation programs (draw programs) and Paint programs. Have students experiment with resizing different bitmapped images and compare the result with drawing objects that have been resized. Ask: How do you suppose graphic artists prevent their paintings from developing jagged edges in a Paint program?

Assign the feature in the *Performing Arts Handbook*, page 577.

CAREERS IN ART If time permits, have interested students investigate the career information in the *Careers in Art Handbook*, page 594.

*inter*NET Have students go online and learn more
CONNECTION about artists on preselected Web sites with the Internet activity for this chapter.

Developing a Visual Vocabulary

ADDITIONAL CHAPTER RESOURCES

Activities

- 📁 Application 2
- 📁 Advanced Studio Activity 2
- 🖱 Chapter 2 Internet Activity
- 📁 Studio Activities 2, 3

Fine Art Resources

🕹 **Transparencies**

Art in Focus Transparency 3

Marc Chagall. *Birthday.*

Art in Focus Transparency 4

Joseph Stella. *Battle of Lights, Coney Island.*

🖼 **Fine Art Prints**

Focus on World Art Print 2

Jean-Leon Gérôme. *The Carpet Merchant.*

Assessment

- 📁 Chapter 2 Test
- 📁 Performance Assessment

Multimedia Resources

- 🎭 Artsource® Performing Arts Package
- 💿 National Gallery Laser Disc
- 💿 National Museum of Women in the Arts CD-ROM
- 📼 Arts & Entertainment Videos

NATIONAL STANDARDS FOR ARTS EDUCATION

The National Standards for Arts Education provide guidelines for grade-appropriate competency in the visual arts. The Content Standards for grades 9–12 are:

1. Understanding and applying media, techniques, and processes.
2. Using knowledge of structures and functions.
3. Choosing and evaluating a range of subject matter, symbols, and ideas.
4. Understanding the visual arts in relation to history and cultures.
5. Reflecting upon and assessing the characteristics and merits of their work and the work of others.
6. Making connections between visual arts and other disciplines.

Listed below are the National Standards for the Visual Arts addressed in this chapter. For a breakdown of the categories listed under each content standard, refer to the *Reproducible Lesson Plans* booklet in the TCR.

1. (a, b) **2.** (b, c) **3.** (a, b) **4.** (a) **5.** (a, b) **6.** (a)

HANDBOOK MATERIAL

Lewitzky Dance Company
(page 578)

Art Director *(page 595)*

Beyond the Classroom

The American Alliance for Arts Education is a national organization providing teachers with valuable arts resources. You can join the alliance or find out about their projects and programs by visiting our Web site at *www.glencoe.com/sec/art.*

🕐 **Out of Time?** If time does not permit teaching this chapter in its entirety, you may wish to preview the artwork and captions with students. Scan the heads in each lesson with students. Discuss the Looking Closely features and examine The Color Wheel in Art on page 29.

Developing a Visual Vocabulary

INTRODUCE

Chapter Overview

CHAPTER 2 introduces students to the visual vocabulary of art. It explains how artists combine elements and principles to achieve unity in art.

Lesson One One contains an introduction to the elements of art and focuses on color, line, texture, shape, form, and space.

Lesson Two concentrates on the principles of art and shows how a chart can be used to map design relationships in an artwork.

Studio Lesson guides students in creating a still life using the elements.

Art & Mathematics

Ask students to name some basic plane geometric shapes (e.g., circle, rectangle, triangle). Ask volunteers to come to the chalkboard and draw the shapes named. Then have students working in pairs study the mixed-media artwork in Figure 2.1. Challenge each pair to isolate as many geometric shapes as they can. Ask what objects or parts of objects these shapes are used to represent?

Developing a Visual Vocabulary

Art & Mathematics

■ **FIGURE 2.1** While other painters working in the same style worked more intuitively, Gris exercised his interest and skill in mathematics when creating his paintings. He planned his works with preliminary drawings in which geometric structures were used to help define spatial relationships. He destroyed these drawings when the paintings were completed, but his geometric approach is still evident in his works.

Juan Gris. *Breakfast.* 1914. Cut and pasted paper, crayon, and oil over canvas. 80.9 × 59.7 cm (31$^7/_8$ × 23$^1/_2$″). The Museum of Modern Art, New York, New York. Acquired through the Lillie P. Bliss Bequest.

CHAPTER 2 RESOURCES

Teacher's Classroom Resources

📁 Advanced Studio Activity 2

📁 Application 2

📂 Chapter 2 Internet Activity

📁 Studio Activities 2, 3

Assessment

📁 Chapter 2 Test

📁 Performance Assessment

Fine Art Resources

🖼 *Art in Focus* Transparencies
   3, Marc Chagall. *Birthday*
   4, Joseph Stella. *Battle of Lights, Coney Island.*

 Focus on World Art Print 2
   Jean-Leon Gérôme. *The Carpet Merchant.*

*When looking at works of art, you see different colors,
values, lines, textures, and shapes. You see
countless ways in which artists combine and organize
these elements so their ideas and feelings can be
communicated and understood by viewers. Looking at works
of art, however, doesn't mean you "see" them.
To fully understand a painting, a sculpture, or a building,
you need to understand a visual vocabulary and recognize
how it is used to produce successful works of art.*

YOUR Portfolio

Look through the chapter and choose an artwork that appeals to you, or look around the room or outside the classroom for a subject to draw. Notice the lines, colors, textures, and shapes that make up the object. In your sketchbook, draw a rough sketch of the object in pencil. Consider the use of the elements and principles of art. How would you develop this sketch into a finished piece of art? Write a brief plan for the design and include your goals. What qualities of the subject do you want to emphasize? What media would be more appropriate for this emphasis? Why? What must you know about your preferred medium that would help you plan your designs?

Focus ON THE ARTS

DANCE
Among the earliest surviving efforts to classify the patterned rhythms and movements of dance are those found in Catalan manuscripts dating to 1468. In these manuscripts, vertical and horizontal strokes were used to designate dance steps.

LITERATURE
Many writers have sought to establish a vocabulary of their craft. One was Edgar Allan Poe, who dedicated his "Poetic Principle," published a year after his death, to future generations of writers and readers.

MUSIC
Composer Johann Sebastian Bach's 1749 *The Art of Fugue*, his final composition, was meant not only to entertain but to help listeners and musicians appreciate the intricacies of harmony and tone.

25

Introducing the Chapter

Ask students what colors come to mind when they think of the word *breakfast*. Direct students' attention to the art-work in Figure 2.1, taking notice of the work's title. Ask: Which breakfast colors are included in this work? Explain that in this chapter, students will learn about the role of color in art, as well as other aspects of the language artists speak through their works.

A R T S O U R C E **Dance.** Help students notice how Bella Lewitzky manipulates elements and principles in her dance choreography that compare to those used by visual artists.

Focus ON THE ARTS

Explain that every art has its own unique language, adding that the vocabulary of literature, for example, includes syllables, words, sentences, and paragraphs. Challenge volunteers to name examples for dance (e.g., steps, dips, leaps) and music (e.g., notes, rhythm, harmony).

Point out that some of the terms used in one art are common to others. Note that the term *rhythm*, for example, is used in poetry, music, dance, and the visual arts.

DEVELOPING A PORTFOLIO

Creating Mood through Color. Point out to students that one of the chief ways in which color is used by artists is to capture mood in a work. Have students again examine the work in Figure 2.1, and ask them to brainstorm a list of adjectives and other descriptive words that convey the mood. Challenge students to create a colored-pencil sketch of a breakfast that conveys an entirely different mood. Note that these sketches are to focus primarily on the element of color. Students need not go to an extreme effort to make the objects in the work lifelike. At the artists' discretion, the sketch may or may not include people. Before they begin, elicit from students which colors tend to be associated with which moods or feelings. Allow time for students to share and analyze their works. Have students keep their sketches in their portfolios.

The Elements of Art

Focus

Lesson Objectives

After studying this lesson, students will be able to:
- Discuss the importance of knowing the language of art.
- Identify the elements of art.

Building Vocabulary

Write the term *element* on the chalkboard. Challenge students to name an element. To start students' creativity, say "oxygen" and "hydrogen." Ask whether students know what these elements have in common. Reveal that these elements are basic units of all matter. Explain that the elements of art—like the chemical elements in the Periodic Table—are basic units—in this case, to works of art.

Motivator

Challenge students to name objects with the following shapes: circle, rectangle, triangle. As they brainstorm, write the headings *Shapes* and *???* on the board, placing correctly identified shapes under the first and placing incorrectly identified forms (e.g., spheres, cubes) under the second. Inform students that in this lesson they will learn your rationale for dividing their responses.

Introducing the Lesson

Ask students how they would convert a line to a square, and how they would create a cube based on the square. Inform students they will be learning about the use of line, shape, and form, as well as the other elements of art.

The Elements of Art

Vocabulary
- elements of art
- principles of art
- unity
- color
- intensity
- value
- line
- axis line
- texture
- shape
- form
- space

Discover
After completing this lesson, you will be able to:
- Discuss the importance of knowing the language of art.
- Identify the elements of art.

*W*orks of art are unique arrangements of the obvious and the not so obvious. In order to understand any art object, you must be willing to go beyond the obvious and examine the not so obvious as well. You need to know what to look for; you must understand the language of art. Art has a language of its own: words that refer to the visual elements, or basic parts, and the principles, the various ways of putting these parts together.

Elements and Principles of Art

One of the most important things to look for in works of art is the way those works have been designed, or planned. This involves knowing what the elements and principles of art are and how they are used to create art objects.

The **elements of art** are *the basic components, or building blocks: color, value, line, texture, shape, form, and space.* Artists use the elements of art to express their ideas. These elements are not the media the artist uses— paint or clay or stone, for example—but the visual vocabulary used by the artist.

The **principles of art** are *the different ways the elements can be used in a work of art: balance, emphasis, harmony, variety, gradation, movement, rhythm, and proportion.*

We can make a comparison with writers who must do more than just select and randomly arrange words if they are to communicate their ideas to others. The elements of art can be compared to words. How writers organize those words is similar to using the principles of art. Writers form phrases, sentences, and paragraphs. Then they must carefully arrange these into meaningful sequences. The words must be organized so that readers can understand and appreciate their ideas.

Unity

When organizing their works of art, artists use the principles of balance, emphasis, harmony, variety, gradation, movement, rhythm, and proportion. They select and use these art principles to arrange the elements. In this way, they are able to achieve unity in their works. **Unity** is *the look and feel of wholeness or oneness in a work of art.* In works where unity is evident, the elements and principles work together. Where unity is lacking, the works may look disorganized, incomplete, or confusing.

When artists recognize that a color, a shape, or some other element does not contribute to unity in a work, they eliminate or change it. Artists strive to make their works appealing to viewers, and few people are willing to view and respond favorably to disorganized works of art.

Teacher's Classroom Resources
- Appreciating Cultural Diversity 2
- Art and Humanities 2
- Reproducible Lesson Plan 3
- Reteaching Activity 3
- Study Guide 3

Style

Artworks owe much of their uniqueness to the ways artists have used the elements and principles. No doubt you have heard people talk about an artist's "style." More often than not, they are referring to the special way an artist uses the elements and principles to organize a work. Just as there are different styles in writing, there are different ways to achieve unity in painting, sculpture, or architecture.

Some artists deliberately select and organize the elements using the principles. These artists are not satisfied until a certain combination of elements and principles looks right to them. Other artists choose to use the elements of art in a more spontaneous or intuitive manner. They do not make deliberate decisions regarding the principles of art. Rather, these artists instinctively select and organize the art elements in their works.

The Elements of Art

People looking at a painting or other work of art often stop looking once they have examined the subject matter. They recognize the people, objects, and events shown, but they pay little attention to the elements of art to create the people, objects, and events. They overlook the fact that a painting is made up of colors, values, lines, textures, shapes, and spaces (Figure 2.2).

In a realistic landscape painting, for example, the art elements are combined to look like trees, hills, fields, and sky. Although you may admire the realistic scene, you should not limit your attention to the subject matter alone. If you do, you might miss other important and interesting things, such as the manner in which the elements of art are used to create that realistic scene. If the subject matter in a painting is not apparent, you should be prepared to examine what is shown in terms of color, value, line, texture, shape, and space.

You are already familiar with the elements of art, even if you have never taken an art course or read a book about art. Imagine that, in a phone conversation, you are listening to a description of an object. Could you guess what that object is after hearing a description that includes the following list of art elements?

- It has height, width, and depth and occupies actual *space.*
- Abrupt changes in light and dark *values* indicate that it is made up of flat planes at right angles to each other.
- It is a flat, three-dimensional *form* with six sides.

■ FIGURE 2.2 Works of art are made up of the elements of color, value, line, texture, shape, form, and space. **Can you identify the different colors, lines, and shapes used in this painting?**

Sonia Terk Delaunay. *Study for Portugal.* 1937. Gouache on paper. 36.2 × 94 cm (14¹/₄″ × 37″). The National Museum of Women in the Arts, Washington, D.C. Gift of Wallace and Wilhelmina Holladay.

TEACH
Aesthetics

Divide the class into groups. Draw a horizontal line on the board, and write *more realistic* at one end and *less realistic* at the other. After questioning students to be sure they understand the term *realistic,* instruct groups to look at every painting and sculpture in Chapter 2 and decide where on the realism continuum each work might be placed. Encourage groups to share and explain their opinions.

Art Criticism

Have students select a work of art in Chapter 2 and list words that describe the feelings or mood that the work suggests to them. Then, working in pairs, have students challenge their partners to identify a particular work based on the list of mood words associated with it. Ask: In what way does the artist's success in capturing unity in the work affect your sense of the mood?

Cross Curriculum

MUSIC. Write the names of several art principles that have well-known counterparts in the world of music on the board, such as *harmony* and *rhythm.* Challenge students to brainstorm examples and definitions of the musical terms. Have students discuss the principles and help them understand that our ability to distinguish one musical composition from another depends in part on how these principles are applied. Emphasize the point by playing tape recordings of short passages that cover the musical spectrum (e.g., a rendition by a barbershop quartet, a heavily syncopated jazz work). Finally, ask students how principles like these could be extended into other areas.

 ## Technology ▌

National Gallery of Art Videodisc Use the following images as examples of more works by artists introduced in this lesson.

Giorgione
The Adoration of the Shepherds

Search Frame 329

Jean-Auguste-Dominique Ingres
Madame Moitessier

Search Frame 1122

Botticelli
The Adoration of the Magi

Search Frame 152

Use Glencoe's *Correlation Bar Code Guide to the National Gallery of Art* to locate more artworks.

Art Criticism

Have groups of students work together to make charts for the works in Chapter 2. Students should identify for each piece (1) the warm colors used, (2) the cool colors used, (3) the amount of surface area in the work occupied by each color (expressed as a percentage), and (4) the overall sense communicated by the color scheme.

Studio Skills

Have students draw two small squares on a piece of paper with pencil. Explain that they are to draw a quick scribble design with highly contrasting values in one square. In the other square, they are to draw a design that shows low contrasting values. (In the first square, students should have very dark areas drawn next to very light areas. In the second square, all areas of the drawing should be similar in value.)

Critical Thinking

Provide the class with black-and-white photographs, and ask them to guess the colors of various objects within a given photo. After allowing time to record their guesses, hand out color versions of the same photos and have students check their hunches. Ask them to think about and discuss what this experiment reveals about the value of a color (i.e., if a color appears dark in a photograph, then its value is dark; if it appears light, then its value is light). Have students think about how they might devise similar experiments that would highlight critical aspects of other properties of color.

- It is rectangular in *shape* when viewed directly from any side or from the top or bottom.
- Three sides are a rich, leather-brown *color;* the remaining three sides are white.
- Three sides are hard and smooth in *texture;* this contrasts with the fine ridged texture of the remaining three sides.
- The three sides with the ridged texture are made up of a series of thin, parallel *lines.*

Did you correctly identify the object as a book?

There can be problems of interpretation with any language; this seems to be especially true with a visual language. When you use the term *line*, for example, you want to be sure that the person to whom you are talking has the same understanding of the term as you do. If this bond of understanding is missing, confusion will occur. In order to avoid confusion and misunderstanding, each of the elements of art is defined and examined in this chapter.

Color

Color is *an element made up of three distinct qualities: hue, intensity, and value.* When talking about a color or the differences between two or more colors, you can refer to any one or all of these qualities.

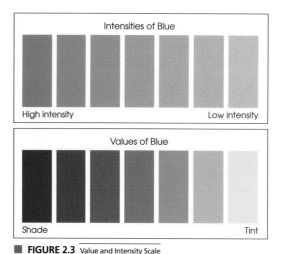

■ FIGURE 2.3 Value and Intensity Scale

Hue

Hue refers to the name of a color. The term is used to point out the difference between a blue and a green, or a red and a yellow. Imagine that you have gone into a department store and have asked to see a selection of blue sweaters. The word blue should be a clear enough description for the salesperson to know what color you have in mind. Examples of 12 different hues are shown in the Color Wheel in Figure 2.4.

Intensity

Now assume that, while checking the store's stock of sweaters, the salesperson discovers a variety of blue sweaters in your size. Some seem to be a brighter, purer blue than others. This is a color's **intensity,** or *quality of brightness and purity.*

When a hue is strong and bright, it is said to be high in intensity. When that same color is faint and dull, it is said to be low in intensity. Perhaps the salesperson brings out a selection of blue sweaters for you to see. Unsure which you like best, you arrange them on the counter in a row, from those that are the brightest to those that are the dullest. The differences in color intensity of these sweaters might resemble the range of intensities shown in Figure 2.3.

Value in Color

The salesperson now brings out more blue sweaters. Some of these sweaters are darker and some are lighter than those you have just seen. You arrange this second group of sweaters in a row from darkest to lightest. Your awareness of the lightness and darkness of the blues means that you have recognized the differences in their color values.

When describing a hue, the term **value** refers to *that hue's lightness or darkness.* Value changes are often obtained by adding black or white to a particular hue. The value chart in Figure 2.3 shows the range of dark and light values created when various amounts of black and white were added to blue. The differences in color value that you found in the sweaters might resemble the range of color values shown in this chart.

About the *Artwork*

Study for Portugal. Explain that the artist of the work on the previous page, Sonia Terk Delaunay, was a Russian-born painter who spent most of her life in Paris. Like her husband, French painter Robert Delaunay, she produced abstract works that are notable for their dynamic use of color.

The work shown here was created for the 1939 Paris World's Fair. Emphasize the ways in which the colors in the work serve a decorative function, as well as suggest a sense of movement. In addition to her painting, Delaunay produced designs for books and clothing might be mentioned.

The Color Wheel in *Art*

$\mathcal{A}$n understanding of color is aided by the use of a color wheel.

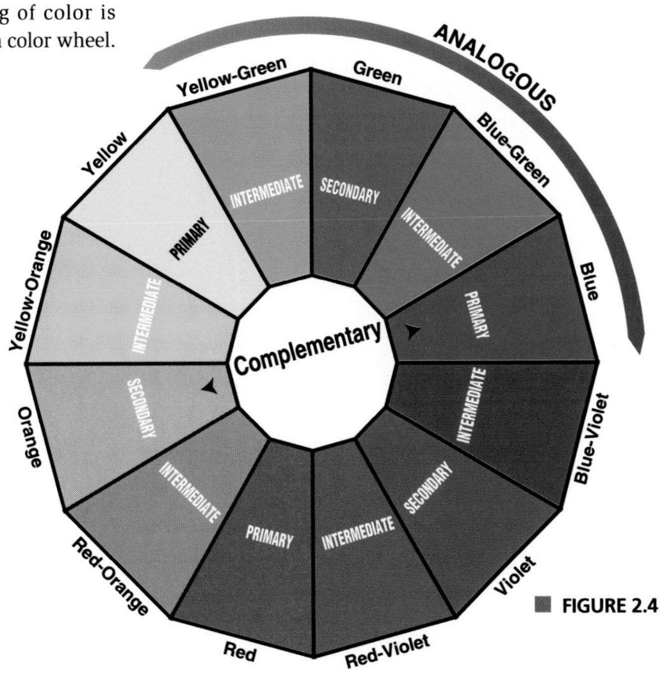

FIGURE 2.4 Color Wheel

①

Notice the three *primary colors:* red, yellow, and blue. These are called primary colors because they are mixed to make all the other colors, but they cannot be made by mixing the other colors.

②

The *secondary colors,* orange, green, and violet, are located midway between the primary colors on the wheel. Each of the secondary colors is made by mixing two primary colors. Orange is made by mixing red and yellow; green, by mixing blue and yellow; and violet, by mixing blue and red.

③

Adding more red to the combination of red and yellow produces a red-orange. Adding more yellow produces a yellow-orange. Red-orange and yellow-orange are examples of *intermediate colors.* By varying the amounts of the two primary colors used, it is possible to create a number of these intermediate hues, or *tertiary colors.* Both terms, *intermediate* and *tertiary,* refer to the colors found between the primary and secondary colors.

④

Colors that are opposite each other on the color wheel are called *complementary colors.* Thus, red and green are complementary colors. These hues are opposites in a more fundamental way, however: There is no green hue in red, and no red hue in green.

⑤

The addition of only a small amount of a hue's complement lowers its intensity. In other words, a green can be made to look less green—and move by degrees closer and closer to a neutral tone—by the addition of its complement, red.

⑥

Colors that are next to each other on the color wheel and are closely related are called *analogous colors.* Examples of analogous colors are blue, blue-green, and green.

Chapter 2 *Developing a Visual Vocabulary* **29**

Color Wheel In *Art*

Examine the feature on this page and discuss the concepts with students. Reinforce the idea of complementary colors by asking students to isolate several examples of complementary colors on the Color Wheel in Figure 2.4. Ask students to state the fundamental difference between two such colors (i.e., red has no green in it, and green has no red in it). Inform students about the role of the eye in perceiving color. Introduce the concepts of reflection and absorption of light, and discuss how these phenomena significantly determine what we see.

Art History

Use two paintings to illustrate the way media can affect the intensity and value of a hue. Have students compare and contrast Figures 2.2 and 2.10 (pages 27 and 34). Observe that the first of the works that students previously considered was done with gouache (a form of watercolor painting) on paper. The second painting was done with egg tempera (a slow-drying paint) on wood. Ask students to point out specific ways in which the hues in the paintings are similar and different. Suggest that an artist must consider this important relationship when preparing to start a piece of work.

Cross Curriculum

COMPUTERS. Explain to students that gradations of color exhibited in the painting in Figure 2.2 on page 27 actually depend on the ability of color receptors in the eye to resolve discrete colors into shades and tints. To illustrate this point, invite a group of volunteers to experiment with color depths on the classroom computer. Have students open (or scan) a color photo. Have the group set the computer's color depth at each of the following calibrations: 16 million colors (24-bit), 64,000 (16-bit), 256 (8-bit), and 16 (4-bit). As students change color depths, they should note differences in the appearance of the image.

Have the group test its findings on a second image, then share what they have learned with the class. Conclude by noting that the grainy effect evident at 256 and, especially, 16 simultaneous colors is a technique called *dithering,* which has a parallel—stippling—in art.

Studio Skills

Ask students to imagine they are art directors for a major recording company. They have been asked to design posters for two of the company's hottest performers. One is a musician whose music is intended to motivate radical political action, and the other is a musician who sings romantic ballads. Tell them to begin by sketching out their designs in their sketchbooks, noting the color schemes they intend to use. They may then execute their designs using felt-tip markers.

Art Criticism

Point out to students that value is a function of color and black and white as well. Direct their attention to the photograph in Figure 2.6. Ask which areas of the work display the darkest values of gray (the central structure of the flower, the shadows on the left). Which areas reveal the lightest values? (The petals in the upper right portion of the picture plane.) Have students brainstorm adjectives this image conjures up (e.g., delicate, fragile).

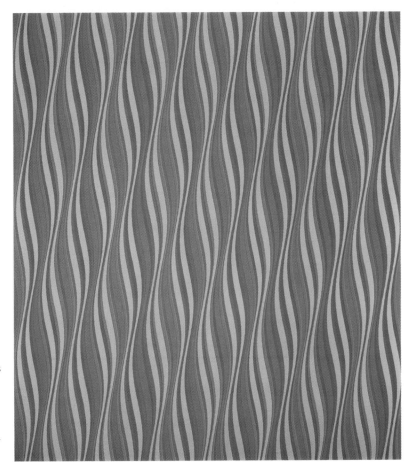

■ **FIGURE 2.5** Notice how the lines of color in this painting create a surface that seems to have a life of its own. **What effect does this use of line have on you?**

Bridget Riley. *Entice 2.* 1974. Acrylic on canvas. 154.3 × 137.5 cm (60³/₄ × 54¹/₈″). Photo courtesy Sidney Janis Gallery, New York, New York.

The terms *warm* and *cool* are applied to certain colors on the color wheel. *Cool colors* are often associated with water and sky. These are colors that contain blue and green and appear on the side of the wheel opposite the warm colors. Warm colors are often associated with fire and sun. These are colors that contain red and yellow and appear on the side of the wheel opposite the cool colors. Cool colors appear to recede in space, whereas warm colors seem to advance.

Over the centuries, artists have used color in many different ways. Some have tried to reproduce exactly the colors of the objects they have painted. Others have freely changed colors in order to emphasize a certain feeling or mood. Bridget Riley, a contemporary British artist, creates works that are composed of completely unexpected changes in color (Figure 2.5). Sometimes these color changes are sudden, sometimes gradual, but they are found everywhere in her paintings. If you look into one of her pictures long enough, you find that your eye begins to wander over waving lines of color. Eventually the surface seems to rise and fall, and you find it difficult to think of the painting as flat and still.

About the *Artwork*

Entice 2. Explain that Bridget Riley is a member of the Op Art movement, a mode of artistic expression concerned with the psychological and physical processes of vision. If possible, display examples of well-known optical illusions (e.g., some in which figure and ground seem constantly to shift, some in which curved lines appear straight and vice versa). Point out that the optical illusion created by Riley in *Entice 2* is a suggestion of movement. Ask students to discuss how substitution, elimination, or addition of colors would alter this illusion.

Value

Sometimes *value* is an important element in works of art even though color appears to be absent. This is the case with drawings, woodcuts, lithographs, and photographs. It is true, too, with most sculpture and architecture.

Abrupt or gradual changes in value can add greatly to the visual effect of these art forms. Abrupt value changes can suggest planes, or flat surfaces at various angles to each other. Gradual value changes can indicate concave or convex surfaces. They can do even more, however. Changes in value can help the artist express an idea. Imogen Cunningham, who specialized in portraits of famous celebrities, also took photographs of plants and flowers. Notice how she used gentle changes in value to capture the unique personality of a flower (Figure 2.6).

■ **FIGURE 2.6** Notice how the photographer captured the essence of a blossom's form by using value contrast. **How does the use of value in this black-and-white photograph differ from the use of value in a color painting?**

Imogen Cunningham. *Magnolia Flower.* 1925. Photograph. 22.5 × 29.5 cm (8⁷/₈ × 11⁵/₈″). Denver Art Museum, Denver, Colorado.

Chapter 2 *Developing a Visual Vocabulary* **31**

Studio Skills

Have students select an object in the classroom with a single solid color (e.g., a wastebasket, a storage cabinet) and make three separate pencil sketches of it. With colored pencils or watercolors, have them color one of the sketches a primary color from the color wheel, one an adjacent secondary color, and one a nearby intermediate color. Ask students to exchange sketches with their neighbor, then ask each student to identify the position on the color wheel each hue used.

Critical Thinking

Ask students to discuss the qualities and traits they would expect to find in a person described as intense (very serious, focused, determined). Ask them for adjectives that would be used to describe the opposite type of person. Have students think of mnemonics, (memory aids) based on these associations, that will help them remember a bright color is more intense than a dull color.

Did You Know?

Landscape photographer Ansel Adams developed a specific darkroom approach for controlling values in fine art prints. Adams mastered ways to create expressive images in black and white with a full range of values, clear delineation of form and texture, and a satisfactory print "color."

Technology

Overhead Projector. An overhead projector and ordinary found objects can be combined to create an invaluable aid in teaching about elements and principles. Consider projecting strands of yarn with different thicknesses and textures to reinforce the notion of line, or arrange opaque objects of different sizes to help students grasp the relationship between form and space. Shifting the objects to different positions can be an effective tool for teaching the principle of balance, which is discussed later in Lesson 2.

Aesthetics

Have students study the painting in Figure 2.7, taking note of the specific kinds of lines the artist used. Ask them to discuss the work and then react to the following questions: How do you think Marie Laurencin went about creating these lines? What adjectives would you use to describe these lines? What message or mood do you feel is communicated by the use of such lines? Do you feel the painting is successful? Why, or why not?

Studio Skills

Using pencil and sheets of white paper, have students create a real or imaginary landscape that makes use of vertical, horizontal, and diagonal lines. Ask students to identify ways in which the three types of lines capture movement.

Art History

Invite students to compare and contrast the use of line and texture in any painting in the lesson created before 1900 (i.e., Figures 2.10, 2.11, 2.13, and 2.14) with any work created after that date. Ask: How were the goals and objectives of artists working in past ages different from those of more recent years? How are they similar? Which group of artists seems more concerned with the depiction of realistic figures? Finally, ask students to consider the factors that may have brought about these changes in artistic style (e.g., restlessness, or a spirit of experimentation).

Line

Line is an element that is difficult to describe, although most people know what it is and can easily think of several ways to create it. Perhaps the simplest way to define **line** is to refer to it as a *continuous mark made on some surface by a moving point*. The marks made by a ballpoint pen moving across a sheet of paper are lines. So are the marks made on canvas by a moving paintbrush, or the marks made by the sculptor's finger moving across a clay surface.

Artists use several different types of line in their works to identify and describe objects and their movements. Different effects are obtained by using these different types of line.

Emphasizing Line

One type of line is used to show the edges, or contours, of an object. This is called a *contour line*. Such a line is familiar to anyone who has tried to draw. It is, in fact, one of the most common forms of line used by children. When children pick up pencils or crayons to draw, they use lines to create figures, houses, trees, and flowers. Usually, children draw these objects in outline form.

Artists often use contour lines in much the same way to identify and describe objects in their drawings and paintings. They do this even though they know that these outlines are not actually a part of the real object. The contour line separates the object from the background and from other objects in the same work.

Some artists place great importance on contours or outlines. They use them as a way of adding interest or unity to their paintings. The works created by such artists are frequently called *linear*. Notice, for example, how the French artist Marie Laurencin (law-rahn-**san**) has used black outlines to add clarity and interest to her portrait of a woman wearing a hat (Figure 2.7). Because of these outlines, every object is clearly defined and stands out on its own. More importantly, the black outlines add a decorative accent that increases the picture's appeal.

De-emphasizing Line

Some artists try to eliminate or conceal the outline of objects in their pictures. The term *painterly* is often used when describing works by these artists. Claude Monet (**kload** mow-**nay**) was such an artist, and you can see why when you look at his paintings of haystacks (Figures 21.14 and 21.15, page 481). Monet was interested in recording the fleeting effect of light on the various surfaces of objects. He used short brush strokes to create a shimmering effect in which the contour lines seem to disappear.

Line and Sculpture

The terms *linear* and *painterly* are not reserved only for discussions about paintings. They are also applied to sculptures. Henry Moore, for example, used a continuous flowing contour line in his sculpture of a standing figure (Figure 2.8).

Terms such as *linear* and *painterly* can help you see more clearly a particular quality found in works of art. Thus, when a painting or sculpture is described as linear, you know immediately that the element of line has been stressed.

■ **FIGURE 2.7** The black outlines help define the shapes in this portrait. How would the impact of the painting be different without the use of these lines?

Marie Laurencin. *Woman with Hat (Femme au Chapeau)*. 1911. Oil on board. 35 × 26 cm (13³⁄₄ × 10¹⁄₄"). The Museum of Fine Arts, Houston, Texas. The John A. Jones and Audrey Jones Beck Collection.

COOPERATIVE LEARNING

Working with Line. Divide the students into small groups or pairs of students: Each group or pair should select one of the types of lines described in the section. In two minutes (time them with a stopwatch or clock with a second hand), they are to write as many real-life analogs as they can find (e.g., eyebrow for curved line, doughnut for circle). Ask groups to read aloud their lists and compare entries. Point out that brainstorming exercises of this kind can also be put to good use by an individual in search of creative inspiration for a given art assignment.

The word *linear* produces a mental image quite different from the image that comes to mind when a work is described as painterly.

Line and Movement

In addition to defining objects in works of art, line can also suggest movement. This movement might be horizontal, vertical, diagonal, or curved. Certain feelings or sensations are associated with each of these movements.

Vertical, or straight up and down, suggests strength and stability. *Horizontal*, or from side to side, suggests calmness. *Diagonal* suggests tension. Curved suggests a flowing movement. Sometimes the feelings suggested by the lines in a picture can influence your reactions to it. The lines in one picture may help you feel calm and relaxed (Figure 21.9, page 474), whereas the lines in another may create a tense and uneasy feeling (Figure 19.9, page 427).

An **axis line,** *an imaginary line that is traced through an object or several objects in a picture,* can be helpful when you are trying to identify movement and the direction of movement in a work of art. It can show you whether the object or objects have been organized in a particular direction. For example, examine the painting by Jacob Lawrence in Figure 2.9. Use

■ **FIGURE 2.8**
Notice how the sculptor has used the element of line in this work. Describe the movement your hand would make if you could trace around this sculpture. Does it change direction suddenly or move in a smooth, flowing manner?

Henry Moore. *Large Interior Form.* 1953, cast 1981. Bronze. 5 × 1.4 × 1.4 m (195 × 56 1/4 × 56 1/4"). The Nelson-Atkins Museum of Art, Kansas City, Missouri. The Hall Family Foundation Collection.

■ **FIGURE 2.9** The axis line in this painting moves from the lower left corner toward the upper right corner. How do the contour lines help to emphasize the strong diagonal movement of these figures?

Jacob Lawrence. *War Series: Another Patrol.* 1946. Egg tempera on composition board. 40.6 × 50.8 cm (16 × 20"). Collection of Whitney Museum of American Art, New York, New York. Gift of Mr. and Mrs. Roy R. Neuberger.

Cross Curriculum

MATH. Ask a volunteer to read aloud the definition of *axis line.* Remind students they have, in all likelihood, encountered the term *axis* before. Point out that, in mathematics, one plots coordinates on a grid with respect to two axes—one horizontal and one vertical. Have them study the work by Jacob Lawrence in Figure 2.9. How do the axis lines here differ from the x and y axes used in math? In what ways are these imaginary lines similar?

Art Criticism

Write *War Series: Another Patrol* on one part of the board, *The Adoration of the Magi* on another. Direct students' attention to the two paintings (Figures 2.9 and 2.10, page 34). Ask students to brainstorm associations that come to mind when they look at each of the paintings. Create word webs by noting their responses on lines radiating outward from the name of the work in question. Point out that the impressions recorded in the word webs are reinforced by the two paintings' axis lines.

CULTURAL DIVERSITY

Flags of the World. Students can choose several particularly colorful or unusual national flags from an encyclopedia or almanac that illustrates flags of the world, then research the origins and significance of the colors on each. Students may look further into the importance attached to color in the nation's culture (e.g., does the leader of the nation live in a building associated with a particular color, such as the White House?), then discuss their findings. Encourage students to work together to create a design and color scheme for a class flag.

Art Criticism

Refer students to Botticelli's work *The Adoration of the Magi* (Figure 2.10). Ask them to describe the quality of the lines the artist used. Are the lines bold or are they mere suggestions of the element of line? Have students concentrate on the types of lines used. What dual function is served by the diagonal lines in the structure above the Christ Child? (Where do these lines direct the viewer's eye, and what impact do they have on the implication of depth of space in the work?)

Studio Skills

Have students bring various small objects with different textures to class. Tell students to glue these objects to a large sheet of tag board. Examples of objects might include sandpaper, wool, silk, cotton, corkboard, rock, metal, glass, aluminum foil, plastic, velvet, leather, and beaded cloth. After assembling a large and varied collection, shine a light source on the objects and have students draw the different textures. Move the source of light, and repeat the activity.

your finger to trace the movement and direction of the three sailors trudging up the gangplank of their ship. Notice that your finger moves upward diagonally, from the lower left-hand corner to the upper right-hand corner of this painting. The axis line is the line your finger would have made if it had left a mark on the picture. It is an imaginary line that you invent and use to trace the direction of movement in a work.

Some artworks make use of a single axis line; others make use of several. In a work with more than one axis line, you should determine how the lines relate to one another. For example, in Figure 2.10 four axis lines combine to form a large W that ties the various parts of the picture together while pointing out the most important figures. Observe how two diagonal axis lines are used to arrange the figures at either side of the painting. These join two other diagonal axis lines that lead upward to complete the W. At the center point are the Christ child and His mother. Even though they are not the largest figures in the work, they are the most important. The artist has skillfully used axis lines to guide your eye to them.

Axis lines can be as important in sculpture and architecture as they are in painting. They can help you recognize the rigid, vertical pose of one sculpture (Figure 8.15, page 178) or the active, twisting pose of another (Figure 8.18, page 182). In architecture, axis lines can also help you define the principal vertical emphasis of one building or the horizontal emphasis of another.

■ **FIGURE 2.10** The religious figures in this painting are dressed in garments of the artist's own time. In addition to the axis lines discussed, can you find other *actual* lines, both diagonal and vertical, that direct attention to the main figures?

Sandro Botticelli. *The Adoration of the Magi.* c. 1481–82. Tempera on wood. Approx. 70.1 × 104.1 cm (27⅝ × 41″). National Gallery of Art, Washington, D.C. Board of Trustees, Andrew W. Mellon Collection.

34 **Unit One** *Creating and Understanding Art*

More About... **Color.** Mention the importance given to color by artists throughout history. Point out that some artists have even felt compelled to write about it. For example, Henri Matisse explained that in painting "an autumn landscape, I will not try to remember what colors suit the season; I will be inspired only by the sensation that the season gives me, [and] . . . the sensation itself may vary: autumn may be soft and warm . . . or quite chilly with a cold sky and lemon-yellow trees." Mention that Matisse founded an art movement called Fauvism, which was devoted to the expressive qualities of color.

Texture

Whenever you talk about the surface quality, or "feel," of an object, you are discussing its texture. **Texture** is *the element of art that refers to the way things feel, or look as if they might feel if touched.* In painting, some works have an overall smooth surface in which even the marks of the paintbrush have been carefully concealed. There are no textural "barriers" or "distractions" to get in the way as your eyes sweep over the smooth, glossy surface.

Other paintings have a more uneven surface. This is the case when a heavy application of paint produces a rough texture that you sense with your eyes and feel with your fingers. Both types of painting are examples of actual texture because you actually feel the smooth surface of one and the rough surface of the other.

There are many paintings, however, in which the surface is smooth to the touch but the sensation of different textures is suggested by the way the artist painted some areas. In a portrait of the Princess de Broglie (Figure 2.11), the artist, J.A.D. Ingres, obviously delighted in painting as accurately as possible a range of different textures. There is a distinctive "feel" to the rich satin and lace of the woman's gown. Other textures are shown in the brocade chair and the smooth, soft skin of the sitter. Yet if you were to pass your fingers lightly over this painting, you would find that it is smooth all over. When artists try to make different objects in their pictures appear rough or smooth, they are using simulated or artificial texture.

■ **FIGURE 2.11** Notice the variety of simulated textures in this painting. What other elements of art did the artist use to add variety to the many surfaces?

Jean-Auguste-Dominique Ingres. *Princesse de Broglie.* 1853. Oil on canvas. 121.3. × 90.8 cm (47³/₄ × 35³/₄"). The Metropolitan Museum of Art, New York, New York. Robert Lehman Collection, 1975. (1975.1.186).

Chapter 2 *Developing a Visual Vocabulary* **35**

Cross Curriculum

LANGUAGE ARTS. Using a book of familiar quotations, consider compiling a list of literary allusions that have to do with texture (e.g., "the dank tropical night . . . pressed its thick, warm blackness in upon the yacht," from Richard Connell's *The Most Dangerous Game*). Divide the list of allusions among students, and have them work in pairs to devise paraphrases for each excerpt. Invite the whole class to discuss their literary allusions and paraphrases, noting which involve real (actual) texture and which involve imagined texture.

Aesthetics

Ask students to choose cards randomly from a box in which you have placed index cards that are equally labeled: *Imitationalist, Formalist, Emotionalist.* Allow time for students to form groups with similar card holders. Then have groups study Jean-Auguste-Dominique Ingres' *Princesse de Broglie* (Figure 2.11). Challenge groups to debate the strengths and limitations of the work according to their own aesthetic view. Then ask groups to rotate labels and repeat the activity with another work from the chapter.

More About... **Texture.** Explain to students that two of the senses—vision and touch— are responsive to the sensation of texture. Emphasize that careful observation of detail, through whatever means available, is the hallmark of any successful artist. Note that students can work at improving their perceptual powers—and, in so doing, improve their painting and drawing abilities—by examining under magnification objects whose surfaces give different readings to the eyes and fingers (e.g., fabrics that appear coarse but which are, in fact, smooth).

Art Criticism

Ask a volunteer to browse through the textbook and choose an artwork. Instruct the rest of the class to turn to this artwork. Ask students in turn to identify instances of space in the picture. As they do, record on the board the word or words the student uses (e.g., *the space formed by the two red shapes*). Encourage students to see that space, unlike other elements of art, relies on other elements (shapes and forms) for its very existence.

Aesthetics

Divide the class into groups. Draw a horizontal line on the board and write *more emotional* at one end and *less emotional* at the other end. Instruct each group to look at every painting and sculpture illustrated in Chapter 2 and decide where on the line each work of art might be located. Explain to the class that, although there are no right or wrong answers, groups will be asked to justify their decisions to the rest of the class.

Texture and Sculpture

Because three-dimensional forms seem to invite touch, texture is especially important to sculptors. They recognize the urge to touch a sculptured surface and often encourage this by providing rich textural effects. José de Creeft creates obvious contrasts in rough and smooth textures in his sculpture of *The Cloud* (Figure 2.12). These different textures are emphasized by the effect of light playing across the surface of the work.

Sculptors recognize that wood, marble, and bronze all have unique textural qualities. They must keep this textural quality in mind when choosing the material for a particular work.

Shape and Form

The term **shape** refers to *a two-dimensional area clearly set off by one or more of the other visual elements, such as color, value, line, texture, and space.* Shapes are flat. They are limited to only two dimensions: length and width. This two-dimensional character of shape distinguishes it from form, which has depth as well as length and width. Thus, a **form** is *an object with three dimensions.*

Shapes can be created deliberately in drawing and painting by joining a single continuous line or several lines to enclose an area. For example, when two parallel horizontal lines are joined to two parallel vertical lines, a square or rectangular shape is made.

Usually, when you try to visualize a shape, the first thing that comes to mind is an area surrounded by lines. Yet line is not always needed to create shapes. Many shapes are formed in a more indirect manner without the aid of lines. When an artist paints an area of a picture with a particular color, a shape is created. An artist can also create shape by isolating or setting off an area that is texturally different from its surroundings.

■ **FIGURE 2.12** Notice how light emphasizes the textures in this three-dimensional piece. What other element of art has been used to provide variety?

José de Creeft. *The Cloud.* 1939. Greenstone. 42.5 × 31.4 × 25.4 cm (16³/₄ × 12³/₈ × 10″). Collection of Whitney Museum of American Art, New York, New York. Purchase. 41.17a–b. © Estate of José de Creeft/Licensed by VAGA, New York, New York.

36   **Unit One** *Creating and Understanding Art*

CULTURAL DIVERSITY

Texture. Invite students to explore the ways texture is used by artists from different cultures. They can accomplish this task by researching the following topics: Native American pottery and blankets, Spanish lace, African sculpture, and Japanese woodcuts. Have them compare the similarities and differences, and have them compare the effects texture has on artworks from different cultures. Encourage students to record their findings, along with original pencil illustrations, in an art journal or sketchbook.

Many painters have tried to create the illusion of solid, three-dimensional forms in their works. Frequently, the look of solidity and depth is achieved by painting shapes with light and dark values. For example, a circular shape can be made to look three-dimensional by gradually changing its value from light to dark. This technique can be used to reproduce the effect of light on the surface of a round object. When combined with a dark shadow cast by the round object, the desired three-dimensional effect is created (Figure 2.13).

Because it possesses the added dimension of depth, a form can be thought of as a shape in three dimensions. You cannot actually feel around a form in a painting, but you are able to do so with the forms found in sculpture and architecture.

Mass and Volume

Two important features of form are *mass* and *volume*. Mass refers to the outside size and bulk of a form, and volume refers to the space within a form.

Any discussion of the mass of a sculpture or building uses the vocabulary of solid geometry. This allows you to describe more clearly a three-dimensional work as resembling a cube, a sphere, a pyramid, a cylinder, or a cone. This does not mean that a sculpture or a building must be solid. You can also describe a contemporary sculpture made of transparent plastic and wire as having mass and resembling a sphere, cylinder, or cone.

The term *volume* is used during discussions of interior space. In architecture, volume refers to the space within a building. This inside space is determined by the exterior mass of the building. Sometimes volume can be small and confining, as in a tiny chapel. At other times it can be huge and expansive, as in an enormous cathedral. You should not limit your concern for volume to buildings alone, however. You can also refer to the volumes created between and within sculptural masses.

Occasionally, it is helpful to describe a sculpture or a building in terms of its shape as well as its form. For example, you might be concerned with the two-dimensional outline or silhouette of a sculpture or building seen from a fixed position. In this way, a sculpture may offer several interesting shapes as you walk around it and view it from different angles. A building that looks small and square when viewed directly from the front might prove to be large and rectangular when viewed from one side.

■ **FIGURE 2.13** You might feel that you could pick up one of the oranges in this painting. **How did the artist make the flat shapes look like round, three-dimensional forms?**

Luis Meléndez. *Still Life with Oranges, Jars, and Boxes of Sweets.* c. 1760–65. Oil on canvas. 48.2 × 35.3 cm (19 × 13⁷/₈″). Kimbell Art Museum, Fort Worth, Texas.

Art Criticism

Have students examine the ways texture is used in other works in the lesson, directing their attention In particular to Figure 2.10 (page 34). How would they describe the texture of the masonry in the ruined structure in the painting? Would they use a different set of terms to describe the apparent texture of the robes on the various figures? Help students recognize that a comprehensive evaluation of any artwork depends on a complete analysis of all elements and principles.

Studio Skills

Provide students with a variety of small found objects with different textures, and invite them to make collages. Afterward, they may choose their own media and draw or paint reproductions of their collages, simulating each of the textures as well as they can. Display the collages alongside the two-dimensional representations of them, allowing time for students to share tips on technique and skills.

Teacher Notes

LOOKING Closely

Examine the feature during class with students. Have students make a chart summarizing the various techniques Gorgione used to capture the illusion of space. Then invite students to make simple sketches of familiar objects that exemplify one or more of the techniques without labeling the technique shown. Have students exchange sketches with a partner and each partner should attempt to assign the appropriate technique from their charts.

Cross Curriculum

MATH. Display a shoebox and, alongside it, a side panel cut from a second, identical box. Point out that in math the two types of objects are referred to as solid and plane figures respectively. Ask a volunteer to provide a definition of the two terms (solid objects are three-dimensional, plane shapes exist in two dimensions). Then ask students to reinterpret the shoebox and box panel in terms of shape and form using the elements of art (the box has form, the panel has shape).

Study Guide

Distribute *Study Guide* 3 in the TCR and review key concepts with students. 📁

Art and Humanities

Distribute *Art and Humanities* 2, "Applying the Elements and Principles to Other Arts," in the TCR. Ask students to select books or stories that are descriptive in nature. Then ask students to determine how the authors of these works use literary elements similar to the elements of art to express ideas to the reader. 📁

Space

Space can be thought of as *the distance or area between, around, above, below, or within things.* In art, space is an element that can be either three-dimensional or two-dimensional.

Three-dimensional space, which has height, width, and depth, is known as *actual* space. It is the type of space found in art forms that are three-dimensional such as sculpture, ceramics, and architecture. For example, if you could study José de Creeft's sculpture of *The Cloud* (Figure 2.12, page 36) in its museum setting, you would be able to move about freely in the space that surrounds the sculpture. You could see the way this

LOOKING Closely

CREATING THE ILLUSION OF THREE-DIMENSIONAL SPACE

Giorgione created a sense of three-dimensional space by using the techniques below:

- **Size.** Distant shapes are made smaller; closer shapes are made larger.
- **Placement.** The shapes within the work overlap, suggesting that some are in front of others. Distant shapes are placed higher in the picture; closer shapes are placed lower.
- **Detail.** Distant shapes are shown with less detail; closer shapes are shown with greater detail.
- **Color.** Distant shapes are colored with hues that are duller and appear bluer to suggest the layers of atmosphere between the viewer and those shapes.
- **Line.** The horizontal lines of shapes (buildings and other objects) are slanted to make them appear to extend back into space.

■ **FIGURE 2.14** Giorgione. *The Adoration of the Shepherds.* c. 1505–10. Oil on panel. Approx. 91 × 111 cm (35³/₄ × 43¹/₂″). National Gallery of Art, Washington, D.C. Board of Trustees, Samuel H. Kress Collection.

38 **Unit One** *Creating and Understanding Art*

COOPERATIVE LEARNING

Shape and Form. Help students clarify the difference between shape and form by stressing that form refers to an object (something that has weight, occupies space, and can be manipulated). To aid students in grasping this important distinction, divide the class into pairs. One partner is to name an object (e.g., a child's building block, a square), and the other is to state whether the item exists in three or two dimensions. Pairs can take turns naming and classifying objects in this fashion.

work changes when viewed from different positions. The work presents not only different shapes, but different images and meanings as well. From one angle, the sculpture resembles a cloud. From a second, it changes to look like a woman. From a third, it appears to be a mother and child. The work does more than just occupy space. Certainly an understanding of this sculpture would be incomplete for a viewer who insisted on examining it from a single point of view.

Architecture is an art form devoted to the enclosure of space. To truly appreciate this art form, you must carefully consider the way in which space is treated in different structures.

Unlike three-dimensional works of art, the space in flat, two-dimensional works is limited to height and width. There is no *actual* depth or distance in such works. Despite this, artists have devised several techniques to create the *illusion* of depth or distance on flat or nearly flat surfaces. Many of these techniques were used by Giorgione (jor-**joh**-nay) when he painted *The Adoration of the Shepherds* (Figure 2.14).

With these techniques, the flatness of the picture plane seems to be destroyed. The viewer is transported into what appears to be a world of actual space, atmosphere, and three-dimensional forms. Giorgione's picture may be an illusion, but it is a very convincing one.

Working with the Elements

Typically, artists are faced with the challenge of considering several elements with each step they take in creating a work of art. They cannot, for example, work effectively with color without considering other elements. They realize that the selection and application of one hue in one part of a painting will have an impact on the hues, shapes, lines, and textures used in other parts of the work.

Some artists respond to this challenge in a deliberate, thoughtful manner, whereas others are more spontaneous and intuitive. To understand and appreciate artists' various responses, you need not only to be familiar with the elements of art, but also to understand how the principles of art are used to organize those elements.

LESSON ONE REVIEW

Reviewing Art Facts
1. List the seven elements of art.
2. Give an example of an analogous color scheme.
3. What is the benefit of identifying the axis line in a work of art?
4. Name four techniques artists can use to create the illusion of three-dimensional space in a two-dimensional work of art.

Activity... *Expressing Mood with Color*
Artists create ideas and feelings in their works through the use of color. Identify a painting from the text that emphasizes the use of color. Describe how the color creates a mood or feeling in the work. Is the color warm or cool, loud or soft?

Create a work of art that expresses mood using color. Use a brayer and a large piece of glass. Choose primary colors and black and white to create a monoprint that expresses the mood you wish to create. Share your work with the class. After your monoprint dries, combine other elements and principles of art to enhance your work.

Chapter 2 *Developing a Visual Vocabulary* **39**

LESSON ONE REVIEW

Answers to Reviewing Art Facts
1. Color, value, line, texture, shape, form, space.
2. Answers, which will vary, might include green, blue-green, blue.
3. It helps in recognizing direction of movement.
4. Answers, which will vary, can include possibilities from the list featured on page 38.

Activity... *Expressing Mood with Color*
Review with students the elements of art and the how color is used in artworks. As students work with the materials for their monoprint, be sure to provide a work area that is equipped with brayer, ink, water, towels, and a place to clean up.

CHAPTER 2
LESSON ONE

ASSESS
Checking Comprehension
Have students complete the lesson review questions. Answers appear in the box below.

Reteaching
Assign *Reteaching* 3, found in the TCR. Have students complete the activity and review their responses. 🗀

Enrichment
Have students read about the symbolism of color in different cultures as explained in *Appreciating Cultural Diversity* 2, "Color as Symbol and Identification," in the TCR. Then have them work in small groups to brainstorm symbolic use of color in their own experiences. Groups should be encouraged to share their findings with the class. 🗀

Extension
Before students come to class, place a common, odorless, noiseless item in a paper bag (e.g., a kitchen utensil). Ask a volunteer to come forward and examine but not reveal the contents of the bag. Using only one element of art, the student attempts to offer as many clues as possible in an effort to get classmates to guess the object. Challenge a second volunteer to choose another element and continue the process until the class is able to identify the object.

CLOSE
Direct students' attention to the interior space of your classroom. Remind them that this interior volume is defined by the room's walls. Encourage dialogue on how the "feel" of the space would change if the walls were placed at different angles or at different points in space.

39

The Principles of Art

Focus

Lesson Objectives

After studying this lesson, students will be able to:
- Explain how the principles are used to organize the elements of art.
- Analyze how successful works of art achieve unity by using the elements and principles.
- Demonstrate how a design chart can be used to identify the elements and principles in a work of art.

Building Vocabulary

Call students' attention to the Vocabulary list on this page. Note that each of the terms in the list has a second meaning that is beyond the realm of art. Have students divide a page of their art journal into two columns. In one column, they are to write a rough definition of each of the terms as it is used in a non-art sense. (*Balance*, for example, might be defined as "one's ability to stand erect and walk without falling over.") Explain that as words are encountered during the reading of the lesson, students are to provide the "art" definition of each term in the second column.

Motivator

Devise a makeshift balance scale using a long strip of heavy cardboard and the palm of your hand as a fulcrum. Challenge students to balance different classroom objects (e.g., a chalkboard eraser, a book) on the ends of the cardboard strip. Point out that they will shortly learn about the role of balance—and other modes of organization—in art.

The Principles of Art

Vocabulary
- design
- balance
- emphasis
- harmony
- variety
- gradation
- movement
- rhythm
- proportion

Discover

After completing this lesson, you will be able to:
- Explain how the principles of art are used to organize the elements of art.
- Analyze how successful works of art achieve unity by using the elements and principles of art.
- Demonstrate how a design chart can be used to identify the elements and principles in a work of art.

*A*rtists "design" their works by controlling and ordering the elements of art in some way. When trying to combine these different elements into an organized whole, they use certain principles, or guidelines. These principles of art are balance, emphasis, harmony, variety, gradation, movement, rhythm, and proportion. A unified **design**—*a skillful blend of elements and principles*—results when all the parts hold together to produce the best possible effect. Without this overall principle of unity, the work would "fall apart," or appear disorganized and confusing to the viewer.

The principles of art, then, describe the different ways artists can use each element. When working with any element, artists seek variety without chaos and harmony without monotony. The elements must fit together and work together to make a complete and unified whole.

In order to understand works of art, you need to know how the principles of art are used. You will use this knowledge whether you are examining works by artists who deliberately use a variety of art principles, or works by artists who use their instinct. Learning the principles will help you recognize and enjoy one of the most fascinating things about works of art: how they are put together.

The following principles should help you determine how the elements of art can be used to create art. Remember, each of these principles describes a unique way of combining or joining art elements to achieve different effects.

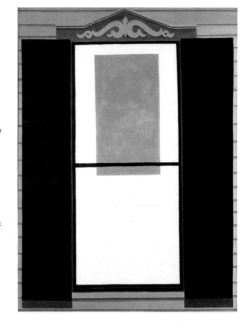

■ **FIGURE 2.15**
All the parts of this picture are equally distributed on either side of an imaginary vertical line in the center. Can you find any other paintings in this book that use this kind of symmetrical balance?

Georgia O'Keeffe. *Lake George Window.* 1929. Oil on canvas. 101.6 × 76.2 cm (40 × 30"). The Museum of Modern Art, New York, New York. Acquired through the Richard D. Brixey Bequest.

40

Balance

Balance refers to *a way of combining elements to add a feeling of equilibrium or stability* to a work of art. Balance can be of three kinds: symmetrical, asymmetrical, or radial.

Symmetrical balance means a formal balance in which two halves of a work are identical; one half mirrors exactly the other half (Figure 2.15). This is the simplest kind of balance.

Asymmetrical balance is more informal and takes into account such qualities as hue, intensity, and value in addition to size and shape. All these qualities have an effect on the apparent weight of objects shown in a work of art. It is possible to balance a large white shape on one side of a picture with a similar large shape of a light hue on

LESSON TWO RESOURCES

Teacher's Classroom Resources

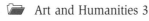 Appreciating Cultural Diversity 3

 Art and Humanities 3

 Cooperative Learning 2, 3

 Enrichment Activities 4, 5

 Reproducible Lesson Plan 4

 Reteaching Activity 4

 Study Guide 4

■ **FIGURE 2.16** The figure of the woman on the far left of this picture is balanced by the large white shape of the fireplace on the right. Do you consider the "felt" balance here more—or less—interesting than the symmetrical balance found in Figure 2.15?

Mary Cassatt. *The Tea.* c. 1880. Oil on canvas. 64.8 × 92.1 cm (25¹/₂ × 36¹/₄"). Museum of Fine Arts, Boston, Massachusetts. M. Theresa B. Hopkins Fund.

the other side (Figure 2.16). A smaller dark shape, though, may accomplish the same result. The dark value of the smaller shape makes it appear heavier and equal to the task of balancing the larger white shape. The result is a "felt" balance.

Radial balance occurs when objects are positioned around a central point. The daisy, with its petals radiating from the center of the flower, is a good example. Notice how the stained-glass window (Figure 2.17) was designed using radial balance.

■ **FIGURE 2.17** The colored glass shapes of this window radiate from the center like the spokes of a wheel. What other kind of balance is demonstrated in this work?

Stained-glass window (West rose window). Chartres Cathedral, France. 1153–1260.

Chapter 2 *Developing a Visual Vocabulary* **41**

TEACH
Introducing the Lesson

Ask a volunteer to relate the mythical account of Sir Isaac Newton's encounter with a falling apple. After establishing that Newton discovered the law of gravity, ask students whether they know synonyms for *law* (e.g., *regulation, principle, rule*). Help students recognize that some laws, chiefly the empirical law of science, are also known as principles and that a principle is a way of organizing information.

Studio Skills

Volunteers can seek out examples of symmetrical, asymmetrical, and radial balance in your community. They can sketch or photograph buildings or structures that exhibit one of these categories of balance and share their photos with the class.

Cross Curriculum

SCIENCE. Explain to students that the sense of physical balance in human beings is controlled in the middle ear. You might display a technical drawing of the ear. Have students brainstorm activities and pursuits in which balance is critical, not only from an aesthetic but from a practical standpoint (e.g., in building construction, in sports). Invite interested groups to research and prepare a presentation on the relationship between an object's base of support and its center of gravity.

Art Criticism

Display examples of the intricately cut paper designs found in Polish and other central European cultures. Invite students to examine and discuss the types of balance in these works.

Technology

National Gallery of Art Videodisc Use the following images as examples of more works by artists introduced in this lesson.

Mary Cassatt
The Boating Party

Search Frame 2016

Mary Cassatt
Children Playing on the Beach
Search Frame 2006

Mary Cassatt
Girl Arranging Her Hair

Search Frame 2010

Use Glencoe's *Correlation Bar Code Guide to the National Gallery of Art* to locate more artworks.

Cross Curriculum

LANGUAGE ARTS. Remind students that humans have the means to add emphasis to a word or idea (i.e., we can italicize the printed word, raise the volume of the voice when speaking). Have teams experiment with the differences in meaning that arise when the same sentence is spoken with an emphasis on a different word. After experimenting with several sentences (e.g., "She said I could go"), have them share their discoveries.

Art Criticism

Have students study *Rainy Night Downtown* by Georgia Mills Jessup (Figure 2.18), which illustrates the principle of emphasis. Ask students whether the work also makes use of the principle of harmony. Which colors blend well (i.e., harmonize) with other colors in the work? Which elements besides color have been organized in a harmonic fashion?

Cross Curriculum

MUSIC. Ask students with musical training to explain the role harmony plays in a composition. Have several volunteers illustrate harmony by performing a well-known round, such as "Row, Row Your Boat." Ask the class as a whole to discuss differences and similarities in harmony as it is applied in this musical number and in the work in Figure 2.19.

■ **FIGURE 2.18**
The vertical shapes in the center of this work contrast with the larger round shapes at the sides. Can you also find contrasts of hue and line in this painting?

Georgia Mills Jessup. *Rainy Night Downtown.* 1967. Oil on canvas. 111.8 × 120 cm (44 × 48"). The National Museum of Women in the Arts, Washington, D.C. Gift of Savanna M. Clark.

■ **FIGURE 2.19**
Notice the shapes in this painting. What has the artist done to add variety to the painting?

Liubov Popova. *Painterly Architectonics.* 1918. Oil on cardboard. 59.4 × 39.4 cm (23³⁄₈ × 15¹⁄₂"). Dallas Museum of Art, Dallas, Texas. General Acquisition Fund and gifts from Mrs. Edward Marcus, James H. Coker and Ann Addison, Margaret Ann Bolinger, George and Schatzie Lee, Elizabeth B. Blake and an anonymous donor.

42 **Unit One** *Creating and Understanding Art*

Emphasis

Emphasis, or *contrast,* is *a way of combining elements to stress the differences between those elements.* Contrasting elements often are used to direct and focus the viewer's attention on the most important parts of a design. Artists try to avoid making works of art in which the same colors, values, lines, shapes, forms, textures, and space relationships are used over and over again. They know that such works may be monotonous and uninteresting. To avoid this, artists introduce obvious contrasts that establish centers of interest in their works.

In *Rainy Night Downtown* (Figure 2.18), Georgia Mills Jessup creates a center of interest by painting a compact collection of vertical, abstract shapes to represent the crowds of people in a busy downtown area at night. Around the edges she uses larger shapes that are brighter and more loosely defined. The contrast between both the colors and the shapes gives the scene vitality. Try to imagine how this picture would look without these contrasts—the picture would lack its visual interest.

Harmony

Harmony refers to *a way of combining similar elements in an artwork to accent their similarities.* It is accomplished through the use of repetitions and subtle, gradual changes. Complex, intricate relationships are avoided in favor of a more uncomplicated, uniform appearance. A limited number of like elements often are used in an effort to tie the picture parts together into a harmonious whole. This is certainly evident in Liubov Popova's work *Painterly Architectonics* (Figure 2.19). Notice how the repetition of similar colors, shapes, and values emphasizes the overall unity of the picture's surface.

COOPERATIVE LEARNING

Harmony. Divide the class into two groups, and assign one group the principle of harmony and one the principle of variety. Each group should browse through the book and write down the name and page number of ten works—besides those in Chapter 2—that exhibit the principle they have been assigned. The groups are then to trade lists and analyze the works named in an effort to find evidence of their own principle in a work that was singled out as containing the opposite principle. Allow time for a discussion of the reciprocal relationship between harmony and variety.

Variety

Variety is *a way of combining elements in involved ways to create intricate and complicated relationships.* It is achieved through diversity and change (Figure 2.20). Artists turn to this principle when they want to increase the visual interest of their works. A picture made up of many different hues, values, lines, textures, and shapes would be described as complex.

A carefully determined blend of harmony and variety is essential to the success of almost any work of art. Both principles must be taken into account during the creative process. Harmony blends the picture parts together to form a unified whole, and variety adds visual interest to this unified whole. It is this visual interest that attracts and holds the attention of viewers.

Gradation

Gradation refers to *a way of combining elements by using a series of gradual changes in those elements.* Examples of gradation include a gradual change from small shapes to large shapes or from a dark hue to a light hue. Unlike emphasis, which often stresses sudden and abrupt changes in elements, gradation refers to an ordered, step-by-step change (Figure 2.21).

■ **FIGURE 2.20** Notice the combination of rounded and angular shapes in this painting. **Describe the different textures in the work. Where is the greatest concentration of texture?**

Max Weber. *Chinese Restaurant.* 1915. Oil on canvas. 101.6 × 121.9 cm (40 × 48″). Collection of Whitney Museum of American Art, New York, New York. Purchase.

■ **FIGURE 2.21** Notice the step-by-step change from large to smaller shapes. **What does this gradual change from large to smaller shapes accomplish?**

Antonio M. Ruiz. *School Children on Parade.* 1936. Oil on canvas. 24 × 33.8 cm (9¹/₂ × 13¹/₄″). Secretaria de Hacienda y Credito Publico, Mexico City, Mexico. © Antonio M. Ruiz/SOMAAP México, 1999.

Chapter 2 *Developing a Visual Vocabulary* **43**

Art Criticism

Have students study *Chinese Restaurant* by Max Weber (Figure 2.20, page 43). Then ask these questions: How does the artist create variety through his use of the elements of line and color? What sense, feeling, or mood does he communicate through his use of line? What role does color play in the painting's message?

Studio Skills

Divide the class into groups of three or four students and have groups brainstorm different kinds of gradation (e.g., dark to lighter hues, sharp angularity to smoothness of shape). After groups have shared and pooled the results of their brainstorming sessions, students can work independently to arrange on a sheet of paper examples of the different kinds of gradation mentioned. Students may either cull their examples from magazine photos and illustrations or create them from scratch.

Aesthetics

Invite students to browse figuratively through the art gallery represented by the works reproduced in this lesson. After their "stroll," students are to debate statements like the following: *Beauty is in the eye of the beholder; Something can be offensive to the eye and still be called a work of art; The purpose of art is to fill the world with beauty.*

■ **FIGURE 2.22** The shapes in this painting appear to be moving. Describe the direction and speed of the apparent movement.

Marcel Duchamp. *Nude Descending a Staircase #2.* 1912. Oil on canvas. 147.3 × 89 cm (58 × 35"). Philadelphia Museum of Art, Philadelphia, Pennsylvania. Louise and Walter Arensberg Collection.

Movement

Movement is *the principle of art used to create the look and feeling of action and to guide the viewer's eye throughout the work of art.* Of course, in a two-dimensional artwork, any look or sensation of action or motion is only an illusion: A horse shown in full gallop gives only the impression of motion. There are some three-dimensional artworks, however, that actually do move. They allow the viewer to study the constantly changing relationships of colors, shapes, forms, lines, and textures found in the artworks.

Movement is also used to direct the viewer's attention to a center of interest, or to make certain that the main parts of the work are noted. This movement is achieved through placement of elements so that the eye follows a certain path, such as the curve of a line, the contours of a shape, or the repetition of certain colors, textures, or shapes.

Rhythm

Closely related to movement is the principle of rhythm. **Rhythm** is created by *the careful placement of repeated elements in a work of art to cause a visual tempo or beat.* These repeated elements invite the viewer's eye to jump rapidly or glide smoothly from one to the next. For example, the same shape may be repeated several times and arranged across the picture to create the sensation of movement in a certain direction. As the viewer's eye sweeps from shape to shape, this sensation is heightened, as seen in Marcel Duchamp's *Nude Descending a Staircase #2* (Figure 2.22).

Sometimes visual contrasts set up a rhythm, in which elements are repeated and combined with contrasting colors, values, shapes, lines, or textures. A certain color may rush forward, then backward, or light values may clash with darker values, all the while moving the viewer's eye through the work.

Teacher Notes

Visual Imaging. Students can develop a better understanding of how the elements and principles of art are present in their lives through exercises in *visual imaging.* This is a technique used by athletes to improve their game. To help students better appreciate movement, ask them to close their eyes and imagine a perfectly calm, placid lake. Make sure each student has in his or her mind's eye a vivid picture of glassy water under a blue sky. Then ask them to imagine a thrown pebble slowly arcing downward toward the surface and the succession of ripples radiating outward from its point of contact with the water. Then ask students to discuss their perceptions of various elements and principles.

Proportion

Proportion is *the principle of art concerned with the relationship of certain elements to the whole and to each other.* Proportion often is closely connected with emphasis. If in a certain portion of a painting, there are more intense hues than dull hues, or more rough textures than smooth, emphasis is suggested. In a similar manner, the large size of one shape compared with the smaller sizes of other shapes creates visual emphasis. The viewer's eye is automatically attracted to the larger, dominant shape.

In the past and in other cultures, artists often relied on the principle of proportion to point out the most important figures or objects in their works. The more important figures were made to look larger than the other, less important figures. This was the case in the bronze sculpture created by an artist of the Benin Empire in Africa (Figure 2.23). This relief was made to decorate the wooden pillars of the palace in the Court of Benin. The powerful king of the tribe is shown on horseback. The sculptor has made the king the largest figure, emphasizing his importance. The king's various servants are shown proportionately smaller, indicating their relative lack of importance. The size of the king in relation to the others is as effective as a spotlight in emphasizing his importance.

■ **FIGURE 2.23** The size of the figures in this work indicates their importance. What principles of art have been used to give this bronze sculpture a unified look?

Kingdom of Benin, Edo people, Nigeria. *Mounted King with Attendants.* c. 16th–17th century. Bronze. 49.5 × 41.9 × 11.3 cm (19$\frac{1}{2}$ × 16$\frac{1}{2}$ × 4$\frac{1}{2}$"). The Metropolitan Museum of Art, New York, New York. The Michael C. Rockefeller Memorial Collection. Gift of Nelson A. Rockefeller, 1965. (1978.412.309).

Chapter 2 *Developing a Visual Vocabulary* **45**

Cross Curriculum

MATH. Remind students that in math one speaks of the phenomenon of proportion in reference to, among other things, fractions. Write the fraction 1/4 on the chalkboard. Then draw a circle, divide it into four equal parts, and shade an open part. Point out that a fraction is a relationship that indicates a *proportion of the whole.* Suggest, finally, that students keep fractions (and percents) in mind as a memory aid when discussing and analyzing the principle of proportion in art, since proportion involves the relationship of certain elements to the whole and to each other.

Art Criticism

Have students consider Duchamp's classic *Nude Descending a Staircase #2* (Figure 2.22). Ask them to discuss which element besides shape is most fundamental in conveying a sense of movement.

Studio Skills

Have students fold a sheet of white paper in half vertically, then flatten the sheet out. Holding the page sideways (i.e., with the long edge facing them), they are to draw five circles of varying size across the top half, gradually widening the space between circles. Then do the same with rectangles or squares along the bottom half. Ask students to compare their efforts and note the way in which changes in size and spatial relations appear to create rhythm and movement.

COOPERATIVE LEARNING

Principles of Art. Divide the class into groups and explain that they are about to become a group of experts. Assign each group a different art principle. Explain that the group's task is to analyze every artwork reproduced in Chapter 2 and show how that principle was used to organize the elements. Form new discussion groups made up of one student from each expert group, and give these new groups an unfamiliar work to analyze. Encourage each student to use his or her new-found expertise to contribute to the discussion group.

Studio Skills

Have students examine the bronze sculpture in Figure 2.23. Ask a volunteer to read aloud the analysis of the work on page 270. Then, using markers, bits of colored paper, and glue, students are to construct plaques on paper plates celebrating themselves as individuals. Each student's plaque is to show him- or herself surrounded by prized possessions, as well as symbolic representations of personal skills, character traits, and other features of self-identity. Like the Benin sculpture, the plaques should reveal an interesting sense of proportion.

Art History

Point out that works like the bronze relief in Figure 2.23 represent an important chapter in the history of art. Invite a group of interested students to research and report orally to the class on the *ciré perdue* method of casting in bronze. Challenge students in their report to reveal when this method was perfected in the West and in what other non-Western cultures this method has been used. Students should display visual examples of bronze castings from the Benin and other African cultures.

Study Guide

Distribute *Study Guide* 4 in the TCR and review key concepts with students. 🖿

Art and Humanities

Assign *Cooperative Learning* 2, "The Elements in the Media," in the TCR. 🖿

Achieving Unity in a Work of Art

Although unity was discussed earlier, its importance demands additional comment here. Unity may be thought of as an overall concept—or principle. It refers to the total effect of a work of art. All artists draw from the same reservoir of elements and principles, but few are able to take those elements and principles and fashion works of art that are unique, exciting, and complete. Those who do achieve unity. Any of the works illustrated in this book can be studied in relation to this overall principle.

Discovering Design Relationships in Art

The Design Chart (Figure 2.24) can help you identify the many possible relationships between elements and principles in works of art. The first step in determining how a work is put together is to ask the right questions about it. The Design Chart helps you identify these questions.

	PRINCIPLES OF ART						
ELEMENTS OF ART	Balance	Emphasis	Harmony	Variety	Gradation	Movement/ Rhythm	Proportion
Color: Hue							
Intensity							
Value							
Value (Non-Color)							
Line							
Texture							
Shape/Form							
Space							

UNITY

Note: Do not write on this chart

■ **FIGURE 2.24** Design Chart

More About... **Using a Design Chart.** The design chart is useful not only in analyzing extant works of art but may be used to help students become more acute observers. Equipped with such a chart, students might be invited to examine in detail a familiar object or scene as though for the first time—for example, the front of the school building or a well-known landmark in the community. Instruct students to note the elements of art called into play by the architect, as well as the principles he or she used to organize them. Have students compare their completed charts. Encourage each to alter his or her perceptions where necessary.

Using the Design Chart

Begin with any element and then, referring to the chart, ask yourself how this element is used in a work. Your questions will link the element with each principle. For example, you might begin an examination of a painting by looking at hue. Then, referring to each principle in order, you would ask and then answer such questions as these about the work:

- Are the hues in the picture *balanced* formally or informally?
- Are contrasting hues used to direct the eye to areas of *emphasis*?
- Is *harmony* achieved through the use of similar hues that are repeated throughout the picture?
- Are different hues used to add *variety* to the composition?
- Do any of the hues change gradually, or in a *gradation* from one to another?
- Are the hues arranged to create a feeling of *movement* or *rhythm*?
- Is the presence of any one hue out of *proportion* to the other hues used in the picture?

Once you have completed an examination of hue, you would turn to the next quality of color, which is intensity, and repeat the procedure with all the principles. An analysis carried on in this manner can help you gain the knowledge and understanding needed to determine how the parts of a picture have been put together to achieve *unity*. In Chapter 4, you will find that the Design Chart can be a very helpful aid when you are trying to learn as much as you can from a work of art.

A work of art is made up of many different colors, values, lines, textures, shapes, forms, and space relationships. The artist who creates it must combine these elements into an organized whole, and this takes a great deal of knowledge and skill. When viewing a work of art, you must determine how the artist has done this, and that too takes a great deal of knowledge and skill. When you have this knowledge and skill, you are able to do more than merely *look* at art; you can *see* it—and fully appreciate it.

LESSON TWO REVIEW

Reviewing Art Facts

1. How are the principles of art used in creating works of art?
2. Name and define the three types of balance.
3. How can harmony be achieved in creating a work of art?
4. What principle of art leads a viewer to sense action in a work?

Activity... *Working with Elements and Principles*

Combining the elements and the principles of art allows endless variations that make art an exciting challenge for the artist. In all art periods, cultures, and movements, artists work with the elements and principles.

Have one student read these statements to the class: *If I were a color, I would be...; If I were a line, I would be...; If I were a value, I would be...* (continue with all elements of art). Have another student sketch the responses on the board. When the board is filled with various sketches, discuss with classmates how a unified design can be created using the sketches. Create your own design on a sheet of paper that combines the sketched items using the principles of art.

Art and Humanities

Distribute *Appreciating Cultural Diversity* 3, "Design in Different Cultures," in the TCR. Instruct individual students to look for differences in the way various cultures approach the phenomenon of design. 📁

Studio Activities

Distribute *Studio* 3, "Imagine Artists as Fabric Designers," in the TCR. 📁

ASSESS
Checking Comprehension

Have students complete the lesson review questions. Answers appear in the box below.

Reteaching

Assign *Reteaching* 4, found in the TCR and review key concepts with students. 📁

Enrichment

Distribute *Cooperative Learning* 3, "Design Elements in Your Natural Environment," in the TCR to small groups of students. Challenge groups to analyze how the elements and principles of art are present in a natural environment. 📁

Extension

Students can find and sketch examples from nature that illustrate the principles of balance, proportion, rhythm, and variety.

CLOSE

Have students open their textbooks and randomly select an artwork. Invite students to discuss how the elements and principles have been used to achieve unity.

LESSON TWO REVIEW

Answers to Reviewing Art Facts

1. To control or order the elements of art.
2. Radial, symmetrical, and asymmetrical.
3. By combining similar elements to accent similarities.
4. Movement.

Activity... *Working with Elements and Principles*

Work with students as they begin the discussion on the use of elements and principles. This discussion can lead students to understand how to create a unified design using the elements and principles. Have each student describe how the principles were used to unify their designs. Display the results.

Still Life Emphasizing Line, Shape, and Color

Objectives
- Experiment with different qualities and line variations to create a still life.
- Use positive and negative space to create interest.

Motivator
Collect as many different media and tools as you can find, including sharpened bits of mineral containing natural pigment, and demonstrate line variations and line quality and the effects of hue on each. Then give students the opportunity to experiment with the media and have them identify the tool that produced a line with even thickness; a line that changed from light to dark; and areas that appear to be interrupted or broken in places.

Aesthetics
Turn students' attention to the still life created by Luis Meléndez, Figure 2.13, page 37. Tell students that a still life is composed of familiar objects and drawn as accurately as possible. Have them identify the items that the artist used for this particular composition (boxes, fruit, jars) and explore other objects that the students could use to create their own still-life arrangements. Ask: Which aesthetic theory would be best to use when judging this work of art? (Imitationalism.)

Critiquing
Have students apply the steps of art criticism to their own artworks using the "Examining Your Work" questions.

Still Life Emphasizing Line, Shape, and Color

Materials
- Pencils and sketch paper
- Ruler
- White drawing paper or mat board, 15 × 22 inches
- Colored pencils

Using colored pencils, complete a drawing of a close-up view of a still life. Include all or parts of four or more objects. Draw these objects in outline and overlap the shapes. Use four different types of line: 1) even weight; 2) light to dark; 3) thick to thin; 4) broken.

Fill in two or more parts of your composition with hues that are low in intensity. Identify the focal point of your composition, and emphasize it by using a third, high-intensity hue.

Inspiration
Examine the paintings and drawings in *Art in Focus,* noting the different kinds of lines used in each. Can you find a work in which the lines are of an even or equal weight or thickness throughout? Change from light to dark? Change from thick to thin? Appear to be interrupted or broken in places?

The areas representing the figures and other objects in a composition are known as *positive shapes.* The areas that remain after the positive shapes have been created are known as *negative shapes.* Select a work in which you can identify the positive and negative shapes.

Look for a painting in the text that demonstrates how a contrast of intensities can be used to emphasize an important part of the composition.

■ **FIGURE 2.25** Student Work

Process
1. Complete several pencil sketches of a still-life arrangement consisting of four or more interesting objects. Overlap the objects in your sketches.
2. Study your sketches carefully and, with a ruler, draw a box around the most interesting sections of each. On white drawing paper, complete a line drawing of the area represented in the best of your boxed sections. Use four types of lines in this drawing: even weight; light to dark; thick to thin, and broken.
3. Select at least *two negative shapes* in your composition and, with colored pencil, carefully fill these in with hues of low intensity. Identify a *single positive shape* in your composition that you want to emphasize. Color this in with a hue of high intensity.

Examining Your Work
Describe. Point out and name the four or more still-life objects in your drawing. Are others able to identify these objects?

Analyze. Does your drawing include four different kinds of line? Show where each is used. Did you color two or more negative shapes with dull or low-intensity hues? Did you also emphasize one positive shape by coloring it with a bright or high-intensity hue?

Interpret. Do you think you solved the artistic problems pertaining to line, shape, and color called for in this studio exercise?

Judge. Do you think your composition is successful? What is its most appealing feature? If you were to do it again, what would you change?

48

ASSESSMENT

Examining Your Work. Divide the class into two groups, each to serve as a review committee for the artworks of the students in the other group. Instruct each group to begin by restating the assignment in its simplest terms (i.e., to create a still life with a minimum of four objects using pencils and paper as media). Ask which of the four steps in art criticism this restatement corresponds to (description). Have groups determine whether each work under review meets these basic criteria. From there, groups are to proceed to the more analytical steps of the critiquing process. Instruct groups to be as fair and impartial as possible. Allow the groups to reunite and devise a rubric for assessing the works as a whole.

Reviewing the Facts

Lesson One

1. What is the relationship between the elements and principles of art?
2. Which of the three qualities of color refers to a color's name and its location on the color wheel?
3. How do works of art described as *linear* differ from those described as *painterly*?
4. Identify the five kinds of line, and describe the effect each kind is intended to achieve in an artwork.
5. How does actual texture differ from simulated texture?
6. How can painters create the illusion of solid, three-dimensional objects?

Lesson Two

7. What kind of balance is shown in a work with one half that mirrors the other?
8. What can happen when an artist avoids the use of emphasis in a work?
9. How is unity achieved?

Thinking Critically

1. **ANALYZE.** What would you do if you were interested in changing a color's intensity? How would you change a color's value?
2. **COMPARE AND CONTRAST.** Look at Figure 2.10 on page 34 and Figure 2.14 on page 38. List the techniques the two artists used to create the illusion of depth or distance.

 DANCE. Use the *Performing Arts Handbook*, page 578 to learn about the Lewitsky Dance Company and "Impressions #2."

■ CAREERS IN Read about a career as an art director in the *Careers in Art Handbook*, page 595.

*inter***NET** **CONNECTION** Visit Glencoe Art Online at *www.glencoe.com/sec/art*. Explore images from art collections, learn about the language of art, and try some interesting activities.

Technology Project

Design Basics

The talents that artists seem to possess come from their ability to make thoughts and feelings visible as pictures and images. Most people use verbal language as communication. Artists use the visual language of art to represent, depict, or symbolize an idea, concept, feeling, or emotion. To do so, they must understand how to arrange the art elements according to the art principles to achieve a unified design. The art elements and principles form a universal visual language in the arts. No matter what the time period, the culture, or the personal style of the artist, all artists work with the art elements and principles. As a computer artist, you will find that the art elements appear as tools and options that can be manipulated according to art principles in many computer programs.

1. Create a nonobjective design that allows you to use the following tools and options: lines, unfilled and filled objects, gradients, geometric and free-form objects, grayscale, color. Choose at least three art elements that you will arrange according to three art principles in order to achieve a unified design.
2. Experiment with various commands until you are satisfied with your design. Before printing a copy of it, be sure that you can identify and describe the art elements you have used. Analyze how you have arranged the art elements according to the art principles to create a unified design.
3. Print a copy of your design to present to the class or keep in your portfolio or sketchbook.
4. Write a critique describing, analyzing, and judging whether or not you achieved a unified design, and discuss your results with the class or with your work group.

Reviewing the Facts

1. Elements are the building blocks of art; principles are the ways in which the elements can be used.
2. Hue.
3. Linear works make use of contour lines; painterly works de-emphasize lines.
4. Vertical lines suggest stability; horizontal lines suggest calmness; diagonal lines suggest tension; curved lines suggest flowing movement. An axis line is imaginary and identifies movement or direction.
5. Actual texture appeals to vision and touch; simulated texture to vision.
6. Making distant shapes smaller, placing distant shapes higher, less detail on distant shapes, duller hues for distant shapes, coloring distant shapes to suggest atmosphere, and slanting lines.
7. Symmetrical.
8. Avoiding emphasis causes boredom.
9. It is the application of principles to elements to create a complete, aesthetically appealing artwork.

Thinking Critically

1. Intensity could be changed by seeking out either livelier or duller variants of a hue; value could be changed by adding black or white.
2. Answers should include: distant shapes smaller and closer shapes larger, distant shapes higher, using blue to suggest atmosphere, less detail in distance, slanting horizon lines for Giorgione; distant shapes smaller, less detail on distant shapes.

Teaching the Technology Project

Review the concepts and commands in the assignment. Make sure they understand the importance of "closing" any objects they intend to fill. If students are using a paint program and wish to include gradient fills, they may need some guidance. Remind students that errors and unintended commands can be corrected by using the Undo Command.

 Assign the feature in the *Performing Arts Handbook*, page 578.

CAREERS IN ART If time permits, have interested students investigate the career information in the *Careers in Art Handbook*, page 595.

*inter***NET** **CONNECTION** Have students go online and learn more about artists on preselected Web sites with the Internet activity for this chapter.

Creating Art: Media and Processes

ADDITIONAL CHAPTER RESOURCES

Activities

- 📁 Application 3
- 📁 Advanced Studio Activity 3
- 🖱 Chapter 3 Internet Activity
- 📁 Studio Activity 4

Fine Art Resources

 Transparencies

Art in Focus Transparency 5
Umberto Boccioni. *Unique Forms of Continuity in Space.*

Art in Focus Transparency 6
The J. Paul Getty Museum and Institute.

🖼 **Fine Art Print**

Focus on World Art Print 3
Rufino Tamayo. *Toast to the Sun.*

Assessment

- 📁 Chapter 3 Test
- 📁 Performance Assessment

Multimedia Resources

- 🎭 Artsource® Performing Arts Package
- 💿 National Gallery Laser Disc
- 💿 National Museum of Women in the Arts CD-ROM
- 📼 Arts & Entertainment Videos

 NATIONAL STANDARDS FOR ARTS EDUCATION

The National Standards for Arts Education provide guidelines for grade-appropriate competency in the visual arts. The Content Standards for grades 9–12 are:

1. Understanding and applying media, techniques, and processes.
2. Using knowledge of structures and functions.
3. Choosing and evaluating a range of subject matter, symbols, and ideas.
4. Understanding the visual arts in relation to history and cultures.
5. Reflecting upon and assessing the characteristics and merits of their work and the work of others.
6. Making connections between visual arts and other disciplines.

Listed below are the National Standards for the Visual Arts addressed in this chapter. For a breakdown of the categories listed under each content standard, refer to the *Reproducible Lesson Plans* booklet in the TCR.

   1. (a, b)   **2.** (a, b, c)   **3.** (a)   **4.** (a, b, c)   **5.** (b, c)   **6.** (b)

HANDBOOK MATERIAL

A R T S O U R C E Lewitsky Dance Company *(page 579)*

 **CAREERS IN** Art

Graphic Designer *(page 596)*

Beyond the Classroom

The Kennedy Center for Arts Education and ArtsEdge is an invaluable resource. The ArtsEdge site is a comprehensive and diverse collection of visual and performing arts, lesson plans, exhibits, and forums. Connect to ArtsEdge by visiting our Web site at *www.glencoe.com/sec/art.*

🕐 **Out of Time?** If time does not permit teaching this chapter in its entirety, you may wish to preview the artwork and captions with students. Scan the heads in each lesson with students. Discuss the Looking Closely features and examine Subject Matter in Art on page 56.

Creating Art: Media and Processes

CHAPTER 3

Creating Art: Media and Processes

INTRODUCE

Chapter Overview

CHAPTER 3 introduces students to the materials and processes used to create art.

Lesson One covers the media and processes of drawing and painting.

Lesson Two examines printmaking and photography and introduces technologies of video and digital media.

Lesson Three discusses the media of sculpture.

Lesson Four introduces architecture media and processes.

Studio Lessons guide students to experiment with different media.

Art & Language Arts

Discuss with students the importance of stories and traditions that are preserved in the art of quilting. Ask volunteers to share information about quilts in their families or quilts they may have seen. Ask: How does this form of storytelling or record-keeping reflect the history and traditions of American families?

Art & Language Arts ■ **FIGURE 3.1** Family histories can be recorded in many ways. Records are kept in diaries or orally passed down from generation to generation. Sometimes family stories are preserved as a visual narrative in a quilt, like the one being created in the artwork shown here. Quilt blocks may show images of actual people, places, or events or they may contain symbols with meanings known only to the maker.

Romare Bearden. *Maquette for Quilting Time.* 1985. Paper on board. Detroit Institute of the Arts, Detroit, Michigan. Founders Society purchase with funds from the Detroit Edison Company. © Romare Bearden Foundation/Licensed by VAGA, New York, New York.

50

National Standards

This chapter addresses the following National Standards for the Arts.
1. (a,b)   4. (a,b,c)
2. (a,b,c)   5. (b, c)
3. (a)   6. (b)

CHAPTER 3 RESOURCES

Teacher's Classroom Resources
- 📁 Advanced Studio Activity 3
- 📁 Application 3
- 🖱 Chapter 3 Internet Activity
- 📁 Studio Activity 4

Assessment
- 📁 Chapter 3 Test
- 📁 Performance Assessment

Fine Art Resources
- 🔖 *Art in Focus* Transparency 5
  Boccioni. *Unique Forms of Continuity in Space.*
  Art in Focus Transparency 6
  The J. Paul Getty Museum
- 🖼 *Focus on World Art* Print 3
  Rufino Tamayo. *Toast to the Sun.*

*A*lmost as important as the elements and principles of art are the media and processes that artists choose to express their ideas and feelings. Taking the materials that time and place provide for them, visual artists, musicians, writers, and artists in all fields respond to the urge to create. The products of their efforts rank among the high points of human achievement.

Introducing the Chapter

Point out that when many people hear the term artist, they instinctively think of painters. Ask students if they know of tools other than paint and brushes that artists use to express themselves.

A R T S O U R C E **Dance.** Help students recognize how choreographer, Bella Lewitzky found inspiration for her dance, "Impressions #1 (Moore)" on page 579 of the *Performing Arts Handbook.*

YOUR Portfolio

Work in pairs or small groups. Choose a subject for a three-dimensional sculpture. Consider what medium and process would best suit the content. Why is the medium appropriate for the design? Try to anticipate any problems with the medium. Draw a rough sketch of your design and briefly describe the medium and process you have chosen. Exchange sketches. Draw another sketch of the subject using a different medium and process. Again, briefly describe the design. Continue exchanging and revising the designs and then return to the original group. Discuss any new ideas that came from the exercise. Keep your sketches and notes in your portfolio.

Focus ON THE ARTS

THEATRE
The relative importance of props and scenery—the media of the modern theatre—is driven home by their absence in *Our Town* by Thornton Wilder. This play takes a microcosmic look at life in a small New England town.

MUSIC
Several composers have attempted to present the instrumental "media" of music—strings, brass, woodwind, and percussion—to the listener through compositions that teach as well as entertain. Consider Benjamin Britten's *Young Person's Guide to the Orchestra.*

LITERATURE
Many writers discuss the creative process in their works. A fine example of this is the whimsically titled "Beware: Do Not Read This Poem," by African-American poet Ishmael Reed.

Focus ON THE ARTS

Ask students to develop an "idea web" of artifacts families maintain as living histories. (Answers might include photograph albums, video and audio tape recordings of family events and get-togethers, and assorted mementos and memorabilia.) Note that, in a sense, the items named are the "media" of family memories. Note that artists of all persuasions have used media of their own to capture the family theme. Ask a volunteer to read aloud the three passages in the student text, while everyone else reads along silently.

Conclude by asking selected volunteers to perform a scene from Our Town. The play should be easy to do since it requires no props, costumes, or scenery. Ask the audience to write critiques of the piece(s) performed.

51

DEVELOPING A PORTFOLIO

Self-Reflection. Remind students that creative people often study their work habits in an effort to understand their natural cycles of creativity. For example, a person might discover that ideas and inspiration come freely at a particular period of the day. Wisely then, that person would work on art projects during hours that match their creative peaks. Ask students to keep a daily journal for a period of several weeks for the purpose of observing their individual creative times. When do they feel inspired? Do they have rituals such as playing specific background music, wearing a favorite paint smock, or using a preferred tool? What can they learn about their work habits to help them develop as artists?

Drawing and Painting

Focus

Lesson Objectives

After studying this lesson, students will be able to:
- Identify and define various two-dimensional art processes and media.
- Explain where artists find ideas for their works.
- Describe the three basic components of paint.

Vocabulary

Have students list each of the Vocabulary terms for this lesson on a sheet of paper. Then ask them to look up each of the words in the text or using the Glossary, and write the definitions. Have them keep the definitions in their portfolios.

Motivator

Divide the class into two groups. Distribute to one group an assortment of familiar drawing media (e.g., crayons, pencils), distribute to the other group an assortment that is probably unfamiliar to them (e.g., charcoal pencils, oil pastels, ink and fine brushes). Ask students to experiment with the various drawing implements.

Introducing the Lesson

Have students examine the artworks in this Lesson. Ask them to decide which of the works they find most appealing. Are they more attracted to the artist's style or to the subject matter? How is their reaction influenced by the media used in the work?

Drawing and Painting

Vocabulary
- dry media
- wet media
- still life
- pigment
- binder
- solvent

Discover
After completing this lesson, you will be able to:
- Discuss the processes of drawing and painting.
- Explain how artists find ideas for their artworks.
- Name and describe the three basic ingredients in paint.

*D*rawing and painting are two important means through which artists give visible form to their ideas and feelings. A knowledge of the media and processes used to create drawings and paintings will prepare you to recognize and respond to those ideas and feelings. It will also help you give form to your own ideas and feelings.

Drawing

Drawing is a process of portraying an object, scene, or form of decorative or symbolic meaning through lines, shapes, values, and textures in one or more colors. This process involves moving a pointed instrument such as a pencil, crayon, or stick of chalk over a smooth surface, leaving behind the marks of its passage. The generally accepted name for this mark is *line*. Although their styles differ (Figures 3.2 and 3.3), all drawings have a common purpose: to give form to an idea and express the artist's feelings about it.

■ **FIGURE 3.2** The artist used this ink drawing to express his ideas and feelings about a religious subject. Which elements and principles of art do you identify as most important in this drawing?

Guercino. *Saint Jerome and the Angel.* c. 1640. Brown ink on paper. 24 × 21.6 cm (9⁷/₁₆ × 8¹/₂"). University of Iowa Museum of Art, Iowa City, Iowa. Museum Purchase.

52

■ **FIGURE 3.3** Notice how the artist used fine, carefully placed lines in this drawing. Which part of the drawing is emphasized? How is the emphasis achieved?

Jean-Auguste-Dominique Ingres. *Charles Francois Mallet, Civil Engineer.* 1809. Graphite on cream wove paper. 26.8 × 21.1 cm (11 × 8"). The Art Institute of Chicago, Chicago, Illinois. The Charles Deering Collection, 1938.166.

LESSON ONE RESOURCES

Teacher's Classroom Resources
- 📁 Appreciating Cultural Diversity 4
- 📁 Cooperative Learning 4
- 📁 Enrichment Activity 6
- 📁 Reproducible Lesson Plan 5
- 📁 Reteaching Activity 5
- 📁 Study Guide 5

The seventeenth-century Italian artist Guercino (guair-**chee**-noh) used his drawing skills to capture the strong religious feelings that dominated his time and place. With a style featuring spontaneous and vigorous lines, he gives visual form to his idea of St. Jerome listening intently to an angel in Figure 3.2.

In this work, the rapidly drawn lines add excitement and action to the scene. Compare these to the fine, carefully placed lines found in Figure 3.3 created by a French artist almost 200 years later. Jean-Auguste-Dominique Ingres (zhahn oh-**gust** doh-min-**eek ahn**-gr) used the lines in his drawing to capture the exact appearance and scholarly dignity of a French civil engineer.

Clearly, the artist's purpose is important in determining the style of a drawing. The choice of a drawing medium, often based on the artist's purpose, can also contribute to style.

Drawing Media

The media for drawing can be divided into two types: dry and wet. **Dry media** are *those media that are applied dry;* they include pencil, charcoal, crayon, and chalk or pastel. An example of a drawing created with a dry medium is Mary Cassatt's (kuh-**sat**) pastel in Figure 3.4.

TEACH
Art Criticism

Have students study the works in Figures 3.1 (page 50), 3.2 (page 52). What emotion or mood does each of these works evoke? To what extent does the expressive quality depend on the drawing media used? Have students discuss and explain their responses.

Studio Skills

Remind students that drawing media can be divided into the categories of wet or dry. Have them bring to class non-traditional drawing media. Possibilities include twigs, roots, grasses, crumpled paper (this can be dipped into ink), bits of charcoal, tree bark, and soft rocks. Have students experiment with these media to discover the qualities of the lines each produces. After displaying the results of their experiments, students can discuss which of the media create the most interesting results.

LOOKING Closely

Direct students' attention to the drawing in the Looking Closely feature, Figure 3.4. What mood or feeling is evoked by this image? Have those students who worked with oil pastels in the Motivator activity for this lesson (page 52) recall the characteristics of this medium. What effect is achieved when pastels are smeared with tissue or other soft paper? How might the use of this medium have enhanced the mood or emotion that Cassatt captured?

LOOKING Closely

DRY MEDIA

The subject here is one the artist used over and over during her career: a mother and her children.

- **Medium.** The artist employed a favorite medium: pastels.
- **Technique.** Cassatt abandoned her more familiar smooth, even surface in favor of one composed of swiftly applied strokes of bright colors.
- **Purpose.** The finished drawing looks as if it were done quickly, suggesting that the artist wanted to capture a fleeting moment shared by a mother and her children.

■ **FIGURE 3.4** Mary Cassatt. *Young Mother, Daughter, and Son.* 1913. Pastel on paper. 110 × 84.5 cm (43¼ × 33¼"). Memorial Art Gallery of the University of Rochester, Rochester, New York. Marion Stratton Gould Fund.

Chapter 3 *Creating Art: Media and Processes* **53**

Technology

National Gallery of Art Videodisc Use the following images as examples of more works by artists introduced in this lesson.

Thomas Gainsborough
A Wooded Landscape with Two Country Carts and Figures

Search Frame 3271

Thomas Gainsborough
Landscape with a Bridge

Search Frame 1621

Jacob Van Ruisdale
Park with a Country House

Search Frame 942

Use Glencoe's *Correlation Bar Code Guide to the National Gallery of Art* to locate more artworks.

Aesthetics

On the board, draw a Venn diagram showing the relationship in adjoining circles among the three aesthetic qualities discussed in Chapter 1.

After explaining the meaning of the diagram, have students make large copies of it and, working in small groups, determine the aesthetic qualities that are most important in each work in the chapter. Figure numbers should be indicated inside the appropriate circle or, in the case of works that satisfy more than one aesthetic criterion, at the appropriate intersection. Have groups share and justify their decisions.

Studio Skills

Have students focus on an object in the classroom that has an organic form (e.g., a flag, a window blind). Ask them to do a rapid pencil sketch of the object's contours. As students work, encourage them to imagine that their pencil is working in sync with their eye; that is, the point is actually touching the lines of the object. Have students put their completed sketches aside. Next, provide them with pens and an assortment of nibs, and allow them enough time to experiment and determine the different results obtained by varying nib thickness and pressure. Once students feel comfortable with the medium, have them use pen and ink to convert their sketches into finished drawings by emphasizing various contour lines.

Wet media are *those media in which the coloring agent is suspended in a liquid;* they include ink and paints. The wet medium most commonly used in drawing is ink in various colors, applied with pen or brush. Paints can also be used as a drawing medium. The drawing of fishing boats (Figure 3.5) demonstrates the skill with which the artist, Vincent van Gogh (van **goh**), worked with a wet medium. Using a reed pen and brown ink, van Gogh created a drawing that features a variety of different lines. These lines give an exaggerated sense of movement to an otherwise simple scene.

Recognizing the advantages offered by both dry and wet media, many artists have combined them in their drawings.

Drawings in Sketchbooks

Artists have long recognized the value of maintaining sketchbooks to record their ideas. Earlier artists used drawings mainly as a way of developing the ideas they wished to express in their paintings and sculptures. More recently, artists have used drawings in two ways: as finished works of art and as preliminary studies to develop ideas.

Thomas Gainsborough regarded both the preliminary drawing (Figure 3.6) and the final painting of *Repose* (Figure 3.7) as among his best works. When the painting was completed, he set it aside as a wedding gift for his daughter.

■ **FIGURE 3.5** The artist based this drawing on a similar oil painting completed earlier. How is the principle of variety demonstrated in this work? What gives the drawing its spontaneous appearance?

Vincent van Gogh. *Fishing Boats at Saintes-Maries-de-la-Mer.* 1888. Reed pen and brown ink and graphite on paper. 24.3 × 31.9 cm (9¹/₂ × 12¹/₂"). The Saint Louis Art Museum, St. Louis, Missouri. Gift of Mr. and Mrs. Joseph Pulitzer Jr.

54 **Unit One** *Creating and Understanding Art*

𝒯eacher 𝒩otes

Pen and Ink. In arranging for students to work with pen and ink for the first time, use an ordinary bond paper or any paper that does not bleed. Avoid packaged papers billed as "calligraphy paper," since the quality of such papers tends to be unpredictable. A pen with a Speedball C-2 nib and basic drawing ink are good choices for beginners. Any student who has experience with pen and ink could be recruited as a peer monitor. Remind students that pens need to be cleaned with water and a coarse-bristled brush (e.g., a toothbrush).

■ **FIGURES 3.6 and 3.7**
Many artists prepare preliminary sketches for their paintings. In these drawings, they plan and test out ideas before beginning to paint. Identify details in Gainsborough's painting that he did not include in the drawing.

■ **FIGURE 3.6**

Thomas Gainsborough. *Preliminary Study for "Repose."* Charcoal and white chalk on blue paper. 25.4 × 32 cm (10 × 12⅝"). The Nelson-Atkins Museum of Art, Kansas City, Missouri. Gift of Thomas Agnew & Sons.

■ **FIGURE 3.7**

Thomas Gainsborough. *Repose.* c. 1777–78. Oil on canvas. 122.2 × 149.5 cm (48⅛ × 58⅞"). The Nelson-Atkins Museum of Art, Kansas City, Missouri. Nelson Fund.

Painting

Painting is one of the oldest and most important of the visual arts. An artist creates a painting by arranging the art elements on a flat surface in ways that are sometimes visually appealing, sometimes shocking or thought-provoking. By presenting us with unique design relationships, offering new ideas, and giving form to the deepest feelings, the painter awakens us to aspects of life that we might otherwise overlook or ignore.

Chapter 3 *Creating Art: Media and Processes* **55**

Cross Curriculum

HUMANITIES. Point out that the creation of sketches and drawings as "studies" for major artistic projects is a fairly common practice. Ask students whether they suspect this phenomenon exists in other areas of the humanities, or is it unique to the visual arts? Have volunteers research this question, determining the form that studies take in fields such as music and literature.

Art History

Have students investigate the use of sketchbooks and notepads by artists other than the two mentioned on this page. Have them seek an answer to this question: Were the artists' reasons for maintaining a sketchbook one of the two outlined on these pages (i.e., to develop a keener eye, to plan projects), or was there another motive (e.g., to capture fleeting images such as rainbows)? Have students share their findings and, if possible, obtain reproductions of sketchbook pages.

Critical Thinking

Direct students' attention to the charcoal drawing in Figure 3.6 done by Gainsborough as a study for his oil painting, *Repose.* Then have them choose sides and debate the following proposition: *If I had viewed this drawing in isolation,* with *no knowledge of its history and purpose, I would consider it to be a finished work of art.* Have students refer to specific details of the work and its execution in support of their positions.

More About... | **Sketches.** Many painters, sculptors, and other artists use drawings to improve their perception and to plan their works. As a case in point, one of the greatest painters and sculptors of all time, Michelangelo (1475–1564), used sketches to master his representation of the body in motion. His drawings, which reveal a close attention to the shapes and movements of muscles, make it clear that he was interested only in the human form itself. It is these studies that gave rise to the remarkable realism in Michelangelo's depiction of the human form in such works as his renowned *David.*

Art History

Have students note the prominence that people that have been subjects of artworks have received. Then have students work as a team to prepare a file titled "A Cavalcade of People in Art." The file should consist of references and, if possible, reproductions of the human form as it has been represented in different cultures and at different times throughout history. Students may use both this text and library resources for the project. When they have completed their file, ask them to consider which periods, and which cultures, typically represent humans as lifelike, and which represent them as stylized.

Did You Know?

The word pencil comes from the Latin word *penicillus,* meaning "a little tail." The first pencils were actually fine brushes of hair or bristles.

Subject Matter in *Art*

The subjects that artists select for their paintings often depend on the time and place in which they live. They are influenced by their own personal experiences, by the lives of the people around them, and by the interests and attitudes of their society. Throughout history, artists have discovered subjects for their paintings in the real world of people, places, and events around them, and the imaginary world within themselves.

Landscapes. Landscape paintings without figures were rare in Europe before the seventeenth century. Although artists used landscapes as backgrounds for their figures, they rejected the idea of using natural scenes as the main subject for their paintings. This certainly was not true in Asia, where landscape painting enjoyed a long and glorious tradition.

European practices changed in the seventeenth century when Dutch painters recognized that nature could serve as a beautiful and often dramatic subject for their art. Jacob van Ruisdael's (van **rise**-dahl) paintings, for example, are more than realistic—they also communicate the artist's emotional reaction to the scene.

■ **FIGURE 3.8** Jacob van Ruisdael. *Forest Scene.* c. 1655. Oil on canvas. 105.5 × 131 cm (41¹/₂ × 51¹/₂″). National Gallery of Art, Washington, D.C. Widener Collection.

Nature. During the seventeenth century, Japanese artists were perfecting an art style that catered to the demands of a growing number of wealthy landowners. It was the age of decorative screen painting, when artists created dreamlike landscapes set against glowing gold backdrops.

■ **FIGURE 3.9** Artist unknown. *The River Bridge at Uji.* Momoyama Period, 1568–1614. Six-fold screen. Ink, colors, and gold on paper. 171.5 × 338.5 cm (67¹/₂ × 133¹/₄″). The Nelson-Atkins Museum of Art, Kansas City, Missouri. Purchase: Nelson Trust.

56 **Unit One** *Creating and Understanding Art*

Subject Matter in *Art*

Have students examine the feature and discuss where ideas for art come from. Point out that various cultures throughout history, beginning with the ancient Greeks, have drawn inspiration for their art from the Muses, the goddesses that presumably watch over and guide the creative act. Have students work individually, or in groups, to learn more about the classical Greek Muses. After the students have shared and discussed their findings, let each student draw his or her own version of one of the Muses.

■ FIGURE 3.10

Alice Neel. *Portrait of Ellen Johnson.* 1976. Oil on canvas. 111.8 × 81.3 cm (44 × 32"). Allen Memorial Art Museum, Oberlin College, Oberlin, Ohio. R.T. Miller, Jr. Fund and gift of the artist in honor of Ellen Johnson on the occasion of her retirement, 1977.

❸

People. It would be difficult to find a subject that is more fascinating for painters than people. Peering out at us from the pages of art history are the countless smiling, frowning, crying faces of people painted in many different ways. Some are famous and easily recognized, but a great many more are long forgotten or may never have been identified.

■ FIGURE 3.11

John Frederick Peto. *The Old Violin.* c. 1890. Oil on canvas. 77.2 × 58.1 cm (30³/₈ × 22⁷/₈"). National Gallery of Art, Washington, D.C. Gift of the Avalon Foundation.

❹

Still Lifes. Painting a **still life,** *an arrangement of inanimate objects such as food, plants, pots, and pans,* has appealed to many artists. One of these, the American John Frederick Peto (**pee**-toh), delighted in presenting authentic-looking objects arranged in shallow spaces. The violin was a favorite subject because he admired the beauty of its shape, and because it gave him an opportunity to pay homage to another art form he admired and practiced: music. Peto's paintings remind us of the beauty to be found in the simple things in life, things that we might otherwise consider outdated or insignificant.

❺

Historical Subjects. At one time historical pictures were considered the highest form of painting. They often take the form of dynamic, colorful pictures depicting dashing military leaders engaged in epic battles. Although it may lack the dynamic force of other historical pictures, John Trumbull's painting *The Declaration of Independence* is no less important or stirring. Of the 48 figures included in the work, 36 were painted from real life. Shown in a momentary lull, the faces of these figures reveal the significance of their actions.

■ **FIGURE 3.12** John Trumbull. *The Declaration of Independence, 4 July 1776.* 1786. Oil on canvas. 53.6 × 79 cm (21¹/₈ × 31¹/₈"). Yale University Art Gallery, New Haven, Connecticut. Copyright Yale University Art Gallery.

Chapter 3 *Creating Art: Media and Processes* **57**

Art History

Have groups of students research more about the role the Church played in Western art. When did the Church become a major influence? How long did its influence last? Which artists and movements were products of this period? What subjects did they focus on repeatedly? Groups can compile their findings in a file called "Art and the Church," which may be retained as a classroom resource for use later in the term.

Study Guide

Distribute *Study Guide* 5 in the TCR. Assist students in reviewing key concepts. 🗁

Art and Humanities

Have students complete *Appreciating Cultural Diversity* 4, "The Diversity of Media," in the TCR. This activity calls upon students to explore the media used in different cultures and seek examples in contemporary settings. 🗁

Studio Activities

Ask students to complete *Studio* 4, "Contour Drawing," found in the TCR, in which students experiment with their own personal drawing style. 🗁

Enrichment

Assign *Cooperative Learning* 4, "Developing Perceptual Awareness," in the TCR. In this activity, students explore how the elements and principles of art are used in their natural environment. Students proceed to document examples in their sketchbooks. 🗁

𝒯eacher 𝒩otes

Developing Perceptual Skills. Instructors can help students improve their perceptual powers by having them perfect the technique of gesture drawing. This technique calls upon the individual to draw lines quickly and loosely in an effort to capture the essence of the subject. Have students practice this technique by placing an everyday object in plain view of the class (e.g., a sneaker, a notebook). Explain that the technique makes use of the whole arm, not just the hand. Encourage students to practice this method often, using the same object each time. After several attempts, ask them to evaluate their progress by examining the rough sketches in the order they were made.

ASSESS

Checking Comprehension

Have students complete the lesson review questions. Answers appear in the box below.

Reteaching

Assign *Reteaching* 5, found in the TCR. Have students complete the activity and review their responses. 📁

Enrichment

Assign students *Enrichment* 6, "The Medium Is the Message," in the TCR. In this worksheet, students examine the use of various drawing, painting, and printmaking media. 📁

Extension

Reveal that the first plastic polymer was created in 1901, by Dr. Leo Baekeland, a chemist. Add that as a result of this discovery, a process for making acrylic paint was available as early as 1915, but was abandoned because it was too costly. Have groups of students research more about the development of acrylic paint. When was a process developed that enabled acrylics to be manufactured at affordable prices? What properties in the polymer have made it popular among artists?

CLOSE

Have small groups of students compare the drawings and paintings they created while studying this lesson. What characteristics of the media used in each work can they identify?

The Media and Tools of Painting

Clearly, artists can draw on a great many sources for ideas. They also have a variety of media and tools from which to choose when expressing their ideas in visual form. Several kinds of paint can be used to achieve different results. All are composed of three basic ingredients: pigment, binder, and solvent.

The **pigment** is *finely ground powder that gives a paint its color.* Some pigments are produced by chemical processes; others, by grinding up some kind of earth, stone, or mineral. The **binder** is *a liquid that holds together the grains of pigment* in a form that can be spread over a surface, where it is allowed to dry. Some tempera paints use the whites of eggs as a binder. (See Figure 24.20, page 558.) Encaustic uses melted wax. Oil paint uses linseed oil. Watercolor uses a mixture of water and gum arabic. A relatively new painting medium, known popularly as acrylics, makes use of acrylic polymer as a binder. The **solvent** is *the material used to thin the binder.*

Brushes are by far the preferred tools for painters. These come in a variety of shapes and sizes: pointed or flat, short and stiff, or long and flexible. Some artists also use a palette knife to spread their paint. This painting method results in rough, heavy strokes that can add to the textural richness of their paintings.

Using Media and Processes

Your own efforts in creating two-dimensional art forms depend in large measure on what you learn about the media and processes introduced in this chapter. As important as it is to know about media and processes, however, it is even more important to know what to do with what you know. Art offers you the opportunity—and the challenge—of making personal choices at every stage of the creative process.

Many of these choices involve the media and the processes you use. To express your thoughts, feelings, and ideas most effectively, you have to make these choices carefully and thoughtfully. Take the time to experiment with art media and processes whenever you can. Your experiments will help you learn to use art media and processes to express your ideas in unique and stimulating ways.

LESSON ONE REVIEW

Reviewing Art Facts

1. Name at least three dry media used in drawing.
2. What types of subjects do artists depict in their works?
3. What is a still life?
4. What are the three basic ingredients in paint?

 ### Activity... *Drawing a Visual Record*

Drawings and paintings provide a record of man's past. These visual records provide many artists with inspiration for their work.

Create a visual-verbal record of your classroom. Using a small sketch pad or a number of small sheets of paper stapled together, walk around the room, viewing things from different perspectives. Sit on the floor and look up. Lie on a tabletop and look down. Look into, through, and out of objects and places. Every five minutes, listen and look for images, sounds, patterns, lines, colors, shapes. Record each impression both visually with sketches and verbally with written notes. Assemble as much information as you can in the time given.

LESSON ONE REVIEW

Answers to Reviewing Art Facts

1. Pencil, charcoal, crayon, chalk, pastels.
2. Subjects in the real world of people, places, and events around them as well as in their imaginations.
3. Still life refers to a painting of inanimate objects.
4. Pigment, binder, and solvent.

Activity...*Drawing a Visual Record*

Before students begin this assignment, ask them to take a look around the classroom to get an impression of the things they may wish to sketch. Allow groups of 4 to 6 students at a time to walk around the room, and limit each group to 10 minutes of sketching time so that everyone has a turn.

Printmaking, Photography, Video, and Digital Media

Vocabulary
- relief printing
- intaglio
- burin
- lithography
- screen printing
- serigraph
- photography
- digital media

Discover

After completing this lesson, you will be able to:
- Describe the four basic print-making methods.
- Explain what photography is, and discuss photography as an art form.
- Recognize the advances in video and digital media in the world of art.

*P*rintmaking, photography, video, and digital media are different from other art media and processes in two respects. First, they involve the creation of an image through an indirect process. Second, they give the artist an opportunity to create multiple images. In printmaking, the artist does this by repeatedly transferring an original design from one prepared surface to other surfaces. The printmaker handles the paper and can "draw" directly on a print.

In photography, black-and-white or color images are recorded as light on frames of film. These images can be reproduced to serve specific purposes. One of these purposes is to portray people, objects, and events accurately in newspapers, books, and magazines. Another purpose—the one you will learn about in this chapter—is the use of photography as an art form.

Video is also used as an art medium. With the aid of computer technology, artists can alter and edit what they have recorded on videotape. Artists can capture a narrative sequence of events or other images on videotape. There is no need to go to a film development lab, because the results can be reviewed immediately on a videocassette recorder.

The use of the computer in the creation of art allows artists great flexibility. When using a computer, images and imaginary objects created by artists are stored in the computer's memory in an electronic form. With the computer, artists can easily manipulate, transfer, and reproduce these images in a variety of ways. There are computer programs available that enable artists to use the computer as an art tool and art medium.

Printmaking

Printing has a long history. Chinese artists were printing with carved wooden blocks more than 1,000 years ago. At first the process may have been used to create repeated designs on textiles. Later it was applied to paper as well.

Printmaking did not develop in Europe until the fifteenth century, in time to meet the growing demand for inexpensive religious pictures and playing cards. Later it was used to provide illustrations for books produced with movable type (Figure 3.13). This printing process, invented by a German printer named Johannes Gutenberg, made it possible to print different pages of a book by using the same metal type over and over again.

Eventually artists began to recognize the value of printmaking applied to the production of fine art. This led to a variety of printmaking processes, ranging from

■ **FIGURE 3.13** This artist's works are said to be as important to the history of the natural sciences as they are to the history of art. **Why do you think this may be so?**

Maria Sibylla Merian. *Dissertation in Insect Generations and Metamorphosis in Surinam, Plate 12.* 1719. The National Museum of Women in the Arts, Washington, D.C. Gift of Wallace and Wilhelmina Holladay.

59

Focus

Lesson Objectives

After studying this lesson, students will be able to:
- Describe the origins and historical developments of printmaking.
- Identify the processes used in printmaking, video, and digital media.
- Discuss the origins of photography as an art form.

Building Vocabulary

Ask students to find each of the Vocabulary terms in the text and determine to which process each term is related.

Motivator

Write the word *printing* in a circle on the board and ask students to free-associate around this term. As students call out words and phrases, write these at the end of spokes radiating outward from the circle to create a word web. After students have produced a fairly elaborate web, place a check mark next to terms that emphasize the connection between the printing process and art. Tell students they are about to learn about the art of printmaking.

Introducing the Lesson

Point out that students learned in the previous lesson about two very old forms of artistic expression—drawing and painting. Tell them that in the lesson they are about to read, they will be learning about one art form that has been around for only the last century.

Teacher's Classroom Resources
- 📁 Art and Humanities 4
- 📁 Enrichment Activity 7
- 📁 Reproducible Lesson Plan 6
- 📁 Reteaching Activity 6
- 📁 Study Guide 6

TEACH

Studio Skills

Point out that truly dedicated artists know no boundaries when it comes to tests of creativity. Illustrate this point by having students use the common potato as a printing plate. Have students make two different relief prints. In one case, they are to cut a positive design; in the other case, cut a negative design. Provide fine-bladed cutting knives for the activity, and challenge students to make their designs as intricate as they can.

Studio Skills

Show students a picture of a burin. An illustration may be found in a dictionary or art supply catalog, or you might draw a picture on the board. Explain how the tool is held. Point out that it is designed to fit into the palm of the hand. Continue describing how the tool cuts into the metal plate as it is pushed forward. Then ask the students to consider how much control the engraver has using this type of tool.

As an experiment, have the students use their pencils and make a straight line by starting at a point and drawing down. Then ask them to start at another point, but this time, draw up to make a line. Discuss which way offers more control—pulling down or pushing up. Remind students that a less-controlled line is not a judgment but a description. Sometimes a great variation of line quality can be achieved when the artist uses a process that allows more room for uncertainty.

■ **FIGURE 3.14** It may take a moment for you to notice the human figures here. Why do you think the artist minimized the importance of the figures?

Katsushika Hokusai. *The Kirifuri Waterfall at Mt. Kurokami, Shimozuke Province.* c. 1831. Color woodblock print. 37.2 × 24.5 cm (14⅝ × 9⅝″). The Nelson-Atkins Museum of Art, Kansas City, Missouri. Purchase: Nelson Trust.

relatively simple to quite complicated. The four basic printmaking methods are relief, intaglio, lithography, and screen printing.

Relief Printing

In **relief printing,** *the image to be printed is raised from the background.* This method requires that the artist cut away the sections of a surface not meant to hold ink. The remaining raised portion is then covered with ink and becomes the printing surface. Paper is laid on it, pressure is applied, and the ink is transferred to the paper.

Printing with carved wooden blocks originated in China and spread to Japan where, in the seventeenth century, it became a highly developed art form. At first, Asian prints consisted of inked outlines that were filled in with color by hand. Later, separate blocks were created for each color in a design. Each block was inked, carefully aligned on the paper, and printed to produce a design with multiple, rich colors (Figure 3.14).

Intaglio

A printing process that is exactly the reverse of relief printing is intaglio. The name comes from the Italian word meaning "to cut into." **Intaglio** is *a process in which ink is forced to fill lines cut into a metal surface.* The lines of a design are created by one of two methods: etching or engraving.

In *etching*, a copper or zinc plate is first covered with a coating made of a mixture of beeswax, asphalt, and resin; the mixture is called a *ground.* The artist uses a fine needle to draw an image through this protective coating. Then the plate is placed in acid, which bites—or etches— the lines of the image into the metal where the ground has been removed. The remaining ground is then removed, and the plate inked. The unetched surface is cleaned, and damp paper is pressed

 ## Technology

National Gallery of Art Videodisc Use the following images as examples of more works by artists introduced in this lesson.

Edward Hopper	**Albrecht Dürer**	**Albrecht Dürer**
Cape Cod Evening	*Apocalypse: The Four Horsemen*	*Melancholia*

Search Frame 2106	Search Frame 3119	Search Frame 3125

Use Glencoe's *Correlation Bar Code Guide to the National Gallery of Art* to locate more artworks.

Edward Hopper. *Night Shadows.* 1921. Etching. 17.6 × 21 cm (6¹⁵/₁₆ × 8¹/₄″). McNay Art Museum, San Antonio, Texas. Gift of the Friends of the McNay.

CHAPTER 3
LESSON TWO

Art History

Have students examine the print by Dürer in Figure 3.16, page 62. Ask students to research major events in Europe during the time when this artist was working. What influence may these events have had on his work? What was the social environment in which he worked?

Art Criticism

Refer students to the prints illustrated in this lesson. Ask them to describe the colors, lines, shapes, and other elements of art emphasized in the works. Identify the print(s) in which the elements have been used to achieve balance, variety, or harmony. What mood or feeling is communicated by the work by Hopper (Figure 3.15), and by the one by Orozco (Figure 3.17)?

Critical Thinking

Read the following quotation by Robert Henri: "Because a line is beautiful in one picture is no argument that it will be beautiful in another. It is all a matter of relation." Have students draw an analogy from Henri's statement to other aspects of life. For example, suggest that a person's behavior might be acceptable in one situation but inappropriate in another.

onto the plate with a press. This forces the paper into the inked grooves, transferring the image (Figure 3.15).

In an *engraving,* the lines are cut directly into the metal plate with a **burin,** or *engraving tool.* The lines made in this way are more pronounced and clear (Figure 3.16) than the fine lines produced by the etching process. When the prints have been made, you can actually feel the lines of raised ink.

Lithography

Another printing process is based on the principle that grease and water do not mix. **Lithography** is a *printmaking method in which the image to be printed is drawn on limestone, zinc, or aluminum with a special greasy crayon.* When the drawing is completed, it is chemically treated with a nitric acid solution. This makes the sections that have not been drawn on resistant to the printing ink. The surface is dampened with water and then inked. The greasy printing ink sticks to the equally greasy crayoned areas but is repelled by the wet, blank areas. Finally, the surface is covered with paper and run through a press to transfer the image.

■ **FIGURE 3.16** Works like this made Dürer one of the outstanding figures in the history of German art. **How do the lines in this engraving compare to the lines in the etching (Figure 3.17, page 62)?**

Albrecht Dürer. *St. Eustace.* c. 1501. Engraving in plate. 35.6 × 25.9 cm (14 × 10³/₁₆″). The Saint Louis Art Museum, St. Louis, Missouri. Purchase.

Chapter 3 *Creating Art: Media and Processes* **61**

Teacher Notes

Classroom Display. To add immediacy to the discussion of terms and materials used in printmaking, prepare a classroom display that includes tools, surface materials, definitions, and illustrations. Have students help organize the display and select new items for inclusion as the lesson progresses. Encourage students to refer to the display during class discussion and relevant chapter review activities. Remember that students themselves often are resources for materials and knowledge. For example, ask your class if anyone has the hobby of printmaking.

Critical Thinking

Have students examine the works in Figures 3.14 (page 60), 3.15, 3.16, and 3.17. Have them speculate about the source of inspiration for each of the works. Then have them discuss which source they feel provides the most interesting subject matter for works of art.

Art Criticism

Divide the class into two groups. Have one group study the painting in Figure 3.16, while the other examines the work in Figure 3.17. Ask each group to brainstorm adjectives and phrases that might describe the artists' use of the elements of color and line. When groups have completed their lists, ask them to switch paintings and repeat the task. Have the groups compare the lists they devised for each of the paintings. How many of the same words and phrases for a given work did the two groups come up with? Were any of the terms in any way contradictory? Allow time for the groups to discuss and explain their choices.

Aesthetics

Have students compare the prints in this lesson with commercially printed pictures in magazines. Discuss the differences and similarities between the two. Ask: Which are works of art? How would you classify the other works? Were artists involved in their production?

Among the many artists attracted to the direct drawing methods of lithography was the Mexican painter José Clemente Orozco (hoh-**say** kleh-**men**-tay oh-**ross**-koh). He used this printing method to create the powerful image of a monk and a starving Indian seen in Figure 3.17.

Screen Printing

Screen printing is a more recent printmaking process. In **screen printing,** *paint is forced through a screen onto paper or fabric.* This technique uses a stencil placed on a silk or synthetic fabric screen stretched across a frame. The screen is placed on the printing surface, and a squeegee is used to force the ink through the porous fabric in areas not covered by the stencil. If more than one color is needed, a separate screen is made for each color. A **serigraph** is a *screen print that has been handmade by an artist* (Figure 3.18).

Photography

Photographs appear everywhere—in newspapers, magazines, books, and on the Internet. In fact, their popularity may be one of the main reasons why photography has had difficulty being accepted as a serious art form. After all, anyone can point a camera, trip the shutter, and obtain a fairly accurate image. This simple description, however, ignores the many concerns of the serious photographer. These include decisions regarding subject, light conditions, and point of view, and the creative work done by the photographer in developing and printing. Other decisions, made before a single photograph is taken, concern the type of camera, film, and lens to be used.

Photography is *a technique of capturing optical images on light-sensitive surfaces.* The best photographers use this technique to create an art form powerful enough to teach others how to see, feel, and remember. Alfred Stieglitz (**steeg**-litz) used his talent and his camera to place viewers on a bridge spanning a canal in Venice. There they share with the artist a brief, magical moment in time (Figure 3.19).

■ **FIGURE 3.17** These two figures have been arranged to fit comfortably within the overall arched shape of the composition. **How do you think this work would have been different as a painting?**

José Clemente Orozco. *The Franciscan and the Indian.* 1926. Lithograph. 31.4 × 26.3 cm (12³/₈ × 10³/₈″). McNay Art Museum, San Antonio, Texas. Margaret Bosshardt Pace Fund. © Estate of José Clemente Orozco/Licensed by VAGA, New York, New York.

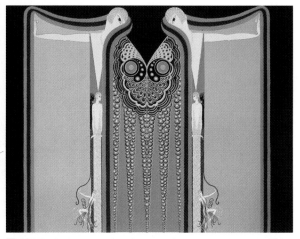

■ **FIGURE 3.18** This work makes use of symmetrical balance. **What problem must the artist overcome when using this type of balance? How has this artist succeeded in overcoming that problem?**

Erté. *Twin Sisters.* 1982. Print (serigraph). 86.4 × 124.5 cm (34 × 29″). © 1998 Sevenarts Ltd. Granted by Chalk & Vermilion Fine Arts, Greenwich, Connecticut.

More About... **Albrecht Dürer.** Point out that fifteenth-century German printmaker Albrecht Dürer and twentieth-century Swiss painter Paul Klee are generally considered to be masters of the element of line. Dürer, in his brief lifetime, created thousands of engravings like the one shown here, as well as woodcuts, paintings, and drawings. All of his works were noted for their intricate detail and expressive use of line. Klee, by contrast, used simplified lines and minimal details to achieve an effect not unlike what a child might produce. An example of Klee's work is shown in Figure 24.5, page 548.

Works like this inspired other artists, including Ansel Adams. Stieglitz, old and in poor health, urged Adams to continue from where Stieglitz was forced to leave off. Adams responded with thousands of photographs that marked a career covering nearly half a century. He photographed scenes from the unsettling stillness of a New Mexico moonrise to the majesty of a Yosemite winter storm (Figure 3.20).

Video and Digital Media

The development of video and computer technology has extended the creative powers of artists. These two innovations have enhanced artists' abilities to generate multiple versions of images, integrate images with other forms of art media and processes, and reproduce images in many ways.

Video Technology

In video technology, artists use a video camera loaded with a cassette of videotape to record images. Patterns of light beams from the subject or objects being videotaped are translated into electric waves, which are then imprinted magnetically on the videotape. Artists can use a videocassette recorder to immediately play back the tape.

Since its development in the first half of the twentieth century, video technology has been prominently used in the television industry. Entertainment and news reports recorded in a broadcasting studio or live on the street and other locations are transmitted directly to viewers.

■ **FIGURE 3.19** The photographer avoided the busy tourist centers of Venice and captured this quiet scene on film. How does this work succeed in pulling the viewer's eye into it?

Alfred Stieglitz. *Reflection-Venice.* c. 1897. Photogravure. 17.8 × 12.3 cm (7 × 4⁷⁄₈″). The Art Institute of Chicago, Chicago, Illinois. Gift of Daniel, Richard and Jonathan Logan, 1984. 1621.

■ **FIGURE 3.20** Adams is perhaps the best-known photographer of the twentieth century. Trained as a concert pianist, he turned to photography in 1930. How does the mood or feeling expressed in this work differ from that expressed in Figure 3.19?

Ansel Adams. *Clearing Winter Storm, Yosemite Valley.* 1944. Silver print. 26.7 × 33.7 cm (10¹⁄₂ × 13¹⁄₄″). The Saint Louis Art Museum, St. Louis, Missouri. Purchase.

Chapter 3 *Creating Art: Media and Processes* **63**

Aesthetics

Have students examine the photograph by Ansel Adams in Figure 3.20 (page 64). Then ask them to discuss which of the aesthetic theories could be applied to this work. Can students devise any other aesthetic criteria that could be used in evaluating photographs?

Critical Thinking

Emphasize that some people have trouble thinking of photography as a serious art form, and ask students why that might be so. Ask them how they might respond to this statement: *For something to be art, it must be either a painting or a drawing.* Is a preschooler who is working with finger paints a "true" artist? Can the same be said about an individual scribbling idly with a pencil as she or he speaks on the phone? How have their personal definitions of the word artist changed since they began this class?

Cross Curriculum

SCIENCE. Point out that the technology of photography has been changing at an amazingly rapid pace. Have students investigate these changes by contacting several manufacturers of photographic equipment and obtaining information on the state of the art. One area students should be sure to investigate is the use of specially designed digital cameras that use microchips to capture a visual image and transmit it onto a floppy disk. Have students share their findings. Whenever possible, ask students with some electronics background to share their expertise with the class.

Teacher Notes _____

Study Guide

Distribute *Study Guide* 6 in the TCR. Assist students in reviewing key concepts. ☞

Art and Humanities

Have students complete *Art and Humanities* 4, "Music Video—Combining Media," in the TCR. In this activity, students study the design of a music video in an effort to grasp the relationship between music, dance, theater, painting, and other art forms.

Studio Activities

Have students place a thin sheet of paper over a wadded newspaper and, pressing hard, draw the first initial of their names. Have students turn the paper over and use the negative image as a guide. They next should carve a letter stamp from a cube of modeling clay. Have students apply ink or paint to the stamp and press several impressions on a single sheet. Ask students whether all impressions are identical, or do they perceive differences? Does this factor enhance or detract from the interest generated by their pattern of printed images?

ASSESS

Checking Comprehension

Have students complete the lesson review questions. Answers appear in the box on the next page.

■ **FIGURE 3.21** This artist claimed that the television tube would one day replace the canvas in art. What meaning do you attach to the artist's placement of television sets in a cathedral-like form?

Nam June Paik. *Technology.* 1991. 25 video monitors, 3 laser disc players, in steel and plywood cabinet with aluminum sheeting and details of copper, bronze, plastic, and other materials. Approx. 3.6 × 1.4 × 1.3 m (11 × 4 × 4'). National Museum of American Art at the Smithsonian, Washington, D.C.

Video cameras were first used artistically in the 1960s by Nam June Paik, one of the first video artists in America (Figure 3.21).

The Art of Video

What advantages do artists find in using video technology? Video technology provides the excitement of recording events as they happen. Video cameras can capture sights, sounds, and the dynamics of motion. Artists who are interested in exploring narrative, or storytelling, can use video technology as an art medium to tell their stories as a continuous stream of images and sounds. In addition, by integrating video technology with computer technology, artists can import, alter, and edit their own images using imagery and sound from other sources. This permits them to create many of the special effects of cinematic film, without the need for expensive equipment.

Digital Media

The development of computer technology and the digital media associated with it represents one of the most exciting frontiers for artists in the second half of the twentieth century. Digital media is any type of material that can be processed by a computer. Computers transform and read text and images as information translated into digits, the combinations of strings of 1s and 0s that represent "on" and "off" electronic switches for a computer system. So, *any kind of material that can be used, processed, and transformed by a computer system* is called **digital media.** Images are actually stored in the computer's memory in electronic form and artists can direct the computer to transform these images in a variety of ways (Figure 3.22). Artists are able to build layers of video or images. The special effects in current popular movies are often created by using this process. Many magazine covers currently do the same, but in two dimensions. Many covers that you see have been constructed from different images—photos, drawings, and computer graphics.

Three-dimensional software programs allow artists to create images in the computer's memory that look as though they have three dimensions. Objects and space are created through a series of mathematical instructions, that resemble the techniques artists use in linear perspective. While we can move around a sculpture to look at it from different points of view, a three dimensional program provides the same opportunity by presenting various views of an object on the monitor screen. Computer animation programs permit artists to animate or move their two or three-dimensional images.

Artists can use a graphics tablet with a stylus, or a mouse connected to the computer, in the same way they would a pencil or paintbrush. The motions of the artist's arm as it draws with these tools result in strokes of electronic light on the computer monitor screen. Text, images, and sound also can be entered into a computer system by using a variety of devices, including cameras, scanners, and audio and video equipment. Whenever artists use a computer's capabilities

64   **Unit One** *Creating and Understanding Art*

CULTURAL DIVERSITY

Media. Point out that although societies in the West are most familiar with paintings done on canvas or paper, other cultures have used other materials. The Chinese, for example, have been painting on silk since at least 400 B.C., and the people of the Pacific Islands have long used tapa cloth, which is made from tree bark, as a painting surface. Have teams of students investigate these painting surfaces and other unique examples. Ask them to learn, in particular, the styles of the works created on such surfaces and what types of paints best adhere to and complement the surfaces.

to design and combine text, graphics, video, and sound into one artwork, it is called multimedia art production.

The Art of Digital Media

The computer is a remarkably versatile tool and medium for artists. Artists can extend their capabilities for creative problem-solving.

The computer can generate a number of options and solutions, including the following:

- Time efficiency in repetitive tasks.
- Visually checking what colors might work best for a painting before actually painting.
- Saving one or more stages of the image as it develops for future reference.
- Altering art elements and art principles.
- Enlarging or reducing the size of images.
- Animating images to move in time.
- Scanning and entering images from other sources to combine with your own images.
- Distorting images in order to create unusual effects.
- Reproducing the images in other forms of art media.

■ **FIGURE 3.22** This image was created by importing photos into a computer. How does the subject of all the tiny photos relate to the large image of two workers?

Robert Silvers. Based on Diego Rivera's *The Flower Carrier,* 1935, in the collection of the San Francisco Museum of Modern Art. Photomosaic (TM) 1997.

LESSON TWO REVIEW

Reviewing Art Facts

1. Explain the difference between the two intaglio processes—etching and engraving.
2. Explain the importance of the principle that grease and water do not mix to the process of lithography.
3. List five concerns of a serious photographer.
4. List some of the options a computer can present to an artist.

Activity... *Photographing Images*

Printmaking and the development of photography offered the ability to create multiple images. When printmaking first developed in Europe, it allowed the common man to possess works of art. Modern photography in its many forms, still, moving, and digital, helps us see and use images in new and different ways.

Using a digital camera, take a series of still-life pictures that emphasize the use of a particular element or principle. Choose one image and print it using a computer program that lets you print the image in grayscale. You might want to carry this experiment further by placing your image into an application that allows you to manipulate the image. Exhibit your work and share your experience with your class.

LESSON TWO REVIEW

Answers to Reviewing Art Facts

1. In etching, a ground of wax, asphalt, or resin is painted on a copper or zinc plate and scratched through, then exposed to acid; when engraving, a burin scratches into the metal.
2. Ink sticks to greasy areas but not to water.
3. Answers may include: subject, light, point of view, darkroom, equipment.
4. Answers should include at least 3 items listed.

Activity...*Photographing Images*

If students do not have access to digital cameras and appropriate computer equipment and software, they may still complete this activity. Have them use black-and-white film and a 35mm camera to take several photos of a single subject. Have them vary the setting, lighting, and focus.

Reteaching

➤ Assign *Reteaching* 6, found in the TCR. Have students complete the activity and review their responses. 📁

➤ Have students review the four basic methods of printmaking outlined in the Lesson. Then have them make charts noting ways in which the methods are similar and different.

Enrichment

Assign students *Enrichment* 7, "Woodblock Printing," in the TCR. In this worksheet, students trace the various techniques and styles of woodblock printing through the ages. They then create a woodblock print of their own. 📁

Extension

Encourage a team of interested students to research the evolution of the printing press. What are the differences between presses used for commercial purposes and the ones that artists use? Have a member of the team create a drawing to illustrate and help explain the mechanics of how a simple press works. Have the team share its research with the class.

CLOSE

Have students compare and contrast the printmaking experiences they have gained in this chapter. What challenges did they encounter in preparing printing plates, in working with mirror images, or in transferring the image to paper?

Sculpture

FOCUS

Lesson Objectives

After studying this lesson, students will be able to:

■ Identify the three types of sculpture as well as the media used in various types.

■ Explain why the choice of materials used in a sculpture is important to both the sculptor and the viewer.

Building Vocabulary

Instruct students to head three journal columns as follows: *Types of Sculpture, Processes of Sculpture, Tools of Sculpture.* Have them look at the list of vocabulary terms and decide which of the terms they believe fits under which of the three headings. After completing the chapter, go back and correct any misconceptions they may have had.

Motivator

Direct students' attention to the artwork in Figure 3.23, and ask a volunteer to read the credit line. Reinforcing that the medium is bronze, ask students to conjecture on how an artist might go about creating a bronze sculpture. Do students suppose such a work begins with a block of "raw" bronze and a sharp chisel? What do students know about this metal? How much does bronze weigh?

Introducing the Lesson

Have students browse through the chapter and note the different styles of sculpture as well as comparative sizes of work and media used. Do sculptors have at their disposal as rich a range of materials as painters? Are their works as varied?

Sculpture

Vocabulary
- bas relief
- high relief
- sculpture in the round
- modeling
- carving
- casting
- assembly
- kinetic art

Discover
After completing this lesson, you will be able to:
- Identify the materials and tools used in sculpture.
- Name and describe the four major techniques used to create sculpture.

$\mathscr{T}$hroughout history, artists in every culture and society have created sculpture of some kind. The works they created come in various sizes and shapes, are made with all kinds of materials and processes, and satisfy many different purposes.

Unique Quality of Sculpture

As an art form, sculpture differs from painting in that it exists in space. It can be seen, touched, and often viewed from all sides. Painting may suggest on a flat surface the *illusion* of space, but sculpture is concerned with *actual* space. A sculptor sets out to fill space with original, visually appealing forms. These forms may echo reality, express powerful emotions, or communicate ideas.

■ **FIGURE 3.23** Although very low, flat relief is used, the figures look as if they exist in space. Do these figures look lifelike? If so, what gives them this appearance?

Follower of Donatello. *Madonna and Child Within an Arch.* Mid-fifteenth century. Gilt bronze. 20 × 15 cm (8 × 6"). National Gallery of Art, Washington, D.C. Samuel H. Kress Collection.

■ **FIGURE 3.24** Here, exceptionally high relief is used, causing portions of the sculpture to project outward into space. Do you think the addition of color enhances this work?

Andrea della Robbia. *Madonna and Child.* c. 1470–75. Glazed terra-cotta. 95 × 55 cm (37³/₈ × 21⁵/₈"). The Metropolitan Museum of Art, New York, New York. Gift of the Edith and Herbert Lehman Foundation, 1969. (69–113).

66

LESSON THREE RESOURCES

Teacher's Classroom Resources

📁 Art and Humanities 5

📁 Enrichment Activities 8, 9

📁 Reproducible Lesson Plan 7

📁 Reteaching Activity 7

📁 Study Guide 7

Relief Sculpture

Not all sculptures can be viewed from all sides. Relief sculptures, for example, are similar in some ways to paintings. Their three-dimensional forms are attached to a flat surface. Like paintings, these works are designed to be viewed from the front. In low relief, or **bas relief,** the *sculptured forms project only slightly from the background* (Figure 3.23). In **high relief,** the *sculptured forms extend boldly out into space* (Figure 3.24).

Sculpture in the Round

Sculpture in the round is *any freestanding work surrounded on all sides by space.* Not all freestanding sculptures are meant to be seen from all sides, however. Many are designed to be viewed only from the front, much like a painting or a relief sculpture. An example of such a work is the striking Buddha image in Figure 3.25. Imagine for a moment that you encounter this golden-colored statue in a darkened temple. You would notice immediately that the figure of the seated religious leader stares straight ahead. Your presence in no way disturbs his quiet meditation, and you find yourself taking a position directly in front of him. There, as the artist intended, you experience the full impact of the Buddha towering over you.

The delicately poised head in Figure 3.26, on the other hand, invites viewers to examine it from all sides. Highly polished, simplified forms flow into each other, spiraling completely around the figure and tempting the viewer to follow.

Materials and Tools for Sculpture

Place yourself in the position of an artist about to transform an idea into three-dimensional form. A number of important questions must be answered before you begin. For example, what material will you use—clay, wood, stone, metal? What tools and processes are best suited for the

■ **FIGURE 3.25** Viewers see this huge figure emerging from the shadows of a darkened temple. Why is it clear that this figure is intended to be viewed only from the front, even though it is an example of sculpture in the round?

Seated Buddha from Wat Phanan Choeng. Ayutthaya, Thailand. c. 14th century.

■ **FIGURE 3.26** The artist may have arrived at the spiral design for this work after studying a dancer's pose. Do you think he succeeded in giving his sculpture a sense of movement? Explain your ideas.

Constantin Brancusi. *Mlle Pogany* (Margin Pogany). (Version 1, 1913, after a marble of 1912). Bronze. 43.8 × 21.5 × 31.7 cm (17$\frac{1}{4}$ × 8$\frac{1}{2}$ × 12$\frac{1}{2}$"). The Museum of Modern Art, New York, New York. Acquired through the Lillie P. Bliss Bequest.

TEACH
Aesthetics

Divide the class into groups, assigning each group one of the three theories of art identified in Chapter 1. Adopting the perspective of their assigned theory, groups are to decide which sculptures in this chapter are the most successful. Allow time for discussion and debate.

Art Criticism

Direct students' attention to the works in Figures 3.25 and 3.26. Challenge them to perform a comprehensive description of the two works, noting the subject of each, the size, the medium, and the date. Have students prepare two lists—one of similarities between the two works, the other of differences. Which list is longer? What item do they feel accounts most for the differences between the sculptures?

Art History

Ask students to research Constantin Brancusi, the sculptor of the works in Figures 3.26 and 3.27, and the times and circumstances under which he worked. Who is the subject of these sculptures? What details or qualities of the individual so fascinated the artist that he did a dozen separate sculptures based on her? Is the degree of abstraction in these sculptures typical of sculpture or painting in the early 1900s?

 # Technology

National Gallery of Art Videodisc Use the following images as examples of more works by artists introduced in this lesson.

Constantin Brancusi
Maiastra

Search Frame 2561

Tilman Riemenschneider
Saint Burchard of Würzburg

Search Frame 2437

Use Glencoe's *Correlation Bar Code Guide to the National Gallery of Art* to locate more artworks.

Studio Skills

Ask students to collect a variety of natural objects, such as pebbles, twigs, and leaves. Then have them work in small groups to create relief sculptures using clay and the materials they have found. Encourage students to share and discuss their sculptures. How did the various materials feel to the touch? What visual texture do they add to the sculpture?

Art Criticism

Review with students the processes of modeling and carving. Explain that the first is an additive process (increasing amounts of a medium are added as the work progresses), the second is a subtractive process (material is removed). Have students look back at the sculptures in Lesson One. Which were created using the process of modeling and which used the process of carving? Have students extend the activity to other sculptures in the text.

Art History

Have small groups of students complete descriptions of the work in Figure 3.28 from the point of view of an art historian. They may use information found in this textbook and in library resources. Encourage groups to share and compare their descriptions.

material selected? Answers to questions like these will determine how your finished sculpture will look.

Look again at the sculpture illustrated in Figure 3.26, page 67. Try to imagine how this work would look if it were made of clay or wood or marble rather than bronze. Instead of a work with a slick, shiny surface, picture this sculpture as a clay piece bearing the signs of the sculptor's fingers, or a rough-hewn wood carving. Would its appearance—and its impact on the viewer—be different if it had been carved in a light-colored marble?

The artist, Constantin Brancusi (bran-**koo**-see), created three marble and nine bronze versions of this sculpture over a 19-year period. Take a moment to compare one carved in marble (Figure 3.27) with the version cast in bronze. Did you react to both works in the same way? Which of the two versions do you find more appealing?

Clearly, the choice of materials is an important one for both the sculptor and the viewer. Sculptors choose a particular material because of what they can do with it and what it can contribute to the finished work.

■ **FIGURE 3.27** The artist carved this version of his sculpture in marble. What are the most significant differences between this marble sculpture and the bronze work (Figure 3.26)? Which do you prefer?

Constantin Brancusi. *Mlle Pogany.* 1913. White marble. 44.5 × 15.2 cm (17$\frac{1}{2}$ × 6"). Philadelphia Museum of Art, Philadelphia, Pennsylvania. Given by Mrs. Rodolphe Meyer de Schauensee.

Processes of Sculpture

Artists use a variety of different processes or techniques to create sculptures from the materials they choose. These processes include modeling, carving, casting, and assembling.

Modeling

Modeling is *a process in which a soft, pliable material is built up and shaped into a sculptural form.* The artist uses a material such as clay, wax, or plaster. Because the sculptor gradually adds more and more material to build a three-dimensional form, modeling is referred to as an additive process.

■ **FIGURE 3.28** The sculptor ignored details in favor of creating a figure that appears to be moving in space. Why do you think clay was a good choice of material for this work?

Gianlorenzo Bernini. *Angel with the Superscription.* 1667–69. Terra-cotta with traces of gilding. 30.2 cm (11$\frac{7}{8}$"). Kimbell Art Museum, Fort Worth, Texas.

More About... **Marble.** Refer students to Figure 3.27, and ask them to name the medium the sculptor used (marble). Explain that marble is a type of metamorphic rock formed from limestone. Divide the class into five groups and have each research one of the following relevant topics: the rock cycle, the formation of metamorphic rock, the mechanics of mining marble, and locations on the globe where marble is found. Also, ask them to find examples of marble used in their homes or school. Have the groups share their findings in a class forum.

More than 200 years ago, the Italian sculptor Gianlorenzo Bernini (jee-ahn-loh-**ren**-zoh bair-**nee**-nee) made excellent use of the modeling process to create the clay figure of an angel in Figure 3.28. This was one of several small figures created as models for ten life-size marble statues intended to decorate a bridge in Rome. Working in clay, Bernini formed the figure quickly, trying to capture a sense of movement. Notice how the body turns in space, causing its garments to swirl about. Notice, too, how a rich pattern of light and shadow seems to energize the figure.

Carving

Carving is *cutting or chipping a form from a given mass of material to create a sculpture.* Unlike modeling, which is an additive technique, carving is subtractive. Material is removed until the sculpture is completely exposed.

Stone carving is a process that has changed little over the centuries. In fact, even the tools remain essentially the same today as in ancient times. Modern stone carvers, have the advantage of power tools that can cut away excess material and polish finished works. This speeds up the carving process, but does not reduce its challenges. Despite its hardness, stone can shatter, leaving the artist with little more than the broken pieces of a dream to show for hours of hard work.

Every kind of stone has its own unique character, and artists must take this into consideration when deciding which to choose for their sculptures. Marble is often selected because it offers a variety of colors and interesting vein patterns. It can also be polished to a glasslike surface, or left rough and heavily textured. A mythological figure carved in marble by a student of Michelangelo illustrates the range of different textures possible with this material (Figure 3.29).

Different textured surfaces can also be realized in another favorite sculpture material: wood. For thousands of years, carvers have turned to this medium for its warmth, color, and grain. A work from fifteenth-century Germany shows what a skilled carver can accomplish with this versatile material (Figure 3.30).

■ **FIGURE 3.29** Pan, the mythological god of woodlands and pastures, is often shown with a human torso and goat legs and horns. How did the artist use texture to add interest to the work?

Giovanni Angelo Montorsoli. *Reclining Pan.* c. 1535. Marble. 63.9 × 134.6 cm (25³/₁₆ × 53"). The Saint Louis Art Museum, St. Louis, Missouri. Purchase.

■ **FIGURE 3.30** When this work was carved, it was customary to paint wooden sculptures. This artist, however, chose to leave his work uncolored. How does the carved material add to the visual appeal of this sculpture?

Hans Tilman Riemenschneider. *Three Holy Men.* c. 1494. Lindenwood. 53.3 × 33 cm (21 × 13"). Würzburg, Germany. The Metropolitan Museum of Art, New York, New York. The Cloisters Collection, 1961. (61.86).

Chapter 3 *Creating Art: Media and Processes* **69**

Aesthetics

Provide each student with a set of index cards bearing one of the following numbers: 1, 3, 7, or 10. Explain that the numbers represent a scale, where "1" is *abstract* and "10" is *realistic.* Have students go through the sculptures in the lesson and, for each, hold up a card. Tally the results and have students discuss and explain their reactions. Then repeat the process, this time redefining the scale so that "1" is *unexpressive* and "10" is *highly expressive.*

Critical Thinking

Have students examine, compare, and contrast the sculptures in Figures 3.29 and 3.30. Remind them that both works are carvings. Ask them to brainstorm why the sculptors of the works chose the media they did. What characteristics can students find that are common to both marble and wood as art media? What generalizations can students make regarding the variety of media available to the sculptor?

Cross Curriculum

SCIENCE. Divide students into groups and ask each group to make an exhaustive list of the media used in the sculptures in this section. Ask them to circle those media they believe to be synthetic (i.e., human-made). After correcting any misconceptions that may arise, have individual students choose and investigate one of the synthetic media. In their research, students should focus on the substance's origins and the process by which it is manufactured. Findings should be shared in the form of brief, illustrated oral reports.

More About... | **Wood Carving.** Reveal to students that wood may be classified as either soft or hard. Emphasize that soft woods can easily be sawed, planed, and bored and, as such, are used chiefly for structural work. Hard woods, favored by many artists, are notable for the handsome grain patterns they exhibit. Have students conduct a local search for wooden objects that show a grain pattern, and have them sketch the grain. You might also contact merchants who carry wood floor coverings and ask for samples to keep in the classroom for sketches. Maintain student sketches in a classroom resource folder.

Art History

Have students investigate the origins of the "lost wax" process of bronze casting in an effort to answer questions such as the following: When and where did this process originate? What were the earliest kinds of works produced using the method? How did this process spread to other cultures? What other metals has it been used with? Have students share their findings.

Studio Skills

Review with students the process of assembly, pointing out that this is a relatively recent innovation. Supplement the assembled sculptures shown in this section with a reproduction of one of the most imaginative assemblages of the twentieth century, Picasso's *Bull's Head.* After establishing that the work consists of nothing more elaborate than a bicycle seat and handlebars, provide students with an assortment of found objects with different forms and textures.

Challenge students to look for human or animal features suggested by single objects or a combination (e.g., a light bulb might suggest a human head, a pin cushion the body of a frog). Have students complete sketches of a creature assembled from found objects.

■ **FIGURE 3.31** The rings at the four corners of the base may have held poles used to carry this image in ceremonial processions. **What advantages does the metal casting process provide to the artist?**

Indian. *Standing Vishnu.* Tamil Nadu. Chola dynasty, 10th century. The Metropolitan Museum of Art, New York, New York. Purchase: John D. Rockefeller 3rd gift, 1962 (62.265).

Casting

In **casting,** *a melted-down metal or other liquid substance is poured into a mold to harden.* This method allows the artist to duplicate an original sculpture done in wax, clay, plaster, or some other material. The technique is practiced today much as it has been for hundreds of years. Known as the *cire-per-due,* or "lost wax" process, it was used well over a thousand years ago by an unknown Indian artist to create the graceful figure of a Hindu god seen in Figure 3.31.

This complex casting procedure involved many steps. First a clay model was created. Then plaster (or gelatine) was applied to the model in sections. A layer of melted wax was brushed onto the inside surface of each plaster section. The thickness of this wax layer determined the thickness of the bronze walls of the finished hollow sculpture. The wax-lined plaster sections were then reassembled and filled with a solid core of fireproof material. Ultimately the layer of wax and the core were encased in a fireproof mixture of plaster and silica. This created a fireproof mold known as an *investment.* The wax layer was then melted and drained off and then replaced with molten metal poured into the cavity that the "lost wax" created.

Casting offers several advantages to the sculptor, including the opportunity to work with a soft, pliable medium to create the original sculpture. By casting the clay portrait in bronze, the artist can maintain the textured surface of the clay. Moreover, the artist may have been able to make several versions of the work.

Assembly

In the process of **assembly,** *the artist gathers and joins together a variety of different materials to construct a three-dimensional work of art.* Unlike the other sculpture processes, assembly is a modern technique. Marisol chose to use wood, plaster, and other common materials to construct an amusing sculpture that pokes fun at military heroes (Figure 3.32).

CULTURAL DIVERSITY

Casting Methods. Reinforce that the lost wax method of casting is generally ascribed to the ancient Chinese. Then ask: With what other art production methods are the Chinese credited? What type of sculptures did the Benin tribe of Africa specialize in? What is significant about the heads carved by the Olmec civilization of ancient Mexico? Divide the class into groups and have each investigate the artistic technologies of a different culture. Groups can share their findings. Ask students to look for examples of contemporary sculpture using the lost wax method, and bring illustrations of these sculptures to share with the class if possible.

Humor in *Art*

This sculpture is a remarkable break with the statues of the past, which showed grand military leaders advancing boldly into battle on their mighty steeds.

 1 ▷

Marisol paints the serious and digni-fied faces of her "heroes" on wooden blocks that serve as their heads.

 2 ▷

Their mighty steed is nothing more than a barrel mounted on legs that were once part of an ordinary table.

 3 ▷

Presented in this manner, the heroes appear ridiculous, the subjects of humor or jeers rather than cheers.

■ **FIGURE 3.32**

Marisol. *The Generals*. 1961–62. Wood and mixed media. 221 × 72.4 × 193 cm (87 × 28$\frac{1}{2}$ × 76"). Albright-Knox Art Gallery, Buffalo, New York. Gift of Seymour H. Knox, 1962. © Marisol Escobar/Licensed by VAGA, New York, New York.

Another type of assembly, **kinetic art,** is *a sculptural form that actually moves in space.* This movement continually changes the rela-tionships of the shapes and forms that have been assembled to make up the sculpture. Movement can be caused by such forces as the wind, jets of water, electric motors, or the actions of the viewer. For example, the wire arms and attached metal shapes of Alexander Calder's sculpture can be set in motion by a current of air. (See Figure 24.28, page 565.) As they move, they continually create new relationships to each other and to their back-ground whether it be a museum hall or an outdoor setting.

Humor in *Art*

Have students examine the artwork and read the feature on this page. Discuss the figures in Marisol's carving of *The Generals*. Ask students what they find to be humorous about the figures and the way they are portrayed by the artist. Explain that the artist may have been trying to make a political state-ment, and that the humorous treatment uses satire. Have students look through the textbook and other sources to locate examples of military figures or heroes portrayed by artists of differ-ent times and cultures. Encourage students to share and compare their examples to Marisol's work.

Critical Thinking

Have students research var-ious ways in which each of the sculpting processes are used in industrial operations or as manufacturing techniques. For example, students might each select an item that they sus-pect might have been made using one of these techniques and then contact the manu-facturer to check their hypoth-esis. Allow students time to share and compare findings.

Aesthetics

Direct students' attention to the sculptures by Chryssa (Fig-ure 3.33, p. 72). Note that works such as these are often the target of harsh criticism by untrained observers of art. Ask students how they would respond to a dismissal of either or both of these works as "not art." What details would stu-dents point to in defense of the artistic integrity of these sculptures? What kinds of his-torical information would help them in explaining the works' inclusions in the collections of major museums?

Study Guide

Distribute *Study Guide* 7 in the TCR. Assist students in reviewing key concepts. ▱

Art and Humanities

Have students complete *Art and Humanities* 5, "A Different Viewpoint," in the TCR. This activity calls upon students to consider how the human form has been sculpted through the ages. Students are asked to examine a particular sculpture in detail and then to write a story assuming the viewpoint of the sculptural form. ▱

ASSESS

Checking Comprehension

Have students complete the lesson review questions. Answers appear in the box below.

Reteaching

➤ Assign *Reteaching* 7, found in the TCR. Have students complete the activity and review their responses. 📁

➤ Have students divide a piece of paper into five columns and label each column: *clay, wood, stone, metal, mixed media, other.* Have students browse through the text and list the first ten sculptures they find in the appropriate columns.

Enrichment

➤ Assign students *Enrichment* 8, "Approaches to Sculpture," in the Teacher's Classroom Resources. In this activity, students consider the many different methods of sculpture available to artists working with three-dimensional media. 📁

➤ Assign students *Enrichment* 9, "Sculpture Media Through the Ages," in the TCR. In this worksheet, students are introduced to the media and tools sculptors use. 📁

CLOSE

Encourage students to discuss the existence and availability of sculpture in their community. Ask them to debate the merits of having this art form available to the general public.

■ **FIGURE 3.33** An essential part of this work—the changing pattern of brightly colored lights—cannot be captured in a still photograph. What elements and principles of art would you name in describing this work?

Chryssa. *Fragment for "The Gates to Times Square" (Analysis of Letter "A")*. 1966. Neon, plexiglass, steel, and painted wood. Overall: 191.1 × 88.6 × 70.2 cm (75¼ × 34⅞ × 27⅝"). Whitney Museum of American Art, New York, New York. Purchase, with funds from Howard and Jean Lipman.

Movement in sculpture is not limited to the gyrations of actual shapes and forms in space. The Greek-born American sculptor Chryssa shaped and assembled neon light tubes inside a transparent box to create a sculpture of moving lights (Figure 3.33). The flip of an electric switch sets in motion a constantly changing pattern of brightly colored lights that turn on and off in a predetermined sequence. This is an art form clearly rooted in the twentieth century. Her unique and colorful works are said to have been inspired by the illuminated lights of New York's famous Times Square.

Today's sculptors, given the advantage of new materials and processes, are creating artworks that go beyond the wildest dreams of artists of just a generation ago. No one can predict what the sculptures of the future will look like. In one important way, however, they will be like those of the past and present: They will continue to record the full range of human experience in ways that are sometimes shocking, sometimes touching, but always thrilling to see, to touch, and to appreciate.

LESSON THREE REVIEW

Reviewing Art Facts

1. Which sculpture process is additive, and which is subtractive?
2. What materials are used in casting?
3. Describe the assembly process, and list five possible materials suitable for use in an assemblage.
4. What is kinetic art?

▶ Activity... *Relief Sculpture*

The two basic types of sculpture, relief and in the round, allow artists to create in three dimensions. The use of negative space and light and shadow is very important. Look at the examples in the text and try to determine where the artist has made negative space an important part of the work. Research sculptures in the text to identify the use of negative space and light and shadow.

Make a relief sculpture that uses different levels to create light and shadow. Work with small scraps of white mat board. Start with a small square or rectangle and add shapes using white glue. Consider ways of including some negative space in your work. When your work is complete, create a classroom display.

LESSON THREE REVIEW

Answers to Reviewing Art Facts

1. Modeling is an additive technique, carving is subtractive.
2. Wax, clay, or plaster.
3. Answers will vary, but should indicate that the student knows the basic steps in the process described.
4. Kinetic artworks actually move in space.

Activity...*Relief Sculpture*

You may wish to have students work in small cooperative groups to plan and create their relief sculptures. Have them sketch their ideas and discuss the design of their sculpture before they begin glueing the final project.

Architecture

Architecture

Vocabulary
- architecture
- tensile strength
- barrel vault
- groin vault
- dome

Discover
   After completing this lesson, you will be able to:
- Explain the functions of architecture.
- Discuss the materials and processes of architecture.
- Describe modern construction techniques.

*A*rchitecture is *the art and science of designing and constructing structures that enclose space for a variety of human needs.* The history of architecture begins in the distant past, when prehistoric cave dwellers left their caves to build shelters out of tree branches. Since then, architects in every land have faced the challenge of erecting structures that are both functional and visually appealing.

Unique Qualities of Architecture

Architecture, like sculpture, involves the organization and manipulation of three-dimensional forms in space. Both deal with form, space, line, texture, proportion, and color. Indeed, many examples of architecture can be thought of as large sculpture pieces (Figure 3.34).

Architecture differs from sculpture in two important ways, however. First and most obvious, in addition to being viewed from the outside as sculpture is, architecture can be viewed from the inside. Second, architecture is a functional art form. Buildings are erected to serve practical purposes, while sculptures are made to express ideas and feelings that evoke an appreciative response in viewers. Of course, architects also hope viewers find their buildings visually appealing, but their first concern is the challenge of enclosing space for specific human needs.

Materials and Processes of Architecture

Early architects usually chose building materials that were readily available. The appearance of the structures they erected was due in large measure to the limitations imposed by those materials. Wood was probably the first building material used, but we know little about the earliest wood constructions because wood burns and decomposes. As a result, few early wood structures remain to indicate how they were built or what they looked like.

Fortunately, a more durable material, stone, was used by builders wherever it was available. In addition to being permanent and fireproof, stone was found to be well suited to the construction of impressive structures; many of these have survived in whole or in part to the present day.

■ **FIGURE 3.34** Built in the city's harbor, this building has the appearance of a great clipper ship under full sail. **How is this building similar to a sculpture in the round?**

Jörn Utzon. Sydney Opera House. Sydney, Australia. 1957–73.

73

FOCUS
Lesson Objectives
   After studying this lesson, students will be able to:
- Explain the materials, processes, and functions of architecture
- Discuss modern construction methods

Building Vocabulary
   Have students look up each of the definitions of the vocabulary terms in the glossary and write them on a sheet of paper. Then ask them to compare the sketches in the lesson to the definitions they have written and to keep their notes in their portfolios.

Motivator
   Divide the class into small groups of three or four students. Tell each group that they are a team of architects hoping to win a contract to remodel a building in the community. (This could be the courthouse, a church, a place of business, or the school itself.) Identify the building and tell each group to study it closely and describe its features.

Introducing the Lesson
   As a follow-up to the motivator, have students read about the qualities of architecture described on this page. Then have them consider the building they chose above and list its strengths and weaknesses. Tell them that in this lesson they learn to make recommendations that would improve the building's functional efficiency and its appearance.

TEACH

Studio Skills

Refer students to Figure 3.39 and ask them to express their opinions about this monument. Tell them to sketch their designs for a monument that would pay tribute to "A Great Contemporary American."

Art History

Point out that Sir Charles Barry's fame as an architect rests mainly on his plans for the Houses of Parliament, constructed in 1840-1890 in London. Barry was commissioned to execute his plans after winning a competition in 1836. He devoted the rest of his life almost entirely to this project, for which he made about 8000 drawings. Barry was assisted by another architect, Augustus W. Pugin, who was responsible for much of the exterior appearances of the structures. At Barry's death in 1860 the buildings were still unfinished and it was his son Edward, also an architect, who supervised the completion of the work. Have interested students find out more about this building and how it was constructed.

Did You Know?

Antonio Gaudi's unique apartment building in Barcelona (Figure 3.35) avoids any use of straight lines or flat surfaces. Inside, no two rooms are alike. Among the many names give to the building is "House of Bones" because of the bonelike columns used in the floor terrace that projects outward.

Architecture and Art

The functions of architecture can be identified in the photographs below. Architecture serves a variety of human needs.

 1 Some buildings are intended to shelter life. This apartment building does this in a unique way, without straight lines or flat surfaces.

■ FIGURE 3.35

Antonio Gaudi. Casa Mila. Barcelona, Spain. 1905–10.

■ FIGURE 3.36

Charles Barry and A.W.N. Pugin. Houses of Parliament. London, England. Designed 1835.

 2 Other buildings are designed to house governments. This impressive structure reflects the importance of the government activities that take place inside.

■ FIGURE 3.37

Philip Johnson. Sony Building. New York, New York. 1985.

 3 The purpose of other buildings, like this skyscraper, is to house commercial or business activities.

 4 Some buildings provide space devoted to the worship of gods. This Temple of Dawn is one of the most celebrated landmarks of Bangkok, Thailand.

■ FIGURE 3.38

Wat Arun (Temple of Dawn). Bangkok, Thailand. c. 18th century

 5 Building such as this are designed to honor leaders and their contributions.

■ FIGURE 3.39

Henry Bacon. Lincoln Memorial. Washington, D.C. 1914–22.

Architecture in Art

Have students examine the different types of architectural structures in the feature. Instruct students to conduct a library search in which they examine buildings from various periods and places. Instruct them to identify one of these buildings that they would like most to visit and write a paragraph explaining their reasons. Have each student bring to class an illustration of the building they selected and read their explanation. Did ancient buildings outnumber modern buildings? What was the most unusual building mentioned and what made it unusual?

■ FIGURE 3.40 Post and lintel construction

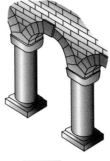

■ FIGURE 3.41 Round arch

Post and Lintel Construction

One of the earliest and simplest methods of building with stone is the post and lintel system, which involves placing a horizontal beam or lintel across the open space between two posts or other vertical supports (Figure 3.40). The size and shape of a building is determined by the number and placement of these post and lintel units.

Examples of post and lintel construction are found throughout history in all parts of the world. Egyptian temples dating back to 2700 B.C. made use of this method of construction. The houses of medieval Europe and the one-room cabins of early American colonists were built with this same system, using wood rather than stone. It was also used in China, Japan, and India, as well as the Yucatán Peninsula.

As a building material, however, stone has certain limitations. The most important of these is its lack of **tensile strength,** *the capacity of a material to withstand bending.* Stone, of course, does not bend. It can span only a narrow space before it cracks in the middle. If you were to walk into a building constructed with posts and lintels, you would find much of the interior space filled with columns or walls. (See Figure 7.6, page 154.) Thus the post and lintel system dictates how a building looks both from the inside and from the outside.

Arch and Vault Construction

Eventually architects discovered they could span larger areas by placing a round arch made of stone blocks on top of two supports.

■ FIGURE 3.42 Later converted into a church, this building was originally constructed for a Spanish king as part of his palace. **What method of construction made buildings like this possible?**

Santa Maria del Naranco, Oviedo, Spain. Ninth century.

The arch transferred the weight outward from its center, or keystone, to the vertical supports (Figure 3.41). The use of the **barrel vault,** *several arches placed front to back to enclose space,* made it possible to construct buildings with stone roofs that could span a wide space, as seen in the view of Santa Maria del Naranco (Figure 3.42).

Chapter 3 *Creating Art: Media and Processes* **75**

Art History

Ask students to browse through the textbook, noting different examples of architecture from a variety of centuries and cultural boundaries. What changes are students able to discern among works of architecture from a particular culture? Do any structures remind them of buildings they have seen in their own community? What culture is responsible for examples of "imitated" works of architecture they may find? During what period of history were those structures built?

Art Criticism

Tell students that the building shown in Figure 3.37 is crowded in on all sides by other tall structures. Ask students to identify the kinds of problems faced by architects who must design buildings for confined spaces like this. How has this architect solved the problem of providing ample space for a large number of people? What has he done to make his building stand apart from those around it? Explain that this building's exterior appearance has not been warmly received by all critics. Ask students whether they would expect positive critiques from critics of the other buildings shown on this page.

Technology ■

National Gallery of Art Videodisc Use the following images as examples of more works by artists introduced in this lesson.

Giovanni Paolo Panini
Interior of Saint Peter's, Rome

Search Frame 510

Giovanni Paolo Panini
The Interior of the Pantheon

Search Frame 512

Use Glencoe's *Correlation Bar Code Guide to the National Gallery of Art* to locate more artworks.

Studio Skills

Divide the class into four or five small groups. One group is to role-play the school board, the others are rival interior design firms who have been asked by the school board to submit proposed plans for a student lounge at the school.

Before they begin work on their designs, firms should be encouraged to consider the following issues: the best location for such a room; its capacity to serve many different functions (e.g., parties, club meetings, rehearsals, and so on); the size of the gatherings that will be centered there; and the room's aesthetic relationship to the rest of the school buildings. Firms can then proceed to make sketches. They may also include paint chips and samples of wallpaper and floor covering to show color schemes.

Did You Know❓

Gothic cathedrals like the one in Figure 3.45, required an average building time of from 40 to 80 years, while the average life expectancy at that time was about 30 years. As a consequence, during the twelfth and thirteenth centuries most of the inhabitants of medieval cities lived in the shadow of unfinished cathedrals under construction.

Like the post and lintel system, the barrel vault had limitations. Builders were reluctant to pierce the thick walls of vaulted buildings with windows; they feared that the openings would weaken the vault. Consequently, without many windows the interiors of buildings with barrel vaults tend to be dark and gloomy.

A partial solution to this problem was found in the third century. Roman builders began using a **groin vault,** *two barrel vaults placed at right angles.* A groin vault provides four separate openings to the interior space (Figure 3.43).

In the Middle Ages, church builders sought other solutions to the problem of letting light into and raising the height of the churches they built. They met both objectives by using a pointed arch rather than a round one. Because the curve of a pointed arch is more vertical, the weight is directed downward to slender supporting columns, or piers, within the building. Additional support is provided by buttresses outside the building (Figure 3.44). Because they often had to reach out over the side aisles of the church, these supports came to be known as *flying buttresses.* The use of pointed arches, piers, and flying buttresses created a thrust-counterthrust system that supported the stone ceiling of massive cathedrals without the need for thick walls. It also enabled builders to fill the spaces between the

supporting piers with spectacular stained-glass windows (Figure 3.45).

Dome Construction

A **dome** is *a hemisphere placed on walls that enclose a circular or square space.* Domes were developed first in the Middle East and later in ancient Rome. A dome has the same downward pressure as the arch and the vault, but the thrust is distributed around its circular rim.

Because the base of a dome is a circle, it can be used most easily on a cylindrical building. The Roman Pantheon (Figure 9.17, page 205) is one of the largest domed structures ever built. This structure, along with the dome of Hagia Sophia in Constantinople (Figure 13.7, page 292, and Figure 13.10, page 293) and the dome of the Florence cathedral designed by Filippo Brunelleschi (brewnell-**less**-kee) (Figure 16.13, page 364), have inspired architects throughout the centuries.

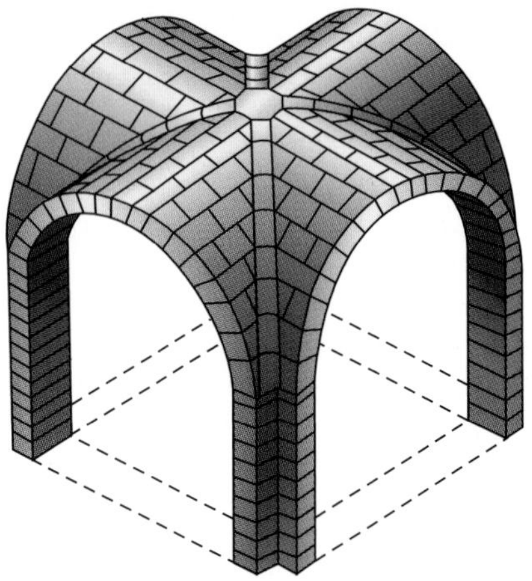

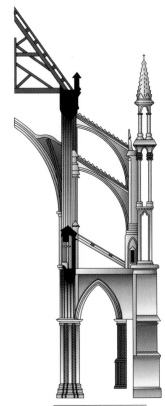

■ **FIGURE 3.43** Groin vault

■ **FIGURE 3.44** Gothic construction features

𝒯eacher 𝒩otes

Developing Perceptual Skills. Architecture is the most difficult of all areas of art to appreciate through photographic reproductions alone. It is virtually impossible for a single photo to convey the sense of space, the quality of light, and the many different viewpoints of a structure. If your community has any interesting buildings that could help students understand twentieth-century developments in architecture, arrange a field trip for students to see these structures. The architecture need not be the product of a pioneer such as Wright or Sullivan. Any structure will suffice so long as it enables students to sense developments of the modern era of building design.

FIGURE 3.45 Notice the immense size of this chapel's stained glass windows. **What architectural development enabled builders to use so much glass?**

Sainte-Chapelle. Paris, France. 1248.

FIGURE 3.46 Balloon framing

Modern Construction Processes

The industrial revolution of the nineteenth century brought about major changes in the materials and processes used by architects. First iron and then steel became common building materials, and mass-production techniques were introduced.

Wood Framing

Wood construction, which had previously been based on the post and lintel system, changed dramatically beginning in the 1800s, when metal nails were manufactured in quantity and sawmills began to provide lumber in standard sizes. A more efficient method of wood construction, known as balloon framing, replaced the slow process of cutting, fitting, and fastening heavy posts and beams in place. With this new method, factory-cut lumber is easily nailed together at the construction site (Figure 3.46). Each part of the building provides support to every other part. Added strength is provided when the outer wall is nailed to this framework.

Iron and Steel Frame Construction

With the development of iron technology in the nineteenth century, this metal was used more and more frequently to construct the framework for large buildings and monuments such as the Eiffel Tower (Figure 23.25, page 536). Architects, recognizing its great strength, used iron to construct buildings with spacious, post-free interiors illuminated by light pouring through vast areas of glass.

The success of early iron structures paved the way for the steel-frame buildings introduced at the end of the nineteenth century. To construct these buildings, a complete skeleton of light, narrow steel beams with great tensile strength is

Art History

Ask students to compare the modern skyscraper in Figure 3.47, page 78, with the medieval French church seen in Figure 3.45. Discuss the similarities in construction methods enabling architects to erect walls of glass. Ask students to explain how the glass walls of each building reflect the time and place in which they were constructed.

Critical Thinking

Assign groups of students to observe different areas in their community. Challenge each to do an in-class presentation on the use of architectural space. Whenever possible, choose areas that contrast with each other, such as the center of town and a vacant pasture. Students can describe the feelings communicated by sparsely settled areas (i.e., barren versus open), commercial areas with high-rise buildings (i.e., lofty versus claustrophobic), and so on. If possible, groups should accompany their presentations with original photographs, photos obtained from local newspapers, and original sketches.

COOPERATIVE LEARNING

Field Trip. If your community boasts any examples of public sculpture, arrange a field trip to view one or more works. (Alternatively, encourage students to make the trip themselves.) Have students write descriptions of and/or draw sketches of a favorite sculpture. Then have them research the sculptor who created the work, gathering information on the artist's life and where other works by this artist are displayed. Ask students to present their findings to the class in the form of an oral presentation. Encourage students to share their experiences with the class. Whenever possible, ask students to write a summary of their field trips to be kept in a class resource file called "Art Field Trips."

Art Criticism

Instruct students to examine closely the illustration of the TWA Terminal Building (Figure 3.48). Have them identify the elements and principles of art evidenced in this building. Ask students if they feel the building *functions* effectively as an airline terminal. Do they feel the design is appropriate? What aspects of the design suggest a soaring bird?

Critical Thinking

Ask students if they feel Saarinen's TWA Terminal Building (Figure 3.49) will withstand the test of time and continue to be appreciated in the future in the same way as the Parthenon (Figure 8.1, page 166) and other famous buildings of the past. If, for some reason, Kennedy International Airport were abandoned, should the TWA Terminal be preserved? If so, what function could it serve?

Studio Activities

Assign *Studio* 5, "Designing a Building," in the TCR. In this activity, students learn about the methods used by architect Frank Gehry in planning a design. They then follow similar steps to design and create a structure from paper.

Study Guide

Distribute *Study Guide* 8 in the TCR. Assist students in reviewing key concepts.

■ **FIGURE 3.47** Still regarded as one of the most impressive of the early skyscrapers, this office building rises above 1000 feet. How were buildings like this constructed?

William Van Alen. Chrysler Building. New York, New York. 1930.

■ **FIGURE 3.48** Eero Saarinen. Interior, TWA Terminal, John F. Kennedy International Airport, New York, New York. 1962.

■ **FIGURE 3.49** The rounded shapes and sweeping roof suggest flight, making this building especially appropriate as an airport terminal. Which elements and principles of art contribute to the unity of this work?

Eero Saarinen. Exterior, TWA Terminal.

78 **Unit One** *Creating and Understanding Art*

riveted together. Then the walls, floors, and interior partitions are added. This steel skeleton is a self-supporting cage, not unlike the stone framework of a medieval cathedral. Because the exterior walls provide no structural support, they can be made of glass or thin panels to enclose space and keep out the weather.

By the beginning of the twentieth century, steel-frame buildings were being constructed in all parts of the world. The invention of the elevator and improvements in construction methods led to the towering urban structures we refer to as skyscrapers (Figure 3.47).

Reinforced Concrete Construction

Concrete, an important building material in ancient Rome, was not used again until the end of the eighteenth century. At that time, it was found to be an acceptable material for the construction of lighthouses. Its full potential, however, was not realized until the following century, when a method was developed to increase its strength. Builders found that they could strengthen concrete by embedding metal rods into it before it hardened. This method produced what is known as ferroconcrete, or reinforced concrete.

Concrete sections in various sizes and shapes can be made by pouring the material into molds and allowing it to harden. When the molds are removed, the concrete retains its shape while exhibiting the same structural advantages of stone. The TWA Terminal Building at New York's John F. Kennedy International Airport,

CULTURAL INFLUENCES

Construction Methods. Ask students to look through the text and identify examples of buildings using the following types of construction: post and lintel, round arch, pointed arch, and dome. As an out-of-class assignment, assign each student the task of locating a building in the community that makes use of at least one of these structural features. Ask students why architects today continue to make use of these early structural features even though new materials and techniques are available. Would the ancient buildings we admire today be as appealing if their architects had available to them the materials and techniques used by contemporary architects?

designed by Eero Saarinen (**air**-oh **sahr**-ih-nen), uses rounded shapes cast in concrete to create an interior space broken only by curving balconies and staircases (Figure 3.48). The exterior of this same building reveals a sweeping design with a wing-shaped concrete roof that suggests flight (Figure 3.49).

Lightweight Structural Systems

The development of lightweight metals and plastics offers contemporary architects new and exciting materials. These new materials enabled Buckminster Fuller to create the geodesic dome for which he is best known (Figure 3.50). This structure uses a lightweight, yet strong frame formed with an intricate network of metal rods. The spaces between these metal rods can be filled in with metal, glass, or other light material. A dome formed in this manner can be assembled quickly to enclose a vast area without interior support. Fuller was so confident of his novel approach to construction that he proposed using it to construct a weather-controlled, transparent dome over a large portion of Manhattan. Deemed impractical, his proposal was never given serious consideration. In architecture, however, the "impractical ideas" of the present often turn out to be the exciting innovations of the future.

■ **FIGURE 3.50** This innovative design relies on the use of light-weight metals and plastics. **What are the advantages of using this kind of design?**

Buckminster Fuller. Geodesic Dome. U.S. Pavilion, Expo 1967, Montreal, Quebec, Canada.

ASSESS
Checking Comprehension
➤ Have students complete the lesson review questions. Answers appear in the box below.
➤ Distribute *Application* 3, "All's Fair," in the TCR, to assess students' understanding of the material in this chapter. 🗁

Reteaching
Assign *Reteaching* 8, found in the TCR. Have students complete the activity and review their responses. 🗁

Enrichment
Assign *Enrichment* 8, "Architecture Through the Ages," in the TCR. 🗁

Extension
Remind students that it is only recently that the ecology movement has made Americans aware of vitally important terms such as *biodegradable* and *recyclable*. Have students research artists who have made statements in their work about consumerism or land, water, air, or sound pollution.

CLOSE
Ask students to prepare a time line of architecture, and on it note the methods of construction that have developed throughout history.

LESSON FOUR REVIEW

Reviewing Art Facts
1. In what way is the round arch an improvement over the post and lintel?
2. Why is it possible to span only a narrow space with stone?
3. How is a barrel vault constructed? Why were buildings constructed with barrel vaults dark and gloomy inside?
4. What brought about the dramatic change in wood construction in the nineteenth century?

▶ ### Activity... *Architectural Design*
Imagine that you are an architect selected to design a tall building. You are challenged to create a design that makes maximum use of a site with limited building space in a modern city.

Use toothpicks or soda straws and glue to construct a preliminary model of your building. Make your design to fit on a cardboard base that is 6 × 6 inches square. Be sure to use at least three of the structural features discussed in this lesson to create the tallest structure you can.

Chapter 3 *Creating Art: Media and Processes* **79**

LESSON FOUR REVIEW

Answers to Reviewing Art Facts
1. The curve in the arch directs the weight downward.
2. Stone will crack.
3. Several arches are placed front to back.
4. The use of metal nails and lumber produced in sawmills.

Activity...*Architectural Design*
Encourage students to sketch a simple plan for their architectural design before they begin constructing their models. Remind them to consider the elements of balance and harmony and how these elements will affect the success of their work.

Studio LESSON
Relief Sculpture

Objectives

■ Construct foam plastic relief sculptures in either high or low relief.

■ Create a surface pattern with contrasts of light and dark values caused by advancing and receding three-dimensional forms.

■ Achieve harmony through the use of an overall textured surface.

Motivator

After discussing the examples of relief sculpture provided in the text, demonstrate the process involved in cutting, assembling, and plastering the foam pieces used to create a relief sculpture. Be certain to explain each step in detail as it is being demonstrated. Following the demonstration, provide students with small pieces of foam plastic with which to experiment. Discuss the various kinds of subject matter that might be used in a relief sculpture. Advise students to avoid designs that are too intricate or make use of fine details, since they are difficult or impossible to achieve with plaster. Explain that plastered surfaces should be kept fairly even to make it easier to apply additional layers.

Aesthetics

Ask students to examine the relief sculptures illustrated in this chapter. Which of these works do they think is most successful? Have them explain why they think it is successful. Which work is considered to be the least successful, and why? Do their explanations take into account all the aesthetic qualities? If not, point out the qualities they have overlooked.

Studio LESSON   Relief Sculpture

Materials

- Pencil and sketch paper
- Sheet of plastic foam, 15 × 15 inches
- Hacksaw blade
- Pieces of plastic foam in assorted shapes and sizes (Packaging material can be cut up and used for this purpose.)
- Several sheets of rough and smooth sandpaper
- Toothpicks, white glue
- Plaster of paris
- Large plastic mixing bowl
- Small spatula for applying plaster

Using pieces of plastic foam covered with plaster, create a relief sculpture. This sculpture can be done in either high or low relief; it can be abstract or make use of recognizable subject matter. The finished sculpture should exhibit an interesting pattern of contrasting light and dark values created by forms extending outward from the background. The marks of the spatula used to apply the plaster provide an overall texture that adds harmony to the work. This surface should be both appealing to the eye and inviting to the touch.

Inspiration

Examine the low-relief and high-relief sculptures illustrated in this chapter (Figures 3.23 and 3.24, page 66). What are the advantages of this particular form of sculpture? What are the disadvantages? Which of the two relief sculptures appeals more to you? Why?

Process

1. Complete several sketches for a relief sculpture. This sculpture can be either abstract or realistic. As you work out your design in pencil, decide whether you want to create a work in low or high relief.

2. Use the large sheet of plastic foam for the background of your relief. Then cut out the various forms for your relief from other pieces of foam. These can be cut easily with a hacksaw blade. Handle the saw carefully. Make the sawing motions away from your face, and keep your other hand away from the cutting area. Wear a mask and protective goggles.

3. Arrange the pieces of your relief on the large foam sheet. Try out various arrangements by fastening the pieces in place with toothpicks. When you are satisfied with the design, glue the sections together with white glue.

4. Mix the plaster in a large bowl; wear a dust mask when mixing powdered plaster. Apply the plaster quickly to the surface of your relief with a spatula. The process is similar to that of frosting a cake. Keep the surface smooth, but recognize that the spatula marks add an interesting texture. Cover the entire sculpture, including the background, with plaster.

■ **FIGURE 3.51** Student Work

Teacher *Notes*

Building Self-Esteem. Research shows that small groups of students working together often accomplish more learning than students working alone. With this in mind, have the class first arrange the completed reliefs in a row, ranging from the most realistic to the most abstract. Break the class into small groups and ask one group to prepare a critique on the most realistic, another on the most abstract. Other groups should be instructed to critique works found at or near the center of the row of sculptures. Have each group present their critiques in class adhering to the four steps of art criticism. Encourage every member of each group to participate.

If you need more than one session to finish the plastering, remember to dampen all the previously plastered surfaces before beginning anew. This prevents separation and cracking.

5. Using fine sandpaper, lightly smooth the surface of the finished sculpture. Wear a dust mask while sanding, and sand only in an area that is well-ventilated. After sanding, examine your sculpture and decide whether a bronze finish, or patina, would add to its visual appeal. *Patina* is a film that can form on bronze and copper naturally (through long exposure to air) or artificially (through the application of acid, paint, etc.) You can achieve a simulated bronze patina on your relief sculpture by using powdered tempera paint and shellac (white or orange) in the following manner.

a. Pour generous portions of black, blue-green, and green powdered tempera paint into separate piles on sheets of newspaper spread over a tabletop in a large, well-ventilated room.

b. Pour a *small* amount of shellac into a flat container. Limit the amount, since any unused shellac will be too contaminated for future use.

c. Dip a stiff brush into the shellac and then into the black powdered tempera paint. Brush this mixture thoroughly over the entire relief, including the edges.

d. When the entire surface of the relief is blackened and while it is still tacky to the touch, lightly brush a small amount of green or blue-green powdered tempera over the entire surface. This highlights the raised portions of the relief and gives it the appearance of bronze.

e. You can repeat the patina process on any section of the relief that fails to look bronzelike.

SAFETY TIP Use shellac and alcohol only in well-ventilated areas and only while wearing protective rubber gloves and a mask. Wear a dust mask and rubber gloves when mixing and handling shellac and powdered tempera.

Optional Materials

- Powdered tempera paint (black, blue-green, and green)
- Shellac (white or orange)
- Stiff brush
- Alcohol to clean brush

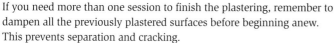

Studio Skills

Have students use a large plastic bowl and a small, flat wood slat to mix the plaster. They should add the plaster to the water in the bowl by sifting it through the fingers. The plaster should be distributed over the entire surface of the water until a mound begins to form. They then stir slowly until the plaster begins to set, making it possible to apply it to the foam plastic surface with a large spatula.

Use large plastic bowls to mix plaster. Allow the excess to dry in the bowl and then twist it to break up the dry plaster. Do not pour unused plaster down a drain.

Extension

Have students complete a sculpture in the round with the same materials and techniques used in creating their reliefs. Have them identify problems experienced in creating a relief sculpture and a sculpture in the round.

Critiquing

Have students apply the steps of art criticism to their own artwork using the "Examining Your Work" questions on this page.

— Examining Your Work

Describe. Is your work best described as abstract or realistic? If realistic, is the subject matter easily recognized? Is your sculpture done in high or low relief?

Analyze. Does your work exhibit an interesting pattern of contrasting light and dark values? Is there an actual texture created by the marks of the spatula?

Interpret. Does your sculpture appeal to the viewer's sense of touch?

Judge. Do you consider your relief sculpture a success? What do you regard as its most appealing feature?

81

— ASSESSMENT

Examining Your Work. As students describe their work, have them explain how they created either an abstract or a realistic appearance to their relief sculpture. Help them to describe the way they incorporated light and dark contrasts of value. As they analyze their work, have students again refer to the two works on page 66. Ask them to compare and contrast the appearance of their relief sculptures to the effects achieved in the bronze or the terra cotta works illustrated. Have them keep notes on the analysis and comparison of their artworks, and how they would make changes in a second relief sculpture project. Students should keep their notes and a photo of their relief sculpture in their portfolios.

Studio LESSON

Whimsical Sandwich Painting

Studio LESSON

Whimsical Sandwich Painting

Objectives

- Design a unique, whimsical sandwich painting consisting of five or more items.
- Use large, proportioned shapes throughout.
- Emphasize the sandwich by using light values and bright intensities that contrast with the darker values and duller intensities in the background.

Motivator

Discuss imaginative works that are identified in the text by students. Ask them to explain why the people or objects depicted are so unusual. Ask them how artists responsible for these works might approach the task of creating a whimsical painting. Tell students to avoid both the conventional and the expected, and give their imaginations free reign.

Aesthetics

Direct attention to the student work illustrated. Ask if items included in the sandwich are represented realistically. What other aesthetic qualities should be taken into account, and why? Which aesthetic theory seems most appropriate when judging the work? Ask them to defend their decisions. Explain how a reference to all three theories can add to their understanding and appreciation of this work.

Critiquing

Have students apply the steps of art criticism to their own artwork using the "Examining Your Work" questions on this page.

Materials

- Pencil and sketch paper
- Large sheet of white mat board, 12 × 18 inches
- Tempera or acrylic paint
- Brushes, mixing tray, and paint cloth
- Water container

■ FIGURE 3.52 Student Work

Using tempera or acrylic, paint a picture of a large, whimsical sandwich seen from the side. Your creation will include items that are not the kinds of things one might be expected to find in a sandwich. Your sandwich will be as unusual and whimsical as your imagination allows.

Inspiration

Examine the two-dimensional works illustrated in this chapter and throughout the book. Notice that the subjects in these works range from those that are realistically represented to others that are based upon images drawn from the artist's imagination.

Process

1. Discuss ideas to include in a unique, whimsical sandwich, unlike any sandwich seen in real life. List "ingredients" for such a sandwich on the chalkboard. Avoid familiar items in favor of unlikely ingredients such as: an assortment of candy bars or items not normally associated with food and eating, such as books, articles of clothing, or tools.
2. Prepare several sketches of a whimsical sandwich. Show the sandwich from the side in order that five or more items can be more easily shown between two slices of bread or the top and bottom half of a bun. Develop a theme for your sandwich, such as "undersea treasure sandwich" (Figure 3.52).
3. Transfer your most successful sketch to the mat board making certain to fill the entire sheet with your drawing. Use acrylic or tempera to paint your composition. Light, bright colors should be used for the sandwich and a contrasting dark, dull color for the background.

Examining Your Work

Describe. Is your painting easily recognized as a sandwich? Is it seen from the side? Does it contain five or more ingredients? Can these be readily identified?

Analyze. Does your sandwich fill the space on which it is painted? Did you use light, bright hues that contrast with the dark, dull background to emphasize the sandwich?

Interpret. Does your painting present a highly imaginative version of a sandwich? Are others able to recognize the whimsical nature of your creation?

Judge. Do you feel that your painting is successful? Is it successful because it is painted in a realistic style, or because it uses the elements and principles of art to achieve an overall sense of unity?

82

ASSESSMENT

Examining Your Work. As students answer the questions in Examining Your Work, ask them to provide a written description of their sandwich. Have them explain how they came up with the plan for the sandwich, and in their descriptions, ask them to describe their use of the elements and principles of art. In their written descriptions, students should explain whether their painting is successful and why they feel it is or is not. Have them keep their notes in their portfolios along with their artworks.

Reviewing the Facts

Lesson One

1. Name two examples of wet media and two examples of dry media.
2. What is the purpose of a binder in paint? What materials are used as the binders in tempera paint, encaustic, oil paint, watercolor, and acrylics?

Lesson Two

3. Who were the first people to develop and use the relief printing process?
4. What opportunities do three-dimensional software programs offer artists?

Lesson Three

5. What is the difference between relief sculpture and sculpture in the round?
6. Name and describe the sculpture process used by Marisol in *The Generals* (Figure 3.32, page 71).

Lesson Four

7. How is architecture similar to sculpture? How is it different?
8. What advantages does stone have over wood as a building material?

Thinking Critically

1. **EXTEND.** From time to time, the expression "Painting is dead" is heard. Examine the possible meanings of this statement. Then organize your thoughts in outline form to argue for or against the statement.
2. **COMPARE.** Michelangelo held that sculpture was the greatest of the visual art forms while Leonardo da Vinci argued in favor of painting. Take a position in this argument and explain why you agree with either Michelangelo or Leonardo. Present your views in class along with other students.

A R T S ○ U R C ▣ ARTSOURCE DANCE. Use the *Performing Arts Handbook*, page 579 to learn more about the Lewitsky Dance Company in "Impressions #1."

CAREERS IN **Art** Read about a graphic design career in the *Careers in Art Handbook*, page 596.

*inter*NET CONNECTION Visit Glencoe Art Online at *www.glencoe.com/sec/art*. Examine prints and photography collections and learn about art media.

Technology Project

Media and Processes

Throughout history, artists have seized upon technological advances and incorporated them into their works. The first artists drew and painted images, and fashioned forms with whatever materials were available—sticks, charcoal, berries, clay, wood, or bone. As time passed, artists discovered image-making materials, techniques, and processes that allowed them to become more versatile in their artistic expression. With the development of the printing press and movable type, graphic artists and printmakers of the Middle Ages found a whole new market for their work as book illustrations.

As you experiment with digital art, it is important not to get swept away by the novelty of it all. Remember that no matter what the time period, culture, tool, or medium, the visual arts originate in the mind of the artist and find appreciation in the eye of the observer.

1. Choose one of your favorite sketches from your sketchbook or create new ones from observation.
2. Complete a small painting from this sketch using a traditional painting medium such as watercolor, tempera, or acrylics.
3. Take your traditional artwork to the computer and re-create it in digital form. Experiment with paint and draw programs. Pay close attention to the fact that as with any traditional medium, the same standards for creating a unified composition should apply. Your use of the art elements such as line, shape, color, value, texture and space, arranged according to the art principles such as balance and rhythm—will not change when you use a computer.
4. When you have completed your work, print it and display it along with your traditional work. In what ways are the works alike? How are they different?
5. Critique your works using the four steps of description, analysis, interpretation, and judgment.

Reviewing the Facts

1. Wet media: ink, paints. Dry media, any two: pencil, charcoal, crayon, chalk, pastels.
2. Binder holds pigment together; egg white, wax, linseed oil, water and gum arabic, acrylic polymer.
3. The Chinese.
4. The artist can present various views of an object on a computer monitor screen.
5. Relief sculpture projects slightly from the background. Sculpture in the round is surrounded on all sides by space.
6. Marisol used the assembly process, combining wood, plaster, and found materials.
7. Similarities: both use organization of three-dimensional forms in space.
   Differences: architecture can be viewed from outside and inside; is functional.
8. Stone is durable, permanent, and fireproof so artworks will survive.

Thinking Critically

1. Possible interpretations will include the following: Art of the twentieth century is so non-representational, that one no longer can apply any criterion for evaluating the merits of a given work. Outlines should note several aesthetic criteria in addition to imitationalism by which works of art may be judged.
2. Both works emphasize the element of line; students should indicate an understanding of how line is used according to each principle.

Teaching the Technology Project

Arrange for a local professional computer artist to come to the classroom to speak with students about some of the issues raised in the activity. Have the person address in particular the kinds of tasks for which he or she might choose a paint program over a draw program and vice versa. Prior to the visit, have students make a list of questions.

A R T S ○ U R C ▣ ARTSOURCE Assign the feature in the *Performing Arts Handbook*, page 579.

CAREERS IN ART If time permits, have interested students investigate the career information in the *Careers in Art Handbook*, page 596.

*inter*NET CONNECTION Have students go online and learn more about artists on preselected Web sites with the Internet activity for this chapter.

Art Criticism and Aesthetics

LESSON ONE
(pages 86–90)

Art Criticism: A Search for Aesthetic Qualities

Classroom Resources

📁 Art and Humanities 6
📁 Enrichment Activity 10
📁 Reproducible Lesson Plan 9
📁 Reteaching Activity 9
📁 Study Guide 9

Features

Using the Design Chart to Analyze *Art*

The Sleeping Gypsy
(pages 88–89)

LESSON TWO
(pages 91–101)

Using Aesthetics and Art Criticism

Classroom Resources

📁 Appreciating Cultural Diversity 5
📁 Art and Humanities 7
📁 Cooperative Learning 6
📁 Enrichment Activity 11
📁 Reproducible Lesson Plan 10
📁 Reteaching Activity 10
📁 Study Guide 10

Features

Nonobjective *Art*

(page 100)

END OF CHAPTER
(pages 102–103)

Studio LESSON

• Painting a Representational Still Life *(page 102)*

ADDITIONAL CHAPTER RESOURCES

Activities
- 📁 Advanced Studio Activity
- 📁 Application 4
- 🖱 Chapter 4 Internet Activity
- 📁 Studio Activities 5, 6

Fine Art Resources
- 🎞 **Transparency**
  Art in Focus Transparency 7
  Magritte. *Human Condition*
- 🖼 **Fine Art Print**
  Focus on World Art Print 4
  Pablo Picasso. *Mandolin and Guitar.*

Assessment
- 📁 Chapter 4 Test
- 📁 Performance Assessment

Multimedia Resources
- Artsource® Performing Arts Package
- 💿 National Gallery Laser Disc
- 💿 National Museum of Women in the Arts CD-ROM
- 📼 Arts & Entertainment Videos

NATIONAL STANDARDS FOR ARTS EDUCATION

The National Standards for Arts Education provide guidelines for grade-appropriate competency in the visual arts. The Content Standards for grades 9–12 are:

1. Understanding and applying media, techniques, and processes.
2. Using knowledge of structures and functions.
3. Choosing and evaluating a range of subject matter, symbols, and ideas.
4. Understanding the visual arts in relation to history and cultures.
5. Reflecting upon and assessing the characteristics and merits of their work and the work of others.
6. Making connections between visual arts and other disciplines.

Listed below are the National Standards for the Visual Arts addressed in this chapter. For a breakdown of the categories listed under each content standard, refer to the *Reproducible Lesson Plans* booklet in the TCR.

  1. (a, b) **2.** (a, b, c) **3.** (a, b) **4.** (a, c) **5.** (a, b, c) **6.** (a)

HANDBOOK MATERIAL

 Alfredo Rolando Ortiz *(page 580)*

CAREERS IN *Art*

Art Critic *(page 597)*

Beyond the Classroom

Through programs sponsored by the Young Audiences National Organization, teachers will have opportunities to bring students face to face with professional performing and visual artists. Find them by visiting our Web site at *www.glencoe.com/sec/art.*

🕐 **Out of Time?** If time does not permit teaching this chapter in its entirety, you may wish to preview the artwork and captions with students. Scan the heads in each lesson with students. Discuss the features on Using the Design Chart to Analyze Art on pages 88 and 89, Nonobjective Art, page 100.

Art Criticism and Aesthetics

INTRODUCE

Chapter Overview

CHAPTER 4 provides an introduction to the evaluative approaches to art taken by art critics and their search for aesthetic qualities in art.

Lesson One deals with the four steps used by the critic in evaluating a work of art.

Lesson Two discusses three aesthetic theories and their application to artworks.

Studio Lesson calls upon students to paint a representational still life.

Art&Science

Begin by explaining that tsunamis are not really tidal waves, noting that they are in fact ocean waves generated by undersea earthquakes. Reveal that tsunamis reach speeds of about 450 to 500 mph and produce waves 50 feet high. Ask: Do you think the wave depicted in Figure 4.1 is a tsunami? After affirming that it is not, ask students: How has the artist captured its ferocity?

Art Criticism and Aesthetics

Art&Science ■ **FIGURE 4.1** Mt. Fuji, one of the tallest volcanoes in the world, is one of a string of volcanoes known as the Ring of Fire that surrounds the Pacific Rim. Japan is made up of several volcanic islands. The earth's crust below the waters that surround these islands is unpredictable, making the island nation subject to giant tsunami, or seismic tidal waves.

Katsushika Hokusai. *The Great Wave at Kanagawa* (from the series The Thirty-Six Views of Fuji). c. 1823–29. Polychrome woodblock print. 25.7 × 38 cm (10 1/8 × 14 15/16").The Metropolitan Museum of Art, New York, New York. The H.O. Havemeyer Collection, bequest of Mrs. H.O. Havemeyer, 1929. (JP 1847).

National Standards

This chapter addresses the following National Standards for the Arts.

1. (a,b)	**4.** (a,c)
2. (a,b,c)	**5.** (a,b,c)
3. (a,b)	**6.** (a)

CHAPTER 4 RESOURCES

Teacher's Classroom Resources

📁 Advanced Studio Activity 4

📁 Application 4

🖱 Chapter 4 Internet Activity

📁 Studio Activities 5, 6

Assessment

📁 Chapter 4 Test

📁 Performance Assessment

Fine Art Resources

 *Art in Focus* Transparency 7
   Magritte. *Human Condition.*

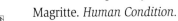 *Focus on World Art* Print 4
   Pablo Picasso. *Mandolin and Guitar.*

*O*ften, people who wish to learn about art are tempted to rely on accepted authorities who tell them what to value and why. Unfortunately, if they do this, they can never experience the satisfaction and pleasure that come with a direct interaction with a work of art. Their experience must always be second hand. Learning to see and understand a work on their own requires that viewers know two things: how to look and what to look for. To learn these two things they must turn to art criticism and aesthetics.

Introducing the Chapter

Ask students to examine Figure 4.1 and share their impressions. Does the work appear to tell a story? Does it capture a feeling or mood? Are the parts of the work arranged in a way that arouses visual interest? Note that questions such as these guide the art critic in judging the success of any artwork. Explain that in this lesson, students will learn about this process.

Music. While studying this chapter, use *Performing Arts Handbook* page 580. Help students appreciate how Alfredo Rolando Ortiz interprets and creates music that touches the aesthetic intelligence of listeners, as well as their emotions.

YOUR Portfolio

Assume the role of an art critic after studying this chapter. Examine the work in Figure 4.1 using the four steps of art criticism. For each step, prepare a brief response to present to the class. Describe the work and its features. How does the artist use the elements of art? What principles are used to organize those elements? Explain how the elements and principles give unity to the design. Explain the mood created by the artwork. A critic of which aesthetic viewpoint would favor this work: imitationalism, formalism, or emotionalism? Tell whether you feel the work is successful. Keep your notes in your portfolio with a copy of the artwork if available.

Focus ON THE ARTS

MUSIC

Just as artists at the turn of the twentieth century began to explore the possibilities of nonobjective art—art without any recognizable subject matter—so musicians began creating music lacking any recognizable tone center, or key. A notable figure in this movement was Austrian-born composer Arnold Schoenberg, who perfected the "twelve-tone system" of musical composition.

LITERATURE

Philosophers have long attempted to answer the questions of what art is and how it relates to the notion of beauty. Among the earliest to put pen to paper in an effort to answer these questions was the Greek philosopher and writer, Plato.

THEATRE

Ever since early cultures sought to communicate a lesson through actions rather than words, the dramatic arts have flourished—and so has the desire to develop a system for objectively judging the merits of dramatic works. An example of this quest is found in George Bernard Shaw's *Quintessence of Ibsenism*, a commentary on the works of playwright Henrik Ibsen.

Focus ON THE ARTS

Bring to class a recording of twelve-tone music—if possible, Schoenberg's first major work, the tone poem *Verklärte Nacht* (*Transfigured Night*). Divide the class into two groups. Direct one group's attention to the Jackson Pollock painting in Figure 4.19. The other group is to listen to a short musical passage. Group members are each to write their reactions on a sheet of paper. After several minutes, groups are to compile member reactions, and the class is to reunite and share their lists. Note similarities among the terms on the two lists. Ask: What about this painting or composition makes it _____?

85

DEVELOPING A PORTFOLIO

Self-Evaluation. Ultimately, students must come to terms with the limitations set on the number of artworks included in a portfolio. They cannot submit everything they have done. Consequently, they learn to be qualitatively sensitive about their work. Stress the value of setting standards, especially through informed judgments, that is, developing the ability to assess their own work on the basis of accepting criteria. Through self-evaluation, students take control of decision-making and feel increasingly responsible for the quality of their work.

Art Criticism: A Search for Aesthetic Qualities

Focus

Lesson Objectives

After studying this lesson, students will be able to:
- Identify the four steps in the process of art criticism.
- Use the first three steps—description, analysis, and interpretation—to gather specific kinds of information from a work of art.

Building Vocabulary

Hand out to each student two slips of paper, one with the word *literal*, the other with the word *expressive*. After ensuring they have a working definition of each, present a slide show of works that may be described as literal, expressive, or both. (Cassatt, Courbet, Degas, and Chuck Close are artists whose works you might consider for this activity.) Without speaking, students are to raise one or both slips in reaction to each slide.

Motivator

Have students select a reproduction of a painting in the text and make a complete list of observations regarding the work (i.e., elements of art emphasized, whether the subject is realistic, and so on). When students feel their lists are complete, ask them to sketch the work they chose. What details did they miss on the list that were brought to their attention in the act of sketching?

Art Criticism: A Search for Aesthetic Qualities

Vocabulary
- aesthetic qualities
- literal qualities
- design qualities
- expressive qualities

Discover
After completing this lesson, you will be able to:
- Identify the four steps in the process of art criticism.
- Use the first three steps—description, analysis, and interpretation— to gather specific kinds of information from a work of art.

*A*rt critics have their own methods of studying works of art. They use these methods to learn as much as possible from artworks representing a variety of styles and techniques. They carefully examine these works, searching for **aesthetic qualities,** *the qualities that can increase their understanding of the works and serve as the criteria on which their judgments are based.* Identifying and assessing these aesthetic qualities enables art critics to make judgments and to defend those judgments with intelligent reasons. In the pages that follow, you will learn that the aesthetic qualities include the literal, design, and expressive qualities.

The methods used by art critics to identify these qualities often involve four operations: description, analysis, interpretation, and judgment. Learning how these operations are used will help you develop your own skills in examining and discussing works of art. These examinations and discussions will help you make your own personal decisions about those works and greatly increase your enjoyment of them.

The Art Criticism Approach

Art criticism is not a matter of casual observation and impulsive expressions of likes or dislikes. It is a reasoned activity of the mind. Art critics use the operations of description, analysis, interpretation, and judgment to gain information *from* the artwork, rather than gathering facts about the work and the artist who created it. Used by a critic, these operations direct attention to *internal clues,* that is, clues found *in* the work itself. When examining any work of art, critics ask and answer questions such as these:

- What is seen in the artwork?
- How is the artwork designed?
- What does it mean?
- Is it a successful work of art?

To understand more clearly how a critic gathers information from an artwork, follow an imaginary critic named Robert as he examines a painting (Figure 4.2). You will learn how a critic uses the operations of description, analysis, interpretation, and judgment. It is the same approach you will use to gain a more complete understanding of the artworks you encounter. It is also an approach that can help you as you examine and try to improve your own works of art.

■ **FIGURE 4.2** When Rousseau first exhibited this picture, viewers greeted it with smiles and laughter. **What was *your* first impression of it?**

Henri Rousseau. *The Sleeping Gypsy.* 1897. Oil on canvas. 129.5 × 200.7 cm (51 × 79"). The Museum of Modern Art, New York, New York. Gift of Mrs. Simon Guggenheim.

86

LESSON ONE RESOURCES

Teacher's Classroom Resources

 Art and Humanities 6

 Enrichment Activity 10

📁 Reproducible Lesson Plan 9

📁 Reteaching Activity 9

📁 Study Guide 9

Description

Robert begins by making a thorough inventory of everything he sees in the work. In other words, he identifies the **literal qualities,** or *realistic presentation of subject matter,* and the elements of art found in the work.

Identifying the Literal Qualities

Focusing first on the literal qualities, Robert observes that the painting depicts an incident taking place in a silent desert landscape illuminated by a perfectly round, cool moon. A few stars twinkle in the blue night sky. In the foreground, a lion sniffs at a gypsy asleep on the sand next to the still water of an oasis. The gypsy, not yet aware of the lion, sleeps peacefully on a carpet of some sort. Beside him rest a mandolin and a large jug. His right hand still grips the staff he used in his trek across the desert.

Looking more closely, Robert observes that there are no footprints in the sand around the gypsy. Could this be an oversight, a detail the artist merely forgot to include in his picture? Robert decides to file this question away in his mind, to be considered later when he attempts to interpret the work. Directing his attention to the lion, he notices that it does not look entirely like a real animal. The tail extends outward gracefully, perhaps too gracefully, and the mane appears to have been carefully arranged. Although it does appear menacing—it is, after all, a lion—Robert finds that it reminds him of the stuffed animals he has seen in toy shops. The lion stares with buttonlike eyes at the gypsy, who slumbers on despite looking stiff and not altogether comfortable. He wears no sandals and is clothed in a colorful striped garment that shows no sign of a hard day's travel.

Identifying the Elements of Art

Satisfied that he has taken into account the realistic details in the painting, Robert turns his attention to the elements of art, making note of the different hues, values, lines, and shapes and of the way space is represented.

Robert is surprised to find that the artist painted with simple, unmixed colors. Most of these colors are found in small amounts in the gypsy's costume and the carpet on which he rests. There, narrow stripes of red, blue, yellow, green, orange, and violet can be identified. The same dark orange noted on the mandolin is also used to color the jug. The sky is blue, and neutral browns and tans bordering on yellow are used for the sand, the lion, and the feet, arms, and face of the gypsy. Light and dark values of blue, brown, and tan can be identified throughout the work.

Robert notes that each shape is clearly defined, making it stand out prominently from the background. Gradual changes in value within each make these shapes look like solid, three-dimensional forms. He also observes that long, short, straight, and curved lines of different thicknesses have been used on the lion's mane and for the narrow stripes of the gypsy's garment and carpet. A series of straight lines represents the strings of the mandolin.

Satisfied that he has made a thorough description of the literal qualities and the elements of art, Robert is ready to move on to the second step of the art criticism process: analysis.

Analysis

During analysis, Robert uses the principles of art to determine how the elements of art used in the picture are organized. By focusing on the relationship of principles and elements, he hopes to gain an understanding of the work's **design qualities,** or *how well the work is organized, or put together.* This understanding will enable him to determine if the work has an overall sense of unity.

Using the Design Chart

Robert uses a design chart as an aid in analyzing the painting. With the chart, he can identify the most important design relationships linking the elements and principles in the work. If you were to look over his shoulder, you might see Robert recording these design relationships on a chart similar to the one in Figure 4.3, page 88.

Robert reviews the design chart and concludes that he has identified the most important design relationships. He knows that, if necessary, he might have identified other, more subtle relationships. He also knows that another art critic, with a different background

TEACH

Introducing the Lesson

Ask students to imagine that while walking, they see an object lying on the pavement in front of the them that looked like a pocket-size computer. Ask: What would you do to learn more about this object? Elicit that they would most likely pick it up, inspect it from all sides, attempt to press buttons on it, and even possibly open it to look inside. Explain that the job of the art critic is similar. That is, a critic takes a work of art apart in order to learn more about it.

Aesthetics

Have students examine the painting by Henri Rousseau in Figure 4.2. What mood or feeling does this work evoke? What literal qualities of the work are responsible for this mood? What role does color play in helping to evoke this mood? What other elements are emphasized?

Studio Skills

Provide students with a variety of objects that yield interesting images under magnification (e.g., an orange, a leather shoe, a baseball). Have students choose and draw one of the objects and then write a detailed description of their drawing. Then have them examine their objects under a magnifying glass or a hand-held microscope and write a second description. Ask whether they now "see" the object in a different way than they saw it before they attempted their drawings. Have them do a second drawing based on their revised perception.

 # Technology

National Gallery of Art Videodisc Use the following images as examples of more works by artists introduced in this lesson.

Henri Rousseau
Tropical Forest with Monkeys

Search Frame 1588

Use Glencoe's *Correlation Bar Code Guide to the National Gallery of Art* to locate more artworks.

Studio Skills

Have students complete sketches of a still life from different angles in preparation for the studio lesson they will attempt later in this chapter. Explain that they should concentrate on the still-life arrangement while drawing. Their eyes should be moving constantly back and forth from the still life to their drawing rather than focusing attention for long periods of time on their drawing. In this way, a continuous comparison can be made between the still life and the drawing to determine if accuracy is being realized.

Art Criticism

Divide the class into small groups. Allow each group to choose a slip of paper bearing a chapter number from 1 to 24. The group is then to select the chapter-opening figure for that chapter. Have groups copy the Design Chart (Figure 4.3) onto a sheet of paper and do a complete art-criticism analysis of the work. Groups should compare and discuss analyses.

Aesthetics

Ask students to assume that they are art critics. Working independently, students are to identify a work of art in the text that they feel is especially successful in its use of the design qualities. Allow time to discuss their choices. Did two or more students select the same work? What about the works chosen communicates a strong sense of design? What elements and principles contribute to this overall sense?

Using the Design Chart to Analyze *Art*

DESIGN CHART

	Balance	Emphasis	Harmony	Variety	Gradation	Movement/ Rhythm	Proportion
Color: Hue		#1	#2				
Intensity							
Value		#3			#4		
Value (Non-Color)							
Line		#5		#6			
Texture			#7				
Shape/Form		#8			#9		
Space							

ELEMENTS OF ART (vertical axis label) — *PRINCIPLES OF ART* (top heading) — UNITY (right side label)

■ **FIGURE 4.3** Design Chart

1 Robert begins his analysis by placing his first check mark (#1) at the intersection of hue and emphasis. Perhaps, like Robert, you noticed that many of the hues in this painting have been used on the gypsy's colorful costume and carpet (Fig. 4.4). This emphasizes the gypsy's importance and makes him, along with the lion, the painting's center of interest.

2 Robert's next check mark (#2) links hue with harmony. This reflects his decision that large areas of the artwork have been painted with a limited number of hues. A relatively simple arrangement of blue, brown, and tan distributed throughout the work ties the parts together into a harmonious whole. At the same time, it makes the gypsy's colorful costume appear more pronounced.

3 A check mark (#3) at the intersection of value and emphasis is an important one. Robert recognizes how contrasts of light and dark values help emphasize not only the lion and the gypsy, but important details like the mandolin and the moon as well. Notice, on the one hand, how the lion's dark form is boldly silhouetted against the lighter sky (Figure 4.5). This clearly establishes the animal's importance. On the other hand, the light values of the gypsy, mandolin, and moon make them stand out against the darker values around them.

4 Robert made another check mark (#4) at the intersection of value and gradation. The gradual change from dark to light values is obvious. This change of value is most clear in the large areas of sky and sand and in the methods the artist used to make the lion and the gypsy look three-dimensional.

Using the Design Chart to Analyze *Art*

Students will be more apt to use the Design Chart grid in their analyses of artworks if you provide them with a supply of blank grids. If you have access to a word processor with a tables feature, a spreadsheet or charting program, or page layout software, you can easily replicate the grid shown in Figure 4.3. Be sure to make the cells large enough to accommodate a check mark, as well as any notes and self-reminders the student may wish to jot down. A copy of this chart is also provided in the *Focus on World Art Prints* package, Print 25.

■ FIGURE 4.4

Henri Rousseau. *The Sleeping Gypsy* (detail).

■ FIGURE 4.5

Henri Rousseau. *The Sleeping Gypsy* (detail).

 5

Robert's decision to place a check mark (#5) linking line and emphasis reveals the importance he attaches to the principle of emphasis in this composition. Already he has made three check marks identifying this principle, and he has not yet completed his analysis. The check here refers to the concentration of lines or stripes that decorate the gypsy's garment and carpet. These lines clearly contrast with the large, unadorned areas of sand and sky and help emphasize the sleeping figure.

 6

Another of Robert's check marks (#6) ties the element of line to the principle of variety. The thick and thin, straight and curved, long and short lines in the lion's mane, the gypsy's costume and carpet, the strings of the mandolin, and the outlines of distant sand dunes provide the variety needed to make the painting visually interesting.

 7

Noticing the painting's consistently smooth surface, Robert placed a check mark (#7) at the intersection of texture and harmony. This reflects his decision that the glossy surface helps pull the painting together to make a harmonious whole.

8

Robert's next two check marks (#8 and #9) link the elements of shape and form with the principles of emphasis and gradation. He saw that the artist emphasized the shapes of the gypsy and the lion by making them look more like three-dimensional forms. A gradual change from dark to light values gives each the appearance of a solid form occupying real space. Notice how the form of the gypsy overlaps that of the lion, which in turn overlaps the water and the sand dunes. Behind the sand dunes is the night sky. This overlapping of forms draws Robert's eye to the desert stretching back as far as the eye can see—a landscape filled with nothing more than sand dunes and silence.

Studio Skills

Ask students to use images torn from consumer magazines to create a composition that subtly expresses a single message or emotion. They can begin by gluing the torn shapes onto a sheet of paper, 9 × 12 inches. They may then use markers either to enhance or obscure parts of the composition. Display completed works, challenging students to interpret the intended message. Conclude with a discussion of whether art critics invariably interpret an artwork as the artist intended.

Aesthetics

Have students choose one of the projects they have completed in one of the Studio Lessons of the previous three chapters. (As an alternative, they may select one of the "Studio Skills" activities encountered thus far in the text.) Ask them to judge the merits of the work in terms of its literal, formal, and expressive qualities. In terms of which of these qualities does the work most succeed? Point out how the work least succeeds. Ask students to defend their critiques.

Cross Curriculum

CAREERS. Invite an industrial designer to speak to the class about the manner in which he or she evaluates the design of goods that are being considered for mass production. If possible, the speaker should represent a company that manufactures goods used primarily by individuals in your students' age group. Make sure the designer discusses how cost considerations are balanced, as well as functionality, consumer preferences, and the aesthetic appeal of a potential product.

𝒯eacher 𝒩otes

Some students may not be familiar with the term *intersection* used in the discussion of the Design Chart in Figure 4.3. Ask if any students recognize this term from their study of coordinate mapping in geometry. To facilitate students' work with the chart, ask a volunteer to read aloud the text that discusses and demonstrates the use of this chart on these pages. Then have students gain practice by working as a group to apply the chart to other artworks in the text. Encourage students to assist one another in filling out the chart so that those familiar with this process can assist others in the class.

Study Guide

Distribute *Study Guide* 9 in the TCR. Assist students in reviewing key concepts. 📁

Art and Humanities

Have students complete *Art and Humanites* 6, "Art Criticism, A Changing Art," in the TCR. 📁

ASSESS

Checking Comprehension

Have students complete the lesson review questions. Answers appear in the box below.

Reteaching

Assign *Reteaching* 9, found in the TCR. Have students complete the activity and review their responses. 📁

Enrichment

Assign students *Enrichment* 10, "Microstudy of an Artist's Style," in the TCR. 📁

Extension

Explain to students that some of the artwork in the textbook is done in the abstract style. Ask them to explain what is meant by the term *abstract*. If they have difficulty, refer them to the Glossary. Have students find examples of paintings and sculptures created in an abstract manner. Ask them if their study of this section changed their opinions about works like these.

CLOSE

Have students discuss the distinctions between literal, design, and expressive qualities when using the steps of art criticism.

and different experiences, might come up with a different list of design relationships for the same work. This is one of the benefits of analysis. It opens the door for interesting discussions that enable two critics to learn even more about the work in question.

Having described and analyzed the painting, Robert is ready for the third art criticism operation: interpretation. He knows that this is the most exciting and the most personal step in the art criticism process.

Interpretation

When interpreting the meaning of an artwork, Robert must refer to everything he learned from the work during description and analysis. His concern centers on identifying the **expressive qualities,** or the *meaning, mood, or idea communicated to the viewer.* Robert knows, however, that a work of art is often very complicated and may be interpreted in different ways by different people. He realizes that his interpretation of the painting will be a personal one, based on the information he has gathered from the picture.

As he described and analyzed the painting, Robert became more and more conscious of its uneasy mood. He attributed this to the manner in which the elements and principles were used to depict a strange, haunting subject: a helpless gypsy asleep in a mysterious landscape, unaware of the lion hovering over him. The absence of footprints in the sand seems to support the idea that the picture represents a dream rather than reality. Viewers who identify the helplessness of the gypsy will recognize their own feeling of helplessness when they find themselves alone and facing the unexpected in a dream. But whose dream is it, the gypsy's or the viewer's? Robert is unsure—but then decides that each person looking at the painting must make that decision on his or her own.

Robert's examination of the painting's literal, design, and expressive qualities is now complete. The only thing left to do is determine whether the work is—or is not—successful.

Judgment

Judgment is an important part of the art criticism process, not only for Robert, but also for anyone who wants to demonstrate a genuine appreciation for art. Indeed, the act of making a judgment and defending that judgment with good reasons demonstrates that a person understands and appreciates a work of art.

How Robert or any other critic judges a work of art depends in large measure on the theory or theories of art he or she favors. These theories help identify the different aesthetic qualities found in the artwork. They are important because they represent the criteria or proof on which judgments are based. To better understand these aesthetic theories, it is necessary to examine the important role aesthetics plays in art criticism.

LESSON ONE REVIEW

Reviewing Art Facts

1. During which art criticism operation is concern directed to the expressive qualities?
2. What are the literal qualities?
3. Explain how a design chart can aid someone in analyzing a work of art.
4. How does a person demonstrate that he or she understands and appreciates an artwork?

▶ Activity... *Critiquing a Design*

When using the art criticism approach, you describe how the artist used the elements and principles. Which chapter in your text describes the elements and principles?

Create a "personality design." Choose a piece of construction paper to express the color of your personality. Add lines, shapes, colors, values, textures, spaces with scraps of cut and folded or curled paper, or other found materials to show your personality in visual terms. Then apply the art criticism steps. Describe—which elements were used? Analyze—which principles were used? Interpret—what moods, feelings, or ideas does the work express? Judge—is your work successful? What would you improve if you were to create it again?

LESSON ONE REVIEW

Answers to Reviewing Art Facts

1. Interpretation.
2. Realistic presentation of subject matter.
3. It can help a critic analyze a work and act as a check sheet for how the principles of art have been used to organize the elements of art.
4. By making a judgment based on sound observations with respect to aesthetic qualities contained in the work.

Activity...*Critiquing a Design*

Have students work independently on this activity. As students critique their designs, ask them to write their responses. Have them keep their notes and their artwork in their portfolios.

Using Aesthetics and Art Criticism

Vocabulary
- aesthetics
- nonobjective art

Discover

After completing this lesson, you will be able to:
- Identify and discuss three major aesthetic theories.
- Explain how statements of like and dislike differ from judgments about artworks.
- Use the steps of the art criticism process to examine a work of art.
- Discuss how the process of art criticism can be used to examine nonobjective artworks.

*A*esthetics is *a branch of philosophy concerned with identifying the clues within artworks that can be used to understand, judge, and defend judgments about those works.* There are many different aesthetic theories, but no single theory takes into account all the aesthetic qualities found in artworks. Three of these theories are imitationalism, formalism, and emotionalism.

Imitationalism

Some aestheticians and art critics feel that the most important thing about a work of art is the realistic presentation of subject matter, or the literal qualities. They feel that a successful work must look like, and remind viewers of, what can be seen in the real world. People with this view feel an artwork should imitate life, that it should look lifelike before it can be considered successful (Figure 4.6). This theory, stressing the importance of the literal qualities, is called *imitationalism.*

Formalism

Not all aestheticians and art critics place importance on the literal qualities. Many feel that the success of a work depends on the design qualities, or the way it is organized. They favor a theory of art known as *formalism,* which holds that the most important aspect of a work of art is the effective use of the principles of art to arrange the elements of art. They believe that an effective design depends on how well the artist has arranged the colors, values, lines, textures, shapes, forms and space relationships used in the work (Figure 4.7, page 92). For these critics, a successful work of art need not look lifelike, but it must use the elements and principles effectively to achieve an overall unity.

FIGURE 4.6 Imitationalism requires that a work of art look real, or lifelike, in order to be considered successful. **Explain why this painting would be appreciated by someone using that theory of art.**

Marie-Louise-Élisabeth Vigée-Lebrun. *Self-Portrait.* c. 1781. Oil on canvas. 65 × 54 cm (25¹/₂ × 21¹/₄"). Kimbell Art Museum, Fort Worth, Texas.

91

FOCUS
Lesson Objectives

After studying this lesson, students will be able to:
- Identify and discuss three major aesthetic theories.
- Use the steps of the art criticism process to examine a work of art.
- Discuss how the processes of art criticism is used to examine nonobjective works.

Building Vocabulary

Direct students' attention to the word *nonobjective.* Point out that the prefix non- is already familiar to them and that the root objective may be as well, though probably not in the sense it is used here. Explain that *nonobjective art* is art with no recognizable subject matter.

Motivator

Ask students how they go about deciding whether they like a new song they hear. Point out that a four-step process similar to the ones they learned about earlier in this chapter could help them better understand the music and their judgments.

Introducing the Lesson

Have students review the three aesthetic qualities that art critics look for in works of art. Ask which of these qualities is present in Figure 4.6. Is the work most striking for its realism, for the strength of its design, or for the mood or message it communicates?

LESSON TWO RESOURCES

Teacher's Classroom Resources

- 📁 Appreciating Cultural Diversity 5
- 📁 Art and Humanities 7
- 📁 Cooperative Learning 6
- 📁 Enrichment Activity 11

- 📁 Reproducible Lesson Plan 10
- 📁 Reteaching Activity 10
- 📁 Study Guide 10

TEACH

Art Criticism

Divide the class into three panels. One panel is to be made up of imitationalists, one of formalists, and one of emotionalists. The panels are to participate in an open forum in which they debate the relative merits of the works in Figures 4.6 (page 91) 4.7 (page 92), and 4.10 (page 93). You may wish to initiate the debate by asking them to discuss which of the works is the most lifelike, which is most expressive, and which is characterized by the most unified design. Explain that artworks often succeed on more than one of these theoretical planes. After allowing ample time for discussion, ask each panel to adopt a different aesthetic theory and continue the debate with three new artworks selected from the text.

Critical Thinking

Ask students to imagine they are at an art exhibit and overhear someone make the following remark with respect to the painting in Figure 4.7: "That picture is awful. It looks like it was done by a child. You can hardly tell it's a picture of a woman." Tell students: Write your response to this person. In it, use one or more of the aesthetic theories and/or your knowledge of the process of art criticism to explain why this work has merit.

■ **FIGURE 4.7** Notice the artist's use of the elements and principles of art in this painting. Why would this work be appreciated by a viewer using the theory of art known as formalism?

Henri Matisse. *The Rumanian Blouse.* 1937. Oil on canvas. 73.3 × 60.6 cm (29 × 24"). Cincinnati Art Museum, Cincinnati, Ohio. Bequest of Mary E. Johnston.

■ **FIGURE 4.8** This realistic painting also succeeds in expressing a certain feeling or mood. What is that feeling or mood? What has the artist done to focus your attention on the woman's face and expression?

Georges de la Tour. *Magdalen with Smoking Flame.* 1638–1640. Oil on canvas. 117 × 91.76 cm (46¹/₁₆ × 36¹/₈"). Los Angeles County Museum of Art, Los Angeles, California. Gift of the Ahmanson Collection.

Emotionalism

Other aestheticians and art critics contend that the success of an artwork depends on its ability to communicate an emotion or idea to the viewer. This theory, called *emotionalism,* places greatest importance on the *expressive qualities,* or the feeling, moods, and ideas communicated to the viewer by a work of art (Figure 4.8).

These three theories of art, summarized in Figure 4.9, can be useful when you look for different aesthetic qualities in works of art. Keep in mind, though, that each theory embraces certain aesthetic qualities and rejects others.

Using More than One Theory

During judgment, the last art criticism operation, Robert must make a decision about the merits of the painting *The Sleeping Gypsy* (Figure 4.2, page 86). Robert realizes that if he relies on a single theory of art, with its emphasis on either the literal, design, or expressive qualities of the work, he may be doing the work an injustice. He might take into account the aesthetic qualities favored by the theory he selected, but in doing so he would overlook other important qualities stressed by the other two theories.

 Technology

National Gallery of Art Videodisc Use the following images as examples of more works by artists introduced in this lesson.

Elisabeth Vigée-Lebrun
The Marquise de Pezé and the Marquise de Rouget

Search Frame 1089

Elisabeth Vigée-Lebrun
Portrait of a Lady

Search Frame 1091

Piet Mondrian
Lozenge in Red, Yellow, and Blue

Search Frame 2255

Use Glencoe's *Correlation Bar Code Guide to the National Gallery of Art* to locate more artworks.

Keep Robert's concern in mind when you examine works of art. If you rely on a single aesthetic theory, you limit your search for information to those qualities favored by the theory you are using. This limitation places you at a disadvantage, especially when you examine works representing different styles. Imitationalism, for example, may be helpful when you examine works that are realistically painted. It would be useless, however, if you were examining paintings with no realistic subject matter. In such cases, it would be wise to turn to one or both of the other theories.

To illustrate this last point, examine the painting by the Dutch artist Piet Mondrian (peet **mohn**-dree-**ahn**) (Figure 4.10). Clearly, there is no recognizable subject matter in this painting. It is a work in which colors, lines, and shapes have been used to create simple vertical and horizontal units. These units have been arranged in a precise and formal order. Because there is no subject matter, imitationalism, which emphasizes literal qualities, would not be useful here. Insisting on using this theory would result in rejecting Mondrian's painting as a successful work of art because it fails to portray a realistically rendered subject. To gain an understanding of this painting, you would have to turn to another theory for help. Of the two remaining theories discussed, formalism and emotionalism, which do you think would be more useful in helping you understand this painting?

Formalism, with its emphasis on the elements and principles of art, is the most appropriate theory to apply here. Why? The reason is because Mondrian's painting lacks both realistic subject matter and the expression of mood or feeling. Instead, it uses carefully selected and arranged lines, shapes, and colors to achieve an overall sense of unity.

	THEORIES OF ART		
	Imitationalism	Formalism	Emotionalism
Aesthetic Qualities	Literal Qualities: **Realistic presentation** of subject matter.	Design Qualities: **Effective organization** of the elements of art through the use of the principles of art.	Expressive Qualities: **Vivid communication** of moods, feelings, and ideas.

■ **FIGURE 4.9** Theories of Art and Aesthetic Qualities

■ **FIGURE 4.10** Notice the artist's use of colors, lines, and shapes in this work. **Why is it appropriate to use formalism rather than imitationalism when examining this painting?**

Piet Mondrian. *Tableau No. IV: Lozenge Composition with Red, Gray, Blue, Yellow and Black.* c. 1924–25. Canvas on hardboard. 1.43 × 1.42 m (56¼ × 56"). National Gallery of Art, Washington, D.C. Gift of Herbert and Nannette Rothschild.

Chapter 4 *Art Criticism and Aesthetics* **93**

CHAPTER 4
LESSON TWO

Critical Thinking

Have students consider the expression, "Beauty is in the eye of the beholder." Have them discuss this expression in terms of its relevance to art and to the discussion of three aesthetic theories discussed on this page.

Cross Curriculum

LANGUAGE ARTS. Point out to students that in a very real sense all the arts are connected. Note that lyric poets, for example, often paint pictures in words. Have students investigate this proposition by reading a selection of easily accessible lyric poets, such as Robert Frost and William Carlos Williams. Working in small groups, students are to apply the steps of art criticism to a selected work. Explain that at the analysis stage, they are to look for poetic and rhetorical devices (e.g., metaphor, alliteration, assonance) used by the poet to communicate the work's essential idea or image. Allow groups to share their critiques.

Did You Know?

Had it not been for an attack of appendicitis, Henri Matisse might never have become an artist. While bedridden, Matisse was provided with a supply of paints to help him pass the time. So great was his interest in this newfound pastime that he abandoned his plans to become a lawyer and devoted his life to art.

More About… **Élisabeth Vigée-Lebrun (1755–1842).** Vigée-Lebrun, whose self-portrait appears in Figure 4.6, was court painter for Marie Antoinette. In this capacity, she completed some twenty paintings of the queen. When the French Revolution erupted in 1789, Vigée-Lebrun fled Paris. To her good fortune, her career continued to flourish in other European capitals, where her skills as a portrait painter were much in demand. By the time she had reached the age of thirty-five, Vigée-Lebrun had earned over a million francs—a regal sum for an artist working in the late eighteenth century.

Art Criticism

Have students discuss why it is important to use more than one aesthetic theory in judging a work of art. Encourage them to consider the works illustrated in Chapters 17, 23, and 24 in support of their views. Ask: In the works of which chapter is imitationalism the most useful theory for making a valid critical judgment? In which chapter is it the least useful theory? What properties of the works are responsible for these assumptions?

Aesthetics

Direct students' attention to the work by Hokusai in Figure 4.1, on page 84, and then to Louis Gugliemi's painting in Figure 4.11. Ask which of the three aesthetic qualities is present in each of these works? Is either striking for its realism? Which work depends solely on the strength of its design, its mood, or the message it communicates? Have students select any two works elsewhere in the program and repeat these questions.

Consider, however, the painting by Louis Guglielmi in Figure 4.11. Although the subject is recognizable, it is hardly true to life. For this reason it might be dismissed if imitationalism is used to measure its success. At the same time, the painting seems to ignore many of the rules of good design stressed by formalism. It would still be regarded as an outstanding work of art if another theory, emotionalism, was used. Indeed, this painting succeeds in communicating a powerful message to the viewer. Examine it closely. Can you identify the clues that enable you to understand that message?

■ **FIGURE 4.11** By using emotionalism as a guide, the viewer is able to read and understand this painting's powerful emotional story—and be better prepared to judge it. **Did you notice the dagger-like lamppost? Why are the women crying and dressed in black?**

Louis Guglielmi. *Terror in Brooklyn.* 1941. Oil on canvas mounted on composition board. 86.4 × 76.2 cm (34 × 30"). Whitney Museum of American Art. New York, New York. Museum purchase.

94   **Unit One** *Creating and Understanding Art*

It is important to take all three theories into account during every encounter with art. Keep in mind that a single theory of art can point out certain qualities in some works, but it cannot point out all the qualities in all works of art.

An Art Critic's Judgment

Robert has decided that Rousseau's *The Sleeping Gypsy* is a successful work of art. Moreover, he is confident that he can defend that decision by referring to the aesthetic qualities favored by each of the three theories of art. He became aware of each of these qualities while describing, analyzing, and interpreting the work.

While focusing on the literal qualities during description, Robert noted that the objects depicted in the painting could be easily identified, even though they were not completely convincing. He recognized some stiffness in the figure of the sleeping gypsy, and felt that the lion did indeed bear a resemblance to a child's stuffed toy. This helped reinforce the idea that the scene took place in a dream rather than in the real world. Robert doubted that an accurately painted lion and gypsy would have been successful in capturing the same magical, dreamlike quality.

Robert was pleased with the design qualities he identified during analysis. The work demonstrated both harmony and variety in the use of hue, texture, and value. He was also impressed by the way hue, value, line, and form were used to emphasize the most important parts of the composition, the sleeping

About the *Artwork*

Terror in Brooklyn. Who are the three mourning women in the scene? Why are they crying, and what is the significance of the dagger-like lamppost? Point out that a mirror image of the scene is provided further back in the painting. The same buildings, automobile, and capsule lead to the horizon, leaving the viewer with the feeling that the scene is repeated endlessly into the distance. Could the women be related to a victim of foul play? By providing a mirror image of the foreground scene in the background, is the artist trying to tell us that tragic events like this take place over and over again?

gypsy and the lion. What pleased him most was the way gradations of value created the illusion of three-dimensional forms existing in real space. This made the scene look incredibly real, even though it was not entirely lifelike. In Robert's opinion, this was a painting in which the art elements and principles worked together effectively to produce a startling image that is also a unified composition.

The expressive qualities noted during his interpretation of the painting were especially appealing to Robert. At first, while attempting to interpret the work, he tried to determine just what was happening in this mysterious, silent desert landscape. Finally, he decided that the work illustrates a dream, although it is by no means an ordinary dream. It is a dream so vivid and captivating that its images and the feelings those images evoke remain fixed in the mind well after the dream has ended.

Learning from External Clues

His examination of the painting completed, Robert might now want to find out what other critics have said about it. Certainly he would want to know what art historians have written about the work. At this point, Robert directs his attention to external clues, facts and information about the work and the artist who created it. This information includes the name of the artist, when and where the painting was done, and the artistic style it represents. Of course, as an experienced critic with an extensive background in art, Robert knew many of these things before he began his examination of the work. He recognized the work as an oil painting completed in France during the latter part of the nineteenth century. He also knew that it was painted by Henri Rousseau, a retired customs official who started to paint at the age of 40. Rousseau was a so-called primitive artist, one who is untrained or self-taught. Rousseau knew little about how to draw, and he was not familiar with color theory. But the pictures he created were so simple, innocent, and poetic that in time, Rousseau came to be regarded as a genius.

Although Robert might choose to consider these and other external clues after his examination of Rousseau's painting, it is important to point out that he made a conscious effort to disregard these and other external clues during his critique of the work. He knew that if he took these clues into consideration while critiquing it, they might influence his perception and ultimately his judgment.

Robert's main objective in critiquing any work of art is to gain a thorough understanding of it. You should set the same objective for yourself whenever you decide to examine an artwork closely. The four-step approach of description, analysis, interpretation, and judgment summarized here can help you achieve this objective (Figure 4.12). Using this approach enables you to identify the aesthetic qualities in a work and prepares you to make and defend your own decisions about it. Just as important, it makes your encounters with art more personally rewarding.

	ART CRITICISM OPERATIONS			
	Description	**Analysis**	**Interpretation**	**Judgment**
Internal Cues	Focus: **Subject matter and/or elements of art** noted in the work.	Focus: **Organization**—how principles of art have been used to arrange the elements of art.	Focus: **Moods, feelings, and ideas** communicated by the work.	Focus: **Decision-making** about the work's artistic merit.

■ **FIGURE 4.12**

Art Criticism Operations

Art History

Assign teams of students to find descriptions and explanations of Rousseau's painting in books and articles in the school or community library. Have teams present their findings in class and record the main points on the chalkboard. Ask students to identify the features mentioned most often by the authors. Did any one author identify details, elements or principles, or ideas not mentioned by the others? Did the authors express a judgment about the overall success or the work? If so, on what aesthetic qualities did they base their decision?

Art Criticism

Ask students to express their judgment of Rousseau's painting of *The Sleeping Gypsy.* Then tell them to suppose that the painting is discovered to have been painted by someone other than Rousseau. It was, in fact, painted in jest by a friend of the artist who never painted another picture in his lifetime. Ask students if this discovery alters their judgment of the picture. Have them provide reasons for their decision. Determine if these reasons took into account the aesthetic qualities of the painting.

CULTURAL DIVERSITY

Aesthetics. Point out that appreciation for literal, design, and expressive qualities in art can vary from culture to culture. Add that it is easy to misinterpret art from a culture whose aesthetic frame of reference is unfamiliar. Japanese music, as a case in point, often sounds strange and even unmusical to the uninitiated Western ear. Have students select and research the visual arts as practiced by a contemporary African or Far Eastern culture. (One possibility is Cameroon figurative sculptures.) Invite them to share their findings with the class in an oral presentation. Ask students to determine what an art critic would need to know about the culture and its art before proceeding with an evaluation.

Aesthetics

Tell students to imagine that they are attending a museum exhibition featuring Rousseau's *The Sleeping Gypsy* and Goya's *Don Manuel Osorio Manrique de Zuñiga* when a fire breaks out. They are in a position to save one of these two paintings. Which one will it be? Have them explain, in terms of aesthetic qualities, why they selected one picture over the other.

Art Criticism

Instruct each student to look through the pages of the text and identify the work that they dislike the most. List these on the chalkboard. Discuss the choices identified to determine if they have anything in common. (Are there more abstract or nonobjective works identified?) Ask the class to vote on these choices to determine the one work that is most disliked. Use the steps of description, analysis, and interpretation to arrive at a judgment. Ask students if they find it difficult critiquing a work that they dislike. Have them explain why it is often necessary to do this.

Did You Know?

Francisco Goya often worked in an impatient frenzy. Ignoring conventional methods, he used whatever odd objects came to hand including sponges, spoons, and even a small broom to apply paints to canvas. He took delight in using the accidental blots or splotches that came about as a result.

Using Aesthetics and the Art Criticism Operations

The art critic uses the art criticism steps to identify the aesthetic qualities in a work. These aesthetic qualities, in turn, are keys to judging the work's success. Now, consider using this process to your own advantage when examining and judging a work of art.

Acting as an Art Critic

Imagine you are standing in front of the painting illustrated in Figure 4.13. Because

■ FIGURE 4.13 Point to things in this work that suggest innocence. What has the artist added to suggest the forces of evil? Why is it possible to say that this painting hints at the passing of time?

Francisco Goya. *Don Manuel Osorio Manrique de Zuñiga*. 1784–1792. Oil on canvas. 127 × 101.6 cm (50 × 40"). The Metropolitan Museum of Art, New York, New York. The Jules Bache Collection, 1949. 49.7.41.

you are now familiar with the literal, design, and expressive qualities, you can determine whether these qualities are in the work. The four art criticism operations—description, analysis, interpretation, and judgment—form a search strategy that will help you find those aesthetic qualities. The first three operations are used to identify the different aesthetic qualities stressed by imitationalism, formalism, and emotionalism. Make sure that you take into account the aesthetic qualities favored by each of these theories when you examine the painting. Using this method helps you make intelligent judgments about the work and enables you to defend those judgments with sound reasons.

Emotional Reactions to Art

Before you begin your examination of the painting in Figure 4.13, ask yourself whether you like it or dislike it. This expression of like or dislike is an emotional reaction to the artwork; all viewers find themselves doing this when they confront works of art. An emotional reaction to art is often deeply felt, and it deserves to be cherished.

Why, then, is it necessary to study the work further, using your knowledge of the art criticism operations and aesthetic qualities? The understanding you derive from a careful study of a work of art often can add to your enjoyment of that work. Sometimes a careful examination can reveal things about the work that may change your initial reaction to it. You may, for example, find that a work you first considered dull and unexciting is in fact lively and satisfying.

There is a difference, though, between expressions of like or dislike and judgment. Emotional like and dislike statements do not require good reasons to support them. Judgments are a reasoned activity of the mind and, as such, can be challenged. For this reason, judgments *do* require support in the form of good reasons. It is possible to dislike a painting and still judge it a successful work of art, just as it is possible to like a painting you judge unsuccessful. An emotional reaction to a work differs from a reasoned judgment—but both are important.

More About... **Francisco Goya.** Goya was born in Saragossa, Spain, in 1746. As a young man he traveled to Italy. He was not impressed by the artworks created by Renaissance masters, so he returned home. There he went to work as a portrait painter for the ruling class, where his paintings flattered the Spanish court subjects. He soon was named personal painter to King Charles IV. An illness four years later left the artist deaf. Instead of plunging into despair, Goya found his handicap fueled his imagination. When war broke out in 1808, Goya created a series of prints unlike anything done before. His view of war has no heroes or acts of glory. The prints in this series speak, rather, of senseless waste and brutality. Later on, his works drew more and more on his own inner dreams and visions.

Description

Begin your examination of the painting in Figure 4.13 by describing the literal qualities or subject matter observed in the painting. To do this, answer the following description questions:

- How is the boy in this painting dressed?
- Does the boy appear to be relaxed and natural, or stiff and posed? Where is he looking?
- Where are the cats located in the picture? What are they doing?
- What is the boy holding in his hands? To what is it attached?
- The bird holds a card in its beak. What is shown on that card (Figure 4.14)?
- What is seen on the floor to the right of the boy?

Your description of this work also should include an inventory of the elements of art in the work. To do this, ask yourself what colors and shapes have been used? What is the most intense or brightest of these hues? Is the space deep or shallow? Answer questions regarding the use of hue, shape, and space in this work.

Analysis

During analysis, your attention is directed toward identifying the design qualities in the painting. Analysis questions are intended to help you identify the principles of art used to organize the elements of art noted during description. By referring to the design chart

on page 88, you can formulate the kinds of questions you should ask and answer in order to understand how this work is structured. (Refer to Chapter 2, pages 46 and 47, to review the way questions are formulated using the design chart.) Ask and answer questions regarding the use of the principles of balance, emphasis, harmony, and gradation of value in this work. Are the shapes balanced symmetrically or asymmetrically? How do the background colors contribute to harmony?

Do your questions take into account all the principles employed in this painting? You may well feel that there are other principles at play in this work. If so, make note of these before moving on to the next art criticism operation.

Interpretation

Your efforts in interpretation focus on identifying the expressive qualities in the work. Interpretation questions are intended to reveal the feelings, moods, and ideas communicated to the viewer by the work of art.

Answer the following interpretation questions:

- Why do you think the boy in this picture looks so stiff and unnatural?
- You have identified the boy, the cats, and the birds in this painting. What clues suggest that someone else was present a short time ago?
- The child appears to be looking at something or someone outside the picture. Do

■ **FIGURE 4.14**

Francisco Goya. *Don Manuel Osorio Manrique de Zuñiga* (detail).

Art History

Appoint a team of students to identify the important historical event that took place in France in 1789, a short time after Goya painted his portrait. (The French Revolution begins.) Ask students if Goya's painting could be interpreted as anticipating the turbulent times that would be unleashed by the revolution in France. Have them point to clues in the work to support such a hypothesis. Discuss reasons why it may be possible to advance several hypotheses regarding the meaning of a particular work of art.

Studio Skills

Remind students that the boy in Goya's painting is not looking at the viewer. Clearly something outside the picture has caught his attention. Tell students to quietly speculate on what the child may be looking at. Then tell students to complete an ink drawing of it. Place the completed drawings on display. Which seem to be especially imaginative or unusual? Do any show the artist, Goya, working on the boy's portrait?

CULTURAL DIVERSITY

Symbolism in Art. Goya's famous portrait depicts a fashionably dressed child holding a string tied to a magpie, a favorite children's pet since the Middle Ages. In the background, three cats focus their attention on the bird, long recognized as a Christian symbol of the soul. Renaissance artists often painted the Christ Child holding a bird tied to a string, and Baroque artists painted caged birds as symbols of innocence. Have interested students look ahead to Chapters 13 through 17 for more information about symbolism in artworks of different periods. Refer them also to the Symbolism in Art features throughout the text to investigate how symbolism is used.

Art Criticism

Divide the class into teams consisting of three students each. Instruct each team to identify any work of art illustrated in the previous three chapters and prepare a critique in which one student provides a description of the literal qualities, a second an analysis of the design qualities, and the third an interpretation or interpretations of the expressive qualities. Each student should be prepared to offer their own judgment of the work and to point out the reasons for their judgment. Provide time class time for teams to prepare their critiques. Have each team present their critiques in class.

Aesthetics

Tell students to examine the nonobjective painting illustrated in Figure 4.15. Ask students to identify qualities and features that nonobjective paintings have in common with earlier representational art forms. Are the differences greater than the similarities? Ask students to assume that nonobjective paintings have little in common with earlier representational art forms. Then ask them if this could be one of the reasons why contemporary artists chose to move in that direction in the first place. Ask students if they find it difficult to do an examination of a nonobjective work. If so, encourage them by explaining that this can contribute to greater viewer involvement with the artwork.

the clues in the painting suggest what or who this might be?

- How do the three cats provide an indication of what is likely to happen in just a few moments?
- How has the artist suggested the passage of time in this work? Can you explain what happened earlier and what is likely to happen in a minute or two?

Judgment

Judgment involves carefully thought out decision making. Remember that judgment does not mean an expression of like or dislike. Instead, you are asked to make a personal decision about a work's success or lack of success. In addition, you must be prepared to offer good reasons to support your judgment.

Judgment questions should focus attention on the aesthetic qualities identified during description, analysis, and interpretation. These aesthetic qualities form the basis for an intelligent judgment and provide you with the evidence you need to defend that judgment. Answer the following judgment questions: Is this a successful work of art? Is it successful because of its literal, design, or expressive qualities? Perhaps, after posing and answering all the art criticism questions, you have

discovered that a painting can be judged in terms of *all three aesthetic theories.* That is, it can be regarded as a success because of the literal qualities favored by imitationalism, the design qualities emphasized by formalism, and the expressive qualities stressed by emotionalism. It is important to note that some works can be judged successful even if they feature the aesthetic qualities championed by only two or even one of these theories.

Examining Nonobjective Artworks

Nonobjective art is *any artwork that contains no apparent reference to reality.* Artists who create these works place primary importance on the manner in which the elements and principles of art are used. When you examine nonobjective artworks, follow the same procedure you would use with a realistic work. The only difference occurs during description. Because there is no recognizable subject matter to identify, begin this operation with an inventory of the art elements.

Look at the nonobjective artwork in Figure 4.15. Is this painting really so different from one that is a literal representation of some part of the world, such as the work

■ **FIGURE 4.15** Notice the way the artist applied paint to her canvas. **How do you think it was done—slowly and deliberately, or swiftly and impulsively?**

Joan Mitchell. *Low Water.* 1969. Oil on canvas. 79 × 113 cm (31¹/₈ × 44¹/₂"). Carnegie Museum of Art, Pittsburgh, Pennsylvania. Patrons Art Fund.

98 **Unit One** *Creating and Understanding Art*

■ **FIGURE 4.16**
Notice that the details of the buildings exposed to the full sun seem indistinct. How would you feel if you found yourself in the foreground of this picture? Would you feel differently if you were somewhere in the background area? Why?

Jean-Baptiste-Camille Corot. *View of Genoa.* 1834. Oil on paper mounted on canvas. 29.5 × 41.7 cm (11¹/₂ × 16¹/₂"). Art Institute of Chicago, Chicago, Illinois. Mr. and Mrs. Martin A. Ryerson Collection, 1937.1017.

Studio Skills

Instruct students to draw a nonobjective composition composed entirely of curvilinear shapes. Tell them to create large shapes first and then divide these into smaller ones. Carefully fill in the shapes with a variety of light and dark values made by mixing black and white tempera paint. Negative shapes should be identified by making them lighter or darker than positive shapes. Caution students to make certain that their compositions are well balanced in terms of color and shape. Light and dark lines can be used to define shapes and provide additional visual interest. Place finished compositions on display and discuss them in terms of the visual qualities.

Critical Thinking

Recite or write the following statement on the board: *In approaching a work of art, an art critic works from the inside out.* Remind students of the brief glimpse they had in Chapter 1 of the work carried out by critics. Ask them to discuss the observation based on this knowledge.

shown in Figure 4.16? Both can be described as a careful arrangement of colors and shapes, lines and textures used to create a visually pleasing effect. In one, this arrangement of art elements is used to create a picture that reflects the real world. In the other, the challenge of using the art elements to create a visually stimulating composition is more important than trying to portray a realistic-looking subject.

Assume for a moment that you have the opportunity to question the artist who created the nonobjective painting in Figure 4.15. If you were to ask why she painted her nonobjective work, she might answer with a question of her own. Pointing to a flower—perhaps a tulip— she might ask why you find it appealing. Perhaps you would mention the flower's ruby-red color, the shape of the individual petals, and the way these shapes join to create an attractive symmetrical form. You might also mention the gradual change from light to dark values evident on each petal, the overall soft texture of the flower, and the graceful curve of the stem. Finally, you might say that you admire it simply because it is a tulip, a flower that you find pleasing to look at. It bears no

resemblance to a pair of stylish shoes or a stately oak tree, and you would never think of comparing it to them. You value it as a flower—for its color, its shape and form, its light and dark values, and its texture.

Then the artist might explain that her nonobjective painting also makes use of colors, shapes, forms, values, and textures. She might ask you to appreciate it for the same reasons that you appreciate the tulip. She would probably discourage you from comparing her work to something else. It is, after all, a painting, nothing more or less, and it should be viewed and valued as such.

Careful examination can help you understand and appreciate nonobjective paintings— and distinguish between the works of different artists employing this style.

The three paintings shown in Figures 4.17, 4.18, and 4.19 on page 100 have one important thing in common: They all reject realistic subject matter. To understand them, you must do the same. When you do, you may discover that nonobjective paintings and sculptures can provide as much visual excitement and delight as any realistically rendered art form.

Chapter 4 *Art Criticism and Aesthetics* **99**

More About... **Corot.** Direct student's attention to Figure 4.16 and tell them that Corot's sense of humor matched his skills as an artist. When he sold his first picture after painting more than 20 years he pretended to be upset and sighed, "Up to this time I have had a complete collection of Corots, and now, alas, it has been broken." A stranger once came to Corot to verify the authenticity of a painting bearing the artist's signature. Corot saw immediately that it was a forgery. The art buyer's disappointment was equaled by Corot's distress at his misfortune. Corot asked if he might borrow the worthless canvas and made it genuine by painting over the fake. Believing the public would not be interested in his paintings of human figures, Corot kept them hidden away in his studio. All 300 of them were discovered there after his death in 1875.

Art History

Have small groups of students examine *The Royal Pavilion* by John Nash in Figure 4.20. Before they begin their examinations, encourage students to brainstorm questions that might be asked when working with architectural structures. How would they apply the art criticism operations to an examination of this building?

Study Guide

Distribute *Study Guide* 10 in the TCR and review key concepts with students. 📂

Art and Humanities

Distribute *Art and Humanities* 7, "Guide to Perceptive Listening," in the TCR. Ask students to read the instructions and complete the worksheet on evaluating music. 📂

Enrichment

Assign *Enrichment* 11, "Comparing Content," in the TCR to help students practice the concepts they have learned. 📂

Nonobjective *Art*

*T*hese three works share a "family resemblance": All three are nonobjective. This is the same kind of resemblance you might identify in three landscape paintings done by different artists.

The three nonobjective painters used a variety of media and techniques. They worked with different elements and principles of art to create three works that would be visually appealing. In the process, they created paintings that differ from each other as much as three landscape paintings might differ.

 Here the artist used oil paints (Figure 4.18). Notice the broad, sweeping strokes of black paint. Notice, too, the bold contrast of white and black values. The painting suggests the strong steel skeletons of modern skyscrapers and bridges.

1 In this work, the artist used tempera paint on paper (Figure 4.17). He created an intricate pattern of white lines and shapes that suggest the written form of a mysterious language.

■ **FIGURE 4.18** Franz Kline. *Mahoning*. 1956. Oil and paper collage on canvas. 203.2 × 254 cm (80 × 100"). Whitney Museum of American Art, New York, New York. Purchase with funds from the friends of the Whitney.

3 This work was created with a combination of oil paints and enamel (Figure 4.19). The artist dripped, poured, and splashed paints from sticks and brushes as he walked around and on a canvas tacked to the floor. This painting is so large that it seems to wrap itself around viewers, commanding their complete attention.

■ **FIGURE 4.17** Mark Tobey. *Echoes of Broadway*. 1964. Tempera on paper. 132.7 × 64.7 cm (52¼ × 25½"). Dallas Museum of Art, Dallas, Texas. Gift of the artist.

■ **FIGURE 4.19** Jackson Pollock. *One (Number 31, 1950)*. 1950. Oil and enamel on unprimed canvas. 269.5 × 530.8 cm (8' 10" × 17' 5⅝"). Museum of Modern Art, New York, New York. Sidney and Harriet Janis Collection Fund (by exchange).

Nonobjective *Art*

Have students look at Figure 4.19 and read the passage in the text that explains how one could go about critiquing a nonobjective work of art such as the images shown on this page. Then have them carry out a critical examination of each of the works. Have students work in teams to examine each of the artworks on this page. As students work, they should keep the following questions in mind: Which elements are used in the work? How did the artist use the principles of art to combine these elements? Then have students continue with the art criticism operations.

Art Criticism Operations and Architecture

You can use the same art criticism operations in a critical examination of architecture. During description, concentrate on identifying the principal features of a building—doors, windows, towers, and building materials. Then list the elements of art used—the colors, lines, textures, shapes, and forms you observe. In analyzing a building, note how the principles of art have been used to organize the elements. Consider the meaning or purpose of the building during interpretation. At this point, you may be surprised to discover that some buildings, like paintings and sculptures, can communicate unmistakable moods and feelings (Figure 4.20).

Your judgment about any kind of architecture—like your judgment of other forms of visual art—should be based on how well the various aesthetic qualities have been used.

■ **FIGURE 4.20** This royal pleasure palace was designed for a prince who later became King George IV of England. **Using description and analysis, try to interpret the feeling or mood you get from this building. Is it serious and forbidding, or light-hearted and inviting?**

John Nash. The Royal Pavilion, Brighton, England. c. 1816–22. Topham Picture Source, Edenbridge, Kent, UK.

LESSON TWO REVIEW

Reviewing Art Facts

1. What name is given to aestheticians who feel the most important thing about a work of art are its design qualities?
2. Why is it impossible to consider the literal qualities when examining nonobjective works?
3. Why is it important to take all three art theories into account during every critical encounter with art?
4. What is the difference between a like/dislike statement and a judgment?

▶ **Activity... *Examining Aesthetic Theories***

The three aesthetic theories provide guidance in understanding how artists work. Most art students begin their study of the visual arts by first being able to appreciate works of art that are primarily based on imitationalism. As they continue to study, they begin to understand and appreciate the formal and emotional aspects of works of art.

Select a photo from a magazine that is an example of imitationalism. Cut out the photo and glue it onto a sheet of drawing paper after tracing around it two times to create two picture planes the size of the photo. Using markers or colored pencils, experiment with creating a formalistic and an emotionalistic work based on the photo.

Chapter 4 Art Criticism and Aesthetics **101**

ASSESS

Checking Comprehension
Have students complete the lesson review questions. Answers appear in the box below.

Reteaching
Assign *Reteaching* 10, found in the TCR. Have students complete the activity and review their responses. 📁

Enrichment
Have students read about Japanese aesthetics in *Appreciating Cultural Diversity* 5, "Ikebana, Interpreting the Mood," in the TCR. 📁

Extension
Remind students that in addition to works of fine art, which include the majority of works they have examined so far, the art world also includes many works of applied art. Ask: What criteria do you think are used by art critics in evaluating applied artworks? Why are criteria beyond those addressed in this lesson necessary?

CLOSE
Ask students to stage a debate in which they argue the relative importance of the work done by art critics. Urge them to use information obtained from the section.

LESSON TWO REVIEW

Answers to Reviewing Art Facts

1. Formalists.
2. They have no recognizable subject matter.
3. Because some works cannot be analyzed in terms of subject and would be readily dismissed by critics subscribing solely to the imitationalist viewpoint.
4. Like/dislike statements are opinions based solely on subjective criteria. Judgments include certain objective facts about a work.

Activity...*Examining Aesthetic Theories*

Have students discuss how they might manipulate their photo to demonstrate the aesthetic theories. Have them mount their results for a class display.

Studio LESSON

Painting a Representational Still Life

Objectives:

■ Complete a still-life paint-ing consisting of at least five objects.

■ Draw and paint the still life as accurately as possible.

Motivator

A discussion of student-selected artworks is an impor-tant learning activity and should be viewed as such. Students can be instructed to work alone or in small groups. Students should be informed that they can learn a great deal from studying and discussing the works of other artists, then applying what is learned from such discussions to their own creative efforts.

Aesthetics

Direct attention to the art-work that students identified as especially appealing. Ask if there are members of the class who do not respond positively to the work. Then ask if it is reasonable to expect that every-one will react in the same way to every work of art. Discuss the factors that might contribute to different reactions. Ask stu-dents if they can think of any value to be gained from dis-cussing differing opinions about art. Discussions of this kind can often expose students to qualities in artworks that they may have failed to notice on their own.

Critiquing

Have students apply the steps of art criticism to their own artwork using the "Examining Your Work" questions.

Studio LESSON Painting a Representational Still Life

Materials

- Minimum of five familiar objects to use in a still life
- Pencil
- Sheet of white drawing paper, 9 × 12 inches
- Tempera or acrylic paint
- Brushes, mixing tray, and paint cloth
- Water container

Complete a still-life painting consisting of at least five familiar objects. Draw and paint these items as realistically and accurately as possible. Your finished painting will exhibit a concern for the literal qualities favored by imitationalism.

Inspiration

Look through *Art in Focus* for illustrations of artworks that emphasize literal qualities effectively. Select one that you find especially appealing. Compare your selection to those made by other members of your class. Was one work mentioned more often than any other? If so, discuss the rea-sons for its popularity.

■ **FIGURE 4.21** Student Work

Process

1. Working with other members of your class, arrange a still life made up of at least five familiar objects. Select objects that have different forms, textures, and colors. Arrange the items so the display is interesting from all sides.
2. Draw the still life as accurately as possible on the sheet of white drawing paper.
3. Use tempera or acrylics to paint your still life. Mix your colors to match those of the still-life objects. Paint care-fully, trying to reproduce the shapes, forms, and textures of each object.

Examining Your Work

Describe. **Point out and name the objects in your still-life composition. Are these objects realistically repre-sented? Were other students able to identify them?**

Judge. **Do you think your painting would be favorably received by a critic focusing exclusively on the literal qualities?**

ASSESSMENT

Examining Your Work. When students have com-pleted their still lifes, arrange a gallery display, and invite the class to browse the collected works, mak-ing notes about each. Be sure to emphasize the phrase in the instruction line, "as realistically and accu-rately as possible." Observe that every artwork is to be critiqued in the context of its own merits and limitations as should individual artists. Suggest that, before students render judgment, they begin by seeking each work's strengths. Works that have been skillfully composed (perhaps shown as looking up or shown from another original vantage point) should be assessed in that light, as well as in terms of their literal qualities.

Reviewing the Facts

Lesson One

1. What are the aesthetic qualities?
2. When examining an artwork, for what kinds of questions does a critic seek answers?
3. How did the lack of footprints in the sand around the gypsy influence Robert's interpretation of *The Sleeping Gypsy?*
4. Why is judgment such an important step in the art criticism process?

Lesson Two

5. Why is no single theory of art adequate when examining and judging different works of art?
6. Where do critics turn to find out more about a work after they have examined it using the art criticism operations?
7. Why does the critic typically avoid referring to external clues while critiquing a work?
8. On what do nonobjective artists place emphasis when creating their works?

 ART SOURCE. MUSIC. Use the *Performing Arts Handbook,* page 580 to learn about Alfredo Rolando Ortiz and the South American harp.

 **Technology Project**

Art Criticism and Aesthetics

Each of us responds to our experiences of the world and to the ways works of art might reflect that experience, in our own unique way. What is "important" to be represented or expressed in art for one person or culture may not be important to another. This makes the study and creation of the visual arts endlessly fascinating. As you decide what your own personal preferences in art may be, research artworks using the following plan.

1. Choose a theme based upon an abstract concept such as love, war, peace, joy, grief, justice, truth, beauty, power. Gather several examples of the theme you choose. Books, the Internet, CD-ROMs and laser discs are good resources. Try to find works from different time periods and cultures.

Thinking Critically

1. **ANALYZE.** Two aestheticians are looking at one of the paintings illustrated in this chapter. One claims that the work is a success because it records accurately the features and expression of the subject. The other says it is a success because the contrast of light and dark values helps direct attention to the most important parts of the work. Which work are they examining? What aesthetic theory is held by each aesthetician?

2. **EXTEND.** Imagine one day you have discovered a painting that seems to be just blobs of paint, but it is pleasing to you. Then you discover that you have been holding the painting sideways and that it is a picture of a fruit basket. Held correctly, the painting doesn't seem interesting or well done. You hang it on your wall sideways. Explain which aesthetic qualities you found successful in this work.

CAREERS IN Read about a career as an art critic in the *Careers in Art Handbook,* page 597.

inter NET CONNECTION Visit Glencoe Art Online at *www.glencoe.com/sec/art.* Explore art museums, learn about viewing art online, and challenge yourself with an activity.

2. Decide which art theories—imitationalism, formalism, or emotionalism—apply to each work. Examine each of your examples using the steps of art criticism.
3. Using available technology resources in your school, create a collage of your thematic works. You might do this by using one of these methods.
   - Using an image manipulation program, create a digital collage that includes parts of each of your choices. Print your collage and display it.
   - Copy each of your choices using a color or black and white copier. Cut and paste elements from each to a cardboard surface to create a collage. You might want to unify your collage by drawing and painting on it as well. Display your work.
4. How are your personal preferences for art reflected in your collage?

103

Teaching the Technology Project

If students will be using the Internet for source material, you may wish to prescreen various Web sites and then provide a list of addresses to students. Allow students to practice until they are able to control the direction of the drawing tool. Point out, also, that the Cut and Paste commands are useful in duplicating an area or areas of the image.

ART SOURCE Assign the feature in the *Performing Arts Handbook,* page 580.

CAREERS IN ART If time permits, have interested students investigate the career information in the *Careers in Art Handbook,* page 597.

inter NET CONNECTION Have students go online and learn more about artists on preselected Web sites with the Internet activity for this chapter.

Reviewing the Facts

1. The qualities art critics use to increase their understanding of artworks and serve as the criteria on which their judgments are based.
2. These might include: What is seen in the artwork? How is the artwork designed or put together? What does it mean? Is it a successful work of art?
3. The lack of footprints supported his interpretation that the picture represented a dream rather than reality.
4. Because making and defending a judgment with good reasons demonstrates an understanding and appreciation of the work of art.
5. No single theory takes into account all the aesthetic qualities in all works of art.
6. To art history and external clues—facts and information about the work and the artist who created it.
7. Because they might influence his or her perception and ultimately his or her judgment.
8. Thy place primary importance on the manner in which the elements and principles of art are used.

Thinking Critically

1. Figure 4.8, *Magdalen with Smoking Flame.* One critic is an imitationalist, one is a formalist.
2. The formal qualities were successful. The literal and perhaps expressive qualities were unsuccessful.

LESSON ONE
(pages 106–115)

Art History: A Search for Information

Classroom Resources

- 📁 Appreciating Cultural Diversity 6
- 📁 Reproducible Lesson Plan 11
- 📁 Reteaching Activity 11
- 📁 Study Guide 11

Features

Cultural Influences in *Art*

Waves at Matsushima Northeaster (page 112)

LESSON TWO
(pages 116–120)

Using Art History

Classroom Resources

- 📁 Art and Humanities 8
- 📁 Cooperative Learning 7, 8
- 📁 Enrichment Activity 12
- 📁 Reproducible Lesson Plan 12
- 📁 Reteaching Activity 12
- 📁 Study Guide 12

END OF CHAPTER
(pages 121–123)

Studio LESSONS

- Painting an Abstract Still Life *(page 121)*
- Creating an Expressive Collage *(page 122)*

ADDITIONAL CHAPTER RESOURCES

Activities

- 📁 Advanced Studio Activity 5
- 📁 Application 5
- 🖱 Chapter 5 Internet Activity
- 📁 Studio Activity 7

Fine Art Resources

🖱 **Transparency**

Art in Focus Transparency 8

George Caleb Bingham.

Fur Traders Descending the Missouri.

🖼 **Fine Art Print**

Focus on World Art Print 5

Thomas Cole. *The Architect's Dream.*

Assessment

- 📁 Chapter 5 Test
- 📁 Performance Assessment

Multimedia Resources

- 🎭 Artsource® Performing Arts Package
- 💿 National Gallery Laser Disc
- 💿 National Museum of Women in the Arts CD-ROM
- 📼 Arts & Entertainment Videos

NATIONAL STANDARDS FOR ARTS EDUCATION

The National Standards for Arts Education provide guidelines for grade-appropriate competency in the visual arts. The Content Standards for grades 9–12 are:

1. Understanding and applying media, techniques, and processes.
2. Using knowledge of structures and functions.
3. Choosing and evaluating a range of subject matter, symbols, and ideas.
4. Understanding the visual arts in relation to history and cultures.
5. Reflecting upon and assessing the characteristics and merits of their work and the work of others.
6. Making connections between visual arts and other disciplines.

Listed below are the National Standards for the Visual Arts addressed in this chapter. For a breakdown of the categories listed under each content standard, refer to the *Reproducible Lesson Plans* booklet in the TCR.

  1. (b)   **2.** (a, b)   **3.** (a, b)   **4.** (a, b, c)   **5.** (a, b)   **6.** (a, b)

🕐 **Out of Time?** If time does not permit teaching this chapter in its entirety, you may wish to preview the artwork and captions with students. Scan the heads in each lesson with students. Discuss the Looking Closely feature and examine Cultural Influences in Art on page 112.

HANDBOOK MATERIAL

Eugene Loring
(page 581)

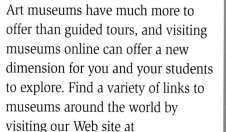

CAREERS IN Art

(page 594)

Beyond the Classroom

Art museums have much more to offer than guided tours, and visiting museums online can offer a new dimension for you and your students to explore. Find a variety of links to museums around the world by visiting our Web site at *www.glencoe.com/sec/art.*

Art History

Art History

INTRODUCE

Chapter Overview

CHAPTER 5 provides an introduction to the evaluative approaches to art taken by art historians and art critics.

Lesson One discusses the steps in the art history approach and tests the students' ability to apply the process.

Lesson Two explains how art criticism and art history can be combined to examine artworks.

Studio Lesson gives directions for creating a woodblock print.

Art & Social Studies

Ask students to examine and read the feature. Ask how many students have experienced a visit to an art museum or gallery. Have volunteers share their experiences and tell what they enjoyed most about viewing a display of artworks from different styles and periods. Discuss the information in the feature that indicates how museums originally developed as an elitist entertainment. Have students describe ways that communities have now taken steps to ensure that art is available to be enjoyed by everyone.

Art & Social Studies ■ **FIGURE 5.1** During the seventeenth and eighteenth centuries, private collections of art and curiosities of nature became a popular hobby of the wealthy in Europe. Emphasis was placed on their entertainment value. Objects were displayed that, because of their uniqueness or rarity, excited viewers. However, these early museums were not open to the public. Only friends of the wealthy owners were admitted. For this reason, museums were regarded as elitist institutions.

Cornelis de Baellieur and Jan Jordaens III. *Galerie eines Sammlers* (in the manner of Frans Franken II). c. 1635. Oil on wood. 115.5 × 148 cm (45¹/₂ × 58¹/₄″). Residenzgalerie Salzburg, Austria. Collection Schöborn-Buchheim.

104

National Standards

This chapter addresses the following National Standards for the Arts.

1. (b)	**4.** (a,b,c)
2. (a,b)	**5.** (a,b)
3. (a,b)	**6.** (a,b)

CHAPTER 5 RESOURCES

Teacher's Classroom Resources

- 📁 Advanced Studio Activity 5
- 📁 Application 5
- 🖱 Chapter 5 Internet Activity
- 📁 Studio Activity 5

Assessment

- 📁 Chapter 5 Test
- 📁 Performance Assessment

Fine Art Resources

- *Art in Focus* Transparency 8
  George Caleb Bingham.
  Fur Traders Descending the Missouri.
- Focus on World Art Print 5
  Thomas Cole. *The Architect's Dream*

Too often, art criticism and art history are treated as only vaguely related methods of inquiry. The knowledge and understanding gained from one, however, can and should assist efforts in the other. Both approaches concentrate on works of art, although from different points of view. They often make use of similar search strategies. We can stress the similarities of these two methods of inquiry and thus emphasize their usefulness to each other. At the same time, identifying their differences in viewpoint can expand your knowledge and understanding of art.

Introducing the Chapter

Ask students to examine Figure 5.1 and share their impressions. Does the work appear to tell a story? Does it capture a feeling or mood? Can they tell when it was painted? Explain that questions like these will be the focus of the chapter.

ART SOURCE Assign the feature on *Performing Arts Handbook*, page 581. Explain that choreographer Eugene Loring broke with classical ballet traditions by creating a ballet based on purely American themes and movements.

YOUR Portfolio

Think of an event that is connected to your own life and heritage. As an artist, what would you choose to record? What decisions must you make regarding media, materials, and subject? In your sketchbook, sketch a design of a historical artwork. Share your sketches in small groups, then select one sketch to be shown to the class. Explain the historical background for the design and the way the medium is used to record that history. Finally, consider the criteria for evaluating a historical artwork. What aspects would be more important than others? What would you want someone who finds this in future generations to understand about your subject?

Focus ON THE ARTS

THEATRE

In dramatic literature, as in all the arts, works are often based on historical precedents. Twentieth-century French playwrights Jean Anouilh and Jean Cocteau looked to history for their inspiration. Both created updated versions of Sophocles's classic fifth-century Greek play, *Antigone*.

DANCE

Throughout the long history of dance, we find tributes to the origins of modern dance forms. A shining example is the ballet *Apollo Musagetes* (Apollo, Leader of the Muses), by Russian composer Igor Stravinsky. This ballet pays homage not only to the foundations of artistic inspiration—the muses—but to ancient Greek dance.

MUSIC

Understanding the historical context of a work can add greatly to your appreciation of it. Franz Joseph Haydn's *Farewell Symphony*, for example, was not the composer's final work. It was a hint to his patron that the court musicians needed a vacation. This is why the last movement concludes with the orchestra members rising and leaving one by one.

105

Focus ON THE ARTS

On the chalkboard list the names of legends and events that have inspired works in various areas of the arts. Possibilities might include the Celtic legend of Tristram and Iseult (immortalized by Tennyson in his epic poem and by Richard Wagner in his opera *Tristan and Isolde*) and the biblical story of Samson and Delila (in the poem by John Milton, and in the opera by George Frederic Handel).

Divide the class into teams, and challenge teams to select one of the legends or events and develop a "family tree" diagram. Have them note the names of works of art that have grown out of this event or legend. Explain that having a familiarity with a work's "genealogy" can often enhance one's appreciation.

DEVELOPING A PORTFOLIO

Written Summaries. Art assessment involves an evaluation technique that challenges students to think critically and to see and understand the range of possibilities. Students need to know how to support these possibilities through opinions, based on reasonable rationales. They can do this by answering questions, such as those in the art criticism and art history operations. When giving students the opportunity to write about works of art, be sure to assess the quality of the responses not the quality of the written expression. You may want to develop a rubric, which is a guide for scoring or passing judgment on the art assignment. For more information for developing a rubric, refer to the *Portfolio and Assessment* booklet in the *Art in Focus* program.

Art History: A Search for Information

LESSON ONE

Art History: A Search for Information

Focus

Lesson Objectives

After studying this lesson, students will be able to:
■ Explain the steps art historians use in evaluating works of art.
■ Apply the art-history approach to an artwork.

Motivator

Display a photographic slide of an individual unfamiliar to students. Ask students to suppose they were interested in learning about the subject of this photo. Can they tell anything about the individual from the photo itself? What sources could they turn to for additional information? Now ask students to suppose that, instead of a photo, you had displayed a work of art. How would they go about answering the same questions? Tell them they are about to learn where the professionals known as art historians turn for answers.

Introducing the Lesson

Have students imagine that the artworks in Figures 5.2 and 5.3 (page 98) were hanging side by side in a museum. Ask: Which picture is the casual viewer least likely to understand or, conversely, most likely to dismiss as "not art"? What do such opinions and sentiments reveal about the untrained observer of art? What do they reveal about the study of art?

Vocabulary
■ style

Discover
After completing this lesson, you will be able to:
■ Identify and discuss the four steps in the process of art history.
■ Explain the value of using art history operations to examine artworks.

*A*rt critics, on the one hand, focus attention on gaining information *from* works of art. Art historians, on the other hand, are concerned with gathering information *about* works of art and the artists who created them. The methods used by critics and historians often involve the same four operations: description, analysis, interpretation, and judgment.

Historians, however, work from a different point of view when they apply these four operations to their study of art. During their examinations, they try to find answers to questions such as these:

● When, where, and why was the artwork created?
● What style of art does it represent?
● What artists, works of art, or other influences inspired the artist?
● What impact did the artist or the artwork have on the history of art?

Historians provide us with dates and other biographical and social information about art. Because of their efforts, we know what was created at a certain time and place by a particular artist. We also know why it was created, how people responded to it when it was first exhibited, and how they continued to respond to it over time. Art historians view artworks as visual documents reflecting the ideas, values, fears, beliefs, superstitions, and desires that have characterized every society in every era from prehistoric times to the present.

The Art History Approach

To gain a better understanding of art history and learn how art historians gather information about art, follow along as an imaginary art historian named Helen studies a painting. The work she is currently examining is a rousing painting of a parade in New York City (Figure 5.2).

Recognizing the need for a plan of action, Helen decides to use the same steps of description, analysis, interpretation, and judgment used by many art critics. Her method will differ in that she will use these steps to gather facts and information about the work and the artist who created it. Because Helen is applying these steps from an art historian's point of view, they are referred to here as art history operations.

In Helen's plan:

● Description involves discovering when, where, and by whom the work was done.
● Analysis involves discovering the unique features of an artwork that determine its artistic style.
● Interpretation involves discovering how the artist is influenced by the world around him or her.
● Judgment involves making a decision about a work's importance in the history of art.

106

LESSON ONE RESOURCES

Teacher's Classroom Resources

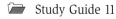 Appreciating Cultural Diversity 6

📁 Reproducible Lesson Plan 11

📁 Reteaching Activity 11

📁 Study Guide 11

Description

During description, the first operation, Helen tries to determine who painted the work and when and where it was created. In this instance, her knowledge of art history enables her to identify the artist as an American painter named Childe Hassam (**hah**-sem). The painting's title includes the date of the event pictured as well as the year it was painted. Because Hassam was born in 1859, Helen knows that this picture was done when the artist was 58 years old.

■ **FIGURE 5.2** Like contemporary French painters, Hassam chose a high vantage point overlooking a crowded street. **How did this vantage point help him create a feeling of space?**

Childe Hassam. *Allies Day, May 1917.* 1917. Oil on canvas. 92.7 × 76.8 cm (36^1/$_2$ × 30^1/$_4$"). National Gallery of Art, Washington D.C. Gift of Ethelyn McKinney in memory of her brother, Glenn Ford McKinney.

TEACH
Aesthetics

Direct students' attention again to the painting in Figure 5.2. Ask what adjectives best describe the style of this painting. If students are at a loss, start them off by suggesting words like *misty* and *dreamlike.* What qualities suggest these impressions? What techniques do they suspect the artist may have used to achieve this effect?

Art History

Have a group of volunteers gather information about Impressionism, an art movement that developed as a new desire for realism. Who were the founders of this movement? How did the movement come to be called *Impressionism?* What were the goals of artists who adopted this style of painting? Allow time for the group to share findings with the class in the form of a pictorial report.

 Technology ▬▬▬▬▬▬▬

National Gallery of Art Videodisc Use the following images as examples of more works by artists introduced in this lesson.

Childe Hassam
Allies Day, May 1917

Search Frame 2086

Camille Pissarro
The Artist's Garden at Eragny

Search Frame 1482

Arshile Gorky
The Artist and His Mother

Search Frame 2303

Use Glencoe's *Correlation Bar Code Guide to the National Gallery of Art* to locate more artworks.

Art Criticism

Have students compare the styles of the paintings in Figures 5.4 (page 109) and 5.5 (page 110). What do the two styles have in common? In what ways are they dissimilar? Which style seems more concerned with the emotional impact of the work? Which seems most concerned with imitating reality?

Art History

Have students investigate the life and work of Claude Monet, the man considered by most scholars to be the chief founder of the Impressionist movement. Have students learn in particular about Monet's methodology as a painter and his practice of painting the same scene many times under different atmospheric conditions. Urge students to share and compare their findings in a class forum.

Did You Know?

The term *Impressionism* was coined not by any member of the movement but by a critic attending one of the group's earliest showings in Paris in 1874. The label, which was used to ridicule and dismiss the work of these painters, was borrowed from a painting by Monet titled *Impression: Sunrise.*

At other times, Helen might not recognize the artist so easily. Then she would need to examine the work carefully to see whether it contained a signature. If a signature is found, it might be the name of an artist with whom Helen is unfamiliar. In that case, she would have to conduct research on the artist. Information usually can be found in readily available sources. Occasionally, however, a great deal of time and effort must be devoted to research before all the important facts about an artist are uncovered.

There are other times, of course, when no signature is found on the work. Even after a long investigation, it might be impossible to say for certain who created it. In those cases, Helen would be required to make a well-informed guess, based on the information she was able to gather. For example, there is no positive identification of the artist who created the handscroll shown in Figure 5.3.

Analysis

Skilled artists have a special way of seeing and develop their own unique ways of showing us what they see. Historians refer to this as the artist's individual **style,** or *personal way of using the art elements and principles to reproduce what they see and to express their ideas and feelings.* For example, Georges Rouault's (**zhorzh** roo-**oh**) style includes the use of a bold, dark outline around brightly colored shapes (Figure 5.4). Most paintings by this artist can be easily recognized because they look very much like stained-glass windows. In this case, the artist's painting style is as personal and distinctive as his signature. (See also Figure 23.4, page 518, another illustration of a Rouault work.)

Following many years of study, historians are able to recognize the main features of an artist's style. They also learn that this style often develops gradually as the artist's special way of seeing matures and as his or her artistic skills are perfected. A historian who has studied the development of an artist's style can usually tell if a work of art was done early or late in the career of that artist.

■ **FIGURE 5.3** There is no positive identification of the artist who created this early Chinese landscape, but for centuries it has been attributed to the tenth-century master Dong Yuan. **Do you think museums should exhibit works created by unknown artists? Why or why not?**

Anonymous (formerly attributed to Dong Yuan). *Clear Weather in the Valley.* Thirteenth century. Handscroll, ink and light color on paper. 37.5 × 150.8 cm (14³/₄ × 59³/₈"). Courtesy, Museum of Fine Arts, Boston, Massachusetts. Chinese and Japanese Special Fund.

108 **Unit One** *Creating and Understanding Art*

More About... **Childe Hassam (1859–1935).** Tell students that Childe Hassam is known as the American artist who most fully incorporated the French Impressionist spirit and style into his artwork. He developed his skill in art long before he visited France. He left high school before graduation to help support his family. Hassam made an unsuccessful attempt at accounting, but his supervisor noticed Hassam had a talent for drawing and suggested a career in art. He apprenticed with a wood engraver and then took lessons in drawing and painting. His art studies led him to spend three years in Paris developing his style in Impressionism.

■ **FIGURE 5.4** The dark outlines and brightly colored shapes in this painting remind viewers of stained-glass windows. **How have color and value been used to emphasize the face of the woman?**

Georges Rouault. *The Italian Woman.* 1938. Oil on panel. 79.37 × 61.44 cm (31¼ × 24¹³⁄₁₆″). Dallas Museum of Art, Dallas, Texas. Gift of Mr. and Mrs. Vladimir Horowitz.

■ **FIGURE 5.3** (continued)

CHAPTER 5
LESSON ONE

Art Criticism

Point out that art historians are sometimes called upon to determine whether an artwork is a forgery. Display a variety of reproductions in the style of Hassam or Rouault, taking care to cover any credit lines. Ask students to pick out which, if any, of the reproductions are legitimate. Have them explain what descriptive and analytical (e.g., stylistic) criteria they used to arrive at their assumptions.

Art History

Bring to class a number of print resources that could be used in applying the four art-history operations listed in the text (e.g., a biographical dictionary, an almanac, a one-volume encyclopedia). Have students review the questions an art historian might ask when performing a description. Then divide the class into groups of three or four students. Invite each group to select a work from another chapter of the text and perform a description. (To avoid duplication of effort, have groups indicate the title and the figure number of the work they have chosen. Record this information on the board.) As groups proceed, they use any resources at their disposal, including this textbook, to help them learn about the artwork they have selected. When groups have completed their descriptions, they should share methods used in gathering information.

Art Criticism

Have students again study the work in Figure 5.4. What image first catches their eye when they look at this work? What elements has the artist emphasized? What principles has he used to organize those elements?

COOPERATIVE LEARNING

Share and Compare. You may enlarge upon the Art Criticism activity on this page by having groups target for description a work already described by one of the other groups. After completing this follow-up activity, groups should share and compare their descriptions. Have the class discuss questions such as the following: Did the two groups turn up identical information about the same artwork? If not, what sources did each group use? What other sources might they find useful in carrying out this type of task?

Critical Thinking

Have students think about and discuss the influence the following events might have on the art of a given period: war, an end to war, natural disaster, civil unrest, and celebrations indigenous to a people's culture. Have students confirm or refute their assumptions by examining works of art created at times that coincide with such historical landmarks.

Studio Skills

Provide students with recent copies of news magazines and ask them to browse through the pages noting headlines and photographs. Then, using pencil, students should sketch on scrap paper or in their sketchbooks a design for an expressive work that captures an event of the times. Before students begin, have them think about symbols that may play a role in their work's theme (e.g., an eagle as a symbol of the United States, balloons as a symbol of celebration). When students are satisfied with the sketches, they can transfer them to white paper and complete their works using oil pastels. Have students exhibit completed works and attempt to guess the themes expressed in their classmates' efforts.

■ **FIGURE 5.5** Late in life Pissarro's eyesight began to fail and he was unable to paint outdoors. He then painted city street scenes viewed through a hotel window. **How is it possible to say that Pissarro used a "painterly shorthand" when creating works like this?**

Camille Pissarro. *Boulevard des Italiens, Morning, Sunlight.* 1897. Oil on canvas. 73.2 × 92.1 cm (28⁷/₈ × 36¹/₄"). National Gallery of Art, Washington, D.C. Chester Dale Collection.

■ **FIGURE 5.6** Dubuffet applied his paint in heavy, thick layers, like a rough coating of plaster. **Why do you think the artist grouped city dwellers crowded together yet never touching each other?**

Jean Dubuffet. *Business Prospers,* (from the *Paris Circus* series). 1961. Oil on canvas. 165.1 × 220 cm (5'5" × 7'2⁵/₈"). The Museum of Modern Art, New York, New York. Gift of Mrs. Simon Guggenheim.

110 **Unit One** *Creating and Understanding Art*

To further illustrate this point, examine the three paintings of cities in Figures 5.5, 5.6, and 5.7. Each illustrates the individual artist's personal view of the same subject rendered in his own unique style.

During analysis, the historian tries to identify the style of an artwork by studying its distinguishing features. When Helen examines the painting by Hassam (Figure 5.2, page 107), she recognizes features that characterize the artist's individual style. For example, she notes that he uses strong, pure hues. Reds, yellows, and greens are placed close together to capture the vibrant and brilliant sunlight of a spring day. When viewed at a distance, these hues mingle and blend just as they do in nature. Helen also observes that the details and the edges of shapes seem to be blurred (Figure 5.8). Moreover, there is no emphasis or center of interest to which the viewer's eye is directed.

Helen realizes that these features characterize a particular style of art in which the artist attempts to depict exactly what the eye sees in a moment of time. From the painting's vantage point high above Manhattan's Fifth Avenue, looking down at the enthusiastic crowd, the exhilarating music of marching bands, and the colorful display of flags waving in the breeze, most viewers would find it difficult to know where to look first. They gain a general impression of the whole rather than a thorough knowledge of any part. It is this impression that Hassam sought to capture in his painting.

During analysis, Helen also tries to group Hassam's painting with works that have the same stylistic features but are painted by other artists. She knows that many works of art have a "family resemblance," which enables historians to group them as part of an art movement. Artists within a given art movement share a similar style.

An art movement quickly becomes apparent to Helen as she continues her study of Hassam's painting. She observes that the picture is composed of brightly colored paint applied in short, side-by-side brushstrokes that give it a sketchy appearance. Because they are created with abrupt strokes of color, the forms in the work lose much of their solidity.

𝒯eacher 𝒩otes

Developing Perceptual Skills. Give students an opportunity to understand the effect of outside influences on artworks. Have students select a site that they will observe at different times of the day and night in order to gain a vivid sense of how changing light affects the quality of a scene. They may choose either an indoor or an outdoor scene, but be sure the illumination (artificial or natural) changes during a 24-hour period. Students should observe the scene at different hours over several days. Have them record in their sketchbooks the times that they make their observations, the quality of light present, and how it altered the mood of the scene. Have them sketch the scene under different light conditions.

Looking more closely, she observes that the shadows and highlights are not painted in black and white. Instead, they are rendered in dark and light values of various hues.

Helen knows Hassam's reason for using short strokes of paint and carefully selecting and placing the intense hues in his picture. He was trying to capture the flickering effect of sunlight on buildings and banners. Once she has reached that conclusion, Helen is able to group the painting with other works in which the effect of sunlight on subject matter is a major stylistic feature. Paintings of this kind were first created in the nineteenth century by a group of French painters now known as Impressionists. No other American painter was as successful in adopting the Impressionist style as Childe Hassam.

Interpretation

When interpreting this work of art, Helen focuses attention on the influences of time and place on the artist. She realizes that pictures of the same subject, created at different times—or in different locations—may have little in common. Their differences reflect the contrasting traditions and values that influenced each artist. For example, the paintings in Figures 5.9 and 5.10 on page 112 both portray waves crashing against rocks.

■ **FIGURE 5.7** Leger included certain recognizable urban details to describe the excitement of the city. **What details associated with the city can be identified in this painting?**

Fernand Léger. *The City.* 1919. Oil on canvas. 2.31 × 4.5 m (7'7″ × 14'9″). Philadelphia Museum of Art, Philadelphia, Pennsylvania. A. E. Gallatin Collection.

■ **FIGURE 5.8**

Childe Hassam. *Allies Day, May 1917* (detail).

Aesthetics

What words would students use to describe each of the paintings of cities exhibited in Figures 5.5 and 5.6 (page 110)? What differences do students perceive in the way the two artists use the element of line? How has shading been used to create depth?

Cross Curriculum

SCIENCE. Have students learn more about the science of optics and the theories of light that were advanced during the nineteenth century. Have a volunteer summarize these theories in an oral report that answers the following questions: What were the names of the scientists responsible for these views? What immediate effect did the theories have on the work of the Impressionists?

Critical Thinking

Students interested in the areas of art restoration or conservation should be encouraged to follow the accounts of people and projects in this field. For example, look for articles in publications such as *Tech Talk* and *ArtNews.* Efforts to preserve and restore artworks are often ongoing at major musems. If possible, arrange a field trip to a restoration facility or plan a classroom visit by a person who works in this field.

Teacher Notes

Providing Resources. A familiarity with research tools is indispensable to the type of information-gathering art historians are called upon to do. To help students succeed with activities in this lesson, you may want to take them on a tour of the school library and explain the arrangement of titles by reference number. Make sure, too, that students have an understanding of the nature and importance of the parts of a reference book such as indexes and tables of contents. Give students an opportunity to practice research skills in the library. Assign an artwork, or ask students to choose a work from the text. Have each student locate one piece of art-history information from the library.

Art History

Remind students that one of the joys of being an art historian is discovering a lost or unknown artwork. As a point of comparison, read to them the description of the tomb of Tutankhamen when it was first opened. Include other accounts of discovery that you are familiar with.

Next, ask the class to imagine that a locked vault in an old warehouse has been recently opened, and in the vault was found a collection of artworks of various forms and media. The only information available about the contents is an inventory of artists and titles. Your students have been asked to head a research team to investigate the history of each piece and determine the authenticity and value of the collection. Ask them to brainstorm methods and materials that would be necessary in their research. What have they learned about art history that will help them organize the search and validate their conclusions? What resources are available? What new areas of discovery might result from their research?

Did You Know?

Winslow Homer was once told by a long-time friend that he used too much brown in his paintings, making them look dull. Homer bet his friend $100 that he could paint a successful dull-brown picture and his friend quickly accepted the wager. When the finished painting, entitled *West Wind*, was placed on exhibit, it was highly praised by critics and the public. Homer wasted no time writing to his friend, saying, "The 'West Wind' is brown. It is darn good! Send me your check."

Cultural Influences in rt

These two works were painted at different times and in different parts of the world.

1

This screen painting (Figure 5.9) reveals the delicate lines and foam-shaped waves favored by many Japanese artists. Although reflecting a deep appreciation for nature, the painting makes no effort to mirror nature. Instead, it serves to inspire quiet contemplation and meditation on the part of the viewer.

■ FIGURE 5.9

Ogata Korin (attributed to). *Waves at Matsushima.* Edo Period. Eighteenth Century. Six-panel folding screen; ink, colors, and gold on paper. 155 × 370 cm (5'8" × 12'13"). Courtesy, Museum of Fine Arts, Boston, Massachusetts. Fenollosa-Weld Collection.

■ FIGURE 5.10

Winslow Homer. *Northeaster.* 1895. Oil on canvas. 87.6 × 127 cm (34¹/₂ × 50"). The Metropolitan Museum of Art, New York, New York. Gift of George A. Hearn, 1910. (10.64.5).

2

This painting (Figure 5.10), however, captures in a realistic fashion the drama of a powerful storm concentrated in a single crashing wave. The ominous force of this wave inspires both awe and fear in the viewer.

Cultural Influences in *Art*

Have students examine the feature on this page and discuss the historical origins of each of the artworks. Point out that aesthetic theories can vary from culture to culture and that it is easy to misinterpret art from a culture whose aesthetic frame of reference is unfamiliar. Japanese music often sounds strange to the uninitiated Western ear. Have students select and research the visual arts as practiced by a contemporary African or Far Eastern culture. Ask students to determine what an art critic would need to know about the culture and its art before proceeding with an evaluation.

The real-world settings of time and place have a powerful influence on artists. They affect the ideas and feelings artists form, and influence the manner in which artists express those ideas and feelings. Time and place even influence the tools and materials artists use to transform their ideas into visual form.

In an effort to determine how time and place influenced Hassam, Helen turns to several sources. She refers to history books, biographies, magazine articles, and published interviews with the artist or with people who knew him. From these she learns that Hassam discovered Impressionism during a trip to Europe from 1886 to 1889. He admired the Impressionists' attempts to view and paint the world with a new freshness. Influenced by scientific research into color and light and the recently discovered camera, the Impressionists were painting pictures that looked like unstudied, candid views of contemporary scenes. (See Figure 5.5, page 110.) In their effort to capture the momentary effects of light on different surfaces, they developed a painting style that used bright colors and sketchy brushwork. Traditionalists greeted this new style with bewilderment, but Hassam appreciated and adopted it.

Inspired by the patriotic atmosphere that marked America's entry into the First World War, Hassam painted the first of many flag paintings around 1916. The title of the painting Helen has been examining reveals that it was painted a year later, in the spring of 1917. On May 9 and 11 of that year, representatives of France and Great Britain had arrived in New York to help formulate plans for America's participation in the war. This sparked a patriotic frenzy in midtown Manhattan. Parades were held on Fifth Avenue, and buildings were decked out with the British, French, and American flags, symbolizing the unity of the three nations in the fight for democracy. Hassam's painting presents a spectacle of brightly colored banners that fills the clear blue sky and the canyon between the city's tall buildings. Almost hidden from view are the marchers, onlookers, and vehicles on the busy street below.

Hassam did not limit himself to a single painting of this scene. He painted several different views, including one that shows flags viewed from a lower vantage point (Figure 5.11). In 1918, just four days after the armistice was signed, all of Hassam's colorful flag paintings were placed on exhibition in a New York gallery. It seems appropriate that the paintings created to commemorate America's entry into the war also marked its victorious conclusion.

■ **FIGURE 5.11** Each city block along the parade route was decorated with the flag of one nation. How is space and movement suggested in this work? What happens when you shift from a close-up examination of this picture to a more distant view?

Childe Hassam. *Avenue of the Allies. Brazil, Belgium, 1918.* 1918. Oil on canvas. 92.2 × 61.8 cm (36⁵/₁₆ × 24⁵/₁₆"). Los Angeles County Museum of Art, Los Angeles, California. Mr. and Mrs. William Preston Harrison Collection.

Critical Thinking

Tell students to imagine that Winslow Homer was somehow persuaded to teach a painting class in which Ogata Korin was a student. Ask students to speculate on the words of advice Homer might offer Korin after critically examining his painting of Matsushima (Figure 5.9). If their roles were reversed and Korin was Homer's teacher, what pointers might he give Homer to improve his work?

Studio Skills

Ask students to assign a personality to the two versions of the sea depicted in Figures 5.9 and 5.10. Instruct them to use watercolors to paint a full-face portrait of a person exhibiting the same qualities as one of these paintings. Tell them that when doing this they should use the same painting technique as the artist.

Study Guide

Distribute *Study Guide* 11 in the TCR. Assist students in reviewing key concepts.

Teacher Notes

Art and Humanities

Have students complete *Cooperative Learning* 6, "Artists Recording Art History," in the TCR. In this activity, students are made aware of how artists document history through their works. 📁

Studio Activities

Assign *Studio* 7, "Creating an Abstract Self-Portrait," in the TCR. Students are invited to make a cardboard cut-out self-portrait that expresses their own personality. 📁

ASSESS
Checking Comprehension

Have students complete the lesson review questions. Answers appear in the box below.

Reteaching

➤ Assign *Reteaching* 11, found in the TCR. Have students complete the activity and review their responses. 📁

➤ Have students work in pairs. As one member of the pair names an art-history operation, the other is to list questions the historian would ask during that operation. Partners are then to switch roles.

Judgment

Helen's examination of Hassam's painting draws to a close as she makes a decision about its historical significance. Some artworks are considered more important because they are the first expressions of a new style or technique. As such, they inspire artists who follow. Other works are valued because they are excellent examples of a great artist's fully developed style.

The date of Hassam's painting in 1917 reveals that it was painted when Hassam had reached his full potential as an artist. It demonstrates convincingly the artist's complete command of the Impressionist style to capture the look and feel of a contemporary event as seen in a quick glance. With paintings like this, Hassam established his importance as one of America's foremost Impressionist painters. It is not surprising, then, that Helen declares Hassam's painting a success.

Helen's examination of Hassam's painting demonstrates that it is possible to gather a great deal of information about a work of art by using the four art history operations, or steps. You can use these same steps whenever you want to learn more about a particular work of art and the artist who created it.

Figure 5.12 illustrates the kind of information, or external clues, you should look for during each of these art history steps.

Value of Art History

Some people may avoid the challenge of conducting a historical examination by saying, "I like (or dislike) the work, and consequently see no reason to learn anything about it." Let's assume for a moment that they are shown the work illustrated in Figure 5.13. Even viewers who felt no initial interest might be tempted to take a closer look if they learned about the unusual circumstances that led the artist to paint it. A closer look might even cause them to change their opinion of the painting.

The artist, Arshile Gorky, was born in the mountain forests of Turkish Armenia in 1905. When he was four years old, his father emigrated alone to the United States to avoid serving in the Turkish army. He left Gorky and his sisters in the care of their young mother. Four years later, Gorky and his mother posed for a photograph that was mailed to his father in Providence, Rhode Island. Then, in 1915, a bloody conflict between Turks and Armenians

	ART HISTORY OPERATIONS			
	Description	**Analysis**	**Interpretation**	**Judgment**
External Cues	Determine **when, where,** and **by whom** the work was done.	Identify **unique features** to determine artistic style.	Learn how **time and place** influenced the artist.	Use information to **make a decision** about the work's importance in the history of art.

■ **FIGURE 5.12** Art History Operations

About the *Artwork*

The Artist and His Mother. Point out to students that this work, which was completed while the artist was in his twenties, is one of Arshile Gorky's earlier efforts. Like other early works, this one contains traces of Surrealism, a movement that affected the artist as a young man. By the time Gorky reached his middle years, he had become immersed in Abstract Expressionism, a school he helped to found. Gorky's Abstract Expressionist paintings are notable for their bold, seemingly random splashes of bright color.

living within Turkish borders caused the frightened mother, her son, and her daughters to flee Turkey. They trekked 150 miles to reach safety in Russian Armenia. The difficult march over rough terrain and the hardships they endured in Russia were too much for Gorky's mother. In 1919, just four years after their arrival, she died of starvation in her son's arms. She was only 39 years old, and her son was just 14.

Not long after his mother's death, Gorky managed to emigrate to the United States. There, using the photograph taken years before as his inspiration, he painted the haunting double portrait of himself and his mother. Certainly this knowledge would add to anyone's understanding of the painting.

Of course, not every work of art has a story behind it. Viewers who do not search for such stories, however, risk missing out on important and often fascinating information about art and artists.

■ **FIGURE 5.13** Notice the haunting quality in the face of the young man in this painting. **What feelings or moods does the painting communicate?**

Arshile Gorky. *The Artist and His Mother.* c. 1926–36. Oil on canvas. 152.4 × 127 cm (60 × 50"). Whitney Museum of American Art, New York, New York. Gift of Julien Levy for Maro and Natasha Gorky in memory of their father.

Enrichment

Ask teams of students to identify an artwork in this lesson and have each team describe the work they have chosen as an art historian would. Have them research the subject and the artist and make notes following the rest of the art history operations for that work.

Extension

Have students look once again at the city paintings on pages 110 and 111. Then have them research other examples of this subject in different times and places. Discuss why artists might elect to re-create the same subject. What differences can students find between the way different artists portray cities in different cultures.

CLOSE

Gather as many postcard-size reproductions of well-known artworks as there are students in your class. With white contact tape, cover the credit line on each card and distribute one card to each student. Challenge the students to apply the four steps in the art-history approach to the work presented to them.

LESSON ONE REVIEW

Reviewing Art Facts

1. What are the four steps of the art history operations?
2. How do these four steps differ when used by art historians and art critics?
3. What is meant by an artist's personal style and what role does it play in the historian's efforts to identify artworks as representative of art movements?
4. On what does the art historian focus attention during interpretation?

▶ **Activity... *Examining the Art History Operations***

Works of art are never created in a cultural vacuum. The political, social, religious, and economic developments of the time in which the artwork is created almost always influence the artist. Examining a work of art through the art history operations makes the work more meaningful.

Choose a work of art that you do not completely understand but find interesting. Follow the operations that an art historian would use: description, analysis, interpretation, and judgment. Determine the style of the work as well as the influence of time and place on the artist. Use the art history table in this lesson. Share your findings with the class.

LESSON ONE REVIEW

Answers to Reviewing Art Facts
1. Description, analysis, interpretation, judgment.
2. Art historians gather information about the artworks, not from the artwork.
3. The artist's personal way of expressing feelings and ideas.
4. The influence of time and place on the artist's style.

Activity... *Examining the Art History Operations*

Have students review the art history operations in the chart on the previous page before beginning this activity. Have them begin by looking at the credit line and finding out as much information as they can from that. Encourage students to research the work they chose to complete the steps.

Using Art History

Focus

Lesson Objectives

After studying this lesson, students will be able to:

■ Use the steps of art history to understand a work of art.

■ Explain the relationship between art criticsim and art history when examining a work of art.

Motivator

Have students select a reproduction of a painting in the text and make a complete list of observations regarding the work (i.e., elements of art emphasized, whether the subject is realistic, and so on). When students feel their lists are complete, ask them to sketch the work they chose. What details did they miss on the list that were brought to their attention in the act of sketching?

Introducing the Lesson

Remind students that while art historians attempt to learn *about* works of art, art critics attempt to learn *from* art. Then review with students the four art-history operations. Ask which of these operations students feel might be equally adaptable to art criticism. Then proceed with the reading.

Discover

After completing this lesson, you will be able to:

■ Use the four steps of the art history operations to gather information about a work of art.

■ Explain how both the art criticism operations and the art history operations can be used to examine a work of art.

*H*aving learned how an art historian examines a work of art, you may be eager to do the same. Unlike the art criticism operations, which draw information exclusively from the work of art, the art history operations require that you have access to historical resources. Your best sources for historical information are books and articles on art. Reading these will expand your knowledge of art history and eventually enable you to draw on this knowledge when seeking answers to questions posed by the art history operations.

Acting as an Art Historian

Pretend for a moment that you are visiting an art museum and have purchased an illustrated guide to the museum's collection. Guides of this kind frequently provide information on the works and the artists who created them. With your guide in hand, you set forth, examining the many paintings and sculptures on display and reading the relevant notes in your guide. You soon discover that your pace has quickened and you are reading less and less. Realizing that you cannot study every work at length, you decide to focus your attention on a few works and examine them using the art history operations. Looking through the museum's illustrated guide, you select a painting of a young girl with a dog as the first work to examine in this way (Figure 5.14).

Description

You begin your historical operations with description, which requires that you answer the following questions:

● Who created the work?
● Where was it done?
● When was it done?

Fortunately, this information is provided on the label next to the painting. You learn that the work was done by Berthe Morisot (**bairt** maw-ree-**zoh**), a French painter who completed it around 1887. You also learn that Morisot titled her painting *Jeune Fille au Chien*, or *Young Girl with a Dog*. Looking in your guide, you learn that Morisot was born to a well-to-do family in Bourges, France, in 1841. She died in Paris in 1895.

Analysis

During analysis, you are concerned with answering the following kinds of questions:

● What are the main features or characteristics of the work?
● Does it represent a particular style of art? If so, what is that style?

116

LESSON TWO RESOURCES

Teacher's Classroom Resources

📁 Art and Humanities 8

📁 Cooperative Learning 7, 8

📁 Enrichment Activity 12

📁 Reproducible Lesson Plan 12

📁 Reteaching Activity 12

📁 Study Guide 12

Have you noticed something familiar about the manner in which Morisot painted her picture? Look closely. Like Hassam's painting (Figure 5.2, page 107), this work exhibits the same dabs and dashes of paint, the blurred edges and details that make much of the work seem fuzzy and out of focus. Looking even more closely, you see that Morisot does use more detail when painting her subject's face, with its amused, fleeting expression.

■ **FIGURE 5.14** This painting has a spontaneous, vibrant quality. Does this picture seem to suggest movement? If so, how is this illusion created?

Berthe Morisot. *Jeune Fille au Chien* (Young Girl with a Dog). c. 1887. Oil on canvas. 72.8 × 60.1 cm (28³/₄ × 23³/₄"). Armand Hammer Museum of Art and Cultural Center, Los Angeles, California. Armand Hammer Collection.

TEACH
Art Criticism

Divide the class into small groups, and ask each group to select one of the artworks pictured in Lesson Two. Ask groups to describe the people and objects they see in the work and make a complete list of the details. Allow the groups to share their lists as a lead-in to a discussion of whether it is more difficult to describe a nonobjective work than a representational one. Is sculpture, similarly, more difficult to describe than paintings? Have students extend the activity to works from other cultures appearing in later chapters of the text. What special challenges surround attempts to describe works such as these?

Art History

Explain to students that art historians often disagree about the interpretation or importance of particular artworks and movements. Art historians may even change their minds during the course of their careers. In fact, it was not until a few decades ago that works by female artists were given the same scholarly attention that was accorded art made by their male peers. Major textbooks on the history of Western art were published without inclusion of female artists. Other art that has received increased respect from art historians includes medieval art, which was once thought to be childish and unsophisticated, and Third World art, which used to be relegated to museums of natural history instead of art museums.

 Technology

National Gallery of Art Videodisc Use the following images as examples of more works by artists introduced in this lesson.

Berthe Morisot
The Artist's Sister at a Window

Search Frame 1260

Berthe Morisot
Girl in a Boat with Geese

Search Frame 1270

Berthe Morisot
The Artist's Sister Edma with Her Daughter Jeanne

Search Frame 2932

Use Glencoe's *Correlation Bar Code Guide to the National Gallery of Art* to locate more artworks.

CHAPTER 5
LESSON TWO

Critical Thinking

Recite or write the following statement on the board: *In approaching a work of art, an art historian works from the outside in, while an art critic works from the inside out.* Ask students to discuss the validity of this observation based on what they have learned about the work of art historians and critics.

Studio Skills

Provide students with a variety of objects that yield interesting images under magnification (e.g., an orange, a leather shoe, a baseball). Have students choose and draw one of the objects and then write a detailed description of their drawing. Then have them examine their objects under a magnifying glass or a hand-held microscope and write a second description. Ask whether they now see the object in a different way than they saw it before they attempted their drawings. Have them do a second drawing based on their revised perception.

Art Criticism

Divide the class into small groups. Allow each group to choose a slip of paper bearing a chapter number from 1 to 24. The group is then to select the chapter-opening figure for that chapter. Have groups copy the Design Chart (Figure 2.24, page 46) onto a sheet of paper and do a complete art-criticism analysis of the work. Groups should compare and discuss analyses.

The rest of the composition, including the young woman's right hand and the dog on her lap, is painted with rapidly applied brushstrokes (Figure 5.15). These brushstrokes provide little more than a general impression of forms. The result is a scene as it might look with a momentary glance rather than a steady stare. The background is barely distinguishable. It only hints at foliage, suggesting an outdoor scene bathed in sunlight. Indeed, the artist was clearly concerned with capturing the effects of natural light on her subjects.

Berthe Morisot was a member of the Impressionists, and her works exhibit all the characteristics of the Impressionist style.

Interpretation

During interpretation, your attention centers on identifying various influences on the artist. Here you are interested in finding answers to questions such as these:

- Which artists or works of art inspired the artist?
- What other influences affected the artist?
- Does the work reveal something about the world in which it was painted?

Art is often difficult to understand completely unless we know the circumstances of its creation. Answers to interpretation questions are important because they provide knowledge of this kind.

Referring to your museum guide, you learn that as a young woman Morisot was certain that she would become a painter. Her grandfather was a famous painter, and she was brought up in a cultured atmosphere. She learned to paint by copying artworks in the famous Louvre museum in Paris, the traditional training ground for aspiring French artists. Later she studied with a well-known artist named Jean-Baptiste-Camille Corot, who taught her to recognize the effects of natural light and ambience, or atmosphere. Her greatest influence, however, was the painter Édouard Manet, whom she met in 1868 when she was 27 years old. Morisot was fascinated by Manet's rapid brushwork (Figure 5.16) and soon began to paint with the same bold, irregular, and rapid strokes of paint.

In 1874, Morisot joined a group of young painters in their first group show—a show scorned by critics who labeled the artists "Impressionists." That same year she married Manet's brother. Morisot continued her association with the Impressionists and participated in their exhibitions.

■ **FIGURE 5.15**

Berthe Morisot. *Jeune Fille au Chien* (detail).

118 **Unit One** *Creating and Understanding Art*

𝒯*eacher* 𝒩*otes*

Technology in the Classroom. Students will be more apt to make use of the design grid in their analyses of artworks if you provide them with a supply of blank grids. If you have access to a word processor with a tables feature or page layout software, you can easily replicate the grid shown on page 46. Be sure to make the cells large enough to accommodate a check mark, as well as any notes and self-reminders the student may wish to jot down. A copy of this chart is also provided in the *Focus on World Art* Print Supplement, Print 25.

Morisot's paintings illustrate the leisurely side of French life in the nineteenth century. Her figures live in a quiet dream world of summer afternoons and carefree moments spent in the cool shade of a garden or by a lake. Her most familiar and admired works are gentle domestic scenes, painted in a delicate, fresh lightness that sets her work apart from that of the other Impressionists. *Jeune Fille au Chien* is an excellent example of her mature painting style.

Judgment

Once you have answered questions dealing with the three previous art history operations, you are able to provide a knowledgeable answer to this judgment question: Does the artwork have historical importance?

Morisot's importance can be easily determined by referring to books on art history. Your museum guide may also provide information about her reputation, although you have probably concluded that the museum must hold her in high regard, since they are exhibiting one of her paintings. Most sources reveal that because of her social status and because she was a woman, Morisot's achievements as a painter were often ignored or treated lightly during her lifetime. Her fellow artists, however, recognized her talent and encouraged her when she expressed doubts about her own ability. Today, her work is acclaimed and her reputation as an important member of the Impressionists is beyond question.

When to Use Art Criticism and Art History

When you are standing in front of a painting or looking at the reproduction of a painting in a book, what should you do first? Should you begin by identifying the aesthetic qualities and deciding whether these qualities have been used to create a successful work of art? Or should you first determine who created it, where and when it was created, and what artistic style it represents?

If a work of art is going to mean anything special to you, you must become personally

involved with it. You should avoid turning immediately to what others have said about it. Instead, you should prepare yourself to make your own decisions about it. After you have made these personal decisions, you can turn to what others have discovered about the work. You may recall that Robert, our imaginary critic in Chapter 4, did not refer to what others had to say about Rousseau's painting *The Sleeping Gypsy* until he had completed his own examination of it.

When you examine a work of art, begin with aesthetics and the art criticism operations. Concentrate on identifying the internal clues, or aesthetic qualities in the work. Then use these as your criteria when making a subjective and tentative decision about its success. When you have done this, you are ready to turn to the objective art history operations. They will help you uncover the external clues,

Chapter 5 *Art History* **119**

CHAPTER 5
LESSON TWO

Art History

Have small groups of students perform the art-history operations they learned about in this lesson on one of the architectural images in Chapter 3, Lesson Four. Before they begin their examinations, encourage students to brainstorm questions that might be asked when working with architectural structures.

Study Guide

Distribute *Study Guide* 12 in the TCR. Assist students in reviewing key concepts. ⮕

Art and Humanities

Have students complete *Art and Humanities* 8, "Art History, Informing the Public," in the TCR. ⮕

Studio Activities

Ask students to look at Figure 5.11 (page 113) and to note the artist's use of both blurred shapes and the effect of strong hues to create emphasis in the painting. Working with tempera paints, have students create an original painting in which emphasis is similarly achieved through the elements of blurred shapes and color. Have students display their finished compositions.

Art and Humanities

Assign *Cooperative Learning* 8, "Charting Art History and Art Criticism," in the TCR. This worksheet calls upon students to complete a worksheet reviewing the art history operations as explained in this chapter.

Teacher Notes _____

Checking Comprehension

Have students complete the lesson review questions. Answers appear in the box below.

Reteaching

➤ Assign *Reteaching* 12, found in the TCR. Have students complete the activity and review their responses. 📁

➤ Have students write a paragraph summarizing the four steps in the art-criticism process and indicating questions that the critic should ask him- or herself at each step.

Enrichment

Distribute *Enrichment* 12, "Art Through the Ages," in the TCR. 📁

Extension

After pointing out that advertisements in consumer magazines often make use of sophisticated design principles, have students examine full-page ads from several such publications. For each layout, ask them to identify the principles that have been used. They may then create layouts of their own for products popular to young people.

CLOSE

Ask students to stage a debate in which they argue the relative importance of the work done by art historians and art critics. Urge them to use information obtained from the lesson.

A SEQUENCE OF ART CRITICISM AND ART HISTORY OPERATIONS		Description	Analysis	Interpretation	Judgment
1.	Art Criticism	Subject matter and/or elements of art noted in the work.	Organization: how principles of art have been used to arrange the elements of art.	Moods, feelings, and ideas communicated by the work.	Personal decision about the degree of artistic merit.
2.	Art History	Determine when, where, and by whom the work was done.	Identify unique features to determine artistic style.	Learn how time and place influenced the artist.	Make decision about work's importance in the history of art.

■ **FIGURE 5.17** A Sequence of Art Criticism and Art History Operations

facts and information about the work of art and the artist who created it. The information you gather during the art history operations will enable you to confirm, modify, or even change the decisions you made during the art criticism operations.

Combining what you learn from aesthetics and art criticism with what you learn from art history will enable you to make a final judgment. This judgment balances information that is both subjective and objective. Bear in mind, however, that no judgment in art can be considered absolutely final. Judgments are always subject to change as you continue learning *from* and *about* works of art with continued viewing and study. Remember that the final judgment is always yours to make. Without this personal involvement, it is unlikely that you will regard the artwork as something special.

In your reading about art and during visits to museums, you will encounter many works that you will want to examine closely. These examinations will be more rewarding if you follow the sequence of art criticism and art history operations outlined in Figure 5.17.

LESSON TWO REVIEW

Reviewing Art Facts

1. What must viewers do if works of art are to become special to them?
2. When you examine a work of art, should you begin with the art criticism operations or the art history operations? Why?
3. What kinds of information must you have before you can make a final judgment about a work of art?
4. Why is it impossible to say judgments in art can be considered absolutely final?

Activity... *Virtual Art Exhibit*

The study of art from a historical point of view can enrich your appreciation and understanding of many of the great masterpieces in art.

Create a virtual exhibit on the Internet or a multimedia presentation. Demonstrate your knowledge and understanding of the work of one artist, a single art style, or an art movement. Identify one work of art that represents the work of the artist or movement you chose. Work with the textbook and prepare your exhibit using each step of the art history operations. Share your work with the class.

LESSON TWO REVIEW

Answers to Reviewing Art Facts

1. Viewers must become personally involved in a work to make it meaningful to them.
2. Examination should begin with aesthetics and the art criticism operations.
3. You must learn from aesthetics and art criticism and combine that information with what you learn from an art history analysis.
4. As you learn more from and about works of art, your final judgment can change.

Activity...*Virtual Art Exhibit*

If your classroom is equipped with a computer and multimedia presentation software, encourage students to create their presentations using one of these programs. Your school may already have a school Web site where students might exhibit.

Studio LESSON Painting an Abstract Still Life

Complete a still-life painting in which attention is focused on the design qualities rather than on realistic representation. Your painting will illustrate a concern for harmony of line, variety of shapes, and emphasis realized by the use of contrasting complementary hues.

Inspiration

Look through *Art in Focus* for illustrations of artworks that make effective use of the design qualities. Select one of these works and examine it closely. Which elements of art are used? How are the principles of art used to organize these elements? Do you feel that the overall effect realized by the use of these elements and principles is unified?

Process

1. Working with other members of your class, arrange a still life made up of at least three familiar objects. Make a pencil sketch of the still life.
2. Draw this still life lightly with pencil on the sheet of white drawing paper. To create harmony of line, use a ruler to straighten every line in your drawing. (If you prefer, make all the lines in your composition curved rather than straight.) Extend these lines to divide the background and the still-life objects into a variety of large and small angular shapes.
3. Select two complementary hues. Paint all the shapes in your still life with hues obtained by mixing these two colors. You can create different values by adding white or black.
4. Emphasize the most important or interesting shapes in your picture by painting them with hues and values that contrast with the hues and values of surrounding shapes.

Materials

- Minimum of three familiar objects to use in a still life
- Pencil and sketch paper
- Sheet of white drawing paper, 9 × 12 inches
- Ruler
- Tempera or acrylic paint
- Brushes, mixing tray, and paint cloth
- Water container

■ **FIGURE 5.18** Student Work

Examining Your Work

Analyze. Are all lines in your composition straight (or curved)? How does the use of the same type of line throughout add harmony to your painting? Does your picture exhibit a variety of large and small shapes? Are these shapes painted with hues obtained by mixing two complementary colors? Did you use these contrasting hues to emphasize certain important shapes in your composition? Were other students able to identify these important shapes?

Judge. Do you think your painting would be favorably received by a critic relying exclusively on the design qualities?

121

Studio LESSON

Painting an Abstract Still Life

Objectives
- Complete a still-life painting consisting of at least three objects.
- Use similar lines throughout to achieve harmony.
- Add variety by making use of large and small shapes.
- Use contrasting hues and values to emphasize the most important and interesting shapes in the composition.

Motivator

Explain to students that art is a visual language consisting of the elements and principles of design. As students discuss the elements and principles in the work selected for examination, list these on the board. When they have finished, refer to each element and principle in turn and ask students to identify another artwork in the text that makes use of the same element or principle.

Studio Skills

After adding the lines to their compositions, students will discover that their still-life objects are lost in a complex maze of lines and shapes. They should be told that their task is to paint those shapes so they will stand out clearly. They will accomplish this by using hues and values that contrast with the hues and values applied to background shapes.

Critiquing

Have students apply the steps of art criticism to their own artworks using the Examining Your Work questions on this page.

ASSESSMENT

Examining Your Work. As students complete the questions, have them check the objectives to be certain they included each of these objects using the elements and principles in their still lifes. Have students carefully describe their use of line and harmony in their works. Have students work with classmates to determine whether others can identify the shapes they wished to emphasize. Ask students then to make notes about what they would do differently in creating another abstract still life.

Creating an Expressive Collage

Objectives

■ Complete a nonobjective paper collage.

■ Express as clearly as possible a one-word idea in visual form.

Motivator

Discuss possible one-word ideas that might serve as a theme for a nonobjective collage. (Possibilities might include joy, confusion, and despair.) List these on the board as they are suggested by students. Encourage them to proceed beyond the more obvious ideas that are mentioned first. Another approach involves reading a short story, poem, or newspaper article in class. Ask students to identify in their own minds the emotion or feeling it aroused in them. They should be cautioned not to tell other students what that emotion or feeling might be. Later, during discussions centering on the finished works, students will attempt to determine the various feelings and emotions represented.

Critiquing

Have students apply the steps of art criticism to their own artworks using the Critiquing questions on this page.

Creating an Expressive Collage

Materials

- Pictures and print material torn from magazines and newspapers
- Mat board or poster board, 12 × 18 inches or larger
- White glue
- Brushes, mixing tray, and paint cloth
- Water container
- Colored tissue paper
- Watercolor paints

Complete a nonobjective *papier collé,* or "collage," that communicates a one-word idea such as *lonely, lost, joyful, afraid, excited.* Your finished composition will exhibit a concern for the expressive qualities favored by emotionalism.

Inspiration

Look through *Art in Focus* for illustrations of artworks that stress the communication of ideas, moods, and feelings. Identify one of these that is highly abstract or nonobjective. How does this work succeed in communicating an idea, mood, or feeling without the use of realistic subject matter?

Process

1. Identify a one-word idea to use as the theme for your collage. From magazines and newspapers, tear out pages that contain images, words, colors, and textures you associate with this idea.

2. Tear the pages into a variety of large and small irregular shapes, and arrange them on the mat board. Establish a focal point or center of interest for your composition. To do this, contrast the hues, intensities, and values of the shapes placed at this center of interest with the hues, intensities, and values of the surrounding shapes.

3. When you are satisfied with your composition, glue the shapes in place. Use white glue thinned with water and apply with a brush.

4. Use colored tissue paper and applications of opaque and transparent watercolor paint to tone down some areas or highlight others. You may want to accent the center of interest even more with the tissue paper or paint. Choose colors that you associate with the idea, mood, or feeling you want to communicate. You may need to apply several layers of paper and paint to achieve the effect you want.

5. Display your finished collage along with those completed by other members of the class. Try to determine the one-word idea each collage attempts to communicate.

■ **FIGURE 5.19** Student Work

Examining Your Work

Interpret. Does your collage succeed in communicating a one-word idea? Are other students able to identify this idea?

Judge. Do you think that your collage would be favorably received by a critic focusing exclusively on the expressive qualities?

ASSESSMENT

Art Critic Exercise. Place the student works on display and assign a number to each. Place these same numbers on index cards and give one to each student. Tell them to identify the artwork with the number on their card and study it closely. Then, acting as a critic favoring the theory of emotionalism, they are instructed to list the idea, mood, or feeling they derive from the painting. The card is placed next to the artwork. Each student artist is asked to reveal the idea they hoped to communicate with their work. Remind students that different interpretations of art in no way minimize a work's aesthetic value.

Reviewing the Facts

Lesson One

1. During which art history operation does the historian attempt to discover the qualities of an artwork that determine its artistic style?
2. What is an art movement?
3. Where do historians turn to learn how time and place may have influenced an artist?
4. What two factors help determine a work's success to an art historian?

Lesson Two

5. What kinds of art history questions must you answer during description?
6. What should you do before trying to find out how others have judged a work of art?
7. What must you have available in order to successfully complete the art history operations?
8. Where do artists such as Morisot typically find inspiration for their art?

 A R T S O U R C E **DANCE.** Use the *Performing Arts Handbook*, page 581 to learn about Eugene Loring and "Billy the Kid."

Thinking Critically

1. **EXTEND.** Every artist has a unique style that becomes more consistent as the artist gains more experience. Brainstorm to make a list of other things that can be identified by a particular style. Examples might include: typefaces (or fonts), clothing styles, or singing styles.
2. **ANALYZE.** You are a radio commentator in 1917 covering the parade illustrated in Figure 5.2 on page 107. What *highly descriptive* statement will you make to introduce your listeners to the colorful event? Phrase your statement so that it arouses your listeners' interest while capturing the historical significance of the event. Along with other members of the class, read your statement as you might over the radio. Which statement is the most effective?

CAREERS IN If you enjoy studying or creating art, read about a fascinating art-related career opportunity in the *Careers in Art Handbook*, page 594.

*inter*NET
CONNECTION Visit Glencoe Art Online at *www.glencoe.com/sec/art*. Explore art history, artworks, and museums. Learn more about art and artists in an online activity.

 ## Technology Project

Media and Art History

The basic types of sculpture—bas relief, high relief, and in the round—figure prominently in the history of art, and have done so for thousands of years. The processes that the sculptor works with—modeling, carving, casting, and assembly—are equally old. Tackle this problem with members of a group to help you to better understand these sculptural types and processes and how they relate to art history.

1. Using a word-processing program, and an image scanning program, create files on your computer for each of the time periods and cultures listed in the table of contents of this book.

2. With the help of resources such as books, the Internet, CD-ROMs and laser discs, look for a visual example of a sculpture for each period and culture.
3. Using a scanner, scan in an image of one sculpture from each period/culture, and store it in an image file.
4. Examine the style and form of sculptures over the centuries. Critique each piece by writing your responses to the questions that follow.
5. What type of subject matter is seen in the artwork? How has the artist used the art elements, organized according to the art principles, to put the work together? What do you think it means? Do you think it is a successful work of art?
6. Next, using the art history operations, find information about the artists and origins of these artworks. Prepare a multimedia presentation to share with the class.

 ## Teaching the Technology Project

Assist students in locating art image archives on the World Wide Web by directing them to appropriate pre-screened sources, and at using the "Import" command in your presentation software to introduce the various file formats. Keep in mind that this file will take up disk space. Restart the computer prior to each presentation.

A R T S O U R C E Assign the feature in the *Performing Arts Handbook*, page 581.

CAREERS IN ART If time permits, have interested students investigate the career information in the *Careers in Art Handbook*, page 594.

*inter*NET **CONNECTION** Have students go online and learn more about artists on preselected Web sites with the Internet activity for this chapter.

Reviewing the Facts

1. During analysis.
2. This term describes a group of artists who share a similar style.
3. Historians refer to several sources including history books, biographies, magazine articles, and published interviews.
4. If it is the first expression of a new style or technique, or if it is an outstanding example of an artist's fully developed style.
5. Description questions are: Who created the work? Where was it done? When was it done?
6. You should first make your own decisions about it.
7. You must have access to historical resources such as books and articles.
8. Most artists find inspiration in the works of others. Morisot, for example, was greatly influenced by the works in the Louvre, her studies with Corot, and her close association with Manet.

Thinking Critically

1. Answers, which will vary, should reveal a grasp of the essential points of the chapter.
2. Statements, which will vary, might include the following: *vibrant, hectic, bright, blurred, hushed.*

UNIT 2

Art of Early Civilizations

Unit Two introduces the beginnings of human art, from the earliest cave paintings, rock carvings, and prehistoric structures to the highly developed art of the ancient Egyptians.

Chapter 6 *Art of Earliest Times* concentrates on cave paintings in France and Spain, with an introduction to rock carvings and megaliths such as Stonehenge in England, and introduces students to the civilization, cultures, and artworks from ancient Mesopotamia.

Chapter 7 *The Art of Ancient Egypt* covers the history of and art discoveries from this early civilization, including the great Sphinx, pyramids, and artifacts such as portrait sculpture and relief carvings.

124

More About...   **Cave Painting.** Ask students to imagine that they unexpectedly came upon a painting like this in a hidden cave in or near their own community. What would their reaction be? What words would they use to describe the work? What would they imagine the artist or artists intended when this work was created? Would they assume the work could have originated thousands of years ago? Why or why not?

Art of Early Civilizations

"I could not dream of painting as well as these cave men painted before the dawn of time."

Henri Matisse
French painter (1869–1954)

Cave paintings. c. 15,000 to 10,000 B.C.
Near Bilbao, Spain.

125

Introducing the Unit

Write the term *prehistoric* on the board, and ask students to analyze the term into its parts (i.e., *pre-* and *historic*). Ask: When did history begin? What was the cutoff point between prehistory and history? Then ask students to brainstorm possible explanations for why men and women of primitive societies might have produced the kind of artworks that have been discovered dating back as far as 10,000 years. Have students imagine what life was like for prehistoric human beings. Ask: What were the priorities and goals of people living in undeveloped societies? How did these people spend their days? Did they have any forms of entertainment?

Discussing the Quotation

Ask students to find examples of Matisse's works in Chapter 23. In what ways do this artist's paintings exhibit qualities found in the prehistoric painting? Point out that Matisse's work, like those of prehistoric artists, strips away unnecessary details to create easy-to-recognize images. Instruct students to make a drawing of a still life consisting of three intricate objects in which they eliminate all unnecessary details but still make it possible for viewers to identify each object.

Teacher Notes

Art of Earliest Times

ADDITIONAL CHAPTER RESOURCES

Activities

- 📁 Advanced Studio Activity 6
- 📁 Application 6
- 🖱 Chapter 6 Internet Activity
- 📁 Studio Activity 8

Fine Art Resources

📇 **Transparency**

Art in Focus Transparency 9
  Group of Votive Statuettes, from the Square Temple of
  the god Abu. Tell Asmar, Iraq

🖼 **Fine Art Print**

Focus on World Art Print 6
  Lion Passant. Babylon, Temple of Ishtar

Assessment

- 📁 Chapter 6 Test
- 📁 Performance Assessment

Multimedia Resources

- 🎭 Artsource® Performing Arts Package
- 💿 National Gallery Laser disc
- 💿 National Museum of Women in the Arts CD-ROM
- 📼 Arts & Entertainment Videos

NATIONAL STANDARDS FOR ARTS EDUCATION

The National Standards for Arts Education provide guidelines for grade-appropriate competency in the visual arts. The Content Standards for grades 9–12 are:

1. Understanding and applying media, techniques, and processes.
2. Using knowledge of structures and functions.
3. Choosing and evaluating a range of subject matter, symbols, and ideas.
4. Understanding the visual arts in relation to history and cultures.
5. Reflecting upon and assessing the characteristics and merits of their work and the work of others.
6. Making connections between visual arts and other disciplines.

Listed below are the National Standards for the Visual Arts addressed in this chapter. For a breakdown of the categories listed under each content standard, refer to the *Reproducible Lesson Plans* booklet in the TCR.

1. (a, b)   **2.** (a, b)   **3.** (a, b)   **4.** (a, b, c)   **5.** (a, b, c)   **6.** (a)

HANDBOOK MATERIAL

ARTSOURCE Performing Arts
(page 576)

CAREERS IN *Art*

(page 596)

Beyond the Classroom

The Getty Institute for the Arts in Education and ArtsEdNet provides valuable teaching strategies and curriculum ideas. Connect to them by visiting our Web site at *www.glencoe.com/sec/art*.

🕐 **Out of Time?**   If time does not permit teaching this chapter in its entirety, you may wish to preview the artwork and captions with students. Scan the heads in each lesson with students. Discuss the Looking Closely features and examine Symbolism in Akkadian Art on page 138.

Art of Earliest Times

Art of Earliest Times

CHAPTER 6

INTRODUCE

Chapter Overview

This chapter traces the growth of art from its origins in prehistoric times to a small, fertile plain between the Tigris and Euphrates Rivers in southwest Asia, the birthplace of Western civilization.

Lesson One Introduces students to life during prehistoric times and to the art and architecture of the earliest humans.

Lesson Two Helps students learn from and about the art produced by civilizations in the Tigris-Euphrates Valley.

Studio Lessons Have students draw and then make a model of an animal in motion.

Art & Language Arts

Have students read the Language Arts feature as they begin this chapter. Tell students that the earliest pictures created by humans are seen in cave paintings illustrated in Lesson One. In Lesson Two they will examine an early form of writing (Figure 6.11). Discuss with them how written communication developed in early civilizations.

Art & Language Arts ■ **FIGURE 6.1** About the time this relief sculpture was carved, an alphabet with similar origins in the Middle East was being spread throughout the Mediterranean area by traders. Known as the Phoenician alphabet, it consisted of 22 letters, written from left to right. Around 88 B.C. the Greeks adopted it. Today it is recognized as the ancestor of all modern European alphabets.

Ishtar Gate, Dragon of Marduk. Neo-Babylonian-Mesopotamian. c. 604 B.C. Terra cotta. 115.6 × 167 cm (45 1/2 × 65 3/4"). The Detroit Institute of Arts, Detroit, Michigan. Founders Society Purchase, General Membership Fund.

126

National Standards

This chapter addresses the following National Standards for the Visual Arts.

1. (a,b)	**4.** (a,b,c)
2. (a,b)	**5.** (a,b,c)
3. (a,b)	**6.** (a)

CHAPTER 6 RESOURCES

Teacher's Classroom Resources

📁 Advanced Studio Activity 6
📁 Application 6
🖱 Chapter 6 Internet Activity
📁 Studio Activity 8

Assessment

📁 Chapter 6 Test
📁 Performance Assessment

Fine Art Resources

 Art in Focus Transparency 9
    Group of Votive Statuettes
 Focus on World Art Print 6
    Lion Passant

*A̶rt is one of humankind's earliest and highest achievements.
Long before they could write or fashion crude metal
tools, our prehistoric ancestors were creating images on the walls of
cave dwellings. Eventually, people learned to extend their
control over nature and began to use it for their own purposes.
Abandoning cave dwellings, they built homes,
domesticated animals, and raised crops. They gathered together
as families, clans, and tribes, and these grew into villages,
towns, and cities. An advanced stage of human development marked
by a high level of art, religion, science, and social and
political organization gradually evolved. Civilization was
born. One of the first great civilizations developed in Mesopotamia.*

YOUR Portfolio

Create a replication of cave art for your portfolio by rolling a large piece of blank paper into a ball. Flatten the paper and note the creases and lines that resemble the uneven surface and texture of a cave's wall. First, study the pattern of the lines and creases and imagine how you would trace the surface lines to resemble the shape of an animal. After taking time to study the paper, use felt markers or pencils to sketch the outline of an animal. Keep your sketched cave art in your portfolio to compare to works you will be preparing in later chapters.

Focus ON THE ARTS

LITERATURE
In Babylonia, the great poem, *The Epic of Gilgamesh,* influenced Mesopotamian literature and the Greek *Iliad* and *Odyssey.* Babylonian writers, inspired by the Phoenicians, invented a written system that helped pave the way for modern alphabets.

MUSIC
In Sumeria, around 3000 B.C., a great musical tradition developed. Songs were sung with harps, reed pipes, drums, trumpets, and tambourines. Secular works included love songs, victory songs, and work songs. Musical instruments were buried with kings to accompany them in death.

DANCE
From the Neolithic period through the eras of Mesopotamian kingdoms, dance arose as a form of religious expression and as a way of honoring and communicating with the dead. It incorporated pantomime, masks, and storytelling.

127

Introducing the Chapter

Divide the class into two groups and identify one as "prehistoric cave dwellers," and the other as "city dwellers in a newly emerging ancient civilization." Have students in each group identify the things they might see around them. Ask them to describe the various activities they might be involved with during a typical day. Ask them to speculate on the role the arts might play in their lives.

Focus ON THE ARTS

Tell students that early civilizations took part in what is called an "image dance," a dance whose gestures, steps, and masks symbolically represented the renewal of life. Divide the class into four teams. Ask each team to design a dance representing the eclipse of the sun, in three sections: before, during, and after the eclipse. They can use masks, a drum, and a flute. They can incorporate all or some of the village members. Remind them that dance can include forming circles, and hand movements. Afterward, have each group report on their experiences.

| **DEVELOPING A PORTFOLIO** | **Assessment.** Because portfolios ultimately are evaluated in one form or another, students should understand how a knowledge of aesthetics will help set standards for success. The art criticism operations in "Examining Your Work" in the Studio Lessons, and the various approaches to evaluation of artworks found in the | lessons are principally designed to help students understand and develop criteria for assessment. Their active involvement in critical evaluation processes teaches them that evaluation is not an arbitrary judgment; rather, it reinforces the concept of standards as a definition of performance within accepted boundaries. |

Prehistoric Art in Western Europe

Focus

Lesson Objectives

After studying this lesson, students will be able to:
■ Offer a reasonable explanation as to why prehistoric people created art.
■ Recognize and examine examples of prehistoric cave paintings.

Building Vocabulary

Write the word part *-lith* on the board and ask students to think of words they have seen that contain this stem. Explain that this word part means "stone." Challenge students to brainstorm definitions of *megalith* and *Paleolithic period*.

Motivator

Bring to class a selection of natural materials representing primitive art media (for example, rock, stick, piece of charcoal, colored leaves, roots). Display the items and ask students to think about what kind of art could be created using these natural materials. Ask students to discuss whether they feel it would be possible to create artworks that would last thousands of years using these primitive tools.

Introducing the Lesson

Direct students' attention to the cave painting in Figure 6.2 and to the credit line. Have students note both the estimated date of completion of the painting and the fact that no media are listed. Ask: What tools and media do you suppose artists of this era used to paint? What was their purpose in creating works like this one?

128

Prehistoric Art in Western Europe

Vocabulary
■ Paleolithic period
■ megaliths
■ post-and-lintel construction

Discover
After completing this lesson, you will be able to:
■ Explain why prehistoric cave paintings may have originated.
■ Explain how prehistoric paintings survived.
■ Describe the manner in which prehistoric paintings were created.

*M*uch of our knowledge about the lives of early human beings comes from their art. Before people could write or use metal to make tools, they were painting and scratching pictures of animals on the uneven walls of caves and rock shelters. This was a remarkable achievement when you consider what it must have been like to live in a world in which each person fought a daily battle for survival. The lives of prehistoric people were filled with danger, hunger, and fear.

Art of Prehistoric People

It is difficult to understand why our prehistoric ancestors took time to produce art. Certainly it would be reasonable to expect that the artworks they did create would be primitive and crude, but are they? Before you answer this question, take the time to examine an example of prehistoric art.

The Cave Paintings of Altamira
■ FIGURE 6.2

One noteworthy example of prehistoric art is a painting of a bison from the ceiling in Altamira (Figure 6.2). Notice the accurate proportions of the animal. Look for any indication of what the bison might be doing.

As you examine the bison from Altamira, notice that the animal is not placed in a setting. There is no hint of the ground beneath its hooves, nor are there signs of trees, hills, or sky behind the bison. What effect does this have on the animal's apparent size and its position in space?

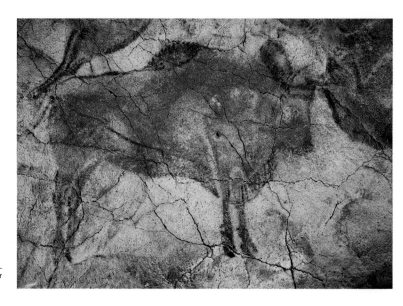

■ **FIGURE 6.2** Examine this painting carefully. Does the animal look lifelike? Can you identify its main feature?

Bison. Cave painting. Altamira Caves. Near Santillana, Spain. c. 15,000–10,000 B.C.

128

LESSON ONE RESOURCES

Teacher's Classroom Resources

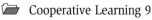 Appreciating Cultural Diversity 7

📁 Cooperative Learning 9

📁 Enrichment 13

📁 Reproducible Lesson Plan 13

📁 Reteaching 13

📁 Study Guide 13

Determining the Age of Prehistoric Art

There is much uncertainty among historians and archaeologists about the early dates of human development. Many experts believe that the earliest known works of human achievement were made during an age that began some 30,000 years ago.

The age of cave paintings and artifacts produced thousands of years ago can be determined by several means. One way is to date the artifact according to the age of the surrounding earth layer. Another way is radiocarbon dating of once-living objects found near the artifact. In general, all living organisms maintain a known amount of radioactive carbon 14. After an organism's death, the carbon 14 loses its radioactivity at a known rate. By measuring how much radioactivity is left in charcoal or carbonized bones, for instance, it is possible to determine their age.

When these objects are found in caves where prehistoric paintings are located, scholars are able to determine the approximate date the paintings were produced. Since dating methods are constantly being improved, scholars may eventually have to revise some of their estimates.

The Paleolithic Period

Because a study of the history of art must start somewhere, we can look back in time to a period known as the Paleolithic period. The **Paleolithic period**—also called the Old Stone Age—is *the historical period believed to have lasted from 30,000 B.C. until about 10,000 B.C.* There you will find these earliest works—the vivid, lifelike pictures of animals painted on the rough ceilings and walls of caves.

The Cave Paintings of Lascaux
■ **FIGURE 6.3**

In caves in southern France and northern Spain are numerous paintings, so skillfully created and so well preserved that they caused great controversy among scholars when they were discovered. Those who examined the animal paintings in the cave of Lascaux in the Dordogne region of southern France questioned whether cave people, working with the most primitive instruments, could have produced such splendid works of art (Figure 6.3). Some suggested that these paintings might be the work of skilled artists from a more recent time.

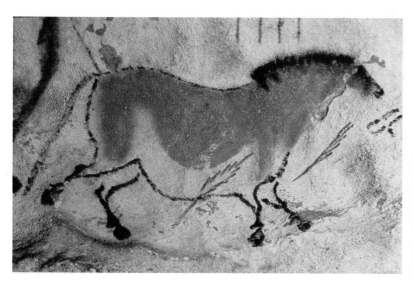

■ **FIGURE 6.3** When this and other paintings were first discovered, many people doubted they could be the work of prehistoric artists. How has the artist suggested action in this work?

Chinese Horse. Cave painting. Lascaux Caves, Dordogne, France. c. 15,000–10,000 B.C.

Chapter 6 *Art of Earliest Times* **129**

CHAPTER 6
LESSON ONE

TEACH
Critical Thinking
Ask students to consider the beginning paragraph of the lesson about lifestyles of early humans. Ask them: Why did primitive humans take time out to create works of art?

Cross Curriculum
SCIENCE Point out that before the discovery of carbon 14 dating, archaeologists relied on other techniques to prove the antiquity of artifacts. Have groups of students investigate some of these early methods, such as indications of geological activity within the cave itself, the growth of moss on the surfaces of the drawings, and the appearance in the drawings of long-extinct animals like the auroch. Set aside class time for an information exchange during which groups share their findings.

Art Criticism
Review with students the four art-criticism operations. Then walk them through these steps as they examine the Chinese horse painting in Figure 6.3. Direct students to the painting of a bison completed at approximately the same time (Figure 6.5, page 132). Divide the class into groups and challenge them to perform a similar examination. Have groups compare their observations.

More About... | **Paleolithic Peoples.** The people of the Paleolithic times are called Cro-Magnon. They lived during a period that geologists today call the Ice Age or Pleistocene era, so called because of the great sheets of ice moving over parts of what is now North America and northern Europe. During the earlier part of the Ice Age, the Cro-Magnons used rocks as tools. Later, they discovered that bone, which was not as brittle, was more useful for their purposes. They used bone to manufacture eating utensils, small weapons, and the needles with which they made cloth. It is believed that they even constructed homes from the rib bones and skins of the mammoth.

Art Criticism

Have students examine the wall paintings in this chapter. Display works done by artists of the early 1900s, such as Picasso, Modigliani, and Matisse. Ask students whether they notice any similarities between the prehistoric paintings and one or more of these artists of recent vintage. Have students comment on the use of shape and other art elements. What role might these similarities play in the difficulty some critics have had in accepting the apparent age of cave paintings?

Art History

Direct students' attention to the cave paintings in this lesson. Point out that works like these represent a capacity for abstraction in human thought. Ask students to consider the development of this thinking process. What event or events may have triggered the abstract thoughts required to create art? How did artwork intermingle with the physical, emotional, and spiritual aspects of the lives of primitive peoples? Have students share their thoughts and theories.

Cross Curriculum

SCIENCE Point out to students that scientists are constantly revising the dates when the first hominids (early humans) were present. Have interested students research the 3.5-million-year-old partial skeleton dubbed Lucy. In a report to the class, volunteers should attempt to find illustrations or descriptions of Lucy's appearance and indicate the species to which she belonged.

Today scholars agree that the paintings discovered at Lascaux and at Altamira are the work of prehistoric artists. It is unlikely that they are the first works of art ever created. They are too sophisticated for that. No doubt they were preceded by hundreds, perhaps thousands, of years of slow development about which nothing is yet known.

Use of Paintings in Hunting Rituals

During prehistoric times, cave painting was limited almost entirely to the depiction of animals. This was probably due to prehistoric people's dependence on animals for food. The painting of animals almost certainly played a part in magic rituals performed before a hunt.

Before taking up their clubs and spears, prehistoric hunters may have turned to magic to place a spell over their prey. This was intended to weaken it and make it easier to hunt. The magic may have involved a ceremony in which an image of the animal was painted on the wall or ceiling of the cave. The hunters probably believed that, by drawing a lifelike picture of an animal, they were capturing some of that animal's strength and spirit.

Such prehistoric hunting rituals probably bolstered the confidence and the courage of the hunters, who were convinced that their prey would be weaker and easier to kill. In some ways, these prehistoric rituals were like some of the rituals we practice today. A high school pep rally with its rousing cheers and inspiring music serves much the same purpose. It builds confidence and courage in team members just as the hunting ritual may have done for prehistoric hunters.

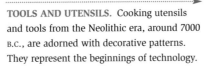

CONNECTIONS
Prehistoric Art
c. 15,000–1000 B.C.

PETROGLYPHS. Symbols carved in stone by settlers in prehistoric North America give us a glimpse into belief systems and ways of life just as the cave paintings of Lascaux and Altamira do.

TOOLS AND UTENSILS. Cooking utensils and tools from the Neolithic era, around 7000 B.C., are adorned with decorative patterns. They represent the beginnings of technology.

Photos © Ara Guler/Magnum Photos, Inc.

ARCHAEOLOGY SITE. Evidence of the movements of early people are found in these footprints. They were fossilized into volcanic ash millions of years ago in Africa.

*A*ctivity **Diary Entry.** Imagine you are at an archaeology site and have discovered an artifact similar to the ones pictured here. Write notes about what you have found, and then prepare a report to a museum curator who may be interested in your discoveries.

Time & Place
CONNECTIONS
Prehistoric Art

Have students examine the images in the Time & Place feature and assign the activity. Students should include in their diary entry a description of the artifact they have found. Encourage them to follow the description step in the art criticism operations outlined in Chapter 4. Students may include information describing the conditions or a fictitious location where they made their discovery. Suggest to students that they examine credit lines and captions of images in this chapter to get ideas on what to include in their reports to the museum.

Survival and Discovery of Cave Paintings

Utensils, bones, and charcoal from numerous campfires found at the mouths of caves suggests that the Stone Age occupants lived there to take advantage of the daylight and ventilation. A special place farther back in the cave was set aside for magic rituals, and this was where the paintings were done. There they were protected from the wind and rain, and for this reason many paintings have survived to the present day. Unfortunately, many others were washed away by underground rivers.

The discoveries of prehistoric paintings at both the caves of Lascaux in 1941 and Altamira in 1879 were quite accidental. The Lascaux cave was found by two boys playing in a field with their dog. The dog fell down a hole and was trapped in a cave. Frantically searching for a way to reach the dog, the boys discovered another, larger hole nearby. Cautiously they crawled down into it. They lit matches and illuminated the magnificent paintings of animals on the cavern surfaces.

Some 70 years earlier near the village of Santillana (Figure 6.4), another dog played a similar key role in discovering the cave of Altamira. A hunter's dog fell into a hole that proved to be the blocked entrance to an unknown cave.

Several years later, Marcelino de Sautuola, an amateur archaeologist excavated inside the cavern, uncovering a number of flint and stone tools made in prehistoric times. One day de Sautuola's five-year-old daughter went along with him to the cave. The father had to bend over as he went into the chamber, but the little girl was able to walk upright. She glanced up at the ceiling and screamed for joy. Her father raised his own

■ **FIGURE 6.4** Most of the cave sites used by prehistoric people were situated on a rise offering a view of the surrounding countryside. **How do you think this view helped them as hunters?**

View of countryside around the Altamira Cave. Near Santillana and Picos, Spain.

Aesthetics

Direct students' attention again to the cave paintings in Figures 6.3 (page 129) and 6.5 (page 132). Ask them to imagine that the artists of these works had assigned titles to them, and have individual students devise possibilities based on aesthetic qualities of the paintings. Indicate these titles on the board and have students decide which is best suited for each of the works.

Studio Skills

Have students attach large sheets of butcher paper to a wall of the classroom with masking tape, leaving one side of the paper untaped to form a pocket. After stuffing the pocket with tightly wadded newspaper, have students tape the fourth side.

Have students place chairs and other potentially hazardous obstacles on one side of the classroom. Then, darkening the room, lead students by dim flashlight or candle light to the textured "cave wall" they have created. Holding the light source aloft to illuminate the wall, provide students with crayons in various earth hues and invite them to create their own cave drawing. Challenge them to include the art elements and principles emphasized in the paintings of Lascaux and Altamira. When students have completed their work, they may "sign" it by blowing baking soda through a drinking straw to produce an outline of their hand.

CULTURAL DIVERSITY

Families. Point out to students that, although we know little of the origins and way of life of prehistoric peoples, it is generally assumed that prehistoric societies were made up of small family groups not unlike the family units we know today. Have interested groups investigate anthropologists' speculations on the nature and quality of family life four thousand years ago. (The school librarian and/or reference catalog should help them isolate the necessary print resources.) Have students determine what motivated the first families to stay together. What was a typical day like for members of a family? Did children work? Were there leisure activities? Have groups make presentations to the class.

Did You Know?

The early artists painted high on the cave walls and ceilings. The cave ceiling in Altamira, Spain, has been called the Sistine Chapel of Paleolithic culture.

LOOKING **Closely**

Have students examine the Looking Closely feature and read the details about materials and techniques used by prehistoric artists. Direct students' attention to the animals in Figure 6.5. Have them note the way in which the artist used earth tones to lend unity to this work. Ask what other elements of art are emphasized. Apart from harmony, what principles are used to organize these elements?

Art History

Ask students whether they have ever gazed up at the sky and watched slowly moving clouds. What shapes did they see in the clouds? Explain that just as they saw shapes in the clouds, early people saw shapes in the rocks of their cave homes. Add that the flickering of the firelight may have enhanced those images and inspired the imaginations of prehistoric artists.

Aesthetics

Have students note the size of the cave paintings indicated on this page, and have them imagine they are viewing the paintings in this lesson at their original size. How would this add to the dramatic impact of the works? What mood or sensations might the works convey at their original size that they fail to communicate through reproductions in a book?

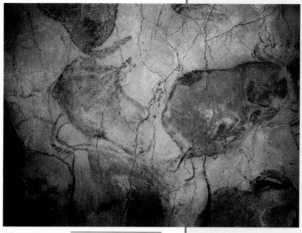

■ **FIGURE 6.5** Two Bison (one crouching). Hall of the Bison. Altamira Caves, Spain. c. 15,000–11,000 B.C.

LOOKING **Closely**

MATERIALS AND PROCESSES

A close examination of this cave painting at Altamira reveals some of the details about how the artist worked with available materials to create this work.

- **Pigment.** The fresh, vivid color makes it seem as if the animals had just been painted. The pigments, or coloring mixture, were made from lumps of clay and soft stone that were ground into fine powder. They were then mixed with animal fat, blood, or some other medium.
- **Brushes.** The pigment was applied to the smoothest surfaces with the fingers, although more advanced techniques— perhaps involving some kind of reed or bristle brush—were also used.
- **Technique.** The artist scratched the outline of the animal on the stone and then filled in the lines with black or dark brown pigment to give it a firm edge. Next, the animal was filled in with different shades of reddish brown hue. This shading technique helped create the impression of a three-dimensional form.

gaze to the ceiling just above his head. There he saw for the first time the painted images of bison, boar, wild horses, and deer.

De Sautuola knew that the cave had been visited by only a few hunters since its discovery. He was convinced from the outset that the paintings dated from the Stone Age. He believed they were the work of the same prehistoric people who had made the tools found earlier in the cave. After similar paintings were uncovered in southern France in 1896, de Sautuola's amazing discovery was recognized as authentic.

Skills of the Prehistoric Artists

At Altamira the low cave ceiling is covered with animals painted in shades of red, brown, and black (Figure 6.5). At

least 16 bison are grouped in the center of the ceiling. Surrounding them are two boars and a deer. A smaller deer painted over a horse is located nearby. It was not uncommon for Stone Age artists to paint on top of earlier paintings when they ran out of space.

Perhaps the most surprising thing about the paintings is their size. A deer at the far end of the chamber is almost 6.5 feet long, while most of the other animals average around 5 feet. The way in which many of the animals have been painted on the uneven rock surfaces seems to accent the swelling muscles and hollows of their bodies.

Though their tools were crude, prehistoric artists were able to demonstrate a knowledge and an affection for the animals they hunted. What they knew and felt was combined with a sensitive artistic instinct. This

COOPERATIVE LEARNING

Time Lines. To help students grasp the full import of the findings described in this lesson, have them devise a time line covering the period from 35,000 B.C. through the New Stone Age (1,000 B.C.). The time line may begin with the dates of early cave paintings. Then have students research and include such milestones as the invention of the potter's wheel and the discovery of writing in Sumerian temples. Encourage students to include events of the New World at this time, such as the rise of Olmec culture in Mexico (Chapter 11). Once students have completed their time line, have them conduct an informal debate in which each student states what he or she considers to be the most important event of the period, and why.

enabled them to capture in paint the power of a bison, the fleetness of a horse, the gentleness of deer.

Prehistoric Builders

Eventually prehistoric peoples ventured out of their caves to begin building more comfortable shelters. Small communities developed, and hunters replaced their weapons with crude farming tools and shepherds' staffs. In time, communities grew into organized villages surrounded by cornfields and grazing animals.

Rock Carvings and Standing Stones

Abstract symbols were carved into stone by prehistoric people during the Paleolithic period. Spirals and concentric arcs appear etched in standing stones, as well as on flat rock surfaces. Detailed relief sculptures carved in stone or horn survive as evidence of prehistoric artists' carving skills (Figure 6.6). Rock carvings have been discovered throughout England, Spain, France, and Germany, as well as Malta and the Canary Islands.

Today ancient **megaliths,** or *large monuments created from huge stone slabs,* lie scattered across Europe, India, Asia, and even the Americas. Remnants of primitive stone art have been discovered all across the globe. Archaeologists once thought that the skills in building and design demonstrated by the megalith builders had originated from more advanced civilizations in the Near East. As more accurate research becomes available, it appears that the architectural methods of prehistoric peoples developed independently in several geographical areas, perhaps earlier than previously believed.

Stonehenge
■ FIGURE 6.7

As early as 4000 B.C., unusual circular arrangements of huge, rough-hewn stones were being erected in western Europe. The most famous of these is at Stonehenge in England (Figure 6.7, page 134). Built in several stages around 2000 B.C., Stonehenge consists of a large ring of stones with three progressively smaller rings within. The outermost ring is nearly 100 feet in diameter. Of the 30 original upright stones, more than half are still standing. The tallest of these is about 17 feet and weighs over 50 tons. Stonehenge is an early example of **post-and-lintel construction,** in which *massive posts support crossbeams, or lintels.*

■ **FIGURE 6.6** This relief sculpture, executed on a piece of horn, exhibits the artist's skill in sculpting and incising to show form and value. **What other elements of art can you identify in this work?**

Bison Licking its Back. Magdalenian Era, Early Middle Stone Age. Bone. 10.5 cm (4¹/₈"). From La Madeleine, Dordogne, France. Musée des Antiquités, St. Germain-en-Laye, France.

Chapter 6 *Art of Earliest Times* **133**

COOPERATIVE LEARNING

Petroglyphs. Point out that numerous prehistoric petroglyphs and pictographs on stone outcroppings have been found in the southwestern United States. Add that these artifacts, which were used to ensure both a bountiful harvest and human fertility, are strikingly similar to objects unearthed in Europe. Have a group of interested students investigate this curious phenomenon. Is it possible that tribes traveled between continents? What other theories have been advanced to account for the presence of these artifacts on land masses separated by vast bodies of water? Have the group share its findings in the form of an illustrated report.

Critical Thinking

Point out that, in addition to the cave paintings shown here, archaeologists have uncovered prehistoric examples of jewelry made from animal teeth and polished stone. Explain to students one commonly held theory is that this jewelry was used as an emblem of rank or status. Ask students to name objects in contemporary cultures that are used for the same purposes. In particular, what are some of the indicators of status among people their own age? Are these material possessions a fair estimation of a person's value?

Aesthetics

Have a student report on the Japanese art form called *nesuke,* which is the carving of tiny animals in a stylized form. The report should include illustrations of these extremely delicate creations, some of which are found in museums throughout the world. The report should also draw parallels between *nesuke* and the tiny sculptures created by prehistoric artists.

Aesthetics

Architecture has been called the "mother of all the arts." Have students decide whether the prehistoric artifacts covered in this chapter support this contention. In other words, is Stonehenge (Figure 6.7, page 134) a greater monumental artistic achievement than the cave paintings, or is the reverse true?

Study Guide

Distribute *Study Guide* 13 in the TCR. Assist students in reviewing key concepts. ▱

Studio Activities

Assign *Studio* 8, "Painting with Natural Pigments," in the TCR. ▱

Studio Activities

Assign *Cooperative Learning* 9, "Exploring Artistic Styles," in the TCR. Students examine the ways artists throughout history have used movement to draw and paint. 📁

ASSESS

Checking Comprehension

➤ Have students complete the lesson review questions. Answers appear in the box below.

➤ Distribute *Application* 6, "Arti-FACTS," in the TCR. The activity provides students with facts and figures relating to artifacts from prehistoric times. 📁

Reteaching

Assign *Reteaching* 13, found in the TCR. Have students complete the activity and review their responses. 📁

Enrichment

Have students complete *Enrichment* 13, "Figure Drawing," in the TCR. 📁

Extension

Ask students to investigate crafts of the New Stone Age (Neolithic period). Ask: What crafts did primitive peoples create? Do these crafts make use of designs similar to those found in the cave paintings and carvings?

CLOSE

Have students select one of the artworks from the chapter and use it as the basis of a one-page essay titled "Why Prehistoric Art Is Worth Studying."

134

Questions concerning Stonehenge have baffled scholars for centuries. What purpose did this prehistoric monument serve? How did people working with the most primitive tools quarry and transport these huge stone blocks across many miles? How did they raise the blocks into position? Today most scholars think it served as a kind of astronomical observatory, enabling prehistoric people to make accurate predictions about the seasons.

Whatever its purpose, the impact of Stonehenge is undeniable. Mysterious, massive, and silent, it is a durable testament to the emerging ingenuity of our prehistoric ancestors.

■ **FIGURE 6.7**
Scholars still do not know how or why the huge stone blocks of this monument were erected. **What feeling or emotions does it arouse?**
_____
Stonehenge. Wiltshire, England. c. 2000 B.C.

LESSON ONE REVIEW

Reviewing Art Facts

1. How did prehistoric artists give their cave paintings a three-dimensional look?
2. Within the caves where prehistoric paintings have been found, where are the paintings located? What does their location indicate?
3. What is a megalith?
4. Give an example of post-and-lintel construction.

▶ **Activity . . . *Prehistoric Images in Plaster***

Realism in prehistoric paintings came from the artist's attention to three-dimensional form and the addition of essential details.

Create an animal image in plaster. Fill a medium-size plastic bag with wet plaster and hold it until the plaster has set. Remove the plaster form and examine it closely, looking for bulges and hollows that suggest an animal form. Outline the shape of the animal with black tempera or acrylic paint. Fill it in with a single color of paint. Use gradual changes of value to emphasize the animal's rounded form. With a small brush, add details to help identify the animal. Construct a simulated cave wall by using plaster to join your animal painting with those made by classmates.

LESSON ONE REVIEW

Answers to Reviewing Art Facts

1. By outlining and then filling with shading and gradation.
2. Rituals were held deep in the caves where paintings were protected.
3. A large monument created from a huge stone slab.
4. Stonehenge; megalith posts supporting a large crossbeam.

Activity...*Prehistoric Images in Plaster*

You may wish to prepare the plaster for this activity just before class begins. Use caution when working with dry plaster by wearing a dust mask. Use a plastic mixing bowl and add the water to the bowl first, following measuring directions on the package.

Art of the Fertile Crescent

Vocabulary
- ziggurat
- stylus
- cuneiform
- stele

Discover

After completing this lesson, you will be able to:
- Name the different civilizations that were born, flourished, and declined in Mesopotamia beginning around 4500 B.C.
- Discuss the kinds of artworks created in those civilizations.

$\mathscr{C}$ivilization developed in a few great river valleys where deposits of rich soil produced abundant harvests. It was there that people first settled, and villages and cities began to rise. One of these river valleys extended about 170 miles north of the Persian Gulf, between the Tigris and Euphrates Rivers (Figure 6.8). In time, the flat plain of this valley, with its rich soil, warm summers, and mild winters, came to be known as the Fertile Crescent.

Origins of Civilization in Mesopotamia

Mesopotamia—the eastern part of the Fertile Crescent—attracted settlers from many different areas. Successive tribes fought to possess the land between the Tigris and Euphrates Rivers. Thus, the history of ancient Mesopotamia is a long series of conquests by a variety of peoples.

Sumerian Civilization

Sometime before 4500 B.C., a people from the east known as Sumerians abandoned their wandering, tent-dwelling lifestyle to settle in Mesopotamia. The region they settled was called Sumer. They formed agricultural communities with markets that eventually grew into towns built around high temples. These Sumerian temples served as centers of both spiritual and community life.

Although we know little about who the Sumerians were or exactly when they first appeared in Mesopotamia, we do know that they were a highly gifted and creative people. Before recorded history, they tilled the soil, built houses, constructed levees to control the floodwaters of the Tigris River, drained marshes, and dug irrigation canals. They are believed to have invented wheeled transportation and the potter's wheel. In a land of blazing sun with little rainfall, farming could be carried on only with irrigation. Widespread cooperation was needed to build the irrigation works, keep them in repair, and allocate the water. This need led to the formation of government and laws—and the birth of a civilization.

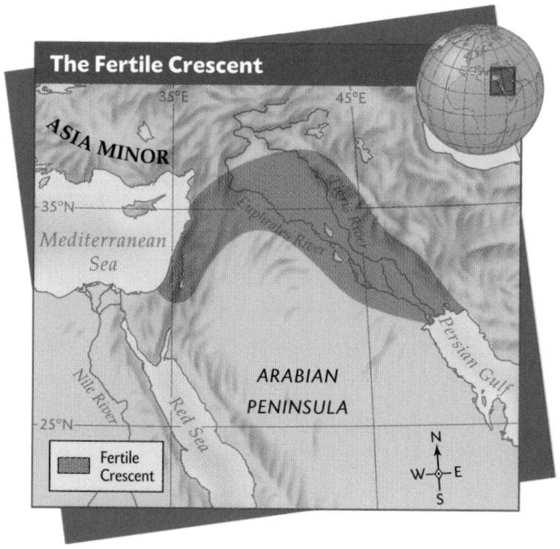

Ziggurats: Symbolic Mountains

There was no Sumerian nation, only small city-states. Each of these city-states grew up around the shrine of a local god. As a city grew in wealth and power, its shrine became more and more elaborate. The name given to these Sumerian shrines was the **ziggurat**, *a stepped mountain*

The Fertile Crescent

ASIA MINOR
Mediterranean Sea
ARABIAN PENINSULA
Nile River
Red Sea
Persian Gulf

Fertile Crescent

MAP SKILLS

■ **FIGURE 6.8** The area between the Tigris River and the Euphrates River has become known as the Fertile Crescent. **What factors might have made this an attractive area for settlement?**

135

LESSON TWO RESOURCES

Teacher's Classroom Resources
- 📁 Appreciating Cultural Diversity 8
- 📁 Art and Humanities 9
- 📁 Enrichment Activity 14
- 📁 Reproducible Lesson Plan 14
- 📁 Reteaching Activity 14
- 📁 Study Guide 14

Art of the Fertile Crescent

FOCUS

Lesson Objectives

After studying this Lesson, students will be able to:
- Explain why civilization took hold on the plain between the Tigris and Euphrates Rivers.
- Identify the Sumerians as the people responsible for establishing the first civilization in Mesopotamia.

Building Vocabulary

Write the term *civilization* on the chalkboard and ask students what it means to them. Tell them that the word comes from the Latin "civis" meaning citizen. Therefore it means that a civilized person is a member of an organized community. Inform them that among the very first of these organized communities were those that appeared in Mesopotamia at the dawn of history.

Motivator

Ask students if they can point to any signs that exist today of a widespread interest in the past. (Examples could include songs of the 1950s, the popularity of historical movies and novels.) Ask them what aspects of the past they are most curious about? Have they ever wondered about the origins of civilization itself?

Introducing the Lesson

Discuss the various reasons why prehistoric peoples may have joined together to form organized communities. Ask students how the art of prehistoric times might change to reflect this new way of life.

135

TEACH

Art Criticism

Have students examine the reconstructed ziggurat illustrated in Figure 6.9. Explain that much of the mud-brick superstructure has been eroded, and only the base remains. Ask for a volunteer to draw a large outline of a complete ziggurat on the chalkboard. Encourage other students to make improvements or changes to this drawing until the class is satisfied with its appearance. Ask students to identify the elements and principles of art exhibited in this drawing. Ask students to speculate on the impact this huge structure might have on a person viewing it for the first time.

Aesthetics

Ask students to identify the most impressive features of the ziggurat. Does the design of the structure complement its function? What does this building tell us about the religious fervor of the people who built it? Is this structure worthy of admiration? Why or why not?

Aesthetics

Direct student's attention to the Lyre Soundbox illustrated in Figure 6.10. Ask students to distinguish between the human and animal features of this work. Have students speculate on the reasons why human and animal features would be combined in a single work of art. Ask students to render a judgment of this work. Did this judgment take into account the fact that this work could be viewed as an example of applied art? Which "label" do they feel more comfortable applying to this work, fine or applied art? Have them explain their reasons.

■ **FIGURE 6.9** At the center of every Sumerian city-state, a ziggurat stood on a huge platform made from clay reinforced with brick and asphalt. Here, one of three stairways, each with a hundred steps, led to the top of the platform. **What role did the ziggurat probably play in the daily lives of the local people?**

Stairway of the reconstructed Ziggurat. Ur, Iraq. c. 2100 B.C.

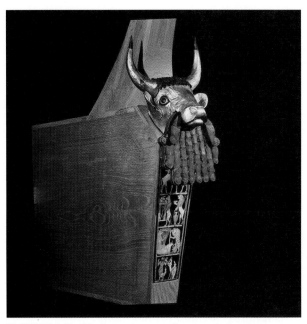

■ **FIGURE 6.10** This elegant lyre soundbox reveals that the Sumerians created music and musical instruments. It also testifies to the skill of early Sumerian artists. **What else can you learn from this work of art?**

Bull-headed lyre soundbox. Ur, Iraq. c. 2685 B.C. Gold, lapis lazuli, shell on wooden reconstruction. University of Pennsylvania Museum, Philadelphia.

made of brick-covered earth. As a towering symbolic mountain, the ziggurat satisfied the desire to create a monument that appeared to span the space between earthbound worshipers and their heavenly gods. The most famous ziggurat, the biblical Tower of Babel, no longer exists, but the still-impressive ruins of others can still be seen rising above the flat plain (Figure 6.9).

Sumerian Decorative Arts

Archaeologists have unearthed evidence of a rich and flourishing civilization at the site of the Sumerian city of Ur. Much of this evidence comes from the ancient cemetery where burial sites were found filled with chariots, jewelry, headdresses, sculpture, and musical instruments.

An impressive sound box from a lyre found in the tomb of a queen testifies to the imagination and skill of Sumerian artists (Figure 6.10). It is decorated with a striking bull's head finished in gold leaf. Lapis lazuli, a semiprecious blue stone, was used to fashion a human beard and other smaller details.

The practice of combining human and animal features in a single work is not uncommon in the art of the ancient Near East. The bull in particular is often represented. The fascination for this animal might be traced to early herders who recognized the animal's power against the wild beasts that threatened their cattle.

Evolution of Writing

Although it is impossible to say with certainty that the Sumerians were the first to develop writing, their writing is the oldest that has come down to us. Like that of other early peoples, the writing of the Sumerians first took the form of picture writing (Figure 6.11). They wrote on clay tablets, pressing rather than scratching lines into the soft, wet clay. To draw their pictures they used a **stylus,** or *writing instrument.* The Sumerian stylus was probably a straight piece of reed with a three-cornered end. With this stylus they could produce triangular forms or wedges, as well as straight lines. Curved

More About... **Sumerian Writing.** On the Sumerian tablets that have been discovered in this century, we find school examinations, ledgers, legal codes, and even lullabies. Also recorded is the heroic epic tale of Gilgamesh who yearns for eternal life. Tell students that an epic is a long poem describing the adventures of a legendary hero. The epic poem, *Gilgamesh,* was recorded before 1800 B.C. Scholars believe that it may be the oldest story in the world. The author or authors probably based the stories of Gilgamesh, a man with superhuman powers who performed heroic deeds, on an actual king of the Sumerian city of Uruk.

lines were made by combining a series of straight strokes. Over time, pictures created through this process lost their form as pictures and became stylized symbols.

The ancient Sumerians were probably the first to develop **cuneiform** writing, or *writing with wedge-shaped characters*. When the writing was completed, the clay tablets were fired, or baked, to make them more durable. In this manner the Sumerians kept records, executed contracts, and created a culture in which the stylus became as important to them as computers are to us today.

Akkadian Period

North and west of the Sumerians, in a region called Akkas, lived a Semitic people eager to add to their territory. By 2340 B.C. an Akkadian king had succeeded in establishing his control over Sumer. Eventually the Akkadian Empire included the entire region between the Mediterranean and the Persian Gulf. This vast empire was short-lived, but while it lasted art and literature flourished. (See Figure 6.13, page 138.)

■ **FIGURE 6.11** Clay tablets like this proved to be very durable when fired. Archaeologists have unearthed thousands of them. **Point out individual marks made in this tablet by a wedge-shaped stylus.**

Clay tablet with cuneiform text. Cast of original from Kish, Iraq. c. 3100 B.C. The British Museum, London, England.

Neo-Sumerian Period

The Akkadian dominance in Mesopotamia ended around 2150 B.C. with a revival of Sumerian culture. This revival, referred to as the Neo-Sumerian period, lasted more than 300 years.

The best-known of the Neo-Sumerian rulers was Gudea. His people honored him for his devotion to religion, literature, and good works. He built temples, promoted learning, and demanded mercy for the weak and helpless. After his death, he was worshiped as a god. Gudea's appearance is known from the many sculpture portraits that have survived to the present.

Seated Gudea
■ **FIGURE 6.12**

One portrait shows the seated ruler with his hands folded as if in prayer (Figure 6.12). The figure is solid, with no openings between the arms and body. The pose is stiff and the proportions squat, but the face appears to be a portrait. The nose, cheeks, and chin are realistically formed, although the eyebrows are incised and stylized. The overall effect is one of quiet dignity—an appropriate effect for a sculpture intended to be placed in a temple.

■ **FIGURE 6.12** In this portrait, the king sits on a low chair in a position of prayer. His hands, with their long fingers, are tightly clasped together. **Identify the most realistic features of the face in this sculpture.**

Seated Gudea. Neo-Sumerian. 2144–2124 B.C. Diorite. 44 cm (17⁵/₁₆"). The Metropolitan Museum of Art, New York. Harris Brisbane Dick Fund, 1959. 59.2.

Chapter 6 *Art of Earliest Times* **137**

Critical Thinking

Tell students that a great quantity of Sumerian art was uncovered at the royal cemetery at Ur by the British archaeologist, Sir Leonard Woolley who conducted excavations there from 1922 to 1934. One of Woolley's most interesting finds was a layer of mud eight feet thick separating an earlier Sumerian town from a later one. Ask students if they can provide any explanation for this.

Studio Skills

Review the manner in which the Sumerians created their form of picture writing. Note especially how they used a series of *straight* strokes to create curved lines. Tell students to cut sheets of different colored construction paper into narrow 1/4-inch strips. Instruct them to complete a picture with recognizable subject matter by cutting these strips to different lengths and gluing them to a sheet of white or black construction paper 12 × 18 inches. Tell them that they must use a series of short strips to create all the curved lines in their pictures.

Did You Know?

The earliest known civilizations developed around the great river valleys in Sumer, Egypt, India, and China between 5,000 and 1,000 B.C.

More About... **The Bull-Headed Lyre Soundbox.** Inform students that a lyre is a stringed instrument of the harp family. Ask them to describe in a single word the sound made by a lyre. Ask them to identify sounds associated with other musical instruments and list these on the chalkboard. As students examine Figure 6.10, explain to them that the bull was revered throughout the Near East and the Mediterranean. Perhaps this animal may have been admired because herdsmen recognized its power against wild beasts and other natural enemies of their flocks.

Studio Skills

Have students examine Figure 6.13 and indicate that Sumerian writing first took the form of picture writing. Over time, their pictures lost their form and became stylized symbols. Instruct students to use india ink and pens to write a sentence in which no fewer than five small pictures are substituted for words. Place the completed works on display and ask the class to read each of the sentences.

Did You Know?

The ancient Akkadians are often referred to as Semites. This word describes the descendents of Shem, one of Noah's three sons.

Symbolism in Akkadian Art

From early times it was the custom of Mesopotamian kings to commission monuments celebrating their military victories such as the one to King Naram-Sin.

The importance of the victorious Akkadian king is emphasized by his large size and his central position at the top of the relief.

 1

The king wears a horned helmet symbolizing his status as a god. He is placed before a triangular mountain with stars shining down on him as he tramples the body of a defeated foe.

 2 Two enemy soldiers confront the Akkadian king, one begging for mercy and another, mortally wounded, attempting to pull an arrow from his neck.

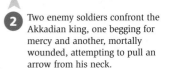 **3** The king's victorious army marches up the mountain. The only casualties shown are those of the king's enemy.

■ **FIGURE 6.13** King Naram-Sin of Akkad in Horned Tiara Near Mountain Summit with Soldiers. 2230 B.C. Sandstone stele. Originally from Mesopotamia, found in Susa, Iran. The Louvre, Paris, France.

138 **Unit Two** *Art of Early Civilizations*

Symbolism in Akkadian Art

Have students examine the illustrations and the text explanations in the feature. Then, write the word *propaganda* on the chalkboard and ask students to provide a definition for it. Direct their attention to the Monument of King Naram-Sin (Figure 6.13) and ask them if this term could be used to describe this work. Have them point to images in the relief that support the claim that this is an example of propaganda art. Refer students to Jacques Louis David's portrait of *Napoleon in His Study* (Figure 21.3, page 468), and ask them to point out how these works are similar.

Babylonian Civilization

Around 1800 B.C., after centuries of warfare between the various Mesopotamian city-states, the Babylonians under the rule of their king, Hammurabi, gained control of Mesopotamia.

Babylonian Sculpture

King Hammurabi (ha-muh-**rah**-bee) owes his fame to the code he published to unify legal practices in his empire. This code was recorded on a **stele** (**stee**-lee), *an inscribed stone pillar,* placed in a public area for all to see (Figure 6.14). At the top of the stele, the king receives the laws from the seated sun god. The god wears the horned helmet of divinity and holds a ring and a rod, symbols of his power.

The Code of Hammurabi
■ **FIGURE 6.14**

The code, or set of laws, was inscribed below the relief sculpture and included a listing of punishments for certain crimes. These specified punishments in kind, similar to the biblical "an eye for an eye." Thus, if a person knocked out an eye or a tooth or broke a limb of another, the same thing was done to that person as punishment. If a house collapsed and killed the purchaser, the architect or builder was sentenced to death. If the accident killed the buyer's son, the son of the architect or builder had to die. From such harsh beginnings, traditions and habits of law and order were established, modified, and changed over thousands of years to form the basis of Western civilization.

Assyrian Civilization

Following Hammurabi's death in 1750 B.C., the Babylonian period came to an end. Warring peoples swept across Mesopotamia, plunging the civilized world into a long period of turmoil. This turmoil came to a close when the powerful Assyrians from the north rose to power around 900 B.C. They ruled until early in the seventh century B.C.

Assyrian Relief Sculptures
■ **FIGURE 6.15**

The most impressive visual records of the Assyrians are the stone reliefs used to cover the mud-brick walls of their royal palaces. On one of these, a winged deity or genie is shown performing what appears to be a magic ritual before a sacred date palm tree (Figure 6.15, page 140). The figure holds a ritual container in his left hand and a conelike object in his right. His firm stance and well-developed

■ **FIGURE 6.14** Hammurabi succeeded in unifying legal practices throughout his empire. Here he is shown receiving the laws from the sun god. How would you describe Hammurabi's behavior before the sun god?

The Code of Hammurabi. 1792–1750 B.C. Engraved black basalt. 225 cm (7'4 3/5"). Originally from Babylon, found at Susa, Iran. The Louvre, Paris, France.

Art Criticism

Direct attention to the *Seated Gudea* illustrated in Figure 6.12. Divide the class into three groups and ask the first group to describe this figure in as much detail as possible. Have the second group discuss the design relationships evident in the work. Instruct the third group to interpret the feeling or mood associated with the figure. Then have each group judge the work solely in terms of the aesthetic qualities they were asked to deal with. Ask the class as a whole to identify what they regard as the most significant of the aesthetic qualities discussed.

Aesthetics

Divide the class into two groups and write the following statement on the chalkboard: *Artworks that serve as instruments of propaganda should not be taken seriously as fine art.* Have each group take a position, pro or con, and present arguments in favor of their point of view.

Did You Know ?

Some of the tombs discovered at the Cemetery at Ur date back to 2500 B.C., a time when the practice of sending a king's servants to death along with him was still carried on. In the chamber containing a king and queen, archaeologists discovered the remains of 59 servants dressed in splendor and surrounded by gold and silver vessels, headdresses, jewels, and countless other treasures. Apparently the servants entombed with their masters had music to the last; one musician was found with fingers spread over the strings of a lyre.

Teacher Notes

Classroom Discussions. As an aid to conducting effective classroom discussions, point out to students that they should listen to what others have to say, wait to be recognized before speaking, and plan ahead what they will say. If possible, arrange seating assignments during discussions so students can make eye contact and can clearly hear each other's remarks. Encourage all students to share their thoughts during discussions.

Art History

Have students refer to the seated Buddha in Chapter 10, Figure 10.17, page 226. Ask them to point out similarities and differences in these two sculptures.

Art Criticism

Ask students to examine closely the *Winged Genie Fertilizing a Date Tree* shown in Figure 6.15. Have them identify the elements of art found in this work. Is there one element in particular that contributes to the overall success of this design? Does the figure exhibit any sign of movement? If so, what word best describes that movement? Ask students to use their imaginations and place themselves before this figure. What feelings would they experience? Ask students if they feel this work is valuable because of its historical importance or because it is a well-designed, expressive work of art.

Art History

Tell students that the Stele of Hammurabi was unearthed among the ruins of an ancient city (Susa) in southwestern Iran in 1901. It had been carried from Babylon as a trophy of war. The scene at the top of the stele calls to mind the presentation of the Ten Commandments to Moses as a gift from heaven.

Did You Know ?

Because durable stone for carving was rare in Mesopotamia, Sumerian sculptures were typically small. Small figures were probably placed in temples to act as substitutes for worshipers.

■ **FIGURE 6.15** This figure's horned helmet and wings identify him as a god, not a human being. What makes the figure seem so powerful?

Winged Genie Fertilizing a Date Tree. From Nimrud, Assyrian. 884–860 B.C. Limestone. 231.8 × 181.0 cm (91¼ × 71¼"). The Nelson-Atkins Museum of Art, Kansas City, Missouri. Purchase: Nelson Trust.

muscles suggest power and strength, whereas the horned helmet and wings identify him as a god. His actions, however, remain a mystery. Perhaps, as some suggest, the image is intended to symbolize the god's power to provide for his earthly subjects.

Neo-Babylonian Period

Early in the seventh century B.C. King Nebuchadnezzar (neh-byuh-kud-**neh**-zer) rekindled Babylonian supremacy. This era has become known as the Neo-Babylonian period. Under Nebuchadnezzar, some of the splendor of the past was restored to Babylon. Unfortunately, the temples and other structures erected during the Neo-Babylonian period were made of clay bricks, which crumbled quickly. The only example of architecture from this period is a single arched gateway once located within the city.

The Ishtar Gate
■ **FIGURE 6.16**

Named after a goddess, the Ishtar Gate (Figure 6.16) was one of eight gateways marking a procession route that curled

■ **FIGURE 6.16** Royal processions passed through this gate during the Neo-Babylonian period. Identify the different kinds of animals that make up the figures on the gate.

Ishtar Gate, Main Gate of Babylon. Built during the reign of Nebuchadnezzar II. c. 605–562 B.C. Enameled tiles. Staatliche Museen, Berlin, Germany.

MEETING INDIVIDUAL NEEDS

Language Proficiency. If you have students who experience language difficulties, try the following strategies: Permit students to use a buddy system. Pair these students with native speakers of English and allow students' individual strengths to complement each other as they complete the lessons.

Have students focus on the section headings first. The headings in each section are designed to help students understand what ideas will be presented and tell them what to focus on as they read. Such information may prove invaluable to students with a limited grasp of English.

through Babylon. The round-arched gateway is covered with blue-glazed bricks and edged with geometric designs in white and gold. Contrasting with the blue background are rows of identical long-necked dragons and bulls in white with yellow details.

A dragon from this gate exhibits features of several different kinds of animals. (See Figure 6.1, page 126.) It has a scaly body, a serpent's head, the front feet of a cat, the hind feet of a bird, and a scorpion's tail. Created in low relief to project out from the wall, these creatures walk toward or away from the arched opening.

End of the Neo-Babylonian Period

Tradition has it that Nebuchadnezzar, after a long reign marked by military conquest and prosperity and after adorning his city with roads, palaces, and temples, suffered from insanity. He thought of himself as some kind of animal, walked on all fours, and ate grass. Nebuchadnezzar died in 562 B.C., and within 30 years his empire was in shambles.

Persian Empire

Egypt, Babylonia, and Assyria were many centuries old when a vigorous people appeared on the eastern border of the civilized world. These newcomers called themselves Irani and their new homeland Irania (now Iran). They were mistakenly called Persians because later Greek geographers named them after a territory known as Parsa, or Persis, where their early kings had their capital.

In 539 B.C., the Persians advanced into Mesopotamia. That same year they captured the city of Babylon without a fight and made it their capital. The Persians remained in power until 331 B.C., when they were conquered by Alexander the Great.

Persian Architecture and Relief Carving

Persian architecture found its highest accomplishment in palaces. The best example is at Persepolis in modern Iran. It was built on a stone platform with magnificent rooms and wooden ceilings supported by huge columns. The most important room was the enormous Audience Hall, where the Persian king formally received official visitors from every corner of the known world (Figure 6.17). The room contained 100 columns 65 feet high. Nothing remains of it today but a few columns and the outlines of the general plan.

■ **FIGURE 6.17** Even now in its ruined state, the Audience Hall of this great Persian palace is impressive. The flights of steps were so spacious that ten horsemen riding side by side could mount them. Describe the impression this hall might have made on representatives of other lands who came here for an audience with the Persian king.

Audience Hall of Darius and Xerxes, (Apadana), East Stairway. c. 500 B.C. Persepolis.

Studio Skills

Have students examine the relief carving illustrated in Figure 6.15, page 140, noting in particular the manner in which a variety of different textures have been used to add interest. Instruct students to create a full-figure *line* drawing of a powerful king or queen measuring at least 15 inches high. Tell them to divide this figure into ten or more distinct shapes and cut them out. Next, have them collect a variety of magazine illustrations that exhibit a variety of textures, place the cut-out shapes over the magazine shapes and cut them out. They should trim each shape on all sides to reduce it slightly. Glue the shapes on a sheet of black construction paper leaving a *narrow* space between each. The finished design must exhibit no less than eight different textures.

Did You Know?

The surviving records of the fierce Assyrians are filled with boastful claims detailing their cruelty to enemies. In one instance a king proudly proclaims that he dyed mountains red with the blood of his enemies and erected pillars with their decapitated heads.

Study Guide

Distribute *Study Guide* 14 in the TCR. Assist students in reviewing key concepts. 🗂

> *More About...* **The Persian Empire.** In the decisive battle with Alexander the Great, Darius III, the Persian king, gathered an army of 600,000. Alexander's army consisted of no more than 30,000 warriors. Yet, when the battle was over, the Persians had lost 110,000 men while Alexander's casualties amounted to about 450. Eventually Darius was killed by one of his own generals, and Alexander declared himself King of Kings and ruler of the Persian Empire. Alexander died eight years later in Babylon, probably of malaria. He was just 33 years of age.

ASSESS

Checking Comprehension

Have students complete the lesson review questions. Answers appear in the box below.

Reteaching

Assign *Reteaching* 13, found in the TCR. Have students complete the activity and review their responses. 🗂

Extension

➤ Assign *Appreciating Cultural Diversity* 8, "Paying Tribute to a Culture," in the TCR. 🗂

➤ Have students compare the *Winged Genie* shown in Figure 6.15 with the Egyptian relief caving in Chapter 7, Figure 7.12 on page 159. On the chalkboard, have students list the ways these two carvings are similar. Then have them list the ways they differ. Ask students to identify the most significant difference between these two ancient relief carvings.

CLOSE

Ask students to review the images in this lesson and notice the dates these works were created. Discuss the fact that we learn about ancient cultures through artworks that have been preserved over centuries.

The top portion of each column in the Audience Hall was decorated with the figures of two bulls facing in opposite directions (Figure 6.18). With their heads lowered and legs tucked under their bodies, these animals have a powerful appearance. They surely must have impressed visitors with the king's power.

Further emphasizing the king's power are the reliefs lining the walls and stairways leading to the Audience Hall. Unlike the military scenes shown on Assyrian reliefs, Persian carvings portray people bringing tributes and offerings to the king.

Today, little remains of the grandeur of the palace at Persepolis. When Alexander the Great marched into the city in 331 B.C., he destroyed the magnificent palace and made off with its huge treasure. This event marked the beginning of a new era in history—an era that saw the rise of Greek civilization. Alexander, however, was not destined to witness this new era. He met death in the palace of Nebuchadnezzar.

In the next chapter we will turn back the pages of history to visit the early civilization that paralleled in time the great civilizations of the fertile crescent. Ancient Egypt was destined to be conquered by Alexander as well, but not before recording nearly 3000 years of glory.

■ **FIGURE 6.18** This is one of two bulls, facing in opposite directions, which decorate the top of the surviving column from the Audience Hall. What features contribute to the powerful impression this bull creates?

Capital in the shape of a Bull. Persian. c. 518–460 B.C. Bituminous limestone. 71.1 × 76.2 × 30.5 cm (28 × 30 × 12"). The Nelson-Atkins Museum of Art, Kansas City, Missouri. Purchase: Nelson Trust.

LESSON TWO REVIEW

Reviewing Art Facts

1. Describe the writing instruments used by Sumerians.
2. For what accomplishment is Hammurabi famous?
3. Where was the Ishtar Gate erected and what was its purpose?
4. What type of building is regarded as the highest accomplishment of Persian architecture?

▶ Activity... *Drawing an Imaginary Creature*

The vivid imagination of Neo-Babylonian artists is clearly evidenced by the animals they created for the Ishtar Gate. The dragons depicted there exhibit the features of several different kinds of animals. Examine the dragon in Figure 6.1, page 126 and notice the way animal features are shown.

Create an imaginary creature for display in your classroom. With colored chalk or oil pastels, make a drawing that combines familiar features associated with at least three different animals. Use light colors for the animal. Use a contrasting dark color for the background.

LESSON TWO REVIEW

Answers to Reviewing Art Facts

1. The stylus was a reed with a three-cornered end used to produce wedges and straight lines.
2. Hammurabi's fame rests on the code of laws he proclaimed.
3. The Ishtar Gate was erected in Babylonia. It was one of eight gateways marking a procession route through the city.
4. Their palaces are ranked as the highest accomplishment of Persian architecture.

Activity...*Drawing Imaginary Creature*

To get ideas for their own drawings, have students review the dragon in Figure 6.1. Then have them look closely at the image in the relief carving shown in Figure 6.15, as well as the other animals that appear on the gate in Figure 6.16, page 140.

Studio LESSON Contour Drawing of an Animal in Motion

Complete a large, simple contour drawing of a familiar animal in motion that fills an entire sheet of gray construction paper. Color your drawing using a single stick of dark chalk. Create light and dark values of this single hue by varying the pressure when applying the chalk to your paper. Gradual changes of value will make your animal appear three-dimensional rather than flat.

Materials
- Pencil and sketch paper
- Sheet of gray construction paper, 18 × 24 inches
- Single stick of dark-colored chalk

Inspiration

Look at the paintings of bison (Figures 6.2, page 128 and 6.5, page 132). What have the prehistoric artists done to make these animals look three-dimensional? Was it necessary for them to include a great many details to make the animals appear lifelike?

Process

1. Complete several pencil sketches of a familiar animal in motion (rearing, running, jumping). Keep these drawings simple by eliminating all but the most important details of the animals.
2. Reproduce your best drawing to completely fill the sheet of gray construction paper. Select a single dark color of chalk. Press down hard on the chalk when coloring the outer edges of the animal. Gradually reduce the pressure as you color further into the animal form. Using this procedure will make the animal appear three-dimensional. (You may wish to practice this procedure using the side and the point of the chalk stick.) Emphasize the necessary details in your drawing by using the tip of your chalk stick.

■ **FIGURE 6.19** Student Work

— Examining Your Work

Describe. Is your animal easily recognized? What features were most helpful to others in identifying it?

Analyze. Does your animal completely fill the paper on which it is drawn? Is it colored with a single hue? Did you use gradations of value to make the animal seem three-dimensional?

Interpret. What is your animal doing? Are other students able to identify its actions? What clues were most helpful to them in doing this?

Judge. Using the literal qualities as the basis for judgment, do you think that your chalk drawing of an animal is successful? Does it look lifelike? If so, what contributes most to its realistic appearance?

143

— ASSESSMENT

Examining Your Work. As students answer the questions in "Examining Your Work," have them focus on the gradations of value they were able to create with the use of chalk in their drawings. The blending should be done carefully to avoid muddy-ing the colors. Ask students if they were careful to apply colors in separate strokes to allow color blending to take place in the viewer's eye. Ask them how this careful blending gives a three-dimensional look to the drawing.

Contour Drawing of an Animal in Motion ____

Objectives
■ Complete a large contour drawing of a familiar animal in motion.
■ Color the drawing with a dark color of chalk.
■ Use gradations of value to give the animal a three-dimensional appearance.

Motivator
Provide pictures of various types of animals that might be used as subjects for this drawing before students begin their preliminary sketches. Demonstrate the simplicity of form they should attain in the finished drawing. On the board, illustrate how gradations of value, achieved by varying the pressure on the chalk as you hold it flat, can create the illusion of a three-dimensional form.

Art History
Prehistoric art owes its realistic appearance to the artists' powers of observation. Ask students if they think this power of observation was limited to artists. Explain that keen observation (being sensitive to the people, objects, and events around them) can provide them with ideas for their own art.

Critiquing
Have students apply the steps of art criticism to their own artworks using the "Examining Your Work" questions on this page.

Modeling an Animal in Clay

Objectives

■ Model a compact clay sculpture of an animal based on one of three geometric forms.
■ Create an animal that exhibits specific traits.
■ Use contrasts of actual textures to add interest to the surface of the sculptures.

Motivator

Draw a sphere, cylinder, or cone and discuss the various animals that might be created from each. Ask students to add heads, legs, tails, and other features.

Studio Skills

Demonstrate for students the steps required to attach various features to the basic geometric form. Explain that the two pieces of clay being joined must be of the same consistency or they will shrink irregularly and separate during the drying process. Show students how to score, add slip, and join clay pieces with a clay modeling tool. Explain how to hollow out the sculptures from the bottom when clay is leather hard so the thickest sections will not exceed one inch. Hollowing allows the piece to dry evenly and reduces the possibility of air bubbles that can cause a piece to explode during firing.

Critiquing

Have students apply the steps of art criticism to their own artworks using the "Examining Your Work" questions on this page.

Materials

● Pencils and sketch paper
● Clay (a ball about the size of a grapefruit)
● Piece of canvas, muslin, or cloth about 14 × 14 inches for each student to cover tabletops
● Clay modeling tools
● Slip (a liquid mixture of clay and water)

Using the modeling process described in Chapter 3, create a compact clay sculpture of an animal based on one of the basic geometric forms (sphere, cylinder, cone). This animal must exhibit a trait commonly associated with it, such as power, grace, gentleness, or fierceness. Use contrasting rough and smooth textures to add interest to the surface of the animal.

Inspiration

Look again at the examples of prehistoric animal paintings in Figures 6.2 and 6.5. Notice how the artists have avoided the use of unnecessary details. What has been done to show the animals' power, grace, or gentleness?

■ **FIGURE 6.20** Student Work

Process

1. With the other students in your class, compile a list of different animals.
2. Select an animal from the list, and complete several pencil sketches of it in a *compact* reclining or sitting position. Each sketch should attempt to show the trait associated with the animal.
3. Choose your best sketch, and use that sketch as a guide for modeling the animal in clay:
   ● Identify and fashion in clay a *geometric form* that resembles the body of the animal in your sketch.
   ● Attach the head, legs, tail, and other large features to the basic form.
   ● Keep turning the sculpture as you continue to work on it. Once the larger features have been joined to the basic body form, use the modeling tools (not your fingers) to refine the features.
   ● Finish your sculpture with a clay modeling tool. Add details and textures.
   ● When the sculpture is firm but not dry, hollow it out with a clay tool. Allow it to dry thoroughly, and fire it in a kiln.

Examining Your Work

Describe. Is your sculpture easily identified as an animal? What features are most useful in helping others identify the animal it represents?

Analyze. What geometric form did you use as the starting point for your animal sculpture? Point to areas of contrasting rough and smooth textures.

Interpret. Does your animal exhibit a trait commonly associated with it? Are other students in your class able to recognize this trait?

Judge. What aesthetic qualities would you refer to when making and defending a judgment about your sculpture? Which of these aesthetic qualities is most appropriate in this case? If you were to make another sculpture of an animal, how would it differ from this one?

144

ASSESSMENT

Examining Your Work. As students examine their work using the questions on this page, have them review the Inspiration statement above. Have them check their completed sculptures to see if they were able to create a sense of power, grace, or gentleness without the use of details. Does their work exhibit the same qualities of the animals found in prehistoric sculptures?

Reviewing the Facts

Lesson One

1. When describing the painting of a bison from Altamira, what did you discover about the setting in which the animal is placed?
2. How is line used in this prehistoric painting?
3. Where were prehistoric paintings done, and how did this contribute to their survival?
4. Why was the discovery of prehistoric paintings at Altamira first greeted with disbelief?
5. List at least three unusual aspects of the megalith construction at Stonehenge.

Lesson Two

6. What kind of material was used to construct the ziggurats?
7. What is cuneiform writing? Who developed it?
8. Who was Gudea? How do we know about his appearance?
9. Why do almost no examples of Neo-Babylonian architecture remain?
10. How many columns were in the Audience Hall of the Persian palace at Persepolis? How was the top of each column decorated?

Thinking Critically

1. COMPARE AND CONTRAST. Look at the bison (Figure 6.2, page 128) and the horse depicted on a Chinese handscroll (Figure 10.15, page 225). Describe the gradation of value in each and tell how they differ. Tell how the media used contribute to the difference.
2. ANALYZE. Pretend you are a noted art critic. You disagree with another scholar who insists that prehistoric cave paintings are simple and childlike. A friendly debate is scheduled, and you must now prepare for it. List all the arguments you will use to demonstrate that prehistoric cave paintings were expressive and skillfully done.

▲ R T / S ● U / R C ◼ Use the *Performing Arts Handbook*, page 576, to learn about music, dance, and theatre from many diverse cultures and times.

■ CAREERS IN Art If you enjoy studying or creating art, read about a fascinating art-related career opportunity in the *Careers in Art Handbook*, page 594.

*inter*NET
CONNECTION Visit Glencoe Art Online at *www.glencoe.com/sec/art*. Explore ancient caves online, learn more about archaeology, and complete an exciting activity.

Technology Project

Exploring Prehistoric Structures

Prehistoric builders created many megaliths around the globe. Today these megaliths stand as architectural symbols constructed by early civilizations to fulfill unknown, mysterious functions. One of the most famous of these is Stonehenge, Figure 6.7, page 134. Located in Salisbury Plain, England, this massive structure has been the focus of curiosity for many years. Who were the builders, and why did they build this structure in the middle of an open plain? Many theories have been proposed, but no clear answers have been found. Other structures, located all over the world, are just as puzzling. Working in groups, find out more about some of these mysterious architectural wonders.

1. Using library resources, the Internet, CD-ROMs, and laser discs, select one of these ancient structures and research it. Using the art history operations, answer questions about the structure to determine where it was built and who built it, what materials were used, how it was designed, and why the structure might have been created.
2. After gathering information about the structure, use a computer draw program to create a diagram of the structure and its site. Label the parts of the structure. Then write a short description of the structure, including all the information that your group discovered about the structure and the culture that produced it. Print your document and exchange with other groups so that classmates will have information on prehistoric architecture to include in their art portfolios.

145

Teaching the Technology Project

Help students find ideas for other megaliths and prehistoric structures. First have them look through their textbooks to find works by Egyptian civilizations (Chapter 7), and stone sculptures by pre-Columbian artists (Chapter 11). Have them compare these to the megalith at Stonehenge. Students should use multimedia presentation software, if available, to do their reports.

▲ R T / S ● U / R C ◼ Assign the feature in the *Performing Arts Handbook*, page 576.

CAREERS IN ART If time permits, have interested students investigate the career information in the *Careers in Art Handbook*, page 594.

*inter*NET
CONNECTION Have students go online and learn more about artists on preselected Web sites with the Internet activity for this chapter.

Reviewing the Facts

1. There is no setting; students should explain that there is no indication of ground beneath, nor signs of trees, hills, or sky behind.
2. To outline and define the simple, compact shape.
3. Far back in cave shelters; this location protected them from wind and rain.
4. Most people thought the paintings were too sophisticated to be the work of primitive people.
5. Large ring of stones with three smaller rings inside; more than half of the stones still stand; tallest stone is 17 feet high and weighs over 50 tons.
6. Clay, reinforced with brick and asphalt.
7. Writing with wedge-shaped characters; developed by Sumerians.
8. A Neo-Sumerian leader. Because he was preserved in many sculpture portraits.
9. They were made of clay bricks that crumbled easily.
10. One hundred columns. Figures of bulls topped the columns.

Thinking Critically

1. Answers will vary, but should indicate that the bison shows less subtle gradation because media were crudely applied to textured cave walls; the horse shows delicate changes because of ink applied to smooth paper.
2. Answers, which will vary, might include: the prehistoric artist used fresh, vibrant colors; the images were lifelike; the natural contours of the rock suggest the curve of muscles and body tissues.

145

The Art of Ancient Egypt

LESSON ONE
(pages 148–154)

The Growth of Egyptian Civilization

Classroom Resources

- 📂 Appreciating Cultural Diversity 9
- 📂 Art and Humanities 10
- 📂 Cooperative Learning 10
- 📂 Reproducible Lesson Plan 15
- 📂 Reteaching Activity 15
- 📂 Study Guide 15

Features

Time & Place CONNECTIONS
(page 152)

LOOKING Closely ↓
(page 154)

LESSON TWO
(pages 155–161)

Egyptian Sculpture and Painting

Classroom Resources

- 📂 Cooperative Learning 11
- 📂 Enrichment Activity 15
- 📂 Reproducible Lesson Plan 16
- 📂 Reteaching Activity 16
- 📂 Study Guide 16

Features

Symbolism in Egyptian *Art*
Pharaoh Khafre
(page 156)

Time & Place CONNECTIONS
(page 159)

END OF CHAPTER
(pages 162–163)

Studio **LESSON**

- Designing and Painting a Sarcophagus Cover
(page 162)

ADDITIONAL CHAPTER RESOURCES

Activities
- 📁 Studio Activity 9
- 📁 Advanced Studio Activity 7
- 🖱 Chapter 7 Internet Activity

Fine Art Resources
- 🕹 **Transparency**
  Art in Focus Transparency 10
  Outer Coffin of Henettaway
- 🖼 **Fine Art Print**
  Focus on World Art Print 7
  Sphinx of Amenhotep III

Assessment
- 📁 Application 7
- 📁 Chapter 7 Test
- 📁 Performance Assessment

Multimedia Resources
- 🎭 Artsource® Performing Arts package
- 💿 National Gallery Laser Disc
- 💿 National Museum of Women in the Arts CD-ROM
- 📼 Arts & Entertainment Videos

NATIONAL STANDARDS FOR ARTS EDUCATION

The National Standards for Arts Education provide guidelines for grade-appropriate competency in the visual arts. The Content Standards for grades 9–12 are:

1. Understanding and applying media, techniques, and processes.
2. Using knowledge of structures and functions.
3. Choosing and evaluating a range of subject matter, symbols, and ideas.
4. Understanding the visual arts in relation to history and cultures.
5. Reflecting upon and assessing the characteristics and merits of their work and the work of others.
6. Making connections between visual arts and other disciplines.

Listed below are the National Standards for the Visual Arts addressed in this chapter. For a breakdown of the categories listed under each content standard, refer to the *Reproducible Lesson Plans* booklet in the TCR.

1. (a, b) **2.** (a, b) **3.** (a, b) **4.** (a, b, c) **5.** (a, b, c) **6.** (a)

HANDBOOK MATERIAL

Performing Arts
(page 596)

CAREERS IN Art

(page 598)

Beyond the Classroom

Encourage young artists with the opportunites provided by the National Society of Arts and Letters. Connect to them through our Web site at *www.glencoe.com/sec/art.*

🕐 Out of Time?
If time does not permit teaching this chapter in its entirety, you may wish to preview the artwork and captions with students. Scan the heads in each lesson with students. Discuss the Looking Closely features and examine Symbolism in Egyptian Art on page 156.

The Art of Ancient Egypt

The Art of Ancient Egypt

INTRODUCE

Chapter Overview

CHAPTER 7 introduces students to the art and culture of ancient Egypt.

Lesson One deals with the origins of Egyptian civilization and the evolution of pyramids and temples.

Lesson Two addresses developments in Egyptian sculpture and painting.

Studio Lesson guides students in designing and painting a sarcophagus cover.

Art & Social Studies

Have students examine and discuss the mask of Tutankhamen shown in Figure 7.1. Explain that Tutankhamen was both a ruler and a god—one of many—for the people of ancient Egypt. Encourage students to consider the implications of a human ruler who is considered divine: What are the implications for the ruler and the ruler's family? What are the implications for nonroyal members of the society? Ask volunteers to read about other cultures in which rulers were considered gods; let these volunteers report their findings to the rest of the class.

Art & Social Studies ■ FIGURE 7.1 This golden mask was created as a funerary mask for the ruler Tutankhamen when the pharoahs of Egypt were considered gods. Within a few hundred years of the time this work was created, two ancient cultures underwent similar changes in their belief systems. The Egyptians, as well as the Hebrews in Palestine, advanced the notion of a monotheistic religion—a religion with a belief in one supreme diety.

Mask of Tutankhamen. c. 1352 B.C. Gold with lapis lazuli, carnelian, and precious stones. 54 × 39.3 cm (21¼ × 15⁷/₁₆"). Egyptian Museum, Cairo, Egypt.

146

National Standards

This chapter addresses the following National Standards for the Visual Arts.

1. (a,b)	**4.** (a,b,c)
2. (a,b)	**5.** (a,b,c)
3. (a,b)	**6.** (a)

CHAPTER 7 RESOURCES

Teacher's Classroom Resources
- 📁 Advanced Studio Activity 7
- 📁 Application 7
- 🖱 Chapter 7 Internet Activity
- 📁 Studio Activity 9

Assessment
- 📁 Chapter 7 Test

- 📁 Performance Assessment

Fine Arts Resources
- 🖽 Transparency 10
    Outer Coffin of Hennettaway
- 🎞 *Focus on World Art* Print 7
    Sphinx of Amenotep III

Traveling up the Nile River in Egypt today, you would be amazed to see the mighty monuments at almost every bend in this great river. Most of these huge stone structures are tombs and temples, reminders of a once-powerful ancient Egyptian civilization. It might also surprise you to know that the people who built these imposing-looking structures invented the harp, loved to sing and dance, and organized huge theatrical events. Who were these Egyptians who were able to build such impressive monuments? Where did they come from? What were they like? Your search for answers to these questions will lead you back to prehistoric times when people first came to inhabit the lands bordering the Nile.

Introducing the Chapter

Have students look at Figure 7.4 (page 151) and Figure 7.7 (page 155) and, without reading the credit lines, try to name the works. Point out that many people cannot think of ancient Egypt without picturing these Wonders of the World. At the same time, most are unaware of when or why the works were built. Tell students they are about to explore these and other aspects of the art of ancient Egypt.

YOUR Portfolio

Choose one symbol from this chapter to be used as a design element for an original artwork to include in your portfolio. You might include the mastaba, hieroglyphics, obelisk, or sarcophagus. Make notes or sketches describing how you would use the design. Determine what qualities are associated with the symbols, and how you might combine two symbols to create a single design. Complete your project and keep it together with the sketches in your portfolio.

Focus ON THE ARTS

THEATRE
In ancient Egypt, actors performed a mystery play recounting the god Osiris's life, death, and resurrection. The play lasted several weeks and encouraged participation by the entire community.

DANCE
Dancers performed in religious rites for the benefit of the gods. The Dance of the Stars symbolically reproduced the rotation of the stars and planets.

MUSIC
Ancient Egyptians invented the harp. They played double reed pipes similar to the flute, drums, and small trumpets. Permanent troupes of singer-dancers were retained for religious events and for royal entertainment.

Focus ON THE ARTS

Tell students that once a year, towns throughout ancient Egypt performed a mystery play honoring the god Osiris who was represented by a statue. Describe the scenes that were included: A procession greeting Osiris's boat; foes attacking the boat. One man scares them off; the procession resumes. Osiris is worshipped in the temple. The people hear that an enemy has killed Osiris. He is dressed for burial and carried by boat down the Nile.

Divide the class into groups and tell them that the pharaoh has asked each group to explain how they would stage each of the scenes described. Plan as much audience participation as possible.

147

DEVELOPING A PORTFOLIO

Choosing a Project. A portfolio should exhibit strong, confident examples of a student's work. Typically, college evaluators would rather see fewer competent works than many that are mediocre and would call into question the student's overall ability. However, a diversity of artistic skill is also critical, so students must learn to balance both objectives. Encourage them to approach each assignment as a potential project for their portfolios and as a method of isolating their strengths and weaknesses. Students can then concentrate on improving those areas that are weaker while continuing to develop the stronger ones.

LESSON ONE

The Growth of Egyptian Civilization

The Growth of Egyptian Civilization

Focus

Lesson Objectives

After studying this lesson, students will be able to:
■ Identify the three major periods of Egyptian history.
■ Explain the role religion played in the development of the pyramids.

Building Vocabulary

Explain that Egyptian kings lived in palaces known as *Per'ao*, a word meaning the Great House. Ask students to identify a related Vocabulary term in the lesson (pharaoh). Then have students find a picture of an obelisk in the lesson. Ask whether they can name any obelisks in North America.

Motivator

Ask students to consider what future historians would think about our modern life in North America if only a few artifacts and the most solidly built architecture survived (for example, reinforced concrete sports stadiums and office buildings). Tell students that they will be using similar clues to learn about the lives and beliefs of ancient Egyptians.

Introducing the Lesson

Have students examine the artworks and captions in this lesson. Ask students for their impressions of life in ancient Egypt. Tell them that it will be important to use their imagination to understand how the massive Egyptian monuments pictured in this lesson were the backdrop to the daily life of people who lived 5,000 years ago.

Vocabulary
■ pharaoh
■ dynasty
■ sarcophagus
■ mastaba

Discover
After completing this lesson, you will be able to:
■ Name the three major historical periods of ancient Egypt.
■ Explain the relationship of religion to the development of the pyramids.

Around 5000 B.C., prehistoric hunters and their families settled in the fertile valley of the Nile River (Figure 7.2). As far as experts can tell, these people came from western Asia. Because there is no evidence that they moved on or died out, they are regarded as the direct ancestors of most Egyptian peoples. The Nile River valley in which they settled was about 750 miles long but measured no more than about 31 miles at its widest point. It was lined on both sides by cliffs ranging in height from around 300 to 1000 feet. Beyond these cliffs was nothing but desert.

Early Inhabitants Along the Nile

Each summer the Nile River flooded its banks and deposited layers of fertile soil in the valley. This soil had been carried for thousands of miles from the African interior. In some places, the rich soil deposits reached a depth of more than 30 feet. In this fertile environment, people gradually changed from food gatherers to food producers. Discovering that the wild vegetables and grains they gathered grew from seeds, they began to collect these seeds and planted them in the fertile soil of the valley.

Although the people continued to hunt animals for food, they came to rely more and more on the animals they raised themselves. This gave them an advantage over their ancestors. They were no longer entirely dependent on the game they hunted for survival. Because they did not have to move from one location to another in search of food, they began to build more permanent houses of mud, wood, and reeds.

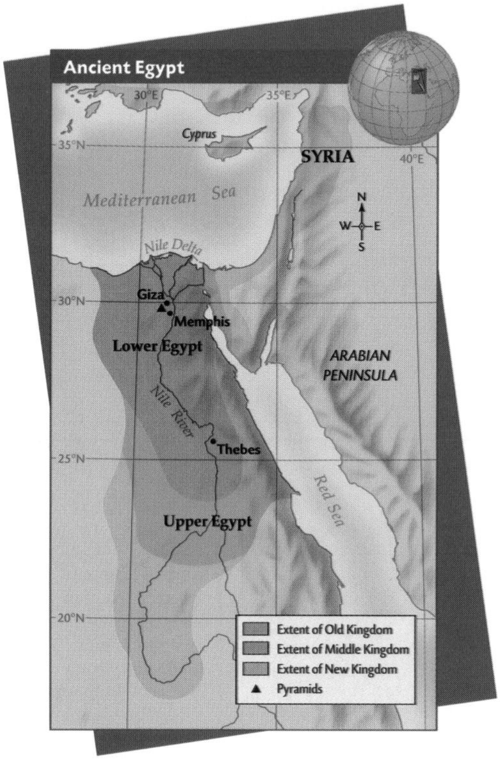

The Formation of Kingdoms

This settled existence brought about an increase in their population and led to the growth of villages and towns. Some towns grew so large that they took control of neighboring villages and, in this way, formed kingdoms. As the prehistoric period came to a close, there were only two large kingdoms in Egypt. One of these was Lower Egypt, which included the fan-shaped delta region at the mouth of the Nile. The other was Upper Egypt, which was the valley carved in the desert by the river (Figure 7.2).

MAP SKILLS
■ **FIGURE 7.2** People first settled in the valley of the Nile River about 7,000 years ago. How do you think the Nile River affected the daily life of the ancient Egyptians? How do you imagine it affected the artworks they created?

148

LESSON ONE RESOURCES

Teacher's Classroom Resources
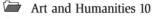 Appreciating Cultural Diversity 9
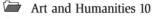 Art and Humanities 10
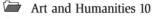 Cooperative Learning 10

 Reproducible Lesson Plan 15
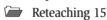 Reteaching 15
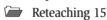 Study Guide 15

Thus, an Egyptian civilization emerged along the banks of the Nile more that 3,000 years before the birth of Christ. It continued to exist for nearly another 3,000 years. During that period, Egypt became a thriving nation in which a **pharaoh,** or *ruler,* governed with complete authority. Agriculture and trade grew, art flourished, and majestic monuments and temples were constructed.

The Three Major Periods of Egyptian History

The history of Egypt can be divided into three periods: the Old Kingdom, the Middle Kingdom, and the New Kingdom, or Empire. Each kingdom is further divided into dynasties. A **dynasty** was *a period during which a single family provided a succession of rulers.*

One reign ended with the death of a pharaoh and another began with the crowning of a successor from the same royal family. For this reason, every precaution was taken to keep the blood of the family pure. One of these precautions was to forbid the pharaoh to marry outside of the immediate family.

The Old Kingdom

The earliest dynastic period began around 3100 B.C. when Upper and Lower Egypt were united by a powerful pharaoh named Menes. Menes established his capital at Memphis and founded the first of the 31 Egyptian dynasties. The Old Kingdom dates from the start of the third of these dynasties, in about 2686 B.C. It ended about 500 years later, when the strong centralized government established by the pharaohs was weakened by the rise of a group of independent nobles. These nobles split the country into small states. Civil war and disorder soon broke out between these states, and the authority of the reigning pharaoh collapsed.

The Middle Kingdom

After a long period of turmoil, the nobles in Thebes, a city on the upper Nile, were able to gain control of the country. They managed to unify Egypt once again into a single state, and order was restored to their troubled land. The success of these nobles marked the beginning of the Middle Kingdom, a period of about 250 years from around 2050 to 1800 B.C.

The Middle Kingdom was a time of law and order and prosperity in Egypt. This was true even though the pharaoh, while still the supreme head, was not as powerful as pharaohs had been during the Old Kingdom. Around 1800 B.C., Egypt was overrun for the first time by foreign invaders. Using horses and chariots, the Hyksos from western Asia swept across the country. They easily defeated the Egyptians, who fought on foot. The Hyksos inhabited Lower Egypt and for 200 years forced the Egyptian people to pay them tribute. Finally, the Egyptians, having learned how to use horses and chariots, drove the invaders from their country and restored independence.

The New Kingdom

The third and most brilliant period of Egyptian history, which began in 1570 B.C., is known as the New Kingdom, or Empire. Warrior pharaohs used their expertise with horses and chariots to extend Egypt's rule over neighboring nations.

Under one of these pharaohs, Amenhotep III, the New Kingdom reached the peak of its power and influence. Thebes, the royal capital, became the most magnificent city in the world. Suddenly Amenhotep's son and heir, Amenhotep IV, broke with tradition. He tried to bring about changes in Egyptian religion that for centuries had recognized many different gods. Amenhotep IV moved the capital from Thebes to Tel el-Amarna. There he established Aton, symbolized by the sun disk, as the one supreme god. In honor of his god, Amenhotep IV changed his name to Akhenaton, which meant "it is well with Aton." Unfortunately, while Akhenaton was absorbed in his new religion, Egypt's enemies began to whittle away pieces of the once-mighty nation.

 ## Technology

Transparencies. An overhead projector enlarges images to make materials easily visible to a large group while leaving the teacher free to observe and interact with the class. Printed illustrations can be lifted from clay-coated magazine pages by adhering the printed side to a sheet of clear, adhesive-backed acetate and soaking off the paper from the back. The overhead provides a good way to illustrate the visual elements and to experiment with composition. Glencoe's *Art in Focus* Fine Art Transparency package provides a variety of fine artworks and technique tips that can be used with this textbook.

TEACH
Using Map Skills

Have students look at the map of Egypt and locate the Nile River Valley. Help students understand the importance of the Nile River in the life of ancient Egyptians. Point out that the Nile River valley is met by vast expanses of desert on both the eastern and western sides. Ask students to imagine what kinds of hardships a scarcity of fertile farm land and space for homes might cause.

Art Criticism

Have students examine the work in Figure 7.3 on page 150. Ask them to describe the figures representing King Tutankhamen and his queen. Students should note that the artist showed all parts of the body clearly. This was based upon the belief that paintings and sculptures could serve as substitutes for the body. A complete image was always necessary. If an arm or leg were concealed behind the body, the king would be forced to spend eternity with one arm or one leg. Ask students to discuss the limitations these rules imposed on imaginative artists living in ancient Egypt.

Art History

Explain to students that the tomb of Tutankhamen was discovered in 1922. The treasures inside revealed the luxury of the New Kingdom. Among the treasures found in the tomb was a throne decorated on the back with a low relief made from a sheet of pure gold, illustrated in Figure 7.3. Have students write a news story from the point of view of a journalist living at the time of this amazing discovery. How would they inform the world in a news story about this find?

Art History

Remind students that the god Aton was symbolized by a sun disk. Explain how the same image can mean different things in different times and places. Have students discuss why the sun would seem like an appropriate symbol for a divinity in Egypt. Then look through art books to see how the sun has been used as a symbol in other times and places. Direct students' attention to Figure 19.5, page 423, in which Bernini used rays of light to symbolize the presence of God. Students might also research the variety of other symbols that suggest divinity in Western art (for example, the dove, cross, or six-pointed star).

Art Criticism

Have students examine Figure 7.4 and imagine the pyramid in its original state. Ask them to describe how the elements of art work together in this pyramid. Would a pyramid have the same effect if it were brightly colored or ornately textured? How would the visual impact of the work change if it did not come to a point?

Did You Know?

It is possible that the pyramids served a secondary purpose as monuments dedicated to the sun god, Re. As the tallest structures in Egypt, they received the first rays of the sun each morning. This was a daily reminder to the people that Re was constantly watching over them.

The Decline of Ancient Egypt

Akhenaton's new religion did not survive after his death. Tel el-Amarna was destroyed by Egypt's enemies, the capital was returned to Thebes, and the old religion was restored. Although other pharaohs after Akhenaton tried to recapture the glories of the past, Egypt's long chapter in history was coming to an end. In 332 B.C., Alexander the Great of Macedonia conquered Egypt, bringing the New Kingdom to a close. Several centuries of Hellenistic rule followed.

Finally, in 30 B.C., Egypt was made a province of Rome.

The greatness of ancient Egypt has not been forgotten over the centuries. Works of art of all kinds remain. They range from huge pyramids and tombs to skillfully formed stone statues, wall paintings, and carved and painted reliefs (Figure 7.3). These and other treasures are fascinating reminders of the magnificent civilization that flourished on the banks of the Nile. (See Figure 7.1, page 146.)

■ FIGURE 7.3
Tutankhamen followed Akhenaton, or Amenhotep IV, as pharaoh. He restored the practice of traditional religious beliefs. Why and how were artworks such as this throne preserved?

The Golden Throne of Tutankhamen (ruled 1361–52 B.C.), detail. Wood overlaid with gold, silver, semiprecious stones, and glass paste. Egyptian Museum, Cairo, Egypt.

More About...   Tomb of Tutankhamen. Archaeologist Howard Carter described his impressions upon gazing for the first time into the tomb of Tutankhamen: "At first I could see nothing, the hot air escaping from the chamber causing the candle flame to flicker; but presently, as my eyes grew accustomed to the light, details of the room within emerged slowly from the mist, strange animals, statues, and gold—everywhere the glint of gold. For the moment—an eternity it must have been to the others standing by—I was struck dumb with amazement, and when Lord Carnarvon, unable to stand the suspense any longer, inquired anxiously, 'Can you see anything?' it was all I could do to get out the words, 'Yes, wonderful things.'"

The Pyramids

Try to picture the pyramids as they once were: covered with a smooth layer of polished white limestone. They were massive, pure-white monuments standing against a backdrop of constantly shifting brown sand and blue sky. What purpose did the pyramids serve? How were they built? What is inside?

The Pyramid of Khufu

■ **FIGURE 7.4**

Before considering these questions, consider one example of these great monuments. The Pyramid of Khufu (Figure 7.4) presents rigid, straight contour lines that clearly define and accent the simple triangular shape of this monumental structure.

Its size is truly massive: The Pyramid of Khufu covers an area of almost 13 acres. This means that the five largest cathedrals in the world could be placed within its base with room to spare. It was made by piling 2.3 million blocks of stone to a height of 480 feet. This makes the pyramid about as high as a modern 48-story building.

The Design of Pyramids

Each pyramid was built on an almost perfectly square ground plan. The pyramid base is much greater than the height. Because the pyramid is wider than it is tall, it lacks an upward movement. Rather than a vertical, soaring quality, the shape and proportions of the pyramid suggest solidity and permanence.

■ **FIGURE 7.4** The visual impact of this huge structure conveys a feeling of permanent solidity. What response do you think this pyramid evoked in the people of ancient Egypt?

Pyramid of Khufu, Giza, Egypt. c. 2545–2520 B.C.

Aesthetics

Explain that the topmost element of a pyramid is a pointed capstone. Discuss the importance of nonstructural, finishing details in architecture. Would a pyramid have the same effect without its capstone? Have students look closely at buildings in their town or community. Then ask them to decide which parts were added to the building after completion of the basic structure to strengthen the building's aesthetic appeal. Have students make sketches to document their findings and then present their sketches to the class.

Studio Skills

Have students construct a pyramid out of sugar cubes and white glue, carefully scraping the sides to achieve as smooth a surface as possible. Have them build models of the great pyramid built for King Khufu and its accompanying small pyramids and mortuary temples. They may use sand to landscape the areas between the various structures.

Art Criticism

To help students gain a more concrete understanding of the size of the pyramid, consider having groups of them pace off an area that corresponds roughly in size to the square base of the structure (that is, about 750 feet per side). Then have students pace off the base of the school building and determine how many such buildings could fit inside the pyramid.

More About... **Pyramid of Khufu.** Ask students to consider the question in the caption to Figure 7.4. Discuss how the pyramid's design addresses both its symbolic purpose as a monument to a pharaoh and its practical purpose as a fortress to protect the pharaoh's remains and belongings. Discuss the features that were intended to make a pyramid impregnable to thieves and whether there were other measures that could have been taken to protect the burial chambers from intruders. Encourage interested students to find out more details about the design and construction of the pyramid. Have them share their discoveries with the class.

Art History

Remind students that tomb construction has played a central role in the history of art. Point out that when, during the Renaissance, Pope Julius II commissioned Michelangelo to design a tomb for him, the artist conceived a design containing forty statues. One of the completed statues, that of Moses, is shown in Figure 16.22, page 371. How is such a grand design reminiscent of the final resting places of pharaohs?

Critical Thinking

Call students' attention to the step pyramid of King Zoser in Figure 7.5. Have volunteers offer theories as to how the huge blocks of limestone in such structures might have been lifted and fitted together. Challenge groups of students to solve an engineering problem of their own by devising and then executing a plan for constructing a scale model of the structure using only corrugated cardboard and scissors.

Did You Know?

Egyptian temples were known for their immense proportions. The temple at Karnak was about 1,300 feet long and covered the largest area of any religious structure ever built. The great hall could accommodate almost any of the great cathedrals in Europe.

Looking at it from the outside, you might expect the inside of the pyramid to be spacious. This is not the case. Except for passageways and a few small rooms called galleries, the pyramid is made of solid limestone. Why build such a massive structure and then provide such little space inside? To answer this question, you must first learn something about the religious beliefs of the ancient Egyptians. As you will see, religion influenced every phase of Egyptian life.

Influence of Religion

Egyptian religion placed great importance on the resurrection of the soul and eternal life in a spirit world after death. The Egyptians believed that the soul, or *ka,* came into being with the body and remained in the body until death. At death, the *ka* would leave the body for a time and eventually return and unite with the body again for the journey to the next world and immortality. If the body were lost or destroyed, the *ka* would be forced to spend eternity wandering aimlessly. For this reason, the Egyptians went to great lengths to preserve and protect the body after death. Following a complicated

embalming process, the body was wrapped in strips of cloth and placed in a fortress-like tomb, where it would be safe until the *ka's* return. Such a tome served as a kind of insurance against final death.

The Pyramids as Tombs

The most impressive tombs were built for the pharaohs. Each pharaoh was more than a king; in the eyes of the people, he was also a god. When he died, the pharaoh was expected to join other gods, including *Re,* the sun god; *Osiris,* the god of the Nile and ruler of the underworld; and *Isis,* the great mother god.

Each pyramid was built to house and protect the body of the pharaoh and the treasures he would take with him from this world to the next. His body was sealed in a **sarcophagus,** *a stone coffin.* It was then placed in a burial chamber located in the center of the pyramid. Dead-end passages and false burial chambers were added to the building. These were meant to confuse tomb robbers and enemies who might try to destroy the pharaoh's body. To an Egyptian, the destruction of the body was the most horrible form of vengeance.

Time & Place
CONNECTIONS

Ancient Egypt
c. 3,100–300 B.C.

STONE PALETTE OF NARMER. This flat stone palette shows images and symbols of King Narmer, also called Menes. The other side of the palette has a small indentation in the center, used for mixing eye paint.

SHIPPING TRADE. Egyptians traveled in boats up the Nile to other Mediterranean cities. Their cargo boats could be filled with items for trade with cities in Mesopotamia and Arabia.

Activity **Map Skills.** Locate a map showing Egypt and the Mediterranean Sea. Trace water routes that linked cities along the Nile River with other settled areas that carried on trade with Egypt.

Time & Place
CONNECTIONS

Ancient Egypt

Have students examine and discuss the images in the Time & Place feature. Then assign the activity. Suggest that students work with partners or in small groups to create their own maps, showing suggested trade routes. Students can draw or trace basic maps, or they can use computers to print prepared maps or to draw and print their own maps. After they have shown possible trade routes on their maps, some students may want to write directions for following these trade routes or write descriptions of trading expeditions.

■ **FIGURE 7.5** Structures of this kind were one step in a long tradition of Egyptian tomb building. Why were tombs such an important concern for the Egyptians?

Step Pyramid of King Zoser. Saqqara, Egypt. c. 2681–2662 B.C.

Evolution of the Pyramid Shape

The pyramid shape developed gradually. Originally, the Egyptians buried their dead in hidden pits and piled sand and stone over the top. Later this practice changed, and the Egyptians began to use sun-dried bricks to build mastabas. A **mastaba** is *a low, flat tomb.* These rectangular tombs had sloping sides and contained a chapel and a false burial chamber in addition to the true one hidden deep inside. In time, several mastabas of diminishing size were stacked on top of each other to form a step pyramid (Figure 7.5). Finally, they were built without steps, and a point was added on the top, thus creating the true pyramid form.

Construction of the Pyramids

Thousands and thousands of workers toiled for decades to build a single pyramid. Limestone was quarried and dragged to the construction site and then carefully fitted into place. How the Egyptians managed to lift and fit these huge blocks of stone, each averaging 2.5 tons, into place remains unclear.

By the time of the Middle Kingdom, the weakened position of the pharaohs and the threat of invasion made construction of

large-scale structures such as the pyramid impractical. Many small pyramids and mastabas may have been built during this period. However, these were probably made of mud bricks, which soon crumbled and disintegrated. More permanent tombs prepared for the pharaoh were cut into the rock cliffs of a valley across the Nile from the capital city of Thebes.

The Temples

If the pyramids are evidence of the skill of Old Kingdom builders, then the great temples are proof of the genius of New Kingdom architects.

The practice of burying pharaohs and nobles in tombs hidden in the cliffs west of the Nile continued throughout the New Kingdom. Meanwhile, architects took on more important tasks. Temples were erected along the eastern banks of the river near Thebes, and these became more and more elaborate. Each of these temples was built by command of a pharaoh and was dedicated to the pharaoh's favorite god or gods. When the pharaoh died, the temple became a funeral chapel where people brought offerings for the pharaoh's *ka.*

Chapter 7 *The Art of Ancient Egypt* **153**

CULTURAL DIVERSITY

Cultural Traditions. Have students choose a particular culture and research its beliefs and practices concerning death, burial, and an afterlife. Some possible choices are Native American, Christian, Hindu, Tibetan Buddhist, Balinese, and Orthodox Jewish. Have students present their findings and then discuss how the various cultural traditions differ from Egyptian beliefs and practices. Students may wish to create a display of their findings to be set up in the classroom and shared with other students.

Have students examine the Temple of Amon (Figure 7.6) on page 154. Let them read about each detail identified in the Looking Closely feature. Then ask: What type of construction was used? In what structures previously studied have you come across this technique? Encourage students to browse through subsequent chapters looking for other structures that make use of post-and-lintel construction.

Extension

Display several types of building stone, including limestone, and have students use simple carving implements to attempt to carve each. List the qualities of each type of stone on the board. Invite students to speculate about why Egyptians built pyramids and other structures out of limestone. Discuss what other choices were available in the Nile River valley environment.

CLOSE

Ask a volunteer to explain the development of the pyramid, while other volunteers draw examples of step pyramids and the later pyramids on the board. Have students identify the functions the structures served.

The Temple of Amon

■ **FIGURE 7.6**

A temple built to honor a particular god often was enlarged by several pharaohs until it reached tremendous proportions. The ruins of the Temple of Amon at Karnak dedicated to the all-powerful chief god of Thebes, will give you an idea of what these gigantic structures must have looked like.

■ **FIGURE 7.6**

Hypostyle Hall, Temple of Amon. Karnak, Egypt. c. 1279–1212 B.C.

DETAILS OF THE TEMPLE OF AMON

A wide avenue led directly to the front of this massive temple complex.

- The great doorway was flanked by **obelisks**, *tall, four-sided, pointed stone shafts.*
- Statues of the pharaoh and huge banners opened onto an uncovered courtyard.
- Entry to the great hall lies beyond the courtyard.
- Massive stone columns reached a height of nearly 70 feet.
- The sanctuary was the small, dark, and mysterious chamber where only the pharaoh and certain priests were allowed to enter.

LESSON ONE REVIEW

Reviewing Art Facts

1. How did the fertile soil of the Nile River valley influence the lives of the people in ancient Egypt?
2. When did an Egyptian civilization develop along the banks of the Nile, and how long did it continue to exist?
3. What are the three major historical periods of ancient Egypt?
4. Why and for whom were the pyramids built?

Activity . . . *Your Name in Hieroglyphics*

Ancient Egyptians developed a complex language containing more than 600 characters. This language of pictures and sounds remained a mystery until Napoleon invaded Egypt in 1799. An officer in the army found a stone, now known as the Rosetta Stone, with an account of the crowning of Ptolemy V, an Egyptian ruler, carved in three languages. The first was Egyptian hieroglyphics; the second was Demotic, a popular language; and the third was Greek. By comparing these three languages, scholars were able to finally break the code of hieroglyphics.

Learn more about Egyptian hieroglyphics. Do research at the library or on the Internet to find an example of simple translated characters. Try writing your name or a sentence with these characters, and share the meaning of the characters with your class.

LESSON ONE REVIEW

Answers to Reviewing Art Facts

1. They changed from food gatherers to food producers.
2. 3000 B.C.; for 3,000 years.
3. The Old, Middle, and New Kingdoms.
4. They were built to honor and house the spirit of the pharaoh.

Activity...*Your Name in Hieroglyphics*

Suggest that students work with partners to learn more about hieroglyphics. Some students may have access to popular games and publications that present simplified versions of the hieroglyphic symbols; these can be shared as appropriate. Provide time for students to compare and discuss their hieroglpyhic messages.

Egyptian Sculpture and Painting

Vocabulary
■ hieroglyphics

Discover
After completing this lesson, you will be able to:
■ Discuss the uses of sculpture, relief sculpture, and painting in ancient Egypt.
■ Explain the strict set of rules imposed on Egyptian artists.

*A*ncient Egypt's most impressive achievements in the field of art were the publicly visible pyramids and temples. Within the pyramids, however, were sculptures and paintings. Many of these treasures have survived over the centuries.

Sculpture

Despite every precaution taken by the Egyptians, the fortress-like pyramids and tombs of the pharaohs were soon robbed of their treasures. Frequently the mummified bodies of the pharaohs were mutilated or destroyed in the process. To make certain the *ka* still would have a body to unite with, sculptors were ordered to carve the pharaoh's portrait out of hard stone. These sculptures were placed in the tomb near the sarcophagus, where they acted as substitutes for the body inside. The Egyptians believed that even if the real body were destroyed, the *ka* would be able to enter the stone substitute for the journey to the next world.

The Great Sphinx
■ FIGURE 7.7

The strength and dignity that were a trademark of the pyramids also characterized the sculptures produced during the Old Kingdom.

Perhaps the most familiar and impressive example of Old Kingdom sculpture is the Great Sphinx (Figure 7.7). Carved from rock at the site, the Sphinx presents the head of a pharaoh, probably the Fourth Dynasty pharaoh, Khafre, placed on the body of a reclining lion. It towers to a height of almost 65 feet.

Portrait of Khafre
■ FIGURE 7.8

In the seated portrait of Khafre, the figure has the solid, blocklike form of the hard diorite stone from which it was carved. (See Figure 7.8, page 156.)

The pharaoh is shown sitting-erect and attentive. His body appears stiff and rigid, but the head has a more lifelike appearance.

■ **FIGURE 7.7** The massive size of the Great Sphinx was intended to demonstrate the power of the pharaoh. Why do you think the pharaoh's head was placed on the body of a lion?

Great Sphinx, Giza, Egypt. c. 2600 B.C.

155

LESSON TWO RESOURCES

Teacher's Classroom Resources
📁 Cooperative Learning 11
📁 Enrichment Activity 15
📁 Reproducible Lesson Plan 16
📁 Reteaching Activity 16
📁 Study Guide 16

CHAPTER 7
LESSON TWO

Egyptian Sculpture and Painting

FOCUS
Lesson Objectives
■ After studying this lesson, students will be able to:
■ Evaluate Egyptian sculpture and painting.
■ Describe the strict set of rules imposed on Egyptian artists.

Building Vocabulary
Let volunteers share what they already know about hieroglyphics. Then have students check the meaning of the term as presented in the Glossary, and ask a volunteer to explain the derivation of the word, as presented in a dictionary.

Motivator
Exhibit photographs that exemplify frontal and profile views. After establishing that the figure in Figure 7.12 (page 159) is shown in profile, challenge students to identify the single facial feature that is shown as it would appear from the front (the eye). Point out that this apparent "mistake" was quite intentional-that it was part of a system of rules followed by Egyptian artists.

Introducing the Lesson
Ask students to think about reasons people have portraits painted or photographed (to honor them and to preserve their memory among those who care about them). Ask students to imagine a society in which only nobility or the very wealthy are featured in portraits. What does this reveal about the culture? Reveal that ancient Egypt was such a culture.

Aesthetics

Divide the class into groups and have them debate whether it is better for a ruler to commission idealized, authoritative portraits like Figure 7.8 or portraits that are more lifelike and informal, such as the one in Figure 7.9. Encourage students to consider the viewpoints of the rulers who commission portraits and of the subjects meant to view them. You may wish to conclude this activity by examining recent political campaign posters and flyers that include photographs. Discuss whether present-day political leaders want to appear dignified and aloof or friendly and informal. Would a politician desire the same sort of image for both a campaign poster and a painted portrait to be hung in a museum? Why or why not?

Did You Know?

The sculpture of Khafre shown on this page was one of several carved for the pharaoh's temple located near his pyramid and the Sphinx at Giza.

Symbolism in Egyptian Art

In studying Khafre's portrait, you may have the feeling that the pharaoh is aware of, but above, the concerns of ordinary mortals. He looks straight ahead, yet the eyes seem alive to events taking place around him. It is this quiet aloofness that makes this portrait a symbol of eternal strength and power—befitting a king and a god. Look below at some of the uses of symbolism in this sculpture.

3 A falcon, which represents Horus, the god of the sky, was placed behind Khafre's head to remind viewers of the pharaoh's divinity. Khafre was considered to be the descendent of Re, the sun god.

2 His right hand forms a fist, which must have once gripped some symbol of his high office.

1 The pharaoh's throne is inscribed with symbols proclaiming him the king of Upper and Lower Egypt.

■ **FIGURE 7.8** Pharaoh Khafre, (front view only). c. 2600 B.C. Diorite. 1.7 m (66") high. Egyptian Museum, Cairo, Egypt.

Symbolism in Egyptian Art

Examine the feature on this page with the class. Guide students in identifying and discussing the specific symbols included in the seated portrait of Khafre, Figure 7.8. The falcon, with wings slightly spread, is hidden behind the cloth headdress worn by the pharaoh. Hieroglyphic markings appear on the side and foot of the throne. Ask students to discuss how these symbols contribute to the strength and dignity portrayed in the work.

Portrait of a Middle Kingdom Ruler
■ **FIGURE 7.9**

The Middle Kingdom, which lasted from around 2050 to 1800 B.C., was a time of law and order that ended when Egypt was invaded by the Hyksos. Much of the sculpture produced during this period was destroyed by the invading Hyksos and by the New Kingdom rulers who followed.

The works that survived have a wide range of quality. A fragment of a portrait of King Sesostris III (Figure 7.9) is an example of the skill and sensitivity demonstrated by the best of the Middle Kingdom carvers. The expression on this surprisingly realistic face suggests none of the confidence and aloofness noted in the portrait of Khafre. In this work, the firmly set mouth and the "worry" lines above the eyes convey a look that is troubled and weary.

The great pharaoh Khafre never would have been portrayed with the expression seen on the sculpture of Sesostris III, but Khafre ruled during the Old Kingdom— a time when no one dared question the pharaoh's divine power or authority. Conditions had changed by the Middle Kingdom, when this pharaoh's portrait was carved. The sculptor captured a look of concern and resignation on the face of this ruler, whose authority depended largely on his personality, strength, and cleverness.

Egyptian Empire Expands

By about 1570 B.C., all of the conquering Hyksos who had not been killed or enslaved had been driven out of the country. Egypt then entered a period of expansion and prosperity known as the New Kingdom.

The Egyptians maintained their powerful army, which had been formed to defeat the Hyksos invaders. They waged a series of successful raids both to the east and into the rest of Africa.

Eventually, Egypt found itself in control of a vast territory.

The expansion of the Empire, which now extended from the upper Nile to the Euphrates River, brought new wealth to the country, and this wealth encouraged artistic activity. During the New Kingdom, sculptors were commissioned to complete a variety of works. These ranged from huge tomb sculptures carved in the native rock to smaller pieces used to decorate temples. Statues of pharaohs were often gigantic, reaching heights of 90 feet. Some statues were painted and had eyes made from rock crystal, which heightened their realistic appearance.

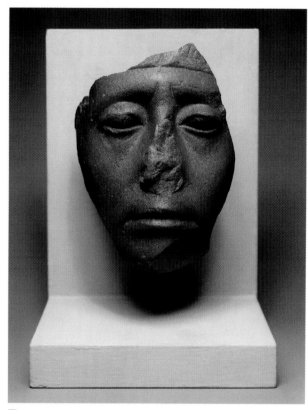

■ **FIGURE 7.9** The sculptor recognized that King Sesostris III was a careworn individual as well as a ruler and a god. **Compare this portrait with a formal photograph of a current head of state.**

Fragment of Head of King Sesostris III. 1887–49 B.C. Red quartzite. 16.5 cm (6¹/₂") high. The Metropolitan Museum of Art, New York, New York. Purchase, Edward S. Harkness Gift, 1926. (26.7.1394).

Chapter 7 *The Art of Ancient Egypt* **157**

TEACH
Art History

Point out that the falcon on the figure of Khafre and the lion's body at the base of the Great Sphinx are two examples of gods that took the form of animals. Then have students assemble a chart that lists as many ancient Egyptian gods and goddesses as they can discover. The chart should include the name of each deity, a drawing, and information about its powers and how it was worshiped by the Egyptians.

Studio Skills

Remind students that the Great Sphinx's head was a portrait of the pharaoh who commissioned the sculpture. Have students use colored markers and paper to draw portraits of themselves with the body of an animal. Invite students to share their drawings with the class and explain why they chose a certain animal to be part of their self-portrait.

Art History

Have students research the regalia and ornaments appearing in the representations of the pharaoh Khafre (Figure 7.8, page 156) and Queen Nefertiti (Figure 7.11, page 158). Is the pharaoh wearing ordinary or ceremonial garments? What is the cylindrical shape beneath his chin? What materials were used in the queen's necklace? Is she wearing eye makeup or has the artist simply exaggerated the outline of Nefertiti's eyes for artistic effect? Is she wearing a crown or is it a stylized version of hair?

More About... **Egyptian Monuments.** Explain to students that although the Sphinx and other Egyptian monuments have endured for centuries, their future survival is now in jeopardy. The sources of potential harm include pollution, which erodes stone, and technological advances. The completion of the Aswan High Dam in 1970 led to an increase in underground water, which has seeped into the limestone walls of temples. The most unlikely—and most harmful threats—are human beings themselves! When tourists crowd into ancient tombs, the humidity rises, causing walls to dampen and paint to chip.

Studio Skills

Have students create miniature models of a room from an Egyptian tomb and its contents. They should begin by researching a list of the items that might be buried with a pharaoh. They may fashion the walls and various artifacts of cardboard, painting them with colored markers before assembly. Ceilings should be omitted so that viewers can see inside the tombs.

Art History

Have students research the role of a pharaoh's wife, particularly Queen Nefertiti. Did any pharaoh's spouse also rule Egypt? Were wives regarded as goddesses just as their husbands were considered gods? Students may also wish to explore the career of Hatshepsut, who led the Egyptian government for about 20 years.

Aesthetics

Direct students to Figure 7.13 (page 161) and explain the concept of *horror vacui,* or fear of empty space. Discuss this term and ask: Why were tomb painters reluctant to leave blank space on the walls? Then ask students to find other works in this book that reflect the aesthetic principle of horror vacui. (Several possibilities appear in Chapter 15, for example, stained-glass windows in Figure 15.6, page 335 and the cathedral portal in Figure 15.15, page 340.) Discuss whether all works embracing this principle share a particular mood or feeling.

Portrait of Akhenaton

■ **FIGURE 7.10**

During the New Kingdom, the pharaoh Amenhotep IV, or Akhenaton, refused to follow the religious customs of his ancestors. Many of Akhenaton's portraits depict him realistically, with an elongated head, pointed chin, heavy lips, and a long, slender neck (Figure 7.10). Much of the art created during Akhenaton's reign also took on a more realistic look. Instead of the solemn, stiff likenesses favored by earlier pharaohs, Akhenaton's portraits are more natural and lifelike. They often show him in common, everyday scenes in which he is playing with his daughters or strolling with his wife, Nefertiti (Figure 7.11).

■ **FIGURE 7.10**

Akhenaton (Amenhotep IV). 18th Dynasty. 1348–1336 B.C. Fragment of a limestone statue from the Temple of Aton, Karnak. Egyptian Museum, Cairo, Egypt.

158 **Unit Two** *Art of Early Civilizations*

Although Akhenaton's revolutionary religious ideas died with him, much of the art produced after his death continued to exhibit the realistic, relaxed poses favored during the reign of this unusual king.

Relief Sculpture

About 4,500 years ago, a relief panel was carved showing a man of that period and two of his children (Figure 7.12). This panel illustrates an artistic style practiced without change throughout the long history of Egyptian art.

■ **FIGURE 7.11** Notice the similarities in the expressions shown on the faces of Akhenaton (Figure 7.10) and his wife, Queen Nefertiti. **How did the sculptors convey a feeling of authority?**

Queen Nefertiti. c. 1360 B.C. Limestone. Approx. 51 cm (20″) high. Äeyptisches Museum, Staatliche Museen, Berlin, Germany.

CULTURAL DIVERSITY

Animals in Artworks. Discuss with students how animals symbolically represent certain qualities in various cultures. For example, just as the lion was associated with the pharaoh's courage and strength, the bald eagle is often used to suggest the vision and power of the United States. Discuss how animals that are not so prized in one culture can be very important and esteemed in another (for example, fish are revered by certain Eastern cultures). Have students write a short essay that explores why a culture chooses a particular animal as a symbol.

Methethy with His Daughter and a Son
■ **FIGURE 7.12**

Notice the unusual appearance of the figure of Methethy. His head, arms, legs, and feet are in profile, but his shoulders and eye are shown as seen from the front. The man even appears to have two left feet, since there is a big toe on the outside of each foot. Furthermore, the figure seems to have been twisted in some way, making it look flat. All parts of the body seem to be at the same distance from the viewer's eye.

Did the artist who carved this panel simply lack the skill needed to make his portrait more lifelike? A close examination of the figure reveals that this explanation is not reasonable. The head, for instance, is skillfully modeled and looks realistic. The body is correctly proportioned, and details on the other parts of the panel show that the sculptor could carve realistically when he chose to. He also knew how to achieve effective design relationships. The detailed areas at the top and left edge of the panel offer a pleasing contrast to the large area occupied by the figure of the man.

■ **FIGURE 7.12**
This limestone relief conforms to the rules governing ancient Egyptian art. Why does this figure look appealing and familiar, in spite of the distortions required by the rules of Egyptian art?

Methethy with His Daughter and Son. c. 2565–2420 B.C. Polychromed limestone relief. 143 × 76 cm (56¹⁄₄ × 30″). The Nelson-Atkins Museum of Art, Kansas City, Missouri. Purchase: Nelson Trust.

Time & Place CONNECTIONS
Ancient Egypt
c. 3,100–300 B.C.

NECKLACE. This gold and jeweled ornament represents the falcon god Horus. Small statues and symbols like these were created to honor and protect the pharaohs.

CARTOUCHE. Early Egyptians used a form of picture writing to create a pictogram called a cartouche. These carved oval symbols represent the name of an important person.

*A*ctivity **Compare and contrast.**
Symbols were significant to society and were used in various forms in the Egyptian culture. Look through the text and identify two other cultures that used symbolism in writing and ornamentation. How do these symbols differ and how are they similar?

Chapter 7 *The Art of Ancient Egypt* **159**

CHAPTER 7
LESSON TWO

Art History
Remind students that the ancient Egyptians were not the only people to paint the inside of tombs. The early Christians also painted pictures on the interiors of catacombs in Rome. Display color photos of Christian catacomb art. Discuss why the images seem relatively crude and unsophisticated. Compare the experience of Egyptian artists with the plight of early Christian artists. The first group was paid by the king to prepare an elaborate tomb, while the second group worked in cramped, secret quarters to escape persecution.

Art Criticism
Have students bring in comic strips from a local newspaper. Review how the various elements and principles of art are used in both the comics and in Egyptian tomb painting.

Art History
Have students find the figures of the servants in Figures 7.13 and 7.14 (page 161). Then have them compare the Egyptian images with the servants in Figures 19.8 (page 426) and 19.17 (page 434). Discuss the differences between the representation of servants in ancient Egypt and those by European artists. Ask why each group wanted to paint servants and why servants were, or were not, considered worthy of being made the main subject of a painting.

Time & Place CONNECTIONS
Ancient Egypt

Guide students in describing and discussing the images in the Time & Place feature. Ask: What is the relationship between these special symbols and the Egyptian rulers? How do the symbols relate to Egyptian gods? What do such symbols tell about the culture and the daily life of ancient Egyptians?

Assign the activity, and let students meet in groups to compare and discuss their results. In addition, encourage volunteers to learn more about Egyptian scarabs: What did they symbolize? How and why were they used? Have volunteers report their findings to the rest of the class.

159

Studio Skills

Explain to students the pictographic nature of the Egyptian system of writing. Show some of the symbols and their definitions. Then have students devise a pictographic language of their own. The language must be complete enough so that students can write a short description of what they did during a recent weekend. Have students display their work and invite classmates to interpret the texts.

Study Guide

Distribute *Study Guide* 16 in the TCR and review key concepts with students. 📁

Cooperative Learning

Remind students that much of the art they have examined in this lesson is available for inspection thanks to the efforts of archaeologists. Then distribute *Cooperative Learning* 11, "Uncovering Ancient Life," in the TCR. Challenge each group of students to take responsibility for planning a different facet of an imaginary archaeology excursion. 📁

Studio Activities

Ask students to review the wall paintings in Figures 7.13 and 7.14, noting in particular the position of different anatomical parts in the various figures depicted. Then distribute *Studio* 9, "Designing a Mural in the Egyptian Style," in the TCR. Have students complete the activity and display their finished murals. 📁

Rules of Egyptian Art

The carving's unusual features adhere to a strict set of rules followed by all Egyptian artists. These rules required that every part of the body be shown from the most familiar point of view. For this reason, the head, arms, legs, and feet were always shown in profile, whereas the eyes and shoulders were presented as seen from the front. Following these rules meant that paintings and relief sculptures of the body looked distorted and unnatural. It is a credit to the skill of Egyptian artists, however, that this distortion was kept to a minimum and did not detract from the appealing appearance of their works.

The Egyptians were greatly concerned about life after death. Paintings and relief sculptures of the dead were meant to serve as substitutes for the body. When artists created images of the pharaoh, they wanted to make sure that all parts of the body were clearly shown. This was more important to them than making the image beautiful or accurate. A complete image was vital. After all, if an arm were hidden behind the body in a relief sculpture or painting, it would mean that the *ka* would enter a body that was without an arm. It would then be forced to spend eternity in a deformed body. Thus, a strict set of rules was developed over the years to make sure that all parts of the body were shown—and shown correctly—in sculptured and painted images.

Art in Egyptian Tombs

At one time, it was customary for a pharaoh to have his wife, servants, and slaves sealed in the tomb with him when he died. Then, when he arrived in the next world, he would have his loved ones and servants with him for eternity. They would make sure that his new life would be just as pleasant as the old one. In time, this practice of burying others with the pharaoh was discontinued. Instead, painted relief sculptures or sculptures in the round were substituted for real people and placed in the tomb with the dead king.

Painting

Eventually the tomb of every important or wealthy person was enriched with painted relief sculptures. When it became difficult and costly to carve reliefs on the rough, hard walls of cliff tombs during the Middle Kingdom, painting came into its own as a separate art form.

First, the walls of the cliff tombs were smoothed over with a coating of plaster. When the plaster was dry, the artist went to work, drawing a series of horizontal straight lines on the plastered wall. Figures and animals were carefully arranged along these lines to tell a story, usually an event from the life of the deceased. The pictures were then colored with rich red and yellow hues, with black and blue-green added for contrast. Typically, little shading was used, so the figures tend to look flat, as if they had been cut from paper and pasted on the wall. This method of arranging pictures in horizontal bands and using bright colors with little shading resulted in a style similar to that of contemporary comic strips.

Nakht and His Wife
■ FIGURE 7.13

A look inside a New Kingdom tomb prepared for a priest named Nakht will add to your understanding of Egyptian painting.

Portraits of Nakht and his wife are found on one wall of this tomb (Figure 7.13). They are surrounded by busy servants engaged in various hunting and fishing activities on the priest's land.

The way in which the figures have been painted should look familiar. This artist, like the relief sculptor who created the portrait of Methethy, was bound by the standard rules of ancient Egyptian art.

The figures of the priest and his wife are much larger than the other figures, to show that Nakht and his wife are more important. They are also stiff and solemn because the Egyptians believed that such a pose was fitting for people of high rank. In contrast, the smaller servants are shown in more natural positions as they hunt and fish.

More About...   **Art Styles.** Help students understand why a particular culture requires artists to work under strict rules. Ask volunteers to find out more about the rules that guided Egyptian tomb painters, the limitations placed on Byzantine icon painters, and the requirements for state-sponsored art in the former Soviet Union. Volunteers might also research the current controversy surrounding the National Endowment for the Arts (that is, whether the organization should dictate policies of acceptability of style and content among artists to whom it awards grants).

Hieroglyphics

Under the border at the top of the painting in Figure 7.13 are rows and columns of small birds and other shapes. These are Egyptian **hieroglyphics,** *an early form of picture writing.* These symbols, some of which represented objects, communicated information and were included in wall paintings and other art forms to help tell the story. The signs were generally spaced to form attractive patterns, frequently clusters of squares or rectangles.

False Door Stela
■ FIGURE 7.14

Painted on another wall of the small chapel within Nakht's tomb is a false door. The priest's *ka* was expected to pass through this door in search of offerings. Arranged in bands on either side of the door are painted substitutes for servants bearing food and drink for the *ka*. An assortment of offerings is painted in the section directly below the door where the *ka* would be sure to find them when it entered.

Egyptian artists were content to echo the art of the past until they encountered new ideas from outside sources, such as Greece and Rome. As the influence of these new ideas grew, Egyptian art lost much of its unique character, and Egyptian artists ceased to create the unique art of the pharaohs.

■ **FIGURE 7.13** Several scenes are shown in this wall painting. What does this painting indicate about the social structure of ancient Egypt?

Nakht and His Wife. Copy of wall painting from Tomb of Nakht. c. 1425 B.C. 2 × 1.53 m (6.5 × 5'). Egyptian Expedition of the Metropolitan Museum of Art, New York, New York. Rogers Fund, 1915. 15.5.19e.

■ **FIGURE 7.14** The priest's *ka* was expected to pass through the door painted on the wall of his tomb. **How does this false door demonstrate the important relationship between religion and art in ancient Egypt?**

False Door Stela. Copy of a wall painting from the Tomb of Nakht. Thebes, Egypt. c. 1425 B.C. 1.69 × 1.54 m (5.5 × 5'). 1:1 scale with original. Egyptian Expedition of the Metropolitan Museum of Art, New York, New York. Rogers Fund, 1915. 15.5.19c.

LESSON TWO REVIEW

Reviewing Art Facts
1. Why were sculptures of the pharaoh created?
2. How are the portraits of Akhenaton different from portraits of earlier pharaohs?
3. Describe the rules that Egyptian artists were required to follow when painting or sculpting a figure.
4. What is the purpose of a false door painted on the wall of an Egyptian's tomb?

Activity... *Creating Egyptian Wall Scenes*

Ancient Egyptian wall paintings depict the customs, dress, and events in Egyptian life. Like other art forms, Egyptian wall paintings were done according to strict rules. The paintings have a distinctly flat look and were organized into cells that show the passage of time. Find other examples of Egyptian wall painting and study their distinctive design motifs.

Using sketch paper, develop a storyboard of several cells that tells of an event in your life. Transfer your sketches to drawing paper and add color using colored pencils or markers. Write an explanation of your story and share it with the class.

Chapter 7 *The Art of Ancient Egypt* **161**

CHAPTER 7
LESSON TWO

ASSESS
Checking Comprehension
➤ Have students respond to the lesson review questions. Answers are given in the box below.
➤ Distribute *Application* 7, "A Journey Up the Nile," in the TCR. 🗁

Reteaching
➤ Assign *Reteaching* 16, found in the TCR. 🗁
➤ Write the names of artworks covered in the lesson on flash cards. Challenge students, as you hold up a card, to identify the work named as an example of a wall painting, relief sculpture, or sculpture in the round.

Enrichment
➤ Have a student find a translation of *The Egyptian Book of the Dead,* which includes information that can guide the deceased through his or her travels in the afterlife. The student can either give a presentation that explains the contents of this book or provide a dramatic reading of a passage or two.
➤ Distribute *Enrichment* 15, "The Great Sphinx at Giza," in the TCR. 🗁

Extension
Students interested in archaeology can learn about colleges and universities that offer courses in this field.

CLOSE
Have students look through their textbooks and find an example of a portrait that violates most or all of the Egyptian rules for depicting a person, and explain how their choice departs from Egyptian rules.

LESSON TWO REVIEW

Answers to Reviewing Art Facts
1. They were substitute homes for the *ka* in case the tomb was robbed.
2. He was portrayed realistically.
3. Head, arms, legs, and feet were shown in profile, eyes and shoulders shown as in frontal view.
4. A priest's *ka* was to pass through this door in search of offerings.

Activity...*Creating Egyptian Wall Scenes*
Help students discuss the customs, dress, and events shown in the painting in Figure 7.13, page 161. Then guide students in planning their own wall scenes. Ask: What event do you want to show? Which separate parts of the event will you depict? What details of modern life do you want to include?

Studio LESSON

Designing and Painting a Sarcophagus Cover___

Objectives

■ Draw and paint a sarcophagus cover featuring the full figure of a deceased king or queen.

■ Design the figure to conform to the same rules imposed upon ancient Egyptian artists.

■ Use intense hues to paint the figure and duller hues to paint the background.

Motivator

Divide the class into three groups. Provide each group with a one-word identification of a ruler: scholar, tyrant, or spiritual leader. Have the members of each group discuss and determine the appearance, personality, and accomplishments of their ruler, and then draw and paint this image.

Studio Skills

Use the board or an overhead projector to demonstrate how the drawing of the ruler should be designed to fit comfortably within the designated shape of the sarcophagus cover. Review the rules students must follow when drawing the head, arms, legs, feet, eyes, and shoulders. Emphasize how contrasts of bright and dull hues can be used to separate the image of the ruler from the background.

Critiquing

Have students apply the steps of art criticism to their own artworks using the "Examining Your Work" questions on this page.

162

Studio LESSON

Designing and Painting a Sarcophagus Cover

Materials

- Pencil
- White drawing paper, 9 × 24 inches
- Ruler
- Mat board, 9 × 24 inches
- Tempera or acrylic paint
- Brushes, mixing tray, and paint cloth
- Water container

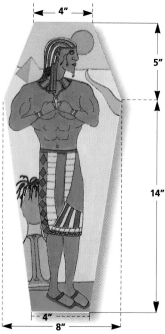

■ **FIGURE 7.15** Student Work

Complete a pencil drawing of a fictional deceased ruler designed to fit within a shape representing the lid of a sarcophagus. Use only the element of line in your drawing and include: the head, arms, legs, and feet of the ruler in profile and the eyes and shoulders as seen from the front; clues about the ruler's appearance, personality, and major triumphs.

Use tempera or acrylic to paint your sarcophagus design. Paint the ruler with intense hues and light values. Use dull hues for the background to provide contrast and emphasize the figure. Avoid gradation of value to make the shapes in your painting appear two-dimensional.

Inspiration

Study the relief sculpture of Methethy (Figure 7.12, page 159) and the wall painting from the tomb of Nakht (Figure 7.13, page 161). How did Egyptian rules for painting and sculpture contribute to the way the figures were painted and carved? Identify the intense hues and values employed. What did the Egyptian artists do to emphasize the most important parts of their paintings?

Process

1. Working with several other students, identify a fictional ruler as a scholar, a spiritual leader, a military hero, or a vicious tyrant. Discuss the ruler's appearance, personality, and triumphs. Make a list of the visual clues that help illustrate these features.

2. On the drawing paper, complete an outline for a sarcophagus lid conforming to the measurements shown in the student artwork.

3. In pencil, draw your version of the ruler to fit in this space. Follow the same rules imposed on ancient Egyptian artists.

4. Transfer your drawing to the mat board. Paint your design with tempera or acrylic. Use intense and light values for the figure that will contrast with the dull background hues to achieve emphasis. Paint shapes without gradation to reproduce the flat quality in Egyptian painting. Place your finished painting on display with those of other students.

Examining Your Work

Describe. Does your painting follow the Egyptian rules of art? Are the head, arms, legs, and feet shown in profile? Are the eyes and shoulders presented as seen from the front? Is it possible to determine whether the ruler was a scholar, a spiritual leader, a military hero, or a tyrant?

Analyze. Point out areas in your painting where intense colors are used. Where are dull hues employed? Where are light values used? How does the contrast of these

hues and values help emphasize portions of the painting? Do the shapes appear flat and two-dimensional?

Interpret. Can your classmates read the visual clues in your painting and correctly identify the personality of your ruler? What clues helped them recognize the ruler's accomplishments?

Judge. Do you think this is a successful painting? What aesthetic qualities did you use to determine whether or not it was successful?

162

ASSESSMENT

Examining Your Work. After students have assessed their own artwork, you may want to have them work in small groups to examine and discuss the works of their classmates. Display the paintings in three groups, according to the original assignment. (See Motivator above.) Encourage students to discuss and compare the paintings in each group: Which attempts

to portray the identity and personality of the ruler are most successful? Why? Which works most closely follow the Egyptian rules of art? With what effect?

After they have considered their classmates' paintings, you might have students write brief journal entries, discussing what they have learned from this assignment.

Reviewing the Facts

Lesson One

1. How long did each of the three major historical periods of ancient Egypt last?
2. How did the Egyptians view the pharaoh?
3. Name three other gods that the Egyptians believed the pharaoh would join when he died.
4. Why were dead-end passages and false burial chambers added to pyramids?
5. Describe the development of the true pyramid form.
6. Why and when were temples built?

Lesson Two

7. How did the expansion and prosperity of the New Kingdom affect artistic activity?
8. Explain why Egyptian paintings show the head, arms, legs, and feet in profile, but show the eyes and shoulders as seen from the front.
9. Why were sculptures or painted relief sculptures buried in the tomb with the dead king?

Thinking Critically

1. **COMPARE AND CONTRAST.** Compare the reigns of Menes, Amenhotep III, and Amenhotep IV. Which reign do you think contributed the most to the development of Egyptian arts? Support your opinion.
2. **ANALYZE.** What clues do sculptures such as the portrait of Khafre (Figure 7.8, page 156) provide about the Egyptians' beliefs concerning the afterlife and the pharaoh's divinity?

 ART SOURCE Use the *Performing Arts Handbook* on page 576 to learn about music, dance, and theatre from many diverse cultures.

CAREERS IN Art After studying about the pyramids, read about a career as an architect in the *Careers in Art Handbook*, page 598.

interNET CONNECTION Visit Glencoe Art Online at *www.glencoe.com/sec/art*. Take a virtual tour of ancient Egyptian sites and learn more about Egyptian artifacts in an activity.

Technology Project

Egyptian Portraits

Egyptian art is filled with portraits that were made to preserve the subject for eternity. As in all other Egyptian art, portraits were painted and sculpted according to strict rules. Examine the Egyptian relief portrait in this lesson. Compare it to the Byzantine portraits in Chapter 13. How are Egyptian portraits similar to the Byzantine portraits? How are they different?

Throughout history, portraits have been an important part of the art of many cultures. What functions do you think portraits of the pharaoh and his queen served in Egyptian culture? Do you think that portraits of rulers might have shared similar functions in both Egyptian and Byzantine cultures? In what ways?

1. Ask a classmate to use a digital camera to take two full-length portrait views of you, one frontal view and one profile view. Save these images in a computer paint or draw program. Experiment and manipulate your image to create a digital full-length self-portrait that follows the strict rules of Egyptian art .
2. Look closely at the Egyptian symbols, hieroglyphics, and design motifs that surround the figures portrayed in Figures 7.11, 7.12, and 7.14 on pages 158–161. Research the meanings of some of these symbols. Choose some of these elements that you think might relate to aspects of your identity, and include them in your work.
3. Print your Egyptian self-portrait and display it in your classroom. Describe your work to your class using the four steps of art criticism.

163

CHAPTER 7
REVIEW ANSWERS

Reviewing the Facts

1. The Old Kingdom lasted approximately 500 years, the Middle Kingdom 250 years, and the New Kingdom over 1,200 years.
2. As part king, part god.
3. Re, Osiris, and Isis.
4. To confuse tomb robbers.
5. It began with a flat tomb called a mastaba. In time, mastabas were stacked to form step pyramids. Eventually, the structures were built without steps and a point was added to the top.
6. They were built during the New Kingdom, as proof of the genius of the architects.
7. Sculptures were commissioned, and emphasis was placed on realistic appearance.
8. It was a way of ensuring that the body, as a vessel for the ka, was complete for the journey to the next life; otherwise, it would be doomed to spend eternity in a deformed state.
9. They were substituted for the real people who used to be placed in the tomb with the pharaoh.

Thinking Critically

1. During the reign of Menes, Egypt was established as a powerful force and majestic pyramids were constructed; Amenhotep III brought Egypt to the peak of its power and influence; Amenhotep IV, broke with tradition and helped launch new directions in art.
2. Answers should indicate awareness of the pose suggesting omnipotence, strength, and power, and the presence of the falcon as a symbol of deity.

Teaching the Technology Project

Provide class time during which students can examine the Egyptian portraits in this chapter and compare them with Byzantine portraits, such as those shown in Figures 13.11 and 13.13 on pages 293–295. Encourage students to consider portraits in other chapters—Chapter 12, Chapter 17, and Chapter 24, for example—as well.

 ART SOURCE Assign the feature in the *Performing Arts Handbook*, page 576.

CAREERS IN ART If time permits, have interested students investigate the career information in the *Careers in Art Handbook*, page 594.

interNET CONNECTION Have students go online and learn more about artists on preselected Web sites with the Internet activity for this chapter.

Art of Rising Civilizations

Unit Three acquaints students with "the glory that was Greece and the grandeur that was Rome," with special attention to the cultural and artistic legacies of these great ancient civilizations.

Chapter 8 *Greek Art* introduces students to the origins of this birthplace of Western civilization and its contributions to sculpture, painting, and especially architecture, as evidenced by temples like the Parthenon.

Chapter 9 *Roman Art* examines the innovative improvements Roman architects brought to the building processes devised largely by the Greeks and also traces the Greek influence in painting and sculpture.

National Museum of Women in the Arts

You may wish to use the National Museum of Women in the Arts videodisc and/or CD-ROM. The videodisc features a bar code guide, and the interactive CD-ROM provides stimulating activities.

164

<hr />

More About...

Doves. Tell students that the work on these pages is a mosaic from the villa of the Roman Emperor Hadrian. Mosaics became a very popular way to decorate homes in Roman times. Ask volunteers to explain this technique. Point out that small pebbles or small, uniformly shaped pieces of stone, marble, or colored glass were pressed into a soft cement-like material called grout. Spaces between the pebbles or stones were then filled with the same material which hardened as it dried. Mosaics were first used because they formed a durable, waterproof surface for floors and pavements. Eventually they became popular as wall coverings for outdoor fountains and gardens, and to decorate the interior walls of homes.

Art of Rising Civilizations

A description of Hadrian's villa:
" . . . a palace with every
variety of room, and
gardens so crowded
with famous works of
art that every major
museum in Europe has
enriched itself from the ruins."

Will Durant
The Story of Civilization,
Volume 3 (1944)

Doves. From the villa of Emperor Hadrian at Tivoli.
2nd century A.D. Mosaic. 85 cm (33$^1/_2$") high.
Capitoline Museum, Rome, Italy.

165

Introducing the Unit

Bring an almanac to class, and ask a volunteer to look up the country of Greece. Have the student share highlights of the demographic information contained, (e.g., the country has a population of approximately ten million, is located on the Balkan Peninsula, and is roughly the size of New York state). Then have another student do the same with Rome. Point out that these facts, though useful, reveal nothing of the mighty empires once known as Greece and Rome. Explain that in the chapters to come students will gain a better understanding of the role of Greece and Rome in world history and, at the same time, develop a sense of the world's artistic debt to those places.

Discussing the Quotation

Tell students that the illustration is a mosaic discovered on a wall in a villa near Rome, Italy, that was built in the second century A.D. Ask students if they know who Hadrian was and why he is famous. Explain that Hadrian was one of the Roman Emperors. He was an intellectual and had an interest in Greek culture. He traveled throughout the Roman provinces, and brought back artworks and ideas from his travels that he used to decorate his lavish home and gardens. Have them discuss the quotation and ask if they can imagine the palace and artworks collected by Hadrian. Direct students' attention to the work and ask them to speculate on where the mosaic might have been located.

Teacher Notes

Greek Art

ADDITIONAL CHAPTER RESOURCES

Activities

- 📁 Advanced Studio Activity 8
- 📁 Application 8
- 🖱 Chapter 8 Internet Activity
- 📁 Studio Activity 10

Fine Art Resources

- 🔖 **Transparency**
  Art in Focus Transparency 11
  Laocoon
- 🖼 **Fine Art Print**
  Focus on World Art Print 8
  Panathenaic Amphora

Assessment

- 📁 Chapter 8 Test
- 📁 Performance Assessment

Multimedia Resources

- 🎭 Artsource® Performing Arts package
- 💿 National Gallery Laser Disc
- 💿 National Museum of Women in the Arts CD-ROM
- 📼 Arts & Entertainment Videos

NATIONAL STANDARDS FOR ARTS EDUCATION

The National Standards for Arts Education provide guidelines for grade-appropriate competency in the visual arts. The Content Standards for grades 9–12 are:

1. Understanding and applying media, techniques, and processes.
2. Using knowledge of structures and functions.
3. Choosing and evaluating a range of subject matter, symbols, and ideas.
4. Understanding the visual arts in relation to history and cultures.
5. Reflecting upon and assessing the characteristics and merits of their work and the work of others.
6. Making connections between visual arts and other disciplines.

Listed below are the National Standards for the Visual Arts addressed in this chapter. For a breakdown of the categories listed under each content standard, refer to the *Reproducible Lesson Plans* booklet in the TCR.

1. (a, b) **2.** (a, b) **3.** (a, b) **4.** (a) **5.** (a, b, c) **6.** (b)

HANDBOOK MATERIAL

Faustwork Mask Theater
(page 582)

 Art

Scenic Designer *(page 599)*

Beyond the Classroom

Teachers can find professional development resources and a collection of excellent lesson plans created by teachers by connecting to the resources at Ask ERIC. Find them by visiting our Web site at *www.glencoe.com/sec/art.*

🕐 **Out of Time?** If time does not permit teaching this chapter in its entirety, you may wish to preview the artwork and captions with students. Scan the heads in each lesson with students. Discuss the Looking Closely features and examine the Three Orders of Decorative Style on page 172.

Greek Art

CHAPTER 8

Greek Art

INTRODUCE

Chapter Overview

CHAPTER 8 introduces students to the artistic accomplishments of ancient Greece.

Lesson One describes the rise of Greek civilization and its contributions to art and architecture.

Lesson Two traces the evolution of Greek sculpture.

Studio Lessons focus on drawing and painting features of Greek architecture.

Art & Mathematics

Guide students in examining and discussing the work that opens this chapter. Then have students read and discuss the introduction to the Golden Section: In what portions of the Parthenon can you see the application of this mathematical concept? How do you explain the visual appeal of the proportions described in this rule? How could you express the concept in a mathematical formula?

Encourage a small group of interested students to learn more about the Golden Section and its application in architecture. Let these volunteers report their findings to the rest of the class.

National Standards

This chapter meets the following National Standards for the Arts:

1. (a,b)	**4.** (a)
2. (a,b)	**5.** (a,b,c)
3. (a,b)	**6.** (b)

Art & Mathematics ■ **FIGURE 8.1** Scholars believe that Greek architects used a concept known as the Golden Section to design and construct buildings such as the Parthenon. The Golden Section is a mathematical process in which shapes grow larger according to a fixed ratio as they rotate around a central axis. Greek architects used the Golden Section to determine the proportions of building elements such as columns.

The Parthenon (view from the west). Acropolis. Athens, Greece. c. 447 B.C.

CHAPTER 8 RESOURCES

Teacher's Classroom Resources
- Advanced Studio Activity 8
- Application 8
- Chapter 8 Internet Activity
- Studio Activity 10

Assessment
- Chapter 8 Test
- Performance Assessment

Fine Art Resources
- *Art in Focus* Transparency 11
  Laocoon
- *Focus on World Art* Print 8
  Panathenaic Amphora

*W*hy do historians place so much importance on events that
happened more than 30 centuries ago in an area not
much larger than the state of Arizona?
Why are the names of such artists as Myron,
Phidias, and Polyclitus still held in esteem, even though none of
their works is known for certain to exist today?
Why are plays by Sophocles still performed all over the world?
Why do people still find the comedy of
Aristophanes funny after thousands of years?
The answer is simple: That area—Greece—was the birthplace of
Western civilization. Furthermore, its contributions
to art, literature, and theatre, have had a profound effect on
artists up to the present day.

Introducing the Chapter

On the board, write the phrase *Ancient Greece.* Beneath it, write the subheadings *philosophy, literature, mathematics,* and *sports.* Challenge students to brainstorm contributions of this once mighty power in each of these areas. Record their ideas on the board.

A R T S O U R C E **Theatre** While studying this chapter, use *Performing Arts Handbook* page 582 to help students understand how the masks, expressions, and human characters portrayed by Robert Faust have their roots in the masks and dramas of the ancient Greek theatre.

YOUR Portfolio

In your sketchbook, plan a design for a vase, a bust, or a temple. Begin by writing a brief description of your proposed design. Be sure to consider subject, media, size, color, and detail in your design description. Now make a thumbnail sketch of your design. After completing this chapter, analyze your design and compare it with the Greek style of art. Consider making changes in your design. Keep your notes and sketches in your portfolio.

Focus ON THE ARTS

LITERATURE
Ancient Greek poetry was usually recited to music. Epic poems like Homer's *Iliad* and *Odyssey,* and Greek plays, created by Aeschylus and Sophocles, were spoken to music.

DANCE
Dance was an integral part of Greek drama. Dances were performed by men and incorporated graceful hand movements. In Sparta, dance was considered a part of gymnastic exercise.

THEATRE
Plays in ancient Athens were presented on a semicircular, open-air stage surrounded by seats that were set into a sloping hillside. These outdoor stages are known as amphitheaters.

Focus ON THE ARTS

Explain to students that theatre in Greece was more than just entertainment. Greeks expressed their religious beliefs through a combination of music, poetry, and dance. Plays written by Aeschylus, Sophocles, and Euripides defined tragedy as an art form that would last for centuries. Have interested students locate passages from a Greek tragedy. Have them take on individual parts and read for the class.

167

DEVELOPING A PORTFOLIO

Personal Style. The success of a portfolio is based in part on the ability of the student to impress evaluators with his or her style. Personal talents are showcased in the portfolio, but can only be effective when students learn to set long-term goals and sustain projects that eventually meet those ambitions. Ask them regularly to evaluate their constructive efforts toward the complete portfolio. How aware is each student of his or her style? What do students know about their style that will help them strengthen the portfolio's presentation? Have they chosen pieces that emphasize their style?

The Birthplace of Western Civilization

Focus

Lesson Objectives

After studying this lesson, students will be able to:
■ Identify the contributions of the Greeks to architecture.
■ Describe the three orders of decorative style that originated in Greece.

Building Vocabulary

Ask students to locate the cities of Corinth and Doris on a detailed map of Greece. Then, have them search the chapter for boldfaced terms related to these place names. Ask a volunteer to read aloud the definitions of Corinthian Ionic, and Doric orders. Have students compare and contrast features of these styles in Figure 8.7, page 172.

Motivator

Direct students' attention to the photograph of the Parthenon in Figure 8.1, and ask them to name some qualities of the work. Point out that, as with other works from ancient Greece, this one exhibits a concern for harmony, grace, and precision. Ask students to examine other works in the lesson, looking for details in each that reinforce these qualities.

Introducing the Lesson

Ask students to describe the purpose of the United Nations. Have them think of other organizations, past or present, that have carried out similar functions (e.g., the League of Nations, NATO). Tell students they will be learning about another such organization of early Greek civilization, the Delian League.

The Birthplace of Western Civilization

Vocabulary
■ raking cornice
■ cornice
■ frieze
■ lintel
■ capital
■ shaft
■ stylobate
■ pediment
■ entablature
■ column
■ colonnade
■ Doric order
■ Ionic order
■ Corinthian order

Artist to Meet
■ Exekias

Discover
After completing this lesson, you will be able to:
■ Identify the contributions of the ancient Greeks to the history of art.
■ Describe the three orders of decorative style that originated in Greece.

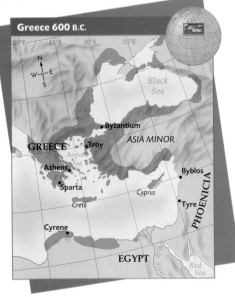

Greece 600 B.C.

MAP SKILLS
■ **FIGURE 8.2** The Greek city-states were separated from each other by mountains, valleys, and the sea. How do you think these separations affected interactions between the city-states?

168

The history of ancient Greece begins around 2000 B.C. At that time the earliest people probably entered the land. The descendants of these primitive peoples remained there, and in about 500 years a strong culture known as the Mycenaean had formed. However, the power of the Mycenaeans eventually gave way to that of a stronger people.

After a series of invasions, the warlike Dorians took over the land in about 1100 B.C. This event changed the way of life in many areas as the conquerors mingled with the native populations. Towns eventually grew into small, independent city-states. Unlike many other civilizations, which developed as collections of city-states that formed kingdoms or empires, the Greek city-states remained fiercely independent.

The independence of Greek city-states can be accounted for, at least in part, by geography. Greece is divided by mountains, valleys, and the sea. (See map, Figure 8.2.) These physical separations made communication difficult. In addition to these natural barriers, social barriers of local pride and jealousy also divided the city-states. These factors combined to keep the Greek city-states from uniting to form a nation.

History of Greek City-States

There was continuing rivalry among the city-states, but none ever succeeded in conquering the others. The rivalry was so intense that the city-states could not even agree to work together toward common goals. Fear alone finally united them long enough to fight off invaders from Persia during the fifth century B.C.

Suspecting further invasions by the Persians, several city-states joined together to form a defensive alliance. This alliance came to be known as the Delian League because its treasury was kept on the island of Delos. The larger cities contributed ships and men to this alliance, while the smaller cities gave money.

Because it was the most powerful member of the Delian League, Athens was made its permanent head. Athenian representatives were put in charge of the fleet and were authorized to collect money for the treasury.

Pericles, the Athenian leader, moved the treasury from Delos to Athens. Before long, Pericles began to use the Delian League's money to rebuild and beautify Athens, which had been badly damaged by the Persian invaders.

The Peloponnesian War

The greatness of Athens was not destined to last long. Pericles' actions were bitterly resented by the other members

LESSON ONE RESOURCES

Teacher's Classroom Resources

📁 Art and Humanities 11, 12

📁 Cooperative Learning 12

📁 Enrichment Activity 16

📁 Reproducible Lesson Plan 17

📁 Reteaching Activity 17

📁 Study Guide 17

of the Delian League, especially Sparta and Corinth. Finally, in 431 B.C., this resentment led to the Peloponnesian War. At first, Pericles successfully withstood the challenge of Sparta and the other city-states, but in 430 B.C. a terrible plague killed a third of the Athenian population. A year later, Pericles himself was a victim of this plague. With the death of its leader, Athens was doomed.

After Athens was defeated, a century of conflict followed. One city-state, then another gained the upper hand. This conflict so weakened the city-states that they were helpless before foreign invaders. In 338 B.C., Greece was conquered by Macedonia.

Despite a history of rivalry, wars, and invasions, the Greek people made many important contributions to art. Their accomplishments in architecture, particularly temple architecture, were among their most enduring legacies to Western civilization.

Greek Architecture

The Greeks considered their temples dwelling places for the gods, who looked—and often acted—like humans. The Greeks believed that the gods controlled the universe and the destiny of every person on Earth. The highest goal for the Greeks was doing what the gods wanted them to do. As a result, fortune tellers and omens, which helped people discover the will of the gods, were important parts of religious practice.

Early Greek Temples

The earliest Greek temples were made of wood or brick, and these have since disappeared. As the economy prospered with the growth of trade, stone was used. Limestone and finally marble became the favorite building materials.

The basic design of Greek temples did not change over the centuries. Greek builders chose not to alter a design that served their needs and was also pleasing to the eye. Instead, they made small improvements on the basic design in order to achieve perfection. Proof that they realized this perfection is represented in temples such as the Parthenon. (See Figure 8.1, page 166 and Figure 8.3.) It was built as a house for Athena, the goddess of wisdom and guardian of the city named in her honor.

The Parthenon
■ FIGURE 8.3

In 447 B.C., using funds from the treasury of the Delian League, Pericles ordered work to begin on the Parthenon. Ten years later the building was basically finished, although work on the exterior carvings continued until 432 B.C. The construction of such a building in just a decade is impressive. Still, it was finished none too soon. The last stone was hardly in place before the Peloponnesian War started.

■ **FIGURE 8.3** Greek architects used the post-and-lintel method of construction. Identify the posts and lintels in this temple. **How would you describe the overall balance of this building? What adjective best describes this temple?**

The Parthenon, Acropolis, Athens, Greece. c. 447 B.C.

Chapter 8 *Greek Art* **169**

TEACH
Using Map Skills

Have students refer to the map in Figure 8.2 and, if possible, also locate Greece on a relief map or globe. Ask them to identify mountains, rivers, and other natural barriers or obstacles. Guide students in discussing how such barriers helped prevent the Greek city-states from becoming unified. Ask the students to consider how ancient Greeks communicated with each other over long distances, pointing out that it would be difficult, for example, to send a messenger over mountains. Have students also discuss how such natural barriers might have insulated communities and made them alert to the presence of outsiders and strangers.

Critical Thinking

Point out that the Greek word for "architect" is *architekon*, which means "chief builder." Explain that in ancient Greece, an individual with this job description was responsible for a building's design and also for administrative and technical decisions, such as how to move the heavy blocks used in construction. Ask students to discuss, and then research, the job title of an individual who carries out these tasks in present-day society. Then ask: Why in modern society are the jobs of architect, engineer, and site manager differentiated? Conversely, why might the Greeks have assigned engineering responsibilities to the same person who designed a structure?

Teacher Notes _____

Cross Curriculum

TECHNOLOGY. Call students' attention to the date in the credit line of Figure 8.3. Explain that, around the time of the Parthenon's completion, a number of important milestones in science and technology were occurring, such as the invention of the compass in China, the Phoenicians' circumnavigation of Africa, and the completion of the Shwe Dragon Pagoda in Burma.

Art Criticism

Point out that the Greeks painted their marble buildings in much the same way we paint our houses today. The colors used, moreover, were usually bright. Ask students to imagine the Parthenon as a brightly colored building. Have them discuss the impact that the element of color might have had on a viewer's perception of the structure. Which hues and color schemes would have made the structure seem less imposing? Which, if any, would have contributed to its stateliness and grandeur? What sort of pattern or design might have been used to help the Parthenon retain a sense of harmony?

LOOKING Closely

Let students work with partners or in small groups to read and discuss Details of Greek Temple Construction. What is the purpose of each feature? Which are structurally necessary? What purposes do they serve? Which features are simply decorative? Then encourage students to identify as many of these features as possible in the Parthenon, shown in Figure 8.3.

The Parthenon made use of the most familiar features of Greek architecture: post-and-lintel construction; a sloping, or gabled roof; and a colonnade. Like all Greek buildings, the parts of the Parthenon were carefully planned to be balanced, harmonious, and beautiful.

Greek Temple Construction

Like most Greek temples, the Parthenon is a simple rectangular building placed on a three-step platform (Figure 8.4).

The Parthenon consisted of two rooms (Figure 8.5). The smaller held the treasury of the Delian League, and the larger housed a colossal gold-and-ivory statue of Athena. (See Figure 8.17, page 180.) Few citizens ever saw this splendid statue. Only priests and a few attendants were allowed inside the sacred temple. Religious ceremonies attended by the citizens of Athens were held outdoors in front of the buildings.

Exterior Design of the Parthenon

Because few people were allowed inside the temple, there was no need for windows or interior decorations. Instead, attention centered on making the outside of the building as attractive as possible.

LOOKING Closely

DETAILS OF GREEK TEMPLE CONSTRUCTION

Examine the illustration and locate each of the following:

- **Raking cornice.** The raking cornice is *a sloping element that slants above the horizontal cornice.*
- **Cornice.** A cornice is *a horizontal element above the frieze.*
- **Frieze.** This is *a decorative band running across the upper part of a wall.*
- **Lintel.** The lintel is *a cross-beam supported by columns.*
- **Capital.** *The top element of a column.*
- **Shaft.** The shaft is *the main weight-bearing portion of a column.*
- **Stylobate.** Find the stylobate at *the top step of the three-step platform.*
- **Pediment.** This is *the triangular section framed by the cornice and the raking cornice.*
- **Entablature.** The entablature is *the upper portion, consisting of the lintel, frieze, and cornice.*
- **Column.** A column is *an upright post used to bear weight.*
- **Colonnade.** A colonnade is formed by *a line of columns.*

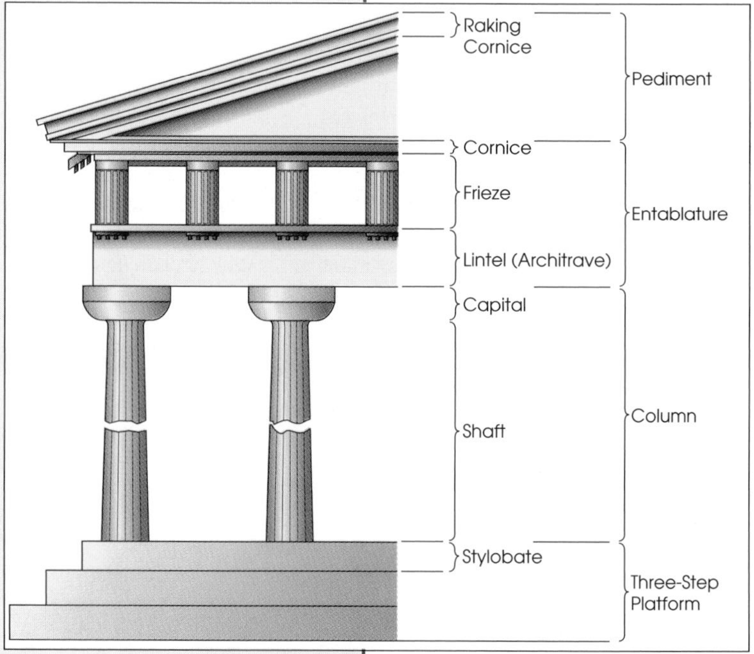

■ **FIGURE 8.4**

Features of Temple Construction

More About... **Pericles.** Pericles, known as the father of democracy, was born about 495 B.C. and died of the plague in 429 B.C. Once he gained power, Pericles made many reforms. He limited the power of the aristocracy and passed laws that allowed common people to serve in any public office. He also required pay for public officials, so that those who were poor could also participate. He wanted to create a democracy, but he also wanted Athens to be a great power, so he fought wars with other countries, including Egypt and Sparta.

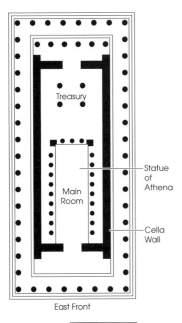

■ **FIGURE 8.5** Plan of the Parthenon

It is hard to see with the naked eye, but there are few, if any, perfectly straight lines on the entire structure. The three-step platform and the entablature around the building *look* straight but actually bend upward in a gradual arc, so that the center is slightly higher than the ends. This means that the entire floor and ceiling form a low dome that is slightly higher in the middle than at the edges. The columns also curve slightly outward near their centers. Like muscles, they seem to bulge a bit as they hold up the great weight of the roof. In addition, each column slants inward toward the center of the building. The columns were slanted in this way to prevent a feeling of top-heaviness and to add a sense of stability to the building.

Use of Color

The Greeks preferred bright colors to the cold whiteness of their marble buildings. For this reason, they painted large areas of most buildings. Blue, red, green, and yellow were often used, although some details were coated with a thin layer of gold. Exposure to the weather has removed almost all of the color from these painted surfaces. If you look closely at the more protected places of these ancient buildings, however, you still might find a few faint traces of paint.

The Parthenon has been put to a variety of uses over its long history. It was a Christian church in the fifth century and a mosque in the 15th century. Its present ruined state is due to an explosion that took place in the 17th century. The ruins have now been restored as much as possible with the original remains.

The Acropolis

■ **FIGURE 8.6**

The Parthenon was only one of several buildings erected on the sacred hill, or *Acropolis,* of Athens. The Acropolis (Figure 8.6) is a mass of rock that rises abruptly 500 feet above the city. Like a huge pedestal, it was crowned with a group of magnificent buildings that symbolized the glory of Athens.

Covering less than 8 acres, the Acropolis was filled with temples, statues, and great flights of steps. On the western edge was a huge statue of Athena so tall that the tip of her gleaming spear served as a beacon to ships at sea. The statue was created by the legendary sculptor Phidias, and it was said to have been made from the bronze shields of the defeated Persians. Today, the crumbling but still impressive ruins of the Acropolis are a reminder of a great civilization.

■ **FIGURE 8.6** The sacred hill, or Acropolis, was crowned with a group of buildings symbolizing the glory of Athens. Why do you think the Athenians chose this location for their religious buildings?

View of the Acropolis today. Athens, Greece.

Studio Skills

Working in pencil, students can create a plan for a school building in the style of an ancient Greek architectural structure. Have them include various views. Sketches should use a post-and-lintel system and any number of the features delineated in Figure 8.4. Make sure students consider the function and existing floor plan of their building.

Art Criticism

Have students consider the floor plan (Figure 8.5) and the exterior (Figure 8.3, page 169) of the Parthenon. Ask them to identify elements of art within the work and to evaluate the use of the principles of art.

Cross Curriculum

LITERATURE. Remind students that many writers have commented on Greek works of architecture (e.g., Henry James in *Transatlantic Sketches,* Cellini in his autobiography). Have students develop bibliographies of works throughout the centuries with this common theme. (As a starting point, groups might consult the catalog in the library under the subject headings architecture and Greece.) Encourage volunteers to report to the class on the views and comments of different writers.

Critical Thinking

Remind students that the ancient Greeks were gifted mathematicians. Their mathematical aptitude is revealed in the columns of the Parthenon which, although they give the illusion of being straight-sided, bulge outward slightly at the center. Ask a volunteer to research and report on the phenomenon responsible for this illusion, known as compensation.

Teacher Notes

Providing Resources. Often, students are asked to find out more about certain artists, artworks, and artistic styles. To help students research and organize their reports, ask the school librarian to lead a tour of the library, explaining specifically how students can locate and use sources of art information. Have students draw a floor plan of the library summarizing this information. The floor plan, along with notes on the information provided by the librarian, should facilitate research.

Art Criticism

Have students study the three orders of columns in Figure 8.7. What differences and similarities can they find in the use of line? What type of balance can students identify in the three stylistic orders?

Aesthetics

Direct students' attention to the picture of the Temple of Athena Nike (Figure 8.8). What features can students identify that were added purely in the interest of beauty? Which features do they see that serve a structural function?

Studio Skills

Using sketch paper and pencils, students can design an original style of decorative column. In preparing to work, they should consider the following questions: Will the column be tall and slender or short and stout? Will the shaft be ribbed or plain? Will the capital be ornate, as in the Corinthian order, or plain as in the Doric? After considering these questions, students can proceed to make scale models of their columns working with either pastels and paper or clay and modeling tools. Students should display completed efforts.

Did You Know?

In the mid-sixth century B.C., writers began to compose architectural treatises detailing solutions to technical problems and describing such matters as how to transport and place large blocks of stone. These were among the earliest Greek prose works. One such work by Theodorus, describes the square, the level, and the lathe, all of which are still important tools in modern building.

The Three Orders of Decorative Style

Over the centuries, the Greeks developed three orders, or decorative styles (Figure 8.7). Examples of these orders can be seen in various structures that were built by ancient Greeks and still survive today.

The Doric Order

The Parthenon was built according to the earliest decorative style, the Doric Order. In

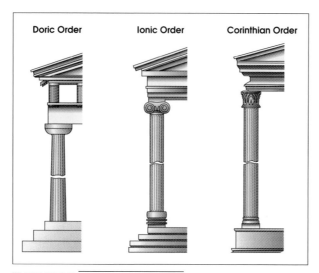

■ FIGURE 8.7 Three Orders of Decorative Style

the **Doric order,** *the principal feature is a simple, heavy column without a base, topped by a broad, plain capital.*

The Ionic Order

The Greeks later began using another order, the Ionic. This order employed columns that were thinner and taller than those of the Doric. In the **Ionic order,** *columns had an elaborate base and a capital carved into double scrolls that looked like the horns of a ram.* This was a more elegant order than the Doric, and for a time architects felt it was suitable only for small temples. Such a temple was the little shrine to Athena Nike (Figure 8.8), built on the Acropolis between 427 and 424 B.C.

The more they looked at the new Ionic order, the more the Greeks began to appreciate it. Soon they began using it on larger structures such as the Erechtheum (Figure 8.9), a temple located directly opposite the Parthenon. This building was named after Erechtheus, a legendary king of Athens who was said to have been a foster son of Athena.

An unusual feature of the Erechtheum is the smaller of two porches added to its sides. On the Porch of the Maidens, the roof is supported by six caryatids, or columns carved to look like female figures.

■ FIGURE 8.8 Compare this temple with the Parthenon (Figure 8.3). How are the two temples alike? What are the most important differences? What do you think accounts for those differences?

Temple of Athena Nike, Acropolis, Athens, Greece. 427–424 B.C.

COOPERATIVE LEARNING

Architecture. Show students illustrations of St. Peter's Basilica in Rome and the Cathedral of St. Paul in London. Point out that both are well-known examples of the Greek influence on architecture. Working in pairs, students can investigate other structures that exhibit these influences, either in your own city (usually in official structures built in the early part of the twentieth century) or in photographs of buildings in Washington, D.C., of similar vintage. During in-class presentations, partners can display photos of the work in question, explaining which stylistic features the works borrow.

FIGURE 8.9 Notice the two types of columns on this building. What order of columns is found on the stylobate?

Erechtheum, Acropolis, Athens, Greece. 421–405 B.C.

The Corinthian Order

The most elaborate order was the Corinthian, developed late in the fifth century B.C. In the **Corinthian order,** *the capital is elongated and decorated with leaves.* It was believed that this order was suggested by a wicker basket overgrown with large acanthus leaves found on the grave of a young Greek maiden.

At first, Corinthian columns were used only on the inside of buildings. Later, they replaced Ionic columns on the outside. A monument to Lysicrates (Figure 8.10) built in Athens about three hundred years before the birth of Christ is the first known use of this order on the outside of a building. The Corinthian columns surround a hollow cylinder that once supported a trophy won by Lysicrates in a choral contest.

FIGURE 8.10 The columns on this monument are the first known example of the Corinthian order on the outside of a building. Describe the form of this structure. How does it differ from the form used for the Temple of Athena Nike (Figure 8.8)?

Monument to Lysicrates, Athens, Greece. c. 334 B.C.

Chapter 8 *Greek Art* **173**

Art Criticism

Divide the class into small groups. Ask groups to complete detailed descriptions of the columns found in the photograph of the Erechtheum in Figure 8.9. They should note, in particular, the order of the columns used and which columns represent an exception to the three orders studied. Then have the class work jointly to complete a critique of the structure.

Aesthetics

Ask students to compare the three Greek temples in Figure 8.3, Figure 8.8, and Figure 8.9, and the Monument to Lysicrates (Figure 8.10). Point out that each structure, true to Greek design, contains features that serve a purely decorative function; perhaps the most pronounced example of this is the carved female figures, or caryatids, supporting the small porch of the Erechtheum. Ask students to debate which of the structures is the most heavily embellished. What effect does this design decision have on the viewer? Make sure students offer support for their contentions.

Studio Skills

Students can test the assumptions of the previous activity by selecting one of the structures shown and creating a quick sketch of it, minus the decorative features. Have students conclude with a discussion of the function of decorative detail in present-day society. Where is this type of detail used most? What purpose does it serve?

More About... **The Parthenon.** The Parthenon is remarkable for the astonishing technical skill of its construction. No mortar was used anywhere in the building. The stones were cut so precisely that, when fitted together, they form a single smooth surface. The columns, which appear to be carved from single blocks of stone, are actually composed of sections called drums. These are joined together by square pegs in the center. These sections are fitted together so tightly that the cracks between them are scarcely visible.

Explain to students that the Parthenon was built as a temple to the Greek goddess Athena. Remind them that throughout history religion has played a significant role in art. Have groups of students brainstorm, and then find specific examples in other chapters of the textbook of forms of artistic expression with religious influences.

Art History

Point out that the figures on Greek vases were often set in storytelling scenes; art that tells a story is called "narrative art." Ask students to browse through the artworks illustrated in this text in an effort to find other works that could be considered narrative. What do these works have in common with the Greek vases shown in this lesson? What qualities, if any, can be found in all examples of storytelling art?

Cross Curriculum

LITERATURE. Provide students with copies of John Keats's poem "Ode on a Grecian Urn." Ask a volunteer to read the poem aloud as students consider the illustrations of Greek vases in this lesson. Ask whether reading the poem enhances their appreciation of the art. Conversely, does viewing the art enhance their understanding of the poem?

Studio Skills

On sheets of white paper, have students draw the silhouette of a Greek vase using thick black lines. They may choose to use any of the vases shown in this chapter as models, but designs should complement the shape and proportions of the vase. Once the students are satisfied with their pencil sketches, have them paint their designs using tempera or acrylic paint. Remind students to limit the number of colors, as the Greeks did. When the students have completed the project, ask them to exhibit and compare their vase designs.

Greek Vase Decoration

■ **FIGURES 8.11 and 8.12**

The earliest Greek vases were decorated with bands of simple geometric patterns covering most of the vessel. Eventually the entire vase was decorated in this way (Figure 8.11). The years between 900 and 700 B.C., when this form of decoration was being used, are called the Geometric period.

Early in the eighth century B.C., artists began to add figures to the geometric designs on their vases (Figure 8.12). Some of the best of these figures were painted on large funeral vases. These vases were used in much the same way as tombstones are used today, as grave markers. The figures on these vases are made of triangles and lines, and look like simple stick figures. Several figures often appear on either side of a figure representing the deceased, as though they are paying their last respects. Their hands are raised, pulling on their hair in a gesture of grief and despair.

■ **FIGURE 8.11** During the Geometric period, patterns of this kind were found on Greek vases and jugs. What details help you recognize this jug as an example created late in the Geometric period?

Geometric Jug. Seventh century B.C. Terra cotta. 41 cm (16"). Indiana University Art Museum, Bloomington, Indiana.

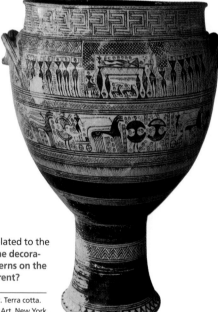

■ **FIGURE 8.12** The figures here are related to the purpose of this funeral vase. How are the decorations here similar to the geometric patterns on the vase in Figure 8.11? How are they different?

Funerary Vase. Athens, Greece. c. Eighth century B.C. Terra cotta. H: 108.2 cm (42 5/8"). The Metropolitan Museum of Art, New York, New York. Rogers Fund, 1914. (14.130.14)

174 **Unit Three** *Art of Rising Civilizations*

CULTURAL DIVERSITY

Religious Traditions. The Parthenon was constructed to meet the unique requirements of ancient Greek religious ceremonies. Religious practices today vary greatly within and between cultures. Instruct groups of students to research different religions in the West and the East to determine how diverse practices influence the design of the structures used for worship. Each group should present their findings in class. Presentations should include visuals illustrating how the interior of each structure is organized.

Realism in Vase Decoration

In time, vase figures became more lifelike and were placed in storytelling scenes. An excellent example of this kind of painting is provided by a vase showing two figures engrossed in a game (Figure 8.13). It was created by an artist named Exekias (ex-**ee**-kee-us) more than 2,500 years ago.

Vase with Ajax and Achilles Playing Morra (Dice)
■ FIGURE 8.13

Have you ever become so caught up in a game that you failed to hear someone calling you? It happens to everyone, no matter how important the person being called or how urgent the summons. Exekias painted such an event on a vase.

■ **FIGURE 8.13** Notice how the artist has arranged this scene to complement the shape of the vase. **What makes this an effective design? What kinds of changes in vase decoration had taken place between the time of the vase shown in Figure 8.12 and this vase by Exekias?**

Exekias. *Vase with Ajax and Achilles Playing Morra (Dice).* c. 540 B.C. Museo Gregoriano Etrusco, Vatican, Rome, Italy.

Study Guide
Distribute *Study Guide* 17 in the TCR and review key concepts with students. 📁

Art and Humanities
Distribute *Art and Humanities* 11, "Words of Greek Philosophers," in the TCR. The activity calls on students to read statements by Greek philosophers, then write interpretations of how the words relate to their own lives. 📁

Studio Activities
Distribute *Cooperative Learning* 12, "Threatre Design through the Ages," in the TCR. Students study the development of theatre space from Greek times through today's conventional theatre. Afterward, they work in teams to build models of different theatre designs. 📁

Art and Humanities
Assign *Art and Humanities* 12, "Music in Greek Cultures," in the TCR. Students compare Greek musical styles with music from other cultures. 📁

More About... **Greek Painting.** Although no great paintings from ancient Greece have survived, it is likely that Greek painters placed great importance on realism. The Roman historian Pliny the Elder supports this notion. He tells of a great competition that took place in the fifth century B.C. The purpose of this competition was to determine which of two famous painters was more skilled in producing lifelike works. The painters, Zeuxis and Parrhasius, faced each other with their works covered by curtains. Zeuxis confidently removed his curtain to reveal a painting of grapes so natural that birds were tricked into pecking at it. Certain that no one could outdo this feat, he asked Parrhasius to reveal his work. Parrhasius answered by inviting Zeuxis to remove the curtain from the painting. When Zeuxis tried, he found he could not—the curtain was the painting.

ASSESS

Checking Comprehension

Have students respond to the lesson review questions. Answers are given in the box below.

Reteaching

➤ Assign *Reteaching* 17, found in the TCR. Have students complete the activity and review their responses. 📁

➤ On a piece of poster board, draw outlines of the features of a Greek temple, including the three orders of columns, the stylobate, the lintel, the frieze, the cornice, and the raking cornice. Cut these features out and use them as flash cards, asking the students to identify the features.

Enrichment

➤ Distribute *Enrichment* 16, "An Ancient Aesthetic," which asks students to read about and research further the Minoans of Crete. 📁

➤ Ask students to research the goddess Athena, patron deity of the Greek city of Athens. Encourage them to share their findings with the class.

Extension

Students can trace the developments of pottery in Native American and other cultures. In what ways are design developments similar to, and different from, those found in Greek vases?

CLOSE

Review the three decorative orders with students. Ask them to describe the basic architectural features of a typical Greek temple. Then ask them which of these features the Parthenon possesses.

Exekias's vase shows two Greek generals playing a board game, probably one in which a roll of the dice determines the number of moves around the board. The names of the generals are written on the vase. They are two great heroes from Greek literature, Ajax and Achilles. The words being spoken by these warriors are shown coming from their mouths just as in a modern cartoon strip. Ajax has just said "tria," or "three," and Achilles is responding by saying "tessera," or "four." Legend says that these two great heroes were so involved in this game that their enemy was able to mount a surprise attack.

Exekias shows the informality of this simple scene. The warriors' shields have been set aside, and Achilles, at the left, has casually pushed his war helmet back on his head. Ajax, forgetting briefly that they are at war, has removed his helmet and placed it out of the way on top of his shield. For a few moments, the Greek heroes are two ordinary people lost in friendly competition.

Exekias's Use of Realism

Exekias also has added details to make the scene as realistic as possible. An intricate design decorates the garments of the two generals. The facial features, hands, and feet are carefully drawn, although the eyes are shown from the front as they were in Egyptian art.

Exekias was not so concerned with realism that he ignored good design, however. The scene is carefully arranged to complement the vase on which it was painted. The figures lean forward, and the curve of their backs repeats the curve of the vase. The lines of the spears continue the lines of the two handles and lead your eye to the board game, which is the center of interest in the composition.

At this stage in Greek vase design, decorative patterns became a less important element, appearing near the rim or on the handles. Signed vases also began to appear for the first time in the early sixth century B.C., indicating that the potters and artists who made and decorated them were proud of their works and wished to be identified with them.

LESSON ONE REVIEW

Reviewing Art Facts

1. Name two factors that contributed to keeping the Greek city-states from uniting to form a nation.
2. What three features of Greek architecture were used in the construction of the Parthenon?
3. Define *frieze*.
4. What decorative style is used on the Erechtheum?

➤ Activity . . . *Greek Vase Design*

We learn about ancient Greeks from vases painted with mythological stories, historical events, and scenes from everyday life. The Greeks used the vessels to carry and store things and for ceremonial purposes. Examine Figure 8.13, page 175, to see how these decorated vases tell us about ancient dress, games, and mythology. Study other examples of Greek vase painting.

Create a design for a vase that tells a story about the present, your life or your experiences. Include some of the distinctive design motifs in your design. Add color to your design and display it in your classroom.

LESSON ONE REVIEW

Answers to Reviewing Art Facts

1. Pride and jealousy; natural boundaries.
2. Post-and-lintel construction, a gabled roof, colonnades.
3. Decorative band running across the upper part of a wall.
4. Ionic.

Activity... *Greek Vase Design*

Have students work in groups to examine the Greek vase and to discuss ideas for their own vase designs. Suggest that they respond to questions such as these: What story or event is worth preserving in this way? Why? What details should you include to make your message clear? What kinds of details should be left out?

The Evolution of Greek Sculpture

Vocabulary
■ contrapposto

Artists to Meet
■ Myron, Phidias, Polyclitus

Discover
After completing this lesson, you will be able to:
■ Explain how Greek sculpture changed over time from the Archaic period, through the Classical period, to the Hellenistic period.
■ Discuss the contributions of Myron, Phidias, and Polyclitus to Greek sculpture.

DETAIL:
Head of Kouros

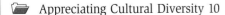
■ **FIGURE 8.14** The stiff figure of this Kouros recalls ancient Egyptian sculpture. Do you think this Kouros was intended to represent a god or an athlete? Explain your reasons.

Kouros. c. 530 B.C. Marble. 200 cm (6'7") high. The J. Paul Getty Museum, Malibu, California.

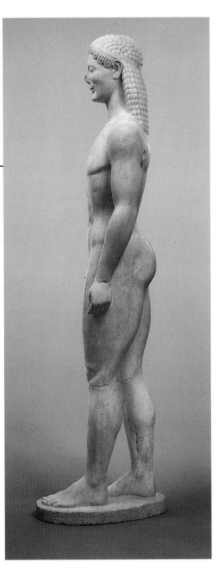

*T*he buildings on the Acropolis were constructed during the fifth and fourth centuries B.C. This was a time in Greek history known as the Classical period. Like architecture, Greek sculpture also reached its peak during this period. To understand and appreciate Greek accomplishments in sculpture, it is necessary to look back to an even earlier time known as the Archaic period.

Sculpture in the Archaic Period

From around 600 to 480 B.C., Greek sculptors concentrated on carving large, freestanding figures known as *Kouroi* and *Korai.* Kouroi is the plural form of Kouros, meaning "youth," and Korai is the plural of Kore, or "maiden."

Kouros
■ **FIGURE 8.14**

The *Kouros* was a male youth who may have been a god or an athlete. This example is from the Archaic period (Figure 8.14). In some ways, the stiffness and the straight pose of this figure bring to mind Egyptian statues. The only suggestion of movement is in the left foot, which is placed slightly in front of the right foot.

Even though the Kouros is stepping forward, both feet are flat on the ground. Of course, this is impossible unless the left leg is longer than the right. This problem could have been corrected if the right leg had been bent slightly, but it is perfectly

177

The Evolution of Greek Sculpture

FOCUS

Lesson Objectives
After studying this lesson, students will be able to:
■ Identify the different periods of Greek sculpture.
■ Identify changes that occurred as Greek sculpture evolved.
■ Discuss the contributions made by Myron, Phidias, and Polyclitus to Greek sculpture.

Building Vocabulary
Let students use their knowledge of language (or dictionaries) to identify the prefix *contra-* in the vocabulary term contraposto. Ask: What is the meaning of the prefix? (against or in opposition to) How does this help you understand the meaning of contraposto?

Motivator
Remind students that art is an expression of a culture. Point out that events that occur in a culture can influence an artist. Have students give examples of political events that have influenced art in our own century. Tell them they are about to learn how the military conquests of a warrior named Alexander the Great influenced Greek culture and art.

Introducing the Lesson
Direct students' attention to the photo of the Kouros (Figure 8.14). Point out that this work, from the earliest period of Greek sculpture, represents the beginning of a process that ended with sculptures that changed the course of art history.

LESSON TWO RESOURCES

Teacher's Classroom Resources
📁 Appreciating Cultural Diversity 10
📁 Art and Humanities 13
📁 Cooperative Learning 13
📁 Reproducible Lesson Plan 18
📁 Reteaching Activity 18
📁 Study Guide 18

TEACH

Art History

Have students page through the lesson, examining the artworks and reading the credit lines. Point out that the sculptures they will learn about here were instrumental in shaping Western art. Challenge groups of students to find out more about a sculpture of equal importance that is not shown here, suggesting the following list of possibilities: the *Venus de Milo;* the *Berlin Goddess;* the portrait statue of *Mausolus;* or the *Cindian Aphrodite.* Each group can give a presentation on the works, including a description, history, name of sculptor (if known), and period.

Art Criticism

Ask students to consider the ways in which the medium and size affect a work of art. Point out that the Hera of Samos (Figure 8.15) is 6 feet tall and quite imposing. What would the effect be if the statue were only 1 foot tall? Have students next turn to the replica of the statue of Athena (Figure 8.17, page 180). After pointing out that the original was made of ivory and gold, ask how different the emotional impact would have been if the work had been carved from limestone or marble. How different would the impact have been if the original were lifesize, rather than 42 feet tall?

178

■ **FIGURE 8.15** Notice how this figure's pose differs from that of the Kouros. Which element of art seems most important here?

Hera of Samos. c. 570–560 B.C. 1.8 m (6′) tall. The Louvre, Paris, France.

straight. Later, Greek artists learned how to bend and twist their figures to make them appear more relaxed and natural.

Except for the advancing left foot, the Kouros is symmetrically balanced. Details of hair, eyes, mouth, and chest are exactly alike on both sides of the figure, just as they are on Egyptian statues. Unlike Egyptian figures, the arms of the Kouros are separated slightly from the body and there is an open space between the legs. These openings help to break up the solid block of stone from which it was carved.

No one knows for certain what the Kouros was meant to be. Some say he represents the sun god Apollo, whereas others insist that he is an athlete. The wide shoulders, long legs, flat stomach, and narrow hips may support the claim that he is an athlete.

The face of the Kouros has a number of unusual features that were used over and over again in early Greek sculptures (Figure 8.14, detail, page 177). Among these are bulging eyes, a square chin, and a mouth with slightly upturned corners. This same mouth with its curious smile can be found in many early Greek sculptures. Greek sculptors wanted their figures to look more natural, and this smile may have been a first step toward greater realism.

The *Hera of Samos*
■ **FIGURE 8.15**

Korai were clothed women, often goddesses, that were also carved during the Archaic period. One of these goddesses, the *Hera of Samos* (Figure 8.15), looks like a stone cylinder. It has the same stiff pose as the *Kouros,* but its right arm is held lightly against the body and the feet are placed tightly together. The missing left arm was bent and may once have held some symbol of authority. There is no deep carving here, and there are no open spaces. Instead, a surface pattern of lines suggests the garments and adds textural interest to the simple form.

 Technology

Cameras. A collection of simple cameras can be very useful in the classroom. With a little instruction, students can use them to explore subject matter, record images, and illustrate reports. Some students who are hesitant about their artistic talents in other media find the medium of photography considerably less intimidating. By carrying a camera, students may become more aware of the visual details of their environment and more apt to record them. Students may also use cameras to record images that will be used later in a studio project, a multimedia presentation, or to record artworks for their portfolios.

Use of Line

Straight vertical lines are repeated to suggest a light lower garment. These contrast with the more widely spaced and deeper lines of a heavier garment draped over her shoulders. The folds of the garments gently follow the subtle curves of the figure. There is little to suggest action or movement. More than 6 feet tall, the *Hera of Samos* must have been an impressive symbol of authority and dignity to all who saw it.

Sculpture in the Classical Period

With each new generation, Greek artists became more bold and skillful. During the Classical period, they abandoned straight, stiff poses and made their figures appear to move in space.

LOOKING Closely

SHOWING ACTION IN SCULPTURE

- The discus thrower is about to put all his strength into a mighty throw, yet his face is completely calm and relaxed. In this respect, the figure is more idealistic than real.

- The athlete's throwing arm is frozen for a split second at the farthest point of the backswing.

- Details reveal that Myron had a thorough understanding of anatomy (how the body is structured).

- The athlete's right leg bears all his weight. His left leg is poised and ready to swing forward.

Myron's *Discus Thrower*

■ **FIGURE 8.16**

You can see how successful the sculptors were by examining a life-size statue of a discus thrower, or *Discobolus* (Figure 8.16), by a sculptor named Myron (**my**-run). Gone is the blocky, rigid pose of the earlier *Kouros.* Myron has skillfully captured an athlete in action.

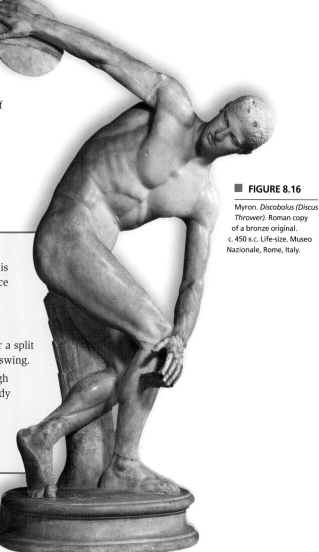

■ **FIGURE 8.16**

Myron. *Discobolus (Discus Thrower).* Roman copy of a bronze original. c. 450 B.C. Life-size. Museo Nazionale, Rome, Italy.

Chapter 8 *Greek Art* **179**

About the *Artwork*

Hera of Samos. Explain that in Greek mythology, Hera is the wife and sister of Zeus, the most powerful god. The figure shown here is a representation of the supreme Greek goddess of heaven. Legend depicts Hera as a notoriously jealous and vindictive individual. Many stories tell of her methods for retaliating against Zeus when he misbehaved. Hera is portrayed as gracious in only one account. It may have been this account that inspired so benign and graceful a sculpture as the Hera of Samos.

Art Criticism

Review with students the steps of art criticism. Remind them that these steps include describing, analyzing, interpreting, and judging. Ask students to select a sculpture from this chapter and to write a short criticism of it. Remind them that the description section should include the size of the work, the medium and process used, and the art elements that the artist emphasized in the work.

Art History

Explain that around the same time Myron was creating his *Discus Thrower,* other developments were taking place in Greek culture. Most notable among them was the redefining of the pictorial representation in three dimensions. Apollodorus is often considered the first master of this technique, having used background landscape in his portraits to suggest deep space.

LOOKING Closely

Guide students in examining Myron's *Discus Thrower* (Figure 8.16). Encourage them to describe each feature identified in the steps of Showing Action in Sculpture, and ask students to relate the figure shown here with real athletes or photographs of real athletes: How did the artist succeed in making this work so realistic? Why do you think he portrayed the athlete's face idealistically, rather than realistically? Have students compare this work with the Kouros shown in Figure 8.14. What kinds of details are included in the later work? With what effect?

Aesthetics

Along the top of the board, write the title and figure number of each sculpture illustrated in this lesson. Divide the class into pairs. Have pairs in turn select an illustration and then study it in an effort to identify the mood of the work. Ask partners to come to the board and list, beneath the appropriate title, adjectives corresponding to the emotions conveyed. After all partners have had a turn, have the pairs switch to a different work and attempt to expand the list of adjectives for the work. Finally, ask students to generalize about the human attributes the Greeks most prized. Do these attributes differ from period to period?

Studio Skills

Remind students that many of the sculptures they are seeing in this lesson are free-standing, or sculptures in the round. Point out that, in creating three-dimensional sculpture, the artist must view the model from all angles.

Place a vase or other object on a table that is convenient for all students to see. Have students draw sketches of the object from various angles. Explain that they should not touch or move the vase, but should draw three or more sketches of it, each from a different point of view. When students have completed their sketches, have them share the sketches with one another. Students should be able to identify the angle from which each sketch was drawn. Discuss whether some sketches seem more accurate than others and why this is so.

■ **FIGURE 8.17** To prevent the head of this colossal Athena from appearing tiny when viewed from floor level, the proportions have been expanded from the waist up. **Do you think that this careful re-creation of an ancient statue is a work of art in its own right? Why or why not?**

Alan LeQuire. *Athena Parthenos.* c. 1993. Fiberglass and gypsum cement, marble, paint, and gold leaf. 13 m (42′) high. The Parthenon, Nashville, Tennessee.

Roman Reproductions

Myron's chief material was bronze. As far as is known, he never worked in marble. Knowledge of his sculptures, however, comes from marble copies produced in Roman times. Not a single certified original work by Myron or any of the great sculptors of Greece exists today. Bronze works, which once numbered in the thousands, were melted down long ago. Even marble sculptures were mutilated, lost, or ruined by neglect. What is known of the ancient Greek works comes from copies made later by Romans, who used them to decorate their public buildings, villas, and gardens.

Sculptures for the Parthenon

It is through Roman copies and descriptions by ancient writers that the works of Phidias (**fhid**-ee-us) are known. He was one of the greatest Greek sculptors and the creator of the gigantic statue of Athena in the Parthenon.

Athena Parthenos
■ **FIGURE 8.17**

Anyone who walked into the darkened room of the Parthenon would have faced Phidias's colossal goddess, towering to a height of 42 feet. Her skin was of the whitest ivory, and over 1 ton of gold was used to fashion her armor and garments. Precious stones were used for her eyes and as decorations for her helmet. A slight smile softened a face that looked as if it could turn cruel and angry at any moment.

Today a full-scale re-creation of this statue stands in the Nashville Parthenon (Figure 8.17). Sculptor Alan LeQuire worked with an international team of scholars to ensure that his work would accurately represent the original. You can see this colossal *Athena Parthenos,* goddess of the Athenians, in a re-creation of the temple originally built for her in 447 B.C.

CULTURAL DIVERSITY

Symbols. Explain that the olive tree is a symbol of the goddess Athena and of the city of Athens. Ask students to think about symbols that other places and cultures have adopted (for example, the eagle as a symbol of the United States). Have them give some examples of symbols with which they are familiar.

Ask students to consider how such symbols might have come into existence and what purpose they serve. You may wish to have students bring examples of these symbols, or make sketches of them, for a classroom display of symbols from different cultures.

Other Sculptures by Phidias

In addition to creating the original statue of Athena, Phidias supervised the decorations on the outside of the Parthenon. One of these decorations was a large relief sculpture that shows 350 people and 125 horses taking part in a religious parade.

Every four years, the citizens of Athens held a great celebration in honor of Athena. The celebration included a procession in which people carried new garments and other offerings to Athena in the Parthenon. These gifts were given as thanks to the goddess for her divine protection. The procession was formed in the city below the Acropolis and moved slowly up a winding road through a huge gateway, the entrance to the sacred hill. Then it wound between temples dedicated to various gods and goddesses and past the huge bronze statue of Athena. The procession finally stopped at the entrance to the Parthenon where, during a solemn ceremony, the presentations were made.

On a 525-foot band, or frieze, Greek sculptors, under the direction of Phidias, show how that parade looked more than 2,400 years ago. The frieze, which was over 3 feet high, ran around the top of the Parthenon walls like a giant stone storyboard.

The processional frieze is no longer on the Parthenon. Badly damaged parts of it are housed in museums in London, Paris, and Athens. This is unfortunate, since they were intended to go together to form a single work of art.

In its original form, the scene begins on the western side of the Parthenon. There the procession is seen taking shape in the city. Riders prepare to mount their prancing horses. Others, preparing to march on foot, stand impatiently, lacing their sandals or adjusting their garments. Farther on, the parade is under way.

Studio Skills

Remind students that the Greeks sometimes painted their statues. Ask students to select one of the sculptures from the lesson and imagine how it would look if it were painted. What colors would seem to fit the action or emotion conveyed? Which hues would most complement the elements and principles emphasized? Have students sketch the sculpture on a sheet of white paper. After reviewing the color schemes used in Greek vase painting (see Lesson 1), students should paint the figures, using acrylic paints.

Did You Know?

The Parthenon is bordered by a decorative frieze which, when taken together with the other carvings on the outside of the famed structure, represents the largest surviving group of Classical sculpture.

Time & Place
CONNECTIONS

Ancient Greece
c. 800 B.C.–50 B.C.

DISCUS. In Greece, the champion discus thrower was considered the greatest of athletes. In ancient times the disc was made of stone or metal. It is now made of wood with a smooth metal rim.

OLYMPICS. The ancient Olympics were first held in 776 B.C. in Athens, to honor the god Zeus. In 1896, the first modern Olympics were held.

COSTUMING IN PLAYS. When performing this Greek drama, "Antigone," written by Sophocles in the fifth century B.C., players from all cultures wear the dress of early Greeks. This image is of a Roman troupe recreated in a mosaic found in Pompeii.

*A*ctivity **Discussing.** The Greeks were concerned with the harmony of physical and mental development. Discuss how this attitude is or is not present in today's entertainment and sports events.

Time & Place
Ancient Greece

CONNECTIONS Have students examine, read about, and discuss the images in the Time & Place feature. Then let students meet in groups to discuss their responses to the activity. Encourage students to explore the differences and similarities between the attitudes of ancient Greece and the attitudes common in modern society. Ask: Why are star athletes and entertainers so influential in our society? What qualities in these stars are considered most admirable? Which qualities and activities are often overlooked? Why? At the close of the discussion, have students write a short journal entry, summarizing what they consider the most important points.

Studio Skills

Direct students' attention to the frieze in Figure 8.18. Have them sketch a frieze design modeled after the Greek style. When they are satisfied with their sketches, have students create relief sculptures of their design in plaster. Plaster should be poured into a lined pie pan or shallow dish to harden.

When the mixture is dry and hard, students can transfer their designs onto the plaster and carve their friezes by scraping away the negative areas. Encourage students to add texture and details by using pointed tools. If they wish, students can paint the finished product with tempera or acrylic paints. When the project is complete, have students view each other's work and comment on those that seem most to resemble the Greek style.

Art Criticism

Have students note the reference in the text to the similarities between the sculpture in Figure 8.19 and Myron's *Discus Thrower* (Figure 8.16, page 179). Ask pairs of students to divide a sheet of paper into two columns. In one they are to list differences, beginning with such superficial distinctions as the fact that the *Discus Thrower* is sculpture in the round and *Nike Fastening Her Sandal* is a relief sculpture. In the other column, have students list the similarities. Have teams share and compare their lists.

Procession of Horsemen

■ **FIGURE 8.18**

As they move, the figures bunch up in some places and spread out in others. At one point, an irritated horseman turns and raises his hand in warning to the horseman behind him, who has come up too quickly and jostled his mount (Figure 8.18). The rider behind responds by reining in his rearing horse. All along the parade, a strong sense of movement is evident in the spirited prancing of the horses and the lighthearted pace of the figures on foot. This pace seems to quicken as the procession draws closer to its destination.

Perhaps movement is best suggested by the pattern of light and shadow in the carved drapery. This pattern of alternating light and dark values creates a flickering quality that becomes even more obvious when contrasted with the empty spaces between the figures.

Sculpture from the Temple of Athena Nike

Another relief sculpture, this one from the Temple of Athena Nike, may remind you of Myron's discus thrower, since it also shows a figure frozen in action (Figure 8.19). The unknown sculptor has carved the goddess of victory as she bends down to fasten her sandal. A graceful movement is suggested by the thin drapery that clings to and defines the body of the goddess. The flowing folds of the drapery and the line of the shoulder and arms create a series of oval lines that unifies the work. If you compare the handling of the drapery here with that of the *Hera of Samos*, you can appreciate more fully the great strides made by Greek sculptors over a 150-year period.

■ **FIGURE 8.18** Find two axis lines in this relief sculpture. Notice how the use of these repeated diagonals suggests movement. **What other elements and principles of art has the sculptor used to give this work a sense of unity?**

Procession of Horsemen, from the west frieze of the Parthenon. c. 440 B.C. Marble. Approx. 109 cm (43″) high. British Museum, London, England.

182   **Unit Three** *Art of Rising Civilizations*

𝒯eacher 𝒩otes

Safety. Impress upon students the importance of taking appropriate measures when disposing of unused plaster. Stress, in particular, that plaster should never be poured down a drain, since doing so can create a plumbing problem once the plaster hardens. The correct procedure for getting rid of unused plaster is to pour it into a trash receptacle lined with newspaper. Small amounts of plaster on the hands and art tools should be removed with a paper towel before washing with soap and water.

Nike Fastening Her Sandal, from the Temple of Athena Nike. c. 410 B.C. Marble. 107 cm (42") high. Acropolis Museum, Athens, Greece.

■ **FIGURE 8.20** The contrapposto pose makes this figure appear lifelike. Is this a successful work of art?

Polyclitus. *Doryphoros (Spear Bearer).* Roman copy of Greek original. c. 440 B.C. Life-size. Vatican Museums, Vatican, Rome, Italy.

Polyclitus's *Spear Bearer*
■ **FIGURE 8.20**

Another famous Classical Greek sculptor was Polyclitus (paw-lee-**kly**-tus). His specialty was creating statues of youthful athletes such as his *Doryphoros* (or *Spear Bearer*) (Figure 8.20). Polyclitus often showed these figures in **contrapposto,** *a pose in which the weight of the body is balanced on one leg while the other is free and relaxed.* In the *Doryphoros,* the left leg is bent and the toes lightly touch the ground. The body turns slightly in a momentary movement that gives the figure a freer, more lifelike look. The right hip and left shoulder are raised; the head tips forward and turns to the right. The result is a spiral axis line, or line of movement, that begins at the toes of the left foot and curves gently upward through the body to the head.

Action is kept to a minimum, but there is a feeling of athletic strength and prowess here. Perhaps the figure is waiting his turn to test his skill in a spear-throwing competition. If so, he looks relaxed and confident that he will be victorious.

Art Criticism

Divide the class into two groups. Assign one an analysis of *Spear Bearer* (Figure 8.20). The other group is to analyze *Discus Thrower* (Figure 8.16, page 179). As groups work, guide them by asking questions such as the following: What is the subject of the work? What elements and principles of art have been used in this sculpture? What feeling or mood is conveyed in the work? How lifelike is the sculpture? After groups have completed their analyses, have them compare their answers. Conclude with a discussion of the inferences one might draw about Greek sculpture of the Classical period.

Studio Skills

Have students note that, like other sculptures in this chapter, *Nike Fastening Her Sandal* (Figure 8.19) is fragmented, missing much of the head and face. Based on the position of the body and its suggestion of precarious balance, ask students to make a pencil sketch of a head and face for the figure. To stimulate their imaginations, encourage students to review the facial features and expressions on other sculptures in the chapter.

More About... **Phidias.** There are many legends about Phidias, but few reliable facts about his life. One story says Phidias was accused of stealing gold that was to be used for the statue of Athena. This charge was apparently not proved, but it was followed by another—that he had included his portrait and that of Pericles in the design on Athena's shield. For this act of blasphemy, Phidias was thrown into prison. According to this story, he died in prison—perhaps of poison. Recent excavations indicate that Phidias was working on a statue of Zeus at Olympus after he left Athens and that he died in exile.

184

Critical Thinking

Direct students' attention to Figure 8.22, *Nike of Samothrace*. Remind students that this sculpture was found in 118 pieces and had to be restored to its present condition. Point out that archaeologists and other experts are often called upon to piece together fragments in this way. Ask students to share their ideas on how they think such restorations are accomplished. Why are such restorations done? What mood or feeling does the work suggest? Would the inclusion of the missing parts of the statue add to or detract from this mood? Ask students to explain their answers.

Cross Curriculum

MUSIC/LITERATURE. Point out that attempts are made from time to time to finish artworks that, like the *Nike of Samothrace,* for some reason are incomplete. Mention that several composers in this century have attempted to "put closure" on Franz Schubert's *Unfinished Symphony.* More recently still, Charles Dickens' last (and unfinished) novel, *The Mystery of Edwin Drood,* was made the basis of a Broadway musical. Ask students to research and report on other famous unfinished works from the fields of music, literature, or the visual arts. Reports should focus on why the works were left incomplete and what attempts, if any, have been made to complete them.

Sculpture in the Hellenistic Period

The Peloponnesian War left the Greek city-states weakened by conflict. To the north, Macedonia was ruled by Philip II, a military genius who had received a Greek education. Having unified his own country, Philip turned his attention to the Greek city-states. Their disunity was too great a temptation to resist; in 338 B.C. Philip defeated them and thus realized his dream of controlling the Greek world.

The Spread of Greek Culture

Before Philip could extend his empire further, he was assassinated while attending his daughter's wedding. His successor was his 20-year-old son, Alexander the Great, who soon launched an amazing career of conquest.

Alexander, whose teacher had been the famous Greek philosopher Aristotle, inherited his father's admiration for Greek culture. Alexander was determined to spread this culture throughout the world. As he marched with his army from one country to another, the Greek culture that he brought with him blended with other, non-Greek cultures. The period in which this occurred is known as the Hellenistic age. It lasted about two centuries, ending in 146 B.C. when Greece fell under Roman control.

Expression in Hellenistic Sculpture

Sculptors working during the Hellenistic period were extremely skillful and confident. They created dramatic and often violent images in bronze and marble. The sculptors were especially interested in faces, which were considered a mirror of inner emotions. Beauty was less important than emotional expression. Because of this new emphasis, many Hellenistic sculptures lack the precise balance and harmony of Classical sculptures.

The *Dying Gaul*
■ FIGURE 8.21

Many of the features of the Hellenistic style can be observed in a life-size sculpture known as the *Dying Gaul* (Figure 8.21). A Roman copy shows a figure that was once part of a large monument built to celebrate a victory over the Gauls, fierce warriors from the north. In this sculpture, you witness the final moments of a Gaul who was fatally wounded in battle.

Blood flows freely from the wound in his side. The figure uses what little strength he has remaining to support himself with his right arm. He has difficulty supporting the weight of his head and it tilts downward. Pain and the knowledge that he is dying distort the features of his face.

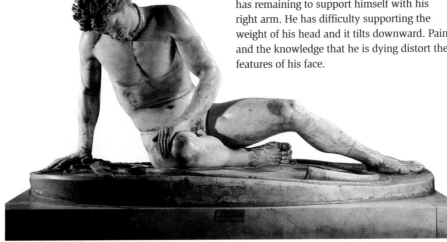

■ **FIGURE 8.21** Observe how this Hellenistic sculpture combines realistic detail and the expression of powerful feelings. What thoughts and feelings does this sculpture evoke in you? What aesthetic theory of art seems especially appropriate to use in judging this piece?

Dying Gaul. Roman copy of a bronze original from Pergamum. c. 240 B.C. Life-size. Museo Capitolino, Rome, Italy.

COOPERATIVE LEARNING

Greek Artists. Divide the class into research committees, and challenge them to compile a class reference file containing information on "Ancient Greek Artists." One committee can be responsible for researching bibliographical data on architects, one on painters, and one on applied artists (makers of pottery). A good starting source would be the *Cambridge History of Greek Art,* available in most libraries. Students can feel free to use the reference file for use in the preparation of reports and papers.

■ **FIGURE 8.22** Notice the excitement and action suggested by this figure. How has the artist created a feeling of forward movement?

Nike of Samothrace (Victory of Samothrace). c. 190 B.C. Marble. Approx. 2.4 m (8'). The Louvre, Paris, France.

■ **FIGURE 8.23** Compare this figure with the *Kouros* created some 600 years earlier. Notice how the abilities, interests, and intentions of sculptors developed over that period. What are your feelings about this figure? Is emotionalism an appropriate theory to use in judging this work?

Seated Boxer. c. 50 B.C. Bronze. Roman copy. Museo Nazionale Romano delle Terme, Naples, Italy.

Expression of Emotion

Works such as the *Dying Gaul* were intended to stir the emotions of the viewer. You are meant to become involved in this drama of a dying warrior, to share and feel his pain and loneliness and marvel at his quiet dignity at the moment of death.

The *Nike of Samothrace*
■ **FIGURE 8.22**

About 2,100 years ago, an unknown sculptor completed a larger-than-life marble work to celebrate a naval victory. The finished sculpture of a winged Nike (goddess of victory) stood on a pedestal that was made to look like the prow of a warship. She may have held a trumpet to her lips with her right hand while waving a banner with her left. A brisk ocean breeze whips Nike's garments into ripples and folds, adding to a feeling of forward

movement. Her weight is supported by both legs, but the body twists in space, creating an overall sense of movement.

It is not known for certain what great victory this sculpture was meant to celebrate. Also uncertain is its original location. The sculpture was found in 1875 on a lonely hillside of Samothrace, headless, without arms, and in 118 pieces. Pieced together, it is now known as the *Nike of Samothrace* and commonly called the Winged Victory. It stands proudly inside the main entrance to the Louvre, the great art museum in Paris.

The *Seated Boxer*
■ **FIGURE 8.23**

Ten years after the *Nike of Samothrace* was found, a bronze sculpture of a seated boxer (Figure 8.23) was unearthed in Rome. It is not as dramatic as the *Dying Gaul* nor as spirited

Chapter 8 *Greek Art* **185**

CULTURAL DIVERSITY

Animals in Subject Matter. Explain that, despite the obvious fascination among Greek sculptors with the human form, animals were another prime subject. Add that other cultures throughout history have made abundant use of animal subjects in their art. Invite groups of students to investigate animal art in the cultures of Mesoamerica (especially the Inca and the Aztec), Africa, and Egypt. While conducting their research, groups should consider the following questions: Were the animals considered sacred? Were they symbolic of some force of nature or fate? How were they represented artistically?

ASSESS

Checking Comprehension

➤ Have students respond to the lesson review questions. Answers are given in the box below.

➤ Assign *Application* 8, "Tour de Force," which tests students' knowledge of ancient Greek art and culture. 📁

Reteaching

➤ Assign *Reteaching* 18, found in the TCR. Have students complete the activity and review their responses. 📁

➤ Divide the class into three groups, assigning each a different period: Archaic, Classical, and Hellenistic. Have the groups select a sculpture that they feel is a typical representation of that period and list attributes of the period it represents.

Extension

Assign *Appreciating Cultural Diversity* 10, "Preserving Greek Culture," in which students learn about the Hellenic Museum in Chicago. Then have students explore and report on manifestations of Greek culture in their own community (e.g., Greek restaurants and cultural centers). 📁

CLOSE

Review the evolution of Greek sculpture, from the Archaic period through the Hellenistic period. On the board, draw a time line and list the characteristics of each period.

as the Winged Victory, but its emotional impact is undeniable.

The unknown artist presents not a victorious young athlete but a mature, professional boxer, resting after a brutal match. Few details are spared in telling about the boxer's violent occupation. The swollen ears, scratches, and perspiration are signs of the punishment he has received. He turns his head to one side as he prepares to remove the leather boxing glove from his left hand. The near-profile view of his face reveals his broken nose and battered cheeks. There is no mistaking the joyless expression on his face, suggesting that he may have lost the match.

Stylistic Changes in Sculpture

The development of Greek sculpture can be traced through an examination of the gods, goddesses, and athletes created from the Archaic period to the Hellenistic period. Sculptured figures produced during the Archaic period were solid and stiff. The *Kouros,* for example, was created at a time when artists were seeking greater control of their materials in order to make their statues look more real.

By the Classical period, sculptors had achieved near perfection in balance, proportion, and sense of movement. The *Discus Thrower* demonstrates the sculptor's ability to create a realistic work. A later Classical work, the *Spear Bearer,* is an example of the balance, harmony, and beauty achieved by Greek sculptors.

During Hellenistic times, sculptures such as the *Seated Boxer* reveal the artists' interest in more dramatic and emotional subjects.

The Demand for Greek Artists

The Romans defeated Macedonia and gave the Greek city-states their freedom as allies, but the troublesome Greeks caused Rome so much difficulty that their freedom was taken away and the city-state of Corinth burned. Athens alone continued to be held in respect and was allowed a certain amount of freedom. Although the great creative Hellenistic period had passed its peak, Greek artists were sought in other lands, where they spread the genius of their masters.

LESSON TWO REVIEW

Reviewing Art Facts

1. What features are characteristic of early Greek sculptures?
2. Which aspects of Myron's *Discus Thrower* are realistic? Which aspect is idealistic?
3. What famous artist oversaw the work on the Parthenon's frieze? What other contribution to the Parthenon did he make?
4. Briefly describe the Hellenistic period, and explain how it originated and how it ended.

Activity . . . *Debating the Fate of Artifacts*

Many treasures from ancient cultures have been taken from their country of origin and now reside in museums in other areas. An example is the Elgin Marbles, fragments taken from the Parthenon in Athens, Greece, by Lord Elgin of Great Britain. The marbles are viewed by thousands of people at the British Museum in London. Do you believe that treasures taken from their origins should be returned? Research other examples of important artifacts that were removed.

Work in two groups: for and against returning the artifacts. Prepare arguments and present each position to the class. You may wish to role-play people with different points of view (artist, museum director, government official, art student) and debate the issues.

LESSON TWO REVIEW

Answers to Reviewing Art Facts

1. Stiffness and solidity, with little suggestion of movement.
2. The pose of the body, especially the arms and legs, and the musculature are realistic. The facial expression is idealistic.
3. Phidias; he created the great statue of Athena.
4. The Hellenistic period was a time of important Greek influence in many different countries. It began with Alexander the Great, and it ended about 200 years later when Greece fell under Roman control.

Activity...*Debating the Fate of Artifacts*

Provide time for students to research this question. Remind them of the importance of preparing arguments for both sides before beginning to debate.

Studio LESSON Drawing Features of Greek Architecture

Complete a detail drawing in pencil of a section of a building in your community that exhibits features of Greek architecture. Fill the entire sheet of paper. Make your drawing entirely of firm, clear lines that define a variety of large and small shapes. Try to communicate the unified, dignified appearance associated with such Greek buildings as the Parthenon.

Materials
- Pencils
- Sketch paper
- Sheet of white drawing paper, 12 × 18 inches or larger

Inspiration

Review the features of the Greek orders illustrated and discussed on page 172. Examine pictures of Greek buildings in this and other books available in your school or community. With other members of your class, discuss the different features and details observed on these buildings.

Process

1. Search your community for buildings that exhibit some of the architectural features found on Greek structures. Complete sketches of the parts of those buildings that best demonstrate these features. Bring your sketches to class, display them, and discuss the Greek influences demonstrated in each.
2. Select your best sketch and reproduce it as a precise line drawing on the sheet of drawing paper. Add as many details as possible to make the Greek architectural features easy to identify. Fill the entire sheet with your drawing, using a variety of large and small shapes.

■ **FIGURE 8.24** Student Work

Examining Your Work

Describe. Does your drawing clearly illustrate the different features of Greek architecture found on buildings in your community? Name the features. Can other students in class identify these features?

Analyze. Did you fill the entire picture surface with your drawing? Explain how the firm, clear lines in the drawing define a variety of large and small shapes.

Interpret. Does your drawing communicate the same dignified look observed in Greek buildings? Do the

details illustrated in your drawing bear a resemblance to details noted in a particular Greek building? If so, which building is it?

Judge. Explain how your drawing achieves an overall sense of unity. If you were to do it again, how would you improve on this unity?

187

Studio LESSON

Drawing Features of Greek Architecture

Objectives
- Complete a detailed pencil drawing of a section of a building in the Greek style.
- Use lines to create a variety of large and small shapes.
- Concentrate on capturing a unified, dignified appearance.

Motivator

Direct students' attention to the illustration of the Parthenon (Figure 8.3, page 169). Ask whether students feel the Parthenon deserves its reputation as one of the most beautiful buildings in the world. Demonstrate how a portion of this building could serve as the basis for an interesting line drawing. (For example, a drawing of a section including the top of a column, the capital, lintel, and a portion of the frieze.)

Aesthetics

Ask students whether they believe buildings are capable of communicating moods or feelings. Can they identify any buildings illustrated in the text that succeed in doing this? Discuss the appropriateness of considering expressive qualities when judging architecture.

Critiquing

Have students apply the steps of art criticism to their own artwork, using the "Examining Your Work" questions on this page.

ASSESSMENT

Examining Your Work. After students have examined their own drawings, have them work with partners to discuss one another's completed projects. Suggest that they use the Examining Your Work questions as discussion guidelines. Remind students to point out positive aspects of their partner's work in response to each question. If appropriate, model

forms of constructive criticism, and show students how to offer suggestions that can help their partners improve their work. As a follow-up to this work with partners, have each student write one paragraph describing what changes he or she would make if starting this project over.

Studio LESSON

Painting Using Analogous Colors

Objectives

■ Paint the drawings from the previous lesson using analogous colors.

■ Use a variety of light and dark values to emphasize the most interesting or important part of the composition.

■ Select colors that will help communicate a mood or feeling.

Motivator

Initiate a discussion on the expressive power of color. Ask whether students know any popular songs that link emotions with colors. Can they recall any common expressions that do the same thing? Instruct students to identify artworks in the text that use color to express feelings or emotions.

Aesthetics

Direct students' attention again to the illustration of the Parthenon and ask them to express their personal judgments about it. Then ask them to picture the building as it must have looked in ancient times. Do they find the bright colors disturbing? Can they identify any contemporary buildings that make use of bright colors? Are the colors used on such buildings put there for aesthetic reasons?

Critiquing

Have students apply the steps of art criticism to their own artwork, using the "Examining Your Work" questions on this page.

Studio LESSON — Painting Using Analogous Colors

Materials

- The drawing you completed in the previous studio lesson
- Tempera or acrylic paint
- Brushes, mixing tray, and paint cloth
- Water container

Use tempera or acrylic to paint a line drawing of the features of Greek architecture. Select an analogous color scheme consisting of three or more hues that lie next to each other on the color wheel. Mix white and black with these hues to produce a variety of light and dark values. Use contrasting values to emphasize the most interesting or important parts of your painting. Choose hues that give your painting a definite mood or feeling, such as pleasant and inviting, somber and forbidding, or dark and frightening.

■ **FIGURE 8.25** Student Work

Inspiration

Examine Figures 8.3, 8.9, and 8.10 on pages 169 and 173. Use your imagination to picture how these Greek buildings might have looked when they were painted with bright colors. How would those colors have contributed to the mood or feeling associated with those buildings?

Process

1. Identify three or more neighboring hues on the color wheel (Figure 2.4, page 29) to make up your analogous color scheme. Select hues that you associate with a particular mood or feeling.

2. Use the colors selected to paint your detail drawing of a building exhibiting Greek architectural features. Add white and black to your hues to obtain a variety of light and dark values. Use contrasting values to emphasize the portions of your drawing that you consider most important or interesting.

Examining Your Work

Describe. Point out and name the three or more hues you selected for your analogous color scheme. Are the shapes in your composition painted precisely?

Analyze. Does your painting include a variety of light and dark values? Did you use contrasting values to emphasize the most interesting or important parts of your composition? Explain how the use of light and dark values adds to the visual interest of your painting.

Interpret. Does your painting communicate a mood or feeling? If so, what did you do to achieve this? Are other students in class able to correctly identify the mood you were trying to communicate?

Judge. Do you think your painting is successful? What aesthetic quality or qualities did you turn to when making your judgment?

188

ASSESSMENT

Class Discussion. Display students' painted drawings, and provide time for informal examination and discussion. Then assign students to select one painting—other than their own—to examine more carefully. Have students write brief essays, devoting one paragraph to each of the art criticism operations (using the questions presented in Examining Your Work). In addition, you may want to have volunteers photograph local colorful buildings or find photographs of other colorful buildings. Display these photos, along with students' painted drawings; encourage students to discuss the effects of various color choices.

Reviewing the Facts

Lesson One

1. How did Athens rise to greatness? What caused it to fall from power?
2. Describe how the following features are used in Greek temples: stylobate, capitals, lintels, frieze, and cornice.
3. Name and describe the three orders of decorative style that originated in Greece.
4. What types of designs were painted on early Greek vases?
5. What features characterize the figures found in later Greek vase painting produced by artists such as Exekias?

Lesson Two

6. Explain why Myron's *Discus Thrower* would be described as more idealistic than realistic.
7. Since the works of ancient Greek sculptors no longer exist, how do we know what they look like?
8. What does the frieze on the Parthenon represent?
9. Describe a pose that is considered contrapposto.
10. How did Alexander the Great influence the spread of Greek culture to neighboring countries?

Thinking Critically

1. **ANALYZE.** List similarities and differences between the way the Egyptians and the Greeks thought of their temples. Explain how the worship of the Greek gods influenced Greek architecture and art.
2. **INTERPRET.** Look again at the sculpture in Figure 8.21 on page 184. What do you think this figure is doing? How would you describe his feelings at this moment? Explain your answer.

ARTSOURCE **THEATRE.** Use the *Performing Arts Handbook,* page 582 to find out more about the "The Mask Man" and the Faustwork Mask Theater.

CAREERS IN Read about a career as a scenic designer who creates sets for plays. See the *Careers in Art Handbook,* page 599.

interNET CONNECTION Visit Glencoe Art Online at *www.glencoe.com/sec/art*. Explore museum exhibits of Greek antiquities and discover more about Greek culture and art.

Technology Project

Greek Architectural Contributions

The Greeks created some of the most perfectly proportioned buildings the world has ever known. This is because the Greeks relied on mathematics and the study of proportion to arrive at the dimensions used in their buildings. Even today, many people judge architectural beauty by the standards set by the Greeks. Working in small groups, review the section on Greek architecture on page 169 of your text and make a list of as many of the architectural developments of the Greeks as you can. Complete one of the following projects.

1. Using a digital camera, 35-mm camera, or a camcorder, go into your neighborhood, town or city and create a visual record of all the examples you can find of architecture that is inspired by the legacy of the Greeks. Be sure to capture such things as cornices, capitals, and other details. Bring your visual records to class and, using available technology, create a presentation for the class.
2. Using the Internet or library as a resource, research the Golden Section or Ratio and learn about the use of the Golden Section and mathematics in Greek architecture. In what ways does this show a connection between art and math?
3. Using resources such as your textbook, CD-ROMs, laser discs, or the Internet, collect images that are examples of modern architecture inspired by the architecture of the ancient Greeks. With the information you find, create a Web page, tutorial page, or a multimedia presentation.

 Teaching the Technology Project

As they consider the architectural contributions of ancient Greece, have students page through the rest of this book—or other books showing buildings from Europe and the Americas—to note and trace various influences. Some students may be interested in focusing on a specific architectural feature as they work on this Project.

ARTSOURCE Assign the feature in the *Performing Arts Handbook,* page 582.

CAREERS IN ART If time permits, have interested students investigate the career information in the *Careers in Art Handbook,* page 599.

interNET CONNECTION Have students go online and learn more about artists on preselected Web sites with the Internet activity for this chapter.

Reviewing the Facts

1. Under Pericles, who used Delian money to restore it, Athens rose to unprecedented greatness until the death of Pericles.
2. Stylobate—top step of the three-step platform; capitals—top elements of columns; lintels—crossbeams supported by columns; frieze—decorative band running across the upper part of a wall; cornice—horizontal element above the frieze.
3. Answers should include desriptions found on page 172.
4. At first geometric and later realistic.
5. Realism, attention to fine points of detail, well-balanced design.
6. The face is calm, while the muscles of the body are tense and strained.
7. They were copied by Romans and are described in the writings of Romans.
8. It commemorates a procession held in Athens every four years to honor the goddess Athena.
9. The body weight is balanced on one leg, while the other leg is free and relaxed.
10. He marched through one country after another blending Greek and non-Greek cultures.

Thinking Critically

1. Responses will vary. Students should note that many surviving buildings are temples and that early sculptures may show the figures of gods.
2. He is gazing down at a wound that will prove mortal; anguish, pain, and remorse.

Roman Art

ADDITIONAL CHAPTER RESOURCES

Activities
📁 Advanced Studio Activity 9
📁 Application 9
🖱 Chapter 9 Internet Activity
📁 Studio Activities 11, 12

Fine Art Resources
🖈 **Transparency**
Art in Focus Transparency 12
   Constantine the Great
🎞 **Fine Art Print**
Focus on World Art Print 9
   Mural in the Villa, Boscoreale, near Pompeii

Assessment
📁 Chapter 9 Test
📁 Performance Assessment

Multimedia Resources
🎭 Artsource® Performing Arts Package
💿 National Gallery Laser Disc
💿 National Museum of Women in the Arts CD-ROM
📼 Arts & Entertainment Videos

NATIONAL STANDARDS FOR ARTS EDUCATION

The National Standards for Arts Education provide guidelines for grade-appropriate competency in the visual arts. The Content Standards for grades 9–12 are:

1. Understanding and applying media, techniques, and processes.
2. Using knowledge of structures and functions.
3. Choosing and evaluating a range of subject matter, symbols, and ideas.
4. Understanding the visual arts in relation to history and cultures.
5. Reflecting upon and assessing the characteristics and merits of their work and the work of others.
6. Making connections between visual arts and other disciplines.

Listed below are the National Standards for the Visual Arts addressed in this chapter. For a breakdown of the categories listed under each content standard, refer to the *Reproducible Lesson Plans* booklet in the TCR.

   1. (a)   **2.** (a, b)   **3.** (a, b)   **4.** (a, b, c)   **5.** (a, b)   **6.** (b)

🕐 **Out of Time?**   If time does not permit teaching this chapter in its entirety, you may wish to preview the artwork and captions with students. Scan the heads in each lesson with students. Discuss the Looking Closely features and examine Styles Influencing Styles on page 202.

HANDBOOK MATERIAL

 Performing Arts *(page 576)*

Urban Planner *(page 600)*

Beyond the Classroom
At the National Endowment for the Humanities, teachers may find ideas and educational programs combining arts and humanities. Connect to their Internet resources by visiting our Web site at *www.glencoe.com/sec/art.*

Roman Art

Roman Art

INTRODUCE

Chapter Overview

CHAPTER 9 discusses ancient Roman civilization and art.

Lesson One introduces Roman portrait sculpture, painting, and architectural innovations.

Lesson Two deals with public structures and with buildings used for recreation.

Studio Lesson guides students in construction of a poster-board relief sculpture of a Roman structure.

Have students examine the work that opens this chapter. Discuss with them the subject shown here: What does this work indicate about the role of music in the society of ancient Rome? Suggest that volunteers form hypotheses based on this artwork and then do research to confirm or revise their ideas. Ask another group of volunteers to learn more about the musical instrument shown in this work, the cithara: What are the characteristics of the instrument? How was it played? When and where did it probably develop? What instruments developed from the cithara? Let both groups of volunteers share the results of their research with the rest of the class.

 ■ **FIGURE 9.1** The wealthy Pompeiian household of P. Fannius Synistor was known for holding lavish entertainments. Singing, dancing, and playing musical instruments was an important aspect of social life. This woman is playing the cithara, a popular string instrument featuring a broad, wooden soundbox and up to 11 strings.

Lady Playing the Cithara. Pompeian, Boscoreale. Wall painting from villa of P. Fannius Synistor. First century B.C. Fresco on lime plaster. 187 × 187 cm (6'1½" × 6'1½"). The Metropolitan Museum of Art, New York, New York, Rogers Fund, 1903. (03.14.5).

190

National Standards

This chapter meets the following National Standards for the Arts:

1. (a)	**4.** (a,b,c)
2. (a,b)	**5.** (a,b)
3. (a,b)	**6.** (b)

CHAPTER 9 RESOURCES

Teacher's Classroom Resources

- 📁 Advanced Studio Activity 9
- 📁 Application 9
- 🖱 Chapter 9 Internet Activity
- 📁 Studio Activities 11, 12

Assessment

- 📁 Chapter 9 Test
- 📁 Performance Assessment

Fine Art Resources

- 🖼 *Art in Focus* Transparency 12
  Constantine the Great
- 🖼 *Focus on World Art* Print 9
  Mural in the Villa, Boscoreale, Pompeii

*Long before the Roman Empire rose to greatness,
Italy was the home of a mysterious ancient people called the
Etruscans. No one is sure about the origins
of the Etruscans. Of all the peoples in Italy, the Etruscans
were the most civilized and the most powerful. In time,
they conquered much of Italy north of the Tiber River. Among
their conquests was the hill town of Rome. The area conquered by
the Roman Empire was expansive, yet Romans aspired
to create art to rival that of tiny Greece. The Romans
adored Greek art and it is only because of faithful Roman copies
that any Greek art survives. The art of the ancient Romans,
their genius in engineering and architecture,
has directly influenced the art of modern civilizations.*

YOUR Portfolio

Create an artwork for your portfolio that represents the influence of Roman art. Exchange your finished work with a classmate and ask for a peer evaluation. Getting different viewpoints will give you a measure of how successful your work is. Peers can tell you what they like about your work and offer suggestions for revision. Decide whether you wish to revise or change your artwork based on the peer review. Then store the peer evaluation, your preliminary sketches, and the final artwork in your portfolio.

Focus ON THE ARTS

LITERATURE
There were many great writers in ancient Rome, from the subtle poet Horace to the passionate Virgil. Playwrights Plautus and Terrence created dramas, and the poet Lucretius wrote about science and nature.

THEATRE
The Romans developed plays with five acts. They created the first villains and introduced subplots. Roman theatre allowed unlimited actors in a scene.

MUSIC
Romans invented the tuba to accompany battle marches. Horns and organs accompanied wild animal shows, while hundreds of trumpeters played at chariot races and gladiator contests.

191

Introducing the Chapter

Have students examine the works of art and architecture in the chapter. Ask volunteers to read the information in the credit lines. Can students infer from this information when the Roman Empire flourished and how far it spread?

Focus ON THE ARTS

Roman theatre expanded on the Greek theatre tradition. Explain that only one actor appeared on stage at a time in Greek tragedy. Then they allowed two actors in a scene; then three. The Romans added four, and eventually as many as needed. Divide the class into four teams. The first team will think about the one-actor situation, the second team will think about two actors, etc. Have each team write dramatic situations that can be acted, given their limited number of actors. After all four teams report, ask: What did Rome contribute to modern drama?

DEVELOPING A PORTFOLIO

Self-Reflection. A well-maintained art journal or sketchbook provides a permanent record of personal and creative growth. Students who routinely write about their work in a journal and use a sketchbook to practice designs have more insights into their progress. These impressions, responses, thoughts, and efforts provide students with a means of understanding how willing they are to be challenged as well as recognizing those areas that need improvement. A regular five-minute writing exercise at the beginning or the end of each class gives students the opportunity to observe changes and refinements of their artistic skills.

The Rising Power of Rome

FOCUS

Lesson Objectives

After studying this lesson, students will be able to:
- Identify the inspiration behind much of Roman architecture and art.
- Identify Roman improvements on earlier building processes.
- Describe the exterior of a typical Roman structure.

Building Vocabulary

Let students read the listed Vocabulary terms and share what they already know about the meaning and use of these words. Then have students page through the lesson, looking for illustrations that will help them understand each term.

Motivator

Have students review and list some of the contributions the ancient Greeks made to the fields of art and architecture. Have them browse again through the illustrations in this chapter and note which of these contributions appear to have influenced Roman art.

Introducing the Lesson

Have students look at the portrait sculpture in Figure 9.3, and ask: What makes this man "feel" familiar? Does it surprise to know that this is the portrait of a specific individual? Does it surprise you to know that the man lived nearly 2,000 years ago? What connections does this portrait create between you and the world of ancient Rome? Tell students that they will learn more about such connections as they study this lesson.

The Rising Power of Rome

Vocabulary
- mural
- barrel vault
- keystone
- aqueduct

Discover

After completing this lesson, you will be able to:
- Identify the inspiration for much of Roman art and architecture.
- Identify the quality Romans favored in their sculptures and their paintings.
- Name the ways in which Roman artists improved on earlier building processes.

*U*nder the rule of Etruscan kings, Rome grew in size and importance. By the end of the sixth century B.C., it had become the largest and richest city in Italy. The Romans, however, were never happy under Etruscan rule, and in 509 B.C. they drove the Etruscans from the city and established a republic.

The Roman Republic

Ridding themselves of the Etruscans did not end Rome's problems. Finding themselves surrounded by enemies, the Romans were forced to fight for survival. As nearby enemies were defeated, more distant foes tried to conquer the young republic. Rome managed to defend itself against these threats and extended its reach and influence until all of Italy was under its control.

An early victory over Carthage, its chief rival, won Rome its first overseas province, Sicily. Eventually, Rome controlled territory from Britain in the west to Mesopotamia in the east (Figure 9.2).

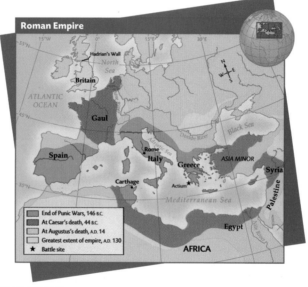

MAP SKILLS

■ **FIGURE 9.2** Notice the wide area influenced by ancient Rome. From this map, what can you conclude about the power and the organization of the Roman Empire?

192

The Greek Influence

Much of Roman art was copied from the Greeks. From the very beginning, well-born and cultured Romans exhibited a great admiration for Greek art forms of every period and style. They imported Greek works by the shipload and even brought Greek artists to Rome to work for them. Generally, it can be said that the Romans became the heirs of Greek art although they also made important contributions of their own, especially in the development of architecture.

Roman Sculpture and Painting

In sculpture and painting, Roman works reflect the tremendous influence exerted by earlier Greek artists.

Portrait Sculpture

A desire for lifelike portraits can be traced back to the earliest period of Rome's history. At that time, wax masks of deceased family members were made to be carried in funeral processions and displayed in small shrines in the home. Masks made of wax were not permanent, though, and a more durable material was sought. Marble and other kinds of stone were found especially suitable. Soon artists who could carve portraits from these materials were in great demand.

Differences Between Greek and Roman Sculpture

Many of the sculptors who worked in Rome came from Greece. These artists worked in the Greek tradition but adapted that tradition to meet Roman demands. The Greeks preferred idealistic portraits; the Romans wanted theirs to look more realistic. Perhaps this was because most Greek portraits were designed for public monuments, whereas Roman portraits were meant to serve private needs.

The Romans wanted their sculptures to remind viewers of specific individuals. This explains why most Roman portraits seem so natural and lifelike. The Romans felt that a person's character could best be shown through facial features and expressions. Therefore, they often commissioned portrait heads rather than sculptures of the entire figure. The Greeks, in contrast, considered a sculpture of a head or bust (head and shoulders) incomplete.

Man of the Republic
■ FIGURE 9.3

A Roman portrait sculpture creates the feeling that the viewer is looking at a real person. The figure may even look familiar. This man (Figure 9.3) could be a high school football coach, a teacher, or a restaurant manager. Like all Roman portrait sculptures, this work is an exact duplicate of a real person, with all wrinkles and imperfections intact and with an expression that suggests the man's personality and character.

Mural Painting

Wealthy Roman families lived in luxurious homes with courtyards, gardens with elaborate fountains, rooms with marble walls and mosaics on the floors, and numerous works of art. They did not, however, like to hang paintings on the walls of their homes. Instead, they hired artists to paint murals. (See Figure 9.1, page 190.) A **mural** is *a large picture painted directly on the wall.* The artists who painted these murals tried to reproduce the world around them as accurately as possible. They painted landscapes and pictures of buildings that suggested a world that lay beyond the walls of the room. These scenes often create the impression

■ **FIGURE 9.3** This portrait shows a real man, complete with wrinkles—not an idealized version of that man. **What kind of personality do you think this man had?**

Man of the Republic. Artist unknown. Late first century B.C. Terra cotta. 35.7 cm (14″). Museum of Fine Arts, Boston, Massachusetts. Contribution, Purchase of E. P. Warren Collection.

TEACH
Using Map Skills

Have students study the map of Rome in Figure 9.2 and discuss whether location may have been a factor in the rise of the Roman Empire. Have students locate the Mediterranean Sea. Ask them whether they think having a border on a major body of water was an advantage or disadvantage. If possible, have students determine Rome's proximity to Greece on a second map. Have students discuss what they have learned about the history of the two civilizations and how and why the proximity of the two powers is significant.

Aesthetics

Remind students that Roman portraits such as the one in Figure 9.3 served private rather than public needs. Point out that this is one way in which the Roman approach to sculpture differs from that of the Greeks. In what other ways is this portrait different from portrait sculptures encountered in Chapter 8?

Did You Know?

Around the time the works like the one in Figure 9.3 were being sculpted, other important cultural developments were underway. In India, the first reliefs depicting Buddha were being completed, while in Segovia, Spain, Roman builders were constructing a great aqueduct.

 Technology

CD-ROMs. The use of digital technology can be particularly instructive in helping students appreciate and analyze works of art. If your classroom has access to a computer with a CD-ROM drive or laser disc player, you may want to investigate some of the art-based packages on the market. Such programs add immediacy to the study of art by displaying works as they were meant to be seen-from various angles and, in the case of outdoor sculptures and works of architecture, in the context of their natural surroundings. Investigate the National Women in the Arts CD-ROM available as part of Glencoe's *Art in Focus* Multimedia Resources.

Aesthetics

Have students study Figure 9.4. Remind them that murals like this were used to decorate walls in much the same way that we use hanging pictures today. Ask students to think about other uses for wall painting they have learned about (e.g., the Egyptians painted murals in the interior of tombs). Ask, finally, what our preference today for hanging pictures—in contrast to the painting of murals—may reveal about contemporary society.

Art History

Tell students that the creation of wall murals has always been a popular form of art. Direct students' attention to famous murals they have probably seen, such as Leonardo da Vinci's *The Last Supper* (Figure 16.18, page 368). Ask students whether they have seen or know of murals in American cities (perhaps their own). In what types of buildings are these murals generally found? What feeling or impression do the works impart?

Studio Skills

Have students create small murals in the Roman style on sheets of poster board. They can begin by drawing a window frame and sketching an outdoor scene within its borders. Urge them to include as much detail as possible. Have them complete the drawing using colored markers.

Art Criticism

Direct students' attention to the mosaic tile floor in Figure 9.4. Have them describe the pattern they see. What elements of art have been emphasized? What principles have been used to organize them?

■ **FIGURE 9.4** This room, with its patterned mosaic floor and murals, was preserved by the eruption of the volcano Vesuvius. How is this room similar to and different from a modern bedroom?

Bedroom from the Villa of P. Fannius Synistor. Pompeian, Boscoreale. First century B.C. Fresco on lime plaster. Mosaic floor, couch, and footstool come from Roman villas of later date. 2.6 × 5.8 × 3.3 m (8'8½" × 19'1⅞" × 10' 11½"). The Metropolitan Museum of Art, New York, New York. Rogers Fund, 1903. 03.14.13.

■ **FIGURE 9.5** This figure has a realistic, graceful appearance. Name the elements and principles of art used by the artist to achieve this effect.

Flora, or Spring. Wall painting from Stabiae, a Roman resort on the Bay of Naples, Italy. First century A.D. Museo Archeologico Nazionale, Naples, Italy.

that you are gazing out a window overlooking a city (Figure 9.4).

Of course, not all Roman paintings were noteworthy. This is evident in many paintings found in houses in Pompeii and neighboring cities, which were covered by ashes when the volcano Vesuvius erupted in A.D. 79. When the well-preserved ruins of these cities were discovered and excavations began, it was found that almost every house was decorated with murals. Many are quite ordinary, created by painters of limited ability.

Maiden Gathering Flowers
■ **FIGURE 9.5**

A surprising number of fine works were also found in the area surrounding Pompeii. Among these is a painting of a maiden pausing in midstride to pluck a flower for her bouquet (Figure 9.5). A breeze stirs her garments as she turns her head and daintily removes a blossom from the tip of a tall bush. Charming and beautiful, this work hints at the level of skill and sensitivity that must have been reached by many Roman painters.

Roman Architecture

Whereas few Roman paintings and murals remain today, many examples of Roman architecture, bridges, and monuments have survived.

Rome ruled an area that extended from present-day Great Britain to the Near East. The Romans built roads, sea routes, and harbors to link their far-flung cities. They designed and constructed city services such as aqueducts and sewer systems, and they erected public buildings for business and leisure-time activities. Because they were excellent planners and engineers, the Romans were destined to make their mark as the first great builders of the world.

The Temples

Many early Roman temples made use of features developed by earlier architects, especially the Greeks. These features, however, were used by Romans to satisfy their own needs and tastes. For example, whereas the Greeks used columns as structural supports, the Romans

About the *Artwork*

Bedroom from the Villa of P. Fannius Synistor. Direct students' attention to Figure 9.4. Ask them to determine which objects in the fresco are closest to the viewer and which appear to be farthest away. Discuss the work's realistic use of space (perspective). Ask students whether they feel this use of perspective in the painting makes it a successful work of art. What do students feel the painting would be like without the use of perspective? What other criteria could one use to judge the painting?

■ **FIGURE 9.6** Notice the similarities between this Roman temple and the Greek Parthenon, Figure 8.1, page 166. Why do you think the Romans did not copy the Greek temple exactly?

Maison Carrée, Nîmes, France. First century B.C.

Aesthetics

Remind students that Romans used columns for decorative more than for structural purposes. Direct students' attention to Figure 9.6. Have students determine which columns on this building most likely serve a structural function and which are purely decorative. Challenge students to devise and sketch other modes of decoration that might replace the columns. Finally, ask students to discuss how the building would look without any columns at all.

Art History

Remind students that the patronage system was in use in ancient Rome and that important, wealthy individuals often had public buildings and temples erected as monuments to themselves. Tell students that experts believe temple design changed little during the period of the Roman Empire because of the conservative nature of patrons. Have students find out about patronage of the arts during different time periods, including the Middle Ages, the Italian Renaissance, and the sixteenth century in Europe. Ask whether modern patronage of the arts is different, and, if so, in what way? Is patronage a positive or negative force on art? Have students discuss their views on the subject.

added columns to their buildings as decoration and not necessarily for structural purposes.

Maison Carrée
■ **FIGURE 9.6**

The Greek influence can be seen in a temple built by the Romans in France during the first century B.C (Figure 9.6). At first glance, the rectangular shape and Ionic columns make this building look like a Greek temple. A closer look reveals that the freestanding columns do not surround the entire building as they do in Greek temples such as the Parthenon. Instead, they are used only for the porch at the front. Along the sides and back of the building, half-columns are attached to the solid walls to create a decorative pattern.

The Roman temple is placed on a podium or platform that raises it above eye level. The Romans borrowed this feature from the Etruscans.

Time & Place
CONNECTIONS

Roman Empire
c. 509 B.C.–A.D. 410

ROMAN COINS. Roman coins were used in trade and commerce throughout the Roman Empire. Imprinted with images of emperors, nobles, and important events, they provide information to researchers about the Roman way of life.

ARMOR. Footsoldiers, called legionnaires, wore protective helmets and metal leg guards. Legionnaires were trained volunteers, marching to distant Roman territory to build forts, camps, and walls to defend conquered lands.

Activity **Identifying Artifacts.**
Both of these artifacts from Roman times give us a glimpse into the expanse and success of the Roman Empire. Identify two artifacts from our society today that reveal aspects of contemporary times.

Time & Place
CONNECTIONS

The Roman Empire

Have students examine and discuss the images in this Time & Place feature. Encourage students to compare the Roman coins with those we use today: How do they probably differ in size? In weight? In value? In availability? Let volunteers share what they know—or do simple research to find out—about the armor and equipment of the Roman legionairres: Of what was it made? How did the soldiers carry and use it? Finally, have students compare the portrait medallion to modern jewelry: How are they alike? How do they differ in size, in use, and in value? Assign the activity, and let students work in groups to prepare exhibits of "modern American artifacts."

Art Criticism

Lead a discussion on the similarities and differences between Greek and Roman architecture. Have students look at the Greek temple of Athena Nike (Figure 8.8, page 172) and then at the Roman temple at Palestrina (Figure 9.7). Have students describe and compare the two structures, listing Roman imitation and original Roman innovations. Conclude by having students evaluate the Roman structure on its artistic merits.

Art History

Ask students to name and list Roman innovations in building structures and materials. To help them better understand the nature of different building materials, provide them with samples of concrete, lime mortar, and mud. Ask students to identify common and unique qualities of the various types of building materials. Then guide them in a discussion to identify which of the qualities unique to concrete may have contributed to the Romans becoming master builders.

Did You Know?

The Emperor Augustus boasted that he found Rome a city of brick and stone and left it a city of marble. His boast was justified. He not only rebuilt the forum, or public square, but restored 82 temples as well.

The Temple Complex in Palestrina

Another early Roman temple that made use of Greek features is found in the foothills of the Apennines, a short distance from Rome. The route to this temple is along an ancient Roman road called the Appian Way. This road was once lined with the grand villas and tombs of wealthy Roman citizens.

The town of Praeneste (now the modern city of Palestrina) was said to have originated when a peasant found a mysterious tablet in the woods nearby. According to legend, the history of the town was recorded on this tablet, even though the town itself had not yet been built. The people in the area were so impressed that they erected a temple (Figure 9.7) to house a statue of Fortuna, the goddess of good fortune; the mysterious tablet was placed within this statue. This temple—the Temple of Fortuna Primigenia—became the home of a famous oracle, and people came from great distances to have their futures revealed.

After Rome became Christianized, the oracle at Praeneste was banished and the temple destroyed. Eventually the temple was forgotten and, after the fall of Rome, a town was built on the site. It was not until a bombing raid in World War II destroyed most of the houses that the ruins of the huge temple were discovered.

Design of the Temple Complex

The Temple of Fortuna Primigenia became part of a large complex, which included circular and semicircular temples, terraces, colonnades, arches, and staircases. To span openings, the builders constructed arches. To roof large areas, they created a **barrel vault,** *a series of round arches from front to back that form a tunnel* (Figure 9.8). This made it possible to cover huge rooms and halls with half-round stone ceilings. Because these ceilings were so heavy, thick, windowless walls were needed to support them.

■ **FIGURE 9.7** Here Roman builders constructed staircases leading to a series of seven terraces built into a hillside. How does this technique differ from the way Greek builders used a hill site for the Acropolis?

Sanctuary of Fortuna Primigenia, Palestrina, Italy. Museo Archeologico Nazionale, Palestrina, Italy. c. 120–180 B.C.

More About... **Fortuna.** Fortuna, the goddess of Fortune, was important to the Romans. They built temples in her honor and felt her influence in every part of their lives. She was believed to bestow good or evil upon a person with no discernible reason and was, therefore, thought to be capricious. It is from the Romans that we derive the expression of fortune "smiling on" individuals. Later, in the Middle Ages, the Wheel of Fortune played a prominent role in theology and literature. Ask volunteers to research more about the Middle Ages and the importance of fortune throughout history. Have them share their findings with the class.

LOOKING Closely

STRUCTURE AND DESIGN

The design of this Roman structure, which has been standing for almost 2000 years, demonstrates how use of the arch and barrel vault creates stability and strength even in large buildings.

- **Round Arch.** A wall or another arch is needed to counter the outward force of the arch. You can see the arch outlined in the picture.
- **Keystone.** The top stone of the arch holds other stones in place. The keystone for one of the arches is outlined at the top of the arch.
- **Barrel Vault.** A half-round stone ceiling is made by placing a series of round arches from front to back. The barrel vault is formed in the dark area under the outlined arch.

■ **FIGURE 9.8** Roman Amphitheater, Arles, France. End of first century A.D.

LOOKING Closely

Guide students in discussing the architectural features illustrated here. Be sure they recognize the features basic to every arch. Let volunteers sketch or use models to show the relationships between a keystone, a round arch, and a barrel vault.

Aesthetics

Have students list specific buildings in their own community that make use of the arch. Now ask students to compile a similar list of buildings that make use of the post-and-lintel construction. Compare the two lists. Are certain kinds of buildings more likely to contain arches than others? Which kind? Why is this so? What impression is conveyed by these works of architecture? For what purposes are the buildings used?

Art History

Have groups of students use sugar cubes and white glue to experiment with different types of building construction. Ask one group to use the information in the book to attempt to construct a simple rounded arch, another a barrel vault, still another a doorway based on post-and-lintel construction. Have students compare the strengths and weaknesses of the different structures they have created.

Innovations in Structure and Materials

The round arch improved on the post-and-lintel system that the Greeks used. The post and lintel limited the space builders could bridge. A stone lintel could not be used to span a wide space because it would break.

Unlike a lintel, an arch (Figure 9.8) is made of a number of bricks or cut stones. During the construction of the amphitheater at Arles, France, Roman builders constructed arches by holding the stones in place with a wooden form until a **keystone,** or *top stone of the arch,* could be placed in position. The space that can be spanned in this manner is much greater than the space bridged by a lintel. An arch, however, needs the support of another arch or a wall. Without that support, the outward force of the arch will cause it to collapse. For this reason, the Romans created a series of smaller arches to replace the single large arch.

Concrete, one of the most versatile of building materials, was used in the Temple of Fortuna Primigenia. Although concrete had been used in the Near East for some time, the Romans were the first to make extensive use of this material. Coupled with their knowledge of the arch, concrete enabled the Romans to construct buildings on a large scale.

The Spread of Roman Architecture

Wherever the Roman legions went, they introduced the arch and the use of concrete in architecture. With these they constructed great domes and vaults over their buildings. Usually, they covered their concrete structures with marble slabs or ornamental bricks. Even today, the remains of baths, amphitheaters (Figure 9.8), theaters (Figure 9.9, page 198), triumphal arches, and bridges (Figure 9.10, page 198) are found throughout countries that were once part of the Roman Empire.

Chapter 9 *Roman Art* **197**

Did You Know?

Around the time the Romans were mastering arch and vault construction, the Syrians were mastering a different form of art-related technology: glass blowing.

CULTURAL DIVERSITY

Temples. Many Roman buildings are temples. Ask students to find out what gods and goddesses these temples were built for and what the priestesses of the temples did. Discuss ways in which Roman religious beliefs were influenced by those of the Greeks. Then have students investigate how these beliefs compare with those of other sects and religions that were in existence at the same time. Possibilities include Christianity, Judaism, and certain Eastern religions. Have students compile this information into a reference file entitled "Roman Gods and Goddesses."

Cross Curriculum

SCIENCE. Point out that, like the Egyptians and Greeks before them, the Romans relied heavily on scientific principles in the creation of structures such as those shown here. (Although, for example, Sir Isaac Newton and his laws of gravity were still several centuries away, the Romans obviously had some understanding of this phenomenon, which was instrumental in the success of the aqueduct as a conveyor of water.) Have groups of students investigate the scientific theories that explain the arch and the vault. Set aside class time for students to share and discuss their findings.

Study Guide

Distribute *Study Guide* 19 in the TCR. Assist students in reviewing key concepts. 📁

Art and Humanities

Have students read *Art and Humanities* 14, "Wisdom from Roman Writers," in the TCR. The worksheet invites students to read and discuss quotations from Marcus Aurelius, Horace, and other Roman philosophers of note, and then develop their own philosophical sayings. 📁

Studio Activities

Assign *Studio* 11, "Making a Face Mask," in the TCR. After completion of the activity, which calls on pairs of students to create a face mask, exhibit finished works and have students evaluate the success of each. 📁

■ **FIGURE 9.9** This theater provided seating and entertainment for many during the time Rome ruled over its vast empire. It was built by Agrippa in 24 B.C. **What does the location of this theater tell about the extent of the Roman Empire?**

Roman theater, Merida, Spain. 24 B.C.

■ **FIGURE 9.10** This bridge near Alcantara, in Spain, was built about A.D. 105. It still stands today, providing a way for traffic to cross the river, in the same way it stood nearly 2,000 years ago. **What can you conclude about the Romans' introduction of the arch and their use of concrete?**

Roman bridge, Alcantara, Spain. A.D. 105–6.

198   **Unit Three** *Art of Rising Civilizations*

COOPERATIVE LEARNING

Roman Oracles. Have groups of students research oracles, assigning each group one of the following specific tasks: (1) discovering what an oracle is; (2) describing how oracles functioned in Roman life and culture; (3) researching the connection between oracles and Roman religion/ mythology. Other areas that could be explored include the Greek influence (i.e., did the Greeks have oracles and, if so, how were they similar and different?) and alternate forms of fortune telling (e.g., astrology).

Roman Aqueducts

Aqueducts demonstrate the Romans' ability to combine engineering skills with a knowledge of architectural form. An **aqueduct,** *a system that carried water from mountain streams into cities by using gravitational flow,* was constructed by placing a series of arches next to each other so they would support each other.

Although attractive, these aqueducts were designed for efficiency rather than beauty. Eleven were built in and around Rome alone. These ranged in length from 10 miles to 60 miles. They carried about 270 million gallons (1 billion liters) of water into the city every day.

One of the best-known aqueducts is found in Segovia, Spain (Figure 9.11). It brought water to the city from a stream 10 miles away. Constructed of granite blocks laid without mortar or cement, the aqueduct consisted of many angles to break the force of the rushing water.

■ **FIGURE 9.11** Many people consider this aqueduct the most important Roman construction in Spain. **Why were aqueducts so important? Why were they constructed as a series of arches?**

Roman aqueduct, Segovia, Spain. A.D. 89–117.

LESSON ONE REVIEW

Reviewing Art Facts

1. From whom did the Romans copy much of their art and architecture?
2. What purpose did Romans want their sculptures and paintings to serve?
3. What did wealthy Romans use to decorate the walls of their homes?
4. How did the Romans adapt columns in temple construction?

Activity . . . *Presenting and Defending Ideals*

When considering art of the Greeks and the Romans, it is important to realize that the two cultures, while very similar, were philosophical opposites. The Greeks were idealists, interested in beauty, harmony, and perfection. Even though they admired everything Greek, the Romans were individualists, interested in glory, power, and practicality.

Form two teams—the Greeks and the Romans. Find out about the philosophies and ideals of each group as reflected in their artworks. Present examples of Greek or Roman architecture and sculpture that demonstrate the strength or importance of each philosophy. Research other areas such as writing, political structure, and mythology in support of your team's position. Present your findings in the form of written or oral reports.

Chapter 9 *Roman Art* **199**

ASSESS
Checking Comprehension

Have students respond to the lesson review questions. Answers are given in the box below.

Reteaching

➤ Assign *Reteaching* 19, found in the TCR. Have students complete the activity and review their responses. 🗀

➤ Have students look at Figure 9.6 (page 195). Ask them to describe the features of this building that the Romans borrowed from the Greeks. Then ask them to identify any features that are original Roman ideas.

Enrichment

Assign students *Appreciating Cultural Diversity* 11, "Scenes from Etruscan Tombs," in the TCR. The worksheet provides information about Etruscan culture and asks students to prepare a large artwork for the walls of their classroom. 🗀

Extension

Have students research and report on different facets of the Roman republic and its influence on modern governments. Students should be encouraged to explore the ways in which these influences are manifested by the architecture and "state art" of modern Western societies.

CLOSE

Have students review and discuss the roles of religion and military conquest in the public works of art and architecture created by the Romans. In what ways are these tendencies similar to and different from those found in ancient Egypt and Greece?

Roman Buildings and Monuments

Roman Buildings and Monuments

FOCUS

Lesson Objectives

After studying this lesson, students will be able to:
- Describe characteristics of Roman public buildings.
- Show how Roman buildings were both structurally sound and beautifully designed.

Building Vocabulary

Have students find the bold-faced term *basilica* in the lesson, and ask a volunteer to read the definition. Explain that this term was borrowed later by builders of early Christian churches, who also borrowed the floor plan. Finally, have students find and discuss other boldfaced terms in the lesson with which they have some familiarity.

Motivator

Show students slides or photographs of present-day Rome. Include shots of ancient and modern structures, traffic, and the business of modern daily life. Let students discuss what they see in the photos. Ask them to describe how Rome compares to other modern cities they have seen.

Introducing the Lesson

Invite students to peruse the artworks of the lesson, encouraging them to read the credit lines and captions. Which structures have modern-day counterparts?

Vocabulary
- baths
- groin vault
- pilasters
- niches
- coffers
- basilica
- nave
- apse
- triumphal arch

Discover

After completing this lesson, you will be able to:
- Describe a Roman bath and explain why this kind of structure was so important to the Romans.
- Describe the characteristics of Roman public buildings.

*R*oman emperors were constantly building and rebuilding the cities of their empire. The emperor Augustus boasted that he had found Rome a city of brick and stone and left it a city of marble.

As long as there was money to do so, the emperors had baths, circuses, forums, and amphitheaters constructed for the enjoyment of the people. By providing beautiful monuments and places for public recreation, the emperors hoped to maintain their own popularity.

The Baths

Roman monuments and public buildings were numerous and impressive. Among the most popular of these public buildings were the baths. These were much more than just municipal swimming pools. **Baths** were *vast enclosed structures that contained libraries, lecture rooms, gymnasiums, shops, restaurants, and pleasant walkways.* These made the baths a social and cultural center as well as a place for hygiene. In many ways, they were like the shopping malls of today.

■ **FIGURE 9.12** The Roman baths at Bath, England, provided recreation and a choice of water temperatures in their pools. This picture shows one of the pools and part of the building as they look today. In what ways were Roman baths like modern shopping malls? What are the most important differences?

Roman Baths. Bath, England. First century A.D.

200

LESSON TWO RESOURCES

Teacher's Classroom Resources
- Appreciating Cultural Diversity 12
- Cooperative Learning 14, 15
- Enrichment Activity 17
- Reproducible Lesson Plan 20
- Reteaching Activity 20
- Study Guide 20

Design of the Baths

Every large Roman city had its baths. Although they differed in ground plan and details, these baths had certain features in common. They all contained a series of rooms with pools of progressively cooler water (Figure 9.12). The calidarium, with its hot water pool, was entered first. From there one walked to the tepidarium, where a warm bath awaited. The last room entered was called the frigidarium, and there a cool bath was provided. The different water and room temperatures were made possible by furnaces in rooms beneath the building. These were tended by scores of workers and slaves.

The Baths of Caracalla
■ FIGURE 9.13

One of the most famous baths was built by the emperor Caracalla in the early part of the third century A.D. It sprawled out over 30 acres and had a bathhouse that measured 750 feet by 380 feet. A huge central hall over 180 feet long and 77 feet wide was spanned with concrete groin vaults (Figure 9.13). A **groin vault** is formed *when two barrel vaults meet at right angles.*

In the Baths of Caracalla, a barrel vault ran the length of the central hall and was intersected at right angles by three shorter barrel vaults, creating the groin vaults. The use of these groin vaults enabled the builders to cover a very large area. It also allowed the placement of windows, which was not possible with barrel vaults requiring thick, solid walls.

Buildings for Sports Events

Although the Romans enjoyed many different athletic events, the chariot races were easily their favorite spectator sport. As many as 150,000 Romans would gather at the Circus Maximus to cheer on their favorite teams. These races became so popular that eventually they were scheduled sixty-four days a year.

■ **FIGURE 9.13** A long barrel vault was intersected by three shorter barrel vaults to make groin vaults, as shown by the white outline. **How did the use of barrel and groin vaults make it possible for Roman architects to build such a large hall?**

Central hall of the Baths of Caracalla. Rome, Italy. A.D. 215. Restoration drawing by G. Abel Blonet.

TEACH
Aesthetics

Have students look at Figure 9.12 and compare the baths with a local shopping mall. Encourage them to explain how the Roman "mall" and the mall of today are similar (i.e., both were divided into small, discrete rooms). Next, ask them to explain how they are different (i.e., contemporary malls must include parking facilities). What aesthetic mood or impression is conveyed by the mall of today? To what degree is functionality an important criterion in mall design?

Art Criticism

Direct students' attention to the picture of the Colosseum in Figure 9.14, page 202. Ask students to identify the elements and principles of art emphasized in the structure. What mood or feeling does the unified work of architecture convey? In what ways is the mood or sense similar to, and different from, that conveyed by a sports stadium of today?

Did You Know ?

The term *coliseum* came into use in the English language in 1708 and continues to be used to designate a large sports stadium or building like the one in ancient Rome. One of the most famous present-day coliseums is the one in Los Angeles, which was built in 1921–1923 to resemble the original Colosseum.

Teacher Notes

Styles Influencing Styles

Help students examine and discuss the details presented in the Styles Influencing Styles feature. What architectural development allowed Romans to adapt the Greek columns to this kind of multilevel structure? What do you think influenced the choice of order for each level of the Colosseum? Why do you think pilasters were used?

Art Criticism

To help students appreciate the size of the Colosseum, point out the reference in the text to its size. Have students compute how many regulation-sized football fields would fit inside the Colosseum. Finally, invite students to compute the area of the school building by pacing off the perimeter and determining how many equivalent structures the Colosseum would house.

The Colosseum
■ **FIGURE 9.14**

Almost as popular as the chariot races were the armed contests. These were held in large arenas or amphitheaters such as the Colosseum (Figure 9.14). The Colosseum was built in the second half of the first century A.D. It owes its name to a colossal statue of the Roman emperor Nero that once stood nearby. The huge structure covers 6 acres. It forms a complete oval measuring 615 feet by 510 feet. The structure is so large that during the Middle Ages people moved within its protective walls and erected a small city.

Over the centuries, rulers, popes, and nobility carried off large masses of stone from the Colosseum to construct new buildings. Only after many of the stones had been removed did Pope Benedict XIV put a stop to this destruction, but it was too late. Today the great amphitheater is little more than a broken shell.

Styles Influencing Styles

GREEK TO ROMAN The exterior of the Colosseum consists of four stories constructed of stone, brick, and concrete.

On the top level are Corinthian **pilasters,** *flat, rectangular columns attached to a wall.* Between these pilasters are small holes. Poles were placed in these holes to support a canvas awning that protected spectators from the sun and rain.

Corinthian columns are used on the third level. These show the most decorative style.

Ionic columns are used on the second level. The capitals are distinguished by their double scroll design.

On the lowest level, the columns are Doric, the heaviest and sturdiest of the column orders.

■ **FIGURE 9.14** Colosseum, Rome, Italy. A.D. 72–80.

CULTURAL DIVERSITY

Cultural Development. Remind students that Greek and Roman cultures existed simultaneously, although the two peaked at different times. Provide students with an approximate time frame; then have small groups trace developments in other cultures during this period. Possibilities include the cultures of India, China, and Japan, which are discussed in Chapter 10.

Have groups present their findings to the class, and record the data on a time line drawn on the board. Ask the students to notice any similarities between the developments of the cultures. What are the differences? What patterns, if any, do they detect? What might account for these patterns?

The Colosseum's Interior

At ground level, 80 arched openings enabled spectators to enter and leave the Colosseum so efficiently that it could be emptied in minutes. Of these openings, 76 were used by the general public. One was reserved for the emperor, and another was used by priestesses. Another, the "Door of Life," was reserved for victorious gladiators. The bodies of the slain gladiators were carried through the "Door of Death."

From inside the Colosseum (Figure 9.15), you can see clearly how it was built. The arches are the openings of barrel vaults that ring the amphitheater at each level. These vaults supported the sloped tiers of seats. The seats are gone now, but once there were enough to accommodate 50,000 people.

The best seats in the Colosseum—those in the first tier—were reserved for the emperor and state officials. Members of the upper classes sat in the second tier, while the general public crowded into the upper tiers. A high stone wall separated the spectators from the gladiators and the wild animals fighting in the arena.

Beneath the floor of the Colosseum were compartments and passages serving a number of purposes. There were places to hold caged animals, barracks for gladiators, and rooms to house the machinery needed to raise and lower stage sets and performers.

■ **FIGURE 9.15** The floor is gone now, but you can still see the passageways and rooms. **How did Roman architects take into account the specific uses of the Colosseum?**

Colosseum, interior. Rome, Italy. A.D. 72–80.

Chapter 9 *Roman Art* **203**

Studio Skills

Have students examine the photographs of the exterior and interior of the Colosseum (Figures 9.14 and 9.15). Have them make pencil sketches of what they think the Colosseum looked like in its heyday. Instruct students to draw both interior and exterior views of the structure. Then have students compare their sketches, allowing each the opportunity to offer a rationale for the details he or she included.

Cross Curriculum

LITERATURE. Point out to students that the Roman Empire has been the focus of many historical novels and other works of literature. Among the most celebrated of these is *Ben Hur,* written by Lew Wallace, a general of the American Civil War, and transformed toward the middle of this century into a screen epic. Invite students to browse through the subject heading of the catalog at the school or local library under the headings Rome, Ancient Rome, and Roman Empire. They can copy relevant titles found there into a resource folder called "Roman Art."

Art History

Have students note the Colosseum's dates of construction in the credit line of Figure 9.14. Point out that a number of historical developments occurred around this time, including the following: A.D. 65—The first persecution of Christians took place in Rome. A.D. 79—Mt. Vesuvius erupted in Pompeii.

COOPERATIVE LEARNING

Roman Sports. Let cooperative learning groups investigate sporting events that were popular in ancient Rome. The members of each group can share their findings with the class in the form of a pictorial report accompanied by either photographs or original illustrations. Reports should detail the rules of the sport, noting, where possible, similar contemporary sports. Encourage groups to describe any social rituals or pomp that surrounded a particular competition, as well as the prizes and penalties facing competitors.

Art History

Remind students that Roman monuments and public buildings were quite numerous. Tell students that the Roman emperors thought they would gain popularity by building these structures. Ask students to consider the functions of buildings such as temples and baths. Ask them how commissioning buildings like these might add to a leader's popularity. Have students think of other examples, perhaps contemporary, of people in power attempting to gain favor by erecting certain types of buildings.

Aesthetics

Have students examine the views of the Pantheon in Figures 9.16 and 9.17. Ask them how they imagine it would feel walking toward this building. What message or feeling does the front (façade) of the building communicate to the viewer? How might the space inside the building make the spectator feel?

Art History

Call students' attention to the dome that caps the Pantheon. Have them compare this dome, both in terms of its appearance and its physical dimensions as described in the text, with the one shown in Figure 16.13, page 364. (dome of Florence cathedral) Point out that Brunelleschi's feat of engineering, which took sixteen years to complete, was based on techniques developed by the Romans.

Gladiator Contests

In the third century B.C., the Romans revived an Etruscan spectacle in which slaves were pitted against each other in battles to the death. These battles became so popular that regular contests between hundreds of gladiators were staged in the Colosseum before thousands of spectators.

Not all Romans approved of these brutal contests, but they were so popular with the masses that most objectors were afraid to express their opinions. The amphitheater was always filled to capacity for events in which as many as 5,000 pairs of gladiators fought to the death and 11,000 animals were killed in a single day.

Public Buildings and Structures

The Roman emperors had great civic pride, and in addition to the buildings provided for public entertainment, they commissioned public squares and civic centers. Magnificent structures were built: meeting halls, temples to Roman gods, markets, and basilicas. Architects and engineers combined their talents to erect huge buildings that were not only structurally sound but also beautifully designed.

The Pantheon
■ FIGURE 9.16

One of the marvels of Roman architecture is the Pantheon (Figure 9.16). Designed as a temple dedicated to all the Roman gods, it was later converted into a Christian church. The building has been in near-continuous use; therefore, it is in excellent condition today.

From the exterior, the Pantheon looks like a low, gently curving dome resting on a cylinder. From street level the building can no longer be viewed as it was originally intended. The level of the surrounding streets is much higher now, and the steps that once led up to the entry porch are gone. The building loses much of its original impact today because you are forced to look straight at it rather than lifting your eyes up to it.

■ FIGURE 9.16
Notice the proportion of the large cylinder capped by a low dome. What impression do you think the Pantheon was intended to create? Do you think it succeeds in creating that impression today? Why or why not?

The Pantheon, Rome, Italy. A.D. 118–25.

204 **Unit Three** *Art of Rising Civilizations*

More About... **Hadrian.** The Roman emperor Hadrian, who is credited with constructing the Pantheon, was by all accounts a brilliant, difficult man with an intense interest in architecture. Like several other Greek and Roman leaders, he exerted a tremendous influence on the course of Roman art. In addition to his architectural inclinations, Hadrian was accomplished in poetry and painting and, because of strong leadership qualities, was known as "the father of his people." Individual students may want to research the role of this emperor and report their findings to the class.

The interior of the Pantheon is certain to have an impact. Passing through the entrance hall, you step suddenly into the great domed space of the interior (Figure 9.17). Looking upward, you discover that the dome, which looked so shallow from the outside, is actually a true hemisphere. Made of brick and concrete, this huge dome soars to a height of 144 feet above the floor. The diameter of the dome is also exactly 144 feet.

The inside of the Pantheon is divided into three zones. The lowest zone has seven **niches,** *recesses in the wall.* These may have contained statues or altars dedicated to the Roman gods of the heavens: Sol (sun), Luna (moon), and gods of the five known planets. Above this, another zone contains the 12 signs of the zodiac. Finally, rising above all, the magnificent dome represents the heavens. The surface of the dome is covered with

coffers, or *indented panels.* These coffers are more than just a decorative touch; they also reduce the weight of the dome.

Illuminating the Pantheon's Interior

The interior of the Pantheon is well illuminated, although there are no windows. Walls up to 20 feet thick were needed to support the dome, and windows would have weakened these walls. In addition to the door, the only source of light is a round opening almost 30 feet across at the top of the dome. It fills the interior with a bright, clear light and lets you see a section of sky through the top of the dome. To solve the problem posed by rain, the Romans built the floor so that it was raised slightly in the center, formed a shallow depression directly under the opening, and created a drainage system to carry away the water.

■ **FIGURE 9.17** The large, round opening at the top of the dome allows light into the interior of the Pantheon. **What is the most surprising feature of this interior? Is this feature suggested by its exterior appearance?**

Giovanni Paolo Panini. *Interior of the Pantheon, Rome.* c. 1734. Oil on canvas. 1.3 × .99 m (50 ¹/₂ × 39″). National Gallery of Art, Washington, D.C. Board of Trustees, Samuel H. Kress Collection.

Chapter 9 *Roman Art* **205**

Cross Curriculum

HISTORY. Ask several volunteers to research and report to the class on the chain of events that led to the collapse of the Roman Empire. If possible, students should include quotes from primary sources.

Study Guide

Distribute *Study Guide* 20 from the TCR and review key concepts with students. 📁

Art and Humanities

Distribute *Cooperative Learning* 14, "Who Is a Hero?" in the TCR. The activity asks small groups of students to consider the meaning of the term hero, as well as the characteristics such individuals generally possess. Groups are then called upon to create original works of art that celebrate a local hero from either the community or school. 📁

Studio Activities

Review with students the characteristics of Roman temple design, perhaps calling their attention once again to the illustrations of temples found in Lessons One and Two of this chapter. Then assign *Studio* 12, "Drawing a Roman Temple," in the TCR. 📁

Art and Humanities

Assign Appreciating *Cultural Diversity* 12, "The Roman Atrium: Past and Present." In this activity, students learn about the atrium, a standard feature of Roman buildings. After students have read the worksheet, challenge them to complete the activity, which calls on them to design an interior that makes use of an atrium. To assist students in their projects, you may wish to show them pictures of modern buildings that feature atriums. 📁

Basilicas

The Romans also constructed spacious rectangular buildings called basilicas. The **basilica** was *a functional building made to hold large numbers of people.* Designed as a court of law and public meeting hall, it was often a part of the forum, or public square. Basilicas combined in one structure many of the architectural advances made by the Romans, but they are important for another reason: They served as models for generations of Christian church builders.

Plan of Basilicas

Inside a basilica, rows of slender columns divided the space into what was later called the **nave,** *a long, wide center aisle,* and two or more narrower side aisles (Figure 9.18). The roof over the center aisle was usually higher than the roofs over the side aisles. This allowed the builders to install windows to let sunlight in. The Roman basilica had a side entrance and at least one area later called an **apse,** a *semicircular area at the end of the nave.*

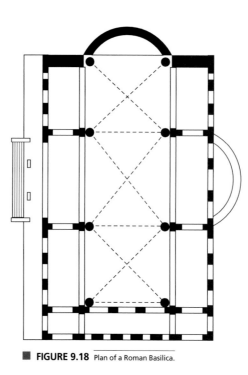

■ FIGURE 9.18 Plan of a Roman Basilica.

Wooden roofs were used for most basilicas. The roof over the center aisle was peaked, whereas roofs over the side aisles sloped gently downward.

Triumphal Arches

Romans loved celebrations and often marked their successful military campaigns by building a monument to the victory: a **triumphal arch** or *heavily decorated arch.* After an important victory, the general and his troops would pass under the triumphal arch while thousands of onlookers cheered. Triumphal arches often consisted of a large central opening and two smaller openings on each side. The general and his officers rode chariots and horses through the central opening, and unmounted troops marched through the smaller ones. It was not unusual for the troops to carry posters showing the major events of the campaign.

The Arch of Constantine
■ FIGURE 9.19

The Arch of Constantine (Figure 9.19) was the largest and most elaborate of these triumphal arches. It was decorated for the most part with sculptures and reliefs taken from earlier monuments dedicated to other emperors. Of course, this meant that the sculptures showing the emperor had to be changed to look more like Constantine.

The Declining Power of Rome

It is difficult to pinpoint exactly what brought about the decline of the great Roman Empire. One important factor was the transfer of the capitol of the Roman Empire from Rome in the west to the site of the ancient Greek city of Byzantium in the eastern provinces.

In A.D. 330 the emperor Constantine I dedicated his new capital, which was renamed Constantinople, in the Eastern Roman Empire. This move marked the beginning of the long history of the Byzantine Empire. From then

---

Emperor Constantine. Ask cooperative learning groups to research different facets of the life and career of Constantine I, the first Christian Roman emperor. An area of particular importance that one group might choose to explore is Constantine's conversion to Christianity, which occurred during an important battle, affecting not only the Roman Empire but Roman culture as well. Another group may want to trace both the causes and effects of the emperor's movement of the capital from Rome to Byzantium. Set aside class time for an information exchange.

■ **FIGURE 9.19** The successful general and his mounted officers would have paraded through the large central arch. The foot soldiers would have marched through the smaller arches on each side. What does this kind of structure indicate about the importance of the army in the Roman Empire?

Arch of Constantine, Rome, Italy. A.D. 312–15.

on, the Western section of the Roman Empire was marked by weakness and decline.

Eventually, invaders from the north came down to overrun the once-powerful Western Roman Empire. In 410, Alaric, king of the Visigoths, took Rome, and wave after wave of barbarian invasions followed. By the end of the fifth century A.D., the Western Roman Empire had come to an end, and the barbarian kingdoms of the Middle Ages took its place.

LESSON TWO REVIEW

Reviewing Art Facts

1. Describe a Roman bath. Why were these structures so popular?
2. What was the Colosseum, and what kinds of events were held there?
3. What are coffers? What two purposes do the coffers in the dome of the Pantheon serve?
4. What were triumphal arches, and how were they used?

Activity...*Recording Examples of Architecture*

The Romans developed architectural methods that are still in use today. Examples can be seen in government buildings in Washington, D.C., and in state capitals, which were often modeled after classical architectural styles.

Look around your school for evidence of the modern-day use of the construction methods of the Greeks and the Romans. (Examples: doorway lintels, columns, skylight domes, and arches.) Keep a written record or draw examples in your sketchbook of any structures you see that could have been inspired by the construction methods of these ancient cultures. As a class, take a tour of the building and point out your findings.

Chapter 9 *Roman Art* **207**

➢ Have students respond to the lesson review questions. Answers are given in the box below.

➢ Have students complete *Application 9*, "Accidental Tourist," which tests their comprehension of terms and concepts presented in the chapter. 📁

Reteaching

➢ Assign *Reteaching* 20, found in the TCR. Have students complete the activity and review their responses. 📁

➢ Ask students to look through the illustrations in this chapter and to identify the different functions served by the buildings shown. Ask students which architectural (or other) features of the buildings help them identify its function.

Enrichment

Assign *Enrichment* 17, "Roman vs Greek Aesthetics," in the TCR. Students are asked to compare Greek and Roman art forms using the descriptive words provided. 📁

Extension

Distribute *Cooperative Learning* 15, "Ancient Rome in American Cities." After students have completed the reading, divide the class into teams to seek out examples of Roman influence in engineering, then document these influences in a poster or video. 📁

CLOSE

Present students with modern guidebooks to Rome and ask them to prepare a report on the information the books contain about the structures that are described in this chapter, such as the Colosseum and the Pantheon.

LESSON TWO REVIEW

Answers to Reviewing Art Facts

1. They were centers of culture and leisure, popular for the many shops and activities offered.
2. An amphitheater, used for races and contests.
3. Coffers are indented panels. They reduced the weight of the dome.
4. Heavily decorated arches built to celebrate successful military campaigns. After an important victory, the general and his troops would pass under the triumphal arch while onlookers cheered.

Activity... *Recording Examples of Architecture*

Discuss the activity with students. Suggest that some students may want to sketch and/or photograph architectural features of other local buildings. Provide time during which these students can share their work with the rest of the class.

Studio LESSON
Relief of a Roman Structure

Objectives

■ Complete a posterboard relief showing the exterior of a Roman temple, aqueduct, colosseum, or arch.

■ Symmetrically balance the architectural features in the relief.

■ Produce a three-dimensional appearance by layering increasingly smaller shapes on top of larger shapes.

Motivator

Ask students to re-examine the examples of Roman architecture illustrated in the chapter and identify the features associated with each. List their suggestions on the board. Then discuss the feature or features common to most of these structures.

Art Criticism

Have individual students select and describe the appearance of one of the Roman structures listed on the board without naming it. Ask the other members of the class to identify the structure. Have other students select and identify one of the structures in terms of its function. Again, ask other students to identify it. Finally, have students identify the structure that they feel is most successful in being both attractive and functional. Discuss their choices.

Critiquing

Have students apply the steps of art criticism to their own artwork, using the "Examining Your Work" questions on this page.

Materials

- Pencil and sketch paper
- Pieces or a sheet of foam-core board or white mat board
- Sheet of white mat board or poster board, 12 × 18 inches
- Scissors or utility knife
- Metal straight edge or ruler
- White glue

Complete a mat board or foam-core board relief showing the exterior of a temple, aqueduct, colosseum, or arch based on a Roman example. Include the same architectural features as the structure that inspired it. Layer increasingly smaller shapes on top of larger shapes for a three-dimensional look. This also provides contrasts of value (light and shadow) that add visual interest to the relief.

Inspiration

Examine the Roman temples, aqueducts, colosseums, and arches illustrated in this chapter. Select one of these for detailed study. If seen directly from the front (or side), would it seem flat or three-dimensional? How many different kinds of shapes can you point out? Which shapes project outward into space? Do the shadows created by the different projections and recessions give the structure a more interesting appearance?

■ **FIGURE 9.20** Student Work

Process

1. Complete several line drawings of the Roman structure you chose. These drawings should show the different shapes you see in this structure. Do not try to draw these as three-dimensional forms, but as simple flat shapes such as triangles, circles, half-circles, squares, and rectangles.

2. Choose your best drawing as a model. Take the foam-core board or white mat board and use scissors or a utility knife and a metal straight edge to cut out the various shapes identified.

3. Carefully arrange the shapes on the sheet of mat board or poster board to create a relief of the structure. The shapes should fill the board. Stack increasingly smaller shapes on top of each other to give your relief a three-dimensional look. Glue the shapes down.

SAFETY TIP Be careful when using sharp tools. Place a sheet of heavy, protective cardboard on your work surface. Keep fingers away from the cutting line. Be sure to use a sharp blade; dull blades can slip.

Examining Your Work

Describe. What features of your relief contributed the most to making it resemble a particular type of Roman architecture?

Analyze. Did you use a variety of large and small shapes on your relief to create a three-dimensional appearance? Does your relief exhibit an interesting pattern of light and dark values? What do these value contrasts contribute to the overall effectiveness of your relief?

Interpret. Do you think viewers can determine the purpose for which your structure might have been built?

Judge. Evaluate your work in terms of its visual qualities. Do you think it demonstrates an overall unity? Which art elements and principles contributed the most in achieving that unity?

208

ASSESSMENT

Peer Review. Let students meet in small groups to examine and discuss one another's completed reliefs. Suggest that each student present his or her relief to the rest of the group, identifying the most successful aspects of the project and discussing what he or she would like to do differently. Encourage other group members to respond honestly yet constructively. Then ask group members to select on relief to present to the class. They might select the work they judge most successful in demonstrating overall unity, or they might choose a relief in which a particular problem was solved in an interesting or unusual way.

Reviewing the Facts

Lesson One

1. What people lived in Italy before 509 B.C.?
2. How did Roman sculpture and painting differ in style from Greek sculpture and painting?
3. How did the Roman arch improve on the post-and-lintel system used by the Greeks?
4. How did Etruscan architecture influence Roman temples?
5. What did the Romans build to transport water to their cities? How did these structures work?

Lesson Two

6. What motivated Roman emperors to construct baths, circuses, forums, and amphitheaters?
7. What features did all the Roman baths have in common?
8. What is a groin vault? How is it made? What special advantage does it offer?
9. Name two unusual aspects of the interior or exterior of the Pantheon's dome.
10. What purpose did Roman basilicas serve? How did they influence later architecture?

Thinking Critically

1. **COMPARE AND CONTRAST.** Using the Parthenon (Figure 8.1, page 166) and the Pantheon (Figure 9.16, page 204) as models, discuss the similarities and differences between Greek and Roman temples.
2. **ANALYZE.** Look closely at the scenes shown in the mural from the Villa at Boscoreale (Figure 9.4, page 194). Then refer to the list of techniques that artists have devised to create the illusion of depth on page 38 in Chapter 2. Which techniques did the Roman artist use?

 R T S U R C Use the *Performing Arts Handbook* on page 576 to learn about music, dance, and theatre from many diverse cultures.

CAREERS IN Art   Read about an art career that began in ancient Rome. Urban planners draw up plans for cities in the *Careers in Art Handbook*, page 600.

interNET CONNECTION Visit Glencoe Art Online at *www.glencoe.com/sec/art*. Learn more about Roman civilization. Visit architecture sites and view artifacts at the Roman Forum.

Technology Project

Mapping Roman Influences

The Romans developed and extended their culture to the entire known world. At one time the Romans controlled the entire area around the Mediterranean Sea, and from what is now Britain to the area called Mesopotamia in the east. The Roman influence was also felt in Egypt and Spain.

When the Romans conquered an area, they did not try to make the inhabitants accept the Roman way of life. They only expected the conquered peoples to be loyal to the Roman rulers and to pay taxes. In return, the practical Romans improved the area with such things as roads, aqueducts, bridges, and public baths. The remains of these structures can still be found in almost every area that the Romans once controlled. The Roman aqueduct featured in Figure 9.11, page 199, still brings water into the city

of Segovia, Spain. Figure 9.12 on page 200 is a Roman public bath located in Bath, England. How old are these structures? What does this tell us about the quality of engineering used by Roman builders?

1. Look at the map on page 192, which shows the locations of major cities in the Roman Empire at the time it was most powerful. Using available resources (books, CD-ROMs, laser discs, the Internet), create a map that also includes other locations such as Britain, Mesopotamia, and Egypt, where remains of Roman rule can be found.
2. Collect images of some of these remains from each location on your map by using cut and paste, scanning, or digital photography. Place copies of the images, with a description, on or with your map at each location.
3. To complete your project, present your map to the class or to your workgroup, or print a copy for class members to place in their art history notes.

Reviewing the Facts

1. The Etruscans.
2. Roman artworks were less idealistic than their Greek counterparts.
3. The arch can span a much greater space.
4. Romans followed the Etruscan example in building temples on a platform that raises the temple above eye level.
5. Aqueducts; they carried water from the mountains to the cities using gravitation.
6. A desire to remain popular.
7. All contained series of rooms with progressively cooler water.
8. The groin vault allows coverage of a larger area and permits the use of windows.
9. Any two: It is actually a true hemisphere; it is divided into three zones; the surface is covered with coffers; there is a large round opening at the top.
10. Basilicas were functional buildings made to hold large numbers of people; they were designed to be law courts and public meeting halls. They later served as models for many Christian churches.

Thinking Critically

1. Similarities: use of columns around a rectangular building; use of a peaked roof. Differences: decorative (versus functional) use of columns, including pilasters; placement of the building on a podium, a feature borrowed from the Etruscans.
2. Overlapping shapes; making distant shapes smaller; placing distant shapes higher in the picture; slanting the lines of shapes inward.

 Teaching the Technology Project

Students may want to work with partners or in small cooperative groups to complete this project. Allow class time during which students can share and discuss their projects. Encourage interested students to extend the project by selecting one geographical area of the Roman empire as a subject for more in-depth research.

R T S U R C Assign the feature in the *Performing Arts Handbook*, page 576.

CAREERS IN ART   If time permits, have interested students investigate the career information in the *Careers in Art Handbook*, page 600.

interNET CONNECTION Have students go online and learn more about artists on preselected Web sites with the Internet activity for this chapter.

Art of Asia, the Americas, and Africa

Unit Four introduces the art of three Far Eastern cultures—India, China, and Japan—and of various civilizations and peoples that flourished in the Americas and in Africa.

Chapter 10 *The Art of India, China, and Japan* treats the religious and cultural forces that have shaped, and in some instances continue to drive, the art and way of life of people in those countries.

Chapter 11 *The Native Arts of the Americas* provides a glimpse at the lasting structures and largely craft-oriented art produced by the mighty Mayan and Inca civilizations, as well as a look at the art of Native Americans to the north.

Chapter 12 *The Arts of Africa* delves into the accomplishments of various peoples and cultures that inhabited or continue to inhabit the African continent, including the remarkable Benin bronze castings and ritualistic wood carvings.

National Museum of Women in the Arts

You may wish to use the National Museum of Women in the Arts videodisc and/or CD-ROM. The videodisc features a bar code guide, and the interactive CD-ROM provides stimulating activities.

210

More About...

Clay Soldiers. The clay soldiers shown in this photograph are located in the Shaanxi province in China. For 2000 years these clay figures were buried in the tomb of the first emperor of Qin, pronounced "chin." They were discovered accidentally when peasants began digging a well in a mound near their home. Archaeologists found the soldiers arranged with their horses as if ready to begin battle. The figures appear gray and colorless now, but were originally painted in vivid colors. Their bodies stand erect, with hand gestures and postures giving a lifelike appearance. Each face was made with unique features and expressions, giving personality to the soldiers guarding the emperor's tomb.

Art of Asia, the Americas, and Africa

"But all the other historic monuments at Xian pale into insignificance beside the discovery made in 1974 to the east of the city, where the vast man-made hill that houses the tomb of Qin Shi Huang, the founder of the Qin dynasty, rises from the valley of the Weihe."

China
Zheng Shifeng and other authors (1980)

Life-size clay soldiers from the tomb of the first Emperor of Qin. c. 246–210 B.C. Xian, China.

211

Introducing the Unit

Direct students' attention to the art on these pages and the chapter openers, and ask them to comment on ways these works differ from others they have encountered in the text thus far. Have students brainstorm possible purposes for which this art was created. Ask: Do you suppose these artworks were created simply to be looked at and admired? Are any of the purposes you attach to these works ones you would also ascribe to Western art?

Discussing the Quotation

Ask students whether their illustration supports the claim of importance made in the quotation. Ask if the significance of these life-size figures would be magnified if they knew that they represent only a fraction of more than 8000 clay warriors guarding the first emperor of China. Tell students that this army, arranged in precise military formation, has been buried since 210 B.C. Ask students what this undertaking tells us about the emperor who commissioned it.

Teacher Notes _____

_____

_____

_____

211

The Art of India, China, and Japan

ADDITIONAL CHAPTER RESOURCES

Activities

- 📁 Advanced Studio Activity 10
- 📁 Application 10
- 🖱 Chapter 10 Internet Activity
- 📁 Studio Activity 13

Fine Art Resources

- 🔖 **Transparency**

  Art in Focus Transparency 13

    Emperor Ming-huang's Flight to Shu.

    Southern Sung Dynasty

- 🖼 **Fine Art Print**

  Focus on World Art Print 10

    Ogata Korin. Yatsuhashi. Six-Fold Screen

Assessment

- 📁 Chapter 10 Test
- 📁 Performance Assessment

Multimedia Resources

- 🎭 Artsource® Performing Arts Package
- 💿 National Gallery Laser Disc
- 💿 National Museum of Women in the Arts CD-ROM
- 📼 Arts & Entertainment Videos

NATIONAL STANDARDS FOR ARTS EDUCATION

The National Standards for Arts Education provide guidelines for grade-appropriate competency in the visual arts. The Content Standards for grades 9–12 are:

1. Understanding and applying media, techniques, and processes.
2. Using knowledge of structures and functions.
3. Choosing and evaluating a range of subject matter, symbols, and ideas.
4. Understanding the visual arts in relation to history and cultures.
5. Reflecting upon and assessing the characteristics and merits of their work and the work of others.
6. Making connections between visual arts and other disciplines.

Listed below are the National Standards for the Visual Arts addressed in this chapter. For a breakdown of the categories listed under each content standard, refer to the *Reproducible Lesson Plans* booklet in the TCR.

1. (a, b)   **2.** (a, b)   **3.** (a, b)   **4.** (a, b, c)   **5.** (c)   **6.** (a, b)

Out of Time?

If time does not permit teaching this chapter in its entirety, you may wish to preview the artwork and captions with students. Scan the heads in each lesson with students. Discuss the Looking Closely features and examine Symbolism in Indian Art on page 221 and Storytelling in Art on page 236.

HANDBOOK MATERIAL

Ranganiketan Manipuri *(page 583)*

 CAREERS IN Art

Landscape Architect *(page 601)*

Beyond the Classroom

The American Arts Alliance home page provides more resources for teachers and links art eucators to a list of state and local organizations supporting the arts. Find them by visiting our Web site at *www.glencoe.com/sec/art.*

The Art of India, China, and Japan

The Art of India, China, and Japan

INTRODUCE

Chapter Overview

CHAPTER 10 treats the religious, intellectual, and artistic achievements that are at the root of Eastern civilization.

Lesson One discusses the architecture and sculpture of ancient India.

Lesson Two presents the scroll painting and sculpture of China.

Lesson Three analyzes Japan's temples, painting, and sculpture.

Studio Lessons guide students to create a drawing composed of a visual symbol and a negative shape painting.

Art & Science

Have students examine and discuss the artwork that opens this chapter. Then focus attention on the cheetahs in the work. Let volunteers share what they know about cheetahs, and about the endangered status of the cats.

Encourage interested students to research the depiction of cheetahs and other large cats in works of art from around the world.

Art & Science ■ **FIGURE 10.1** The spotted cats seen in this work, cheetahs, are the fastest land animals. Running cheetahs have been clocked at 60 miles per hour. Cheetahs once ranged on open plains of the Middle East and Sub-Saharan Africa. Today, due to loss of their natural habitat, they are virtually extinct and are listed as a critically endangered species.

Lal and Sanwlah. *Akbar Hunting with Trained Cheetahs,* from *Akbar Nama.* c. 1590. Gouache on paper. Victoria and Albert Museum, London, England.

212

National Standards

This chapter meets the following National Standards for the Arts:
1. (a,b)   4. (a,b,c)
2. (a,b)   5. (c)
3. (a,b)   6. (a,b)

CHAPTER 10 RESOURCES

Teacher's Classroom Resources
- Advanced Studio Activity 10
- Application 10
- Chapter 10 Internet Activity
- Studio Activity 13

Assessment
- Chapter 10 Test
- Performance Assessment

Fine Art Resources
- *Art in Focus* Transparency 13
  Emperor Ming-Huang's Flight to Shu.
- *Focus on World Art* Print 10
  Ogata Korin. *Yatsuhashi.*

*𝒯he ten centuries beginning in the fifth century B.C. and
ending in the fifth century A.D. are often
considered a formative period in both the West and the East.
During this long period, the seeds for both
halves of our modern world civilization were sown. The
Greco-Roman culture resulted in the formation of
contemporary Western culture. At the same
time, the religious, intellectual, and artistic achievements
that took place in India, China, and Japan combined to form
the basis for contemporary Eastern culture. Dance,
musical instruments, and even dramatic makeup and
gestures evolved in different ways in the East than in the West.
As a result, when Western artists encountered
Eastern art, they sometimes were inspired in new directions.*

Introducing the Chapter

Display posters or photos of several artworks from India, China, and Japan. Let students examine and discuss them, noting similarities and differences. Ask: How are these works different from the most famous examples of Western art? Remind students, as they read the chapter, to correct any misconceptions about Eastern art.

 Dance/Music While studying this chapter, use *Performing Arts Handbook* page 583 to help students appreciate how the dances and music performed by Ranganiketan represent spiritual and cultural aspects of Hindu life.

YOUR Portfolio

As you study this chapter, select one of the cultures that interests you. Begin a page in your sketchbook where you can write information about the art of that culture as you read about it. Make notes and sketches for your portfolio. Work with your class to begin a class resource file to which you and classmates can contribute pictures and facts about the art of different countries and cultures. Each student can then use this resource to research a specific culture.

Focus ON THE ARTS

LITERATURE
In 500 B.C. and 300 B.C., two Hindu plays, Naimiki's *Ramaya* and the *Mahabarata* unfolded epic tales of conflicts between ruling families and their relationships with the gods.

THEATRE
During a thousand years of cultural isolation, Japan developed an extraordinary range of theatre styles, from the religious Nō drama, to bunraku puppet theatre and the popular Kabuki.

MUSIC
Far Eastern music is based on principles different from Western music. The Chinese Opera uses quarter tones. Indian musical structure has a system of alternating parts. Instruments of the East include the gong, sitar, huqin, and bamboo flute.

Focus ON THE ARTS

Explain that Japanese drama makes use of simple gestures that are highly symbolic. If an actor takes one step, it represents a complete journey; if he simply turns his head, it's a refusal; if he touches his sword, he has won the battle. Great stillness and elaborate preparation go into a single gesture. Ask each student to invent a similar gesture, with or without a prop. Then have students read or act out their gestures. Have the class guess their meaning.

213

DEVELOPING A PORTFOLIO

Presentation. Remind students to keep their portfolios up to date, reflecting their progress as artists. Since colleges and art schools may have different requirements, students should be prepared with a variety of pieces, and should be flexible with the contents. If they keep a supply of finished work available for submission, they will be spared any rushed jobs that might affect the overall impact of their portfolio. If possible, have models available for their inspection, showing various ways to meet the requirements students might encounter. Stress attention to detail and overall appearance.

The Art of India

The Art of India

FOCUS

Lesson Objectives

After studying this lesson, students will be able to:
- Explain how the religions of Hinduism and Buddhism influenced the architecture and sculpture of ancient India.
- Identify forms of art and architecture indigenous to this part of the world.

Building Vocabulary

Let volunteers share what they already know about the two Vocabulary terms for this lesson: What is meditation? With what religions and belief practices is meditation usually associated? If the word stupa is entirely new to students, have them turn to page 217 to read the definition and to examine a photograph of a stupa (Figure 10.6).

Motivator

Encourage students to share what they know about modern Indian culture and/or about the culture of ancient India. Then have students brainstorm a list of questions they hope to have answered as they study this focus. Record their ideas on the board, and return to this list later to discuss what they have learned.

Introducing the Lesson

Have students browse through the lesson, taking notice of the works of architecture and sculpture they find. Ask: What adjectives and phrases would you use to describe these works? Are the works similar to those of other civilizations you studied in earlier chapters?

Vocabulary
- meditation
- stupa

Discover

After completing this lesson, you will be able to:
- Describe the development of the Hindu and Buddhist religions in India.
- Explain how the Hindu and Buddhist religions influenced the architecture and sculpture of India.

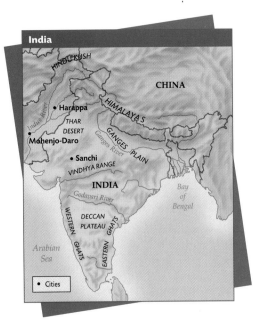

MAP SKILLS

■ **FIGURE 10.2** Two major Eastern religions, Hinduism and Buddhism, began in India. Buddhism spread to China and Japan. **How do you think the spread of religious ideas affected the artworks created in these areas?**

214

The long history of India is also the history of two great and enduring religions. For centuries Hinduism and Buddhism have influenced all aspects of Indian life. Nowhere is this more evident than in the art of India, the birthplace of both.

At times these two religions vied with one another, each producing its own unique art style in architecture and sculpture. At other times the two have existed side by side, resulting in artworks that are both Hindu and Buddhist in character.

When and how did these religions originate? How did they influence the art of India? A search for answers to these questions involves a journey back 4,500 years, to the same period when Egypt's Old Kingdom flourished.

The Indus Valley Civilization

The modern nations of India, Pakistan, and Bangladesh trace their cultural beginnings to the early Indian civilizations. Historians now recognize that an ancient civilization once flourished on the banks of the Indus River in what is now northwest India. (See map, Figure 10.2.)

The Harappans

The Harappans, or people of the Indus Valley, gradually developed a way of life as far advanced as that of Egypt. They used bronze and copper technology and erected multistoried buildings made of fired bricks along streets as wide as 40 feet. The Harappans also built an efficient drainage system and developed a written language based on pictograms, or picture symbols.

While most Harappans raised grain and vegetables in the fields surrounding their cities and towns, others made and traded small clay pottery, bronze and stone figures, and cotton cloth. The production of these items made the Indus Valley an important trading center.

Harappa and Mohenjo-Daro

In modern times, two important sites have been discovered: Harappa in 1856, and Mohenjo-Daro (Figure 10.3) in 1922. Excavations reveal that about 4,500 years ago a civilization rose along the 400-mile route separating these two cities. More than 70 cities, towns, and villages have been discovered; they are believed to have been part of an organized kingdom with a central government.

LESSON ONE RESOURCES

Teacher's Classroom Resources

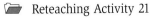

📁 Art and Humanities 15

📁 Enrichment Activity 18

📁 Reproducible Lesson Plan 21

📁 Reteaching Activity 21

📁 Study Guide 21

■ **FIGURE 10.3** This site reveals the ruins of a carefully planned city that thrived about 4,500 years ago. What do these ruins tell you about the people who lived here?

Mohenjo-Daro, India. c. 2500 B.C.

Harappan Art

Many Harappan clay works (Figure 10.4) have been found, most of which were apparently made for trading purposes. Only a few small stone and bronze sculptures from Mohenjo-Daro have survived to the present day. These hint at a fully developed artistic style and provide insights into the religious beliefs of the mysterious Harappan people. Like their clay works, these sculptures indicate that the Harappans worshiped a great many spirits who, they believed, were found in water, trees, animals, and humans.

Decline of the Harappan Civilization

By about 2000 B.C. the Harappan civilization began to decline, and by 1500 B.C. it vanished completely. Most historians believe that invaders from the northwest, known as Aryans, were largely responsible for bringing an end to the Indus Valley civilization.

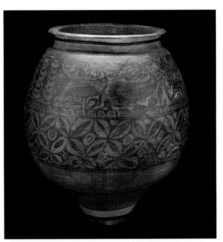

■ **FIGURE 10.4** Notice the images of nature, birds, and flowers decorating this work by Harappan artists. What elements and principles of art would you discuss when analyzing this work?

Large Painted Jar with Birds. Pakistan, Chanhu-daro. 3000 B.C. Terra cotta. 25 × 49.5 cm (9³/₄ × 19¹/₂″). Charihu-daro. Chanhu-daro Expedition. Courtesy of the Museum of Fine Arts, Boston, Massachusetts.

Chapter 10 *The Art of India, China, and Japan* **215**

TEACH
Using Map Skills

Direct students' attention to the map, Figure 10.2, that shows the land of India. Ask students to note the dates of artworks illustrated in this lesson and consider the location on the map in relation to China. Do they imagine that the peoples of these ancient lands had contact with one another, or were they isolated from each other as their individual art styles developed? As they read about the different artworks and locations, have them trace the growth of Hinduism and Buddhism across these lands on the map.

Critical Thinking

Direct students' attention to the photograph of the ruins of Mohenjo-Daro in Figure 10.3. Ask whether students are surprised to learn that a society that flourished 4,500 years ago had the skills to plan such a city. Ask: Are we inclined to assume that ancient cultures could not have had the intelligence or sophistication we see in modern societies? Are we also inclined to think that other cultures are less intelligent or sophisticated than our own? Ask students why they think such beliefs tend to be widespread. How does studying art help us overcome these prejudices?

 Technology

Multimedia Resources. You can find a listing of helpful on-line and multimedia art resources at Glencoe's Online Art Web page on the Internet. Find out about art reference materials, image libraries, and art history resources. Locate distributors of computer art software, CD-ROMs, and art media and supplies for your classroom. If you have resources that you would like to add to our site, send us information with the Contact Us button. Find the Glencoe Online Art home page at: *www.glencoe.com/sec/art.*

Cross Curriculum

HISTORY. Around the time the city of Mohenjo-Daro was under construction, the following cultural milestones were also in progress. The step pyramids and the seated portrait of the pharaoh Khafre were being created in Egypt. The Standard of Ur was nearing completion in Sumer. Have groups of volunteers research each of these accomplishments and present their findings to the rest of the class.

Aesthetics

Ask students to consider the fact that the painted jar (Figure 10.4, page 215) has survived more than 4,000 years. Point out that the substance from which the object was made, terra cotta (Italian for "baked earth"), is still widely used today—for everything from rooftop tiles to flower pots. Ask: What property of terra cotta gives the medium its warmth? What is it about pottery in particular that communicates a sense of intimacy— that makes us feel a personal connection to the artisan who crafted it? Ask students what flora and fauna they recognize in the painted design.

Did You Know?

During the period when the painted jar in Figure 10.4 was being created, the Phoenicians were settling on the Syrian coast.

The Ganges Civilization and the Rise of the Hindu Religion

The Aryans controlled India during the thousand-year period now commonly known as the Ganges civilization. They were warrior-shepherds who relied on their cattle and sheep for livelihood. There is no evidence to suggest that the Aryans were as well organized as the Harappans were. They had no central government and were loosely organized into tribes. Each tribe was ruled by a *raja,* or chief, who was assisted by a council of warriors.

Over time the Aryan religion, which recognized many gods and goddesses, blended with the beliefs of the Harappans to form what eventually became the national religion of India: Hinduism.

Hinduism

Hinduism was not founded on the teachings of a single person. Instead, it developed over a long period of time from a blend of several different beliefs and practices.

The Hindu believe there are three primary processes in life and in the universe: creation, preservation, and destruction. The three main Hindu gods reflect this belief. They are Brahma, the Creator; Vishnu, the Preserver; and Shiva, the Destroyer. In addition to these great gods, Hindus recognize and worship a multitude of other gods that include good and evil spirits, heavenly bodies such as the sun, and birds and other animals. To a devout Hindu, there is no distinction between humans and animals. Both have souls, or spirits, that pass from one to the other through reincarnation, or rebirth.

Reincarnation is a purification process in which the soul lives in many bodies over many lifetimes. To move to a higher, purer state, a person must follow a set of rules governing moral conduct. The ultimate hope of the Hindu is to escape the cycle of reincarnation. When that happens, the soul becomes one with Brahma, the great soul or Force of the World.

The Birth of Buddhism

By 500 B.C. northern India was little more than an on-again, off-again battlefield for a number of feuding kingdoms. During this troubled period, another important religion— Buddhism—emerged. The founder of this new religion was a prince, Siddhartha Gautama, whose holiness and love for all creatures earned him widespread fame throughout India. In time he came to be called the Buddha, which means "the Enlightened One."

The Beliefs of Buddhism

Buddha did not claim to be of divine origin, nor did he claim to receive inspiration from gods. He practiced **meditation,** *the act of focusing thoughts on a single object or idea,* but did not pray to a higher being. After his death in 483 B.C., temples were built in his honor, and his beliefs eventually spread throughout Asia.

Fundamental to Buddhist beliefs is reincarnation. Like Hinduism, Buddhism holds that, after death, a soul returns to life in another form. The two religions differ on the rules one must follow to complete the cycle of reincarnation successfully. Buddhists believe that when completion is achieved, the spirit experiences nirvana, a blissful state free of all desires.

Buddhist Architecture

The importance attached to meditation moved many of Buddha's followers to withdraw from society and live in monasteries, called *vihāras.* At first these monasteries were simple wooden structures or natural caves. Around the third century B.C., more elaborate chambers and meeting halls were carved out of the rock in hillsides and cliffs.

Lomas Rishi Cave
■ **FIGURE 10.5**

One of these chambers was the Lomas Rishi Cave (Figure 10.5) in northeastern India. The exterior of this cave is carved to look like the wooden constructions of that time. This practice continued in monasteries for a thousand years.

More About... | **Buddha.** As students are introduced to the philosophy and teachings of Buddha in the text, explain to them that legends and tales about the way Buddha lived have been passed down through the ages. Tell students it is said Buddha possessed a sense of humor to go along with his many other virtues. Recount the following story to illustrate this: When verbally abused by a foolish man, he listened quietly until the man was finished. Then Buddha asked: "If a man chooses not to accept a gift offered to him, to whom does it belong?" The man answered immediately, "To the giver, of course." Buddha then said to the man, "I decline to accept your abuse and request that you keep it for yourself."

The Stupa

By the end of the second century B.C., another important architectural form appeared: the **stupa,** *a small round burial shrine erected over a grave site to hold relics of the Buddha.* Shrines such as these offered opportunities for the faithful to engage in private meditation, an important element in the Buddhist religion.

The most impressive of these stupas was erected, enlarged, and finally completed in the first century A.D. at Sanchi (Figure 10.6). Buddhists showed their devotion by walking clockwise along a railed path at the base of the dome. This walkway symbolized the path of life that circled the world. As they strolled slowly, contemplating the holy relic within the shrine, believers were transported from the real world and its distractions to the comfort of the spiritual world. In this way they approached the enlightened state sought as a means of moving ever closer to nirvana.

Symbolism in Buddhist Art

The complex carvings and sculptures that adorned the shrine were intended to remind worshipers of Buddha's teaching and aid them in meditation. The figure of Buddha never appears in the shrine, however. His presence is implied by such symbols as an empty throne, a tree under which he sat when meditating, and his footprints. The use of symbols to represent the Buddha reflects a belief in a teacher who had attained nirvana. There was, for the Buddhist, nothing to which such a person could be compared. Still, the religion required images to aid in teaching and to inspire meditation. Symbols were used to fulfill these religious functions.

■ **FIGURE 10.5** This kind of monastery—a cave with a carved exterior—was constructed by Buddhists in India for a thousand years. **From this cave entrance, what can you learn about the wooden structures built in India?**

Entrance, Lomas Rishi Cave. Maurya period. Barabar Hills, India. Third century B.C.

■ **FIGURE 10.6** This impressive stupa was completed in the first century A.D. **How did Buddhists conduct their devotions at shrines like this?**

Great Stupa. Sanchi, Madhya Pradesh, India. c. 150–50 B.C.

Chapter 10 *The Art of India, China, and Japan*   **217**

CHAPTER 10
LESSON ONE

Art Criticism

Point out that we all tend to define the world in terms of our own attitudes and experiences. For example, when people of Western cultures think of art, they may instinctively think of Western art. Have students choose one of the three aesthetic views and apply that view to one of the works illustrated in this lesson. Ask: How will you judge the success of this work of art from an ancient or distant culture using the aesthetic view you have chosen?

Studio Skills

Explain that Buddhist traditions are important to our understanding of Eastern art. Introduce students to the effect quiet contemplation can have on their artistic creativity. Begin by lowering the lights in the classroom. Then ask students to focus on an image, mood, object, or idea of their own choosing. After allowing ample time for reflection, restore the lights. Provide students with drawing paper and colored pencils, and have them create a drawing based on their reflections. Encourage students to be spontaneous—to strive for expressive rather than literal drawings.

Art History

Have students study the monastery entrance to Lomas Rishi Cave in Figure 10.5. Display one or more photographs that focus on Romanesque arches from early medieval churches (a subject students will learn about in Chapter 14). Ask students to compare the two architectural features. Ask: What do the similarities between the two suggest about the possible heritage of at least some features of Western art?

More About...   **Kailasa Temple.** As impressive in its own right as Lomas Rishi cave is the Kailasa temple at Ellora, a village located some 270 miles northeast of the Indian metropolis of Bombay. This monolithic temple, which stands on a lava rock plateau, was hewn (carved) from a single hillside, from the top down. Construction of the temple probably dates to the reign of Rashtrakutan King Krishna I, who ruled from about A.D. 756 to A.D. 773. The identities of the architects of this amazing structure are unknown, since, before the advent of European contact and influence, the artworks of India were created in the service of religion and names of individual artists and artisans were not revealed.

Art History

Have students consider the photograph of the Great Stupa in Figure 10.6. Then have students write a paragraph explaining what religious concept the circular shape of the dome calls to mind.

Art Criticism

Call students' attention once more to the Great Stupa, noting in particular the basketweave motif on the structure atop the dome, on the wall encircling the dome, and on the ground wall surrounding the building. Ask: What other example of Indian art in this lesson employs this motif?

Aesthetics

Point out the many designs and patterns the artist made use of in the relief sculpture in Figure 10.8. Point out these details provide us with a glimpse of the fashions of the day. Would students describe this relief as realistic or symbolic? Can a work of art be both? Have students explain their responses.

■ **FIGURE 10.7** This central aisle in the Chaitya Hall leads directly to the stupa. How is the principle of harmony shown here?

Interior of the Chaitya Hall. Karli Cave, India. c. 2nd century A.D. The Ancient Art and Architecture Collection.

Chaitya Hall at Karli
■ **FIGURE 10.7**

The stupa at Sanchi is recognized as the greatest of the early Buddhist shrines, whereas the cave at Karli is thought to be the finest of cave temples. By the second and first centuries B.C., cave structures had progressed far beyond the earlier efforts at the Lomas Rishi Cave. At Karli an elaborate exterior was carefully carved to look exactly like a wooden building. Inside, a hall nearly 45 feet high and 125 feet long was carved out of a stone cliff (Figure 10.7). This hall is divided into three aisles by rows of closely spaced columns crowned with male and female riders astride elephants. These columns lead up to and around a stupa, forming the pathway Buddhists follow when meditating.

A large window above the main entrance allows light to filter in, dramatically illuminating the interior of the stupa. Walking along the main central aisle toward the sunlit stupa, worshipers experience the sensation that they are moving away from the harsh realities of the world and, with each step, closer and closer to spiritual enlightenment.

Buddhist Sculpture

Early Buddhist relief sculptures depicted various events in the life of the Buddha. An example from a stupa erected in the second century B.C. (Figure 10.8) shows the Buddha being visited by a king. As in all early Buddhist art, the Buddha is represented only by a symbol—here by a wheel placed on an otherwise empty throne. To the faithful, the wheel had several meanings. One of these meanings is that the wheel symbolizes the circle of life, maturity, and death associated with each reincarnation, all leading to nirvana.

COOPERATIVE LEARNING

Art tour. Ask for groups of volunteers to research locations in present-day India that could be visited to view ancient artworks mentioned in this chapter. Have these students choose several artworks that exist today and determine their location and whether they are accessible. Ask the groups to plan a tour of India that would incorporate as many artworks as possible. Students may consult maps, tour books, or travel agencies to plan their itineraries. Have them indicate the sequence of cities to be visited, the most appropriate means of travel between these locations, and any special arrangements that might be necessary to view the artworks they wish to visit.

FIGURE 10.8 This relief has been carved to show very specific details, so that the viewer can see, understand, and share in the homage being shown to the Buddha. **How is space suggested in this relief?**

King Prasenajit Visits the Buddha. Detail of a relief from the Bharhut Stupa. Early second century B.C. Hard, reddish sandstone. 48 × 52.7 × 9 cm (19 × 20³⁄₄ × 3¹⁄₂"). Courtesy of Freer Gallery of Art, Smithsonian Institution, Washington, D.C.

Art History

Have groups of students review the photographs of art and architecture in this lesson. Ask group members to list ways in which the architecture compares, in form and function, with modern houses of worship. Then have group members discuss their responses to this question: What aspects of religious architecture have remained constant throughout the centuries?

By the end of the first century A.D., a number of reforms had taken place in the Buddhist religion. As a consequence of those reforms, artists began to represent the Buddha in human form.

Sculpture in the Gupta Era

Buddhist sculpture reached its peak during the Gupta era, which lasted from A.D. 320 to 600. Sculptures and relief carvings produced during this time combine an appearance of great power with a feeling of inner peace. The standing Buddha image and the Buddha seated cross-legged in meditation were perfected at this time (Figure 10.9). These became the models that sculptors used to portray the Buddha throughout Asia.

The Revival of Hinduism

Although Buddhism was for many centuries the leading religion in India, Hinduism was never completely forgotten. Beginning around the fifth century A.D., Hinduism experienced a revival that ended with its return to prominence in the two centuries that followed. This revival may have been due to the fact that Hinduism offered more varied avenues to spiritual perfection. These included the simple performance of one's daily duties.

FIGURE 10.9 This Buddha is seated upon a lotus flower throne—a representation of nirvana, or enlightenment. **How does the figure's facial expression reveal his emotional state?**

Statuette of Buddha from Northern India. Brought to Sweden in the 5th century A.D. Statens Historiska Museet, Stockholm, Sweden.

Cross Curriculum

MUSIC. Remind students of the commonly held philosophical view that great art, music, and literature share a universal language, that all art reaches out to communicate an idea or feeling. Test this hypothesis by playing a recording of Indian folk music. Ask students to listen uncritically to the music for several minutes, ideally with their eyes closed. Then lead a discussion of the message or mood the music communicates.

Art History

Direct students' attention to the photograph of the *Shiva Nataraja* (Figure 10.11, page 221). Point out that this almost iconic image from Eastern art is widely reproduced—that its likeness appears not only in art books but in advertisements and travel posters. Ask if students can identify images from Western art that have been similarly popularized. Ask: Does this treatment of an artwork or art object somehow diminish its legitimacy? Does it perhaps make the casual viewer more aware of art? Conclude with a discussion of the reciprocal importance of art and culture, the way art helps us understand a culture, and the way a knowledge of culture helps us interpret and appreciate its art.

MEETING INDIVIDUAL NEEDS

Logical/Math Learners. Have students create a Venn diagram to compare and contrast the religions of India—Hinduism and Buddhism. If they are unfamiliar with making their own Venn diagrams, instruct students to draw two overlapping circles that share an area in common. Have students list characteristics and beliefs unique to each religion in the area of the circle not shared, and note elements common to both religions in the area shared by the two circles. This activity helps students organize their understanding of the belief systems and helps them compare the two religions.

Study Guide

Distribute *Study Guide* 21 in the TCR. Assist students in reviewing key concepts. 📁

Art and Humanities

Have students complete *Art and Humanities* 15, "Ravi Shankar—Connecting with the Past," in the TCR. In this activity, students explore an interesting musical form indigenous to India by listening to works of this noted sitarist. 📁

Studio Activities

Assign *Enrichment* 18, "Chikankari Embroidery from India," in the TCR. Students learn about this fine needlework and then create a pattern using unique Chikankari embroidery designs. 📁

ASSESS

Checking Comprehension

Have students respond to the lesson review questions. Answers are given in the box below.

Reteaching

Assign *Reteaching* 21, found in the TCR. Have students complete the activity and review their responses. 📁

■ **FIGURE 10.10** This Hindu temple is similar to ancient Greek temples: Neither was intended to accommodate large numbers of worshipers and was meant to be viewed from the outside. Why is this kind of temple sometimes considered an example of sculpture rather than architecture?

Vishnu Temple. Deogarh, India. Early sixth century A.D.

Hindu Architecture

Nothing remains of monumental Hindu architecture before the fourth century A.D. At that time some Hindu architects began to follow the example of Buddhist builders, carving their temples in caves. Meanwhile, others began erecting temples of stone. One of the earliest of these is a sixth-century temple in north central India constructed during the Gupta era (Figure 10.10). Many of the features found in this building were used in subsequent structures.

Vishnu Temple in Deogarh
■ **FIGURE 10.10**

Like all Hindu temples, this building was never intended to accommodate large numbers of worshipers. Its primary purpose was to serve as a residence for the god Vishnu.

Inside the temple, a sanctuary lined with thick, solid walls and a heavy ceiling housed and protected a statue or relic. Like earlier Greek temples, the Hindu temple was meant to be seen from the outside and appreciated in the same way one would appreciate a fine sculpture. In this early example, however, the "sculpture" is relatively simple. The overall form is little more than a cube once crowned with a tower. Some exterior walls contain relief panels, but these only hint at the ornate carving that characterized later Hindu temples.

Hindu Sculpture

In addition to carving stone sculptures and reliefs to decorate their temples, Hindu sculptors produced bronze works of high quality. A bronze figure of Shiva from the kingdom of Chola demonstrates these artists' skill and sensitivity (Figure 10.11).

Shiva Nataraja
■ **FIGURE 10.11**

Shiva is one of the most important of the Hindu gods. He is shown in various forms in Hindu sculpture; among the most fascinating is his portrayal as the Lord of the Dance. In Figure 10.11 he is seen performing a dance that symbolizes the destruction of the universe, which is then reborn.

The Spread of Indian Art

The great achievements of Indian art were not confined to India alone. Its ties to Indian religious beliefs, especially Buddhism, assured the spread of Indian art as these religious beliefs swept across Asia. Buddhism experienced a decline in India with the introduction of Islam beginning in the tenth century. This new religion, however, brought a rich artistic tradition of its own. Eventually unique Indian forms of Islamic Art were created. (See Figure 10.1, page 212.)

Symbolism in Indian *Art*

Let students examine the feature on page 221 and share their impressions. The god Shiva (Figure 10.11), one of the most important of the Hindu deities, has many aspects and forms—all meant to be perceived in a single sculpture. He is at once graceful and terrible; he is the destroyer of the world in the never-ending cycle of destruction and rebirth.

Shiva is the god of death; he is also the god of dance and love. The dancing Shiva here expresses the rhythmic cycle of destruction and renewal. Every portion of the sculpture is rich with symbolism. Guide students in reading and discussing the explanations of the symbolism in the work.

Symbolism in Indian *Art*

*T*his work echoes the Hindu belief that the human spirit is born again after death, taking on a new form that reflects the state of perfection achieved in previous lives.

 The multiple arms serve a dual purpose. They not only emphasize the god's graceful movements but also permit him to hold several symbolic objects.

2

In this hand he grasps a drum symbolizing creation.

 In this hand he holds the flame of destruction.

4

He raises this hand to protect the faithful.

5

This hand points gracefully to his upraised left foot, which symbolizes escape from ignorance represented by the small figure he crushes beneath his right foot.

■ **FIGURE 10.11**

Shiva Nataraja, the Dancing Lord. Late Chola period. Thirteenth century A.D. Bronze. 87 × 70 × 33 cm (34¹/₄ × 27¹/₂ × 13″). The Nelson-Atkins Museum of Art, Kansas City, Missouri. Purchase: Nelson Trust.

Enrichment

Invite volunteers to learn more about the gods of Hinduism and their representation in sculpture and other art forms. Volunteers should present their findings jointly. If possible, the group should include slides or photographs in their presentation.

Extension

Explain that during the 1960s an entire generation of Westerners was introduced to the richness of Eastern culture and religion through the music of the legendary British rock group known as the Beatles. Ask several volunteers to research this phenomenon. Volunteers should explain how the Beatles' interest in Eastern music developed and what expression it found in their own work. If possible, volunteers should play recordings of the Beatles' earlier grass-roots songs and their later, more easternized music.

CLOSE

Ask students to respond to this statement: "The study of Indian art must ultimately be the study of Indian religion."

LESSON ONE REVIEW

Reviewing Art Facts

1. Name three technologies or building and craft materials used by the Harappans of the Indus Valley.
2. How was the Lomas Rishi Cave used? How was its exterior decorated?
3. What is a Buddhist stupa?
4. What is the primary purpose of Hindu temples?

Activity... *Comparing Language Symbols*

The ancient Harappan civilization developed in the Indus River Valley of India at about the same time that the Egyptian civilization developed along the Nile. Both cultures were able to develop advanced and complex civilizations that included cities, trading systems, religions honoring several gods, and languages. The Harappans developed a language based on picture symbols. The Egyptians developed hieroglyphics, a language based on both sounds and pictures.

Find examples of both the Harappan and the Egyptian language and compare them. How were these languages alike? How were they different? Do you think these two ancient cultures could have had any contact with each other? Share your findings with the class.

LESSON ONE REVIEW

Answers to Reviewing Art Facts

1. Bronze and copper; multistoried brick buildings; drainage systems; written language.
2. A monastery. The exterior was carved to look like the wooden structures of that time.
3. A small, round burial shrine erected over a gravesite to hold relics of the Buddha.
4. To serve as a residence for a god.

Activity... *Comparing Language Symbols*

Let students work independently to find examples of writing from the Harappan and ancient Egyptian civilizations. Schedule class time for students to compare and discuss their examples. Encourage volunteers to learn more about the two forms of writing and to share their research findings with the rest of the class.

The Art of China

The Art of China

Focus

Lesson Objectives

After studying this lesson, students will be able to:

■ Identify the types of art associated with various Chinese dynasties.

■ Identify the influence of religion on Chinese art.

■ Analyze the impact of meditation on Chinese art.

Building Vocabulary

Have students work in cooperative groups to discuss the Vocabulary terms. Let group members begin by sharing any knowledge or understanding of these words they already have. Then have group members work together to find definitions of the terms both in a dictionary and in the text glossary.

Motivator

Write the lesson title, "The Art of China," on the board, and have students jot down five words or phrases the phrase brings to mind. After they have finished studying the lesson, ask students to reread and discuss their notes. How have their ideas about Chinese art changed?

Introducing the Lesson

Have students examine the artworks in the lesson and vote on the one they find the most Chinese in appearance. After asking students to explain their choices, assign the reading of the lesson.

Vocabulary
■ Bodhisattva
■ scroll
■ porcelain
■ vanishing point

Artists to Meet
■ Han Kan
■ Kuo Hsi
■ Ch'ien Hsüan
■ Chao Meng-fu

Discover
After completing this lesson, you will be able to:
■ Identify major Chinese dynasties and discuss the important artworks produced during each.
■ Analyze the impact of meditation on Chinese art.

■ **FIGURE 10.12** This work was created from bronze and decorated with black pigment more than 3,000 years ago. What sculptural techniques were used to produce this vessel?

Ritual Lobed Tripod Cauldron. Chinese, Shang dynasty. Eleventh century B.C. Bronze inlaid with black pigment. 21.3 × 18 cm (8³/₈ × 7¹/₁₆"). The Metropolitan Museum of Art, New York, New York. Gift of Ernest Erickson Foundation, Inc. 1985. (1985.214.3)

222

$\mathcal{T}$he history of India is marked by the rise and fall of dynasties and kingdoms. Recorded in the long history of China is a similar succession of dynasties, each with its own unique problems and its own special contributions to art.

The Beginnings of Chinese Civilization

Chinese civilization, which began some 2,000 years before the birth of Christ, is the oldest continuous culture in the world. As this civilization grew, its people gained skill and knowledge in many different fields. Among Chinese accomplishments are the inventions of the compass, paper, porcelain, and printing with carved wood blocks.

Early Bronze Vessels

Skill in bronze casting was developed at an early date in Chinese history. Bronze vessels found in ancient graves reveal that Chinese artisans were exercising this skill by the First Dynasty. This period, known as the Shang dynasty, began in 1766 B.C. Many of the early bronze vessels show extraordinary technical mastery that probably took centuries to develop (Figure 10.12).

The art of painting is mentioned in Chinese literature several centuries before the birth of Christ and even names a woman named Lei (lah-**ee**) as the first Chinese painter. Unfortunately, no paintings have survived from these early periods of Chinese history. Written reports, however, tell us that paintings of great skill and beauty were created and appreciated.

The Chow dynasty, which followed the Shang dynasty in 1030 B.C., apparently produced few artistic changes. This dynasty eventually disintegrated into warring states and continued to be fragmented until the powerful Han dynasty was founded in 206 B.C.

The Arrival of Buddhism During the Han Dynasty

Near the end of the Han dynasty, the religion of Buddhism, which originated in India, came to China. This religion had a great impact on the way artists approached their work. It also helped raise artists to a position of respect and admiration in Chinese society. The Chinese people were the first to consider the painting of pictures an important and honorable task; they placed artists on the same level as poets, who were very highly regarded.

LESSON TWO RESOURCES

Teacher's Classroom Resources

📁 Appreciating Cultural Diversity 13

📁 Cooperative Learning 16

📁 Enrichment Activity 19

📁 Reproducible Lesson Plan 22

📁 Reteaching Activity 22

📁 Study Guide 22

Buddhism offered comfort to the weary and hope for an eternity of peace in the next world. It recognized the existence of people who had attained a state of enlightenment.

Standing Buddha Statue
■ FIGURE 10.13

Buddhism also recognized those who had either postponed death or made the decision to return to the world for the purpose of bringing comfort and offering guidance to the living. Such a person was known as a **Bodhisattva** (boh-dee-**saht**-vah), or *Buddha-to-be.* Figure 10.13 shows a type of Bodhisattva, one of the largest of its kind to survive to the present day. With a serene smile, he extends his open hands in a sign of welcome and a promise of peace that must have been reassuring and calming to those who saw him.

Unlike ancient Greek sculptors, Chinese sculptors did not regard the body as a thing of beauty. This attitude, combined with the fact that they did not regard sculpture as one of the important arts, caused them to limit their sculpture production to religious portraits such as that of the Bodhisattva.

The Importance of Meditation

Buddhism, like other Eastern religions, places great emphasis on meditation. This emphasis had an important impact on Chinese art.

Meditation is the process of focusing one's thoughts on a single object or idea. It allows one to experience completely the inherent beauty or meaning of that object or idea. Buddhist monks may remain motionless in meditation for hours, or even entire days. They may contemplate a leaf sagging from the weight of raindrops, or the possible meanings of a single word.

Influenced by these monks, Chinese artists found meditation enabled them to recognize the beauty of a leaf, a tree, a rock, or a mountain. They were then better prepared to capture that beauty in their painting.

Increased Concern for Landscape Painting

For more than a thousand years, beginning with the Han dynasty in 206 B.C., the human figure dominated in Chinese painting, just as it did in the West. By the ninth century, though, Chinese artists were beginning to exhibit a greater appreciation for nature. By the eleventh century, this trend was complete. While Western artists continued to focus their attention on people, artists in China preferred to concentrate on nature and landscape painting.

■ **FIGURE 10.13** This unusually tall figure was decorated with a thin covering of gold. **What aesthetic qualities are most appropriate when making a judgment about this work?**

Standing Buddha. Northern Wei Dynasty. A.D. 477. Gilt bronze. 140.3 × 48.9 cm (55¼ × 19½"). The Metropolitan Museum of Art, New York, New York. John Stewart Kennedy Fund, 1926. (26.123)

Chapter 10 *The Art of India, China, and Japan* **223**

TEACH
Critical Thinking

Explain that the ancient Mayas, whom the students will study in the next chapter, had a thriving culture in lands that later became Mexico and Central America. Add that, as a result of a series of regional conflicts and conquests, the civilization disintegrated, leaving behind a wealth of art and architecture for archaeologists and historians to explore. Finally note that ancient China suffered similar conflicts and disruptions, yet managed to survive them. Ask: What conclusions can we draw from this? How does it enhance our appreciation of Chinese art?

Art History

Briefly explain—or let a student volunteer explain—the role of patron saints in Christianity. Then have the class consider ways in which Bodhisattvas might be compared to such saints (for example, did they have special powers to protect humans against various threats or improve their worldly success). Ask: In what way might the Bodhisattva be considered a kind of bridge between the human and the spiritual?

Did You Know?

Few Asian paintings existed for a significant period of time due to the fragile nature of the material on which they were painted. The paintings of the Far East were never done on canvas. Occasionally they were wall frescoes, and in more recent periods they were painted on paper. For the most part, however, they were painted on silk, which is not a durable material.

Teacher Notes _____

Art History

Explain that the invention of paper by the Chinese is an example of the way advancements in a society's technology can affect its art (this invention gave rise to a whole new medium for Chinese artists in the form of parchment scrolls). Ask students to brainstorm and discuss examples in contemporary art where technology has provided new avenues for artists (for example, photography, computer graphics, and videotape/disc technology).

Cross Curriculum

LANGUAGE ARTS. Have students learn about the artistic tastes and temperament of the Mongol leader Kublai Khan by inviting a volunteer to offer a dramatic interpretation of Samuel Taylor Coleridge's poem "Kubla Khan," while the rest of the class reads along. Set aside time for discussion of the grandeur Coleridge describes in his slightly mythologized poem. Ask: Which of the works in the lesson would the Mongol leader most likely have held in the greatest esteem? Why?

Did You Know?

It was during the Han dynasty that the modern period of Chinese civilization is thought to have begun. Although the dynasty survived only 14 years, the Chinese still refer to themselves as the Han people.

Artists, like poets, sought out places in which they could meditate and be inspired to create. They valued every opportunity to do this, taking long, leisurely walks across the countryside.

To gain the knowledge and skills needed to continue in the tradition of painting landscapes, Chinese artists spent years copying the paintings of earlier artists. Although it was common to base a painting on the work of an earlier artist, the painter was expected to add some original touches as well.

Scroll Painting

Other than a few murals on the walls of burial chambers, the earliest Chinese paintings that have survived to the present are of two kinds: hanging scrolls and horizontal scrolls, or handscrolls.

A **scroll** is *a long roll of illustrated parchment or silk.* Scrolls were designed to be rolled up and carefully stored away. When their owners were in the mood for quiet reflection, the scrolls were taken from the shelf, just as we might take down a book to read. Unrolling the scrolls section by section, the viewer gazed at no more than 24 inches or so at a time. In this way it was possible to journey slowly from scene to scene through the entire painting.

The End of the Han Dynasty

The culture of the Han dynasty rivaled that of the Roman Empire, which was flourishing at this same time in history. The Han dynasty extended over a 400-year period, the second longest in Chinese history.

A series of weak emperors brought the Han Empire to an end. There followed a period, beginning at the close of the third century A.D., in which China was divided into a number of smaller states. None of these states became strong enough to conquer the others and restore a unified empire. After a period of chaos, a new dynasty, the Tang dynasty, assumed control in A.D. 618 and ruled for nearly 300 years.

The Powerful Tang Dynasty

During the Tang dynasty, China reached a peak of power and influence. The people enjoyed prosperity, military campaigns extended the boundaries of the empire, foreign trade increased, and Buddhism grew in strength.

■ **FIGURE 10.14** Many clay sculptures like this were found in ancient Chinese tombs. Why do you think these sculptures were placed in tombs?

Saddle Horse. c. A.D. 700–755. Tang dynasty. A.D. 618–907. Earthenware with three-color lead glaze. 76.2 cm (30"). The Nelson-Atkins Museum of Art, Kansas City, Missouri. Acquired through the Joyce C. Hall Estate and various Hall Family Funds.

More About...   **Chinese Gardens.** While painters re-created the natural world in their silken and paper scrolls, gardeners were similarly shaping their plots of ground to reflect the greater cosmos. By using stones and water as symbols and assembling trees, shrubs, and flowers, a skilled gardener could reproduce the variety of relationships that characterized the body and universe according to Chinese tradition. During the early Chou dynasty, kings and lords went so far as to "populate" their gardens with animals as a symbol of status. By 3000 B.C., however, the well-tended garden came to represent spiritual peace rather than economic or social power. To this day, China's gardens remain as examples of this unity and peacefulness.

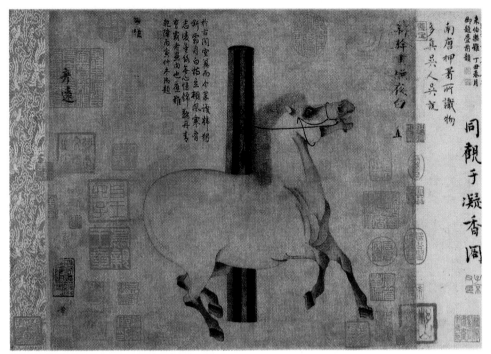

■ **FIGURE 10.15** Notice the delicate lines and the subtle value gradations in this handscroll. **Does this work make good use of the literal qualities? What details help give this work a sense of movement?**

Han Kan (attributed to). *Night-Shining White.* c. 742–56. Tang dynasty. Handscroll, Ink on paper. 30.8 × 34 cm (12¹/₈ × 13³/₈"). The Metropolitan Museum of Art, New York, New York. Purchase, the Dillon Fund Gift, 1977. (1977.78)

Sculpture During the Tang Dynasty

Most of the sculptures produced during the Tang period were religious. Believers in Buddhism, looking forward to a peaceful life in the next world, commissioned thousands of sculptures of Buddha.

Saddle Horse
■ **FIGURE 10.14**

Tomb sculptures, chiefly in clay, were also created to honor the dead. Many of these tomb sculptures were of animals. An excellent example is the earthenware and polychrome-glazed horse illustrated in Figure 10.14.

Tang Handscroll
■ **FIGURE 10.15**

Horses were highly prized by the Chinese. The emperor Ming Huang was said to own more than 40,000. The handscroll illustrated in Figure 10.15 shows one of his favorite horses rearing against the tether that binds it to a post.

Use of Line

One of the chief measures of excellence in Chinese painting throughout its long history is the quality of the brush line, which is evident in Figure 10.15. A delicate use of line is combined with subtle value gradations to give the animal a realistic appearance. The work demonstrates convincingly that the artist, Han Kan (**hahn kahn**), knew his subject well and could apply this knowledge effectively to his art.

The many inscriptions and seals on Han Kan's painting were placed by collectors who wished to express their approval of the work. These inscriptions and seals, which are found on many Chinese paintings, add their own ornamentation and meaning.

Chapter 10 *The Art of India, China, and Japan* **225**

CHAPTER 10
LESSON TWO

Aesthetics
Direct students' attention to the horse in Figure 10.15, and in particular to the following details: (1) the emotion on the horse's face; (2) the way the artist successfully conveyed the animal's movement, strength, and fury in its attempt to escape the tether. Ask: What feature of the horse's face is your eye first drawn to? What other features has the artist used to make us sense the animal's restlessness?

Art History
Have students examine both the scrolls in Figure 10.15 and Figure 10.19 (page 229), paying particular attention to the brush-strokes in the two works. Ask what words students would use to describe the use of the brush in the two paintings? Ask what this observation suggests about the Chinese regard for perfection in art.

Critical Thinking
Have students note the reference to the personal seals and inscriptions collectors of T'ang handscrolls affixed to the works of Han Kan. Ask: In what ways might such seals have been reminiscent of the personal monograms or logos people often use today to identify property as their own? Ask: Considering the Chinese approach to art, how do you suppose the seals differ from present-day monograms?

More About... **Music and Dance.** The T'ang dynasty was noted for its interest in music and dancing. The royal palace at Ch'ang-an set aside a special lesson to develop a training center for young students to practice the arts. Known simply as the *chaio-fang* (training center), students from areas of Indochina, Korea, India, as well as China, attended this center. Instruction in dancing and traditional musical instruments such as bamboo mouth organs and lutes resulted in performances at the royal court by the most talented students. Graceful glazed clay figures of such musicians and dancers remain as evidence of this interest in the arts from the ancient dynasty.

Studio Skills

As a follow-up to the Critical Thinking discussion on the previous page, ask students to design their own personal seals, based on their initials. Suggest that students work with colored pencils or use computer programs with a font collection. Display students' seals, and allow time for comparisons and discussion.

Cross Curriculum

HISTORY. Suggest that interested students research the following events, which were occurring at the same time artisans of the Sung dynasty were crafting bowls like the one shown in Figure 10.16: the First Crusade, launched by Pope Urban II; the conquest of Jerusalem by the Crusaders.

Art Criticism

Emphasize that the human side of Buddha was depicted in statues of the *lohans,* or disciples, of Buddha, who were devoted to introspection and meditation. Have students study the face of the *Seated Lohan* (Figure 10.17), that of the *Bodhisattva* (Figure 10.18, page 227), and that of *Standing Buddha* (Figure 10.13, page 223).

Ask students to compare and contrast the expressions of the three figures and describe how visual differences reflect their roles. How would students compare the lohan's face to that of the others? Is it more humanistic or more vulnerable? Does it show the wisdom of age? How would students describe the unique smile on the Buddhas and Bodhisattvas of Eastern art? How does the smile make students feel? Does it help the viewer to understand the religious function of this art?

■ **FIGURE 10.16** This bowl was created as a useful vessel. It is now part of a museum art collection. **Is the bowl now an artwork? If so, when and how did it become art?**

Bowl with mold stamped lotus design.Ting ware. Sung dynasty. A.D. 1127–1179. Porcelain with pale blue glaze. 6.1 cm (2¹⁄₄″) high; 18.1 cm (7″) diam. Asian Art Museum of San Francisco, San Francisco, California. The Avery Brundage Collection. B80S3, B62P177.

■ **FIGURE 10.17** This seated figure is shown in a pose similar to that in many Buddha sculptures. **What mood does this work convey to you?**

Seated Lohan. Late Tang Dynasty. Ninth century A.D. Earthenware with three-color glaze. 104.7 cm (41¹⁄₄″). The Metropolitan Museum of Art, New York, New York. Frederick C. Hewitt Fund, 1921. (21.76).

The Stable Sung Dynasty

Following the collapse of the Tang dynasty in 906, China experienced a period of confusion. Finally, reunification was realized in 960 under the Sung dynasty. The rule of this dynasty proved to be a period of great stability that produced a series of artists whose works were admired the world over for centuries.

The Production of Porcelain

During the Sung period, the production of porcelain ware was carried to new heights. **Porcelain,** *a fine-grained, high-quality form of china,* is made primarily from a white clay known as kaolin. This clay is relatively rare and can be found in only a few locations in China, Europe, England, and North America.

After a vessel is made from this clay, which has been mixed with other types of clay to give it a more workable quality, it is fired in a kiln to a high temperature. The work is then coated with a glaze containing feldspar, a crystalline mineral, and fired again. The result is a vessel with a hard, translucent surface of great beauty.

CULTURAL DIVERSITY

Religions. Emphasize the fact that during turbulent periods of China's history, Buddhism offered hope for peace in the next world. By contrast, this religion also flourished during times of prosperity, such as the T'ang dynasty. Ask students to discuss concepts of life after death as they appear in the art of various cultures—Egyptian, Early Christian, Chinese, and Indian. Ask: What can we conclude about human nature from the fact that virtually all religions throughout history have embraced some interpretation of an afterlife? How does this universal concept make art of other periods and cultures accessible to our understanding and appreciation, despite their distance in time or place?

An excellent example of Sung porcelain ware is illustrated in Figure 10.16. Bowls like this were the first of the classic pieces that were widely imitated but seldom equaled by later artists. The bowl's delicate shape and beautiful, translucent surface are enhanced with a subtle floral pattern.

Sculpture During the Sung Dynasty

Sung sculpture remained strongly tied to Buddhism, although the figures were more informal and natural than those created earlier. A painted and glazed ceramic sculpture of a follower of Buddha (Figure 10.17) is an example of this more relaxed and natural style which began to appear in the Tang dynasty.

The Water and Moon Guanyin Bodhisattva

■ **FIGURE 10.18**

This same relaxed attitude is noted in a carved wood Bodhisattva figure traditionally associated with mercy and compassion (Figure 10.18). Prayers to this Buddha-to-be were answered in the form of protection against any possible misfortune. The figure is seen resting comfortably on a weathered, moss-covered ledge, which contrasts with the splendid garments and jewels. Calm and gentle, the softly smiling figure represents no threat to the devout who approach. The gaze is direct and unwavering, encouraging viewers to feel that the Bodhisattva is concerned exclusively with them.

■ **FIGURE 10.18** This wooden figure may remind you of the ceramic figure in Figure 10.17. What do the two works have in common? What are the most important differences between them?

The Water and Moon Guanyin Bodhisattva. Liao or Northern Sung dynasty. Eleventh to early twelfth century A.D. Wood with paint. 241.3 × 165.1 cm (95 × 65″). The Nelson-Atkins Museum of Art, Kansas City, Missouri. Purchase: Nelson Trust.

Chapter 10 *The Art of India, China, and Japan* **227**

Aesthetics

Have students consider the position of the sculpted figure in Figure 10.18, serenely poised on a rock as if ready and willing to listen, guide, and give solace to all believers. Ask: How does this pose suggest patience and solidity? Call students' attention to the gracefulness of the fingers on his outstretched hand. Ask: How has the artist made the figure appear wise and enlightened, yet human and approachable? How would you characterize the artist's choice of colors?

Art History

Direct students' attention to the Sung landscapes in Figures 10.19 and 10.20 (page 229). Emphasize that the artists' goal appears to have been to induce the viewer to slow down, enjoy, and reflect. Ask groups of students to browse through this textbook and other resources for examples of art from other periods and cultures that are designed not to relax the viewer but to arouse, challenge, or provoke. Ask: What are the subjects of such works? Can any of them be categorized as landscapes?

Cross Curriculum

SCIENCE. Point out that while the Sung dynasty was in power in China, the following breakthroughs in technology were achieved: the first water-driven mechanical clock was built in Japan; Walcher of Malvern recorded an eclipse of the moon. Ask interested students to learn about the most important advances in technology in China and in other parts of the world during this period. Suggest that these students work together to create a display that summarizes the results of their research.

More About... **Kaolin.** The word *kaolin* comes from a Chinese word meaning high hill. The popularity of this ingredient for high-quality porcelain stems from its pure white color and the fact that it can be ground to the finest powder. This clay, made of decomposed feldspar, is mined either with a shovel, as was probably the case in early production methods, or with more modern water-jet pump systems. It is washed and put through a separation process to remove sand, mica, and other impurities. The clay is formed into cakes or dried for shipment. From this fine, powdery clay, artists from the early Sung dynasty to the modern factories in Europe and America have produced lasting, delicate works that are highly prized.

Studio Skills

Provide students with sheets of white paper and a supply of watercolors. Challenge students to create a landscape painting in the manner of those shown in Figures 10.19 and 10.20. To begin, students should make preliminary sketches, taking care to keep their designs airy and uncluttered in appearance. Have students transfer their best sketch onto their sheet of drawing paper and apply color using quick, light brushstrokes. Encourage students to display their finished landscapes and share tips for achieving the graceful and expressive qualities common to the paintings appearing in this section of the text.

Art Criticism

Direct students' attention to the use of color in Figure 10.20. Ask: How does the use of the element of color in this work compare with its use in Figure 10.19? Which colors are more suggestive of those found in nature? Does the presence—or absence—of realistic color affect the success of either painting?

Did You Know?

The art of calligraphy, or fine handwriting, was practiced for years by art students before they became painters.

Landscape Painting

The Sung dynasty was noted for its great landscape artists. Painters like Kuo Hsi (**koo**-oh **see**) claimed that the value of landscape painting lay in its capacity to make viewers feel as if they were really in the place pictured. In the handscroll *Clearing Autumn Skies over Mountains and Valleys* (Figure 10.19), the artist invites you to journey beneath the trees of an enchanted mountain landscape. As you slowly unroll the scroll, you can walk through the forest of towering pine trees, pause beside the gently flowing stream, and gaze up at the mountains that disappear into the fine mist.

Use of Multiple Vanishing Points

Unlike Western paintings, Chinese art makes use of different vanishing points. In perspective drawing, a **vanishing point** is *the point at which receding parallel lines seem to converge.* Thus, as you unroll a handscroll, you may find that the perspective shifts. This makes you feel that you are indeed traveling through the work—journeying over worn paths, under stately trees, in front of distant mountains, and across quaint bridges.

Every opportunity is provided for you to stop and examine a flower heavy with dew or a butterfly perched on a blossom. There is nothing to distract you from your quiet contemplation. Even shadows are eliminated from the picture because they might interfere with your efforts to experience and enjoy the painting.

The End of the Sung Dynasty

In 1224 Genghis Khan and his powerful Mongol army swept into northwest China, bringing an end to the Sung dynasty. Following a period of strife, the Mongols, under Kublai Khan, a grandson of Genghis Khan, took control of the country and established the Yüan dynasty. During this time, artists such as Ch'ien Hsüan (chee-**en** shoo-**ahn**) painted scenes that repeat a familiar Chinese theme: the quiet contemplation of nature (Figure 10.20).

Time & Place CONNECTIONS

Ancient China
c. 2000 B.C.–A.D. 220

TEAPOT. This artifact is from the Ming dynasty. It is both a functional object as well as a piece of fine art.

TOMB SOLDIERS. Life-size terra cotta figures of the army of emperor Ch'in Shih-Huang-ti (Qin) were buried in the emperor's tomb over 2,000 years ago. Their individual decoration and lifelike expressions present these soldiers as real people.

CONFUCIUS. A teacher, philosopher, and scholar, Confucius was born around 551 B.C. His teachings were centered around the importance of keeping order in society and how to live according to principles of ethics.

Activity **Interviewing.** If you traveled in a time capsule to visit China during the time of Confucius or Emperor Qin, what would you ask the people you meet? Prepare five questions you might ask in an interview.

Time & Place CONNECTIONS

Ancient China

Have students examine and discuss the images in this Time & Place feature. Encourage them to note the individuality of the tomb soldier and ask: What do these figures tell us about daily life during the rule of Ch'in Shih Huang-ti? What do they indicate about Chinese society at that time? If you could interview one of these soldiers, what questions would you ask? Assign the activity, and encourage students to select a specific kind of person they would like to interview—a peasant, a soldier, an emperor, or a philosopher, for example. Have a group of volunteers do appropriate research and present possible responses to those interview questions.

■ **FIGURE 10.19** This handscroll is designed to take the viewer on a quiet, contemplative journey through the pictured landscape. **Study this view of the mountains and valleys, and decide whether a mood is conveyed. If so, how does the work make you feel?**

Kuo Hsi. *Clearing Autumn Skies over Mountains and Valleys.* Date unknown. Lesson of handscroll, ink, and colors on silk. 26 cm (10¹/₄") high. Courtesy of the Freer Gallery of Art, Smithsonian Institution, Washington, D.C.

■ **FIGURE 10.20** Handscrolls like this are intended to be examined slowly, quietly, and in private. **What appears to be more important in this work—the figures or the setting?**

Ch'ien Hsüan. *Wang Hsi-chih Watching Geese.* c. 1295. Handscroll, ink, color, and gold on paper. 23.2 × 92.7 cm (9¹/₈ × 36¹/₂"). The Metropolitan Museum of Art, New York, New York. Gift of the Dillon Fund, 1973. (1973.120.6)

DETAIL:
Notice the intricate details of this scene in the handscroll.

Art History

Briefly introduce the use of perspective, directing students' attention to one of the Renaissance paintings in Chapter 16 that exhibit this technique. Then have students view a Chinese landscape painting (e.g., the one from the Sung dynasty in Figure 10.19). Let students point out the various vanishing points of the Chinese work. Have them discuss the way that multiple perspectives affect their experience of looking at the art. Do students find the Chinese method confusing, or does it make the work interesting? Does it leave less or more to the viewer's imagination? Can one approach to art be considered more spiritual than another? Discuss how multiple-perspective art may reflect a view of life different from that depicted in art of the West.

Art Criticism

Point out the dragon motif on the Ming dynasty vases (Figure 10.22, page 231). Then divide the class into three groups, and have each group consider one of the following characteristics of the design: the mythological nature of the subject matter; the use of a single color to focus the viewer's eye on the elements of line and shape; the fluid movement of the dragon's form. Ask each group to explain how its characteristic makes the design eminently suitable for the roundness of a vase. Ask: How might this design be less successful on a flat surface?

About the *Artwork*

Wang Hsi-chih Watching Geese. Explain to students that Ch'ien Hsüan's painting of *Wang Hsi-chih Watching Geese* and Duccio's work in Figure 15.20 (page 344) were done at about the same time in history. Duccio's painting emphasizes the importance of the figures as characters in a religious drama. Ch'ien Hsüan attaches little importance to the people in his painting. Like other Chinese artists of his time, he subordinates the presence of humans to the grandeur of nature. Students should recognize that Duccio's painting was meant to instruct, to provide a clear and easily understood religious lesson. Ch'ien Hsüan made no attempt to teach; his painting is intended to arouse the same poetic response in the viewer he felt when meditating on the beauty of nature.

As students examine the handscroll in Figure 10.21, encourage them to consider the relationship between this work and the practice of meditation. Then have them read and discuss the *Use of Elements and Principles* explanation.

Study Guide

Distribute *Study Guide* 22 in the TCR. Assist students in reviewing key concepts. 📁

Art and Humanities

Have students complete *Appreciating Cultural Diversity* 13, "Comparing Chinese Record of Inventions to the West," in the TCR. In this worksheet, students note some inventions from Western culture that appeared earlier in China. Students then chart the specific dynasty and the use of the invention in China. 📁

Studio Activities

Assign *Studio* 13, "Making a Scroll Painting," in the TCR. As the name suggests, students are given the opportunity to make a scroll painting in the Chinese style. 📁

Art and Humanities

Review with students the order and artistic achievements of the various Chinese dynasties. Then have students work in groups to complete *Cooperative Learning* 16, "Making a Time Line of the Dynasties of China." In this worksheet, students work in teams to create a time line using information provided. 📁

Chao Meng-fu (1254–1322)

The contemplation of nature is also the theme of a painting by Chao Meng-fu (**chow** meeng-**foo**), a pupil of Ch'ien Hsüan's (Figure 10.21). This artist was greatly admired even though he chose to cooperate with the Mongol ruler Kublai Khan.

Twin Pines, Level Distance
■ **FIGURE 10.21**

Chao Meng-fu's painting of pine trees, rocks, and distant mountains was done only after the artist had meditated on the subject at great length. He practiced his skills at representing trees, rocks, mountains, and clouds in a precise style for years before actually painting the picture. Chao Meng-fu did this in the traditional way—by carefully studying the paintings of earlier masters rather than by studying nature. Only when his skills were perfected did he attempt to create a painting based on his own response to the natural world.

Works like this were not done to tell a dramatic story, teach a profound lesson, or decorate a wall of a house. They were intended to inspire in the viewer the same deep thoughts that passed through the mind of the artist while the work was created. A work like this would be unrolled and savored only when the viewer was in the proper state of mind and was certain not to be disturbed.

The Art of the Ming Dynasty

The Ming dynasty, which followed the collapse of the Yüan dynasty in 1368, signified the end of foreign rule and the beginning of another Chinese dynasty. Thus, it was a time in which artists sought to restore the glories of the past.

In painting, nature scenes of great beauty were done on silk and paper. These works mainly continued the traditions of the past.

In ceramics, a range of different styles and techniques developed during the Ming dynasty. The use of a stunning cobalt blue glaze was one of the major accomplishments in the development of Chinese porcelain. An early

USE OF THE ELEMENTS AND PRINCIPLES

■ **FIGURE 10.21**

Chao Meng-fu. *Twin Pines, Level Distance.* c. 1310. Handscroll, ink on paper. 26.9 × 107.4 cm (10 × 42½"). The Metropolitan Museum of Art, New York, New York. Gift of the Dillon Fund, 1973. (1973.120.5)

What is *not* in this painting is as important as what you *do* see. Most of the painting is simply left blank.

- **Unity.** The landscape has been reduced to its barest essentials.
- **Space.** The twin pines rise in the foreground to give a strong sense of space in the landscape.
- **Line.** A few lines depict the hills in the distance and draw your attention to the expanse of the work.
- **Emphasis.** The artist shows concentration and confidence with the emphasis placed on each brushstroke.

COOPERATIVE LEARNING

Oral Descriptions. Divide the class into cooperative learning groups, and have the members of each group work together to plan an imaginary journey through an idyllic landscape as depicted in the scrolls in this lesson. Group members should plan and write a detailed descriptions of the things they might see during each portion of the journey. Then have each group present an "oral scroll painting" to the rest of the class, describing each portion of the scroll in detail. These detailed descriptions should be presented with expression to replicate in words the effect achieved with pictures in a scroll painting.

example of a matched pair of vases (Figure 10.22) is admired for the intricate design that complements the vases' elegant form.

Decline of the Ming Dynasty

Tribes from Manchuria conquered China in 1644. This brought the Ming dynasty to an end and ushered in the Ching dynasty, which continued until 1912. Like other conquerors before them, Manchu rulers were determined to make the Chinese culture part of their own. However, despite the work done by several well-known and talented artists and the encouragement of Manchu emperors, Chinese painting experienced a decline during this period.

Porcelain production fared somewhat better than painting did. During this last great age of Chinese porcelain, many fine works were produced. Unfortunately, rebellion and subsequent warfare in the middle of the nineteenth century resulted in the destruction of most kilns and the flight of talented craftspeople.

■ **FIGURE 10.22** These vases, nearly 600 years old, are decorated with the cobalt blue glaze that was first used during the Ming dynasty. **How does the design complement the form of these vases?**

Pair of Vases. 1426–35. Ming dynasty (1368–1644). Porcelain with underglaze blue decoration. 55.2 × 29.2 cm (21³/₄ × 11¹/₂"). The Nelson-Atkins Museum of Art, Kansas City, Missouri. Purchase: Nelson Trust.

ASSESS
Checking Comprehension

Have students respond to the lesson review questions. Answers are given in the box below.

Reteaching

➤ Assign *Reteaching* 22, found in the TCR. Have students complete the activity and review their responses. 📁

Enrichment

Assign students *Enrichment* 19, "The Buried Clay Army of China," in the TCR. In this activity, students read about the emperor Ch'in Shi Huang Ti, his accomplishments, and his fantastic legacy of clay sculpture. 📁

Extension

Note that the Han dynasty roughly coincided with the Classical Greek period in Western art. Ask interested students to research and compare the themes and visual aspects of the art of these two cultures. Did religion play a significant role in Classical Greek sculpture, as it did in China? How was the human form depicted? Students should also discuss the concepts of humanism, the intellectuality, and the spirituality as they relate to art in both cultures. Students should share their findings with the class.

CLOSE

Lead a discussion on aspects of Chinese art that appear, remarkably, to have remained constant over the centuries. Explore possible reasons for this continuity. Ask students to compile a resource folder of visual symbols and notes on subject matter, styles, and themes.

LESSON TWO REVIEW

Reviewing Art Facts

1. How did Chinese artists make use of meditation?
2. What was considered the primary interest and major accomplishment of Chinese painting?
3. What is a scroll painting and how is it used?
4. Name the element of art that was considered one of the chief measures of excellence in Chinese painting.
5. What is porcelain?

Activity… *Painting with India Ink*

Chinese artists were masters at using the element of line in subtle ways to express the character of their subjects. Examine the use of line and gradation in the painting in Figure 10.15, page 225. How did the artist vary the lines? What was he trying to do by making these subtle changes in the width of the lines?

Use a soft bristle brush that will make a fine point, india ink, water, and parchment or rice paper. Experiment with making lines that change in value and width by adding water to the ink and varying pressure to the brush. Use a variety of lines to create an animal painting inspired by the Chinese painting tradition.

Chapter 10 *The Art of India, China, and Japan* **231**

LESSON TWO REVIEW

Answers to Reviewing Art Facts

1. It enabled them to recognize and capture nature's beauty in their paintings.
2. Landscape.
3. A scroll is a long roll of illustrated parchment or silk designed to be rolled and stored until it is viewed by slowly unrolling it section by section.
4. The element of line.
5. A fine-grained, high-quality form of china, made from a white clay known as kaolin.

Activity… *Painting with India Ink*

Encourage students to work with partners or in small groups to experiment with soft bristle brushes and india ink. Then suggest they brainstorm ideas for appropriate animal subjects. Finally, have students work independently to plan and execute their paintings.

The Art of Japan

Focus

Lesson Objectives

After studying this lesson, students will be able to:
- Trace the influences on Japanese art.
- Identify specific styles of Japanese art.
- Discuss the impact of Buddhism on Japanese art.

Building Vocabulary

Let volunteers discuss what they already know about pagodas and woodblock printing—and, if appropriate, *Yamato-e* and *Ukiyo-e*. Then have students compare their previous knowledge with the definitions presented in the lesson.

Motivator

If possible, obtain a recording of koto music. The distinctive sound of this silk-stringed Japanese zither will be familiar to many students, who will identify the sound with the Japanese culture. Ask students to describe the unique sound of this instrument and of the music in general. Can the music be considered an aid to appreciating Eastern art?

Introducing the Lesson

Display photographs of contemporary Japanese architecture, including interiors and gardens. Ask students how these compare with their Western counterparts. Explain that students are about to learn about the precedents for these exotic structures.

The Art of Japan

Vocabulary
- pagoda
- Yamato-e
- Ukiyo-e
- woodblock printing

Artists to Meet
- Kujaku Myō-o
- Sōami Kangaku Shinso
- Torii Kiyonobu I
- Suzuki Harunobu
- Katsushika Hokusai
- Andō Hiroshige

Discover
After completing this lesson, you will be able to:
- Trace the influences on Japanese art.
- Identify specific Japanese art styles.

Japan owed a debt of gratitude to China for its initial artistic development. Eventually, however, Japan produced an abundance of painting, sculpture, and architecture that was uniquely its own. The accomplishments of its artists added luster to this island empire's ancient and proud history. The first traces of Japanese art date to a culture known as Jomon (c. 12,000–300 B.C.).

Early Development of Japanese Art

During the Kofun period which lasted from A.D. 300–800, the earliest artworks consist mainly of simple, undecorated vessels, figures, and animals made of red clay (Figure 10.23). Curiously, many clay figures and animals have been discovered in the areas surrounding burial mounds. Some experts suggest that they were placed there to ward off evil spirits and protect the dead.

Until the end of the ninth century, the art of Japan was largely modeled on that of China and other Asian cultures. After that time, however, foreign influences became less pronounced, and Japanese artists began to develop their own styles. In the centuries that followed, various subjects grew in favor, faded, and were replaced by new ones. At certain times, scenes of life at court, witty caricatures, and portraits were popular. Other favorite subjects included battle scenes, genre scenes, and landscapes.

Introduction of Buddhism

In A.D. 552, the ruler of a kingdom in Korea sent a gilt bronze figure of the Buddha to the emperor of Japan. Along with the sculpture came

■ **FIGURE 10.23** Small clay figures and animals of this kind have been uncovered in the areas surrounding Japanese burial mounds. What qualities contribute to the appeal of this small work?

Haniwa Falcon. Late Kofun period. Sixth century A.D. Earthenware. 11.1 × 17.8 cm (4³/₈ × 7"). Asian Art Museum of San Francisco, San Francisco, California. B80 S3 B62 P177. The Avery Brundage Collection. Bequest of Mr. Joseph M. Branston.

232

LESSON THREE RESOURCES

Teacher's Classroom Resources

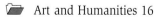 Appreciating Cultural Diversity 14, 15

 Art and Humanities 16

 Reproducible Lesson Plan 23

Reteaching Activity 23

Study Guide 23

Buddhist writings and missionaries. This is how Buddhism was introduced to Japan.

At first there was resistance to the new religion, particularly by those who remained faithful to Shinto, the indigenous religion of Japan. Eventually, though, Buddhism became firmly established throughout the country and came to affect every aspect of Japanese culture.

Temple Construction

In the year 594, the empress Shiko ordered that Buddhist temples be built throughout her kingdom. Architects, wood-carvers, bronze workers, weavers, and other skilled artisans were brought from Korea to build and decorate the temples that soon filled the countryside.

In many respects these temples were similar to those in China. They were, however, more richly decorated and more delicately assembled. Because the Japanese islands were formed from volcanic rock, there was little hard stone suitable for building these temples. Consequently, these and other structures were made of wood.

Japanese builders raised the practice of constructing wooden buildings to a sophisticated art form. Their temples and palaces were built on a stone base, with wooden posts and rafters carefully fitted together in beautifully crafted joints. These buildings had to be especially well designed and constructed to survive the frequent earthquakes and violent storms that plagued the island nation.

The Temple at Horyuji
■ FIGURE 10.24

Among the greatest architectural achievements in Japan was the temple complex at Horyuji, built near Nara about the year 616. The temple was constructed on a square plan surrounded by a double wall. Inside were a number of buildings: the main hall containing a sculpture of the Buddha, a lecture hall, a library, and a bell tower.

In addition there were two pagodas. A **pagoda** is *a tower several stories high with roofs slightly curved upward at the edges.* These structures contained sacred relics. Amazingly, one of these ancient wooden

pagodas has survived countless earthquakes and outlasted thousands of stone edifices. It still stands today as the oldest wooden structure in the world (Figure 10.24). Few buildings in history have surpassed its simple majesty.

The Treasures at Todaiji

Perhaps as beautiful, and only slightly younger, is the temple of Todaiji in Nara, which was erected by the emperor Shomu in 752. Four years after the temple was completed, the emperor died. Not long after his death, his widow, the empress Komoyo,

■ **FIGURE 10.24** This pagoda, built nearly 1,400 years ago, is the oldest wooden structure in the world. **What features does this structure have in common with all pagodas?**

Pagoda from the Temple Complex at Horyuji, near Nara, Japan. c. A.D. 616.

TEACH
Aesthetics

Direct students' attention to the *Haniwa Falcon* in Figure 10.23. Point out that the coarse earthenware makes the viewer want to touch the work and experience its texture. Ask: How does the work's rough-hewn appearance, simplicity, and spareness of detail increase its aesthetic appeal?

Art Criticism

Have students study the pagoda in Figure 10.24, noting the role line plays in giving the structure both a sense of grace and majesty. Ask: In what ways might this structure be said to be an early skyscraper?

Critical Thinking

Have students note the comment in the text regarding the age and composition of the pagoda in Figure 10.24 and the fact that it remains standing today. Have students discuss what these observations suggest about the skills of the architects who designed the structure.

Did You Know?

The temple complex at Horyuji (written sometimes as *Horyu-ji*) was built during a period of Japanese history known as the Asuka period, which spanned the years from 538 to 645. It is customary to name the various periods in Japanese history according to the name of the capital city. The capital at this time was Asuka.

Teacher Notes

Art History

Direct students' attention to the artwork in Figure 10.25, and in particular to the circle surrounding the head of the key figure. Reminding students that this is a religious artwork, ask them to speculate on the significance of this shape. Ask: What feature surrounding the heads of holy figures in Western art does this circle call to mind?

Art Criticism

Refer students again to the painting in Figure 10.25 and help them discuss the work, describing the painting, noting its size, the medium in which it was created, the subject matter contained within it, and the elements of art that have been emphasized. Working as individuals, students are then to complete the art criticism operations, concluding with a short written interpretation of the work. Allow time for students to share and compare their interpretations.

Cross Curriculum

HISTORY. Emphasize that, unlike the largely religious art discussed thus far in this chapter, *Yamato-e* was secular, or nonreligious, finding its themes and subjects in history, literature, and popular romances of the day. Ask interested students to research circumstances and factors in addition to those mentioned in the text that led to this separation between church and art.

■ **FIGURE 10.25** The Buddha is the most important figure in this composition. How did the artist emphasize this figure? What message about the Buddha do you think the painting communicates?

Historical Buddha Preaching on Vulture Peak (Hokkedo Kompon Mandata). Eighth century A.D. Artist unknown. Ink, color, and gold on hemp. 107 × 143.5 cm (42 × 56½"). Courtesy of Museum of Fine Arts, Boston, Massachusetts. William Sturgis Bigelow Collection.

presented the treasures of his court to the Great Buddha enshrined at Todaiji. Other gifts were later added to these treasures and were housed and protected in the temple. As a result, no less than 10,000 works of eighth-century Japanese art were preserved.

Historical Buddha Preaching on Vulture Peak
■ FIGURE 10.25

Among the artworks preserved at Todaiji is a painting on hemp (Figure 10.25) regarded as one of the temple's greatest treasures. It portrays the Buddha, surrounded by Bodhisattvas, preaching in the mountains. Although retouched during the twelfth century, this painting still testifies to the high quality of eighth-century Buddhist painting.

The Heian Period

In 784, Heian (the modern city of Kyoto) was made the capital of Japan. The Heian period is regarded as a golden age for Japanese art. During the next 400 years, numerous new temples and monasteries

were built. In addition, members of the royal court and the heads of great families commissioned painters to create works of art.

The Yamato-e Style

Contacts with China continued until 898 when ties were broken as a consequence of internal strife in Japan. No longer able to draw inspiration from China, Japanese artists developed their own unique style of painting, which was known as **Yamato-e,** or *painting in the Japanese manner.*

Paintings done in this style were the first true examples of pure Japanese art. Yamato is an island near Kyoto and Nara, considered the center of Japanese culture. Artists using this style created decorative wall paintings showing travelers on the road, nobles admiring cherry blossoms or hunting, peasants working in the fields, and other scenes from everyday life. These spirited scenes included clear references to particular seasons of the year. Unfortunately, only a few works dating to this period have survived.

The Kamakura Period

A series of civil wars prompted by corrupt provincial governments brought an end to the Heian period in 1185. Clan leaders waged war with one another until one leader, Minamoto Yoritomo, was able to establish a military government at Kamakura.

A succession of military rulers assumed control over various parts of the country for the next 148 years. These rulers recognized the emperor as little more than a powerless figurehead.

Kujaku Myō-o
■ FIGURE 10.26

During this period, a military spirit dominated the arts as it did politics. Vigor replaced elegance and boldness replaced restraint. This is shown in an expressive painting of a stern Buddha in more or less human form (Figure 10.26). Kujaku-Myō-o, also known as the Peacock King, is seen eating poison grasses and insects representing obstacles to salvation. He sits on the powerful peacock—his identifying symbol.

More About... **Japanese Architecture.** Japanese architects have a goal of making their buildings blend harmoniously with their surroundings. In the beginning, Japanese structures followed the Chinese style of Buddhist temples, with strong colors and heavy materials. Soon, the Japanese developed their own style to reflect their living conditions. Wood and lightweight materials were chosen to withstand earthquakes in the mountain range that makes up the islands of Japan. Architects retained the natural colors of the wood, and added features to allow the structure to blend with gardens and natural surroundings. Porches or narrow platforms make the home seem part of the garden, which is an important part of Japanese family life.

The Great Buddha at Kamakura
■ FIGURE 10.27

A long tradition of creating colossal sculptures continued during this period with such works as the Great Buddha at Kamakura (Figure 10.27), which was cast in bronze in 1252. Viewed from the front, the figure is an example of exact symmetrical balance; the two sides mirror each other. Today the sculpture sits outdoors on a rise surrounded by a pleasant grove of trees. This seems to be an especially appropriate setting for the gigantic Buddha seated in quiet contemplation.

The Burning of the Sanjō Palace
■ FIGURES 10.28 and 10.29

Painting is the most interesting visual art form from the Kamakura period. Advances made in the Yamato-e style reflected the artistic tastes of the new military leaders, who preferred paintings that stressed realism and action. Nowhere is this realism and action more apparent than in a handscroll, *The Burning of the Sanjō Palace.* (See Figures 10.28 and 10.29, page 236.)

The Rise of Zen Buddhism and the Fall of the Kamakura Rulers

During the Kamakura period, new Buddhist sects were formed. One of these, the Zen sect, which was introduced from China, had an important impact on later Japanese art.

The power of the Kamakura military rulers ended in 1333. To their great shame, this loss of power did not occur on the battlefield. Like their predecessors, they too became corrupted by power. Civil war again broke out and continued until 1573. Somehow the arts managed to flourish during this period of almost continuous unrest and conflict.

■ FIGURE 10.26
This painting with its rich color and fine drawing is characteristic of the high level of painting during the Kamakura period. **How does this work differ from religious paintings with which you are familiar?**

Kujaku Myō-o. Kamakura Period (1185–1333). Hanging scroll, ink, color, and gold on silk. 117 × 71 cm (46 × 28″). The Nelson-Atkins Museum of Art, Kansas City, Missouri. Purchase: Nelson Trust.

■ FIGURE 10.27 This gigantic bronze Buddha sits outdoors rather than in a temple. **What does this religious figure appear to be doing?**

Giant Buddha. Kamakura, Japan. c. A.D. 1252.

Chapter 10 *The Art of India, China, and Japan* **235**

CHAPTER 10
LESSON THREE

Art Criticism

Direct students' attention to the *Giant Buddha* in Figure 10.27. Then have them refer back to the Chinese *Standing Buddha* in Figure 10.13, page 223. Have students work together to compile charts listing similarities and differences between the two works. Discuss how each representation of Buddha is in keeping with cultural tenets of the civilization in which it was created.

Did You Know ?

At one time the *Giant Buddha* at Kamakura was housed in a temple, but in 1495 a great tidal wave destroyed both the temple and the nearby city. When the waters subsided, the huge bronze Buddha was found calmly surveying the widespread destruction.

Critical Thinking

On the board, write the following quotation: "Harmony is to be valued." Identify the author of these words as Shotoku Taishi, a Japanese prince (A.D. 573–621) who was an important patron of the arts. Ask students to discuss the quotation as well as artworks from the lesson that they feel reflect the sentiment.

CULTURAL DIVERSITY

Kimonos. The interesting and elegant dress often represented in Japanese art is called a kimono. It is a traditional Japanese dress worn by men and women. Kimonos are still made and worn for special occasions, for praying at a shrine, for the tea ceremony, for marriages, and for other special family events. For funerals, black kimonos with the family crest are worn. The shape of the kimono and its dimensions are carefully prescribed. The fabric must be silk, or cotton for summer, and is decorated with embroidery or intricate batik designs. Lengths of fabric are sewn together to make long, straight panels. Kimonos can be worn for many years; they are often passed along as family treasures.

235

Art Criticism

Observe that *The Burning of the Sanjō Palace* is noteworthy both for its style and subject matter. Add that, in addition to serving as a form of recorded history, the handscroll is an artistic depiction of a violent and horrific series of events and that, in this regard, it is far different from the peaceful landscapes and contemplations of Buddhism students have seen in other artworks of this chapter.

Art History

Ask students if Figure 10.28 can be considered a political statement for its time. Discuss the way the energetic style captures the chaos and inhumanity of the event. Then have students turn to Picasso's *Guernica* (Figure 23.16, page 525). Explain that this work was painted halfway around the world seven centuries later as an expression of the artist's outrage over the Spanish Civil War. Have students write a short essay comparing these two works with respect to details, style, and content.

Did You Know?

Shinto, or "Way of the Gods," originated in early Japan. It is a religion based on ancestor worship and a love of nature, family, and, above all, the ruling family, whose members were regarded as direct descendants of the gods.

Storytelling in Art

This scroll illustrates with shocking realism a revolt that took place on the night of December 9, 1159. On that tragic night, the Sanjō Palace was attacked and the emperor taken prisoner. Unrolling the scroll from right to left, the viewer is immediately swept up in the frantic scene. As the scroll is unrolled further, the viewer is led at a less hectic pace through swarms of soldiers, horses, and carts. Finally, at the very end of the scroll—nearly 23 feet long—the powerful narrative comes to a quiet end.

1 Noblemen and their servants arrive at the palace after hearing of the attack, but they are too late.

2 The palace is engulfed in flame.

3 Warriors surround the palace.

4 Within the palace itself, the horrors of war are presented in graphic and frightening detail: palace guards are beheaded, loyal attendants are hunted down and killed, and ladies-in-waiting are trampled beneath the hooves of horses.

5 In this section of the scroll, the viewer finds the final warrior taking control of his rearing horse.

6 A single archer is the final, quiet figure signaling an end to this story of frantic action.

■ **FIGURE 10.28** *The Burning of the Sanjō Palace.* (Sanjo-den youchi no emaki). Kamakura period. Second half of thirteenth century A.D. Handscroll, eighth view of twelve. Ink and colors on paper. 41.3 × 699.7 cm (16¹/₃ × 144″). Courtesy of Museum of Fine Arts, Boston, Massachusetts. Fenollosa-Weld Collection.

■ **FIGURE 10.29** *The Burning of the Sanjō Palace.* Detail: *Rider and Warriors.* Handscroll, 12ᵗʰ view of 12. Ink and colors on paper. 41.3 × 699.7 cm (16¹/₃ × 144″). Courtesy of Museum of Fine Arts, Boston, Massachusetts. Fenollosa-Weld Collection.

Storytelling in Art

Direct students' attention to the *The Burning of the Sanjō Palace,* Figure 10.28 and Figure 10.29. Let volunteers describe the scenes, and then have students read the explanations as an aid to understanding the actions depicted. Let students share their responses to the work, and ask whether students suspect every artwork created during the violent Kamakura period addressed a similar theme in a similar fashion. Why or why not?

Landscape of the Four Seasons: Fall and Winter
■ **FIGURE 10.30**

The growing appeal of Zen Buddhism resulted in the popularity of art forms associated with that religion. Zen's appeal may have been due to the fact that it offered people an escape from the chaos that marked daily life. A desire to escape reality may have motivated artists as well. For example, when the painter Sōami Kangaku Shinso (soo-ah-mee kahn-gah-koo sheen-soh) took up ink and paper to create a design for a screen, he chose as his subject a peaceful landscape (Figure 10.30).

His finished paintings were mounted on two screens illustrating the four seasons. Reading from right to left in the same manner as a handscroll, the paintings were intended to draw viewers gently into an imaginary world of beauty and peace in which they could forget the real world of unrest and fear.

This same quest for beauty and peace was undertaken by architects. The result can be seen in carefully proportioned pavilions set in the midst of splendid gardens.

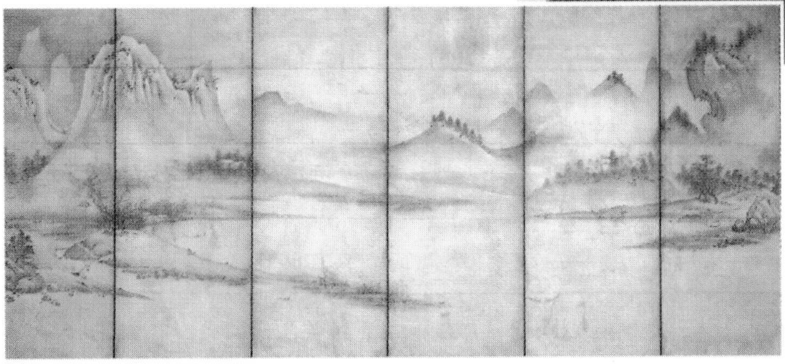

■ **FIGURE 10.30** Like handscrolls, these screen paintings are intended to be viewed slowly and thoughtfully, from right to left. What does this Japanese landscape have in common with Chinese landscapes such as Figure 10.19, page 229?

Sōami Kangaku Shinso. *Landscape of the Four Seasons: Fall and Winter.* Six-fold screen ink on paper. 173.4 × 371 cm (68¼ × 146″). The Metropolitan Museum of Art, New York, New York. Gift of John D. Rockefeller Jr., 1941. (41.59.2)

The Momoyama Period

A period known as the Momoyama marked a time in which a succession of three dictators, or *shoguns,* finally restored unity and brought peace to the troubled land. During this era, huge palaces were built (Figure 10.31). These palaces served two purposes: They were both protective fortresses and symbols of power. Inside these structures, sliding doors and large screens were decorated with gold leaf and delicate paintings.

A Rich Era of Japanese Art

In 1615, Iyeyasu Tokugawa overwhelmed the forces of rival military leaders in a battle that left 40,000 dead. Victory enabled him to build a new capital at Edo (the modern city of Tokyo) and establish the Edo rule, which continued until 1867.

■ **FIGURE 10.31** Japanese castles such as this one were built as protective fortresses and as symbols of power. Compare this castle with a European castle, such as the one in Figure 14.12, page 318. What are the most important similarities and differences?

Hiroshima Castle. Lake Biwa, Japan. Rebuilt after World War II.

Art History
Ask students to discuss the changes in the art of Japan that resulted from the spread of the Zen sect of Buddhism. Have them determine what teachings of the Zen Buddhists were responsible for the shift from violent to peaceful, more contemplative subjects.

Aesthetics
Ask students to study the photo of the Hiroshima Castle, Figure 10.31. Have them consider the feelings its architectural aspects evoke, such as the way the larger base and increasingly smaller upper levels give the building an enormous sense of stability, strength, and permanence. Conclude with a discussion of whether this building succeeds as a "symbol of power." Ask: What effect does the upturned corners create?

Art Criticism
Display a photograph of the Guggenheim Art Museum in New York. Have students compare this iconoclastic work of Western architecture with the Hiroshima Castle. Ask: What feelings does this modern building evoke? What do you think the architect was trying to convey? In what ways might Frank Lloyd Wright's objectives have paralleled those of the architect of the Japanese castle?

CULTURAL DIVERSITY

National Treasures. Artists in Japan today are honored in a special and unique way. A select few are designated as Living National Treasures and are considered "Holders of Important Intangible Cultural Properties." Seventy artists, craftsmen, and performing artists are given this title, and they retain this honor until their death. The significance of this honorable designation is that these artists are given the responsibility to teach, train apprentices, perform or exhibit their arts, and keep their art form alive for future generations. In this way, the people of Japan, the government, and the emperor express the reverence and appreciation for the arts that has long been a tradition in Japan.

Aesthetics

Have students study *A Woman Dancer* (Figure 10.32), noting the way the drapery forms a sculpture exclusive of the lines of the body beneath. Ask: What aspects of style has the artist employed to create a feeling of liveliness and movement? What other feelings or moods does this work convey? How is its tone different from previous works in this chapter, especially those that concern themselves with quiet contemplation?

Art History

Point out that the woodblock print is another example of how technology has transformed the path of art. Then divide the class into two teams, and have them debate this proposition: Replication diminishes the significance or value of an artwork. In developing their arguments, students should address the issues of both artistic merit and actual retail price.

Art Criticism

Explain that, throughout history, Mt. Fuji has been a popular subject for Eastern and Western artists. Add that, although the mountain has most often been viewed—and interpreted in art—as a symbol of the power and permanence of nature, the artist Hokusai (Figure 10.34) chose to depict Fuji in a different way. The long angle causes the mountain to appear as if it were visually engulfed by the enormous wave that also dwarfs the humans and their fishing boats. Discuss what the artist may have been attempting to symbolize about human beings and their relationship to nature.

This period represents one of the longest periods of peace and one of the richest eras for art in Japanese history.

Peace brought about a prosperous middle class. This new middle class demanded artworks that showed the life of the people rendered in new techniques. Demands such as these led to the development of the **Ukiyo-e** style, which means *pictures of the passing world.*

Woodblock Printing

Since painting produced only one picture at a time, artists searched for other ways to satisfy the increased demand for art. A solution, which had been introduced from China in the eighth century, was found in **woodblock printing.** This process involves *transferring and cutting pictures into wood blocks, inking the surface of these blocks, and printing.* Using this technique, an artist could produce as many inexpensive prints as needed.

Prints originally were made with black ink on white paper. If color was desired, it was necessary to add it by hand. In the eighteenth century, a process for producing multicolored prints was developed. This process required the talents of a painter, a wood-carver, and a printer.

The artist first prepared a design in ink, adding color notations to guide the printer. The lines of the design were then transferred to a wood block, and a specialist in wood cutting carved away the wood between the lines. A separate block was prepared for each color. Finally, the printer inked each block and pressed each one against paper, being careful to align the blocks exactly. Since hundreds of

copies could be made from one set of blocks, the prints produced were relatively inexpensive.

Around the middle of the seventeenth century, a designer of dress patterns named Hishikawa Moronobu (hee-shee-kah-wah moh-roh-noh-boo) produced the first woodblock prints. At first these were used as illustrations for books, but later they were sold separately. Moronobu's charming style made his work especially appealing.

Torii Kiyonobu I (1664–1729)

Moronobu paved the way for other artists who soon began producing individual prints with a similar style and technique. One of these was Torii Kiyonobu I (toh-ree kyoh-noh-boo), an actor's son who often selected as his subjects actors from the Kabuki theater. His picture of a woman dancer (Figure 10.32) uses a characteristic bold line that flows across the paper to create a complex yet graceful rhythm of curved lines and patterns.

■ **FIGURE 10.32** This woodblock print was created with black ink on white paper. The colors were added by hand. **Which of the elements—value, line, or texture—seems especially important in this work?**

Torii Kiyonobu I. *A Woman Dancer.* c. 1708. Woodblock print. 55.2 × 29.2 cm (21³/₄ × 11¹/₂″). The Metropolitan Museum of Art, New York, New York. Harris Brisbane Dick Fund and Rogers Fund, 1949. (JP 3098)

COOPERATIVE LEARNING

Reporting. Have students form groups to research the great palaces remaining in Japan today. Begin by asking students to compile a list on the board of the structures mentioned in this lesson. Have each group choose one location to research. Students may then record what artwork this palace is famous for. Have them use encyclopedias and library resources to find more detailed information and compile a report for the class. Reports should include historical information, what dynasties or emperors were responsible for construction of the palaces, what significant events were associated with the location, and what use the structure serves today. Ask groups to share their findings with the rest of the class.

Suzuki Harunobu (1724–1770)

The first multicolored prints were probably done by Suzuki Harunobu (soo-zoo-kee hah-roo-noh-boo). His prints reveal that he endowed the female figure with an almost supernatural grace. In Harunobu's prints (Figure 10.33), female figures appear to have weightless bodies with slender waists and tiny hands and feet. Rarely do their faces betray any sign of emotion or stress.

Harunobu, along with Katsushika Hokusai (kah-tsoo-shee-kah hok-sigh) and Andō Hiroshige (ahn-doh hee-roh-shee-gay) produced many of the works that inspired the French Impressionists in the nineteenth century.

■ **FIGURE 10.33** This is a multicolored wood-block print; the colors were added as part of the printing process, not painted in later. What mood does this work convey?

Suzuki Harunobu. *Girl Admiring Plum Blossoms at Night.* c. 1768. Polychromed woodblock. 32.4 × 21 cm (12 3/4 × 8 1/4"). The Metropolitan Museum of Art, New York, New York. Fletcher Fund, 1929. (JP 1506)

Katsushika Hokusai (1760–1849)

Hokusai was fond of saying that he "was born at the age of fifty." By this he meant that long years of preparation were required before he was able to produce works of art that he considered worthy of admiration.

From about 1825 to 1831, Hokusai published his brilliant Mount Fuji series of prints. In spite of its title, "Thirty-six Views of Mount Fuji," there are actually 46 scenes included in the series. In this group of prints, he adopted a long angle of vision to increase the dramatic impact. One of these prints, *The Great Wave at Kanagawa* (Figure 10.34), shows Mount Fuji in the distance, beyond a huge wave threatening to destroy the fishing boats that are almost lost in the violently churning sea. (See also Figure 4.1, page 84.)

Hokusai was a humble man destined to be ranked among the great artists of history. Shortly before he died at the age of 89, Hokusai is quoted as having said, "If the gods had given me only ten more years I could have become a truly great painter."

■ **FIGURE 10.34** This print is one of 46 scenes in a single series. In what way does the addition of the fishing boats help emphasize the wave's awesome power? What is the only thing in the picture that does not seem to be in motion?

Katsushika Hokusai. *The Great Wave at Kanagawa.* c. 1823–29. Polychrome woodblock print. 25.7 × 38 cm (10 1/8 × 14 15/16"). The Metropolitan Museum of Art, New York, New York. The H.O. Havemeyer Collection, bequest of Mrs. H.O. Havemeyer, 1929. (JP1847).

Chapter 10 *The Art of India, China, and Japan* **239**

Study Guide

Distribute *Study Guide* 23 in the TCR. Assist students in reviewing key concepts. 📁

Art and Humanities

Assign *Art and Humanities* 16, "Sharing Thoughts from Oriental Wisdom," in the TCR. Students read excerpts from the works of four writers in this worksheet. Then have them create a book of sayings, complete with a Japanese-style binding. 📁

Studio Activities

Refer students back to the photograph of the Haniwa Falcon (Figure 10.23, page 232). Point out that the subject matter of the work, despite its high degree of stylization, is unmistakable. Have students use clay and shaping tools to model an animal of their own choosing that exhibits similar properties.

Art and Humanities

Have students complete *Appreciating Cultural Diversity* 14, "Preserving the Culture from Japan to America," in the TCR. In this activity, students practice the paper-folding technique of origami. 📁

Did You Know?

The Kabuki theater provided a popular form of drama. It was developed as a more easily understood, enjoyable form of entertainment than the highly stylized plays favored by the nobility.

More About... **Hokusai.** Explain to students that master Japanese woodblock print artist Katsushika Hokusai (1760–1849) completed over 30,000 artworks in his lifetime. He produced illustrations for novels, calendars, greeting cards, and even the equivalent of Japanese modern comic books. His feeling about life is evident in the approach he took to his art. He once wrote, "I have been in love with painting ever since I was six . . . I will really master the secrets of art at 90. When I reach 100, my work will be truly sublime. My final goal will be attained around the age of 110, when every line and dot will be life itself."

Checking Comprehension

➤ Have students respond to the lesson review questions. Answers are given in the box below.

➤ *Assign Application* 10, "Hold the Presses!" In this activity, students are provided with fictitious newspaper headlines from ancient India, China, and Japan. They are to identify the title and other details about the work of art referenced, along with information about its significance. 📁

Reteaching

➤ *Assign Reteaching* 23, found in the TCR. Have students complete the activity and review their responses. 📁

➤ Have students consider concepts such as size, strength, permanence, and "imperturbability" as they are conveyed by the Giant Buddha in Figure 10.27 (page 235). Ask students to discuss how these properties reinforce the purpose of this sculpture as a work of religious art.

Enrichment

Assign students *Appreciating Cultural Diversity* 15, "Understanding the Japanese Relation to Nature," in the TCR. In this worksheet, students learn about the nature-oriented work of contemporary Japanese sculptors. Students then work on a sculpture of their own to express their own relation to nature. 📁

CLOSE

Have students investigate and report to the class on the influence of Japanese woodcuts on twentieth-century European artists such as Manet, Whistler, and Toulouse-Lautrec.

■ **FIGURE 10.35**
The subdued colors in this work contribute to the quiet atmosphere. What are the most important differences between this work by Hiroshige and the print by Hokusai (Figure 10.34, page 239)?

Ando Hiroshige. *Evening Rain on the Karasaki Pine* from the series "Eight Views of Omi Province." Nineteenth century. Woodblock print. 26 × 38 cm (10¼ × 15"). The Metropolitan Museum of Art, New York, New York. Bequest of Mrs. H. O. Havemeyer, 1929. The H. O. Havemeyer Collection. (JP 1874)

Andō Hiroshige (1795–1858)

Although he greatly admired Hokusai and was strongly influenced by him, the younger Hiroshige did not adopt his predecessor's spirited style. Instead, he used delicate lines and a harmonious color scheme to give nature a more subdued atmosphere.

Hiroshige often unified a work by giving it an overall darkness of tone that captures the sadness of a rainy scene (Figure 10.35). Much of the beauty of his work comes from his sensitive response to variations in the weather and changing seasons.

LESSON THREE REVIEW

Reviewing Art Facts

1. Explain how the Buddhist religion reached Japan.
2. What did a Japanese temple look like? From what material was it made and why?
3. What period in Japanese art was considered the golden age and why?
4. What led to the development of the Ukiyo-e style of art?
5. What prompted the development of woodblock printing in Japan?

➤ Activity... *Designing a Print Image*

Japanese artists focused on beauty and simplicity in their works. This is reflected also in the way they designed woodblock prints. Examine the flowing lines and graceful movement shown in the print in Figure 10.33, page 239. Find other examples of woodblock prints from Japan.

Sketch a simple plan as the basis for a three-color block print design. Use a sheet of paper and pencil to draw your image. Remember that when you prepare a design for a printing plate to be carved, the design you make will be printed as a mirror image. Experiment with sketching various forms and letters in reverse before you work these into your design. Use colored pencils to fill in areas on your design plan to emphasize line, shape, and texture in your design.

LESSON THREE REVIEW

Answers to Recalling Art Facts

1. Japan received a sculpture of Buddha from Korea in 552 A.D.
2. Japanese temples were multistoried wooden structures built to survive earthquakes.
3. The Heian period; many new temples were built and families commissioned artworks.
4. The peaceful middle class demanded works showing the life of the people.
5. Increased demand for inexpensive art.

Activity... *Designing a Print Image*

Have students bring in and share with the class other woodblock prints from Japan. Then let students experiment with sketching forms and letters in reverse. Have students draw their designs independently.

Complete a complex, highly detailed pencil drawing composed of symbols representing a specific person. Use a variety of lines, shapes, simulated textures, and values to add to the complexity of your design and completely fill the paper on which it is made.

Inspiration

Examine the relief carving from the Bharhut Stupa (Figure 10.8, page 219). How is the Buddha represented in this work? What other images were used by Buddhist artists to symbolize the founder of their religion? Would you describe this particular relief as complex or simple? What makes it so?

Process

1. Choose a well-known person to serve as the subject for this drawing. *Do not reveal your choice to any other member of the class.* On the sheet of paper, list as many visual symbols associated with your subject as you can.

2. On the white drawing paper, complete a composition made up of the detailed drawings of each of the symbols on your list. Draw these symbols in a variety of sizes and overlap them to create a complex composition. Use a variety of lines, create different simulated textures, and add shading.

3. Exhibit your drawing with those completed by other members of the class. Try to identify the subject of each drawing by "reading" and interpreting the symbols.

Materials

- Pencil and sheet of paper
- White drawing paper, 9 × 12 inches or larger

■ **FIGURE 10.36**   Student Work

Examining Your Work

Describe. Are the different symbols in your drawing drawn accurately? Are they easily identified by viewers?

Analyze. Is your drawing a complex composition made up of a variety of lines, shapes, simulated textures, and values? Can you point to and describe these different art elements in your work?

Interpret. Can others read the symbols in your composition to determine the person represented? Did viewers find one particular symbol useful in identifying the subject?

Judge. What is most successful about your drawing? Overall, do you think it demonstrates unity? If you were to redo this drawing, what would you do to make it more unified?

241

ASSESSMENT

Peer Review. Suggest that students meet in groups to compare and discuss the visual symbols in their drawings. Have them focus on these questions: What makes this kind of symbol successful? What are some of the most effective ways of combining symbols into a unified drawing? Group members may want to choose another well-known figure and, together,

brainstorm a list of symbols for that person. They can then describe—or sketch—the symbols they think would be most successful.

After this discussion, have students use what they have learned to draw one or two new symbols in their sketchbooks.

Studio LESSON
Creating Visual Symbols

Objectives

■ Complete a pencil drawing of symbols to represent a specific person.

■ Use of a variety of lines, shapes, simulated textures, and values.

Motivator

Ask students to compile a list of prominent people, and have them suggest symbols that might be applied to each. Instruct students to work independently and select a well-known figure. Remind them not to reveal the identity of the person selected to classmates. Have them explore combinations of visual symbols to form an interesting, complex composition. Explain that complexity is achieved by relying on the principle of variety when using the elements of art.

Aesthetics

Direct students' attention to the relief carving from the Bharhut Stupa (Figure 10.8, page 219) and ask them to point out and describe the lines, shapes, and textures evident in this work. Have students explain how the appearance of this work would have been different if it had been carved in low relief. Discuss how contrasts of value can also contribute to a more realistic, three-dimensional appearance and enhance visual interest in a two-dimensional composition.

Critiquing

Have students apply the steps of art criticism to their own artwork, using the "Examining Your Work" questions on this page.

Negative Shape Painting

Objectives

■ Complete an accurate drawing of a branch that runs off the paper on all sides, creating a variety of negative shapes.

■ Create a range of intensities by mixing two complementary colors.

Motivator

Provide a few minutes for students to study their branches closely and then ask them to identify the most interesting or unusual quality or feature. As students draw the outline of their branches, remind them that they are to be as precise as possible, making certain to include every detail. It may be necessary to extend some branches to run off the edge of the paper to create the negative shapes.

Studio Skills

Tell students to choose any pair of complementary colors to mix the different intensities. If either or both of these complementary colors is to be mixed, they should be as accurate as possible. Instruct students to match mixed hues to those shown on the Color Wheel (Figure 2.4, page 29). Demonstrate how small amounts of a complement are added to a hue until a neutral gray is produced. If an intensity scale is to accompany the negative shape painting, this neutral gray should be located in the middle of the scale.

Critiquing

Have students apply the steps of art criticism to their own artwork, using the "Examining Your Work" questions on this page.

Studio LESSON Negative Shape Painting

Materials

- A large branch with a few leaves intact
- Pencil
- White drawing paper, 9 × 12 inches or larger
- Tempera or acrylic paint (two complementary colors only)
- Brushes, mixing tray, and paint cloth
- Water container

Following a period of intense contemplation or study, draw a large branch as accurately as possible. The lines of this branch will run off the paper at the top, bottom, and sides. This creates a variety of negative shapes. These are then painted with hues obtained by mixing two complementary colors. Restricting yourself to these two hues enables you to obtain a range of different intensities.

Inspiration

Examine the paintings by Ch'ien Hsüan (Figure 10.20, page 229) and Chao Meng-fu (Figure 10.21, page 230). What did these artists do before beginning work on a painting? Consider the positive effects that practice could have on your own work.

■ **FIGURE 10.37** Student Work

Process

1. Bring to class a large branch and remove most, but not all, of its leaves. Silently study this branch, noting the way it bends, twists, and divides to form smaller branches.

2. On the drawing paper, slowly draw the outline of the branch with pencil, making your drawing as accurate as possible. Make the drawing large enough so that it runs off the paper on all sides, creating a variety of negative shapes. (The shapes between the branches are negative shapes. The branch itself is a positive shape.)

3. Use tempera or acrylic to paint *the negative shapes only.* Paint these shapes with a variety of intensities obtained by mixing two complementary hues. First, number each negative shape lightly in pencil. Then, paint shape Number 1 with the first of the complementary colors selected. Paint shape Number 2 with the same color to which you have added a small amount of its complement. Add increasing amounts of the complement, and paint the final shape with the second complementary color. Following this procedure enables you to complete a type of intensity scale.

Examining Your Work

Describe. Does your drawing of a branch look accurate? Do the lines of this branch run off the paper on all sides?

Analyze. How were the negative shapes in your picture created? How many different intensities did you obtain by mixing the two complementary colors?

Interpret. Does your finished work offer hints as to the intense contemplation you practiced before beginning your painting? What effect do you think that contemplation had on your work?

Judge. How would you respond to someone who says your picture is "nothing more than a painting of an ordinary branch"? What aesthetic qualities would you want such a person to consider when judging your work?

ASSESSMENT

Examining Your Work. After students have used the "Examining Your Work" questions, suggest that they make a different kind of drawing of the same branch they used in the original work. Instruct students to study the branch briefly and then to make a quick sketch of it, creating as realistic an impression as possible. Students may want to use colored pencils to add details and color to their drawings. Have students meet in cooperative learning groups to compare and discuss the two approaches and the two works each student created. Encourage students to describe how they felt about the calm, slow approach they took to the Studio Lesson project. What have they learned from this comparison?

Reviewing the Facts

Lesson One

1. What two great, enduring religions originated in India?
2. Name the three main Hindu gods and tell what primary process each represents.
3. Explain what the wheel symbolized in Buddhist art.
4. During what years did Buddhist sculpture reach its peak in India?

Lesson Two

5. Who was the first Chinese painter?
6. During which dynasty did China reach its peak of power and influence?
7. Which Chinese dynasty was flourishing at the same time as the Roman Empire?
8. How does a landscape painted on a Chinese scroll differ from a painting of the same subject done in the West?

Lesson Three

9. Would Yamato-e painting, during the Kamakura period, be considered a more symbolic or more realistic style of painting?
10. How might *The Great Wave at Kanagawa* (Figure 10.34, page 239) have differed had it been a painting?
11. What Japanese invention helped to satisfy the increased demand for art among the middle class?

Thinking Critically

1. **COMPARE AND CONTRAST.** Refer to the *Standing Buddha* (Figure 10.13, page 223) and *Nike Fastening Her Sandal* (Figure 8.19, page 183). Discuss the similarities and differences between the two figures. Do you have a feeling that a real human figure exists beneath the drapery?
2. **ANALYZE.** Look closely at the artist's line in Figure 10.15. Make a list of adjectives to describe the quality of this line. Look through the book to find another artist whose lines could be described in much the same way. Finally, find another work showing lines that are very different in quality.

 Use the *Performing Arts Handbook* on page 583 to learn about music and dance of the Ranganiketan Cultural Arts Troupe.

CAREERS IN Art Read about how an appreciation of the beauty in nature can develop into a career as a landscape architect in the *Careers in Art Handbook,* page 601.

*inter*NET CONNECTION Visit Glencoe Art Online at *www.glencoe.com/sec/art*. Take a look at sites from Asian and Indian museums and learn more about the art and cultures of India, China, and Japan.

Technology Project

Chinese Handscroll

Much of the art of India, China, and Japan is based on quiet contemplation of the natural world, focusing on images, ideas, or thoughts. The Chinese culture developed a strong tradition of creating horizontal handscrolls. The subject of these scrolls often was based upon very small items such as a tiny flower or a pebble. This enabled artists to recognize beauty and to capture it in their art. Due to the fast pace of our high-tech culture, this approach may seem very different to us. Study the Chinese scrolls in this chapter. Try this way of working by creating a modern digital handscroll.

1. Using parchment or thin paper and small dowel rods or other similar materials, construct a small handscroll long enough to hold several images horizontally.
2. Using resources such as the Internet, CD-ROMs, laser discs, books, and magazines, choose one image from nature that is interesting or compelling to you. Your choice might be a flower, a leaf, a pattern, or a seashell.
3. Copy or sketch the image and place it into an image manipulation program. Create 10 to 15 versions of the image using various commands to create subtle changes in each image. Print small copies of each image and trim them to fit your handscroll.
4. Attach the images to your scroll.

243

Reviewing the Facts

1. Hinduism and Buddhism.
2. Brahma, the Creator; Vishnu, the Preserver; Shiva, the Destroyer.
3. It represents the circle of life, maturity, and death.
4. From A.D. 320 to A.D. 600, the Gupta era.
5. A woman named Lei.
6. T'ang Dynasty.
7. Han Dynasty.
8. Landscapes painted on Chinese scrolls usually have multiple vanishing points and changing perspective; Western landscapes usually have a single vanishing point.
9. More realistic.
10. Answers will vary but should indicate students know the difference between the effects achieved by the techniques used for woodblock prints and for paintings.
11. Woodblock printing.

Thinking Critically

1. Similarities: depiction of real fabric, suggested by the folds. Differences: fluidity and vitality to the ancient Greek sculpture, suggesting a living and breathing being beneath the cloth; the Buddha sculpture is more posed, artificial, and static.
2. Adjectives students might list are *fine, delicate,* and *graceful.* Selections of works will vary.

 Teaching the Technology Project

Some students may want to add poems or brief prose pieces to the images on their scrolls. These can be original compositions or translations of appropriate Chinese writings. Suggest that students use Internet resources to find poems or paragraphs to use in this way.

 Assign the feature in the *Performing Arts Handbook,* page 583.

CAREERS IN ART If time permits, have interested students investigate the career information in the *Careers in Art Handbook,* page 601.

*inter*NET CONNECTION Have students go online and learn more about artists on preselected Web sites with the Internet activity for this chapter.

The Native Arts of the Americas

LESSON ONE Native American Art ....

(pages 246–253)

Classic Resources

📁 Appreciating Cultural Diversity 16, 17
📁 Art and Humanities 17, 18
📁 Cooperative Learning 17
📁 Enrichment Activities 20, 21
📁 Reproducible Lesson Plan 24
📁 Reteaching Activity 24
📁 Study Guide 24

Features

Map of North America
(page 246)

Time & Place
CONNECTIONS
(page 248)

(page 250)

LESSON TWO Art in Mexico and in Central and South America ....

(pages 254–261)

Classroom Resources

📁 Appreciating Cultural Diversity 18
📁 Art and Humanities 19
📁 Enrichment Activities 22, 23
📁 Reproducible Lesson Plan 25
📁 Reteaching Activity 25
📁 Study Guide 25

Features

Identifying
Icons in Aztec *Art*

The Book of Days
(page 259)

END OF CHAPTER ....

(pages 262–263)

Studio
LESSON

• Abstract Ink Drawing of an Animal, Insect or Fish *(page 262)*

ADDITIONAL CHAPTER RESOURCES

Activities

- 📁 Advanced Studio Activity 11
- 📁 Application 11
- 🖱 Chapter 11 Internet Activity
- 📁 Studio Activities 14, 15

Fine Art Resources

🕹 **Transparencies**

Art in Focus Transparency 14
  Sakid Headdress Frontlet.

Art in Focus Transparency 15
  Pitseolak Ashoona. *To Rescue a Drowning Hunter*

🖼 **Fine Art Print**

Focus on World Art Print 11
  Aztec Stone Sculpture of Coatlicue, the Earth Mother.

Assessment

- 📁 Chapter 11 Test
- 📁 Performance Assessment

Multimedia Resources

- 🎭 Artsource® Performing Arts Package
- 💿 National Gallery Laser Disc
- 💿 National Museum of Women in the Arts CD-ROM
- 📼 Arts & Entertainment Videos

NATIONAL STANDARDS FOR ARTS EDUCATION

The National Standards for Arts Education provide guidelines for grade-appropriate competency in the visual arts. The Content Standards for grades 9–12 are:

1. Understanding and applying media, techniques, and processes.
2. Using knowledge of structures and functions.
3. Choosing and evaluating a range of subject matter, symbols, and ideas.
4. Understanding the visual arts in relation to history and cultures.
5. Reflecting upon and assessing the characteristics and merits of their work and the work of others.
6. Making connections between visual arts and other disciplines.

Listed below are the National Standards for the Visual Arts addressed in this chapter. For a breakdown of the categories listed under each content standard, refer to the *Reproducible Lesson Plans* booklet in the TCR.

  1. (a, b) **2.** (a, b) **3.** (a, b) **4.** (a, b, c) **5.** (c) **6.** (a, b)

HANDBOOK MATERIAL

Chuna McIntyre
(page 584)

CAREERS IN Art

(page 594)

Beyond the Classroom

Arts councils help raise awareness of the need for art education in and out of the classroom. Artists and patrons associated with arts councils can be valuable resources to the teacher interested in promoting and enhancing school arts programs. Track down resources in your area by visiting our Web site at *www.glencoe.com/sec/art*.

🕐 Out of Time?

If time does not permit teaching this chapter in its entirety, you may wish to preview the artwork and captions with students. Scan the heads in each lesson with students. Discuss the Looking Closely features and examine Identifying Icons in Aztec Art on page 259.

The Native Arts of the Americas

CHAPTER 11

The Native Arts of the Americas

Art & **Social Studies** ■ **FIGURE 11.1** Geography has an impact on the lifestyles of many cultural groups. The land along the northwestern coastline of North America provided an abundant supply of food and shelter resources. With these key ingredients of survival readily available, the Native American inhabitants had more time to develop their cultural traditions. The Sun Mask pictured here was used in an elaborate ritual staged by the Bella Coola to tell a mythic story about the creation of human beings and animals.

Sun Mask. Bella Coola, 19th century. Central British Columbia. Red cedar, alder; carved, painted. 108.5 × 106.9 cm (42³/₄ × 42¹/₈"). The Seattle Art Museum, Seattle, Washington. Gift of John Hauberg.

244

INTRODUCE

Chapter Overview

CHAPTER 11 introduces students to the cultural developments and native art of the Americas.

Lesson One discusses the art and crafts produced by native North American groups.

Lesson Two covers developments in the art and civilizations of Central and South America.

Studio Lesson guides students to create abstract ink drawings.

Art & **Social Studies**

Help students examine and discuss the artwork that opens this chapter. Ask students to consider the effect climate and geography had on the people who produced this mask. How do a plentiful supply of food and abundant shelter resources affect the daily lives of people?

Encourage students to research and determine the impact those factors had on the art produced. Provide time for students to share and discuss the results of their research.

National Standards

This chapter addresses the following National Standards for the Arts.

1. (a,b)	**4.** (a,b,c)
2. (a,b)	**5.** (c)
3. (a,b)	**6.** (a,b)

244

CHAPTER 11 RESOURCES

Teacher's Classroom Resources

📁 Advanced Studio Activity 11

📁 Application 11

🖱 Chapter 11 Internet Activity

📁 Studio Activities 14, 15

Assessment

📁 Chapter 11 Test

📁 Performance Assessment

Fine Art Resources

🏛 *Art in Focus* Transparencies

　　14, *Sakid Headdress Frontlet.*

　　15, Pitseolak Ashoona.

　　　　To Rescue a Drowning Hunter.

🖼 *Focus on World Art* Print 11

　　Aztec Stone Sculpture of Coatlicue, the Earth Mother.

While art flourished in India, China, and Japan, it also developed in North and South America. Anthropologists estimate that by the time Europeans arrived on these continents around A.D. 1500, there may already have been as many as 20 million people inhabiting the Americas. Up to 2,000 groups had settled in different areas across the land, and each had its own way of building, worshiping, and celebrating. Their art forms were complex and sophisticated. They included creation myths, symbolic religious rites, striking works of visual art, and a wide variety of musical traditions.

Introducing the Chapter

Ask students to share their own ideas about the first European explorers to reach the Americas. Then help students identify the first inhabitants of the American continents. Which different groups of native peoples are students able to identify? What do they know about the lives, culture, and arts of each group? Students will learn more about various native peoples as they study this chapter.

ART SOURCE **Dance** While studying this chapter, use *Performing Arts Handbook* page 584. Help students recognize how the dance of Chuna McIntyre reflects the traditions and beliefs of Native Americans.

YOUR Portfolio

While studying this chapter, you will create art that expresses something about your personality or a tradition that is meaningful to you. After you complete these artworks, select one and describe how it reflects your personality, traditions, or values. Keep your chosen artwork together with your notes in your portfolio.

Focus ON THE ARTS

LITERATURE
Scholars have decoded a complex system of picture writing from the few Aztec books that survive. These books, known as codices, record Aztec beliefs and myths.

MUSIC
Drums and rattles are the main types of Native American musical instruments. Rattles can be made out of gourds, turtle shells, carved wood, baskets, coconuts, bird beaks, cow horns, or seashells.

DANCE
Native American cultures incorporate dance in their ceremonies to suit many different purposes: to honor their families and their ancestors; to preserve time-honored traditions; and to bring good fortune to their people.

245

Focus ON THE ARTS

Divide the class into teams of two or three students. Assign each team a culture. The teams are to research religious dances practiced by the group and answer the following: (1) What is the name of the dance? (2) What is its purpose? (3) What is at least one thing about the dance that is symbolic? This symbolism can be represented by its form (circle, individuals dancing alone), its steps, hand movements, instruments played, placement of spectators, or anything else. (4) What does the symbolism mean? After the students have finished their brief reports, have the whole class discuss what the dances have in common and how they differ.

DEVELOPING A PORTFOLIO **Self-Evaluation.** Teachers are instrumental in promoting self-evaluation by initiating nonjudgmental dialogue with students. As the class progresses, conferences, annotations in a sketchbook or art journal, and constant encouragement to form critical opinions increase students' ability to recognize relative levels of merit. Stress the four steps for critiquing artworks found in every *Studio Lesson.* This procedure reinforces the idea that standards are real and can be agreed upon. Since portfolio evaluation is often a part of college admissions, students are better prepared to recognize standards when they have practiced self-evaluation procedures.

Native American Art

Focus

Lesson Objectives

After studying this lesson, students will be able to:
■ Identify and describe the contributions to art made by various Native American cultures.
■ Discuss the influence of geography and beliefs on the artworks created by those Native American cultures.

Building Vocabulary

Point out that the names of many of the fifty states are of Native American origin, as well as lakes, mountain ranges, and other features of topography. Explain that in this lesson students will learn other terms to add to their stock of Native American-based words.

Motivator

Prepare and distribute copies of a true-false questionnaire about Native American peoples. Among the statements that might be included are the following: *Some Native Americans produced totem poles. All art produced by Native Americans is applied art. No Native American artists are at work today.* After correcting misconceptions, proceed with the reading.

Introducing the Lesson

Ask students to describe artworks appearing in Lesson One. Have them compare their descriptions. Ask: What ideas and details recur frequently? What generalizations about Native American art can you make at this point? Have students keep notes in their journals and then review these after completing the lesson.

246

Native American Art

Vocabulary
■ Inuit   ■ sipapu
■ shaman   ■ adobe
■ potlatch ■ kiva
■ totem poles

Discover
After completing this lesson, you will be able to:
■ Identify the contributions to art made by Native American cultures in the Arctic, Northwest Coast, Southwest, Great Plains, and Woodland regions.
■ Discuss the influence of geography and beliefs on the artworks created by those Native American cultures.

*A*rchaeologists believe that the first visitors to North America were groups of Asian hunters who crossed an ancient land bridge across the Bering Strait. They began to arrive in what is now Alaska between 20,000 and 40,000 years ago. Gradually these people spread out to cover all parts of North and South America.

Some groups continued to live as hunters, whereas others settled and grew crops. Artifacts found in these regions show that all of the groups created art of some kind, which gives us insight into their cultures.

Arctic Region

The Arctic region, covering the vast coastal area between northeast Siberia and eastern Greenland, was the homeland of the **Inuit,** or *Eskimos.* (See map, Figure 11.2.) Compared to hunters and boat builders, artists played a minor role in Inuit life until recent times. They fished and hunted along with other members of their villages and turned to their art only when the opportunity presented itself. Artists did not imitate each other or criticize each other's work, and they did not consider themselves as belonging to any special group. They took their art seriously, though, and were proud of their accomplishments.

Inuit Art

The images created by Inuit artists reveal the importance attached to the animals they relied on for food: seal, walrus, fish, whale, and caribou. Other animals, such as the fox, wolf, and bear, were also represented in their art. The human figure was depicted in the masks and dolls they created.

Ivory Engraving
■ **FIGURE 11.3**

Figures are also found on engravings done on walrus ivory. In these engravings, Inuit artists used a kind of pictorial writing that described various activities and events associated with everyday life. In one such engraving on an ivory pipestem (Figure 11.3) a series of lively drawings records the activities associated with the daily quest for food.

Because the surfaces of this pipestem are less than one inch wide, the engraving takes the form of tiny, decorative circles and miniature figures. Despite their small size, the artist still managed to present an easy-to-read account of the hunt. To

MAP SKILLS
■ **FIGURE 11.2** Native American cultures developed in many different parts of North America. What differences would you expect to find between the artworks of cultures in these different regions?

246

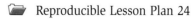

LESSON ONE RESOURCES

Teacher's Classroom Resources
📁 Appreciating Cultural Diversity 16, 17
📁 Art and Humanities 17, 18
📁 Cooperative Learning 17
📁 Enrichment Activities 20, 21

📁 Reproducible Lesson Plan 24
📁 Reteaching Activity 24
📁 Study Guide 24

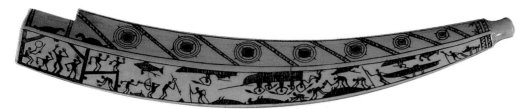

■ FIGURE 11.3 Many familiar activities are illustrated in this engraving. In what ways is this art similar to the Egyptian tomb paintings? How would you describe this style of art?

Inuit. Engraved tobacco pipestem. Norton Sound, Alaska. 19th century. Walrus ivory. 27.3 cm (10³/₄″) long. Arctic Studies Center, National Museum of Natural History, Smithsonian Institution, Washington, D.C.

TEACH
Using Map Skills

On a geographic or topographical map of Asia, have students locate Siberia. Ask them to trace the most logical path early migrating tribes would have taken across the Bering Strait, through Alaska, and into the present-day United States. Point out that, from this point, the dispersal of peoples is a topic of discussion and debate among anthropologists. Some of the oldest remains have been found in the desert in southwestern New Mexico. Ask students to discuss why this area has yielded what are reputed to be the oldest Native American artifacts. Discuss the phenomenon of desert dryness, and its preserving qualities, as opposed to the dampness and humidity of other areas of the country.

accent the engraved lines used in works like this, artists filled them in with color or darkened them with soot.

Inuit Masks
■ FIGURE 11.4

Frequently, Inuit art was created to serve the religious needs of the people. This was the case of a mask carved to represent a moon goddess (Figure 11.4). An Inuit **shaman,** or *leader believed to have healing powers,* wore such a mask during ceremonial dances. While dancing, the shaman would go into a trance and act as a messenger between the world of the living and the spirit world.

■ FIGURE 11.4 A mask of this kind was worn only by a shaman during ceremonial dances. What feelings do you think the mask evoked in viewers?

Inuit. Mask of Moon Goddess. Lower Yukon or Northwest Bering Sea. Before 1900. 63.5 cm (25¹/₄″) high. Hearst Museum of Anthropology, the University of California at Berkeley.

Northwest Coast Region

The vast North American territories below the arctic can be divided into a number of different regions. These regions are determined by similarities in culture and language of the Native Americans who originally inhabited the land.

For food, the Native Americans of the Northwest Coast depended on a plentiful supply of fish. Vast forests provided the timber used to construct their fishing boats and houses. These forests also offered abundant game and a rich variety of food plants. The prosperity and leisure that resulted from this abundant food supply contributed to the rise

of elaborate rituals and ceremonies designed to celebrate and demonstrate rank and status.

The Bella Coola people of British Columbia held masked rituals. They used the sun mask (Figure 11.1, page 244) to represent the sun during an elaborate ceremony about the creation of man.

Secret Societies of the Kwakiutl

The Kwakiutl, one of the Native-American groups inhabiting the Northwest region, identified people of differing rank and wealth according to their affiliation with one of several secret societies. The most distinguished of

Chapter 11 *The Native Arts of The Americas* **247**

Cross Curriculum

GEOGRAPHY. Provide students with a list of questions about the traditional Inuit lifestyle, such as the following: Where and how do the Inuit live? What kinds of work do men and women do? How many individuals today still maintain traditional lifestyles? Have volunteers select and research one of the above questions. Students should share their findings.

Aesthetics

Direct students' attention to the Inuit mask shown in Figure 11.4. Ask a group of volunteers to research similarities between these masks and ceremonial masks of Africa. What common function do the masks of the two different cultures serve? What are the most important differences among them?

◉ Technology ▌

Videocassettes. If you have access to a videocassette player in the classroom, you can take advantage of the many excellent videos available on Native American art and artists. Check with local natural history museums or museum catalogs to find out what they may have about groups near your area. Contact Native American museums of the southwestern states and ask if there are videos of Native American artists at work. Many subjects are available, including basketweaving, pottery, and other Native American crafts being created by authentic Native American artists and craftspeople.

Art Criticism

Direct students' attention to the dance mask in Figure 11.5. Ask them to identify the type of balance reflected in the work. What elements of art have been used to convey this sense of balance? Would students describe the mask as realistic or stylized? How does their answer to this last question reflect the function the mask served in Kwakiutl culture?

Cross Curriculum

LANGUAGE ARTS. Have students review the description of a Hamatsa ritual dance. Then have several volunteers write and stage a short play focusing on the acceptance of a new member into this society. If possible, the production should include appropriate music and props.

Art Criticism

Explain that the campaign to elevate people's awareness of Native American art, which had its roots in the 1970s, has been furthered by organizations like the Institute of American Indian Art located in Santa Fe, New Mexico. The institute is dedicated to education and to marketing fine art produced by young, upcoming Native American artists. Have groups of students investigate the work of this organization and of the more recently opened Institute of American Indian and Alaskan Native Arts and Culture, also based in Santa Fe.

■ **FIGURE 11.5**
Each of the beaks on this mask is movable. **What other design elements did the artist use to add drama to the mask?**

George Walkus. *Secret Society Mask.* Kwakiutl. British Columbia. 1938. Cedar, cedar bark, commercial paint, and string. 53.3 × 129.5 cm (21 × 51"). Denver Art Museum, Denver, Colorado.

these societies was for shamans only. Within this society, the most important members formed a subgroup known as the Hamatsa.

Like other societies, the Hamatsa held annual rituals to initiate new members, reinforce the status of old members, and demonstrate to nonmembers the extent of their magical powers. During these rituals, new members performed by screaming and leaping wildly about as rites were conducted to pacify the spirits. These rites were performed by other members of the society wearing fantastic costumes and masks.

The Hamatsa mask illustrated in Figure 11.5 is composed of several movable hinged pieces. Movement was intended to add surprise and drama to the ritual. Each of the several beaks on this mask could be manipulated to open and close, enhancing its threatening appearance. The eye areas were painted white to reflect the light from a ceremonial fire.

Time & Place
CONNECTIONS

Time Period
Native American
c. 1000 B.C.–A.D. 1900

LIVING SPACES. Unique and functional living spaces were designed to fit the lifestyle of Native Americans. Types of houses evolved and adapted as agriculture developed and the hunting lifestyle changed.

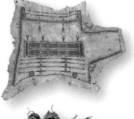

CLOTHING. Wearing apparel was crafted from animal hide and decorated with beads and dyes from natural plant sources. These items are from the Sioux and Arapaho Plains people.

*A*ctivity **Artifact Analysis.**
Imagine that you are employed by the government to document an expedition west of the Mississippi River in the early nineteenth century. The images shown here represent the clothing and habitat of the peoples you have encountered. What do they tell you about the societies from which they came?

Time & Place
CONNECTIONS
Native American Cultures

Have students examine and discuss the images in the Time & Place feature, and assign the activity. Let students meet in groups to discuss their ideas for the artifact analysis. Group members should consider the kinds of artifacts they might collect, the form their descriptions should take, and the conclusions they might draw. Interested students may want to refer to primary source documents as examples, and to share their conclusions with other group members. After planning discussions, have students work independently to write their own artifact analyses.

The Power of Ritual

Hamatsa rituals were carefully staged for dramatic impact. Subdued lighting permitted the use of elaborate props to add mystery and suspense. For example, a woman member might suddenly claim to have supernatural powers and, to prove it, ask another to behead her. The ritual was carried out and a replica of the woman's detached head, carved in wood, was prominently displayed in the dim light. This replica had been so realistically crafted that the audience, caught up in the excitement of the moment, believed they had actually witnessed the beheading. Thus, when the woman appeared with her head still intact, the audience was convinced of her power.

After a Hamatsa ceremony, or to celebrate some other important event, members of a tribe often celebrated with a **potlatch,** *an elaborate ceremonial feast.* This was a clan event, enabling the members of one clan to honor those of another while adding to their own prestige. At a potlatch, the host clan was able to exhibit its wealth and confirm its status by offering enormous quantities of food and valuable gifts to the members of the guest clan.

Totem Poles
■ FIGURE 11.6

The art of the Northwest includes the totem poles created by artists of various clans. **Totem poles** are *tall posts carved and painted with a series of animal symbols associated with a particular family or clan.* They can be thought of as similar to a European family's coat of arms. These poles were erected in front of a dwelling as a means of identification and a sign of prestige.

Totem poles like this one (Figure 11.6) rank among the world's largest and most visually appealing wood carvings. It may have taken a team of carvers as long as an entire year to carve a single totem pole. The amount of effort spent creating these poles can be more fully appreciated when one learns that every house had its own totem pole, each measuring from 30 to 50 feet high. Exceptional examples stand as high as 80 feet above the ground.

■ FIGURE 11.6 Wood carvers worked in teams to create totem poles like this one. What does this work reflect about the life and beliefs of the people who created and used it?

Haida totem pole. Prince of Wales Island. c. 1870. Originally 16.2 m (53') high. Taylor Museum of the Colorado Springs Fine Arts Center, Colorado Springs, Colorado.

The Design of Totem Poles

Each totem pole has a complex design. Every foot, from the bottom of the pole to the top, holds interest for the viewer. Thus, the viewer's eye is constantly engaged as it sweeps upward from one animal symbol to the next. Even more complex are totem poles that are completely painted, often with contrasting colors. This method of painting is a modern innovation. Early artists painted only the eyes, ears, and a few other details, using mainly black, red, blue-green, and occasionally white.

In the nineteenth century, as the wealth and prestige of some families grew, more symbols were added to their totem poles. The more symbols on a pole, the greater the prestige. This meant that the poles had to be built higher and higher. Eventually it was found that a single pole often proved to be inadequate, and additional poles had to be carved to accommodate all the symbols associated with a family.

Chapter 11 *The Native Arts of The Americas* **249**

CHAPTER 11
LESSON ONE

Aesthetics

Have students study the totem pole illustrated in Figure 11.6. What message do they think the totem pole is intended to communicate? What mood or feeling does the object convey? Do students think the individuals who created this pole considered the work to be applied art or fine art? Have students explain their responses.

Art Criticism

Have a volunteer read aloud the passage in the text indicating the measurements of totem poles. To help students fully understand the dimensions of such works, as well as the planning and dedication that must have gone into each, have students pace off 50 feet on the school grounds. Have students imagine that the path they have just paced off is occupied by a large fallen tree. Ask: How would you go about preparing the tree for use as a totem pole? How would you arrange for the work of individual artists to form a unified whole? How long would you allow for the task of converting the raw tree into a finished work of art?

Studio Skills

Provide students with cardboard tubes (paper towel rolls). Instruct them to wrap the tubes securely in sheets of white paper and fasten the sheets with transparent tape. Working with fine-point black felt-tip markers, students are to create designs on the prepared tubes reminiscent of those found on the totem pole in Figure 11.6 but also reflecting personal interests and beliefs. Remind students to use symmetrical balance and geometric shapes in their designs. Have students compare finished totem poles.

More About... **Potlatch.** The potlatch was such an important ceremony that it often took years to prepare for one. Once under way, a potlatch could involve several hundred guests and would continue for ten days or more. The task of providing food and shelter for that many people was in itself a great strain for the hosts, but their responsibilities did not end there. They also had to provide gifts for every guest, and these had to be selected with great care to match the recipient's rank. Sometimes the hosts destroyed leftover gifts, thereby gaining increased prestige. The guests were expected to eat as much food as possible as a sign of honor to their hosts.

Art History

Have students research the twentieth-century architectural innovation of the setback. Ask them to compare examples of contemporary buildings with setbacks to the pueblos that display this feature. Do students suppose Pueblo builders used the setback effect for purely aesthetic reasons? What other motivation may have prompted the decision to construct buildings in this fashion?

Critical Thinking

Have students examine the water jar in Figure 11.9. In what way is this object similar in shape and design to the *amphoras* created by the ancient Greeks? Are the two objects similar in function? Can both be considered as examples of applied art and fine art?

■ **FIGURE 11.7**

Taos Pueblo adobe dwellings. Taos, New Mexico. c. 1300.

■ **FIGURE 11.8**

Kiva. Pecos Pueblo, Pecos National Monument, New Mexico.

Southwest Region

Another cultural region extends from the northern area of Mexico to the southern foothills of the Rocky Mountains. Though many Native American groups lived in this territory, it is most often associated with the Pueblo people.

The Pueblo

Early Spanish explorers used the word *pueblo,* meaning village, to identify groups of people living in large, highly organized settlements. Ancient Pueblo dwellings (Figure 11.7) were built with walls made of **adobe,** or *sun-dried clay.* One of the most important parts of a pueblo was the **kiva,** a *circular underground structure* (Figure 11.8).

Pueblo Pottery
■ **FIGURE 11.9**

The Pueblo people were especially skillful in creating painted pottery (Figure 11.9). Each community developed its own distinctive shapes and painted designs. In the Rio Grande Valley of New Mexico, for example, Pueblo potters used black outlines and geometric shapes to create bold designs over a cream-colored base.

250   Unit Four *Art of Asia, the Americas, and Africa*

■ **FIGURE 11.9** The shape and painted design identify this water jar as a work from the Rio Grande Valley of New Mexico. **What elements of art can you identify in this design? What principles have been used to organize those elements?**

Water jar. Santo Domingo Pueblo, New Mexico. 1910. Pottery, polychrome. 24.13 cm (9½″) high × 24.45 cm (9⅝″) diameter. Denver Art Museum, Denver, Colorado.

■ **FIGURE 11.10** This saddle blanket, created for everyday use, is now on display in a museum. **How are the principles of harmony and variety used in this design? How is rhythm suggested?**

Saddle blanket. Navajo weaving. c. 1890. Wool. 129.5 × 83.8 cm (51 × 33″). Denver Art Museum, Denver, Colorado.

The Navajo

Another Southwestern tribe, the Navajo, learned the art of weaving from male Pueblo weavers. The Navajo weavers, who were women, began making cloth with looms at the beginning of the eighteenth century. As Spanish and Mexican settlers moved into the Southwest, they introduced new designs and patterns, which the Navajo adapted.

By the first half of the nineteenth century, the Navajo were using European cloth and dyes to create weavings that matched the quality of work produced on the best looms in Europe. A saddle blanket (Figure 11.10) exhibits many of the qualities associated with the finest Navajo weavings. These qualities include the closeness of the weave; rich, vibrant colors; and bold design. This kind of design was called an eye-dazzler, because it created the illusion of motion with its brilliant colors and repeated patterns of jagged-edged squares within squares.

Great Plains Region

Our most familiar image of Native Americans comes from the Great Plains. This area between the Mississippi River and the Rocky Mountains stretches from the Gulf of Mexico into Canada. Because their lands were generally not suited to farming, people living there became hunters.

Continually on the move, these tribes followed the great herds of bison that once covered this territory. This movement from place to place made the production of pottery, basketware, or weaving impractical. Work in wood or

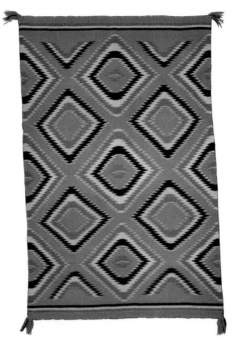

stone was limited mainly to the fashioning of bows and flint-tipped arrows for hunting.

Painted Animal Skins
■ **FIGURE 11.11**

The different tribes of the Plains—including Blackfeet, Crow, Cheyenne, and Sioux—were highly skilled in the preparation of skins used for clothing, footwear, shields, and various kinds of containers. These were painted or embroidered with porcupine quills and, later, glass beads.

Chapter 11 *The Native Arts of The Americas* **251**

CHAPTER 11
LESSON ONE

Art History

Have students compare and contrast the cultures of the Pueblo and Great Plains Native Americans. Ask: What were the most important differences between the lives of people in the two groups? How was the architecture of the two groups different? How do the crafts of the two groups differ? What factors may explain some of these differences, as well as any similarities that exist?

Critical Thinking

Direct students' attention to the photograph of the Adena Serpent Mound in Figure 11.12, page 252. Point out that the subject of the mound builders has long held great appeal for archaeologists and has spawned numerous myths about these peoples. Even today, most Americans fail to recognize the highly advanced civilizations that flourished in the central and southeastern river valleys of North America several centuries before the coming of Columbus. Ask pairs of students to compile a profile of the Adena, based partly on information provided in the text and partly on their own research.

Aesthetics

Have students study the stone pipe in Figure 11.13, page 253. Ask: What does it reveal about the stature and other physical attributes of its creators? How would color affect the impact this object has on the viewer? Would the impact of the object change if it were much larger? Does the fact that it was discovered in a burial mound affect the way it is perceived?

COOPERATIVE LEARNING

Kachina. Another Pueblo tradition is the Kachina. Emanating from a Pueblo belief of supernatural spirits called Kachina that once lived among the people, the sacred hand-carved figures teach children about traditions and rituals. Have pairs of students formulate and then seek answers to questions pertaining to this interesting art form. Questions might include the following: What are the standard features of a Kachina? When were such figures first made? Do they continue to be made? How does their use differ from figures we give to children in your culture?

Study Guide

Distribute *Study Guide* 24 in the TCR. Assist students in reviewing key concepts. 📁

Art and Humanities

Have students complete *Art and Humanities* 17, "Enjoying Native American Poetry," in the TCR. This activity calls on students to read poetry by Native American tribal poets and learn its connection to music, dance, and nature. Students conclude by writing a poem of their own. 📁

Studio Activities

Assign *Studio* 14, "Creating a Totem Image," in the TCR. Students interpret their own interests, personal characteristics and qualities in the form of a representative totem to hang on the door of their room at home. 📁

Art and Humanities

Assign *Art and Humanities* 18, "Probing the Mystery of the Mound Builders," in the TCR. In this worksheet, students learn about the lifestyle of the Adena Indians, builders of the Serpent Mound shown in Figure 11.12. Students proceed to design an earthwork that contains a message to future generations. 📁

Studio Activities

➤ Assign *Enrichment* 20, "Tracing the Path of the Ancient Anasazi," in the TCR. Students investigate the culture of the Anasazi, and then create a split-twig figure in the Anasazi style. 📁

➤ Have students complete *Enrichment* 21, "Symbolism of Native American Rug Weaving," in the TCR. In this activity, students read about and learn to decipher some of the symbols found in Hopi and Navajo woven rugs. 📁

■ **FIGURE 11.11** This robe presents images of success and bravery. It may have been worn to honor past victories and assure future triumphs. **What modern garments may have the same kinds of meaning for their wearers?**

George Washakie. Elkhide painted with design of *Sun Dance Ceremony.* Shoshoni, Wyoming. Purchased from artist about 1900. 175.3 × 152.4 cm (69 × 60"). Courtesy of the National Museum of the American Indian/Smithsonian Institution, New York, New York.

■ **FIGURE 11.12** Notice the size and the intricate shape of this mound. It is most easily appreciated in an aerial photograph. **What does this mound indicate about the technical abilities, interests, beliefs, and organization of the Adena?**

Serpent Mound State Memorial. Adams County, Ohio. c. 1000 B.C.–A.D. 300.

The men of the tribe usually painted the skins used for tepees, shields, and the chief's robes. The events pictured on a robe often were meant to illustrate the bravery of the chief who wore it, reminding everyone of his prowess in war (Figure 11.11). A robe of this kind was highly prized, and it was not unusual for the person wearing it to believe that it would protect him from harm.

Woodlands Region

The Woodlands included the area between the Mississippi River and the Atlantic Coast, and from the Great Lakes to the Gulf of Mexico. The geographic variety of this region resulted in the formation of many different cultures.

The Mound Builders

In prehistoric times, small villages were often clustered around monuments constructed in the form of large earthworks or mounds. Some took the form of high, narrow ridges of earth that encircled large fields. Smaller burial mounds, some conical and others domed, were placed within these large earthworks.

The purpose of these mounds remains a subject of debate among archaeologists. Some contend that they were built to create an impressive setting for spiritual ceremonies.

Among the first of the mound-building peoples were the Adena, who lived chiefly in the Ohio valley. Carbon dating tests reveal that their culture originated more than 2,500 years ago and flourished for about 700 years. The Adena attached great importance to honoring their dead. Early in their history, they built low mounds over burial pits; over time, these funeral mounds were built larger and larger.

The Great Serpent Mound
■ **FIGURE 11.12**

The Great Serpent Mound in Ohio (Figure 11.12) is the most impressive of these later Adena mounds. Formed to look like a huge serpent in the act of uncoiling, the mound is about a quarter of a mile long. A great many workers must have been involved in its creation. This kind of project would have required both organization and leadership.

𝒯eacher 𝒩otes

Classroom Resources. One way to enhance students' appreciation of contemporary Native American art is by creating a well-stocked classroom library of Native American audiovisual and print resources. If you have a videocassette recorder at your disposal, you might purchase one or more of the several available outstanding videotapes about Native American artists, such as *Daughters of the Anasazi,* which traces the life and work of potter Lucy Lewis, and *Maria,* which deals in like fashion with Maria Martinez and her son, Papovi Da. You might also consider subscribing to periodicals such as *American Indian Art* and *Southwest Art,* as well as obtaining brochures from appropriate art galleries.

Some of the Adena mounds were built in several layers and contained, in addition to the dead, a rich assortment of artifacts. Many tools, weapons, ornaments, and pottery pieces have been unearthed, but the most impressive art is the carvings. An excellent example (Figure 11.13) is a pipe in the form of a figure, discovered in a mound in southern Ohio. The mouthpiece for the pipe is above the head, and the bowl is placed between the legs. The pipe is carved of pipestone, a fine-grained, hard clay that has been smoothed, polished, and hardened by heat. Iron in the clay produced the spotty effect over its surface.

The fully rounded form and rigid posture give this work a solid, sturdy appearance. A muscular build with powerful shoulders and arms suggests great physical strength, even though the figure is no more than 8 inches high. A work like this demonstrates that early Native American artists were able to overcome the handicap imposed by primitive tools to create works that were expressive as well as visually appealing.

The Iroquois

One of the largest tribes living in the northeast area of the Woodlands region was the Iroquois. Expert wood carvers, the Iroquois created wooden masks that were usually painted and decorated with horse hair. The best known were created for a society of healers known as the False Faces because of the

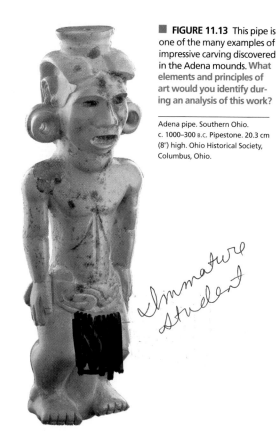

■ **FIGURE 11.13** This pipe is one of the many examples of impressive carving discovered in the Adena mounds. **What elements and principles of art would you identify during an analysis of this work?**

Adena pipe. Southern Ohio. c. 1000–300 B.C. Pipestone. 20.3 cm (8″) high. Ohio Historical Society, Columbus, Ohio.

Immature Student

masks they wore. These sacred masks represented the spirits who gave healers the power they needed to treat illnesses. Because they were considered so powerful, these masks were hidden away when not in use.

LESSON ONE REVIEW

Reviewing Art Facts

1. Who used a mask such as the one representing a moon goddess (Figure 11.4, page 247), and for what purpose?
2. What was the purpose of a kiva, and what are its main features?
3. In which art did the Navajo excel?
4. Explain why the Native American tribes from the Great Plains region did not create such items as pottery or basketware, and tell what they did create.

▶ Activity... *Creating a Symbol*

The Hamatsa of the Northwest Coast region used masks in rituals. Study the masks of various cultures in Figure 11.1, page 244, 11.4, page 247; Figure 11.5, page 248; and Figure 12.19, page 278. Pay special attention to how the artist made use of design motifs with line and texture. Masks were used as symbols, in rituals, and as a way to represent events in nature.

Using clay, create a small symbol that represents your school or symbols from the natural environment. Make your symbol small enough to use as a piece of jewelry to be worn on a cord or chain around your neck. If possible, fire and glaze your work, or finish by painting or staining it.

Chapter 11 *The Native Arts of The Americas* **253**

Art in Mexico and in Central and South America

Focus

Lesson Objectives

After studying this lesson, students will be able to:

■ Explain what is meant by the term *pre-Columbian*.

■ Identify the first great civilizations in Mexico and describe the artworks for which this civilization is best known.

■ Describe the cultural and artistic achievements of the great civilizations of Central and South America.

Building Vocabulary

As they consider the Vocabulary term for this lesson, let students identify the prefix and its meaning. Then have them identify the name on which the word root is based, and ask volunteers to use these word parts to build a definition of the word.

Motivator

Write the phrase *American art* on the board. Then arrange along the chalk rail numbered reproductions of unmistakably American paintings, for example a Winslow Homer painting, along with photographs of Mayan temples, Zapotec funerary urns, and other "American" works of art. Have students record in their journals the numbers of works that meet the description "American art." Then proceed with the reading.

Art in Mexico and in Central and South America

Vocabulary
■ pre-Columbian

Discover
After completing this lesson, you will be able to:
■ Explain what is meant by the term pre-Columbian.
■ Identify the contributions to art made by the Olmec, the Maya, the Aztecs, and the Incas.

*T*he term **pre-Columbian** is used when referring to *the various cultures and civilizations found throughout North and South America before the arrival of Christopher Columbus in 1492.* Many of these civilizations created works of art that give insights into their cultures and ways of life. Discovery and study of these works have helped unravel some of the mysteries of these ancient peoples.

The Olmec

The first great civilization in Mexico was the Olmec, which dates from as early as 1200 B.C. to A.D. 500. These people lived on the great coastal plain of the Gulf of Mexico. They settled mainly in the areas that are now Veracruz and Tabasco. The Olmec are believed by many to have made the first Mexican sculptures. They left the earliest remains of carved altars, pillars, sarcophagi, and statues in Mexico.

The Olmec's most surprising works were gigantic heads carved in volcanic rock (Figure 11.14). Eighteen have been discovered thus far. They may represent the severed heads of losers in an ancient game known as *pelota*. These sculptures measure 8 feet high and weigh up to 40 tons.

■ **FIGURE 11.14** This huge head presents an intimidating image to the viewer. What aesthetic qualities seem most appropriate when making and defending a judgment about this work?

Olmec. Colossal Head. 1200 B.C. –A.D. 500. Basalt. 243.8 cm (8′) high. Anthropology Museum, Veracruz, Mexico.

254

LESSON TWO RESOURCES

Teacher's Classroom Resources

📁 Appreciating Cultural Diversity 18

📁 Art and Humanities 19

📁 Enrichment Activities 22, 23

📁 Reproducible Lesson Plan 25

📁 Reteaching Activity 25

📁 Study Guide 25

■ **FIGURE 11.15** Note the similarities between the face on this jadeite mask and the face on the huge head in Figure 11.15. Do you think that knowing when, where, why, and by whom this mask was created would affect your judgment of it? What does your answer to this question tell you about the value of art history?

Olmec. Mask. Tabasco, Mexico. 900–500 B.C. Jadeite. 18.1 × 16.5 × 10.1 cm (7¹⁄₈ × 6⁹⁄₁₆ × 4"). Dallas Museum of Art, Dallas, Texas. Gift of Mr. and Mrs. Eugene McDermott, the McDermott Foundation, and Mr. and Mrs. Algur H. Meadows and the Meadows Foundation, Inc.

Olmec Sculpture

Some of the same features found on those heads can be seen in a realistic jadeite mask that may have once graced the tomb of an Olmec ruler (Figure 11.15). The huge heads and this striking mask have the same mouth that droops at the corners. The face on this mask is certainly not warm or welcoming. Eyes peer out at you from under heavy eyelids, and the open mouth suggests a snarl rather than speech. These features were intended to convey power, for the king not only ruled over the people but was thought to have a link to the supernatural world.

Although it is reasonable to assume that the Olmec produced architecture of the same high quality as their sculpture, no examples have been discovered.

The Maya

The most elegant of the pre-Columbian cultures was the Mayan. The Maya controlled vast lands that included what are now Yucatan, Guatemala, and Honduras. They never advanced technically beyond the Stone Age but possessed highly developed skills in a number of other areas. They became great builders, devised an elaborate system of mathematics, and invented a precise calendar.

Mayan Religion

In order to understand the chilling rituals that were an important part of Mayan culture, it is necessary to learn about their religious beliefs. The Maya believed that the gods created humans through self-sacrifice and that the first people were formed by mixing maize, or corn, with water. These people were brought to life with the blood of the gods. To repay this debt, humans were required to return blood to the gods, who in turn were expected to maintain the people's strength and nourishment.

The most sacred rituals in the Mayan religion were characterized by efforts to secure blood for the gods. Public ceremonies typically included rituals in which the Mayan ruler and his wife drew their own blood and captives taken in war were sacrificed.

Chapter 11 *The Native Arts of The Americas* **255**

Have students study the Olmec head sculpture in Figure 11.14, noting its size. Ask: What does the capacity to produce larger-than-life works of art such as this reveal about a people? Explain that students will read about several civilizations that functioned in many respects on a very advanced level.

Aesthetics

Direct students' attention to the mask in Figure 11.15. What adjectives would they use to describe the appearance of this face? How many of these words could be applied to the colossal head sculpture in Figure 11.14?

Studio Skills

Remind students that the mask shown in Figure 11.15 was found on a ruler's tomb, and have them discuss what this fact might imply about the purpose and aesthetic statement of such artifacts. Then provide students with slabs of clay, 1 inch thick, and challenge them to carve a negative impression of a face similar to the one depicted in the Olmec mask. Explain that the carving is to serve as a mold for a plaster relief and that concave and convex carved details will be reversed in the final product. When the clay is firm enough to hold its shape, have students pour in mixed plaster. Students may wish to paint their completed plaster reliefs.

More About... **Maya Symbolism.** The Mayas sometimes used animals as artistic subjects, but they avoided offending or mistreating other creatures because, like humans, animals were paid respect in Mayan beliefs. Mayans gave special respect to dogs, which they kept as pets. The serpent was especially significant according to Mayan tradition. The dragon provided shamans with the ability to perceive and interpret revelations during religious ceremonies. Snakes were common in representation of rulers, where they symbolized a governor's right to rule. A feathered and bearded serpent represented the Mayan god Kikulcan, also known as Quetzalcóatl in other pre-Columbian cultures.

Did You Know?

Pelota was a game reserved for the nobility. It made use of a hard rubber ball, called a *pilota*.

Cross Curriculum

COMMUNICATION. After students have been introduced to the Mayan culture, explain that Mayan weavings often contained images of brightly colored animals that functioned as symbols (for example, a snake symbolized the earth, eagles represented life and death). Point out that for centuries people have used various kinds of nonverbal communication to convey their thoughts to others. Have students work in groups to report on specific examples of non-verbal communication. Possibilities include semaphore, international traffic signs, body language, and certain forms of signing used by the hearing impaired.

Art Criticism

Have students compare the heads in Figures 11.15 (page 255) and 11.18. Ask: How do these figures compare in size? Do they exhibit the same types of lines and shapes? Do you see any Olmec influence in the Mayan figure in Figure 11.18? How do you suppose the artwork depicted in Figure 11.14, page 254, evolved into the elaborate reliefs of the Mayans?

Art History

Have students obtain photographs of Mayan and Aztec pyramids and compare these structures with those produced by the Egyptians. Then have them discuss the following questions: How did the three structures differ in function and purpose? Were the building techniques different, and if so, how? What was the unifying element among the various pyramid types? How do you explain the building of such similar structures on two different continents by peoples who clearly never met?

■ **FIGURE 11.16** The Mayan city at Tikal included temples and other structures built with a cement-like compound made from burnt lime. The pyramids here are 230 feet high. **What other ancient culture developed a cement to create buildings that have lasted through the centuries?**

Maya. Great Plaza of Tikal, general view. Tikal, Guatemala. A.D. 150–700.

Mayan Architecture

Mayan cities were constructed with vast central plazas to accommodate the masses of people who gathered to witness these ceremonies. Rich reliefs covered the buildings, monuments, and temples around and within these plazas (Figure 11.16). At first, these carvings were simple and realistic, but later they became more elaborate and complex. Figures were carved with so many ornaments that it is often difficult to separate them from backgrounds filled with symbols and inscriptions referring to various important events.

Mayan architecture and sculpture were painted. Examples have been found in which traces of pigment still cling to the limestone surface. The carved surfaces were painted in contrasting colors, and this may have helped separate the figure from the background. Red commonly was used for the skin areas, blue and green for ornaments, green for feathers, and blue for garments.

Mayan Relief Sculpture
■ **FIGURES 11.17 and 11.18**

This Mayan relief (Figure 11.17) shows a royal priestess dressed in a rich costume and wearing an elaborate plumed headdress. Her face is in profile. The forehead slants back, the large nose dominates, and the chin recedes. These features, found in most Mayan heads, are easily observed in a detail from the Mayan relief illustrated in Figure 11.18.

The Maya built their first cities by A.D. 320. Their civilization reached a peak, declined, revived, and declined again before the arrival

256 **Unit Four** *Art of Asia, the Americas, and Africa*

More About... **Archaeology.** Archaeologists, anthropologists, and prehistorians have argued for years about the precise meaning of the term *civilization.* Archaeologist Charles Redman organized a set of ten primary and secondary characteristics common to all civilizations. Primary characteristics include settlement in cities, full-time specialization among members of the labor force, concentration of surpluses, a well-defined class system, and state organization. Secondary characteristics include monumental public works, trade between parties separated by long distances, standardized monumental artwork, a system of writing, and development of arithmetic, geometry, and astronomy.

■ **FIGURE 11.17** Originally, contrasting colors probably helped the viewer distinguish between this intricately carved figure and its elaborate background. **Do you think attempts to restore the painted surfaces would add to this work of art or detract from it? Explain your ideas.**

Royal Woman. Relief carving, Chiapas or Tabasco, Mexico. A.D. 650–750. Limestone, stucco, paint. 220.3 × 76.8 × 15.2 cm (86³/₄ × 30¹/₄ × 6"). Dallas Museum of Art, Dallas, Texas. Foundation for the Arts Collection, gift of Mr. and Mrs. James H. Clark.

■ **FIGURE 11.18** Note the similarities between this face and the face of the *Royal Woman* in Figure 11.17. **Is this a successful work of art? On what aesthetic qualities did you base your decision?**

Mayan relief (detail). Yaxchilan, Mexico.

of Hernando Cortés in 1519. The Spanish conquest completed the downfall of the Mayan culture.

The Aztecs

When Cortés waded ashore at Veracruz in 1519, a people called the Aztecs had nearly succeeded in conquering Mexico from the

Atlantic Ocean to the Pacific Ocean and as far south as Guatemala. After a campaign lasting less than 200 years (1324–1521), the Aztec conquest was complete. Following a legendary prophecy that they would build a city where an eagle perched on a cactus with a serpent in its mouth, the Aztecs settled in the marshes on the west shore of the great "Lake of the Moon," Lake Texcoco.

Chapter 11 *The Native Arts of The Americas* **257**

Aesthetics

Direct students' attention to the Aztec carving in Figure 11.21, page 260. Have students consider independently how they would complete the following statement concerning the figure: *The aesthetic theory under which this work would be judged the greatest success is _____.* Instruct students with like opinions to form teams, and have teams debate this issue.

Art History

In 1978, one of the greatest Aztec archaeological finds of all time was unearthed. Some 7,200 artifacts were found in the vicinity of a ruined temple. One of the most remarkable of the artifacts turned up was a huge carved circular stone. Called the Coyolxauhqui Stone by scholars, the object depicts a decapitated woman representing the Aztec moon goddess. According to legend, this goddess was murdered by her brother Huitzilopochtli. Ask a group of volunteers to research the Coyolxauhqui Stone and to present their findings to the rest of the class.

COOPERATIVE LEARNING

Oral Reports. In addition to being advanced in mathematics and architecture, the Maya also developed a sophisticated religious world view. Like other tribes of North, Central, and South America, the Maya were governed by shamans, who served as mediums between the spiritual and physical worlds. Although the shamans were almost exclusively male, the Mayan religion emphasized the equal importance of the two sexes. In the Mayan religious view, humans and animals were believed to share the surface of a world confined to a single branch of a ceiba tree. Have a group of students research more of the religious rituals of this civilization and prepare an oral report to be presented to the class.

Critical Thinking

Have students write a paragraph in which they identify the accomplishment covered in Lesson Two that they find to be the most compelling. Students may choose an artistic achievement of one of the civilizations they read about, or they may respond to some other facet of culture. Be sure students explain their choices.

Did You Know?

Though all Aztec artists enjoyed the respect of the people, those known as "painters in red and black" were considered most important; their work involved the mysterious use of signs and symbols.

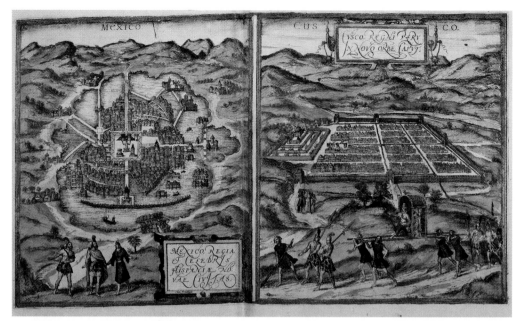

■ **FIGURE 11.19** The city of Tenochtitlán was developed into an agricultural center and marketplace. Explain how the Aztec population made the best use of the limited land when the city was created.

The Aztec City of Tenochtitlán (Mexico City). Left: Tenochtitlán. Right: Cuzco (the Inca City). Etching, tinted by Franz Hogenberg (c. 1538–1590).

Tenochtitlán

The Aztec settlement grew into the splendid city of Tenochtitlán on the site of the present-day Mexico City (Figure 11.19). Built on an island in the lake, it contained huge white palaces, temples, gardens, schools, arsenals, workshops, and a sophisticated system of irrigation canals and aqueducts. City streets and palace walls were scrubbed clean by thousands of slaves. Bridges carried the streets over a network of canals that crisscrossed the city. Raised highways led from the mainland toward a spacious temple complex at the city's heart.

The Aztecs were a warlike people driven to continuous combat by their religious beliefs. They believed that human sacrifices were necessary to keep the universe running smoothly. Against a backdrop of brilliantly painted architecture and sculpture, sacrifices of human hearts were made to ensure that the gods remained in good spirits. At the dedication of the great temple at Tenochtitlán, 20,000 captives were sacrificed. They were led up the steps of the high pyramid-temple to an altar where chiefs and priests waited to slit them open and remove their hearts.

Aztec Sculpture

Art was closely linked to these rituals. Statues to the gods were carved and placed in the temples atop stepped pyramids. There were even statues of priests and celebrants dressed in the skins of flayed victims who had been sacrificed. The sculpture shown in Figure 11.21, on page 260 depicts a man dressed in this way. The artist has shown stylized flay marks and the slash in the skin where the victim's heart was removed.

Aztec Picture Writing

The Aztecs also used a system of picture writing. This writing was done on sheets of parchment that were joined and accordion-folded to form a book. This kind of painted book, later called a codex by the Europeans, was produced by the most highly respected artists in Aztec society (Figure 11.20).

More About... **Aztec Capital.** The Aztec capital was actually made up of two cities built on two different islands, Tenochtitlán, the administrative center, and Tlatelolco, which was primarily an economic center. Tenochtitlán was also a ceremonial center, housing twenty-five pyramids and one massive pyramid topped by twin temples. One temple was dedicated to the god Tlaloc—the god of water, rain and fertility—and the other to Huitzilopochtli, the war god. It was to the great Huitzilopochtli that some twenty thousand victims were sacrificed. The great pyramid of Tenochtitlán was about half the size of the Great Pyramid of Cheops in Egypt.

Identifying Icons in Aztec *Art*

This painting is from *The Book of Days*, a codex from which personal destinies were predicted. This codex reveals a taste for fantastic images created with clear, bright colors and flat shapes. There is no shading or modeling to suggest three-dimensional forms. Heads are large and torsos and limbs short. These paintings were never meant to illustrate people or events associated with the real world. The figures, most with humanlike heads, torsos, and limbs, do not represent human beings. Their poses and gestures communicate ideas and combinations of ideas. These paintings serve as both writings and pictures.

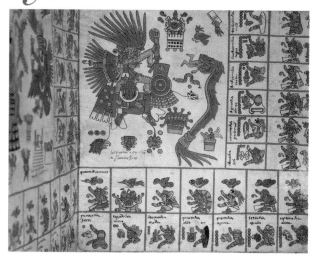

■ **FIGURE 11.20** Aztec. Painting of the gods Tezcalipoca and Quetzalcóatl. From Codex Borbonicus. Early 1500s. Bibliothèque du Palais Bourbon, Paris, France.

1 Tezcalipoca is dressed in the flayed skin of a sacrificial victim. Note that the hands dangling from the god's upraised arms are actually part of the skin of the victim.

3 Quetzalcóatl, the life god, is shown as a feathered serpent. The Aztecs believed that Quetzalcóatl was originally an old priest who set himself on fire in order to purify his people. He returned to life in the form of the planet Venus, promising to return from the east to redeem his people.

2 Tezcalipoca, the war god and god of the night winds, wears a necklace of seashells.

Chapter 11 *The Native Arts of The Americas* **259**

Art History

Have students note the date when Machu Picchu (Figure 11.22, page 261) was completed. Point out that it was within a year of this date that the renowned Renaissance sculptor Michelangelo began work in Florence on his statue of David. Let students work in small groups to research other events around the world during that same time period. Schedule class time in which the groups can compare and discuss their findings.

Art History

Have students note the passage in the text describing the precision with which the Inca fitted together the huge stone blocks of Machu Picchu. Ask what other ancient civilization students have read about that was similarly adept at fitting together large stones. Do the structures of that culture resemble those of the Incas? Have they survived equally well?

Identifying Icons in Aztec *Art*

The Book of Days. Have students examine the painting, and then read and discuss the explanations of the figures and symbols. Suggest that interested volunteers learn more about *The Book of Days* and share the results. Then instruct the class to create a grid chart in which they indicate along one axis the names of cultures they have read about; along the other they should list gods and goddesses that were prominent in those cultures. In each intersecting cell on the chart, students should note: the way dieties were represented in art, the way these representations affected other art of the culture.

Study Guide

Distribute *Study Guide* 25 in the TCR. Assist students in reviewing key concepts. 📁

Art and Humanities

Have students complete *Appreciating Cultural Diversity* 18, "Imagining a Trip to Mexico," in the TCR. In this activity, students plan an imaginary trip to Mexico to learn about the cultures of the ancient Aztecs and Maya, as well as about contemporary Mexican arts. Students are called to make an itinerary for their trip and to record journal entries of their experiences. 📁

Studio Activities

Assign *Studio* 15, "Linoleum Block Print," in the TCR. This worksheet asks students to make a block print working with linoleum. As a source of inspiration for their prints, students consider the dynamic designs of the Inuit stoneblock printers. 📁

Art and Humanities

Assign *Enrichment* 22, "Getting the Feel of Inuit Sculpture," in the TCR. In this worksheet, students study soapstone carvings by Inuit sculptors as a means of learning about this form. Students are then given the opportunity to try creating a "feeling" sculpture of their own. 📁

■ **FIGURE 11.21** Notice that this figure's garment is made from the skin of a flayed victim sacrificed to the gods. How does an understanding of Aztec religious beliefs help you understand this work?

Aztec. *Xipe Impersonator.* 1450–1521. Volcanic stone, shell, and paint. 69.8 × 28 × 22.2 cm (27$^1/_2$ × 11 × 8$^3/_4$"). Dallas Museum of Art, Dallas, Texas. Gift of Mr. and Mrs. Eugene McDermott, the McDermott Foundation, and Mr. and Mrs. Algur H. Meadows and the Meadows Foundation, Inc.

When Cortés, a powerful conqueror from Spain, arrived in November of 1519, he received a friendly welcome from the Aztecs, who believed him to be their legendary redeemer, Quetzalcóatl. Cortés came from the east, just as Quetzalcóatl had promised he himself would. Cortes' arrival heralded the beginning of the end for the Aztec Empire.

Art in Peru: The Incas

The Incas are the best known of all the ancient peoples who inhabited Peru. They were a small tribe who established their rule in the Valley of Cuzco, with the city of Cuzco as their capital. Between the thirteenth and fifteenth centuries, the power of the Incas grew until their empire stretched from Quito in Ecuador to central Chile—a distance of more than 3,000 miles.

The Incas demonstrated great organizational skill and managed to control their far-flung empire even though they had no written language. Their only method of calculating and keeping records was the use of knotted strings of different colors known as *quipu*. These were kept in a secure place at Cuzco.

Inca Engineering and Communication

Skillful engineers, the Inca joined all parts of their empire together with a network of roads and bridges. They also established an efficient system of relay runners who used these roads to carry messages to every corner of the empire. Runners were expected to wait for any royal dispatch and, when it arrived, to race with it to the next village, where another runner waited. This system was so efficient that when members of the royal family at Cuzco wanted fresh fish from the Pacific, runners carried it hundreds of miles through the Andes Mountains in two days. Running in short spurts at breakneck speed, a series of couriers could cover 250 miles a day—faster than the speed of messengers on horseback galloping over the famous roads of Rome.

Inca Architecture

The capital at Cuzco and other Inca cities featured solid structures of stone built on a large scale, some of which have survived to the present day. The durability of these buildings was due to the precision with which each block of stone was fit into place. It is believed that each of these blocks may have been placed in a sling of some kind and then swung against those that were to be placed below and beside it. Swinging continued until the surfaces were ground to a perfect fit. The buildings were not decorated with sculpture or relief carvings, but interior walls were often covered with fabric wall hangings decorated with geometric patterns.

Machu Picchu
■ **FIGURE 11.22**

Machu Picchu (Figure 11.22) was an Inca city built to protect the people from attacks by hostile tribes living in the jungle to the east.

More About... **Incas.** Two aspects of the Incan Empire should be noted when considering current ideas of civilization. First, the cities were not the usual settlement type, and second, the people had no written language. (Their spoken language, Quechua, was imposed upon all they conquered.) Their primary religion was a form of ancestor worship centering on the perpetual care of the mummies of their dead, which were brought to participate in major ceremonies. Unlike the Aztecs, the Inca practiced human sacrifice only rarely; even the sacrifice of animals was relatively unusual. Because the Incan Empire was designed to be ruled by a small, elite group, Francisco Pizarro was able to overtake them with only 168 soldiers.

■ FIGURE 11.22
Machu Picchu was built on a high, isolated site to protect its inhabitants. What does this city tell you about the people who built it?

Inca. Aerial view of Machu Picchu. Peru. c. 1500.

CHAPTER 11
LESSON TWO

One of the world's most magnificent sites, the city is dramatically perched on a ridge between two rugged mountain peaks, 8,000 feet above sea level. Like other Inca buildings, those in Machu Picchu were constructed of huge stone blocks cut and locked into place with such skill that they have withstood centuries of wars and earthquakes.

By the time the Spaniards, under Francisco Pizarro, reached Peru in 1532, the Inca empire had been weakened by civil war. It fell easily to Pizarro and his handful of men.

LESSON TWO REVIEW

Reviewing Art Facts
1. Describe the artworks for which the Olmec were best known.
2. Why were Mayan cities constructed with large central plazas?
3. How was art linked to sacrificial rituals in the Aztec culture?
4. What was Machu Picchu? Where and why was it built?

> ### Activity... *Designing a Calendar*
The Mayan invention of an accurate and precise calendar is evidence of the brilliance of their civilization. Find more information on the Mayan calendar and on the ancient calendars and timekeeping systems of the Babylonians, Egyptians, Greeks, Romans, or Chinese. More modern calendars are the Julian calendar and the Gregorian calendar, which are used today.

Create a calendar to keep accurate records of the passage of time for an imaginary culture. Work in groups and imagine you are forming a new culture (perhaps a space colony). Determine the divisions your calendar will have and what the divisions will be called. Create a unique design for your calendar, and mount it on poster board.

Chapter 11 *The Native Arts of The Americas* **261**

ASSESS
Checking Comprehension
➤ Have students respond to the lesson review questions. Answers are given in the box below.
➤ Assign *Application* 11, "Lost and Found," in the TCR to reinforce what students have learned. 📁

Reteaching
Assign *Reteaching* 25, found in the TCR. Have students complete the activity and review their responses. 📁

Enrichment
Assign students *Enrichment* 23, "Planning an Aztec Calendar," in the TCR. In this activity, students study the imagery, symbolism, and geometry in the Aztec Calendar Stone. They then proceed to plan and construct a large calendar representing the history of the United States in the manner of the Aztec calendar. 📁

Extension
Explain that there are many sculptures of only the human head found in the cultures of the world (for example, in Celtic tribal art, or in the mysterious heads of Easter Island). Have students research these and other representations of the human head in ancient cultures. How do these various types of heads compare with those of the civilizations of the pre-Columbian Americas?

CLOSE
Ask students to retrace the steps of the Spaniards as they came to America, determining ways in which they influenced the art and architecture of the early peoples. Where is their influence most pronounced?

LESSON TWO REVIEW

Answers to Reviewing Art Facts
1. Gigantic heads carved in stone.
2. To accommodate large crowds witnessing religious ceremonies.
3. Statues of gods were placed in temples, atop stepped pyramids; some depicted priests dressed in skins of flayed victims.
4. Inca city built between mountain peaks to protect the inhabitants from attack.

Activity... *Designing a Calendar*
Encourage students to work together in listing ideas about their imaginary culture and then in creating an original design for their culture's calendar. Post the completed work and let students discuss it.

Abstract Ink Drawing of an Insect, Fish, or Other Animal

Objectives

- Complete a design in india ink that combines four identical abstract images of an insect, fish, or other animal.
- Use repetitious, flat geometric shapes and contrasting light and dark values.
- Suggest a sense of movement associated with the insect, fish, or other animal represented.

Motivator

On the board, write the headings *insects, fish, other animals.* Ask students to identify examples of each. For every specific example, have students suggest verbs that describe the different kinds of movements associated with it.

Aesthetics

Ask students to imagine that they are early explorers who unexpectedly come across a totem pole similar to the one illustrated in Figure 11.6 (page 249). Having never seen anything to compare with this huge carving, how would they react? Would they be inclined to regard it as art? Why or why not? Do theories of art such as imitationalism, formalism, and emotionalism help them answer questions of this kind?

Critiquing

Have students apply the steps of art criticism to their own artwork, using the "Examining Your Work" questions on this page.

262

Abstract Ink Drawing of an Insect, Fish, or Other Animal

Materials

- Pencil and sketch paper
- Ruler and compass
- Section of mat board, 10 × 12 inches or larger
- India ink
- Pen and small, pointed brush

Using india ink, complete a design that combines four identical images of an abstract drawing of an insect, fish, or other animal. This drawing should exhibit a pattern of repetitious, flat geometric shapes and contrasting light and dark values. Combine the four images to suggest a sense of movement associated with the insect, fish, or other animal represented.

Inspiration

Examine the totem pole illustrated in Figure 11.6, page 249. What kinds of images are included in this design? Are these images carved to look lifelike, or are they simplified? What term is used to describe works in which artists focus attention on the elements and principles of art and on simplified forms? Can you identify any other artworks in this book that are created in this same manner?

■ **FIGURE 11.23** Student Work

Process

1. Select an insect, fish, or other animal to use as your subject. Complete a series of pencil sketches in which you first eliminate all unnecessary details and then transform the image into a simplified pattern of flat, geometric shapes.
2. Complete a final line drawing of your simplified animal measuring about 8 inches (20 cm) in length. Cut this out and, with the flat side of the pencil, darken the back of it. Place the drawing on a section of mat board and trace four copies of it. Be certain you create a sense of movement through the placement of your drawings. This movement should be characteristic of the animal depicted—hopping, swimming, or running, for example. You may find that this movement can be enhanced by overlapping the four drawings.
3. Use india ink to add light and dark value contrasts to the geometric shapes in your design.

— Examining Your Work

Describe. Does your design consist of four images of the same insect, fish, or other animal? Is the animal easily identified? What features make this identification possible?

Analyze. Do the images in your design present a pattern of repetitious, flat geometric shapes? Are these shapes rendered in contrasting light and dark values? Is a sense of movement realized by the placement of the four images in your design?

Interpret. Is the sense of movement in your composition characteristic of the insect, fish, or other animal represented? What word best describes this movement?

Judge. Why would formalism be the most appropriate aesthetic theory to use when examining and judging your design? Why would imitationalism be unsuitable in this instance? Using the formalist theory, do you feel that your composition is successful? What do you regard as its most visually pleasing feature?

262

— ASSESSMENT

Peer Review. Have students work with partners to review and reconsider the decisions they made in planning and carrying out this project. Partners should discuss ideas raised by questions such as these: What other animal might have been a more appropriate subject for this drawing? What unnecessary details should have been deleted? Which other details—if any—should have been included. What kinds of changes might have created a more convincing sense of movement? Where and how should the use of value contrasts be revised?

To close this peer-review discussion, encourage each student to identify at least three especially successful aspects of his or her partner's work.

Reviewing the Facts

Lesson One

1. What kind of images were created by the Inuit artists of the Arctic region? Why was so much importance attached to those images?
2. What is a potlatch?
3. What purpose were totem poles intended to serve?
4. In what North American region did the Pueblo people live? What kind of art were they noted for?
5. What kinds of monuments did the Adena build?

Lesson Two

6. What is meant by the term *pre-Columbian*?
7. What group was thought to have made the first Mexican sculptures?
8. What made Mayan relief sculpture of figures so elaborate and complex?
9. What features are found in most heads in Mayan sculpture?
10. What method did the Aztecs use to make their painted books?
11. What made Inca buildings so durable?

Thinking Critically

1. **SYNTHESIZE.** Working with another student, select an artwork illustrated in Lesson One in this chapter and prepare a list of ten single-word clues to describe it. These clues should focus on: subject matter (if appropriate); elements and principles of art; idea, mood, or feeling expressed. Present your word clues one at a time in class. How many clues are necessary before others can correctly identify the artwork?
2. **ANALYZE.** Look at the sculpture *Xipe Impersonator* (Figure 11.21, page 260). Describe the art elements found in the work. Discuss how the artist uses these elements according to the principles of harmony, variety, and balance.

 DANCE. Use the *Performing Arts Handbook* on page 584, to learn about the native dance of an Inuit artist, Chuna McIntyre.

CAREERS IN Art If you enjoy studying or creating art, read about a fascinating art-related career opportunity in the *Careers in Art Handbook*, page 594.

*inter*NET CONNECTION Visit Glencoe Art Online at *www.glencoe.com/sec/art*. Explore native arts and have a look at online archaeological expeditions.

Technology Project
Totem Symbols

A totem is a symbol that represents significant ideas, beliefs, and events. Totem poles symbolized the status and history of a clan or a family. They were often extremely complex and took a long time to create. The use of such symbols to stand for families, clans, or individuals is common in many ancient and contemporary cultures.

1. Study the totem in Figure 11.6, page 249. Each section represents an equally important part of the whole. How did the artist use art elements and principles to achieve a sense of unity in the totem pole's overall design?
2. Find examples of other totems that are products of the cultures of the Americas. Research the use of totems or symbols by other cultures. For example,

explore the art symbols used for family crests in medieval Christian Europe, or in feudal Japan.
3. Think about natural and cultural symbols of your own that might symbolize interests, beliefs, and events in your life. In your sketchbook, make notes and sketches of possible designs for totems.
4. Divide into groups of 8 to 10 students. Examine all the preliminary sketches. Make a vertical totem pole design plan that allows each individual to contribute a section. Choose art elements that can be repeated to achieve a sense of unity in the totem pole design.
5. Using a computer draw program that allows the creation of strong black-and-white images, create individual totems. Fill with color, or print in black and white and then add color.
6. Attach the different parts of your group's totem pole design. Display it along with a short explanation of the meanings of the symbols used.

Reviewing the Facts

1. Animals such as seal, walrus, fish, whale, and reindeer; these were animals upon which they relied for food.
2. An elaborate ceremonial feast to honor different clans.
3. Totem poles were used as a means of identification and a sign of prestige.
4. Southwest region; painted pottery.
5. Mounds, or large earthworks.
6. It refers to various cultures and civilizations established throughout North and South America before the arrival of Columbus in 1492.
7. Olmec.
8. They were carved with so many ornaments and symbols that it is difficult to separate the figures from the backgrounds.
9. In most, the forehead slants back, the large nose dominates, and the chin recedes.
10. They used a form of picture writing, done on sheets of parchment. The sheets were joined and accordian-folded.
11. They fitted each block of stone into place with great precision.

Thinking Critically

1. Answers, which will vary, should reveal both an understanding of art criticism operations and of Native American art.
2. The elements are line and texture. The repeated line creates harmony. Variety is introduced through the contrast in smooth and patterned areas. The position of the arms lends the otherwise symmetrical work a sense of asymmetrical balance.

Teaching the Technology Project

Remind students to consider their own interests, beliefs, and experiences. Their sketches should reflect their own individuality and—as such—should not be imitations of totem figures in the figures they have studied. Remind them of the importance of bringing together their own sketches and adapting each to complete a unified design.

 Assign the feature in the *Performing Arts Handbook*, page 584.

CAREERS IN ART If time permits, have interested students investigate the career information in the *Careers in Art Handbook*, page 594.

 *inter*NET CONNECTION Have students go online and learn more about artists on preselected Web sites with the Internet activity for this chapter.

The Arts of Africa

ADDITIONAL CHAPTER RESOURCES

Activities

- 📁 Advanced Studio Activity 12
- 📁 Application 12
- 🖱 Chapter 12 Internet Activity
- 📁 Studio Activity 16

Fine Art Resources

- 🎛 **Transparency**

  Art in Focus Transparency 16

  Bamileke. Throne.

- 🖼 **Fine Art Print**

  Focus on World Art Print 12

  Leopard-shaped aquamanile.

Assessment

- 📁 Chapter 12 Test
- 📁 Performance Assessment

Multimedia Resources

- 🎭 Artsource® Performing Arts Package
- 💿 National Gallery Laser Disc
- 💿 National Museum of Women in the Arts CD-ROM
- 📼 Arts & Entertainment Videos

NATIONAL STANDARDS FOR ARTS EDUCATION

The National Standards for Arts Education provide guidelines for grade-appropriate competency in the visual arts. The Content Standards for grades 9–12 are:

1. Understanding and applying media, techniques, and processes.
2. Using knowledge of structures and functions.
3. Choosing and evaluating a range of subject matter, symbols, and ideas.
4. Understanding the visual arts in relation to history and cultures.
5. Reflecting upon and assessing the characteristics and merits of their work and the work of others.
6. Making connections between visual arts and other disciplines.

Listed below are the National Standards for the Visual Arts addressed in this chapter. For a breakdown of the categories listed under each content standard, refer to the *Reproducible Lesson Plans* booklet in the TCR.

1. (a, b) **2.** (a, b) **3.** (a, b, c) **4.** (a, b, c) **5.** (a, b, c) **6.** (a, b)

🕐 **Out of Time?** If time does not permit teaching this chapter in its entirety, you may wish to preview the artwork and captions with students. Scan the heads in each lesson with students. Discuss the Looking Closely feature and examine Styles Influencing Styles on page 269.

HANDBOOK MATERIAL

Chuck Davis
(page 577)

CAREERS IN Art

(page 594)

Beyond the Classroom

Discover resources and art links that showcase contemporary African and African-American artists at various sites found by visiting our Web site at *www.glencoe.com/sec/art*.

The Arts of Africa

The Arts of Africa

INTRODUCE

Chapter Overview

CHAPTER 12 acquaints students with features of African culture and artworks.

Lesson One provides students with an understanding and appreciation of the beauty and power of African art.

Lesson Two directs attention to more recent artworks produced primarily in wood, including masks and sculptures.

Studio Lesson has students create a ceremonial mask.

Art & Social Studies

Guide students in describing and discussing the artwork that opens this chapter. Encourage them to identify similarities and differences between this work and other forms of sculpture they have studied.

Ask a group of volunteers to learn more about the royal dynasty of the Kingdom of Benin: What is known of the beginnings of this dynasty? What are its major accomplishments? What are the duties and privileges of the current members of Benin's royalty. Have these volunteers share their findings with the rest of the class.

Art & Social Studies ■ FIGURE 12.1 Works of art from the Kingdom of Benin reflect the society's centrally-organized political system. In plaques which once hung in the palace in Benin City, the most politically powerful individual is often the central image, depicted larger and more fully three-dimensional than other figures. The royal dynasty responsible for founding the Kingdom of Benin centuries ago continues uninterrupted to this day.

Kingdom of Benin, Edo people, Nigeria. *Mounted King with Attendants.* c. 16th–17th century. Bronze. 49.5 × 41.9 × 11.3 cm (19 1/2 × 16 1/2 × 4 1/2"). The Metropolitan Museum of Art, New York, New York. The Michael C. Rockefeller Memorial Collection. Gift of Nelson Rockefeller, 1965. (1978.412.309).

264

CHAPTER 12 RESOURCES

Teacher's Classroom Resources

📁 Advanced Studio Activity 12

📁 Application 12

🖱 Chapter 12 Internet Activity

📁 Studio Activity 16

Assessment

📁 Chapter 12 Test

📁 Performance Assessment

Fine Art Resources

🖋 *Art in Focus* Transparency 16
    Bamileke. Throne.

🖼 *Focus on World Art* Print 12
    Leopard-shaped aquamanile.

*A*frica, the second largest continent in
the world, accounts for about 20 percent of the earth's
land area. It is more than three times the size of the
United States, including Alaska. If you were to
board a plane at the northernmost point and
fly to the southern tip of Africa, you would cover
the same distance as a flight between
New York City and San Francisco—and most of
the way back again. The arts created in this
vast continent stand as the creative record of many
great and imaginative cultures.

Introducing the Chapter

Direct students' attention to the artwork in Figure 12.1. Ask students whether they find the work successful or not and take a show of hands. Then ask: If you had encountered this work unexpectedly in another setting, would you have recognized it as an example of African art? Ask students to tell what they know about African art. Do they feel that their knowledge of African art is extensive? Why—or why not? What else would they like to know about African art?

Dance. Help students understand how Chuck Davis and his African American Dance Ensemble bring the message of love, peace, and respect through dance and music in "African Roots in American Soil."

YOUR Portfolio

For your portfolio, create an artwork that shows the influence of African art. Choose an object, place, or animal that interests you. Use the images in this chapter as inspiration and create an artwork using the media of your choice. Explain briefly how African art influenced your final product. Put your name and date on the work and keep it in your portfolio. If your work is three-dimensional, take a picture of it and mount the photo with the date and title and store this in your portfolio.

Focus ON THE ARTS

MUSIC
African music contains sophisticated structures—some more complex than in Western compositions. Music includes complex rhythms with and without melody. Instruments include a wide variety of drums, xylophones or balafons, horns, reeds, and harps.

THEATRE
African communities often do not differentiate between artists and audience. The whole village is asked to enact various roles. Many members of the community engage in role-playing and improvisation, leading individuals through dramatic scenes during initiation ceremonies.

DANCE
Dance is an integral part of life in Africa. As with theatre, African cultures generally do not divide a dance performance into artists and spectators; instead, everybody present participates. Purposes of dance may include celebration, expressions of religious feeling, and communication with ancestors.

Focus ON THE ARTS

Explain to students they will try an intellectual exercise that is part of a ritual practiced by the Ndembu tribe of Zambia. Ask them to list character qualities of the following imaginary creatures: Bear-Man; Grass-Man; Green Man; Purple Man. Might another society see a bear or a green man in another way? Discuss how a person preparing to dance like a lion would have to focus on the animal's personality, movements, mood, and rhythms. Dance encourages us to think about emotions and how movement reflects temperament.

265

DEVELOPING A PORTFOLIO

Assessment. To help students form opinions and develop awareness of critical standards, remind them that assessment is a process of thoughtful, informed engagement of a viewer with a piece of art. Questions designed to generate critical thinking about the relative values of artwork will help them make better judgments about the work they intend to include in a portfolio. Examples are: How does the artwork demonstrate successful use of the elements of art? How are principles of art used to organize the elements? How is media used to enhance the subject of the piece? Does the artwork suggest an innovative use of form, media, or technique?

Art of African Kingdoms

Art of African Kingdoms

FOCUS

Lesson Objectives

After studying this lesson, students will be able to:

■ Describe how artworks made of enduring materials provide information about the technologies and social structures of African peoples who lived centuries ago.

■ Discuss the importance of Yoruba religious beliefs in the creation of Yoruba artworks.

■ Describe the forms of art created in the kingdoms of Benin, Asante, and Ethiopia.

Building Vocabulary

On a sheet of paper, have students list the Vocabulary terms for the chapter. Next to each term, have them write two ideas that they think relate to the term's meaning. After they complete the chapter, have students review the ideas they noted, correcting any inaccurate information.

Motivator

Help students identify and discuss words commonly used to describe African people and societies such as *primitive, underdeveloped,* and so on. Explain that these terms reflect Western prejudices and ignorance regarding African culture and history. Point out that these prejudices are related to a long history of colonization and enslavement.

Vocabulary
■ masquerade
■ griots
■ kente cloth

Discover
After completing this lesson, you will be able to:
■ Discuss how Yoruba religious beliefs are reflected in Yoruba artworks.
■ Identify important features in the art and architecture of the Empire of Mali.
■ Describe metal sculptures created in the Benin kingdom.
■ Explain the importance of gold works and kente cloth in the Asante kingdom.
■ Discuss the creation of crosses in the ancient kingdom of Ethiopia.

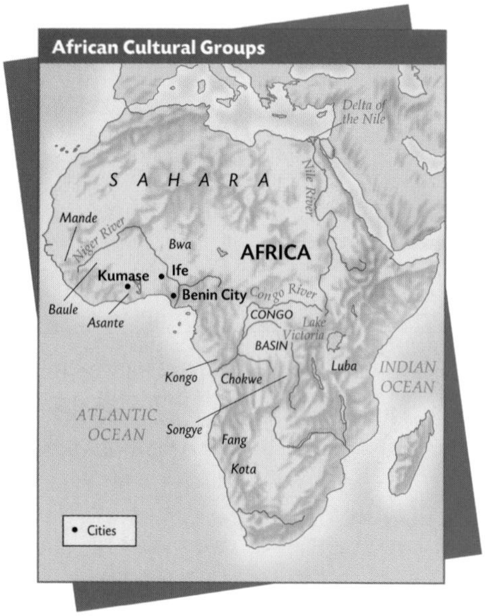

MAP SKILLS

■ **FIGURE 12.2** Artworks created by cultural groups across the African continent reflect the varied traditions and lifestyles of the people. **Find out how natural resources impact the art forms of groups living in different areas of Africa.**

266

$\mathcal{W}$ithin the immense continent of Africa (Figure 12.2), an impressive array of art forms has originated. As you will discover, Africa's ancient civilizations produced refined sculptures and architectural monuments that have endured for centuries. More recent works reflect the vitality of African art today.

The peoples of Africa can boast of long-established, highly developed cultures that have been producing sophisticated art forms for centuries. The court of Ife, the ancient spiritual capital of the Yoruba people, located in what is now southern Nigeria, flourished 1,000 years ago. At that same time, Europe was still working its way through the Middle Ages. Other technologically sophisticated, politically centralized African kingdoms and empires even predate Ife. One was the ancient Egyptian empire. Another was the kingdom of Cush, which conquered Egypt around 700 B.C.

The Role of Art in African Cultures

Throughout Africa, in both the past and the present—even within the context of modern nation-states—the visual arts are well integrated with other art forms, including music, dance, and drama. Art is an important part of people's lives, from birth, through adulthood, to death. In death, the spirit joins the ancestral realm if the individual has led an honorable, productive life. Art addresses not only the concerns of the living, their ancestors, and those yet to be born, but also those of the spirits of nature. A great deal of African art emphasizes the important events of life and the forces in nature that influence the lives of individuals and communities.

Dominant themes in African art include birth and death; the roles of men, women, and children; coming of age; sickness and healing; the importance of food and water; and the human relationship with nature. Artworks are often linked to celebrations and rituals, both secular and sacred. Although it is possible to appreciate works of art from Africa in purely aesthetic terms, a fuller understanding of these forms comes from a knowledge of their cultural context and specific functions.

Art of Ancient Ife

For the Yoruba people of Nigeria, the city of Ife is the place where life and civilization began. Yoruba people now number more than 25 million and live in Nigeria, the neighboring Republic of Benin, and throughout Africa. Large concentrations of people of Yoruba ancestry live in Brazil, Cuba, Haiti, and the United States. One in ten of all African-Americans is of Yoruba descent.

LESSON ONE RESOURCES

Teacher's Classroom Resources
📁 Appreciating Cultural Diversity 19
📁 Cooperative Learning 18
📁 Enrichment Activity 24

📁 Reproducible Lesson Plan 26
📁 Reteaching Activity 26
📁 Study Guide 26

Yoruba Sculpture
■ **FIGURES 12.3 and 12.4**

Yoruba cities developed between the years A.D. 800 and 1000. By 1100, artists of Ife had developed a highly refined, lifelike sculptural style to create portraits of the first Yoruba kings and queens. The display of royal portraits, with their composed, balanced facial features, added a sense of stability in periods of political transition between rulers, or following the death of a ruler.

Metal sculpture exemplifies early African use of the lost-wax process for creating sculptures. Artists in Ife developed this metal-casting process to perfection. Their cast metal sculptures were probably made collaboratively, with women creating the clay forms and men casting them in metal. This is the standard division of labor for artists working throughout the Yoruba region today.

Western scholars did not discover these lifelike terra-cotta and bronze sculptures (Figures 12.3 and 12.4) until 1910. These works are now recognized as a reflection of Yoruba aesthetic values, grounded in their religion and philosophy.

Yoruba Religion and Philosophy

According to Yoruba beliefs, the world consists of two realms: *aye*, the world that can be seen and touched; and *orun*, the supernatural world of ancestors, gods and goddesses, and spirits. Works of art created for the visible world, *aye*, tend to be realistic, whereas works of art created for the invisible world, *orun*, tend to be more abstract.

The Yoruba have a related belief about *ori*, or head, and *ori inu*, or inner head. A Yoruba prayer states, "May my inner head not spoil my outer head." The value the Yoruba place on sound states of mind—inner calm, self-confidence, and dignity—is reflected both in this prayer and in the serene faces of the terra-cotta and bronze sculptures from ancient Ife.

As memorial portraits of Yoruba royalty, these refined sculptures celebrate the lives and accomplishments of individuals. They encourage living generations to match or surpass the cultural accomplishments of previous generations.

■ **FIGURE 12.3** The vertical lines on the face of this figure probably represent ornamental scars made to indicate ethnic identity and to enhance physical beauty. How did the artist use the principles of balance and variety in creating this portrait of a king?

Ife, Nigeria. Portrait of a king. 11th–15th century. Copper alloy. H: 36.2 cm (14¼″). Museum of Mankind, London, England.

■ **FIGURE 12.4** This is a portrait of a Yoruba queen wearing an elaborate beaded crown. In this work, is the queen depicted idealistically or realistically?

Ife, Nigeria. Portrait of a queen. 12th–13th century. Terra-cotta. 25 × 17 cm (9¾ × 6¾″). National Commission for Museums and Monuments, Ife, Nigeria.

Chapter 12 *The Arts of Africa* **267**

TEACH
Introducing the Lesson

Help students study a world map or globe. Point out that Africa is more than three times the size of the United States. Explain that there are approximately as many nations in Africa as there are states in the U.S. Describe the continent's enormous cultural diversity, with many different peoples (or ethnicities) living together within each nation. Tell students that there are more than 1,000 distinct languages spoken in Africa, and that most people speak several languages.

Aesthetics

Divide the class into three groups—imitationalists, formalists, and emotionalists. Direct the attention of all three groups to Figure 12.4. Ask each group to brainstorm the strengths of the work in terms of its assigned aesthetic theory and then to prepare a brief statement expressing the group's views. After groups have shared their statements, ask students which group provided the most convincing argument in favor of the work's artistic success.

Cross Curriculum

LANGUAGE ARTS In Yoruba society, *oriki*, or praise poems, are recited publicly to honor particularly accomplished members of the community. Ask students to write an *oriki* for someone they admire and to recite the praise poem for the rest of the class to hear.

 ## Technology

Videodiscs. An invaluable resource for the art classroom can be found in the many videodiscs available that contain images and collections of artworks, information on artists, and cultures. The National Gallery of Art has a videodisc that you can obtain without charge for use in the classroom. This videodisc contains over 300 images. Glencoe's *Correlation Bar Code Guide to the National Gallery* is correlated to the chapters of *Art in Focus.* You will find bar codes provided throughout this *Teacher's Wraparound Edition* to help you find images on the National Gallery videodisc that enhance many of the lessons in this text.

Art Criticism

Have students look at Figure 12.5. Describe to students how, like the twirling, circular dance movements of the *egungun* masquerade performance, the interlace beadwork adorning the costume emphasizes, abstractly, how the past, present, and future are intertwined in a continuous cycle to encompass birth, life, departure, and return. Then have students meet in groups to discuss the specific use of the elements and principles of art in this work.

Studio Skills

Taking their cue from the interlace patterns in the beadwork that adorns the *egungun* costume in Figure 12.5, have students design their own interlace patterns. Ask them to complete several drawings using colored pencils. In the first drawing have them use two different colors to make a simple interlace pattern, inspired by the one in yellow and blue at the center of the masquerade costume. In the next drawing, have them extend this interlace into a larger pattern, studying the more complex interlace pattern towards the top of the costume. Tell students not to worry about how precisely the interlaces intersect and overlap, but to make it visually interesting, using contrasting colors. Finally, suggest that students outline each section in a third color.

Yoruba Masquerade
■ **FIGURE 12.5**

To the Yoruba, **masquerade** means *a full costume, including a face covering, or mask.* In Yoruba communities today, masqueraders wear *egungun* ensembles (Figure 12.5), or cloth masquerades that include beads and other materials. *Egungun* ensembles are worn to honor ancestors during public dances. Associated with the spirit world, these costumes are abstract creations. When performing, dancers whirl and twirl in circles. These movements symbolically show how the past, present, and the future are intertwined in a continuous cycle encompassing birth, life, departure, and return. These performances are considered a form of play and are fun for all involved. They also have a profoundly serious purpose. They are designed to influence the way people think and to take action to improve world conditions.

■ **FIGURE 12.5** Many different materials were used to create this work. **Describe the different colors and textures you see.**

Yoruba people, Nigeria. Egungun costume. 19th–20th century. Fabric, glass beads, cowrie shells, leather, synthetic leather, plant fiber, string. 173 × 52 × 43 cm (68 × 20½ × 17"). UCLA Fowler Museum of Cultural History, Los Angeles, California. Museum Purchase. X96.3.7.

Art and Architecture of the Empire of Mali

Works of art made centuries ago in Ife and elsewhere in West Africa document the rise of city-states throughout the region. The terracotta sculptures of cavalrymen (Figure 12.6) and foot soldiers from the Inland Niger Delta, near the ancient city of Jenne, date to the early thirteenth century, when the empire of Mali was founded by a powerful military leader and king named Sundiata. These figures reveal proud profiles, with jutting chins and heads held high atop sturdy necks. Their bodies appear straight and tall whether shown standing or seated upright on stallions. The figures represent members of the well-outfitted and well-organized army described in the epic that recounts Sundiata's life history.

The strength of Sundiata's great cavalry and army of foot soldiers enabled him to gain

■ **FIGURE 12.6** Because wet clay is malleable, artists can easily add texture to the overall forms of clay sculptures. **How many different kinds of texture can you identify in this work?**

Inland Delta region, Mali. Equestrian figure. c. 13th century. Ceramic. 70.5 cm (27¾"). National Museum of African Art, Smithsonian Institution, Washington, D.C. Museum purchase, 86-12-2.

COOPERATIVE LEARNING

Monetary Systems. Divide the class into four or five groups, and instruct each to research a different aspect of the subject of money. Among topics groups might investigate are: how trade was conducted before the development of currency (i.e., the barter system), how the practice of using coins evolved, and how and where money is made in the United States today. Take care to monitor the topics groups select as a means of both avoiding duplication of effort and ensuring comprehensive coverage of a given topic. Then set aside time for groups to share their findings along with relevant illustrations and/or photographs in a class "Money Forum."

Styles Influencing *Styles*

IRONWORK IN MALI AND THE UNITED STATES

Just as Mande blacksmiths helped build the empire of Mali, ironworkers helped build the United States of America in its early years.

This solid iron figure shows the strong vertical lines that characterize Mande sculpture.

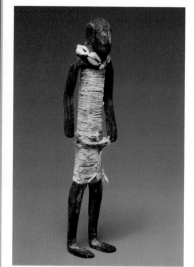

■ **FIGURE 12.7**

Bamana peoples, Mali. Bamana iron figure. Iron, string, cowrie shells. Indiana University Art Museum, Bloomington, Indiana. Gift of Ernst Anspach.

This eighteenth-century iron figure, very similar in form to figures made by Mande blacksmiths in West Africa, was found during excavations at the site of a blacksmith shop in Alexandria, Virginia. It was probably made by a Mande blacksmith who was either born in Africa and a survivor of the Atlantic passage, or a first-generation African-American.

■ **FIGURE 12.8**

African-American, Virginia. Iron figure. Eighteenth century. Iron. 36.8 × 11.4 × 8.9 cm ($14^1/_2 \times 4^1/_2 \times 3^1/_2$"). Collection Jasper Johns.

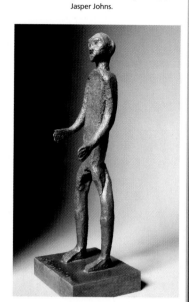

political power. Under his leadership, the empire of Mali became one of the largest and wealthiest kingdoms the world has ever known. The epic of Sundiata is passed on by **griots,** (**gree**-oh) *oral historians who are also musicians and performers,* throughout West Africa to this day.

The Sundiata epic is filled with stories of hunter/warriors accomplishing supernatural feats. Sundiata himself is described as a hunter/warrior-king. His alliance with Mande blacksmiths, men skilled in making iron weapons and tools, enabled Sundiata to build an empire.

The Great Friday Mosque

■ **FIGURE 12.9**

The architecture of the city of Jenne also reflects an emphasis on the vertical. In Jenne, the oldest city in sub-Saharan Africa, the corner pinnacles of house façades are made tall and straight, "like a man." The Jenne mosque (Figure 12.9, page 270) amplifies this principle through repetition. The façade and sides of the mosque feature rows of tall, narrow columns that give the structure its impressive appearance.

The mosque is made of hand-molded adobe brick, a sun-dried mixture of clay and straw. Because heavy rains erode its outer walls, an army of men must climb the mosque every year to refinish its surfaces. Wooden beams project from the sides of the mosque to provide permanent supports for scaffolding. The mosque's proportions are monumental, making even more impressive the accomplishment of workers who built it by hand. Rebuilt in 1907, this mosque retains the style of the thirteenth-century original.

Styles Influencing *Styles*

Let students describe and discuss the two sculptures in Figures 12.7 and 12.8 that exemplify ironwork sculptures from Mali and the United States. What similarities can students identify on their own.

Then have students read and discuss the explanation of the similarities between the two works. Ask: How and why did the Mande blacksmith probably leave West Africa? If the blacksmith was born in Virginia, why is the influence of the work from Mali still so clear in his sculpture?

Did You Know?

A heroic woman, Nana Yaa Asantewa, led a resistance movement against the British in 1900. Her political action was provoked by an incident with the British Governor of what was then the Gold Coast, now Ghana.

More About...

Oral Traditions. In African societies, the spoken word holds special power. Before the imposition of written traditions on African societies during the colonial era, historical information and cultural knowledge was passed from generation to generation primarily by word of mouth. Even now, oral traditions have a particularly important place in African societies. The feature film, *Keita: Heritage of the Griot,* made by Dani Kouyate, set in modern Mali with flashbacks to the past, tells the history of Sundiata Keita. It is available in the Library of African Cinema distributed by California Newsreel, in San Francisco. Arrange for a classroom or auditorium viewing of this film. Or consult Niane's book and have groups of students stage passages from the epic for their classmates.

Art Criticism

Have students examine the relief sculpture detailed in Figure 12.1 on page 264. Point out that the four-leaf motif incised in the background of this plaque represents river leaves, symbol of Olokun, god of the sea, source of the wealth for the Kingdom of Benin, also associated with trade. Suggest that interested students learn more about these and related symbols.

Cross Curriculum

HISTORY. Within the Kingdom of Benin, metal-casters, like ivory carvers and other groups of specialized artists, worked together in artistic guilds controlled by the king. Artworks made of enduring materials, such as copper alloy, document the history of the Kingdom of Benin and its encounters with foreign powers. Ask students to research this history. Then have students work in groups to plan and prepare timelines showing the major events in Benin's history.

Did You Know?

The Sahara has not always been a desert. It began to dry up between about 4000 and 2500 B.C. Trade across the desert, a vast "sea" of sand, remains active. *Sahel*, the Arabic word for the region at the edge of the desert means shore. Towns of the *sahel*, at the end of caravan routes, are like ports, and camels are the "ships" of the desert.

■ **FIGURE 12.9**
The wall with the three tall towers establishes the building's orientation to Mecca. How does the play of light and shadow emphasize the deeply recessed forms of the mosque's walls?

The Great Friday Mosque. Jenne, Mali. Earth, wood, ostrich eggs. 1907 reconstruction of original 13th-century building.

The Kingdom of Benin

The Benin kingdom, situated in what is now southern Nigeria, was a society of many class levels, with an oral tradition that goes back seven or eight centuries. The kingdom reached the peak of its power in the sixteenth century. Like earlier artists in nearby Ife, Benin artists excelled in creating sculptures of metal, specifically a copper alloy with many of the same qualities associated with bronze.

For centuries in the West, European masters had reserved bronze for the most important works. Imagine, then, the excitement created in 1897, when a huge shipment of African metal castings arrived in England. These cast pieces were brought back to England by the leaders of a British expedition that had attacked Benin City earlier that same year. European scholars and artists alike were astounded by the technical proficiency and beauty of the Benin sculptures.

Benin Sculpture

Among the most ambitious of the Benin castings are the high-relief sculptures that once covered the walls and pillars of the royal palace. One of these contains the figure of the *oba,* or king, flanked by two chiefs bearing shields, sword bearers and palace attendants. (See Figure 12.1, page 264.)

In Benin art the most politically powerful person is represented as the largest figure. This representation reflects the central organization of the kingdom. Less powerful individuals are smaller.

Here four social ranks are depicted. The king, or *oba* is placed in the center and is the largest figure. The two chiefs are almost as large as the king. Two sword bearers, one a child, are even smaller. Three tiny figures, one supporting the king's foot and two in the top corners, represent the least powerful members of the court.

The *oba* wears a patterned wrapper, or waist cloth, a six-ringed coral necklace, and sits side-saddle on a horse. In Benin culture, horses are symbols of political power.

Without question, the Benin artist who created this relief was in complete command of metal-casting techniques. Notice how the arms and shields are thrust forward in space, completely free of the background. This not only adds to the three-dimensional appearance of the figures but also creates an interesting pattern of light and dark values. A variety of contrasting textures and a symmetrically balanced design help tie all parts of this complex composition together to form a unified whole.

MEETING INDIVIDUAL NEEDS

Auditory/Musical Learners. Play excerpts of recorded African music. Ask students to listen to the music and identify the use of percussion instruments and repeated rhythms. Have students use both hands to play the rhythm patterns on their laps. Suggest that students can use these rhythm patterns to set a mood for their studio activities.

Kinesthetic Learners. Challenge students to create a dance through which they can teach classmates about some aspect of African culture. Dancing groups may have a narrator who helps interpret the symbolic meaning of the dance steps. Encourage students to bring rhythm instruments, such as hand drums, bells, rattles, or maracas, to play during the dance.

The Asante Kingdom

The Akan people lived in city-states in central and coastal Ghana. In the first half of the eighteenth century, these people joined together to form a powerful confederation of states, that included many cultural groups. The largest of these groups was the Asante.

Gold was the measure of wealth for the Akan, and kings, whose power was thought to come from God the Creator, tightly controlled its use. Items fashioned from the precious metal were made to be worn by these kings as a sign of their divine authority and absolute power.

Asante Gold Jewelry

■ FIGURE 12.10

Asante necklaces, bracelets, and anklets were crafted by stringing cast-gold beads with gold nuggets, glass and stone beads, and other items. In one example, a pendant in the form of a crab is used. This necklace (Figure 12.10) was probably designed for a queen mother, because the crab was widely recognized by the Asante as a symbol for a person of this rank.

The work of goldsmiths in Kumase, the Asante capital, was regulated by the king. Only with his permission were people allowed to commission works of art from these highly skilled craftsmen. Items obtained through the king's court included gold ornaments and gold leaf-covered staffs and swords.

Kente Cloth

■ FIGURE 12.11

The Asante king also controlled the use of special cloth. During the 1600s, weavers created the first **kente (ken-**tay) **cloth,** *a brilliantly colored and patterned fabric* that became the royal cloth. Kente cloth is woven in narrow strips that are then stitched together to form large pieces with complex patterns (Figure 12.11). By the 1720s, Asante weavers were unraveling imported silk fabrics and reweaving them into cloths featuring their own unique designs. Silk cloths woven with special symbolic patterns, such as the gold-dust design, were reserved exclusively for kings.

■ **FIGURE 12.10** Works of art made using the lost-wax casting technique often show finely textured details. What elements of art are especially important in this work?

Akan people, Asante kingdom, Ghana. Necklace. 19th century. Gold. 2.5 × 40 cm (1 × 15 3/4"). Virginia Museum of Fine Arts, Richmond, Virginia. The Adolph D. and Wilkins C. Williams Fund.

■ **FIGURE 12.11** Weavers of kente cloth have invented many different patterns. These patterns often have names that are immediately recognized by members of Akan societies. What elements of art have been used to create the patterns in this cloth?

Asante people, Ghana. Man's cloth (kente cloth). Rayon. L: 314 cm (123 5/8"), W: 217 cm (85 7/16"). UCLA Fowler Museum of Cultural History, Los Angeles, California. Anonymous Gift.

Chapter 12 *The Arts of Africa* **271**

Cross Curriculum

HISTORY. Many people in the United States first became aware of kente cloth when it was worn by the first president of Ghana, Kwame Nkrumah, at meetings of the United Nations in New York City. During the 1960s, kente cloth became closely associated with the black consciousness movement. Today the patterns of kente cloth may be worn in the United States to make both political statements and fashion statements. Ask a small group of interested volunteers to learn more about the uses of kente cloth in the United States and to share their findings with the rest of the class.

Art Criticism

Have pairs of students select one of the crosses illustrated in Figure 12.12 (page 272). Then have partners work jointly to write a detailed description of the cross they have chosen. Allow pairs to share their descriptions while the remainder of the class attempts to identify the cross they chose.

Study Guide

Distribute *Study Guide* 26 in the TCR. Assist students in reviewing key concepts. 📁

Art and Humanities

Assign *Enrichment* 24, "Dahomey Style Appliqué," in the TCR. In this worksheet, students learn the technique of applique and then use this technique to create a wearable object. 📁

Studio Activities

Assign groups of students *Cooperative Learning* 18, "Ceremonies of Life," in the TCR. In this activity, groups learn about the rituals indigenous to African tribal societies. 📁

ASSESS

Checking Comprehension

Have students respond to the lesson review questions. Answers are given in the box below.

Reteaching

Assign *Reteaching* 26, found in the TCR. Have students complete the activity and review their responses. 📁

Enrichment

Assign students *Appreciating Cultural Diversity* 19, "Ibejis—Yoruba Twin Sculptures," in the TCR. In this worksheet students learn about the reverence paid to twins in the Yoruba culture. 📁

Extension

African sculpture had an impact on Western European artists, particularly during the early years of the twentieth century. Have interested students read about the works of Amedeo Modigliani, Henri Matisse, Georges Braque, and Pablo Picasso. Ask students to make short presentations to the class explaining what and how each artist learned and was influenced by African works.

CLOSE

Ask each student to write a sentence identifying the most fascinating fact he or she learned in this lesson. Have students read their statements aloud and compare their responses. What fact was mentioned most often?

The Ancient Kingdom of Ethiopia

In the fourth century, as Christianity was beginning to gain followers in western Europe, the ancient kingdom of Ethiopia, then known as Aksum, was already a center of Christianity. In fact, Ethiopia is the oldest Christian nation in the world. A Moorish invasion in the seventh century, however, drove the Ethiopian Christians to mountain strongholds in search of safety. They remained there for 800 years, forgotten by the world. When Portuguese explorers arrived in the fifteenth century, they thought that they had discovered the kingdom of Prester John, a legendary Christian king of fabulous wealth.

Ethiopian Crosses
■ FIGURE 12.12

In the fifteenth century, an Ethiopian king decreed that all his Christian subjects wear a cross around their necks. Early examples of these crosses were made from iron or bronze, but starting in the nineteenth century, silver was used to create a variety of delicately crafted crosses (Figure 12.12).

The art of Christian Ethiopia included large ceremonial crosses as well. These were made of wood, bronze, or silver in a variety of decorative styles and were used in religious processions. In addition, a great deal of silver jewelry dating from ancient to recent times constitutes an important part of the Ethiopian art heritage.

■ **FIGURE 12.12** Ethiopian crosses are made in many different shapes and sizes. Why are so many crosses found in Ethiopia?

Ethiopian orthodox style, Ethiopia. Pendants. Silver alloy. 7.6 × 4.4 cm (3 × 1³⁄₄″). National Museum of African Art, Smithsonian Institution, Washington, D.C. Gift of Mr. and Mrs. Donald F. Miller, 71–23 mn.

LESSON ONE REVIEW

Reviewing Art Facts

1. How long ago were the sculptural portraits of the first Yoruba kings made? What technique was used to make them?
2. What materials were used in the construction of the mosque in Jenne? Describe the features of this mosque.
3. How is kente cloth assembled?
4. What was the measure of wealth for the Akan people, and who controlled its use?

Activity... *Discovering African Art*

Look at the map on page 266 and note the size of the continent of Africa. There are many kingdoms, nations, and cultural groups that make up the millions of people who live there. African art represents an enormous and diverse contribution to the cultural history of man. Most of the art produced in Africa is closely tied to themes of life and death.

Create a multimedia presentation for your class. Working in small groups, use online or library resources to learn about the art of Africa. Identify some of the major art forms of each of the regions of the African continent and point out their similarities and differences.

LESSON ONE REVIEW

Answers to Reviewing Art Facts

1. Between the eleventh and the fifteenth century; Lost-wax technology.
2. Adobe bricks, made of earth mixed with straw, and wood for scaffolding supports.
3. Kente cloth is woven in narrow strips and then stitched together.
4. Gold, which was controlled by the Akan kings.

Activity... *Discovering African Art*

Have students work together to divide the African continent into four or five general regions. Then let each group select one region, and have group members work together to explore the artworks created there. Suggest that the groups combine their presentations into a longer multimedia presentation about the entire continent.

African Sculpture

Vocabulary
■ adze

Artist to Meet
■ Olowe of Ise

Discover
After completing this lesson, you will be able to:
■ Identify the medium and the technique used in the production of most African sculptures.
■ Name and describe the different types of figures created by African artists, and explain their functions.
■ Explain how works of art serve as a link between generations, living and deceased.
■ Discuss the purposes of African masks.

■ **FIGURE 12.13** Replicas of African masks of all types are mass-produced as decorative items. **How are masks made for tourists different from ones made for traditional use?**

Bwa people, Burkina Faso, village of Ouri. Bomavay Konaté carving a sun mask for sale to tourists. 1984.

*M*uch of Africa's contribution to world art is in the form of sculptures made of wood. These sculptures include powerfully expressive figures, highly stylized masks (Figure 12.13), symbols of royalty, and household furniture. Works of this kind have been admired by artists outside Africa since 1905, when Maurice de Vlaminck, a French painter, was impressed by three African figures displayed in a French café. Other artists, including Henri Matisse, Pablo Picasso, and Ernst Ludwig Kirchner, were subsequently fascinated by African art and borrowed features from it to incorporate in their own work. (See Chapter 23.) In this way, the art of Africa has had an impact on the course of modern art in the West.

African Wood Carvings

Most wood sculptures from Africa in Western museum collections date from the late nineteenth or early twentieth century, the period of European colonization of Africa. Much of the essential information about objects collected during this colonial era—including geographic origin, function, and artists' names—is incomplete or nonexistent. More recent research, consisting primarily of information gathered in Africa since the 1960s, has increased our understanding of these works.

In their original African settings, sculptures made of wood often did not survive beyond several generations of use. Wood-eating white ants and damp climates contributed to the destruction of sculptures. This meant that each new generation of artists had to produce new carvings to replace those that had been damaged or destroyed. Although the lack of early examples makes comparison to more recent works impossible, it can be assumed that artists profited from the efforts of their predecessors. Rather than merely copying earlier models, innovative artists attempted to improve upon them. They continuously revitalized the images and forms used in religious rituals and ceremonies.

Variety of Artistic Styles

The African artworks most familiar to Western viewers are sculptural figures and masks. These vary in style from one ethnic group to another. Because nearly 1,000 cultural groups are distributed throughout the vast continent, there is a large variety of artistic styles. These styles are influenced by cross-cultural contact and exchange. Like artists everywhere, African artists respond to works created by other artists within their own culture and beyond. Artistic traditions often cross geographic boundaries to link different peoples. Thus, the relationship between artistic styles and ethnic identities in Africa is dynamic and complex.

273

LESSON TWO RESOURCES

Teacher's Classroom Resources
📁 Appreciating Cultural Diversity 20, 21
📁 Art and Humanities 20
📁 Enrichment Activity 25

📁 Reproducible Lesson Plan 27
📁 Reteaching Activity 27
📁 Study Guide 27

African Sculpture

FOCUS
Lesson Objectives
After studying this lesson, students will be able to:
■ Identify several different types of African figurative sculptures, and describe their functions.
■ Identify several different types of African masks, and describe their functions.

Building Vocabulary
Show students a photograph of an adze (from an encyclopedia, other reference work, or online resource, for example). Let volunteers name the tool and share what they know about its uses. Then have students read the definition of *adze* provided in the Glossary.

Motivator
Ask students to survey briefly the artworks illustrated in this lesson. Instruct students to use their imaginations to write a detailed description of an African ceremony or ritual in which one of these objects might be used. In their descriptions, students could identify features of the art objects that would help young people learn the meaning of these rites. Have volunteers share their descriptions with the class.

Introducing the Lesson
Ask students to examine the illustrations in this lesson and identify the artwork that most arouses their curiosity. Have students take turns identifying the work they found most interesting, providing reasons for their choices. Have students note which work was singled out most often.

TEACH

Art History

Have students discuss why certain European artists incorporated features of African art in their own works. Inform students that the European artists mentioned on page 273 were primarily interested in the creation of fine art. Ask students to review the meanings of the terms *fine art* and *applied art*. Do students think African artists were concerned with creating fine art? Why, or why not? Tell students that, in later chapters, they will learn that artists in medieval Europe—like the African artists discussed here—had little interest in the creation of fine art.

LOOKING Closely

Let students meet in groups to discuss the carving in Figure 12.14. Encourage group members to share their responses to the figure before they read and discuss the information presented about it.

Art History

Help students understand the creation of carved wooden figures by presenting this information: To fashion a sculpture's basic form, African sculptors use an adze, an axlike tool with an arched blade at right angles to the handle. A chisel or small knife is used for details. Rough leaves, or now, sandpaper, is used to create a smooth finish. Sculptures are generally oiled or painted with pigments made from natural ingredients, or using Western paint. Colors are applied by the sculptor, or by someone else, after it leaves the carver's hands, within the context of later use.

Carved Figures

The carved-wood sculptures of Africa have many different forms, although the most common are based on the human figure. To create them, the carver relies on the **adze,** *an axlike tool with an arched blade at right angles to the handle.* Usually, a figure is carved from a single section of wood and, when finished, reflects the shape of the log from which it is made.

Figurative sculptures, or figures, from different parts of Africa share certain common characteristics. These include:

- proportions that reflect cultural preferences rather than natural proportions;
- frontal symmetrical poses;
- disproportionately large heads, signifying the importance of the head as the center of reason and wisdom;
- little or no suggestion of movement.

African figurative sculptures are made for a variety of purposes. They promote the well-being of individuals, families, social groups, and larger communities. African sculptures address themes that reflect the concerns of the living, as well as the concerns of ancestors and spirits—including spirits of those yet to be born.

The wood carvings of Africa reflect a wide variety of forms and functions. These include ancestors and cultural heroes, guardian figures, and spirit spouse figures.

Ancestors and Cultural Heroes

In many African societies, death is not considered the end of life. Rather, death initiates an individual's spirit into the world of ancestors. When the soul separates from the body, it joins its ancestors and remains nearby to influence the living.

Figurative sculptures serve as pleasant resting places for ancestral spirits. These sculptures are created to *contain* the spirit of the deceased. Although such figures are not

LOOKING Closely

THE MEANING OF AN AFRICAN CARVING

If you study the carving of Chibinda Ilunga closely, you will note a mature, sturdy figure that seems to command attention.

- **Identify.** The treatment of the face shows a notable attention to detail. Each feature is carved with great care. The wide-open eyes suggest the vigilance of the hunter/warrior, and the mouth is firmly fixed to show determination. A beard made of animal hair adds an air of wisdom, suggesting that this person's strength is tempered by good judgment.
- **Compare.** The powerful torso and limbs lack the detail that might divert attention away from their strength.
- **Examine.** The royal headdress and an animal horn held in the left hand are carved with exacting precision.
- **Interpret.** The right hand bears a staff to aid Chibinda Ilunga in his journeys. The most impressive of these may be the journey spanning more than three centuries—the length of time this idealized ruler's reputation and influence was felt by the Lunda and Chokwe peoples.

■ **FIGURE 12.14** Chokwe, Northeastern Angola. *Chibinda (The Hunter), Ilunga Katele.* Mid-19th century. Wood, hair, hide. H: 40.6 cm (16"). Kimbell Art Museum, Fort Worth, Texas.

More About... | **Chibinda Ilunga.** Early in the seventeenth century, at about the time Chibinda Ilunga married the heiress to a powerful ruler, one of the great monarchs in Western Europe, Elizabeth I of England, died and James I ascended to the throne.

Chibinda Ilunga was, through his mother, the bearer of the sacred blood of the Luba royal line. As a younger son, he was so skilled as a hunter and warrior that he represented a threat to his politically powerful father. To avoid conflict, Chibinda Ilunga fled, seeking his fortunes elsewhere. Eventually, around 1600, he married the heiress to a powerful ruler, and from this union came the Lunda aristocracy.

intended to be realistic portraits, they may include identifying features in their details. To assure that the spirit inhabits the figure, offerings and sacrifices are made in ritual ceremonies. The spirit remains within the sculpture until it decides to leave or is summoned to the hereafter. Because the spirit dwells in the figure, members of the family talk to it, especially to discuss difficult situations and ask for assistance. In this way, the sculpture serves as an effective link between the past and the present, the living and the dead.

Even removed from their original contexts, African sculptures project a powerful presence. This is especially true of a figure from northeastern Angola (Figure 12.14). This carving represents an actual historical figure named Chibinda Ilunga, who became the idealized ancestor of the sacred royalty of the Lunda, an agricultural and hunting people. Chibinda Ilunga became a hero to his people and to the nearby Chokwe people, who furnished many of the sculptors who created carvings for the Lunda royal court.

While the sculpture of Chibinda Ilunga has an unmistakable sense of power and strength, another sculpture from central Africa projects a different kind of presence (Figure 12.15). Kongo artists of Angola, Congo, and the Democratic Republic of Congo produced sculptures called *minkisi* (singular: *nkisi*). These figures were used in elaborate rituals to deal with various social problems. They contain ancestral relics or clay from graves, as well as medicines. The powerful forces contained within these carvings are activated by a spiritualist. Once activated, the *nkisi* sculpture draws on these forces to aid those requiring assistance.

The spectacular figure illustrated in Figure 12.15 is nearly four feet high and belongs to a special class of *minkisi* called *nkondi,* a name that means "hunter." *Nkondi* are considered to be the most powerful of all *minkisi.* Nails and iron blades were inserted into these figures as part of a legal process that drew on Kongo ancestral authority. The accumulation of metal blades inserted into these figures documents the history of their divine intervention into human affairs. With its hands on

■ **FIGURE 12.15**
Sculptures like this one, bristling with metal blades, are often misunderstood by viewers unfamiliar with African art. For what purposes were figures like this one made?

Kongo. *Nkisi Nkondi* (Nail figure). 1875–1900. Wood with screws, nails, blades, cowrie shells. H: 116.8 cm (46″). The Detroit Institute of Arts, Detroit, Michigan. Founders Society Purchase, Eleanor Clay Ford Fund for African Art.

its hips, a strong blade-studded chest, and an open mouth, this figure stands alert as if ready to speak and act. As the embodiment of the Kongo system of law, this sculpture dealt with painful, complex issues. It oversaw oaths, treaty negotiations, the punishment of criminals, issues of life and death, and other serious matters.

Chapter 12 *The Arts of Africa* **275**

CHAPTER 12
LESSON TWO

Studio Skills
On the board, list the characteristics associated with African figure carvings found in this lesson. Tell students to use these characteristics as a guide in completing a pencil drawing of a cultural hero or a spirit spouse. Display the finished drawings and ask students to write a description of their favorite work.

Art Criticism
Tell students to examine the Nkisi Nkondi in Figure 12.15. Then have students close their books and write a detailed description of the work. When they have finished, ask several students to read aloud their descriptions. As descriptive adjectives are read, write these on the board. Have students determine which descriptors appear most frequently, noting also whether anyone noticed the open mouth. Ask: Why are mouths on all figures of this kind open?

Critical Thinking
The word *minkisi* does not translate into English. *Minkisi* sculptures represent ancestral authority and are used to heal and protect. Like other African sculptures that play an active role in peoples lives, *minkisi* are "things that do things." Guide students in discussing both these figures and the word itself. Ask: Why don't we have an English word that means minkisi?

Did You Know ❓
About forty percent of the ten million individuals taken from Africa between 1550 and 1850 came from Kongo-influenced Central Africa.

About the *Artwork*

Nkonde Nail Figure. Inform students that *Minkisi* like the one illustrated in Figure 12.15 were the products of many individuals, including the carver, the spiritualist, and clients. The carver was responsible for creating the physical form, but without the aid of the "other-worldly" input from the spiritualist, the figure would have no meaning. It was the job of the spiritualist to fill the carving with the medicinal/magical substances and conduct the ritual performances that gave it its power. An Nkisi Nkondi functions like an altar. Medicines in the stomach protect the enabling spirit of the sculpture. Each nail or blade commemorates a moral issue.

Art Criticism

Direct students' attention to the reliquary figure in Figure 12.16. Ask them to identify the facial feature that appears to be missing (the mouth). What significance, if any, do students attach to this omission?

Studio Skills

Have students examine Figure 12.16 and then attempt to use a computer to create an original drawing that exhibits some of the same properties. Students should begin by creating a half dozen or so geometric shapes. After experiments with resizing, placement, and orientation of these shapes, students should use the software's "snapping" feature to align their shapes vertically along a central axis. Students may fill each shape with a selected color or pattern.

Aesthetics

Introduce the following information to the class, and ask for volunteers to learn more about these topics. The colors most commonly used to paint African sculptures are red, black, and white. These colors generally have symbolic significance, though their precise meaning varies according to social context.

The color white is often associated with purity and coolness, and with the ancestral and spiritual world. In many African societies, white bands are painted across the eyes to show that a person has special visionary power, is able to communicate with the spiritual realm. One of the main sources for the color white is kaolin, a white clay that is also used to make porcelain dishes.

■ **FIGURE 12.16**
Form and function are often interrelated in African works of art. How was this sculpture used?

Kota people, Gabon. Reliquary Figure. c. 19th–20th century. Wood, brass, copper, iron. 73.3 cm (28$^7/_8$"). The Metropolitan Museum of Art, New York, New York. Purchase 1983. (1983.18).

Guardian Figures
■ **FIGURE 12.16**

Other sculptures from central Africa, both figurative and more abstract in form, were created to guard ancestral relics. Guardian figures were placed on top of baskets or bundles containing the relics of the dead. Among the best-known guardian figures are the wood and metal sculptures created by the Kota people of Gabon (Figure 12.16). These abstract sculptures have large oval faces and bodies reduced to open diamond shapes. They are made of wood covered with thin sheets and strips of metal. This metallic trim serves to emphasize portions of the face, neck, and body. The use of copper and brass indicates the importance attached to these figures, since metal was a form of wealth in central Africa. The sculpture's penetrating, steady gaze reflects its supernatural role in linking this world and the world of ancestors.

When this sculpture was made, the Kota were known for their elaborate hairstyles, headdresses, and body painting. The Kota people's great concern for personal beauty is reflected in the infinitely varied forms of their reliquary guardian figures.

Time & Place
CONNECTIONS
African Art
c. 1200–1800

HEADDRESS. Shells, feathers, and animal fur often adorn masks and headpieces. They were designed to shield the identity of the wearer during ceremonies.

Chumbanndu, Buluba, Africa. Face Mask.

TALKING DRUM. The sounds created with the talking drum can imitate the sounds of spoken language. The drummer plays on different parts of the tightly-drawn drum skin to create different sounds.

*A*ctivity **Diary Entry.** Write a first-person narrative as a trader traveling to a trade center in Africa. On the streets you see people wearing headdresses and musicians with percussion instruments. Write a diary entry about your experiences.

Time & Place
CONNECTIONS
African Art

Have students examine the images in the Time & Place feature, and assign the diary entry activity. Be sure students understand that their diary entries should vividly describe the scene of a bustling marketplace and be written in the first person, from the point of view of a specific individual. Suggest these possible beginning sentences: "As I entered the marketplace I saw . . . . I heard the sounds of . . . ." Encourage students to include references to the artifacts pictured here as well as to other items that they might also see in an African trade center of this time period.

Primordial Couples
■ FIGURE 12.17

Sculptures representing primordial couples, made by the Dogon people of Mali, convey a sense of harmony and balance. As images of the first man and woman described in Dogon myths of creation, these sculptures serve as an inspiration to living generations. These figures (Figure 12.17) are seated on a stool with a cylindrical support that symbolizes the link between the earth below and the spirit world above. As a sign of affection and protection, the male figure's arm wraps lightly around the woman's shoulder. Carved from a single piece of wood, the interlocking forms effectively convey Dogon ideas regarding the interdependence of men and women and their complementary social roles.

■ FIGURE 12.17 This sculpture, like most African sculptures, was carved from a single piece of wood. What idea or feeling does this work communicate?

Dogon people, Mali. *Seated Man and Woman.* Wood. 76.2 cm (30″). Photograph © 1993 by the Barnes Foundation, Merion Station, Pennsylvania.

Spirit Spouse Figures
■ FIGURE 12.18

Spirit spouse figures made by the Baule people of the Ivory Coast underscore the often complex relationships between men and women in another African society. For the Baule, everyone has a spirit spouse, a mate who lives in the invisible realm. At birth, a child leaves his or her spirit mate behind in the invisible realm. The invisible realm mirrors the physical world. Spirit spouses usually do not interfere in the affairs of the physical world. If it becomes discontent or jealous, however, the spirit spouse may disrupt the life of the real-world mate.

To please a spirit spouse who desires material form, a sculpture is carved. This sculpture is then cared for in a private shrine in the owner's bedroom. The sculptures help Baule men and women imagine the existence of a different world that is experienced in nighttime dreams. Through sculptures and dreams, people form closer relationships with their spirit mates. This makes it easier to create more harmonious real-world relationships.

Baule spirit spouse sculptures are still being carved today. The sculpture in Figure 12.18 was made during the 1950s.

■ FIGURE 12.18
Spirit spouse sculptures reflect Baule ideas regarding both beauty and goodness. Do you find this work to be visually appealing? Why or why not?

Baule, Ivory Coast. Figure of an Other-World man. c. 1950. Wood, pigments. 25 cm (9³/₄″). National Museum of African Art, Smithsonian Institution, Washington, D.C. Anonymous Gift, 93-1-2.

Chapter 12 *The Arts of Africa* **277**

Cross Curriculum

LANGUAGE ARTS. Ask an interested volunteer to prepare and present to the class an explanation of the term *primordial couples:* What sets a couple apart as "primordial"? What are some examples of primordial couples from other cultures?

Art Criticism

Divide the class into two groups, and assign to one the principle of harmony, assign the other the principle of variety. Instruct each group to identify how its principle is reflected in the works in Figures 12.17 and 12.18. Provide time for both groups to present their findings. Ask students if they think either of these works made more effective use of these two principles than the other.

Cross Curriculum

SOCIAL STUDIES. Have students locate on a map or globe all of the nations represented by works of art included in Lesson Two. Ask students to take out a piece of paper and make columns at the top of the page, one for each of these nations. Under each heading, list which peoples/artists are from this nation.

Did You Know❓

In the past, and sometimes now, African religious beliefs, laws, and customs were/are passed down from one generation to the next during initiation periods that could last from a few months to several years.

Teacher Notes

Aesthetics

Have students examine the figures and masks illustrated in this chapter and select the one that they find most interesting, offering reasons for their choices. Compile a representative list of reasons on the board. Then ask the class to determine if any of the reasons listed pertain to the literal qualities, placing an *L* after those that do. Repeat this procedure with the design and expressive qualities, placing a *D* or *E* next to a listed reason as appropriate. Ask: Which of the three aesthetic theories appears to be most applicable to this work? Which is least applicable? Ask students what this survey reveals about their perceptions of African art?

Critical Thinking

Divide the class into small groups, and instruct each group to bring to class a collection of natural materials and/or discarded items. Have each team decide on a way of combining these materials to produce a three-dimensional artwork that could provide a viewer with information about modern life in the United States. Exhibit the completed works, and have students discuss them in terms both of originality and of their success in communicating information about our way of life.

Did You Know?

Ouagadougou, the capital of Burkina Faso, is an active center for filmmaking. Every other year, the international film festival, FESPACO, takes place there.

■ **FIGURE 12.19**
In many African societies, the color white is associated with the ancestral or spiritual realm. Masks like this one are used in mourning ceremonies. **What do you think the lines that run vertically from the eyes represent?**

Vuvi, Gabon. Mask. Wood, with white and pink pigments. 38.1 × 24.4 cm (15 × 9⅝"). The University of Iowa Museum of Art, Iowa City, Iowa. The Stanley Collection.

■ **FIGURE 12.20**
African masks are generally more than just a face covering. **Imagine wearing a leaf mask like this one. How would it feel?**

Bwa people, Burkina Faso, village of Boni. Leaf mask. 1985.

278 **Unit Four** *Art of Asia, the Americas, and Africa*

Masks

Like African figurative sculptures, African masks take different forms and serve different functions. Many African masks cover only the face. Art historians refer to these as face masks (Figure 12.19).

In Africa, the concept of "mask" includes much more than just the mask itself. Masks are used in performances and are generally part of a full costume. They often have their own songs, dance steps, and sometimes even personal names. With few exceptions, African masks are worn only by men.

Masks are made to be seen in motion during ceremonies or religious rituals. Although they are sometimes used in secular dances, they are generally intended to facilitate communication with the spirit world. Like figurative sculptures, masks can embody powerful forces and are believed to have supernatural abilities. When members of masking societies perform wearing masks, they cease to be themselves. They become mediums, able to communicate directly with the spiritual realm. As sacred objects, such masks should be viewed with honor and respect.

Not all African masks served sacred purposes. Some were created and used purely for entertainment. Today, more and more replicas of African masks of all types are being mass-produced as decorative objects for urban African and Western consumers.

Masks of the Bwa People
■ **FIGURES 12.20 and 12.21**

Although face masks and headdresses carved in wood are the most common, African masks are constructed in different ways using a wide variety of materials. For example, the Bwa people of Burkina Faso make masks of leaves, plant fibers, porcupine quills, and feathers (Figure 12.20). Leaf masks are made at the end of the dry season, before the rains that mark the beginning of the next agricultural cycle. The Bwa people consider leaf masks the most ancient mask form and closely associate them with nature and with life's regenerative power.

CULTURAL DIVERSITY

Traditions. Discuss how African sculpture serves as a link between generations, living and deceased, and ask students if they find this practice unusual. A moment's reflection should suggest to students the parallel customs in our own culture of memorial services and the use of headstones to mark graves. Have students form research committees for the purposes of investigating practices adopted by other cultures as a means of remembering the deceased. Among the cultures students should investigate are Native American and Mesoamerican peoples.

FIGURE 12.21 Though large, plank masks are made of lightweight wood. To help steady the mask, the performer holds a stick between his teeth. This stick projects through a hole at the back of the mask. **How do you think a person wearing a plank mask is able to see?**

Bwa people, Burkina Faso, village of Pa. Plank masks entering performance area, harvest celebration, 1984. Wood, mineral pigments, fiber.

■ **FIGURE 12.22** Mende women commission helmet masks from male carvers, often stipulating exactly how they want the work to be carved. **How is the principle of variety used in this mask?**

Mende, Sierra Leone. Bundu Society mask. Late 19th century. Wood. 43.18 × 19.69 × 22.23 cm (17 × 7³/₄ × 8³/₄"). Denver Art Museum, Denver, Colorado.

The Bwa people also produce wooden masks. These masks are used during village purification ceremonies, initiations, funerals, harvest festivals, and now national holidays. The music of flutes, drums, and gongs accompanies the dancers wearing these masks. These wooden masks take different forms—animal, human, and abstract. All are painted with black, white, and red geometric patterns. Plank masks are among the most abstract of all mask forms made by the Bwa people (Figure 12.21).

Helmet Masks
■ **FIGURE 12.22**

The Mende of Sierra Leone are one of several Guinea Coast people with a separate, exclusive women's association responsible for educating and initiating young women into adult society. At ceremonies marking the end of the initiation process and on other festive and ritual occasions, prominent women in the society wear full costumes and helmet masks (Figure 12.22) that cover the entire head.

Features of this mask, particularly the elaborate hairstyle and the richly textured, lustrous black surface, represent the wealth, beauty, and social status desired for the initiates. These and other characteristics make the mask irresistibly attractive to audiences. The tiny, delicate face and high forehead are found in most masks of this type.

Individual masks have personal names and, like people, exhibit unique personalities. These personalities are expressed through the way dancers wearing the masks perform and interact.

Chapter 12 *The Arts of Africa* **279**

Art Criticism

Discuss with students the plank masks (Figure 12.21) created by the Bwa. Explain that the patterns painted on these tall, vertical masks function as a coded language. To the uninitiated, the checkerboard patterns painted on these masks might be interpreted using Western symbolic systems structured by corresponding sets of opposites: white and black, light and dark, good and evil, and so on. For those initiated into Bwa masking traditions, the black squares of the checkerboard represent the dark, worn animal-hide mats used by knowledgeable elders as they sit watching the mask rituals. The white squares represent the fresh, new, light-colored hides that more junior initiates sit on. Thus, the black squares symbolize wisdom, and the white squares symbolize ignorance, as darkness is associated with the deep knowledge of the elders. Through mask performances, initiates learn the rules of Bwa society.

After these explanations, have students meet in groups to discuss the use of the elements of art in these Bwa masks.

Studio Skills

Direct students' attention to the Bundu Society Mask in Figure 12.22. Have students create initiation masks of their own that, like the Bundu mask, suggest desirable qualities. Students should begin by forming a cylinder from a sheet of colored construction paper and fastening the cylinder with a staple. Have students cut facial features from contrasting shades of construction paper and fasten these with white glue. Attach full costumes of shredded newspaper to the lower rim of the mask. Allow them to share their finished masks.

COOPERATIVE LEARNING

Myths and Legends. The various cultures of Africa have a rich heritage of myths and legends that explain the mysteries of life and death. Ask teams of volunteers to research further the mythology of various African groups. Have each team choose one kingdom or group of people, and use references from the library and/or Internet to find information on the mythological traditions. One excellent resource is *World Mythology* by Larousse. Teams may also find relevant information in collections of legends and stories from various cultures. After completing their research, have teams share their findings with the class in oral presentations.

Critical Thinking

Ask students whether their opinions about African art have been altered as a result of this chapter. Ask them to explain why it is important to consider the society, geographic area, and the age in which a work of art is created.

Study Guide

Distribute *Study Guide* 27 in the TCR. Assist students in reviewing key concepts. 📁

Art and Humanities

Have students complete *Art and Humanities* 20, "The African Roots of Jazz," in the TCR. In this activity, students trace this musical form to its roots in African life. 📁

Studio Activities

Have students complete *Studio* 16, "Creating with African Designs," in the TCR. Students are invited to practice their creativity working with designs based on African styles. 📁

■ **FIGURE 12.23** Many of Olowe of Ise's works have only recently been identified. **Why is it sometimes difficult to identify the names of African artists?**

Olowe of Ise, Yoruba, Nigeria. *Veranda Post of Enthroned King (Opo Ogoga)*. 1910–14. Wood, pigment. 152.5 × 31.7 × 40.6 cm (60 × 12¹/₂ × 16"). The Art Institute of Chicago, Chicago, Illinois. Major Acquisitions Centennial Fund, 1984.550.

280 Unit Four *Art of Asia, the Americas, and Africa*

African Artists

Although no individual artists' names have been associated with works discussed so far, this does not mean that the artists were not well known within their own societies. Information regarding works collected during the colonial era, from the late nineteenth century to the 1960s, is often incomplete. Still, individual styles identify works of art made by particular artists, even though artists' names might not be known.

Sometimes the purpose artworks served was considered more important than the identity of the artist. In the case of some sacred works, the identity of the artists has been suppressed, and the artworks are described as having descended miraculously from the sky. In other cases, an artwork might be more closely associated with the person who commissioned it, rather than the artist who created it.

Olowe of Ise (1875–1938)

Olowe of Ise (oh-**low**-eh of **ee**-say), was an innovative Yoruba artist who lived in Nigeria during the colonial era. During his lifetime, Olowe enjoyed much fame. He was invited by Yoruba kings from throughout a wide region to come to their palaces to carve various objects. Between 1910 and 1914, Olowe carved posts for a veranda in the inner courtyard of a palace in Ikerre, in the Ekiti region of Nigeria (Figure 12.23).

As Olowe worked to honor the aesthetic traditions of Yoruba art, he also developed his own artistic vision. His unique style of carving is recognized by the forcefulness of its fully three-dimensional forms, richly textured details, and painted surfaces. His sculptures of figures in active poses appear energetic and fully animated. Like the veranda posts in Figure 12.23, his works are often large-scale.

Luba Neckrest

■ **FIGURE 12.24**

The name of the Luba artist from the Democratic Republic of Congo who made this neckrest is not known, but he has been called

More About... **Olowe of Ise.** An *oriki*, or praise poem, recited by Olowe's fourth wife, Oloju-ifun Olowe, describes her husband and his achievements:

One with a mighty sword. Handsome among his friends. Outstanding among his peers.
One who carves the hard wood of the iroko tree as though it were as soft as a calabash.
One who achieves fame with the proceeds of his carving . . .
Olowe, you are great! . . . .
Leader of all carvers. He is a great dancer,
Who dances with joy and laughter. I adore you!
You have done well! . . .

the "Master of the Cascading Hairstyle." The small neckrests he carved share similar features; all figures wear the same elaborate hairdo. While this artist's style is easily identified, no two works are exactly alike. In each work, he experimented with new combinations of symmetrical and asymmetrical forms. In Figure 12.24, for example, the sculpture's overall zigzag profile is interrupted by the asymmetrical position of its arms, with one hand caressing the edge of the hairdo.

When this neckrest was made, Luba aristocracy wore very elaborate hairdos as a sign of social rank and marital status. Molded over a frame of cane and shaped with oil and clay, such hairstyles took days to create and were meant to last for months. To avoid crushing these elaborate hairdos, neckrests elevated people's heads as they slept. Finely carved neckrests made by master carvers were highly prized objects of daily use.

Today, African art has taken its rightful place among the art traditions of the world. It was once dismissed for its frequent departures from realism. Regarded as novelties by Western travelers in the eighteenth and nineteenth centuries, African artworks were collected as souvenirs. Now African art is well represented in the collections of many major museums all across the United States.

A great deal has been written about the influence of African art on European artists, who admired its emotionally charged, abstract styles. More recently, African art has begun to be understood and appreciated on its own terms.

■ **FIGURE 12.24** This neckrest was made by an artist whose name is unknown but who developed an easily identified personal style. How are symmetrical and asymmetrical balance exhibited in this work?

"Master of the Cascading Coiffure," Zaire, Luba. Neckrest with female figure. 19th century. Wood, beads. 16.2 cm (6³/₈"). The Metropolitan Museum of Art, New York, New York. Gift of Margaret Barton Plass in honor of William Fagg, C.M.G., 1981. (1981.399).

LESSON TWO REVIEW

Reviewing Art Facts
1. What tool did African artists rely on when creating their wood carvings?
2. What does the use of metal in Kota reliquaries indicate?
3. In what ways does the concept of "mask" include more than just a face covering in African societies?
4. What do leaf masks of the Bwa people represent?

Activity... *Creating a Design Motif*
The art of Africa exhibits a strong sense of design in the way in which lines and shapes are repeated to create rhythm and movement.

On a piece of white poster board rub a heavy layer of crayon or oil pastel over the entire surface. Use different colors and repeated patterns of stripes, circles, diamonds, and lines. Keep your design large, simple, and bright. Then cover the entire colored board with a heavy layer of black crayon or india ink. On tracing paper, create a simple design using repeated design motifs. Transfer your design to the crayoned board. With a sharp-edged tool such as scissors or a craft stick, remove areas of your design to reveal the colors under the layer of black crayon or ink.

ASSESS
Checking Comprehension
➤ Have students respond to the lesson review questions. Answers are given in the box below.
➤ Assign *Application* 12, "Out of Africa," in the TCR to reinforce what students have learned. 📁

Reteaching
Assign *Reteaching 27*, found in the TCR. Have students complete the activity and review their responses. 📁

Enrichment
➤ Assign students *Enrichment* 25, "The Aesthetics of African-American Art," in the TCR. In this activity, students learn about African-American artists whose work is influenced by the art of Africa. Students then prepare an oral report for the class. 📁
➤ Have students complete *Appreciating Cultural Diversity* 20, "Contemporary African Art." In this worksheet, students learn about the kinds of art being produced in Africa today and find similar styles in African-American fashions. 📁

CLOSE
Suggest that students visit a museum with a collection of African art. (Online visits are a good option for students who do not live close to museums.) Ask students to sketch some of the sculptures and then to share and discuss their sketches.

LESSON TWO REVIEW

Answers to Reviewing Art Facts
1. An axlike tool known as an adze.
2. Metal is a symbol of wealth and importance.
3. In Africa, the concept of "mask" includes more than just a face covering. Costumes and performances contribute essential aspects.
4. Leaf masks represent nature's regenerative power.

Activity... *Creating a Design Motif*
Guide students in discussing the strong sense of design they have observed in African art. Then suggest that students work in small groups to complete the activity. Have group members share their plans for each stage of the activity, and encourage them to learn from each other's ideas and experiences.

Creating a Papier-Mâché Ceremonial Mask

Objectives

■ Create a three-dimensional papier-mâché mask inspired by African mask forms and functions.

■ Use clearly defined facial features and expressions to communicate a sense of power and dignity.

Motivator

Have each student cut out a picture of a face from a magazine or newspaper. Instruct them to select faces that suggest the individual's power and dignity. Then have students meet in groups to share and discuss the faces they have selected. Ask: How are these faces similar? What is distinctive about each face? What details in these faces indicate power and dignity?

Aesthetics

Instruct students to look through the text and identify painted and sculpted faces that succeed in revealing personality and feeling. Were there some artists who were especially successful in doing this? Select a work by one of these artists and point out how that artist treated each of the facial features. Ask them if these facial features are depicted realistically. Were they exaggerated or distorted in some way to emphasize personality and emotion?

Critiquing

Have students apply the steps of art criticism to their own artworks using the "Examining Your Work" questions on this page.

Studio LESSON

Creating a Papier-Mâché Ceremonial Mask

Materials

- Pencil and sketch paper
- Aluminum foil
- Newspaper, scissors
- Masking tape
- Sheet of poster board, approximately 10 × 12 inches
- Cellulose wallpaper paste, thinned to be creamy
- Paper towels
- Sheet of fine-grade sandpaper
- Tempera or acrylic paint, water container
- White glue, materials for decorating (pieces of colored cloth, buttons, bottle caps, yarn)

■ **FIGURE 12.26** Student Work

You will create a three-dimensional, papier-mâché mask inspired by African mask forms and functions. Use pronounced facial features in your mask and place them correctly. These features, combined with the expression on the face, should communicate a sense of otherworldliness, dignity, and power. Paint the mask with a variety of hues mixed from the primary colors, using black to add details. Attach various materials to the mask to provide decoration and actual texture.

Inspiration

Examine the masks shown in Figure 12.19, page 278, and Figure 12.22, page 279. What purposes did masks like these serve? Where is actual texture indicated? Note how the eyes, nose, and mouth are made.

Process

1. Sketch your ideas for a mask that has a sense of dignity and power.
2. Fold a sheet of aluminum foil into several layers, forming a rectangle large enough to cover your entire face. Place this over your face and, with your fingers, gently form it around the eyes, nose, mouth, and chin.
3. Remove the aluminum-foil mask and place it on a sheet of poster board. Wad small pieces of newspaper and tuck these under the mask to support it and prevent it from collapsing. Tape the mask to the poster board.
4. Cut more newspapers into ½-inch strips about 2 to 3 inches long. Soak these strips in the wallpaper-paste mixture and apply them carefully to the aluminum foil. Smooth the surface after each strip is added to remove wrinkles.
5. Allow the mask to dry. Use the scissors to cut it away from the poster board. Remove the newspaper. If you wish, cut holes for the eyes and mouth.
6. Cut and assemble various facial features from the poster-board scraps. Use masking tape to assemble and attach these features to the mask. Consider exaggerating all or some of these features. Then add a final layer of papier-mâché to cover the entire face.
7. When the mask is dry, lightly sandpaper it and paint it, using hues mixed from the three primary colors. Add details and decoration.

Examining Your Work

Describe. Are the various facial features of your mask pronounced and accurately placed? Does the mask exhibit any lifelike qualities?

Analyze. Does your mask exhibit skillful use of the papier-mâché medium? Did you use a variety of hues mixed from the primary colors? Was black used to indicate details? Were various materials attached to the mask to add decoration and actual texture?

Interpret. On what occasions would you wear the mask? Is it suitable for such a purpose? Does the mask suggest dignity and power? If so, how does it accomplish this?

Judge. Do you think that your mask is successful? Why? What qualities does it share with the masks illustrated in Figures 12.19 and 12.22? How is it different?

ASSESSMENT

Class Activity. Write these three labels and place them on three separate tables in the classroom: *literal qualities, design qualities,* and *expressive qualities.* Let students work together to examine and discuss each papier-mâché mask. Together, have them determine which aesthetic quality is best represented by the work, and place the mask on the table with the appropriate label. After students have placed all the masks on one of the labeled tables, ask: Which table has the most masks? What do you think explains this grouping? What have you learned from considering your masks in these terms?

Reviewing the Facts

Lesson One

1. How does art function in the lives of African peoples, both past and present?
2. List at least three dominant themes of African art.
3. What material was used in the production of Benin relief sculpture?
4. Describe two ways that gold was used by the Asante artists.

Lesson Two

5. What are the two most common forms of African wood carvings?
6. Describe the forms and functions of three different types of figures created by African artists.
7. Why are nails or other pieces of metal driven into figures carved by the Kongo people?
8. Name the people and the country in which a politically powerful women's association uses masks.
9. Why did the Luba people use neckrests?

Thinking Critically

1. **ANALYZE.** Look at the mask in Figure 12.22, page 279. Describe the art elements that are found in this work. Then discuss how the artist used these elements according to the principles of harmony, variety, and balance.
2. **EXTEND.** Imagine that you are a noted aesthetician writing a newspaper article. In this article, you hope to teach readers with little art background how to understand and appreciate art created in Africa. Identify one work illustrated in this chapter that you feel proves your point. What would you say about this work to show that it has artistic merit? What arguments could you expect to hear in letters from readers who disagree with you? How would you answer those arguments?

■ CAREERS IN *Art* If you enjoy studying or creating art, read about a fascinating art-related career opportunity in the *Careers in Art Handbook*, page 594.

 ▲RT SOURCE **DANCE.** Use the *Performing Arts Handbook*, page 577 to learn about Chuck Davis and the African American Dance Ensemble.

*inter*NET CONNECTION Visit Glencoe Art Online at *www.glencoe.com/sec/art*. Explore exhibits from African artists and galleries, learn about cultural and historical themes in Africa, and try an activity.

 ## Technology Project

African Sculpture

The sculpture of the diverse cultural groups that are a part of the vast African continent include a wonderful collection of works in metal, wood, and precious metals such as gold and silver. The art of Africa is intricately tied to life and nature, to ancestor and family, to spiritual and secular subjects, and to relationships among humans, animals, and nature. Although it is necessary to understand the particular culture that produced each piece in order to interpret the symbols used, the sense of design exhibited in African sculpture is immediately obvious.

1. Working in small groups and using available resources, find an example of African sculpture that you find especially interesting. Find out as much as possible about the symbolism of this piece.
2. Create a multimedia presentation or a lesson on the design qualities in the African sculpture that your group has selected.
3. Include information in your presentation on the elements and principles of design. Pay special attention to how the artist used repetition, pattern, and balance. Study closely the aesthetic qualities of the piece. Does it exhibit literal, design, or expressive qualities?

Reviewing the Facts

1. Art is integrated into the lives of people.
2. Possible responses include birth and death, the roles of men and women, coming of age, sickness and healing, the human relationship with nature.
3. Copper alloy.
4. Gold was used to make jewelry and was pounded into sheets of gold leaf to encase sculpted staff finials.
5. Figures and masks.
6. Cultural heroes, primordial couples, and spirit spouse sculptures.
7. To document the sculpture's divine interventions into human affairs. Each nail or iron blade records a particular incident.
8. Mende people of Sierra Leone.
9. It supported the head and conserved an elaborate hair style.

Thinking Critically

1. Answers will vary. Students should follow the steps of art criticism to describe and analyze this work.
2. Responses will vary. They should reveal an awareness of both aesthetic theory and the artistic purpose underlying the works in this chapter.

283

 ## Teaching the Technology Project

Encourage students to suggest appropriate sculptures, and list their suggestions on the board. Some students might also suggest particular kinds of sculpture or cultures that they would like to explore. Add these suggestions to the list. Then let students use the ideas on the board as the basis for forming cooperative learning groups.

▲RT SOURCE Assign feature in the *Performing Arts Handbook*, page 577.

CAREERS IN ART If time permits, have interested students investigate the career information in the *Careers in Art Handbook*, page 594.

*inter*NET CONNECTION Have students go online and learn more about artists on preselected Web sites with the Internet activity for this chapter.

Art in Quest of Salvation

Unit Five introduces the rise of Christianity as a guiding force in Western art and traces this thread through early Christian and Byzantine art up through the Middle Ages. The art of Islam is also considered.

Chapter 13 *Early Christian, Byzantine, and Islamic Art* details the profound influence the teachings of Christ and Muhammad had on the art and architecture of the Byzantine Empire, the Middle East, and parts of Spain.

Chapter 14 *Early Medieval and Romanesque Art* traces developments in early churches and monasteries, as well as the art created for these structures.

Chapter 15 *Gothic Art* chronicles the advances in architecture that made possible the soaring cathedrals of Europe and the works of the first great painters.

National Museum of Women in the Arts

You may wish to use the National Museum of Women in the Arts videodisc and/or CD-ROM. The videodisc features a bar code guide, and the interactive CD-ROM provides stimulating activities.

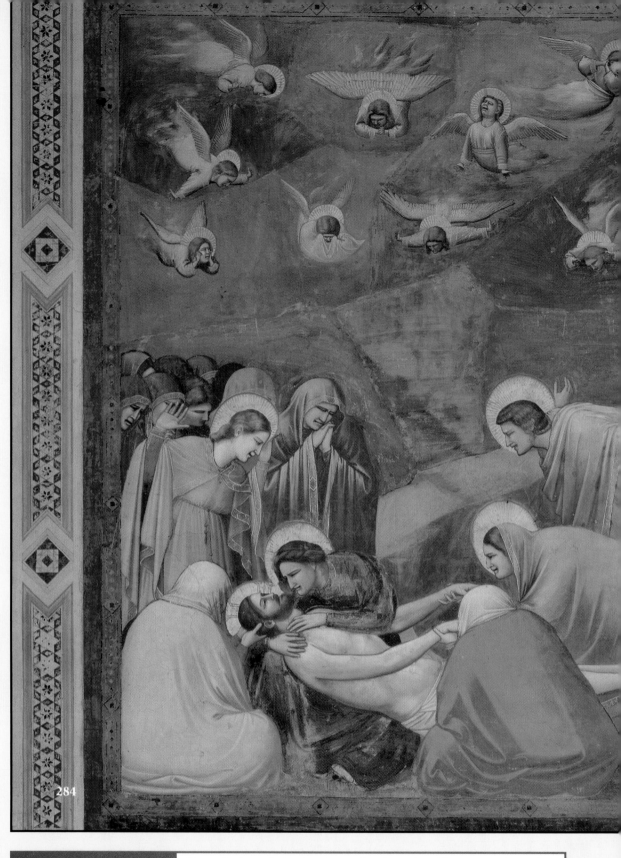

284

More About…   **Giotto.** In the early 1300s, Giotto painted a series of frescoes on the walls of a church in Padua, Italy. His fame eventually spread to Rome where the Pope was preparing to decorate St. Peter's Basilica with paintings. The Pope sent a messenger to Florence to gather information about the artist. When asked for a sample of his work, the artist took a pencil and, with a quick turn of his hand, produced a perfect circle on a scrap of paper. "Is this what you want me to take to the Pope?" the messenger asked. Giotto nodded, saying, "It is enough and more than enough." The messenger returned and presented the drawing with a description of how it was made. The Pope looked at the circle and immediately summoned the artist. Giotto was received with great honor, having demonstrated with a twist of his wrist that he was one of the outstanding artists of his time.

Art in Quest of Salvation

*"Giotto elevated
painting from
the service of
symbolism and
made it a mirror
of mankind."*

Sarel Eimerl
The World of Giotto
(1967)

Giotto. *Lamentation Pietà.* c. 1305.
Fresco. Scrovegni Chapel, Padua, Italy.

Introducing the Unit

Point out that the period beginning with the fall of Rome and ending with the time of great intellectual rebirth known as the Renaissance has been referred to as the "Dark Ages." Emphasize that this period, which witnessed among other things, the emergence of a monumental style of architecture, was anything but dark. Direct students to one of the photographs of Gothic architecture in Chapter 15 and ask if they know what this style is called.

Discussing the Quotation

Have students examine the fresco and describe the appearance and actions of the figures in this picture. How has the principle figure been emphasized? Describe the expressions and behavior of the other figures in this work. Giotto's work focused on familiar stories from the Bible, but, unlike anything ever done before, this artist's paintings were peopled with flesh-and-blood figures. The figures exhibited realistic human characteristics. They moved about in what appeared to be real space. After reading the quotation about Giotto's work, discuss the importance of this fresco in its depiction of people with real feelings and emotions.

285

Teacher Notes _____

_____

_____

_____

_____

Early Christian, Byzantine, and Islamic Art

LESSON ONE Early Christian and Byzantine Art
(pages 288–296)

Classroom Resources

- 📁 Appreciating Cultural Diversity 22
- 📁 Cooperative Learning 19, 20
- 📁 Reproducible Lesson Plan 28
- 📁 Reteaching Activity 28
- 📁 Study Guide 28

Features

Map of Byzantine Empire
(page 288)

Symbolism in Christian Art
> *Good Shepherd, Orants, and the Story of Jonah*
> *(page 289)*

Time & Place CONNECTIONS
(page 294)

LOOKING Closely
(page 295)

LESSON TWO Islamic Art
(pages 297–304)

Classroom Resources

- 📁 Art and Humanities 21
- 📁 Enrichment Activity 26
- 📁 Reproducible Lesson Plan 29
- 📁 Reteaching Activity 29
- 📁 Study Guide 29

Features

LOOKING Closely
(page 299)

END OF CHAPTER
(pages 305–307)

Studio LESSONS
- Byzantine-Style Self-Portrait *(page 305)*
- Creating a Word Design *(page 306)*

ADDITIONAL CHAPTER RESOURCES

Activities

- 📁 Application 13
- 📁 Advanced Studio Activity 13
- 🖱 Chapter 13 Internet Activity
- 📁 Studio Activity 17

Fine Art Resources

🕹 **Transparency**

Art in Focus Transparency 17

The Harbaville Triptypch

▨ **Fine Art Print**

Focus on World Art Print 13

*Bahram Gur with the Indian Princess in
Her Black Pavillion*

Assessment

- 📁 Chapter 13 Test
- 📁 Performance Assessment

Multimedia Resources

- 🎭 Artsource® Performing Arts Package
- 💿 National Gallery Laser Disc
- 💿 National Museum of Women in the Arts CD-ROM
- 📼 Arts & Entertainment Videos

NATIONAL STANDARDS FOR ARTS EDUCATION

The National Standards for Arts Education provide guidelines for grade-appropriate competency in the visual arts. The Content Standards for grades 9–12 are:

1. Understanding and applying media, techniques, and processes.
2. Using knowledge of structures and functions.
3. Choosing and evaluating a range of subject matter, symbols, and ideas.
4. Understanding the visual arts in relation to history and cultures.
5. Reflecting upon and assessing the characteristics and merits of their work and the work of others.
6. Making connections between visual arts and other disciplines.

Listed below are the National Standards for the Visual Arts addressed in this chapter. For a breakdown of the categories listed under each content standard, refer to the *Reproducible Lesson Plans* booklet in the TCR.

1. (a, b) **2.** (a, b, c) **3.** (a) **4.** (a, b, c) **5.** (a, b) **6.** (a, b)

HANDBOOK MATERIAL

Anna Djanbazian
(page 585)

CAREERS IN *Art*

Advertising Artist *(page 602)*

Beyond the Classroom

Resources dedicated to promoting information on arts and architecture can be found at the non-profit center for Islamic and Arabic Arts. Find them by visiting our Web site at *www.glencoe.com/sec/art.*

🕐 **Out of Time?** If time does not permit teaching this chapter in its entirety, you may wish to preview the artwork and captions with students. Scan the heads in each lesson with students. Discuss the Looking Closely features and examine Symbolism in Christian Art on page 289.

Early Christian, Byzantine, and Islamic Art

CHAPTER 13

INTRODUCE

Chapter Overview

CHAPTER 13 examines the history and art of the early Christians, the Byzantine Empire, and the Islamic world.

Lesson One covers Roman and early Christian art and architecture and the Byzantine use of mosaics.

Lesson Two deals with Muhammad's teachings and the development of Islamic art in Spain.

Studio Lessons direct students to complete a Byzantine self-portrait and an india ink design using parts of a word.

Art & Social Studies

Guide students in examining and discussing the artwork.

Then focus attention on the central figure. Theodora. Ask: What indicates that the central figure is a woman of authority?

Interested students might research the depiction of women in artworks at different times and in different cultures.

National Standards

This chapter addresses the following National Standards for the Arts:

1. (a,b)	**4.** (a,b,c)
2. (a,b,c)	**5.** (a,b)
3. (a)	**6.** (a,b)

Early Christian, Byzantine, and Islamic Art

Art & Social Studies ■ **FIGURE 13.1** Theodora, empress and wife to Justinian of the Byzantine Empire, was one of the most powerful and respected women of the early Christian era. As a trusted political advisor, her decisions helped maintain the stability of Justinian's rule. Nearly all the laws passed reflected her influence. After Theodora's death little significant legislation was passed by Justinian.

Theodora and Attendants. c. A.D. 547. Mosaic from San Vitale. Ravenna, Italy.

286

CHAPTER 13 RESOURCES

Teacher's Classroom Resources
- 📁 Advanced Studio Activity 13
- 📁 Application 13
- 🖱 Chapter 13 Internet Activity
- 📁 Studio Activity 17

Assessment
- 📁 Chapter 13 Test
- 📁 Performance Assessment

Fine Art Resources
- 🔨 *Art in Focus* Transparency 17
  The Harbaville Triptych
- 📁 *Focus on World Art* Print 13
  Bahram Gur with the Indian Princess in Her Black Pavilion

*T*he latter part of the second century marked the beginning of a period of rapid decline in the Roman Empire. In spite of capable rulers such as Diocletian and Constantine, the downward spiral continued, fueled by a variety of internal ills and external threats and invasions. The devastating invasions of the fifth century finally brought the collapse of Rome's political structure. As Rome fell, the Christian Church became a powerful influence. Musicians, writers, and artists looked to the empire that had passed and tried to reconcile it with an uncertain but hopeful future. In the Byzantine Empire, Muslims, Jews, and Christians developed a rich culture of philosophy, music, literature, and visual arts.

Introducing the Chapter

Have students imagine they just learned that the United States was planning to adopt an official state religion. Ask how such a development might affect the kinds of art the government would sponsor. Explain that they will learn about the importance of the relationship between governments, society, and organized religion, and about the impact that relationship has on art.

Dance/Music While studying this chapter, use *Performing Arts Handbook* page 585 to help students see how Anna Djanbazian's choreography draws from the ancient cultures of the Middle East. She keeps these traditions alive through the performance of dance and music.

YOUR Portfolio

List symbols associated with your background and/or family heritage. Explain in writing how each symbol is an important part of your life. Create a thumbnail sketch of a larger design of the symbols and people in your life. Your design might be similar to a Byzantine mosaic, or a design of your choice. Arrange the symbols in relation to the people in the design. How will the viewer understand the meaning of the symbols? Could the symbols be misunderstood? How would this mistake affect a viewer's interpretation of a piece of art? Store your notes and completed design in your portfolio.

Focus ON THE ARTS

LITERATURE
Omar Khayyam, a Persian astronomer-poet, wrote *The Rubiyat*. Avicenna and other great Muslim scholars attempted to link the ideas of science, theology, and philosophy.

THEATRE
As Rome fell, critics demanded closure of the Roman theatre, insisting it was one of the decadent pursuits that destroyed the Empire. Christians were forbidden to attend the theatre.

MUSIC
Early church music was sung softly because services had to be hidden from the authorities. This vocal music was based on chants of ancient Greek origin.

Focus ON THE ARTS

Bring in a recording of a Gregorian chant. Tell students that this music originated in Byzantium and was eventually adapted by the church in Rome. Play a selection or two for the students. Ask students what mood this music conveys. Then ask: What parts of a Gregorian chant put you in mind of some other world? Explain that balance, emphasis, intensity, and harmony of this style of music suggest tremendous calmness, away from the strife of the world. The lack of melody or rhythm is different from music that is familiar to us.

287

DEVELOPING A PORTFOLIO

Choosing a Project. Learning to isolate problem areas in an artwork can help the student decide whether or not the project should be included in a portfolio. Show students how a series of critical questions will help them make a decision about the piece. First, they should determine if the project meets the specific requirements given. If not, what adjustments are necessary? Second, have they remained focused on their individual goals for the project? If not, what direction can they take in order to meet their goals? Then have them apply the four steps of art criticism to their work. Last, they should ask themselves if the artwork is a worthy example for their portfolio.

Early Christian and Byzantine Art

FOCUS

Lesson Objectives

After studying this lesson, students will be able to:

■ Explain the early Christian use of symbolism.

■ Describe the relationship between early Christian art and religious beliefs.

■ Describe Byzantine contributions to art.

Building Vocabulary

Ask a student who knows or is studying Italian to identify the word related to *campanile,* or have a volunteer look in an Italian language dictionary for a term that starts with the same letters as *campanile.* The Italian word *campana* means "bell."

Motivator

Draw an octagon on the board and ask students what street sign this shape calls to mind (the stop sign). Ask students to name other popular shapes and symbols they associate with ideas, products, and so on. Explain that, as they study this lesson, students will learn about the role symbols played in early Christian art.

Introducing the Lesson

To set the mood for the reading, dim the lights in the classroom and play a recording of slow, dirge-like mood music, if possible the "Catacombae" movement of Mussorgsky's *Pictures at an Exhibition* or his *Songs and Dances of Death.* Ask students to imagine they have been commissioned to create art for an underground "city of the dead." What kinds of works will they create?

Early Christian and Byzantine Art

Vocabulary
■ catacombs
■ campanile
■ mosaic
■ piers

Discover
After completing this lesson, you will be able to:
■ Explain how early Christians used art to express their religious beliefs.
■ Discuss significant developments in Byzantine architecture and mosaic art.

*I*n the vacuum left by the decline of the Roman Empire, a new source of power was born—the Christian Church. The place of the Roman emperors was taken by popes; the Church was to play the dominant role in the 500 years following the waning of the Classical period. The Church's influence eventually spread to touch on every aspect of life. Nowhere was this more evident than in the visual arts.

Early Christian Art

For many years, the Christian religion was not legal throughout the Roman Empire, resulting in much hardship and persecution for its many followers. Finally, in A.D. 313, Christianity was made legal when the emperor Constantine signed the Edict of Milan. Pictures with hidden Christian meanings were being painted long before that time, however.

Many of those early paintings were made on the stone walls of narrow underground passageways. When persecuted by Roman emperors, the Christians dug **catacombs,** or *underground passageways,* as places to hold religious services and bury their dead. In time, the catacombs grew into a vast maze of tunnels. A painting found on a catacomb ceiling (Figure 13.3) in Rome tells a great deal about the early Christians' outlook on life and offers insights into the characteristics and purpose of their art.

The views of early Christians set them apart from those who believed in the Roman religion. The Christians believed Christ to be the savior of all people; they hoped to join him in heaven after death as a reward for following his teachings. They had little interest in gaining fame and fortune in the world. Instead, they sought an eternal reward in the form of life after death.

Characteristics of Early Christian Art

In their paintings of people, early Christian artists showed little interest in the beauty, grace, and strength of the human body, which were so important to Greek and Roman artists. Christian art was intended to illustrate the power and glory of Christ. It was also meant to tell, as clearly as possible, the story of his life on earth. Christ's life story was important because it was the model for people to follow as the surest way to attain salvation.

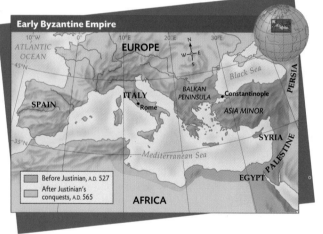

Early Byzantine Empire

■ Before Justinian, A.D. 527
□ After Justinian's conquests, A.D. 565

MAP SKILLS

■ **FIGURE 13.2** In the fourth century A.D., the Roman Empire was divided into a Western and an Eastern empire. **How do you imagine this political separation affected artistic development in the two areas?**

288

LESSON ONE RESOURCES

Teacher's Classroom Resources

📁 Appreciating Cultural Diversity 22
📁 Cooperative Learning 19, 20
📁 Reproducible Lesson Plan 28

📁 Reteaching Activity 28
📁 Study Guide 28

Symbolism in Christian *Art*

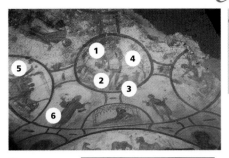

FIGURE 13.3 *Good Shepherd, Orants, and the Story of Jonah.* Catacomb of Saints Peter and Marcellinus. Rome. Fourth century A.D. Archivio PCAS.

 *M*ore than 1,650 years ago, an unknown Christian artist completed a painting on the rough ceiling of a gallery in one of the catacombs. The artist who painted on that rough catacomb wall borrowed heavily from art forms seen all over Rome, but these forms were given new Christian meanings.

5

The arms of the cross end in half-circles in which the biblical story of Jonah and the whale is told. This story illustrates God's power to protect the faithful from danger.

6

Standing figures with their hands raised in prayer represent all the members of the Church pleading for God's assistance and mercy.

1

A great circle was painted to represent heaven. Within this circle is a cross, the symbol of Christ's death and resurrection.

2

The shepherd in the center circle represents Christ.

3

The sheep around him symbolize his faithful followers. Christians believed that Christ, also called the Good Shepherd, was willing to lay down his life for them, his flock.

4

The lamb on Christ's shoulders symbolizes those people who need additional help on the difficult road to salvation.

Symbolism in Early Christian Art

The early Christians' view of life on earth as a preparation for the hereafter is reflected in the artworks they produced. These works may have *appeared* Roman, but the beliefs and ideas they passed on to other Christians were not Roman beliefs and ideas—they were Christian.

Christian artists used symbols as a kind of code. Familiar figures or signs were used to represent something else. Catacomb paintings are filled with images of animals, birds, and plants, which are also found in Roman art. When Romans looked at one of these images, perhaps a painting of a goldfinch, they saw only the goldfinch. Christians looking at the same painting remembered that the goldfinch ate thistles and thorns, and plants of that kind reminded them of Christ's crown of thorns. Thus, the goldfinch was a symbol of Christ's death. Over time, birds, animals, and plants came to symbolize different Christian ideas.

Chapter 13 *Early Christian, Byzantine, and Islamic Art* **289**

TEACH
Using Map Skills

Have students look at the map in Figure 13.2 and point out the port cities in the Roman Empire. Discuss how trade with the East influenced the development of Byzantine art. Can students think of any examples of how trade in modern times has led to the borrowing of artistic styles or other facets of culture? Have them consider the influence of Japanese aesthetics on contemporary North American architecture and, conversely, the Japanese interest in American fashion and European painting.

Art History

Have students examine Figure 13.3, noting in the text the conditions under which it was created. Ask students whether they can imagine any circumstances under which they would be willing to risk punishment or even death to complete a painting. What happens to a group of people if they never are able to express their beliefs and aspirations through the arts?

Symbolism in Christian *Art*

Let students examine the painting in Figure 13.3 and read and discuss the explanation of the symbolism in the work. Invite a student to recount the Old Testament story of Jonah and the whale (or tell the basic story yourself). Then refer students to Figure 13.3 and have them identify which details of the account are illustrated in the catacomb painting. Discuss whether someone who was not already familiar with the tale could understand this picture. What facets of the picture would help a viewer to recognize events in the story? Is the painting realistic? Is it expressive?

Cross Curriculum

HISTORY. Divide the class into research teams, and have each team select a group that, like the early Christians, has been exposed to systematic persecution by another group. Have groups share their findings. What are some common motivating factors behind this mistreatment? What traits in each situation are unique?

Art History

Introduce students to an important art history research tool, the dictionary of symbols in art. Have several copies available (they need not be the same version) and distribute them to groups of students. Have each group use felt-tip markers to create a drawing that incorporates at least three symbols listed in the dictionary. Display each drawing and ask the rest of the class to interpret the pictures.

Aesthetics

Help students understand that symbolism is not restricted to art. Have students browse through magazines and clip images from advertisements that represent symbols in contemporary American culture. Ask them to consider how symbols are used today. What messages are conveyed through the use of symbols? Compare these messages to those communicated through the use of symbols in early Christian art.

A dog was used as a symbol of faithfulness because of its watchfulness and loyalty. Ivy, because it is always green, was associated with eternal life.

The figures in the catacomb painting are sketchy, and there is little to suggest depth or the world in which the figures lived. Clearly, the artist's main interest was in illustrating the Christian story so that followers could "read" it easily and meditate on its meaning.

Basilicas

Not long after the catacomb painting was completed, the status of Christians began to improve. Christianity had spread rapidly across the entire Roman Empire, and the emperor Constantine finally granted Christians the freedom to practice their faith openly. A new kind of building was needed for the large numbers of worshipers. Again, the Christians borrowed from the Romans. Christian builders selected the basilica as their model. This was the long, spacious building that the Romans had used for their public meeting halls.

Christian churches were intended as retreats from the real world, places where worshipers could take part in a deeply spiritual event. The exterior of these churches was quite plain (Figure 13.4), especially when compared to classical temples. The later addition of a **campanile,** or *bell tower,* did little to change the outer simplicity of these early churches.

In contrast to the plain exterior, the inside of the church was designed for dramatic effect (Figure 13.5). As in the Roman basilica, rows

■ **FIGURE 13.4** The exteriors of Christian churches were quite plain. **What do you think this plain exterior indicates about the lives and the religious beliefs of the local people?**

Sant' Apollinare in Classe. Ravenna, Italy. A.D. 533–49.

■ **FIGURE 13.5** Two rows of columns divide the church interior into a nave and two smaller side aisles. **Compare the decoration inside this church with the decoration on the exterior (Figure 13.4). How do you account for the differences?**

Sant´ Apollinare in Classe (interior, looking toward the apse). Ravenna, Italy.

290 **Unit Five** *Art in Quest of Salvation*

Technology

National Gallery of Art Videodisc Use the following images as examples of more works by artists introduced in this lesson.

Pietro Lorenzetti
Madonna and Child with Saint Mary Magdalene and Saint Catherine

Search Frame 36

Attributed to Cimabue
Madonna and Child with the Baptist and Saint Peter

Search Frame 56

XIII Century Byzantine School
Enthroned Madonna and Child

Search Frame 18

Use Glencoe's *Correlation Bar Code Guide to the National Gallery of Art* to locate more artworks.

of columns divided the huge space into a main corridor, or nave, and narrower aisles on either side. Also, as with the earlier model, windows were inserted in the space between the wooden roofs over the side aisles and the higher roof over the nave. At one end of the nave stood the altar. There the priest solemnly celebrated the Mass, while the faithful silently followed each movement with their eyes.

Mosaics
■ FIGURE 13.6

When eyes strayed from the altar, they rose to view walls richly decorated with mosaics (Figure 13.6). A **mosaic** is *a decoration made with small pieces of glass and stone set in cement.* Christian artists placed mosaics on walls where light from windows and candles caused them to flicker and glow mysteriously. This may be one of the reasons why early Christian churches came to be known as "Houses of Mystery."

From the few early Christian churches that have survived, it is clear that they served as the basic model for church architecture in western Europe for centuries.

Growth of Byzantine Culture

After the eastern capital was established in Constantinople in A.D. 330, the Roman Empire functioned as two separate sections, East and West, each with its own emperor. (See map, Figure 13.2, page 288.)

■ **FIGURE 13.6** Like many other early Christian churches, this one is decorated with a colorful mosaic in the apse. Why were mosaics used for decoration? Why were they placed in the apse?

Apse decorations from Sant' Apollinare in Classe. Ravenna, Italy.

In the West, the emperors gradually lost their influence and prestige. After a long struggle, the Western Roman Empire fell to barbarian invaders. This marked the end of the Classical era. As the emperors lost power, the Church, governed by the popes, assumed its place as the central authority in the West.

The eastern part of the Roman Empire remained unified and strong. Now called the Byzantine Empire, it continued to thrive for another 1,000 years. The city of Constantinople soon surpassed Rome in both size and wealth. It became the largest city in the medieval world and was a great cultural center with grand public buildings and art treasures.

In Constantinople, Roman, Greek, and Eastern influences were blended to produce a rich and brilliant art. Above all, this art glorified the Christian religion and served the needs of the Church. It set the standard for artistic excellence in western Europe until the twelfth century.

Chapter 13 Early Christian, Byzantine, and Islamic Art **291**

Art Criticism
Divide the class into two groups. Refer one group of students to Figures 13.4 and 13.5, the other to Figures 9.16 and 9.17 (pages 204 and 205). Have each group prepare a detailed description of the exterior and interior of the structure assigned to them. Then have groups share their descriptions, noting similarities and differences.

Aesthetics
Have students list as many different kinds of architectural spaces as possible, such as houses, shopping malls, sports stadiums, and places of worship. Have students think of specific examples of each type and find the interior height of each structure. Gather the data together and discuss the aesthetic reasons that may govern the height of a structure's interior. Consider both practical factors, such as how sound travels within small versus large spaces, and the different moods generated by intimate rather than expansive settings. Direct students' attention to Figure 13.5. In what way do the interior dimensions contribute to the use and the atmosphere of the building?

Cross Curriculum
HISTORY. Call students' attention to the dates during which Sant' Apollinare in Classe was under construction (A.D. 533–49). Point out that this was a period of intense political activity throughout the world. During this period, the Chi dynasty ended in southern China, and Britain resisted a Saxon invasion. Ask interested students to research and report on these events or on other political developments of the same period.

Art Criticism

Have students study the photograph and floor plan of Hagia Sophia in Figures 13.7 and 13.8. What type of balance has been used in the structure? What adjectives would students use to describe the overall impression conveyed by the building? To what extent is this impression related to the building's use? Would the viewer react differently if the building were reserved for commercial office space? Why or why not?

Critical Thinking

Have students consider the planning and construction of Hagia Sophia. Ask: How has the role of the architect evolved since Justinian selected two mathematicians to design this church? Would a contemporary architect be able to, or want to, create another Hagia Sophia? How much longer is the church likely to remain standing?

Critical Thinking

At the time Christianity was coming into its own right, the seeds for another religion, Islam, were being planted in Mecca where, in A.D. 570, Muhammad was born. During this same period, Buddhism was introduced in Japan. Assign groups of students to research these developments and share their findings with the rest of the class.

Did You Know?

The name *Hagia Sophia* derives from a Greek phrase meaning "Holy (or Divine) Wisdom."

Byzantine Architecture and Mosaics

The best examples of the Byzantine style were great churches. Western architects favored the hall-like basilica plan for their churches, but those in the East preferred a central plan.

Hagia Sophia
■ FIGURE 13.7

Hagia Sophia (Figure 13.7), built in the sixth century A.D. by the emperor Justinian, was the greatest of these centrally planned churches (Figure 13.8). Justinian hired two Greek math experts to design Hagia Sophia. The finished church beautifully blends

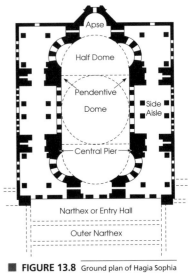

■ **FIGURE 13.7** The Hagia Sophia is one of the finest examples of centrally planned Byzantine churches. **How does this church differ from the basilica plan used in the Western Empire? Of which Roman building does this structure remind you?**

Hagia Sophia. Istanbul, Turkey. A.D. 532–37.

■ **FIGURE 13.8** Ground plan of Hagia Sophia

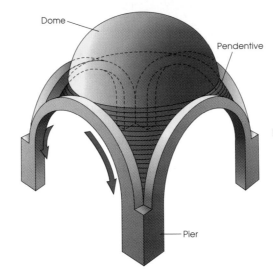

■ **FIGURE 13.9** The use of piers and arches in the construction of Hagia Sophia's dome allows more light to enter the building. Supporting the dome's great weight are four pendentives, the triangular portions at the corners of each arch. **Can you identify how the arches are in turn supported by four piers?**

Plan of Hagia Sophia dome

About the *Artwork*

Hagia Sophia. The central dome of Hagia Sophia was the largest in circumference and the lightest in appearance until twentieth-century techniques of casting concrete were developed. The gentle curve has been likened to the arch of the sky when viewed over the sea. The first version of this dome was, in fact, too shallow and too wide, and it fell down during an earthquake in A.D. 558. The new version was a complete success, but it was never reproduced in its time. Patrons and architects seemed to accept that it was a one-of-a-kind original that was not to be imitated.

the engineering skills of the Romans with a Greek sensitivity for carefully balanced proportions. Its most impressive feature is the huge dome. Almost 200 feet across, it is 31 feet higher than the one used for the Pantheon. The dome over the Pantheon is placed on a massive concrete drum made with thick, concrete walls. Hagia Sophia's dome rests on four huge **piers,** *massive vertical pillars,* that support arches made of cut stone (Figure 13.9).

By using this method of construction, the builders were free to erect thinner walls and add more windows to light the interior of the church. This method also creates the appearance of lighter weight. The great dome seems to soar over a row of windows placed around its base.

The Mosaics of Hagia Sophia

Inside, Hagia Sophia's dim lighting and shimmering surfaces combine to produce a dreamlike setting (Figure 13.10). Walls of stone and marble are decorated with gold, silver, ivory, and gems. Worshipers are treated to a dazzling display of red and green marble piers, polished marble slabs, brilliant murals, and gleaming mosaics.

Churches as large as Hagia Sophia required special decoration on the inside. Works of art had to have bright colors and be large enough to be seen from great distances. Mosaics met these special needs. Brightly colored mosaics became a trademark of Byzantine churches. They were created to tell familiar stories from the Bible using easily recognizable symbols.

■ **FIGURE 13.10** Look carefully at the interior details of this church. **What principles of art help unify the interior? What do you consider its most impressive features?**

Interior of Hagia Sophia. Istanbul, Turkey. A.D. 532–37.

Aesthetics

Have students compare the dome of Hagia Sophia (Figures 13.7 and 13.9) with that of the Pantheon in Figure 9.16 (page 204). What features do the two domes share? In what ways are they dissimilar? What role does surrounding scenery have on the impression each dome makes? Which of the domes is more visually striking? Have students explain their answers.

Studio Skills

Provide students with a variety of magazines and ask them to select photographs of individuals with stances or poses reminiscent of those in Figure 13.11 (page 294). Then have students glue the photos to pieces of scrap lumber and affix transparent plastic jewels, metallic buttons, and silver and gold foil in the manner of jewel-encrusted Byzantine icons. Discuss the effect. Is it possible to re-create the transcendent Byzantine mood using modern American photographs? Why or why not?

Art Criticism

Have students carefully examine the base of the throne in Figure 13.11 (page 294). What is unusual in how it is rendered? Where else in this mosaic can you see an example of skewed perspective? Have students describe the Byzantine use of perspective.

Did You Know?

When he was given the task of replacing St. Paul's Cathedral after the Great Fire of London, architect Christopher Wren sent for the measurements of Hagia Sophia's dome.

CULTURAL DIVERSITY

Houses of Worship. Discuss with students how Hagia Sophia's layout suits the purposes for which the building was used. Ask students to select religious buildings used by members of various faiths and investigate how the special needs of different religious groups dictate the design of houses of worship. For example, how are synagogues designed so that they can accommodate both the large crowds that gather for High Holy days and smaller groups of worshipers at other times of the year? How does the Quaker practice of sharing divine inspiration during times of quiet, group reflection influence the layout of a Quaker meeting house?

Aesthetics

Have students examine Figure 13.13 and Figure 13.1 (page 286). Discuss what sort of images of the emperor and empress are suggested in these portraits. Why might political leaders want to be viewed in this way? Then have students carefully study photos of present-day political leaders. How do contemporary leaders want to be viewed by their people? Discuss why Byzantine and modern politicians take such different approaches to presenting themselves to the public.

Studio Skills

Have students design a group mural in the manner of those of San Vitale. First they will need to decide on a subject. After studying Figures 13.1 and 13.13 for stylistic features, students should use tempera on a sheet of white paper cut from a roll measuring 3 feet high. Colors should typify those of the Byzantine palette. Students can use metallic pigments to imitate gold leaf and apply glitter to the background before the paint dries.

Did You Know?

Justinian and Theodora had more problems with the Church than is suggested in their reverential mosaic portraits at San Vitale. Justinian was tangled in heresy, and Theodora was very sympathetic to the Monophysite belief that Christ has one nature.

FIGURE 13.11 The mosaics in this huge church are large and brilliantly colored. Why do you suppose they were made that way? How do you imagine worshipers responded to these images?

Madonna and Child with the Emperors Justinian and Constantine. A.D. 986–94. Byzantine mosaics from Hagia Sophia. Istanbul, Turkey.

The Virgin and Child
■ FIGURE 13.11

In Hagia Sophia, one notable mosaic shows the Virgin (Christ's mother) and the Christ Child between two figures (Figure 13.11). The figure on the left is the emperor Justinian carrying a small church, while the figure on the right is the emperor Constantine bearing a small city. The meaning of the mosaic is clear: The emperors are proclaiming the loyalty and dedication of church and state to the Virgin and Child.

Refuge at Ravenna

The Byzantine style was not limited to the Eastern half of the empire. When Constantine moved his capital to Constantinople, contacts and trade between East and West were not wholly broken off and were maintained until the middle of the fourth century A.D. Nowhere in Italy is the Byzantine style more obvious than in the Italian city of Ravenna.

Time & Place
CONNECTIONS

Early Christian and Byzantine Periods
C. A.D. 200–1550

CATACOMBS. Early Christians found refuge and religious expression in secret tunnels and underground mazes. Some of these hidden meeting places can still be found under the streets of modern cities with roots in Christianity.

BRONZE WEIGHTS. Merchants of the Byzantine empire carried on trade and weighed goods using small weights made of bronze and decorated with silver inlay. These artifacts represent an item of daily commerce from the Byzantine era.

ASTROLABE. This instrument of ancient astronomers was used to measure the angles of stars above the horizon. It is representative of Middle Eastern advances in measurement and mathematics.

Activity **Double Entry Journal.** Make an analysis of the items on this page. Divide a paper into two columns. In one column, make a sketch of each artifact. In the second column, record notes about the purpose of each item and add information from the text or from other resources. Keep your sheet in your journal or portfolio.

Time & Place   Early Christian and Byzantine Periods

CONNECTIONS Have students examine and discuss the images in this Time & Place feature. Which are familiar? Why? Then let students work with partners to complete the Double Entry Journal activity. Partners can work together to find good research resources and can share and discuss their findings; suggest that students might check the Internet, encyclopedias, reference works and other nonfiction books in the public or school library, and/or talk with informed individuals. When students have completed their activity projects, schedule class time during which they can compare and discuss their work. What differences do they note? What accounts for those differences?

Ravenna had become the capital of the Western Roman Empire early in the fifth century A.D. The Roman emperor moved to Ravenna because it was isolated and seemed a safe refuge from barbarian invaders. He was mistaken. Ravenna was captured in A.D. 476. With this, the last emperor of the West was forced to surrender his authority to the barbarian conquerors. Later, in A.D. 540, Justinian, the Eastern emperor, recaptured the city. It remained under Byzantine control for the next two centuries.

The Mosaics of San Vitale

Justinian had long dreamed of equaling the achievements of early Roman emperors. He saw his chance with the capture of Ravenna. He was determined to erect a great church in the city, one that would rival anything his predecessors had built. Justinian's church, San Vitale, became the most famous church of that time.

Justinian and Attendants
■ FIGURE 13.13

Inside San Vitale, artisans created two mosaics on opposite sides of the apse (Figure 13.12). One of these shows the emperor Justinian with the archbishop, deacons, soldiers, and attendants (Figure 13.13, page 296).

The bodies of the most important people overlap those of the lesser ones. Note, however, that the archbishop beside Justinian places his leg in front of the emperor's cloak, perhaps to show that in spiritual matters the archbishop was the leader of all people, including the emperor.

Theodora and Attendants

On the opposite wall, facing the emperor and his party, are his wife, the empress Theodora, and her attendants. (See Figure 13.1, page 286.) Like Justinian, she is dressed in magnificent robes and wears the imperial crown. Theodora, the daughter of a bearkeeper and a former popular actress, is shown as the equal of any saint in heaven. The great halo around her head is similar to her husband's. It is a symbol of their

■ FIGURE 13.12 Notice the extensive decoration of the interior of this church. **Why are mosaics within the apse especially significant?**

View of the Apse. San Vitale. Ravenna, Italy. A.D. 526–47.

virtue and innocence, and proclaims that they are marked for future sainthood. The emperor and empress are part of a solemn religious procession leading to the altar. They bear items used in the celebration of the Mass.

The figures on the walls of San Vitale and other Byzantine churches cannot be described as realistic or natural. They are flat and stiff, more abstract and formal than early Christian art.

Byzantine artists did not aspire to create figures of beauty and grace. Rather, they intended their pictures to be religious lessons, presented as simply and clearly as possible. Important court dignitaries were an important part of these lessons. They reminded common people that everyone—even members of the highest royalty—had to pay homage to God in order to gain salvation.

Chapter 13 *Early Christian, Byzantine, and Islamic Art* **295**

LOOKING Closely

Direct students attention to the mosaics shown in Figure 13.12 and Figure 13.13. Help them identify the location of the works *Justinian and Attendants* and *Theodora and Attendants* within the apse shown in Figure 13.12. Ask students to share their own ideas about the use of the elements and principles of art within these mosaics before they read and discuss the feature.

Cross Curriculum

MUSIC. Play a recording of canticles used in the Orthodox church. Although relatively little is known about Byzantine music, many of the ancient hymns have survived in altered form into the present, and even the modern versions can be helpful in creating an atmosphere in which to appreciate Byzantine church art.

Study Guide

Distribute *Study Guide* 28 in the TCR. Assist students in reviewing key concepts. 🗁

Art and Humanities

Assign *Appreciating Cultural Diversity* 22, "Mosaics: Art for the People," in the TCR. Ask a volunteer to read aloud the steps involved in planning, creating, and installing a mosaic on a New York City high-rise building. 🗁

Studio Activities

Have students complete *Cooperative Learning* 19, "Creating a Mosaic," in the TCR. For this activity, students are asked to work in groups to create a mosaic design that depicts a significant idea or image for their school. 🗁

Teacher Notes

Developing Perceptual Skills. Ask students to study an object in a mosaic, make a quick guess as to how many different colors are used in the tiles, and then actually count the colors. Then have students attempt to use color tiles to create a decorative pattern of their own. Have them begin by sketching an object of their choosing. Next, they are to glue small squares of colored paper onto the sketch. Although students should feel free to refer back to the photo of the mosaic, encourage them to devise patterns of their own. Allow time for students to compare efforts.

ASSESS
Checking Comprehension
Have students respond to the lesson review questions. Answers are given in the box below.

Reteaching
➤ Assign *Reteaching* 28, found in the TCR. Have students complete the activity and review their responses. 📁
➤ Have students write a paragraph describing the differences between the early Christian catacomb paintings and the Byzantine mosaics at San Vitale.

Enrichment
Find out whether there is a local jeweler or metalworker whose work involves some of the same filigree, paste inlay, cloisonne enameling, silversmithing, or goldsmithing techniques used by the Byzantines. Arrange a visit to the jeweler's studio where students can view these techniques.

Extension
Assign students *Cooperative Learning* 20, "East and West: Bridging Cultures," in the TCR. In this worksheet, students recognize the wealth of material brought to the West from the East during the Middle Ages. 📁

CLOSE
Lead the class in a brief debate on whether early Christian artists had more freedom to paint as they wished before the Edict of Milan (A.D. 313), when Christianity was still illegal, or after the emperor made Christianity the state religion and sponsored church decorations that were not only religiously expressive but also made political statements about the role of the emperor.

296

LOOKING Closely

USE OF THE ELEMENTS AND PRINCIPLES
Many features of Byzantine style can be identified in this mosaic. Notice how the elements and principles of art are used in this style.

- **Emphasis.** The emperor's elegant attire, crown, and halo set him apart from the others.
- **Harmony.** All the figures are tall and slender, with small feet and oval faces. They turn to face the viewer and stare boldly through huge, dark eyes.
- **Space.** The figures seem to float before a gold background, used to add a supernatural, heavenly glow to the scene. A feeling of weightlessness is heightened by the lack of shadows and by the position of the feet, which hang downward.

■ **FIGURE 13.13**

Justinian and Attendants. c. A.D. 547. Mosaics from San Vitale. Ravenna, Italy.

LESSON ONE REVIEW

Reviewing Art Facts
1. What are symbols and what part did they play in early Christian art?
2. What brought about the fall of Rome? When did this happen?
3. What name was given to the Eastern half of the Roman Empire after the fall of Rome in Italy?
4. What are piers? How did the use of piers affect the design of church interiors?

Activity... *Mapping the Roman Empire*
Constantine has gone down in history as the Roman ruler who first embraced Christianity. He issued the Edict of Milan in A.D. 313, making Christianity the official religion. He divided the Roman Empire by establishing an Eastern capital in Constantinople in A.D. 330. These acts established the Eastern Roman Empire (Constantinople) and the Western Roman Empire (Rome) and set the stage for great changes in the history of art. Study the map on page 288 to see the division.

Locate a modern map of the two parts of the ancient Roman Empire. What countries exist there today? Consider the religious, political, social, and cultural forces that influence contemporary art in each area. Present your findings to the class.

LESSON ONE REVIEW

Answers to Reviewing Art Facts
1. Familiar figures or signs used to represent something else; they masked the meaning of Christian religious beliefs.
2. First it was divided into two empires; then the Western Empire was attacked repeatedly and eventually fell in the fifth century.
3. The Byzantine Empire.
4. Massive vertical pillars, allowed windows.

Activity...*Mapping the Roman Empire*
Students might work in groups to create a large wall map showing both the boundaries of the Eastern and Western Roman Empires and the borders of the modern countries within that area. Another group might create displays of various artworks from those areas.

Islamic Art

Vocabulary
- Koran
- mosque
- minaret
- muezzin
- mihrab
- alcazar

Discover
After completing this lesson, you will be able to:
- Discuss the influence of Islam on the art of the Fertile Crescent and Moorish Spain.
- Describe significant features of the Alhambra.
- Explain the importance of book illustrations in Islamic art.

In the seventh century A.D., a religion known as Islam (which means "followers of God's will") emerged in the Middle East. The prophet of Islam was an Arab merchant named Muhammad, who was born in Mecca around A.D. 570.

Following the death of his parents, Muhammad was raised by an uncle. As a hard working young trader, Muhammad learned the habits and languages of the wandering Arabs. His fortunes improved following his marriage to a wealthy widow, whose business he tended. During this time, Muhammad received personal revelations that forced him to challenge the superstitions of the Arabs, who worshiped many different idols.

The Teachings of Muhammad

Following years of meditation, Muhammad heard a divine call to be the last of the prophets and a teacher for all. He taught that there is only one god, Allah (in Arabic, "the God"), whose will should be followed in order for people to live just and responsible lives. At first Muhammad taught in secret, converting his wife, cousin, and adopted son.

In 613, when he began to teach openly, Muhammad was opposed by those who wished to preserve established tribal and religious customs. He persisted, however, and today more than 925 million followers, called Muslims, honor him as the last and greatest of the prophets and as their guide, the Messenger of God.

After Muhammad's death, messages he received from God were assembled into the **Koran** (kuh-RAN), or Qur'an, *the holy scripture of Islam*. For Muslims, the Koran is the final authority in matters of faith. It also offers rules to guide the daily lives of Muslims.

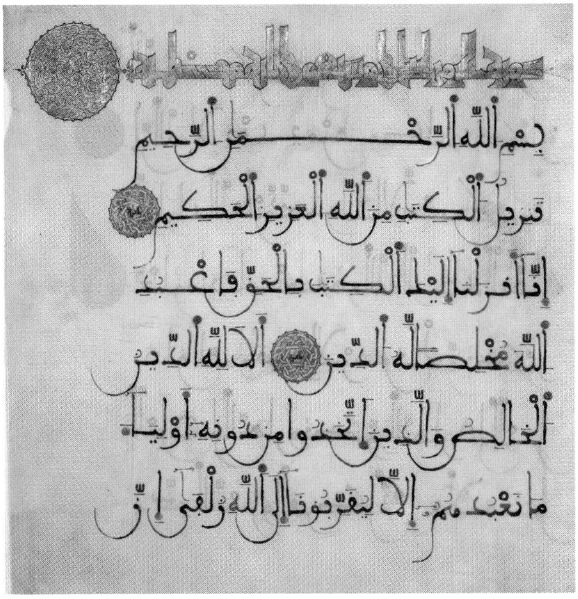

■ **FIGURE 13.14** The writing on this page of the Koran presents a pleasing design. **How do you think this design reinforces the meaning of the words? What does the page communicate to viewers who cannot read the words?**

Leaf from a Koran (Qur'an), in Maghribi script. Islamic. North African. c. 1300. Ink, colors, and gold on parchment. 53.3 × 55.8 cm (21 × 22″). The Metropolitan Museum of Art, New York, New York. Rogers Fund, 1942 (42.63).

The Koran
■ **FIGURE 13.14**

A page from a Koran of the fourteenth century (Figure 13.14) illustrates the skill with which Muslim artists used a decorative script to record Muhammad's revelations, laws, and moral stories. The top line of this page contains a single word written in Arabic, to be read from right to left. This line is designed to fit with the others on the page to form a visually pleasing, unified whole.

CHAPTER 13
LESSON TWO
Islamic Art

Focus

Lesson Objectives
After studying this lesson, students will be able to:
- Describe the origins of Islam.
- Identify features of a mosque.
- Describe the Alhambra and explain its purpose.

Building Vocabulary
Let students read and discuss the Vocabulary terms for this lesson. Ask: To what religion are all these terms related? Have volunteers read the definitions presented in the Glossary.

Motivator
Bring to class a photograph of a Persian rug or, if possible, a small prayer rug. Allow students to examine the rug and describe what kinds of patterns are woven into the rug. What feelings or moods are suggested? Explain that Persian rugs are one of the enduring contributions of Islamic art.

Introducing the Lesson
Display a photograph of the Taj Mahal, and ask students to name this famous structure. Ask whether students can identify what type of building it is. Explain that they will be learning about this structure.

Did You Know?
The period during which the Taj Mahal was completed was one of political turmoil in England: Charles I was beheaded and England was proclaimed a commonwealth (1649); Charles II was defeated by Cromwell and escaped to France (1651).

LESSON TWO RESOURCES

Teacher's Classroom Resources
- Art and Humanities 21
- Enrichment Activity 26
- Reteaching Activity 29
- Reproducible Lesson Plan 29
- Study Guide 29

TEACH
Aesthetics

Have students study Figure 13.14 (page 297), a page from the Koran. Remind students that Muslim scribes, just like Christian scribes, often produced beautiful works in calligraphy. Ask students if they can understand the meaning of the words. Ask them if their inability to understand the words makes it more difficult for them to appreciate the beauty of the script. Does the page create a mood or feeling? Would the ability to read the words alter this mood or feeling?

Cross Curriculum

HUMANITIES. Remind students that Muslims made great contributions to nearly all areas of learning and art; Muslim advances in learning contributed to the conditions that led to the Renaissance in Europe. Then have students select and research one of the contributions made by Muslims in the following areas: mathematics, medicine, architecture, or philosophy.

Using Map Skills

Have students identify the city of Mecca on a map and trace the route of the spread of Islam through the Middle East, on to North Africa and Spain, and finally to France, where the Muslims were defeated. Students should be able to understand the scope of this conversion. Remind students that for hundreds of years the Muslims, called Moors, remained in Spain. Point out that there are very few Muslims in Spain now, but there are still many Muslims in North Africa as well as the Middle East and in countries throughout the world.

Islamic Art in the Fertile Crescent

During the early centuries of Islamic history, the center of the Muslim world was an area known as the Fertile Crescent, composed of parts of present-day Iraq, Syria, and Palestine. (See map, Figure 6.8, page 138.) Here the constant blending of Eastern and Western cultures had left a stunning array of magnificent ruins. To these ruins, Muslim builders soon added their own impressive

■ **FIGURE 13.15**
Most of the mosque is now in ruins. This photograph shows the minaret and one corner of the once-huge prayer hall. **How is the design of a minaret related to its purpose?**

Spiral Minaret. Mosque of Al-Mutawakkil. Samarra, Iraq. Abbasid dynasty. A.D. 848–52.

■ **FIGURE 13.16** A wall now separates worshipers inside the mosque from the orange trees in this patio, but originally the mosque opened onto the patio. **How do you think the atmosphere of the mosque has been changed by the addition of the wall?**

Court of the Oranges. Mezquita, the Mosque at Cordoba, Spain. A.D. 784–988.

structures. Included among these was the **mosque,** or *Muslim place of worship.*

The Mosque of Al-Mutawakkil
■ **FIGURE 13.15**

In the ninth century, the largest mosque in the world was built at Samarra in Iraq. Measuring 384 by 512 feet, it covered 10 acres and could accommodate 100,000 worshipers. Today little remains of this huge prayer hall. Only traces of the 464 brick columns that once supported the flat, wooden roof can be seen. On the north side of the ruins, however, a **minaret,** or *tower attached to a mosque,* still stands (Figure 13.15). From a lofty perch on top of this minaret, a **muezzin,** or *prayer caller,* once summoned the people to group worship each Friday.

Islamic Art in Spain

By 710, the religion of Islam had spread throughout North Africa, at times by persuasion and at times by force. In 711, Muslims crossed the Strait of Gibraltar and entered Spain.

The Muslim army advanced swiftly through Spain, encountering little resistance. After their advances into France were repelled, the Muslims did not attempt additional invasions. Instead, they consolidated their control of Spain and some other parts of southern Europe. The Muslims, known as Moors in Spain, remained on the Iberian peninsula for almost 800 years.

At the height of Moorish power in Spain, the city of Cordoba was one of Islam's most impressive capitals. People from all over Europe came for enlightenment and knowledge. In contrast to many other cities in Europe, Cordoba was a splendid center of learning and art. All that survives today, however, are the remnants of a fortress—and the great mosque known as the Mezquita.

The Mezquita
■ **FIGURE 13.16**

The ancient brown walls of the Mezquita, marked by sealed, arched entries, offer little hint of the pleasures that await inside. Within these walls, however, lies a courtyard known as the Patio of the Orange Trees (Figure 13.16). Originally no walls separated

---

Teacher Notes _____

_____

_____

_____

_____

this courtyard and the interior of the mosque. The courtyard and the mosque were linked by the lines of orange trees outside and the rows of columns inside.

Muslim Worship

Muslims worship five times a day: at sunrise, noon, afternoon, sunset, and evening. Private prayers can be offered anywhere, but group prayer takes place in the mosque at noon on Fridays. In Moorish times, preparing for group worship involved ceremonial bathing. The fountains in the Patio of the Orange Trees were used for this bathing. In

contrast to the courtyard, the mosque interior is dark (Figures 13.17 and 13.18).

Mosque Interiors

The interiors of Islamic mosques are unlike the interiors of Christian churches. Christian artists created religious images as a way of teaching the religion to people who could not read. Islamic artists avoided portraying living creatures in mosques and other religious buildings, because they did not want in any way to diminish the greatness of God's creative power by portraying such forms. Instead, these artists decorated mosques and

■ FIGURE 13.17

The Mezquita Mosque (interior) at Cordoba, Spain.

■ FIGURE 13.18

Mihrab. The Mezquita Mosque at Cordoba, Spain.

LOOKING Closely

ARCHITECTURAL FEATURES

The function of each of these architectural features help to set the mood and guide the worshipers to enhance their experience as they enter the mosque.

- **Columns.** Rows of polished marble columns extend back into the darkness.
- **Arches.** The columns support horseshoe-shaped arches decorated with yellow and red bands.
- **Piers.** The columns also support stone piers that carry a second tier of arches three feet above the first.
- **Aisles.** The direction of the aisles guides the worshiper to the side of the building facing Mecca, the birthplace of Islam. (This is the direction Muslims face when praying.)
- **Mihrab.** The **mihrab,** *a niche in the wall, that indicates the direction of Mecca and is large enough to accommodate a single standing figure,* is the most important part of the mosque.
- **Relief.** Delicate stucco relief, incorporating passages from the Koran, decorate the mihrab.
- **Arches.** In this section of the mosque, the arches are more ornate, and their colors have changed to creamy white and dark brown.

Chapter 13 *Early Christian, Byzantine, and Islamic Art* **299**

LOOKING Closely

Have students examine the mosque interiors in Figures 13.17 and 13.18 and share their reactions to the atmosphere created: What mood do you feel is created here? What elements contribute to the mood?

Then guide students in reading and discussing the Architectural Features explanations. Ask: Which features here are similar to those you have seen in Christian churches, especially Hagia Sophia? Which are different?

Art History

Remind students that the dazzling interiors shown in Figures 13.17 and 13.18 are contained within a building that, when viewed from the exterior, is comparatively plain and fortress-like. Point out that this description might be applied with equal accuracy to early Christian churches, which were examined in the first lesson of this chapter. Have students discuss factors, practical and otherwise, that might have prompted builders of the period to construct edifices in this fashion. In what ways might an unimpressive exterior detract from the total impact of the work? Would such a building decision enhance the viewer's first glimpse of the interior? Have students provide reasons for their opinions.

COOPERATIVE LEARNING

Group Research. Ask students to find out more about the beliefs held by inhabitants of the Fertile Crescent before the arrival of Islam. Point out that some of the people living in this area were Christian and Jewish, and that many of the Arabs adhered to lesser-known beliefs, such as animism, Mithraism, Manichaeism, and Zoroastrianism.

Divide students into groups and assign each group one of these religions. The groups should identify the beliefs or tenets of the religion, isolate key leaders, and uncover other pertinent information. When they have completed their research, have students share the information they have obtained.

Studio Skills

Direct students' attention to Figure 13.19, which illustrates the decorative skills of Moorish artists. Tell students that they will attempt to design a geometric pattern that could be used in a mosque. In their sketchbooks, have students first sketch their ideas and then use acrylic paints to give an intense, clear color to their designs. When students have finished their projects, arrange and display the different artworks and have students evaluate their efforts.

Art History

Have students look once more at Figure 13.19. What other architectural works have they learned about that were created on a grand scale so as to be "like no other . . . in the world"? What other works have they studied that were notable for their domes? In what way does this palace and its dome depart architecturally from those works? What traits do the various structures from different times and cultures share?

Cross Curriculum

HISTORY. Have students research and report on the role of the Moorish ruler called a caliph. Tell them that the word *caliph* is a shortened version of the phrase, "khalifat rasul Allah," which means "successor of the messenger of God." This should help students understand the respect and responsibility that went with the title. In their reports, students should describe the manner by which caliphs rose to power, the type of rule they imposed (for example, were they absolute rulers?), how long their "term of office" lasted, and any other points of interest they find.

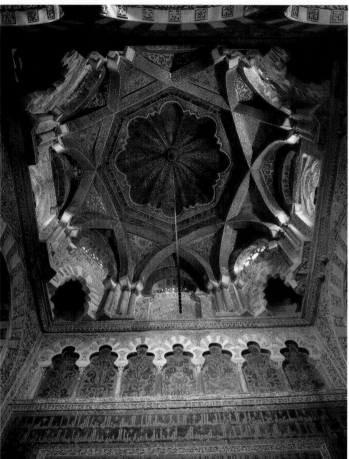

■ **FIGURE 13.19** This photograph allows you to imagine yourself looking directly up into the dome over the mihrab. **What single adjective best summarizes your reaction to this dome?**

Dome over the bay in front of the Mihrab. The Mezquita Mosque at Cordoba, Spain.

■ **FIGURE 13.20** These ruins only hint at the huge fortified palace that once stood here. Contemporary accounts report that 25,000 people worked in the palace. **What does this palace indicate about the power and wealth of the Moorish rulers?**

The Palace at Madinat az-Zahra. Near Cordoba, Spain. Tenth century.

other religious structures with ornate calligraphy, geometric patterns, and stylized plants and flowers. Their skill in doing this is evident in the rich and varied visual effects concentrated around the mihrab.

In the Mezquita, an ornate dome covers the area in front of the mihrab (Figure 13.19). On this dome, the Moorish artists applied their decorative skills to perfection.

Madinat az-Zahra
■ **FIGURE 13.20**

Not far from Cordoba, a tenth-century Moorish ruler, or *caliph*, decided to erect a palace. When it was completed, it was like no other palace in the world—an entire self-contained city extending upward in three levels: a mosque below, gardens in the center, and an **alcazar**, or *fortified palace*, at the top. Today only ruins remain (Figure 13.20).

The palace at Madinat az-Zahra covered an entire hillside. According to contemporary accounts, the caliph's rooms numbered 400. More than 4,000

CULTURAL DIVERSITY

Religious Traditions. Explain to students that the tenets of Islam are based on "The Five Pillars of Islam"—Witness, Worship, Fasting, Tithing (devoting a portion of one's income to furthering the spread of Islam), and Pilgrimage. Divide the class into research groups and invite some groups to find out more about these pillars, while others explore fundamental tenets of other religions and sects (for example, the Ten Commandments of Judeo-Christian tradition). Groups should consider, and then report on, the impact of such rules on culture and society.

marble columns supported the massive roof, and there were so many fountains that it required 800 loaves of bread daily to feed the fish swimming in them.

Occasionally, objects are found among the ruins at Madinat az-Zahra that rekindle the legends of its former greatness. One of these is a small ivory container only 4.5 inches high (Figure 13.21). Deeply carved into its tiny surface are pairs of lions, gazelles, and parrots placed within an elaborate vine scroll.

The Alhambra
■ **FIGURE 13.22**

Granada, which resisted capture by the Christians until 1492, was the last great Moorish city in Spain. During the last centuries of Moorish rule, while Granada was at the height of a long, productive artistic period, the Alhambra was built on a hill overlooking the city. This fortress-palace is considered one of the most impressive examples of Islamic architecture.

The Alhambra is protected by an outer wall that can be entered at several well-fortified gates. The massive Justice Gate (Figure 13.22) received its name from the tribunals that met there to conduct trials of petty thieves. On the keystone of the outer horseshoe arch is carved a great open hand; on the keystone of the smaller arch within, a key is carved. It is likely that these carvings represent Moorish law and faith.

■ **FIGURE 13.21** This carved ivory cup is only 4.5" high. What makes the craftsmanship evident here so noteworthy? What design relationships would you be certain to take into account when making a judgment about this work?

Pyxis. Cylindrical, carved with candelabra trees, parrots, gazelles, rearing lions. Tenth century. Ivory. 11.8 × 10.5 cm (4⁵/₈ × 4³/₃₂″). The Metropolitan Museum of Art, New York, New York. The Cloisters Collection, 1970 (1970.234.5).

■ **FIGURE 13.22** Visitors—or attackers—might have approached the Alhambra through this fortified gate. What impression do you think this gate made when the Alhambra was occupied? What impression does it create now?

Door of Justice. The Alhambra, Granada, Spain. Fourteenth century.

Chapter 13 *Early Christian, Byzantine, and Islamic Art* **301**

Art Criticism

Direct students' attention to Figure 13.21, a detail of the small ivory container from the ruins at Madinat az-Zahra. Ask students to describe what they see. Have them identify the elements and principles of art that are emphasized in the work. Ask them to imagine that the work was one hundred times larger. Would this change in size affect the message or mood the work conveys? If so, how? Ask whether the style of this work reminds students of any other art style they have studied.

Aesthetics

Ask committees of three or four students to brainstorm and then share speculations on what the animals carved on the surface of the pyxis in Figure 13.21 might represent. Was the object probably used for religious purposes? Why or why not? What facts about Islamic culture and art can committees cite in support of their assumptions? What can students infer from the fact that this container was found among the ruins of a palace?

Art History

Direct students' attention to Figure 13.22, the Justice Gate at the Alhambra palace. Ask them to determine the extent to which this structure borrows from building techniques devised by the Romans. How might the structure be regarded as a unique contribution of Islamic builders?

More About... **Islamic Style.** Ivory carvings made by Islamic artists survive in substantial numbers. These are among the finest products of the period. Ivory, though expensive, was also used as an inlay in furniture and to decorate doors. The most popular use of ivory, however, was for containers, such as chests and caskets. Fine detail can be seen in the surviving ivories, some of which are carved in patterns that resemble manuscript illumination. Ask students if they are aware of the regulations recently imposed on the collection and sale of ivory. Have informed students share their information with the class.

Aesthetics

Have students study the Lion Fountain in Figure 13.24. Have them note, in particular, the symmetrical arrangement of the lions around the fountain. Ask: What might an aesthetician of the emotionalist school say about this work? What would be the opinion of someone from the formalist school? Which of the two scholars do students believe would find the work successful? Have students explain their answers.

Aesthetics

Have students look at the miniature illustration in Figure 13.25 (page 304). Ask what adjectives students would use to describe the human figures and objects depicted. What is the tone of the work? What features contained in the work are consistent with those found in other Islamic artworks students have witnessed in this lesson? Finally, have students discuss ways in which nonrealistic art can still represent or reflect the culture of the artist.

Art History

Direct students' attention again to Figure 13.25 and ask them to research the clothing and the surroundings of the figures in this miniature. Are these aspects historically correct? (Do they accurately reflect customs of dress in the sixteenth century?) Ask students to present the results of their research with illustrations to the class.

■ **FIGURE 13.23** This court lies at the heart of the palace, which is protected by heavy walls and fortified gates. What do the differences between the exterior wall of the Alhambra and this interior court tell you about the Moorish rulers?

Court of the Lions and Room of the Kings. The Alhambra. Granada, Spain.

The Court of the Lions
■ FIGURES 13.23 and 13.24

The Court of the Lions (Figure 13.23) at the heart of the Alhambra palace was built by Muhammad V around a massive, low-lying fountain that gave the court its name. A delicate arcade supported by 124 marble columns is a reminder of the covered walkways found in monasteries throughout western Europe.

The fountain in the center of the court, with its crudely carved lions (Figure 13.24), seems out of place in this enchanting setting. Around the rim of the fountain, a poem is carved in Arabic. It describes how fierce the little lions would be if they were not behaving themselves out of respect for the king.

The columns and walls of the arcade and apartments around the Court of the Lions are filled with delicate stucco decorations. These consist of a variety of ornate designs, including bands of inscriptions from the Koran. Impressive today, they must have been especially beautiful in the fourteenth century, when they were brilliantly colored and gilded.

The End of Moorish Rule in Spain

Although they gradually lost parts of their kingdom to the advancing Christian armies, the Moors managed to maintain a presence in Spain until 1492. Following a period of intrigue, the last Moorish king, Boabdil, surrendered Granada and the Alhambra to the Christian monarchs Ferdinand and Isabella.

With the surrender of Granada, the 781 years of Moorish rule in Spain came to an end. Although the Islamic religion had vanished from Spain, its contributions had not. Muslim advancements in mathematics, medicine, architecture, and classical philosophy had profoundly affected European thought and helped make possible the European Renaissance.

302 **Unit Five** *Art in Quest of Salvation*

𝒯eacher 𝒩otes

Providing Resources. Names and terms indigenous to Islamic art and culture may create pronunciation difficulties for some students. To overcome this obstacle and simultaneously increase students' awareness of other cultures, you might have on hand glossaries of biographical and geographical names (gazetteers). Note that resources such as these are often included at the back of many dictionaries intended for school use. Find out whether any students in the class might have access to reference materials on Islamic culture that could be shared.

■ **FIGURE 13.24** Notice the contrast between the lions supporting this fountain and the delicate arcade. What can you conclude about the planning and execution of this court? What adjective best describes the architectural style?

The Lion Fountain, Court of the Lions. The Alhambra. Granada, Spain.

Study Guide

Distribute *Study Guide* 29 in the TCR. Assist students in reviewing key concepts. ☞

Art and Humanities

Assign *Art and Humanities* 21, "The Influence of Islamic Culture," in the TCR. In this worksheet, students have an opportunity to trace the influence of Islamic culture on the Spanish and English languages and on the literature of the Middle Ages. ☞

Studio Activities

Have students complete *Studio* 17, "Abstract Design in the Islamic Style," in the TCR. The activity challenges students to complete an abstract design reminiscent of those they studied in the chapter. Students are invited to work with the tools of geometry as a means of adding the necessary precision to their efforts. ☞

Islamic Book Illustration

The furnishings of palaces and mosques in Spain and other parts of the Islamic empire revealed a love for rich, decorative effects. This same love is evident in the pictures created to illustrate Islamic books. By the year A.D. 1200, the art of book illustration reached its peak, particularly in Iraq and Iran.

Book illustrators were free to depict images that could never have been represented in mosques. Without these limitations, artists printed manuscripts with scenes of everyday pleasures. These included banquets, hunting scenes, incidents inspired by popular romantic stories, and even scenes from mosques.

The Meeting of the Theologians
■ **FIGURE 13.25**

In the sixteenth century, an artist named 'Abd Allah Musawwir painted a miniature illustrating a story (Figure 13.25, page 304). It shows different scenes inside and outside a mosque. Within this mosque, a young man listens intently to the wise words of his teacher. Nearby, seven bearded men sit quietly or talk earnestly among themselves. Outside, another teacher approaches the door to the mosque, where he is met by two beggars with hands outstretched. At the far left a man drinks from a jar, while a youth at the right prepares to follow the custom of washing his feet before entering a holy building.

Did You Know?

The Alhambra's survival owes much to American author Washington Irving, who lived there while on the staff of the United States Embassy in Madrid and was saddened by its poor condition. As a result, he wrote a book titled *Tales of the Alhambra* that motivated the Spanish government to preserve the structure.

Chapter 13 *Early Christian, Byzantine, and Islamic Art* **303**

COOPERATIVE LEARNING

Design Sketches. Tell students that the nomadic Arabs were mobile societies that carried much of their art with them from place to place. It is because of this tendency that many Islamic pendants, pins, rings, and purses found their way to Europe. Have pairs of students design applied artworks in the Islamic style. Before they begin, point out that many of these works were made of gold and ivory and inlaid with garnets, enameling, and precious stones. After sketching their designs, pairs can use markers to decorate them.

ASSESS

Checking Comprehension

➤ Have students respond to the lesson review questions. Answers are given in the box below.

➤ Ask students to complete *Application* 13, "Past-port," in the TCR. The activity calls upon students to identify early Christian and Islamic works of art or architecture solely on the basis of clues provided. 📁

Reteaching

Assign *Reteaching* 29, found in the TCR. Have students complete the activity and review their responses. 📁

Enrichment

Assign *Enrichment* 26, "Creating a Tessellated Pattern," in the TCR. In this activity, students study the meaning of geometric patterns in Islamic art. They then create an original design using tessellation. 📁

Extension

Have students each write a paragraph in response to this question: Which form of Islamic art do you find most interesting? Encourage students to include examples and, if possible, illustrations beyond those found in the chapter. After students have completed the assignment, allow time for them to read and share their preferences and reasons.

CLOSE

Write the phrases *Early Christian Art* and *Islamic Art* on the board. Ask students to compile a list of details highlighting the difference between the two.

Use of Pattern and Color

Delicate flowing lines are used to draw each of these figures, but a lack of shading makes them look flat rather than round. This same flat appearance is noted in the rugs and floor tiles that seem to be hanging vertically. The artist has clearly elected to ignore realistic appearances in favor of rich, decorative patterns and intense, clear colors. A wide range of bright, contrasting colors adds to the freshness and vitality of the scene. Small areas of rich color are skillfully blended to create a work that would challenge the dazzling effects of the most precious jewel in a caliph's treasury.

■ **FIGURE 13.25** Notice the bright colors in this painting. Some of the pigments for the work were made by grinding precious metals such as gold and silver. What was the artist's primary purpose in painting this scene?

'Abd allah Musawwir. *The Meeting of the Theologians.* c. 1540–1550. Watercolor on paper. 33 × 22.9 cm (13 × 9"). The Nelson-Atkins Museum of Art, Kansas City, Missouri. Purchase: Nelson Trust.

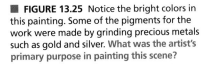

LESSON TWO REVIEW

Reviewing Art Facts

1. What is the Koran, and what role did Muhammad play in its creation?
2. What is the most important part of a mosque? Describe its appearance.
3. What is the Alhambra? Name and describe the architectural feature found at the heart of the Alhambra.
4. What types of images were Islamic book illustrators allowed to depict?

Activity... *Examining Early Eastern Art*

In the days of the early Christian Church, images were forbidden in places of worship in the Eastern Roman Empire. In 726 Emperor Leo III ordered that all images and paintings in churches be covered or destroyed. The prophet Muhammad also forbade the use of images. These events changed the character of Eastern art. Finally, in 843, the Eastern Church reached a settlement permitting pictures but not complete statues or images.

Locate illustrations and images of religious art of this period. Choose one work and examine the way color and symbolism are used. Is the work a product of Eastern or Western influences? Share your findings with the class.

LESSON TWO REVIEW

Answers to Reviewing Art Facts

1. The holy scripture of Islam; it is a compilation of messages Muhammad received from God.
2. The mihrab; a niche in the wall indicating the direction of Mecca.
3. A fortress-palace; the Court of the Lions, built around a massive, low-lying fountain.
4. Banquets, hunting scenes, romantic stories, scenes from mosques.

Activity...*Examining Early Eastern Art*

Suggest that students conduct the first stages of their research in groups, sharing and discussing resources. Once students have chosen individual works, have them meet in groups again to share and discuss their ideas.

Studio LESSON   Byzantine-Style Self-Portrait

Paint a self-portrait, presenting yourself as an attendant in a Byzantine-style mosaic. Show your face as viewed from the front. Compose large, simple, flat shapes to represent your features. Present the solemn, dignified look associated with Byzantine portraits. For emphasis, use intense colors to paint your portrait and colors in contrasting subdued intensities for the background. Cut your painting into small squares and assemble them to simulate a mosaic.

Inspiration

Carefully examine the mosaics showing Justinian and Theodora in Figures 13.1 and 13.13, pages 286 and 296. What words best describe the feelings revealed by their faces? What details are expressed in those faces? Notice how the colors add to a dreamlike dignity.

Process

1. Use the hand mirror to study your face. Complete several pencil sketches of your face, avoiding the use of small details.
2. Select your best sketch and reproduce it lightly in pencil to fill the sheet of white drawing paper.
3. Paint your self-portrait with a variety of intense colors. For the background, select colors in contrasting values to emphasize your self-portrait.
4. Cut your self-portrait into 1-inch (or smaller) squares. Arrange these squares on the sheet of black construction paper so that there is a ¼-inch gap around each, and glue the squares in place.
5. Exhibit your drawing along with those by other members of your class. Can other students pick out your self-portrait from the rest?

SAFETY TIP Paper cutters should be used with caution. Use in a separate, uncrowded area. Hold materials to be cut with the hand away from the cutting blade.

Materials

- Small hand mirror
- Pencil and sketch paper
- Sheets of white drawing paper and black construction paper, 12 × 18 inches
- Tempera or acrylic paint
- Brushes, mixing tray, paint cloth, and water container
- Paper cutter or scissors
- White glue

■ **FIGURE 13.26** Student Work

Examining Your Work

Describe. Is your drawing immediately recognized as a human face seen from the front? Which facial features have been emphasized?

Analyze. Are the features of the face shown as large, simple, flat shapes? Is the face painted with intense colors? Does the use of colors in contrasting subdued intensities for the background help emphasize the face?

Interpret. What gives your "mosaic" self-portrait a solemn and dignified appearance?

Judge. What is most successful about your self-portrait—its resemblance to your actual appearance, or its effectiveness in expressing a solemn, dignified feeling? Do you think your work is successful? Why or why not?

305

ASSESSMENT

Group Discussion. Have students meet in small groups to compare and discuss their completed portraits in the Byzantine style. If possible, have each student bring to this discussion a recent photo of himself or herself (such as a school picture). Direct students to compare their self-portraits and their photos: What does each tell about your appearance? About your personality? About your attitudes? How does the mosaiclike appearance of your self-portrait change the impression made by the work? If you could redo your self-portrait, what changes would you make to your original sketch? To conclude the discussion, have students identify what they like best about each other's self-portraits.

Objectives

■ Complete a large self-portrait as an attendant in a Byzantine mosaic.
■ Use large, simple, flat shapes to create the features of the face viewed from the front.
■ Use intense colors for self-portraits and contrasting colors for the background.

Motivator

Focus students' attention on the mosaics of Thoedora and Justinian in Figures 13.1 and 13.13 (pages 286 and 295). Have students carefully examine both illustrations for two minutes. Instruct them to close their books and respond to these questions:

Are there the same number of figures on either side of Justinian? How is the emperor shown to be both king and future saint? How many faces are shown in profile? What does Theodora hold in her hands? Which figure appears to be taller than the rest? What colors appear in the background?

Studio Skills

Students should be encouraged to refer often to the faces in the two Byzantine mosaics. Stress the fact that the self-portraits should be free of small details and exhibit a solemn, dignified appearance.

Critiquing

Have students apply the steps of art criticism to their own artwork, using the Examining Your Work questions on this page.

Studio **LESSON**

Creating a Word Design

Objectives

■ Complete a design in india ink made up of words and parts of words inspired by a school or community event.

■ Use a variety of large and small shapes to create light, medium, and dark values.

■ Realize simulated textures with closely-spaced ink lines.

Motivator

Ask students to identify school or community events that might provide the words to be used in their designs. List these on the board and write the words students associate with each. As students develop their ideas in sketches, caution them not to reveal the event they have selected.

Aesthetics

Briefly discuss the reasons why Muslim artists did not use images in their art. Muhammad forbade the making of images. Ask students if the lack of images makes it impossible to apply any of the art theories (formalism, imitationalism, emotionalism) to artworks created by Muslim artists. What theory or theories could be used during examinations of such Islamic works as the decorative script in Figure 13.14 (page 297) or the Alhambra stucco decoration in Figure 13.24 (page 303)?

Critiquing

Have students apply the steps of art criticism to their own artwork, using the Examining Your Work questions on this page.

306

Materials

● Pencil, sketch paper, and ruler
● Sheet of white mat board, 12 × 18 inches
● India ink
● Fine-pointed pens and penholders
● Small, pointed paintbrushes

Complete an india ink design made up entirely of words and parts of words inspired by a school or community event. Overlap these words throughout the design to produce a variety of large and small shapes. Paint some of these shapes with india ink and leave others unpainted. Fill some with closely spaced ink lines to create gray areas and provide a simulated texture to your design.

Inspiration

Examine the decorative script from a fourteenth century copy of the Koran illustrated in Figure 13.14, page 297. Why is this script visually pleasing, even to viewers who may not be able to read it? Turn to Figure 13.23, page 302, showing stucco decoration from the Alhambra. Why did Islamic artists use bands of inscriptions like these instead of paintings and relief carvings to decorate their buildings?

■ **FIGURE 13.27** Student Work

Process

1. Identify a current event to serve as the source of ideas for at least five words to use in your design. For example, a school election might suggest such words as *vote, candidate, politics, campaign,* and *ballot.*

2. Make several quick sketches in which you arrange your words into a visually pleasing design. Letters of the words may be in different block styles (upper and lower case), should overlap, and can even run off the page. Overlapping letters results in a range of large and small shapes that adds variety to your design.

3. Using pencil, lightly draw your word design on the mat board. With india ink, paint in some of the letters and shapes produced by overlapping letters. Use a fine-pointed pen to make closely spaced straight and curved lines in other shapes. Leave some letters and shapes white.

Examining Your Work

Describe. Tell how your design is made up entirely of words or parts of words. Is it possible to read any of these words or recognize any of the letters represented?

Analyze. Did you use a variety of values in your design? How did you simulate textures?

Interpret. Were other students able to identify the event that inspired your design? What words or parts of words in the design helped them make this identification?

Judge. What elements and principles contributed most to the success of your design? Are these the same elements and principles that contributed to the success of the Islamic artworks illustrated in Figures 13.14 and 13.23, pages 297 and 302?

306

ASSESSMENT

Examining Your Work. After students have assessed their own word designs, have them meet with partners to discuss and assess each other's work. Suggest that they offer constructive comments in response to these questions: What changes in your choice of event or your choice of words might have improved your design? What changes would have added greater variety to your design? Would those changes improve the work? What changes in technique or approach might have improved the appearance of your india ink lines? What is the most successful aspect of this work? After this peer-review session, have students write journal entries recording what they learned from the activity.

Reviewing the Facts

Lesson One

1. When was the Christian religion made legal by the Roman emperor Constantine?
2. Explain why early Christian paintings showed little interest in the beauty, grace, and strength of the human body.
3. What were the catacombs?
4. Why did the Christians select the Roman basilica as a model for their church?
5. Why were huge churches, such as Hagia Sophia, decorated with mosaics on the inside walls?

Lesson Two

6. What is the significance of the *mihrab*?
7. Discuss the historical importance of Muhammad.
8. Describe the interior appearance of the mosque at Cordoba.
9. List two elements and two principles of art used by the artisans who designed the dome before the mihrab in the mosque at Cordoba (Figure 13.19, page 300).
10. Explain the symbolism behind the great open hand and the key above the Justice Gate at the Alhambra.

Technology Project

Early Christian Symbols

Early Christian art and architecture exhibits many images and symbols. It is important to understand that these images and symbols came from very different sources. Many of the symbols, such as the cross, the lamb, the fish, the lily, originated in the Christian faith. Others, such as the cross-like design seen in the cathedral, with its long central isle, columns, and arches, originated from the structure of the Roman basilica, which in turn had its beginnings in Greek architecture.

Other elements in early Christian art, including the interlace motif and abstract animal symbols, were introduced by the culture of the barbarians that filtered down into the Roman Empire during its long decline. All these influences converged over a long period to form the imagery that we know as early Christian art. Research these three basic contributors to early Christian art.

Thinking Critically

1. **COMPARE AND CONTRAST.** List the similarities and differences between the Byzantine church Hagia Sophia and the Roman Pantheon. Consider the construction techniques of each building, as well as the elements and principles of art.
2. **ANALYZE.** Refer to Figure 13.13, page 296, *Justinian and Attendants*, and Figure 13.1, page 286, *Theodora and Attendants*. What art elements has the artist used to create harmony in these works? In what ways has the artist created variety?

 DANCE/MUSIC. Use the *Performing Arts Handbook,* page 585 to learn about the Persian dance and music of Anna Djanbazian.

CAREERS IN Art Read about a career as an advertising artist in the *Careers in Art Handbook,* page 602.

interNET CONNECTION Visit Glencoe Art Online at *www.glencoe.com/sec/art*. Experience online galleries, visit Christian and Byzantine architectural sites worldwide, and complete an activity.

1. Working in your sketchbook or on drawing paper, collect several images that show examples of each of the three influences: Christian, Greek and Roman.
2. Note how early Christian art relies heavily upon the use of repetition in line and shape to create a sense of rhythm, seen in the mosaics of Figure 13.12, and Figure 13.13, page 296. A tessellation is a design executed in the manner of a mosaic that relies upon the same art elements and principles to create a visual impact.
3. Using an available computer program or Internet site that will allow you to create tessellations, create a design that uses at least one image from each of the three influences on Early Christian art.
4. Critique your work and your use of the elements and principles of design.
5. Print your tessellation and display it in your classroom.

307

Reviewing the Facts

1. In A.D. 313.
2. Early Christians' view of life on earth was in preparation for the hereafter, so they had less interest in the material or physical aspects of this world.
3. Underground Christian burial grounds that were also used to hold religious services.
4. This type of building could accommodate large numbers of people.
5. Because churches this big required art to be brightly colored and large enough to be seen from a distance.
6. It indicates the direction of Mecca.
7. He founded and spread the teachings of Islam and, after his death, came to be recognized as the last and greatest prophet of the Muslims.
8. It is an enchanting building, consisting of rows of polished marble columns.
9. Possible answer: the elements of shape and color, the principles of balance and harmony.
10. One explanation holds that they are magical signs on which the fate of the Alhambra depended.

Thinking Critically

1. Similarities: Both structures feature huge domes and Greek-style columns, both make use of the principle of balance. Differences: The basic structures are radically different, the decorations of Hagia Sophia are far more resplendent and colorful than those of the Pantheon.
2. The elements of line, shape, and color; variety is introduced through the contrasting use of shapes, values, and textures.

307

Teaching the Technology Project

Divide the class into three groups, and assign each group one of these basic sources of imagery in Early Christian art: Christianity, ancient Greece and Rome, barbarian cultures. Have the members of each group work together to compile a list of images and explanations of those images; these should be presented to the entire class.

 Assign the feature in the *Performing Arts Handbook,* page 585.

CAREERS IN ART If time permits, have interested students investigate the career information in the *Careers in Art Handbook,* page 602.

interNET CONNECTION Have students go online and learn more about artists on preselected Web sites with the Internet activity for this chapter.

Early Medieval and Romanesque Art

LESSON ONE
(pages 310–317)

The Early Medieval Period

Classroom Resources

- 📁 Appreciating Cultural Diversity 23
- 📁 Art and Humanities 22
- 📁 Cooperative Learning 21, 22
- 📁 Enrichment Activity 27
- 📁 Reproducible Lesson Plan 30
- 📁 Reteaching Activity 30
- 📁 Study Guide 30

Features

Map of Europe
(page 311)

Time & Place CONNECTIONS
(page 315)

(page 316)

LESSON TWO
(pages 318–327)

The Romanesque Period

Classroom Resources

- 📁 Appreciating Cultural Diversity 24
- 📁 Art and Humanities 23
- 📁 Enrichment Activity 28
- 📁 Reproducible Lesson Plan 31
- 📁 Reteaching Activity 31
- 📁 Study Guide 31

Features

(page 323)

END OF CHAPTER
(pages 328–329)

Studio **LESSON**
- Woodblock Print of an Imaginary Creature
  (p. 328)

ADDITIONAL CHAPTER RESOURCES

Activities
- 📁 Application 14
- 📁 Advanced Studio Activity 14
- 🖱 Chapter 14 Internet Activity
- 📁 Studio Activity 18

Fine Art Resources
- 🕹 **Transparency**
  Art in Focus Transparency 18
  Clasp from the Sutton Hoo Ship Burial.
- 🖼 **Fine Art Prints**
  Focus on World Art Print 14
  Lindau Gospels. (back cover)

Assessment
- 📁 Chapter 14 Test
- 📁 Performance Assessment

Multimedia Resources
- 🎭 Artsource® Performing Arts Package
- 💿 National Gallery Laser Disc
- 💿 National Museum of Women in the Arts CD-ROM
- 📼 Arts & Entertainment Videos

NATIONAL STANDARDS FOR ARTS EDUCATION

The National Standards for Arts Education provide guidelines for grade-appropriate competency in the visual arts. The Content Standards for grades 9–12 are:

1. Understanding and applying media, techniques, and processes.
2. Using knowledge of structures and functions.
3. Choosing and evaluating a range of subject matter, symbols, and ideas.
4. Understanding the visual arts in relation to history and cultures.
5. Reflecting upon and assessing the characteristics and merits of their work and the work of others.
6. Making connections between visual arts and other disciplines.

Listed below are the National Standards for the Visual Arts addressed in this chapter. For a breakdown of the categories listed under each content standard, refer to the *Reproducible Lesson Plans* booklet in the TCR.

1. (a, b)   **2.** (a, b, c)   **3.** (a)   **4.** (a, b, c)   **5.** (b, c)   **6.** (b)

HANDBOOK MATERIAL

 Performing Arts
(page 576)

CAREERS IN *Art*

(page 594)

Beyond the Classroom

Artswire online gives teachers a complete, searchable listing of state arts organizations for your convenience. Connect to them by visiting our Web site at *www.glencoe.com/sec/art*.

🕐 **Out of Time?** If time does not permit teaching this chapter in its entirety, you may wish to preview the artwork and captions with students. Scan the heads in each lesson with students. Discuss the Looking Closely features and examine Styles Influencing Styles on page 323.

Early Medieval and Romanesque Art

INTRODUCE

Chapter Overview

CHAPTER 14 acquaints students with features of Carolingian and Romanesque art.

Lesson One covers the building of monasteries and the creation of manuscript illuminations.

Lesson Two traces the development of Romanesque churches and the revival of relief sculpture and wall painting as ornamentation.

Studio Lesson gives directions for creating a woodblock print.

Art & Language Arts

Have students examine and discuss the artwork and caption that opens this chapter.

Let students who are familiar with *Beowulf* share their knowledge of the work's form, language, and content. Ask a group of volunteers to learn more about *Beowulf* and share the results of their research with the rest of the class.

National Standards

This chapter addresses the following National Standards for the Arts.

1. (a,b)	4. (a,b,c)
2. (a,b,c)	5. (b,c)
3. (a)	6. (b)

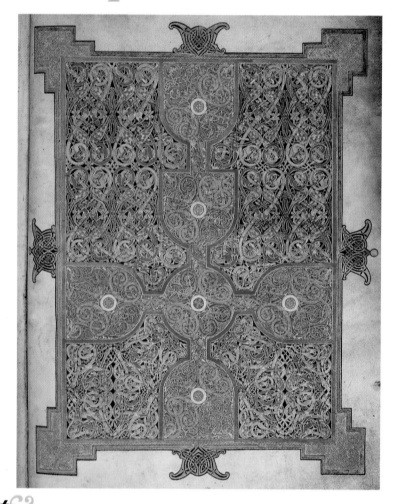

Art & Language Arts ■ FIGURE 14.1

At the same time ornamental manuscripts such as this were being produced in Britain and Ireland, a peasant poet named Caedmon, wrote his *Hymn*, the earliest known English poem. It skillfully uses the long, alliterative non-rhyming line, suggesting that this form of poetry was already well established. Many poems written later, including *Beowulf*, made use of this form.

Ornamental page from the *Book of Lindisfarne*, late 7th century. Illumination. By Permission of the British Library, London, England. (MS Cotton Nero, D.IV. F62V)

CHAPTER 14 RESOURCES

Teacher's Classroom Resources

- 📁 Advanced Studio Activity 14
- 📁 Application 14
- 🖱 Chapter 14 Internet Activity
- 📁 Studio Activity 18

Assessment

- 📁 Chapter 14 Test
- 📁 Performance Assessment

Fine Art Resources

- 🔖 *Art in Focus* Transparency 18
  Clasp from the Sutton Hoo Ship Burial.
- 🖼 *Focus on World Art* Print 14
  Lindau Gospels.

*The Byzantine Empire survived for about 1,000 years,
while the Western Roman Empire rapidly
crumbled. During this period, the court of Constantinople,
with its power, wealth, and knowledge, had no equal
in the West. Christians, Jews, and Muslims were producing
epics, philosophical writings, scientific studies, and
unique visual art. Meanwhile, western Europe
struggled through a period of change, beginning with the fall of
Rome and ending with the start of modern culture
in the fifteenth century. This period, from about A.D. 500 to 1500,
is known as the Middle Ages, or the Medieval period.*

Introducing the Chapter

Write the term Medieval on the board. Have students reveal what they know about medieval times. Is it a time during which students might like to have lived? Have students record their ideas about this period, and then at the close of the chapter, ask if their impressions have changed.

Music Help students understand how Paul Salamunovich's work with Gregorian chants is a direct link to the medieval church.

YOUR Portfolio

Prepare an artwork for your portfolio made from a collection of unusual found objects. Search for unique objects that could be used in a design. Work in small groups and design a piece of art that uses some or all of the objects you collected. Brainstorm several possibilities for using your found object(s). What media will you combine for the design? How will subject and design be related? Arrange the found objects in a pleasing way and make a rough sketch of the final design. Discuss and compare your designs. Store your artwork or a photograph of it in your portfolio.

Focus ON THE ARTS

MUSIC
A new complex musical structure called polyphony began to replace Gregorian chants. This style combined many tones or voices and was adopted in both religious and secular music.

THEATRE
Church fathers forbade theatre, but in A.D. 970, they allowed the reinactment of a brief Easter scene to be held inside a church. One prop was used: a wooden chest representing the tomb of Christ.

LITERATURE
Around A.D. 700 the great Anglo-Saxon epic poem *Beowulf* was written. In Spain, the *Poema del Cid* recounted a national hero's deeds.

Focus ON THE ARTS

Explain that for a long time, leaders of the Church did not allow theatre because they thought it was too worldly. Gradually, they became enthusiastic supporters. Ask the class to brainstorm about ways in which theatre could be used as an aid to spiritual feeling and thought. Some possible answers: Theatrical scenes make religious stories more vivid and memorable; theatre is one way to teach; theatre can make use of many art forms (music, dance, poetry, costumes), each of which can convey a spiritual feeling.

309

DEVELOPING A PORTFOLIO

Personal Style. Careful study of artists, techniques, and media is a way to access models for personal style. Remind students that many of the artists they have learned about first took inspiration from other artists. Ask your students to spend some time reflecting on the style of art that they like best. Remind them to remain aware of what they are most happy about in their work and what they are least happy about. Are they aware of artists who could serve as a source of inspiration? If so, encourage them to research more about those artists and even collect examples of their work to use as models. Then, frequent evaluation of their own sketches and efforts will help them develop their own unique style.

The Early Medieval Period

Focus

Lesson Objectives

After studying this lesson, students will be able to:
■ Describe the role of Charlemagne and monasticism in the art of the Middle Ages.
■ Identify the features of a medieval monastery.
■ Explain the symbols found in medieval manuscript illuminations.

Building Vocabulary

On the board, write the suffix *-ism*. Have students identify and define words that end with this suffix (for example, totalitarianism, vegetarianism). Ask: How does the suffix *-ism* change the form and meaning of a root word? Then have students define the Vocabulary terms that end in *-ism*.

Motivator

Ask students to imagine trying to study art without the benefit of photographs of the artworks discussed. What role in general do pictures play in any book? Inform students they are about to learn about a type of book in which illustrations play an especially meaningful role.

Introducing the Lesson

Acquaint students with the concept of periodization, the attempt of historians to slice up time into distinct units. Help students understand that time is a continuum and that the events of one age tend to blend into those of the next. Have students briefly review the history of the Byzantine Empire as a preface to events of the Middle Ages.

The Early Medieval Period

Vocabulary
■ feudalism
■ serfs
■ transept
■ monasticism
■ cloister
■ illuminations

Discover

After completing this lesson, you will be able to:
■ Identify the three periods of the Middle Ages.
■ Explain the contributions Charlemagne made to learning and the arts during the Early Medieval period.
■ Discuss the importance of monasticism and the contributions of monks to the art and architecture of the Early Medieval period.

*A*t one time the Middle Ages were known as the "Dark Ages," a label suggesting that they represented many blank pages in the history of Western civilization. However, a closer look has helped to fill in those pages with an impressive list of accomplishments.

During this period, many of the important features of our modern world were born, including parliamentary government, common law, present-day languages, and modern nation states. In art, the Middle Ages were anything but dark. It was the most splendid of all periods for bookmaking, a time of a great architectural revival, and an era of important developments in sculpture.

The Age of Faith

Perhaps a more accurate label for this period would be the Age of Faith. The hearts and minds of Medieval people were fixed on one all-important goal—preparation for eternal life after death. The Church, which had grown in power and influence since the collapse of the Roman Empire, guided the people in this quest.

The Church influenced the lives of kings and peasants alike throughout western Europe. Virtually everyone was born into the faith, and all were expected to place loyalty to the Church above everything else.

Three Periods of the Middle Ages

Because of its length, it is helpful to divide the Middle Ages into three overlapping periods. They are the *Early Medieval,* which dates from about the last quarter of the fifth century to the middle of the eleventh; the *Romanesque,* which, in most areas, took place during the eleventh and twelfth centuries; and the *Gothic,* which

MAP SKILLS
■ **FIGURE 14.2** Notice the various kingdoms into which Europe was divided during the Middle Ages. How is Europe during this period different from Europe during the height of the Roman Empire? How do you imagine these changes might have affected the art and architecture of Europe?

310

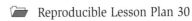

LESSON ONE RESOURCES

Teacher's Classroom Resources

📁 Appreciating Cultural Diversity 23

📁 Art and Humanities 22

📁 Cooperative Learning 21, 22

📁 Enrichment Activity 27

📁 Reproducible Lesson Plan 30

📁 Reteaching Activity 30

📁 Study Guide 30

overlapped the Romanesque and continued in some areas into the sixteenth century. This chapter deals with the Early Medieval and Romanesque periods.

From Charlemagne to Feudalism

The fall of Rome is considered the start of the Early Medieval period. This was a time of great uncertainty because the strong central government that had assured law and order to all Roman subjects was gone. The period was marked by conflicts, open warfare, and mass migrations of foreigners into and across lands formerly controlled by the Romans. Under these trying conditions, the Carolingian dynasty was founded. Although it survived less than 150 years, this dynasty managed to bring about the revival of a strong, efficient government. Furthermore, it stimulated a renewed interest in learning and the arts.

The Role of Charlemagne

One man was largely responsible for the many accomplishments of the Carolingian dynasty. He was Charles the Great, more commonly known as Charlemagne (Figure 14.3). Already King of the Franks, Charlemagne was crowned emperor by the pope on Christmas Day in the year 800 and became the first of the Holy Roman Emperors.

Charlemagne's domain grew until it included all of the Western part of the old Roman Empire except Britain, Spain, southern Italy, and Africa. His subjects enjoyed an efficient government and a remarkable level of law and order.

Beyond creating a great empire, Charlemagne encouraged learning and the arts. He ordered every monastery and abbey to establish a school where students could learn arithmetic, grammar, and the psalms. His most important achievement, however, may have been the preservation of ancient manuscripts. He invited scholars from England and Ireland to his court to rewrite old texts and prepare new ones. It is to

■ **FIGURE 14.3** Charlemagne was King of the Franks until Pope Leo III crowned him the first Holy Roman Emperor. Under Charlemagne's rule, people throughout western Europe were united by his style of government and by a set of common ideas. **How do you imagine this stability and unity influenced artists and their work?**

Equestrian Statuette of Charlemagne. c. 800. Bronze. Carolingian sculpture. 24 × 17.5 × 9.5 cm (9½ × 6¾ × 3¾"). Louvre, Paris, France.

Charlemagne's credit that many of the ancient documents we have today were copied by scholars working under his command.

The center and capital of Charlemagne's empire was Aix-la-Chapelle, now the German town of Aachen. (See map, Figure 14.2.) Here he set up his court and tried to restore the splendors of ancient Rome. Statues were brought from Italy, baths were constructed,

Chapter 14 *Early Medieval and Romanesque Art* **311**

TEACH

Using Map Skills

Refer students to the map in Figure 14.2. Provide a map showing present boundaries in Europe. Help students understand how different the boundaries within Europe today are from those that defined the region in the Early Medieval period. Point out the extent of the Frankish Empire in A.D. 800 and the area held by the Eastern Roman Empire. If possible, have students research one present-day country located within the area shown here whose boundaries have undergone changes.

Art History

Explain that all medieval artwork in this chapter represents the collective desire of people who valued it enough to fashion each work and then preserve it. Consequently, medieval art represents the values of the community, not the individual. Ask students to work in small groups and devise lists of 20 books that are worth preserving by copying by hand. Have the groups share lists and compare their entries to the manuscripts illustrated in Figures 14.8 (page 315), 14.9 (page 316), and 14.28 (page 327). Discuss the values inherently expressed in students' choices.

Cross Curriculum

MUSIC. Recordings of sacred and secular medieval music are widely available. Play one or two Gregorian chants and ask students to characterize the mood of the compositions. Encourage students to explain why this style of music appeals or fails to appeal to them. Does the Gregorian chant seem to have anything in common with the art and architecture reproduced in this chapter?

Aesthetics

Direct students' attention to Figure 14.4. What adjectives does this structure call to mind? How would students describe the use of space? What features are borrowed from the Greeks or the Romans?

Art Criticism

Have students examine Figure 14.4 again. Ask them to describe the interior of the chapel, identify the kinds of shapes that are used in the structure, and analyze the use of color and texture. Ask them: What is the effect of the two-color arches? Have they seen other examples of this use of architectural color in the textbook? (Refer them to Figures 13.17 and 13.18, page 299).

Cross Curriculum

CIVICS. Introduce students to the Burgundian code. Unlike Roman law (the basis of the contemporary North American legal system), which concerned itself with principles that could be applied to changing circumstances, the Burgundian code assigned fixed penalties for well-defined circumstances and allowed trial by ordeal when facts appeared to be contradictory. Have students read the Burgundian code (a modern edition translated by Catherine Fisher Drew is available). Then ask students to select a well-known contemporary legal case and attempt to apply the Burgundian code to it.

Did You Know?

Within a century of the completion of Charlemagne's palace, the first windmills appeared in the Middle East and the Vikings developed the art of shipbuilding.

and a chapel was built (Figure 14.4) that closely resembled the famous Roman church at Ravenna (Figure 13.12, page 295).

Unfortunately, Charlemagne's empire with its strong central government ended shortly after his death in 814. By the close of the ninth century, civilization in western Europe was in a shambles once again. Weak central government and the need for protection led to the formation of a governmental system known as feudalism.

The Rise of Feudalism

Feudalism was *a system in which weak noblemen gave up their lands and much of their freedom to more powerful lords in return for protection.* The lord allowed the former owner to remain on the land as his administrator. The administrator was the servant,

or vassal, to the lord. The vassal pledged his loyalty and military assistance to the lord.

Most of the people, however, were **serfs,** or *poor peasants who did not have land* to give in return for protection. These people worked the land and were handed over with it when the land passed from one nobleman to another.

Churches and Monasteries

Like their early Christian ancestors, Medieval church builders used Roman models. The Roman civic basilica continued to be the most popular type of structure for religious services.

The basilica featured a rectangular plan, which was divided on the inside to form a nave, or central aisle, and two or more side

■ **FIGURE 14.4** The capital of Charlemagne's empire was Aix-la-Chapelle (now Aachen, Germany). It was here that he built his palace and tried to recapture the glories of Rome. What do you think Rome represented for Charlemagne and the rest of Medieval Europe?

Palatine Chapel of Charlemagne. Aachen, Germany. 792–805.

CULTURAL DIVERSITY

Feudal System. Help students recognize that the feudal system has been used in periods other than the Carolingian dynasty. Students may enjoy gaining a sense of how feudalism operated in medieval Japan, for example, by watching one of several films by Japanese director Akira Kurosawa that are set in feudal Japan. (An especially noteworthy film fitting this description is *Ran.*) As an alternative, you may wish to have a volunteer read and report to the class on James Clavell's novel, *Shogun,* also available in a film adaptation. Interested students may wish to record similarities and differences between the Medieval period of Europe and that of Japan.

aisles. Light from windows in the walls of the nave above the side aisles lit the interior of the building. As in early Christian churches, at one end of the nave was the main entrance, and at the opposite end was a semicircular area known as the apse. An altar was placed in the apse in plain view of the people who assembled in the nave.

Changes in Basilica Design

During Charlemagne's time, a few changes were made in the basic plan of the basilica. Some churches were built with a **transept,** *another aisle that cut directly across the nave and the side aisles.* This aisle was placed in front of the apse and extended beyond the side aisles. Seen from above, the addition of this aisle gave the church the shape of a cross.

The transept not only increased the space inside the building but also added to its symbolic appearance. Occasionally, towers were also added to the exteriors of the churches (Figure 14.5). These towers were to influence church construction in western Europe for centuries.

Unfortunately, most of the churches erected during the Early Medieval period were made of timber. Warfare during the ninth and tenth centuries and accidental fires destroyed most of these. Today only a few heavily restored buildings remain.

The Spread of Monasticism

Throughout the long Medieval period, people labored in the service of learning and art. Many were monks, devoted religious men who lived under a strict set of rules in remote communities called monasteries.

Monasticism refers to *a way of life in which individuals gathered together to spend their days in prayer and self-denial.* It had its roots in the Near East as early as the third and fourth centuries A.D. At that time, some people began to feel that the Church had become too worldly. Eventually, groups of men with the same spiritual goals banded together. They formed religious communities far removed from the rest of society where they spent their lives in quiet contemplation and prayer.

■ **FIGURE 14.5** This Romanesque church can be spotted from a distance because of its campanile, or bell tower. What does the existence of this church, and another almost like it, in a small remote village tell you?

Church of San Clemente, Tahull, Spain. 1123.

The Monastery of San Juan de la Peña
■ **FIGURE 14.6**

Monks built their monasteries in remote places, often in deep forests or on the rocky slopes of mountains. Most of the earliest Medieval monasteries have long since crumbled away, but in northern Spain, deep in the forests covering the foothills of the Pyrenees, you can still visit the ruins of the Monastery of San Juan de la Peña (Figure 14.6, page 314).

Characteristics of the Monastery Structure

The history of San Juan de la Peña is shrouded in legend, but no legend is more interesting than the building itself. From the

Chapter 14 *Early Medieval and Romanesque Art* **313**

Aesthetics

Emphasize that medieval aesthetics placed a great deal of value on decoration, a value that has been severely questioned and sometimes derided in the twentieth century. Have students write down all the reasons they can think of to explain why medieval artists were willing to lavish so much time, care, and materials in creating embellished works such as the cloister in Figure 14.7 (page 314) and the detailed tympanum in Figure 14.21 (page 323). Discuss the importance of decoration in medieval art, especially its expressive, religious, recreational, and symbolic roles.

Critical Thinking

Pass around a copy of the *Rule of St. Benedict,* one of the most widely used monastic rules in the Early Medieval period. (Many translations are available. A good one is found in *Western Asceticism,* edited by Owen Chadwick [Philadelphia: The Westminster Press].) *The Rule* contains 73 short sections. Ask each student to select and read one section. Allow students a day or two to think over their passage and then explain it to the class.

Aesthetics

Arrange a panel discussion in which the members debate the contradiction between monks vowing to lead a life of poverty and then creating lavish manuscripts ornamented with expensive pigments and bound with precious metals and gemstones.

More About... **Monasteries.** Enclosure was a part of monasticism for both men and women, but it was usually much stricter for women. Aside from the spiritual benefits of a thick, high wall around the convent, enclosure provided protection against local violence and invasions. Monks were advised not to go to taverns or banquets, embrace a woman, or accept a parish, but they were not strictly prohibited from leaving the monastery enclosure. An abbess, however, often needed the local bishop's permission for her to leave the convent or to grant permission for one of her nuns to leave. Even then, nuns seldom traveled beyond the convent walls alone.

Cross Curriculum

LANGUAGE ARTS. Explain to students that different monastic communities took slightly different religious vows. The most familiar were vows of poverty, chastity, and obedience. Have students research a vow common to one of the orders and write a paragraph or two explaining how it was essential to the well-being of a monastic community.

Studio Skills

Direct students' attention to Figure 14.8 (page 315). Have them look closely at the interlaced arch within which St. John is enclosed. Have students practice drawing interlaced bands on scratch paper first, then have them draw an interlaced border on a piece of white paper. Once they have worked out the sequence of overlapping bands, students can use india ink to create the final outlines and fine-tip felt markers to color the interior of the bands. By using different colors, students can emphasize the interweaving of the several bands. Students may attempt to imitate the pattern shown in Figure 14.8, or they may devise a simpler pattern of their own.

■ **FIGURE 14.6** The ruins of this monastery—now more than 1,000 years old—are isolated and difficult to find. What does the isolated location of this monastery tell you about the lives and activities of Medieval monks?

Monastery of San Juan de la Peña. Near Jaca, Spain. c. 922.

■ **FIGURE 14.7** Cloister. Monastery of San Juan de la Peña. Near Jaca, Spain. Cloister completed in twelfth century.

outside, the thick stone walls and small windows give it the look of a fortress. Inside it is dark and damp. The walls are marked by dark smoke stains from the torches that were once used to light the interior.

A flight of stairs leads to an upper story, where an arched doorway marks the entrance to an open court with the massive, projecting wall of the cliff overhead. This was the **cloister,** *an open court or garden and the covered walkway surrounding it* (Figure 14.7). It is as quiet and peaceful now as it was

centuries ago when the monks came here to contemplate and pray.

Much emphasis was placed on private prayer and contemplation in the monastery. Typically, this was done in the cloister, where the monks spent several hours each day. In general, the cloister was attached to one side of the church, linking it to the other important buildings of the monastery. Here, in all kinds of weather, the monks came to pray, meditate, and read from books they received from an adjoining library.

COOPERATIVE LEARNING

Scrapbooks. Have students look at Figure 14.9 (page 316) and focus on the manner in which St. Matthew's clothing is rendered. Ask students to describe how line and texture have been used to suggest flowing drapery. Then have the class assemble a scrapbook of examples of the many different ways in which fabric can be drawn and painted. The examples can be taken from art and fashion magazines or anywhere else that textiles might be illustrated. Divide the scrapbook into different sections for different kinds of fabric such as velvet, silk, or denim. Discuss how color, value, texture, line, gradation, and movement can be used to describe the various types of cloth.

Art of the Early Medieval Period

A Medieval monastic library bore little resemblance to our modern public libraries. It usually was little more than an alcove located off the cloister, and the number of books on its shelves was modest—probably no more than 20.

Manuscript Illumination

■ FIGURE 14.8

Perhaps no other art form captures the spirit of the Early Medieval period better than the illuminated manuscript. Until the development of the printing press in the fifteenth century, all books had to be copied by hand. This usually was done by monks working in the monasteries.

■ **FIGURE 14.8**
Manuscripts decorated with illuminations like these preserve precious ideas from the past. What do you think motivated the monks who worked so hard to copy and illuminate Medieval manuscripts?

St. John, from the Gospels (in Latin). c. 860. The Pierpont Morgan Library, New York, New York.

Art Criticism

Have students examine Figure 14.8. How is the principle of balance demonstrated in this illumination? Which parts are balanced symmetrically, and which parts are balanced asymmetrically? Is this a successful composition? Have students explain their answers.

Art History

Explain that medieval manuscripts were valuable objects and were sometimes stolen, ripped apart, and rebound in a new style. Sometimes thieves would discard the pages altogether and keep only the manuscript's jewel-encrusted metal covers. Given the abuses of time, changing tastes, poor storage conditions, and lack of knowledge about proper preservation methods, most medieval manuscripts and artworks no longer exist. Ask students to work in small groups and devise a list of artifacts from their own time that they would most want to preserve for future generations. Have the groups share and compare their lists.

Cross Curriculum

TECHNOLOGY. Invite an archivist to class to discuss how documents are preserved today. Point out that paper today has a much shorter shelf life than the vellum used by medieval scribes and that archivists have devised numerous ways to combat the destructive effects on paper of time, light, and moisture. Following the visit, have small groups of students research alternative technologies currently used for preserving information (for example, high-speed personal computers, CD-ROM, and laser disc). Discuss whether any of these techniques will store documentation for as many centuries as monastic copies of books have lasted.

Time & Place
CONNECTIONS

Medieval Period
C. A.D. 500–1500

ARMOR. Knights and warriors during the middle ages were required to wear protective metal suiting during attacks and battles. Sheets of metal attached with moveable joints for flexibility and full-face helmets sometimes weighed 80 pounds or more.

COAT OF ARMS. The coat of arms of a family or royal household contained symbols representing events or strengths of individual families. Often a shield was included, sometimes with animals and decorated with plumes, feathers, and ribbon flourishes. Coats of arms were displayed on shields and flags for identification during battle.

Activity **Illuminated Manuscript.**
Choose from these objects and create a manuscript page for each in the style of early Medieval manuscript illumination. Use the beginning letter of the name of the object in the upper left corner of the page, and describe each of the objects pictured.

Time & Place
CONNECTIONS

Medieval Period

Guide students in examining and discussing the images in the Time & Place feature. Let students share what they already know about medieval armor and coats of arms. Then have students select one of these areas of interest and research it further. After completing their research, students can work independently to create their own "illuminated manuscripts." They should prepare by studying examples in this chapter, as well as other photographs of illuminated manuscripts they may find in art books, reference works, or on the Internet.

Have students examine and discuss the painting in Figure 14.9. Ask: Which elements of art can you identify in this work? What are the important principles of art shown here?

After students have compared and discussed their ideas, have them read and respond to the explanations in the feature, *Creating the Illusion of Movement.*

Study Guide

Distribute *Study Guide* 30 in the TCR. Assist students in reviewing key concepts. 📁

Art and Humanities

Assign *Appreciating Cultural Diversity* 23, "Attend a Medieval Festival," in the TCR. Students learn how festivals in Europe continue traditions that originated during the Middle Ages. Students then have an opportunity to plan a festival commemorating an important school event. 📁

Studio Activities

Assign *Enrichment* 27, "Calligraphy in the Carolingian Style," in the TCR, which calls on students to practice calligraphy with a chisel pen. 📁

Art and Humanities

Have students complete *Cooperative Learning* 21, "Artists of the Middle Ages," in the TCR. In this activity, groups of students learn about the artists' guilds of the Middle Ages and then design symbols for their groups. 📁

Monks often decorated manuscript pages with delicate miniature paintings done in silver, gold, and rich colors. For nearly 1,000 years, these **illuminations,** or *manuscript paintings,* were the most important paintings produced in western Europe. (See Figure 14.1, page 308.) Illuminated manuscripts were created by dedicated men who worked anonymously to record and illustrate history.

Writing painstakingly in Latin, Medieval monks passed on the ideas of classical writers and church fathers. Often they phrased these ideas in beautiful and complex ways. Like painters, sculptors, and architects, they brought inspiration and skill to their work.

Throughout the Medieval period, manuscripts of the Gospels were illustrated with small paintings of the four Evangelists. A symbol was usually used to help the reader identify each of these Gospel writers. Matthew was symbolized by an angel; Mark, by a lion; Luke, by a bull; and John, by an eagle (Figure 14.8, page 315).

St. Matthew
■ **FIGURE 14.9**

A painting of Matthew (Figure 14.9) from a ninth-century Gospel book created in Reims, France, shows the Evangelist seated before a small writing table. His left hand holds an ink container shaped like a horn, while a quill pen is clutched in the right. This is not a picture of a scholar calmly recording his thoughts and ideas, however. It is a painting of an inspired man frantically writing down the words of God.

■ **FIGURE 14.9** *St. Matthew,* from the *Gospel Book of Archbishop Ebbo of Reims.* Carolingian Manuscript. c. 830. Approx. 25.4 × 20.3 cm (10 × 8"). Epernay, France.

CREATING THE ILLUSION OF MOVEMENT

Motion, not form, is the focus in this work. The drapery swirls around the figure, while sketchy lines behind seem to push upward. This motion underscores Matthew's excitement as he works furiously at the moment of inspiration to record the sacred message.

- **Identify.** The wide-open eyes, furrowed brow, and rumpled hair indicate Matthew's intense concentration. His huge, clumsy hand guides the pen rapidly across the pages of his book.

- **Interpret.** An angel, Matthew's symbol, reads the sacred text from a scroll. It is Matthew's responsibility to pass these words on to the world. His expression and actions show that he is painfully aware of this responsibility.

About the *Artwork*

Adam and Eve. Have students look at Figures 14.10 and 14.11 (page 317). Ask: What are the advantages and disadvantages of sculpting figures in relief as opposed to creating sculpture in the round? If possible, show students photographs of other contemporary relief panels. Have students describe the mood conveyed by these figures. Students can also look for similar relief sculpture on the doors of churches, synagogues, and other places of worship in their communities. Encourage them to sketch or photograph examples and bring them to class for display.

■ **FIGURES 14.10 and 14.11** These are two scenes from the story of Adam and Eve. In the first scene, God is looking for Adam and Eve, who cover their ears and try to hide from him. In the second, an angel drives them from the garden of paradise. Adam and Eve clasp their hands and look heavenward for forgiveness. Did you find the story illustrated by these relief carvings easy to understand? What expressive qualities do the works possess?

■ **FIGURE 14.10** *Adam and Eve Eating the Forbidden Fruit.* Relief carving on a capital from the cloister, Santes Creus Monastery. Near Tarragona, Spain. Twelfth century.

■ **FIGURE 14.11** *Adam and Eve Banished from the Garden of Eden.* Santes Creus Monastery. Near Tarragona, Spain. Twelfth century.

The Importance of Illuminations and Other Religious Art

The Church was the center for art and learning as well as religion during the Medieval period. It favored art that could teach and inspire the people in their faith. The written portions of manuscripts were meant for the few people who could read, whereas the illustrations were intended for those who could not. The messages presented in the illustrations had to be simple and familiar so everyone could understand them. The pictures often told the same Scripture stories that the people heard every Sunday in church sermons. These stories were also expressed in carvings and reliefs (Figures 14.10 and 14.11).

LESSON ONE REVIEW

Reviewing Art Facts

1. What is monasticism? Where and when did it originate?
2. Name and describe the decorations used on Early Medieval manuscript pages.
3. Give examples of symbolism used by manuscript illustrators.
4. What type of art did the Church favor during the Medieval period?

▶ **Activity... *Form a Living Cathedral***

The Early Medieval, Romanesque, and Gothic periods form the greatest era of church building in history. Examine a diagram of a Gothic church and notice how parts were added as churches got bigger and higher.

Build a living cathedral with your classmates. Form a row of six students facing another row of six students. Join hands and form a barrel vault. Raise your hands higher to form the pointed arch, the basis for the later Gothic cathedral. Add parts such as buttresses, aisles, and vaults by adding students. "Build" an entire cathedral and see how one part supports another.

LESSON ONE REVIEW

Answers to Reviewing Art Facts

1. A way of life centering on prayer and self-denial; the Near East in the third or fourth century A.D.
2. Illuminations: delicate, miniature paintings.
3. Answers, which will vary, can include: Matthew, an angel; Mark, a lion; Luke, a bull; John, an eagle.

4. Art that could teach and inspire the faithful.
Activity...*Form a Living Cathedral.*

Encourage students to draw their own floor plans and sketches of the interior and exterior of these structures. Then create some space in the classroom or outdoors, and have students work cooperatively to form their own living cathedral.

ASSESS
Checking Comprehension

Have students respond to the lesson review questions. Answers are given in the box below.

Reteaching

Assign *Reteaching* 30, found in the TCR. Have students complete the activity and review their responses. 🗀

Enrichment

➤ Assign students *Cooperative Learning* 22, "Creative Papermaking," in the TCR. Students will learn about the process of papermaking and its effect on manuscript production. 🗀
➤ Point out that sage was an extremely popular medicinal herb throughout medieval Europe and was thought to be an excellent muscle strengthener and a tonic for the stomach, heart, and nerves. Then have students research the role of medieval monasteries in preserving and extending knowledge of the medicinal properties of various plants.

Extension

Have students complete *Art and Humanities* 22, "Dances in Medieval Times," in the TCR, in which students learn about dance as a form of expression and ritual during the Middle Ages. 🗀

CLOSE

Provide students with a photograph of a monastery or medieval church other than those shown in the section. Ask them to identify the key features of the structure, as well as the principles and elements of art emphasized in it.

The Romanesque Period

Focus

Lesson Objectives

After studying this lesson, students will be able to:
- Identify the features of a medieval castle and a Romanesque church.
- Describe the structural changes made in churches during the Romanesque period.
- Describe developments in painting and sculpture during this era.

Building Vocabulary

Have students briefly discuss what they already know about tapestries. Then display photographs of several tapestries and ask: How are tapestries different from paintings? How are they different from rugs? What practical purposes do you think tapestries might have served?

Motivator

Write the word *Romanesque* on the board, and help students identify the root (*Roman*) and the suffix (*-esque*). Ask students to write brief journal entries describing the artistic and cultural developments they would expect of a time period with this name. After reading the lesson, discuss whether their initial impressions were consistent with the facts.

Introducing the Lesson

Ask students to imagine what it would have been like to live in a castle during the Middle Ages. What would their castle have looked like? Have students complete sketches of imaginary castles.

The Romanesque Period

Vocabulary
- tapestries
- pilgrimage
- ambulatory
- tympanum

Discover
After completing this lesson, you will be able to:
- Discuss the effects of feudalism on Romanesque architecture.
- Describe the structural changes made in churches during the Romanesque period.
- Explain the importance of the revival of sculpture during the Romanesque period.

*T*he art of the Early Medieval period began to take on new features and abandon others until a new artistic style known as Romanesque emerged. This new style was especially apparent in architecture. Churches began to dot the countryside in greater numbers, and most of these had many features in common.

By the eleventh century, the Romanesque style appears to have been accepted throughout most of western Europe. It continued to thrive until the middle of the twelfth century, when another style, Gothic, appeared on the scene.

The Effects of Feudalism

The feudal system, which had developed in the ninth century, reached its peak during the Romanesque period. It contributed to the constant disputes and open conflict that continued to mar the Medieval period.

Under the feudal system, land was the only source of wealth and power, but the supply was limited. Nobles, lords, and kings fought constantly to protect or add to the land under their control.

Castles
- **FIGURE 14.12**

With warfare unchecked, nobles found it wise to further fortify their dwellings. Towers of stone were built by the late eleventh century, and by the twelfth century the now-familiar stone castle (Figure 14.12) had evolved. With its tower, walls, moat, and drawbridge, the castle became the symbol of authority during the Romanesque period.

■ **FIGURE 14.12** Notice the thick walls of this castle, without windows that might provide light and ventilation for the inhabitants. What do you imagine life was like for the people who lived in this kind of castle?

Castle ruins near Leon, Spain.
c. Thirteenth century.

318

LESSON TWO RESOURCES

Teacher's Classroom Resources

- 📁 Appreciating Cultural Diversity 24
- 📁 Art and Humanities 23
- 📁 Enrichment Activity 28
- 📁 Reproducible Lesson Plan 31
- 📁 Reteaching Activity 31
- 📁 Study Guide 31

■ **FIGURE 14.13** Walls like this were built to provide protection for the inhabitants of cities during the Romanesque period. How has this old city wall been incorporated into the modern community?

City Wall, overlooking River Adaja. Avila, Spain. Eleventh century.

■ **FIGURE 14.14** Narrow, dark street in Viana, Spain.

Life in the Castles

A noble's castle could hardly have been a comfortable place. Its main purpose was defense, and this eliminated the possibility of windows. The thick outer walls were pierced only by narrow slots through which archers could fire on attackers. Stairs were steep and passageways dark and narrow.

The drafty rooms were usually sparsely furnished and lacked decoration. Occasionally **tapestries,** *textile wall hangings that were woven, painted, or embroidered with colorful scenes,* were hung to keep the dampness out. In cold weather, the only warmth came from fireplaces; the largest fireplace was in the great hall, where family members gathered and meals were served.

The Growth of Cities

Castles remained important as long as the feudal system flourished, but the growth of trade and industry in the thirteenth century brought about an economy based on money rather than land. Cities sprang up, and castles became more and more obsolete.

The still unsettled times made it necessary to erect barricades around the towns. Wooden walls were used at first, but these were replaced during the twelfth and thirteenth centuries by more sturdy stone barricades. An early example of such a stone wall surrounds the historic city of Avila in Spain (Figure 14.13). Often referred to as one of the most ambitious military constructions of the Middle Ages, it measures more than 1.5 miles and includes 88 towers and nine gates.

Town walls succeeded in keeping out intruders, but they created problems as well. As more people moved into a town, space ran out and overcrowding resulted. To solve this problem, buildings were built higher, sometimes reaching seven stories or more. The space inside was increased by projecting each story out over the street. Of course, this method of construction made the narrow streets below very dark (Figure 14.14).

Romanesque Churches

All the towns had one thing in common: In the center of each stood a church. During the Romanesque period, the Church increased its influence on the daily lives of the people. It offered comfort in this life and, more importantly, it provided the means to salvation in the next. The richly decorated stone churches of the eleventh and twelfth centuries are a testimony to the power of the Church, the faith of the people, and the skill of the builders.

Chapter 14 *Early Medieval and Romanesque Art* **319**

CHAPTER 14
LESSON TWO

TEACH
Art Criticism

Have students examine Figure 14.12 and describe it in detail. Would they say that every aspect of the castle's design was created with a practical purpose in mind? Do some parts seem to have an ornamental function? Is this castle a successful building? Is it an attractive one? Have students explain their responses.

Art History

After they have studied Figure 14.12, small groups of students can research and report on other castles. Their reports should include pictures of the castle, an explanation of what type of castle it is, and any special features such as a tower or stronghold. Groups should also furnish information on the present condition of their castle. Some possible choices are: Baños de la Encina in Jaén, Spain; Castel del Monte in central Apulia, Italy; Castle of Chillon in Montreux, Switzerland; Blarney Castle in Cork, Ireland; Chateau Gaillard in Les Andelys, France; Gravensteen in Ghent, Belgium; the Marksburg in Braubach, Germany; Windsor Castle in New Windsor, England; and Harlech Castle, in Merioneth, Wales.

Did You Know?

The tapestries that hung in medieval castles illustrated scenes from the Bible or popular legends. Weavers, both men and women, often spent years completing a large tapestry.

 ## Technology

National Gallery of Art Videodisc Use the following images as examples of more works by artists introduced in this lesson.

Girolamo di Benvenuto
Portrait of a Young Woman

Search Frame 108

Andrea del Castagno
The Youthful David

Search Frame 140

Use Glencoe's *Correlation Bar Code Guide to the National Gallery of Art* to locate more artworks.

Art History

A volunteer with an interest in weaponry may wish to research how the development of cannons transformed the castle from a secure fortress into an obsolete, vulnerable household. The student's report should include information on the kinds of weapons that a castle was originally designed to withstand, such as rams and stone-throwers, and the gradual development of more powerful cannons.

Art History

Have students examine the drawing of the floor plan of a Romanesque church (Figure 14.16). Which of the features identified in the illustration did students also encounter in their study of Roman basilicas and in their study of early Christian churches? How did the use and appearance (dimensions) of these structures change over the course of time?

Did You Know?

The weakest part of a medieval castle was its wooden drawbridge, which could easily burn.

■ **FIGURE 14.15** This famous cathedral was the destination of many pilgrimages. Why did so many people undertake pilgrimages during the Romanesque period? How do you think the experience affected them?

Cathedral of Santiago de Compostela, Spain. Eleventh to thirteenth centuries.

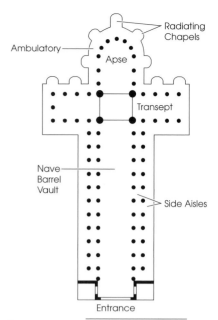

■ **FIGURE 14.16** Plan of a Romanesque Church.

Pilgrimage Churches
■ FIGURE 14.15

The Church at this time placed great importance on piety and encouraged people to take part in pilgrimages. A **pilgrimage** is *a journey to a holy place.* These journeys were a visible sign of religious devotion. People banded together and traveled to pay homage to saints and relics in far-off churches.

Worshipers believed that praying before the sacred remains of a saint could assure a plentiful harvest, cure diseases, solve personal problems, and secure the promise of eternal salvation.

The Holy Land and Rome were the destinations of many early pilgrimages. The long journey to the Holy Land was dangerous, however. A pilgrimage to the shrine of St. James at the Cathedral of Santiago de Compostela (Figure 14.15) in northwest Spain became an acceptable substitute, and churches and shelters were soon being built along this pilgrimage route in southern France and northern Spain. Builders continued to use the Roman basilica plan, but the churches were made larger to hold the great number of pilgrims that visited them.

Modifications to Church Design
■ FIGURE 14.16

To increase the size of a Romanesque church, builders extended both the nave and transept and added two more aisles, one on each side (Figure 14.16). They often added an **ambulatory,** *an aisle curving around behind the main altar,* which made it easier for religious processions and groups of pilgrims to move about inside the building.

About the *Artwork*

Cathedral of Santiago de Compostela. Point out that the cathedral exterior that modern travelers to Compostela see is considerably different from the one seen by pilgrims in the twelfth century. The Romanesque version itself was built over a ninth-century church. An imposing Baroque frontispiece was later added to the west façade, thereby obstructing the original double tower entrance. The entrance to the south transept, however, retains its medieval appearance. Interested students might want to research the evolution of the cathedral and bring photos to class, if available.

To accommodate the many priests who were required to say Mass every day along the pilgrimage routes, additional altars were placed in small curved chapels built along the transept and the ambulatory. The chapels, projecting out from the building, became a familiar part of Romanesque churches (Figure 14.17).

Building stone roofs for these huge Romanesque churches posed a serious problem. The Roman technique of using a series of round arches to construct a barrel vault (Figure 9.8, page 197) provided a solution. Thick, solid walls and huge pillars were needed to support the heavy stone roofs.

The Church of Saint Sernin in Toulouse
■ FIGURE 14.18

It was in France that the Romanesque style reached its peak in architecture. Perhaps no structure better illustrates this style than the Church of Saint Sernin in Toulouse (Figure 14.18). Outside, this church appears large and solid. It is no wonder that churches like this came to be known as fortresses of God.

Inside, the church is spacious but dark and gloomy. A few steps lead down into the wide nave; on either side are two other aisles. Massive, closely spaced piers line the nave and separate it from the aisles on either side. These form a majestic arcade of arches leading from the main entrance to the altar at the far end of the church (Figure 14.19, page 322). Above, barely visible in the dim light, is the rounded ceiling of the barrel vault. The nave, side aisles, transept, apse, and ambulatory are easily identified. A sketch of the building would reveal that the church is laid out in the form of a huge cross.

Many feel that the overall impression of Saint Sernin is one of quiet strength and dignity. The church is simple and direct. With its massive walls, small windows, and durable tower, it has the look and feel of a stone castle.

■ **FIGURE 14.17** Chapels projecting out from churches were a familiar feature of Romanesque architecture. **How did practical requirements affect this design development?**

Santillana del Mar Collegiate Church, apse exterior. Spain. c. Twelfth century.

■ **FIGURE 14.18** The solid exterior of this church may remind visitors of a castle. **Based on this exterior, what kind of interior would you expect?**

Saint Sernin. Facade. Toulouse, France. c. 1080–1120.

Chapter 14 *Early Medieval and Romanesque Art* **321**

More About... **Castles.** Three basic styles of castles were built during the Middle Ages. The motte-and-bailey type was composed of a high mound (motte) of earth on which sat a wooden tower overlooking a courtyard (bailey). Both the motte and the bailey were surrounded by a fence and a moat. A stone keep was a three- or four-story story castle. It was usually square and had square towers at each corner and a carefully defended entrance at the ground level. A concentric castle had two rings of walls for protection. The inner wall was higher than the outer wall so that invaders could be fired on from any side.

Aesthetics

Have students browse through the chapters on twentieth-century art (see Chapters 23 and 24) and find examples of modern, virtually unadorned buildings. Discuss the different historical tastes in architectural ornamentation as exemplified by modern structures and those shown in this lesson. Then have students write a paragraph discussing the strengths and limitations of each style. Which do they prefer and why?

Art History

Explain to students the importance of primary sources in art history. To understand the meaning and function of medieval artifacts, art historians depend heavily upon documents that have been preserved since the Middle Ages.

Have students pretend that they are literate, medieval pilgrims undertaking a journey from their town to the shrine of St. James at the Cathedral of Santiago de Compostela. Students should write a few pages in the diary that they would keep while on this journey. The entries may make reference to their hopes for the trip, what they saw along the way, and the shrine itself. Help students realize that a pilgrim's motives for undertaking such a trip were not always completely spiritual. A pilgrimage could offer a chance to see more of the world, temporarily escape an unpleasant marriage, and experience new adventures.

■ **FIGURE 14.19** The simple interior of the church was lit only by small, high windows and rows of flickering candles. How well do you feel this interior matches the exterior of the church (Figure 14.18)? How is the viewer's eye directed to the apse? What is placed there?

View of central nave, interior of Saint Sernin. Toulouse, France.

■ **FIGURE 14.20** Stories and scenes carved in the tympanum would be seen by everyone who entered the church. What do you imagine was the main motivation of artists who carved relief sculptures on a church tympanum? What type of balance is used in this tympanum design?

West portal and tympanum, Leyre Monastery. Province of Navarra, Spain. Twelfth century.

The Revival of Sculpture and Painting

The revival of the sculptor's craft was one of the important achievements of the Romanesque period. Many of the churches along the pilgrimage routes used relief sculptures as another way to teach the faith to people, many of whom were illiterate. Like manuscript illustrations, these stone carvings reminded people of the familiar stories from Scripture.

Two architectural features were found to be ideal places for relief carvings: the **tympanum,** the *half-round panel that fills the space between the lintel and the arch over the doorway of the church* (Figure 14.20) and the capitals of columns inside.

The tympanum on the exterior of the church was an area to which people naturally lifted their eyes as they entered the building. It was a perfect location for relief sculpture. The shape of the tympanum seemed to demand a large figure in the center, which became the focus of attention. Smaller figures were placed on either side of this central figure. A subject such as the *Last Judgment* (Figure 14.21) was especially well suited for this arrangement.

CULTURAL DIVERSITY

Pilgrimages. Explain that the phenomenon of religious pilgrimage is important to many different religious groups. Working in committees of three or four, each group selecting a different quadrant of the globe, students can research and then mark on large world maps the sites of pilgrimage destinations. Well-known sites include the Ganges River, Mecca, Jerusalem, Lourdes, and Guadalupe, Mexico. Committees should include in their reports such particulars as: Who makes pilgrimages to a given spot? What do they do at the site? How often might a pilgrim go there? What is expected from the undertaking?

Styles Influencing *Styles*

ROMAN TO ROMANESQUE Just as Roman artists used relief sculpture on the triumphal arch to honor important and victorious personalities, Romanesque carvers filled the tympanum with sculptures representing important figures.

The Arch of Constantine (Figure 14.21a) depicts the victories of Constantine I. Relief carvings that appear on the arch show the emperor as the largest and most important of the figures.

Emphasis is used in the Romanesque tympanum (Figure 14.21b) to show the important figures. The large figure in the center represents God the Father. Angels trumpet the news that the final judgment has arrived. He welcomes the chosen on his right, but his left arm points down, condemning the sinners on his left. The chosen stand upright. The sinners fall—or are pulled—to their doom.

The row of figures below includes Mary with the Christ Child in the center. The 12 apostles stand on either side. St. Michael weighs souls to determine who is worthy to enter heaven.

■ **FIGURE 14.21a** Arch of Constantine, Rome, Italy. A.D. 312–15.

■ **FIGURE 14.21b**

Last Judgment. Tympanum, Church of Santa Maria. Sangüesa, Spain. Twelfth to thirteenth centuries.

Chapter 14 *Early Medieval and Romanesque Art* **323**

More About... **Architectural Ornamentation.** The Romanesque interest in ancient Roman culture ultimately led to a revival of carved stone architectural ornamentation. Italian and French sculptors of the Early Medieval period studied local examples of ancient sculpture to develop their technique. The large numbers of churches built in the eleventh century provided masons with the first lucrative and steady labor they had had since antiquity. Gradually specialties developed, and the more experienced masons ceased to cut pillars and stones in favor of constructing friezes, tympana, corbels, arcades, and capitals.

Art History

Have students look at Figure 14.23 and consider how these carvings might have changed since they were originally installed. Ask a volunteer to research the effects of both weather and airborne pollutants on outdoor sculpture, then present the findings to the class. The report should include examples of other artworks that have sustained similar damage. It should conclude with information on measures that can be taken to lessen the damaging effects of nature and environmental pollution.

Art History

Make sure that students understand the differences among various styles of columns and capitals. Have students identify Doric and Ionic orders in illustrations in Chapter 8 (Figure 8.7, page 172) and describe how these classical forms differ from the Romanesque ones seen in this chapter.

Studio Skills

Have students consider the medieval capital decorations as discussed in the text. Then have them devise and create capital decorations of their own. Have them gather materials that will help them convey a message (for example, found objects, pictures clipped from magazines and reinforced with cardboard). Students can then create the structural framework for their capital by cutting a strip of cardboard measuring 8 × 24 inches and forming it into a ring; the two short edges can be fastened with staples. Objects can be attached to the framework with white glue or staples. Encourage students to display and discuss finished capital decorations.

■ **FIGURE 14.22** Romanesque church façades like this one were known as Bibles in Stone. How can you explain that term? What made this kind of Bible in Stone necessary?

Santa Maria façade. Sangüesa, Spain. Twelfth to thirteenth centuries.

■ **FIGURE 14.23** Notice how the figures have been elongated to fit into the spaces between the columns. What messages do you think these figures were intended to convey to worshipers?

Portal sculpture. Santa Maria façade. Detail, Judas. Sangüesa, Spain. Twelfth to thirteenth centuries.

Church of Santa Maria
■ **FIGURES 14.22 and 14.23**

Efforts were made to fit as many stories as possible into the space available on the front of Romanesque churches. This was the case at Santa Maria in Sangüesa (Figure 14.22). There you even find one of the few carvings of the hanged Judas, as shown in Figure 14.23. Judas is the figure to the far right in the bottom row of figures that flank the door on either side.

Carvings of strange creatures can be found on many Romanesque buildings. There lurking among carvings of the Holy Family, church fathers, apostles, and saints are fantastic creatures, half-human and half-animal (Figure 14.24). They may be evil spirits or devils lying in wait to snare the unwary. These grotesque combinations of animal and human forms may be a sign that artists were beginning to use their imaginations once more.

Capital Decoration

Inside churches and in cloisters, the capitals of columns were another excellent place for carvings. Here, where the weight of the ceiling was met by the upward thrust of columns, the roving eyes of the faithful came to rest. Many Medieval sculptors served their

324 Unit Five *Art in Quest of Salvation*

MEETING INDIVIDUAL NEEDS

Verbal/Linguistic Learners. As students study the art of the Middle Ages, read portraits from Chaucer's *Prologue to the Canterbury Tales* aloud to them, or have them read portraits independently or in groups. Help students discuss the details presented by Chaucer, and encourage students to imagine the lives and activities of artists who lived during this time.

Interpersonal Experience. Have students work together to identify some of the technological improvements that date from the Middle Ages, Possibilities include trousers, barrels, skis, horseshoes, and the water mill. Have groups create advertisements for these innovations and display their ads in the classroom.

■ **FIGURE 14.24**
Romanesque sculptors often included fantastic creatures among their carvings. Why do you think Romanesque sculptors created these unusual creatures?

Relief carving from the cloister, Santes Creus Monastery. Near Tarragona, Spain. Twelfth century.

Art History

Appoint a panel of students to role-play members of a museum board of directors at a meeting that will decide which piece illustrated in this chapter should be purchased for the museum's collection. For the sake of this exercise, architectural details such as capitals will be assumed as available but whole buildings are not. The panel should include a chairperson, four directors, a manuscript curator, a curator of sculpture, a curator of architecture, and a museum budget director who has set the price of each piece and determined the dollar amount budgeted for medieval purchases this year. The panelists must defend their choice in terms of which piece would best inform the public about the nature of medieval art. The rest of the class will be museum members who are allowed to question the reasoning and decisions of the panel.

Art Criticism

Divide the class into four groups and assign each group the task of describing and analyzing the relief carvings on one of the following edifices: Leyre Monastery (Figure 14.20, page 322), Church of Santa Maria (Figure 14.21, page 323 and Figures 14.22, and 14.23, Santes Creus Monastery (Figure 14.24), and the Cathedral at Tarragona (Figures 14.25 and 14.26). Have groups discuss the following: What elements and principles of art are emphasized in each work? In what ways are the works unique? Can students arrive at any generalizations with respect to Romanesque church carvings? Have them test their conclusions on other examples.

apprenticeships by carving these capitals with biblical scenes, human figures, birds, and animals. Once they had developed their skills, they moved on to carving larger scenes.

Romanesque capitals are often a curious mixture of skilled craftwork and quaint storytelling. For example, in a capital relief carving in the cloister of the cathedral at Tarragona, Spain (Figures 14.25 and 14.26), rats carry a "dead" cat to its grave. The wily cat, however, is only pretending to be dead as it is carried on the litter. In the next panel, it jumps up to claim its careless victims. Some claim this carving is a rare example of Medieval humor. Others suggest it was inspired by an old Spanish proverb: The mouse is wise, but the cat is wiser. Then again, it may be a reference to the resurrection, indicating that Christ's return from the dead will result in the destruction of his enemies.

■ **FIGURE 14.25 and FIGURE 14.26** There are two scenes to the story being told here. **Reading from left to right, what is happening in each scene?**

Left and right views of capital relief carvings from the cloister, Cathedral at Tarragona, Spain. Twelfth to thirteenth centuries.

Chapter 14 *Early Medieval and Romanesque Art* **325**

More About... **Relics.** The medieval attitude toward saints and their relics is central to an appreciation of medieval life. The tenth century saw a great increase in the number of churches built and the "discovery" of relics. An overwhelming number of churches claimed to have bits of wood that were parts of the cross on which Jesus was crucified. A church that possessed such a treasure could be assured of attracting pilgrims whose offerings were an important source of revenue. Not surprisingly, the religious and economic importance of relics made them a popular target for thieves.

Study Guide

Distribute *Study Guide* 31 in the TCR. Assist students in reviewing key concepts. 📁

Art and Humanities

Have the class as a group undertake *Art and Humanities* 23, "Rhythmic Movement in Art and Music," in the TCR. The worksheet provides students with diagrams of frescoes that were created during the Romanesque period. Students are then asked to compare these artworks with the rhythmic movement of Gregorian plainsong. 📁

Studio Activities

Have students complete *Enrichment* 28, "Drawing with Stitchery," in the TCR, which asks them to plan and execute a stitchery design using stitches similar to those visible in the Bayeaux Tapestry. 📁

Art and Humanities

Invite a professional calligrapher to visit the class and demonstrate at least one of the following medieval scripts: uncial, half-uncial, Carolingian, or black letter. Have the class prepare questions in advance to explore what it is like to be a calligrapher and how much contemporary calligraphers have in common with their medieval counterparts.

Studio Activities

Assign *Studio* 18, "Drawing Using Romanesque Space Techniques," in the TCR. The worksheet encourages students to use disproportionate size relationships and the space-filling techniques of early Romanesque fresco painters as a basis for drawing a contemporary scene of a basketball game. After students have completed the activity, allow time for discussion of results. 📁

■ **FIGURE 14.27** This painting shows Christ with his right hand raised in blessing, while his left holds an open book proclaiming his title as Supreme Ruler. He is surrounded by the four Evangelists. Do you think this is a successful work? Would you support your decision by referring to the literal, design, or expressive qualities?

Christ in Majesty. Wall painting from San Clemente. Romanesque Catalan fresco. Tahull, Spain. Twelfth century. Museo de Arte de Cataluna, Barcelona, Spain.

Church Wall Paintings

Large paintings decorating the inside walls of churches were also done during this period. Artists often were required to fit their paintings into a specific area. At San Clemente in Tahull, Spain, the painter took a familiar Byzantine theme and tailored it to fit within the apse of the church (Figure 14.27).

As Ruler of the Universe, Christ is seated on an arch representing the sphere of the universe with his feet resting on a semicircular shape. A bold use of line, brilliant colors, and a sensitive feeling for pattern are reminders of the manuscript illuminations produced during the same time. It is likely that many works like this one were painted by artists who also decorated the pages of Medieval manuscripts.

Teacher Notes

Developing Perceptual Awareness. Display examples of calligraphic and typeset texts and ask students if they can distinguish between the two. Be sure to include samples of calligraphic alphabets that resemble modern typefaces and printed material that is based on medieval letterforms. Help students become sensitive to the minute variations in form and rhythm that are a part of the charm of calligraphic work. If your samples of calligraphy are original, students may even be able to detect the variations in pressure on the pen and the way in which the paper's texture subtly affects the shape of the letters.

Illuminations in Religious Manuscripts

Illuminations in religious manuscripts continued to be an important form of painting throughout the Romanesque period. The flattened look seen in figures carved in stone is even more obvious in these paintings. There are no shadows and no suggestion of depth.

Common Features of Romanesque Paintings

Certainly Romanesque painters possessed the skill to reproduce more accurately what they saw, but they chose not to do so. They were concerned primarily with the presentation of easy-to-understand religious symbols, not with the imitation of reality. This flattened quality is evident in an illumination from a gospel produced around the middle of the twelfth century in Swabia, a small territory in southwest Germany (Figure 14.28). Here an angel appears before a woman who raises her hands in surprise.

Followers of the Christian religion had no difficulty recognizing this scene as the Annunciation. The angel, with his hand raised to show that he is speaking, has just announced to Mary that she is to be the mother of the Savior. The easy-to-read message, flat, colorful shapes, and bold use of line are common features in this and all other Romanesque paintings.

■ **FIGURE 14.28** This illumination tells a familiar Bible story clearly and completely. How is this work similar to the carved reliefs created during the same period?

The Annunciation. Leaf from a Psalter. German. Twelfth century. Tempera and gold and silver leaf on parchment. 15.2 × 12 cm (6 × 4 ³/₄"). The Metropolitan Museum of Art, New York, New York. Fletcher Fund, 1925. (25.204.1).

LESSON TWO REVIEW

Reviewing Art Facts

1. What was the primary purpose of a Romanesque castle?
2. Why was it necessary to increase the size of Romanesque churches?
3. What part of the church building is the tympanum? Where is it located? Why was this feature added?
4. Name two architectural features found to be ideal places for relief carvings.

Activity... *Designing a Medieval City*

Two major building types in the Middle Ages were castles and cathedrals. Every aspect of life revolved around these two structures. The castle, with its resident lord, offered much needed protection from the unsettled living conditions of the time. The church offered comfort and the promise of a better life in the hereafter.

Find films, books, CD-ROMs, or laser discs on castles and cathedrals and share them with the class. Working in small groups, imagine you live in a Medieval city. Design a plan that includes a castle and a cathedral, and assign everyone in the group a position and a purpose in the city. Base the assignments on your research findings.

Chapter 14 *Early Medieval and Romanesque Art* **327**

LESSON TWO REVIEW

Answers to Reviewing Art Facts

1. Defense.
2. To make room for the large number of people making pilgrimages.
3. The half-round space between the lintel and the doorway arch.
4. Tympana and capitals of columns.

Activity...*Designing a Medieval City*

Have students work in cooperative learning groups to research castles, cathedrals, and life in a medieval city. Suggest that group members draw a detailed plan of their city and that each group member write a short essay describing his or her daily life in the assigned medieval role.

CHAPTER 14
LESSON TWO

ASSESS
Checking Comprehension

➤ Have students respond to the lesson review questions. Answers are given in the box below.

➤ Assign students *Application 14*, "For Crying Out Loud," in the TCR. Students are asked to identify types of medieval architecture on the basis of partial announcements as they might have been given by a town crier during the Middle Ages. 📁

Reteaching

Assign Reteaching 31, found in the TCR. Have students complete the activity and review their responses. 📁

Enrichment

Have students visit a papermaking studio to learn some of the methods by which paper is made. Ask your host to explain the differences between genuine vellum and parchment and the cheaper imitation counterparts that go by the same names in stationery and art supply stores today.

Extension

Have students complete *Appreciating Cultural Diversity 24*, "Updating a Medieval Town Design," in the TCR. Students learn about the goals of medieval town planners. Students then design a modern shopping mall that follows the design of a medieval town. 📁

CLOSE

Ask students to describe the themes and stylistic features that most of the artworks illustrated in this chapter have in common.

327

Studio LESSON

Woodblock Print of an Imaginary Creature

Objectives
■ Complete a woodblock print of a fantastic imaginary creature.
■ Point out and identify the positive and negative shapes within the design.
■ Reveal a variety of simulated textures in the finished print.

Motivator

Have students examine the fantastic medieval creature in Figure 14.24 (page 425) and identify its most unusual features. Ask them to compare medieval creatures with contemporary fictional monsters portrayed in movies and on television. How do modern-day representations of monsters differ in appearance and in purpose from those created by medieval artists?

Aesthetics

Ask students to describe the emotions and feelings aroused by the works illustrated in Figure 14.24 (page 325). How would the religious setting in which works such as this one are found affect a person's reactions to them?

Critiquing

Have students apply the steps of art criticism to their own artwork, using the "Examining Your Work" questions on this page.

Studio LESSON

Woodblock Print of an Imaginary Creature

Complete a woodblock print of a fantastic imaginary creature. Identify the positive and negative shapes in your design. Cut the negative shapes away, leaving the positive shapes to be inked and printed. Include a variety of rich, simulated textures in your final prints.

Materials

- Pencil, sketch paper, and carbon paper
- Newspapers
- Piece of soft pine, approximately 8 × 10 inches
- Wood-carving tools (V- or U-shaped gouges with wooden handles)
- Water-soluble printer's ink
- Shallow pan, brayers
- White drawing paper or colored construction paper, 9 × 12 inches

Inspiration

Examine the example of Romanesque carving in Figure 14.24. Note how Medieval artists often included fantastic creatures in carvings of this kind. What purpose do you think these creatures served? Describe their unusual features.

Process

1. Complete several sketches of fantastic creatures, making each as unique as possible. You might wish to combine the features of several animals with those associated with a human form. Make your sketches on paper cut to the same size and shape as the wood block.

2. Lay down sheets of newspaper to catch your shavings and ink. Transfer your best sketch to the wood block using pencil and carbon paper. Label the positive and negative shapes in your design.

3. With the wood-carving tools, cut away the negative shapes. Make all cuts in the direction of the wood grain. The hand holding the wood block should always be kept away from the path of the carving tool.

4. Check your design by placing a piece of paper over it and rubbing the surface with the side of a pencil.

5. When carving is completed, squeeze a small amount of printer's ink from the tube into the shallow pan. Roll the ink with a brayer until it is spread evenly over the pan. Apply the brayer to the wood block, covering it completely with ink.

6. Place a sheet of white drawing paper or colored construction paper over the inked wood block and rub it firmly with your fingers or the back of a large spoon. Before removing the paper, pull back a corner to see whether additional rubbing is needed. Re-ink your wood block for additional prints. Try printing on various kinds of paper for different results.

■ **FIGURE 14.29** Student Work

Examining Your Work

Describe. What are the most unusual features of your creature? How did you arrive at the idea of using those features?

Analyze. Did you clearly distinguish between the positive and negative shapes of your design before carving your wood block? Did you use a variety of simulated textures?

Interpret. What adjective best describes your fantastic creature? What words do other students use to describe your creature?

Judge. Evaluate your woodblock print in terms of its expressive qualities. Does your work succeed in communicating a particular idea or emotion?

ASSESSMENT

Peer Review. After students have used the Examining Your Work questions to assess their own work, you may want to have them apply the same process to another student's woodblock print. Display the completed prints in the classroom, and have each student choose one print he or she considers especially successful in conveying a specific feeling. Have students write a paragraph, describing the feeling and explaining how that feeling is communicated in the work. Then have students write a second paragraph, making three or more specific suggestions for improving the woodblock print.

Reviewing the Facts

Lesson One

1. What years are considered the Middle Ages, or the Medieval period?
2. What event in history marks the start of the Early Medieval period?
3. Name the main features that would be identified in a plan of a Romanesque church.
4. List several ways the Christian Church taught illiterate people stories from the Bible.

Lesson Two

5. During the Medieval period, when land was the only source of wealth and power, how could a nobleman increase his wealth?
6. Who originated barrel vault construction? How was it used during the Romanesque period?
7. Why did sculpture regain importance during the Romanesque period? What purpose did sculpture serve?
8. What was the subject matter of the sculpture that was produced during the Medieval period?

Thinking Critically

1. ANALYZE. Look closely at each of the illustrations of paintings in Chapter 14. What can you say about Medieval artists' interest in creating a sense of deep space in their paintings? What can you say about their interest in using areas of pattern?
2. EVALUATE. Refer to *Christ in Majesty*, Figure 14.27, page 326. Consider the elements of color, value, line, and shape. How did the artist use the principles of balance, emphasis, harmony, and variety to arrange each of the elements mentioned?

 Use the *Performing Arts Handbook*, page 576 to learn about music, dance, and theatre from many diverse cultures and times.

CAREERS IN Art If you enjoy studying or creating art, read about a fascinating art-related career opportunity in the *Careers in Art Handbook*, page 594.

inter NET CONNECTION Visit Glencoe Art Online at *www.glencoe.com/sec/art*. Examine more artworks from Medieval and Romanesque artists, and learn about the times in which these works were created.

Technology Project

A Modern-Era Illuminated Manuscript Page

For hundreds of years scribes and monks who worked in monasteries copied all books by hand. They preserved much of what we know about ancient history. The creators of these ancient documents took great pride in their work, often embellishing the pages with beautifully designed letters and miniature paintings, encased between elaborate covers. We call these works illuminated manuscripts.

Find examples of these early texts and study them (Internet, CD-ROMs, laser disks, books). Imagine what their makers would think if they could see us at work on our modern computers. The scribes and monks had to carefully form each letter using pen and ink. We can instantly choose a typeface from hundreds of fonts. Try your hand at creating a modern-era illuminated manuscript page using available computer programs.

1. Choose a favorite short piece of writing, about one page in length, that is either your own work or one chosen from another source. Research the texts of some medieval writers to make your selection.
2. Choose a typeface that you think will visually express the content of your writing choice. By looking at examples from medieval illuminated manuscripts, you will see that on many pages, the first word on a page began with a special large and ornate letter. You might wish to design such a letter for the first word on your page either by hand or on the computer.
3. There were often small paintings included on the manuscript pages (Figure 14.1, page 308). You might consider creating one of these using traditional media such as watercolor, tempera, or acrylics, then scanning and sizing it to fit the page you designed.
4. Print your illuminated manuscript page and share it with your class or workgroup.
5. Extend this project by printing a copy of each class member's page and binding them into a handmade book.

329

CHAPTER 14
REVIEW ANSWERS

Reviewing the Facts

1. The Middle Ages extended from A.D. 500 to A.D. 1500.
2. The fall of Rome.
3. A nave, two or four side aisles, an apse, a transept, an ambulatory, and radiating chapels.
4. Possibilities include illustrations on manuscripts, church sermons, and biblical scenes decorating the church building.
5. By marrying someone who had land or by going to war and taking the land.
6. The Romans; to build larger churches.
7. Churches began to use more and more relief sculpture; these were intended to teach the faith to people who could not read.
8. Stories from Scripture.

Thinking Critically

1. The interest in creating space appears to have been lacking, while an interest in creating patterned areas seems to have been of utmost importance.
2. A possible answer: The artist has used symmetrical balance via the use of color, line, and shape; a shift in values among the various earth tones combined with the use of shapes of varying sizes lends harmony; variation in size emphasizes the figure of Christ.

Teaching the Technology Project

As students begin working on this project, have them examine again the illuminations in Figure 14.8, page 315, Figure 14.9, page 316, and Figure 14.28, page 327. Also have them review photographs of illuminated manuscripts, considering both the level of detail included and the mood created by these works.

 Assign the feature in the *Performing Arts Handbook*, page 576.

CAREERS IN ART If time permits, have interested students investigate the career information in the *Careers in Art Handbook*, page 594.

inter NET CONNECTION Have students go online and learn more about artists on preselected Web sites with the Internet activity for this chapter.

329

Gothic Art

LESSON ONE Emergence of the Gothic Style
(pages 332–337)

Classroom Resources

📁 Art and Humanities 24
📁 Cooperative Learning 23
📁 Enrichment Activity 29
📁 Reproducible Lesson Plan 32
📁 Reteaching Activity 32
📁 Study Guide 32

Features

Time & Place CONNECTIONS
(page 334)

LOOKING Closely
(page 335)

LESSON TWO Gothic Sculpture and Illustrated Books
(pages 338–343)

Classroom Resources

📁 Appreciating Cultural Diversity 25
📁 Art and Humanities 25
📁 Reproducible Lesson Plan 33
📁 Reteaching Activity 33
📁 Study Guide 33

Features

LOOKING Closely
(page 340)

LESSON THREE Italian Church Painting
(pages 344–346)

Classroom Resources

📁 Enrichment Activity 30
📁 Reproducible Lesson Plan 34
📁 Reteaching Activity 34
📁 Study Guide 34

Features

Dramatic Effect in Art
Lamentation Pietà
(page 345)

END OF CHAPTER
(pages 347–349)

Studio LESSONS
- Drawing a Landscape Tympanum *(page 347)*
- Carving a Tympanum Landscape Relief *(page 348)*

ADDITIONAL CHAPTER RESOURCES

Activities

- Advanced Studio Activity 15
- Application 15
- Chapter 15 Internet Activity
- Studio Activity 19

Fine Art Resources

Transparency

Art in Focus Transparency 19

Giotto. *The Kiss of Judas.*

Fine Art Print

Focus on World Art Print 15

Nicholas of Verdun and workshop.
Shrine of the Three Kings.

Assessment

- Chapter 15 Test
- Performance Assessment

Multimedia Resources

- Artsource® Performing Arts Package
- National Gallery Laser Disc
- National Museum of Women in the Arts CD-ROM
- Arts & Entertainment Videos

NATIONAL STANDARDS FOR ARTS EDUCATION

The National Standards for Arts Education provide guidelines for grade-appropriate competency in the visual arts. The Content Standards for grades 9–12 are:

1. Understanding and applying media, techniques, and processes.
2. Using knowledge of structures and functions.
3. Choosing and evaluating a range of subject matter, symbols, and ideas.
4. Understanding the visual arts in relation to history and cultures.
5. Reflecting upon and assessing the characteristics and merits of their work and the work of others.
6. Making connections between visual arts and other disciplines.

Listed below are the National Standards for the Visual Arts addressed in this chapter. For a breakdown of the categories listed under each content standard listed, refer to the *Reproducible Lesson Plans* booklet in the TCR.

1. (a, b) **2.** (a, b) **3.** (a) **4.** (a, b) **5.** (a) **6.** (b)

HANDBOOK MATERIAL

 Paul Salamunovich *(page 586)*

CAREERS IN Art

Illustrator *(page 603)*

Beyond the Classroom

Teacher forums, articles, and opportunities for communication between art educators and the arts community can be located at ArtsWire Online. Connect to their extensive database through our Web site at *www.glencoe.com/sec/art.*

Out of Time? If time does not permit teaching this chapter in its entirety, you may wish to preview the artwork and captions with students. Scan the heads in each lesson with students. Discuss the Looking Closely features and examine Dramatic Effects in Art on page 345.

Gothic Art

CHAPTER 15

INTRODUCE

Chapter Overview

CHAPTER 15 focuses on the rise and spread of Gothic architecture and sculpture as well as fourteenth-century developments in Italian church painting.

Lesson One covers the emergence of the Gothic style and the great cathedrals of Europe.

Lesson Two discusses the realistic sculpture used to grace cathedrals.

Lesson Three covers the rise of Italian church painting and, in particular, the frescoes of Giotto.

Studio Lessons focus on creating a landscape tympanum and a tympanum landscape relief.

Art & Social Studies

Guide students in examining and discussing this artwork. Let students share what they know about the Crusades: What Europeans participated? Why? With what results? Then ask a small group of students to research the Crusades and the role Louis IX played. Have them find out the meaning of *canonization* and why Louis IX was canonized. Have them share their findings with the rest of the class.

Art & Social Studies
■ **FIGURE 15.1** Louis IX, a brave warrior, a competent administrator, and a just ruler, lead two Christian crusades to recover the Holy Land from the Muslims. He is shown in this illuminated manuscript seated across from his mother who managed the kingdom in his absence. Although both crusades were unsuccessful, Louis was canonized in 1297.

Page with *King Louis IX of France and Queen Blanche of Castile*, Moralized Bible, France. c. 1230. Ink, tempera, and gold leaf on vellum. The Pierpont Morgan Library, New York, New York. (M.240, F.8).

330

National Standards

This chapter addresses the following National Standards for the Arts.

1. (a,b)	**4.** (a,b)
2. (a,b)	**5.** (a)
3. (a)	**6.** (b)

CHAPTER 15 RESOURCES

Teacher's Classroom Resources
- 📁 Advanced Studio Activity 15
- 📁 Application 15
- 🖱 Chapter 15 Internet Activity
- 📁 Studio Activity 19

Assessment
- 📁 Chapter 15 Test
- 📁 Performance Assessment

Fine Art Resources
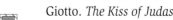
- Art in Focus Transparency 19
  Giotto. *The Kiss of Judas*
- *Focus on World Art* Print 15
  Nicholas of Verdun and Workshop.
  Shrine of the Three Kings

A revival of cities during the late stages of the Romanesque period gradually changed the character and tempo of life in western Europe. These new cities drew large numbers of serfs away from their rural villages with the promise of a better life. By the beginning of the thirteenth century, thriving cities could be found in northern Italy, southern France, and Flanders. By 1200, the Flemish towns of Bruges, Ghent, and Lille boasted populations numbering in the thousands. By the late thirteenth century, the population in Florence, Italy, had reached 45,000. These and other cities were the center of most of the intellectual and artistic progress in music, literature, and the visual arts during the Late Medieval period.

YOUR Portfolio

The contents of your portfolio should be reviewed from time to time. If you have stored your notes, sketches, and final artworks, you may wish to add or remove some of your entries. You may keep artworks because they represent your best example of the use of the elements and principles of art. You may decide to keep other works because they demonstrate growth in use of specific media. You may also choose to keep works that represent a process such as clay sculpture. Remember that your portfolio should contain examples of your best works that demonstrate your strongest skills.

Focus ON THE ARTS

LITERATURE
Italy's greatest poet, Dante Alighieri, wrote the *Divine Comedy.* In England, William Langland wrote *Piers Plowman,* an allegory about the search for truth.

THEATRE
The Catholic Church finally gave its support to theatre. Guilds presented plays in open-air venues. In Italy, universities set up theatres for private college performances.

MUSIC
Gothic composers followed strict rules, often with symbolic meaning. Church music used groups of three beats, or triple meter, to symbolize the three-part division of God in the Holy Trinity.

331

Introducing the Chapter

Have students read the chapter opener. Ask them to think about the changes in social and cultural life that occurred with the growth of cities. Encourage them to speculate about the effects such changes may have had on the artworks created during this period.

ART SOURCE **Music** While studying this chapter, use *Performing Arts Handbook* page 586 to help students experience the beauty of a musical form from the Middle Ages, traditional Gregorian chant by Paul Salamunovich.

Focus ON THE ARTS

Play the music of Guillaume de Machaut for the class—perhaps the Kyrie of The Mass of Nostre Dame and whatever else you have time for (Note: The company Naxos puts out an inexpensive, high-quality CD). Ask the class in what ways de Machaut's music resembles a Gregorian chant. (Mood; deep voices have the important part of the music.) Ask in what ways it resembles Gothic architecture. (Many different parts come together in a unified manner.) In what ways does it show the composer to be an individualist? (Passionate; takes rhythmic liberty; very odd vocal effects.) Explain that these conflicting styles show how different eras overlap in time.

DEVELOPING A PORTFOLIO **Self-Reflection.** Frequent writing tasks, in the form of ungraded reflections about an assignment or individual progress, actively engage students in their learning process. For example, as they respond to a work in progress, they can be encouraged to articulate their goals and evaluate the evolution of an artwork. Writing can also be a means of working out a solution to problems they encounter. Most art schools or colleges require a cover letter to accompany an application and/or portfolio submission; students who constantly write about art keep writing skills practiced and fresh.

Emergence of the Gothic Style

Focus

Lesson Objectives

After studying this lesson, students will be able to:
- Identify the key features of Gothic architecture.
- Explain the architectural innovations that made possible the building of soaring cathedrals.
- Discuss the dual purposes served by stained-glass windows.

Building Vocabulary

Ask students to define the word *vandal,* and have them investigate its etymology. After establishing that the word derives from the name of a barbarian tribe, point out that the name of another tribe, the Goths, was the source of the word *Gothic.*

Motivator

Present students with this challenge: Choose any major historical period (for example, Elizabethan times, the Roaring Twenties) and state the precise year and time at which that period began. Have students discuss why such a task is impossible. Point out that trends in art are similarly impossible to pinpoint and often overlap.

Introducing the Lesson

Show students a slide or large photograph of a Romanesque church and ask them to brainstorm a list of words that describe the structure and the feeling it evokes. Repeat the procedure with a slide or photograph of a Gothic cathedral. Tell students they will learn how architects managed to create such graceful, soaring structures.

Emergence of the Gothic Style

Vocabulary
- Gothic
- buttress

Discover
After completing this lesson, you will be able to:
- Describe the main features of Gothic architecture.
- Explain the relationship between Gothic architecture and the art of stained-glass windows.

*T*hroughout the thirteenth and fourteenth centuries, the growth of trade kept pace with the growth of cities. Trade routes were established between existing cities, and new cities sprang up along these routes. Trade, the growth of cities, and the increasing power of kings combined to bring an end to the feudal system.

What is Gothic?

Gothic is the term used to identify *a period that began around the middle of the twelfth century and lasted to the end of the fifteenth century and, in some places, into the sixteenth.* The name was coined by later critics who scorned the art of the period because it did not hold to the standards of ancient Greek and Roman art.

Because the Goths and other barbarian tribes had brought about the fall of Rome, the term *Gothic* was given to buildings that replaced classical forms. The name, then, is misleading; the Goths did not design or construct Gothic buildings.

The Romanesque style paved the way for the Gothic style and, in most areas, merged with it. In fact, many buildings that were begun as Romanesque were completed as Gothic (Figure 15.2). The lessons learned in producing Romanesque churches were put to good use during the Gothic era. If the greatest of the Medieval arts was architecture, then the Gothic cathedral was Medieval architecture's greatest triumph (Figure 15.3).

■ **FIGURE 15.2** This cathedral, begun in the twelfth century, combines features of Romanesque and Gothic architecture. Point out specific Romanesque features in this structure.

Cathedral of Tarragona, Spain. Begun in the twelfth century.

LESSON ONE RESOURCES

Teacher's Classroom Resources
- 📁 Art and Humanities 24
- 📁 Cooperative Learning 23
- 📁 Enrichment Activity 29
- 📁 Reproducible Lesson Plan 32
- 📁 Reteaching Activity 32
- 📁 Study Guide 32

Innovations in Cathedral Architecture

Gradually, Gothic architecture moved away from Romanesque heaviness and solidity toward structures of lightness and grace. During the thirteenth century, French architects developed the pointed arch, piers, and the flying buttress. These innovations enabled builders to erect the slender, soaring Gothic cathedral.

Pointed Arches and Flying Buttresses
■ FIGURES 15.4 and 15.5

Gothic builders discovered that they could reduce the sideways pressure, or thrust, of a stone roof by replacing the round arch with a pointed one (Figure 15.4). Because the curve of a pointed arch is more vertical, the thrust is directed downward. This downward thrust is then transferred to slender supporting columns, or piers, within the building.

Additional support is provided by buttresses. A **buttress** is *a support or brace that counteracts the outward thrust of an arch or vault.* Because they often had to reach over the side aisles of the church, these braces came to be known as "flying buttresses" (Figure 15.5, page 334). The use of pointed arches, piers, and

■ **FIGURE 15.3** An early Christian basilica was built on this site in the fourth century. It was replaced by this cathedral, built in the Gothic style during the twelfth and thirteenth centuries. **What specific features identify this cathedral as Gothic?**

Cathedral of Chartres, France. Right side and apse. c. Twelfth century.

■ **FIGURE 15.4** The introduction of pointed arches made it possible to use this kind of slender column or pier inside a large cathedral. **In addition to these piers, what else was used to support the heavy stone ceiling of cathedrals?**

Plasencia Cathedral (interior). Plasencia, Spain. Begun in the thirteenth century.

Chapter 15 *Gothic Art* **333**

TEACH
Using Map Skills

On a topographical map of Europe, have students find the following cities: Florence, Italy; Paris, France; and Tarragona, Spain. Have students compute the distances between these cities. Then have them note mountains and other geographical features that may have made travel between the cities difficult. Let students discuss how the Gothic style may have spread from its birthplace in France to these other centers. Have them investigate modes of transportation and communication available at the time.

Art History

Have students examine Figure 15.3, the Cathedral of Chartres. Then have them turn to the Parthenon in Figure 8.3 (page 169) and the Pantheon in Figure 9.16 (page 204). Have students compare and contrast the three houses of worship. In what ways did each serve the needs of its worshipers at the time it was constructed? Do students agree with the fifteenth-century attitude that Gothic cathedrals failed to meet the standards set by Greek and Roman art? What features and aspects of these structures can students point to that refute this position?

Teacher Notes _____

_____

_____

_____

Studio Skills

Instruct students to design and sketch the façade of a Gothic cathedral. First, have them examine the cathedrals illustrated in this lesson. Have students note which architectural features they find most pleasing, and encourage them to plan their own designs around these special features. Tell students to keep in mind the elements and principles of art emphasized in Gothic cathedrals, most notably balance. When students have finished the project, have them share and compare their work. Which sketches seem best to capture the Gothic spirit? Have them explain their reactions.

Art History

Have students summarize in a chart the different systems of structural support they have learned about so far (that is, post-and-lintel construction, the round arch, the vault, the pointed arch, the flying buttress). Then ask them to investigate what advances in structural engineering are in use today. Can students find examples of the pointed arch or the flying buttress in structures other than churches built in the twentieth century? What intent might an architect have when using structural techniques of an earlier age?

Aesthetics

Direct students' attention to the photographs of stained-glass windows in Figures 15.6 and 15.7. Which design would an aesthetician of the emotionalist school find more aesthetically pleasing? Which would a formalist consider more successful? Have students explain their responses.

■ **FIGURE 15.5** A support that reaches out to absorb the outward thrust of the heavy roof of a Gothic cathedral is called a flying buttress. What was placed in the walls between these flying buttresses?

Àvila Cathedral, Àvila Spain. Begun in the twelfth century.

flying buttresses created a thrust-counterthrust system that supported the ceiling. This system eliminated the need for solid walls. As a result, the space between the supporting piers could be filled in with stained-glass windows.

Stained-Glass Windows

The walls of glass, which builders were now free to use between the piers, let light flow into the cathedrals (Figures 15.6 and 15.7). They were also an ideal way to impress and instruct the faithful congregation through images created with pieces of colored glass. The light streaming through the windows made the glass richer and brighter than the dull surface of a wall painting.

Time & Place
CONNECTIONS
Gothic Period
c. 1100–1500

COURT FEASTS. Life at court in Gothic castles included banquet feasts for the wealthy nobles. This scene shows the fashionable headdresses worn by women, and musicians playing in the balcony as servants wait on the guests.

MAGNA CARTA. This thirteenth-century document helped shape the U.S. Constitution and Bill of Rights. Signed by King John of England in 1215, it guarantees freedom and liberties to the common people. It is now housed in the National Archives in Washington, D.C.

Activity **Examining Primary Sources.** Look at this image of the Magna Carta document. Locate a copy and read it. Show evidence from the document that helps you to understand why it was written. What class of people were most affected by it?

Time & Place
CONNECTIONS

Gothic Period

Have students examine and discuss the images in this Time & Place feature. Encourage volunteers to share their reactions: To whom do you think the Magna Carta has special significance? Why do you imagine the original document is preserved in the United States, rather than in England, where it was written?

Let students share what they already know about the Magna Carta. Then have students work with partners to read and discuss the document. Have partners work together to plan and write short essays in response to the Activity questions.

LOOKING Closely

THE MEDIEVAL ART OF STAINED GLASS

With stories depicting the lives of Christ, the Virgin Mary, and saints, stained-glass windows bring to mind the beautifully colored illuminations found in Medieval manuscripts. These stories are preserved in scenes that have lasted for centuries.

- **Size.** In cathedrals such as those at Chartres, Reims, and Paris in France and at León in Spain, huge areas were devoted to stained glass.

- **Color.** For color, artisans added minerals to the glass while it was still in a molten state. In this way, the glass was stained rather than painted; the color was very bright.

- **Design.** Small pieces of this stained glass were then joined with lead strips and reinforced with iron bars. The lead strips and iron bars often were made a part of the design.

■ **FIGURE 15.6** Notre Dame Cathedral, Stained glass. Paris, France. Begun in the twelfth century.

■ **FIGURE 15.7** Mary Magdalene, (detail). Stained-glass window in the Cathedral of León, Spain. Thirteenth to fourteenth centuries.

Chapter 15 *Gothic Art* **335**

LOOKING Closely

If possible, show students several slides of light streaming through stained glass windows; in addition, let students who have seen European cathedrals describe their reactions to the stained glass windows. Then guide students in discussing the windows in Figure 15.6 and Figure 15.7, and in reading and discussing the information in the feature The Medieval Art of Stained Glass.

Aesthetics

Point out that, because cathedrals such as those at Reims and Chartres are so large, they cannot be fully appreciated from a single vantage point. Have students consider the impact of this fact on the process of art criticism. Does the inability to glimpse the entirety of the work all at the same time create a hardship? Does it compromise the critic's ability to judge whether a work has unity? Have students brainstorm and discuss other issues raised by cathedral design that need to be taken into account in a critical assessment (for example, the effect of light filtering through the stained-glass windows at different times of day). Could the way the light looked have been a factor in the decision of Claude Monet, some 500 years later, to paint various scenes (among them the Cathedral at Rouens) numerous times and under different atmospheric conditions?

COOPERATIVE LEARNING

Group Reports. Tell students that in the Middle Ages almost all skilled trades were represented by guilds, which are similar to the trade unions of today. These guilds were often quite wealthy and powerful. Have groups of students each select and research a guild, determining such information as how powerful the organization was, what social welfare events and projects it supported, and details of apprenticeship. If some students wish to research contemporary trade unions, a discussion that follows their presentations might focus on the similarities and the differences between the two types of organized labor. Encourage groups to share their findings in the form of brief reports.

Art History

Provide students with a list of the European countries that adopted the Gothic style, including those represented in the text. Have groups of students each choose a country and research the adaptations it made in French Gothic style to suit the needs and tastes of its inhabitants. Have the groups present their findings in brief oral reports.

Study Guide

Distribute *Study Guide* 32 in the TCR. Assist students in reviewing key concepts. 📁

Art and Humanities

If possible, obtain and play an example of medieval plainsong recorded in a cathedral. Then have students read *Art and Humanities* 24, "The Origins of Plainsong," in the TCR. In this activity students learn how the acoustics of a building impact the dynamics of sound produced within it. 📁

Studio Activities

Assign *Cooperative Learning* 23, "The Many Facets of Stained Glass," in the TCR. This worksheet asks students to research the technique of making colored glass, leaded glass, and the many variations of stained glass. Students then work in teams to make window displays from paper "stained-glass" designs. 📁

Art and Humanities

Point out that the process of using images in medieval stained glass and paintings to enable the illiterate person to "read" is called *iconography*. Have students learn more about this process and its role in the depiction of saints and other religious figures.

■ **FIGURE 15.8**
Notice the use of symmetrical balance on the exterior of this cathedral. **What element of art is used to direct the eye upward?**

West façade, Reims Cathedral (exterior). Reims, France. Begun in 1211.

The Gothic Interior

Gothic interiors required no more decoration than the vertical lines of the architecture, the richly colored stained glass, and the colorful flow of light. Romanesque churches had to be lighted from within by candles and lamps. Gothic interiors, however, were bathed in tinted sunlight passing through walls of stained glass.

A Gothic cathedral such as the Cathedral of Chartres or the Cathedral of Reims (Figure 15.8) is just as impressive on the inside as it is on the outside. It is so huge that it cannot be completely examined from one spot because no single point offers a view of the entire structure.

Walking through such a cathedral, you find your gaze moving in all directions. A beautifully carved relief sculpture captures your attention for a moment, but then an immense expanse of stained glass draws your eyes upward. Tilting your head far back, you see an arched stone ceiling that seems to float overhead.

A Heavenly Light

These Gothic interiors (Figure 15.9) are always striking, but they are even more so at sunset. At that time of day, when the rays of the sun strike low and filter through the many colors of the window, the effect is breathtaking. Not surprisingly, it was once said that the mysterious light in Gothic cathedrals would lead the souls of the faithful to the light of God.

■ **FIGURE 15.9** The pointed arches, slender columns, and large stained-glass windows mark this interior as Gothic. **How does it differ from the Romanesque interior seen in Figure 14.7 on page 314?**

Central nave toward the apse, Reims Cathedral (interior). Reims, France.

336 **Unit Five** *Art in Quest of Salvation*

> *More About...* **The Gothic Period.** Point out to students that this period of history was one that witnessed the production of many literary masterpieces. Among them were *Chaucer's Canterbury Tales* and Mallory's *Morte D'Arthur* in England, Boccaccio's *Decameron* in Italy, and the anonymous *Romain de la Rose* in France. Invite groups of students to select and explore one of these cultural milestones. Groups should determine, through a consideration of their work, the relationship between art and literature during the Middle Ages.

Gothic Church Construction

Gothic cathedrals were both expressions of religious devotion and symbols of civic pride. Unlike the rural settings of Romanesque churches, Gothic cathedrals were products of the new and prosperous cities. They served as churches for bishops. Rival bishops and cities vied for the right to claim that their cathedral was the biggest, the tallest, or the most beautiful. In the growing and prosperous cities of the Gothic period, everyone wanted to participate in the community effort to build these magnificent structures. People of all ranks and backgrounds contributed money, time, or effort toward the common goal of praising God and beautifying their own city.

The Gothic style was not limited to France or to religious structures. Architectural features developed in cathedrals were adapted in the construction of monasteries (Figure 15.10) and secular buildings throughout Europe.

■ **FIGURE 15.10** Gothic monasteries exhibited the same architectural features as cathedrals. **What Gothic feature can you identify in this monastery cloister? Do you recall the purpose served by cloisters?**

Santes Creus Cloister (exterior). Near Tarragona, Spain. Twelfth century.

LESSON ONE REVIEW

Reviewing Art Facts

1. Explain why the term *Gothic* was given to the art of this period.
2. What is a flying buttress?
3. List three ways a Gothic cathedral differed from a Romanesque church.
4. What structural features enabled Gothic builders to add windows to their cathedrals?

▶ **Activity... *Listening to Gothic Music***

A form of music was developed in the Gothic period to accompany the ceremony of the Medieval church. Known as the plainchant, this was music for voices that had no harmony and sounded like sung speech. For many years the plainchant was passed orally from master to pupil. From the ninth century, chant books began to appear, giving us a record of this music.

Obtain some modern recordings of the plainchant and present these unique sounds as the class looks at some of the magnificent church architecture of the Middle Ages. Locate Internet sites containing virtual tours of Gothic cathedrals. Listen to the music and imagine being a worshiper during this remarkable period of history.

Chapter 15 *Gothic Art* **337**

LESSON ONE REVIEW

Answers to Recalling Art Facts

1. Because the Goths and other barbarians brought about the fall of Rome and buildings of this time replaced classical forms.
2. A support or brace that counteracts the outward thrust of an arch or vault and that reaches over the side aisles of the church.
3. Romanesque church was low, thick-walled, and dimly lit; Gothic cathedral was slender, soaring, and light.
4. Pointed arches, piers, and flying buttresses.

Activity...*Listening to Gothic Music*

Have students read about the development and preservation of the plainchant, and discuss what they already know about this musical form. Then have students work in cooperative groups.

ASSESS

Checking Comprehension

Have students respond to the lesson review questions. Answers are given in the box below.

Reteaching

➤ Assign *Reteaching* 32, found in the TCR. Have students complete the activity and review their responses. 📁

➤ Ask pairs of students to list innovations of Gothic architecture. Partners then take turns reading an innovation from the list and identifying the benefit(s) it afforded medieval builders (for example, the use of the pointed arch enabled the construction of walls that permitted an abundance of windows).

Enrichment

Assign students *Enrichment* 29, "Probing the Mystery of the Unicorn," in the TCR. In this worksheet, students study the symbolism and mystery of the unicorn, the mythical beast that appears often in medieval tapestries. 📁

Extension

Ask volunteers to find out about the American Gothic Revivalists. Students' reports should include the aims and purposes of this school, characteristics of its art, the time period when it was most active as a school of art, and the names of artists involved.

CLOSE

Have small groups of students research and summarize events in one of the following cities prominent during the Gothic period: Bruges, Ghent, Lille, and Florence. Students should identify examples of Gothic architecture in the city.

Gothic Sculpture and Illustrated Books

LESSON TWO

Focus

Lesson Objectives

After studying this lesson, students will be able to:

- Explain how sculptures on Gothic cathedrals differed from those found on Romanesque churches.
- Describe how stained-glass art influenced manuscript illumination during the Gothic period.
- Describe features of the International style of painting.

Building Vocabulary

Ask volunteers to give their own informal definitions of the word *gargoyle*. Then have students read the definition in the text and examine the example on page 341.

Motivator

Bring to class and distribute photographs of fantastic creatures from current or recent science-fiction films or television shows. Ask students to identify as many of these creatures as they can and to decide which reveal the most imagination on the part of their creators. Let students guess when creatures of this sort were first created. Tell them they are about to glimpse creations of this kind that date back six or more centuries.

Gothic Sculpture and Illustrated Books

Vocabulary
- gargoyles

Discover
After completing this lesson, you will be able to:
- Explain how the sculptures on Gothic cathedrals differed from sculptures on Romanesque churches.
- Discuss the influence of stained-glass art on manuscript illumination during the Gothic period.
- Describe the features of the International style of painting.

*G*othic sculpture, like the stained glass of the period, was designed as part of one large composition—the cathedral erected to the glory of God. Gradually, sculpture developed along more realistic and individualized lines, but it always complemented the architectural setting in which it was placed.

Sculptural Decorations

Seen from the narrow streets of Medieval cities, the spires of Gothic cathedrals stretched upward to heaven. This upward tendency is noted everywhere, in the pillars, pointed arches, and windows.

A statue of normal size and proportions attached to such a structure would have detracted from this soaring quality. To avoid this, sculptures were elongated, or stretched out (Figure 15.11). The repeated, long folds on their sculptured garments emphasize the vertical movement of these figures. Often, the figures even stand on globes with their toes pointing downward to create the impression that they are rising upward.

■ **FIGURE 15.11** Note the elongated proportions of these figures. With your finger, trace along the repeated lines of these sculptures. In what direction do the lines lead you?

Statues from the Royal Portal façade of Chartres Cathedral, France. Early thirteenth century.

338

LESSON TWO RESOURCES

Teacher's Classroom Resources

- Appreciating Cultural Diversity 25
- Art and Humanities 25
- Reproducible Lesson Plan 33
- Reteaching Activity 33
- Study Guide 33

Romanesque carvers made their figures appear firmly attached to the wall. Gothic sculptors, by contrast, made theirs project outward into space. Further, each figure was clearly identified in some way and easily recognized by anyone familiar with the Bible.

A figure holding keys was immediately identified as St. Peter, who had been entrusted with the keys to the heavenly kingdom. Another bearing stone tablets was recognized as Moses; engraved on the tablets were the Ten Commandments given to him by God on Mount Sinai (Figure 15.12).

The Growing Concern for Reality

Gothic sculptors wanted to do more than present sacred symbols of biblical figures. They wanted to make these figures look like real people. The figures appear to move and look about, and the drapery looks as though it covers a real three-dimensional body. Figures flanking the entrance to the Burgos Cathedral (Figures 15.13 and 15.14, page 340) demonstrate this realism.

■ **FIGURE 15.12** Each of these calm, dignified figures would have been easily identified by worshipers, entering the cathedral during the Gothic period. **Identify specific details that give these figures a realistic appearance.**

Statues from the west portals, Tarragona Cathedral, Tarragona, Spain. Thirteenth century.

■ **FIGURE 15.13** Notice the design of the entrance to the cathedral. **What kind of balance is used here? With what effect?**

Sarmental Portal, Burgos Cathedral. Burgos, Spain. Before 1250.

Chapter 15 *Gothic Art* **339**

Introducing the Lesson

Review with students the features of Gothic cathedrals. Point out that the ability to use stained-glass windows as decorative features rendered wall paintings obsolete, at least for a period of time in much of Europe. Ask students to speculate on what Western artists with interests in areas other than architecture (for example, sculptors) may have focused on during the fourteenth and fifteenth centuries.

TEACH
Aesthetics

Direct students' attention to the sculptures in Figures 15.11 and 15.12. What mood or feeling do the works convey? Is this feeling consistent with the one suggested by the architectural features of the cathedral? Have students explain their responses.

Did You Know?

One of the most richly decorated of all Gothic cathedrals is the Duomo in Milan, Italy, which includes over 3,000 individual sculptures. To this day, visitors can take an elevator to the stepped, gabled roof of the structure in order to admire the uppermost tier of sculptures close up.

Technology

National Gallery of Art Videodisc Use the following images as examples of more works by artists introduced in this lesson.

Canaletto
The Square of Saint Mark's

Search Frame 472

Use Glencoe's *Correlation Bar Code Guide to the National Gallery of Art* to locate more artworks.

339

LOOKING Closely

Have students examine and discuss the portal tympanum in Figure 15.14, referring to Figure 15.13 to understand where and how this work fits into the cathedral's main entrance. Encourage students to explain and elaborate on each statement in the Use of Formal Balance feature.

Art Criticism

Have students examine and compare the tympanum sculptures in Figures 15.14 and 15.15. Ask them to summarize the characteristics of Gothic sculpture exhibited by both works. Which principles of art are emphasized in both tympana? What single principle among those emphasized is also responsible for a key difference between the two works?

Art History

Have students research the role of the Virgin Mary in medieval religious beliefs. Ask students to identify special characteristics people in the Middle Ages ascribed to Mary that would lead to their building churches in her honor.

Art Criticism

Have students look at Figure 15.16, noting in particular the manner in which the Virgin Mary appears to be interacting with her baby. What adjectives would students use to describe this interaction? Have them turn their attention to the small relief sculptures at the base of the column. In what other culture have they seen size used in similar fashion for emphasis?

LOOKING Closely

USE OF FORMAL BALANCE

Although it still recalls the spirit of the Romanesque, the south door of the Burgos Cathedral reveals this growing concern for realism, particularly in the tympanum. Like Romanesque tympana, the one at Burgos makes use of a formal balance.

- **Central focal point.** The large, central figure shows Christ as a majestic, thoughtful, and approachable man.
- **Triangular shape.** The four Evangelists are bent over their writing desks, allowing them to fit into the triangular shape of the tympanum.
- **Symmetry.** Two apostles and their symbols are balanced evenly on each side of Christ. The Twelve Apostles are also symmetrically placed with six on each side below Christ.

■ **FIGURE 15.14** Sarmental Portal tympanum, Burgos Cathedral. Burgos, Spain.

■ **FIGURE 15.15** Notice the informal balance and the realistic emotional expressions in this work. **How does a comparison of this tympanum with the tympanum at Burgos (Figure 15.14) illustrate the development of Gothic sculpture?**

Death of the Virgin. Cloister tympanum, Cathedral of Pamplona, Spain. Fourteenth century.

As the Gothic style developed further, an informal, more natural balance was sought. This informality is observed in a fourteenth-century tympanum in the cathedral cloister in Pamplona, Spain (Figure 15.15). Here fifteen figures surround a bed on which rests the lifeless body of the Virgin Mary. Again, the figures are carefully designed to fit within the tympanum. Christ is the largest figure, and if you look closely, you will see that he holds a small version of Mary. This is her soul, which he is preparing to carry to heaven.

A sign of the growing concern for human emotions is noted in the sorrowful expressions on the faces of the mourners around the deathbed. These are more than mere symbols for religious

More About... **Symbols in Gothic Art.** Figures and symbols were a focus of Gothic art as teaching tools for the uneducated. To enable viewers to interpret the symbolism, people in the Middle Ages who could not read were taught the four levels of meaning in the Bible. The first level is the most obvious, the narrative and descriptive details of a story. The second is the allegorical level, which relates the story to the history of Christ and humanity. The third level is the moral, which extracts the psychological meaning or the "lesson" of the story. The fourth level is called the *anagogic*, which interprets the meaning of the story as a parable for the relationship of one's soul to God.

figures. They are real people expressing genuine grief over the loss of a loved one.

Veneration for the Virgin Mary

Veneration for the Virgin Mary grew steadily during the Gothic period. This was especially true in France, where great cathedrals were erected in her honor.

On the south portal of Amiens Cathedral is an almost freestanding sculpture of Mary holding the Christ Child (Figure 15.16). Originally covered in gold, it came to be known as the *Golden Virgin.* The figure is both elegant and noble. Its gentle human features and friendly expression made it one of the most famous sculptures in Europe.

Gargoyles

■ **FIGURE 15.17**

One of the most interesting sculptural features of Gothic cathedrals was the inclusion of **gargoyles,** *the grotesque flying monsters that project out from the upper portions of the huge churches.* Made of carved stone or cast metal, gargoyles are actually rain spouts, intended to carry rainwater from the roofs of the churches (Figure 15.17). Why were they made to look like frightening monsters? Perhaps because someone thought it would be a good idea to make rain spouts interesting as well as functional. They were made to look like evil spirits fleeing for their lives from the sacred building.

Illustrated Books

A demand for illustrated books containing psalms, gospels, and other parts of the liturgy grew steadily during the thirteenth and fourteenth centuries. These books, called "psalters," were the prized possessions of the wealthy. Artists used tiny, pointed brushes and bright colors to illuminate these psalters with scenes from the life of Christ.

The Influence of Stained-Glass Art

During the thirteenth and fourteenth centuries, manuscript illumination showed the influence of stained-glass art. These

■ **FIGURE 15.16** This figure of the Virgin Mary was noted for its gold covering—now gone—and its warm, welcoming smile. **How is this pose similar to that of such Greek sculptures as the** *Spear Bearer* **by Polyclitus (Figure 8.20, page 183)?**

Golden Virgin. Right door called the Mother of God. Amiens Cathedral. West façade. Amiens, France. c. 1250–70.

■ **FIGURE 15.17** Gargoyles like this appear ready to unfold their wings and fly off to some faraway land of mystery. **How do you think gargoyles might be related to the carvings of fantastic creatures found on many Romanesque churches?**

Gothic gargoyle. Convent of Christ, Tomar, Portugal.

Chapter 15 *Gothic Art* **341**

Aesthetics

Point out that Gothic cathedrals, though intended to capture the essence of faith through their upward, soaring design, were also meant to serve the practical purpose of providing a place of worship. Then direct students' attention to the gargoyle in Figure 15.17. What was the functional purpose behind structures such as these? Did they also have a symbolic function like the cathedrals themselves? Ask students to explain their responses.

Studio Skills

Direct students' attention to the manuscript illuminations in Figures 15.18 (page 342) and 15.19 (page 343). Reinforce the idea that illuminations usually corresponded directly to the story being told or the information being presented in the writing on the same page. Then ask students to choose a popular folktale or fable and create an illumination for it.

Have students begin by sketching their ideas in their sketchbooks. Once they are satisfied, they may transfer the image to white paper or parchment. Have students use colored inks and pens to draw their illuminations. Remind them that medieval illustrations are rich, graceful, and elegant, and urge students to strive for these qualities in their work. When the project is complete, have students display their illuminations and attempt to match classmates' artworks with the stories or fables they are based on.

About the *Artwork*

Gothic Gargoyles. Grotesque figures, like the one depicted here, may have had their roots in the architecture of classical Greece, where marble or terra cotta lions' heads often masked drain pipes. The word *gargoyle* derives from a French word meaning "throat." Point out how the *gargoyle* in Figure 15.17 projects outward several feet from the cathedral, and have students imagine the effect of glimpsing the work against a brilliant blue sky. What other features of Gothic cathedrals depend on atmosphere, and especially daylight, for effect?

Study Guide

Distribute *Study Guide* 33 in the TCR. Assist students in reviewing key concepts. 📁

Art and Humanities

Have students read *Art and Humanities* 25, "Caring for Your Environment," in the TCR. In this timely activity, students read the "Canticle of the Sun" and apply the ideas contained in the work to contemporary environmental issues and concerns. 📁

Extension

Explain that while there are many reasons for the similarities between medieval manuscript illumination and Gothic stained-glass windows, an especially insightful explanation might be that both stained glass and illuminated manuscripts were often made by masters in the same shop. Moreover, some masters were experts in both arts. *The Psalter of Saint Louis*, as a case in point, is thought to have been one of several books created in Paris for Louis IX of France by artisans who also created the stained-glass windows for Sainte Chapelle. Have students look at the work of contemporary stained-glass artisans and find styles that they feel would also lend themselves to a style appropriate for illuminated manuscripts.

Studio Activities

Assign *Studio* 19, "Making a Papier-Mâché Gargoyle," in the TCR. Students create a papier-mâché gargoyle modeled on those adorning Gothic cathedrals. 📁

---

illustrations often were placed within a painted architectural framework that resembled the frames used for stained-glass windows.

In addition, the elegant figures found in these manuscript illuminations were drawn with firm, dark outlines, suggestive of the lead strips used to join sections of stained glass. With these features and their rich, glowing colors, the illuminations closely resembled the stained-glass windows set into Gothic cathedral walls.

The Carrow Psalter

■ **FIGURE 15.18**

The influence of stained glass can be seen in an illumination in a thirteenth-century English book of prayers known as the *Carrow*

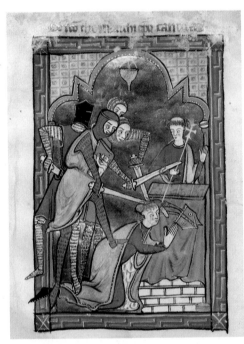

■ **FIGURE 15.18** In 1538 King Henry VIII ordered the destruction of all portraits of Becket. Fortunately, this manuscript page was not destroyed. Instead, it was covered by a sheet of paper glued in place to hide it from view. Later, when the paper was removed, some of the paint on the upper corner was pulled off. **What details in this illumination indicate the influence of stained-glass art?**

The Martyrdom of Thomas à Becket. From the *Carrow Psalter.* Mid-thirteenth century. Walters Art Gallery, Baltimore, Maryland.

Psalter. This full-page illustration (Figure 15.18) shows the assassination of Thomas à Becket, archbishop of Canterbury, before the altar of his cathedral. Four knights are seen attacking the kneeling archbishop with such fury that the blade of one sword breaks. An astonished church attendant looks on as the archbishop is forced to the floor by the swords and the foot of one knight. Two years after his death in 1170, Thomas à Becket was made a saint, and his fame quickly spread throughout England.

The International Style

In the years that followed, painters began to exhibit a greater concern for realistic detail in their works. Even more important, was a desire to make their painted figures more graceful and colorful. They took delight in painting elegant and beautiful subjects with care and precision.

This elegant art style appealed to the tastes of the wealthy throughout western Europe, and the demand for manuscripts illustrated in this manner grew. Because of its widespread popularity, this style of painting came to be known as the International style.

Book of Hours

■ **FIGURE 15.19**

Among the greatest artists working in the International style were the Limbourg brothers. These three brothers from Flanders had settled in France, where their patron was the Duke of Berry, the brother of the French king. Early in the fifteenth century, the Limbourg brothers produced a luxurious book of prayers, or *Book of Hours,* for the duke.

Included in this book was a series of elaborate pictures illustrating the cycle of life through scenes from each of the twelve months. In an illustration for *May* (Figure 15.19), lords and ladies are shown enjoying a carefree ride in the warm sunshine. The cold gray winter months, which meant confinement within castle walls, have finally come to an end. The lords and ladies have donned bright attire and crowned themselves with leaves and flowers to welcome spring. Trumpeters announce the new season's arrival, and horses prance about excitedly.

More About...

The Plague. Both tympana examined in this lesson have death or the Last Judgment as a theme. Remind students that the art of a period frequently reflects the society in which it was produced. Ask them if they can think of any significant event that occurred in the middle of the fourteenth century that might have contributed to a preoccupation with death and the life after death. In the middle of the fourteenth century, the Black Death devastated Europe. A form of bubonic plague, it began in the Black Sea region and spread southwest across Europe. Scholars today estimate that for the area extending from India to Iceland, approximately one-third of the population perished from this disease.

The precision found in paintings of this kind is fascinating. The artists must have relished the chance to demonstrate in paint their powers of observation. The trees of the forest are painted with such exactness that each branch and many of the leaves stand out clearly. The same concern for minute detail is observed in the ornate castle beyond. To paint such detail, the Limbourg brothers must have held a magnifying glass in one hand and a very fine brush in the other.

The desire for rich detail and gracefulness is stressed at the expense of realism. The finely dressed women sit regally on their horses, unmindful of the fact that their positions are not very secure. Of greater importance is that they look graceful, sophisticated, and beautiful. Much of the movement suggested in the work is a result of the flowing lines of the drapery rather than any action on the part of the figures themselves.

■ **FIGURE 15.19** Like the lords and ladies in the center of this work, the bushes in the foreground and the trees in the background are painted in precise detail. **What features make this work a clear example of the International style?**

The Limbourg Brothers. *May,* a page from a *Book of Hours* painted for the Duke of Berry. 1413–15. Illumination. 21.6 × 14 cm (8¹/₂ × 5¹/₂″). Ms. 65/1284, fol. 5v. Museé Condé, Chantilly, France.

LESSON TWO REVIEW

Reviewing Art Facts

1. How do Gothic sculptures differ from sculptures on a Romanesque church?
2. Gothic sculptors were not content with creating sacred symbols of biblical figures. What else did they try to do?
3. Describe two techniques used by Gothic sculptors.
4. In what ways did stained-glass art influence manuscript illumination in the thirteenth and fourteenth centuries?

Activity... *Designing a Gothic Entrance*

The Gothic cathedral was a storybook in stone. Sculptured figures around and over doors and on walls functioned as illustrations of the story of Christianity to educate a population that was largely illiterate. The sculptures were carefully constructed to complement the soaring quality of the Gothic cathedral. Look at the illustrations in this lesson to see some of the sculptural styles of the Gothic period. Imagine that your school needs a new entrance.

Create a design for the entrance of your school that tells the story of the school. Include appropriate jamb figures and a tympanum design. What figures would need to be placed around the sides of the door? What story would be told in the tympanum?

LESSON TWO REVIEW

Answers to Reviewing Art Facts

1. Gothic sculptures project outward into space.
2. Made their figures look more like real people.
3. Possible response: They made the drapery look three-dimensional and let the figures display emotions.
4. Illuminations were often placed in frames like those around stained-glass windows; outlines around figures suggested by lead strips; colors were similar to those found in stained glass.

Activity...*Designing a Gothic Entrance*

Lead students in a brief discussion of the styles and stories of Gothic entrances. Then let students discuss stories that might be told in their school entryway. Finally, have students work independently to sketch and explain their ideas.

ASSESS

Checking Comprehension

Have students respond to the lesson review questions. Answers are given in the box below.

Reteaching

➤ Assign *Reteaching* 33, found in the TCR. Have students complete the activity and review their responses. 📁

Enrichment

Have students complete *Appreciating Cultural Diversity* 25, "The International Style," in the TCR. Ask students to read about the spread of this style across Europe, and then ask them to chart examples from several different countries. 📁

Extension

Explain that one of the most popular subjects of medieval art was the depiction of the Seven Deadly Sins. These sins were symbolized in various ways and were often carved on reliefs in churches, where people could see them and be reminded of them. Have students investigate the Seven Deadly Sins, as well as the Seven Saintly Virtues. If possible, have them locate examples of art featuring each sin and virtue.

Have a volunteer research more about the life of Thomas á Becket, the famous archbishop of Canterbury. Ask the student to deliver a brief oral report about his life.

CLOSE

On the board, write the following question: *Which development in Gothic sculpture do you find the most interesting?* Have students share and discuss their responses to this question.

Italian Church Painting

Focus

Lesson Objectives

After studying this lesson, students will be able to:

■ Explain why painting remained an important form of church decoration in Italy during the Middle Ages.

■ Explain the fresco technique of painting.

■ Discuss the accomplishments of Duccio and Giotto.

Building Vocabulary

After students have read and discussed the definition of fresco presented in the lesson, let a volunteer refer to a dictionary and explain the origin of the word.

Motivator

Have students recall that many manuscript illuminations, such as the one in Figure 15.18 (page 342), were remarkably small. Ask volunteers to identify some of the characteristics of artworks in miniature. Then, in contrast, ask students what characteristics they would expect to find in unusually large works of art. Have students proceed with reading the lesson.

Introducing the Lesson

Ask students to name the most famous artists the world has ever known. List them on the board, placing a check mark next to the names of artists who are, or were, painters. Explain that when many people hear the term art, they automatically think of painting. Tell students they will learn about the work of two painters who changed the course of Western art.

344

Italian Church Painting

Vocabulary
■ fresco

Artists to Meet
■ Duccio di Buoninsegna
■ Giotto di Bondone

Discover
After completing this lesson, you will be able to:
■ Explain the fresco technique of painting.
■ Discuss contributions to painting made by Duccio and Giotto.

𝒢othic architecture did not become popular in Italy. Italian builders continued to construct churches in a modified Romanesque style throughout the Gothic period. Perhaps the warmer climate of their country caused them to prefer the darker, cooler interiors of Romanesque-type buildings. Instead of putting in stained-glass windows, the builders continued to commission artists to decorate their church walls with murals.

Duccio (1255–1318)

Paintings on wooden panels were also used to decorate the interiors of Italian churches. One of the most famous of these panel paintings was created by Duccio di Buoninsegna (**doot**-cho dee **bwo**-neen-**seh**-nya) for the altar at the Cathedral of Siena. It was known as the *Maestà* (or "majesty") *Altarpiece* and was actually a combination of several panel paintings.

The Virgin in Majesty was the subject of the main panel. This painting, on a large central panel almost 11 feet high, showed the Madonna enthroned as the Queen of Heaven. Below and above this panel and on the back was a series of smaller panels on which Duccio painted scenes from the lives of the Virgin Mary and Christ.

The Calling of the Apostles Peter and Andrew
■ **FIGURE 15.20**

One of the *Maestà* panels shows Christ calling to Peter and Andrew (Figure 15.20), inviting them to join him as his apostles. The extensive use of gold in the background of this picture calls to mind the rich mosaics of Byzantine art. The intense colors, two-dimensional figures, and shallow space are further reminders of a Byzantine style that was both familiar and popular in Italy.

The Byzantine style stressed the spiritual and ignored references to the real world. Byzantine artists stripped reality to its essentials and avoided suggestions of depth and volume as they sought to express intense religious feelings in their work.

Duccio's painting avoids the typical Byzantine stiffness and introduces a more realistic, relaxed look. The three figures seem solid; they suggest that Duccio studied real men before he attempted to paint them. The gestures are natural, and the faces express the appropriate emotion: Christ's face is serene, Peter looks startled, and Andrew appears hesitant.

■ **FIGURE 15.20** The influence of the Byzantine style in this Italian painting is not surprising. Italy continued to have contact with the Byzantine Empire throughout the Medieval period. In what ways is this work similar to a Byzantine mosaic? How is it different?

Duccio di Buoninsegna. *The Calling of the Apostles Peter and Andrew.* 1308–11. Tempera on wood panel. 43.5 × 46 cm (17 1/4 × 18 1/8″). National Gallery of Art, Washington, D.C. Samuel H. Kress Collection.

344

LESSON THREE RESOURCES

Teacher's Classroom Resources

 Enrichment Activity 30

 Reproducible Lesson Plan 34

Reteaching Activity 34

Study Guide 34

Giotto (1266—1337)

While Duccio was taking important steps away from Byzantine conservatism, another Italian artist was making a revolutionary break with the flat, unrealistic elements of that style. Giotto di Bondone (**jot**-toh dee bahn-**doh**-nee) painted natural-looking figures who appear to take real actions in real space. A series of Giotto's works in a chapel in Padua presents familiar stories from the lives of Christ and the Virgin. The scenes are surprising, however, because they present realistic figures, actions, and emotions.

Lamentation Pietà Fresco
■ **FIGURE 15.21**

One of Giotto's frescoes in Padua testifies to his monumental talent. Entitled *Lamentation Pietà* (Figure 15.21), it shows a group of mourners around the body of Christ following the crucifixion. The purely spiritual did not interest Giotto. He vigorously pursued a more realistic course. Giotto's concern for realism led him to study human emotions, and he tried to show those emotions in his paintings. In *Lamentation Pietà*, anguish, despair, and resignation are noted in the expressions and gestures of the figures surrounding Christ.

Dramatic Effect in Art

$\mathcal{G}$iotto arranged his scene carefully with an eye for dramatic effect, much like a director placing the actors in a play. He offers a solitary rock ledge rather than a mountain range; he presents a single tree instead of a forest. These objects direct your attention to the players acting out the tragedy of Christ's death. The ledge guides your eye to the most important part of the picture: the faces of Christ and his mother. The tree visually balances the figure of Christ in the opposite corner. You do not "read" this story as you would a Romanesque carved relief. Instead, you *experience* it as a totally involved witness.

1 A natural background of blue sky makes the scene look real. Gone is the flat gold background featured in earlier works.

2 A grieving woman—undoubtedly Christ's mother, Mary—holds the body.

3 A mourner clasps her hands in anguish and suffers in silence.

4 A man throws his hands back in a violent gesture of horror and disbelief.

■ **FIGURE 15.21** Giotto di Bondone. *Lamentation Pietà*. c. 1305. Fresco. Scrovegni Chapel, Padua, Italy.

TEACH
Using Map Skills

Explain to students that Italy was not a unified country during the Gothic period; rather, it consisted of a number of small, independent cities or dukedoms. Have students find a map that shows how this area looked during the Gothic period. Then ask small groups to select a city, dukedom, or region and determine the following: the name and characteristics of its ruling family during the Middle Ages; special events of the region; and artists (both past and present) that the area has produced.

Art Criticism

After noting that the central panel of Duccio's *Maestra* is 11 feet high, have students look through the text for paintings of similarly heroic dimensions. Ask them to imagine how such works would appear when viewed in person. How would the impact of Duccio's work have been different had he painted manuscript illuminations?

Study Guide

Distribute *Study Guide* 34 in the TCR. Assist students in reviewing key concepts. 🗁

Dramatic Effect in Art

Direct students' attention to Giotto's *Lamentation Pietà*, Figure 15.21. Ask them to identify features that are realistic. Which features are not realistic by today's standards? Then ask how Giotto used the elements and principles of art to create a dramatic effect in this work. Finally, have students read and discuss the explanations presented in the feature. Have them think of dramatic scenes from a play they may have experienced. How does the effect of the details in this painting compare to the drama of a play?

Art and Humanities

Have students research more about Duccio's *Maestá* by locating illustrations of the other panels in the work and determining the relationship of the parts to the whole.

Studio Activities

Have students complete *Enrichment* 30, "Creating a Fresco," in the TCR. Students learn about the chemical processes of this ancient medium through firsthand experience with fresco techniques.

ASSESS

Checking Comprehension

➤ Have students respond to the lesson review questions. Answers are given in the box below.

➤ Assign students *Application* 15, "Photo Finish," in the TCR.

Reteaching

Assign *Reteaching* 34, found in the TCR. Have students complete the activity and review their responses.

Extension

Arrange a field trip to a local artist's studio. Arrange for the artist to demonstrate either a technique that students are familiar with or one they have not seen before. Encourage students to ask questions about the technique.

CLOSE

Have students create an exhibition of their favorite or most successful projects from this chapter. Ask them to include an explanation of the purpose and goal of each project, as well as credit lines listing the name of the artist, the title, the medium, and the size of the work.

346

The Fresco Technique

Most of Giotto's works were murals on the inside walls of churches in a form of painting called fresco. **Fresco** is *a painting created when pigment is applied to a wall spread with fresh plaster.* To make a fresco, Giotto first drew with charcoal directly on the wall. Then, covering only as much of the drawing as he could finish before the plaster dried, he spread a thin coat of wet plaster over the dry wall and then retraced the charcoal lines, which he could barely see underneath.

He applied pigment, mixed with water and egg whites, directly to this fresh plaster.

The paint and wet plaster mixed together to form a permanent surface. If an artist tried to paint over this surface after it had dried, the repainting usually flaked off over time. If a mistake was made, the whole surface had to be cleaned off and the section painted again.

Technique Dictates Style

Because the fresco technique required that painting had to be completed before the plaster dried, Giotto did not have time to include many details in his pictures. As a result, his pictures were simple but powerfully expressive (Figure 15.22).

■ **FIGURE 15.22** This work is a fresco; Giotto painted it directly onto the wall of the chapel. How did the techniques of fresco painting affect Giotto's style? What has Giotto done to keep the viewer's eye from wandering off the picture at either side?

Giotto di Bondone. *Death of St. Francis* (detail of mourners). c. 1320. Fresco. Bardi Chapel, Santa Croce, Florence, Italy.

LESSON THREE REVIEW

Reviewing Art Facts

1. What effect did the design of Italian churches during the Gothic period have on the art used to decorate the interiors of those churches?
2. How do Giotto's painted figures differ from those painted by earlier artists?
3. What is a fresco painting?
4. What limitations are imposed on artists who used the fresco technique?

Activity... *Comparing Paintings of the Middle Ages*

Giotto occupies a unique place in art history because he was the first artist in the Middle Ages to paint realistic figures, actions, and emotions taken directly from life. These new goals were the foundation for artists for generations after Giotto lived and worked. Giotto represents the "bridge" between the old painting traditions of the Middle Ages and the new ideas of the modern period.

Find three examples of paintings from the Middle Ages, two of them by Giotto. List the ways Giotto's works differ from the other paintings of the Gothic period. Look for differences that make his work stand out. Choose one of Giotto's paintings and the one from another artist of the Gothic period and present your comparison to the class.

LESSON THREE REVIEW

Answers to Reviewing Art Facts

1. Walls needed to be decorated, so painters were hired to paint murals.
2. The figures are realistic-looking, with human gestures and expressions, and appear to move about in real space.
3. A painting completed on wet plaster that has been applied to a wall.
4. Painting must be completed while the plaster is still wet, so there is no time to include details.

Activity...*Comparing Paintings*

Have students read and discuss the brief review of Giotto's significance. Then assign the Activity, and let students work in cooperative groups to select and compare three works. Have each group plan and give a short presentation.

Complete a pencil drawing of a landscape in which one object is singled out and emphasized by its larger size or by its placement at or near the center of the composition. The landscape should suggest a particular season of the year. Design all the objects in the drawing to fit within a half-round or triangular shape. Indicate in writing whether your landscape will be balanced symmetrically or asymmetrically.

Inspiration

Compare and contrast the examples of Romanesque and Gothic tympana in Figure 14.21, page 323, and Figure 15.15, page 340. Which of these appears more lifelike? How is each balanced?

Process

1. On a sheet of paper, list the kinds of things you are likely to see on a long walk in the country during a particular season of the year. Make several quick sketches of the landscape.
2. On a large sheet of sketch paper, outline a half-round or triangular shape measuring no less than 12 inches in length and 8 inches in height. Cut this out.
3. Look over your landscape sketches and identify one item you want to emphasize. Draw it at or near the center of your composition.
4. Add the other objects to your landscape, making certain that they fit comfortably within the half-round or triangular shape.

Materials

- Pencils and sketch paper, 12 × 18 inches
- Ruler
- Scissors

■ **FIGURE 15.23** Student Work

Examining Your Work

Describe. Point out and name the different objects in your landscape. What is the most unusual object in your drawing?

Analyze. Which object did you choose to emphasize in your composition? Is your composition balanced symmetrically or asymmetrically? Do the objects in your landscape fit comfortably within the half-round or triangular shape?

Interpret. How does your drawing suggest a particular season? Were other students able to identify the season?

Judge. What is the most successful feature of your drawing: its realistic appearance, its use of the elements and principles of art, or its effectiveness in illustrating a particular season?

347

Objectives

■ Complete a pencil drawing of a landscape in which one object is emphasized by its size and placement.
■ Suggest a particular season of the year.
■ Balance the composition symmetrically or asymmetrically to fit within a half-round or triangular shape.

Motivator

Discuss the various objects that students might include in their landscape drawings. Refer students to drawings in their sketchbooks. Discuss how these objects could be represented to indicate a particular season of the year. Because these tympanum drawings will be used in the next Studio Lesson, tell students to avoid the use of shading. Instead, have them concentrate on using a clearly defined line to create their landscape images.

Studio Skills

Emphasize the need for students to tailor their designs to fit the tympanum shapes they have decided upon. Encourage them to think of their drawing as a whole rather than as a collection of parts. Instruct them to sketch in the larger shapes throughout their compositions first and add the details later.

Critiquing

Have students apply the steps of art criticism to their own artwork, using the "Examining Your Work" questions on this page.

ASSESSMENT

Examining Your Work. Once students have examined their landscape drawings, suggest that they consider these drawings as plans for their next studio project, the landscape relief. Will the emphasized object be effective as a center of interest in a relief sculpture? Does the drawing include enough details to make a relief interesting? Does it limit details enough to make a relief sculpture clear? Have students discuss these and other, related issues with partners.

Then ask each student to write a short evaluation of his or her drawing, noting specific changes that might make working on the relief sculpture project easier and more satisfying.

Studio LESSON

Carving a Tympanum Landscape Relief ____

Objectives

- Complete a clay relief sculpture of a tympanum.
- Emphasize clearly one object in the composition.
- Use deep carving techniques to create a rich surface pattern of light and dark values.
- Exhibit five different kinds of actual texture.

Motivator

Explain that students will use the drawings they completed in the previous Studio Lesson. Ask students to examine the landscape drawing they have made and decide which lines they will transfer to the clay for the best emphasis of value and texture.

Aesthetics

After bisque-firing the reliefs, display them on a table. Divide the class into three groups of aestheticians: imitationalists, formalists, and emotionalists. Let the members of each group consider and discuss several of the works.

Critiquing

Have students apply the steps of art criticism to their own artwork, using the "Examining Your Work" questions on this page.

Studio LESSON

Carving a Tympanum Landscape Relief

Materials

- Tympanum drawing from the previous lesson
- Clay
- Two wood slats, 1 inch thick
- Rolling pin and clay modeling tools
- Canvas, muslin, or cloth about 14 × 14 inches to cover table-tops or desktops

Complete a clay relief sculpture of a tympanum landscape. Use deep carving techniques to create the nearly three-dimensional forms of the landscape, resulting in a rich surface pattern of light and dark values. Use a variety of tools to create at least five different actual textures on the relief.

Inspiration

Examine the tympanum from the Sarmental Portal of Burgos Cathedral (Figure 15.14, page 340) and the *Death of the Virgin* tympanum from the Cathedral of Pamplona (Figure 15.15, page 340). Notice how the various forms in these reliefs were created.

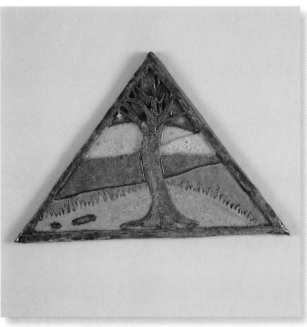

■ **FIGURE 15.24** Student Work

Process

1. Roll out a large slab of clay to a uniform thickness of 1 inch. The clay slab must be large enough to accommodate the 12 × 8 inch tympanum design completed in the previous lesson.
2. Place your tympanum drawing directly on the clay slab. Cut out the half-round or triangular shape of the tympanum. Trace over the lines of your landscape, with a sharp pencil. This will transfer the lines of your drawing to the soft clay slab.
3. Use clay modeling tools to carve your landscape in the clay. Do not use modeling techniques. Instead, use the subtractive carving method to create a panel in high relief. Use only the clay tools—not your fingers—to smooth surfaces and add details.
4. When it is thoroughly dry, bisque-fire the relief and, if you wish, glaze it.

Examining Your Work

Describe. Is the subject of your relief easily identified as a landscape? Can other students name the different objects in your landscape?

Analyze. Did you clearly emphasize one object in your landscape? How did you emphasize that object? Point out five different examples of actual texture in your relief.

Interpret. What season of the year is represented in your relief? What are the most important clues to this season?

Judge. Assume that you are an art critic inclined to judge works of art in terms of design qualities. Would you consider this relief a successful work of art? How would you defend your judgment?

ASSESSMENT

Peer Review. After they have examined and assessed their own relief sculptures, let students meet in cooperative learning groups for a short peer-review session. Have students display both their landscape drawings and their relief sculptures for the rest of the group. For each student's work, suggest that group members identify the drawn features that translated most successfully into the sculpted form. Encourage group members to make constructive suggestions and to note successful uses of the elements and principles of art. Finally, have each student write a short assessment of the relief created by another group member, using the "Examining Your Work" questions as a guide.

Reviewing Art Facts

Lesson One

1. What contributed to bringing an end to the feudal system in Europe?
2. Name three architectural innovations that enabled architects to construct the huge, soaring Gothic cathedrals.
3. Describe the feeling evoked by the interior of a Gothic cathedral.

Lesson Two

4. How were sculpted figures altered to fit into the "upward surge" feeling of Gothic architecture?
5. Would you say that Gothic relief sculptures were higher-relief or lower-relief than those of the Early Medieval period?
6. Compared to Medieval sculptures, were Gothic sculptures more realistic or less realistic? Why?
7. What is a gargoyle?

Lesson Three

8. Which country continued to build churches with solid walls, unlike the new Gothic architecture?
9. Why did Giotto have to work quickly when he was painting a fresco?
10. What new goals did Giotto identify in painting?

Thinking Critically

1. **COMPARE AND CONTRAST.** Refer to Figure 15.11 on page 338 in this chapter and to Figure 14.21 on page 323. Make a list of similarities and differences between the relief sculpture on the Romanesque church and that on the Gothic church. Be sure to consider each element and principle of art.
2. **ANALYZE.** Look closely at the colors used in *May* (Figure 15.19, page 343). Make a list of the colors you see that are intense, or very bright. Then list the colors that are dull or low in intensity. Remember that in some cases the same color will be in both columns.

> **A R T S●U R C∈** MUSIC. Use the *Performing Arts Handbook,* page 586 to learn about Paul Salamunovich and Gregorian Chant.

> ■ CAREERS IN Read about a career as an illustrator in the *Careers in Art Handbook,* page 603.

> *inter*NET CONNECTION Visit Glencoe Art Online at *www.glencoe.com/sec/art*. Learn about the art of fresco, and find an activity to reinforce what you have learned.

Technology Project

Designing Gothic Windows

The evolution of great Gothic cathedrals with buttresses to support the weight of the ceiling allowed builders to transform walls of stone into walls of glass. Stained-glass windows permitted light to penetrate the dark interiors of cathedrals and fill them with shimmering color. These windows still stand in many parts of Europe. The round windows at the top are called rose windows. They often contain a central figure or theme enhanced by surrounding smaller round windows. Together, the windows often provide the visual narrative of a story.

Much of the art of this era had a practical function. The sculpture and stained-glass windows in a church or cathedral provided the clergy with a means to visually tell the story of the Bible to a congregation that was mostly illiterate.

1. Find other examples similar to these Gothic stories in glass. You can find modern examples of stained glass that tell stories (the space window in the National Cathedral, Washington, D.C.; the modern windows of Chagall and Matisse). Use information resources such as the Internet, CD-ROMs, and laser discs.
2. Using your sketchbook or working on drawing paper, design a window that tells a story. Your story might be a personal one about you or your family, or it might be a story of an event familiar to you.
3. Using a computer application that includes paint or draw functions, design your window. Be sure to use line and color in the Gothic style.
4. Using the word processor on your computer, write and print the story visually represented in your window design.
5. Print your window design and display it in your classroom along with the written narrative.

Reviewing the Facts

1. Trade, the growth of cities, and the increasing power of kings.
2. Pointed arches, piers, and flying buttresses.
3. Answers will vary, but may include: light, airy, inspiring, lofty, mysterious.
4. Figures were elongated, or stretched out; toes pointed downward to create the impression that they were rising.
5. Higher.
6. They were more realistic because of their resemblance to real people, the three-dimensional quality, and the emotions they exhibited.
7. A grotesque, flying monster projecting out from the upper portions of a church, serving as a rainspout.
8. Italy.
9. Because frescoes are painted on wet plaster, the painting must be completed before the plaster dries.
10. Realistic figures, actions, and emotions.

Thinking Critically

1. Similarities: the two tympana depict the same image from the Bible; both make use of repetition of form; both exhibit symmetrical balance. Differences: the sculptures on the Romanesque tympanum are contained by a round arch, those on the Gothic tympanum by a pointed arch; the figures on the Gothic tympanum are more realistic; they stand out more in space.
2. Intense colors: red, blue, green; dull colors: blue, green, flesh tones. The blue-gray color of the horse is low intensity.

Teaching the Technology Project

Let students meet in groups to discuss stories that might be appropriate and effective for their window designs. Encourage students to discuss scenes that might be shown clearly and to explore the use of line and color in sketches for their window designs. Schedule class time during which they can examine and discuss the designs and stories.

> **A R T S●U R C∈** Assign the feature in the *Performing Arts Handbook,* page 586..

> **CAREERS IN ART** If time permits, have interested students investigate the career information in the *Careers in Art Handbook,* page 603.

> *inter*NET CONNECTION Have students go online and learn more about artists on preselected Web sites with the Internet activity for this chapter.

Art of an Emerging Modern Europe

Unit Six covers the enormous strides, chiefly in the area of painting, that characterized Western art from the fifteenth through the seventeenth centuries.

Chapter 16 *The Italian Renaissance* addresses the unparalleled contributions of artists of this era of rebirth.

Chapter 17 *Fifteenth-Century Art in Northern Europe* traces the spread of Renaissance ideals.

Chapter 18 *Art of Sixteenth-Century Europe* showcases the art of the great Venetian school and the conflicts that arose in northern Europe.

Chapter 19 *Baroque Art* covers the art and architecture of the Counter-Reformation.

Chapter 20 *Rococo Art* notes seventeenth-century developments in the art of France, England, and Spain.

National Museum of Women in the Arts

You may wish to use the National Museum of Women in the Arts videodisc and/or CD-ROM. The videodisc features a bar code guide, and the interactive CD-ROM provides stimulating activities.

350

More About...

Ceiling of the Sistine Chapel. Direct students' attention to the central panels of the ceiling. Tell them that these panels depict scenes from the Bible, including the creation of the earth, sun, and moon, and the Creation of Adam. Ask students to try to identify some of the scenes visible on this page. The other panels contain portraits of the ancestors of Christ, as well as saints and other biblical and historical figures. Be sure to point out to students that the columns and pointed arches shown here are part of Michelangelo's painting on the curved ceiling and not part of the architecture of the chapel. More information about the painting and more of Michelangelo's works can be found in Lesson 3 of Chapter 16, on pages 370 and 371.

Art of an Emerging Modern Europe

"This work has been and truly is the beacon of our art, and it has brought such benefit and enlightenment to the art of painting that it was sufficient to illuminate the world…"

Giorgio Vasari
Italian art historian
(1511–1574)

Michelangelo Buonarroti. Ceiling of the Sistine Chapel. 1508–12. Fresco (post-restoration). Vatican Museums and Galleries, Vatican City, Rome, Italy.

351

Introducing the Unit

Assign groups the task of developing a "Top Ten" list of the most famous artists who ever lived. If the names Leonardo da Vinci and Michelangelo appear on all the lists, point out that these masters both worked around the same time and in the same place. In the next five chapters, students will be learning about other artists who changed for all time the course of history.

Discussing the Quotation

Bring to class a copy of *Bartlett's Familiar Quotations.* After helping students gain an understanding of how this resource is used, have them make posters focusing on one of the many quotes by either Michelangelo or Leonardo da Vinci. The poster should be decorated with images typical of the artist selected (e.g., a quote by Leonardo may be illustrated by drawings of the type he would have included in his sketchbook). Have students include on the reverse side an explanation of the quote's relevance both to the artist and to viewers of the artist's work.

Did You Know ?

Giorgio Vasari was the first modern art historian. In 1550, he wrote a series of biographies of the Italian artists of the previous three hundred years. Today it is one of the most important, though often debated, sources of information about Renaissance art.

Teacher Notes

The Italian Renaissance

LESSON ONE
(pages 354–360)

The Emergence of the Italian Renaissance ....

Classroom Resources
- 📁 Appreciating Cultural Diversity 26
- 📁 Art and Humanities 26
- 📁 Cooperative Learning 24
- 📁 Reproducible Lesson Plan 35
- 📁 Reteaching 35
- 📁 Study Guide 35

Features

(page 357)

Map of Renaissance Italy
(page 354)

Styles
Influencing
Styles
"Gothic to Renaissance"
(page 359)

LESSON TWO
(pages 361–366)

The Acceptance of Renaissance Ideas ....

Classroom Resources
- 📁 Cooperative Learning 25
- 📁 Reproducible Lesson Plan 36
- 📁 Reteaching 36
- 📁 Study Guide 36

Features

LOOKING Closely
(page 362)
(page 366)

Styles
Influencing
Styles
"Renaissance to Roman"
(page 363)

LESSON THREE
(pages 367–375)

High Renaissance ....

Classroom Resources
- 📁 Enrichment Activities 31, 32
- 📁 Reproducible Lesson Plan 37
- 📁 Reteaching 37
- 📁 Study Guide 37

Features

The School of Athens
(page 372)

END OF CHAPTER
(pages 376–377)

....

Studio
LESSON

- Painting a Cityscape (page 376)

ADDITIONAL CHAPTER RESOURCES

Activities

- 📁 Advanced Studio Activity
- 📁 Application 16
- 🖱 Chapter 16 Internet Activity
- 📁 Studio Activity 20, 21, 22

Fine Art Resources

🕹 **Transparencies**

Art in Focus Transparency 20

Leonardo da Vinci. *Ginevra de'Benci*

Art in Focus Transparency 21

Piero della Francesca. *Federíco Monte Feltro*

◼ **Fine Art Print**

Focus on World Art Print 16

Sofonisba Anguissola. *The Sisters of the Artist and Their Governess*

Assessment

- 📁 Chapter 16 Test
- 📁 Performance Assessment

Multimedia Resources

- 🎭 Artsource® Performing Arts Package
- 💿 National Gallery Laserdisc
- 💿 National Museum of Women in the Arts
- 📼 Arts & Entertainment Videos

NATIONAL STANDARDS FOR ARTS EDUCATION

The National Standards for Arts Education provide guidelines for grade-appropriate competency in the visual arts. The Content Standards for grades 9–12 are:

1. Understanding and applying media, techniques, and processes.
2. Using knowledge of structures and functions.
3. Choosing and evaluating a range of subject matter, symbols, and ideas.
4. Understanding the visual arts in relation to history and cultures.
5. Reflecting upon and assessing the characteristics and merits of their work and the work of others.
6. Making connections between visual arts and other disciplines.

Listed below are the National Standards for the Visual Arts addressed in this chapter. For a breakdown of the categories listed under each content standard, refer to the *Reproducible Lesson Plans* booklet in the TCR.

   1. (a, b) **2.** (a, b) **3.** (b) **4.** (b, c) **5.** (b, c) **6.** (a, b)

HANDBOOK MATERIAL

 Diana Zaslove
(page 587)

 Video Game Designer *(page 604)*

Beyond the Classroom

Museums Collections at The National Gallery of Art in Washington, D.C., include works by Renaissance artists such as Leonardo da Vinci and Raphael. Connect to the National Gallery by visiting our Web site at *www.glencoe.com/sec/art*.

🕐 **Out of Time?** If time does not permit teaching this chapter in its entirety, you may wish to preview the artwork and captions with students. Scan the heads in each lesson with students. Discuss the Looking Closely features and examine Symbolism in Art on page 372.

The Italian Renaissance

The Italian Renaissance

The Italian Renaissance

Chapter Overview

CHAPTER 16 examines the origins and artworks of the Renaissance.

Lesson One discusses the contributions of Masaccio and his use of linear perspective.

Lesson Two deals with refinements in Renaissance style and innovations in sculpture, architecture, and painting.

Lesson Three presents the achievements of Leonardo da Vinci, Michelangelo, and Raphael.

Studio Lesson directs students to paint a cityscape and to create the illusion of deep space.

Art & Social Studies

Have students examine the artwork that opens this chapter. Discuss with them how the images in this fresco are representative of thinking and ideas that were developing during the Renaissance. (See page 372 for more information on the details and symbolism of this work.)

Raphael painted the fresco of *The School of Athens* for Pope Julius II. When Raphael died in Rome the whole city mourned, and a funeral mass was celebrated at the Vatican

Art & Social Studies   ■ **FIGURE 16.1** By 1500, Rome was the leading Renaissance city.
The popes and the cardinals living in Rome's Vatican made up the wealthiest and most powerful class. They commissioned architects to construct ornate churches and palaces. They had artists create magnificent paintings, like the one above, and sculptures to decorate these buildings.

Raphael. *The School of Athens.* 1509–11. Stanza della Segnatura, Vatican Palace, Rome, Italy.

National Standards

This chapter meets the following National Standards for the Arts:

1. (a,b)	**4.** (b,c)
2. (a,b)	**5.** (b,c)
3. (b)	**6.** (a,b)

CHAPTER 16 RESOURCES

Teacher's Classroom Resources

📁 Advanced Studio Activity 16

📁 Application 16

🖱 Chapter 16 Internet Activity

📁 Studio Activities 20, 21, 22

Assessment

📁 Chapter 16 Test

📁 Performance Assessment

Fine Art Resources

🖋 *Art in Focus* Transparencies 20, 21

    da Vinci. *Genevra de' Benci*

    della Francesca. Federíco Monte Feltro

🖼 *Focus on World Art* Print 16

    Anguissola. *The Sisters of the Artist.*

*During the Middle Ages, people in western Europe
thought of the Catholic Church as the center of their existence,
guiding them along the rough road of life to salvation.
By the beginning of the fifteenth century, however, people began
to rediscover the world around them and realize that
they were an important part of it. They had
believed that life in this world was primarily a preparation for heaven,
and this gave way to an interest in the here and now.
This change of view was brought about through
a revival of interest in the art and literature of ancient Greece and Rome.
This period is referred to as the **Renaissance**, a period
of great awakening. The word* renaissance *means "rebirth."*

YOUR Portfolio

Compare and contrast two artworks from the Renaissance period. What is the subject matter? How does each artist use the elements of line, color, texture, space, and shape or form? How does each use the principles of art? What media were used to create the artworks? Describe the mood or feeling of the artworks. Date your written entries and place them in your portfolio. At a later date, compare these artworks with ones created from a different time period.

Focus ON THE ARTS

LITERATURE
Niccolò Machiavelli's *The Prince* advised leaders to rule intelligently but ruthlessly. The invention of the printing press increased publication of books in languages other than Latin.

DANCE
The ballet was invented during the Renaissance. In villages, people performed round dances and "canaries," which included tapping as a special effect.

MUSIC
Martin Luther demanded that each Lutheran church have singers and instruments, paving the way for the German influence on music of later centuries. A Spaniard invented the twelve-note scale we use today. In vocal music, the soprano, instead of the tenor, sang the main melody.

353

Introducing the Chapter

Ask students to compose a short poem that describes the coming of spring. Point out that human culture has experienced a number of rebirths. Tell students they are about to read about an important period of rebirth and the artistic legacy it produced.

 Theatre While studying this chapter, use *Performing Arts Handbook* page 588. Help students see how Jennifer Tipton's directing interpretation emphasizes humanistic experiences represented in Shakespeare's play, *The Tempest.*

Focus ON THE ARTS

As an introduction to this chapter, you may wish to bring a recording of a piece by one of the composers of this period (Gosquin des Prez, Orlando di Lassus, or Giovanni da Palestrina) and have it playing as students come into the classroom. Direct students to read the information about the development music, literature, and theatre during the Renaissance. Ask students if they are familiar with the writings of any of the authors listed.

DEVELOPING A PORTFOLIO **Drawing in Perspective.** Have students practice space-creating techniques in drawing. Arrange several objects on a table, spaced apart so students can see the shape of each object. Have students sketch the individual shapes represented by the objects. Also sketch two or more of the objects in an arrangement using any one of these space-creating techniques: overlapping, size rela- tionship, placement, or intensity and value of color. On another sheet of paper, have them create the illusion of deep space using linear perspective (e.g., a hallway, tunnel, or highway). Next, have them draw the objects from the table arrangement into the linear perspective, placing the objects at various points along the perspective line. Have students compare and discuss their sketches. They may then wish to keep these sketches in their portfolios.

The Emergence
of the Italian
Renaissance

Focus

Lesson Objectives

After studying this lesson, students will be able to:

■ Identify circumstances of the fifteenth century that led to the Renaissance.

■ Explain the impact of the printing press on middle-class people of the time.

■ Explain how linear perspective and aerial perspective are used to create depth and space.

Building Vocabulary

On the board, list these stems and affixes: -(i)al, -spect, per-, -ance, -ive, -(e)ar, and -re. Have students name words that contain these word parts (e.g., inspect, repeat, observance). Challenge students to define the terms.

Motivator

Provide students with hand mirrors. Direct students' attention to the view through the window or an interesting corner of the classroom. Ask students to create contour sketches of the scene working solely from reflected images. Point out that it was just such an experiment that led to one of the most important technical discoveries in the history of art.

Introducing the Lesson

Review the characteristics of art produced during the Gothic period. List these properties in a column headed *Gothic Art* on the board. Head a second column with *Renaissance Art*. Ask students to brainstorm characteristics of this "new art."

The Emergence of the Italian Renaissance

Vocabulary
■ Renaissance
■ humanism
■ linear perspective
■ aerial perspective

Artists to Meet
■ Masaccio
■ Fra Angelico
■ Lorenzo Ghiberti

Discover
After completing this lesson, you will be able to:
■ Explain the impact of the printing press on the period.
■ Analyze how linear perspective and aerial perspective are used to create depth and space.

*T*he fifteenth century was a time of great growth and discovery. Commerce spread, wealth increased, knowledge multiplied, and the arts flourished. In Italy, a number of cities grew to become important trading and industrial centers. Among these was Florence, which rose to become the capital of the cloth trade and boasted of having the richest banking house in Europe. (See map, Figure 16.2.)

The Medici family, who controlled this banking empire, became generous patrons of the fine arts.

Influences that Shaped the Renaissance

During this period, artists and scholars developed *an interest in the art and literature of ancient Greece and Rome*. This interest in the classics was called **humanism**. Humanists—the scholars who promoted humanism—embraced the Greco-Roman belief that each individual has dignity and worth.

Artists greatly admired the lifelike appearance of classical works and longed to capture the same quality in their own works. They turned to a study of nature and the surviving classical sculptures in an effort to make their artworks look more realistic.

In the middle of the fifteenth century, a German printer named Johannes Gutenberg perfected the printing press, an invention that ranks as one of the most important contributions of the Renaissance. Within years, thousands of presses were in operation in Europe, and hundreds of books were printed from these presses. This mass-production capability made available to great numbers of readers the works of ancient Greek and Roman writers, religious books, and volumes of poetry and prose.

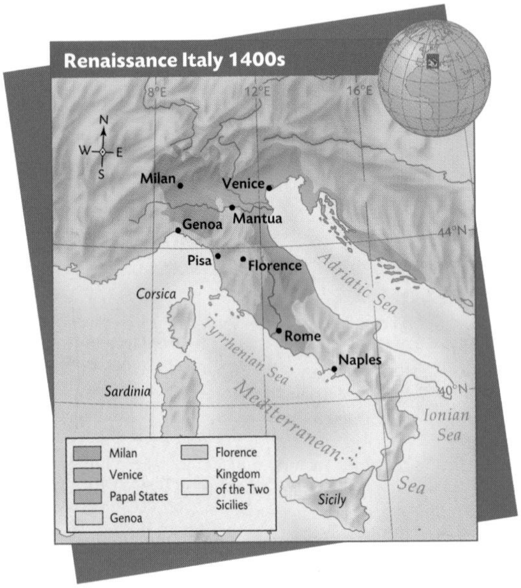

Masaccio (1401–1428)

In Florence, the wealthy and better-educated citizens grew in number and began to show a lively interest in the arts. Beginning in the fourteenth century and continuing through the fifteenth century, they made their city the artistic capital of Italy. It was in Florence that a carefree young painter known as Masaccio (ma-**saht**-chee-oh) brought about a revolution in art equal to that brought by Giotto.

Masaccio is regarded as the first important artist of the Italian Renaissance. He took the innovations of

MAP SKILLS

■ **FIGURE 16.2** Italy was made up of city-states during the 1400s. Why was the location of Florence important to the development and promotion of Renaissance art?

354

LESSON ONE RESOURCES

Teacher's Classroom Resources

📁 Appreciating Cultural Diversity 26

📁 Art and Humanities 26

📁 Cooperative Learning 24

📁 Reproducible Lesson Plan 35

📁 Reteaching 35

📁 Study Guide 35

Giotto and developed them further to produce a style that became the trademark of the Italian Renaissance. It was a style that owed a great deal to the fresco technique that continued to be popular throughout Italy.

The Holy Trinity
■ **FIGURE 16.3**

Masaccio worked in fresco when he created one of his greatest works in the Florentine church of Santa Maria Novella. The painting was *The Holy Trinity* (Figure 16.3). Like Giotto before him, he ignored unnecessary detail and focused his attention on mass and depth.

He wanted his figures to look solid and real, so he modeled them in light and shadow. To show that some of these figures were at different distances from the viewer, he overlapped them. To increase the lifelike appearance of his painting even more, Masaccio created the illusion of a small chapel. In it he placed the Holy Trinity, St. John the Baptist, and the Virgin Mary. On either side of this chapel, he added two figures, members of the wealthy family that had commissioned him to paint the fresco. These two figures are life-size. However, the figures inside the painted chapel are smaller to show that they are farther back in space. As a result, you are made to believe that you are looking into a real chapel with real people in it, when actually the entire scene is painted on a flat wall.

■ **FIGURE 16.3** Masaccio made brilliant use of linear perspective in this work. The lines of the ceiling and capitals of the columns slant downward and inward to meet at a vanishing point below the foot of the cross. **How might viewers have reacted when they saw this realism for the first time in a painting?**

Masaccio. *The Holy Trinity.* c. 1428. Fresco. Santa Maria Novella, Florence, Italy.

TEACH
Art Criticism

Divide the class into groups of three or four students, and provide each group with a shoe box. Instruct students to hold the box close to them, so that the sides appear foreshortened. Have them study their boxes and note that some of the lines appear to slant. Direct students to visualize the imaginary point where these slanting lines would meet if they extended far enough, and ask what this point is called. Refer students to Figures 16.3 and 16.4 (page 356). Ask: How many slanting (i.e., perspective) lines can you trace with your finger? At what point do the sets of lines appear to meet?

Studio Skills

Encourage students to practice drawing in visual perspective as they study the illustration on this page. After completing this Lesson, students may wish to work with *Studio 20*, "Drawing in One-Point Perspective," in the TCR. 📁

Using Map Skills

Ask students to examine the map of Renaissance Italy on the previous page, noting the names of the cities marked on the map. Have them look through the chapter and list the artists who worked during the Renaissance in Italy. Then ask students to determine the city of birth for each of the artists on their lists as well as the locations where they worked. Assign teams to research the history and artistic influences of each of these locations.

Technology

National Gallery of Art Videodisc Use the following images as examples of more works by artists introduced in this lesson.

Masaccio
Profile Portrait of a Young Man

Search Frame 70

Botticelli
Giuliano de'Medici

Search Frame 150

Fra Filippo Lippi
Madonna and Child

Search Frame 126

Use Glencoe's *Correlation Bar Code Guide to the National Gallery of Art* to locate more artworks.

Art Criticism

Write the terms *linear perspective* and *aerial perspective* on the board. Ask students to define the terms and discuss the differences between the two types of perspective. Then have students categorize each painting in this section in one of three ways: as using linear perspective, as using aerial perspective, or as using both. Conclude with a discussion of how the use of perspective adds realism to a work of art.

Cross Curriculum

HEALTH. Have a group of volunteers research what life was like for men and women during the Renaissance. In particular, the group should determine the roles and responsibilities that were appropriate for each gender. Have group members role-play a conversation between men and women today and their Renaissance counterparts.

■ **FIGURE 16.4** Light has been used to make these figures seem round and solid. Notice the perspective lines that lead you into the painting. **Explain how the setting, clothing, and other details in this painting help the viewer understand the story depicted here.**

Masaccio. *The Tribute Money*. c. 1427. Fresco. Brancacci Chapel, Santa Maria del Carmine, Florence, Italy.

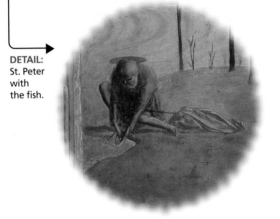

DETAIL:
St. Peter with the fish.

■ **FIGURE 16.5**

An example of linear perspective.

Eye Level — Vanishing Point

Discovery of Linear Perspective

Shortly before Masaccio painted *The Holy Trinity,* an architect named Filippo Brunelleschi (fee-**leep**-poh brew-nell-**less**-kee) made a discovery known as **linear perspective,** *a graphic system that showed artists how to create the illusion of depth and volume on a flat surface.* Based on geometric principles, this system enabled an artist to paint figures and objects so that they seem to move deeper *into* a work rather than across it.

Slanting the horizontal lines of buildings and other objects in the picture makes them appear to extend back into space (Figure 16.5). If these lines are lengthened, they will eventually meet at a point along an imaginary horizontal line representing the eye level. The point at which these lines meet is called a *vanishing point.*

The Tribute Money
■ **FIGURE 16.4**

Not too long after finishing *The Holy Trinity*, Masaccio began working on a number of large frescoes in another Florentine church. *The Tribute Money* (Figure 16.4) is one of these frescoes. In it he grouped three scenes to

CULTURAL DIVERSITY

Clothing Styles. Tell students that during the Renaissance, clothing showed the class status of its wearer; each class wore a particular, well-defined style of clothing. Ask students to investigate and report on the role clothing styles have played in other societies and cultures, including those of the Far East, Middle East, and present-day America. Among questions students should address in their research are: How did these styles come into existence? What factors brought about changes in styles? Has the wearing of particular fashions ever been mandated by the government of a given society? Have students share their findings in the form of pictorial essays.

tell a story from the life of St. Peter. In the center, Christ tells St. Peter that he will find a coin in the mouth of a fish with which to pay a tax collector. The tax collector is shown at Christ's left with his back to you. At the left side of the picture, you see St. Peter again, kneeling to remove the coin from the mouth of the fish. Finally, at the right, St. Peter firmly places the coin in the tax collector's hand.

Aerial Perspective

As in his earlier painting *The Holy Trinity*, Masaccio wanted to create a picture that would look true to life. Depth is suggested by overlapping the figures of the apostles gathered around Christ. With linear perspective, he slanted the lines of the building to lead the viewer's eye deep into the picture. He also made distant objects look bluer, lighter, and duller, heightening the illusion of deep space. This method, known as atmospheric or **aerial perspective**, *uses hue, value, and intensity to show distance in a painting.* In *The Holy Trinity*, aerial perspective was not used because the illusion of space was limited to a chapel interior. In *The Tribute Money*, an outdoor setting offered Masaccio the opportunity of using aerial perspective to create the impression of endless space.

Masaccio's Quest for Reality

Masaccio again modeled his figures so that they seem to be as solid as statues. To achieve this effect, he used a strong light that strikes and lights up some parts of his figures while leaving other parts in deep shadow. Then he placed these figures before a faint background. This makes them seem not only more solid, but also much closer to you. The figures are quite large in relation to the rest of the picture and are shown standing at the front of the scene rather than farther away.

Because these figures are so large and so near, you can see clearly what Masaccio was trying to do. He was concerned with showing how the body is put together and how it moves, but he does not stop here in his quest for reality. Notice the natural and lifelike gestures and poses of the apostles around Christ. Now look at the face of St. Peter at the left and shown in the detail. In his effort to bend over and take the money from the fish's mouth, his face has turned red.

Finally, at the right, observe how St. Peter hands over the coin with a firm gesture while the tax collector receives it with a satisfied expression on his face. The gestures and expressions here are what you might expect from real people.

Time & Place
CONNECTIONS

The Italian Renaissance
c. 1400–1520

MUSIC. During the Renaissance music moved away from having an exclusive Church focus. Non-religious songs were written for musical instruments such as the pear-shaped lute, made with 11 strings.

LITERATURE. The invention of a printing press with movable type came about in Germany in 1440. Books could now be reproduced with greater ease and less cost. Books therefore became more available. A great interest in humanist texts grew during the Renaissance.

Activity **Articles.** The invention of movable type made it possible to quickly print notices and post them on city walls. Today, because of computers and copy machines everyone can be an author. Create your own article or flyer. Add illustrations, copy the results, and share it with classmates.

Critical Thinking

To help students better grasp the concept of aerial perspective, ask them to imagine themselves on a flat desert looking off toward some mountains in the distance. Ask: What colors would you expect to see in the mountains? Would these colors be intense or dull? Would the mountains seem more or less blurred than closer objects? Point out that it is precisely these same effects that artists attempt to capture through the use of aerial or atmospheric perspective.

Cross Curriculum

LITERATURE. Point out that the word *renaissance* has been used to describe periods of human cultural reawakening other than the one that occurred during the fifteenth century. Have volunteers investigate and report on the Harlem Renaissance, the reawakening of interest in African-American culture, art, and literature during the 1920s. Students should chronicle where exactly this renaissance took place, the names of its founders, and the kinds of works they produced.

Time & Place
CONNECTIONS

The Italian Renaissance

Have students examine the images in the Time & Place feature and assign the activity. Have students create a "zine," a popular form of a miniature magazine or pamphlet. Their pamphlet should be made with at least two or three folded pages, written by hand or on the computer. Students may wish to choose a contemporary subject or a topic important to them. Have them print their work and duplicate it to be distributed to classmates.

Art Criticism

Direct students' attention to Figure 16.6. Have students compare this painting with the two by Masaccio (Figures 16.3, page 355, and 16.4, page 356). Ask students to identify the features in Fra Angelico's work indicating that he was influenced by the work and ideas of Masaccio. Then ask students to identify ways in which Fra Angelico's work differs from Masaccio's. Conclude with a discussion of how an artist can be strongly influenced by another artist and still develop his or her own individual style.

Studio Activities

Explain to students that various techniques can be used to achieve the gradual shifts from light to shadow that characterize works of the Renaissance and later. Illustrate the point by drawing a variety of geometric solids on the board and challenging students to create the illusion of three dimensions by using the techniques of hatching, crosshatching, blending, and stippling.

Art and Humanities

Have volunteers read aloud the dramatic monologues *Fra Lippo Lippi* and *Andrea Del Sarto* by Robert Browning. Conduct a roundtable discussion in which students brainstorm what life must have been like during the time when these artists worked. What would it have been like to be a Renaissance artist?

Blending Renaissance and Gothic Ideas

Not all Italian artists accepted the innovations made by Masaccio. Many chose to use some of his ideas and ignore others. Italian art at this time was a blend of the progressive ideas of the Early Renaissance and the conservative ideas of the Gothic period. Two artists who worked in this way were the painter Fra (or "brother") Angelico and the sculptor Lorenzo Ghiberti.

Fra Angelico (c. 1400–1455)

Fra Angelico (**frah** ahn-**jay**-lee-koh) was described by the people who knew him as an excellent painter and a monk of the highest character. A simple, holy man, he never started a painting without first saying a prayer. He also made it a practice not to retouch or try to improve a painting once it was finished. He felt that to do so would be to tamper with the will of God.

The Annunciation
■ **FIGURE 16.6**

A few years after Masaccio's death, Fra Angelico painted a picture in which the angel Gabriel announces to Mary that she is to be the mother of the Savior (Figure 16.6). This painting shows that he was familiar with Masaccio's ideas and did not hesitate to use some of them. Fra Angelico's earlier paintings had been done in the Gothic style and were filled with figures and bright colors. In this painting, there is a simplicity that calls to mind the works by Masaccio. Fra Angelico uses just two figures, placing them in a modest, yet realistic, architectural setting.

Although he makes some use of perspective, it is clear that Fra Angelico was not greatly interested in creating an illusion of deep space in his picture. The figures of Mary and the angel do not overlap as do the figures in Masaccio's paintings. Instead, they are separated and placed within a limited area marked off by arches. Fra Angelico chose not to use Masaccio's modeling techniques to make his figures look round and solid. There is little to suggest that real people exist beneath the garments he paints.

There are no surprises in Fra Angelico's paintings. The gestures and facial expressions are easy to read. Like Gothic artists before him, Fra Angelico painted the religious story so that it could be easily understood. This religious story was more important to Fra Angelico than making his picture seem true to life.

■ **FIGURE 16.6** These figures are presented with more simplicity than figures painted by Masaccio. **How has the artist shown that his most important concern here is telling a clear, recognizable story?**

Fra Angelico. *The Annunciation.* c. 1440–45. Fresco. Museo di San Marco, Florence, Italy.

358 **Unit Six** *Art of an Emerging Modern Europe*

Teacher Notes

Styles Influencing *Styles*

GOTHIC TO RENAISSANCE The transition from Gothic to Renaissance style can be seen in these two works in bronze. Compare the panels and identify details that reflect Renaissance or Gothic style.

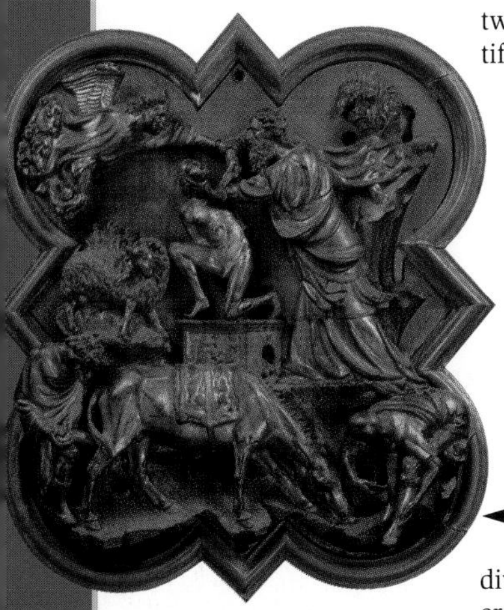

■ **FIGURE 16.7a**

Filippo Brunelleschi. *The Sacrifice of Isaac.* 1401–2. Bronze relief. 53.3 × 43.2 cm (21 × 17″). Museo Nazionale del Bargello, Florence, Italy.

Brunelleschi's panel shows a Gothic flatness. Each object is formed separately, and figures do not relate to each other. The figures have been arranged across the front plane.

Ghiberti's work forms a more unified whole. Objects overlap in a more natural way, representative of the Renaissance style. Figures turn into the work and seem to communicate through glances or gestures.

Brunelleschi's panel can be divided horizontally into three layers that are placed one on top of the other to retain the Gothic style.

Ghiberti's panel can be divided vertically into two scenes that each tell part of the story. This arrangement reflects the Renaissance qualities of harmony and balance.

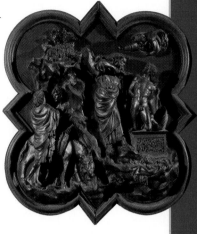

■ **FIGURE 16.7b**

Lorenzo Ghiberti. *The Sacrifice of Isaac.* 1401–2. Bronze relief. 53.3 × 43.2 cm (21 × 17″). Museo Nazionale del Bargello, Florence, Italy.

Lorenzo Ghiberti (1378–1455)

Like Fra Angelico, Lorenzo Ghiberti (loh-**ren**-zoh gee-**bair**-tee) combined elements of the new Renaissance style with the earlier Gothic style. A sculptor, Ghiberti is best known for the works he made for the Baptistry of the Florence Cathedral.

The Contest for the Baptistry Doors

In 1401, the Florence City Council sponsored a contest to find an artist to decorate the north doors of the Baptistry of the cathedral. This Baptistry, built in the twelfth century and dedicated to St. John the Baptist, was one of the most important buildings in the city. It was here that children were baptized and officially brought into the Church. In 1330, an artist named Andrea Pisano had been selected to decorate the south doors of the Baptistry with scenes from the life of St. John the Baptist. Pisano had done so by creating a series of bronze reliefs in the Gothic style of that period.

To decorate the north doors the city offered a challenge to the leading artists of the day. Sculptors were asked to design a sample relief panel in bronze. The subject for the relief was to be the sacrifice of Isaac.

This subject was chosen because it seemed like a good test for an artist. It was a religious scene of great dramatic interest, and it would have to include several figures in motion. Entries were turned in by hopeful artists and were carefully examined. Finally Ghiberti was declared the winner. He spent the next twenty-one years of his life completing the twenty-eight panels used on the doors.

Styles Influencing *Styles*

Encourage discussion of the feature and ask students to examine and compare each of the works. Point out that Brunelleschi's show a Gothic flatness, which you can see in the way the figures have been arranged across the front plane.

Ghiberti, on the other hand, tried to pull the different parts of his work together to form a more unified whole. The figures and objects in his work overlap each other. There is indeed movement in Ghiberti's panel. However, much of this movement is suggested by the flow of the draperies rather than by the figures themselves. Students can see that Ghiberti did not choose to abandon completely the flowing lines and graceful gestures that were the trademarks of earlier Gothic figures.

Critical Thinking

Direct students' attention to the painting in Figure 16.6 and the relief panels in Figures 16.7a and 16.7b. Working in pairs, students are to list details and features of these works that are common to art of the Gothic period. Are any of these features found or hinted at in the works of Masaccio? Have students browse through later chapters of the text. Can they find works created after the Renaissance that exhibit similar features?

Art Criticism

Have students locate a photograph of the relief panels Pisano created for the south doors of the Baptistry. Ask: In what ways are these sculptures similar to those by Ghiberti or to those by Brunelleschi?

CULTURAL INFLUENCES

Developing Perceptual Skills. Explain to students that art historians sometimes disagree about the importance of particular artworks or styles of art. For instance, medieval art, which was once dismissed by art historians as childish and unsophisticated, has recently become a "serious" subject. The same is true of much of so-called "third world" art, which for many years was found in museums of natural history but not art museums. One point on which virtually all historians would agree is the importance of approaching any work of art with an open mind and with as much information as can be obtained about the artist and the environment in which he or she worked.

Study Guide

Distribute *Study Guide* 35 in the TCR. Assist students in reviewing key concepts.

Studio Activities

Ask students to complete *Studio* 21, "Experimenting with Egg Tempera," in the TCR.

ASSESS

Checking Comprehension

Have students complete the lesson review questions. Answers appear in the box below.

Reteaching

Assign *Reteaching* 35, found in the TCR. Have students complete the activity and review their responses.

Enrichment

Assign students *Appreciating Cultural Diversity* 26, "A Little Italy in America," in the TCR.

Extension

Have students read *Cooperative Learning* 24, "Meet the Artists of the Renaissance," in the TCR.

CLOSE

Ask students to describe the difference between linear and aerial perspective. Have them identify ways in which art of the Renaissance was different from the art of earlier periods, especially Gothic art.

■ **FIGURE 16.8** Ghiberti's doors are still referred to as "The Gates of Paradise." **What reaction did Ghiberti's work stir in his peers?**

Lorenzo Ghiberti. *Gates of Paradise.* 1425–52. Gilt bronze. Approx. 4.57 m (15') high. Baptistry of Florence, Italy.

Comparison of Two Panels

When you compare Ghiberti's winning relief panel with one produced by his chief rival in the competition, Filippo Brunelleschi, some interesting similarities and differences are apparent. (See Figures 16.7a and 16.7b, page 359.)

A requirement of the competition was that all the panels had to employ the same Gothic frame used by Pisano on the south doors of the Baptistry. At first glance, this frame makes the panels created by Brunelleschi and Ghiberti both look like pictures from a medieval manuscript. A close inspection, however, reveals that only one panel retains the Gothic style.

The Gates of Paradise
■ **FIGURE 16.8**

Ghiberti drew more heavily on new Renaissance ideas later in his career when he worked on a second set of doors for the Baptistry (Figure 16.8). These doors showed scenes from the Old Testament.

For them, Ghiberti abandoned the Gothic frame used in earlier panels and made the individual reliefs square. He also introduced a greater feeling of space by using linear perspective. This made the buildings and other objects appear to extend back into the work.

Finally, he modeled his figures so that they stand out from the surface of the panel and seem almost fully rounded. When Michelangelo gazed upon these doors, he said they were worthy of being used as the gates to heaven.

LESSON ONE REVIEW

Reviewing Art Facts

1. Identify the contribution Gutenberg's printing press made to the intellectual rebirth of the Renaissance and how it changed the way people viewed life and the world around them.
2. Describe how Masaccio gave his figures mass and showed depth in *The Holy Trinity* (Figure 16.3 on page 355).
3. Define *linear perspective*. Who is given credit for its discovery?

Activity... *Draw a Maze*

With the discovery of perspective, Renaissance artists began to create the illusion of deep space in their works. When Masaccio or Botticelli created a religious painting (Figure 16.3, page 355, and Figure 16.16, page 366), they often included Greek and Roman architectural forms.

Create a drawing of a maze based on two-point perspective. Include as many Greek and Roman architectural forms as possible. Try using arches, columns, and domes in your drawing. If time permits, research modern architectural forms such as the cantilever and include them in your maze. Display your maze in class.

LESSON ONE REVIEW

Answers to Reviewing Art Facts
1. Books and education became more accessible.
2. He modeled his figures in light and shadow; overlapped them.
3. A graphic system based on geometry that creates the illusion of space on a flat surface; Filippo Brunelleschi.

Activity...*Draw a Maze.*
Help students recognize the use of perspective by discussing the examples shown in this lesson. Discuss the drawing of linear perspective on page 356. Provide time in class for students to practice drawing in two-point perspective.

The Acceptance of Renaissance Ideas

Vocabulary
- foreshortening
- contrapposto

Artists to Meet
- Paolo Uccello
- Piero della Francesca
- Donatello
- Filippo Brunelleschi
- Sandro Botticelli

Discover

After completing this lesson, you will be able to:
- Identify the ideas of the Renaissance and their influence on art and artists.
- Recognize how artists looked to earlier works while developing new styles.

A number of changes had taken place during the early 1400s that influenced artists and thinkers. Patrons of the arts such as Florence's Medici family knew who the talented artists were and provided them with generous funding. Scholarship was encouraged and intellectual curiosity spread in both the humanities and the arts.

Development of Renaissance Style

The medieval search for salvation gradually changed to a humanist focus based on the classical culture of ancient Greece and Rome. As a result of this intellectual rebirth, artists acquired additional areas of interest from which to draw ideas for their works and developed techniques that brought an exciting new vitality to their paintings and sculptures.

Paolo Uccello (1397-1475)

Paolo Uccello (**pah**-oh-loh oo-**chell**-oh) was one of the Renaissance artists who eagerly accepted new Renaissance ideas. His concern for perspective is evident when you analyze his painting *The Battle of San Romano* (Figure 16.9). Bodies and broken spears are placed in such a way that they lead your eye into the picture. Notice the fallen figure in the lower

■ **FIGURE 16.9** The figures in this battle scene seem stiff and frozen. The lack of movement makes the scene appear unrealistic. **Find places where contour and axis lines lead the viewer's eye into this work.**

Paolo Uccello. *The Battle of San Romano.* 1445. Tempera on wood. 182 × 323 cm (6′ × 10′5″). National Gallery, London, England.

361

LESSON TWO RESOURCES

Teacher's Classroom Resources

📁 Cooperative Learning 25

📁 Reproducible Lesson Plan 36

📁 Reteaching 36

📁 Study Guide 36

CHAPTER 16
LESSON TWO

The Acceptance of Renaissance Ideas

FOCUS

Lesson Objectives

After studying this lesson, students will be able to:
- Describe the advances in sculpture introduced by Donatello.
- Identify the contributions of Brunelleschi to the field of architecture.

Building Vocabulary

Discuss with students the roots and origins of the two vocabulary terms: *contrapposto* and *foreshortening*

Motivator

Ask students to review the architectural contributions of the ancient Greeks and Romans chronicled in Chapters 8 and 9. Ask: Which techniques or points of design is each of these civilizations credited with? Which techniques and features are most likely to have been borrowed or expanded upon by Renaissance architects? Instruct students to keep these questions in mind as they read the lesson.

Introducing the Lesson

Ask students to perform a quick inventory of all the paintings in this lesson. Then have them divide a sheet of paper into two columns, one headed *Most Like*, the other *Least Like*. Ask students to identify the works that are most and least like those created by Masaccio. Give students time to consider their conclusions. Then, during classroom discussion, have students explain their decisions and offer reasons for the judgments they have made.

TEACH

Direct students' attention to the painting by Piero della Francesca in Figure 16.10. Ask them to describe what they see. On the board, write headings for *elements of art* and *principles of art*. Help students identify the use of elements in the work.

Have students observe how Piero used two gently curving arches to frame and draw your attention to Christ's face. One of these arches curves over Christ's head. It is formed by a tree branch and the hand and arm of John the Baptist. A second arch, representing the horizon line, dips down below Christ's head.

Critical Thinking

Divide the class into two groups. Have one group research names and works by Renaissance artists beyond those in this chapter who found it difficult to break completely with the Gothic style. The other group should do the same for artists, like Paolo Uccello, who were unable to understand the full meaning of the new style and therefore concentrated only on specific aspects or innovations of the new style. Discuss why artists historically have been reluctant to accept new styles or found them difficult to understand. Discuss how these factors sometimes lead to the uneven development and criticism of new art styles.

LOOKING Closely

USE OF THE ELEMENTS OF ART

Observe how Piero used the elements of art to focus the viewer's attention in this work.

- **Shape.** Gently curving arches formed by a tree branch and the hand and arm of St. John the Baptist draw your attention to Christ's face.
- **Line.** The horizon line forms a second arch that dips down below Christ's head.
- **Color.** Piero's use of color gave solidity to the figures and added realism to the space around them.
- **Light.** The clear morning air brightens the landscape, and light flows around the people in the scene.

■ **FIGURE 16.10**

Piero della Francesca. *The Baptism of Christ.* 1445. Tempera on panel. 167.6 × 116.2 cm (66 × 45³/₄"). National Gallery, London, England.

left corner. Here Uccello used a technique known as **foreshortening**, *drawing figures or objects according to the rules of perspective so that they appear to recede or protrude into three-dimensional space.*

Yet, even with all its depth, you would never say that this work looks realistic. It is more like a group of puppets arranged in a mock battle scene. By concentrating on perspective, Uccello failed to make his figures and their actions seem lifelike. The world that he painted is not a real world at all, but an artificial world dictated almost entirely by the rules of perspective.

Piero della Francesca
(1420–1492)

Fra Angelico and Ghiberti could not turn their backs entirely on the Gothic style. Uccello's interest in the Renaissance style

was solely in perspective. It was up to a fourth artist, Piero della Francesca (pee-**air**-oh **dell**-ah fran-**chess**-kah), to break with tradition and fully embrace the new style. By doing so, he carried on the ideas that started with Giotto and were continued by Masaccio.

The Baptism of Christ
■ FIGURE 16.10

The Baptism of Christ (Figure 16.10) shows how Piero painted figures to appear three-dimensional like the figures painted by Giotto and Masaccio. Christ is a solid form placed in the center of the picture. The hand of St. John the Baptist and a dove representing the Holy Spirit are placed directly over his head. The figures show little movement or expression. They are serious, calm, and still. The tree and the figures in the foreground provide a strong vertical emphasis. The effect of this vertical emphasis is softened

More About... **The Medicis.** The Medici family was the ruling family of Florence during the fifteenth century. Giovanni de' Medici (1360–1429), the founder of the family, was a wealthy merchant. His sons Cosimo and Lorenzo were, like their father, devout patrons of the arts. Cosimo, who was a banker by profession, established the Florentine Academy. Lorenzo, known as the Magnificent by his admirers, was a man of varied ideas. It was Lorenzo who encouraged learning in the arts and sciences and patronized numerous artists. The esteem enjoyed by the Medici inspired other ambitious and wealthy Florentine families to try to keep pace with them by commissioning many works. During this period, art in Florence prospered.

by the artist's use of contrasting horizontals and curves. The horizontals are found in the clouds and the dove. The curves are seen in the branches, stream, and horizon line.

Innovations in Painting, Sculpture, and Architecture

A new emphasis on realism inspired by surviving models from classical Greece and Rome revealed itself in various ways in the visual arts of the Italian Renaissance.

In *painting*, more and more artists turned their attention to creating depth and form to replace the flat, two-dimensional surfaces that characterized medieval pictures. Perspective and modeling in light and shade were used to achieve astonishing, realistic appearances.

In *sculpture*, this same concern for realism was manifested in the lifelike figures of Donatello and Michelangelo that seemed to move freely and naturally in space.

In *architecture*, the Gothic style was abandoned by Filippo Brunelleschi and followers in favor of a new architectural style. This style traced its origins back in time to the carefully proportioned, balanced, and elegant buildings of classical times.

Donatello (1386–1466)

Donatello (doh-nah-**tell**-loh), one of the assistants who worked for Ghiberti on the first set of doors for the Baptistry of Florence, would go on to become the greatest sculptor of the Early Renaissance. A good friend of Brunelleschi, he also shared Masaccio's interest in realistic appearances and perspective.

Styles Influencing *Styles*

ROMAN TO RENAISSANCE   Donatello's sculptures became famous for their lifelike qualities. You can see this remarkable realism in Donatello's sculpture *St. George* (Figure 16.11a). The young knight seems to lean forward in anticipation as he stares intently ahead. Perhaps he is watching the advance of an enemy and is preparing for his first move, ready to do battle.

In many ways, *St. George* shows influences of classical Greek sculptures. Its slightly twisting pose, known as **contrapposto**, may remind you of the *Spear Bearer* by Polyclitus (Figure 16.11b). This pose is *a representation of the human body in which the weight is shifted onto one leg, shoulder, and hip to create an uneven balance to the figure.* Even though Donatello's figure is clothed, there is no mistaking the presence of a human body beneath the garments.

■ **FIGURE 16.11a**

Donatello. *St. George.* 1415–17. Marble. Approx. 210 cm (6'10") high. Museo Nazionale del Bargello, Florence, Italy.

■ **FIGURE 16.11b**

Polyclitus. *Doryphoros (Spear Bearer).* Roman copy after Polyclitus. c. 450–440 B.C. Life-size. Museo Archeologico Nazionale, Naples, Italy.

Styles Influencing *Styles*

Direct students' attention to the sculpture in Figures 16.11a and 16.11b, and especially to the facial expressions of the figures. What adjectives would students use to describe the expressions? Can students find examples of Roman works to which these same adjectives might apply?

Have students note how Donatello compensated to ensure that a sculpture would appear as realistic as possible to viewers gazing up at it from below. Ask: In what other cultures and during what periods have you seen similar allowances made by sculptors or architects? What does this reveal about Donatello's artistic purpose?

Art Criticism

Provide students with some background material on the subject of Donatello's *St. George* sculpture. You may wish to share the information featured at the bottom of the page or ask a volunteer to do independent research. Ask students why they think Donatello chose St. George as the subject of a heroic sculpture. Is doing so in keeping with the tradition of the Greek sculptors whom Donatello was attempting to emulate? Then ask students whether understanding more about the subject matter of a work of art can enhance their appreciation of the work.

About the *Artwork*

St. George. The subject of Donatello's sculpture is a legendary warrior and Christian martyr who is thought to have died near the end of the third century. He typically appears in Christian art as either undergoing martyrdom or slaying a dragon, the latter a symbol of evil in early Christianity. According to later accounts of the life of St. George, the martyr is credited with having engaged in combat with an actual dragon in order to rescue a king's daughter. Ask students which of these interpretations seems more consistent with Donatello's starkly realistic depiction of the saint.

Art History

Direct students' attention to the description and photograph of the dome Brunelleschi designed for Florence Cathedral (the "Duomo") in Figure 16.13. Ask students what other great domes they recall learning about in the chapters on Roman and Byzantine art (Figures 9.16, page 204 and 13.7, page 292). What features do those domes share with this one? In what ways is this one unique? Which dome is the largest?

■ **FIGURE 16.12**
Notice that the sculptor stretched the upper part of the body here. What happens when you look up at this sculpture from below?

Donatello. *St. Mark.* 1411–13. Marble. Approx. 236 cm (7'9") high. Orsanmichele, Florence, Italy.

Donatello used perspective in sculpture when carving figures that were to be placed above eye level in churches. He made the upper part of the bodies longer so that when viewed from below, they would seem more naturalistic (Figure 16.12). This kept his sculptures from looking short and awkward.

Filippo Brunelleschi
(1377–1446)

You may be wondering what became of Filippo Brunelleschi. He was, you recall, the artist credited with discovering linear perspective. You may also recall that he was Ghiberti's major rival for the right to design the doors for the Baptistry in Florence. When he lost the contest to Ghiberti, Brunelleschi was very disappointed. In fact, it caused him to abandon sculpture for a career in architecture.

Designing the Dome of Florence Cathedral

Sixteen years later, the two rivals faced each other again in another competition. This time they were asked to submit their designs for a huge dome for the Cathedral of Florence. Work on the cathedral had been under way for generations. Everything had been completed except a dome that would span the huge opening above the altar. No one was able to design a dome to cover such a large opening, however. Many claimed that it could not be done. Brunelleschi was one of those who claimed that it could. He submitted a plan based on Gothic building techniques and was awarded the opportunity to try.

Brunelleschi's plan called for the use of eight Gothic ribs that met at the top of the dome and were joined by horizontal sections around the outside of the dome at its base. The surface between the ribs was then filled in with bricks. In Figure 16.13, four major ribs can be seen on the outside of the dome. For extra height,

■ **FIGURE 16.13** The plan for constructing this dome was based on building techniques developed by Gothic architects. **Explain the significance of artists making use of styles and techniques from earlier eras.**

Filippo Brunelleschi. Florence Cathedral. View of dome. Florence, Italy. 1420–36.

364 **Unit Six** *Art of an Emerging Modern Europe*

More About... **Filippo Brunelleschi (1377–1446)** was one of several architects of the Renaissance who began his art career as a sculptor. Unlike others, however, Brunelleschi displayed an intense interest in details. He showed other artists and architects in this period how to blend the old with the new, and his commissions were many and varied. A listing of his major structures includes the Dome of Santa Maria del Fiore; the Foundling Hospital; the rebuilding of the Church of Santo Spirito, which remained unfinished at the time of his death; the pulpit of the Church of Santa Maria Novella; and the original plan of the Pitti Palace.

the entire dome was placed on a drum. Circular windows in this drum allowed light to flow into the building (Figure 16.14).

It took 16 years to build the dome, but when it was finished, Brunelleschi's reputation as an architect and engineer was made. The towering dome dominated Florence. It soon became a symbol of the city's power and strength. It was so spectacular that later, when designing the great dome for St. Peter's in Rome, Michelangelo borrowed ideas from it.

Striving for Roman Balance

Before he began work on the dome, Brunelleschi agreed to design a chapel for the Pazzi family. They were one of the wealthiest and most powerful families in Florence. In this chapel, he rejected the Gothic style. Instead, he chose a new architectural style based on his studies of ancient Roman buildings.

Inside the Pazzi Chapel (Figure 16.15), you will not see soaring pointed arches or a long, high nave leading to an altar. The vertical movement was not stressed. Rather, Brunelleschi wanted to achieve a comfortable balance between vertical and horizontal movements.

Brunelleschi preferred a gently rounded curve rather than a tall, pointed arch. Dark moldings, pilasters, and columns were used to divide and organize the flat, white wall surfaces. The overall effect is not dramatic or mysterious as in a Gothic cathedral, but simple, calm, and dignified. Its beauty is due to the carefully balanced relationship of all its parts.

■ **FIGURE 16.14** The interior of the cathedral was illuminated by the light coming into the windows below the dome. **Why would an architect need to incorporate light sources when planning a building this size?**

Filippo Brunelleschi. Florence Cathedral, interior.

■ **FIGURE 16.15** The interior of the Pazzi Chapel uses gentle curves and plaster detailing to highlight and organize the space. **How does this interior decoration reflect the mood of a small family chapel rather than the interior of a great cathedral?**

Filippo Brunelleschi. Pazzi Chapel, interior. Santa Croce, Florence, Italy. Begun c. 1440.

Art Criticism

Have students study and compare the two interiors designed by Brunelleschi (Figures 16.14 and 16.15). Which of the designs was executed earlier? Which is more in keeping with the style of art that includes the bronze panels Brunelleschi completed for the Baptistry competition? Which shows greater classical influences? What principles of art are common to both designs?

Studio Skills

Have students note, as stated in the text, that Botticelli uses a letter *W* as the basis for the design of *The Adoration of the Magi* on page 366. Have students each choose a letter of the alphabet to use as an organizing principle for an *Adoration* of their own. Have students begin by creating preliminary design sketches containing rough images of the figures to be depicted. Students are to transfer their best design to a sheet of white paper and finish the work using felt-tip markers. Have students display and compare their efforts.

Study Guide

Distribute *Study Guide* 36 in the TCR. Assist students in reviewing key concepts. 📁

Art and Humanities

Have groups of students complete *Cooperative Learning* 25, "Patrons of the Arts," in the TCR. In this activity, students explore the role of art patrons in the creation of art. They may then form a student art patron committee to commission an artwork for the classroom. 📁

MEETING INDIVIDUAL NEEDS

Auditory/Musical Learners Have students collect and present examples of court, church, and popular music that were common in Europe during the Renaissance period. Suggest they locate recordings by musicians such as Guillaume Dufay, Johannes Ockeghem, Jacob Obrecht, Heinrich Isaac, William Byrd, Thomas Morley, or Thomas Campion.

Visual/Spatial Learners Have students design a bulletin board display that contains a time line and identifies important Renaissance paintings, sculptures, and buildings. Encourage students to use resources from history books and encyclopedias as well as information from this text.

LOOKING Closely

Explain to students that in creating *Adoration of the Magi* Botticelli relied on the element of line to organize and add interest to his painting. Notice what happens when you draw a line around the principal figures. It forms a large triangle with the Madonna and Child at the apex, or top.

ASSESS

Checking Comprehension

Have students complete the lesson review questions. Answers appear in the box below.

Reteaching

Assign *Reteaching* 36, found in the TCR. Have students complete the activity and review their responses. 📁

Enrichment

Have students locate and report on Renaissance paintings that not only exhibit a classical Greek influence but make use of ancient Greek subjects.

Extension

Have students gather reproductions of famous Impressionist paintings and compare them with works by Piero.

CLOSE

Have students imagine themselves to be members of nobility in fifteenth-century Italy. Students should write detailed instructions to an artist they have commissioned to paint a portrait.

Sandro Botticelli
(1445–1510)

Sandro Botticelli (**sand**-roh **bought**-tee-**chel**-lee) was born in 1445 and died quietly in Florence some 66 years later. Forgotten for centuries, the artist's paintings are now ranked among the most admired of the Renaissance period.

In his *Adoration of the Magi* (Figure 16.16), an aisle bordered by kneeling figures leads you to the Holy Family. They are surrounded by the Magi, the kings or wise men who visited the Christ child, and their attendants all dressed in garments worn during Botticelli's time. The Magi are presenting their gifts to the Christ child, seated on Mary's lap.

■ FIGURE 16.16

Sandro Botticelli. *The Adoration of the Magi.* c. 1481. Tempera and oil on wood. Approx. .7 × 1 m (27⅝ × 41″). National Gallery of Art, Washington, D.C. Board of Trustees, Andrew W. Mellon Collection.

LOOKING Closely

USE OF THE ELEMENTS AND PRINCIPLES

Notice how Botticelli's use of line stresses the importance of the central figures in this painting.

- **Line.** The figures are drawn with crisp, sharp, contour lines and their garments have folds that twist and turn in a decorative pattern.
- **Proportion.** A graceful style can be seen in the figure of Mary. Her upper body has been stretched and her head tilted to make her look more elegant.
- **Emphasis.** Line is used to unify the painting and to emphasize the most important parts. A line drawn around the principal figures forms a large triangle with the Madonna and child at the top. If you include the Magi's attendants on both sides, a large W is formed.

LESSON TWO REVIEW

Reviewing Art Facts

1. Explain the technique Piero della Francesca used to give solidity to his figures and realism to the space around them.
2. Identify the interests the sculptor Donatello shares with the painter Masaccio.
3. Describe how Donatello used perspective in his sculptural figures.
4. Explain who the Medici family was, and how they influenced Renaissance art.

Activity... *Preserving Art*

Many of the great masterpieces of the Renaissance, such as the ceiling of the Sistine Chapel (pages 350–351) have been restored. In this way, great works of art can be viewed as they appeared during the Renaissance. Research the difference between restoration and preservation. Consider that some people feel works of art should be preserved rather than restored.

Use the Internet to find out about architectural wonders such as the Great Pyramids in Egypt and the Colosseum in Rome. Do you feel it is important to preserve these treasures? Present your viewpoint to the class.

LESSON TWO REVIEW

Answers to Reviewing Art Facts
1. He studied and captured the effects of sunlight on figures and landscapes.
2. They both showed an interest in realistic appearances and perspective.
3. He elongated the upper bodies of figures to be viewed from below so they would seem more realistic.
4. They were wealthy bankers who supported artists and scholars during the Renaissance.

Activity...*Preserving Art*
Discuss with students the differences between *restoration* and *preservation*. Provide time for students to research some of the architectural works mentioned in the activity.

High Renaissance

Vocabulary
- Pietà

Artists to Meet
- Leonardo da Vinci
- Michelangelo
- Raphael
- Sofonisba Anguissola

Discover
After completing this lesson, you will be able to:
- Identify the artists of the High Renaissance and describe their contributions.
- Discuss the reasons why there were few artworks by women artists before the Renaissance.

*O*ne of the most remarkable things about the Renaissance was its great wealth of artistic talent. Between the years 1495 and 1527, known as the High Renaissance, the master artists Leonardo, Michelangelo, and Raphael created their timeless masterpieces.

All three lived in Italy and were commissioned by the popes of Rome to create ambitious artworks that glorified religious themes. Never before had such a concentrated surge of creative energy occurred simultaneously on three fronts. Like all artists before them, these great masters dreamed of achieving new levels of excellence.

Leonardo da Vinci (1452-1519)

Even when he was a child, people saw that Leonardo da Vinci (lay-oh-**nar**-doh da **vin**-chee) was blessed with remarkable powers. He had gracious manners, a fine sense of humor, and great physical strength.

Leonardo also had a curiosity that drove him to explore everything. As he grew older, he studied architecture, mathematics, sculpture, painting, anatomy, poetry, literature, music, geology, botany, and hydraulics. It is estimated that he completed 120 notebooks filled with drawings surrounded by explanations (Figure 16.17). The subjects range from anatomy to storm clouds to rock formations to military fortifications.

Leonardo dissected cadavers at a time when the practice was outlawed. This enabled him to learn how arms and legs bend and how muscles shift as the body moves. He was especially interested in the head, particularly how the eye sees and how the mind reasons. He searched for that part of the brain where the senses meet, believing that this was where the soul would be found.

The Last Supper
■ FIGURE 16.18

Leonardo left many projects unfinished because the results did not please him or because he was eager to move on to some new task. He was always experimenting, and many of these experiments ended in failure. Perhaps his greatest "failure" is his version of *The Last Supper* (Figure 16.18, page 368). This was a magnificent painting that began to flake off the wall shortly after he applied his final brushstroke because he had used an experimental painting technique.

The Last Supper had been painted many times before, and so Leonardo probably welcomed the challenge of creating his own version. He had an entire wall to work on in a dining hall used by monks in the Monastery of Santa Maria delle Grazie in Milan.

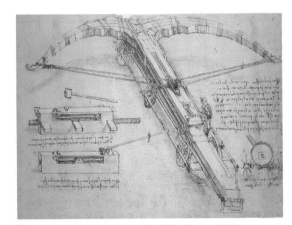

■ **FIGURE 16.17** Leonardo's sketchbooks reveal his remarkable curiosity. **Can you name some of the subjects that interested him?**

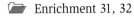

Leonardo da Vinci. Giant catapult. c. 1499. Biblioteca Ambrosiana, Milan, Italy.

367

FOCUS
Lesson Objectives
After studying this lesson, students will be able to:
- Identify the singular contributions of three Renaissance giants—Leonardo da Vinci, Michelangelo, and Raphael.
- Explain why there were few artworks by women prior to the Renaissance.

Using Vocabulary
Discuss with students the roots and origins of the vocabulary term: *Pietà*

Motivator
Before introducing the lesson, display an untitled reproduction of the *Mona Lisa*. Going around the room, ask students in turn to volunteer a piece of information about this famous artwork or its creator, beginning with the work's title.

Introducing the Lesson
Write the phrase *Renaissance Man* on the board. Ask students if they are familiar with this term (or with the more recently coined companion term *Renaissance Woman*). If not, explain that these terms are often applied to living individuals to indicate that they are gifted in many areas. Add that the Italian Renaissance produced two artists who were gifted not only in the visual arts but in literature, poetry, and other fields. After permitting students to guess the names of these two original "Renaissance people," proceed with the reading.

LESSON THREE RESOURCES

Teacher's Classroom Resources
📁 Enrichment 31, 32
📁 Reproducible Lesson Plan 37
📁 Reteaching 37
📁 Study Guide 37

TEACH
Studio Skills

Have students study the sketchbook page by Leonardo da Vinci (Figure 16.17). Emphasize the keen powers of observation and eye for detail this illustration suggests. Then instruct students to select a familiar location (e.g., the school yard, their room at home) and to view it as though for the first time. Ask them to use pencil to create a page of notes and sketches of the location in the manner of Leonardo. Have students share their completed pages. Ask which sketchbook entries they feel most capture the spirit of Leonardo and why. Discuss ways in which this activity stimulated students' imaginations. Did creating the sketchbook pages make them more aware of the world around them? You may want to collect these pages to form a "Classroom Perception Notebook."

Did You Know❓

Giorgio Vasari says that the prior of the monastery became impatient with Leonardo while he was painting *The Last Supper*. He thought the artist was taking much too long to finish the painting. He became especially upset when he noticed that Leonardo spent long periods of time staring at the picture rather than working on it. Angry, the prior went to the Duke of Milan to complain. Leonardo was then summoned to appear before the Duke.

After hearing the complaints made against him, Leonardo said that men of genius sometimes produce the most when they do not seem to be working at all.

■ **FIGURE 16.18** This painting depicts a key scene in the life of Christ and is painted on a wall of an actual dining hall. **Explain why Leonardo grouped the figures around the table so close together.**

Leonardo da Vinci. *The Last Supper.* c. 1495–98. Fresco. S. Maria delle Grazie, Milan, Italy.

Using linear perspective, Leonardo designed his scene so that it would look like a continuation of the dining hall. Christ is the center of the composition. All the lines of the architecture lead to him silhouetted in the window. He has just announced that one of the apostles (Judas) would betray him, and this news has unleashed a flurry of activity around the table. Only Christ remains calm and silent, and this effectively separates him from the others.

The apostles are grouped in threes, all expressing disbelief in his statement except Judas. The third figure on Christ's right, Judas, leans on the table and stares at Christ, his expression a mixture of anger and defiance. He is further set off by the fact that his face is the only one in shadow. The other apostles, stunned, shrink back and express their denials and questions in different ways.

As you examine Leonardo's painting, you may be struck by an unusual feature. All the apostles are crowded together on the far side of the table. Certainly they could not have been comfortable that way, and yet none had moved to the near side, where there is ample room. Leonardo chose not to spread his figures out because that would have reduced the impact of the scene. Instead, he jammed them together to accent the action and the drama.

Leonardo broke with tradition by including Judas with the other apostles. Earlier works usually showed him standing or sitting at one end of the table, apart from the others. Instead, Leonardo placed him among the apostles but made him easy to identify with a dark profile to show that Judas was separated from the other apostles in a spiritual rather than in a physical way.

Mona Lisa
■ **FIGURE 16.19**

Leonardo was a genius who showed great skill in everything he tried. This was his blessing and his curse, for he jumped suddenly from one undertaking to the next. His curiosity and constant experimenting often kept him from remaining with a project until it was completed. A perfectionist, he was never entirely satisfied with his efforts. When he died, he still had in his possession the *Mona Lisa* portrait (Figure 16.19). He

COOPERATIVE LEARNING

Interviews. Divide the class into two groups. Ask the students in one group to imagine that they are reporters assigned to interview Leonardo da Vinci. Have each student in this group write three questions they would like to ask the artist. Students in the second group are instructed to answer these questions as they are read aloud, but they must answer them as they think da Vinci would respond. Encourage students from the second group to take turns answering the questions. When the interview is complete, open a discussion and ask students to evaluate their feelings on the accuracy of answers and to support reasons these answers were given.

had been working on it for 16 years. Yet, he claimed that it was still unfinished. That painting, which he regarded as unfinished, is now one of the most popular works of art ever created.

Michelangelo (1475–1564)

Ranked alongside Leonardo as one of the greatest artists of the Renaissance was Michelangelo Buonarroti (**my**-kel-**an**-jay-loh bwon-nar-**roh**-tee). Like Leonardo, Michelangelo was gifted in many fields, including sculpture, painting, and poetry.

Pietà

■ FIGURE 16.20

A measure of Michelangelo's early genius is provided by his *Pietà* (Figure 16.20), carved when he was still in his early twenties. A **Pietà** is *a work showing Mary mourning over the body of Christ*. In this over-life-size work,

the Virgin Mary is seated at the foot of the cross. She holds in her lap the lifeless form of the crucified Christ. Gently, she supports her son with her right arm. With her left, she expresses her deep sorrow with a simple gesture.

Mary's face is expressionless. It is a beautiful face, but small when compared to her huge body. In fact, you may have noticed that Mary's body is much larger than that of Christ.

Why would Michelangelo make the woman so much larger than the man? Probably because a huge and powerful Mary was necessary to support with ease the heavy body of her son. Michelangelo wanted you to focus your attention on the religious meaning of the figures and the event, not on Mary's struggle to support the weight of Christ's body.

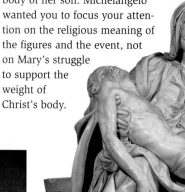

■ **FIGURE 16.20**
Michelangelo brings forth the expression of tenderness and emotion in this marble sculpture. **What is happening in this scene, and how has the artist shown emotion in the position of the figures?**

Michelangelo. *Pietà.* c. 1500. Marble. St. Peter's Basilica, Rome, Italy.

■ **FIGURE 16.19**
The eyes are the windows to the mind, according to Leonardo, and he expressed this idea in his portrait of Mona Lisa. **Tell how the artist has succeeded in demonstrating his idea in the way he painted the portrait.**

Leonardo da Vinci. *Mona Lisa.* c. 1503–06. Oil on wood. 77 × 53 cm (33³⁄₈ × 20⁷⁄₈"). The Louvre Museum, Paris, France.

Chapter 16 *The Italian Renaissance* **369**

CHAPTER 16
LESSON THREE

Aesthetics

Have students study the portrait in Figure 16.19. Ask: What mood or feeling does the painting evoke? What do the eyes suggest about the personality of the subject? Does she seem happy or sad, introverted or extroverted? Does the work contain any clues as to what the artist felt toward his subject? Do students feel he has presented her in an idealized style, or has he provided a faithful (i.e., photographic) record of his subject? What details can students point to in support of their assumptions?

Art Criticism

Have students again examine the portrait by Leonardo in Figure 16.19. Ask: What part of the painting does the artist emphasize? How does he go about emphasizing it? What elements of art play a role in this emphasis?

Critical Thinking

Point out that many Renaissance artists used a geometric shape or solid as a design base for their works. Michelangelo's *Pietà* (Figure 16.20) is underlain by a pyramid with its apex just above Mary's head. Have students choose an artwork from the lesson and execute a rapid gesture drawing of it. Then instruct them to find and superimpose the underlying geometric form or shape on the drawing. Encourage them to compare their results. Ask: Does identifying the organizing shape or form add to an understanding of an artwork and the effect it creates?

Aesthetics

Divide the class into three groups. One group is to function as imitationalists, one as formalists, and one as emotionalists. Explain that the groups are to collaborate on a promotional pamphlet encouraging tourists in Rome to visit the Sistine Chapel. Limited space in the pamphlet dictates that only one paragraph (100 words maximum) be devoted to Michelangelo's ceiling. Have students discuss what information they might include in the allotted space that would be most effective in attracting would-be art lovers. Should they emphasize the incredible realism of the work, the methodical design, or the highly charged emotions it evokes?

Cross Curriculum

LANGUAGE ARTS. Ask a student volunteer to read aloud the section of the text relating the demanding circumstances under which Michelangelo completed his painting of the Sistine Chapel ceiling. Then have students imagine themselves to be the artist during his first months of work on a project which is estimated to take four years. Have students write a diary entry Michelangelo might have written. Entries should express his feelings about the project to date, as well as his plans for filling the balance of the ceiling space.

■ **FIGURE 16.21** This fresco was completed by Michelangelo after four years of working on scaffolding built especially to reach the ceiling of the Sistine Chapel. **Explain what issues the artist would have to consider while working on wet plaster.**

Michelangelo. Ceiling of the Sistine Chapel. 1508–12. Fresco. Vatican Museums and Galleries, Vatican City, Italy.

The Ceiling of the Sistine Chapel

Everything that Michelangelo set out to do was on a grand scale. For this reason, many projects were never completed. Asked by Pope Julius II to design a tomb for the pope himself, Michelangelo created a design calling for 40 figures. Only a statue of Moses and some figures of slaves were ever finished, however.

While Michelangelo was still preparing for this project, the pope changed his mind and decided not to spend any more money for it. Instead, he assigned the artist the task of painting the immense ceiling of the Sistine Chapel in the Vatican (Figure 16.21).

This chapel was about 40 feet wide and about 133 feet long and had a rounded ceiling. The ceiling had been painted with stars on a dark blue background. Because it looked very hard and time-consuming to paint, Michelangelo protested. It was not just the difficulty of the task. No doubt his pride was hurt as well. Ceiling paintings were considered less important than wall paintings, but the walls of the Sistine Chapel had already been painted by Botticelli and other well-known artists.

Furthermore, what could he paint on such an immense ceiling so high above the heads of viewers? Michelangelo's anger was intensified by the fact that he thought of himself as a sculptor and not a painter. In the end, all his protests were in vain. The proud, defiant artist gave in to the pope.

Before he could begin work on the ceiling, Michelangelo had to build a high scaffold stretching the

More About... **Michelangelo.** *The Last Judgment* Between 1536 and 1541, Michelangelo was at work on the fresco *The Last Judgment,* which covers the entire wall behind the altar of the Sistine Chapel. Michelangelo's characteristic mastery and manipulation of the human form is displayed through his representation of the many unclad figures appearing in the work. In his intense interpretation of the Bible story, Michelangelo depicts Christ turning toward the damned as the mouth of hell yawns open immediately over the altar. At the time, the choice of subject was considered a curious one, since this fresco replaced a painting by Perugino of the Assumption of Mary, to whom the chapel had been dedicated.

length of the chapel. Then, refusing the aid of assistants, he bent over backward and lay on his back to paint on the wet plaster applied to the ceiling. He divided the ceiling into nine main sections and in these painted the story of humanity from the Creation to the Flood.

Michelangelo's Sculptural Painting Style

Looking up at this huge painting, you can see that Michelangelo the sculptor left his mark for all to see. It looks more like a carving than a painting. The figures are highly modeled in light and shade to look solid and three-dimensional. They are shown in constant movement, twisting and turning until they seem about to break out of their niches and leap down from their frames.

A Dedicated Artist

For more than four years, Michelangelo toiled on the huge painting over 68 feet above the floor of the chapel. Food was sent up to him, and he climbed down from the scaffold only to sleep.

Perhaps his greatest difficulty was being forced to see and work while bending backward in a cramped position. He claimed that after working on the Sistine ceiling, he was never able to walk in an upright position again.

When Michelangelo was finished, he had painted 145 pictures with more than 300 figures, many of which were 10 feet high. Only a man of superhuman strength and determination—only a Michelangelo—could have produced such a work.

Moses

■ **FIGURE 16.22**

As soon as the Sistine Chapel was finished, Michelangelo returned to work on the pope's tomb. Attacking the stone blocks with mallet and chisel, he said that he was "freeing" the figures trapped inside. In about two years, he carved the life-size figures of two slaves and a seated Moses.

Michelangelo's *Moses* (Figure 16.22) shows the prophet as a wise leader, but capable of great fury. His head turns as if something has caught his attention. It is a powerful and commanding portrait.

Michelangelo's Energy and Spirit

Popes and princes admired Michelangelo, and everyone stood in awe before his works. His talents were so great that people said that he could not be human, but he had some very human characteristics as well. He had strong views about art, and this caused him to disagree with other artists, including Leonardo. A violent temper made it difficult for him to work with assistants. He placed his art above everything else. Only death, at age 89, could silence the energy and the spirit of the man regarded by many as the greatest artist of his time.

■ **FIGURE 16.22**
Moses seems about to come alive and rise up from his marble seat. **Discuss how this work of art demonstrates Michelangelo's strength and abilities as a sculptor.**

Michelangelo. *Moses.* c. 1513–15. Marble. Approx. 244 cm (8') high. San Pietro in Vincoli, Rome, Italy.

Chapter 16 *The Italian Renaissance* **371**

Aesthetics

Have students brainstorm a list of adjectives and phrases that describe the expression on the face of Moses (Figure 16.22). What thoughts do they imagine to be running through the figure's mind? If any of the students are familiar with the biblical story of Moses, permit them to share their knowledge. Then ask: What impact does this information have on your understanding and appreciation of Michelangelo's work?

Art History

Have students select a famous Italian Renaissance painting, sculpture, or work of architecture not illustrated in this chapter. Instruct students to write a brief art-history analysis of the work, including each of the stages—description, analysis, interpretation, and judgment—as well as an explanation of why the work is typical of Renaissance art. Have students present their research and critiques to the class, along with an illustration of the work in question.

Critical Thinking

Remind students that they have studied two religious art forms in this chapter—the Madonna and the Pietà—that have recurred throughout the history of Western art. Provide the class with a large sheet of heavy paper, and have them collaborate on a collage titled *Religious Art Themes of the World.* The collage should include color-enhanced photocopied reproductions and original illustrations of subjects that have been repeated in the art of Western and non-Western religions and cultures of the world. Display the completed collage.

Teacher Notes

Art Criticism. In the context of the cross curriculum diary activity on page 370, you may wish to point out that it was customary for artists of the Renaissance to write their memoirs. Though many of these works have been lost, the surviving documents reveal a great deal about the personality and character of the writer, as well as the circumstances the artist lived in. In fact, it is partly thanks to these writings that the practice of art criticism emerged. The memoirs, more self-analytical than the sketchbooks and notebooks that many artists maintained, provided later ideas about criteria for art criticism.

Aesthetics

Raphael's painting recognizes the visual arts, only recently included among the liberal arts. In classical times, the seven liberal arts, which provided the traditonal curriculum in the education of the rich and powerful, were divided into three language arts and four numerical arts. The language arts were grammar, rhetoric, and logic; the numerical arts were arithmetic, geometry, astronomy, and music.

The visual arts came to be regarded as equal in status to music with the development of scientific perspective in the Renaissance. This is why we can discover in Raphael's fresco what are thought to be portraits of the aged Leonardo as Plato, Michelangelo as Heraclatus, and the architect of St. Peter's, Bramante, as Archimedes.

At the left side of the painting, students are gathered around the mathematician Euclid, who appears to be demonstrating a new theory.

Symbolism in Renaissance *Art*

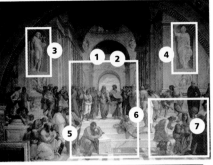

The "school" to which this work refers is actually two opposing schools of thought represented by the two great classical philosophers Plato and Aristotle (Figure 16.23).

Raphael placed these two figures before an open archway. To further emphasize their importance, the artist arranged all the perspective lines so they would converge on a central vanishing point placed between these two figures.

On Plato's side of the composition are the ancient philosophers concerned with the metaphysical, the mysteries that go beyond the here and now. On Aristotle's side are the philosophers and scientists interested in nature and the affairs of humankind.

■ **FIGURE 16.23** Raphael. The School of Athens (detail). 1509–11. Stanza della Segnatura, Vatican Palace, Rome.

2 At the right, Aristotle holds his *Ethics* and gestures earthward to indicate his greater interest in the real and practical world.

1 At the left, Plato holds his classic work *Timaeus* in one hand while pointing skyward with the other to symbolize his concern with an idealistic world.

5 It is thought that Michelangelo is portrayed as the philosopher Heraclitus. He sits pensively on the steps with his head resting on his hand as he writes.

3 To Plato's right a niche contains a statue of Apollo, patron of poetry.

4 A niche to the left of Aristotle holds a statue of Athena, goddess of reason.

6 A portrait of the aged Leonardo is believed to be seen as the philosopher Plato.

7 Raphael included his own portrait as the young man looking at us in the lower far right. He appears among the mathematicians symbolizing the Renaissance belief that geometry and art were strongly linked and that a knowledge of mathematics was essential to an artist's development.

372 **Unit Six** *Art of an Emerging Modern Europe*

Symbolism in Renaissance *Art*

Ask students to examine the painting on page 352 and then to study the symbolism and details of the same painting in the feature on this page. Ask them what techniques have been used to make the figures of Plato and Aristotle the focal point of this composition. Have them explain how space is suggested. Ask students to identify perspective lines that do not converge on the vanishing point between these two figures.

Raphael (1483–1520)

Raphael Sanzio (**rah**-fah-yell **sahn**-zee-oh) was successful, wealthy, and admired throughout his brief but brilliant career. As a child in a small town in central Italy, he was apprenticed to a respected artist. He learned to use soft colors, simple circular forms, and gentle landscapes in his paintings.

The young, ambitious Raphael next traveled to Florence to study the works of the leading artists of the day. From Leonardo he learned how to use shading to create the illusion of three-dimensional form. From Michelangelo he learned how to add vitality and energy to his figures. By blending the ideas of those artists in his own works, he became the most typical artist of the Renaissance.

The School of Athens
■ **FIGURE 16.23**

In 1508, at about the same time Michelangelo began work on the Sistine Chapel ceiling, Pope Julius II summoned Raphael to Rome to decorate a series of rooms in the Vatican Palace. In the first of these rooms, Raphael painted frescoes celebrating the four domains of learning: theology, philosophy, law, and the arts. One of these is *The School of Athens*. (See Figure 16.1, page 352 and Figure 16.23.)

The Alba Madonna
■ **FIGURE 16.24**

It was while Raphael was working on the Vatican frescoes that he probably painted the well-known *Alba Madonna* (Figure 16.24). This is an excellent example of the kind of pictures that were painted in Italy at the peak of the Renaissance.

Interpretation of a Religious Theme

The halos and cross immediately suggest a religious theme. The woman and unclothed child are identified as the Madonna and the Christ child. The second child is St. John the Baptist. The camel's hair garment that he wears fits the description of the garment he wore later while preaching in the desert.

St. John holds a small cross, the symbol of salvation made possible by Christ's death. The Christ child freely accepts the cross and appears to be turning and moving on his mother's lap. He twists around in a way that suggests that he wants St. John, representing all people, to follow him.

There is an undercurrent of tension in the work that is best noted in the faces. All three figures stare intently at this cross, and their thoughts drift to the future. Do they

■ **FIGURE 16.24**
These figures seem round, solid, and lifelike, a result of Raphael's subtle shading technique.
Describe how the Madonna figure in this scene is shown demonstrating care and concern for her holy charges.

Raphael. *The Alba Madonna.* c. 1510. Oil on wood panel transferred to canvas. Diameter, 94.5 cm (37¼"). National Gallery of Art, Washington, D.C. Board of Trustees, Andrew W. Mellon Collection.

Aesthetics

Direct students' attention to the painting by Raphael in Figure 16.24. Have them note the work's high degree of realism and emotionalism, as well as the great care that went into its design. Then have students repeat the "Aesthetics" activity described on page 370, side column, in which groups were to imagine themselves in collaboration on a promotional pamphlet encouraging tourists to view an artwork.

Did You Know ?

In the spring of 1520, Raphael fell ill with a violent fever He died on his 37th birthday and was buried with full honors in the Pantheon in Rome. His epitaph, in Latin, includes the words, "He who is here is Raphael." No other words were needed, his name alone testifies to his greatness.

Aesthetics

Tell students that at first glance they may think that *The Alba Madonna* is little more than a gentle picture of Christ, his mother, and St. John enjoying a pleasant outing in the countryside. A closer look may reveal to students an undercurrent of uneasiness. Point out this evidence in the three faces. Although the world appears calm and peaceful in the painting, the faces reveal little sign of happiness or contentment. A sadness veils Mary's face as she shifts her eyes from her book. All three figures stare intently at the cross, and perhaps their thoughts drift to the future. Do they recognize the meaning of the cross and what it holds in store for them, or are they puzzled by the unexpected uneasiness it stirs up in them?

More About... **Pietro Perugino (c. 1445–1523).** The artist who was teacher to Raphael was Pietro Perugino, a minor artist of the Renaissance. He created several frescoes for the Sistine Chapel. Perugino learned his art from Piero della Francesca and, like many other Renaissance artists, had an interest in classical art. This, however, was not of major importance to him, and in some ways he was forward-thinking. Perugino felt that grace was the most important quality a painting could possess, and his works are therefore peopled with graceful and elegant figures. This philosophy, which went against the prevailing tide, was one that, happily, he passed on to his student, Raphael.

Critical Thinking

Have students read the description explaining the restrictions placed on women during the Renaissance. Ask: In what ways has women's struggle for equality carried on into our own times? Are there still jobs and positions from which women are systematically excluded?

Cross Curriculum

SOCIAL STUDIES. Point out that laws were very different during the Renaissance from those we are accustomed to today. Add that, during the Renaissance, a person could be hanged, for example, for stealing a chicken. Ask an interested student or group of students to find out more about the laws that were in effect during the Renaissance and to give a brief presentation on this subject. Ask the student or group to describe the processes of arrest, trial, and punishment as they were practiced during this period.

Study Guide

Distribute *Study Guide* 37 in the TCR. Assist students in reviewing key concepts. 📁

Art and Humanities

Have students complete *Enrichment* 31, "Restoring the Masterpieces," in the TCR. In this worksheet, students learn about the process of cleaning and restoring centuries-old paintings. 📁

Studio Activities

Have students complete *Studio* 22, "Building a 3-D Space Construct," in the TCR. 📁

recognize the meaning of the cross, or are they concerned only with the unexpected uneasiness it stirs up within them?

Raphael's Mastery of Color and Form

There is a balanced use of hue in the painting. Raphael has used the three primary colors—red, yellow, and blue—which represent a balance of the color spectrum. Blue dominates; it is used throughout the work and, in the background, adds to the illusion of deep space.

This illusion is heightened further by the use of duller hues in the background. A gradual change from light to dark values adds a feeling of roundness and mass.

Renaissance Women Artists

You may have noticed that in the coverage of art periods up to this point, there has been no mention of women artists. The reason for this is that few works by women artists completed before the Renaissance have come to light. Furthermore, it was not until the Renaissance had passed its peak that women artists were able to make names for themselves as serious artists. Even in that enlightened period, it was not easy for women to succeed as artists because of the obstacles that had to be overcome.

Role of Women in the Medieval Period

During the Medieval period, most women were expected to tend to duties within the household. Their first responsibilities were those of wife and mother. If that failed to occupy all their time, they were required to join their husbands in the backbreaking chores awaiting in the fields.

Women were, in general, excluded from the arts because, as women, most of them were prevented from gaining the knowledge and skills needed to become artists. Their

involvement in art was limited, for the most part, to making embroideries and tapestries and occasionally producing illustrated manuscripts.

The Role of Artists

During the Renaissance, the new importance attached to artists made it even more difficult for women to pursue a career in art. Artists at that time were required to spend longer periods in apprenticeship. During this time, they studied mathematics, the laws of perspective, and anatomy.

Serious artists were also expected to journey to major art centers. There they could study the works of famous living artists as well as the art of the past. This kind of education was out of the question for most women in the fifteenth and sixteenth centuries. Only a handful were determined enough to overcome all these barriers and succeed as serious artists. One of these was Sofonisba Anguissola (soh-foh-**niss**-bah ahn-gue-**iss**-sol-ah).

Sofonisba Anguissola
(1532–1625)

Anguissola was the first Italian woman to gain a worldwide reputation as an artist. She was the oldest in a family of six daughters and one son born to a nobleman in Cremona about 12 years after Raphael's death. Sofonisba's father was pleased to find that all his children showed an interest in art or music. He encouraged them all, especially his oldest daughter.

Sofonisba was allowed to study with local artists, and her skills were quickly recognized. Her proud father even wrote to the great Michelangelo about her. The response was words of encouragement and a drawing that Sofonisba could study and copy as part of her training.

Many of Sofonisba's early works were portraits of herself and members of her family. Her father was always eager to spread the word about his talented daughter. He sent several of her self-portraits to various courts, including that of Pope Julius III.

𝒯eacher 𝒩otes

Developing Perceptual Skills. Art historians often have difficulty determining even the most basic information about a piece of art—who made it, when it was made, where it was made. When examining works themselves, students should, therefore, be aware of and mindful of such issues as these:

- Appearance of pigments and media change over time, and sometimes works will be touched up by a restorer or later owner.
- Some works may have been planned by a particular artist and then completed by students or assistants.

In 1559, while she was still in her twenties, Sofonisba accepted an invitation from the King of Spain, Philip II. He asked her to join his court in Madrid as a lady-in-waiting. For ten years, she painted portraits of the royal family. After this time, she met and married a nobleman from Sicily. She returned to Italy with him and a fine assortment of gifts presented to her by the appreciative king.

Double Portrait of a Boy and Girl of the Attavanti Family
■ FIGURE 16.25

Many of Sofonisba's portraits deserve to be included among the best produced during the Late Renaissance. The reason will be clear when you examine her portrait of the son and daughter of a wealthy Florentine family (Figure 16.25). The boy is gazing up thoughtfully from an open book. As he does so, his sister places her arm around him. The artist seems to be telling us that the boy not only knows how to read, but is intelligent enough, even at this young age, to think seriously about what he has read. His sister's gesture and expression are signs of her affection and her pride.

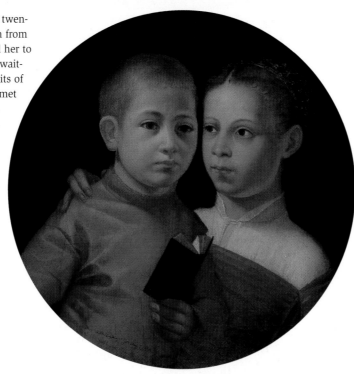

■ **FIGURE 16.25** This artist is set apart from the others you have learned about so far because she is a woman. **Discuss how she was able to become an internationally renowned portrait artist.**

Sofonisba Anguissola. *Double Portrait of a Boy and Girl of the Attavanti Family.* Early 1580's. Oil on panel. Diameter, 40 cm (15³/₄"). Allen Memorial Art Museum, Oberlin College, Oberlin, Ohio. Kress Study Collection, 1961.

LESSON THREE REVIEW

Reviewing Art Facts
1. Identify five of the many different subjects Leonardo studied.
2. Explain why Michelangelo distorted the proportion of the two figures in his *Pietà*.
3. Explain why Michelangelo was not asked to paint the walls of the Sistine Chapel.
4. Describe why Raphael was regarded as the most typical of the Renaissance artists.

▶ Activity... *Painting a Ceiling*
Think about how Michelangelo painted the ceiling of the Sistine Chapel (Figure 16.21, page 370). He mixed his own paints and drew the line drawings for the figures. At the same time, he had to defend himself against critics who did not always agree with his humanistic visions of Christianity.

Create a ceiling painting based on contemporary life. Work in groups of six to eight students. Sketch a concept for the painting. Attach 18-inch squares of kraft paper to the underside of large art tables. Using tempera paints, have each member paint a square and experience painting from the viewpoint of Michelangelo. Attach finished paintings to the ceiling of your classroom.

LESSON THREE REVIEW

Answers to Reviewing Art Facts
1. Answers may include: architecture, mathematics, sculpture, painting, poetry, literature, music, geology, botany, and hydraulics.
2. To focus attention on the religious meaning.
3. Because they had already been painted.
4. Because he so skillfully incorporated the ideas developed by other artists into his own works.

Activity...*Painting a Ceiling.*
For this activity, be sure students wear comfortable clothing for working under the art tables. Allow time for groups to work together first to plan the artwork they will create. Then arrange for students to work separately on their paintings.

ASSESS
Checking Comprehension
➤ Have students complete the lesson review questions. Answers appear in the box below.
➤ Have pairs of students complete *Application* 16, "Master Pieces," in the TCR. The activity provides fragments of actual critical quotations regarding Renaissance artists. 📁

Reteaching
➤ Assign *Reteaching* 37, found in the TCR. Have students complete the activity and review their responses. 📁
➤ Ask students to identify the major artists of the Italian Renaissance. Have them name the contributions of these artists and describe the characteristics of each artist's particular style.

Enrichment
Assign students *Enrichment* 32, "The Last Supper—A Source of Inspiration," in the TCR. In this activity, students compare Leonardo's *The Last Supper* with treatments of the same subject done by artists both before and since Leonardo's time. 📁

Extension
Ask students to consider what they know about the personalities of Leonardo, Michelangelo and Raphael. Then have them write a paragraph on what it would be like if one of these artists were a family member.

CLOSE
Have students discuss what they feel was the greatest contribution of Renaissance artists.

Studio LESSON

Painting
a Cityscape

Objectives

■ Complete a painting of a cityscape using flat, overlapping shapes.

■ Use light and dark values of a single hue when painting the cityscape.

■ Create the illusion of space by using a gradation of value from the light background shapes to the dark foreground shapes.

Motivator

Review the techniques artists use to create the illusion of space on a flat surface. Students might mention gradation of value and transparency, in which two overlapping shapes are seen completely and assumed to be transparent. Explain that in this studio lesson they will be required to concentrate on two techniques: overlapping shapes and gradation of value.

Aesthetics

Ask students why aestheticians concerned with the literal qualities would be inclined to respond favorably to artworks that make effective use of space-suggesting techniques.

Critiquing

Have students apply the steps of art criticism to their own artwork using the "Examining Your Work" questions on this page.

376

Studio LESSON Painting a Cityscape

Materials

- Pencil and sketch paper
- White drawing paper, 9 × 12 inches
- Tempera or acrylic paint (one hue plus white and black)
- Brushes, mixing tray, and paint cloth
- Water container

Paint a cityscape in which buildings and other objects are shown as flat, overlapping shapes. Paint these shapes with a variety of values obtained by mixing white and black with a single hue. To create an illusion of deep space, apply the darkest values to shapes in the foreground and the lightest to those in the background.

Inspiration

Examine paintings by Masaccio (Figures 16.3 and 16.4), Botticelli (Figure 16.16), and Raphael (Figure 16.1, and 16.24). What methods did these artists use to create an illusion of deep space in their pictures? What is the name given to this method of showing space? How do changes of value contribute to this effort to suggest space on a two-dimensional surface?

Process

1. Complete several sketches of city buildings. Then simplify these sketches by transforming the buildings into flat, overlapping shapes. Make certain that each of the buildings maintains some of its own unique features.
2. Reproduce the best of your sketches on the sheet of drawing paper. Make all the lines of this drawing as precise as possible.
3. Choose a single hue to paint your cityscape. Mix white and black to this hue to create a range of values. Apply the darkest value to the building or object in the immediate foreground. As you paint each object farther back in the picture, use a lighter value. The lightest value should be reserved for the building or object farthest back in the composition.

■ **FIGURE 16.26**   Student Work

Examining Your Work

Describe. Is your painting easily recognized as a cityscape? Is each building in your painting unique in terms of shape and detail, or do they all look alike? Did you use different values of a single hue to paint your picture?

Analyze. Are the building shapes in your picture flat? Do they overlap each other? Did you use a variety of different values in your painting? Do these values become gradually lighter as they are applied to buildings and objects located farther and farther back into

space? Does this method of using value gradation help create the illusion of space in your picture?

Interpret. Does your painting communicate a feeling of deep space filled with city buildings?

Judge. What is the best feature of your painting? What is its least effective feature? If you relied only on the visual qualities, do you think you could consider your picture a success? Why or why not?

ASSESSMENT

Examining Your Work. Have students apply the steps of art criticism to their cityscape painting using the questions in Examining Your Work. Students may benefit from peer review of their work on this studio lesson. Have pairs of students exchange completed artworks and take turns critiquing one another's work. This exercise will help students develop skills in listening, discussing assignments, and learning from comments by classmates. Encourage pairs to carefully apply the questions to describe, analyze, interpret, and judge the work of their partner. Have them discuss their findings and keep notes for their portfolios.

Reviewing the Facts

Lesson One

1. What invention was most responsible for helping to educate the middle classes during the Renaissance?
2. Were Renaissance artists and scholars more interested in studying the artistic accomplishments of the Medieval period or those of the Greeks and Romans?
3. Who is regarded as the first important artist of the Italian Renaissance?
4. Name the graphic system, based on geometry and developed during the Renaissance, that gave artists a method for creating the illusion of depth on a flat surface.

Lesson Two

5. Refer to Piero della Francesca's *The Baptism of Christ* (Figure 16.10 on page 362). How is the main figure made to look most important?
6. Who was the greatest sculptor of the Early Renaissance? What quality did his sculptures exhibit?
7. Name the artist who is given credit for inventing the system of linear perspective.

Lesson Three

8. List six fields, other than painting, that Leonardo da Vinci studied.
9. Who painted the *Mona Lisa* and how long did he work on it?
10. What does the word *Pietà* mean?

Thinking Critically

1. **ANALYZE.** Look at Masaccio's *The Holy Trinity* (Figure 16.3 on page 355). Then refer to the techniques that create the illusion of depth on pages 38–39 in Chapter 2. Identify the techniques that Masaccio has used.
2. **EVALUATE.** Artists can make objects in their pictures look like they are far away by painting them bluer, lighter, and duller. Locate examples of this use of atmospheric, or aerial, perspective. Explain why this technique is appropriately named. Compare your choices with those made by other members of your class.

 R T S U R C ARTSOURCE **MUSIC.** Use *Performing Arts Handbook* page 587 to find out about the Renaissance singing style of Diana Zaslove.

CAREERS IN Art Read about a career as a video game designer, where you might use what you have learned about perspective, in *Careers in Art Handbook*, page 604.

interNET CONNECTION Visit Glencoe Art Online at *www.glencoe.com/sec/art*. Investigate the works and lives of Renaissance artists.

Technology Project

Linear Perspective

Linear perspective, perfected during the Renaissance, reflects the sense of reality experienced from our point of view, at eye level. The entire picture plane is constructed as a series of lines, known as guidelines, that converge at one or more vanishing points. These guidelines are able to create the illusion of three-dimensional space displayed on the two-dimensional picture plane of a computer monitor.

1. With a pencil and ruler, first make a sketch of the composition of a painting of your choice. Using the linear perspective diagram on page 356 as a guide, construct a diagram of the linear perspective system that you think the artist used.

2. Then, using a computer draw program, draw this perspective as a diagram on your computer. Choose a tool in the program that allows you to set anchor or end points, then connect them with a straight line. Use a stylus or computer drawing pen if available.
To proceed:
   a. Following your sketched diagram, first create a straight line to establish a horizon line.
   b. Place one or two points on the horizon line to set your vanishing point(s).
   c. Next, create the guidelines that radiate from the vanishing point toward you, the viewer.
   d. Align vertical lines of walls, edges, and doors.
   e. Connect horizontal lines to indicate the edges of the ground, floors, or ceiling.
3. Print out and examine your computer diagram.

Reviewing the Facts

1. Gutenberg's printing press made books widely available.
2. Greeks and Romans.
3. Masaccio is considered the first important artist of the Renaissance.
4. Linear perspective.
5. The figure of Christ is a solid form placed in the center of the picture.
6. Donatello; his sculptures were famous for their life-like qualities.
7. Filippo Brunelleschi.
8. Any six: architecture, math, anatomy, literature, poetry, geology, botany, hydraulics.
9. Leonardo; 16 years.
10. Pietà is the name given to a picture or sculpture of the Virgin Mary mourning over the dead body of Christ.

Thinking Critically

1. Techniques include: overlapping shapes; making distant shapes smaller; placing distant shapes higher in the painting; using greater detail on closer shapes; slanting lines of shapes to make them appear to recede into space.
2. Answers, which will vary, should reflect an understanding of material covered in the chapter.

 ## Teaching the Technology Project

As an option to the design project above, have students import the file of their computer diagram to a Paint program. Instruct students to select a paintbrush and airbrush tool. They can add color to the original drawing that shows changes in value, from foreground to background. Have them compare it to the first diagram.

 R T S U R C ARTSOURCE Assign the feature in the *Performing Arts Handbook,* page 587.

CAREERS IN ART If time permits, have interested students investigate the career information in the *Careers in Art Handbook,* page 604.

interNET CONNECTION Have students go online and learn more about artists on preselected Web sites with the Internet activity for this chapter.

Fifteenth-Century Art in Northern Europe

ADDITIONAL CHAPTER RESOURCES

Activities

- 📁 Advanced Studio Activity 17
- 📁 Application 17
- 🖱 Chapter 17 Internet Activity
- 📁 Studio Activity 23

Fine Art Resources

📌 **Transparency**

Art in Focus Transparency 22

Petrus Christus. *St. Eloy (Eligius) in His Shop.*

🖼 **Fine Art Print**

Focus on World Art Print 17

Jan van Eyck. *Ghent Altarpiece.*

Assessment

- 📁 Chapter 17 Test
- 📁 Performance Assessment

Multimedia Resources

- Artsource® Performing Arts Package
- National Gallery Laser Disc
- National Museum of Women in the Arts CD-ROM
- Arts & Entertainment Videos

NATIONAL STANDARDS FOR ARTS EDUCATION

The National Standards for Arts Education provide guidelines for grade-appropriate competency in the visual arts. The Content Standards for grades 9–12 are:

1. Understanding and applying media, techniques, and processes.
2. Using knowledge of structures and functions.
3. Choosing and evaluating a range of subject matter, symbols, and ideas.
4. Understanding the visual arts in relation to history and cultures.
5. Reflecting upon and assessing the characteristics and merits of their work and the work of others.
6. Making connections between visual arts and other disciplines.

Listed below are the National Standards for the Visual Arts addressed in this chapter. For a breakdown of the categories listed under each content standard, refer to the *Reproducible Lesson Plans* booklet in the TCR.

1. (a, b) **2.** (b) **3.** (a, b) **4.** (a, b) **5.** (b) **6.** (b)

🕐 **Out of Time?** If time does not permit teaching this chapter in its entirety, you may wish to preview the artwork and captions with students. Scan the heads in each lesson with students. Discuss the Looking Closely features and examine Symbolism in Flemish Art on page 383.

HANDBOOK MATERIAL

Diana Zaslove
(page 587)

CAREERS IN Art

Video Game Designer *(page 594)*

Beyond the Classroom

For information on Community Arts Partnerships, musical arts, and integration of the arts, the California Institute of the Arts has student and teacher resources available on their Internet home page. Find them by visiting our Web site at *www.glencoe.com/sec/art.*

Fifteenth-Century Art in Northern Europe

Fifteenth-Century Art in Northern Europe

INTRODUCE

Chapter Overview

CHAPTER 17 discusses developments in northern European painting during the Renaissance.

Lesson One covers the origins of oil painting and the achievements of Jan van Eyck.

Lesson Two deals with the works of Rogier van der Weyden and Hugo van der Goes.

Studio Lesson direct students to create an expanded detail drawing and design a visual symbol.

Art & Mathematics

Ask students to explain what they already know about the use of perspective. Ask students to consider why linear perspective remained "one of the foundations of European painting" only until the late nineteenth century: What developments in painting changed the importance of linear perspective?

Art & Mathematics ■ FIGURE 17.1

Geometric perspective, as shown in Campin's work, presented some problems for artists up until this period. The use of perspective was being perfected by Italian artists at the time this picture was done. Brunelleschi invented geometric or linear perspective in painting, which was explained by Piero della Francesca in 1435 in his book entitled *On Painting*. This method of creating the illusion of space on a flat surface remained one of the foundations of European painting until the late nineteenth century.

Robert Campin (Master of Flémalle), *Merode Altarpiece, The Annunciation* (Central panel). 1425–28. Oil on wood. 64.1 × 63.2 cm (25¼ × 24⅞"). The Metropolitan Museum of Art, New York, New York. Cloisters Collection, 1956. (56.70)

378

CHAPTER 17 RESOURCES

Teacher's Classroom Resources

 Advanced Studio Activity 17

 Application 17

  Chapter 17 Internet Activity

  Studio Activity 23

Assessment

  Chapter 17 Test

  Performance Assessment

Fine Art Resources

  Art in Focus Transparency 22
  Petrus Christus. *St. Eloy in His Shop.*

  Focus on World Art Print 17
  Jan van Eyck. *Ghent Altarpiece.*

The fifteenth century saw commerce and industry thrive in northern Europe, just as they did in Italy. This contributed to the growth of cities and a vigorous middle class. The people of this new middle class did not exhibit the same interest in the spiritual life as had their medieval ancestors. Their thoughts were fixed on the here and now rather than on an eternal life after death. They placed their faith in a future on earth and preferred to enjoy the pleasures and material possessions of this world instead of preparing for spiritual rewards in the next. Northern European art reflected this practical attitude. Artists did, however, represent spiritual feelings through symbolism. Symbols and emotions were expressed in literature and theatre, as well as in secular and religious music.

Introducing the Chapter

Have students bring in objects that symbolize something important to them (for example, a lucky article of clothing). They should explain what the item symbolizes and why it has that meaning for them. Then tell students that, as they study this chapter, they will examine symbols used in works of art.

A R T S O U R C E **Music** While studying this chapter, use *Performing Arts Handbook* page 587 to help students see how Diana Zaslove's interpretation of Renaissance songs breaks away from religious music, combining poetry and music for the purpose of expressing a variety of emotions, especially aspects of love.

YOUR Portfolio

Create a still life demonstrating visual textures for your portfolio. Assemble a collection of objects of varying size and textures. Possibilities include coarse or smooth fabric, clay pottery, a mirror, a baseball, and a sea shell. Make a still life arrangement of the objects on a table. Sketch the arrangement, noticing what techniques are necessary to reproduce textures. Now use a strong light to illuminate the still life. Describe how the added light affects visual textures. What adjustments in your techniques must you make to accommodate the new textures? Sketch the still life again, this time capturing the new textures.

Focus ON THE ARTS

THEATRE

Italian Commedia dell'Arte troupes wore symbolic costumes and masks, improvised lines, and made extensive use of pantomime. The English Masque involved pageantry, songs, and elaborate dances.

LITERATURE

Satire became a popular form of literature as a way of pointing out the follies of society. Dutch scholar Desiderius Erasmus was a humanist who blended a rational outlook with religious feeling in his satires.

MUSIC

Dutch composers Johannes Ockegham and Josquin de Prez wrote masses and psalm compositions with melodic voice parts. Their complex style influenced both secular and religious composers.

379

Focus ON THE ARTS

Tell the class that Johannes Ockeghem (Ock'-eh-gomm) and other composers from the Netherlands revolutionized music. They introduced "polyphony," four voices, each singing a separate tune, that blend. Our modern music is different; it is based on chords. Ockeghem and others inserted symbols into their work, just like painters did. To demonstrate, play "Alma Redemptoris Mater." Pass around a copy of the words that come with the recording (in Latin and English). Ask students to follow the words and make a mark any time the music sounds unusual or appears to mirror the words' meaning.

DEVELOPING A PORTFOLIO

Self-Evaluation. Peer review helps students establish priorities for revision of their work through feedback from other students. When expected to articulate responses to the work of others, basic concepts are reinforced and a student learns to trust his or her artistic insights. Often a cooperative environment encourages a mutual exchange of ideas that help students progress at an accelerated rate. Peer review is also a source of ongoing reflection that refines judgment. Students often see the relationship between ideas and design in another's work more easily than in their own; likewise, suggestions from peers are sometimes less intimidating than from teachers.

Renaissance Painting in Northern Europe

Focus

Lesson Objectives

After studying this lesson, students will be able to:
- Explain why the change from medieval to a more modern style occurred more slowly in northern Europe than in Italy.
- Discuss the development of oil-painting.
- Discuss the precision and color that mark the works of Jan van Eyck.

Building Vocabulary

Point out that two of the Vocabulary terms—*tempera* and *oil paints*—have appeared in earlier chapters. Have students create a Venn diagram showing the relationship of these terms.

Motivator

On the board, write and circle the phrases *Renaissance* art and *International style*. Direct students' attention to the chapter-opening painting (Figure 17.1), and ask them to identify features of the work reminiscent of each approach to painting. Create two word webs using the features students identify.

Introducing the Lesson

Bring to class several contemporary photos of couples at their wedding ceremonies. Direct students' attention to the painting in Figure 17.4 (page 383). Have students compare the photos with this wedding portrait. Tell students they will learn about the culture of the period and their impact on art.

Renaissance Painting in Northern Europe

Vocabulary
- tempera
- gesso
- oil paints

Artists to Meet
- Jan van Eyck
- Robert Campin (Master of Flémalle)

Discover
After completing this chapter, you will be able to:
- Explain the effects of the introduction of oil paints.
- Discuss the precision and color that mark the works of Jan van Eyck.

*T*hroughout the fifteenth century, most artists in northern Europe (Figure 17.2) remained true to the traditions of the Late Medieval period. This was especially true in architecture. The progress of painting in the North during this time was more complicated, however.

Continuation of the International Style

The change from a medieval art style to a more modern art style began later and progressed more slowly in northern Europe than it did in Italy. While Italian artists were busy studying the classical art of ancient Greece and Rome, Northern artists further developed the International style. For this reason, their paintings continued to show a great concern for accurate and precise details.

Artists spent countless hours painting a delicate design on a garment, the leaves on a tree, or the wrinkles on a face. At the same time, symbolism, which was so important in Gothic art, grew even more important. Many of the details included in a picture had special meanings. For example, a single burning candle meant the presence of God, and a dog was a symbol of loyalty.

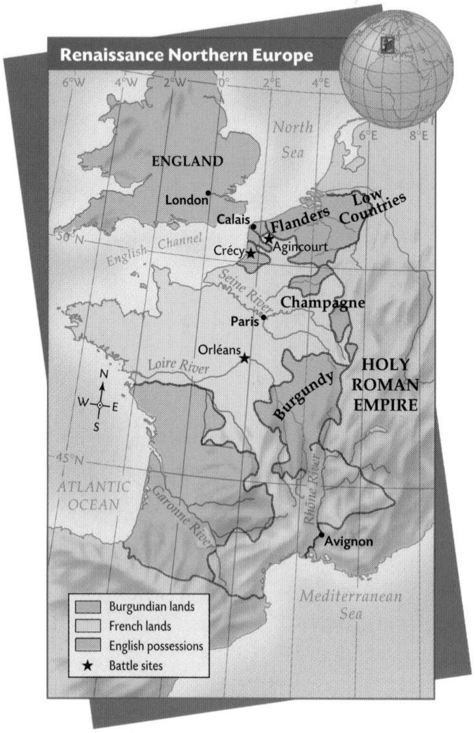

New Developments in Painting Techniques

Up to this time, European artists were accustomed to using **tempera,** *a paint made of dry pigments, or colors, which are mixed with a binding material.* A binder is a liquid that holds together the grains of pigment in paint. Typically, this binder was egg yolk, although gum and casein were also used.

Tempera paint was applied to a surface, often a wooden panel, which had been prepared with a smooth coating of **gesso,** *a mixture of glue and a white pigment such as plaster, chalk, or white clay.* This painting method, which produced a hard, brilliant surface, was used for many medieval altarpieces.

Development of Oil Paints

In the fifteenth and sixteenth centuries, the Northern artists' concern for precision and detail was aided by the development in Flanders of a new oil-painting technique. **Oil paints** consist of *a mixture of dry pigments with oils, turpentine, and sometimes varnish.*

MAP SKILLS
■ **FIGURE 17.2** During this time, the Hundred Years' War between England and France was fought over conflicting claims to the land areas shown on this map. **Find a map of present-day France. Compare the area controlled by England and France today to what they controlled in the 1400s.**

LESSON ONE RESOURCES

Teacher's Classroom Resources
- Art and Humanities 27
- Cooperative Learning 26
- Enrichment Activity 33
- Reproducible Lesson Plan 38
- Reteaching Activity 38
- Study Guide 38

With such a mixture, artists could produce either a transparent, smooth glaze, or a thick, richly textured surface.

The change from tempera paint to oil was not a sudden one. At first, oil paints were used as transparent glazes placed over tempera underpaintings. The solid forms of figures and objects in a painting were modeled with light and dark values of tempera. Oil glazes were then applied over them, adding a transparent, glossy, and permanent surface. Later, artists abandoned the use of an underpainting and applied the oil paint directly to the canvas, building up a thick, textured surface in the process.

Advantages of Oil Paints

One of the more important advantages of the oil-painting technique was that it slowed down the drying time. This gave artists the chance to work more slowly, so they had time to include more details in their pictures, time that Italian artists working in fresco, did not have. Also, the layers of transparent glazes added a new brilliance to the colors, so that finished paintings looked as if they were lit from within.

Robert Campin (c. 1378–1444)

One of the first artists to use the new medium of oil paint was the Master of Flémalle, now identified by most scholars as the Flemish painter, Robert Campin. His most famous work, the *Merode Altarpiece*, consists of three panels showing, from left to right, the donors of the work kneeling in a garden, Mary receiving the news that she is to be the mother of Christ from the angel Gabriel (Figure 17.1, page 378), and Joseph working in his carpentry shop (Figure 17.3). Attention to detail and the use of familiar contemporary settings noted in this work are typical of Campin's religious pictures. Many of the objects shown are not only realistically rendered but possess symbolic meaning as well. For example, Joseph is seen constructing mousetraps. This symbolized the belief that Christ was the bait with which Satan would be trapped.

■ **FIGURE 17.3** This and other works are judged by experts to be the work of Robert Campin. Along with Jan van Eyck, he is credited with breaking away from the elegant International style. What features suggest that this artist was concerned with making his painting look real?

Robert Campin (Master of Flémalle). *Joseph in His Workshop*, Right panel from *The Mérode Altarpiece*. c. 1425–28. Oil on wood. 64.5 × 27.3 cm (25³/₈ × 10³/₄″). The Metropolitan Museum of Art, New York, New York. Cloisters Collection, 1956. (56.70)

TEACH
Using Map Skills

Direct students' attention to the map of Renaissance Northern Europe, Figure 17.2. Explain that this map shows the area of northern Europe that was affected by the more modern approach of the International style and the use of realism. As students look at the illustrations in this chapter, ask them to locate on the map the cities or countries where the featured artists lived and worked. Assign individual students to research: the relationship between Flanders and Belgium; the history of Luxembourg during the fifteenth century. Have these students report their findings to the class.

Aesthetics

Direct students' attention to the painting in Figure 17.3. Have them note the artist's use of perspective. What would an aesthetician of the imitationalist school say about this work? How would an aesthetician of the formalist school view it?

Studio Skills

Explain that the development of different paint formulas has largely been a matter of trial and error on the part of artists and scientists, a situation that continues to the present day. Have students bring to class a variety of foods and other substances that could be used as part or all of a paint formula. The goal is not necessarily to select ingredients that will yield a perfect product but to guide students in evaluating the advantages and disadvantages of various paint media. Have students test their "paints" on a variety of surfaces such as paper, canvas, and wood and note their results. Have students share their conclusions.

Technology ▌

National Gallery of Art Videodisc Use the following images as examples of more works by artists introduced in this lesson.

Jan van Eyck
The Annunciation

Search Frame 576

Jan van Eyck
The Annunciation

Search Frame 577

Jan van Eyck
The Annunciation

Search Frame 580

Use Glencoe's *Correlation Bar Code Guide to the National Gallery of Art* to locate more artworks.

Critical Thinking

Prepare a demonstration in which two stretched canvas panels are painted with oil paints. Prime one of the panels with gesso and leave the other panel unprimed. After oil paints have been applied and have had time to dry, have students observe the panels and discuss the long- and short-term effects of not using gesso.

Art Criticism

Have students closely examine Figure 17.4, especially the bride. Point out that, despite van Eyck's keen interest in realism, he has idealized certain features of the woman. In particular, he has given her tiny hands and a high forehead; the second of these was an especially prized characteristic among fifteenth-century ladies of that region. Ask: What might have been the artist's motivation for idealizing these features?

Did You Know?

Jan van Eyck's portrait of Giovanni Arnolfini is thought to have inspired Sir John Tenniel's picture of the Mad Hatter in *Alice's Adventures in Wonderland.*

The Flemish Influence: Jan van Eyck (c. 1390–1441)

The artist usually given credit for developing this new painting technique was the Flemish master, Jan van Eyck (yahn van **ike**). The art of Jan van Eyck and his successors, Rogier van der Weyden and Hugo van der Goes, made Flanders the art center of northern Europe. Throughout the fifteenth century, the art produced by Flemish artists was a great influence on other artists in Europe, from Germany to Spain.

Although Jan van Eyck was a product of the late Middle Ages, he went beyond the older traditions of the exceedingly detailed International style to introduce a new painting tradition. Like other Northern artists, he used the International style as a starting point.

The Arnolfini Wedding
■ FIGURE 17.4

One of van Eyck's best-known works is a painting of two people standing side by side in a neat, comfortably furnished room (Figure 17.4). Who are these people and what are they doing? The man is Giovanni Arnolfini, and the woman at his side is his bride.

Giovanni Arnolfini was a rich Italian merchant who lived in Flanders. It is probable that he became wealthy by selling silk brocade and other luxury goods; he may also have worked as a banker. When Giovanni Arnolfini decided to marry Jeanne de Chenay in 1434, he looked for the best artist available to paint a picture of their wedding. He found that artist in Jan van Eyck, who made him, his bride, and their wedding immortal.

Time & Place CONNECTIONS

Northern Renaissance
c. 1400–1500

MECHANICAL CLOCK. During the late 1400s, mechanical clocks like this were in use. They worked with weights, had only one hand and some had a bell that struck on the hour.

Photograph courtesy of The Time Museum, Rockford, Illinois.

PLUMED HATS. The Renaissance opened the door for more decorative fashion. People dressed in fancier clothing. Wide brimmed hats were worn by both men and women, and were often trimmed with feather plumes.

Activity **Listing Artifacts.** The new middle class was concerned more with commerce and material goods than ever before. If you lived during this time you would be wearing the style of the day and would want the latest in home furnishings and decoration. What other items besides the clock pictured here might be available to you? Look at the details in the artworks in this chapter for ideas, research technological advances during this period, and make yourself a shopping list.

Time & Place CONNECTIONS

Northern Renaissance

Have students examine the images in the Time & Place feature and assign the activity. Discuss with students the changing focus of middle class Europeans toward industry during this time. Point out details of furnishings and artifacts, especially in the room in Figure 17.4. Encourage them to research the period for more details about the lifestyle of the times. After each student has created his shopping list, have groups share and compare their ideas.

Symbolism in Flemish *Art*

 1 The wedding couple solemnly faces the witnesses to the ceremony. Giovanni raises his right hand as if he is saying an oath, while his bride places her right hand in his left. Both figures look real, but frozen in their poses.

 4 The single burning candle is a symbol of God's presence.

2 The mirror shows a reflection of the room, the backs of Giovanni and his bride, and two other people standing in the doorway. These two people face the bride and groom and are probably the witnesses to the exchange of vows.

DETAIL: Mirror and inscription.

5 Innocence is suggested by the fruit on the table and windowsill.

6 The couple have removed their shoes as a sign that a holy event is taking place.

3 Above the mirror is a Latin inscription that reads, "Jan van Eyck was here."

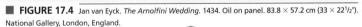

■ **FIGURE 17.4** Jan van Eyck. *The Arnolfini Wedding.* 1434. Oil on panel. 83.8 × 57.2 cm (33 × 22½"). National Gallery, London, England.

 7 The little dog represents the loyalty that the husband and wife pledge to each other.

Art History

Ask students how an art historian who had never heard of Jan van Eyck would go about placing Figure 17.4 within its historical context. As students isolate relevant details and clues, list these on the board. Have students consult a history of fashion and a book on the history of furniture to confirm their assumptions.

Aesthetics

Have students examine Figure 17.5 (page 384) and describe what art historians mean when they call van Eyck's style highly realistic. Is there more than one type of realism in art? Have students look through the text and other art resources to identify as many forms of realism as possible. What in Figure 17.5 might be considered romanticized, idealized, pre-arranged, or otherwise lacking in realism?

Symbolism in Flemish *Art*

Have students examine the painting in Figure 17.4. Encourage students to speculate on the meaning of various details, such as the shoes and the dog. Ask: How does an understanding of these symbols affect your appreciation of the artwork? Jan van Eyck's painting was one of the first examples in art of the effects of atmospheric diffusion of light. Have students trace the effects of light in the painting, beginning at the light source (the window on the left), continuing with the soft illumination of the back wall, and noting finally the way light is used to accentuate the bride.

Art History

Display a reproduction of the full Ghent Altarpiece, which is widely reproduced in art history books and works on fifteenth-century art. Have students identify where Figure 17.5 fits into the plan of this complex work. Make sure students understand how the movable elements of the altarpiece can be arranged either to expose or conceal the *Adoration of the Lamb.* Ask: Does Figure 17.5 make more sense when seen in the context of the whole altarpiece, or is the weight of theological symbolism in this work (which has been called a "theological machine") too overwhelming for modern viewers?

Study Guide

Distribute *Study Guide* 38 in the TCR. Assist students in reviewing key concepts. 📁

Art and Humanities

Have students complete *Art and Humanities* 27, "Symbolism of Greek Mythology" in the TCR. In this activity, students learn how the mythology of ancient Greece exemplifies an early use of visual symbols in art. 📁

Did You Know?

Until 1563, it was customary for the Church to allow a man and a woman to exchange marriage vows in private if they chose, with no need for religious or civil officials to be present.

Adoration of the Lamb
■ **FIGURE 17.5**

Van Eyck's painting *Adoration of the Lamb* (Figure 17.5) is the central lower panel of a large (14.5 × 11 feet) altarpiece containing 12 panels. It shows angels, saints, and earthly worshipers moving through a green valley toward a sacrificial altar. A lamb, one of the symbols of Christ, stands on this altar. Blood from the lamb flows into a chalice. In the foreground is a fountain from which flows the pure water of eternal life.

This painting most likely was inspired by a Bible passage that refers to Christ as the *Paschal,* or sacrificial, Lamb. The symbolism in the picture conveys the belief that eternal salvation is possible for all because Christ sacrificed his life on the cross, and that his death made possible the water of salvation received by the faithful at baptism.

The scene is carefully organized so that the lamb is the obvious center of interest. The placement of the angels kneeling at the altar and the prophets and other worshipers around the fountain leads your eye to this center of interest. Other groups of saints and worshipers move toward it from each of the four corners of the painting.

Like Masaccio, van Eyck controls the flow of light and uses atmospheric perspective to create the illusion of deep space in his work. Unlike that in Masaccio's work, however, the light in van Eyck's painting is crystal clear. It allows you to see perfectly the color, texture, and shape of every object.

Mastery of Detail

The details in van Eyck's picture are painted with extraordinary care. Every object, no matter how small or insignificant, is given equal importance. This attention to detail enabled van Eyck to create a special kind of realism—a realism in which the color, shape, and texture of every object were painted only after long study.

■ **FIGURE 17.5** Notice how the figures have been arranged in this work. **Point to the center of interest. How is your attention directed to that center?**

Jan van Eyck. *Adoration of the Lamb,* central panel from *The Ghent Altarpiece.* 1432. Tempera and oil on wood. Cathedral St. Bavo, Ghent, Belgium.

384 **Unit Six** *Art of an Emerging Modern Europe*

COOPERATIVE LEARNING

Interviews. Divide the class into two groups. Ask the students in one group to imagine that they are reporters assigned to interview Jan van Eyck. Have each student in this group write three questions they would like to ask the artist. Students in the second group are instructed to answer these questions as they are read aloud, but they must answer them as they think van Eyck would respond. Encourage students from the second group to take turns answering the questions. When the interview is complete, open a discussion and ask students to evaluate their feelings on the accuracy of answers and to support reasons these answers were given.

In van Eyck's *Saint Gerome in His Study* (Figure 17.6), you will see how skillfully he painted even the smallest details. The books and articles on the table seem to glow softly in the mellow light. Notice the deep colors of green in the tablecloth, the reds and blues of the cloak and drapery. Even the texture in the paper, wool, leather, and glass add to the precise detail of van Eyck's work, a style that has never been equaled.

It is still not known how van Eyck was able to achieve many of his effects. Somehow, by combining a study of nature with a sensitive use of light and color, he was able to produce paintings that others could not duplicate. No painter has ever been able to match van Eyck's marvelous precision and glowing color.

■ **FIGURE 17.6** This work is rich in details. Notice the variety of textures in the objects and figures. **How many different kinds of textures can you find?**

Jan van Eyck. *Saint Gerome in His Study.* c. 1435. Oil on linen paper, mounted on oak panel. 20.6 × 13.3 cm (8¹/₈ × 5¹/₄"). The Detroit Institute of Arts, Detroit, Michigan. City of Detroit Purchase.

LESSON ONE REVIEW

Reviewing Art Facts

1. In what way did the interests of Italian artists differ from those of northern European artists during the fifteenth century?
2. Name two characteristics of the International style used widely by northern European artists.
3. What is gesso? How is it used?
4. List two advantages of oil paints over tempera.

▶ Activity... *Creating a Symbol*

The use of symbols continued to be an important part of Renaissance art in northern Europe. Artists used symbols in paintings of seemingly everyday events to convey many meanings and ideas. Study Figure 17.4 on page 383 and read about symbolism in artworks. Almost any painting from this time contains messages in the form of symbols. Many of them may be recognizable to you.

Look for other Northern Renaissance paintings that use symbols and do research to determine their meanings. Using tempera paint, create a small painting of an everyday event, using the detailed Northern Renaissance style. Make your painting more interesting and meaningful by including several symbols in your work. Display your finished work in the classroom.

ASSESS

Checking Comprehension

Have students respond to the lesson review questions. Answers are given in the box below.

Reteaching

Assign *Reteaching* 38, found in the TCR. Have students complete the activity and review their responses. 🗁

Enrichment

➤ Assign students *Enrichment* 33, "The Science of Oil Painting," in the TCR. In this worksheet, students read about the scientific research and experimentation that contributed to the discovery of oil as a painting medium. 🗁

➤ Have groups of students work together to complete *Cooperative Learning* 26, "Symbolism in Contemporary Artworks," in the TCR. 🗁

Extension

Have a student do a dramatic reading of Renaissance art historian Giorgio Vasari's 1550 account of how van Eyck experimented with an enormous number of ingredients to develop a formula for oil paint. This passage is found in Vasari's *The Lives of the Painters, Sculptors and Architects*, reprinted in 1977, by Harry N. Abrams.

CLOSE

Ask students to state briefly whether they prefer paintings that include symbols to be decoded. Ask: Do symbols make an artwork more interesting or fun to look at? Are symbols a prominent part of the visual material twentieth-century people see, such as advertisements and films?

LESSON ONE REVIEW

Answers to Reviewing Art Facts

1. Italian artists studied the classical art of ancient Greece and Rome. Northern Europeans were interested in the International style.
2. Precise details, items of symbolic meaning.
3. A mixture of glue and a white pigment such as plaster, chalk, or white clay. It was used to prepare a surface for tempera paints.
4. Slower drying time and the brilliant colors resulting from transparent glazes.

Activity...*Creating a Symbol*

Let students meet in groups to share and discuss other Northern Renaissance paintings. Have group members brainstorm lists of everyday events appropriate for their paintings and symbols that might be successfully included in those paintings.

Realism and Emotionalism

Focus

Lesson Objectives

After studying this lesson, students will be able to:
- Identify the contributions of Rogier van der Weyden.
- Describe differences in paintings done by Rogier and van Eyck.
- Identify innovations introduced by Hugo van der Goes.

Building Vocabulary

Ask students what the prefix *tri-* means, and let them give examples of familiar words with that prefix. Let them use that knowledge to speculate about the meaning of the Vocabulary term *triptych* and then refer to the Glossary for a formal definition of the word.

Motivator

Have students note the unusual shape of the painting in Figure 17.7. Ask small groups to brainstorm reasons the artist may have had for choosing this shape. Encourage groups to use clues that are readily at hand, such as the painting's title.

Introducing the Lesson

Refer students back to van Eyck's portrait of *The Arnolfini Wedding* (Figure 17.4, page 383. Inform students that the lesson they are about to read contains information on two artists of northern Europe whose approach to subject matter and emotion was often very different from that of van Eyck.

Realism and Emotionalism

Vocabulary
- triptych

Artists to Meet
- Rogier van der Weyden
- Hugo van der Goes

Discover

After completing this lesson, you will be able to:
- Describe the differences in paintings done by Jan van Eyck and Rogier van der Weyden.
- Discuss the artistic contributions of Hugo van der Goes.

*G*radually, Northern fifteenth-century art developed into a style that combined the realism of Jan van Eyck with the emotionalism and attention to design found in works done during the late Gothic period. This style is best seen in the works of another Northern artist.

Rogier van der Weyden (c. 1399–1464)

Jan van Eyck had been concerned with painting every detail with careful precision. Rogier van der Weyden (roh-**jair** van der **vy**-den) continued in this tradition, but also emphasized the emotional impact of his subject matter.

Descent from the Cross
■ **FIGURE 17.7**

Rogier's painting *Descent from the Cross* (Figure 17.7) was probably the center part of a **triptych,** *a painting on three hinged panels that can be folded together.* In this painting you see more emotion and a greater concern for organization than you find in van Eyck's pictures. Organization is achieved through the use of repeating curved axis lines. Observe how the two figures at each side of the picture bend inward and direct your attention to Christ and his mother. In the center of the picture, Christ's lifeless body forms an S curve, which is repeated in the curve of his fainting mother.

Use of Emphasis

Unlike van Eyck, van der Weyden made no attempt to create a deep space. He managed to group ten figures in this shallow space without making them seem crowded. By placing these figures on a narrow stage and eliminating a landscape behind, he forces you to focus on the drama of Christ's removal from the cross.

The figures and the action are brought very close, forcing you to take in every detail. The faces clearly differ from one another, just as the faces of real people do. Every hair, every variation of skin color and texture, and every fold of drapery are painted in with care.

Use of Emotionalism

Equal attention is given to the emotions exhibited by the different facial expressions and gestures. The entire work is a carefully designed and forceful grouping of these different emotional reactions to Christ's death. Yet, one of the most touching features is also one of the easiest to miss. The space between the two hands—Christ's right and Mary's left—suggests the void between the living and the dead.

LESSON TWO RESOURCES

Teacher's Classroom Resources

📁 Appreciating Cultural Diversity 27

📁 Reproducible Lesson Plan 39

📁 Reteaching Activity 39

📁 Study Guide 39

■ **FIGURE 17.7** The narrow stage and the elimination of background landscape help focus attention on the two central figures in this work, Christ and his mother. **Point out the repeated, curved axis lines in this work, and explain their importance.**

Rogier van der Weyden. *Descent from the Cross* (Deposition). c. 1435. Tempera and oil on wood. Approx. (7' 2⅝" × 8' 7⅛").
Museo del Prado, Madrid, Spain.

TEACH
Art Criticism

Explain that the majority of the figures in *Descent from the Cross,* Figure 17.7, are figures from the New Testament. Let students research the figures or present the following information: The man in the red tunic and hose supporting Christ's body from behind is Joseph of Arimathea. St. John, the figure at the left and dressed in red, is stooping to help the Virgin Mary, who wears a white head covering and blue gown. Nicodemus faces the viewer and wears a gold brocade robe. The anguished woman at the far right side of the painting is Mary Magdalene. The woman covering her eyes at the left side of the work is Mary, the mother of James and Joseph. Have students discuss how these identifications affect their understanding of the artwork.

Art History

Have students refer back to *The Tribute Money* (Figure 16.4, page 356). Then have them work in small groups to devise charts noting features of fifteenth-century Italian paintings, as exemplified by Masaccio's work, and of fifteenth- century northern European paintings, as exemplified by the works in this chapter. (You may wish to point out that *The Tribute Money* was painted at about the same time as van Eyck's *Adoration of the Lamb.*) Encourage groups to compare and discuss charts.

Portrait of a Lady
■ **FIGURE 17.8**

Rogier van der Weyden was a popular portrait artist. His portrait of a young woman (Figure 17.8, page 388), who is unknown to us today, was painted some 20 years after *Descent from the Cross.* The woman's face, framed by a white, starched headdress, stands out boldly against a dark background. Light flows evenly over the portrait, revealing a pleasant facial expression. The headdress is thin and transparent, allowing you to see the line of her shoulder.

Look closely at this remarkable portrait. What does the painting tell you about the personality of the woman? Do you think she was loud and outgoing, or was she quiet, shy, and devout? Van der Weyden provided you with clues. The lowered eyes, tightly locked fingers, and frail build all suggest a quiet dignity. The young woman is lost in thought, her clasped hands seemingly resting on the frame. She must have been wealthy, but a gold belt buckle and rings are the only signs of luxury. Even though we do not know this woman's name, van der Weyden has left us with a vivid impression of her.

Chapter 17 *Fifteenth-Century Art in Northern Europe* **387**

 Technology ▬▬▬

National Gallery of Art Videodisc Use the following images as examples of more works by artists introduced in this lesson.

Rogier van der Weyden
Portrait of a Lady

Search Frame 592

Use Glencoe's *Correlation Bar Code Guide to the National Gallery of Art* to locate more artworks.

Art Criticism

Have students study *Portrait of a Lady,* Figure 17.8. Ask: Is this a virtually photographic representation of this woman? What features may have been idealized? Why is her left ear placed so high on her neckline? Are her hands peculiarly small? Then ask students to look through contemporary fashion magazines and identify the subtle and not-so-subtle ways in which an "ideal" appearance is created (for example, photographs of models are airbrushed to create the illusion of flawless skin). To what extent might Rogier's motives have been the same as those of fashion photographers today?

Studio Skills

Have students examine Figure 17.8 and discuss the effects of using a black background for a bust portrait. If possible, display a reproduction of van Eyck's 1433 portrait *Man in a Red Turban* for comparison. Ask: What mood is created by a black background? How does a dark background draw attention to the face and headwear of the sitter? Have students use felt-tip markers and sheets of white paper to create self-portraits with a black background.

Aesthetics

Direct students' attention to *The Adoration of the Shepherds* in Figure 17.9. Ask students to consider how an emotionalist might react to this work. Then divide the class into two teams and have them debate the following proposition: The disproportionate size of the figures in the work detracts from its emotional appeal.

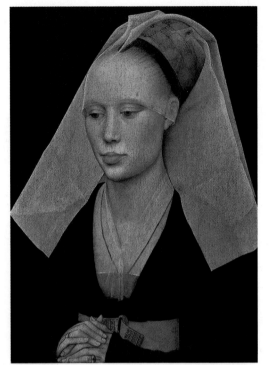

■ **FIGURE 17.8** Set against a dark background, the face—with its quiet, dignified expression—stands out in this painting. **Point out examples of both sharp and subtle contour lines in this work.**

Rogier van der Weyden. *Portrait of a Lady.* c. 1460. Oil on panel. 34 × 25.5 cm (13³/₈ × 10¹/₁₆"). National Gallery of Art, Washington, D.C. Andrew W. Mellon Collection.

Van der Weyden's Influence

Rogier van der Weyden performed a valuable service by preserving the Gothic concerns for good design and vivid emotion. Those concerns could have been lost in the rush to use van Eyck's new oil-painting technique to produce highly detailed pictures. Van der Weyden's paintings however, set an example for other artists. When he died in 1464, van der Weyden had been the most famous painter in Flanders for 30 years; his influence was second to none outside Italy.

Hugo van der Goes (1440–1482)

One of the artists who continued in the direction taken by van der Weyden was Hugo van der Goes (**hoo**-go van der **gose**). Van der Goes rose to fame as an artist in Bruges, one of the wealthiest cities in Flanders. He combined the emotionalism of van der Weyden with the realistic detail of Jan van Eyck. In addition, he made his own unique contribution: He altered nature and the proportions of people or objects when those changes added to the emotional impact of his picture.

Time & Place
CONNECTIONS

Northern Renaissance
c. 1400–1500

TEXTILES AND CLOTHING. Beautifully woven textiles were fashionable in the 1400s and 1500s. Garments were often sewn with intricate threads and rich-textured cloth acquired through trade with distant lands.

EARLIEST MAPS. Maps such as this are a record of the voyages of early explorers. Each voyage took sailors to further shores and led to progress in mapmaking during the 1500s.

Activity **Role Play.** Have one student play the owner of a trading company and another pretend to be a ship owner. The trading company owner is trying to convince the ship owner to sail to a far-off land to obtain exotic threads and fabrics. One student should use the clothing shown as an example of potential wealth, the other should use the map to explain potential dangers.

Time & Place
CONNECTIONS
Northern Renaissance

Have students examine and discuss the images in this Time & Place feature: What do these elegant garments bring to mind? What do they indicate about the daily life of those who wore them? Who wore such garments? What kinds of clothing do you think other people wore?

Who probably took most interest in maps like this one? What did they hope to learn from them? How and why were such maps updated and improved?

Have partners choose roles and plan the details they want to include in their dialogue. Then ask each pair to role-play their discussion for the rest of the class.

The Portinari Altarpiece

■ FIGURE 17.9

Van der Goes' most ambitious work was an altarpiece completed in 1476 for the Italian representative of the Medici bank in Bruges. This huge work is known as *The Portinari Altarpiece* after the name of this banker. It was sent to Florence soon after it was completed. There it was a great influence on late fifteenth-century Italian artists, who were deeply impressed by van der Goes ability to portray human character and feeling.

Emotionalism over Realism

Unlike van Eyck, van der Goes decided not to organize the space in his picture so that it would look real. Instead, he took liberties with space to increase the emotional appeal of his picture. In the central panel of his altarpiece showing *The Adoration of the Shepherds* (Figure 17.9), he tipped the floor of the stable upward. This not only gives you a better view but also brings you into the scene as a witness. Both Joseph and Mary seem strangely withdrawn, even sad, in spite of the joyous event. Van der Goes' picture succeeds in

arousing your curiosity. He makes it difficult for you not to think ahead in time to the tragic events awaiting the Christ child.

Use of Symbolism

Like Jan van Eyck, van der Goes used symbolism to enrich *The Portinari Altarpiece*. A sheaf of wheat in the foreground symbolizes the communion bread. The bouquets of iris and columbine are traditional symbols for the sorrows of Mary. The shoe at the left, like the shoes in van Eyck's *The Arnolfini Wedding*, is a reminder that the event makes this holy ground. It is a reminder of God's words to Moses from the burning bush on

LOOKING **Closely**

USE OF THE PRINICIPLES OF ART

Notice the unusual differences in the sizes of the figures. Perhaps van der Goes painted the scene as if he were seeing it in a dream or a vision, since the figures in a dream do not have to follow the rules of logic.

- **Proportion.** The angels closest to you should be much larger than the figures farther back in space. Instead, they look much smaller. The three shepherds at the right are about the same size as Mary even though they are farther away.
- **Movement.** Note how the placement of figures leads your eye throughout the work. The central figures draw your eye first. Then the highlighted faces and circular placement of the onlookers guides you to notice each group gathered around Mary and the Child.

■ FIGURE 17.9 Hugo van der Goes. *The Adoration of the Shepherds,* central panel of *The Portinari Altarpiece.* c. 1476. Approx. (8'3" × 10'). Galleria degli Uffizi, Florence, Italy.

Chapter 17 *Fifteenth-Century Art in Northern Europe* **389**

LOOKING **Closely**

Let volunteers describe the figures in *The Adoration of the Shepherds,* Figure 17.9. Ask: Are the sizes of these figures realistic? Which are closest to the viewer? Which are farthest away? How should their size reflect their positions? After a brief discussion, have students read the explanation in the Use of the Principles of Art feature.

Study Guide

Distribute *Study Guide* 39 in the TCR. Assist students in reviewing key concepts. 📁

Art and Humanities

Have students complete *Appreciating Cultural Diversity* 27, "Images of Religious Beliefs," in the TCR. In this worksheet, students read about the symbols and images of religions around the world. Students determine the ways in which these symbols have been incorporated into the artworks of different cultures. 📁

Studio Skills

To emphasize differences among painting media, have students complete a watercolor painting of one of the shepherds' faces in the detail from *The Adoration of the Shepherds* in Figure 17.10. Have students begin by making a contour sketch of the face, attempting to capture not only the prominent lines but the facial expression of the figure. In choosing paints, students should come as close as possible to the color scheme Hugo employed. When students' works are dry, encourage them to display and discuss their results.

Teacher Notes

Developing Perceptual Skills. When looking at photographs of altarpiece panels, students may easily ignore the fact that these works were part of a large, decorated altar, which in turn was just one part of the entire church interior. Remind students of the importance of reading credit lines to determine if a work is self-contained or part of a larger work. Point out that details of individual paintings are sometimes reproduced for purposes of instruction and are so marked. (An example is Figure 17.10.) Encourage students, finally, to attempt whenever possible to view works in the total context in which they were created.

ASSESS
Checking Comprehension
➤ Have students respond to the lesson review questions. Answers are given in the box below.

➤ Assign *Application 17*, "Off the Wall," in the TCR. In this activity, students are asked to imagine that various figures in the paintings in this chapter could speak. Based on imaginary quotes, students determine the artwork, the artist, and his or her contribution. 📁

Reteaching
➤ Assign Reteaching 39, found in the TCR. Have students complete the activity and review their responses. 📁

➤ Have students compare Rogier's *Descent from the Cross* (Figure 17.7, page 387) with Figure 15.15 (page 340), the Gothic relief sculpture of the *Death of the Virgin* on the Cathedral of Pamplona. Using the elements and principles of art, ask groups of students to list all of the similarities between the two works. Then have them discuss how Rogier's painting represents a departure from the Gothic style.

Extension
Have students visit a graphic design firm that specializes in "corporate identity design," the creation of logos and other materials that express the purpose and personality of a particular company. Have students compare corporate logos in terms of function and design with the symbols they learned about in this chapter.

CLOSE
Have students debate whether the artists profiled in this chapter would have been happier as photographers than as painters.

390

Mount Sinai: "Put off your shoes from your feet, for the place on which you are standing is holy ground."

The donkey and the ox have symbolic meaning, too. The donkey—busily eating and too stupid to understand the meaning

■ **FIGURE 17.10** Hugo van der Goes. *The Adoration of the Shepherds*, (detail).

of Christ's birth—symbolizes people who fail to recognize Christ as the savior. The ox, solemnly surveying the scene, represents faithful Christians.

Use of Expression
More than anything else, the behavior and expressions of the three shepherds set this painting apart from other Nativity scenes (Figure 17.10). Van der Goes's shepherds are not saints or angels or elegant noblemen. They are ragged peasants from the lowest level of society. Each shepherd shows his surprise at finding himself a witness to this grand and glorious event. One kneeling shepherd clasps his hands reverently. The other kneeling shepherd spreads his hands in wonder. The standing shepherd presses forward to peer over their heads, his mouth open in amazement. With these shepherds, van der Goes presents a new kind of piety—the piety expressed by the ordinary uneducated people of the world, the piety based on blind faith rather than on knowledge and understanding.

The art of Hugo van der Goes marks the end of a period. The innovations of Jan van Eyck and Rogier van der Weyden began to lose ground by the end of the fifteenth century. They were replaced by new ideas spreading northward from Renaissance Italy.

LESSON TWO REVIEW

Reviewing Art Facts
1. How do Rogier van der Weyden's paintings differ from those of Jan van Eyck?
2. In his painting *Descent from the Cross* (Figure 17.7, page 387), what does van der Weyden achieve by placing the figures on a narrow stage without a landscape behind them?
3. Describe one way Hugo van der Goes altered nature to add to the emotional impact in his painting *The Adoration of the Shepherds* (Figure 17.9, page 389).
4. What caused the innovations of Northern artists to lose ground by the end of the fifteenth century?

▶ Activity... *Developing a Time Line*
During the time in which Northern artists Rogier van der Weyden and Hugo van der Goes were creating their artworks, other parts of the world were undergoing great change. Look at the credit lines for artworks included in this chapter and study the dates. Can you name other important events that took place during this time?

Work in teams to find as much information as possible within an agreed-upon time span. Using a long strip of paper, construct a time line with the dates 1400–1500 listed. Note at least five historical or cultural developments on your time line. Compare your team's effort with those of other teams in your class. Which team identified the most events?

LESSON TWO REVIEW

Answers to Reviewing Art Facts
1. Rogier's paintings exhibit more emotion and a greater organization than van Eyck's.
2. Viewers focus their attention on the drama of Christ's removal from the cross.
3. The floor of the stable appears tipped upward; he distorted the sizes of the figures.

4. They were replaced by new ideas spreading northward from Renaissance Italy.

Activity...*Developing a Time Line*
Have students work in cooperative learning groups to complete the Activity. Encourage group members to consult a variety of resources and to learn about events in various parts of the world. Students might illustrate their time lines.

Complete a highly detailed and precise pencil drawing by starting with a small detail found on an interesting and intricate object. Your drawing will expand in all directions from this starting point until it runs off the paper on all sides. A complex assortment of values, shapes, lines, and textures will illustrate every detail as accurately as possible.

Materials

- Pencil
- White drawing paper, 9 × 12 inches or larger

Inspiration

Study closely the paintings by Jan van Eyck and Rogier van der Weyden illustrated in this chapter. Are you inclined to like pictures like these? If so, why do you like them? What did both of these artists do to make their pictures look so lifelike? What new painting technique enabled them to do this?

Process

1. Bring to class an interesting and complicated object to draw. Among the things you might consider are a kitchen appliance; an old, laced boot; a kerosene lantern; a piece of complex machinery.
2. Beginning at or near the center of your paper, draw one part of the object as accurately as possible. Maintain precision as you add each new detail to the drawing, allowing it to "grow" in all directions until it reaches all four edges of the paper. The shapes, lines, and textures in your drawing should be complex, reflecting your effort to illustrate the intricate nature of the object you are drawing. Use both abrupt and gradual changes of value to suggest three-dimensional forms and show shadows. Draw slowly and carefully, creating on paper what your eye observes after a close examination of every detail in the object before you.
3. Exhibit your drawing, along with those by other members of your class.

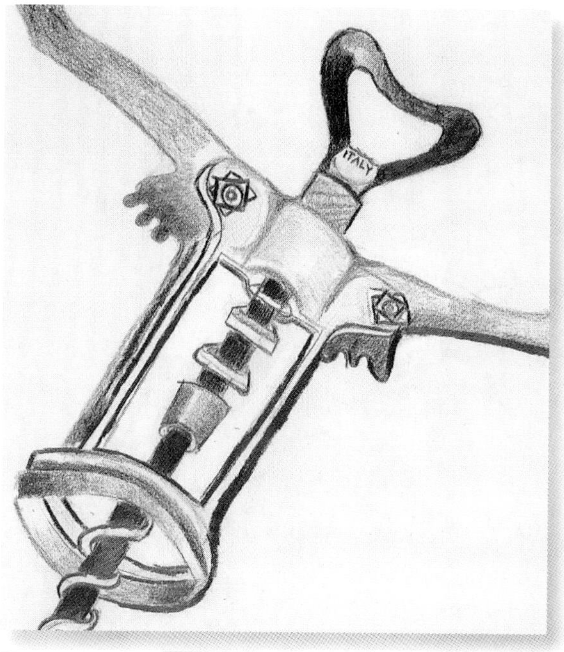

■ **FIGURE 17.11** Student Work

Examining Your Work

Describe. Is your drawing accurate and precise in every detail? Does it look like the object you selected to draw? Point to the detail on this object that you used as your starting point.

Analyze. Did you use a complex assortment of values, shapes, lines, and textures in your drawing? Do these elements contribute to the realistic appearance you were seeking?

Interpret. What adjective would you use to describe your drawing? What adjectives do others use when describing your drawing?

Judge. Limiting yourself to a consideration of the literal qualities only, is your drawing successful? What was the most important thing you learned from this studio experience?

391

ASSESSMENT

Peer Review. Once students have completed the project, including their assessment of their own work, let them work with partners to reconsider and evaluate the choices they made. Partners should respond to questions such as these: How appropriate was the object I chose to draw? What other objects would have been good subjects for this draw-

ing? Would my drawing have been more successful if I had chosen a different starting point? What part of the object might have been better? Should I have used greater variety of values? Shapes? Lines? Textures? How could I have improved that variety? With what effects? What could I have done to improve the details at the edges of my drawing?

Objectives

- Complete a highly detailed, precise pencil drawing of an interesting and intricate object.
- Expand the drawing in all directions from a starting point representing a small detail in the object.
- Use a complex assortment of values, shapes, lines, and textures.

Motivator

Students should develop the habit of keeping their eyes open for possible subjects to use in their art. They may find interesting subjects in the most unusual places—in a garage, basement, tool box, hardware store, or beneath the hood of an automobile. Instruct students to keep this in mind as they conduct a search for "an interesting and complicated object" to draw in this studio lesson.

Aesthetics

Instruct students to examine Jan van Eyck's painting *Adoration of the Lamb* (Figure 17.5, page 384). Inform them that some writers, when discussing van Eyck's work, indicate that he faithfully reproduced every detail. Ask students if they agree completely with that statement. Ask them to point to things in the artwork to support their decision.

Critiquing

Have students apply the steps of art criticism to their own artwork, using the "Examining Your Work" questions on this page.

Designing a Visual Symbol

Objectives

■ Design and construct a container for a familiar household product.
■ Design the container to serve as a visual symbol for the product within.
■ Use simplified colors, forms, and shapes.
■ Use bold contrasts of hue, value, and intensity.

Motivator

Display several packages of different products in class, some well designed and others poorly designed. Instruct students to point out the more successful ones. Ask them to provide reasons for their choices. Move some of the packages farther away from students and ask them to identify the ones that stand out best from a distance. Ask if this should be an important consideration for the designer. If so, why?

Studio Skills

Tell students that a great deal of planning and experimentation will be necessary to arrive at a design for a container with an original shape. Explain that a box cannot be regarded as original and is not acceptable. Point out that part of the challenge involves the construction of a container with the proper dimensions to hold exactly the items that will go into it. Once work is underway, students may not add to or subtract from these items.

Critiquing

Have students apply the steps of art criticism to their own artwork, using the "Examining Your Work" questions on this page.

Materials

● A familiar household product to be repackaged
● Pencil and sketch paper
● Mat board
● Scissors and/or paper-cutting knife
● White glue
● Tempera or acrylic paint
● Brushes, mixing trays, and paint cloth
● Water container

Design and construct with mat board a three-dimensional container for a familiar household product. This container not only holds the product, but it also serves as a visual symbol for that product. Along with the name, it will help others identify the product quickly. Use simplified colors, forms, and shapes. Draw attention to the package by using bold contrasts of hue, value, and intensity.

Inspiration

Examine the works by Jan van Eyck and Hugo van der Goes in this chapter. The works of both artists include a great many symbols. Are you aware of the different uses of symbols today? Are there certain symbols that you automatically associate with specific products? What are those symbols?

■ **FIGURE 17.12** Student Work

Process

1. Bring to class a small package containing a familiar product, such as toothpicks or dry cereal.
2. Make several pencil sketches of a new container for your product. This container must act as a visual symbol for the product inside, so consider carefully its overall shape and the images placed on this shape. The name of the product must be prominently displayed on the container.
3. When you have a satisfactory design, construct the container. Cut sections of mat board to the desired shapes and glue these together to make the three-dimensional container. Remember to include a lid of some kind so the container can be opened easily and closed securely.
4. When your container has been assembled, use tempera or acrylic to paint it. Use simplified colors and shapes; do not focus on small details that cannot be seen from a distance.
5. Place your product in the container. It should fit with no room to spare.

Examining Your Work

Describe. Did you design and construct a three-dimensional container for a familiar household product? Does the product you brought to class fit in this container?

Analyze. Does your design include simplified colors, forms, and shapes? Did you use bold contrasts of hue, value, and intensity? Do these help draw attention to your container?

Interpret. Do you think your package is an effective symbol for the product inside? Can others readily identify this product by looking at the package, or must they rely on the name to identify it?

Judge. Do you think your container can be regarded as a successful symbol for a particular product? What could you have done to make it more effective? What is the most pleasing feature of your design?

ASSESSMENT

Examining Your Work. After students have used the "Examining Your Work" questions to assess their own product containers, have them meet in peer-review groups to compare and discuss their containers. Ask students to present their own containers to the rest of their group, identifying the aspects of the project they consider most successful and explaining how they think they could have improved their work.

Then suggest that group members select one product and its container and, together, create an ad campaign for that newly packaged product using billboard designs, radio ads, or television commercials.

Reviewing the Facts

Lesson One

1. In the works of fifteenth-century northern European painters, what does a single burning candle mean?

2. Until the fifteenth century, what type of paints did European artists use?

3. Why would an artist using oil paint be more inclined to include small details than an artist painting a fresco?

4. What two effects are especially remarkable in the paintings of Jan van Eyck?

Lesson Two

5. Does Rogier van der Weyden's painting *Descent from the Cross* give the illusion of deep space or shallow space? What does this treatment of space add to the work?

6. How did van der Weyden influence other painters in Europe?

7. What was unusual about the three shepherds that Hugo van der Goes included in his painting *The Adoration of the Shepherds?*

8. What gives van der Goes's painting *The Adoration of the Shepherds* a dreamlike quality?

Thinking Critically

1. **ANALYZE.** Discuss the color scheme of Jan van Eyck's painting *The Arnolfini Wedding* (Figure 17.4, page 383). Consider the following in your discussion: complementary colors, intensity of the colors, and value contrasts.

2. **EVALUATE.** Look again at *The Adoration of the Shepherds* by Hugo van der Goes (Figure 17.9, page 389). Explain the success, or lack of success, of the painting from the perspective of each of the art theories: imitationalism, formalism, and emotionalism.

> ▲ R T
> S ● U
> R C ■ **MUSIC.** Use the *Performing Arts Handbook,* page 587 to learn how Diana Zaslove's singing style reflects Northern Renaissance ideas.

■ CAREERS IN If you enjoy studying or creating art, read about a fascinating art-related career opportunity in the *Careers in Art Handbook,* page 594.

> *inter*NET
> CONNECTION Visit Glencoe Art Online at *www.glencoe.com/sec/art*. Explore more images from the artists of the Northern Renaissance. Discover the meanings of symbolism in artworks.

Technology Project
Designing a Triptych

The tradition of the triptych, which had its beginnings in the Early Christian period, continued to be an important part of Renaissance art in northern Europe. The triptych is a work of art painted or carved on one central panel with two hinged wings that could close shut. It often served as an altarpiece in many churches. As with most artwork of the medieval era, the content of the artwork depicted on the triptych was spiritual in nature and filled with religious symbols. One of the most famous, the Ghent Altarpiece, is an excellent example of the complexity of these works of art.

1. Imagine you are a designer with the task of designing a modern triptych. Your triptych might function as a decorative work of art for a specific type of room, or as a screen to divide a room. You may want to adopt a concept to unify each of the three panels. For example, you may choose an overall theme of "Time," with each of the three panels standing for "Past," "Present," and "Future."

2. Collect several images that you choose to use in your triptych design. Find images on the Internet, copy the images and save them to a file for later use. You may scan images found in books, prints or other sources.

3. Create a plan for your triptych using a computer program with a draw function.

4. Construct a small model of your triptych using cardboard, mat board, paint, paper, or other available materials. Think of a way to hinge the three panels together so that the wings open and close.

5. Print copies of some of your images to use as a collage technique on your model.

6. Present your triptych to the class and invite members to critique your work.

Reviewing the Facts

1. A burning candle indicated the presence of God.

2. Tempera.

3. Oil paint dries much more slowly than the plaster of a fresco, so the artist has time to include details.

4. His attention to detail and the effects created through his use of light and color.

5. All figures are placed in shallow space. This enables viewers to focus on emotions shown by the figures.

6. His works preserved Gothic concerns for good design and vivid emotion.

7. It was the first time peasants had been represented in a painting.

8. Figures are out of proportion to each other, and realistic space seems unimportant.

Thinking Critically

1. The color scheme of the painting consists predominantly of medium- to low-intensity members of the complementary red and green families. A sense of depth and shadow are suggested by gradual shifts in value within a given hue.

2. Answers will vary, but should indicate knowledge of criteria used in each theory.

Teaching the Technology Project

Suggest that students share images they are considering for their triptychs and ask other group members for their responses: Which images are most effective? Why? What combinations of images convey the intended mood and message most clearly? Establish guidelines for crediting original artists when students choose to copy works for their projects.

> ▲ R T
> S ● U
> R C ■ Assign the feature in the *Performing Arts Handbook,* page 587.

CAREERS IN ART If time permits, have interested students investigate the career information in the *Careers in Art Handbook,* page 594.

*inter*NET Have students go online and learn more
CONNECTION about artists on preselected Web sites with the Internet activity for this chapter.

Art of Sixteenth-Century Europe

ADDITIONAL CHAPTER RESOURCES

Activities

- 📁 Application 18
- 📁 Advanced Studio Activity 18
- 🖱 Chapter 18 Internet Activity
- 📁 Studio Activity 24

Fine Art Resources

- 🎨 **Transparency**
  Art in Focus Transparency 23
  Albrecht Dürer. *Self-Portrait with Gloves*
- 🖼 **Fine Art Print**
  Focus on World Art Print 18
  Rosso Fiorentino. *Descent from the Cross*

Assessment

- 📁 Chapter 18 Test
- 📁 Performance Assessment

Multimedia Resources

- 🎭 Artsource® Performing Arts Package
- 💿 National Gallery Laser Disc
- 💿 National Museum of Women in the Arts CD-ROM
- 📼 Arts & Entertainment Videos

NATIONAL STANDARDS FOR ARTS EDUCATION

The National Standards for Arts Education provide guidelines for grade-appropriate competency in the visual arts. The Content Standards for grades 9–12 are:

1. Understanding and applying media, techniques, and processes.
2. Using knowledge of structures and functions.
3. Choosing and evaluating a range of subject matter, symbols, and ideas.
4. Understanding the visual arts in relation to history and cultures.
5. Reflecting upon and assessing the characteristics and merits of their work and the work of others.
6. Making connections between visual arts and other disciplines.

Listed below are the National Standards for the Visual Arts addressed in this chapter. For a breakdown of the categories listed under each content standard, refer to the *Reproducible Lesson Plans* booklet in the TCR.

1. (a, b) **2.** (a, b) **3.** (a) **4.** (a, b, c) **5.** (a, c) **6.** (a, b)

HANDBOOK MATERIAL

Jennifer Tipton
(page 588)

Fashion Designer *(page 605)*

Beyond the Classroom

The California Alliance for Arts Education (CAAE) is actively involved in community, professional, and educational development to increase awareness and interest in arts education. Find them by visiting our Web site at *www.glencoe.com/sec/art*.

🕐 Out of Time?

If time does not permit teaching this chapter in its entirety, you may wish to preview the artwork and captions with students. Scan the heads in each lesson with students. Discuss the Looking Closely features and examine Styles Influencing Styles on page 399 and Symbolism in Art on page 412.

CHAPTER 18

Art of Sixteenth-Century Europe

INTRODUCE

Chapter Overview

CHAPTER 18 traces major developments in Western art of the sixteenth century.

Lesson One treats the contributions of two Venetian masters, Giorgione and Titian.

Lesson Two deals with the departure from Renaissance harmony that characterizes the works of the Mannerists.

Lesson Three discusses the conflicts in style and artistic theory reflected in the works of northern European artists.

Studio Lessons instruct students to create a painting of a bizarre creature and a humorous face using expanded shapes.

Art & Language Arts

Encourage students to examine the artwork in Figure 18.1.

Ask students to discuss what they have learned about daily life during the late sixteenth and early seventeenth centuries from the works of William Shakespeare. Have volunteers research Shakespeare's life and specific aspects of his work.

Art & Language Arts ■ **FIGURE 18.1** Bruegel's vision of life in sixteenth-century Holland reveals a rich understanding of the range of human experience almost rivaling that of William Shakespeare, who was born in England in 1564. Shakespeare's ability to develop timeless plots and characters developed during the next century and influenced the world of drama and literature for all time.

Pieter Bruegel, the Elder. *Children's Games.* 1560. Oil on oakwood. 118 × 161 cm (46^1/$_2$ × 63^1/$_3$"). Kunsthistorisches Museum, Vienna, Austria.

394

National Standards

This chapter addresses the following National Standards for the Arts.

1. (a,b)   4. (a,b,c)
2. (a,b)   5. (a, c)
3. (a)   6. (a,b)

CHAPTER 18 RESOURCES

Teacher's Classroom Resources

📁 Advanced Studio Activity 18
📁 Application 18
🖱 Chapter 18 Internet Activity
📁 Studio Activity 24

Assessment

📁 Chapter 18 Test
📁 Performance Assessment

Fine Art Resources

🎮 *Art in Focus* Transparency 23
　　Albrecht Dürer. *Self-Portrait with Gloves*
🖼 *Focus on World Art* Print 18
　　Rosso Fiorentino. *Descent from the Cross*

*L*acking the classical monuments of Greece and Rome,
which had inspired artists in Rome and Florence,
Venetian artists relied on other sources of inspiration.
One of the most important of these sources was
their beautiful and unique island city. As the sixteenth century
progressed, a series of disturbing events in Europe lead
artists in Florence and Rome to reject the goals of the Renaissance.
This resulted in a new artistic style known as Mannerism.
Meanwhile, in Northern Europe, a conflict of styles was
occurring as some artists embraced the new Renaissance
style while others continued to work in the traditional Gothic style.

Introducing the Chapter

Have students examine and share their impressions of the artworks pictured in this chapter. Point out that the art styles vary from lesson to lesson because the art styles varied from region to region. Ask students to suggest reasons, either historical or cultural, for these differences.

ART SOURCE **Theatre.** While studying this chapter, use *Performing Arts Handbook* page 588. Help students understand how Jennifer Tipton's directing interpretation emphasizes humanistic experiences represented in Shakespeare's play, *The Tempest*.

YOUR Portfolio

Practice line and shading techniques to create the illusion of movement and depth in a drawing for your portfolio. Ask a classmate to be your model. This student should pretend to be frozen in the middle of an action and may use a prop. Ask the model to hold the pose for about 30 seconds and quickly make a sketch of the model. Use loose, free lines that build up the shape of the model. The lines should be drawn quickly in order to capture movement. After completing the rough sketches, fill in the outlined shape with shading to give the drawing a sense of depth.

Focus ON THE ARTS

THEATRE
In an attempt to re-create classical Greek drama, the first opera was created in Italy. This early form of opera included musical tones and chanted speech. Later the plot was brought back into prominence, but was enhanced with solos, choruses, and songs.

LITERATURE
English writer Thomas More created an idealistic island in his book *Utopia*, written in 1516. In it he imagined a place, unlike sixteenth-century Europe, where there was no money, war, or poverty.

MUSIC
The Protestant Reformation brought a new approach to music within the church as well as in daily life. Music became more personal and passionate. Compositions were written for instruments such as the lute, instead of for voices, for the first time.

395

Focus ON THE ARTS

Discuss the events under the theatre, music, and literature headings with students. Ask if any students are familiar with the work by Thomas More. If students have read *Utopia*, have volunteers summarize the theme of the book. Ask students to name other works that dealt with the idealistic or fantastic stories and places that may have been fashioned after More's work (e.g., *Gulliver's Travels*).

DEVELOPING A PORTFOLIO

Assessment. When submitting a portfolio for evaluation or admission to a school, students must be careful to pay special attention to details. When is the deadline for submitting the work? What are the stylistic preferences of a particular art school or college? Whenever possible, encourage them to visit the campus they are considering and interview professors and administrators who are involved with portfolio assessment. Other details to be addressed are the requirements for a high school transcript and a cover letter. In both cases, remind students to allow enough time for the processing of documents and revision of their writing.

The Art of Venice

Focus

Lesson Objectives

After studying this lesson, students will be able to:
- Identify the source of inspiration that fueled the imaginations of Venetian painters.
- Explain how Giorgione's use of landscapes in his paintings differed from that of earlier artists.
- Discuss the most important features of Titian's works.

Building Vocabulary

Have students identify the base word in the Vocabulary term *painterly* and discuss the two suffixes (-er and -ly) that have been added to form the word. Let students speculate about the meaning of painterly and then check their ideas against the definition presented in the Glossary.

Motivator

Point out that in this lesson students will be meeting an artist who died at 33, yet during his short life, this artist made a contribution that has assured him a permanent place of honor in the annals of art history. Proceed with the reading.

Introducing the Lesson

Direct students' attention to the artwork that opens this chapter (Figure 18.1). Then divide the class into two groups, and challenge one group to list as many similarities as they can between this work and art of the Renaissance, while the other group lists differences. Have groups compare lists.

The Art of Venice

Vocabulary
- painterly

Artists to Meet
- Giorgione da Castelfranco
- Titian

Discover

After completing this chapter, you will be able to:
- Identify sources of inspiration for the works of Venetian painters.
- Explain how Giorgione's use of landscapes differed from that of earlier painters.
- Discuss the most important features of Titian's works.

*D*uring the sixteenth century, as now, Venice could be described as a city of constantly changing lights and reflections. Surrounded by colorful buildings, shimmering sunlight, and the rippling water of the canals, Venetian artists were inspired to paint works that glowed with color.

Influences on Venetian Art

Centuries of close contact with the East left their mark on the appearance of Venice. The dazzling mosaics that decorated Venetian churches and the Venetians' pervading love of color, light, and texture can be traced to the Byzantine art style of the East. The Byzantine influence on Venetian art was far different from that of classical Greece and Rome on the Renaissance cities of Florence and Rome.

Unlike their classical counterparts, Byzantine artists were not primarily interested in portraying a world of solid bodies and objects existing in space. Instead, they sought to present a world of carefully designed surfaces and brilliant colors. Byzantine art did not try to mirror the present world. It wanted to offer a glimpse of the next.

Venetian artists skillfully adapted the Byzantine use of color, light, and texture to their own painting. At the same time, they were aware of the new Renaissance concern for reality that characterized the art of Florence and Rome. Near the end of the fifteenth century, Venetian artists had successfully combined the best of the Byzantine with the best of the Renaissance. This produced a new school where emphasis was placed on color and painting technique.

Giorgione da Castelfranco (1477–1511)

One of the first great Venetian masters was Giorgione da Castelfranco (jor-**joh**-nay da cah-stell-**frahn**-koh), who died of the plague while he was still in his early thirties. Art historians can point to no more than a handful of pictures that were definitely painted by Giorgione.

Giorgione's paintings reveal that he was among the first artists in Europe to place importance on the landscape. Before his time, artists had used the landscape to fill in the spaces around their figures. Giorgione used it to set the stage and to create a mood in his paintings.

The Advantages of Oil Paint

Giorgione used oil paint to add a new richness to his colors. This medium was more suited to the Venetian taste than the cold, pale frescoes of Florence and Rome. It was more vivid and allowed the artist to create delicate changes in hue, intensity, and value. Further, the artist could linger over a painting to produce a glowing effect with colors that stayed

LESSON ONE RESOURCES

Teacher's Classroom Resources
- 📁 Art and Humanities 28
- 📁 Enrichment Activity 34
- 📁 Reproducible Lesson Plan 40
- 📁 Reteaching Activity 40
- 📁 Study Guide 40

■ **FIGURE 18.2** Giorgione used landscape to provide a mood in this painting. Why is it possible to say that "music sets the mood for this scene"? How many ways is music suggested?

Giorgione (possibly Titian). *The Concert.* c. 1508. Oil on canvas. Approx. 105 × 136.5 cm (41³/₈ × 53³/₄"). The Louvre, Paris, France.

wet and workable for days. Inspired by his radiant Venetian surroundings, Giorgione avoided hard edges and lines and bathed his subjects in a soft, golden light.

The Concert
■ **FIGURE 18.2**

One of Giorgione's most beautiful and haunting paintings is *The Concert* (Figure 18.2). The work shows two travelers who meet alongside the road. One is dressed simply and is barefoot. He listens intently as the second, dressed in rich garments, plays a lute. The men are accompanied by two women, who may not be flesh and blood at all. Perhaps they exist only in the minds of the two young men. One appears to be pouring water into a well while the other holds a flute-like instrument. The women may

represent the sound of water churning in a nearby brook and the hum of the breeze through the tree.

The uncertainty of the subject is part of the charm of this painting. More important than this mystery however, is the calm, gentle mood that the work creates.

Giorgione's scene appears to glow in the warm rays of a setting sun. The edges of his figures are blurred as though a light mist is settling around them. This mist surrounds and blends together the green and blue shadows and softens the red accents of a cloak and a hat. It also dulls the other colors found farther back in space. Giorgione's treatment of the landscape and his use of color enabled him to create a haunting picture.

 Technology ■

TEACH
Art Criticism
Remind students that Venetian artists used the city around them, with its constantly changing lights and reflections, for much of their inspiration. Ask students to describe their own city, stating ways in which the place is unique and special. Have them list some of these characteristics on paper. Conclude with a discussion of ways these qualities might influence artists and how this influence might be reflected in art.

Studio Skills
Use the above observations as an introduction to a studio activity in which students create paintings based on unique characteristics of their city or town. To begin, students should sketch a local building, event, or scene that draws upon one or more of the features they listed in the previous activity. Once they have completed their sketches, have students use acrylics to complete their work. They may decide how they want to use color based on literal or expressive qualities of their city (e.g., bright, vibrant colors for the hectic life typical of a major urban center).

Aesthetics
Direct students' attention to the illustration of Giorgione's *The Concert* in Figure 18.2. Point out the artist's use of color, contrast, and lighting in the painting. Discuss the mood or feeling these three properties convey. What other aspects can students identify (e.g., subject matter) that help contribute to the mood of the painting?

Using Map Skills

Have students locate the city of Venice on a large map of Italy. Point out where the city lies in relation to Rome and Florence. Ask: How difficult would it have been for Venetian artists to journey to these cultural centers for inspiration and instruction? Would topographical features have made this trip an easy or difficult one? If a map of Venice is available, have students note the city's layout and physical makeup. Ask how this arrangement may have facilitated trade with other powers.

Critical Thinking

Have students examine Titian's *The Entombment* (Figure 18.3); focus their attention on the fact that Titian obscured the face of the work's principal subject. Ask students to discuss how this same curiosity-inspiring effect could be accomplished in other areas of the arts, such as literature. Then challenge students to test their hypotheses by writing short narrative pieces without ever mentioning the name of their main character.

Cross Curriculum

HISTORY. Remind students that Venice was located in a pivotal position between Christian Europe and Muslim invaders. Point out that Venetian citizens had to defend against these invaders, and most of Europe depended on them. Have a group of students find out more about this Christian-Muslim conflict and the place Venice occupied in it. Ask them to supply dates and other details and to present their findings to the class. One student or group can find out more about Doge Andrea Gritti and furnish a brief biography of the ruler.

Titian (1490–1576)

After his untimely death, Giorgione's approach to painting was carried on by another Venetian artist, Titian (**tish**-un).

Unlike Giorgione, Titian lived a long life. He died not of old age but of the plague. A noble's artist, Titian had many wealthy patrons and painted the portraits of many royal and privileged individuals.

The Entombment
■ **FIGURE 18.3**

From Giorgione, Titian learned how to use landscape to set a mood. He also learned to use oil paints to make works that were rich in color and texture. However, whereas Giorgione's figures always seem to be inactive—sleeping, dreaming, or waiting—Titian's are wide awake, alert, and active. Notice that the figures in his painting *The Entombment* (Figure 18.3) are more powerfully built and more expressive than those of Giorgione.

When Titian combined Giorgione's lighting and color with these sturdy figures, he created a highly emotional scene. The mourners carrying the crucified Christ to his tomb turn their eyes to him and lean forward under the weight of the lifeless body. This helps to direct your gaze to Christ between them.

Use of Light and Shadow

The rapidly fading light of day bathes the scene in a mellow glow. It heralds the approach of night and accents the despair of the figures in this tragic scene. Curiously, Titian placed the head and face of Christ in deep shadow.

Look again at Giorgione's painting of *The Concert* (Figure 18.2, page 397), and notice that the faces of the two young travelers also are in shadow. Both artists used this technique to arouse your curiosity and to involve you with their paintings. They challenge you to use your imagination to complete the most important part of their pictures: the faces of the main characters.

■ **FIGURE 18.3** Compared with Giorgione's figures, Titian's figures appear active and powerful. **Identify the ways that the artist has put emphasis on the figure of the dead Christ.**

Titian. *The Entombment.* c. 1520. Oil on canvas. 149.2 × 215.3 cm (58³/₄ × 84³/₄"). The Louvre, Paris, France.

COOPERATIVE LEARNING

Talk Show. Remind students that the years from 1250 through the time of the Reformation were years of intense global exploration. Assign one student the role of talk-show moderator and four others the roles of the following explorers: Christopher Columbus, Vasco da Gama, Prince Henry of Portugal, and Bartolomeu Dias. The rest of the class may be divided into four groups that will serve as research teams for the explorers. After sufficient material about these men and their contributions has been compiled, stage a talk show in which the explorers and host assess the impact of discovery on all aspects of human culture, including the visual arts.

Styles Influencing *Styles*

MICHELANGELO TO TITIAN The powerful right hand of Titian's *Doge Andrea Gritti* was modeled after the hand on Michelangelo's heroic statue of Moses. Titian knew of this hand from a cast that had been made of it and brought to Venice by a sculptor named Jacopo Sansovino. Titian realized that such a hand could communicate as well as any facial expression. That hand is as strong and tense as the Doge himself.

■ **FIGURE 18.4a**

Titian. *Doge Andrea Gritti.* c. 1546–48. Oil on canvas. 133.6 × 103.2 cm (52¹⁄₂ × 40⁵⁄₈"). National Gallery of Art, Washington, D.C. Samuel H. Kress Collection.

■ **FIGURE 18.4b**

Michelangelo. *Moses* (detail). c. 1513–15.

Doge Andrea Gritti
■ **FIGURE 18.4a**

Titian's greatest fame was as a painter of portraits. One of his most forceful was of Andrea Gritti, the doge, or ruler, of Venice (Figure 18.4a). Gritti ruled during troubled times, when Venice was involved in a series of wars and conflicts. In spite of his advanced age—he was more than 80 years old when Titian painted his portrait—Gritti took an active role in the fighting. It was this fierce

determination and power that Titian captured in his portrait.

The doge is shown as if he is about to burst out of the frame. A curving row of buttons curls up the robe leading to the stern, defiant face. Titian leaves no doubt that this was a fierce, iron-willed leader. The visible brushstrokes in this portrait are representative of Titian's **painterly** technique, which *involves creating forms with patches of color rather than with hard, precise edges.*

Chapter 18 *Art of Sixteenth-Century Europe* **399**

Guide students in examining and discussing Titian's *Doge Andrea Gritti* and then in comparing the hand in Titian's painting with the hand in Michelangelo's statue. Ask: What do you think Titian learned from the cast of the sculpted hand? Why do you think Sansovino brought the cast to Venice? How did Titian adapt what he learned from Michelangelo's work to suit his own work?

Art History

Ask students to note other similarities between Titian's painting of *Doge Andrea Gritti* (Figure 18.4a) and Michelangelo's *Moses* (Figure 16.22, page 371). Have pairs of students collaborate on charts noting specific features that the two works have in common. Then let students share and compare their charts.

Study Guide

Distribute *Study Guide* 40 in the TCR. Assist students in reviewing key concepts. 📁

Art and Humanities

Have students complete *Art and Humanities* 28, "Creating a Sound Score of Your Name," in the TCR. In this worksheet, students are called on to plan a polyphonic musical score and then create a sound score to depict how their name would sound if it were sung. 📁

Teacher Notes

Developing Perceptual Skills. Ask students what it means to *appreciate* art. A variety of responses can be expected, since students are likely to interpret the term in different ways. Ask students to provide a behavioral definition for the word (i.e., a definition that describes the kind of actions one must exhibit to demonstrate he or she is appreciating a work of art). Appreciation can be defined as the act of making a decision about a work of art and backing up that decision with good reasons. Then have students describe their responses to Titian's painting of Doge Andrea Gritti (Figure 18.4a). Statements should show that they appreciate—or do not appreciate—the work.

ASSESS

Checking Comprehension

Have students respond to the lesson review questions. Answers are given in the box below.

Reteaching

➤ Assign *Reteaching* 40, found in the TCR. Have students complete the activity and review their responses. 📁

➤ Have students write facts and information from the lesson on index cards. One partner then reads a statement, while the other places it in context. For example, the statement: "Venice is a city of colorful buildings and reflections," would be assigned the following context: *This atmosphere influenced local artists of the sixteenth century.*

Enrichment

Assign students *Enrichment* 34 "Comparing Styles of Painting," in the TCR. In this activity, students compare and contrast paintings by Giorgione and Manet. 📁

Extension

Have a group of students learn about Venice's glass-blowing industry, which endures to this day on the Venetian island of Murano. Questions to explore include: When did this industry get its start? What kinds of glass objects are created?

CLOSE

Remind students that Venetian art was influenced by both Byzantine and Renaissance art. Have students list some characteristics of Venetian art that illustrate these influences.

400

Titian's Enduring Fame

All the important people of his day were eager to have their portraits painted by Titian. Titian's patrons included Lucrezia Borgia, the Duchess of Farrara; Pope Paul III; and the Emperor Charles V, who made Titian a knight and a count. According to Vasari, there was hardly a noble of high rank, scarcely a prince or lady of great name, whose portrait was not painted by Titian. See Figure 18.5 for a portrait of the young son and heir of Charles V, Philip II.

As a result of his wealthy patrons, Titian lived like a prince, traveling far and wide to complete his commissions, accompanied by numerous servants, admirers, and students. In his lifetime he became nearly as famous as the legendary Michelangelo, and his fame has not lessened over the centuries.

■ **FIGURE 18.5** Titian's painterly technique is visible in this full-scale oil sketch of Spanish king Phillip II. **Where in the painting is this technique most recognizable?**

Titian. *Portrait of Philip II.* c. 1549–51. Oil on canvas. 106.4 × 91.1 cm (42 × 35⅞"). Cincinnati Art Museum, Cincinnati, Ohio. Bequest of Mary M. Emery.

LESSON ONE REVIEW

Reviewing Art Facts

1. Venetian artists used Byzantine color, light, and texture in their work. What did they incorporate from Renaissance art?
2. What were Giorgione's most important contributions to painting?
3. What characterizes the figures in Titian's *Entombment* (Figure 18.3, page 398)?
4. List three ways Titian conveyed the power of Doge Andrea Gritti in his portrait of the 80-year-old ruler.

Activity... *Painting Your Environment*

The city of Venice offered endless variations of light and color, allowing artists to try to capture this light on their canvases. Many artists of different time periods have used their surroundings as the subject of their work. One example is the later Impressionist artists who used their surroundings as subjects.

Create a drawing or painting of your environment. Consider going outside your school and capturing the surroundings as a subject. You may make sketches of your neighborhood and choose one as a subject. Another possibility is to use the classroom as your subject. Display your finished work.

LESSON ONE REVIEW

Answers to Reviewing Art Facts

1. The new concern for reality.
2. He used landscape to set the stage and to create a mood; he used oil paint to add a new richness to his colors.
3. Figures are powerfully built and expressive.
4. By painting him as if he were about to burst from the frame; showing fierce determination in the face; giving him a powerful right hand.

Activity...*Painting Your Environment*

Have students begin by discussing their classroom as the subject of a painting. What details would they want to include? Why? What mood or feeling would they want to convey? What medium and what colors would they choose? Why?

Mannerism

Vocabulary
- Mannerism
- Protestant Reformation

Artists to Meet
- Parmigianino
- Tintoretto
- El Greco

Discover

After completing this chapter, you will be able to:
- Explain what Mannerism is and why it developed.
- Identify Mannerist characteristics in the works of Parmigianino, Tintoretto, and El Greco.
- Discuss the attitude of the Church toward the works of Mannerist artists.

*A*rtists such as Giorgione and Titian made Venice a great art center that rivaled and then surpassed Florence and Rome. In Rome, artists were challenged to find new avenues of expression in the vacuum left by the passing of Leonardo, Michelangelo, and Raphael while facing a world filled with increasing unrest and uncertainty. It was that unrest and uncertainty that contributed to a style of art known as Mannerism.

Mannerism

Today, **Mannerism** is considered *a deliberate revolt by artists against the goals of the Renaissance.* Why would Mannerist artists turn against the art of the Renaissance? To answer this question, you must compare the Italy in which the Renaissance masters lived with the Italy in which Mannerist artists lived.

Cultural Influences

When Raphael painted the *Alba Madonna* around 1510, Italy was at peace and the Church was the unchallenged seat of authority. It was a period of confidence and hope, and this was reflected in the artworks that were created. Artists such as Raphael produced works that were carefully thought out, balanced, and soothing.

Then, within the span of a few decades, the religious unity of Western Christendom was shattered. The **Protestant Reformation,** *a movement in which a group of Christians led by Martin Luther left the Church in revolt to form their own religion,* began in 1517. This movement, along with the French invasion of Italy in 1524 and the French defeat of Rome in 1527, brought about an era of tension and disorder. It was in this setting that Mannerist art was born and matured.

Where the art of the Renaissance tried to achieve balance, Mannerism preferred imbalance. The calm order found in works such as the *Alba Madonna* (Figure 16.24, page 373) was replaced by a restlessness. Mannerism was a nervous art, created to mirror a world filled with confusion. Its artists painted the human figure in impossible poses and with unreal proportions. Mannerist artists preferred figures that were slender, elegant, and graceful. Gradually, these figures began to look less natural and more supernatural.

Parmigianino (1503–1540)

The Mannerist style is evident in the work of Francesco Mazzola, called Parmigianino (par-mih-jah-**nee**-noh), who was among the first generation of Mannerists in Rome.

401

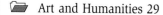
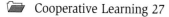
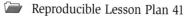
FOCUS

Lesson Objectives

After studying this lesson, students will be able to:
- Define the term Mannerism.
- Identify key artists of the Mannerist movement.
- Explain why the works of Mannerist artists were welcomed by the Church.

Building Vocabulary

Write the word *manners* on the board, and ask students to list words and phrases that come to mind, using a thesaurus if necessary. Ask students what qualities they expect to find in Mannerist art.

Motivator

Ask whether any students in the class have ever participated in a protest (e.g., an effort to get city officials to clean up a dump site). Ask: What were some of the feelings that go along with a movement protesting the status quo? What are some ways of expressing these feelings so as to appeal to—and involve—a larger audience? Explain that students will learn about a protest against the Church during the sixteenth century and the changes it brought about in art of the period.

Introducing the Lesson

Review with students the role the Church played during the Renaissance. Explain that in the early 1500s, a group of Christians led by Martin Luther split off from the Church to follow religious convictions of their own. Have students brainstorm the effects that an opposition movement might have had on Western art.

TEACH
Art History

To help students better appreciate the goals and ambitions of the Mannerists, review with them the goals and characteristics of art created during the Renaissance. Divide the class into two groups, and have one list goals, the other characteristics. Combine the lists in a classroom resource file called "Mannerist and Renaissance Styles," and encourage students to refer back to it periodically during their reading and discussion of this lesson.

Art Criticism

Ask students to examine the painting by Parmigianino in Figure 18.6. In spite of the difference of approach, in what ways, superficially, does this Mannerist painting resemble works created during the Renaissance? Have students compare the work directly with Raphael's *Alba Madonna* (Figure 16.24, page 373), noting that Parmigianino has, like this artist of Renaissance style, tried to make his figures look rounded and solid. What other common traits can students discover?

Cross Curriculum

SOCIAL STUDIES. Discuss with students Martin Luther's role in the Protestant Reformation. Point out that Martin Luther believed that some of the practices of the monks, such as the selling of indulgences, were proof of the greed and corruption that had overtaken the Church. Have students research other reform movements in history.

The Madonna with the Long Neck
■ FIGURE 18.6

Parmigianino studied the works of other painters and developed his own personal art style. His best-known work is *The Madonna with the Long Neck* (Figure 18.6).

Description and Analysis

A description of this painting raises a number of disturbing questions. For example, is this an interior or an exterior setting? It is difficult to say for certain because the drapery at the left and the columns at the right suggest a background that is both interior and exterior.

The figure of the Madonna is also unusual. She is enormous and towers over the other figures in the picture, even though she is seated and they are standing. She looks as if she is about to stand; the baby already seems to be slipping from his mother's lap. Curiously, the mother shows no concern. Her eyes remain half-closed, and she continues to look content and quite pleased with herself.

The Christ child looks lifeless; his flesh is pale and rubbery, and his proportions are unnatural. His neck is concealed by the Madonna's left hand and his head looks as if it is not attached to the body.

Crowding in tightly at the left side of the picture are a number of figures who have come to admire and worship the Christ child. They pay little attention, however. Instead, they look about in all directions—one even stares out of the picture directly at you. Within that group, notice the leg in the left corner. To whom does this leg belong?

The foreground space occupied by the Madonna and other figures is crowded; everyone seems jammed together here. When your gaze moves to the right side of the picture, you plunge into a deep background. Notice the small figure of a man reading from a scroll. The size of this man indicates that he is far back in space, but there is no way of determining the distance between him and the foreground

figures. Who is this man and what is he doing? It is impossible to know, since the artist gives no clues to his identity.

Interpretation

The questions continue as you move on to interpretation of the work. Is it just an accident that the Christ child looks lifeless, or that his arms are outstretched in the same position he would take later on the cross? Could the mother be a symbol of the Church? If so, why does she seem unconcerned that her child is slipping from her grasp? Why are all those people crowding in at the left—and apparently not even noticing the child?

■ **FIGURE 18.6** This painting is an early example of the Mannerist style, which was intended to reflect the instability and tensions of European life. **Point out specific ways in which the figures of the Madonna and the baby are distorted.**

Parmigianino. *The Madonna with the Long Neck.* c. 1535. Oil on panel. 220 × 130 cm (85 × 52"). Galleria degli Uffizi, Florence, Italy.

 Technology ▬▬▬

National Gallery of Art Videodisc Use the following images as examples of more works by artists introduced in this lesson.

El Greco
Saint Martin and the Beggar

Search Frame 523

Use Glencoe's *Correlation Bar Code Guide to the National Gallery of Art* to locate more artworks.

What is Parmigianino trying to say? Could he be criticizing the Church and the people for their growing worldliness? Was he trying to say that they were becoming so concerned with their own well-being that they had forgotten the sacrifices made for them by Christ?

Parmigianino's painting raises a great many questions and offers few answers. No doubt that is exactly what it was intended to do.

Tintoretto (1518–1594)

Mannerism established itself later in Venice than in other parts of Italy. The best-known Venetian artist to work in this style was Tintoretto (tin-toh-**reh**-toh). Tintoretto's real name was Jacopo Robusti, but he was the son of a dyer and he became known as "Tintoretto," the Italian word for "little dyer." He was able to combine the goals of Mannerism with a Venetian love of color. His style featured quick, short brushstrokes and a dramatic use of light.

Presentation of the Virgin
■ FIGURE 18.7

In Tintoretto's painting *Presentation of the Virgin* (Figure 18.7), you can see the qualities that make it a Mannerist work. Among these are the elongated figures with their dramatic gestures, the odd perspective, and the strange, uneven light that touches some parts of the picture and leaves other parts in deep shadow.

Almost everyone in the picture is watching the young Mary as she climbs solemnly up the stairs to the temple. The woman in the foreground points to the small figure of Mary silhouetted against a blue sky. Without that gesture you might not notice her at all. Mary may be the most important person in the picture, but Tintoretto made her look small and unimportant. The viewer becomes actively involved in finding her and is led to her with visual clues.

Tintoretto wanted to do more than just describe another event in the life of the Virgin. He tried to engage the viewer and capture the excitement of that event. He wanted you to feel as though you were actually there, on the stairs to the temple.

■ **FIGURE 18.7** Mary, the main character in this picture, is the small figure near the top of the stairs. How does Tintoretto draw the viewer's attention to that small figure? Do all the figures exhibit an interest in what is happening? If not, how does this make you feel?

Tintoretto. *Presentation of the Virgin.* c. 1550. Oil on canvas. 4.3 × 4.8 m (14′1″ × 15′9″). Church of Santa Maria dell' Orto, Venice, Italy.

Aesthetics
Ask students to compare Tintoretto's *Presentation of the Virgin* (Figure 18.7) with spiritual paintings from previous centuries. Discuss the similarities and differences among the works. Have students identify the mood or feeling of the paintings, as well as the ways the artists of the various periods went about achieving these effects. Conclude with a discussion of how changes in history affected the expression of spirituality in art.

Art Criticism
Have students compare the way Tintoretto draws the viewer into the painting in Figure 18.7 with the way Giorgione and Titian achieve the same result. How does each artist arouse the curiosity of the viewer? Which of the artists is most successful in this area, and why?

Critical Thinking
Tell students that, while he was in Rome, El Greco became familiar with the works of Michelangelo, which he did not much admire. El Greco is said to have declared that, though Michelangelo was a good man, he did not know how to paint. Ask: Was this remark merely an indication of El Greco's ignorance, or was it a function of his own artistic purpose and the Mannerist viewpoint?

More About... **Mannerism.** Some of the features of Mannerist painting carry over into Mannerist sculpture. Among them can be found a passion for the abnormal, a love of the fantastic, a preoccupation with restless, complex movement, and a dominating concern for line. Nowhere are these features more evident than in the Park of Monsters, created about 1580 as the park of the Palazzo Orsini. One enters the park through the "Mouth of Hell," a huge grotesque figure with a gaping mouth, carved from a natural stone wall. In this park, nature and art are combined. One of the concerns of the Mannerist style was the relationship of art to nature, and in this case, art neither represents nor distorts nature but incorporates it.

Art History

Ask students to recall other artists who displeased, or had stormy relationships with, their patrons. Possibilities include Leonardo da Vinci and Michelangelo. What effect, if any, did these interpersonal difficulties have on the work of these artists?

Cross Curriculum

LITERATURE. Point out that during the time El Greco worked, William Shakespeare was writing many of the world's greatest dramas in England. To help students gain both a sense of the history of this period and an appreciation of Shakespeare's craft, have a group of volunteers select a scene from one of the historical dramas, perhaps *Henry VIII*, and stage a dramatic reading for the class. It may be useful to have the group listen to a professional recording of the passage on tape or compact disc as they prepare.

Art History

Tell students that El Greco's art was forgotten for centuries and that he was treated as nothing more than an interesting footnote in the history of art. Some writers even went so far as to call him "the painter of the weird." Add that it was not until the beginning of the twentieth century that El Greco and his works were rediscovered and historians and critics finally realized how important he was. Ask students to isolate properties in the works and the theory of art embraced by El Greco that may have been responsible for his lack of recognition for three centuries.

■ **FIGURE 18.8** El Greco's elongated treatment of the human figure may have been inspired by Tintoretto, and his use of light and dark contrasts to heighten drama may have been learned from Titian. **Point out specific qualities in this work that may represent the influences of Tintoretto and Titian.**

El Greco. *The Martyrdom of St. Maurice and the Theban Legion.* 1580. Oil on canvas. 4.4 × 3m (14′6″ × 9′10″). The Escorial, near Madrid, Spain.

El Greco (1541–1614)

Highly emotional religious pictures by Mannerists like Tintoretto were welcomed by the Church during this troubled period. The Church was placing a renewed emphasis on the spiritual in order to counter the Reformation.

Art could aid this effort by working on the emotions of the people, reminding them that heaven awaited those who followed the Church's teachings. Nowhere was this more evident than in Spain. There you will find the last and most remarkable of the Mannerist artists, El Greco (el **greh**-koh). El Greco was born on the Greek island of Crete and christened Domeniko Theotocopoulos. He received the nickname El Greco (the Greek) after settling in Toledo, Spain in 1577.

The Martyrdom of St. Maurice and the Theban Legion
■ FIGURE 18.8

In 1580, El Greco was commissioned to paint two pictures for King Philip II of Spain. One of these, *The Martyrdom of St. Maurice and the Theban Legion* (Figure 18.8), so displeased the king that he refused to have it hung in his palace. Today that painting is regarded as one of El Greco's greatest works.

The painting depicts the fate of Maurice and his soldiers, who were loyal subjects of the pagan Roman emperor and faithful Christians. When the emperor ordered everyone in the army to worship the Roman gods or face execution, Maurice and his soldiers chose death.

El Greco blends the three parts of this story into a single scene. In the foreground, Maurice is seen explaining the situation to his officers. Farther back, he and one of his officers are shown watching their men being beheaded. They calmly offer encouragement, knowing that they will soon face the same end. At the top of the picture, the heavens open up and a group of angels prepares to greet the heroes with the laurels of martyrdom.

COOPERATIVE LEARNING

Guide to Artists. Divide the class into three groups. Assign each group one of the artists from this lesson—Parmigianino, Tintoretto, or El Greco. Tell students that they will be creating a guide to the artist they have been assigned. Have each group begin by finding illustrations of at least five works of art created by their artist. Then have groups identify and record on paper as many details as they can about: the chronology of the works selected; the circumstances under which each was created; how well each work typifies the artist's style; and what changes are discernible between the artist's earliest and latest efforts. Have groups combine their research into a resource folder entitled "Lives of the Mannerist Artists."

The Burial of Count Orgaz
■ FIGURE 18.9

Disappointed after his experience with Philip, El Greco went to Toledo, where he spent the rest of his life. There the Church of St. Tomé hired him to paint the burial of a man who had died 200 years earlier. The huge painting, entitled *The Burial of Count Orgaz* (Figure 18.9), took two years to complete; El Greco considered it his greatest work.

The Count of Orgaz was a deeply religious man who commanded his subjects to contribute money, cattle, wine, firewood, and chickens to St. Tomé each year. When the count died, so it was said, St. Stephen and St. Augustine came down from heaven and placed the count in his tomb with their own hands.

The villagers of Orgaz continued to pay their annual tribute to St. Tomé for generations. Eventually, however, they felt that they had done enough and stopped. Officials at St. Tomé protested, and a church trial was held. After all the testimony was heard, it was decided that the villagers should continue making their payments. El Greco's painting of the count's funeral was meant to remind the villagers of their eternal debt to St. Tomé. In his contract, El Greco was instructed to show witnesses to the miracle, a priest saying Mass, and heaven opened in glory.

LOOKING Closely

THE USE OF AXIS AND CONTOUR LINES

With the aid of axis and contour lines, El Greco takes you on a journey from the bottom of the painting to the top.

- **Examine.** A horizontal axis line made up of the heads of the witnesses divides the painting into two parts, heaven and earth.

- **Inspect.** The two parts are united by another axis line that begins at the right shoulder of St. Stephen. Tracing this line, you find that it passes down the arm of the saint and through the arched body of the count. It continues to curve upward through the body of St. Augustine to the wing of the angel and on to the soul of the dead count.

- **Identify.** The contour lines of the clouds at either side of the angel guide your eye even higher to the figure of Christ.

■ **FIGURE 18.9** El Greco. *The Burial of Count Orgaz.* 1586. Oil on canvas. 4.9 × 3.7 m (16 × 12′). Church of St. Tomé, Toledo, Spain.

Chapter 18 *Art of Sixteenth-Century Europe* **405**

CHAPTER 18
LESSON TWO

Art Criticism
Direct students' attention to *The Burial of Count Orgaz* (Figure 18.9). Ask: What elements does the artist use to communicate a sense of calm dignity in the bottom portion of the painting? How does he create a sense of almost frenzied action in the top portion?

LOOKING Closely
As students examine *The Burial of Count Orgaz* and read the explanations in the feature, encourage them to trace each line with their fingers. Ask: What do you think El Greco intended to achieve with this use of axis and contour lines? How fully do you think he succeeded?

Study Guide
Distribute *Study Guide* 41 in the TCR. Assist students in reviewing key concepts. 🗁

Art and Humanities
Ask students to complete Art and *Humanities* 29, "Education in Fifteenth-Century Italy," in the TCR. In this worksheet, students discover an innovative school in Italy in the fifteenth century. 🗁

Studio Activities
Have students complete *Studio* 24, "Modeling Expressive Figures in Clay," in which students are encouraged to create a three-dimensional figure that expresses an emotion. 🗁

Art and Humanities
Invite an art historian to class to discuss the different media and tools that artists in the sixteenth century used (i.e., silverpoint, egg tempera, and oil paint).

CULTURAL DIVERSITY

City Life. Divide students into groups and have each group select and research one of the European cities mentioned in this lesson. Each group should determine: what life was like in the city of their choice during the sixteenth century; what other famous artists (if any) came from this area; in what ways it pays homage to the artists it was home to; other reasons for its fame; and how it has changed in the intervening centuries. Groups can consult books and travel agents to obtain information, as well as photographs of their city in its present-day state. Set aside class time for students to share their findings in the form of informative travelogues.

ASSESS

Checking Comprehension

Have students respond to the lesson review questions. Answers are given in the box below.

Reteaching

➤ Assign *Reteaching* 41, found in the TCR. Have students complete the activity and review their responses. 📁

➤ Create two decks of flash cards, one deck containing a word or phrase that characterizes Renaissance art (e.g., balance, harmony), the other containing the same for Mannerist art (e.g., imbalance, confusion). Shuffle the two decks and quiz students. They may also use the flash cards to test themselves.

Enrichment

Assign students *Enrichment* 35 "Impact of the Protestant Reformation," in the TCR. 📁

Extension

Have students read *Cooperative Learning* 27, "Counter the Reformation." Students find out what action the Church took to counter the Protestant Reformation. Then, working in groups, they are to imagine that they are living during the sixteenth century and that their job is to convince artists of the period to create artworks to help further the cause of the Counter-Reformation. 📁

CLOSE

Remind students that the Mannerist style was a deliberate break with the goals of the Renaissance. Have students write a short essay in which they identify characteristics of the Mannerist style, the artists, and their works

406

You will discover a great deal when you study a complicated painting like *The Burial of Count Orgaz.* As a starting point, notice the young boy in the lower left of the painting who seems to introduce you to the scene. His pointed finger directs your attention to the richly dressed figures of the two saints, St. Stephen and St. Augustine. Together, the two saints lower the body of the count into his grave. His lifeless pose and pale color show that the count is dead. The gaze of this priest leads your eye to a winged angel, who carries the soul of the dead count. The clouds part, giving the angel a clear path to the figure of Christ, seated in judgment at the top of the painting. Saints and angels have gathered before Christ to ask that the count's soul be allowed to join them in heaven.

El Greco may have painted his own self-portrait in this work (Figure 18.10). He may be the central figure here, looking out directly at the viewer. Details about El Greco's life are sketchy. In addition to including his self-portrait in this work, some people think that the woman, shown as the Virgin, may have been his wife. That is uncertain, although it is quite likely that the boy in the picture is his son. On a paper sticking out of the boy's pocket, El Greco has painted his son's birthdate.

El Greco and Mannerism

El Greco carried Mannerist ideas as far as they could go. His intense emotionalism and strong sense of movement could not be imitated or developed further. Thus, the final chapter in the development of the Mannerist style was written in Spain. In Italy, the new Baroque style was already developing, and in northern Europe, conflicts arose between Late Gothic and Italian Renaissance styles.

■ **FIGURE 18.10** El Greco. *The Burial of Count Orgaz* (detail).

LESSON TWO REVIEW

Reviewing Art Facts

1. Why did Mannerist artists seek imbalance and restlessness in their work?
2. Why did the Church welcome the highly emotional religious pictures created by Mannerist artists such as Tintoretto?
3. List three ways Mannerist artists distorted reality in their works.
4. In their paintings, Mannerist artists often depicted many things happening at the same time. Select one of the Mannerist paintings by Parmigianino, Tintoretto, or El Greco, and list at least four events taking place simultaneously.

Activity... *Recognizing Cultural Changes*

The Mannerist style, which features distortion of reality and intense emotionalism, was a revolt of artists against the goals of the Renaissance. This development was a result of many changes, such as the Protestant Reformation, that were challenging the established order. This mirroring of change has been a part of art in other times as well.

Find other art styles that developed as a result of change in the culture. Choose one art movement from the nineteenth or twentieth century. Examine the art style, and review the historical and social events happening at that time. Show how these events are reflected in the artworks and style of the period. Present your findings to the class.

LESSON TWO REVIEW

Answers to Reviewing Art Facts
1. To mirror the world in which they lived, a world of imbalance and confusion.
2. It felt this art could aid in the efforts to counter the Reformation.
3. Elongated figures; odd proportion; unusual perspective; uneven light; optical illusion.
4. Answers will vary according to piece chosen.

Activity... *Recognizing Cultural Changes*
Have students work together to brainstorm a list of art movements they might study for this Activity assignment. Then let students form cooperative learning groups in which to research one of those art movements. Group members should work together to plan a presentation for the rest of the class.

The Art of Northern Europe

Vocabulary
■ parable

Artists to Meet
■ Matthias Grünewald
■ Albrecht Dürer
■ Hieronymus Bosch
■ Pieter Bruegel
■ Hans Holbein

Discover
After completing this chapter, you will be able to:
■ Identify the two painting styles favored by northern European artists in the sixteenth century.
■ Discuss the styles and works of Matthias Grünewald, Albrecht Dürer, Hieronymus Bosch, Pieter Bruegel, and Hans Holbein.

*D*uring the fifteenth century, most of the artists north of the Alps remained indifferent to the advances made by the Italian Renaissance. Since the time of Jan van Eyck, they had looked to Flanders and not to Italy for leadership. This changed at the start of the next century, however. Artists began to make independent journeys to Italy and other countries. Eventually, the lure of Italian art became so strong that a trip to Italy to study the great Renaissance masters was considered essential for artists in training.

The Spread of the Renaissance Style

The spread of the Renaissance style across western Europe was further aided by powerful monarchs with a thirst for art. These monarchs invited well-known artists to come and work in their courts. As Italian artists moved throughout western Europe, and as other European artists visited Italy, ideas about artistic styles were shared and revised.

Early in the sixteenth century, a conflict of styles developed between Northern artists who remained faithful to the style of the Late Gothic period and those who favored adopting Italian Renaissance ideas as quickly as possible. This conflict continued until the Renaissance point of view triumphed later in the century.

Matthias Grünewald (c. 1480–1528)

A comparison of the works of two great Northern painters of that time, Matthias Grünewald (muh-**tee**-uhs **groon**-eh-vahlt) and Albrecht Dürer (**ahl**-brekt **dur**-er), brings this conflict of styles into focus. Both these German artists felt the influence of the Italian Renaissance. They understood the rules of perspective and could paint figures that looked solid and real.

Matthias Grünewald, however, continued to show a preference for the dreams and visions of Gothic art. He used Renaissance ideas only to make his pictures of these dreams and visions more vivid and powerful.

The Small Crucifixion
■ FIGURE 18.11

In his painting *The Small Crucifixion* (Figure 18.11, page 408), Grünewald created a powerful version of this Christian subject. Like earlier Medieval artists his aim was to provide a visual sermon.

Grünewald's sermon forcefully describes Christ's agony and death. It spares none of the brutal details that Italian artists preferred to avoid. The pale yellow of Christ's body is the color of a corpse. The cold, black sky behind the figures is a dark curtain against which the tragic scene is played, emphasizing the people in the foreground with its contrasting value and hue.

407

FOCUS

Lesson Objectives
After studying this lesson, students will be able to:
■ Identify factors that caused artists of northern Europe to be divided in their stylistic preferences.
■ Describe the contributions of Matthias Grünewald, Albrecht Dürer, Hieronymus Bosch, Pieter Bruegel, and Hans Holbein.

Building Vocabulary
Let volunteers give informal definitions of the Vocabulary word, *parable,* and offer brief examples. Then have students read the formal definition given in the Glossary.

Motivator
Remind students that in Italy during the fifteenth century, a conflict in art styles emerged. Ask students to recall and describe the conflict (i.e., some artists quickly accepted the new, progressive ideas of the Renaissance, while others stubbornly held fast to the more conservative ideals of the Gothic style). Explain that students will be learning about a similar conflict that developed during the sixteenth century.

Introducing the Lesson
Divide the class into groups. Have each group study the artworks in the lesson and choose one of the following categories: (1) literal; (2) expressive; (3) literal and expressive. Have them compare descriptions before beginning the lesson, which focuses on conflicts in style and artistic purpose.

LESSON THREE RESOURCES

Teacher's Classroom Resources

📁 Appreciating Cultural Diversity 28

📁 Art and Humanities 30

📁 Reproducible Lesson Plan 42

📁 Reteaching Activity 42

📁 Study Guide 42

TEACH

Using Map Skills

Remind students that before the sixteenth century, artists of northern Europe relied on Flanders, not Italy, for their inspiration and leadership. Have students locate the Low Countries on a map of Europe and indicate their general geographic location. Have them do the same for Italy. Next, have students skim the lesson, looking for names of cities and/or countries where artists were born or lived, and have students record the sites of these places on the map.

Discuss the role geography can play in the spread of culture and tastes from one place to another. Ask: What do you think travel between northern Europe and Italy, the seat of the Renaissance, might have entailed during the sixteenth century?

Art History

Ask students to identify the two main art styles that influenced artists of northern Europe during the sixteenth century (i.e., late Gothic and Renaissance). Have students review the characteristics of the two styles. Then divide the class into groups, and have each select a work from this lesson. Challenge groups to identify which of the styles the work they have selected most conforms to, noting as many details as they can in support of their claim.

Attention is focused on the central figure of Christ. The ragged edge of his cloth garment repeats and emphasizes the savage marks of the wounds covering his body. His fingers twist and turn in the final agony of death. Like everything else in the work—color, design, brushwork—this contributes to an expression of intense pain and sorrow. The calm balance of the Renaissance has been rejected. Instead you see a representation of the Crucifixion that seeks to seize and hold your emotions.

■ **FIGURE 18.11** This work depicts the intense agony and sorrow of the Crucifixion. **Identify specific details that contribute to the emotional impact of this painting.**

Matthias Grünewald. *The Small Crucifixion.* c. 1511–20. Oil on wood. 61.3 × 46 cm (24^1/$_8$ × 18^1/$_8$"). National Gallery of Art, Washington, D.C. Board of Trustees, Samuel H. Kress Collection.

Time & Place
CONNECTIONS
Sixteenth-Century Europe
c. 1500–1600

STUDY OF ASTRONOMY. Three hundred years before people actually traveled in space, astronomers were seeking answers to mysteries of the solar system. Jan Vermeer painted this astronomer poring over his charts.

SAILING SHIPS. Advances in shipbuilding gave explorers better vessels for travel to distant shores. The caraval, shown here, allowed for cargo storage and had room for weapons. This ship could navigate in shallow waters to make landing easier.

Activity **Writing.** You are a writer of historical fiction. Create the first page of an adventure novel set in the sixteenth century. Incorporate the objects on this page into your description of the setting and the thoughts of the main character.

Time & Place
CONNECTIONS
Sixteenth-Century Europe

Let students meet in cooperative learning groups to examine and discuss the images in this Time & Place feature. Have the members of each group work together to write about specific developments in the study of astronomy and advances in ship building: What was the sixteenth-century understanding of the solar system? Which planets were identified, and how were they observed? How were ships powered and organized? How large were they? How far did they sail? Have the students in each group find and share answers to these and other questions.

Albrecht Dürer
(1471–1528)

Almost every German artist at this time followed the same course as Grünewald. Only Albrecht Dürer turned away from the Gothic style to embrace the Renaissance.

After a trip to Italy, Dürer made up his mind to make the new Renaissance style his own. He studied perspective and the theory of proportions in order to capture the beauty and balance found in Italian painting. Then he applied what he learned to his own art.

Knight, Death, and the Devil
■ FIGURE 18.12

Dürer's studies enabled him to pick out the most interesting and impressive features of the Italian Renaissance style and combine them with his own ideas. In his engraving entitled *Knight, Death, and the Devil* (Figure 18.12), the horse and rider exhibit the calmness and the solid, round form of Italian painting.

Dürer's Use of Symbolism

The figures representing death and the devil, however, are reminders of the strange creatures found in Northern Gothic paintings. The brave Christian soldier is shown riding along the road of faith toward the heavenly Jerusalem, seen at the top of the work. The knight's dog, the symbol of loyalty, gallantly follows its master. The knight is plagued by a hideous horseman representing death, who threatens to cut him off before his journey is complete. Behind lurks the devil, hoping the knight will lose his courage and decide to turn back. However, the knight rides bravely forward, never turning from the Christian path, no matter how frightening the dangers along the way.

■ **FIGURE 18.12** Dürer selected certain features of the Italian Renaissance style and combined them with his own ideas to create his own personal style. **Point to features in this work that show how Dürer was influenced by the Italian Renaissance.**

Albrecht Dürer. *Knight, Death, and the Devil.* 1513. Engraving. 24.6 × 19 cm (9⅝ × 7½"). Staedelsches Kunstinstitut, Frankfurt, Germany.

Art Criticism

Direct students' attention to *Knight, Death, and the Devil,* the engraving by Albrecht Dürer in Figure 18.12. Ask: How does the artist take advantage of this medium? How would the overall impression of the work differ if it had been created as a painting?

Studio Skills

Ask students to create an original symbol that relates to one of the following: being a member of their age group, being a student at the school they attend, being a citizen of planet Earth. Like the symbols appearing in artworks in this lesson, students' efforts should be realistic representations of objects meant to stand for some abstract ideal or belief. Have students sketch their ideas on scrap paper and then transfer their best sketch onto a sheet of white paper, completing the work with pastels. Have students display finished works and attempt to identify the symbolic interpretation of their classmates' creations.

Art Criticism

Point out that both Albrecht Dürer and Hieronymus Bosch used fantastic creatures and symbols in their works of art. Ask students to name other art styles and/or artists that made use of one or both of these devices. Have students discuss their responses and then compile them in a chart featuring the names of artists, the period in which they worked, specific images and symbols used in their work, and the meaning of each.

 ## Technology

National Gallery of Art Videodisc Use the following images as examples of more works by artists introduced in this lesson.

Albrecht Dürer
Melancholia

Search Frame 3125

Pieter Bruegel, the Elder
Landscape with the Penitance of Saint Jerome

Search Frame 2779

Hieronymus Bosch
Death and the Miser

Search Frame 628

Use Glencoe's *Correlation Bar Code Guide to the National Gallery of Art* to locate more artworks.

Art History

Point out that many of the artworks in this lesson tell stories. Have students list the titles of works that fit this description and the artists who painted them. Ask: In what other period that you have studied was storytelling a goal of art? What kinds of stories did works of art during this period tell? In what medium did the artists work? Finally, ask individual students to select one of the storytelling paintings from their list and restate in their own words the story or object lesson.

Critical Thinking

Have students note that various artists mentioned in this lesson influenced, or were themselves influenced, by other artists (e.g., Bruegel was influenced by Bosch, who, in turn, was influenced by both Rogier van der Weyden and Hugo van der Goes). Have students form teams to create "artist family trees" that illustrate this lineage of influence. Like family genealogies, the trees should be constructed as series of hierarchical perpendicular lines, with sources of influence appearing higher up in the tree. Allow time for teams to share and compare their trees.

Hieronymus Bosch
(1450–1516)

One of the most interesting artists of the late fifteenth and early sixteenth centuries was the Flemish painter Hieronymus Bosch (heer-**ahn**-ni-mus **bosh**). Bosch's paintings, like those of the Italian Mannerists, mirrored the growing fears and tensions of the people during that uneasy period.

An Era of Religious Conflict

Many felt that the increasing religious conflicts were a sign that the evil in the world had reached new heights. It was only a matter of time, they felt, before an angry God would punish them all. This religious and moral climate gave artists subject matter for their works of art.

Bosch's Mysterious Symbols

Bosch's pictures were meant to be viewed in two ways—as stories and as symbolic messages. His stories clearly focused on the subject of good and evil. The meanings of many of his symbols have been forgotten over the years. Many probably came from magical beliefs, astrology, and the different religious cults that were popular in his day.

Even though his paintings are often frightening or difficult to understand, they are not without traces of humor. Bosch often pictured the devil as a fool or a clown rather than as the sinister Prince of Darkness.

Death and the Miser
■ FIGURE 18.13

Bosch's skills as a storyteller, as well as his sense of humor, are evident in his painting *Death and the Miser* (Figure 18.13). He uses the picture to tell you that no matter how evil a man has been during his life, he can be saved if he asks for forgiveness before dying.

An old miser is shown on his sickbed as a figure representing death enters the room and prepares to strike. Even at this final moment, the miser is torn between good and evil. An angel points to a crucifix in the window and urges the miser to place his trust in the Lord. At the same time, a devil tempts him with a bag of money. The miser seems about to look up at the crucifix (detail of Figure 18.13), although his hand reaches out for the money at the same time.

At the bottom of the picture is a scene from an earlier period in the miser's life. Here, too, Bosch shows that the miser cannot decide between good and evil. The man fingers a rosary in one hand, but adds to his hoard of money with the other.

DETAIL:
Crucifix that the miser looks upon.

COOPERATIVE LEARNING

Danube School. You can encourage students' understanding of the art of the North during the sixteenth century by helping them become familiar with the artists and works of the so-called "Danube School." Have groups of students investigate and share the results of their research on different aspects of this school, which included the artists Lucas Cranach, Jorg Brue the Elder, and Albrecht Altdorfer. Point out that, although the members of the movement ultimately branched out in separate directions, they all at first shared an enthusiasm for landscapes and painted in a romantic fashion emphasizing a love of nature. Have students fit the information they have compiled into the larger context of this chapter.

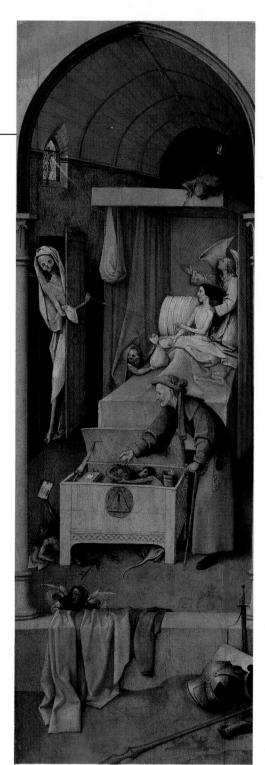

■ **FIGURE 18.13** This picture tells a story but does not give it an ending—the man in the bed has to make an important decision. Which figures help you understand the miser's dilemma? Why must the miser make his decision immediately rather than taking time to think it over?

Hieronymus Bosch. *Death and the Miser.* c. 1485–90. Oil on panel. 93 × 31 cm (36 5/8 × 12 3/16″). National Gallery of Art, Washington, D.C. Board of Trustees, Samuel H. Kress Collection.

Pieter Bruegel (1525–1569)

Bosch's unique art style did not end with his death in 1516. Forty years later, a Flemish artist named Pieter Bruegel the Elder (**pee**-ter **broi**-gl) turned away from the landscapes he had been painting to create pictures that owe a great deal to Bosch's influence.

The Parable of the Blind
■ **FIGURE 18.14**

Bruegel's work *The Parable of the Blind* (Figure 18.14, page 412) shows five blind beggars walking in a line. The sixth—their leader—has stumbled and is falling over the bank of a ditch, and the others are destined to follow. Like Bosch's work, Bruegel's painting can be seen as a **parable,** *a story that contains a symbolic message.* It illustrates this proverb: "And if the blind lead the blind, both shall fall into a ditch."

His concern for detail ties Bruegel more firmly to Jan van Eyck and other Flemish painters than to any Italian Renaissance artist (Figure 18.1, page 394). Also, Bruegel used symbolism much as the medieval artist did in illustrating stories from the Bible. His blind men are symbols painted with accurate details to give them a more lifelike appearance.

CHAPTER 18
LESSON THREE

Art Criticism

Have students note the helmet in the foreground of *Death and the Miser,* Figure 18.13. In what other painting in this lesson have students seen a similar helmet? What may have been the artist's reasons for including it? Is the helmet literal or symbolic?

Cross Curriculum

LANGUAGE ARTS. Point out that the parable is a well-established literary genre, having its roots in antiquity. Review with students the definition of parable provided in the text. Then ask individual students to create parables for their own time. The compositions, which are to run no longer than one page, may treat a school-related theme, one that relates to young people of the late twentieth century, or a topic of their own choosing. Allow time for volunteers to share their parables with classmates.

Did You Know**?**

Michelangelo was a contemporary of Bruegel, even though he painted the Sistine Chapel ceiling more than a decade before the Flemish painter was born. Michelangelo died just five years before Bruegel's death in 1569.

CULTURAL DIVERSITY

Cultural Differences. Point out to students that the artists discussed in this lesson were the products of different cultures, each with its own system of laws, food, clothing, and social customs. Ask students to research and explore the cultures of the different areas mentioned in this lesson, including Flanders, the Netherlands, and England. (Point out that Germany was not unified during this period but consisted of a number of small duchies and principalities, each with its own distinct culture.) When students have completed their research, have them give brief presentations summarizing the culture they have chosen. Conclude with a discussion of the similarities and differences.

Art Criticism

Direct students' attention to Hans Holbein's portrait of Edward VI, Figure 18.15. Emphasize that the work is meant to be the portrait of a two-year-old child. Then pass around a photograph of a two-year-old child, and ask students to compare the picture with Holbein's portrait. Ask students to identify characteristics in the painting that makes it less realistic and more idealistic than the photo. Ask: In what other ways are the painting and photograph different? Why did Holbein paint the portrait as he did?

Art History

Have students compare the two portraits by Holbein (Figures 18.15 and 18.16, pages 413–414). Considering the circumstances under which the works were created, how much can we infer about the appearance (i.e., facial features, mode of dress) of people living in northern Europe in the sixteenth century? Remind students that Holbein created his portrait of Anne of Cleves in a week's time. Ask: Were students surprised to learn this? What does this fact reveal about the artist's skills?

Symbolism in Sixteenth-Century Art

Bruegel's beggars follow a road leading to eternal suffering rather than the road leading to salvation. In their blindness they stumble past the distant church, cleverly framed by trees and the outstretched staff of one of the beggars.

1 The ditch they are about to tumble into could represent hell. It would represent the only possible end for those who allow themselves to be led down the path of wickedness.

■ **FIGURE 18.14**

Pieter Bruegel. *The Parable of the Blind.* 1568. Tempera on canvas. 86 × 152 cm (34 × 60"). Museo Nazionale di Capodimonte, Naples, Italy.

2 Bruegel warns that anyone can be misled; even the blind man wearing a showy cross as proof of his piety is being led astray.

3 Bruegel demonstrates a keen sense for detail. A French physician once identified the symptoms of five different eye diseases on the faces of these beggars.

4 The faces of the figures show expressions that range from confusion (the man at the far left) to fear (the figures at the right).

Symbolism in Sixteenth-Century Art

Before students read the explanation in this Symbolism in Art feature, let them point out likely symbols in the work. Ask: Given the proverb that the work illustrates, what do the blind men probably symbolize? What kind of building is shown in the background? Why do you think Bruegel included it?

After students have discussed their initial ideas, have them read and discuss the information in the feature. Ask: Under which aesthetic theory—formalism or emotionalism—does the work most succeed? Have students explain their responses.

Hans Holbein (1497–1543)

Several years after the deaths of Grünewald and Dürer, another German artist named Hans Holbein the Younger (hans **hole**-bine) left his native country to settle in England. Holbein hoped to escape from the strife of the Reformation. Known for his lifelike portraits, he became the court painter for King Henry VIII.

Edward VI as a Child

■ **FIGURE 18.15**

As a New Year's gift in 1539, Holbein presented Henry with a portrait of his 14-month-old son, Edward. The birth of this son had been widely acclaimed in England because the king finally had a male heir to the throne.

Holbein painted the young Edward in royal garments and placed a gold rattle in his hand (Figure 18.15). Even though the face and hands are childlike, Edward does not look like a young child. The artist probably wanted to impress Henry by showing the child's royal dignity rather than his infant charms.

The Latin verse below Edward's portrait asks him to follow the path of virtue and to be a good ruler. Unhappily, he had little opportunity to do either. Never healthy or strong, Edward died of tuberculosis when he was 16.

Anne of Cleves

■ **FIGURE 18.16**

The year after the painting of young Edward VI was completed, Henry VIII asked Holbein to paint a most unusual portrait (Figure 18.16, page 414). The king, who was looking for a new bride, had heard that Anne, the young daughter of the Duke of Cleves in Germany, was available. He decided to send a delegation to look her over. Included in this delegation was Holbein, who was to paint a portrait of Anne. Taking the artist aside, Henry confided, "I put more trust in your brush than in all the reports of my advisers."

Sir Thomas Cromwell, one of the king's most powerful ministers, was anxious to see a marriage between Anne and Henry for political reasons. Cromwell instructed Holbein that he must, without fail, bring back a most beautiful portrait of Lady Anne.

When Holbein met Anne in her castle in Germany, he found that she was good-natured, patient, and honest; unfortunately,

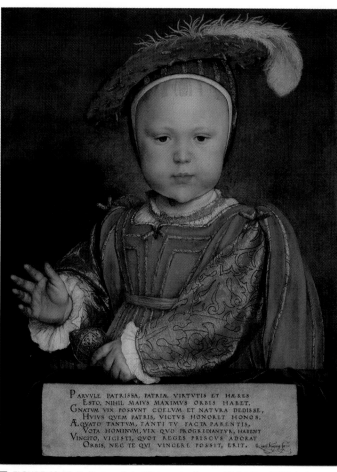

■ **FIGURE 18.15** Holbein painted this portrait as a gift for the child's father, King Henry VIII. **Identify the childlike features and the adult qualities in this portrait of the young prince.**

Hans Holbein, the Younger. *Edward VI as a Child.* c. 1538. Oil on panel. 56.8 × 44 cm (22³/₈ × 17³/₈″). National Gallery of Art, Washington, D.C. Board of Trustees, Andrew W. Mellon Collection.

CHAPTER 18
LESSON THREE

Art History

Let several volunteers research the life Anne led after her marriage to King Henry VIII was dissolved. Ask another group of volunteers to research the fate of Thomas Cromwell. Have these students share their findings in oral presentations.

Study Guide

Distribute *Study Guide* 42 in the TCR. Assist students in reviewing key concepts.

Art and Humanities

Have students complete *Art and Humanities* 30 "Traveling the Road to Canterbury," in the TCR. Through this activity, students discover the mosaic of humanity that Chaucer wrote about in his poetry.

Enrichment

Assign students *Appreciating Cultural Diversity* 28, "Art Portraying Good and Evil," in the TCR, in which students explore the expression of goodness and evil in art.

Art and Humanities

Ask volunteers to read selected parables in *The Miner's Pale Children,* a collection of works in this genre by twentieth-century American author and poet W.S. Merwin. Many of the works in the anthology address ills of contemporary society, such as apathy and pollution. Encourage students to give a dramatic interpretation of one of the shorter selections (e.g., "Take This Simple Test") and then interpret its meaning.

More About...

Hans Holbein. Although Hans Holbein is now best-known as a portraitist (*Edward VI as a Child, Anne of Cleves*), he was famous in his own time for woodcuts, such as *The Alphabet of Death* and *The Dance of Death.* The second of these is a series of forty-one woodcuts that were widely popular among Holbein's contemporaries, because, like Dürer's *Apocalypse* series, they reflected the preoccupation with death that characterized this time period. Each of the scenes Holbein created portrays a skeletal figure triumphing over a human one, suggesting that every person, regardless of status, wealth, or faith, must face death. The first in the series *Expulsion from Paradise* portrays man's first encounter with death outside the Garden of Eden.

ASSESS

Checking Comprehension

➤ Have students respond to the lesson review questions. Answers are given in the box below.

➤ Have students complete *Application* 18, "Credit Where Credit Is Due." This activity asks students to assign credit lines to sixteenth-century artworks based on descriptions of subject matter and/or technique. 📁

Reteaching

➤ Assign *Reteaching* 42, found in the TCR. Have students complete the activity and review their responses. 📁

➤ Ask students to review the conflict of styles in northern art of the sixteenth century. Have them describe the characteristics of each style. Then ask students to name an artist who represents each style.

Extension

Ask a student to find out more about the great scholar Erasmus, an important figure in the Renaissance, and an acquaintance of artist Hans Holbein. Have the student give a brief oral report on the life and work of Erasmus and to explain to the class why Erasmus was a significant figure in the sixteenth century.

CLOSE

Have students plan and write a brief essay titled "Life and Strife in the Sixteenth Century." The composition should include relevant facts and dates from the lesson.

---

she was also dull, lifeless, and plain. This presented a problem for the artist. If he painted Anne to look beautiful, he would please Cromwell but risk the anger of the king. If he painted her plain, he would offend both Cromwell and the woman who might become queen.

Apparently Holbein decided to let his brush make the decision for him; he completed the portrait in less than one week. Returning to England, he showed the painting to Henry, who took one look at it and signed the marriage contract. Arrangements were soon under way for a marriage ceremony that would dazzle all of Europe.

When the king finally met Anne, he was stunned and enraged that the person did not match the portrait. Still, he was forced to go ahead with the wedding to ensure that Anne's father would remain England's ally. The marriage took place on January 6, 1540, and was legally dissolved on July 7 of the same year.

Surprisingly, Holbein suffered no ill effects for his part in the arrangements, although Henry chose his next two wives after close personal inspection. Holbein remained in Henry's good graces and had begun painting a portrait of the king when he fell victim to the plague. Holbein died in London in the fall of 1543.

■ **FIGURE 18.16** The different textures in this painting contribute to the elegant and lifelike appearance of the subject. **Who is the subject of this painting? How did this portrait change her life?**

Hans Holbein. *Anne of Cleves.* 1539. Tempera and oil on parchment. 65 × 48 cm (25⅝ × 18⅞"). The Louvre, Paris, France.

LESSON THREE REVIEW

Reviewing Art Facts

1. Which German artist showed a preference for the dreams and visions favored by Gothic art?
2. Which German artist turned away from the Gothic style to embrace the ideas of the Italian Renaissance?
3. Tell how the paintings of Hieronymus Bosch are similar to those of the Italian Mannerists.
4. For what kind of painting was Hans Holbein best known?

Activity... *Writing About an Artwork*

Albrecht Dürer and Hieronymus Bosch are two of the most fascinating and mysterious artists of all time. Their works are a curious mixture of Northern Renaissance concern for detail, emotionalism, and symbolism. Much of the original meaning of the works of these artists, especially Bosch, is lost to us.

Study the two works by these artists in this chapter. Can you interpret the meaning of each work? Find other examples of the work of Dürer and Bosch. Choose one that is interesting to you. Imagine that you are the artist and write an explanation of the work. Share your work with the class.

LESSON THREE REVIEW

Answers to Reviewing Art Facts

1. Matthias Grünewald.
2. Albrecht Dürer.
3. They mirrored growing fears and tensions of the people during an uneasy period.
4. Portraits.

Activity...*Writing About an Artwork*

Let students work with partners to find and examine other works by Dürer and Bosch. Encourage interested students to read more about these artists and their works. Then have partners or group members discuss what one of the artists might think and feel about a particular work. How would he be likely to express his thoughts and feelings?

Complete a highly imaginative tempera painting of a bizarre creature. Create the starting point for this painting by manipulating a length of colored yarn on a sheet of paper. Use a variety of hues, intensities, and values obtained by mixing the three primary colors and white and black.

Inspiration

Did you notice the strange creatures lurking in the works of Dürer and Bosch (Figure 18.12, page 409 and Figure 18.13, page 411)? Which of these creatures did you find especially bizarre? Can you find earlier works illustrated in this book that may have influenced the two artists in creating these unusual creatures?

Process

1. Begin by experimenting with a length of yarn, dropping and manipulating it on a sheet of paper. Use your imagination to see this yarn line as the starting point for a drawing of a bizarre creature. The creature might have human or animal characteristics, or it could combine characteristics of both.

2. When you are satisfied that you have a starting point for your drawing, glue the yarn in place on the paper. Use a pencil to continue this line at both ends to create your creature.

3. Paint your picture. Limit yourself to the three primary colors, but do not use any of these colors directly from the jar or tube. Instead, mix them to obtain a variety of hues and intensities. Add white and black to these hues to create a range of different values. Do not paint over the yarn line. Allow it to stand out clearly as the starting point in your picture.

Materials

- A length of colored yarn, about 10 inches long
- White drawing paper, 9 × 12 inches
- White glue
- Pencil
- Tempera or acrylic paint
- Brushes, mixing tray, and paint cloth
- Water container

■ **FIGURE 18.17** Student Work

Examining Your Work

Describe. Does your painting feature a bizarre, highly imaginative creature? Point out and name the most unusual features of this creature.

Analyze. Is the yarn line used to start your picture clearly visible? Does your painting include a variety of hues, intensities, and values?

Interpret. How is the creature you created unusual? What feelings does it evoke in students viewing your picture for the first time? Were these the feelings you hoped to evoke?

Judge. Evaluate your picture in terms of its design qualities. Is it successful? Then evaluate it in terms of its expressive qualities. What was the most difficult part of this studio experience?

415

Objectives

■ Complete a tempera painting of a bizarre creature.

■ Begin with a line created by manipulating a length of yarn.

■ Include a variety of hues, intensities, and values.

Motivator

Show students a length of yarn and demonstrate how, when stretched out, it becomes a straight line. Place the yarn on an overhead projector and have a student move it about until an unusual line is made. Ask students what they could draw using this line as a starting point. Emphasize that this can be a great deal more challenging than one would expect—it requires imagination to visualize the possibilities.

Aesthetics

Direct students' attention to the paintings by Grünewald, Dürer, and Bosch illustrated in this chapter. Ask whether students think it is possible to understand these works completely if the expressive qualities are ignored. Discuss the role of emotion in the appreciation of art—is it always relevant? Ask students to identify artworks in this textbook that do not appeal to the emotions.

Critiquing

Have students apply the steps of art criticism to their own artwork, using the "Examining Your Work" questions on this page.

ASSESSMENT

Group Discussion. After students have examined and assessed their own paintings, let them meet in small groups to discuss and reconsider the process of the project, responding to questions such as these: How did the shape of the yarn line affect my painting? What other yarn line might I have used? What kind of painting might I have done with that line? Given the yarn line I started with, how could I have created an even more bizarre and imaginative creature? If I had not started with a yarn line, what kind of creature might I have painted? What could I have done at any stage of this project to improve the design qualities of my work?

Studio LESSON

Humorous Face from Expanded Shapes

Objectives

■ Create a face composed of a variety of large and small shapes cut from a single, free-form shape.

■ Make certain the face is humorous in both appearance and expression.

Motivator

Have students use their imaginations to "walk into" Bruegel's painting of *The Parable of the Blind*. What could they expect to hear each of the blind men saying? How many students would feel pity for these men? How many would smile or even laugh at their foolishness? What would they tell the men as they lay in a tangle at the bottom of the ditch? Is there one face in particular that students find interesting? What makes it so?

Art Criticism

Instruct students to write a brief humorous paragraph that provides additional information about the characters they created. Collect the paragraphs and randomly redistribute them to class members. Students should be instructed not to accept statements they wrote themselves. Place the works on display and ask students to examine them, read the statement, and then try to match it to the correct artwork.

Critiquing

Have students apply the steps of art criticism to their own artwork, using the "Examining Your Work" questions on this page.

Studio LESSON

Humorous Face from Expanded Shapes

Materials

- Sheet of white construction paper, 6 × 9 inches
- Sheet of colored construction paper, 12 × 18 inches
- Scissors and white glue
- Scrap pieces of colored construction paper

Using a variety of large and small shapes cut from a single, free-form shape, create a face that is humorous in both appearance and expression.

Inspiration

Examine Bruegel's painting *The Parable of the Blind* (Figure 18.14, page 412). Observe the different expressions on the faces of the blind men. Do the faces suggest that these men are clever or foolish? How is this indicated? Do you find yourself feeling sorry for these characters, or are you more inclined to smile at their predicament? Do you think humor is acceptable in art?

Process

1. Cut a simple, free-form, solid shape from the white sheet of construction paper. Then cut this into three shapes of approximately the same size. Cut each of the three into five shapes, producing a total of 15.

2. Arrange all 15 shapes on the sheet of colored construction paper. Let each shape touch—in just one place—the shape that had been next to it before you cut them apart. Spread the shapes slightly, leaving gaps between the pieces.

3. Glue all the shapes in place, and study your design carefully. Use your imagination to "see" the beginnings of a humorous face. When you have discovered such a face, add hair, eyes, ears, nose, mouth, and other details cut from scraps of colored paper. Try to make your face as humorous as possible.

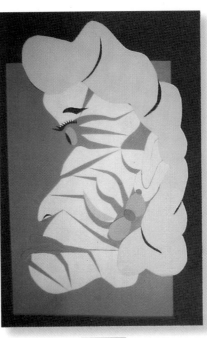

■ **FIGURE 18.18** Student Work

Examining Your Work

Describe. Can viewers easily identify the subject of your picture as a face? Are the eyes, nose, mouth, and other features clearly indicated?

Analyze. Is your picture composed of a variety of large and small shapes? Were all these cut from a single, free-form shape?

Interpret. Is the face you have created humorous? What makes it so? Do you think others will find it humorous?

Judge. Do you think your picture is successful? Did you find that making a humorous work of art is just as challenging as making one that is more "serious"?

416

ASSESSMENT

Peer Review. Following students' individual assessment of their humorous faces, have them meet in peer-review groups to examine and discuss one another's work. Encourage group members to identify the most successful aspects of each work and to make constructive suggestions for improving other aspects. Then ask students to write entries in their art journals, discussing what they have learned from creating the humorous face and from examining it with the other members of their peer-review group.

Reviewing the Facts

Lesson One

1. How did Giorgione use the landscape in his paintings?
2. What is a *painterly* technique?
3. For what subject matter was Titian most famous?

Lesson Two

4. List five unsettling or ambiguous aspects of Parmigianino's painting *The Madonna with the Long Neck* (Figure 18.6, page 402).
5. What qualities in Tintoretto's *Presentation of the Virgin* (Figure 18.7, page 403) identify it as a Mannerist work?

Lesson Three

6. What was Matthias Grünewald's goal in creating *The Small Crucifixion* (Figure 18.11, page 408)?
7. What does the dog at the bottom of Dürer's engraving *Knight, Death, and the Devil* (Figure 18.12, page 409) symbolize?
8. In what two ways were Hieronymus Bosch's and Pieter Bruegel's paintings meant to be viewed?

Thinking Critically

1. **ANALYZE.** Identify two works in this chapter in which the artists understate the main subjects in the works. Explain, in each case, how understating the subject seems to have the effect of drawing attention to it.
2. **COMPARE AND CONTRAST.** Refer to Parmigianino's *Madonna with the Long Neck* (Figure 18.6, page 402) and to Raphael's *Alba Madonna* (Figure 16.24, page 373). Describe the similarities and differences between the works. Explain how current events played a role in each artist's interpretation of essentially the same subject.

 THEATRE. Use the *Performing Arts Handbook,* page 588 to learn about Jennifer Tipton and *The Tempest.*

CAREERS IN Art Read about a career as a fashion designer in the *Careers in Art Handbook,* page 605.

*inter*NET
CONNECTION Visit Glencoe Art Online at *www.glencoe.com/sec/art*. Explore more artworks from the sixteenth century and investigate the times in which these works were created.

Technology Project

Sixteenth-Century Artists

Art of the sixteenth century, created in both the northern and the southern sections of Europe, reflects the contrasting concerns of artists who lived in the same era. While the artists of such southern cities as Florence and Rome continued to turn to classical ideals for their inspiration, the artists of the north followed a much different path. Their works reflect conflicting values and influences. Northern artists grappled with accepting new humanistic ideas and styles emerging from the Italian Renaissance, while retaining the religious concerns of the late Gothic period.

1. Examine the works of Pieter Bruegel and of another fascinating artist of the north, Hieronymus Bosch, which provide a look into a world of symbols whose meanings have been mostly lost. What do you think is the symbolic significance of the people, creatures, and objects in the painting?
2. Working in small groups, investigate some of the other interesting artists of northern Europe during the sixteenth century such as Hans Holbein, Matthias Grünewald, and Lucas Cranach. Plan a presentation on one of these artists. Using art criticism and art history operations, compare and contrast these artists' works.
3. Create a multimedia presentation, short videotape, or slide show, and present your information to the class.

417

Teaching the Technology Project

Have students work independently to examine artworks by various northern European artists of the sixteenth century, using CDs, the Internet, reference works, and other print resources. Ask each student to select the artist he or she wants to examine more closely. Encourage them to make their presentations as visually interesting as possible.

 Assign the feature in the *Performing Arts Handbook,* page 588.

CAREERS IN ART If time permits, have interested students investigate the career information in the *Careers in Art Handbook,* page 605.

*inter*NET
CONNECTION Have students go online and learn more about artists on preselected Web sites with the Internet activity for this chapter.

Reviewing the Facts

1. To create a mood.
2. Technique of creating forms with patches of color rather than with hard, precise edges.
3. For his portraits.
4. Answers will vary, but may include any five of the following: whether the setting is interior or exterior; what purpose the columns serve; what the Madonna is sitting on, the Madonna is too large; she seems unconcerned that the Christ Child is about to fall; Christ Child is out of proportion; uncertainty about the unidentified leg.
5. The elongated figures with dramatic gestures, odd perspective, and strange, uneven light.
6. Grünewald wanted to create a visual sermon.
7. Loyalty.
8. As stories and as symbolic messages.

Thinking Critically

1. Answers might include: Giorgione's *The Concert,* Titian's *The Entombment,* and Tintoretto's *Presentation of the Virgin.* In the first two, the technique has the effect of arousing the viewer's curiosity. Tintoretto's work involves the viewer in a search for Mary by rendering her small and unimportant.
2. Similarities: both artists create solid, round forms through the use of light, perspective, and proportion. Differences: the subjects of Dürer's work are reminiscent of the strange features typical of northern Gothic paintings.

Baroque Art

LESSON ONE
(pages 420–428)

Baroque Art of Italy and Flanders

Classroom Resources

- 📁 Art and Humanities 31
- 📁 Enrichment Activity 36
- 📁 Reproducible Lesson Plan 43
- 📁 Reteaching Activity 43
- 📁 Study Guide 43

Features

Time & Place CONNECTIONS
(page 424)

LOOKING Closely
(page 425)

Finding Axis Lines in Art
The Raising of the Cross
(page 427)

LESSON TWO
(pages 429–436)

Dutch Art

Classroom Resources

- 📁 Appreciating Cultural Diversity 29
- 📁 Cooperative Learning 28
- 📁 Reproducible Lesson Plan 44
- 📁 Reteaching Activity 44
- 📁 Study Guide 44

Features

Storytelling in Art
The Love Letter
(page 434)

LESSON THREE
(pages 437–440)

Spanish Art

Classroom Resources

- 📁 Art and Humanities 32
- 📁 Reproducible Lesson Plan 45
- 📁 Reteaching Activity 45
- 📁 Study Guide 45

Features

The Viewer's Position in Art
The Surrender of Breda
(page 438)

END OF CHAPTER
(pages 441–443)

Studio LESSONS

- Painting a Shape Moving in Space *(page 441)*
- Charcoal Figure Drawing *(page 442)*

ADDITIONAL CHAPTER RESOURCES

Activities

- 📁 Advanced Studio Activity 19
- 📁 Application 19
- 🖱 Chapter 19 Internet Activity
- 📁 Studio Activity 25

Fine Art Resources

🕹 **Transparency**

Art in Focus Transparency 24

Claude Lorrain. *The Marriage of Isaac and Rebecca.*

🖼 **Fine Art Prints**

Focus on World Art Print 19

Rachel Ruysch. *Flower Still Life.*

Assessment

- 📁 Chapter 19 Test
- 📁 Performance Assessment

Multimedia Resources

- 🎭 Artsource® Performing Arts Package
- 💿 National Gallery Laser Disc
- 💿 National Museum of Women in the Arts CD-ROM
- 📼 Arts & Entertainment Videos

NATIONAL STANDARDS FOR ARTS EDUCATION

The National Standards for Arts Education provide guidelines for grade-appropriate competency in the visual arts. The Content Standards for grades 9–12 are:

1. Understanding and applying media, techniques, and processes.
2. Using knowledge of structures and functions.
3. Choosing and evaluating a range of subject matter, symbols, and ideas.
4. Understanding the visual arts in relation to history and cultures.
5. Reflecting upon and assessing the characteristics and merits of their work and the work of others.
6. Making connections between visual arts and other disciplines.

Listed below are the National Standards for the Visual Arts addressed in this chapter. For a breakdown of the categories listed under each content standard, refer to the *Reproducible Lesson Plans* booklet in the TCR.

1. (a, b)   **2.** (a, b)   **3.** (a, b)   **4.** (a, b, c)   **5.** (a, b)   **6.** (b)

HANDBOOK MATERIAL

ARTSOURCE

Los Angeles Baroque *(page 589)*

CAREERS IN

Careers in Art *(page 594)*

Beyond the Classroom

The International Society for the Performing Arts Association promotes and encourages involvement in all the performing arts for students and teachers. Find them by visiting our Web site at *www.glencoe.com/sec/art.*

🕐 **Out of Time?** If time does not permit teaching this chapter in its entirety, you may wish to preview the artwork and captions with students. Scan the heads in each lesson with students. Discuss the Looking Closely feature and examine Finding Axis Lines in Art, page 427, and Storytelling in Art on page 434.

Baroque Art

Baroque Art

INTRODUCE

Chapter Overview

CHAPTER 19 acquaints students with features of Baroque art.

Lesson One introduces stylistic features of Baroque art in Italy, Flanders, the Netherlands, and Spain.

Lesson Two introduces Dutch genre painters.

Lesson Three focuses on Spanish artists of the time and their preference for religious subject matter.

Studio Lessons instruct students to paint a moving shape and execute a charcoal figure drawing.

Art & Social Studies

Have students describe and discuss the artwork that opens this chapter. How is it similar to or different from paintings they have examined in previous chapters? Then let students identify details in the painting that indicate the status of artists in seventeenth-century Europe. Ask a group of interested volunteers to learn more about the role of artists in seventeenth-century society and to share the results.

National Standards

This chapter addresses the following National Standards for the Arts.

1. (a,b)	**4.** (a,b,c)
2. (a,b)	**5.** (a,b)
3. (a,b)	**6.** (b)

418

Art & Social Studies ■ **FIGURE 19.1** Clues to the status of artists in the seventeenth century can be found in this painting. The palette and brushes in the hands of the artist identify his trade. The sheen of fine fabric and the fur edging that decorate the girl's clothing suggest that his students are from a wealthy background. The statue of the cow symbolizes the ox of St. Luke, the patron saint of artists. Each detail in the painting suggests the artist was regarded as an important mentor in the education of future generations.

Jan Steen. *The Drawing Lesson.* c. 1665. Oil on panel. 49.3 × 41 cm (19³/₈ × 16¹/₄"). J. Paul Getty Museum, Los Angeles, California.

418

CHAPTER 19 RESOURCES

Teacher's Classroom Resources
- 📁 Advanced Studio Activity 19
- 📁 Application 19
- 🖱 Chapter 19 Internet Activity
- 📁 Studio Activity 25

Assessment
- 📁 Chapter 19 Test
- 📁 Performance Assessment

Fine Art Resources
- 🖼 *Art in Focus* Transparency 24
  Claude Lorrain. *The Marriage of Isaac and Rebecca.*
- *Focus on World Art* Print 19
  Rachael Ruysch. *Flower Still Life.*

Late in the sixteenth century and early in the seventeenth century, a more relaxed and confident attitude replaced the tension and doubts of the Mannerist period. By the start of the seventeenth century, the Catholic Church had gained back much of its power in Italy. It was now answering the challenge of the Protestant Reformation with a reform movement of its own. In the visual arts, artists began turning out works of stunning originality. Literature and music created during this period represent some of the greatest works of all time.

Introducing the Chapter

Direct students' attention to Figure 19.1. Ask whether this painting might have been done during the Renaissance, and have students record their answers in their journals. Review students' answers after the reading of the chapter.

ART SOURCE

Music. While studying this chapter, use *Performing Arts Handbook* page 589 to help students understand how Gregory Maldonado and the L.A. Baroque Orchestra recapture the sound of music created during the Baroque period.

YOUR Portfolio

Work in groups with half the group taking the role of art critics while the other half will be art historians. Students acting as art critics should study Figure 19.8 on page 426 based on the four steps, or operations, of art criticism. Students acting as art historians should use the art history operations. Although you use the same four steps, you use different sources and criteria when reviewing an artwork. Share the results, then discuss the similarities and differences that arise. Create a dramatic artwork for a portfolio entry. Then examine the work using the art criticism steps. Keep notes with your work in your portfolio.

Focus ON THE ARTS

THEATRE

In England, permanent open-air theaters were devoted to the performance of plays. These theaters were decorated, but no real scenery existed. Actors wore costumes and used props to enhance the scenes.

LITERATURE

English playwright and poet William Shakespeare steadily developed his writing to become the most influential dramatist the world has known. His dramas and poems demonstrate an unequaled mastery of the English language.

MUSIC

Johann Sebastian Bach, German organist and choir director, composed organ preludes, fugues, and tocattas. His musical style paralleled the harmony and variety of Baroque art.

Focus ON THE ARTS

In the Middle Ages, European plays were performed in churches and marketplaces. Then in 1576, some London actors bought a building and called it "The Theatre." It was the first building in England devoted only to plays. Divide students into groups of theater managers. Have them imagine it is 1600, and they have bought such a building. Have them list the advantages, for practical and artistic reasons. What kinds of plays will they put on and why?

Practical advantages of an indoor theater: It is easier to store costumes, scenery, jewelry, props, and special effects; it is easier to control stage lighting; provides shelter; there is room for a large orchestra; it contains trap doors (for dramatic reasons and for hiding scenery).

419

DEVELOPING A PORTFOLIO

Choosing a Project. When preparing a portfolio for evaluation, students are often expected to follow precise guidelines. Remind them that their choice of specific subjects and techniques will demonstrate their artistic imagination as well. For example, if they are expected to include a still life that exhibits both transparency and reflection, they might choose a clear glass vase filled with tinted water. Also, making decisions about subjects often leads to further research. They can browse through print material, like this textbook, looking for models that successfully demonstrate the necessary criteria for the project.

Baroque Art of Italy and Flanders

Baroque Art of Italy and Flanders

Focus

Lesson Objectives

After studying this lesson, students will be able to:

■ Explain what is meant by Counter-Reformation and how art played a part in it.

■ Compare and contrast Baroque and Italian Renaissance art.

■ Describe the qualities Baroque architects and sculptors sought in their work.

Building Vocabulary

Let students who know—or are studying—French and Italian share their understanding of the Vocabulary terms *façade* and *chiaroscuro.* Then have students check the formal definitions of these terms.

Motivator

Ask students to brainstorm words that begin with the prefix *counter-* (e.g., *counterclockwise, counterproductive*). Ask students to infer the meaning of this word part. Then tell them that around the turn of the sixteenth century, the Church began a Counter-Reformation movement in an effort to regain its power base in Italy.

Introducing the Lesson

Ask students to volunteer examples from their own experience of telling a story in an effort to persuade someone of something. Draw a parallel between student responses and the contention of the Church that emotionally charged accounts from the Bible were needed to persuade members to stay with the Church.

420

Vocabulary
■ Counter-Reformation
■ Baroque art
■ façade
■ chiaroscuro

Artists to Meet
■ Francesco Borromini
■ Gianlorenzo Bernini
■ Michelangelo da Caravaggio
■ Artemisia Gentileschi
■ Peter Paul Rubens

Discover
After completing this lesson, you will be able to:
■ Explain what the Counter-Reformation was and discuss the role art played in this movement.
■ Describe the qualities Baroque architects and sculptors sought in their work.
■ Discuss the styles and innovations of Baroque artists, including Caravaggio, Gentileschi, and Rubens.

The **Counter-Reformation** was *an effort by the Catholic Church to lure people back and to regain its former power.* Art played a major role in this movement to stamp out heresy and encourage people to return to the Church. Artists and architects were called to Rome to create works that would restore religious spirit and make the city the most beautiful in the Christian world. A style emerged that had dramatic flair and dynamic movement. It was **Baroque art,** *a style characterized by movement, vivid contrast, and emotional intensity.* Once again, Rome became the center of the art world, just as it had been during the height of the Renaissance a century earlier.

A New Style in Church Architecture

In architecture, the Counter-Reformation brought about a revival of church building and remodeling. One of these new Roman churches, Il Gesú (Figure 19.2), was among the first to use features that signaled the birth of the new art style. The huge, sculptured scrolls at each side of the upper story are a Baroque innovation. They are used here to unite the side sections of the wide **façade,** or *front of the building,* to the central portion. This sculptural quality on buildings such as Il Gesú was an important feature of the Baroque architectural style. Over the next hundred years, this style spread across a large part of Europe.

■ **FIGURE 19.2** This church was an early example of the new Baroque style. Point to a feature on this building that marks it as uniquely Baroque.

Gíacomo della Porta. Il Gesú, Rome, Italy. c. 1575.

420

Teacher's Classroom Resources

📁 Art and Humanities 31

📁 Enrichment Activity 36

📁 Reproducible Lesson Plan 43

📁 Reteaching Activity 43

📁 Study Guide 43

Francesco Borromini (1599–1667)

An excellent example of the mature Baroque style in architecture is a tiny Roman church designed by the architect Francesco Borromini (fran-**chess**-koh bore-oh-**mee**-nee).

San Carlo alle Quattro Fontane
■ **FIGURE 19.3**

The church that made Borromini famous worldwide was San Carlo alle Quattro Fontane (Figure 19.3). The façade of this church is a continuous flow of concave and convex surfaces. This makes the building seem elastic and pulled out of shape.

The push and pull that results creates a startling pattern of light and shadow across the building. The façade is three-dimensional, almost sculptural. The moldings, sculptures, and niches with small framing columns add three-dimensional richness and abrupt value contrast. Borromini boldly designed this façade to produce an overall effect of movement, contrast, and variety.

■ **FIGURE 19.3** This building is said to produce an effect of movement. **How is this effect achieved?**

Francesco Borromini. San Carlo alle Quattro Fontane, Rome, Italy. 1665–76.

Chapter 19 *Baroque Art* **421**

TEACH
Critical Thinking

To reinforce the underlying principles in the Church's Counter-Reformation efforts (i.e., presenting itself anew through art by emphasizing features such as realism, strong emotion, and the theme of repentance), ask students to bring in examples of product packaging that has been redesigned to express the item's new "personality" (e.g., a changing logo style). Have students share their discoveries and discuss why companies periodically present themselves and their products in new ways.

Aesthetics

Direct students' attention to the work of architecture illustrated in Figure 19.3. What adjectives or phrases do students feel best describe this structure? How would an aesthetician of the formalist school react to the structure? What would an aesthetician of the emotionalist school think?

Did You Know?

Some historians suggest that the word *Baroque* comes from the Portuguese word *barroco*, which means "irregularly-shaped pearl." At first, the term was used to label works that were felt to be bizarre or grotesque. This has changed, and now *Baroque* is used when referring to the period from 1600 to about 1700, and the style of art that was practiced during this period.

Technology

National Gallery of Art Videodisc Use the following images as examples of more works by artists introduced in this lesson.

Peter Paul Rubens
Daniel in the Lions' Den

Search Frame 776

Peter Paul Rubens
Saint Catherine of Alexandria

Search Frame 3164

Peter Paul Rubens
A Lion

Search Frame 2831

Use Glencoe's *Correlation Bar Code Guide to the National Gallery of Art* to locate more artworks.

Cross Curriculum

SCIENCE. Point out that not only was the world of art in great transition during the period from about 1500 to 1700, but that the field of science was also undergoing an unprecedented revolution. Divide the class into research teams. Have each team investigate the theories of one of the following: Nicolaus Copernicus, Galileo, Johannes Kepler, Andreas Vesalius, Sir Francis Bacon, and Sir Isaac Newton. Have each team present itself as a panel of experts and have them field questions from the rest of the class. Permit teams to take turns as panel members and spectators.

Art Criticism

Have students examine Figure 19.5 on page 423, paying particular attention to Bernini's use of voluminous drapery. Then refer students to Figure 8.19 (page 183), which illustrates the Classical Greek use of drapery on a figure. Ask: How does his use of form, line, texture, and rhythm differ from that of the Greeks? How important was it for Bernini to suggest St. Theresa's body beneath the drapery? Can you tell what position her legs are in? Where does Bernini place the emphasis instead?

Cross Curriculum

LITERATURE. Have a student read the lesson in St. Theresa's *Autobiography*, in which she describes the mystical vision portrayed by Bernini in Figure 19.5. Ask the student to give a dramatic reading of this passage and discuss whether Bernini's sculpture successfully conveys the details and spirit of St. Theresa's amazing experience.

■ **FIGURE 19.4** The artist who painted this ceiling placed a small mark on the floor beneath it. When people stood on this mark and looked up, they had the best view of this amazing painting. **Can you tell where the building ends and the painting begins? What makes this painting Baroque?**

Fra Andrea Pozzo. *The Entrance of St. Ignatius into Paradise.* 1691–94. Ceiling fresco. Sant' Ignazio, Rome, Italy.

Emphasis on Mood and Drama in Sculpture

Throughout the Baroque period, sculptors showed the same interest in movement, contrast, and variety as did architects. They placed great importance on the feeling expressed in their work and tried to capture the moment of highest drama and excitement.

Sculptors showed less interest in portraying ideal or realistic beauty. Drapery, for example, no longer suggested the body beneath. Instead, it offered artists a chance to show off their skills at complex modeling and reproducing different textures. Deep undercutting was used to create shadows and sharp contrasts of light and dark values. Colored marble replaced white marble or somber bronze as the preferred sculptural medium.

During this time, sculptors created works that seemed to break out of and flow from their architectural frames. This effect is similar to that found in murals and ceiling paintings done at the same time (Figure 19.4). The results overwhelm and even confuse the viewer. Sometimes the viewer has trouble seeing where the painting or sculpture ends and reality takes over.

CULTURAL DIVERSITY

Architecture. Have groups of students research and provide presentations to the class on Indonesian architectural styles that embody the "sculptural" aesthetic also seen in Baroque building façades. Some possibilities include the Great Palace (sometimes called the Grand Palace) in Bangkok, Thailand; Sri Mariamman, Singapore's oldest Hindu temple; and the temple of Angkor Wat in Cambodia. In their presentations, which should include reproductions of the structures, students should characterize the way in which the façades of these buildings share some of the same elastic, rhythmic, and three-dimensional qualities as Il Gesù and San Carlo alle Quattro Fontane.

Gianlorenzo Bernini (1598–1680)

This merging of Baroque sculpture and architecture is seen in Gianlorenzo Bernini's (jee-ahn-low-**ren**-zoh bair-**nee**-nee) altar containing the famous *Ecstasy of St. Theresa* (Figure 19.5). It was dedicated to St. Theresa, a sixteenth-century Spanish saint of the Counter-Reformation. The inspiration for this sculpture is St. Theresa's vision in which an angel pierced her heart with a fire-tipped golden arrow symbolizing God's love.

Bernini's Use of Space and Light

The angel and the saint are carved in white marble and placed against a background of golden rays radiating from above. This scene is lit from overhead by a concealed yellow glass window that makes the figures seem to float in space within a niche of colored marble. The figures appear to move about freely within that space. This new relationship of space and movement sets Baroque sculpture apart from the sculpture of the previous 200 years.

■ **FIGURE 19.5** The figures in this Baroque work appear to float in space. Which elements and principles of art did Bernini employ when creating this sculpture?

Gianlorenzo Bernini. *The Ecstasy of St. Theresa.* 1645–52. Marble. Life-size. Cornaro Chapel, Santa Maria della Vittoria, Rome, Italy.

Chapter 19 *Baroque Art* **423**

Aesthetics

Have students again study Figure 19.5, this time observing how Bernini designed his sculpture of St. Theresa and the angel specifically to fit into a niche above the altar of the Cornaro Chapel. Ask: Does the sculpture seem at home in its space? Might Bernini have changed anything in the positioning of the figures if the sculpture were to fit in a shorter but wider niche? Have groups of students look through books on contemporary sculpture and ask them to select a work that was designed to be "site-specific" (such as Richard Serra's notorious *Tilted Arc*). Each group should present its choice to the class and explain how the artist took the work's proposed site into account when designing it. Ask students whether they think, in each instance, the sculpture is successfully integrated with its particular site.

Art History

On the board, list the techniques Baroque architects and artists used to create the most exciting environment possible. Discuss which of these ideas are still used today to enliven a particular setting. Then, with students' help, create a second list that includes contemporary approaches to dramatizing art and architectural space (e.g., the use of sound and special effects such as laser beams and holographs).

More About... **Gianlorenzo Bernini.** Gianlorenzo Bernini (1598–1680) was more than just a great Baroque sculptor. He also had a reputation as an extraordinary architect, a reputation so widespread that Louis XIV asked him to come to Paris and work out the plans for an enlargement of the Louvre Palace. Among Bernini's architectural achievements in Rome, where he spent most of his career, were the famous colonnaded *piazza* (square) in front of St. Peter's Basilica and the huge and impressive bronze *baldachino* (canopy) above the altar inside the church. Bernini was also responsible for San Andrea al Quirinale and the Scala Regia at the Vatican.

Art Criticism

Have students leaf through consumer magazines featuring photographs of athletes and find examples of each of two types of photos: (1) those that maximize the sense of the athlete's movement, and (2) those that show sports figures in repose. Compare the results of the search with Figures 16.11 (page 363) and 19.6. Discuss the circumstances under which a sports photographer might prefer a Bernini-style image versus occasions when Donatello's aesthetic approach better suits the purpose. Does one or the other style necessarily better convey a sense of power or drama?

Aesthetics

Have a student read aloud in *Samuel I*, 17:1-58, the biblical story illustrated in Figure 19.6. What is the focal figure of Bernini's sculpture attempting to do? How would students describe the look on the figure's face? Is the look consistent with what they would expect of an individual in this situation?

Cross Curriculum

MUSIC. Help students understand the Baroque temperament by playing selections of Baroque-era music. Explain to students that, as is the case in so many comparisons of art historical and musical styles, Baroque music developed at least fifty years after Baroque art and architecture. Compositions by Vivaldi, Bach, Torelli, and Telemann (all of whom were born near the end of what art historians consider the Baroque period), would all be excellent choices to play while viewing slides or prints of Italian Baroque art and architecture.

424

■ **FIGURE 19.6** If you compare this work with a Renaissance sculpture such as Donatello's *St. George* (Figure 16.11a, page 363), you will quickly recognize the Baroque sculptor's love of movement within space. How was this work designed to encourage a viewer to move around it rather than view it from one spot?

Gianlorenzo Bernini. *David.* 1623. Marble. Life-size. Galleria Borghese, Rome, Italy.

David
■ **FIGURE 19.6**

This new relationship between active figures and space is observed in Bernini's sculpture *David* (Figure 19.6). The theme in Bernini's work is movement. David's body is twisting in space as he prepares to hurl the stone at the mighty giant, Goliath. The coiled stance, flexed muscles, and determined expression are clues to his mood and purpose. Although Goliath is not shown, his presence is suggested by David's action and concentration. The dramatic action of the figure forces you to use your imagination to place Goliath in that space in front of David.

Baroque Painting

Like Baroque architects and sculptors, painters of this period used more action in their works than had their predecessors, and this increased the excitement of their creations. Furthermore, they used dramatic lighting effects to make vivid contrasts of light and dark. This magnified the action and heightened the excitement.

Time&Place
CONNECTIONS
Baroque Period
c. 1600–1700

SALON SOCIETY. In France during the Baroque period, upper class society gathered for games and discussions of daily events

and intellectual ideas. These gatherings, known as Salons, often included artists and writers.

GALILEO'S TELESCOPE. This telescope was perfected by Italian astronomer and mathematician Galileo in 1609. It allowed him to watch the paths of the planets.

MOLIÈRE. French playwright Molière is known for his satire. His comedies made fun of the foolishness and false values of the society of his time. His work greatly influenced other writers.

Activity **Personality Research.** Write an "I am" poem about Galileo, Molière, or another personality from the period. Complete the following lines from the point of view of that person: I am a…; I wonder…; I hear…; I see…; I want…; I understand…; I say…; I dream…; I hope…; My name is….

424 **Unit Six** *Art of an Emerging Modern Europe*

Time&Place
CONNECTIONS
Baroque Period

Have students examine and discuss the images in this Time & Place feature. Encourage volunteers to explain what they know about the lives and accomplishments of Moliere and Galileo. Then have students brainstorm a list of other important figures in the arts, sciences, and politics of seventeenth-century Europe; record their ideas on the board.

Allow time for group members to discuss their poem ideas. Have students work independently to draft and compose their poems.

Michelangelo da Caravaggio (1571–1610)

More than any other artist, Michelangelo da Caravaggio (mee-kel-**ahn**-jay-low da kar-ah-**vah**-jyoh) gave Baroque art its unique look and feel.

Caravaggio chose to study and paint the world around him instead of reworking the subjects of Renaissance artists. He made light an important part of his painting, using it to illuminate his figures and expose their imperfections. By showing their flaws, he made his figures seem more real and more human.

The Conversion of St. Paul
■ FIGURE 19.7

Caravaggio's *The Conversion of St. Paul* (Figure 19.7) is a fine example of his painting

style. Only St. Paul, his horse, and a single attendant are shown. The entire scene is pushed forward on the canvas, so you are presented with a close look. There is no detailed landscape in the background to distract your attention from this scene, only darkness. Instead of stretching back into the picture, space seems to project outward from the picture plane to include you as an eyewitness to the event.

Controversial Portrayal of Religious Subjects

Caravaggio's desire to use ordinary people in his portrayal of religious subjects met with mixed reactions. Some of his paintings were refused by church officials who had commissioned them. They disliked the fact that Christ and the saints were shown in untraditional ways. The people of Caravaggio's time were

■ FIGURE 19.7

Caravaggio. *The Conversion of St. Paul.* c. 1601. Oil on canvas. Approx. 228.6 × 175.3 cm (90 × 69"). Santa Maria del Popolo, Rome, Italy.

LOOKING Closely

Let students examine Caravaggio's painting, *The Conversion of St. Paul*, Figure 19.7, and describe the artist's use of light. What is the source of the light? Which parts of the painting are in light, and which are in darkness? What are the effects of this use of light? Then have students read and discuss the information presented in the feature.

Art History

Have students read the *Acts of the Apostles* 9:1-9, the biblical passage that describes the conversion of Saul (later known as Paul) illustrated in Figure 19.7. Discuss how Caravaggio translated this story from text to an image. Why did Caravaggio position Saul on his back?

Art History

Explain to students that the technique of chiaroscuro, popularized by Caravaggio, won favor among a number of his contemporaries, including the so-called "Caravaggisti" of Utrecht, Holland, in northern Europe. Have groups of students each research an artist from this group, which includes Gerrit van Honthorst, Hendrick Terbrugghen, and Dirk van Baburen. Ask each group to present reproductions of several works and point out where the artist makes use of Caravaggesque dramatic contrasts of light and dark.

LOOKING Closely

USING THE ART CRITICISM OPERATIONS

There is something unreal and mysterious about this scene.

- **Description.** A powerful light illuminates a figure on the ground with arms upraised and another standing figure gripping the bridle of a horse. The light makes them stand out boldly against the dark background. Like a spotlight, it originates outside the picture.

- **Analysis.** Caravaggio uses this mysterious light to add drama to the scene. This technique is **chiaroscuro,** the *arrangement of dramatic contrasts of light and dark value.* In Italian, *chiaro* means "bright" and *scuro* means "dark."

- **Interpretation.** The figure on the ground is St. Paul, who, as Saul, was once feared as a persecutor of Christians. The brilliant flash of light reveals St. Paul at the exact moment when he hears God's voice with a message that changes his life.

- **Judgment.** Do you think this artwork is successful in using light to increase the visual impact of the scene?

COOPERATIVE LEARNING

Chiaroscuro. Point out that, although the practice of modeling figures in light and shadow was certainly a hallmark of Baroque art (the word *chiaroscuro* was itself coined in 1686), the technique had its roots in works of art as early as the Renaissance. Divide the class into research committees and ask them to choose one of the following topics as the basis for an oral presentation: (1) the origins of chiaroscuro (i.e., who coined the term?); (2) the history of chiaroscuro in art; and (3) different color models (e.g., process color, the RGB model) and their role in gradations of light and dark. Set aside time for committees to present their findings.

Studio Skills

Set up a scene in the classroom that is illuminated by a single candle or lamp, arranging for the light to fall diagonally across the subject selected. If possible, include in the scene a student model engaged in a tense or exciting action. Have students draw the scene using oil pastels. Encourage them to render the shadows and dramatic lighting in the manner of Gentileschi's painting in Figure 19.8. Have students share and compare their completed works.

Art Criticism

Help students note the four artists who had important influences on the work of Peter Paul Rubens. Have pairs of students divide sheets of paper into four columns and, at the top of each column, write the name of one of the four artists mentioned. Then ask them to locate a work by Rubens not featured in this chapter and list, in the appropriate column, details that reveal the influence of that artist.

Did You Know?

The world's largest collection of Rubens's paintings outside the Netherlands is in Sarasota, Florida, located at the Ringling Museum of Art.

used to seeing religious figures pictured as majestic and supernatural beings. Often Caravaggio's figures looked like peasants and common beggars.

Caravaggio's reckless life was as shocking to the public as many of his pictures. During the last decade of his life, he was in constant trouble with the law because of his brawls, sword fights and violent temper.

Caravaggio's dynamic style of art and dramatic use of chiaroscuro, however, helped to change the course of European painting during the seventeenth century. Spreading north into Flanders and Holland, these techniques and new approaches to religious subject matter provided inspiration for Rubens, Rembrandt, and other artists.

■ FIGURE 19.8 A single candle is the only source of light in this scene. How does this work show Caravaggio's influence on the artist?

Artemisia Gentileschi. *Judith and Maidservant with the Head of Holofernes*. c. 1625. Oil on canvas. 184.2 × 141.6 cm (72 × 56″). The Detroit Institute of Arts, Detroit, Michigan. Gift of Mr. Leslie H. Green.

Artemisia Gentileschi
(1593–1653)

Artemisia Gentileschi (ar-tay-**mee**-zee-ah jen-tih-**less**-key) became the first woman in the history of Western art to have a significant impact on the art of her time. Her debt to Caravaggio is evident in her works. A good example is *Judith and Maidservant with the Head of Holofernes* (Figure 19.8), painted when she was at the peak of her career.

Judith and Maidservant with the Head of Holofernes
■ FIGURE 19.8

The biblical story of Judith is one of great heroism. She used her charms to capture the fancy of Holofernes, an important general and an enemy of the Jewish people. When Holofernes was asleep in his tent, Judith struck suddenly, cutting off his head. Gentileschi captures the scene just after this act. Judith stands with the knife still in her hand as her servant places the severed head in a sack. A mysterious noise has just interrupted them and Judith raises a hand in warning.

The dark, cramped quarters of the tent are an effective backdrop for the two silent figures illuminated by the light from a single candle. Judith's raised hand partially blocks the light from this candle and casts a dark shadow on her face. Her brightly lit profile is thus emphasized and this adds force to her anxious expression.

Gentileschi's lifelike treatment of the subject matter, her use of light and dark contrasts for dramatic effect, and her skill as a forceful storyteller are all evidenced in this painting. As did Caravaggio, Gentileschi captured the moment of highest drama and excitement and intensified it for the viewer with chiaroscuro.

Peter Paul Rubens (1577–1640)

Of all the European artists of the seventeenth century, Peter Paul Rubens most completely captured the dynamic spirit of the Baroque style. Returning to his native Antwerp after an eight-year stay in Italy, Rubens created paintings that were influenced by Titian, Tintoretto, Michelangelo, and Caravaggio. His works reveal the rich colors of Titian, the dramatic design of Tintoretto, and the powerful, twisting figures of Michelangelo. Also evident is Caravaggio's use of light to illuminate the most important parts of his paintings. To all this, Rubens added the realistic detail favored by earlier Flemish painters to create works of great dramatic force.

The Raising of the Cross

■ FIGURE 19.9

Rubens's preference for powerful subjects is evident in his sketch *The Raising of the Cross* (Figure 19.9). The action in this painting is so intense that it embraces the viewer—you are made to feel as though you are part of it. This is a trademark of the Baroque style. You will see it demonstrated in architecture and sculptures as well as in painting.

By avoiding stiff, geometric forms, Rubens gave his pictures a feeling of energy and life. You will rarely find straight contour lines or right angles in a painting by Rubens. Instead, he used curving lines to create a feeling of flowing movement. Then he softened the contours of his forms and placed them against a swirling background of color. The effect is one of violent and continuous motion.

Study Guide

Distribute *Study Guide* 43 in the TCR. Assist students in reviewing key concepts. 📁

Art and Humanities

Have students complete *Art and Humanities* 31, "Art as Theater," in the TCR. In this activity, students learn about the connections between theater and art throughout history. 📁

Studio Activities

Assign *Studio* 25, "Ink Drawing Emphasizing Value Contrasts," in the TCR. Students will work in india ink to create a drawing of a figure in an action pose. 📁

Art and Humanities

Obtain a copy of the film *Caravaggio* directed by Derek Jarman, and arrange for the class to view it. The film should serve to convey both a sense of the historical period and Caravaggio's reputedly fiery temperament. After viewing, initiate a discussion of these and other facets of the period and art covered in this lesson of the text.

Finding Axis Lines in *Art*

 1 Rubens carefully arranged his figures to form a solid pyramid of twisting, straining bodies.

2 His pyramid tips dangerously to the left, and the powerful figures seem to push, pull, and strain in an effort to restore balance.

3 Like many other Baroque artists, Rubens makes use of a strong diagonal axis line in this picture. It follows the vertical section of the cross through the center of the pyramid.

4 Notice how the diagonal axis line runs from the lower right foreground to the upper left background. The axis line not only organizes the direction of movement in the painting, but also adds to the feeling of space. It serves to draw your eye deep into the work.

■ **FIGURE 19.9**

Peter Paul Rubens. *The Raising of the Cross* (sketch). 1609–10. Oil on board. 68 × 52 cm (26⁴/₅ × 20¹/₂"). The Louvre, Paris, France.

Chapter 19 Baroque Art **427**

Finding Axis Lines in *Art*

Let students begin by examining *The Raising of the Cross,* Figure 19.9, independently and noting their own understanding of Rubens's use of axis lines. Then guide students in reading and discussing the feature; encourage students to trace the lines with their fingers. Point out that the oil sketch painted by Rubens that is shown in Figure 19.9, now hanging in the Louvre, shows a deep, receding background, whereas the final version features a rock wall as a backdrop. Ask students to consider factors that may have prompted this alteration (e.g., the preference of a patron).

ASSESS

Checking Comprehension

Have students respond to the lesson review questions. Answers are given in the box below.

Reteaching

➤ Assign *Reteaching* 43, found in the TCR. Have students complete the activity and review their responses. 📁

➤ Display a variety of Baroque and Renaissance paintings that clearly demonstrates the differences between the two styles. Ask students to pretend they are connoisseurs who have been asked to authenticate these works by a museum interested in buying Baroque art. Acting as a team, the students are to decide which paintings the museum ought to buy.

Enrichment

Assign students *Enrichment* 36, "Experimenting with Chiaroscuro," in the TCR. In this activity, students use lamps or floodlights to cast strong shadows on objects assembled for a still life. 📁

Extension

Have students visit a masonry supply house to become acquainted with the wide variety of stone materials that an artist may use as sculpting media. Follow up the visit with a discussion of which of the materials encountered were popular among Baroque sculptors.

CLOSE

Invite students to comment on the Italian Baroque tendency to emphasize pain, cruelty, and dramatic moments. Ask students to state whether they prefer the Baroque style or the more meditative quality found in much of Renaissance art.

428

■ **FIGURE 19.10**
Before painting this work, Rubens spent time at a nearby zoo, making chalk drawings of the lions. What details make the depiction of these lions realistic?

Peter Paul Rubens. *Daniel in the Lions' Den.* c. 1613. Oil on linen. 224.3 × 330.4 cm (88¼ × 130⅛"). National Gallery of Art, Washington, D.C. Board of Trustees, Ailsa Mellon Bruce Fund.

Daniel in the Lions' Den
■ **FIGURE 19.10**

One of Rubens's best-known paintings illustrates the biblical story of *Daniel in the Lions' Den* (Figure 19.10). The prophet, illuminated by the light coming in from a hole overhead, stands out against the dark interior of the lions' den. He raises his head and clenches his hands in an emotional prayer. God's answer is indicated by the behavior of the lions—they pay no attention at all to Daniel. His faith in God has saved him. As in all of Rubens's works, there is a great deal of emotion here, but not at the expense of realism. The lions are accurately painted and arranged at different angles in natural poses.

LESSON ONE REVIEW

Reviewing Art Facts

1. What role was art intended to play in the Counter-Reformation movement?
2. What was the name given to the new art style exemplified by Il Gesú and San Carlo alle Quattro Fontane?
3. What qualities did Baroque sculptors like Bernini feel were most important in their work?
4. Which Italian artist's revolutionary style of painting helped change the course of European painting during the seventeenth century?

Activity... *Comparing Sculpture*

The Baroque style is characterized by emotional intensity combined with movement and great contrasts. This spirit is vividly illustrated in the sculpture of Gianlorenzo Bernini. To understand that the theme of Bernini's work is demonstrated through movement and emotion, study Figures 19.5 and 19.6 on pages 423–424. Bernini's *David* is one of three famous sculptures of this biblical character.

Find reproductions of sculptures by Michelangelo and Donatello and compare and contrast them. How does each work express the culture of the time in which it was created? Share your findings with the class.

LESSON ONE REVIEW

Answers to Reviewing Art Facts

1. Art was seen as an important weapon in the struggle to stamp out heresy and lure people back to the Church.
2. They exemplified the Baroque style.
3. The mood or feeling expressed in their works and capturing the moment of highest drama and excitement.
4. Caravaggio's style.

Activity . . . *Comparing Sculpture*

Suggest that students work with partners or in small groups to find reproductions of the Michelangelo and Donatello sculptures; encourage them to do research on the two artists and their sculptures. Guide students in discussing the similarities and differences.

Dutch Art

Vocabulary
■ genre

Artists to Meet
■ Frans Hals
■ Rembrandt van Rijn
■ Jan Steen
■ Jan Vermeer
■ Judith Leyster

Discover
After completing this lesson, you will be able to:
■ Explain why the Baroque style had little impact on Dutch art.
■ Name several important Dutch painters and describe the kinds of subject matter for which they are best known.

*I*n 1648, a treaty with Spain divided the Low Countries into two parts. Flanders in the south remained Catholic and a territory of Spain. Holland in the north, which was largely Protestant, finally gained its independence from Spain.

In Holland, the Baroque style had little impact. Although some features appear in Dutch art, the Baroque was limited mainly to Catholic countries, where it was the style of the Counter-Reformation.

Dutch Genre Paintings

Religious sculptures and paintings had little appeal for the Dutch Protestants. They did not want this art in their churches. This presented a radical shift in focus for artists. Since early Christian times, the art of western Europe had primarily been religious in nature. Now there was no market for such paintings. Instead, Dutch citizens wanted secular artworks that portrayed their comfortable homes and profitable businesses. Realizing this, Dutch artists began to paint people and places, city squares and streets, the countryside and the sea. Many of these works were **genre** paintings, *scenes from everyday life*. The market for portraiture, landscape, still life, and genre paintings grew to such an extent that artists began to specialize. For instance, some painted only pictures of the sea, while others portrayed views of the city or interior scenes of carefree groups in taverns and inns.

■ **FIGURE 19.11** This portrait captures a single moment and makes the subject look relaxed and natural. What does this painting have in common with a photograph? How is it different from a photograph?

Frans Hals. *Portrait of a Member of the Haarlem Civic Guard.* c. 1636/1638. Oil on canvas. 86 × 69 cm (33³/₄ × 27″). National Gallery of Art, Washington, D.C. Board of Trustees, Andrew W. Mellon Collection.

Frans Hals
(c. 1580–1666)

One artist, Frans Hals (frahns **hahls**), specialized in portraits. He was one of the busiest and most prosperous portrait painters in Holland. Hals's *Portrait of a Member of the Haarlem Civic Guard* (Figure 19.11) presents a completely natural view. The officer looks as if he has just turned to glance over at the painter. Flashing a sly grin, he appears to be saying, "Really, Mr. Hals, aren't you finished yet?"

429

FOCUS
Lesson Objectives
After studying this lesson, students will be able to:
■ Describe what is meant by genre painting.
■ Identify several important Dutch painters of the period.
■ Explain how Dutch painters incorporated moralistic messages into their art.

Building Vocabulary
Students may be familiar with the term *genre* from their study of literature; let volunteers explain the word in that context. Then have a student find and read aloud the definition given in the lesson. Ask: How are the definitions related?

Motivator
Ask students to think about the role body language and facial expression play in the conveying of emotion. Have students experiment with conveying several common emotions (e.g., impatience, surprise, sadness) solely through nonverbal cues. Explain that in this lesson they will encounter artworks that depend largely on such cues.

Introducing the Lesson
List on the board contemporary genre scene subjects that could never have been painted in the seventeenth century. Discuss why genre paintings are so popular even though they illustrate subjects that are ordinary and familiar to viewers. Then discuss the value of genre paintings as a record of everyday life for future generations. What kinds of genre paintings would best capture life in the present decade?

LESSON TWO RESOURCES

Teacher's Classroom Resources
📁 Appreciating Cultural Diversity 29
📁 Cooperative Learning 28
📁 Reproducible Lesson Plan 44
📁 Reteaching Activity 44
📁 Study Guide 44

TEACH

Using Map Skills

Have students locate the Low Countries on a present-day map of Europe. Explain that the term *Low Countries* comes from the word *Netherlands,* which means "lowlands"—an appropriate label, since much of that country is below sea level. On the map, have students locate the "Catholic countries" of seventeenth-century Europe, which were located in the southern portion of western Europe and included Portugal, Spain, France, Flanders, and Italy.

Aesthetics

Ask students to examine closely the sitter's clothing in Figure 19.11 and the men's clothing in Figures 19.12 and 19.13. Then have a volunteer research the history of men's clothing during the seventeenth century in Holland and discuss why lace and ruffles were considered appropriate and fashionable for men. What customs have replaced these as standard accessories in men's apparel?

Art Criticism

Have students study Figures 19.12 and 19.19 (page 436) and characterize the style of each work, paying special attention to the elements and principles of art that Hals and Leyster use in the same way. Summarize the findings into a brief description of the style of Dutch Baroque portraiture. Then refer students back to Figures 17.4 (page 383) and 17.7 (page 387). Would students rather be painted by van Eyck and Rogier van der Weyden or by Hals and Leyster? Why?

Other subjects of Hals's portraits include laughing soldiers, brawling fish vendors, and happy merrymakers (Figure 19.12). Hals used quick, dashing brush strokes to give his works a fresh, just-finished look. His portraits are so successful in capturing a fleeting expression that they look like candid photographs. His genius lies in the illusion that, in an instant, he has caught a characteristic expression of the subject and recorded it in paint.

■ **FIGURE 19.12** Merrymakers such as this happy couple were a common subject for Frans Hals. **How does a diagonal axis line tie the important parts of this picture together?**

Frans Hals. *Young Man and Woman in an Inn.* 1623. Oil on canvas. 105.4 × 79.4 cm (41¹⁄₂ × 31¹⁄₄"). The Metropolitan Museum of Art, New York, New York. Bequest of Benjamin Alman, 1913. (14.40.602).

Rembrandt van Rijn
(1606–1669)

No discussion of Dutch seventeenth-century art could be complete without mention of Rembrandt van Rijn (**rem**-brant vahn **ryne**), often called the greatest Dutch painter of his era. Like other artists of his time, Rembrandt painted portraits, everyday events, historical subjects, and landscapes. Unlike most artists, though, he refused to specialize and was skilled enough to succeed in all subjects.

The Night Watch
■ **FIGURE 19.13**

If Rembrandt specialized at all, it was in the study of light, shadow, and atmosphere. Observe the light in one of his best-known paintings, *The Night Watch* (Figure 19.13), originally titled *The Company of Captain Frans Banning Cocq.*

Light can be seen throughout *The Night Watch,* although it is brightest at the center. There an officer in charge gives instructions to his aide. The shadow of the officer's hand falls across the aide's uniform, telling you that the light comes from the left. The light falls unevenly on the other figures in the picture. Several, including a young woman and a drummer, are brightly illuminated, whereas others are barely visible. Rembrandt's skill in handling light for dramatic effect, so obvious in this painting, was one of his most remarkable accomplishments.

Use your imagination to add movement and sound to this scene. When you do, you will find that you become a spectator at a grand pictorial symphony. Light flashes across the stage, a musket is loaded, lances clatter, and boots thud softly on hard pavement. At the same time, a dog barks at a drummer and instructions are heard over the murmur of a dozen conversations.

Rather than paint a picture showing continuous movement, Rembrandt has frozen time, allowing you to study different actions and details. The visual symphony

---

⊙ Technology ▌

National Gallery of Art Videodisc Use the following images as examples of more works by artists introduced in this lesson.

Frans Hals
A Young Man in a Large Hat

Search Frame 832

Rembrandt van Rijn
A Girl with a Broom

Search Frame 862

Jan Steen
The Dancing Couple

Search Frame 924

Use Glencoe's *Correlation Bar Code Guide to the National Gallery of Art* to locate more artworks.

Rembrandt van Rijn. *The Night Watch (Group portrait of the Amsterdam watch under Captain Frans Banning Cocq).* 1642. Oil on canvas. 359 × 438 cm (12'2" × 14'7"). Rijksmuseum, Amsterdam, Holland.

Aesthetics

Have students compare the paintings in Figures 19.14 and 19.19 (page 436). Both are portraits of Dutch painters at their easels, but the artists seem to have very different temperaments. Have pairs of students write a dialogue between Rembrandt and Leyster in which the two artists discuss what it is like to be a painter. If students wish, they may add Frans Hals to the dialogue. Have students read their dialogues aloud. Note the dates of the two paintings and discuss how an artist's experience is colored by whether he or she is young or old, successful or struggling.

Art History

Explain to students that an artist's self-portrait may say as much about that person's dreams and aspirations as it does about the person's actual life. Have students explore this idea by finding as many of Rembrandt's self-portraits as possible. Examine the paintings together, for comparison. Have students note, among other details, the different types of clothing styles.

before you is not as loud and emotional as one created by Rubens. This melody is quieter and more soothing. *The Night Watch* holds your attention with highlights and challenges your imagination with hints of half-hidden forms.

Artist in His Studio
■ **FIGURE 19.14**

Early in his career, Rembrandt painted a small picture of an artist in his studio (Figure 19.14). It may be a self-portrait—he painted more than 90 in his lifetime—or it could be a picture of one of his first students. In the picture, the artist is not actually working on his painting, nor is the painting visible to you. Instead, the artist stands some distance away and seems to be studying his work. This could be Rembrandt's way of saying that art is a deliberate, thoughtful process, requiring much more than one's skill with a brush.

■ **FIGURE 19.14** Notice that, although the painting on it is not visible, the artist's easel stands in the foreground. **What do you think the artist shown in the painting is doing? What idea or message do you receive from this work?**

Rembrandt van Rijn. *Artist in His Studio.* c. 1627. Oil on panel. 24.8 × 31.7 cm (9 3/4 × 12 1/2"). Courtesy of Museum of Fine Arts, Boston, Massachusetts. The Zoe Oliver Sherman Collection. Given in memory of Lillie Oliver Poor.

Chapter 19 *Baroque Art* **431**

About the *Artwork*

The Night Watch. In 1715, Rembrandt's painting suffered unwitting vandalism when it was cut to fit a new frame. It was trimmed on all four sides when it was transferred from its original site to the Amsterdam town hall. Fortunately, the Dutch artist Gerrit Lundens had made a careful copy in the late 1640s, enabling art historians to deduce how much of Rembrandt's original work was excised. It appears that three figures on the left were eliminated, and the balance was distorted by losses on the remaining three sides.

Aesthetics

Have students examine Rembrandt's *The Mill*, Figure 19.15. Help them discuss the work by asking questions such as these: What mood or feeling does this work evoke? What literal qualities of the work are responsible for this mood? What role does color play in the painting's aesthetic statement? What other elements are emphasized?

Art History

Discuss with students the wealth of hidden moral messages in *St. Nicholas' Day*, Figure 19.16 on page 433. Point out that many of Jan Steen's artistic peers sought likewise to include a moralizing precept in their pictures. Have small groups of students research other seventeenth-century Dutch paintings, such as those created by Gerard Ter Borch and Pieter de Hooch, to find out what moral teachings were popular among artists of the period and place. Discuss why the Dutch liked art that simultaneously presented scenes of wrong-doing and an admonition to behave correctly. Ask: Might the Dutch have been vicariously or unconsciously enjoying the activities they admonished themselves to avoid?

The Mill
■ FIGURE 19.15

Few artists have been as successful as Rembrandt in arousing the viewer's curiosity and rewarding it with a warm and comfortable feeling. Nowhere is this more evident than in his painting *The Mill* (Figure 19.15). This is his largest and probably most famous landscape.

Deeply saddened by the death of his wife, Saskia, in 1642, Rembrandt took long walks in the country where the peace and quiet helped him overome his grief. It was during this period that he painted this haunting landscape.

Here darkness advances to envelop a drowsy world. In the shadows, half-hidden figures can be seen moving slowly as though weary from a long day's activity. The only sounds are the occasional creaking of the old mill, the muffled voice of a mother talking to her child, and the gentle splash of oars as a boat glides into the picture at the far right. Peaceful and still, the picture expresses an overpowering feeling of

solitude and loneliness. This feeling is traced to the solitary windmill outlined dramatically against the fading sunset. The great sweep of the sky seems to overwhelm the windmill, further emphasizing its isolation. Perhaps, with this painting, Rembrandt expresses his own sense of isolation and loneliness at the loss of his beloved wife.

Jan Steen (1626–1679)

During the same period in which Hals and Rembrandt were working, a group of artists doing only genre paintings supplied the Dutch with pictures for their fashionable homes. These artists are now called the Little Dutch Masters. This name is not intended to imply that the artists lacked skill or sensitivity. Indeed, one of the greatest painters of the period, Jan Vermeer, is often associated with this group. Before discussing Vermeer, let's examine a painting by another Little Dutch Master, Jan Steen (**yahn styn**).

■ **FIGURE 19.15** Notice how Rembrandt has made the mill the focal point in this painting. **How many people can you identify? How does contrast of value add to the emotional impact of this painting?**

Rembrandt van Rijn. *The Mill*. 1645/1648. Oil on canvas. 87.6 × 105.6 cm (34¹/₂ × 41⁵/₈"). National Gallery of Art, Washington, D.C. Board of Trustees, Widener Collection.

COOPERATIVE LEARNING

Panel Discussion. Ask a group of students to research the many different Protestant movements that flourished during the seventeenth century in Europe. The group should make a panel presentation of its findings to the class, with each panel member summarizing the beliefs and practices of one of the Protestant groups. Some of the Protestant sects that could be researched are the Quakers, Calvinists, Lutherans, Puritans, Jansenists, Anglicans, and the radical British sects known as the Diggers, the Ranters, and the Levellers. Encourage students to find as much information as possible concerning each group's attitude toward and patronage of the fine arts.

St. Nicholas' Day
■ **FIGURE 19.16**

Steen's painting *St. Nicholas' Day* (Figure 19.16) tells a simple story involving common people and familiar events. It is the Christmas season, and St. Nicholas has just visited the children in this Dutch family. At the right, a young man holding a baby points up to something outside the picture. The child beside him looks upward, his mouth open in wonder. You can almost hear the man saying, "Look out the window! Isn't that St. Nicholas?"

This is not a joyous occasion for everyone in Steen's picture. The boy at the far left has just discovered that his shoe is not filled with gifts. Instead, it contains a switch. This means he did not behave well during the year and now must suffer the consequences. A child in the center of the picture smiles at you and points to the shoe's disappointing contents. This child makes you feel like a welcomed guest.

Steen uses diagonal lines to lead you into and around his picture. The long cake at the lower left guides you into the work, and the diagonal lines of the table, chair, and canopy direct your attention to the crying boy at the left. Jan Steen recognized a good story—and knew how to tell it.

■ **FIGURE 19.16** This scene tells a complex story, with several important characters. Point to the diagonal lines in this work. Where do they direct your attention?

Jan Steen. *St. Nicholas' Day.* c. 1660–65. Oil on canvas. 82 × 70 cm (32 1/4 × 27 3/4"). Rijksmuseum, Amsterdam, Holland.

Jan Vermeer (1632–1675)

With Jan Vermeer (**yahn** vair-**meer**), Dutch genre painting reached its peak. For more than 200 years, however, Vermeer was all but forgotten, until his genius was recognized during the second half of the nineteenth century.

Fewer than 40 pictures are known to have been painted by Vermeer. Of these, most illustrate events taking place in the same room. Because so many of his paintings show inside scenes, Vermeer is often thought of as a painter of interiors. Even though there are people in his paintings, they seem to be less important than the organization of the composition and the effect of light on colors and textures.

The Love Letter
■ **FIGURE 19.17**

The Love Letter (Figure 19.17, page 434) demonstrates Vermeer's mastery as an artist. He has taken an ordinary event and transformed it into a timeless masterpiece of perfect poise and serenity. Everything seems frozen for just a moment as if under some magic spell.

Studio Skills

Have students use felt-tip markers to create a contemporary version of one of Steen's many chaotic household scenes, one of which is illustrated in Figure 19.16. You may wish to display other reproductions of Steen's genre scenes including his *The Topsy-Turvy World* and *Merry Company.* Have students include several children and at least two adults who are inattentive in their supervision of the children. Allow time for students to share and compare efforts.

Art History

Point out to students that few details are meaningless in Dutch art, noting in support of the claim that the woman in Vermeer's *The Love Letter,* Figure 19.17, holds a musical instrument. Have a volunteer research the significance of musical instruments in Dutch genre paintings (i.e., they were symbols of love). Among the questions the researcher should seek to answer is how the presence of a lute is a visual cue to the viewer about the nature of the letter.

More About... **Jan Steen.** In addition to his painting, Jan Steen (1626–79) was an innkeeper and amateur actor. Good-humored and sharply observant as an artist, Steen consistently created paintings that carried an obvious moral message, one that was often repeated in the form of an inscription tacked to the wall in the painting. At least half of Steen's works lament the folly to which children are prey when their parents and other adults do not raise them properly. Other typical Steen themes include lovesick maidens and groups of merry, carefree people. Despite the somber nature of Steen's outlook, he was sympathetic rather than cruel to those who erred, and many of his paintings are quite humorous.

Art History

Direct students to the description in the text of Judith Leyster and her contribution (page 435). Some students may enjoy researching the lives and careers of other prominent seventeenth-century Netherlander women artists, including the still-life painters Clara Peeters and Maria van Oosterwyck and the flower painter Rachel Ruysch. These and many other historical women artists are profiled in the 1976 exhibition catalog *Women Artists: 1550–1950,* by Ann Sutherland Harris and Linda Nochlin.

Critical Thinking

Review the text's discussion of the relationship between Hals and Leyster. Discuss what it implies about how artists were educated in seventeenth-century Holland. Tell students that formal art schools were not organized until the eighteenth century when the Royal Academy in Paris began to offer regular drawing classes. Discuss the advantages and disadvantages of apprenticeship under one artist such as Rembrandt, Hals, or Leyster for several years compared with taking classes taught by many different instructors.

Storytelling in Art

*Y*ou are made to feel that you are actually in the painting, standing in a darkened room that looks very much like a closet. The doorway of this closet acts as a frame for the scene in the next room. Thus, the foreground is an introduction to the story unfolding deeper in the work.

■ **FIGURE 19.17** Jan Vermeer. *The Love Letter.* 1666. Oil on canvas. 44 × 39 cm (17³⁄₈ × 15¹⁄₄"). Rijksmuseum, Amsterdam, Holland.

1 The black and white floor tiles lead your eye into this room, where you see two women.

2 The clothes of the standing woman suggest she is a servant. A basket of laundry rests on the floor beside her. She has just handed a letter to the seated woman.

3 This woman is richly dressed and, until this moment, has been amusing herself by playing the lute. The facial expression and exchange of glances tell you that this is no ordinary letter. The young woman holds the letter carefully but avoids looking at it. Instead, she glances shyly up at the face of the servant girl.

4 Words are unnecessary, a reassuring smile from the servant girl is enough to tell the young woman that it is indeed a very special letter, no doubt from a special young man.

5 The two figures seem to be surrounded by light and air. This contributes to a feeling of space, which is increased by placing the viewer in the darkened closet.

6 The marine painting shows ships at sea. It may suggest that the letter is from someone at sea or someone who has been transported afar by sea.

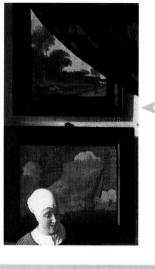

7 The landscape on the wall curves to repeat the diagonal sweep of the curtain above the door. In this way, it connects the foreground and the background.

Storytelling in Art

Let students begin their examination of *The Love Letter* by describing what they see in the painting and discussing the story as they understand it. Then guide them in reading and discussing each item in the feature. Ask: How does an understanding of these details help you appreciate this work? Display another work by Vermeer exploring a similar theme. (A good choice for the exercise is *Allegory of the Art of Painting.*) Challenge students working in teams to list all of the ways in which the artist uses line, shape, color, space, and rhythm to focus the viewer's attention.

Judith Leyster (1609–1660)

In 1893, officials at the great Louvre museum in Paris were surprised when they cleaned a work long thought to have been painted by Frans Hals (Figure 19.18). They discovered that the signature on the painting belonged to a woman—Judith Leyster (**lie**-stir).

It was soon discovered that there was little written information available on Judith Leyster. At first, some historians considered her to be just an imitator of Hals. In the years since, however, Leyster has been recognized as a unique and talented artist whose work had its own impact on Dutch art of the seventeenth century.

Women artists at the time were expected to paint delicate still lifes. Leyster did paint still lifes, but chose in addition to do genre subjects and portraits.

Influences on Leyster's Art

A serious student of art, Leyster studied the works of others and skillfully applied what she learned to her own painting. From artists who had visited Italy, she learned about Caravaggio's dramatic use of light and dark. This sparked her own interest in the effects of light on her subjects under varying conditions.

Leyster also learned from the pictures painted by her fellow Dutch artists. Not only was she familiar with Hals's work, but she was also his friend. It is clear that she saw much to be learned from his remarkable brushwork. The influence of Hals on Leyster's style was not far-reaching, though. The majority of her works give less an impression of the fleeting moment and more the feeling that care and time have been taken to achieve an overall elegant effect.

■ **FIGURE 19.18** Judith Leyster was not only influenced by the work of Frans Hals, she was a close friend—until Hals coaxed one of her students to study with him. **What similarities do you see in the work of these two artists?**

Judith Leyster. *Merry Company.* 1630. Oil on canvas. 68 × 57 cm (26³/₄ × 22¹/₂"). The Louvre, Paris, France.

Art Criticism

Have students closely compare Figures 19.11 (page 429) and 19.12 (page 430) with Figures 19.18 and 19.19 (page 436). Remind students that in the past Leyster's work was often mistaken for that of Hals. Ask: Why did curators and art historians make this mistake? Then have students list the art elements and principles common to both Hals's and Leyster's paintings. After carefully considering the four works, ask students whether they would have confused works by the two artists.

Study Guide

Distribute *Study Guide* 44 in the TCR. Assist students in reviewing key concepts. 📁

Art and Humanities

Have students complete *Cooperative Learning* 28, "Artists Examining Space," in the TCR. In this activity, students consider the results that the scientific understanding of the universe has had on artists' representation of space. 📁

Enrichment

Assign *Appreciating Cultural Diversity* 29, "Dutch Art—Genre Painting," in the TCR, in which students explore the cultural impact of this art style. 📁

Art and Humanities

The lute, pictured in Vermeer's *The Love Letter* and numerous other Dutch Baroque paintings, was an extremely popular instrument during the seventeenth century. Students may enjoy listening to period lute compositions, such as contemporary English lutist John Dowland's *The King of Denmark's Galliard.*

CULTURAL DIVERSITY

Women Artists. Tell students that, while women artists such as Artemisia Gentileschi and Judith Leyster experienced great difficulty in both establishing and continuing their careers as artists, in some cultures the making of art (or at least certain kinds of art) is the special province of women. Have volunteers or groups of students research the ritual paintings made by the women of Mithila, India (see *The Women Painters of Mithila* by Yves Vequaud), the molas made by Cuna Indians of the San Blas Islands in Panama, the *arpilleras* created by Peruvian women, and the West African wall paintings documented in Margaret Courtney-Clarke's *African Canvas.*

ASSESS

Checking Comprehension

Have students respond to the lesson review questions. Answers are given in the box below.

Reteaching

Assign *Reteaching* 44, found in the TCR. Have students complete the activity and review their responses. 📂

Enrichment

Arrange a visit to the conservation department of a local museum to see how works in all media are cleaned and repaired, or invite a professional conservator to visit the class and show examples of his or her projects. Ask how conservators probably went about cleaning Rembrandt's *The Company of Captain Frans Banning Cocq (The Night Watch)* and repairing Vermeer's *The Love Letter.*

Extension

Have students write a dialogue among family members depicted in Steen's *St. Nicholas' Day.*

CLOSE

Have students imagine that the date 1150 was found on the back of the painting in Figure 19.19. Challenge them to state reasons for assuming the date to be erroneous. They may use what they know about art styles, the history of fashion, the role of women painters, and the types of subject matter preferred.

Self-Portrait
■ **FIGURE 19.19**

Although the subjects in Leyster's portraits often smile and gesture toward the viewer as they do in Hals's pictures, they do so more quietly and with greater dignity. Nowhere is this more evident than in a self-portrait she did as a young woman (Figure 19.19). Here you feel as if you have been looking over her shoulder while she worked on a painting of a laughing fiddler. She has just turned to see how you like it. Her smile is friendly, and she seems completely at ease. It was just this kind of psychological interaction between subject and viewer that Leyster sought in her paintings of people, and in this self-portrait, she succeeded in achieving it.

■ **FIGURE 19.19** Here, the artist's manner convinces viewers that they are in the company of a good friend. **How is this painting similar to Rembrandt's *Artist in His Studio* (Figure 19.14, page 431)? What are the most important differences between the works?**

Judith Leyster. *Self-Portrait.* c. 1630. Oil on canvas. 72.3 × 65.3 cm (29³/₈ × 25⁵/₈"). National Gallery of Art, Washington, D.C. Board of Trustees, Gift of Mr. and Mrs. Robert Woods Bliss.

LESSON TWO REVIEW

Reviewing Art Facts

1. Why did the highly religious Baroque style have little impact in Holland?
2. What is genre painting?
3. What type of picture did Frans Hals prefer to paint?
4. How did Rembrandt succeed in arousing the viewer's curiosity?

▶ Activity... *Discussing Baroque Music*

The qualities of Baroque art are also characterized in the music of the period. This music was made not for the commoners, but for the aristocrats and the patricians who had formal training in music. It was a common complaint during that time that ordinary people did not understand the elaborate church music. These musical works have since become music that was not for an age, but for all times.

Find and listen to Baroque music by composers of the time, including Bach, Vivaldi, Torelli, Handel, Purcell, and Albinoni, as you view Baroque works of art. Discuss how these two art forms combine to express the ideas of the Baroque period.

LESSON TWO REVIEW

Answers to Reviewing Art Facts

1. Dutch Protestants did not want religious sculptures or paintings in their churches.
2. Paintings illustrating scenes from daily life.
3. Frans Hals painted portraits of people.
4. By placing large parts of his paintings in shadow.

Activity... *Discussing Baroque Music*

Let a group of interested volunteers plan and present a short discussion—with examples—of Baroque music. Then divide the class into three or four groups, and have each group prepare a slide show of Baroque artworks set to Baroque music. Provide time during which each group can share its show with the rest of the class.

Spanish Art

Vocabulary
■ prodigal

Artists to Meet
■ Jusepe de Ribera
■ Diego Velázquez
■ Bartolomé Esteban Murillo

Discover
After completing this lesson, you will be able to:
■ Identify the most common subjects of Spanish paintings during the seventeenth century.
■ Describe the style and the most important works of Jusepe de Ribera, Diego Velázquez, and Bartolomé Esteban Murillo.

While Dutch artists painted portraits, landscapes, and genre subjects, Spanish artists continued to paint saints, crucifixions, and martyrdoms. Religious subjects always interested Spanish artists more than other subjects. The seventeenth century brought a slight change, however. Artists at this time often used the same religious subjects as El Greco did, but their works had a more realistic look.

Jusepe de Ribera (1591–1652)

One of the first Spanish painters to show greater realism in his works was Jusepe de Ribera (zhoo-**say**-pay day ree-**bay**-rah).

In his painting *The Blind Old Beggar* (Figure 19.20), Ribera used Caravaggio's dramatic lighting and realism to paint an old man and a young boy standing together in the shadows. Their faces stand out clearly against a dark background.

A light originating outside the painting illuminates these faces and allows you to see every detail. The wrinkles, creases, and rough beard of the old man's face contrast with the smooth freshness of the boy's. The old man's unseeing eyes are tightly closed, but the lively eyes of the boy stare directly at the viewer.

The figures in this work may be the main characters from the autobiography of a penniless wanderer named Lazarillo de Tormes. When he was a boy, Lazarillo was given to a blind man. The child was to act as the man's guide and, in return, was to be fed and cared for. The relationship between the crafty, often cruel old man and the innocent boy was unhappy from the beginning. Gradually the boy became just as shrewd and hardened as his master. Nothing could shock or surprise or frighten Lazarillo, and the same could be said for the boy who stares boldly from the shadows of Ribera's painting.

Baroque painters such as Rubens liked to paint large, complicated pictures filled with masses of active people. Ribera's paintings, however, were much simpler. He preferred to paint a single tree rather than a forest, one or two figures instead of a crowd. He also avoided excitement and action in favor of calmness in most of his works.

Diego Velázquez (1599–1660)

Diego Velázquez (dee-**ay**-goh vay-**lahs**-kess) was born in Seville to a noble family. Since it was considered improper at that time for a nobleman to earn his living as a common artist, Velázquez could only pursue a career as a painter if he found a position at the royal court.

■ **FIGURE 19.20** The light here highlights the details in the faces of both figures, and illuminates the cup the beggar holds out to passersby. **Point out specific details that indicate the influence of Caravaggio on this painter's style.**

Jusepe de Ribera. *The Blind Old Beggar*. c. 1632. Oil on canvas. 124.5 × 101.7 cm (49 × 40¹/₁₆"). Allen Memorial Art Museum, Oberlin College, Oberlin, Ohio. R. T. Miller Jr. Fund, 55.9.

437

FOCUS

Lesson Objectives
After studying this lesson, students will be able to:
■ Explain how Spanish Baroque painting differs from Dutch Baroque art.
■ Identify the most common subjects of Spanish paintings during the seventeenth century.
■ Describe the style and the most important works of three major Spanish painters of the period.

Building Vocabulary
Encourage volunteers to offer informal definitions of the Vocabulary word for this lesson, *prodigal*. Then have students find and read the definition given in the Glossary.

Motivator
Divide the class into four groups, and assign each group one of the following four paintings: Figures 19.20, 19.21, 19.22, 19.23. Have each group write a brief paragraph identifying how their work is similar to and different from Italian works of the same period.

Introducing the Lesson
Direct students' attention to the painting in Figure 19.21, noting the title of the work. Ask how a viewer who knew nothing of the event depicted would know which side won and which lost. Ask students to describe everyday examples of how standing upright, leaning over, or even handing something to a person can communicate who has authority in a situation and who does not. Tell students that concerns such as these were guiding forces in the work of Diego Velázquez.

LESSON THREE RESOURCES

Teacher's Classroom Resources
📁 Art and Humanities 32
📁 Reproducible Lesson Plan 45
📁 Reteaching Activity 45
📁 Study Guide 45

TEACH
Studio Skills

Have students examine Figure 19.20 (page 437), paying particular attention to how Ribera contrasts a young face and an old one. Then provide students with photos of young and old people to serve as models, and have students use oil pastels or charcoal pencils to create original drawings that contrast youth and old age. Afterward, have students share their drawings with the class.

Aesthetics

Direct students to this sentence in the text about Velázquez's *Las Meninas:* "Generations of curious viewers have tried to discover what is happening in the picture—but is it really so important?" Organize the students into two debate teams, each of which appoints two or three speakers. Have teams argue the proposition that realistic art can be enjoyed without necessarily understanding the details of the event depicted. Remind students to use specific examples to support their arguments.

Did You Know?

Many Spaniards had misgivings about handing over the restoration of Velázquez's *Las Meninas* to a foreigner, John Brealey, of The Metropolitan Museum of Art in New York City. The national honor was thought to be at stake. Brealey's work was superb, however, and the tremendously popular painting has enjoyed renewed attention.

The Viewer's Position in *Art*

*V*elázquez composed the figures in *The Surrender of Breda* (Figure 19.21b) so that they can be seen best when you are looking straight ahead at the center of the painting. How did he arrange the figures to establish this position for the viewer?

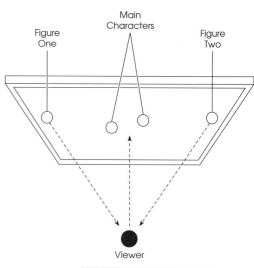

■ **FIGURE 19.21a** Diagram of the viewer's position before *The Surrender of Breda.*

The two commanders are the main characters in this scene. They are placed directly in the center.

The figures at the far left and far right both stare directly at you. Their gaze, coming from different places in the picture, pinpoints your position in front of the painting, as shown in the diagram (Figure 19.21a). From this position, you can observe the meeting of the two rival commanders.

The key to the city is being passed from one commander to the other. Velázquez silhouetted the key against a light background to place emphasis on it.

The position of a horse leads your eye deeper into the painting, to the point where you see the lances and the flag of the Spanish army. The soldiers of this army proudly hold their lances erect; they are the victors.

The defeated Dutch soldiers hold their lances carelessly. Smoke rises from the captured city in the background. The angle of this smoke repeats the diagonal movement of the Spanish flag on the right and unites the triumphant army with the city it has conquered.

■ **FIGURE 19.21b**

Diego Velázquez. *The Surrender of Breda.* 1634–35. Oil on canvas. 3.07 × 3.65 m (10'1" × 12'). The Prado, Madrid, Spain.

438 Unit Six *Art of an Emerging Modern Europe*

The Viewer's Position in *Art*

Guide students in examining *Surrender of Breda* as they read and discuss the information in this feature. Have them follow the numbered items as they examine the work, taking in each detail in the way that their attention is guided around the work. Ask: Why do you think Velázquez wanted to influence the position of the viewer? How are students affected by the scene as they view each section of the painting? How do you think the painter would have arranged his work to place the viewer in a different position?

With this in mind, the young artist went to Madrid, where his talent was soon recognized, and he was asked to paint a portrait of the king, Philip IV. When it was finished, Philip was so pleased that he said no one but Velázquez would ever again paint his picture. In all, Velázquez painted Philip 34 times. No other artist ever painted a king so often.

Velázquez's painting *The Surrender of Breda* (Figure 19.21) celebrated the Spanish victory over the Dutch city of Breda. The picture, the largest the artist ever created, shows the moment when the commander of the Spanish army receives the key to the conquered city.

Las Meninas
■ **FIGURE 19.22**

Later in his career, Velázquez painted one of his best-known works, *Las Meninas,* or *The Maids of Honor* (Figure 19.22). Here he shows the young daughter of the king surrounded by ladies-in-waiting, attendants, and a dog. The artist also shows himself standing at his easel. Farther back in the picture, the faces of the king and queen are reflected in a mirror.

Velázquez's use of a mirror in this way may remind you of Jan van Eyck's picture of Giovanni Arnolfini and his bride (Figure 17.4, page 383). It is quite possible that Velázquez was influenced by van Eyck's painting, since it was part of the Spanish royal collection at that time.

What is happening in this picture? The princess may have just entered a room in which the artist is painting a portrait of the king and queen. Or, the artist may be trying to paint the princess while the king and queen watch; but the princess, tired of posing, turns her back to him. Generations of curious viewers have tried to discover what is happening in this picture—but is it really so important? If one sees the painting as simply a picture of everyday life at the palace, it is still interesting. The scene is peaceful, quiet, and natural.

One of the most striking things about Velázquez's painting is the way he creates the illusion of space. You see the scene stretched out before you and, by looking in the mirror, you see the scene continuing behind you, as well.

Velázquez also suggests the world beyond the room, which he allows you to glimpse through an open door. Light from a window illuminates the foreground, while the background is veiled in soft shadows. You not only see space here—you can almost feel it. If you could enter that room, you would first pass through the bright, warm sunlight in the foreground and, with each step, move deeper and deeper into the shadowy coolness of the interior. If you wished, you could walk through the open door, up the steps, and out of the room.

■ **FIGURE 19.22** Notice the light from the open door at the back of the room. **From which direction does additional light come?**

Diego Velázquez. *Las Meninas (The Maids of Honor).* 1656. Oil on canvas. 3.18 × 2.76 m (10'5" × 9'). The Prado, Madrid, Spain.

Chapter 19 *Baroque Art* **439**

CHAPTER 19
LESSON THREE

Art History
Point out the presence of a dog in both Figures 19.22 and 19.23 (page 440). Ask: How do Velázquez's and Murillo's use of this animal differ from that by van Eyck in Figure 17.4 (page 383) and Dürer in Figure 18.12 (page 409)? Ask for a volunteer to research the changing role of the dog in Western art. Have the student present his or her findings to the class.

Art Criticism
Have students examine how Murillo's composition in Figure 19.23 (page 440) helps the viewer focus on the central characters (i.e., all the secondary figures either lean toward or face the father and son, the background contains no distractions). Play a videotape of a feature film familiar to most students. "Freeze" the tape at moments where the scene has been composed to focus the viewer's attention on the action. Have students explain how the cinematographer used the elements and principles of art as Murillo did, to dramatize the action.

Study Guide
Distribute *Study Guide* 45 in the TCR. Assist students in reviewing key concepts. 📁

Art and Humanities
Have students complete *Art and Humanities* 32, "*Don Quixote*—The Spirit of Sixteenth-Century Spain," in the TCR. In this activity, students discover how publication of Cervantes's novel *Don Quixote* represented the changing spirit of sixteenth-century Spain. 📁

More About... **Cleaning and Restoration.** Point out that the cleaning and restoration of a painting can greatly affect its visual impact. Add that Velázquez's *Las Meninas* was cleaned and repaired in the mid-1980s. Obtain and show students "before" and "after" versions of the work (these were pictured in many art magazines during early 1986, including *Connoisseur,* March 1986). Ask how many changes students can find. Students may also enjoy comparing examples of other famous paintings that have been cleaned, such as Veronese's *The Feast in the House of Levi,* Titian's *Presentation of the Virgin,* Michelangelo's Sistine Chapel paintings, and Masaccio's fresco cycle at the Brancacci Chapel in Florence.

ASSESS

Checking Comprehension

➤ Have students respond to the lesson review questions. Answers are given in the box below.

➤ Assign students *Application 19,* "Ask the Librarian," in the TCR. Students are provided with a listing of fictitious art titles and with short descriptions of topics for art-class term papers. Students are called upon to determine which books would be useful for which assignments. 📁

Reteaching

➤ Assign *Reteaching* 45, found in the TCR. Have students complete the activity and review their responses. 📁

➤ Ask students to select one of the artworks illustrated in this lesson and state how it is similar or dissimilar to one of the Italian or Dutch Baroque works illustrated in earlier lessons of the chapter. Encourage students to share and compare their responses.

Enrichment

Have students create a diagram similar to that in Figure 19.21a (page 438) for another artwork from the text in which several figures surround the main character(s). How does this compare to the work of Velázquez?

CLOSE

Ask students briefly to explain whether they prefer Italian, Dutch, or Spanish Baroque art. Encourage them to explore artworks not illustrated in the text.

Bartolomé Esteban Murillo (1617–1682)

While Velázquez was working at the royal court in Madrid, another artist, Bartolomé Esteban Murillo (bar-toh-loh-**may ess**-tay-bahn moo-**ree**-yoh), was building a reputation for himself in Seville.

Many of Murillo's paintings were done for monasteries and convents. One of these tells the familiar story of The Prodigal Son (Figure 19.23). You see the father welcoming the **prodigal,** or *recklessly wasteful* son; the calf to be prepared for the celebration feast; and servants bringing a ring, shoes, and new garments. Notice the contrast between excited and calm feelings in the picture. You see a little dog

barking excitedly and servants conversing in an earnest manner. Yet, the tone of the reunion between father and son is tender and quiet.

Murillo avoided sharp lines and color contrasts in order to keep his composition simple and harmonious. In this way, the viewer would not be distracted from observing the joy associated with the son's return.

The subject of *The Return of the Prodigal Son* reflects the attitude of the Catholic Church during this period of the Counter-Reformation. Like the forgiving father, it welcomed back those who had followed Martin Luther and other Protestant reformers. Many did return, but others did not.

The religious map of Europe was now complete, and it has stayed about the same ever since. This meant artists could no longer seek out or depend on a universal Church for commissions. At the same time, they experienced a new freedom to paint, carve, and build for a variety of patrons. Their freedom also extended to subject matter, for most of these patrons did not request religious works. In fact, most of them taxed the artists' ingenuity with demands for art that was not inspired by religion.

■ **FIGURE 19.23** The central figures in this work are clearly the father and the son. **How did the artist use light and position to identify the central figures?**

Bartolomé Esteban Murillo. *The Return of the Prodigal Son.* 1667–70. Oil on canvas. 236.3 × 261.0 cm (93 × 102³/₄"). National Gallery of Art, Washington, D.C. Board of Trustees, Gift of the Avalon Foundation.

LESSON THREE REVIEW

Reviewing Art Facts

1. How did the subject matter of Spanish Baroque painters differ from that of Dutch Baroque artists?
2. Tell how Caravaggio's style influenced Jusepe de Ribera.
3. Look at *The Surrender of Breda* (Figure 19.21, page 438) and tell how Velázquez used line to express the pride of the victors.
4. List at least three ways Velázquez used space to intrigue the viewer in *Las Meninas* (Figure 19.22, page 439).

Activity… *Exploring Court Life through Artworks*

The painting *Las Meninas* (Figure 19.22, page 439) by Diego Velázquez is an example of the work of an artist who was attached to a royal court. Many artists in history have been a part of royal or noble households that became patrons and supporters of the arts. The works of these artists reveal many details of court life that would otherwise be lost.

Identify other artists who were attached to a royal court or were in the service of a member of the church or the nobility. Research their work and bring an example to class that illustrates what life was like at the time the artist worked. Share your findings with the class.

LESSON THREE REVIEW

Answers to Reviewing Art Facts

1. Spanish painted religious subjects; Dutch painted genre.
2. Caravaggio's use of chiaroscuro.
3. By painting their spears as vertical lines.
4. Highlighting figures; showing the king and queen reflected in a mirror; silhouetting a man against an open door; dark shadows.

Activity… *Exploring Court Life*

Have students work in small groups to explore various artists who were attached to royal courts or served members of the church. Then have each student select a specific artist for further research. Let students explore what the artists' works reveal about the lives of noble individuals or households.

Complete a painting that records, in repeated overlapping shapes and gradual changes in intensity, the movement of a falling, bouncing object as it turns and twists along an axis line through space. Select two complementary hues to obtain a range of color intensities.

Inspiration

Study Peter Paul Rubens's *The Raising of the Cross* (Figure 19.9, page 427). Can you trace your finger along the axis line in this picture? Explain how this line helps organize the placement of shapes and contributes to the illusion of movement.

Process

1. On the piece of cardboard, draw the outline of a small, simple object such as a key, large coin, or eraser. Cut this shape out with scissors.
2. With the ruler and pencil, make a straight, horizontal line about one-half inch from the bottom of the sheet of white drawing paper positioned lengthwise. This line can represent a tabletop or the floor.
3. Position your cardboard shape at the top left corner of your paper and trace around it with the pencil. Draw the same shape near the lower right corner of the paper so that it appears to rest on the horizontal line.
4. Imagine that the object you have drawn is made of rubber. The two drawings represent the first and last positions of this object. It has been dropped, strikes the floor, and bounces through space. To indicate this movement, lightly draw an axis line from the object at the top of the paper to the one at the bottom.
5. Using your cardboard shape as a pattern, complete a series of *overlapping* drawings showing your object as it twists, turns, and bounces through space along the axis line.
6. Select two *complementary* colors of tempera or acrylic and paint the shapes you have created. Use your imagination and gradations of intensity to show movement.

Materials

- Small piece of cardboard or mat board
- Scissors, ruler, and pencil
- White drawing paper, 9 × 12 inches
- Tempera or acrylic paint
- Brushes, mixing tray, and paint cloth
- Water container

■ **FIGURE 19.24** Student Work

Examining Your Work

Describe. Is the object in your painting easily identified? Did you show that it has bounced on the floor at least twice? Did you use two complementary colors?

Analyze. Can you trace the movement of your shape along an axis line? Do repeated, overlapping shapes and gradual changes of intensity add to the illusion of a falling object twisting, turning, and bouncing through space?

Interpret. What adjective best describes the movements of the object pictured in your painting? Is the idea of a falling, bouncing object clearly suggested?

Judge. Which theory of art, formalism or emotionalism, would you use to determine the success of your painting? Using that theory, is your painting successful?

441

ASSESSMENT

Peer Review. Once students have assessed their own paintings, suggest that they meet in small groups to examine and assess each other's work. As each group member shows his or her painting, have other group members respond to questions such as these: What is the most successful aspect of the original shape? What, if anything, might have been done to improve the shape itself or the choice of object for that shape? How clear is the axis line in this work? What might have improved the use of the axis line? What makes the bouncing motion of the object clear in this painting? Students should conclude the discussion of each painting by identifying what they like most about that work.

Objectives

■ Complete a painting of a falling, bouncing object as it moves along an axis line.

■ Use repeated overlapping shapes and gradual changes in intensity.

■ Limit the range of color intensities obtained by using two complementary colors.

Motivator

Ask students to identify other works illustrated in the text that make use of one or more diagonal axis lines to organize the art elements in a composition. Ask if axis lines must always follow a straight line. Have students point out works that use axis lines charting a different type of movement.

Art History

Ask students to compare and contrast Rubens's painting of *The Raising of the Cross* with Rogier van der Weyden's *Descent from the Cross* (Figure 17.7, page 387), completed almost 200 years earlier. Discuss the ways the styles of these two artists differ. Point out that Rubens uses an axis line to organize the art elements and draw viewers into the work. Rogier pushes his figures forward and arranges them across the picture plane so that viewers can observe the scene without feeling as if they are a part of it. Ask: Are any similarities noted in the two paintings?

Critiquing

Have students apply the steps of art criticism to their own artwork, using the "Examining Your Work" questions on this page.

Charcoal Figure Drawing

Objectives

■ Complete a series of large charcoal drawings of figures in action.

■ Use contrasts of value to indicate areas illuminated by light and other areas left in shadow.

Motivator

Review the term *chiaroscuro*. Ask each student to identify the work in the chapter that they think uses chiaroscuro most effectively to enhance its dramatic impact. Was one work selected more than any other?

Studio Skills

Explain to students that charcoal is a versatile, easy-to-use drawing medium. Show them the different ways it can be used, pointing out that it can be erased easily and smoothed and smudged to create different effects. Tell them that these qualities make charcoal an especially good medium for beginning artists who are often hesitant to make large bold marks that will be permanent. Provide ample time for students to experiment with the medium. Make certain that they use both the tip and the side of a charcoal stick. Discuss the different effects achieved by varying the pressure with which the charcoal is applied to a paper surface.

Critiquing

Have students apply the steps of art criticism to their own artwork, using the "Examining Your Work" questions on this page.

Materials

- Pencil
- Several sheets of white drawing paper, 18 × 24 inches
- Charcoal

■ **FIGURE 19.25** Student Work

Complete a series of charcoal drawings of figures in action. Each of the figures will fill a large sheet of drawing paper and will be spotlighted so that contrasts of light and dark values are clearly indicated. These light and dark values will add drama to your drawings.

Inspiration

Examine the Baroque paintings by Caravaggio, Gentileschi, Rubens, Rembrandt, Ribera, and Velázquez illustrated in this chapter. What do these works have in common? How has each artist used light and dark value contrasts to increase the dramatic effect of his or her picture?

Process

1. Take turns acting as models for this series of drawings. Each model should stand on a raised platform or table and assume an active pose (throwing, chopping, pulling, pushing). Complete a large drawing of the model lightly in pencil, concentrating on contours and the action noted in the model's pose.
2. Darken the room and direct a spotlight on the model, who continues in the same action pose. Use charcoal to shade in the dark areas.
3. Vary the pressure on the charcoal to obtain a range of dark and light values. Use the tip of the charcoal stick to indicate the most important contour lines of the figure.
4. Complete several other drawings of figures in action poses. When you gain skill and confidence, eliminate the preliminary pencil drawing and use charcoal exclusively. Select your best drawing for assessment.

Examining Your Work

Describe. Is your drawing easily identified as a human figure in action? Does this figure completely fill the paper on which it is drawn?

Analyze. Did you use charcoal to create areas of dark value? Do these contrast with areas of light value? Does the use of these value contrasts show that the figure was illuminated by a spotlight?

Interpret. Is the action of the figure easily identified? Do the contrasts of value in your drawing add to its dramatic impact?

Judge. Do you think that your drawing is successful? Is its success based mainly on its literal qualities, design qualities, or expressive qualities? Compare the first drawing you did with the last. In what ways have your figure-drawing skills improved?

ASSESSMENT

Personal Essay. After students have used the lesson questions to assess their projects, have them work independently to plan and write brief essays about their charcoal figure drawings. Suggest that students use their responses to these questions as the basis for their essays: How are your first drawing and your final drawing alike? What are the most significant differences between the two drawings? Of all your drawings, which do you consider most successful? Why? What did you learn from this Studio Lesson? What specific things do you think you can do to improve your contour drawings?

Reviewing the Facts

Lesson One

1. What was the Counter-Reformation?
2. How do Baroque artworks suggest a sense of movement or stillness?
3. How did Caravaggio paint his figures to remind the viewer that they were not supernatural beings?

Lesson Two

4. While artists in the Catholic countries were painting religious subjects, what were the Dutch Protestants painting?
5. What kind of subject matter did Vermeer generally paint?
6. Where has Vermeer placed the viewer in his painting *The Love Letter* (Figure 19.17, page 434)?
7. How does Judith Leyster involve the viewer in her *Self-Portrait* (Figure 19.19, page 436)?

Lesson Three

8. What purpose is served by the two side figures that stare out at the viewer in Velázquez's painting *The Surrender of Breda* (Figure 19.21, page 438)?
9. What freedoms were artists experiencing by the end of the seventeenth century?

 MUSIC. Use the *Performing Arts Handbook*, page 589 to learn about the music of Los Angeles Baroque.

Thinking Critically

1. **COMPARE AND CONTRAST.** Look at Bernini's *David* (Figure 19.6, page 424). Then refer to Myron's *Discus Thrower* (Figure 8.16, page 179). What can you say about the similarities and differences between these two sculptures? Closely examine details such as the hair and facial expressions.
2. **ANALYZE.** Look closely at the lighting in Rembrandt's *The Night Watch* (Figure 19.13, page 431). Turn your book upside down and squint at the painting so everything except the light areas are blocked out. Trace along the light areas with your finger. Now turn the book right side up and, on a sheet of paper, draw a rectangle the same size as the illustration in the book. Then diagram the location of the light areas in the painting.

■ **CAREERS IN** If you enjoy studying or creating art, read about a fascinating art-related career opportunity in the *Careers in Art Handbook*, page 594.

*inter*NET
CONNECTION Visit Glencoe Art Online at *www.glencoe.com/sec/art*. Investigate Baroque artworks and explore chiaroscuro techniques.

Technology Project

Exploring Baroque Art

The Baroque period produced an interesting and unique style of art that reflected the forces of a powerful struggle at work. The Protestant Reformation and the Counter-Reformation, launched by the Catholic Church, vied for religious dominance. In every form of the arts, from painting to architecture, artists selected dramatic subject matter. They heightened the expression of emotional intensity through the use of exaggerated gesture and extreme contrasts in art elements and principles such as color, value, movement, and rhythm.

1. Study some seventeenth-century painters such as Caravaggio, Peter Paul Rubens, Rembrandt, and Jan Vermeer, whose works demonstrate the exciting and dramatic style of the Baroque period.

2. Using available resources (Internet, CD-ROMs, laser discs), look for artworks by other Baroque artists. Then create a digital work of art that combines twenty-first-century technology with the dramatic vision of seventeenth-century Baroque artists.

3. Scan an image that exhibits the dominant and dramatic aesthetic qualities of art of the Baroque period. You might use an original sketch, a magazine image, or a part of a famous work of art.

4. Place your scanned image into a computer program that features digital tools. Use these tools to manipulate the art elements and art principles in order to achieve the expressive aesthetic qualities seen in Baroque art. Experiment with using filters to create special effects in gradients, textures, and pixellation.

5. Print a copy of your work.

443

Reviewing the Facts

1. The Catholic Church's reform movement in answer to the Protestant Reformation.
2. By showing figures that twist and turn and by using dramatic lighting to magnify action.
3. Showed flaws to remind viewers his figures were not supernatural beings.
4. People, places, and everyday events.
5. Interior scenes.
6. In a darkened closet.
7. The subject turns and looks over her shoulder as if suddenly interrupted by the viewer.
8. The gaze pinpoints the viewer's position in front of the main subjects in the painting.
9. The freedom to paint for a variety of patrons and choice of subject matter.

Thinking Critically

1. Similarities: Both works depict athletic-looking individuals in action poses; both works reveal meticulous attention with respect to anatomy and the realistic depiction of musculature. Differences: The chief difference is in the improbably placid facial expression on Myron's *Discus Thrower* as opposed to the look of determination and defiance on the face of David. The hair in Bernini's sculpture is tousled, the hair in the Greek statue looks contrived.
2. Student efforts should reveal an understanding of the artist's use of light and shadow and its importance to the art of the seventeenth century.

Teaching the Technology Project

Have students describe and discuss—and, if possible, show—additional Baroque works they have found in other resources. Then pose the question: How can you use your own drawings and computer program manipulations to create a work that exhibits these same qualities? Have students discuss and assess one another's work.

▲ R T
S ● U
R C ▣ Assign the feature in the *Performing Arts Handbook*, page 589.

CAREERS IN ART If time permits, have interested students investigate the career information in the *Careers in Art Handbook*, page 594.

*inter*NET Have students go online and learn more
CONNECTION about artists on preselected Web sites with the Internet activity for this chapter.

443

Rococo Art

LESSON ONE ## Art in France
(pages 446–451)

Classroom Resources

📁 Appreciating Cultural Diversity 30
📁 Art and Humanities 33
📁 Cooperative Learning 29
📁 Enrichment Activity 37
📁 Reproducible Lesson Plan 46
📁 Reteaching Activity 46
📁 Study Guide 46

Features

Time & Place CONNECTIONS
(page 447)

LOOKING Closely ↓
(page 449)

LESSON TWO ## Art in England and Spain
(pages 452–458)

Classroom Resources

📁 Art and Humanities 34
📁 Reproducible Lesson Plan 47
📁 Reteaching Activity 47
📁 Study Guide 47

Features

Social Commentary in Art

Scene 1 from Marriage à la Mode
(page 454)

END OF CHAPTER
(pages 459–461)

Studio **LESSONS**
• Still-Life Chalk Drawing *(page 459)*
• Expressive Self-Portrait Collage *(page 460)*

ADDITIONAL CHAPTER RESOURCES

Activities

- 📁 Application 20
- 📁 Advanced Studio Activity 20
- 🖱 Chapter 20 Internet Activity
- 📁 Studio Activity 26

Fine Art Resources

- 🕹 **Transparency**

  Art in Focus Transparency 25

    Jean Baptiste Simeon Chardin. *The House of Cards.*

- ◼ **Fine Art Print**

  Focus on World Art Print 20

    Louis Carmontelle. *Mozart's Father and His Two Children.*

Assessment

- 📁 Chapter 20 Test
- 📁 Performance Assessment

Multimedia Resources

- 🎭 Artsource® Performing Arts Package
- 💿 National Gallery Laser Disc
- 💿 National Museum of Women in the Arts CD-ROM
- 📼 Arts & Entertainment Videos

NATIONAL STANDARDS FOR ARTS EDUCATION

The National Standards for Arts Education provide guidelines for grade-appropriate competency in the visual arts. The Content Standards for grades 9–12 are:

1. Understanding and applying media, techniques, and processes.
2. Using knowledge of structures and functions.
3. Choosing and evaluating a range of subject matter, symbols, and ideas.
4. Understanding the visual arts in relation to history and cultures.
5. Reflecting upon and assessing the characteristics and merits of their work and the work of others.
6. Making connections between visual arts and other disciplines.

Listed below are the National Standards for the Visual Arts addressed in this chapter. For a breakdown of the categories listed under each content standard, refer to the *Reproducible Lesson Plans* booklet in the TCR.

1. (a, b)　**2.** (a, b, c)　**3.** (a)　**4.** (a, b, c)　**5.** (b, c)　**6.** (b)

HANDBOOK MATERIAL

Performing Arts *(page 576)*

CAREERS IN Art

(page 594)

Beyond the Classroom

For a link to a comprehensive listing of street addresses, phone numbers, and individuals to contact for national arts education services, visit our Web site at *www.glencoe.com/sec/art.*

🕐 **Out of Time?** If time does not permit teaching this chapter in its entirety, you may wish to preview the artwork and captions with students. Scan the heads in each lesson with students. Discuss the Looking Closely feature and examine Social Commentary in Art on page 454.

Rococo Art

INTRODUCE

Chapter Overview

CHAPTER 20 explains the origins and spread of Rococo ideals in painting and architecture.

Lesson One One traces the new directions in French painting initiated by Watteau and others.

Lesson Two treats portraiture in England and Spain.

Studio Lessons guide students to create a still life in chalk and an expressive self-portrait collage.

Art &Social Studies

Have students examine the painting and ask: From this artwork, what can you conclude about the subject matter and the style of the artworks of the Rococo period? Then have students focus on the evidence in this painting of sentiment between men and women that marked this period in European history. Ask: Why is it important to understand the relationships between men and women during any particular period of history? What does that indicate about daily life, society and politics of the period?

Art &Social Studies ■ **FIGURE 20.1** The arts of this era focused on the pursuit of pleasure. Painters like Antoine Watteau introduced the concept of sentiment between men and women in their works. After Watteau's death, his elegant, delicate form and use of pastel color influenced artists all over Europe. This delicate style is also seen in the buildings and churches designed at the time.

Antoine Watteau. *The Game of Love.* 1717. Oil on canvas. 51 × 59 cm (20 × 23¹⁄₄"). The National Gallery, London, England.

444

National Standards

This chapter addresses the following National Standards for the Arts.
1. (a,b)   4. (a,b,c)
2. (a,b,c) 5. (b, c)
3. (a)   6. (b)

Teacher's Classroom Resources

📁 Advanced Studio Activity 20
📁 Application 20
🖱 Chapter 20 Internet Activity
📁 Studio Activity 26

Assessment

📁 Chapter 20 Test
📁 Performance Assessment

Fine Art Resources

 Art in Focus Transparency 25
Jean Baptiste Simeon Chardin. *The House of Cards.*

Focus on World Art Print 20
Louis Carmontelle. *Mozart's Father and His Two Children.*

The end of the seventeenth century witnessed the decline of Dutch and Spanish naval power and political influence. This was matched by a similar decline in the quality of the art produced in both countries. At the same time, a new art style emerged to replace the Baroque. The drama and movement that characterized the Baroque gave way to artworks marked by a new concern for elegance and gaiety. This new movement, known as Rococo, also influenced the development of music, dance, and theatre. This new style first appeared in France and was responsible for elevating that country to a position of leadership in the art world. France was destined to maintain that position for the next three centuries.

Introducing the Chapter

Have students imagine that they were required to spend their days attending one formal function after another. Ask them whether they would eventually become bored. What might relieve some of the tedium? Draw a parallel between the students' responses and the eighteenth-century French court's fascination with romance, elaborate ornament, and extravagant expenditures.

YOUR Portfolio

Brainstorm a list of social problems that are important to you as an individual. Narrow the list to three issues that seem most important. In your sketchbook, begin thumbnail sketches of images and ideas related to each of the issues. As you progress on the sketches, pay attention to the issue that inspires you with the most images. After several minutes, stop and choose one topic to be the subject of a future piece of art. Write a proposal for the artwork in which you set goals and describe the media and techniques you would use. Keep notes and sketches in your portfolio for a future project.

Focus ON THE ARTS

DANCE
This was the age of the minuet. The minuet was a court dance involving dancers in a huge room moving together in small, precise steps. The dance required lessons and it could take as long as a year to learn the steps.

LITERATURE
Samuel Johnson published the first *Dictionary of the English Language* in 1755. He also wrote philosophical works that encouraged the development of literary criticism.

MUSIC
Music reflected the lighter style of the period, as typified by the airy quality and musical wit of Wolfgang Amadeus Mozart. Another German composer, George F. Handel, inspired a national love of opera in England when he visited London in 1739.

445

Focus ON THE ARTS

Play recordings of Bach's *Prelude I in C Major* (first piece of the *Well-Tempered Clavier*) and some of Mozart's *Sonata No. 1 in C Major*. Discuss: Does each piece of music sound religious, secular, serious, or humorous? How does the music communicate this?

Explain that although both pieces are written for a stringed keyboard instrument, and are in the key of C, they are very different. Bach's music is abstract. It has a slow and stately rhythm, eliciting a serious mood. Its sudden dissonances inspire awe. In contrast, Mozart's sonata is bright and happy. It has a quick pace. The piano sections are almost childlike in their playfulness. It has a rococo mood, aimed at those who might hear it at court or play it at home for fun. Some of Mozart's music does have a religious feeling. His music was so joyous and sweet that people said he was the only composer who talked to the angels.

DEVELOPING A PORTFOLIO

Personal Style. Encourage students to observe the evolution of individual pieces of art as a way of identifying their developing style. Remind them that creative people take risks and see failure as an indication of where the creative process needs modification. For example, if they are not happy with a sketch, instead of discarding it, have students make notes about their displeasure with the design or make corrections without erasing the old. Their increased awareness of the process of artistic creation will help them recognize their choices about style. During private conferences, encourage students to articulate progress in the style of their work.

Art in France

Art in France

FOCUS

Lesson Objectives

After studying this lesson, students will be able to:
■ Understand how royal tastes influenced the development of Rococo painting.
■ Explain the differences between Baroque and Rococo art.
■ Name the greatest Rococo painter and describe features of his work.

Building Vocabulary

Have students use a dictionary to look up the etymology of the word *aristocracy* (i.e., it derives from *aristo,* which means "best" in Greek, and *kratos,* which means "strength" or "power"). Direct students' attention to the text definition of *aristocracy.* Discuss how it relates to these root words.

Motivator

Have students imagine they are reigning monarchs. Ask them to develop their own personal insignia. After allowing time for students to share their work, have them discuss why they chose the symbols and images they did. Inform them that they are about to read of a monarch whose chosen symbol was the sun.

Introducing the Lesson

Have students examine the pictures of Versailles and works by Watteau and Fragonard. Refer students back to the Cornaro Chapel (Figure 19.5, page 423) and Rubens' energetic style (Figure 19.9, page 427). Point out that although both Baroque and Rococo art are highly ornamental, there are nevertheless differences between the two styles.

Vocabulary
■ aristocracy
■ Rococo art

Artists to Meet
■ Antoine Watteau
■ Jean-Honoré Fragonard
■ Jean-Baptiste Siméon Chardin

Discover
After completing this lesson, you will be able to:
■ Identify the differences between Baroque and Rococo art.
■ Discuss how the works of Antoine Watteau and Jean-Honoré Fragonard conform to the Rococo style.
■ Explain how the works of Jean-Baptiste Siméon Chardin differ from those of other French eighteenth-century painters.

*A*t the beginning of the eighteenth century, a new style of art and architecture became evident in France. The royal court had become increasingly important, and the **aristocracy**—*persons of high rank and privilege*—took their place in the pageantry of court life. The new style reflected this luxurious and idle way of life. It was marked by a free, graceful movement, a playful use of line, and delicate colors. Sometimes referred to as Late Baroque, the style differed enough from the Baroque that it deserved its own label. It received one when artists at the beginning of the next century disrespectfully called it *Rococo.*

Rococo art *placed emphasis on the carefree life of the aristocracy rather than on grand heroes or pious martyrs.* Love and romance were thought to be more fitting subjects for art than history and religion. At a time when poets were creating flowery phrases of love, painters were using soft, pastel colors to express the same sentiment. Both showed a zest for describing a lighthearted world filled with people seeking little more than pleasure and happiness.

The Palace at Versailles

■ **FIGURE 20.2**

At Versailles, a short distance from Paris, King Louis XIV embarked on the greatest building project of the age. It was to be the largest, most elegant palace in the world—the king's home as well as the capital of France (Figure 20.2). The royal family moved into it in 1682, but the palace continued to undergo numerous changes. Louis and his successors lavished money, time, and attention on the palace, constantly making improvements and adding new decorations.

■ **FIGURE 20.2** Large forests were planted and statues of marble and bronze decorated the magnificent gardens of Versailles. Looking at it from the outside, what do you think the interior of this palace looked like?

The Palace of Versailles, near Paris, France. 1668–85.

446

Versailles was considered to be an example of the Baroque style in France. However, in this elegant, aristocratic setting which was under constant renovation during Louis XIV's long reign, were also the seeds of the new Rococo style. In architecture, the style was marked by delicate interior decorations, including fancy curving ornamentation.

Within the palace, King Louis XIV was treated as if he were a god. He chose the sun as his emblem and was known as the Sun King. To make sure there was always an audience for the royal display of power and wealth, people were free to enter and wander about the palace, as long as they were properly dressed. There they could gaze at the artworks, the tapestries, and the mirrors and even watch the royal family eat their spectacular meals (Figure 20.3).

New Directions in French Painting

In painting, the dramatic action of the seventeenth century gave way to this new, carefree style. The constant movement of the Baroque lost its force in Rococo art, which favored greater control and elegance. Paintings made greater use of delicate colors and curved, graceful patterns. When seen in the palaces and châteaus for which they were intended, these paintings added a final touch of gaiety and elegance.

■ **FIGURE 20.3** The elaborate decorations, gilded and painted ceiling, and architectural detail in the Hall of Mirrors is typical of the palace interior. **Identify familiar architectural features in this hall.**

Jules Hardouin Mansart. Hall of Mirrors in the Palace at Versailles, Versailles, France. 1678–89.

Time & Place CONNECTIONS

Rococo Period
c. 1700–1800

COTTON GIN. After cotton was picked, the fiber had to be separated by hand from the seed. Eli Whitney's invention in 1793 helped speed the process. The cotton gin had revolving saws to pull cotton from the seed and ribs between the saws to prevent the seeds from passing through with the cotton fibers.

MANCHESTER FACTORIES. One of the largest industrial centers in England, Manchester became a world center of the cotton and wool trade. The Industrial Revolution brought economic growth as well as damaging smoke from the factories.

Activity **Historical reporter.**
You are a reporter covering conditions of the Industrial Revolution. Write an article chronicling the conditions in a factory of the time. Comment on events of the period such as working conditions, child labor, women's rights.

TEACH
Critical Thinking

Share with students the view held by Madame du Châtelet, a product of the eighteenth-century high style of living. "We must begin," the Madame wrote, "by saying to ourselves that we have nothing else to do in the world but seek pleasant sensations and feelings." Discuss how this philosophy of life relates to Rococo art. Then ask students to write a page that compares Madame du Châtelet's point of view with the aesthetic philosophy of any other artist or art period covered thus far in the text.

Cross Curriculum

MATHEMATICS. Have students locate and study photos of the gardens at Versailles. Ask students to discuss the characteristics of Versailles landscaping. Then, working as a team, have them analyze the geometric forms present in the design of the gardens. Using rulers, squares, and protractors, have students draw on graph paper the patterns they see in photographs of the gardens.

Aesthetics

Tell students that the great majority of eighteenth-century intellectuals strongly objected to Rococo art on the grounds that it was frivolous and lacking in serious moral purpose. Divide students into three debating teams. One should defend paintings such as those by Watteau, highlighting the works' artistic merits. The second should explain why such works are morally harmful. The third team should make a case for supporting all art, whether it entertains a serious theme (e.g., Baroque art) or dwells on more pleasurable moments.

Time & Place CONNECTIONS

Rococo Period

As students examine and discuss the images in this Time & Place feature, pose questions such as these: What difference did the invention of the cotton gin make in the speed and efficiency with which cotton fiber could be separated from the seed? How do you think the invention affected consumers? How do you think it affected cotton workers? What were the advantages and disadvantages of this change? After a brief class discussion, have students explore the conditions of the industrial revolution and consider information they might include in their articles.

Art History

Ask volunteers to research the Venus statue that appears in Figure 20.4. The students may report on the role played by Venus in the mythological pantheon—how Cythera came to be known as the island of love and the stories and legends that center on Venus. Students may also wish to present other artworks that feature the goddess of love.

Art Criticism

Have students write down the inner thoughts of an eighteenth-century visitor to Versailles who, during a tour of the palace, happens upon the painting in Figure 20.4. Before students write, have them brainstorm a range of reactions, reminding them that the individual's idea of "art" up to this point has been synonymous with works by "serious" painters like Rubens and Caravaggio. Is the viewer shocked by the sight of Watteau's painting, or relieved?

Art History

Explain to students that many art historians believe that the roots of Rococo art can be traced to the work of Rubens. Display a reproduction of Rubens's painting *Garden of Love,* which features couples in love strolling around a shrine to Venus. Ask students to point out as many similarities as they can between this work and the Rococo paintings.

Did You Know?

Many of Watteau's works hint at the fleeting nature of happines. This may reflect the artist's own poor health. Watteau died four years after completing *Embarkation for Cythera;* he was only 37 years old.

Antoine Watteau (1684–1721)

The greatest of the Rococo painters was Antoine Watteau (an-**twahn** wah-**toh**). Watteau began his career as an interior decorator and rose to become the court painter to King Louis XV. He is best known for paintings of characters or scenes from the theater as well as for paintings that show the French aristocracy at play.

Embarkation for Cythera

■ **FIGURE 20.4**

In *Embarkation for Cythera* (Figure 20.4), Watteau demonstrates the elegance of the Rococo style. The subject of this painting comes from a play and shows a group of happy young aristocrats about to set sail from Cythera, the legendary island of romance.

(For 200 years this painting has been known by the wrong name! It has always been called "Embarkation for Cythera" but recent interpretations point out that it shows a departure *from* the mythical island.)

The soft, dreamlike atmosphere, luxurious costumes, dainty figures, and silvery colors give the picture its dreamy feeling, or mood. The figures move with graceful ease. Arranged like a garland, they curl over a small hill and down into a valley bordering the sea. A similar garland made of cupids playfully twists around the mast of the ship.

Like many of Watteau's other works (Figure 20.1, page 444), which hint at the fleeting nature of happiness, *Embarkation for Cythera* is tempered by a touch of sadness. One figure in particular seems to sum up this

■ **FIGURE 20.4** It is said that this painting depicts a happy occasion. **Can you detect another mood in any of the members of the party?**

Antoine Watteau. *Embarkation for Cythera.* 1717–19. Oil on canvas. 1.3 × 1.9 m (4′3″ × 6′ 4¹/₂″). The Louvre, Paris, France.

Technology

National Gallery of Art Videodisc Use the following images as examples of more works by artists introduced in this lesson.

Antoine Watteau
Italian Comedians

Search Frame 1015

Jean-Honoré Fragonard
The Happy Family

Search Frame 1071

Jean-Baptiste-Siméon Chardin
The Kitchen Maid

Search Frame 1031

Use Glencoe's *Correlation Bar Code Guide to the National Gallery of Art* to locate more artworks.

feeling: The woman in the center casts a final backward glance as she reluctantly prepares to join her companions boarding the boat. Along with her friends, she has spent a carefree day on the island paying homage to Venus, the goddess of love, whose flower-covered statue is seen at the far right of the picture. The woman lingers for just a moment, but her companion reminds her to hurry—the dream is ending.

Jean-Honoré Fragonard
(1732–1806)

Ignoring the growing signs of unrest that led to the French Revolution, the upper class continued to devote their lives to pleasure. They liked to frolic in parklike gardens, pamper their pets, play on elegant swings, and engage in idle gossip. All of these trivial pastimes are found in a painting by Jean-Honoré Fragonard (**jawn** oh-no-**ray** frah-goh-**nahr**).

The Swing
■ **FIGURE 20.5**

Fragonard, like Watteau, was a court painter. He painted pictures about love and romance using glowing pastel colors applied in a sure, brisk manner. These pictures reveal that Fragonard was a master designer as well. In *The Swing* (Figure 20.5), he used axis lines and contour lines to tie the parts of his composition together.

The French Revolution brought a swift end to Fragonard's popularity. All but forgotten, he died of a stroke while eating ice cream. Today his works are reminders of a bygone era and an outdated, luxurious way of life.

LOOKING Closely

ACHIEVING UNITY THROUGH THE USE OF LINE

● **Axis lines.** The arrangement of the figures, the ropes of the swing, the water from the lion fountains, even the position of the telescope form a series of parallel diagonal lines in the lower part of the picture.

● **Contour lines.** The sky and the landscape are united with repeated, rounded contours; the clouds at the right repeat the curved contours of the trees at the left.

■ **FIGURE 20.5**

Jean-Honoré Fragonard. *The Swing.* c. 1765. Oil on canvas. 215.9 × 185.5 cm (85 × 73"). National Gallery of Art, Washington, D.C. Board of Trustees, The Samuel H. Kress Collection.

Chapter 20 *Rococo Art* **449**

Art Criticism

In his old age, Chardin gave up oil painting in favor of pastels. This change may have been motivated by the artist's failing eyesight. Some historians suggest that the artist opted for this medium because it allowed him to work more quickly than did oil paints. Since pastels require less time and effort for preparation, Chardin may have found them more relaxing to work with. Have students research the drying time of oil paints and determine facets of Chardin's works that lend credence to the above theory.

Study Guide

Distribute *Study Guide* 46 in the TCR. Assist students in reviewing key concepts. 📁

Art and Humanities

Have small groups of students work jointly to complete *Cooperative Learning* 29, "Commedia dell'Arte—The Traveling Theater," in the TCR. In this activity, students learn about the development of the Commedia dell'Arte during the Rococo period. Students then create character masks that express familiar personalities. 📁

Studio Activities

Assign *Studio* 26, "Designing a Formal Garden," in the TCR. Students will plan a geometric design for a garden patterned after the precision of the Versailles gardens. 📁

Jean-Baptiste Siméon Chardin (1699–1779)

Jean-Baptiste Siméon Chardin (jawn-bahp-**teest** see-may-**ohn** shahr-**dahn**) rejected the delicately painted subjects of the court artists. He preferred subjects that were more in keeping with those painted by the Little Dutch Masters. His works show peasants and members of the middle class going about their simple daily chores.

Art about Common People

Chardin's mature work reveals that, in the arrangement of simple objects, he saw the symbols of common working people. He painted still lifes of humble everyday items (Figure 20.6). Earthenware containers, copper kettles, vegetables, and meat were his subjects. Chardin took delight in showing slight changes of color, light, and texture. The way he painted these everyday objects made them seem important and worthy of close examination.

Toward the middle of his career, Chardin began to paint simple genre scenes. One such scene is *The Attentive Nurse* (Figure 20.7). This work exhibits a gentle, homespun quality that is unforced and natural. Chardin's brush illuminates beauty hidden in the commonplace. He shows you a quiet, orderly, and wholesome way of life. You are welcomed into a comfortable household where a hardworking nurse is carefully preparing a meal.

■ **FIGURE 20.6** Chardin selected simple everyday objects for this still life. What was his purpose in painting this kind of subject? How did his intentions in painting differ from those of court artists such as Watteau and Fragonard?

Jean-Baptiste Siméon Chardin. *Still Life with a Rib of Beef.* 1739. Oil on canvas. 40.6 × 33.2 cm (16 × 13¹/₁₆″). Allen Memorial Art Museum, Oberlin College, Oberlin, Ohio. R. T. Miller Jr. Fund, 1945.

450 **Unit Six** *Art of an Emerging Modern Europe*

Fashion. Point out to students that women's clothing styles during this period, were, like the male fashions described in the text, unusual in their own right, especially when judged against today's standards. Note that hairdos, for example, grew taller and taller until they made a woman's face appear to be located in the middle of her person. Have a group of volunteers consult an encyclopedia of fashion and obtain illustrations of a variety of clothing styles of the period. Instruct the group to include these illustrations in a presentation to the class, in which they discuss materials most commonly used, how long a given costume took to create, and who were the foremost designers of the day.

Light filters in the room to fall softly on the figure and the table in the foreground. The rest of the room is partly hidden in the shadows. The light reveals the rich textures and creates the changes of value on cloth, bread, and kitchen utensils. The colors are silvery browns and warm golds, which add to the sense of calm and the poetry of this common domestic scene.

In his old age, Chardin gave up oil painting in favor of pastels because of his failing eyesight. Other reasons have been suggested for Chardin's decision to work in pastels. Some historians have indicated that he used pastels because they allowed him to work more quickly than did oil paints. Because pastels require less time and effort for preparation, Chardin may have found them more relaxing to work with. Weakened by illness, he died in 1779.

■ **FIGURE 20.7** This picture creates a quiet, peaceful mood in a simple domestic setting. **How does the use of light contribute to that mood?**

Jean-Baptiste Siméon Chardin. *The Attentive Nurse.* c. 1738. Oil on canvas. 46.2 × 37 cm (18¹/₈ × 14¹/₂"). National Gallery of Art, Washington, D.C. Board of Trustees, Samuel H. Kress Collection.

LESSON ONE REVIEW

Reviewing Art Facts

1. What subject did French Rococo artists consider most suitable for their paintings?
2. How did the style of Rococo art differ from that of Baroque art?
3. Who was considered the greatest of the French Rococo painters?
4. How did Fragonard tie together the parts of his composition *The Swing* (Figure 20.5, page 449)?

Activity... *Comparing Points of View*

The Rococo style of art mirrored the time in which it was produced. Examine the artworks in the chapter. These paintings represent different points of view shown in art during this period. Jean-Honoré Fragonard was a popular court painter who painted elegant scenes with disregard for the plight of the common people of France. Jean-Baptiste Siméon Chardin created paintings that depicted the objects, scenes, and symbols of the common people.

Compare two works by artists in this chapter. Point out examples of how subject matter has been depicted differently in each of the paintings. Identify two contemporary artists and show how their different styles represent today's culture.

ASSESS

Checking Comprehension

Have students respond to the lesson review questions. Answers are given in the box below.

Reteaching

Assign *Reteaching* 46, found in the TCR. Have students complete the activity and review their responses. 📁

Enrichment

Assign students *Enrichment* 37, "Art Representing the Common People," in the TCR. In this worksheet, students are called upon to compare artworks that depict the struggles of the poor. Students then create collages that make a statement about today's lifestyles. 📁

Extension

Have students complete Appreciating *Cultural Diversity* 30, "Bag Wigs Three Feet High," in the TCR. In this activity students read about the splendid wigs fashionable during the Rococo period.

CLOSE

Display photographs of the gardens at Versailles. Have small groups of students discuss how the topiary and orderly, intricate arrangements reflect the ritualized life of the royal court.

LESSON ONE REVIEW

Answers to Reviewing Art Facts

1. The carefree life of the aristocracy and scenes of love and romance.
2. Baroque art featured movement and drama; Rococo was marked by playful use of line and bright colors.
3. Antoine Watteau.
4. With axis lines and contour lines.

Activity... *Comparing Points of View*

Have students meet in cooperative learning groups to examine and compare pairs of Rococo works and pairs of contemporary works. Then have each student work independently to plan and write a short essay in response to the Activity assignment.

Art in England and Spain

FOCUS

Lesson Objectives

After studying this lesson, students will be able to:
■ Describe the kinds of paintings preferred in England during the eighteenth century.
■ Identify and describe the best-known work of Sir Christopher Wren.
■ Explain how Goya opened up the visual arts to include highly personal and subjective vision as subject matter.

Building Vocabulary

Let students explain their own understanding of the Vocabulary term, *satire,* and ask a volunteer to read aloud the definitions given in a dictionary. Ask: Which definition is probably closest to the one given in this lesson? Then let students read and discuss the definition in the text.

Motivator

Ask students to browse through magazines and find examples of satirical pictures, cartoons, headlines, jokes, or other statements. Have students brainstorm to identify common features of these various print phenomena. Explain that in this lesson they will discover how the traits they have isolated were successfully incorporated into the work of at least one eighteenth-century painter.

Art in England and Spain

Vocabulary
■ satire

Artists to Meet
■ Sir Joshua Reynolds
■ Thomas Gainsborough
■ William Hogarth
■ Sir Christopher Wren
■ Francisco Goya

Discover
After completing this lesson, you will be able to:
■ Identify the kind of paintings preferred in England and offer reasons to explain their popularity.
■ Identify and describe the best-known work of Sir Christopher Wren.
■ Discuss the development of Francisco Goya's style.

*A*rtists in England and Spain responded in different ways to the elegant and decorative Rococo style that emerged in France. Most rejected the artificial subjects preferred by Watteau and Fragonard but adopted those artists' delicate, light-washed painting techniques. In England, artists made use of this technique to paint portraits, scenes and events from daily life, and still lifes.

As the century progressed, these paintings became more and more realistic. The century came to a close with a Spanish artist, Francisco Goya, who turned away completely from the Rococo style to paint pictures that drew their inspiration from a new source: his own personal thoughts and feelings.

The Art Movement in England

Until this time, England could boast of only a few outstanding painters and sculptors. No doubt the Protestant Reformation was partly to blame. Reformers were against religious images, and this had a crushing effect on art. With the return of the fun-loving Stuarts to the English throne and the growth of a wealthy aristocracy, however, the visual arts gained in importance.

Portrait painting in particular grew in popularity. Instead of making use of English artists, however, wealthy people invited foreign portrait painters such as Hans Holbein to England. This practice continued until around the middle of the eighteenth century. By then the talents of native English painters were finally being appreciated.

■ **FIGURE 20.8** This portrait shows a fashionable—but very natural looking— five-year-old. Where has the artist used warm and cool colors in this painting? With what effect?

Sir Joshua Reynolds. *Lady Elizabeth Hamilton.* 1758. Oil on canvas. 116.8 × 83.8 cm (46 × 33"). National Gallery of Art, Washington, D.C. Board of Trustees, Widener Collection.

452

Sir Joshua Reynolds (1723–1792)

Sir Joshua Reynolds (**ren**-uhldz) was one of a number of English artists who painted the fashionable portraits that the English nobility desired. He was especially skillful in capturing on canvas the sensitive and fleeting expressions of children. His appealing portrait of the five-year-old daughter of the Duke of Hamilton (Figure 20.8) shows that he could make his young subjects seem completely natural and at ease.

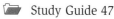

Thomas Gainsborough

(1727–1788)

Reynolds's great rival was Thomas Gainsborough (**gainz**-bur-oh), who began his career by painting landscapes. Ultimately he became the favorite portrait painter of English high society. Gainsborough was admired for his delicate brushwork and rich, glistening pastel colors. His works showed the shining silks and buckles, fragile lace, and starched ruffles of fashionable clothing.

The Blue Boy

■ FIGURE 20.9

A professional rivalry with Reynolds resulted in one of Gainsborough's best-known paintings, *The Blue Boy* (Figure 20.9). In a lecture to the Royal Academy of Art, Reynolds had stated that blue, a cool color, should always be used in the background. He said it should never be used in the main part of a portrait. When Gainsborough heard this, he accepted it as a challenge and began planning a blue portrait. The finished portrait shows a princely looking boy dressed in a shimmering blue satin suit standing in front of a warm brown background. The work was an immediate success in the eyes of most viewers—although Reynolds never publicly admitted that Gainsborough had proved him wrong.

The story does not end here, however. Later, when Gainsborough was dying, Reynolds paid him a visit. What they said to one another is unknown. However, when Gainsborough died, Reynolds with tears in his eyes, delivered another lecture to the Royal Academy, this time praising the rival who had challenged him.

■ **FIGURE 20.9** This child, though older than the subject of Reynolds's portrait, also looks both fashionable and natural. How does the use of warm and cool colors here differ from the use of warm and cool colors in Reynolds's picture of Lady Elizabeth Hamilton (Figure 20.8)?

Thomas Gainsborough. *The Blue Boy.* c. 1770. 177.8 × 121.9 cm (70 × 48"). The Huntington Library Art Collections and Botanical Gardens, San Marino, California.

William Hogarth (1697–1764)

Other artists in England at this time refused to cater to the tastes of the aristocracy in the manner of Reynolds and Gainsborough. William Hogarth (**hoh**-gahrth) was one of these. He was more interested in painting the common people he found on London streets and in taverns than he was in painting portraits for wealthy patrons. Nothing gave him more pleasure than exposing the immoral conditions and foolish customs of his time.

Hogarth used his art to tell a story, scene by scene, picture by picture, with great wit and attention to detail. His pictures were a stage filled with colorful performers from every level of society: lords, ladies, lawyers, merchants, beggars, and thieves.

Chapter 20 *Rococo Art* **453**

TEACH
Introducing the Lesson

Ask students to bring in a variety of formal and informal photographs of themselves as children. Have them compare these images with that in Figure 20.9. Discuss the factors that go into making a successful picture of a child. Ask: What makes this painting a work of art? Is the difference between the painting and the photos purely a matter of technique? Urge students to seek answers to these questions as they read.

Art Criticism

Let students meet in groups to examine and discuss the two portraits, *Lady Elizabeth Hamilton* in Figure 20.8 and *The Blue Boy* in Figure 20.9. Have group members follow the steps in the art criticism operation to compare the two works.

Art History

Display a variety of portraits of children from different periods of art, and have students compare these with Figure 20.9. Possibilities include the Dutch Baroque artist Gabriel Metsu's *The Sick Child,* Mary Cassatt's *Two Children at the Seashore,* and *American Surrealist* Dorothea Tanning's *Maternity.*

Studio Skills

Have students use oil pastels to create portraits of themselves as younger children. Encourage students to consider how a childhood portrait can sum up many experiences, emphasize a particular personality trait, or show a child as a member of a larger family structure. Invite students to share their self-portraits with classmates.

Cross Curriculum

SOCIAL STUDIES. Have students research the practice of arranged marriage, which is satirized in Figure 20.10. Student reports should focus on the similarities and differences between arranged marriages in various cultures and religions. After students have presented their findings, re-examine Hogarth's satirical picture of an arranged marriage. Which aspects did he choose to emphasize in order to make his point?

Art History

Students may enjoy researching the work of Honoré Daumier, a nineteenth-century French heir to the tradition of Hogarth's sarcastic and witty art. Have groups of students locate and prepare critiques of several of Daumier's lithographs, which satirize a variety of types of people, especially rich people and lawyers. Conclude with a discussion of the similarities and differences between the works of Daumier and Hogarth.

Social Commentary in *Art*

*I*n a series of six paintings entitled *Marriage à la Mode,* Hogarth criticized the accepted practice of arranged marriages. In the first of this series, *The Marriage Contract* (Figure 20.10), he introduces the main characters in his story.

■ **FIGURE 20.10** William Hogarth. *Scene I from Marriage à la Mode, The Marriage Contract.* 1742–1744. Oil on canvas. The National Gallery, London, England.

 The future bride and groom, their backs to each other, seem uninvolved and uninterested in what is going on around them. A lawyer flirts with the young woman, while her bored fiancé prepares to take a pinch of snuff.

 The father of the bride, a wealthy merchant eager to have his daughter marry into a noble family, studies the marriage agreement as if it were nothing more than another business contract.

 The father of the groom, a nobleman with gout, points proudly to his family tree.

 The other five pictures in this series show the progress of the marriage from this unfortunate start. It moves from boredom to unfaithfulness to death. Each scene is painted with the same brilliant, biting **satire,** *the use of sarcasm or ridicule to expose and denounce vice or folly.*

5 The paintings demonstrate Hogarth's uncanny ability to remember and use what he saw in the world around him. The gestures and expressions he portrays were learned during long observations of the way real people behave in different situations.

Social Commentary in *Art*

Let students begin by examining *Scene I* from *Marriage à la Mode,* Figure 20.10, and describing what they see. Ask: What mood do you think this work communicates? How? Then guide students in reading and discussing the information presented in this feature.

Have a group of student actors and a few prop coordinators work together to stage a skit based on Hogarth's satire in this work. The script should alternate between the flirtatious conversation of the bride-to-be and the lawyer and the haggling over the marriage contract.

Sir Christopher Wren
(1632–1723)

Although it took English painters a long time to gain acceptance in their native country, this was not the case with architects. In fact, many of the most impressive buildings in London are due to the efforts of a single English architect: Sir Christopher Wren.

In 1666, the Great Fire of London burned for four days. It destroyed 89 churches, the city gates, a large number of public buildings, and some 14,000 houses. For years after this fire, Sir Christopher Wren was responsible for designing churches and other buildings to replace those that had been destroyed. St. Paul's Cathedral and 51 parish churches were built according to his designs.

Revising Church Architecture

It was not easy to design churches to fit comfortably within specified areas. Many of these areas were small and awkward, yet Wren was able to design buildings ideally suited for their settings. He often used a tall, slender steeple to crown these churches. Soaring proudly above surrounding buildings which threatened to hide the church, this steeple became an inspiration for later architects in England and North America.

The best known of Wren's work is St. Paul's Cathedral (Figure 20.11). Before the fire, he had been hired to restore the old cathedral, which had been built in the late eleventh century. The fire, however, destroyed the building, and Wren was asked to design a new cathedral instead.

The façade of St. Paul's is marked by a pattern of light and dark values. This pattern is created by the use of deep porches at two levels. Each porch is supported by huge columns arranged in pairs. The top porch is narrower than the one below and draws your eye upward to the tympanum and the great dome above. Two towers flank the façade and frame the dome.

Unity of Design

One of the most impressive features of St. Paul's is its overall unity. All of the parts are joined together to form a symmetrically balanced whole that is a striking reminder of classical structures such as the Parthenon. (See Figure 8.1, page 166.) Much of this unity is no doubt due to the fact that this building is the only major cathedral in Europe to be erected under the watchful eye of a single architect.

The London skyline is Wren's legacy—and his monument. The Latin inscription on his tomb calls attention to this skyline with a simple statement that reads in part: "If ye seek my monument, look around."

■ **FIGURE 20.11** The deep porches on this cathedral create a pattern of light and dark values. **What characteristics does this cathedral have in common with classical structures?**

Sir Christopher Wren. St. Paul's Cathedral, London, England. 1675–1710.

Critical Thinking

Divide the class into groups, and ask each group to research a disaster, such as a fire, hurricane, or earthquake, in which buildings were destroyed. The event may have occurred locally or in another city, or even country. The groups should find out exactly what buildings were destroyed and what kinds of buildings later replaced them. If at all possible, groups should assemble diagrams or photos of the "before" and "after" versions of their chosen site. After all the groups have presented their findings, compare the results and discuss how funding, demographics, and the needs of a community influence the way an area is rebuilt and whether the same structures are re-created.

Studio Skills

Review the challenge faced by Christopher Wren to design churches that suited awkward or small sites. Then divide the class into groups, and have each choose or imagine an odd-sized lot in the local community, preferably one that is currently vacant so that students can more easily appreciate the problems of designing for it. Each group's goal is to design a particular building type to suit their lot, such as a school, a convenience store, or medical offices. Groups are to prepare both floor plans and elevation views of their building design. Have students present their work to the class and explain factors in addition to lot size and shape that affected their design. Discuss whether these constraints helped jog the students' architectural creativity to find innovative solutions, as in Christopher Wren's case.

More About... **Sir Christopher Wren.** Although Sir Christopher Wren is famous for his architectural designs, he was never formally trained in architecture, masonry, sculpture, or engineering. Wren's principal interest during his youth was science and, following studies at Oxford, he taught astronomy, illustrated a technical study of brain anatomy, and was responsible for dozens of inventions, theories, discoveries, and technical improvements. At the request of Oxford University, he designed a theater in 1663. This early foray into architecture showed that Wren had a great deal yet to learn about architectural design, but the theater's timber roof is considered an ingenious work of engineering.

Aesthetics

Direct students' attention to the portrait by Goya in Figure 20.12. Apart from the obvious hints about the artist's feelings for the subject alluded to in the text, what visual clues can students find that carry the same message? Does the subject's facial expression carry any suggestion of the feelings that existed between her and Goya? Does body language help convey these feelings, and, if so, how?

Art History

Have students locate a reproduction of Goya's *The Marquesa de Pontejos*. Have them determine whether this portrait was painted earlier or later than the one in Figure 20.12. What is the history behind Goya's painting of the marquesa? Can students isolate differences of style between the two works? Does one of the portraits reveal a more mature style?

Art Criticism

Have students closely examine the artworks in Figures 20.12 and 20.13. Emphasize that, even though Goya has used very different subject matter for these two works, there is still a similarity in his use of the elements and principles of art. Ask students to identify common features of style. Ask: If these two works were unidentified, would curators be able to say that they had been created by the same artist?

Cross Curriculum

LITERATURE. Suggest that interested students research and report on these milestones in English literature, achieved during Goya's lifetime: Thomas Gray penned *Elegy Written in a Country Churchyard;* Samuel Johnson began work on his *Dictionary of the English Language.*

Francisco Goya (1746–1828)

This discussion of eighteenth-century art ends in Spain with the work of Francisco Goya (frahn-**seese**-koh **goh**-yah), an artist who eventually rejected the past and looked to the future.

Early in his career, Goya adopted the Rococo style to gain considerable fame and fortune.

Appointed court painter to King Charles IV, he painted portraits of the royal family and the aristocracy, using the same soft pastel colors favored by Watteau and Fragonard.

The Duchess of Alba
■ **FIGURE 20.12**

Later in his career, Goya met and was completely captivated by the most celebrated woman of the day, the thirteenth Duchess of Alba. While under her spell, Goya painted a portrait of the duchess pointing confidently to the artist's name scrawled in the sand at her feet (Figure 20.12).

In addition to being one of the wealthiest people in Spain, she was also one of the most controversial. At the time Goya painted her, the duchess was in exile from Madrid for having once again embarrassed her queen, Maria Luisa. She had announced a great ball in honor of the queen and then sent spies to Paris to learn what kind of gown the queen was planning to wear. When the queen arrived at the Alba palace, she was greeted by a score of servant girls—each wearing the same gown as the queen!

In Goya's portrait, the duchess gazes directly at the viewer with large eyes under black eyebrows. She wears two rings on the fingers of her right hand. These bear the names Goya and Alba and, like the inscription in the sand, are meant to illustrate the union of artist and model. However, the fickle duchess soon turned her attention elsewhere while the artist never forgot her. Before he died in 1828, Goya turned over all his belongings to his son. Goya had only kept two of his many paintings. His portrait of the duchess was one of these. In a recent cleaning of the picture, the word *solo,* or *only* was discovered written in the sand before the artist's name. (Goya died wishing it had been so.)

Goya the Rebel

Goya was satisfied to be a fashionable society painter until he reached middle age. Then, following an illness and after witnessing the brutality and suffering caused by war, his art changed and he became Goya the Rebel.

■ **FIGURE 20.12** The duchess points to the artist's name in the sand, with the word *solo,* or "only" painted in front of it. What impression of the duchess does this portrait convey?

Francisco Goya. *The Duchess of Alba.* 1797. Oil on canvas. 210.2 × 149.2 cm (82³/₄ × 58³/₄″). Courtesy of the Hispanic Society of America, New York, New York.

456 **Unit Six** *Art of an Emerging Modern Europe*

MEETING INDIVIDUAL NEEDS

Language Proficiency. Bringing the lessons alive can often aid in students' understanding of a different life style or historical period. If possible, arrange a class visit to a local art museum to view some eighteenth-century decorative arts. Viewing the actual household furnishings of aristocrats of the period and relating these to those pictured in Rococo paintings can help students—especially less capable readers—to gain a more vivid sense of daily life in the eighteenth century. Point out that many Rococo painters also worked in the decorative arts. For example, François Boucher created designs for tapestries and porcelain, the latter a particularly popular medium since the West was being flooded by Chinese goods.

The Third of May, 1808

■ **FIGURE 20.13**

Goya was in Madrid when the French invaded Spain. One of his most memorable paintings commemorates an uprising of the people of Madrid after the French had occupied their city. On May 2, 1808, people gathered in anger before the royal palace. They had heard that the children of the king were to be taken to France. A fight broke out, and Spanish civilians and French soldiers were killed. That night and the next morning, French troops executed the Spanish patriots they had taken prisoner.

Goya's painting (Figure 20.13) captures the drama of the event. The morning sky is almost black. A lantern placed on the ground lights the scene. The patriots are lined up, about to be shot. The French soldiers lean forward, pointing their rifles like lances. Their faces are hidden from view, but their faces are unimportant here. The soldiers are like robots—cold, unfeeling, unthinking. The wedge of light from the lantern reveals the different reactions of the men facing death. The central target is a figure in white with his arms raised. His pose suggests an earlier sacrifice—Christ on the cross. To his right, a monk seeks refuge in prayer. One man stares blindly upward, another covers his ears, and a third buries his face in his hands.

Goya's painting does not echo the traditional view of war. Unlike his countryman Velázquez (Figure 19.21, page 438), he placed no importance on chivalry and honor or bravery and glory. To him, war meant only death and destruction, and he used his art to express his feelings to others.

Goya's Later Years

As he grew older, Goya became more bitter and disillusioned. Increasingly he turned away from the subject matter found in the real world because it could not be used to express his thoughts and feelings. Instead, he turned to his dreams and visions for subject matter.

■ **FIGURE 20.13** Repeated shapes and axis lines have been used to create a sense of movement. What is the direction of that movement?

Francisco Goya. *The Third of May, 1808.* 1814. Oil on canvas. Approx. 2.64 × 3.43 m (8'8" × 11'3"). The Prado Museum, Madrid, Spain.

Chapter 20 *Rococo Art* **457**

About the *Artwork*

The Third of May, 1808. Several features in Goya's painting reveal the artist's despair that the Church could offer no help against the forces of Napoleon's invading army. One of the victims is a monk, and a church depicted in the background appears remote and helpless in the face of the crisis. The central figure takes on Christ-like qualities by extending his arms outward in the guise of a crucifixion. His right hand even bears a wound not unlike Christ's stigmata. Yet, this beleaguered figure lacks the power to rescue the hapless victims. Goya depicts a brand of suffering that does not end in immortality.

Art History

Emphasize that Goya's explorations into unromanticized realism and the territory of visions and dreams opened up new paths for the artists who came after him. Then ask whether art history might conceivably have followed a different course had Goya never lived. Have students write a page that defends the view either that the existence of a single artist such as Goya could alter the direction of art history or that the visual arts eventually would have developed in that direction.

Art History

Direct students' attention to the etching in Figure 20.16. Have students research images of monsters and other horrific beings in the art of different cultures.

Study Guide

Distribute *Study Guide* 47 in the TCR. Assist students in reviewing key concepts. 📁

Art and Humanities

Assign *Art and Humanities* 33, "Enjoying the Satire of Voltaire," in the TCR. Through this activity, students discover the wit, irony, and satire in Voltaire's Candide. Students then apply their insights by identifying the satire in current political cartoons. 📁

Extension

Divide the class into two teams. Have them use Gainsborough's *The Blue Boy* (Figure 20.9, page 453) as a starting point for a debate on the topic of whether it is true that clothes make the person. Review the circumstances under which the model came to be dressed in such finery, and then expand the debate to include the significance and importance of clothing today.

Checking Comprehension.

➤ Have students respond to the lesson review questions. Answers are given in the box below.

➤ Assign *Application 20*, "Doing Your Bidding," in the TCR to reinforce what students have learned. 📁

Reteaching

Assign *Reteaching 47*, found in the TCR. Have students complete the activity and review their responses. 📁

Enrichment

Assign students *Art and Humanities 34*, "Musical Innovation in the Eighteenth Century," in the TCR. In this worksheet, students learn about musical innovation during the eighteenth century. 📁

Extension

Have students research and report on one of the women artists of the Rococo era (e.g., Italian pastel portraitist Rosalba Carriera, French society portraitist Marie Anne Loir, and German painter Anna Dorothea Lisiewska-Therbusch). All these women are profiled in Ann Sutherland Harris and Linda Nochlin's 1976 book, *Women Artists 1550–1950*.

CLOSE

Have students read about the Royal Academy of Art in an effort to learn when the institution began, who belonged, how an artist gained membership, and how it influenced the creation and exhibition of art.

Art of Personal Inspiration

The drawings, paintings, and etchings Goya produced were unlike anything that had been created before. For the first time, an artist reached deep into his own mind for inspiration. By doing this, Goya made it difficult for others to understand exactly what he was trying to say. At the same time, he challenged

■ **FIGURE 20.14** Like Goya's other late works, this print challenges viewers to use their imaginations and arrive at their own interpretations. What mood do you think this figure creates? Whom or what do you think he represents?

Francisco Goya. *The Giant.* c.1818. Burnished aquatint, first state. 28.5 × 21 cm (11¼ × 8¼"). The Metropolitan Museum of Art, New York, New York. Harris Brisbane Dick Fund, 1935. (35.42).

them to use their imaginations to arrive at their own interpretations of his work.

One of Goya's most unforgettable prints shows a giant sitting on the edge of the world (Figure 20.14). A small landscape in the foreground is dwarfed by the towering presence of this giant. This could be Goya's vision of war—a giant who could, with one swipe of his mighty hand, cause widespread destruction and suffering. He glances up as if something or someone has summoned him. Perhaps he is being instructed on what action to take with regard to the unsuspecting world sleeping peacefully in the moonlight.

Breaking with Tradition

The eighteenth century began with artists such as Watteau and Fragonard creating works that emphasized the lightheartedness and fancy of court life. A more middle-class view of life was presented in the works of Chardin and Hogarth. Goya's works ranged from the courtly Rococo style to the more realistic and finally to the realm of his imagination.

By using his own visions and dreams as the inspiration for his art, Goya opened the door for others to follow. From that point on, artists no longer felt bound by tradition. Like Goya, they could rely on their own personal visions to move in any direction they wished. For this reason, Goya is regarded as the bridge between the art of the past and the art of the present.

LESSON TWO REVIEW

Reviewing Art Facts

1. What kind of painting grew in popularity in eighteenth-century England? What contributed to its popularity?
2. Which artist ultimately became the favorite portrait painter of English high society? Why?
3. Name an English artist who was not interested in catering to the tastes of the aristocrats. Tell what he preferred to paint and how he got his message to the viewer.
4. For which type of work is Sir Christopher Wren best known? Name the best-known example of his work.

Activity... *Creating an Imaginative Artwork*

Rococo artists who came after the French painters Fragonard and Watteau rejected the elegant style and subject matter inspired by court life. Chardin and Hogarth created paintings depicting everyday scenes and events, while Goya turned to his visions and dreams for subject matter. Goya's works mark an important shift between the art of the past and the art of the present.

Find and examine the works of other artists such as Joan Miró and Salvador Dali. Recognize how these artists have relied on dreams and visions as subjects for their work. Create a work of your own using ideas from your own imagination. Share it with the class.

LESSON TWO REVIEW

Answers to Reviewing Art Facts

1. Portrait painting; the growing wealthy aristocracy desired fashionable portraits.
2. Thomas Gainsborough; he was skilled at showing intricate details of fashionable clothing.
3. William Hogarth preferred painting the common people; his paintings exposed the immoral conditions and foolish customs of his time.
4. Architecture; St Paul's Cathedral in London.

Activity... *Creating an Imaginative Artwork*

Have students work in cooperative groups to find and examine works by Miro, Dali, and other artists whose works show imaginative subjects. In these groups, encourage students to discuss their own ideas for such paintings and techniques that might help them depict their dreams or visions effectively.

Studio LESSON Still-Life Chalk Drawing

Using colored chalk, complete a drawing showing a close-up view of a selected portion of a still-life composition. This drawing should include gradations of value to emphasize three-dimensional forms. It should also contain at least three different examples of simulated texture.

Inspiration

Compare the Rococo painting style of Watteau (Figure 20.4, page 448) with the style of Chardin (Figures 20.6, page 450). How do these styles differ? Which artist's works do you think would be most appreciated by an art critic favoring the theory of imitationalism? What has that artist done to make his works look so lifelike?

Process

1. Working with other members of your class, set up a still-life arrangement of common everyday objects.
2. Make a simple "viewfinder" by cutting the poster board, cardboard, or paper into two L shapes and attaching the ends to form a flat square frame. By manipulating the viewfinder, you will be able to alter the views of the still-life arrangement. You may find that a close-up view of a small portion of the still life is more appealing than a view that includes all the objects.
3. Using the large sheet of neutral-tone construction paper and white chalk, draw the view that you find most pleasing when looking through the viewfinder.
4. Complete your drawing using colored chalk. First, apply base colors, then change the values by carefully blending in white and dark chalk where needed. Add textures and the darkest shading last.
5. Exhibit your drawing in class along with those made by other students.

Materials

- Poster board, cardboard, or heavy paper, about 6 × 6 inches
- Scissors, ruler, and pencil
- Neutral-tone construction paper, 18 × 24 inches
- White chalk and colored chalk (pastels)

■ **FIGURE 20.15** Student Work

Examining Your Work

Describe. Are the still-life objects in your drawing easily recognized even if they are not shown completely?

Analyze. Did you use gradations of value to emphasize the three-dimensional forms of still-life objects? Does your drawing show at least three different examples of simulated texture?

Interpret. Do you feel that your picture provides an interesting close-up view of the still life?

Judge. Would an art critic favoring the theory of imitationalism be pleased with your drawing? What feature of your drawing do you think such a critic would appreciate most?

459

ASSESSMENT

Peer Review. After students have assessed their own chalk drawings, have them meet with partners to compare and discuss their work. Have them discuss their ideas in response to questions such as these: Which different views did we find with our viewfinders? How did our choice of views affect our finished drawings? How could I have changed my view to select a more interesting close-up of the still life? Which colors did we both select to show the objects in the still life? What is most effective about each color choice? Have partners conclude their discussion by identifying the specific aspects of each other's drawing they most admire and explaining why.

Objectives

- Complete a chalk drawing of a lesson of a still-life composition.
- Make use of gradations of value to emphasize three-dimensional forms.
- Include four different examples of simulated texture.

Motivator

Divide the class into two groups and assign Watteau's *Embarkation for Cythera* to one and Chardin's *Still Life with Rib of Beef* to the other. Instruct students in each group to write the reasons why their painting should be considered more successful than the other. Ask them to present and discuss these in class. Were the reasons of either group more persuasive than the others? If so, ask students why they were more persuasive.

Aesthetics

Have students remain in the same groups and ask them to review the reasons they presented when championing the painting assigned to them. Ask each group to discuss these reasons by referring to the literal qualities, design qualities, and expressive qualities. Have each group determine which aesthetic qualities they relied on most. Did either group rely on two or more aesthetic qualities? If so, did this strengthen their argument in favor of the artwork?

Critiquing

Have students apply the steps of art criticism to their own artwork, using the "Examining Your Work" questions on this page.

Studio LESSON

Expressive Self-Portrait Collage _____

Objectives

■ Create a self-portrait collage to express characteristics of individual, unique personalities.

■ Arrange colors, lines, shapes, and textures in harmonious or varied ways to reflect their personalities.

Motivator

Allow students time to determine the personal traits they wish to emphasize in their self-portraits. Have them identify as many traits as possible before turning to magazines and newspapers of pictures, words, and phrases that suggest these qualities. Remind students that the size, color, and letter style of words selected can represent subtle clues to their personalities. Caution them not to choose illustrations that are too obvious. Putting the collage together is the most creative part of this lesson and should be carefully planned using preliminary sketches.

Art History

Present students with the questions listed below. Instruct each student to show Goya's *The Giant* to a person not in an art class and ask them to answer these questions: Do you think the artist lived during a peaceful or a troubled period in history? What clues in the work caused you to respond in this way?

Critiquing

Have students apply the steps of art criticism to their own artwork, using the "Examining Your Work" questions on this page.

460

Studio LESSON Expressive Self-Portrait Collage

Materials

● Magazines and newspapers
● Pencil and sketch paper
● Colored construction paper or mat board, 12 × 18 inches
● Scissors and white glue

Create a self-portrait collage that expresses characteristics of your own unique personality, rather than a portrait that shows how you look. From magazines and newspapers, cut pictures, phrases, and words that say something about you. Assemble these as a collage that illustrates your "real inner self."

Inspiration

Examine Goya's print *The Giant* in Figure 20.14, page 458. How does a picture like this differ from other pictures of people, such as those created by Reynolds (Figure 20.8, page 452) or Gainsborough (Figure 20.9, page 453)?

■ **FIGURE 20.16** Student Work

Process

1. Look through magazines and newspapers for pictures, phrases, and words that say something about you—your hopes, aspirations, and feelings. Tear these out and set them aside.

2. Make several sketches showing the general outline of your face viewed from the front or in profile. Redraw the best of these lightly to fill the construction paper or mat board.

3. Cut the magazine and newspaper items into various shapes and assemble these within and around your face drawing. If you prefer, you can draw certain parts of your portrait. Do not draw the entire face, however.

4. Exhibit your self-portrait along with those created by other students. Can you determine which student created which portrait? Are other students able to correctly identify your self-portrait?

— Examining Your Work —

Describe. Can viewers readily identify your collage as a portrait? Are the different features of this portrait clearly evident?

Analyze. Is the arrangement of colors, lines, shapes, and textures in your portrait harmonious or varied? Did you do this intentionally? If so, why?

Interpret. Does your self-portrait present an accurate picture of what you are like inside? Do you think others can read the clues you have provided to learn more about your thoughts and feelings?

Judge. A critic known to favor the expressive qualities is asked to judge your self-portrait. How do you think this critic will respond to your work? Do you think a critic favoring the theory of imitationalism would be impressed with your effort? Why or why not?

460

ASSESSMENT

Extension Activity. After students have used the "Examining Your Work" questions to assess their collages, encourage them to create a different kind of self-portrait collage. This second collage should make use of a variety of different materials in addition to the printed items from magazines and newspapers— small items that have some personal meaning or that tell something about the student. Then have students meet in small groups to compare and discuss the two collages each has created. Ask: Which collage does the student consider most meaningful? Which collage tells the other group members most about the student?

Reviewing Art Facts

Lesson One

1. Explain why Louis XIV was called the Sun King.
2. Did Rococo art place a greater emphasis on religious subjects or scenes from aristocratic life? Why?
3. Describe how Watteau's *Embarkation for Cythera* (Figure 20.4, page 448) typifies Rococo art.
4. What subject matter did Fragonard paint?
5. What kinds of objects did Chardin typically include in his still-life paintings?

Lesson Two

6. Which English artist painted scenes that exposed the foolish customs of the time?
7. What event gave Sir Christopher Wren the opportunity to design more than 50 churches in London?
8. What features cause the light and dark pattern on the façade of St. Paul's Cathedral?
9. How does Goya identify the main character in *The Third of May, 1808* (Figure 20.13, page 457)?
10. Why is Goya regarded as the bridge between the art of the past and the art of the present?

 Use the *Performing Arts Handbook,* page 576 to learn about music, dance, and theatre from many diverse cultures and times.

Thinking Critically

1. **EXTEND.** Imagine a film that includes Watteau's *Embarkation for Cythera* (Figure 20.4, page 448) as an important scene in the narrative. Outline an appropriate plot for this film. Indicate when Watteau's scene would occur, and explain why it is such an important scene. Also, identify what you feel would be suitable background music for this particular scene. Finally, give your film a title. Share your ideas with other members of the class.
2. **ANALYZE.** Refer to Chardin's painting *The Attentive Nurse* (Figure 20.7, page 451). Describe how the art elements—color, value, line, texture, shape, form, and space—are used in the painting. Which elements are emphasized? Which are less important?

CAREERS IN Art If you enjoy studying or creating art, read about a fascinating art-related career opportunity in the *Careers in Art Handbook,* page 594.

*inter*NET CONNECTION Visit Glencoe Art Online at *www.glencoe.com/sec/art*. Visit museum sites to view Rococo artworks, and take a virtual tour of Versailles.

Technology Project

Linking Cultures and Concepts

Some artists have successfully made a transition in their artwork that creates a cultural link between two eras. Their work may undergo a shift in the way they visually represent subject matter, make use of art elements and principles, or convey emotional responses to a changing world. The work of such artists may create a visual connection between established concepts and values of the past and those of the future. Sometimes their work may influence a dawning art movement. Goya was such an artist. He departed from the Rococo style and explored the use of images inspired by his innermost feelings. Goya's later work influenced artists who came after him.

1. Imagine you are destined to become the artist whose artwork provides a link between two eras, as

Goya's did in his time. The digital options for creating images provide you with many ways to experiment with this exciting challenge. Consider these questions: What form will this art assume? What media and process will you use? What subject matter will you choose? Will your work continue to make use of the traditional art elements and principles? What will be the ideas, values, mood, and emotions you convey in your work?

2. Begin by studying some of the work of contemporary artists who are working in new ways with new media. Bring your findings to a class discussion.
3. Create a work of art that links two eras by using digital media. Your solution might take one of many forms—multimedia, digital, video, performance art or anything that you can imagine.
4. Display or present your work of art in your classroom.

461

 Teaching the Technology Project

Have group members brainstorm a list of contemporary artists whose works they might consider, and suggest that members work cooperatively to gather examples of and information about those artists' works. As students work independently on their own works of art, provide time for several group meetings to discuss progress and compare ideas.

ART SOURCE Assign the feature in the *Performing Arts Handbook,* page 576.

CAREERS IN ART If time permits, have interested students investigate the career information in the *Careers in Art Handbook,* page 594.

*inter*NET CONNECTION Have students go online and learn more about artists on preselected Web sites with the Internet activity for this chapter.

CHAPTER 20
REVIEW ANSWERS

Reviewing the Facts

1. He chose the sun as his emblem.
2. Life of the aristocracy; love and romance were more fitting subjects for art than history and religion.
3. It shows the French aristocracy at play.
4. He painted pictures about love and romance; The Swing is one example.
5. Humble, everyday items, such as earthenware containers, copper kettles, vegetables, and meat.
6. William Hogarth.
7. A huge fire destroyed thousands of homes, more than 80 churches, and other public buildings.
8. The deep porches and huge columns.
9. The figure is bathed in light and has a Christ-like pose.
10. Because he was the first to use his own visions and dreams as inspiration for his art.

Thinking Critically

1. Outlines should reveal awareness of the subject matter and Watteau's aesthetic statement.
2. Descriptions should show knowledge of art elements. Value is the most important element; form, shape, and texture are next; color and line are least important.

Art of the Modern Era

Unit Seven introduces the multitude of art styles and movements that have characterized Western art in the last two centuries.

Chapter 21 *New Styles in Nineteenth-Century Art* treats the theory and works of the Neoclassicists, Romanticists, Realists, and Impressionists.

Chapter 22 *Art of the Later Nineteenth Century* presents the contributions of the Post-Impressionists and artists working in the United States during this period.

Chapter 23 *Art of the Early Twentieth Century* treats the largely movement-oriented art of the period and the rise of New York as an international art center.

Chapter 24 *Modern Art Movements to the Present* discusses innovations in art and architecture in our own time.

National Museum of Women in the Arts

You may wish to use the National Museum of Women in the Arts videodisc and/or CD-ROM. The videodisc features a bar code guide, and the interactive CD-ROM provides stimulating activities.

462

More About... **Staffelsee in Autumn.** Gabrielle Münter began working in the Impressionist style, then began to assimilate the principles of Post-Impressionism and Fauvism to create her own personal style which became part of the German Expressionist movement. Point out to students the way this painting is organized in blocks of color to accentuate the cutout effect of the landscape. Explain how color is used to create unity. The blue hue of the houses in the foreground is repeated in the color of the lake and then again in the mountains and sky in the background. Explain that Münter used intense and expressive color contrasts to create an expressive mood in her work. Their choice of color communicates many things to the viewer, depicting the Staffelsee as a quiet, clean, and picturesque setting.

UNIT 7

Art of the Modern Era

"Nature should be greater to me than humanity. It speaks louder than I. I should feel small before its greatness."

Gabriele Münter
German painter
(1877–1962)

Gabriele Münter. *Staffelsee in Autumn.* 1923. Oil on board. 34.9 × 48.9 cm (13³/₄ × 19¹/₄"). National Museum of Women in the Arts, Washington, D.C.

463

Introducing the Unit

Ask students if they are familiar with "step puzzles," brain teasers in which a person is provided with the first and last word in a series and called upon to fill in intermediate words by altering one letter at a time. (You may wish to demonstrate by converting the word *HELP* to *ROAR* in five steps as follows: *HELP, HEAP, REAP, REAR, ROAR*). Explain to students that the world of art in the last two hundred years has undergone a similar series of step-like changes.

Discussing the Quotation

Ask students to explain how the artist's statement is reflected in her painting. Does it appear that Münter was concerned with recording all the details in the scene she was painting? Ask students to identify feelings or emotions they associate with this picture. In judging it, what aesthetic qualities would they rely on the most?

Teacher Notes

New Styles in Nineteenth-Century Art

LESSON ONE
(pages 466–470)

Neoclassicism

Classroom Resources

- 📁 Appreciating Cultural Diversity 31
- 📁 Art and Humanities 35
- 📁 Cooperative Learning 30
- 📁 Enrichment Activity 38
- 📁 Reproducible Lesson Plan 48
- 📁 Reteaching Activity 48
- 📁 Study Guide 48

Features

LOOKING Closely ↓
(page 469)

LESSON TWO
(pages 471–479)

Romanticism and Realism

Classroom Resources

- 📁 Art and Humanities 36
- 📁 Cooperative Learning 31
- 📁 Reproducible Lesson Plan 49
- 📁 Reteaching Activity 49
- 📁 Study Guide 49

Features

Interpreting Realism in *Art*
Burial at Ornans.
(page 476)

Time & Place CONNECTIONS
(page 478)

LESSON THREE
(pages 480–489)

Impressionism

Classroom Resources

- 📁 Art and Humanities 37
- 📁 Enrichment Activities 39, 40
- 📁 Reproducible Lesson Plan 50
- 📁 Reteaching Activity 50
- 📁 Study Guide 50

Features

Identifying Styles in *Art*
Le Moulin de la Galette.
(page 483)

END OF CHAPTER
(pages 490–491)

Studio LESSON

- Watercolor Still Life in a Painterly Style *(490)*

ADDITIONAL CHAPTER RESOURCES

Activities
- 📁 Application 21
- 📁 Advanced Studio Activity 21
- 🖱 Chapter 21 Internet Activity
- 📁 Studio Activity 27

Fine Art Resources
- 🎨 **Transparencies**
  Art in Focus Transparency 26
    Edward Degas. *Four Dancers.*
  Art in Focus Transparency 27
    Mary Cassatt. *Little Girl in a Blue Armchair.*
- 🖼 **Fine Art Print**
  Focus on World Art Print 21
    Eugène Delacroix. *Arabs Skirmishing
    in the Mountains.*

Assessment
- 📁 Chapter 21 Test
- 📁 Performance Assessment

Multimedia Resources
- 🎭 Artsource® Performing Arts Package
- 💿 National Gallery Laser Disc
- 💿 National Museum of Women in the Arts CD-ROM
- 📼 Arts & Entertainment Videos

NATIONAL STANDARDS FOR ARTS EDUCATION

The National Standards for Arts Education provide guidelines for grade-appropriate competency in the visual arts. The Content Standards for grades 9–12 are:

1. Understanding and applying media, techniques, and processes.
2. Using knowledge of structures and functions.
3. Choosing and evaluating a range of subject matter, symbols, and ideas.
4. Understanding the visual arts in relation to history and cultures.
5. Reflecting upon and assessing the characteristics and merits of their work and the work of others.
6. Making connections between visual arts and other disciplines.

Listed below are the National Standards for the Visual Arts addressed in this chapter. For a breakdown of the categories listed under each content standard, refer to the *Reproducible Lesson Plans* booklet in the TCR.

1. (a)   **2.** (a, b,)   **3.** (a, b)   **4.** (a, b, c)   **5.** (a, b)   **6.** (b)

HANDBOOK MATERIAL

Natividad Nati Cano
(page 590)

Photographer *(page 606)*

Beyond the Classroom

Arts councils help raise awareness of the need for arts education in and out of the classroom. Artists and patrons associated with arts councils can be valuable resources to the teacher interested in promoting and enhancing school arts programs. Track down resources in your area by visiting our Web site at *www.glencoe.com/sec/art.*

🕐 **Out of Time?**   If time does not permit teaching this chapter in its entirety, you may wish to preview the artwork and captions with students. Scan the heads in each lesson with students. Discuss the Looking Closely features and examine Interpreting Realism in Art, page 476, and Identifying Styles in Art on page 483.

New Styles in Nineteenth-Century Art

INTRODUCE

Chapter Overview

CHAPTER 21 introduces students to major developments in European art in the nineteenth century.

Lesson One covers the origins of the Neoclassical movement.

Lesson Two addresses Romanticism, Realism, and English landscape painting.

Lesson Three is devoted to the quest of the Impressionists.

Studio Lesson guides students to create a still life in the painterly style.

Art & Language Arts

Guide students in examining and discussing the artwork that opens this chapter. Encourage students to share what they know about the subject of the painting, the Athenian philosopher Socrates. Also ask about the use of the philosopher's name in familiar terms, especially *Socratic method* and *Socratic irony*. Ask interested students to learn more about Socrates and his teachings and to share their findings with the class.

New Styles in Nineteenth-Century Art

Art & Language Arts ■ **FIGURE 21.1** The Greek philosopher Socrates is shown in this painting calmly accepting death by drinking poison hemlock. He was condemned because he taught young people to live their lives by making reasoned, logical judgments rather than blindly following the worship of pagan gods. An account of his last days can be read in *Phaedo,* written by his pupil, Plato.

Jacques-Louis David. *The Death of Socrates.* 1787. Oil on canvas. 129.5 × 196.2 cm (51 × 77¹/₄"). The Metropolitan Museum of Art, New York, New York. Catharine Lorillard Wolfe Collection, Wolfe Fund, 1931 (31.45).

National Standards

This chapter addresses the following National Standards for the Arts.

1. (a,b)   4. (a,b,c)
2. (a,b)   5. (a,b)
3. (a,b)   6. (b)

CHAPTER 21 RESOURCES

Teacher's Classroom Resources

📁 Advanced Studio Activity 21
📁 Application 21
🖱 Chapter 21 Internet Activity
📁 Studio Activity 27

Assessment

📁 Chapter 21 Test
📁 Performance Assessment

Fine Art Resources

🖋 *Art in Focus* Transparency
    26, Edward Degas, *Four Dancers.*
    27, Mary Cassatt. *Little Girl in a Blue Armchair*
🖼 *Focus on World Art* Print 21
    Eugène Delacroix. *Arabs Skirmishing in the Mountains.*

The growth of academies, or art schools, in France and England during the seventeenth and eighteenth centuries changed the way artists were taught. No longer were they apprenticed to established masters to learn their craft. Instead, art was taught in schools, just as other school subjects were. These schools encouraged students to look to the past and led to the Neoclassical style of painting. In music, dance, literature, and theatre, a new era was sweeping the world—the Romantic movement. This new way of thinking and feeling would eventually revolutionize all art forms, including the visual arts.

YOUR Portfolio

Self-evaluation is an important skill to develop when choosing works for your portfolio. Use the Design Chart in Figure 2.24, page 46, to examine the painting in Figure 21.4. Record as much information as possible about how the principles of art are used to organize the elements. Remember the relationship indicated by the design chart helps you to *see* art, not just *look* at it, and exercises like this help sharpen your evaluation skills. Finally, evaluate the artwork based on your conclusions reached while working with the design chart. Keep your notes in your portfolio for future reference.

Focus ON THE ARTS

LITERATURE
Romantic poets William Wordsworth and John Keats focused on imagination and emotion in their works. Novelists such as Émile Zola and Charles Dickens protested social conditions brought on by the Industrial Revolution.

DANCE
The controlled minuet was replaced in popularity by the passionate waltz. Choreographers focused on a dance form taken from opera called ballet to express a Romantic view of the world.

MUSIC
Romantic composers considered symphonic music as a poetic form, enabling them to express more feeling. German-born Ludwig van Beethoven, a child prodigy at the age of eight, went on to compose symphonies for large orchestras.

465

CHAPTER 21
LESSON ONE

Neoclassicism

Focus

Lesson Objectives

After studying this lesson, students will be able to:

■ Explain how the growth of academies in France and England changed the way artists were taught.

■ Identify the main features of Neoclassicism.

Building Vocabulary

Write the word *Neoclassicism* on the board, and have students analyze its prefix, base, and suffix. (*neo, classic,* and *-ism*) What does this analysis of word parts indicate about the meaning of the term? Encourage students to speculate about the kinds of artworks that might be considered examples of Neoclassicism.

Motivator

Ask students to free-associate with the word *academy.* Point out that the appearance of academies, or formal art schools, in the nineteenth century changed the nature of art education. To add visual impact to the point, obtain and display a reproduction of Johann Zoffany's painting *The Academicians of the Royal Academy,* which shows the members of the Royal Academy in London.

Introducing the Lesson

Direct students' attention to the painting by David in Figure 21.1. Ask whether the work compares more closely to art styles of the past that students have studied or to contemporary art. Have them proceed with the reading.

466

Neoclassicism

Vocabulary
■ academies
■ Salons
■ Neoclassicism
■ propaganda

Artists to Meet
■ Jacques-Louis David
■ Marie-Louise-Élisabeth Vigée-Lebrun
■ Jean-Auguste-Dominique Ingres

Discover
After completing this lesson, you will be able to:
■ Explain how the growth of academies in France and England changed the way artists were taught.
■ Describe the Neoclassic style and discuss the works of artists who practiced this style.

466

$\mathcal{T}$he **academies,** or *art schools,* urged their students to study the famous works of the past as the best way of developing their own skills. The people who bought paintings also showed a preference for artworks produced by the great masters. For example, a wealthy French merchant interested in buying a new painting usually chose a work by one of the old masters rather than one by a living artist.

To encourage interest in contemporary artists, the Royal Academies in Paris and London began to hold yearly exhibitions. These **Salons,** or *exhibitions of art created by Academy members,* became important social events and aroused great interest and even controversy. Reputations were made and destroyed during these annual events. The artists who won honors at these exhibitions were not always the most gifted, however. Those who best reflected the tastes of the academies were acclaimed, while others risked being ignored or ridiculed.

Neoclassic Artists

In France, the Academy endorsed a new style of art based on the art of classical Greece and Rome. This style had been born late in the eighteenth century. When the buried ruins of Pompeii and Herculaneum were found in the 1730s and 1740s, the world gained renewed interest in the Classical period and art forms.

This interest was true of artists as well. They studied and copied classical sculptures hoping that, in time, their works would equal those of legendary ancient artists. These French artists rejected the earlier Baroque and Rococo styles and turned to classical forms to express their ideas on courage, sacrifice, and love of country. Their new art style, known as **Neoclassicism,** *sought to revive the ideals of ancient Greek and Roman art, and was characterized by balanced compositions, flowing contour lines, and noble gestures and expressions.*

Jacques-Louis David (1748–1825)

One of the first artists to work in this style was the painter Jacques-Louis David (zhjahk loo-**ee** dah-**veed**). David's involvement in politics, his love of ancient art, and his skill as a painter are all apparent in his picture *The Death of Marat* (Figure 21.2).

The Death of Marat
■ FIGURE 21.2

David admired the noble simplicity and calm beauty of Greek art and tried to achieve the same qualities in this tribute to Jean-Paul Marat, one of the major figures of the French Revolution.

LESSON ONE RESOURCES

Teacher's Classroom Resources

📁 Appreciating Cultural Diversity 31

📁 Art and Humanities 35

📁 Cooperative Learning 30

📁 Enrichment Activity 38

📁 Reproducible Lesson Plan 48

📁 Reteaching Activity 48

📁 Study Guide 48

This shocking painting shows the dead figure of the political leader slumped over the side of his bathtub. The murder weapon still lies on the floor where it was dropped by the assassin. The clear, cool lighting illuminates a room that is almost bare. The textured wall contrasts with the smooth skin of the dead politician. Marat, wearing a white turban, leans back against a white cloth that lines the tub. His color is pale except for the red around the small wound. Throughout the work, color has been used sparingly.

Influence of Classical Sculpture

David's study of Greek and Roman sculptures taught him how to paint figures that look realistic and noble. He also learned to avoid details that could interfere with the simple, direct statement he wanted to make in a work of art. (See Figure 21.1, page 464.) Like the *Dying Gaul* (Figure 8.21, page 184), David's picture was meant to stir your emotions. He wanted you to become involved in the drama, to share the pain and anger he felt at the "martyrdom" of Marat.

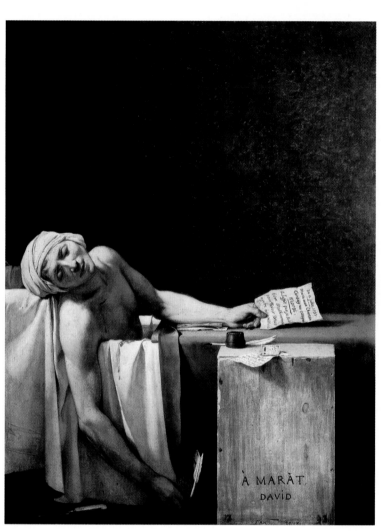

■ **FIGURE 21.2** This work shows the body of an important political leader moments after he was murdered. **What makes this painting an example of propaganda?**

Jacques-Louis David. *The Death of Marat.* 1793. Oil on canvas. Approx. 1.6 × 1.24 m (5'3" × 4'1"). Musée d'Art Ancien, Brussels, Belgium.

TEACH
Studio Skills

Have the class visit an art museum or gallery Let students each choose a painting that they will closely observe and draw, just as art students did in nineteenth-century academies. Provide students with charcoal pencils and sketchbook or sketch paper clipped to a firm backing. After this exercise, have students discuss their experience. What insights are made available to the student through this teaching method? How does the method compare with the apprenticeship practice of earlier centuries?

Art History

Have volunteers research the organizations modern artists have formed to promote their work, from artists' unions to watercolor societies to artist-owned galleries. Help students draw a parallel between these organizations and the salons created by academy members. Emphasize that in the absence of widespread patronage by a central power base, such as the church, artists since the early nineteenth century increasingly have found the need to create other markets for their artworks.

Art Criticism

Have students compare Figure 21.2 with David's 1783 painting *Andromache Mourning Hector,* which also features a hero who has died for his country. Have students list differences between the two paintings. Which painting is more powerful?

Technology

National Gallery of Art Videodisc Use the following images as examples of more works by artists introduced in this lesson.

Jacques-Louis David
Napoleon in His Study

Search Frame 1100

Elisabeth Vigée-Lebrun
The Marquise de Pezé and the Marquise de Rouget

Search Frame 1089

Jean-Auguste-Dominique Ingres
Madame Moitessier

Search Frame 1122

Use Glencoe's *Correlation Bar Code Guide to the National Gallery of Art* to locate more artworks.

Critical Thinking

Have students search through print advertisements, illustrated political literature, and posters for contemporary examples of visual propaganda. Have students set up a simple display of the materials. Ask in what ways present-day propagandistic art is similar to and different from David's painting of Napoleon. Discuss whether propaganda is necessarily evil. Ask: Do supporters of a cause or organization ever refer to their own public-relations material as "propaganda"?

Art History

Have students compare the differing interpretations of Napoleon and his career as suggested in David's dignified portrait of Napoleon and in Goya's painting of the mayhem and bloodshed wrought by troops under Napoleon's command (Figure 20.13, page 457). Have students research the invasion of Spain by France and then write a dialogue between Goya and David on the subject. Then discuss whether David could have painted Figure 20.13. How might he have illustrated this incident if Napoleon had wanted it painted in the Neoclassic style?

Aesthetics

Have students examine Figure 21.4 (page 469) and then locate other examples of portraits in which the sitter appears to have been captured in the midst of some activity. What mood or sensibility is common among such portraits? What about portraits in which the undistracted sitter gazes directly out at the viewer?

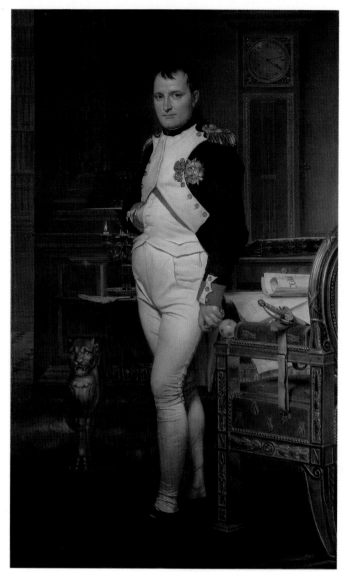

■ **FIGURE 21.3** The emperor is shown in his study, surrounded by his work, in the middle of the night. **What statement does this painting make about the efforts and accomplishments of Napoleon?**

Jacques-Louis David. *Napoleon in His Study*. 1812. Oil on canvas. 203.9 × 125.1 cm (80¼ × 49¼″). National Gallery of Art, Washington, D.C. Board of Trustees, The Samuel H. Kress Collection.

David's work gives you only one side of the story, however. Like many photographs you may have seen, David's painting is a form of **propaganda,** *information or ideas purposely spread to influence public opinion.*

Napoleon in His Study
■ **FIGURE 21.3**

Under Napoleon, David became the court painter. Napoleon recognized the value of propaganda, and David knew how to produce it.

In a portrait of Napoleon (Figure 21.3), David presents the emperor standing by a desk covered with important papers of state. The clock tells you that it is after four o'clock and the candle tells you that it is nighttime. The message here is clear: While his subjects sleep peacefully, the emperor toils far into the night for their well-being.

Marie-Louise-Élisabeth Vigée-Lebrun
(1755–1842)

David chose to stay in France and take an active part in the revolution. Another artist, Marie-Louise-Élisabeth Vigée-Lebrun (mah-**ree** loo-**eez** ay-**lee**-zah-bet vee-**zhay** luh-**bruhn**), left France and did not come back until peace was restored.

Vigée-Lebrun is one of history's most celebrated women artists. She was a portrait painter for members of the French aristocracy, including Queen Marie Antoinette. After she left Paris, she was able to continue painting with equal success in other capitals of Europe.

Many of Vigée-Lebrun's portraits were extremely favorable to the sitter. Especially in her self-portraits, Vigée-Lebrun tended to be quite flattering. (See Figure 4.6, page 91.) To all of her sitters, the artist gave large, expressive eyes, and she played down the less attractive details of the face.

More About... **The Academies.** Aspiring artists, like David, who trained at the academy followed a rigorous program that began with the copying of drawings and engravings of anatomical details such as heads, eyes, arms, mouths, and noses. Later a pupil would copy pictures of whole figures. After a year of such training, students studied casts of famous ancient sculptures and works by noted modern artists. Only then would students be permitted to attend classes in live drawing with a male nude model, with students seated in a strict hierarchy that gave preference to sons of academy members. Courses on anatomy, perspective, geometry, literature, and religious and ancient history rounded out the curriculum.

LOOKING Closely

USE OF THE ELEMENTS OF ART

- **Line.** The artist used repeating contour lines to achieve harmony in this picture. The sweeping contour of the hat is repeated by the curve of the sofa back, and the angle of the forearm is duplicated by the edge of the pillow. The diagonal of the upper arm is found again in the deep crease of the skirt.
- **Color.** The color scheme is softened by the extensive use of a dark gray for the background and of a dull white for the dress. Needed contrast is provided by the green velvet sofa, the blue-gray sash, and the gold trim on the pillow.

■ **FIGURE 21.4** Marie-Louise-Élisabeth Vigée-Lebrun. *Madame de la Châtre.* 1789. Oil on canvas. 114.3 × 87.6 cm (45 × 34½″). The Metropolitan Museum of Art, New York, New York. Gift of Jessie Woolworth Donahue, 1954. (54.182).

LOOKING Closely

Let students examine and discuss the portrait of Madame de la Châtre. Before they read they feature, have students identify the use of art elements they can recognize in the work. Then have students read and discuss the Use of the Elements of Art feature: Which of their ideas do students find confirmed in this explanation?

Art History

Have students compare Ingres's *Apotheosis of Homer* (Figure 21.5, page 470) with Raphael's *School of Athens* (Figure 16.1, page 352). Ask: In what specific ways do you think Raphael's painting influenced Ingres's work?

Study Guide

Distribute *Study Guide* 48 in the TCR. Assist students in reviewing key concepts. 🗀

Art and Humanities

Assign *Cooperative Learning* 30, "Taking Sides in the Beauty Battle." In this activity, students are called upon to examine works of art, read poetry, and listen to music to distinguish between Classical and Romantic modes. Then, working as groups, they are to impose a similar categorization on artists covered in the text. 🗀

Studio Activities

Discuss with students the many different approaches to portrait painting covered in the lesson. Then assign *Appreciating Cultural Diversity* 31, "The Many Faces of Portraiture," in the TCR. 🗀

Madame de la Châtre
■ **FIGURE 21.4**

Madame de la Châtre was just 27 years old when she had her portrait painted by Vigée-Lebrun (Figure 21.4). The artist selected a simple, direct pose. Madame de la Châtre glances up from an open book and turns slightly to face in your direction. She takes little notice of you, however. Instead, there is a faraway look in her eyes, and it seems as though her thoughts still linger on the words she has been reading.

Jean-Auguste-Dominique Ingres (1780–1867)

By the beginning of the nineteenth century, the art of Europe was influenced by France, and the art of France was influenced by the Academy. The Academy itself was influenced by Neoclassic artists who followed David. The Neoclassic style was carried to its highest point by Jean-Auguste-Dominique Ingres (zhjahn oh-**gust** doh-min-**eek ahn**-gr), the best known of David's students.

Chapter 21 *New Styles in Nineteenth-Century Art* **469**

COOPERATIVE LEARNING

Room Models. The painting in Figure 21.3 provides, among other things, a glimpse of the style of furnishings popular in the late eighteenth and early nineteenth centuries. Have groups of students research this style of furnishing and then create small models of period rooms. The walls of the room should be made by taping together pieces of cardboard at right angles. Students can glue cut shapes of lightweight cardboard to make the furniture, which can be decorated with pen and colored ink or fabric. A piece of heavy fabric in an appropriate print can serve as a carpet, draperies, and so on; tiny art reproductions can be hung on the wall. Have groups compare their finished models.

ASSESS

Checking Comprehension.

Have students respond to the lesson review questions. Answers are given in the box below.

Reteaching

➤ Assign *Reteaching* 48, found in the TCR. Have students complete the activity and review their responses. 📁

➤ Review the characteristics of Neoclassical art using Ingres's painting. Then, after concealing the credit lines, present students with reproductions of Ingres's *Napoleon on His Imperial Throne* and Antoine-Jean Gros's *Napoleon in the Penthouse at Jaffa.* Ask students if they can identify the picture by Ingres.

Enrichment

Have students complete *Art and Humanities* 35, "William Blake—Poet, Visionary, Artist," in the TCR. In this activity, students learn more about this eighteenth-century "Renaissance" figure and then express their feelings about current concerns. 📁

Extension

Assign *Enrichment* 38, "Comparing Artistic Styles," in the TCR. Students are asked to compare the styles of Neoclassicism and Romanticism and then write in the spirit of these periods. 📁

CLOSE

Have several volunteers pretend to be posing either for a Neoclassic-style painting or a Baroque-style painting. Challenge the remainder of the class to guess the style of work for which the subject is posing, stating reasons for their guesses.

470

The Apotheosis of Homer
■ **FIGURE 21.5**

Although today his portraits are ranked among his most impressive works, Ingres preferred to paint large pictures glorifying historical and imaginary events and people. One of these, *The Apotheosis of Homer* (Figure 21.5) was commissioned as a ceiling mural in the Louvre museum. In a work that brings to mind Raphael's *The School of Athens* (Figure 16.1, page 352), Ingres presents viewers with an impressive assembly of immortals representing all the arts.

In the place of honor sits the enthroned Homer. The facade of an Ionic temple acts as a backdrop, and a figure representing the *Nike of Samothrace* (Figure 8.22, page 185) prepares to crown Homer with a laurel wreath. Seated below Homer are two female figures symbolizing his classic works, the *Iliad* and the *Odyssey.* The names of both epics can be seen engraved on the step on which the figures are seated.

The figures surrounding Homer are his successors—the poets, playwrights, philosophers, critics, painters, and sculptors who have championed the arts through the ages. Among those represented are Phidias, Virgil, and Fra Angelico. Aeschylus, credited with writing the first tragedy, is seen unrolling a scroll listing his plays. At the lower right, Racine and Molière, wearing the wigs fashionable during the time of Louis XIV, extend in tribute the masks of tragedy and comedy. The profile of Raphael is seen at the upper left. In the lower left corner, almost crowded out of the picture, are Dante and Shakespeare.

Use of Line

In this painting, Ingres demonstrates his love for carefully planned compositions and his preference for crisply outlined figures that exhibit little emotion. For Ingres, line was the most important element in painting; color was secondary.

■ **FIGURE 21.5** Notice the similarities and differences between this painting and *The School of Athens* (Figure 16.1, page 352). Which painting do you prefer?

Jean-Auguste-Dominique Ingres. *Apotheosis of Homer.* 1827. Oil on canvas. 386 × 512 cm (12¹/₂ × 16²/₃'). The Louvre, Paris, France.

LESSON ONE REVIEW

Reviewing Art Facts

1. How did the academies of Paris and London change the way artists were taught?
2. What were the Salons, and on what basis were the artworks judged?
3. What events created renewed interest in the Classical period and its art forms?
4. Name two artists who practiced the Neoclassic style.

▶ **Activity... *Recognizing Art Patronage***

Artists often were appointed as court painters and remained in the service of rulers or figures of wealth and status. Neoclassic artist Jacques-Louis David, for instance, was the painter to Emperor Napoleon in the French court. This practice helped further an artist's career and ensured that his or her work would be recognized.

Identify five other artists who have earned a place for themselves and their works. List the art period in which each artist worked, and who their patrons were, and note what influence the patron had on the work and fame of the artist. Share your findings with the class.

LESSON ONE REVIEW

Answers to Reviewing Art Facts

1. Artists were no longer apprenticed; art was taught in schools.
2. Yearly exhibitions of art; art reflecting academy tastes.
3. Discovery of Pompeii and Herculaneum ruins.
4. David and Ingres.

Activity... *Recognizing Art Patronage*

Suggest that students work in small cooperative learning groups to complete this Activity. Group members should gather information about various artists and their patrons, select the individuals they want to feature, and prepare a chart or other visual presentation of their findings.

Romanticism and Realism

Romanticism and Realism

FOCUS

Vocabulary
- Romanticism
- Realism

Artists to Meet
- Théodore Géricault
- Eugène Delacroix
- John Constable
- Joseph M. W. Turner
- Gustave Courbet
- Édouard Manet
- Rosa Bonheur

Discover

After completing this lesson, you will be able to:
- Define Romanticism and discuss some of the works created by artists associated with this style.
- Identify the two major English landscape painters of the period and compare their works.
- Define Realism and identify some artists associated with this style of painting.

*E*ven though the Neoclassic style of David and Ingres became the official style of the Academy, it did not go unchallenged. Not all artists shared these painters' enthusiasm for classical art forms, noble subject matter, balanced compositions, and flowing contour lines.

Some artists chose to focus on dramatic events; others preferred to represent everyday scenes and events. The two new styles were Romanticism and Realism.

The Romantics

In 1819, a painting called the *Raft of the Medusa* (Figure 21.6) was exhibited for the first time. This work signaled the birth of a new art style in France. Known as **Romanticism,** this style *portrayed dramatic and exotic subjects perceived with strong feelings.*

Théodore Géricault (1792–1824)

This early example of the Romantic style was painted by a young French artist, Théodore Géricault (tay-oh-**door** zhay-ree-**koh**).

Géricault's *Raft of the Medusa* shows a dramatic, contemporary event as it actually happened, not a scene from the classical past. When the French ship *Medusa* was wrecked, 149 passengers and crew members tried to reach safety on a large raft towed by officers aboard a lifeboat. Only 15 men on the raft survived, and claims were made that the officers had cut the raft adrift.

■ **FIGURE 21.6** Notice the two opposite diagonals Géricault used to organize and balance this composition. **How does this painting differ from works created by Neoclassic artists?**

Théodore Géricault. *Raft of the Medusa.* 1819. Oil on canvas. 4.9 × 7 m (16 × 23′). The Louvre, Paris, France.

471

Lesson Objectives

After studying this lesson, students will be able to:
- Understand the attitudes and themes associated with the Romantic movement.
- Identify the two major English landscape painters of the period and compare their works.
- Describe the characteristics of Realism and identify artists associated with this style.

Building Vocabulary

Write the words *Romanticism and Realism* on the board. Let students analyze the two terms and share their ideas about what might be involved in each art movement.

Motivator

Ask students to describe their associations with the words *romance* and *romantic.* Record their responses in a word web on the board. Then, next to the web, write the words *lion hunt.* After pointing out that *The Lion Hunt* is the title of one of the artworks students will encounter in this lesson, have them brainstorm which of the responses from the word web could be compatible with the subject of a lion hunt.

Introducing the Lesson

Have students discuss periods of art history they have studied where different groups of artists pursued divergent interests and theories. Explain that they are about to learn about two movements that ran counter to the ambitions and ideals of the Neoclassicists.

Teacher's Classroom Resources

 Art and Humanities 36

 Cooperative Learning 31

Reproducible Lesson Plan 49

 Reteaching Activity 49

 Study Guide 49

TEACH
Studio Skills

Have the class develop a group composition centering on a modern-day event or scene that expresses dramatic emotions. The class should begin by selecting a current event as the theme of the picture and then work out the most dramatic arrangement of the figures. Have students compare the spirit of the finished result with that of *Raft of the Medusa* (Figure 21.6, page 471). Could the joint effort be fairly described as a Romantic painting? Have students defend their answers.

Art History

Have a group of volunteers find out as much as they can about what Delacroix would have seen when he visited North Africa in 1832. Students should attempt to locate reproductions of pages from the sketchbook the artist kept during his trip. These should be displayed as part of a presentation to the class in which the volunteers also point out the relative locations of Morocco, Tangiers, and Algiers on a map.

Studio Skills

Have students select a subject and then, using oil pastels and sheets of drawing paper measuring 9 × 12 inches, draw the subject in the manner of either Ingres or Delacroix. When students have finished, display all the "Ingres" pictures in one part of the room, and all the "Delacroix" works in another. Lead a discussion on whether each group of pictures as a whole expresses the style of Neoclassicism or Romanticism, respectively.

■ **FIGURE 21.7** Delacroix is known as a great Romantic painter. Why is this a Romantic painting? Which of the following adjectives would you use when interpreting this work: rigid, calm, ordinary, swirling, dramatic?

Eugène Delacroix. *The Lion Hunt.* 1860/61. Oil on canvas. 76.5 × 98.5 cm (30 × 38³/₄"). The Art Institute of Chicago, Chicago, Illinois. Potter Palmer Collection, 1922.404.

Géricault's picture reflects the diagonal compositions of Rubens and the sculpturesque painted figures of Michelangelo. Géricault arranged his figures in a design based on two opposite diagonals. The major diagonal, from lower left to upper right, carries you into the work and leads you over a series of twisting figures expressing emotions ranging from despair to hope. A second diagonal, from the corpse at the lower right to the mast of the crude raft at the upper left, balances the composition.

The diagonal design, twisting figures, strong emotion, and dramatic use of light are important characteristics of the Romantic style. They marked Géricault's break with the Neoclassic style, which stressed calmness and balance.

Eugène Delacroix (1798–1863)

When Géricault died suddenly at age 33 from a fall from a horse, his position of leadership in the Romantic movement fell to Eugène Delacroix (oo-**zhen** del-lah-**kwah**). Glowing colors and swirling action are marks of Delacroix's style. Ingres and his Neoclassical followers disliked such work, however. They found it violent, crude, and unfinished. This disagreement resulted in a long rivalry between Delacroix and Ingres.

The Lion Hunt
■ **FIGURE 21.7**

Delacroix's love of dramatic action and exotic settings is evident in his painting *The Lion Hunt* (Figure 21.7). A six-month trip through Morocco, Tangier, and Algiers in 1832, fired his enthusiasm for the Near East and provided the inspiration and subject matter for many of his works, including *The Lion Hunt.*

The theme of this work is action. The frantic movement of hunters, horses, and lions is arranged in a circular pattern placed within an oval of light. The violent action is made more convincing by the use of blurred edges, rapidly applied brushstrokes, and spots of bold color, reminders of Rubens. Everything has been swept up into the swirling spiral, making colors and forms blur as they whirl around and around.

Color was the most important element in painting for Delacroix. Unlike Ingres, he did not begin his paintings with lines. When painting a figure, for example, he did not draw the outline first and then fill it in with color. Instead, he began painting at the center

---

⊙ Technology ▬

National Gallery of Art Videodisc Use the following images as examples of more works by artists introduced in this lesson.

Théodore Géricault
Trumpeters of Napoleon's Imperial Guard

Search Frame 1112

Eugène Delacroix
Arabs Skirmishing in the Mountains

Search Frame 1131

John Constable
Wivenhoe Park, Essex

Search Frame 1697

Use Glencoe's *Correlation Bar Code Guide to the National Gallery of Art* to locate more artworks.

of the figure and worked outward to the edges to complete it. The artist learned a great deal from studying the work of the English landscape painter John Constable, who used patches of color placed side by side instead of blending them smoothly together. When Delacroix did this, however, he was criticized for the rough finish of his works.

English Landscape Painters

By 1800, qualities that were to characterize English painting throughout the nineteenth century could be found in the works of John Constable and Joseph M. W. Turner. Both artists were primarily landscape painters, although they took different approaches to their works.

John Constable (1776–1837)

Like the seventeenth-century Dutch masters, John Constable wanted to paint the sky, meadows, hills, and streams as the eye actually sees them. He delighted in trying to capture the light and warmth of sunlight, the coolness of shadows, and the motion of clouds and rain. He painted wide-open landscapes with great detail, re-creating the exact look and feel of the scene.

During long walks through the fields, Constable carried a small pocket sketchbook. The pages of this sketchbook measured little more than 3 × 4 inches. On these tiny pages he drew views of the landscape from different angles. He was especially interested in the effects of changes in sunlight. Later, when working on his large paintings, he referred over and over again to these sketches.

The Dell at Helmingham Park
■ FIGURE 21.8

Constable's *The Dell at Helmingham Park* (Figure 21.8), with its sparkling color and dewy freshness, is a scene of quiet charm. When you examine the painting closely, you recognize that the artist used tiny dabs of pure color, stippled with white and applied with a brush or palette knife. This technique creates a shimmer of hue and light across the work, and effectively captures the fleeting effects of nature.

■ **FIGURE 21.8** The viewer can "listen" to the sounds in this scene—the murmur of the stream, the gentle splashing of the cow's hooves, the rustle of the leaves in the summer breeze. Taking into account what you see and what you "hear," what feeling does this painting evoke?

John Constable. *The Dell at Helmingham Park.* 1830. Oil on canvas. 113.4 × 130.8 cm (44⅝ × 51½"). The Nelson-Atkins Museum of Art, Kansas City, Missouri. Purchase: Nelson Trust.

Art Criticism

Display pictures or slides of Ingres's and Delacroix's widely reproduced, but strikingly different, portraits of the famous violinist Niccolò Paganini. Ask students to compare the artists' use of the elements and principles of art. While students perform the necessary art-criticism operations, you may wish to play a recording of some of Paganini's music, such as selections from his *Twenty-four Caprices for Solo Violin.*

Studio Skills

Have students visit a park or other outdoor location and make small sketches from many different angles of various aspects of the surroundings (e.g., a tree, a pond, a pathway). Back in the classroom, challenge students to create a unified sketch of the entire scene. Conclude with a discussion of whether making numerous preliminary sketches, as Constable did, can be instrumental in the creation of a unified, harmonious landscape.

Did You Know?

Students may note that the top of *Raft of the Medusa* appears blackened. The reason is that Géricault, in an act of poor judgment, mixed his pigments with a kind of coal tar that proved to have poor lasting quality.

Teacher Notes

Developing Perceptual Skills. Students will more easily appreciate the themes and styles associated with the parallel movements described in this chapter if they are exposed to some of the art trends in northern Europe during this period. Two artists who would be especially good examples to introduce are Caspar David Friedrich and Philip Otto Runge. In contrast to Constable's sunny, picturesque landscapes, Friedrich's landscapes, such as *Woman in Morning Light* and *Abbey Under Oak Trees,* have a sense of supernatural power. Runge, meanwhile, was obsessed with images of utopian purity, and he painted children as though they inhabited a mysterious, magical world and were bursting with a sort of animal vigor.

Art History

Explain that some art historians contend that landscape painting as an independent genre began as early as the fifteenth century. In support of this contention, have students examine the manuscript illumination by the Limbourg brothers (Figure 15.19, page 343). Can students discern why some scholars claim to find the seeds of Constable's landscapes in the backgrounds of artworks such as these? Ask: Why did it take centuries for landscape painting to become an accepted genre in its own right?

Studio Skills

Direct students' attention to the clouds in Constable's landscape, Figure 21.9. Then, over the span of several days, have students maintain "cloud sketchbooks" in which they record original sketches of cloud types. Have students share their sketchbooks, discussing which types of clouds are hardest and easiest to render.

■ **FIGURE 21.9**
Constable wanted to paint scenes from nature as the eye actually sees them. Identify details and techniques that make this scene appear real.

John Constable. *Wivenhoe Park, Essex.* 1816. Oil on canvas. 56.1 × 101.2 cm (22¹/₈ × 39⁷/₈"). National Gallery of Art, Washington, D.C. Board of Trustees, Widener Collection.

Wivenhoe Park, Essex
■ **FIGURE 21.9**

In *Wivenhoe Park, Essex* (Figure 21.9), Constable offers his view of an estate belonging to a friend of his father. The landowner commissioned the painting and asked that certain things be included in it. In fact, because he thought Constable had not included everything, the artist was required to sew pieces of canvas to each side of the painting to enlarge the scene.

The painting conveys the look and feel of the scene as Constable saw it. He caught the light airiness of the atmosphere and the sweeping movement of the clouds. The sparkle of light across the dark green leaves of the trees and the light green of the rolling hills is shown. In addition, the artist captured the stately look of the red brick house emphasized by the break in the trees and light reflection in the water. The entire scene has a feeling of the momentary—as though you have been given a quick glimpse of nature as it exists at a particular moment in time.

Joseph M. W. Turner
(1775–1851)

Joseph M. W. Turner began his career as a watercolor painter and later turned his attention to painting landscapes in oils. As his career progressed, he became less and less interested in showing nature in realistic detail. Instead, he concentrated on the effects that light and atmosphere have on subject matter.

In time, light and atmosphere became the most important part of Turner's works. He painted a glowing atmosphere as a way of arousing the viewer's curiosity and luring the viewer closer for a longer look. The blurred forms and intense colors would be changed by the viewer's imagination. In the indistinct forms one could see a blazing sunset, violet mountains, and the silhouette of a medieval castle.

Snow Storm: Steamboat off a Harbor's Mouth
■ **FIGURE 21.10**

Turner's painting entitled *Snow Storm: Steamboat off a Harbor's Mouth* (Figure 21.10) is his view of nature at its most violent. He captures this violence with a bold use of sweeping light and color, rather than with detail. When this painting was exhibited at the Royal Academy in London, critics were shocked and angered. They were used to traditional pictures of ships at sea, and failed to find any value in this painting of blurred and violent impressions.

COOPERATIVE LEARNING

Drawing Expressions. Students at the academy copied engravings of facial expressions drawn in the late seventeenth century by Charles Le Brun. It was Le Brun's theory that all the passions of the soul were revealed through bodily posture and facial expressions, and, as a result, he codified a range of emotions into visual formulas for the use of artists. It was not until the Romantic period that artists began to extend Le Brun's master list of facial expressions in painting. Students may enjoy devising their own typologies of expressions. Divide the class into groups of four to six students. Let each group determine a set of about ten different facial expressions and divide up the task of drawing them.

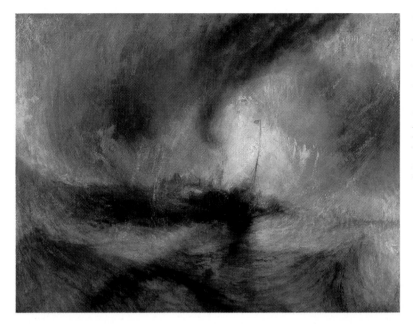

■ **FIGURE 21.10** Turner was more interested in depicting the effects of light and atmosphere than in showing realistic details. Why were critics shocked when this work was first exhibited? Describe the mood created by the swirling colors.

Joseph M. W. Turner. *Snow Storm: Steamboat off a Harbor's Mouth.* 1842. Oil on canvas. 92 × 122 cm (36 × 48″). Clore Collection, Tate Gallery, London, England.

The critics failed to understand that Turner was painting things that have no shape or form—things like speed, wind, and atmosphere. Turner's later paintings of space and light became even more abstract. They were so formless that he had to attach rings to the frames so galleries would know which way to hang them.

Turner died on December 19, 1851, a death listed simply as "natural decay." His last words were, "The sun is God."

The Realists

Meanwhile, in France, many young artists were looking for subject matter that did not glorify the past or offer romantic views of current events. They rejected both Neoclassicism and Romanticism.

To understand this reaction to both Neoclassicism and Romanticism, you must consider conditions in France around the middle of the nineteenth century. Factories were expanding, using new machines to increase production. Great numbers of people moved from rural areas to the cities to work in these factories. Factory workers, who were usually unskilled and poorly paid,

lived in crowded conditions in drab, unhealthy slums.

These changes had an effect on some artists. They realized that classical models and romantic subject matter were out of place in their world. A peasant, they felt, was as good a subject for their brush as a Greek goddess was, and the life of a factory worker offered as much inspiration as a lion hunt in some far-off land did.

These artists also knew, however, that they could not use old techniques to paint the world around them. They would have to invent new techniques. So they discarded the formulas of Neoclassicism and the theatrical drama of Romanticism to paint familiar scenes and trivial events as they really looked.

Gustave Courbet (1819–1877)

Gustave Courbet (**goo**-stahv koor-**bay**) was in the forefront of this group of artists. He and his followers became known as *Realists.* Their art style, known as **Realism,** *represented everyday scenes and events as they actually looked.*

In *Burial at Ornans* (Figure 21.11, page 476), Courbet painted the funeral of an ordinary villager.

Art Criticism

Have students leaf through the text searching for other works that, like Turner's, emphasize the quality of light and atmosphere. A volunteer may also be interested in exploring and preparing a presentation on twentieth-century artists whose work focuses on light, such as the contemporary light sculptor James Turrell, whose environmental artworks alter the viewer's perception of light and space.

Cross Curriculum

MUSIC. After reinforcing the unkindness of critics' reception of Turner's *Snow Storm,* ask a volunteer to investigate parallels from the world of music. One possibility is the 1913 Paris debut of Igor Stravinsky's *The Rite of Spring,* which nearly incited a riot and led to characterizations of the avant-garde composer as "a monster." If possible, the volunteer should obtain and play a recording of the first movement of the composition for the class.

Studio Skills

Have students use oil pastels and sheets of drawing paper to create a local scene based on the stormiest weather they have ever experienced or could imagine. Students who wish, may make their pictures nearly abstract renderings of light and atmosphere, in the manner of Turner. Encourage students to focus on the weather itself rather than the details of the scene. Have students compare efforts.

More About... **Joseph M. W. Turner.** Art critic John Berger has proposed an unusual theory for what may have inspired Turner's swirling renditions of a stormy sea. Turner was the son of a barber in London, and Berger hypothesizes that some of the visual details of a barbershop may have found expression in the artist's seascape. Berger writes: "Consider some of his later paintings and imagine, in the backstreet shop, water, froth, steam, gleaming metal, clouded mirrors, white bowls or basins in which soapy liquid is agitated by the barber's brush and detritus deposited. Consider the equivalence between his father's razor and the palette knife which, despite criticisms and current usage, Turner insisted upon using so extensively."

Aesthetics

Have students find paintings in the text that include angels. Reminding them of Courbet's attitude about painting only images visible to his eye, have students debate whether artists should attempt only to represent what they know from personal experience and through the five senses.

Art History

Discuss with students the fact that part of the cultural background that influenced Realist painters was the development of science as a logical inquiry. There was an excitement revolving around the belief that virtually everything could, in time, be known through scientific means. In many fields, people sought to emulate the virtues of scientific discipline and the scientist's agenda to impartially collect the raw facts, reject metaphysical prejudices, and closely observe empirical phenomena. The Realist painters were also inspired by these goals. In the spirit of scientific fair-mindedness, they criticized traditional distinctions between beauty and ugliness and they regarded truth as the highest criterion of beauty.

Interpreting Realism in *Art*

*T*his funeral (Figure 21.11) is a common scene. Unlike El Greco's *Burial of Count Orgaz* (Figure 18.9, page 405), there are no saints assisting at this burial. Courbet shows only a large group of almost full-size figures standing beside an open grave in front of a somber landscape.

 There is no mystery or miracle here; the painting communicates little in the way of grief or piety. Indeed, not one person looks at the cross or at the grave. The people attending this funeral do so out of a sense of duty.

 The priest routinely reads the service. The kneeling gravedigger looks bored and impatient to get on with his work.

 The women at the right go through the motions of mourning, but they are not very convincing.

■ **FIGURE 21.11** Gustave Courbet. *Burial at Ornans.* 1849–50. Approx. 3 × 6.7 m (10 × 22′). Musée d'Orsay, Paris, France.

 Courbet's friends had posed for the painting, and, in most cases, they could be identified. He used them because they were important to him and were a part of his life. However, when he exhibited his painting in Paris, he was criticized for using his friends as models. He had dared to use plain, ordinary people painted on a scale that was by tradition reserved for important people or great events.

 Courbet felt that an artist should draw on his or her own experiences and paint only what could be seen and understood. That is what he did in painting this funeral. It is an actual scene painted honestly. The work shows real people behaving the way real people behave.

Interpreting Realism in *Art*

Have students examine and discuss Courbet's painting in Figure 21.11. Then ask them to turn to page 405 and examine El Greco's painting in Figure 18.9. Encourage students to identify techniques and details that mark Courbet's work as an example of Realism and distinguishes it from El Greco's depiction of a similar subject. Have students read and discuss the information in the feature. Then have students choose one of the individuals pictured in Figure 21.11 and write a fictionalized diary account of the day of the funeral, including before, during, and after the funeral.

Édouard Manet (1832–1883)

Among the artists who took part in the Realist movement was Édouard Manet (ay-doo-**ahr** mah-**nay**). He exhibited with Courbet and was often attacked by critics for the same reasons. Unlike Courbet, however, Manet was more concerned with *how* to paint than with *what* to paint.

The Railway
■ FIGURE 21.12

In *The Railway* (Figure 21.12), Manet uses his knowledge and skill to paint a simple everyday scene. A woman with a sleeping puppy in her lap has just looked up from a book. You feel as though you have come upon her by chance, and she looks up to see who it is. As you exchange casual glances with her, your eye takes in the black fence of a railway station.

Use of Pattern and Shape

A little girl stands with her back to you, peering through this fence at the steam and smoke left by a passing locomotive. The girl's left arm unites her with the figure of the woman; it also breaks up the strong vertical pattern of the fence. The curving shapes of the figures contrast with the repeated verticals of the railings. In this way, Manet adds variety and interest to his composition.

Manet did not pose the figures in his pictures. He painted them as he found them. He avoided details because he wanted his picture to show what the eye could take in with a quick glance. His concern with technique is seen in his methods of placing colors on the canvas. In some places, the paint is stroked on carefully. In others, it is dabbed on or pulled across the canvas. The result is a richly textured surface that adds even more to the variety and interest of the picture.

■ **FIGURE 21.12**
Although Manet participated in the Realist movement, he was more interested in *how* to paint than in *what* to paint. **Describe the lines in this picture. How have these lines been used to tie the composition together?**

Édouard Manet. *The Railway.* 1873. Oil on canvas. 93.3 × 111.5 cm (36³/₄ × 43⁷/₈″). National Gallery of Art, Washington D.C. Gift of Horace Havemeyer in memory of his mother, Louisine W. Havemeyer.

Chapter 21 *New Styles in Nineteenth-Century Art* **477**

Aesthetics

Have students pretend that they are collectors with a taste for realistic art. Their budget permits them to purchase any five paintings reproduced in this chapter. Which ones would they choose? Compare students' lists of choices. Did any students include Neoclassical or Romantic works? Use this exercise to introduce a discussion of the many different interpretations of "realism" and to clarify exactly what Courbet and the Realists meant by this word.

Art Criticism

Invite students to imagine themselves to be nineteenth-century salon critics. Challenge them to write abrasive and insulting reviews of Figure 21.12. If possible, show students an example of a more traditional painting that hung in the same salon during the same period, such as Jan Matejko's *Stephen Báthory After the Battle of Pskov.* Student critiques should make use of each of the four art-criticism operations.

Cross Curriculum

HISTORY. Point out that the period during which Manet was at work on his painting *Gare Saint-Lazare* was one of technological progress. For example, Alexander Graham Bell invented the telephone in 1876, and Thomas Edison patented the gramophone in 1877. Ask interested volunteers to research technological developments from this period. Provide time during which these students can share their findings with the rest of the class.

More About... | **Rosa Bonheur.** Rosa Bonheur, discussed on page 478, came from an unusual family, a fact that surely contributed to both her pursuit of the arts and her fondness for animal subjects. Bonheur's father belonged to a sect known as the St. Simonians, who believed in the complete equality of women and men and a feminine element in God. The St. Simonians anticipated the coming of a female messiah and wanted a society based on love, with no war or class distinctions. The French government eventually forced the St. Simonians to disband, but Bonheur and her family continued to support these ideals. Bonheur's fondness for animal subjects may have stemmed in part from her family's curious habit of keeping animals in the household.

Art History

Have students locate other examples of animal paintings by Rosa Bonheur and present these to the class. Then conduct a discussion on the artist, guiding student participation with questions like the following: What sort of animals did Bonheur prefer to paint? Would you expect to find a Bonheur painting of a cat or dog? Why or why not?

Study Guide

Distribute *Study Guide* 49 in the TCR. Assist students in reviewing key concepts. 📁

Extension

Have students complete *Cooperative Learning* 31, "Tracing the Effects of the Industrial Revolution." In this worksheet, groups of students read and discuss responses of artists and writers to the Industrial Revolution, comparing their thoughts to present-day attitudes toward social conditions. 📁

Studio Activities

Assign *Studio* 27, "Expressive Paper-Cylinder Portrait," in the TCR. Students will find ways to express different moods using paper as a medium. 📁

Did You Know❓

During the development of Romanticism and Realism, the countries of Western Europe and the United States entered a great age of industrialization. The period from 1780 to 1880 produced more astounding advances in technology and invention than the world had ever known.

Rosa Bonheur (1822–1899)

An artist who effectively combined the flair of Romanticism with the accuracy of Realism was Rosa Bonheur (**roh**-zah bah-**nur**). Few artists were as successful or as admired in their lifetime as this woman. She received her first painting lessons from her father, who was a painter and art teacher. When her mother died, the young Rosa was forced to leave school and help her father raise her two brothers and a sister. This did not prevent her from continuing to paint, however. The family had moved to Paris when she was seven years old, and Bonheur often copied the works of the masters found in the many galleries there.

Bonheur showed a preference for sketching live animals however, rather than copying paintings. She journeyed to country fields and stockyards outside Paris to draw the animals. She also found subjects for her works at cattle markets and fairs where horses were traded. To be more comfortable when working, Bonheur wore men's clothing instead of the restrictive women's clothing of the day. (However, this was done only after permission had been obtained from the authorities.) Men's clothing was much more suitable for walking and sketching among the animals, and it helped her avoid the jeers of the workers and spectators.

When she was just nineteen, two of Bonheur's paintings were chosen for exhibition at the Salon. Four years later, she was given a medal. This was the first of many honors and awards she earned during her long career. Eventually, she was made an officer of the Legion of Honor, the first woman to be so recognized.

The Horse Fair
■ FIGURE 21.13

Bonheur's accurate anatomical studies of animals enabled her to paint such large, convincing works as *The Horse Fair* (Figure 21.13). Here she combines her knowledge and admiration of horses with an understanding of the emotion and vigor found in paintings by Géricault and Delacroix.

Bonheur shows horses being led by their handlers around the exhibition area of a fair. The scene is crackling with tension and excite-

Time & Place
CONNECTIONS

Early Nineteenth Century
c. 1800–1850

DAGUERREOTYPE. In 1839, Louis J.M. Daguerre devised a method of exposing light to a silver coated copper plate to make a photographic image. This became a popular portrait medium because minute details could be captured on the image.

BUSTLES. Women's clothing, such as bustles, was increasingly made in factories rather than by hand. Waistlines were laced tightly, and bustles made of padding or wire framing were worn to make skirts fuller in back.

Activity **Postcard.** Design a postcard that might have been written by a traveler in the American west to family back home. On one side draw a scene from this period that depicts the clothing styles pictured on this page. On the other side write a note home about the trip.

Time & Place
CONNECTIONS
Early Nineteenth Century

Let students meet in groups to examine and discuss the images in this Time & Place feauture. Have group members share what they already know about bustles and daguerreotypes; encourage interested students to research the topics and share their findings with other group members. Before students begin working on the Activity, have group members discuss specific locations that might be shown on their postcards. Ask students to learn about scenery, structures, and activities that might accurately be shown in postcards from those locations.

■ **FIGURE 21.13** Her accurate and exciting animal paintings made Bonheur one of the most popular European artists of her time. In what ways does this painting remind you of the works of Géricault and Delacroix? How is it similar to Realist paintings by Courbet and Manet?

Rosa Bonheur. *The Horse Fair.* 1853–55. Oil on canvas. 244.5 × 506.8 cm (96¹/₄ × 199¹/₂"). The Metropolitan Museum of Art, New York, New York. Gift of Cornelius Vanderbilt, 1887. (87.25).

ment. High-strung horses rear up suddenly and flail the air with their hooves. Others trot and prance about, barely held in check. The result is a thrilling blend of movement, drama, and reality that echoes the accomplishments of both Romantic and Realist artists.

Bonheur's animals are painted boldly with a heavy, rich application of paint. She pos-

sessed the skill and the confidence to paint pictures of great size. *The Horse Fair,* for example, is more than 16 feet wide.

Her animal paintings made Bonheur one of the most popular painters in Europe. It is a mark of her talent that her popularity has not diminished over the years.

LESSON TWO REVIEW

Reviewing the Facts

1. Define *Romanticism* and tell how the subject matter of artworks in this style differed from that of the Neoclassicists.
2. Name three characteristics of the Romantic style used by Théodore Géricault in his painting *Raft of the Medusa* (Figure 21.6, page 471).
3. Identify two characteristics of Eugène Delacroix's style.
4. What aspect did Joseph M. W. Turner consider most important in his landscapes and seascapes?

Activity... *Comparing Realists and Romantics*

Artists of this time had differing approaches to creating artworks. They formed two groups, the Romantics and the Realists, and each felt that art should function differently.

Consider whether you are a Realist or a Romantic. Using information from the lesson, make a list of the characteristics of each style. Identify paintings that represent examples of each style. Work in groups of either Realists or Romantics to create a presentation to your class expressing your viewpoint, and explain why you chose to represent that group.

LESSON TWO REVIEW

Answers to Reviewing Art Facts

1. A style portraying dramatic and exotic subjects, while Neoclassicists used classical forms to express their ideas on courage, sacrifice, and patriotism.
2. Diagonal design, twisting figures, strong emotion, and dramatic use of light.
3. Glowing colors and swirling action.

4. Mood.

Activity . . . Comparing Realists and Romantics

Have students work together to brainstorm two lists of characteristics—one of the Romantic style, the other of the Realist style. Then let students form two groups, each to represent one of the styles. Ask groups to work cooperatively in planning and sharing their presentation.

ASSESS

Checking Comprehension

Have students respond to the lesson review questions. Answers are given in the box below.

Reteaching

Assign *Reteaching* 49, found in the TCR. Have students complete the activity and review their responses. 📁

Enrichment

➢ Have a volunteer research the subject matter of Figure 21.7 (page 472). Was the hunting of lions in North Africa merely a matter of sport? Were they hunted for food or for personal safety? Information should be shared with the class.

➢ Assign *Art and Humanities* 36, "Comparing Styles in Literature," in the TCR. Students compare styles of poetry and writings from Romantic and Neoclassic writers. 📁

Extension

A volunteer may be interested in finding out more about the woman who appears in Figure 21.12 (page 477). Her name is Victorine Meurent, and she appears in many of Manet's paintings. A good source of information on this woman, who was herself a painter, is Eunice Lipton's *Alias Olympia: A Woman's Search for Manet's Notorious Model and Her Own Desire* (New York: Scribner's, 1993).

CLOSE

Ask students to state whether they would have preferred to be a Neoclassical, Romantic, or Realist painter in the nineteenth century. Have them explain their responses with information from the lesson.

Impressionism

Focus

Lesson Objectives

After studying this lesson, students will be able to:

■ Understand the goals of the Impressionists.

■ Explain the painting techniques artists of the movement developed to meet their goals.

■ Identify major outside influences on Impressionist painters.

■ Name notable Impressionist painters and describe some of their works.

Building Vocabulary

Ask students: What is an impression? How is it different from a detailed study? How do you usually get an impression of a person or a place? Taking their responses to these questions into account, have students describe qualities they think might be associated with the art style called Impressionism.

Motivator

Have students bring in examples of two types of photographs depicting human subjects— ones that are candid (e.g., news photos from magazines or newspapers, personal snapshots) and ones in which the subjects appear posed (school portraits, fashion photos). Have students set up a display of the two groups of pictures. What adjectives would students use to describe the mood communicated by each type of photo?

Introducing the Lesson

Ask students to page through the lesson, noting especially the paintings shown there. Ask: What makes these artworks different from those you studied in earlier lessons?

Impressionism

Vocabulary
■ Impressionism
■ candid

Artists to Meet
■ Claude Monet
■ Pierre Auguste Renoir
■ Gustave Caillebotte
■ Edgar Degas
■ Mary Cassatt
■ Berthe Morisot
■ Auguste Rodin

Discover
After completing this lesson, you will be able to:
■ Identify the objectives of the Impressionists and describe the painting technique they developed to achieve those objectives.
■ Identify major Impressionist painters and describe some of their works.
■ Discuss two important influences on Impressionist artists.
■ Describe the sculptures of Auguste Rodin and explain his relationship to the Impressionists.

*T*he generation of artists that followed Courbet and were associated with Manet carried even further the quest for realism. They took their easels, paints, and brushes outdoors to paint rather than work from sketches in their studios.

A New Style Emerges

These artists contributed to a new style of painting that stressed the effects of atmosphere and sunlight on subject matter. They tried to capture this effect by using quick, short brushstrokes. Their paintings are made up entirely of small dabs, or spots, of color that, when viewed from a distance, blend together to create the desired effect.

Because these artists were concerned with momentary effects, they avoided posed or staged compositions. Instead, they preferred an informal, casual arrangement in their paintings. In many ways, their pictures have the same natural look as quickly snapped photographs. This "snapshot" approach to composition added a lively, more realistic appearance to their paintings.

Claude Monet (1840–1926)

In 1874, a group of artists using this new style of painting held an exhibition of their works in Paris. One of these artists was Claude Monet (**kload moh-nay**), who exhibited a picture entitled *Impression: Sunrise.* Outraged critics took the word *Impression* from Monet's title and used it as a label when referring, unkindly, to all the works in this exhibition. This label, **Impressionism,** described *an art style that tried to capture an impression of what the eye sees at a given moment and the effect of sunlight on the subject.*

Monet's Haystacks
■ **FIGURES 21.14 and 21.15**

In 1891, Monet stood in a field near Paris, working on a painting of haystacks. When he realized that the sunlight had changed, he put down his unfinished work and began another painting of the same subject. Why create many paintings of the same subject? When you learn the answer to this question, you will have a better understanding of what the Impressionists tried to accomplish with their paintings.

By sunset Monet had started more than a dozen paintings of the same haystacks. Each of these captures a different moment of light (Figures 21.14 and 21.15).

For months, Monet worked in the field painting the same haystacks. Often he worked on several pictures at once, rushing from one to another as the light changed. He painted the haystacks at all hours of the day,

480

LESSON THREE RESOURCES

Teacher's Classroom Resources

📁 Art and Humanities 37

📁 Enrichment Activities 39, 40

📁 Reproducible Lesson Plan 50

📁 Reteaching Activity 50

📁 Study Guide 50

■ **FIGURE 21.14**
Monet painted the same haystacks at different times of day, trying to capture the effects of changes in the lighting. How are these two paintings different? (See Figure 21.15 below.) What aspects of sunlight has the artist depicted?

Claude Monet. *The Haystack, End of Summer, Giverny.* 1891. Oil on canvas. Musée d' Orsay, Paris, France.

TEACH
Art Criticism

Point out that the invention of the tin paint tube around 1840 opened up new possibilities for artists by permitting them to work outdoors for long periods of time. Have students appreciate the advantages of painting "at the source" by displaying a photograph of a familiar nearby subject (e.g., the front of the school building, a tree on the school grounds). Escort the class outdoors to the location in the photo. Have them record in their sketchbooks brief descriptions of the way sunlight, shadow, and other aspects of atmosphere play on the subject. Ask how many of these details are present in the photo. Conclude with a discussion of how being outdoors influenced the style of Impressionist works such as Figures 21.14, 21.15, 21.16, and 21.17.

always trying to record in paint the exact colors he saw reflected off them. Sometimes the sun was so brilliant that the outlines of the haystacks became blurred and seemed to vibrate. Monet tried to capture this effect in his pictures, painting exactly what his eye saw rather than what he knew to be there.

When Monet exhibited his haystack paintings later in Paris, though, most critics responded in anger. They claimed that Monet's works looked crude and hastily completed, as if they were no more than sketches.

Monet refused to be discouraged. Instead, he began work on another series of paintings showing a row of poplar trees along a river. This time he was interested not only in painting the colors reflected from the subject, but also in showing how these colors looked in the rippling water of the stream.

Later, when they were shown in Paris, Monet's poplar trees were more warmly received than his haystacks had been. Monet, however, was unimpressed. "What do the critics know?" he asked.

Critical Thinking

If you have access to a computer moniter that requires the use of "dithering" (i.e., tiny dots of color to simulate different hues), try the following experiment. Have students stand at least four paces from the monitor, and display a richly colored image or scene. Ask students to make a complete list of all the "true" colors they see. After students have compiled their lists, allow them to approach the screen and see which colors are actually composites. Ask: Which colors are used to suggest other colors?

■ **FIGURE 21.15**

Claude Monet. *Stack of Wheat (Thaw, Sunset).* 1890/91. Oil on canvas. 64.9 × 92.3 cm (25^1/$_2$ × 36^1/$_3$"). The Art Institute of Chicago, Chicago, Illinois. Gift of Mr. and Mrs. Daniel C. Searle, 1983. 166.

Chapter 21 *New Styles in Nineteenth-Century Art* **481**

Technology ▬▬▬

National Gallery of Art Videodisc Use the following images as examples of more works by artists introduced in this lesson.

Claude Monet
The Artist's Garden at Vétheuil

Search Frame 1388

Auguste Renoir
A Girl with a Watering Can

Search Frame 1300

Edgar Degas
Ballet Dancers

Search Frame 2928

Use Glencoe's *Correlation Bar Code Guide to the National Gallery of Art* to locate more artworks.

Aesthetics

Remind students that Monet and the other Impressionists did not have all of the same media that are available to artists today. Black-and-white photography was in its infancy in the nineteenth century, and color photography was nonexistent. Have students consider Monet's artistic goals and then write a page on whether they believe Monet would have been happier working in color photography if it had been a possibility in the late nineteenth century. Invite students to read their essays aloud.

Critical Thinking

Emphasize that critics of the period were less than encouraging to Monet. Ask: If you had been the artist, would you have been more inclined to heed the allegedly expert opinions of the critics or pursue your own ideas? What characteristics of the individual does each decision reveal? What role may the support of fellow artists have played? To help students answer these questions, have volunteers role-play Monet discussing one of his paintings with both a critic and a supportive fellow artist.

■ **FIGURE 21.16** Monet devoted three winters to painting the doorways and towers of this cathedral. At the end of the second winter, he wrote, "What I have undertaken is very difficult. . . . The more I continue, the more I fail." Why did Monet continue to paint the same subject over and over, in spite of the difficulties of his project?

Claude Monet. *Rouen Cathedral, Full Sun, Blue Harmony and Gold.* 1894. Oil on canvas. 107 × 73 cm (42 1/8 × 28 3/4"). Musée d' Orsay, Paris, France.

Rouen Cathedral
■ **FIGURE 21.16**

Monet's painting of the west façade of Rouen Cathedral (Figure 21.16) shows the famous building bathed in bright, shimmering sunlight. The artist made 26 paintings of this same church.

One winter Monet visited his brother, who lived in the cathedral city of Rouen. Late one afternoon, he looked through a shop window and saw the towers and the doorway of the great church looming in the twilight. He sent home for his canvases and set up his easel in the window of the little shop and for the next three winters painted the facade of the cathedral.

One of Monet's paintings of Rouen Cathedral uses complementary colors—blues and oranges. These colors were applied in separate brushstrokes, which look like an uneven mixture of colored dabs and dashes when seen up close. Viewed from a distance, however, they blend together. As a result, what the viewer sees is not solid form, but a rich visual impression.

When critics saw Monet's pictures of Rouen Cathedral, they marveled at last. The highest tribute to Monet's genius, however, may have come from another great artist. Paul Cézanne said, "Monet is only an eye, but what an eye!"

> *More About...* | **Salons.** Salons offered painters their most important opportunities to exhibit their artworks publicly. Once the academy determined which works were admitted to the great exhibition, the person hired to hang the works (called a *tapissier*) took charge of arranging them in the gallery space, a thankless task that inevitably met with criticism by artists and visitors alike. The paintings were hung almost from floor to ceiling, making it difficult to view works in the higher rows, especially if they were small. The best positions were given to artists of good reputation within the academy. The show lasted about three weeks, and sometimes important works commissioned by the king were moved to a more easily viewed position.

Pierre Auguste Renoir
(1841–1919)

All the characteristics of Impressionism can be noted in a painting by Pierre Auguste Renoir (pee-**air** oh-**gust** ren-**wahr**), *Le Moulin de la Galette* (Figure 21.17). It shows a crowd of young people enjoying themselves on a summer afternoon at an outdoor dance hall in Paris. Rather than portraying the larger-than-life subjects favored by earlier artists, Renoir and other Impressionists found their subjects in the world around them. In *Le Moulin de la Galette*, Renoir makes us feel that we just happen to be walking by. We take in the scene as we stroll, our eyes darting over the carefree throng. Sunlight filters unevenly through the leafy trees overhead, creating a pattern of light and shade on the scene.

Like the majority of Renoir's works, this is a happy painting, which lets us experience the pleasures of a summer day in Paris. Renoir delighted in showing the joyful side of life. You will never find anything evil or ugly in his pictures. He even avoided painting night or winter scenes, which he considered depressing.

Renoir loved to paint and did so up to the day he died. Even though he was crippled by rheumatism during his final years, Renoir continued to paint—using a paintbrush tied to his wrist.

Identifying Styles in Art

*T*he important features of Impressionism can be identified by examining the elements and principles in this work.

 Bright colors are applied in dabs and dashes that seem to blend together as you look at them.

 Blues and violets are used in place of grays, browns, and blacks, even in the shadows.

 Smooth, slick surfaces are replaced by richly textured surfaces made up of many short brushstrokes.

 Because they are composed of strokes and patches of color, solid forms lose some of their solidity.

 Hard, precise outlines are replaced by blurred edges.

 Often there is no emphasis or center of interest to which your eye is guided by perspective lines. Details are missing because the artist includes only what can be taken in with a single glance. This gives the picture a casual, almost accidental look.

The subject matter comes from the contemporary world, which may seem unimportant when compared to the grand subjects painted by earlier artists.

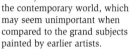
■ FIGURE 21.17

Pierre Auguste Renoir. *Le Moulin de la Galette*. 1876. Oil on canvas. 131 × 175 cm (51¹/₂× 69″). Musée d'Orsay, Paris, France.

Art Criticism

Have students select a pet, plant, or other natural object and spend time observing it closely, listing all the colors seen under different forms of light. Invite students to share their lists and then work jointly on a list of the many colors used in the painting in Figure 21.17.

Studio Skills

Have groups of three or four students each select a painting from an earlier period of art. Challenge each group to collaborate on an interpretation of the work as it might have been done by one of the Impressionists discussed in this lesson. Have groups share and compare their work.

Did You Know?

Romanticism, though prominent in the visual arts of the nineteenth century, was by no means confined to art. The movement was also evident in literature, music, and the philosophy of the age.

Identifying Styles in Art

Have students examine and discuss *Le Moulin de la Galette*, Figure 21.17. Ask them to identify characteristics that mark this painting as an example of Impressionism. Then have students read and discuss the explantion of the elements and principles in the work. Read to students this statement by Renoir: "For me, a picture must be an amiable thing. Joyous and pretty—yes, pretty! There are enough troublesome things in life without inventing others." Ask: How might this information help an art historian confirm whether Renoir painted Figure 21.17?

Aesthetics

Reinforce the idea that, during the nineteenth century, Japanese prints were used as packing material. Then have students brainstorm all of the kinds of visual art that are not considered worth saving today, such as Sunday comics, photographs printed in newspapers and magazines, and product packaging. Ask: Might another culture value such "artworks"?

Art Criticism

Show students a reproduction of Monet's *La Japonaise.* Call to their attention the painting's undeniably Western flavor, despite its obvious Japanese theme. Then have students compare this painting with the work in Figure 10.33 (page 239) to clarify how differently line and form are used in nineteenth-century French and Japanese art.

Art History

Have students examine Figure 21.18, pointing out that this is one of several Paris street scenes painted by Gustave Caillebotte featuring the architectural work of Baron Haussmann. This shows his bridge over railroad tracks. Have a group of students research the work of Haussmann and present their findings to the class. If possible, their presentation should include a reproduction of Caillebotte's *Street in Paris, A Rainy Day,* which shows one of the thoroughfares designed by Haussmann.

Major Influences

Monet, Renoir, and the other Impressionists sought inspiration everywhere. Certainly, one source of inspiration was the Japanese print.

Japanese Prints

A century before, the Japanese had perfected an inexpensive way of printing pictures in several colors. This process made it possible to produce huge quantities of prints that could be sold at modest costs to large numbers of people. The process involved using several wood blocks, each inked with a different colored ink and all applied to the same piece of paper.

The prints produced in this way were usually landscapes or genre scenes. (See Figure 10.33, page 239.) They were done with an elegant pattern of lines and with delicate, flat colors. No attempt was made to create an illusion of depth by using perspective or shading. Further, Japanese printmakers did not hesitate to show only part of a figure. Sometimes a curtain or even the edge of the print was used to "cut off" a figure so that part of it could not be seen. This was something that European artists had never done.

In time, the Impressionists discovered the prints. Awed by their beauty, the artists began to collect them. Before long, some of the features found in the Japanese prints began to appear in Impressionist paintings.

Photography

In addition to Japanese prints, the Impressionists were influenced by the new art of photography. The camera opened artists' eyes to the possibilities of **candid,** or *unposed,* views of people. Snapshots showed familiar subjects from new and unusual points of view.

Gustave Caillebotte (1848–1894)

The influence of both Japanese prints and the art of photography on the Impressionists is readily apparent in a painting by Gustave Caillebotte (**goo**-stahv **kigh**-bott) (Figure 21.18). Three men are seen on a bridge that spans the same railroad tracks indicated in Manet's picture *The Railway* (Figure 21.12, page 477). In Caillebotte's work, as in Japanese prints, the setting and the people reflect everyday life.

Notice how the figures are shown. Their unposed actions at a particular moment in time seem frozen as though captured in a photograph. One leans casually over the rail to view the scene below. Another pauses briefly to glance in the direction of the railroad station. A third walks by so rapidly that he is about to pass completely beyond out of the picture. No European artist would have shown a cutoff figure like this before the appearance of Japanese prints and the development of modern photography.

■ **FIGURE 21.18** The figures in this painting are shown unposed in an everyday setting. How was this work influenced by Japanese prints? By the new art of photography?

Gustave Caillebotte. *On the Europe Bridge.* 1876–77. Oil on canvas. 105.7 × 130.8 cm (41⅝ × 51½"). Kimbell Art Museum, Fort Worth, Texas.

484 **Unit Seven** *Art of the Modern Era*

More About... **Art Collectors.** The collecting of Japanese goods became extremely popular in France during the late nineteenth century. Wealthy people had been procuring lacquers, porcelains, and ivories since the 1840s, but after the Exposition Universelle in 1867, middle-class French were at last able to purchase such items as well. The popularity of Japanese wares was so great that it spawned a local industry dedicated to forging the prized objects. Some critics felt that even the genuine articles were devalued by being made accessible to the general public. Edmond de Goncourt stated that Utamaro prints had become "vulgar merchandise in the hands of editors desirous of making money and addressing the taste of a low class of people."

Edgar Degas (1834–1917)

Another artist who found inspiration in these new discoveries was Edgar Degas (ed-**gahr** day-**gah**). The same cutoff figures, unusual points of view, and candid poses noted in Caillebotte's picture can be found in many of Degas's paintings. Many of these features are evident in his painting *The Glass of Absinthe* (Figure 21.19).

Beginning with the slightly out-of-focus items on the nearest table, you are led indirectly to the two figures at the upper right. A folded newspaper acts as a bridge, enabling your eyes to cross from one table to the next and from there across to the woman and man. Degas wanted nothing to interfere with this journey into and across his painting. He decided not to paint legs on the tables because they might lead your eye away from the route he wanted you to travel.

Degas's carefully planned tour is well rewarded. Your eye is led to a woman you will not soon forget. Lonely, sad, lost in her own thoughts, she is seated next to a man who ignores her to look at something outside the picture.

Interest in Drawing

Degas's great interest in drawing set him apart from the other Impressionists. His drawings, and the paintings he developed from those drawings, show that Degas was concerned with the line, form, and movement of the human body. They offered him the chance to capture the split-second movement of a dancer in the many ballet scenes he painted. Along with scenes of the racetrack, these views of ballerinas became his favorite subject.

■ **FIGURE 21.19** Degas painted the café tables without legs to avoid distracting the viewer from the central figure in this work. **What does the work communicate about the relationship between this central figure and her companion?**

Edgar Degas. *The Glass of Absinthe.* 1876. Oil on canvas. 92 × 68 cm (36 × 27″). Musée d' Orsay, Paris, France.

Cross Curriculum

LANGUAGE ARTS. Have students examine the painting in Figure 21.19, noting in particular the work's intriguing female subject. Challenge students to write either the story of this woman's life or a monologue of her thoughts as she sits with her glass of absinthe. Invite students to read their compositions aloud.

Studio Skills

Have students again study *The Glass of Absinthe.* Then ask them to sketch an original scene that illustrates people engaged in a leisure activity (e.g., a group of students seated at a favorite after-school hangout). As in Degas's painting, the edge of the paper should cut off a full view of one or more of the people. They may use charcoal or pastels to complete their drawings.

Did You Know❓

Edgar Degas has been described as an aloof perfectionist who was often dissatisfied with his work. Legend holds that on one occasion, he said that he wished he were rich enough to buy back all his early pieces and put his foot through them. Fortunately, he never became rich enough to carry out his plan.

COOPERATIVE LEARNING

Art Critic Discussion. To enable students to better understand the reaction of critics to the art movement sneeringly dubbed "Impressionism," share with them this description of the movement by a critic of the time: "The Impressionists take a canvas, some paint, and brushes, throw some tones onto the canvas, and then sign it. This is the way in which lost souls . . . pick up pebbles from the roadway and believe they have found diamonds." Have pairs of students work jointly to paraphrase this indictment. Have partners share their paraphrases as a lead-in to a discussion of why critics reacted as they did.

Aesthetics

Direct students' attention to Figure 21.20. Divide the class into six groups, two groups for each of the three aesthetic theories. For each aesthetic theory, one group is to function as "detractors," noting aspects of the work an aesthetician of the school in question would find troublesome, the other group as "enthusiasts," noting details the same aesthetician would find praiseworthy.

Art History

Remind students of the difficulty Berthe Morisot had in achieving recognition for her art. Then have students research whether the situation for women artists has improved much during the intervening century since Morisot's time. The resource *Making Their Mark: Women Artists Move into the Mainstream, 1970–1985* contains excellent material on this subject, including statistics that compare the funding and exhibition of works by male and female artists. Students interested in researching the topic can report to the class on their findings.

Did You Know?

A critic once said of Morisot's loose handling of paint, "That young lady is not interested in reproducing trifling details. When she has a hand to paint, she makes exactly as many brushstrokes lengthwise as there are fingers, and the business is done."

Mary Cassatt (1845–1926)

Degas played an important role in the development of one of America's finest painters, Mary Cassatt (cuh-**sat**). After studying art in the United States, Cassatt journeyed to Paris to continue her training. She soon found that, as a woman, she had to work twice as hard to gain recognition in the competitive nineteenth-century Paris art world.

Cassatt developed an admiration for Degas's work claiming later that her first exposure to one of his paintings in a shop window changed her life. Later, her paintings attracted his attention, and the two artists became good friends. Degas introduced her to the Impressionists, and they liked her paintings so much that she was invited to show her work at their exhibitions.

The Boating Party
■ FIGURE 21.20

Cassatt's most famous and popular painting may well be a work she completed while on summer vacation on the French Riviera (Figure 21.20). The painting is beautifully designed, with the curved contours of the boat and the sail directing the viewer's gaze to the center of interest, the woman's face and the figure of the child. If you trace the oarsman's gaze with your finger, you will find that it leads down to his arm and the oar, then up to the curved sail and back to the woman and child.

Notice that the mother and child are seen at eye level. In fact, the scene is presented as if the viewer were sitting on a seat at the back of the boat. From that vantage point, we can see all of these two central figures, but only parts of everything else in the work. Behind the mother and child we notice the vibrant blue color of the sea, with just the right touches of green to suggest the sparkle of sunlight on water. We are aware of the dark figure of the oarsman leaning into his task—and it seems that he is about to row the boat right out of the painting!

Many of Cassatt's paintings are tender, peaceful scenes of mothers and their children. Painted in bright colors, they help us see and appreciate the beauty of common, everyday events.

As both a painter and an adviser to American collectors, Cassatt had an important influence on American art. She persuaded many wealthy Americans to purchase artworks by old and new masters—especially the Impressionists.

■ **FIGURE 21.20** Like many of Cassatt's works, this painting focuses on the figures of a mother and her child. Use your finger to trace the line from the oarsman's gaze, along the oar, and back up the curved sail to the central figures of this work.

Mary Cassatt. *The Boating Party.* 1893–94. Oil on canvas. 90 × 117 cm (35⁷/₁₆ × 46¹/₈″). National Gallery of Art, Washington, D.C. Board of Trustees, Chester Dale Collection.

More About... **The Influence of Japanese Art.** The strong influence of Japanese prints that is evident in the works of Edgar Degas and Mary Cassatt can be attributed to their first exposure to this art form during a visit to an 1890 exhibition of Japanese woodblock prints at the Ècole des Beaux-Arts in Paris. This famed school of fine arts was founded in 1648, and sponsored by the French government. The Ècole is world-renowned, and has been a foundation of technical training for such artists as Manet, Matisse, Monet, Renoir, as well as Degas. It currently houses a large collection of artworks and an impressive compilation of drawings.

Berthe Morisot (1841–1895)

Mary Cassatt was not the only woman artist included in the Impressionist group. Berthe Morisot (**bairt** maw-ree-**zoh**) had a long and important career and took part in the Impressionist exhibitions.

Morisot's entire life was entwined with art. A great-granddaughter of Jean-Honoré Fragonard, she was born into a family with a rich artistic tradition. By the time she was 16, she was studying painting by copying pictures in the Louvre. At that time, it was common practice to learn from the masters of the past by copying their works. In the Louvre, Morisot often saw Édouard Manet. They met and became good friends. Several years later, she married Manet's brother Eugène.

The Sisters
■ **FIGURE 21.21**

Like Manet, Morisot concentrated on portraits and interior scenes. She added a fresh, delicate vision that was entirely her own. In *The Sisters* (Figure 21.21), two young women dressed in identical ruffled gowns sit quietly on a sofa. They are almost exactly alike in appearance and manner. They lower their gaze shyly and hold their pose patiently. It is unlikely that they had to do so for very long. Morisot usually posed her models for short periods of time and then painted them largely from memory. In that way she was able to capture the more natural but fleeting expressions of her sitters. She avoided the stiff, artificial expressions displayed when poses were held over long periods.

As with so many fine women artists throughout history, Morisot's achievements as a painter were largely overlooked in her day. Her fellow Impressionists, however, regarded her as a serious, talented artist and considered her work equal to theirs. It was not until after her death at age 54 that Morisot's work finally received the widespread acclaim it deserved.

■ **FIGURE 21.21** The two fans in this work—one held by a sister and the other framed and hanging over the sofa—bridge the space between the two subjects and tie them together. **What makes this painting an Impressionist work? How is it different from the works of other Impressionists?**

Berthe Morisot. *The Sisters*. 1869. Oil on canvas. 52.1 × 81.3 cm (20¹/₂ × 32″). National Gallery of Art, Washington, D.C. Board of Trustees, Gift of Mrs. Charles S. Carstairs.

CHAPTER 21
LESSON THREE

Art Criticism
Have students examine Figure 21.22, page 488. Tell students that the city fathers of Calais who had commissioned this monument were extremely disappointed with Rodin's final version, which failed to emphasize the heroism of the six citizens who voluntarily sacrificed themselves for the sake of their fellow townspeople. Discuss the mood of Rodin's interpretation. Then have students work in small groups to develop chalk sketches of a monument that students believe would have pleased Rodin's sponsors. How do the results differ from Figure 21.22?

Aesthetics
Help students examine and then discuss the sculpture in Figure 21.23, page 489. Ask: Who is the subject of this work? What message or mood does the work communicate? How does a knowledge of the significance of the subject add to or detract from the work's message?

𝒯eacher 𝒩otes

Technology in the Classroom. Students tend to become easily discouraged when they have difficulty isolating nuances of style. This situation may be remedied if you can feature slides of artworks. While few high schools maintain a slide library, you may be able to rent slides for a nominal fee from a local college or the education department of a local museum. If these options are not available in your community, consider purchasing slides from a supply company that specializes in art slides. You will find addresses in photography magazines or through local photography shops or clubs.

Cross Curriculum

FILM STUDIES. Students may enjoy viewing a video of the 1990 film *Camille Claudel,* which chronicles the life of a nineteenth-century woman sculptor closely associated with Rodin and who has achieved renown for her sculpture only a century after her death. After viewing the film, students interested in learning more about Claudel's life and career may read and give book reports on several of the recently published volumes on the free-spirited artist.

Study Guide

Distribute *Study Guide* 50 in the TCR. Assist students in reviewing key concepts. 📁

Art and Humanities

Have students complete *Art and Humanities* 37, "Impressionism in Music," in the TCR. In this worksheet, students are asked to listen to works by Impressionist composers Debussy and Ravel and find parallel characteristics between these compositions and Impressionist paintings. 📁

Extension

Assign *Enrichment* 39, "The Search for Color and Light," in the TCR. Students explore artists' new fascination with ways to represent color and light in painting. 📁

Auguste Rodin (1840–1917)

One man dominated the world of sculpture at the end of the nineteenth century and beginning of the twentieth. He was Auguste Rodin (oh-**gust** roh-**dan**). Like the Impressionists, he was able to capture in his work the most fleeting moments of life.

Rodin's technique in sculpture was similar to that of the Impressionists in painting. As he modeled in wax or clay, he added pieces bit by bit to construct his forms, just as the painters added dots and dashes of paint to create their pictures.

The Burghers of Calais
■ FIGURE 21.22

The uneven surfaces of Impressionist paintings are also found on Rodin's sculptures. The *Burghers of Calais* (Figure 21.22) was designed for public display in the French city of Calais. The work commemorates an event from the city's medieval past. In 1341, six citizens presented themselves before the conquering King of England, Edward III, dressed in sackcloth with nooses around their necks. They offered their own lives in order that their city and its inhabitants might be spared from destruction.

Rodin depicts the men not as a compact group of stalwart heroes, but as ordinary people reacting in different ways to impending doom. Some stride defiantly forward, others appear desperate, while still others seem to hesitate in fear. Their facial expressions and gestures, captured at a particular moment in time, echo these different emotions (Figure 21.22a).

Rodin's sculpture was meant to be viewed at street level, enabling the viewer to walk up to and around it, thus making the encounter direct and immediate. The emotional impact of this encounter serves as an unforgettable reminder of humankind's boundless capacity for love and self-sacrifice.

■ **FIGURE 21.22** Rodin wanted viewers to walk up to and around this sculpture. **Which emotions can you identify in the figures in this group?**

Auguste Rodin. *The Burghers of Calais.* 1884–89, cast c. 1931–47. Bronze. 2 × 2 × 1.9 m (79³/₈ × 80⁷/₈ × 77¹/₈"). Hirshhorn Museum and Sculpture Garden, Smithsonian Institution, Washington, D.C. Gift of Joseph Hirshhorn, 1966.

488   **Unit Seven** *Art of the Modern Era*

CULTURAL DIVERSITY

Prodigal Son. Point out that the biblical tale of the prodigal son has been "retold" in visual terms by artists of virtually every Western culture. Have students consult indexes to a number of art anthologies and other print resources and locate other works from different times and places based on this theme. You may wish to remind students that they have already studied one of the more famous paintings exploring the return of the prodigal son by the Spanish painter Bartolomé Esteban Murillo in Chapter 19 (page 440). Another particularly interesting rendering of the parable is that by nineteenth-century American primitivist Mary Ann Willson, which depicts the principal figures in American colonial garb.

Auguste Rodin. *The Burghers of Calais* (detail).

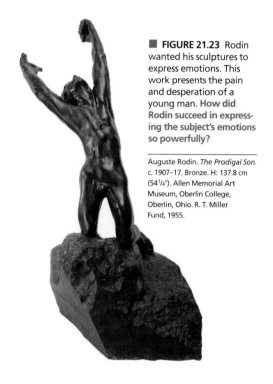

■ **FIGURE 21.23** Rodin wanted his sculptures to express emotions. This work presents the pain and desperation of a young man. **How did Rodin succeed in expressing the subject's emotions so powerfully?**

Auguste Rodin. *The Prodigal Son.* c. 1907–17. Bronze. H: 137.8 cm (54¼"). Allen Memorial Art Museum, Oberlin College, Oberlin, Ohio. R. T. Miller Fund, 1955.

The Prodigal Son
■ **FIGURE 21.23**

The way light and shadow play over the uneven surface of the figure of *The Prodigal Son* (Figure 21.23) gives it life and vitality.

Rodin said he wanted to express joy and sorrow and pain as he saw them. The prodigal son, with head and arms reaching upward, is a powerful image. His wealth and self-esteem gone, at the edge of despair, he pleads for forgiveness. Rodin's vision of pain and desperation is so effective here that, like the father to whom the son pleads, you are moved to show forgiveness.

LESSON THREE REVIEW

Reviewing Art Facts

1. What was stressed by the Impressionist style of art?
2. What painting technique did the Impressionists use to achieve their objective?
3. List at least three characteristics of Impressionist artworks.
4. What two famous women artists were associated with the Impressionists? Which of these artists was an American?

➤ Activity... *Examining Women Artists*

During the Impressionist period, two women artists became well known in artistic circles. Mary Cassatt, an American, fought against family and tradition to become a leading artist of the period. Berthe Morisot, although born into a rich artistic tradition, was never recognized during her lifetime. It was only after their deaths that the works of these women artists have been given wide recognition.

Examine the contributions of other women artists throughout history. Work in groups and research the lives and artworks of at least three other women artists. Locate examples of their works, if possible, and present your findings to the class.

ASSESS
Checking Comprehension

➤ Have students respond to the lesson review questions. Answers are given in the box below.

➤ Assign *Application* 21, "Art-Talk," in the TCR, to help students apply what they have learned in the chapter. 🗀

Reteaching

➤ Assign *Reteaching* 50, found in the TCR. Have students complete the activity and review their responses. 🗀

➤ Distribute magnifying glasses to pairs of students, and have them examine one of the Impressionist paintings reproduced in the text. Prior to the examination, partners should make a list of the colors they see in the work. After examining the works under magnification, students should indicate the components of each listed color.

Extension

Assign *Enrichment* 40, "Building a Camera Obscura," in the TCR. In this activity, students learn about the earliest "dark room" and then create an original pinhole camera. 🗀

CLOSE

Have students state which artist profiled in this chapter they would most like to invite to their home for dinner and what they would expect to discuss with him or her.

LESSON THREE REVIEW

Answers to Reviewing Art Facts

1. The effects of sunlight on a subject.
2. Quick, short brushstrokes of different colors to capture the effect of sunlight on the subject.
3. Smooth surfaces replaced by textured surfaces; solid forms lose solidity; blurred edges; no center of interest; details are missing; subject matter from contemporary world.
4. Berthe Morisot and Mary Cassatt.

Activity . . . *Examining Women Artists*

Have the class work together to compile a list of women artists. Then ask each group to select artists from the class list, avoiding repetition from group to group. Remind group members to work together in researching and examining the artworks created by their selected artists.

Studio LESSON

Watercolor Still Life in a Painterly Style

Objectives

■ Complete a watercolor painting in which the shape of each object is represented as an area of color.

■ Add a variety of thick and thin lines to define the contours of each object.

Motivator

Ask students to take two or three minutes to examine the paintings by Ingres and Delacroix. Have students describe the features they find most impressive, and list those features on the board. Compare and contrast the features in the two lists. Can students arrive at a single word to sum up the features listed in each column?

Studio Skills

Explain that many beginning students approach painting by drawing the outlines of the shapes in their pictures, and then filling these in with color. Delacroix reversed this procedure by blocking in the colors of each shape, often leaving the edges blurred as a way of showing figures in action. Tell students that in this lesson they will follow this approach. The edges or contours of the shapes in their paintings will be defined with ink lines since they are painting motionless still-life objects rather than figures in action.

Critiquing

Have students apply the steps of art criticism to their own artwork, using the "Examining Your Work" questions on this page.

490

Studio LESSON

Watercolor Still Life in a Painterly Style

Materials

- Three or more objects to use in a still-life arrangement.
- Several sheets of white drawing paper or watercolor paper
- Watercolors
- Brushes, mixing trays, and paint cloth
- India ink
- Pens and penholders
- Water container

Paint a still life in which the shape of each object is shown as an area of color. Create these areas of color by using a painterly technique in which still life objects are painted quickly, without the aid of preliminary outlines. Paint each object by beginning at the center and working outward to the edges. Add a variety of contrasting thick and thin contour lines only after all painting has been completed.

Inspiration

Examine the paintings by Ingres and Delacroix illustrated in Figure 21.5, page 470 and Figure 21.7, page 472. How do these works differ? Which appears to place more emphasis on line? Which on color?

■ **FIGURE 21.24** Student Work

Process

1. Set up a still-life arrangement consisting of three or more objects. A variety of sizes, shapes, and colors should be represented.

2. Paint the still-life arrangement with watercolors, beginning with the object closest to you. As you paint each object, start in the center and work outward to the edges. Work with lighter values first and then paint in the darker values. Paint rapidly, with your eye moving continuously from the still life to your paper and back again. Fill the entire paper with paint.

3. When the paint has dried, outline the various shapes of the still-life objects with a variety of thick and thin ink lines. These ink lines should be as accurate as possible in defining the objects. Some colors will extend beyond these outlines, while others will fail to reach the contour lines. Add more ink lines to show specific details in the still-life objects.

Examining Your Work

Describe. Are the still-life objects in your painting easily identified? Which of these is especially successful in terms of the literal qualities?

Analyze. Did you use a variety of thick and thin lines in your painting? Where is variety evidenced in your painting? How did your use of line in this painting differ from your use of line in earlier paintings?

Interpret. Does your painting give the impression that it was done rapidly? Does this give it a more relaxed, informal appearance?

Judge. Are you pleased with the results of this painting style? Compare your work with that of Ingres and Delacroix. Which artist's work more closely resembles your own? What theory or theories of art seem most appropriate to use when judging your painting?

490

ASSESSMENT

Extension Activity. After students have examined their still life watercolors, ask them to complete a series of quick watercolor studies of a figure in action, using student models in action poses. Instruct students to paint the figure in the same way they painted their still-life objects—starting in the center and working outward to the edges. However, in this case, they will *not* add contour lines. Instead, the blurred edges of the figures will be retained as a way of accenting movement. When they have completed these studies, let students meet in groups to examine and discuss all their watercolor projects.

Reviewing the Facts

Lesson One

1. What characterized the Neoclassic style?
2. Refer to Vigée-Lebrun's painting of *Madame de la Châtre* (Figure 21.4, page 469). The angle of the subject's arm is repeated somewhere else in the picture. Where?
3. Which element of art did Ingres believe was most important in a painting?

Lesson Two

4. Which element of art did Delacroix believe was most important in a painting?
5. What were Realist artists such as Courbet attempting to do that is reminiscent of Hugo van der Goes's break with the tradition of his time?
6. Name the artist who painted *The Horse Fair*, and tell what was unusual about this particular artist's choice of subject matter.

Lesson Three

7. Why did Monet make many different paintings of the same subject?
8. At the end of the nineteenth century, who was the most important sculptor? What did his technique have in common with Impressionist painters?

Thinking Critically

1. **COMPARE AND CONTRAST.** Refer to Jacques-Louis David's *The Death of Marat* (Figure 21.2, page 467) and to the Roman copy of the *Dying Gaul* (Figure 8.21, page 184). Discuss the aesthetic qualities that seem most important to each artist. Then identify similarities and differences between the two works.

2. **EXTEND.** Imagine that you are a well-known television reporter noted for your probing interviews of famous people. Select an artist discussed in this chapter, and prepare a list of questions that you might ask him or her during an interview. Ask another student to play the role of the artist. In class, conduct your "interview."

 Use the *Performing Arts Handbook*, page 576 to learn about music, dance, and theatre from many diverse cultures and times.

CAREERS IN Art Read about an art career as a photographer in the *Careers in Art Handbook*, page 606.

*inter*NET
CONNECTION Visit Glencoe Art Online at *www.glencoe.com/sec/art*. Explore sites that showcase nineteenth-century art and artists and complete an interactive project.

Technology Project

Nineteenth-Century Styles

As the established pattern of training artists through apprenticeship began to give way to the nineteenth-century schools of art called academies, artists began to form loose groups that sought to determine the nature, function, and value of art. The academies sponsored exhibitions, called Salons, which encouraged artists to compete for recognition. In addition to these developments, many scientific discoveries in photography and the scientific study of color had profound effects on the artists of the period. The major styles of Neoclassicism, Romanticism, Realism, and Impressionism are the result.

1. Using art criticism steps as your guide, study the different styles of the works of art that are included in your text. Using art history steps, analyze and interpret the works of art to determine the goals of the artists who created these works. Using online resources, CD-ROMs, or laser discs, investigate other examples of these styles.

2. If you were an artist living and working during this period which style would you adopt? Are you a Neoclassicist, a Realist, a Romantic, or an Impressionist? Be ready to defend your choice.

3. Using computer resources, create a multimedia presentation, performance piece, or tutorial page that uses art criticism and art history operations to assess the differences between these styles. You might also investigate these styles in other art forms such as literature and music.

491

CHAPTER 21
REVIEW ANSWERS

Reviewing the Facts

1. Neoclassic style was characterized by balanced compositions, flowing contour lines, and noble gestures and expressions.
2. The angle of the arm is repeated in the folds of the skirt at the bottom of the painting.
3. Ingres believed the element of line was the most important.
4. Delacroix believed color was the most important element in a painting.
5. Realists painted familiar scenes or trivial events as they really looked.
6. Rosa Bonheur. Animal paintings were not customarily done by women.
7. He was trying to capture the effects of changes in the lighting.
8. Rodin. He added bits of wax or clay to the surface of his pieces, just as painters added dots and dashes of paint to create their pictures.

Thinking Critically

1. Like *Dying Gaul*, David's painting makes a strong statement in an effort to stir the viewer's emotions; both artists seem intent, moreover, in portraying a starkly realistic scene. The key difference between the two works is that David's is an "act of propaganda," whitewashing Marat's fanatical support of violence and terror during the French Revolution.
2. Approaches, which will vary, should reveal a grasp of the content of the chapter.

Teaching the Technology Project

Ask students to select two artworks that they consider representative of each of the period's four styles—Neoclassicism, Romanticism, Realism, and Impressionism. For each style, have students select one work from the text and another from an online resource. Students should use these examples in their explanation of their own style preference.

 Assign the feature in the *Performing Arts Handbook*, page 590.

CAREERS IN ART If time permits, have interested students investigate the career information in the *Careers in Art Handbook*, page 606.

*inter*NET Have students go online and learn more
CONNECTION about artists on preselected Web sites with the Internet activity for this chapter.

Art of the Later Nineteenth Century

LESSON ONE Europe in the Late Nineteenth Century ....
(pages 494–500)

Classroom Resources

📁 Enrichment Activity 41, 42
📁 Reproducible Lesson Plan 51
📁 Reteaching Activity 51
📁 Study Guide 51

Features

LOOKING Closely ↓
(page 495, 499)

LESSON TWO America in the Late Nineteenth Century ....
(pages 501–510)

Classroom Resources

📁 Appreciating Cultural Diversity 32
📁 Art and Humanities 38
📁 Cooperative Learning 32
📁 Enrichment Activity 43
📁 Reproducible Lesson Plan 52
📁 Reteaching Activity 52
📁 Study Guide 52

Features

Time & Place CONNECTIONS
(page 503)

Storytelling in *Art*
Jonah
(page 505)

END OF CHAPTER
(pages 511–513)

Studio **LESSONS**
- Painting Emphasizing Aesthetic Qualities *(page 511)*
- Tempera Batik in the Style of Gauguin *(page 512)*

ADDITIONAL CHAPTER RESOURCES

Activities

- 📁 Application 22
- 📁 Advanced Studio Activity 22
- 🖱 Chapter 22 Internet Activity
- 📁 Studio Activity 28

Fine Art Resources

🎨 **Transparency**

Art in Focus Transparency 28

Edward Mitchell Bannister. *Approaching Storm.*

🖼 **Fine Art Print**

Focus on World Art Print 22

Georges Seurat. *A Sunday on La Grande Jatte*

Assessment

- 📁 Chapter 22 Test
- 📁 Performance Assessment

Multimedia Resources

- 🎭 Artsource® Performing Arts Package
- 💿 National Gallery Laser Disc
- 💿 National Museum of Women in the Arts CD-ROM
- 📼 Arts & Entertainment Videos

NATIONAL STANDARDS FOR ARTS EDUCATION

The National Standards for Arts Education provide guidelines for grade-appropriate competency in the visual arts. The Content Standards for grades 9–12 are:

1. Understanding and applying media, techniques, and processes.
2. Using knowledge of structures and functions.
3. Choosing and evaluating a range of subject matter, symbols, and ideas.
4. Understanding the visual arts in relation to history and cultures.
5. Reflecting upon and assessing the characteristics and merits of their work and the work of others.
6. Making connections between visual arts and other disciplines.

Listed below are the National Standards for the Visual Arts addressed in this chapter. For a breakdown of the categories listed under each content standard, refer to the *Reproducible Lesson Plans* booklet in the TCR.

1. (a, b) **2.** (a, b) **3.** (a) **4.** (a, c) **5.** (a, b) **6.** (a, b)

🕐 **Out of Time?** If time does not permit teaching this chapter in its entirety, you may wish to preview the artwork and captions with students. Scan the heads in each lesson with students. Discuss the Looking Closely features and examine Storytelling in Art on page 505.

HANDBOOK MATERIAL

AMAN International Folk Ensemble *(page 591)*

CAREERS IN Art

Medical Illustrator *(page 607)*

Beyond the Classroom

Guest speakers can provide an important dimension to the students' experience in the classroom. Guest speakers can come from a variety of art-related areas and discuss a wide range of topics. Resources for local or community speakers can be located by visiting our Web site at *www.glencoe.com/sec/art.*

Art of the Later Nineteenth Century

INTRODUCE

Chapter Overview

CHAPTER 22 introduces students to trends in Western art of the late nineteenth century.

Lesson One treats the new styles of painting that evolved from Impressionism.

Lesson Two discusses American artists whose work incorporated aspects of Neoclassicism, Romanticism, and Realism.

Studio Lessons include painting emphasizing aesthetic qualities and a tempera batik in the style of Gauguin.

Art & Science

Have students examine and discuss the artwork that opens this chapter. Ask: Do you think this work represents what the artist saw or what he felt? Then have students discuss the possible explanation of the appearance of the sky in van Gogh's painting. Have interested students gather additional information about what the artist might actually have seen—and what his state of mind might have been—in 1889.

National Standards

This chapter addresses the following National Standards for the Arts.

1. (a,b)	4. (a,c)
2. (a,b)	5. (a,b)
3. (a)	6. (a,b)

492

Art of the Later Nineteenth Century

Art & Science ■ **FIGURE 22.1** The sky in this painting appears fantastic and beyond the limits of visual reality. Some have even claimed that it reflects the Milky Way and constellations shining in 1889 over the valley of the Rhone River in France, where it was painted. Van Gogh experienced harsh weather conditions while living there. He depicted the hard blue of the sky, the bright sun, and the *mistral*—the cold, violent wind that blows down the valley of the Rhone to the Mediterranean.

Vincent van Gogh. *The Starry Night.* 1889. Oil on canvas. 73.7 × 92.1 cm (29 × 36¼″). The Museum of Modern Art, New York, New York. Acquired through the Lillie P. Bliss Bequest.

492

During the last two decades of the nineteenth century,
some artists who had been associated with
Impressionism began to find fault with it.
They felt that this style sacrificed too much by trying
to capture the momentary effects of sunlight on forms and colors.
Creative individuals began to search for ways to set
aside what they saw as limitations on their art.
Writers in France, America, and England
explored new genres. Composers experimented with
unusual scales and harmonies.

YOUR Portfolio

Bring to class a magazine picture or photo of an animal that was a part of your childhood experience. Using pencils and working in your sketchbooks, sketch an animal. You might continue to add other animals, people, or a landscape; or you can show the same animal in different poses. Make the drawings fanciful and spontaneous. Repeat the drawing on another piece of paper, this time using a felt marker to outline the animal that is the center of interest. With pastels or chalk, color the figures, creating a sharp contrast between the primary figure and the secondary ones. Keep drawings and your final work in your portfolio.

Focus ON THE ARTS

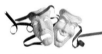

LITERATURE
Playwrights and novelists moved away from romantic subjects to concentrate on realism. American short-story writer Edgar Allan Poe, and British author Arthur Conan Doyle, perfected the detective story, while French writer Jules Verne wrote science fiction.

THEATRE
Thomas Alva Edison perfected electric stage lighting, expanding possibilities for scenic design and lighting in drama, opera, and dance. Up to this time, gas lamps, candles, or unreliable electric arcs had been used to light the stage.

MUSIC
In Europe, Franz Liszt began experimenting with abstract music. Giuseppe Verdi and Richard Wagner produced grand operas. African Americans revolutionized popular music worldwide with the evolution of blues and ragtime.

493

Introducing the Chapter

Have groups of students browse through the chapter and list any Impressionist ideals they see reflected in the art. Explain that they will now learn about differences between the work of the Impressionists and the work of late nineteenth-century artists.

A R T
S O U
R C E **Music/Dance.** While studying this chapter, use *Performing Arts Handbook* page 591 to help students learn how the AMAN International Folk Ensemble preserves cultural dance and musical forms introduced to America during the late nineteenth century.

Focus ON THE ARTS

Divide the class into groups of "theater managers." Have each group brainstorm and report on how electric lights and machinery will change the way they run their theaters. Some possible ideas: More realistic lighting is now possible to represent all times of day and night. Spectacular special effects can be created. Theaters can be larger and stages can be deeper because audiences can see more clearly. Machines can make stunningly rapid scene changes, lifting scenery up and down, moving stage sets in and out.

DEVELOPING A PORTFOLIO

Personal Style. Encourage students to observe the evolution of individual pieces of art as a way of identifying their developing style. Remind them that creative people take risks and see failure as an indication of where the creative process needs modification. For example, if they are not happy with a sketch, instead of discarding it, have them make notes about their displeasure with the design or make corrections without erasing the old. Their increased awareness of the process of artistic creation will help them recognize their choices about style. During private conferences, encourage students to articulate progress in the style of their work.

Europe in the Late Nineteenth Century

Focus

Lesson Objectives

After studying this lesson, students will be able to:

■ Understand how Impressionism influenced Post-Impressionist artists.

■ Describe the paintings of Paul Cézanne.

■ Explain how Cézanne, van Gogh, and Gauguin influenced the artists who followed them.

Building Vocabulary

Have students brainstorm words that begin with the prefix *post-* (e.g., *postscript*, *postpone*). Then ask them to define the word part (i.e., "after or later"). Ask: What features would you expect to find in an art movement called *Post-Impressionism?*

Motivator

Bring to class a carpenter's plane and a section of a wooden two-by-four plank. Let students use the carpenter's tool to shave slivers from the board and feel how it flattens and smooths the board's surface. (See *Teacher Notes,* page 496.) Discuss the term *plane* and its reference to flat surfaces in a picture. Point out that the idea of picture plane was vital to the work of at least one of the artists students will meet in this lesson.

Europe in the Late Nineteenth Century

Vocabulary
■ Post-Impressionism
■ plane

Artists to Meet
■ Paul Cézanne
■ Vincent van Gogh
■ Paul Gauguin

Discover
After completing this lesson, you will be able to:
■ Define and explain Post-Impressionism.
■ Describe the painting styles of Paul Cézanne, Vincent van Gogh, and Paul Gauguin.
■ Discuss how the major Post-Impressionist painters influenced artists who followed them.

*A*rtists painting during the 1880s and 1890s wanted to continue painting the contemporary world but hoped to overcome some of the problems they saw in the Impressionist style. They felt that art should present a more personal, expressive view of life rather than focusing on the changing effects of light on objects. Although their works continued to exhibit an Impressionistic regard for light and its effect on color, they also included a new concern for more intense color and a return to stronger contours and more solid forms.

Post-Impressionism

The most important artists who searched for solutions to the problems of Impressionism were Paul Cézanne, Vincent van Gogh, and Paul Gauguin. Each of these artists wanted to discover what was wrong or missing in Impressionism. Their search for an answer led them in different directions and had an important effect on the course of art history.

These painters belong to a group of artists who are now called *Post-Impressionists.* **Post-Impressionism** was *the French art movement that immediately followed Impressionism.* The artists who were a part of this movement showed a greater concern for structure and form than did the Impressionist artists.

Paul Cézanne (1839–1906)

Early in his career, Paul Cézanne (say-**zahn**) was associated with the Impressionists. His studies of the great artists in the Louvre led him to believe, however, that Impressionist paintings lacked form, solidity, and structure. He spent the rest of his life trying to restore those qualities to his paintings. His goal was to make Impressionism "something solid, like the art of museums."

The style that Cézanne worked so hard to perfect was not realistic. He was not concerned with reproducing exactly the shapes, colors, lines, and textures found in nature. He felt free to discard anything he considered unnecessary. Further, he carefully arranged the objects in his works rather than painting them as he found them.

Cézanne's Technique

Cézanne's effort to change this representational style began with experiments in still-life painting, followed by pictures with figures and landscapes. He often painted the same object over and over again until he was completely satisfied. In time, his patience paid off; he arrived at a technique in which he applied his colors in small, flat patches.

494

LESSON ONE RESOURCES

Teacher's Classroom Resources

📁 Enrichment Activities 41, 42

📁 Reproducible Lesson Plan 51

📁 Reteaching Activity 51

📁 Study Guide 51

These patches of color were placed side by side so that each one represented a separate **plane,** or *surface.* When he painted a round object such as an apple, these planes were joined together to follow the curved form of the object.

Each of these planes had a slightly different color as well, because Cézanne knew that colors change as they come forward or go back in space. So he used cool colors that seemed to go back in space and warm colors that seemed to advance in space to make his painted objects look more three-dimensional.

With this technique, Cézanne was able to create the solid-looking forms that he felt were missing in Impressionist pictures.

Cézanne's Still Lifes
■ **FIGURE 22.2**

Cézanne developed his painting technique with still-life pictures (Figure 22.2). Unlike paintings of people in which the subject moved, still-life painting gave him the chance to study and paint objects over long periods of time.

■ **FIGURE 22.2**

Paul Cézanne. *Still Life with Peppermint Bottle.* c. 1894. Oil on canvas. 65.9 × 82.1 cm (26 × 32³⁄₈″). National Gallery of Art, Washington, D.C. Board of Trustees, Chester Dale Collection.

LOOKING Closely

USE OF THE ELEMENTS AND PRINCIPLES

Notice how every object in this still life has been carefully positioned. All the pieces fit neatly together to form a unified design.
- **Value.** The dark vertical and horizontal bands on the wall hold the picture together and direct your eye to the most important objects in the center of the composition. To balance the strong horizontal lines at the right, Cézanne has strengthened the contour of the white napkin at the left by placing a shadow behind it.
- **Line.** Because the firm line on the wall to the right of the glass jug might compete with the jug, he blends it out. Then he adds a dark blue line to strengthen the right side of the jug.
- **Variety.** To add interest and variety, Cézanne contrasts the straight lines with the curved lines of the drapery, fruit, and bottles.
- **Color.** The blue-green hue used throughout helps to pull the parts together into an organized whole. Cézanne often chose blue tones to show depth. The pieces of fruit in the middle seem to float forward toward you and away from the blue-green cloth and wall. This illusion is due to the warm reds and yellows used to paint the fruit. These hues are complements to the cool blue-green.

TEACH
Introducing the Lesson

Have students turn to Figure 22.4 (page 496). Suggest students hold the text a few inches from their faces, and ask them to explain what they see (i.e., more or less rectangular blotches of color). Now instruct them to hold the text at a comfortable distance and repeat the activity. After noting that, as with works of the Impressionists, this one uses the eye's capacity to resolve bits of color into a unified whole, point out that there are monumental differences between this painting and one by, for instance, Monet.

LOOKING Closely

Have students examine *Still Life with Peppermint Bottle,* Figure 22.2. let volunteers describe the careful positioning of the items and the neat manner in which the pieces fit together. Based on their own observations, students should discuss their ideas about Cézanne's use of the elements and principles of art. Then have them read and discuss the feature.

Art History

Appoint three students to act as curators at a museum that is considering the acquisition of one of Cézanne artworks illustrated in this lesson. Each curator should select one of the artworks and explain why it would be a valuable addition to the museum's collection. The rest of the students should act as the board of trustees, carefully consider the curators' statements and then take a vote on which piece the museum will purchase.

Aesthetics

Have pairs of students role-play a scene in which a contemporary art dealer attempts to convince a collector to purchase the painting in Figure 22.2. Reveal that the collector is the sort who wants to enjoy his or her purchases (not just store them away until they increase in resale value) and is not sure that still-life paintings are relevant to modern life or that *Still Life with Peppermint Bottle* would be interesting to view on a daily basis. Can the dealer persuade this collector to buy a Cézanne still life?

Cross Curriculum

LANGUAGE ARTS. Tell students that art historians are still unsure about why Cézanne felt compelled to paint Mont Sainte-Victoire so many times. Have students fabricate a historical document that clears up this mystery for art historians. Encourage students to be inventive in their explanations of the power that this mountain held for Cézanne. Possible types of art-historical documents include a diary entry, a letter from Cézanne to a friend, a long-lost article that includes an interview with Cézanne, and journal notes that Cézanne kept on the progress of his paintings.

Studio Skills

Have students use tempera paints and sheets of paper measuring 9 × 12 inches to create their own Cézanne-style landscapes or still lifes. You may set up a simple still life in the classroom, have students work from photographs of a landscape, or have students venture outdoors to complete this exercise. Begin by reviewing the features of Cézanne's style, emphasizing his use of flat patches of color to define planes.

Up close, everything in Cézanne's still life seems flat, because your eye is too near to see the relationships between the colored planes. When viewed from a distance, however, these relationships become clear, and the forms take on a solid, three-dimensional appearance.

Cézanne's still life does not look very realistic; the drapery fails to fall naturally over the edge of the table, and the opening at the top of the jug is too large. However, he was willing to sacrifice realism in order to achieve another goal. He wanted the apples to look solid and heavy and the napkin and tablecloth to appear as massive and monumental as mountains.

Cézanne's Landscapes
■ **FIGURES 22.3 and 22.4**

This same solid, massive quality is found in Cézanne's landscapes. Notice that the rock in the foreground of his *Pines and Rocks*

■ **FIGURE 22.3** Cézanne's love for painting caused him to continue painting in a rainstorm. Finally he collapsed and was taken home. A few days later he died of pneumonia. **How did the artist show form and solidity in this work?**

Paul Cézanne. *Pines and Rocks (Fontainebleau?).* 1896–99. Oil on canvas. 81.3 × 65.4 cm (32 × 25³/₄"). The Museum of Modern Art, New York, New York. Lillie P. Bliss Collection.

(Figure 22.3) looks heavy and solid. Small brush strokes have been used to suggest the form of this rock, giving it the weight and volume of a mountain. The foliage of the trees is painted as a heavy mass of greens and blue-greens. Like everything else in the work, the foliage is created with cubes of color.

The work has the appearance of a three-dimensional mosaic. Some cubes seem to tilt away from you, whereas others turn in a variety of other directions. They lead your eye in, out, and around the solid forms that make up the picture.

Cézanne did his best to ignore the critics who scorned or laughed at his work. Even the people in the little town where he lived considered him strange. What sort of artist would stand for long periods of time, staring at a little mountain? Further, when he finally put his brush to canvas, he sometimes made no more than a single stroke before returning to his study. Cézanne painted more than 60 versions of the little mountain known as Sainte-Victoire (Figure 22.4). In each, he used planes of color to build a solid form that is both monumental and durable. (See also Figure 1.17, page 20.)

■ **FIGURE 22.4** Cézanne, like Claude Monet, often painted the same subject over and over again. **How were the objectives of these two artists the same? How did they differ?**

Paul Cézanne. *Mont Sainte-Victoire.* 1902–06. Oil on canvas. 63.8 × 81.5 cm (25¹/₈ × 32¹/₈"). Nelson-Atkins Museum of Art, Kansas City, Missouri. Purchase: Nelson Trust.

Teacher Notes

Safety Tip. If, as suggested in the "Motivator" activity for the lesson, you have students use a carpenter's plane to reinforce the meaning of the term plane, you will need to enforce a few safety guidelines. Begin by clamping the two-by-four into place. Set the tool's blade for a very fine cut (i.e., one that produces light and feathery shavings) and keep students from tampering with the setting. Instruct students to plane along the grain of the wood, holding the front knob with the left hand and the rear grip with the right hand to control the action of the tool. Finally, as when using any sharp-bladed instrument in the classroom, have a well-stocked first-aid kit handy.

Vincent van Gogh (1853–1890)

The familiar story of Vincent van Gogh's (van **goh**) tragic life should not be allowed to turn attention away from his powerfully expressive paintings.

As a young man, this Dutch artist worked as a lay missionary in a poor Belgian coal-mining village, but he realized he was a failure at this vocation. He began to withdraw into himself and turned to the one thing that made life worth living for him: his art. He loved art; wherever he went he visited museums, and he drew and painted at every opportunity. His early pictures, painted in browns and other drab colors, showed peasants going about their daily routines.

When he was 33, van Gogh moved to Paris to be with his younger brother, Theo, an art dealer. Recognizing his brother's raw talent, Theo provided encouragement and an allowance so van Gogh could continue painting.

During this stay in Paris, van Gogh met Degas and the Impressionists. Their influence on him was immediate and dramatic. Soon his pictures began to blaze with color. He even adopted the Impressionists' technique of using small, short brushstrokes to apply his paint to canvas.

Self-Portrait
■ FIGURE 22.5

The influence of the Impressionists is seen clearly in a self-portrait van Gogh completed a year after his arrival in Paris (Figure 22.5). Observe how the dots and dashes of paint in the background create a whirling dark pool against which the flame-bright head stands out with a powerful force. Study this face closely. What does the artist tell you about himself? Notice that he turns his head away slightly to avoid eye contact. Perhaps this is a defensive move, the act of a person who wants to avoid hearing the kind of personal questions for which he has no answers.

Indeed, at this point in his life, Vincent van Gogh was asking himself difficult questions. Although he found the Impressionist style fascinating, he was beginning to wonder whether it allowed him enough freedom to express his inner feelings. Somehow he had to find a way to combine what he learned from the Impressionists with the raw power of his earlier works. His search continued after he left Paris and moved to the city of Arles in southern France.

■ FIGURE 22.5 This painting reveals that at this point in his life van Gogh was withdrawn and unsure of himself. **How does this painting show the influence of the Impressionists on van Gogh?**

Vincent van Gogh. *Self-Portrait.* 1886–87. Oil on artist's board mounted on cradled panel. 41 × 32.5 cm (16 × 12³⁄₄"). The Art Institute of Chicago, Chicago, Illinois. Joseph Winterbotham Collection, 1954.326.

Aesthetics

Direct students' attention to van Gogh's *Self-Portrait* in Figure 22.5. Ask: What is the mood of the work? How does the artist convey this mood? How concerned was van Gogh with portraying a realistic image? How can you tell?

Cross Curriculum

HUMANITIES. Ask a volunteer to prepare a report on van Gogh's early and not entirely successful career in the ministry. The presentation should include a description of how the poor reacted to van Gogh's intense style of preaching and information on why van Gogh gave up the ministry and turned to a career in art.

Art History

Working as a group, students are to consider the three paintings in this lesson by van Gogh (Figures 22.1, 22.5, and 22.6). After allowing time for discussion and reflection, have students complete a chart indicating differences in style, subject matter, and artistic purpose that the works, as a whole, reflect. Ask: Which work is van Gogh's most mature?

𝒯eacher 𝒩otes

Building Self-Esteem. To help students learn to accept and even benefit from positive criticism directed toward their work, reveal that no less an artistic luminary than Paul Cézanne suffered from the lifelong conviction that he and his art were unfairly criticized. In his later years, he stated that his own generation (i.e., the Impressionists) had deserted him. He resented the fact that most of his former fellow Impressionists had been accepted in the Salon by the early 1880s. He was often argumentative, especially when the subject of a conversation was his work. Because of such behavior, Cézanne has been labeled a misanthrope, even though he was gentle and patient with young artists who sought his advice.

Art History

Explain to students that many nineteenth-century artists, including van Gogh, painted nature not so much to illustrate it, but as a kind of metaphor for intense human emotions. An artist of the era might, for example, paint a drooping tree to suggest the melancholy mood of a person sitting beneath it. Show students several examples of works that exemplify this approach to painting. Some possibilities are Francis Danby's *Disappointed Love* (1821) and Thomas Cole's *Landscape with Dead Tree* (c. 1827–28). Then have students examine the painting by van Gogh in Figure 22.1 (page 492) and discuss how the artist painted the cypress trees, the stars, and the moon to convey human emotion.

Art History

Have pairs of students locate and give a dramatic reading of passages from letters that Vincent van Gogh exchanged with his brother, Theo.

Studio Skills

Discuss with students the technique of *impasto*—the application of paint in thick, buttery layers—practiced by van Gogh in his later works. Have students create their own impasto paintings of a scene in the manner of van Gogh. First have students sketch their ideas on scratch paper. Then have them use acrylic paints in tubes and small pre-stretched canvas panels measuring about 5 × 7 inches, to create the final version. Students may use a combination of brushes and fingers and may even squeeze the paint tube directly onto the canvas to achieve a rich impasto surface. Have students compare their finished works.

Bedroom at Arles

■ **FIGURE 22.6**

In Arles, van Gogh hoped to find the brilliant colors he saw in Japanese woodblock prints. These prints, like Impressionism, had a deep impact on his painting style. He began to use large, flat areas of color, and he tilted his compositions to create a strange new kind of perspective. In one of these works, van Gogh combines features found in Japanese prints with his own desire to express his most personal feelings. At first, you might see just a picture of the sparsely furnished room van Gogh rented in Arles (Figure 22.6). Look more closely and you will discover that the artist uses the work to express his emotions as well. Why are two pillows on the bed? What need is there for *two* chairs? Why are the pictures arranged in pairs on the walls? All these clues testify to van Gogh's loneliness and his desire for companionship.

Van Gogh eventually realized that the Impressionist painting technique did not suit his restless and excitable personality. He developed his own style, marked by bright colors, twisting lines, bold brushstrokes, and a thick application of paint. He began to paint fields bathed in sunlight, and trees and flowers that twisted and turned as if they were alive. In his eagerness to capture these dazzling colors and spiraling forms in his pictures, he squeezed the paint from tubes directly onto his canvas. Then he used his brush and even his fingers to spread the paint with curving strokes.

During this period, the last two years of his life, van Gogh painted his best works—portraits, landscapes, interiors, and night scenes, including *The Starry Night*. (See Figure 22.1, page 492.) You can see how van Gogh used quick slashes of paint to create the dark cypress trees that twist upward like the flame from a candle. Overhead the sky is alive with bursting stars that seem to be hurtled about by violent gusts of wind sweeping across the sky. Short, choppy brushstrokes are combined with sweeping, swirling strokes, which gives a rich texture to the painting's surface.

Unlike Cézanne, van Gogh did not try to think his way through the painting process. He painted what he felt. Here he felt and responded to the violent energy and creative force of nature.

A Troubled Life

Van Gogh's personality was unstable, and he suffered from epileptic seizures during the last two years of his life. Informed that there was no cure for his ailment, he grew more and more depressed. Finally, on a July evening in 1890, in a wheat field where he had been painting, van Gogh shot himself; he died two days later. Theo, his faithful brother, was so heartbroken that he died six months after the artist did.

Although van Gogh's art was not popular during his lifetime, it has served as an inspiration for many artists who followed. Today the works of this lonely, troubled man are among the most popular and most acclaimed in the history of painting.

■ **FIGURE 22.6** Notice van Gogh's use of large, flat areas of bright color and a strange new perspective in this work. **What details in this work express the artist's emotions?**

Vincent van Gogh. *Bedroom at Arles.* 1888. Oil on canvas. 73.6 × 92.3 cm (29 × 36″). The Art Institute of Chicago, Chicago, Illinois. Helen Birch Bartlett Memorial Collection, 1926.417.

498 **Unit Seven** *Art of the Modern Era*

More About... **Vincent van Gogh.** *The Starry Night* (Figure 22.1, page 492) may reflect van Gogh's optimistic feelings about death. The artist had written of "a terrible need of religion" that compelled him "to go out at night to paint the stars." One art historian has suggested that the work is based on *Revelations* 7:1-4, while another contends that van Gogh was inspired by *Genesis* 37:9-11. In both biblical tracts, a star-filled sky is the setting for other-worldly happenings. The sum of this work's references to death, faith, and the infinity of the cosmos is a statement about the limits of earthly life and the eternal richness of the hereafter.

LOOKING Closely

LOOKING Closely

USE OF THE ELEMENTS OF ART

Gauguin was more interested in creating a decorative pattern than a picture that looked real.

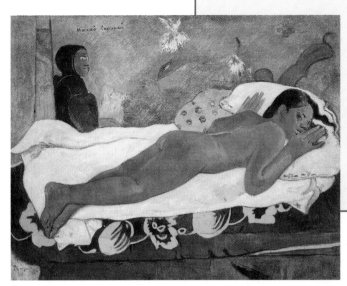

- **Color.** Flat areas of bright colors are combined with forms that look round and solid.
- **Shape.** Notice how the shapes that surround the girl are arranged in a relatively flat pattern, while the body of the girl looks three-dimensional.
- **Light.** Gauguin felt that artists should be free to use light and shadow when and where they wanted, but that they should never feel bound to do so.

■ **FIGURE 22.7** Paul Gauguin. *Spirit of the Dead Watching.* 1892. Oil on burlap mounted on canvas. 72.4 × 92.4 cm (28¹/₂ × 36³/₈″). Albright-Knox Art Gallery, Buffalo, New York. A. Conger Goodyear Collection, 1965.

Paul Gauguin (1848–1903)

Like Cézanne and van Gogh, Paul Gauguin (goh-**gan**) passed through an Impressionistic period before moving in another direction. He was a successful businessman who began painting as a hobby. Under the influence of some of the Impressionists, he exhibited with them. Then, at the age of 35, he left his well-paying job and turned to painting as a career. His paintings did not sell, and he and his family were reduced to poverty. Still, Gauguin never lost heart.

Throughout his career, Gauguin moved from one location to another, searching for an earthly paradise with exotic settings that he could paint. His quest took him to the South Seas, where he lived with the natives and shared their way of life.

Spirit of the Dead Watching
■ **FIGURE 22.7**

In Tahiti, Gauguin painted a haunting picture entitled *Spirit of the Dead Watching*

(Figure 22.7). In a letter to his wife, the artist explained that he had painted a young girl lying on a bed, frightened by the spirit of a dead woman appearing behind her.

Gauguin's pictures started with the exotic subject matter he searched for in his travels. As he painted, however, he allowed his imagination to take over. "I shut my eyes in order to see," he said. What he saw were crimson rocks, gold trees, and violet hills.

Gauguin's novel ideas about color are demonstrated in another picture he did in Tahiti entitled *Fatata te Miti* (Figure 22.8, page 500). This title means "by the sea" in the Maori language. Beyond a huge twisted tree root, two young women wade out into the blue-green sea for a swim. A fisherman with spear in hand stalks his quarry. Flat areas of bright colors give the picture the look of a medieval stained-glass window.

Except for the figures, the forms are flattened into planes of color that overlap to lead you into the work. Gauguin is not interested

Chapter 22 *Art of the Later Nineteenth Century* **499**

Art History

Have students work in small groups to develop a conversation among Cézanne, van Gogh, and Gauguin. Have students pretend that the three artists are taking a trip together to paint. Ask: Can the artists agree on where to go? Would they get along? If you wish, ask some students to research the actual friendship between van Gogh and Gauguin and see what they thought of each other and one another's art.

Study Guide

Distribute *Study Guide* 51 in the TCR. Assist students in reviewing key concepts. 📁

Studio Activities

Assign *Enrichment* 41, "Figure Study in Motion," in the TCR. 📁

Art and Humanities

Explain to students that Cézanne was not the only artist to have spent many years making pictures of the same landscape feature. As evidence, display prints from Japanese printmaker Katsushika Hokusai's series of prints titled *Thirty-six Views of Mount Fuji.* Invite teams of students to research the importance of Mount Fuji to the Japanese people.

LOOKING Closely

Let students meet in groups to examine and discuss *Spirit of the Dead Watching*, Figure 22.7. Have group members share their own ideas about Gauguin's use of the elements of art and about his interest in creating a decorative pattern. Then have group members read and discuss the information about the elements of art in the feature.

𝒯eacher 𝒩otes

Developing Perceptual Skills. Review the reproductions of Gauguin's paintings, emphasizing his ability to transform three-dimensional objects into relatively flat, decorative patterns. Then ask students to keep simple sketchbooks in their journals. The sketchbooks should include two parts. First, students should use watercolor markers to practice rendering a wide variety of objects as flat patterns. Second, students should observe as many two-dimensional patterns as they can find in their daily life, such as textile and packaging designs, and copy them into their journals. Invite students to share their sketches with the class and discuss the many decorative patterns they found.

ASSESS

Checking Comprehension

Have students respond to the lesson review questions. Answers are given in the box below.

Reteaching

➤ Assign *Reteaching* 51, found in the TCR. Have students complete the activity and review their responses. 📁

➤ Show students reproductions of paintings by Cézanne, van Gogh, Gauguin, Cassatt, and Degas, taking care to exclude any works students have already studied. Then have students try to identify which are Impressionist paintings and which are Post-Impressionist.

Enrichment

Assign *Enrichment* 42, "Comparing Landscape Paintings," in the TCR. Students are called upon to compare landscape paintings from different periods in order to discover the different interests and approaches of artists. 📁

Extension

Have students locate a copy of *Noa Noa,* the journal that Gauguin kept while he lived in the South Seas, and select passages for a dramatic reading. Afterward, conduct a class forum on what the journal passages reveal about the artist and his goals.

CLOSE

Ask students to write a paragraph stating which artist profiled in this lesson they would have wanted to be apprenticed to as an aspiring artist in the late nineteenth century.

in creating the illusion of real space here. He is more concerned with combining flat, colorful shapes and curving contour lines to produce a rich, decorative pattern.

Gauguin always believed he would be a great artist, and he was right. His contribution to the history of art is unquestioned. He succeeded in freeing artists from the idea of copying nature. After Gauguin, artists no longer hesitated about using a bright red color to paint a tree that was touched only with red or

■ **FIGURE 22.8** Gauguin selected colors to make his paintings visually exciting rather than realistic. **How is this painting similar to a medieval stained-glass window?**

Paul Gauguin. *Fatata te Miti (By the Sea).* 1892. Oil on canvas. 67.9 × 91.5 cm (26³/₄ × 36″). National Gallery of Art, Washington, D.C. Board of Trustees, Chester Dale Collection.

to change the curve of a branch or a shoulder to the point of exaggeration.

Influence of the Post-Impressionists

Cézanne, van Gogh, and Gauguin saw the world in different ways and developed their own methods to show others what they saw.

Cézanne sought weight and solidity in his carefully composed still lifes, landscapes, and portraits. He used planes of warm and cool colors that advance and recede to model his forms, creating a solid, enduring world with his brush.

Van Gogh used vibrating colors, distortion, and vigorous brushstrokes to show a world throbbing with movement and energy.

Gauguin took the shapes, colors, and lines he found in nature and changed them into flat, simplified shapes, broad areas of bright colors, and graceful lines. Then he arranged these elements to make a decorative pattern on his canvas.

Each of these three artists experienced loneliness, frustration, and even ridicule, but their work had a tremendous influence on the artists of the twentieth century. Cézanne inspired Cubism. Van Gogh influenced the Fauves and the Expressionists. Gauguin showed the way to different groups of primitive artists and American Abstract Expressionists.

LESSON ONE REVIEW

Reviewing Art Facts

1. What was the name of the French art movement that immediately followed Impressionism?
2. What did Cézanne believe was lacking in Impressionistic paintings?
3. Describe van Gogh's later painting style and tell how it differed from the style of his early paintings.
4. What was Paul Gauguin searching for by moving from one location to another? Where did he paint *Spirit of the Dead Watching*?

➤ **Activity... *Studying an Artist in Depth***

Cézanne, van Gogh, and Gauguin, all Post-Impressionists, were driven to create their artworks by unique and individual circumstances. Cézanne carefully placed planes of color on canvas. Van Gogh expressed strong emotion in his images. Gauguin presented an exotic, perfect world through the use of color.

Study one of these three artists whose work speaks strongly to you. Work with others in your class who chose the same artist. Create a multimedia presentation about this artist and his works. Your presentation may be created using a computer, video, or traditional class presentation with visuals.

LESSON ONE REVIEW

Answers to Reviewing Art Facts

1. Post-Impressionism.
2. Form, solidity, and structure.
3. Early: He used dull colors. Later: He used bright colors, bold brushstrokes, and thick paint.
4. An earthly paradise with exotic settings; Tahiti.

Activity... *Studying an Artist in Depth*

Review with students the possible forms of presentation for this Activity. Then let students select the artist about whom they want to learn more, and help students form cooperative learning groups based on their choices. It may be useful to have more than one group researching the works of each artist, so that the groups are not too large.

America in the Late Nineteenth Century

Vocabulary
- philanthropy

Artists to Meet
- Winslow Homer
- Thomas Eakins
- Albert Pinkham Ryder
- Edward Mitchell Bannister
- Henry Tanner
- Edmonia Lewis

Discover

After completing this lesson, you will be able to:
- Identify two of the first Realists in American painting, and describe their styles.
- Describe the particular interests and style of Albert Pinkham Ryder.
- Discuss the contributions African-American artists made to the growth of American art.

*T*he nineteenth century was a time of great growth and change in the United States. There was growth westward, growth in trade and industry, growth in population, and growth in wealth. Although the Civil War stopped the rate of progress for a time, it continued with a new vigor after the war ended.

American scientists, inventors, and businesspeople provided new products such as the typewriter, sewing machine, and electric lamp. Meanwhile, immigrants from all over Europe brought their knowledge and skills to the New World.

Great fortunes were made. Wealthy entrepreneurs, including Carnegie, Rockefeller, and Morgan, funneled some of their riches into schools, colleges, and museums. This practice of sharing the wealth is known as **philanthropy,** or *an active effort to promote human welfare.* Interest in education also grew. The first state university was founded in 1855 in Michigan, and others quickly followed. By 1900, the United States had become a world leader.

Changes in American Art

Change and growth were also noted in American art. A great many works were produced by self-taught artists traveling from village to village. Other works were created by more sophisticated artists who studied in the art centers of Europe. Some chose to remain there, where they became part of European art movements. Others returned to the United States to develop art styles that were American in subject matter and technique.

Winslow Homer (1836–1910)

One of these American artists was Winslow Homer. As a child, Homer developed a love of the outdoors, which lasted throughout his lifetime and which he expressed in his paintings.

Homer's interest in art began while he was quite young. His family encouraged him to pursue this interest. When he was 19, he was accepted as an apprentice at a large printing firm. He soon tired of designing covers for song sheets and prints for framing, however, and decided to become a magazine illustrator.

For 17 years, Homer earned his living as an illustrator, chiefly for *Harper's Weekly* in New York. During the Civil War, *Harper's* sent him to the front lines, where he drew and painted scenes of army life.

After the war, Homer decided to strike out on his own as a painter. He painted the American scene: pictures of schoolrooms, croquet games, and husking bees—pictures that were popular with everyone but the critics. They felt his works were too sketchy and looked unfinished.

501

After studying this lesson, students will be able to:
- Recognize several late nineteenth-century American artists.
- Explain where Winslow Homer turned most often for ideas for his work.
- Identify the contributions made by African-American artists to the growth of American art.

Building Vocabulary

Ask volunteers to give their own informal definitions of the Vocabulary term, *philanthropy.* Have them analyze the word parts, referring to a dictionary if necessary. (The prefix *philo-* or *phil-* means "loving"; *anthropo-* means "human.")

Motivator

Provide an array of everyday objects, including items found in the classroom (e.g., a chalk eraser), and ask students to make drawings of the items. As students work, urge them to draw exactly what they see— nothing more and nothing less. When students have finished, allow them to share their drawings. Ask: What movement and period that you have studied do artworks such as these embody? Point out that students are about to learn about another group of artists whose "calling card" was realism.

LESSON TWO RESOURCES

Teacher's Classroom Resources

TEACH
Introducing the Lesson

Direct students' attention to Figures 22.9 and 22.10. Challenge students to find other paintings they have studied to which these works bear a stylistic resemblance. Perceptive observers will point to works of the Realists in Chapter 21. Explain that students will presently read about other trends in American art of the late nineteenth century that borrowed from and enlarged upon earlier styles.

Aesthetics

Have students note that Winslow Homer began his career as an illustrator and only later in his life turned to painting. Let students work in small groups to discuss whether Homer was an "artist" only during the period that he painted or whether his work as an illustrator demanded just as much of his artistic skills and sensibility as his painting did. Groups should begin by discussing the differences between commercial illustration and painting as a fine art. When students have concluded their discussion, have each group present its views to the class.

The Fog Warning
■ **FIGURE 22.9**

From 1883 until his death, Homer lived in Prout's Neck, Maine, where the ocean crashing against majestic cliffs inspired many of his great seascapes. Long regarded as one of the most skillful and powerful painters of the sea, Homer is seen at his best in works such as *The Fog Warning* (Figure 22.9).

In this painting, a lone fisherman rests the oars of his small dory and takes advantage of his position on the crest of a wave to get his bearings. He turns his head in the direction of a schooner on the horizon, although his eyes are locked on the fog bank beyond. The sea is very rough. Whitecaps are clearly visible, and the bow of the light dory is lifted high in the air, as the stern settles deep into a trough of waves.

Dramatic Use of Line

Different values separate the sea, sky, and fog. The horizontal contour lines of the oars, boat seats, horizon, and fog bank contrast with the diagonal axis lines of the dory and portions of the windblown fog.

Notice in particular how effectively Homer directs your attention to the right side of the picture. A diagonal line representing the crest of the wave on which the dory rests leads your eye in this direction. Furthermore, the curving axis line of the fish in the dory guides you to the same destination. There you discover the schooner and the advancing fog bank.

Homer has caught the exact moment when the fisherman recognizes his danger. Even the dory seems frozen at the top of a wave as the fisherman calculates whether or not he can reach the schooner before it is hidden by the windswept fog. You know that, in the next instant, he will begin rowing as he has never rowed before in a desperate race to beat the fog to the schooner. His survival depends on whether or not he can win that race. If he loses, he will be lost, alone, and at the mercy of the storm.

■ **FIGURE 22.9** The central figure in this painting is the fisherman, but the title of the work indicates the importance of the fog. **How are diagonal axis lines used to tie the boat and the fog together?**

Winslow Homer. *The Fog Warning*. 1885. Oil on canvas. 76.2 × 121.9 cm (30 × 48″). Courtesy of Museum of Fine Arts, Boston, Massachusetts. Otis Norcross Fund.

 ## Technology

National Gallery of Art Videodisc Use the following images as examples of more works by artists introduced in this lesson.

Winslow Homer
Breezing Up

Search Frame 2032

Thomas Eakins
The Biglin Brothers Racing

Search Frame 2022

Henry O. Tanner
The Seine
Search Frame 2056

Use Glencoe's *Correlation Bar Code Guide to the National Gallery of Art* to locate more artworks.

Right and Left
■ **FIGURE 22.10**

Homer's unique imagination and organizational skills are further shown in a painting finished a year before his death, *Right and Left* (Figure 22.10). The horizontal and diagonal lines of the waves and clouds provide a backdrop for two ducks. One is plunging into the sea while the other rises upward and is about to fly out of the picture. As the viewer, your vantage point is in the sky, near the two ducks. You are looking back at a hunter in a boat who has already shot the duck at the right and is, at this moment, firing at the second duck. Homer has placed you at the same height as the ducks, so you can look down at the stormy sea and the hunter.

■ **FIGURE 22.10** The falling duck on the right has already been shot; a white pin feather, dislodged by the blast, can be seen at the far left. Can you find the single, small spot of red in this picture? What does it represent?

Winslow Homer. *Right and Left.* 1909. Oil on canvas. 71.8 × 122.9 cm (28¹/₄ × 48³/₈"). National Gallery of Art, Washington, D.C. Board of Trustees, Gift of the Avalon Foundation.

Time & Place CONNECTIONS

Later Nineteenth Century
c. 1850–1900

RAILROAD. The first steam locomotive arrived in America in 1830 in Charleston, South Carolina. Passengers first traveled by rail on the Baltimore & Ohio Railway. In 1869, the first trans-contintental rail line was completed, linking the eastern and western states.

PHONOGRAPH. Thomas Edison's invention in 1877 used electricity to record sound vibrations. A tin foil sheet was wrapped around a cylinder on which the sound was recorded. Only limited sound waves and pitches could be recorded on this early device.

WOMEN'S DRESS. Frontier life in America required sturdy garments to be worn day after day. A simple wool or cotton dress could withstand many years of wear.

Activity
Venn Diagram Comparison. Use a Venn diagram to compare your life and times to life during this period in history. Consider dress, transportation, and sources of entertainment.

Art Criticism

Review the ways in which Eakins's art was influenced by his studies of Rembrandt. Then have students compare *The Gross Clinic* (Figure 22.11) with Rembrandt's *The Night Watch* (Figure 19.13, page 431), finding examples in each work showing how the artist uses light and dark values to create lifelike figures and to draw the viewer's attention to specific areas of the canvas.

Art History

Tell students that Eakins was indebted to Rembrandt not only for features of style but for subject matter. Have a volunteer find a reproduction of Eakins's painting *The Agnew Clinic* and Rembrandt's *Anatomy Lesson of Doctor Tulp* (1632), a group portrait in the guise of a demonstration of dissection. Compare how both Rembrandt's and Eakins's paintings emphasize the gravity of the procedure and the esteem in which the lead physician is held by other figures.

Critical Thinking

Have students who have performed dissections in a biology class describe the experience and discuss whether the activity would be good subject matter for a painting. Then have the class consider why the subject of surgery is no longer a popular theme in painting today.

Thomas Eakins (1844–1916)

Winslow Homer and Thomas Eakins (**ay**-kins) are considered to be among the first Realists in American painting. Both were firmly rooted to their time and place and drew on these roots for their work, but the subjects they chose differed. In contrast to Homer, Eakins was mainly interested in painting the people and scenes of his own Philadelphia setting.

Early in his career, Eakins studied in the Paris studios of a Neoclassic artist and was certainly influenced by the realism of Courbet. His most important teachers, however, were the seventeenth-century masters Velázquez, Hals, and the painter he called "the big artist," Rembrandt. From Rembrandt, Eakins learned to use light and dark values to make his figures look solid, round, and lifelike.

When he returned to the United States, Eakins found that Americans did not appreciate his

■ FIGURE 22.11 The cringing figure at the left is a relative of the patient required by law at that time to be present as a witness. **Point out the detail in this work that some viewers considered objectionably realistic. Why did the artist feel it was necessary to include this detail?**

Thomas Eakins. *The Gross Clinic.* 1875. Oil on canvas. 244 × 198 cm (96 × 78"). The Jefferson Medical College of Thomas Jefferson University, Philadelphia, Pennsylvania.

highly realistic style. They preferred sentimental scenes and romantic views of the American landscape. Many felt his portraits were too honest, too lifelike. Eakins insisted on painting only what he saw and would not consent to flattering his subjects. Even though it reduced his popular appeal, Eakins never varied his realistic style during a career that spanned 40 years.

The Gross Clinic
■ FIGURE 22.11

One of Eakins's best works and one of the great paintings of the era was *The Gross Clinic* (Figure 22.11). The famous surgeon, Dr. Gross, has paused for a moment during an operation to explain a certain procedure. Eakins draws attention to the head of the doctor by placing it at the tip of a pyramid formed by the foreground figures.

The artist's attention to detail and his portrayal of figures in space give this painting its startling realism. For some viewers, it was too real. They objected to the blood on the scalpel and hand of the surgeon.

Throughout his life, Eakins was fascinated by the study of the human body. He was a knowledgeable, enthusiastic student of anatomy by dissection and required his own students to dissect corpses to learn how to make their figures look more authentic. It was this knowledge that enabled Eakins to paint figures that looked as if every bone and muscle had been taken into account.

Albert Pinkham Ryder (1847–1917)

Eakins and Homer painted realistic scenes from everyday American life. Albert Pinkham Ryder, however, was inspired by the Bible, Chaucer, Shakespeare, and nineteenth-century romantic writers. Although Ryder visited Europe several times, he exhibited little interest in the works of other artists. He lived as a hermit, apart from the rest of the world, and looked within himself for inspiration.

In *Jonah* (Figure 22.12), Ryder shows the Old Testament figure in a sea made turbulent by a raging storm.

More About... **Thomas Eakins.** Eakins's fervent belief in the importance of anatomical study was a source of endless trouble for the artist. When he presented a nude male model to a women's art class, Eakins was fired for breach of propriety. An editorial criticized the artist as having "for a long time entertained and strongly inculcated the most 'advanced' views. . . . Teaching large classes of women as well as men, he holds that, both as to the living model in the drawing room and the dead subject in the anatomical lecture and dissecting room, Art knows no sex."

Storytelling in *Art*

*T*his painting by Albert Pinkham Ryder depicts a scene from the biblical story of Jonah and the whale. Artists often use their artworks to tell a story.

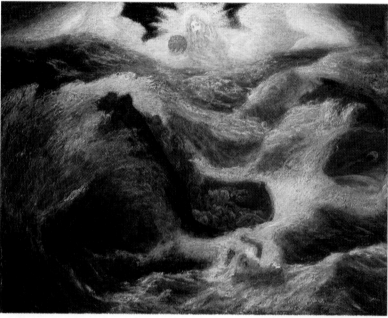

Art Criticism

Direct students' attention to the painting in Figure 22.13, page 506. Ask: What art elements are common to this work and the one in Figure 22.12, also by Ryder? In what other ways are the paintings related?

Studio Skills

Reinforce the observation that Ryder found inspiration in literature, especially in the works of Romantic writers. Provide the class with literary anthologies that include works of the British Romantic period. Then divide the class into groups, and have each group study a poem by a noted Romantic writer that contains rich visual imagery (e.g., William Blake's "The Tyger," Samuel Taylor Coleridge's "Kubla Khan"). After groups have familiarized themselves with both the theme and content of the poems, students are to work individually to create artworks in the manner of Ryder that express the mood of the poem. Allow time for students to share finished works.

■ **FIGURE 22.12**

Albert Pinkham Ryder. *Jonah.* c. 1885. Oil on canvas. 69.2 × 87.3 cm (27¼ × 34⅜″). National Museum of American Art, Smithsonian Institution, Washington, D.C. Gift of John Gellatly.

DETAIL: The whale

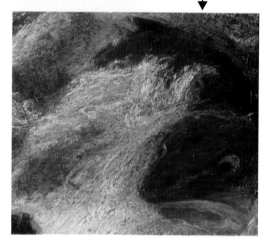

1

Jonah has been tossed from the frail boat by frightened crew members who hold him responsible for their misfortune. He flails about helplessly in the rough waters.

2

At the top of the picture, barely visible in a golden glow, God, Master of the Universe, looks on.

3 ➤

The whale, in whose stomach Jonah will spend three days, is fast approaching at the right. It is almost lost in the violent action of the water. Ryder's version of the whale may look strange to you. He had never seen the real thing, so he had to rely on his imagination when painting it.

Chapter 22 *Art of the Later Nineteenth Century* **505**

Storytelling in *Art*

Let students describe and discuss Ryder's *Jonah,* Figure 22.12. Then have them read and discuss the explanation of the story told in the painting. Ask: Why do you think artists often use their artworks to tell a story? What kinds of stories do you consider most appropriate for artworks? Why? How does an understanding of the story shown in *Jonah* affect your appreciation of the painting? As students examine Ryder's use of the elements of art in *Jonah,* ask: To what extent does color help create, or at least affect, the mood of the work? What other elements are used?

Art Criticism

Ask students to compare the two paintings by Ryder, *Jonah* (Figure 22.12, page 505) and *Flying Dutchman* (Figure 22.13). How is Ryder's use of the elements and principles of art similar in the two works? What are the most important differences between these two paintings?

Cross Curriculum

MUSIC. Have a volunteer determine the source of the title of Ryder's painting *Flying Dutchman* (i.e., the name was appropriated from an 1843 opera by Wagner), as well as the artist's reason for creating a work so named (i.e., he was a devotee of opera). You might wish to share the legend behind Wagner's work and then play a recording of the forceful overture while students view Ryder's painting. Discuss whether the painting in Figure 22.13 seems to capture the spirit of the music.

Emphasis on Color and Texture

Color and texture were as important to Ryder as the objects or events he painted. His small pictures were built up carefully over months and even years, until the forms were nearly three-dimensional. At one time these simple, massive forms had the rich color of precious stones. Now, because Ryder's paints were of poor quality or were applied improperly, the colors have faded.

There is more to Ryder's pictures than texture, form, and color. If you have seen the fury of a storm at sea, you will be excited by his pictures. Even if you have never seen or experienced a stormy sea, Ryder's paintings act as a springboard for your imagination. This would please Ryder, who relied on his own imagination for inspiration. In this way, he discovered a dream world where mysterious forests are bathed in an unearthly light and dark boats sail soundlessly on moonlit seas (Figure 22.13).

African-American Artists

African-American artists have contributed a great deal to the growth of art in the United States. In colonial times, many of these artists traveled from one town to the next, creating and selling their artworks.

One such artist, Joshua Johnston of Baltimore, was in demand among wealthy Maryland families who sought him out to paint their portraits. After his death, other artists were often given credit for pictures that were actually painted by Johnston. Such mistakes are now being corrected, and Johnston's place in history is being confirmed.

■ **FIGURE 22.13** Troubled with poor eyesight, Ryder remained indoors during the day and roamed the streets of New York City at night. In what ways does this picture seem more like a scene from a dream than an event from real life?

Albert Pinkham Ryder. *Flying Dutchman.* c. 1887. Oil on canvas. 36.1 × 43.8 cm (14¼ × 17¼"). National Museum of American Art, Smithsonian Institution, Washington, D.C.

CULTURAL DIVERSITY

Religious Images. Have students examine the painting *Jonah* (Figure 22.12, page 505) and note that it includes a representation of God holding a globe. Discuss what this detail suggests about the nature of God according to Ryder. Then ask students to research and locate images of deities from as many different cultures as possible—such as Hindu statues, Tibetan mandalas, Yoruban wood carvings, pre-Columbian metalwork, and Indonesian temple carvings. Some students may wish to research reasons why certain religious groups, such as Muslims and Jews, have, for the most part, discouraged the representation of divine figures. Set aside time for students to share their findings.

■ **FIGURE 22.14** Bannister captured a single moment in the workday of this newspaper seller. How did the artist communicate emotion in this work?

Edward Mitchell Bannister. *Newspaper Boy.* 1869. Oil on canvas. 76.6 × 63.7 cm (30¹/₈ × 25″). National Museum of American Art, Smithsonian Institution, Washington, D.C. Gift of Frederick Weingeroff.

Art History

Have students work in cooperative groups to learn more about the life of Edward Mitchell Bannister. Encourage group members to discuss how Bannister's experiences affected his art.

Cross Curriculum

SOCIAL STUDIES. Ask several volunteers to learn more about the Bannister Gallery at Rhode Island College; encourage them to gather information about current and recent exhibits there. Have these volunteers share what they have learned with the rest of the class.

Studio Skills

Guide students in examining Tanner's *The Banjo Lesson* (Figure 22.15, page 508), which illustrates an older person passing on his craft to a younger person. Then have students use charcoal pencil and sheets of white drawing paper to create original pictures of someone teaching music, sports, or any other subject to a younger person. The pictures can be purely imaginary or students can illustrate someone who personally has taught them an important skill. Invite students to share their drawings and explain them to the class.

Edward Mitchell Bannister (1828–1901)

Two years after the Civil War, African-American artist Edward Mitchell Bannister from Providence, Rhode Island, was angered by an article in a New York newspaper. The writer of the newspaper story claimed that African-Americans were especially talented in several arts, but not in painting or sculpture. Bannister later shattered that claim by becoming the first African-American painter to win a major award at an important national exhibition. When the judges learned that he was African-American, they considered withdrawing the award. The other artists in the show, however, insisted that Bannister receive the award he had earned.

Newspaper Boy
■ **FIGURE 22.14**

Although he preferred to create romantic interpretations of nature in pictures of the land and sea, Bannister also painted portraits and other subjects. One of these, painted in 1869, shows a well-dressed newsboy clutching a bundle of newspapers (Figure 22.14). The boy stares intently ahead while reaching into his pocket with his left hand. Perhaps he has just sold a newspaper and is pocketing the coins received. However, his facial expression and his action suggest that he may be checking his pocket to determine how much money is there. Bannister captured the serious expression of a young man concerned with earning his way.

Chapter 22 *Art of the Later Nineteenth Century* **507**

MEETING INDIVIDUAL NEEDS

Interpersonal Experience. Have groups of students work together to plan an issue of a newspaper recounting the industrial, economic, social, and artistic changes taking place in the United States during the late 1800s. Have students divide the tasks of writing, editing, illustrating, and laying out various sections of the newspaper. Encourage them to check history books and other sources for further information about the period. Illustrations may include reproductions of artworks photocopied from books or catalogs. Have students plan and organize the contents of each section, and be sure all students contribute equally to the final product.

Art History

Remind students that Tanner studied with Eakins, who was greatly influenced by Rembrandt. Ask whether students see any similarities between Tanner's work and that of Rembrandt. Then compare Figure 22.15 with reproductions of paintings by the northern Baroque artist. Ask: How are light and shadow used? What is the mood of each piece?

Art History

Students may be interested in researching the contributions of the sculptors Harriet Hosmer and Anne Whitney and the painters Anna Lea Merritt and Lilly Martin Spencer. Have students present their findings to the class.

Did You Know?

Henry Tanner came from a family of high achievers. Not only was his father a bishop in the African Methodist Episcopal Church, but his mother founded one of the first black women's organizations in the United States. His sister was one of the first women doctors in Alabama.

■ **FIGURE 22.15** This simple scene tells the story of the relationship between the old man and his young banjo student. How would you answer someone who claimed that this picture is too sentimental?

Henry Tanner. *The Banjo Lesson.* 1893. Oil on canvas. 124.5 × 90.2 cm (49 × 35½"). Hampton University Museum, Hampton, Virginia.

Henry Tanner (1859–1937)

The most famous African-American artist of the late nineteenth and early twentieth centuries was Henry Tanner. Tanner was born and raised in Philadelphia. His father was a Methodist minister who later became a bishop. Tanner's interest in art began when, as a 12-year-old, he saw a landscape painter at work.

Against his father's wishes, Tanner later enrolled at the Pennsylvania Academy of the Fine Arts where he studied with Thomas Eakins. They became friends, and Eakins influenced Tanner to turn from landscapes to genre scenes. Eakins also convinced his student to stay in the United States rather than go to Europe. Tanner took his advice and went south to North Carolina and Georgia.

The Banjo Lesson
■ **FIGURE 22.15**

Tanner's painting of *The Banjo Lesson* (Figure 22.15) grew out of his experience among the blacks of western North Carolina. Here, under the watchful eye of an old man, a boy strums a tune on a worn banjo. This music lesson represents more than just a pleasant way to pass the time. For the old man, music is his legacy to the boy, one of the few things of value he has to pass on. For the boy, music may represent the one source of pleasure he can always rely on in a world often marked by uncertainty and difficulty. Tanner tells this story simply and without sentimentality, and because he does, it is not likely to be forgotten.

In time, Tanner decided to ignore Eakins's advice to remain in the United States. He was not enjoying financial success. Furthermore, his strong religious upbringing made him eager to paint biblical subjects. So, following the route of many leading artists of his day, Tanner journeyed to Paris when he was 32 years old. Five years later, his painting of *Daniel in the Lion's Den* (Figure 22.16) was hanging in a place of honor in the Paris Salon. The next year, another religious painting was

More About... **Henry Tanner.** Henry Tanner faced a great deal of discrimination as an African-American painter in the United States, which is the main reason he left at the age of thirty-one, never to return. In each of his early endeavors—as an art student, painter, magazine illustrator, and photographer—Tanner suffered from prejudice, finally writing: "With whom should I study? No man or boy to whom this country is a land of 'equal chances' can realize what heartaches this question caused me." Fortunately, the artist showed enormous resilience, never losing sight of his mission, and eventually was befriended by the older artist C. H. Shearer, who, in Tanner's words, "encouraged me to put bitterness out of my soul and to cultivate the best in me."

■ **FIGURE 22.16** Tanner chose as the subject for this work a familiar Bible story. **Compare this painting to the work with the same name by Rubens (Figure 19.10, page 428). How did each artist portray Daniel?**

Henry Tanner. *Daniel in the Lion's Den.* c. 1907–1918. Oil on paper on canvas. 104.5 × 126.7 cm (41³/₁₆ × 49⁷/₈″). Los Angeles County Museum of Art, Los Angeles, California. Mr. and Mrs. William Preston Harrison Collection.

awarded a medal and purchased by the French government. The recognition Tanner failed to receive in his homeland was finally his.

Edmonia Lewis (1845–1890)

Tanner's European success as a painter surpassed that achieved earlier by the American sculptor Edmonia Lewis, an artist whose life and death were marked by mystery. Half Native American, half African-American,

Lewis was born in Greenhigh, Ohio, and raised by her mother's people, the Chippewa.

In 1856, Lewis received a scholarship to Oberlin College, where she studied such traditional subjects as Greek and zoology. In her fourth year, Lewis found herself at the center of controversy. Two of her best friends were poisoned, and Lewis was charged with their murder. Her celebrated trial ended in a not-guilty verdict, and Lewis was carried triumphantly from the courtroom by friends and fellow students.

Art Criticism

Guide students in examining and discussing *Forever Free* (Figure 22.17, page 510). Encourage students to identify the elements of art Lewis used and the principles of art with which she organized those elements.

Study Guide

Distribute *Study Guide* 52 in the TCR. Assist students in reviewing key concepts. 📁

Art and Humanities

Assign *Art and Humanities* 38, "Perspectives by African-American Poets," in the TCR. In this worksheet, students read poetry written by African-American poets. 📁

Studio Activities

Assign *Studio* 28, "Making an Expressive Watercolor," in the TCR. In this activity, students express a quiet, still mood in their painting. 📁

Art and Humanities

Have students work jointly to complete *Cooperative Learning* 32, "Art Making News." In this activity, students consider how increased communication via newspapers has affected rapidly changing ideas and developments in art. After discussion, groups create their own newspapers. 📁

More About... **Women Artists.** Women artists of the late nineteenth century suffered from the public perception that female artistic talent and ambition were somehow a violation of nature. The sculptor Vinnie Ream Hoxie, for example, was subjected to a demeaning congressional debate when she was nominated to create a statue of Abraham Lincoln. Ultimately, she prevailed, but after the statue was unveiled, critics charged that the work was not her own. Fellow artist Harriet Hosmer came to her defense, stating, "We women artists will not hear that we are impostors without asking for proof. . . . We resent all such accusations." Edmonia Lewis, too, was sensitive to allegations that her work was not her own.

ASSESS

Checking Comprehension

➤ Have students respond to the lesson review questions. Answers are given in the box below.

➤ Assign *Application* 22, "Hands Across the Ocean," and evaluate students' understanding of what they have learned. 📁

Reteaching

➤ Assign *Reteaching* 52, found in the TCR. Have students complete the activity and review their responses. 📁

➤ Have students each select one artwork from this lesson and explain how it is similar in style to an artwork studied in an earlier chapter.

Enrichment

Assign students *Enrichment* 43, "Opening Japan to the World," in the TCR. In this worksheet, students learn about the opening of Japan's trade relations with Europe and America in the nineteenth century and how, since that time, the Eastern nation has become a world leader in trade. 📁

Extension

Have students complete *Appreciating Cultural Diversity* 32, "Tracing the Growth of African-American Art," in the TCR. In this activity, students are provided with information on African- American artists to supplement information conveyed in this lesson. 📁

CLOSE

Ask each student to state briefly which artist studied in this chapter is his or her favorite and to explain the choice.

After the trial, Lewis turned her attention to marble carving. In 1867, with money she received for a bust of a famous Civil War officer, she purchased a boat ticket to Europe and settled in Rome.

Forever Free
■ **FIGURE 22.17**

Shortly after her arrival in Rome, Lewis completed *Forever Free* (Figure 22.17). The work was done in celebration of the Thirteenth Amendment to the U.S. Constitution, which ended slavery forever. For a time her works sold for large sums and her studio became a favorite place for tourists to visit.

Unfortunately, Lewis's fame and prosperity were fleeting. A taste for bronze sculpture developed, and the demand for her marble pieces declined. Edmonia Lewis dropped out of sight, and the remainder of her life remains a mystery.

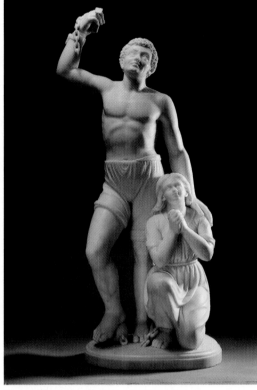

■ **FIGURE 22.17** A visitor to Lewis's studio in Rome described her as one of the most fascinating representatives of America in Europe. **Compare this sculpture with bronze works, such as those by Rodin (Figures 21.22 and 21.23, pages 488 and 489). How do you think the decision to work in marble affected the expressive qualities of Lewis's work?**

Edmonia Lewis. *Forever Free*. 1867. Marble. H: 104.8 cm (41¼"). The Howard University Gallery of Art, Permanent collection. Howard University, Washington, D.C.

LESSON TWO REVIEW

Reviewing Art Facts
1. Which two painters are considered to be among the first Realists in American art?
2. Why did some viewers object to Eakins's painting of *The Gross Clinic*?
3. Where did Albert Pinkham Ryder find inspiration for his art?
4. Discuss how Henry Tanner's roots influenced his choice of subject matter.

Activity... *Painting a Mural Scene*
Artists like Edmonia Lewis illustrate in their artworks the trials and triumphs of real people. The man and woman in her marble statue *Forever Free* (Figure 22.17) show these emotions in expressions and body language.

Work in teams to create an artwork that represents the triumphs of humanity. Consider groups of people around the world today who have recently achieved liberation. You may instead choose to represent those who have yet to realize their freedom. Research the historical impact of the experiences of this group. Use tempera paints and white shelf paper to create a mural that illustrates this theme. Display your work in the classroom.

LESSON TWO REVIEW

Answers to Reviewing Art Facts
1. Winslow Homer and Thomas Eakins.
2. Some viewers found the details too realistic.
3. In literary works and within himself.
4. Tanner spent time in the South; he was the son of a minister and liked to paint biblical subjects.

Activity... *Painting a Mural Scene*
Let students begin by meeting in cooperative groups to examine and discuss Lewis's statue. What emotions do the figures in the artwork express? How do they express those emotions?

Then have group members work together to plan, sketch, and paint their mural.

Studio LESSON   Painting Emphasizing Aesthetic Qualities

Complete a painting guided by your answers to questions about Henry Tanner's painting *The Banjo Lesson* (Figure 22.15, page 508).

Inspiration

With other members of your class, examine Henry Tanner's painting *The Banjo Lesson*. Answer the following questions dealing with the different aesthetic qualities noted in this painting.

Literal Qualities: How many people are in this picture? What are these people doing? What kind of clothing are they wearing? How would you describe the environment and the economic condition of these people?

Design Qualities: What kinds of colors, values, textures, and space dominate? What has the artist done to direct the viewer's eyes to the main parts of the painting?

Expressive Qualities: Do you think the environment in this painting is warm and cozy, or cold and uncomfortable? What word best describes the people's expressions? How do you think the people in this picture feel? What feelings or moods does this work evoke in viewers?

Process

1. Examine the questions about Tanner's painting once again. Select two or more questions in each of the three categories and answer them as if you were talking about a painting of your own—a painting you are about to do. For example:
   - Literal Qualities: How many people will I include in *my* picture?
   - Design Qualities: What kinds of colors will dominate *my* painting?
   - Expressive Qualities: Will the environment in *my* painting be warm and cozy, or cold and uncomfortable?

2. Use your answers to the six questions you chose as a guide, and complete several sketches. Transfer your best sketch to the mat board, and paint it with tempera or acrylic.

Materials

- Pencil and sketch paper
- White mat board, about 12 × 18 inches
- Tempera or acrylic paint
- Brushes, mixing tray, and paint cloth
- Water container

■ **FIGURE 22.18**   Student Work

Examining Your Work

Exhibit your painting in class along with those created by other students. Use the same kinds of questions applied to Tanner's painting to conduct a class critique.

Describe. Ask and answer questions that focus attention on the literal qualities.

Analyze. Ask and answer questions that focus attention on the design qualities.

Interpret. Ask and answer questions that focus attention on the expressive qualities.

Judge. Discuss the success of the works on display in terms of the literal, design, and expressive qualities.

511

ASSESSMENT

Group Discussion. After students have used the "Examining Your Work" questions to assess their own projects, display the completed paintings in the classroom. Ask each student to choose one of the paintings (other than his or her own) and write an analysis of its aesthetic qualities, responding to the questions posed in the *Inspiration* section of this lesson. After students have completed this writing activity, let them meet with others who analyzed the same painting to compare and discuss their conclusions.

Studio LESSON

Painting Emphasizing Aesthetic Qualities ____

Objectives
- Complete a painting based on answers to questions about *The Banjo Lesson*.
- Determine the subject matter, use of elements and principles, and the mood and feelings to be depicted.

Motivator
Have students answer and discuss the questions pertaining to *The Banjo Lesson* posed in this lesson. Record the responses on the board. Ask students to identify the types of questions they found easiest to answer. Discuss the reasons for this.

Studio Skills
Inform students that they must abide by certain limitations in completing this studio lesson. The most important of these is that their pictures must show a specified number of people doing something in a room of some kind. Tell them to keep the questions and answers prepared to guide them in creating this painting near at hand while they are working. These should be referred to often and, if changes are required, they should be discussed with the teacher before being implemented.

Critiquing
Have students apply the steps of art criticism to their own artwork, using the "Examining Your Work" questions on this page.

Studio LESSON

Tempera Batik in the Style of Gauguin

Objectives:

- Complete a tempera batik using flat shapes of intense color, overlapping shapes to suggest shallow space.
- Outline shapes with a variety of thick and thin lines.
- Create a flat, colorful, decorative design rather than a picture marked by representational accuracy.

Motivator

Ask students to identify images that they associate with modern American life. List these on the board. Have students point out the images that they think would appear most unusual to a visitor from a remote South Seas island.

Art History

Tell students that art historians often remark that Gauguin's style of painting is reminiscent of pre-Renaissance works. Ask whether they agree with this observation. Have students compare Gauguin's painting of *Fatata te Miti* with Egyptian paintings in Chapter 7 and Romanesque paintings in Chapter 14. Are they able to identify any similarities in the painting styles noted in Gauguin's work and those created earlier? Point out that the earlier works, like Gauguin's, avoid modeling and perspective in favor of flat, simplified shapes outlined with black shapes.

Critiquing

Have students apply the steps of art criticism to their own artwork, using the "Examining Your Work" questions on this page.

Studio LESSON — Tempera Batik in the Style of Gauguin

Materials

- Pencil and sketch paper
- Sheet of lightly colored construction paper, 9 × 12 inches or larger
- White chalk
- Tempera paint
- Brushes, mixing tray, and paint cloth
- India ink
- Food tray or some other large, flat surface
- Water container

■ **FIGURE 22.19** Student Work

Complete a tempera batik in which you present your view of life in contemporary America. This work is intended to enlighten viewers who are unfamiliar with our modern society. Make sure to use large shapes, bright colors, and a variety of thick and thin lines.

Inspiration

Examine Gauguin's painting of *Fatata te Miti* (Figure 22.8, page 500). How are the shapes used to suggest space? Are the colors bright or dull? Would you describe this as a realistic-looking picture? What does this painting tell you about life on a South Pacific island?

Process

1. Complete several sketches in which you present your version of life in twentieth-century America. Direct your view of contemporary life to viewers who live on a remote South Sea island.
2. Reproduce your best sketch to fill the sheet of colored construction paper. Overlap the shapes in your drawing to suggest shallow space.
3. Go over the main lines in your picture with white chalk, making some lines thick and others thin.
4. Paint your picture with a *heavy* application of tempera paint. Choose bright, rather than dull, colors. Paint up to—but not over—the chalk lines. A thick coating of tempera is needed because some of the paint will wash off later. Avoid overlapping paint layers, since the top layer will be lost during the final operation. Tempera paint details should never be applied to a previously painted surface.
5. As soon as the tempera paint is dry, cover your picture completely with a brushed-on coat of india ink.
6. When the ink is completely dry, place your picture on a food tray to prevent it from tearing. At the sink, gently wash the ink from the surface. Use a light stream of water, and rub carefully with your fingers. Do not remove all the ink, or you will lose the batik-like look you are trying to achieve. To retouch your work, apply small amounts of tempera paint with a sponge or crushed paper towel while the picture is still damp.

Examining Your Work

Describe. Does your batik present viewers with your ideas about life in contemporary America? What typically American people, objects, or events did you include?

Analyze. Did you use large, flat shapes? Were these shapes painted with bright, intense colors? How is space suggested in your picture? Did you use a variety of thick and thin lines?

Interpret. Did you include enough visual clues to help viewers form an accurate opinion about life in contemporary America? What single idea about America does your picture communicate?

Judge. What type of critic or critics would be most pleased with your picture: those favoring the theory of imitationalism, formalism, or emotionalism? Explain your answer.

ASSESSMENT

Class Discussion. After students have responded to the "Examining Your Work" questions, help them discuss what they have learned about using the tempera batik technique. What effects does the technique produce? In which kinds of art projects might it be most effective? To assure the success of future projects using this technique, tell students that it is important to use a good quality of liquid tempera, rather than powder or cake tempera. The paint should be mixed to a consistency of heavy cream. If they use tempera that is too thin, the ink will penetrate it and neutralize the hue.

Reviewing the Facts

Lesson One

1. During what time period did French artists begin to become dissatisfied with the Impressionist style?
2. What principle of art did Cézanne use when he combined straight lines and curved lines within a painting?
3. How did van Gogh create a new kind of perspective in *Bedroom at Arles* (Figure 22.6, page 498)?

Lesson Two

4. Refer to Winslow Homer's painting *The Fog Warning* (Figure 22.9, page 502). How does the artist direct the viewer's eyes to the schooner and fog bank on the horizon? Why was it important to direct attention to these two items?
5. How would you describe the colors in Homer's painting *Right and Left* (Figure 22.10, page 503)?
6. Thomas Eakins learned to use light and dark values to make his figures look solid by studying the work of what artist?
7. Refer to Henry Tanner's painting *The Banjo Lesson* (Figure 22.15, page 508). Would you say there is a greater contrast in hue or value in this painting?

Thinking Critically

1. **ANALYZE.** Look again at Vincent van Gogh's painting *The Starry Night* (Figure 22.1, page 492). Discuss the elements of color, line, texture, and shape. Tell how they have been used according to the principle of movement. What elements of art do you think were most important to van Gogh?
2. **EXTEND.** After the African-American artist Joshua Johnston died, others were often given credit for pictures that were actually painted by him. This sometimes happened to women artists, too. You might recall, from Chapter 19 for example, that Frans Hals was given credit for a painting by Judith Leyster. Discuss the reasons why this might have happened to African-American and women artists.

▲ **R T** DANCE. Use the *Performing Arts Handbook*, page 591 to learn about The AMAN International Folk Ensemble.
S ● U
R C ▣

CAREERS IN Art Read about a career as a medical illustrator in the *Careers in Art Handbook*, page 607.

*inter*NET
C O N N E C T I O N Visit Glencoe Art Online at *www.glencoe.com/sec/art*. View more works by van Gogh and Cézanne. Explore American art at online museums.

Technology Project

Examining Artists' Lives

As artists of the Western world in the late nineteenth century directed the path of their own artistic exploration, they continued to change their ideas about the nature, value, and function of art. This period produced several of the best-known artists in all of modern art history. Few people have not heard about the art and lives of Vincent van Gogh and his friend Paul Gauguin. These artists left the world artworks that are priceless. They sacrificed a great deal in order to pursue their artistic quest to achieve individual artistic expression.

1. The tragic yet heroic lives of these artists were recounted in books, films, or videos. Locate and share parts of these with your class.
2. Consider whether you think the choices these artists made were worth the price they paid. Using a word processor, record your feelings about whether the aesthetic legacy of their artwork is significant enough to compensate for the moral or financial sacrifices they might have made. What do you feel was the right thing for each of them to do? If you could rewrite their lives, how would the script read?
3. Using available technology media, prepare a short presentation, performance, or tutorial to share images of the works of these artists and to defend your position to your class.

513

Reviewing the Facts

1. French artists began to express dissatisfaction with the Impressionist style during the 1880s and 1890s.
2. Cézanne uses the principle of variety when he uses straight lines and curved lines within a painting.
3. Van Gogh tilted the composition to create a new kind of perspective.
4. The fish in the boat forms a curve that leads up to the schooner, and a wave forms a diagonal line that points in the same direction. Students might also mention the direction of the man's gaze. The distance to the schooner and the moving fog bank emphasize the danger the fisherman faces.
5. The colors in Homer's *Right and Left* are cool, low in intensity, and for the most part, monochromatic.
6. Eakins studied the work of Rembrandt to learn about light and dark values.
7. There is a greater contrast in value.

Thinking Critically

1. The elements of line and color were most important to the artist. In *The Starry Night*, he uses progressions of curving, swirling lines and short dabs of hot color against a backdrop of cool ones to create dynamic tension.
2. Student answers, which may vary, should address the ongoing struggle for civil and human rights.

Teaching the Technology Project

Let students work in cooperative learning groups to explore available videotapes depicting the lives of specific artists. Have group members select appropriate sections of these videotapes and show them to the rest of the class. Allow students to work either independently or with partners to plan and share their point-of-view presentations.

▲ **R T** Assign the feature in the *Performing Arts Handbook*,
S ● U page 591.
R C ▣

CAREERS IN ART If time permits, have interested students investigate the career information in the *Careers in Art Handbook*, page 607.

*inter*NET Have students go online and learn more
C O N N E C T I O N about artists on preselected Web sites with the Internet activity for this chapter.

Art of the Early Twentieth Century

LESSON ONE
(pages 516–527)

Many Movements in European Art

Classroom Resources
- 📁 Appreciating Cultural Diversity 33
- 📁 Cooperative Learning 33
- 📁 Reproducible Lesson Plan 53
- 📁 Reteaching Activity 53
- 📁 Study Guide 53

Features
Identifying
Styles in *Art*

Guernica
(page 525)

(page 527)

LESSON TWO
(pages 528–535)

Contributions from Mexico and the United States

Classroom Resources
- 📁 Art and Humanities 39
- 📁 Cooperative Learning 34, 35
- 📁 Enrichment Activity 44
- 📁 Reproducible Lesson Plan 54
- 📁 Reteaching Activity 54
- 📁 Study Guide 54

Features

(page 530)

Discovering
Movement in *Art*

Backyards,
Greenwich Village
(page 533)

LESSON THREE
(pages 536–540)

European and American Architecture

Classroom Resources
- 📁 Reproducible Lesson Plan 55
- 📁 Reteaching Activity 55
- 📁 Study Guide 55

Features
LOOKING Closely ↓
(page 538)

(page 539)

END OF CHAPTER
(pages 541–543)

Studio
LESSONS
- Abstract Cut-Paper Figures *(page 541)*
- Cubist-Style Painting *(page 542)*

ADDITIONAL CHAPTER RESOURCES

Activities
- 📁 Application 23
- 📁 Advanced Studio Activity 23
- 🖱 Chapter 23 Internet Activity
- 📁 Studio Activity 29

Fine Art Resources
🕹 **Transparencies**

Art in Focus Transparency 29
    Henri Matisse. *Still Life with Goldfish.*

Art in Focus Transparency 30
    José Clemente Orozco. *The Family.*

🖼 **Fine Art Print**

Focus on World Art Print 23
    Lois Mailou Jones. *The Ascent of Ethiopia.*

Assessment
- 📁 Chapter 23 Test
- 📁 Performance Assessment

Multimedia Resources
- 💿 Artsource® Performing Arts Package
- 💿 National Gallery Laser Disc
- 💿 National Museum of Women in the Arts CD-ROM
- 📼 Arts & Entertainment Videos

NATIONAL STANDARDS FOR ARTS EDUCATION

The National Standards for Arts Education provide guidelines for grade-appropriate competency in the visual arts. The Content Standards for grades 9–12 are:

1. Understanding and applying media, techniques, and processes.
2. Using knowledge of structures and functions.
3. Choosing and evaluating a range of subject matter, symbols, and ideas.
4. Understanding the visual arts in relation to history and cultures.
5. Reflecting upon and assessing the characteristics and merits of their work and the work of others.
6. Making connections between visual arts and other disciplines.

Listed below are the National Standards for the Visual Arts addressed in this chapter. For a breakdown of the categories listed under each content standard, refer to the *Reproducible Lesson Plans* booklet in the TCR.

  1. (a, b) **2.** (a, b, c) **3.** (a) **4.** (a, b, c) **5.** (b, c) **6.** (b)

HANDBOOK MATERIAL

ARTSOURCE American Repertory Dance Company *(page 592)*

CAREERS IN Art

Cinematographer *(page 608)*

Beyond the Classroom

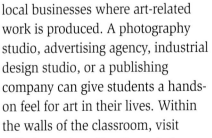

You can arrange for students to tour local businesses where art-related work is produced. A photography studio, advertising agency, industrial design studio, or a publishing company can give students a hands-on feel for art in their lives. Within the walls of the classroom, visit galleries and studios through the Internet by visiting our Web site at *www.glencoe.com/sec/art.*

🕐 **Out of Time?** If time does not permit teaching this chapter in its entirety, you may wish to preview the artwork and captions with students. Scan the heads in each lesson with students. Discuss the Looking Closely feature and examine Identifying Styles in Art on page 525, and Discovering Movement in Art on page 533.

Art of the Early Twentieth Century

INTRODUCE

Chapter Overview

CHAPTER 23 introduces students to the multiplicity of movements that typified early twentieth-century art and architecture in Europe and North America.

Lesson One focuses on the works and theories of the Fauves, German Expressionists, Blaue Reiter, and Cubists.

Lesson Two introduces the Mexican muralists and Ashcan painters.

Studio Lessons guide students to create abstract cut-paper figures and Cubist-style paintings.

Art & Social Studies

Ask students what identifies this as a twentieth-century work. Have one group of volunteers research and present a brief report on the rapid growth of industry at the beginning of the twentieth century. Ask another group to research the economic conditions in the United States during the 1930s.

Art of the Early Twentieth Century

Art & Social Studies   ■ **FIGURE 23.1** America was emerging as an industrial giant at the time this painting was done. Ample resources of petroleum and steel combined with a more efficient use of human labor made this possible. Henry Ford devised a mass production method in which workers on an assembly line fitted standardized parts together to assemble automobiles. His Ford Motor Company, founded in 1903, produced its one-millionth car 12 years later.

Diego Rivera. *Mural: Detroit Industry.* 1932–1933. Fresco. 2.57 × 2.13 m (8¹/₂ × 7'). The Detroit Institute of Arts, detail of north wall, Detroit, Michigan. Gift of Edsel B. Ford.

514

National Standards

This chapter addresses the following National Standards for the Arts.

1. (a,b)   4. (a,b,c)
2. (a,b,c)   5. (b, c)
3. (a)   6. (b)

CHAPTER 23 RESOURCES

Teacher's Classroom Resources

📁 Advanced Studio Activity 23
📁 Application 23
🖱 Chapter 23 Internet Activity
📁 Studio Activity 29

Assessment

📁 Chapter 23 Test
📁 Performance Assessment

Fine Art Resources

🖋 *Art in Focus* Transparency
    29, Henri Matisse. *Still Life with Goldfish.*
    30, José Clemente Orozco. *The Family.*
▦ *Focus on World Art* Print 23
    Lois Mailou Jones.
    The Ascent of Ethiopia.

The beginning of the twentieth century is recognized today as a period of revolution and change in art. Artists introduced a variety of new art styles that not only broke with the artistic traditions of the past but also pointed the way for future innovations. At first, Europe was the birthplace for these new art styles—styles that greatly influenced the art created later in America. However, as the century progressed, American art began to exhibit a bold new character of its own. Ultimately, the artworks created by American artists became the models to which artists in Europe and other parts of the world turned for inspiration.

YOUR Portfolio

Perfect your watercolor technique in a painting to keep in your portfolio. First choose a subject that you feel will lend itself to watercolor wash. On watercolor paper, paint washes of watercolor for the background. Then, using colored pencils, add details of the subject. Concentrate on areas of fine detail while leaving other areas with less. Keep your pencil points sharp when working on the finer details. Critique your own work according to the four steps of art criticism: describing, analyzing, interpreting, and judging. Speculate about other media and techniques that would give successful results.

Focus ON THE ARTS

DANCE
Modern dance was introduced in America by Isadora Duncan, Loïe Fuller, and Ruth St. Denis. Later, American choreographer Martha Graham, created a style of modern dance that continues to influence choreographers and dancers.

LITERATURE
The Expressionist art style was adapted by playwrights in America. Eugene O'Neill's *The Hairy Ape* and Elmer Rice's *The Adding Machine* used symbolism, exaggeration, and direct language to explore inner emotions.

MUSIC
In America, jazz music was influenced by the blues and musical styles from Africa. Jazz was quickly adapted internationally by classical and popular composers.

515

Introducing the Chapter

Have students browse through the chapter, identifying characteristics that distinguish the artworks shown from those studied in previous chapters. Explain that many of the changes introduced resulted from an attempt to elevate art to an intellectual plane.

ART SOURCE **Dance.** Use *Performing Arts Handbook* page 592 to let students enjoy the American Repertory Dance Company. Tell them they will experience the work of dance pioneers in the early twentieth century.

Focus ON THE ARTS

Write the following lines on the board from the poem *The Red Wheelbarrow,* by Wallace Stevens, 1923: *so much depends upon/ a red wheel barrow/ glazed with rain water/ beside the white chickens.*

Explain that twentieth-century writers sometimes adapt art theories to expand the boundaries of literature. Have the class analyze this poem. Ask: Is this a poem or just words strung together? Note that the poem has *color:* the wheelbarrow is bright red and shiny. It has *contrast:* the red contrasts to the white chickens. It has *balance, rhythm,* and *proportion* in its words and images. The use of expressive language makes this a poem with strong visual images.

DEVELOPING A PORTFOLIO

Self-Evaluation. Students should be encouraged to critique their progress regularly on specific pieces of art as well as their entire portfolio. Routine self-assessment fosters growth, decision-making skills, and an increased awareness of their personal style. Internal dialogue and critiquing is vital to their success as independent learners. For example, they could routinely ask themselves a series of questions such as: How have I progressed? Where do I want to go? What areas remain weak and need more attention? What are the expectations for my portfolio? What do I need to know in order to continue?

Many Movements in European Art

FOCUS

Lesson Objectives

After studying this lesson, students will be able to:
- Discuss the objectives of the Fauves, German Expressionists, Nonobjectivists, and Cubists.
- Identify some of the important artists identified with these movements.

Building Vocabulary

Have students identify the proper nouns in the Vocabulary terms for the chapter. Ask: Which of these terms do you think were the result of abrasive reactions by critics?

Motivator

Have students list the kinds of activities that filled their days when they were toddlers (e.g., playing, eating, napping). Then ask students to list activities that typically fill their days now. Point out that, as we mature, our interests branch out in many different directions. Draw a parallel between human development and art, which, by the early twentieth century, had grown in many directions.

Introducing the Lesson

Have students examine the painting in Figure 23.2. Draw their attention in particular to the unorthodox use of color. Ask them whether color is used to create a realistic view of a room that resides in deep space. Have students brainstorm possible motives for this defiant use of color.

Many Movements in European Art

Vocabulary
- Fauves
- Expressionism
- nonobjective art
- Cubism
- collage

Artists to Meet
- Henri Matisse
- Georges Rouault
- Paula Modersohn-Becker
- Ernst Ludwig Kirchner
- Käthe Kollwitz
- Edvard Munch
- Wassily Kandinsky
- Gabriele Münter
- Pablo Picasso
- Georges Braque
- Aristide Maillol

Discover
After completing this lesson, you will be able to:
- Explain the style and objectives of the Fauves and identify two artists associated with this movement.
- Discuss the objectives of the Expressionists and name some of the artists associated with this art movement.
- Define nonobjective art.
- Describe the ideas underlying Cubism and identify artists associated with this style.

*T*he turn of the century saw the end of the academies' influence and the beginning of a new series of art movements in Europe. The first of these movements came to public attention in 1905. A group of younger French painters under the leadership of Henri Matisse exhibited their works in Paris. Their paintings were so simple in design, so brightly colored, and so loose in brushwork that an enraged critic called the artists **Fauves,** or *"Wild Beasts."*

The Fauves

The Fauves carried on the ideas of Vincent van Gogh and Paul Gauguin. They took the colors, movement, and concern for design stressed by those earlier artists and built an art style that was unrealistic, free, and wild. They were more daring than van Gogh in their use of color, and bolder than Gauguin in their use of broad, flat shapes and lively line patterns. They tried to extend and intensify the ideas first expressed by those Post-Impressionists.

Henri Matisse (1869–1954)

Henri Matisse (ahn-**ree** mah-**tees**), the leader of the Fauves, turned to art when he was a 20-year-old law student. He spent a brief period as a student of an academic painter, but found this experience almost as frustrating as studying law.

Then Matisse studied with another artist, Gustave Moreau (**goo**-stahv maw-**roh**), who was not as rigid and strict. Moreau encouraged Matisse to exercise greater freedom in his use of color. While studying with Moreau, Matisse met Georges Rouault and some of the other artists who became associated with him in the Fauve movement.

The Red Studio
■ FIGURE 23.2

By 1905, Matisse had developed a style using broad areas of color that were not meant to look like the shapes or colors found in nature. This style is shown in his painting entitled *The Red Studio* (Figure 23.2). Like many artists before him, Matisse uses his studio as a subject; although unlike those earlier artists, he does not include himself in the picture. Instead he shows a number of his paintings, which hang from or lean against the walls in a haphazard way. He welcomes you into his studio by using linear perspective. A table at the left and a chair at the right direct you into the room and invite you to look around.

In this work, the room has been flattened out into a solid red rectangle. The walls do not have corners; round objects look flat; and there are no

---

LESSON ONE RESOURCES

Teacher's Classroom Resources

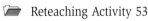 Appreciating Cultural Diversity 33

Cooperative Learning 33

Reproducible Lesson Plan 53

Reteaching Activity 53

Study Guide 53

shadows. Red is found everywhere—it covers the walls, floor, and furnishings. It is a strong, pure red selected for its visual impact, not for its accuracy.

Emphasis on Design

Matisse was mainly interested in organizing the visual qualities in this picture rather than providing a lifelike view of his studio. The studio itself suggested the colors, shapes, lines, and textures that were then used in new and exciting ways to create a colorful decorative pattern. The objects in his work seem to be suspended by the intense red hue. This illusion allows you to glance casually about the room where surprising contrasts of greens, pinks, black, and white serve to attract and hold your interest. Unnecessary details are stripped away. The result is a balanced design in which tables, dresser, and chairs exist as colors, lines, and shapes.

Today it is difficult to understand why Matisse's paintings were so shocking when they were first exhibited. Perhaps critics were upset by the simplicity of his pictures, but Matisse used simplicity because he wanted a more direct form of personal expression. In a way, he is like a writer who uses a few sentences and simple, easy-to-understand words to make his or her message as precise and direct as possible.

Nowhere are Matisse's simple, direct forms more obvious than in his version of a circus knife thrower (Figure 23.3). With simple shapes and a few colors, Matisse playfully contrasts the furious actions of a knife thrower with the inactive pose of his female assistant.

During the last years of his life, Matisse devoted most of his efforts to making paper cutouts from papers that he had painted earlier. Matisse spent days and even weeks arranging and rearranging his cut shapes until he was satisfied with the results.

Matisse had no complicated theories to explain his paintings or cutouts. He claimed they had only one purpose: to give pleasure. "Art," he once said, "is something like a good armchair which provides relaxation from physical fatigue."

■ **FIGURE 23.2** Matisse used this red for its strong visual impact, not because his studio was actually this color. **How does Matisse use linear perspective to welcome you into his studio?**

Henri Matisse. *The Red Studio.* Issy-les-Moulineaux (1911). Oil on canvas. 181 × 219.1 cm (71¼ × 86¼"). The Museum of Modern Art, New York, New York. Mrs. Simon Guggenheim Fund.

■ **FIGURE 23.3** The forms here are simplified but easily identified. The bright, active knife thrower on the left presents a contrast to the pale, still assistant on the right. **What do the other shapes add to this work?**

Henri Matisse. *The Knife Thrower,* from *Jazz.* 1947. Stencil. 40.3 × 64.7 cm (15⅞ × 25½"). Philadelphia Museum of Art, Philadelphia, Pennsylvania. John D. McIlhenny Fund.

Chapter 23 *Art of the Early Twentieth Century* **517**

TEACH
Aesthetics

Emphasize the reaction of critics to the work of the Fauves. Then ask students to respond to the following statement: *New ways of making art require new evaluative criteria.* Invite students to debate the proposition, referring to the three main aesthetic theories they have studied in the text.

Art Criticism

Review with students Matisse's artistic goals, which he summarized by declaring that he wanted to create "an art of purity and serenity without depressing subject matter." Then ask students to attempt to encapsulate the goals of other artists covered in the lesson by referring to the way their works use the principles of art to organize the elements.

Critical Thinking

As a follow-up to the previous activity, ask students to try to explain why artists working in the same time period under similar conditions might develop radically different artistic goals. Ask whether students think this phenomenon is the result merely of personal preference or whether there are other factors to consider.

Studio Skills

Ask students to study Matisse's *The Red Studio* (Figure 23.2) and then try to use color as Matisse used it. Have them begin by drawing a large simple object, such as a desk, using broad outlines. Explain that they do not need to include small details. Have students use acrylic paints to fill in their object, selecting a color that is not usually associated with the object but which expresses a personal feeling or sense of it.

Technology

National Gallery of Art Videodisc Use the following images as examples of more works by artists introduced in this lesson.

Henri Matisse
Large Composition with Masks

Search Frame 2212

Edvard Munch
The Scream

Search Frame 3333

Pablo Picasso
Family of Saltimbanques

Search Frame 2275

Use Glencoe's *Correlation Bar Code Guide to the National Gallery of Art* to locate more artworks.

Art Criticism

Point out that, despite the largely negative critical response to many of the works shown in this lesson, early critics were nevertheless divided in their views—that some critics of the period went so far as to praise works shown here. Have groups of students assume the role of early, forward-thinking critics attending an exhibition featuring one of the works illustrated in the lesson. The group is to collaborate on a critique of the work making use of each of the four art criticism operations, ultimately explaining why the work is successful.

Art History

Remind students that many modern artists were influenced by the art of other cultures. For instance, Matisse's art was greatly influenced by Egyptian, Greek, and Oriental art. Have students review what they have learned about the art of these other cultures, listing specific details about the goals of indigenous artists and the way in which they went about meeting those goals. Then have students correlate details from their lists with specific details of the artworks in Figures 23.2 and 23.3 (page 517).

Art History

Direct students' attention to the painting by Rouault in Figure 23.4, emphasizing the thick lines and glowing colors that the artist used in this painting. Then have students turn to Figure 15.7 (page 335) and compare the stained-glass window with Rouault's painting. Can students find a greater number of similarities or dissimilarities between the two artworks?

Georges Rouault (1871–1958)

Matisse's attitude toward art was not shared by Georges Rouault (**zhorzh** roo-**oh**), another artist associated with the Fauves. Instead of trying to show happiness and pleasure in his art, Rouault chose to illustrate the more sorrowful side of life. His works were bold visual sermons condemning the world's injustices and suffering.

When he was a boy, Rouault was apprenticed to a stained-glass maker. Later he used heavy, dark lines to surround areas of thick, glowing colors, creating paintings that look like medieval church windows. In this manner, he painted clowns, landscapes, and biblical figures.

FIGURE 23.4 The dark, heavy lines in this painting emphasize the sorrowful expression on the king's face. What other art form do these lines suggest?

Georges Rouault. *The Old King.* 1916–36. Oil on canvas. 76.8 × 54 cm (30¼ × 21¼"). Carnegie Museum of Art, Pittsburgh, Pennsylvania. Patrons Art Fund.

The Old King
■ **FIGURE 23.4**

Rouault's heavy lines do more than make his painting of *The Old King* (Figure 23.4) look like stained glass. They also tie his picture together while stressing the sorrowful expression of the figure. Rouault may have been trying to arouse your curiosity. Certainly this is no proud, joyful ruler. Is Rouault trying to tell you that even a king, with all his power and wealth, cannot find comfort in a world of suffering, or is he suggesting that no king is powerful enough to offer his subjects the happiness needed to guarantee his own happiness?

Rouault sometimes kept his pictures for as long as 25 years, during which he endlessly studied and changed them, hoping to achieve perfection. Like Cézanne before him, he did not hesitate to destroy a painting if it failed to please him. It did not bother him in the least that a picture he casually threw away could have been sold for thousands of dollars.

German Expressionism

Rouault and Matisse considered art a form of personal expression. It was a way for them to present their own thoughts and feelings about the world. In Germany, this view was eagerly accepted by several groups of artists. These artists, who were interested in communicating their deep emotional feelings through their artworks, were called *Expressionists.* Their art movement, **Expressionism,** *resulted in artworks that communicated strong emotional feelings.*

Paula Modersohn-Becker
(1876–1907)

In Germany, Paula Modersohn-Becker has long been recognized as an extraordinary artist. Over a brief career, she created some 400 paintings and more than 1,000 drawings and graphic works. Her paintings demonstrate the depth of her feelings and her ability to communicate those feelings in a highly personal, expressive style.

COOPERATIVE LEARNING

Group Forum. Tell students that Matisse's use of simplicity can be compared to a writer's use of simple language and syntax to strip a work of literature down to its bare essentials. Have groups of students research the power of simplicity as a statement in other movements in twentieth-century art, literature, and music. One group might concentrate on the decep-tively simple sentences in works by Ernest Hemingway (e.g., *The Old Man and the Sea*), another on the minimalist compositions of contemporary composer Philip Glass, and a third on the minimalist paintings of Barnett Newman. In a class forum, groups can note similarities in each of these approaches to artistic expression.

Old Peasant Woman

■ **FIGURE 23.5**

In the only example of Modersohn-Becker's work in the United States, the viewer is presented with a haunting image of a peasant woman (Figure 23.5). Seated, with her arms crossed and clutched to her chest, the old woman stares ahead as if in prayer. Her lined face, rough hands, and coarse clothing speak of the hardships she has endured, although these hardships have failed to shake her faith or temper her dignity.

Ernst Ludwig Kirchner (1880–1938)

Street, Berlin (Figure 23.6) is a painting by the German Expressionist Ernst Ludwig Kirchner (**airnst lood**-vig **keerk**-ner). Here Kirchner uses clashing angular shapes to express one of his favorite themes: the tension and artificial elegance of the city. The people here are jammed together on a street, part of a never-ending parade. They look strangely alike, as if cut from the same piece of cardboard with slashes from a razor-sharp knife. They appear to be concerned only with themselves and going their own way. Or are they? It is hard to tell because their faces look like masks.

Historical Context

Behind those masks are the *real* faces. The faces remain hidden, though, because they might betray the people's true feelings. This picture was painted in Berlin just before the outbreak of World War I. It may be the artist's

■ **FIGURE 23.5** The subject of this work may be praying. Perhaps she is also staring back into her memories—or trying to see into the future. **What makes this painting a good example of German Expressionism?**

Paula Modersohn-Becker. *Old Peasant Woman*. c. 1905. Oil on canvas. 75 × 57 cm (29¹/₂ × 22¹/₂"). The Detroit Institute of Arts, Detroit, Michigan. Gift of Robert H. Tannahill.

■ **FIGURE 23.6** These elegant people, who all look so much alike, have hidden their real faces—and their real feelings—behind masks. **What statement does this painting make about the people of Berlin just before World War I?**

Ernst Ludwig Kirchner. *Street, Berlin*. 1913. Oil on canvas. 120.6 × 91.1 cm (47¹/₂ × 35⁷/₈"). The Museum of Modern Art, New York, New York. Purchase.

Chapter 23 *Art of the Early Twentieth Century* **519**

Art Criticism

Reveal two facts about Ernst Ludwig Kirchner: (1) He began his career by studying architecture; (2) Some of his early works as a painter followed the style of Matisse, especially with regard to color. Then refer groups of students to the paintings in Figures 23.6 and 23.7 (page 520). Have students discuss whether either of these works hints at Kirchner's early artistic goals.

Art History

Point out that a number of wars occurred during the first half of the twentieth century, including World War I, World War II, and the Spanish Civil War. Have groups of students research and report on details of these wars (e.g., how long the conflict lasted, what nations were involved, examples of the suffering and devastation that resulted). Students are then to discuss the manner in which these wars affected, directly or indirectly, the art of the period.

More About... **Ernst Ludwig Kirchner.** Like all Expressionists, Ernst Ludwig Kirchner (1880–1938) was interested in making strong personal statements—indeed, Expressionism demanded strong personal statements. Kirchner's later works include a door he carved for a studio he intended to build. One side of the door, which is titled *Man Dancing Between Two Women,* shows just that; it is thought that this image represents Kirchner himself as a young man. The other side of the door, *Ascent of the Alps,* shows rural life in Switzerland, where the artist spent most of his life after World War I. The door seems to serve as a symbol of both the past and the present. The carving shows the influence of Gauguin, as well as European folk art and Romanesque carving.

Art History

Remind students that, while Hitler condemned and destroyed many works of art, he and other officials captured many thousands of works of art from occupied countries during the Second World War. Add that after these works were recovered, the task of identifying them fell to art historians and art critics commissioned specifically for this undertaking. Have students imagine they are such a panel of art critics and historians faced with the task of categorizing each of the works in this lesson. Ask students to examine the works one at a time and note visual and stylistic qualities of each that enable them to identify the artist.

Cross Curriculum

HISTORY. Ask students to read about the life of Käthe Kollwitz. Then encourage them to work in groups to compare their findings and respond to these questions: How did social events in Europe affect Kollwitz's work? What kinds of statements besides those alluded to in the text did she hope to make with her art? How might her artwork have differed had she lived at a different time?

Aesthetics

Have students locate a reproduction of *Death and the Mother*, another lithograph by Käthe Kollwitz. Have them develop a chart showing parallels and points of departure between that print and the one in Figure 23.8. Ask: Which work delivers the more poignant message? Which is more grotesque in the starkness of its commentary?

■ **FIGURE 23.7** Kirchner used yellow for the face here, not because it is realistic but because it is expressive. **Where does this young woman seem to be staring? With what expression?**

Ernst Ludwig Kirchner. *Seated Woman*. 1907. Oil on canvas. 80.6 × 91.1 cm (31³/₄ × 35⁷/₈"). The Minneapolis Institute of Arts, Minneapolis, Minnesota.

■ **FIGURE 23.8** The woman in this lithograph extends her hand in acceptance to Death. **What purpose do the two children serve here? Why does the woman accept death so willingly?**

Käthe Kollwitz. *Woman Greeting Death*. 1934. Lithograph. Private Collection. New York.

attempt to suggest the tension lurking just beneath the phony elegance of the German capital on the brink of war.

Seated Woman
■ **FIGURE 23.7**

Kirchner's colorful, decorative, and highly expressive style is apparent in the haunting portrait of a young woman titled *Seated Woman* (Figure 23.7). Actually, the model was a street urchin named Franzi who appeared one day at the artist's studio and remained to serve as a model and do odd jobs in return for food and lodging. Franzi stares calmly out of the picture, directly at the viewer, with large, sad eyes. Blue shadows below the eyes contrast with the yellow face, attesting to the hardships that marked her past and hinting at those that lie ahead. Franzi disappeared during World War I and was never heard from again. The only clue to her existence is Kirchner's painting; he never parted with it.

In 1938, Kirchner's works were condemned by Hitler. The artist, ill and upset about the conditions in Germany, was unable to face up to this insult and took his own life.

Käthe Kollwitz (1867–1945)

Käthe Kollwitz (**kah**-teh **kole**-vits) was another of Germany's great Expressionists. She used her art to protest against the tragic plight of the poor before and after World War I. Hoping to reach the greatest number of viewers, she chose to express her ideas with etchings, woodcuts, and lithographs.

Her lithograph *Woman Greeting Death* (Figure 23.8) is an example of this work. It shows a woman—frail, weak, and defeated— extending her hand to Death. Too weak even to show fear, she reaches out with one hand while gently pushing her children forward with the other. One child, terrified, turns away, but the other stares directly at Death. Perhaps he is too young to recognize the stranger who takes his mother's hand and will soon reach out for his.

Kollwitz and many of the other German Expressionists were greatly influenced by Vincent van Gogh, the Fauves, and a Norwegian painter named Edvard Munch.

More About... **German Expressionism.** The term *German Expressionism* is in a sense an umbrella term for a number of art movements that formed in the early modern period. The formation of *Die Brucke (The Bridge)* in 1905 signals the beginning of German Expressionism. Ernst Ludwig Kirchner was one of the founding members of this group, which moved in a direction diametrically opposed to most movements of the day. Kirchner himself created the Brucke Manifesto, carving it on a wood block and printing it by hand. The manifesto holds that the young and new should replace the old and established and that art should be, first and foremost, about life. Soon, other Expressionist groups formed, each with different theories about the goals of modern art.

Edvard Munch (1863–1944)

The childhood of Edvard Munch (**ed**-vard **moonk**) was marked by the deaths of some of his family members and by his own poor health. The fear, suffering, and experience of death in his own life became the subject matter for his art.

The Sick Child
■ FIGURE 23.9

How much his own suffering contributed to his work can be seen in a picture entitled *The Sick Child* (Figure 23.9) which was inspired by the death of his older sister. Munch captures the pale complexion, colorless lips, and hopeless stare of a child weakened and finally conquered by illness. Beyond caring, she looks past her grieving mother to a certain, tragic future.

Pictures like this shocked viewers at first. Munch's figures seemed crude and grotesque when compared to the colorful and light-hearted visions of the Impressionists, who were enjoying great popularity at the time. Munch's works, however, were in keeping with the period in which he lived, a period when writers and artists were interested in exploring feelings and emotions rather than describing outward appearances.

Before, artists showed people in anguish as they appeared to a rational, objective viewer. With Munch and the other Expressionists, this point of view changed. Instead, they showed the world *through the eyes of the people in anguish*. When seen that way, the shapes and colors of familiar objects change. Trees, hills, houses, and people are pulled out of shape and take on new, unexpected and often disturbing colors.

The Scream
■ FIGURE 23.10

The painting style based on this view of the world is illustrated in Munch's painting *The Scream* (Figure 23.10). The curved shapes and

■ **FIGURE 23.9** Munch's choice of subject here was influenced by his own experiences with illness and the early death of a beloved sister. **What are the similarities between the sick child here and the central figure in Kollwitz's *Woman Greeting Death* (Figure 23.8)?**

Edvard Munch. *The Sick Child.* 1907. Oil on canvas. 118.7 × 121 cm (46³/₄ × 47²/₃"). The Tate Gallery, London, England.

■ **FIGURE 23.10** The body of the central figure bends and twists as a scream builds and erupts from deep within. **How did Munch show that the figures in the background are unaffected by the emotions of the central figure?**

Edvard Munch. *The Scream.* 1893. Tempera and pastels on cardboard. 91 × 73.5 cm (36 × 29"). National Gallery, Oslo, Norway.

Chapter 23 *Art of the Early Twentieth Century* **521**

CHAPTER 23
LESSON ONE

Art Criticism

Direct students' attention to Munch's *The Scream,* Figure 23.10. Then divide the class into two groups, assigning one group the art element of color, and the second the element of line. Each group is to consider and then explain how its element contributes to the strong emotion conveyed by the work.

Critical Thinking

Share with students the views of French poet and modern art critic Guillaume Appollinaire, who once attempted to explain the purpose of Expressionism to a skeptical fellow critic by commenting that "Exactitude is not truth." Have students analyze his statement and then apply it to the artworks on these pages. Ask: What truth is expressed in each work?

𝒯eacher 𝒩otes

Technology in the Classroom. If your classroom computer includes a CD-ROM player, you might investigate the acquisition of compact discs of several of the early twentieth-century periodicals in which numerous artists covered in this chapter shared their opinions, theories, and ideas on modern art. Some of the more noteworthy periodicals include Hans Arp and Robert Delaunay's *Abstraction-Creation,* Piet Mondrian's *Cercle et Carre (Circle and Square),* the architect Le Corbusier's *L'Esprit Nouveau (The New Spirit),* and Art Concret, which had only one issue—though that issue included the very important Constructivist Manifesto.

Aesthetics

Remind students that Kandinsky, like many modern artists, felt that expression, and not literal depiction, was the ultimate purpose of art. Then divide the class into two groups. Have one group assume the role of a panel of aestheticians who subscribe to the imitationalist theory, have the other group be a panel adhering to the emotionalist theory. Have the two panels confer on the relative merits of Figure 23.11, and then stage a debate on the subject.

Art Criticism

Call to students' attention that few art movements are more misunderstood by the majority than nonobjective art. Point out that works such as Figure 23.11 are often dismissed as "scribbles" or "random doodling" by individuals who fail to understand the place of such paintings in art history. Have groups of students collaborate on letters supposedly written to an individual who has leveled such misguided criticisms. In defending such works, groups may rely on both critical and historical data to support their contentions.

colors in this work are expressive rather than realistic. Everything is distorted to communicate an overpowering emotion. The subject of this picture is fear. There is no mistaking the fact that the person in this painting is terrified. The scream that comes from the open mouth is so piercing that the figure must clasp its hands tightly over its ears.

Nonobjective Art

Until the nineteenth century, artists used recognizable images in their works. This approach changed when artists began to alter the appearance of the objects they painted. Cézanne painted jugs with openings that were too large, Gauguin created crimson trees and rocks, and Matisse stripped unnecessary details from the figures and objects in his pictures.

By the beginning of the twentieth century, more and more artists were veering away from literal interpretations of subject matter to focus attention on the formal qualities in their art. Eventually, some of these artists decided to remove the figures and any other objects that might interfere with their desire for a unified and visually appealing design.

■ **FIGURE 23.11** Notice that the title of this work suggests a musical composition. Why is this work a clear example of nonobjective art?

Wassily Kandinsky. *Improvisation 28 (Second Version)*. 1912. 111.4 × 162.1 cm (43⁷/₈ × 63⁷/₈″). The Solomon R. Guggenheim Museum, New York, New York. Gift, Solomon R. Guggenheim, 1937. The Solomon R. Guggenheim Foundation. (FN37.239).

Wassily Kandinsky
(1866–1944)

Perhaps the first artist to reject the use of figures and objects was a Russian, Wassily Kandinsky (vah-**see**-lee kahn-**deen**-skee). When Kandinsky, then a 29-year-old lawyer, visited an exhibit of French Impressionist paintings in Moscow, he was overwhelmed by the works he saw. Months later, he abandoned his legal career and went to Munich, Germany, to study painting.

For several years, Kandinsky experimented unsuccessfully with several different styles: Impressionism, Post-Impressionism, Fauvism, and Expressionism. Then, around 1909, he turned away from these outside influences and listened to his own instincts. A year later he finished a watercolor painting that changed the course of art history. It was brightly colored and may have been based on some earlier landscape studies. Most importantly no subject matter could be seen in the work. Kandinsky's painting marked the start of a new style—**nonobjective art,** *a style that employs color, line, texture, and unrecognizable shapes and forms. These works contain no apparent references to reality.*

Kandinsky went on to do more paintings that rejected subject matter even as a starting point (Figure 23.11). His main goal was to convey moods and feelings. This effect could be achieved, he felt, by arranging the elements of art in certain ways. Colors, values, lines, shapes, and textures were selected and carefully arranged on the canvas for a certain effect.

Kandinsky felt that art elements, like musical sounds, could be arranged to communicate emotions and feelings. In fact, Kandinsky believed that a painting should be the "exact duplicate of some inner emotion." He did not believe that art should be an illustration of objects as they appear in nature.

CULTURAL DIVERSITY

Der Blaue Reiter. Provide students with more information about Wassily Kandinsky and the splinter group called Der Blaue Reiter ("The Blue Rider"), which he helped found. Point out that the group was very conscious of artistic theory and artistic duty and felt that a connection between the artists and their audience was necessary. Then ask several volunteers to research the "Blaue Reiter Almanac," an almanac devoted to essays and illustrations of art and music. Have volunteers locate and bring to class reproductions of illustrations from the almanac, many of which were not commonly considered art (i.e., folk art, Bavarian paintings on glass, Russian religious prints, and children's art).

Gabriele Münter (1877–1962)

In 1911, Kandinsky and several other painters banded together in Munich to form a group known as the *Blaue Reiter* (Blue Rider), a name taken from a painting by Kandinsky. The members of this group differed widely in their artistic styles but were united by a desire to express inner feelings in their paintings. One of the founding members of this group was a former student of Kandinsky's, Gabriele Münter (**moon**-ter). As a mature artist, Münter made use of the intense colors, heavy outlines, and simplified shapes associated with the Fauves to express the kind of inner emotions Kandinsky sought to capture in his nonobjective paintings.

This mature style is seen in her *Schnee und Sonne (Snow and Sun)* (Figure 23.12), painted in the same year that the Blue Rider was founded. It shows a solitary figure walking along the snow-covered street of a small village. Despite the bright colors, bitter cold is suggested by the leaden sky and the heavily clothed figure. The painting illustrates the simple, slow-paced life of a small village. In this respect, Münter's painting echoes those of other twentieth-century artists who believed that modern culture had become too complicated, too mechanized, and too detached from real feelings.

Cubism

German Expressionism, with its concern for expressing moods and feelings, can be traced back to the works of van Gogh and Gauguin. Another twentieth-century art movement can be linked in much the same way to the work of Paul Cézanne in the nineteenth century.

Artists such as Pablo Picasso (**pah**-bloh pee-**kah**-soh) and Georges Braque (zhorzh **brahk**) started with Cézanne's idea that all shapes in nature are based on the sphere, the cone, and the cylinder. They carried this idea further by trying to paint three-dimensional objects as if they were seen from many different angles at the same time. They developed a style of painting, called **Cubism,** *in which artists tried to show all sides of three-dimensional objects on a flat canvas.*

The Cubist Approach

The Cubist approach to painting can be illustrated with the simple sketches provided in Figure 23.13. In the first sketch, an ordinary coffee cup has been drawn from several different points of view. After these first sketches have been done, the artist studies them to find the parts of the cup that are most interesting and most characteristic of coffee cups. These parts are then arranged in a composition. Thus, parts from the top, sides, and bottom of the cup are blended together to complete the picture. This illustration is very simple, but it may help you to understand the

■ **FIGURE 23.12** In spite of the bright colors, this work suggests bitter cold weather and a somber mood. **How is the lone figure emphasized?**

Gabriele Münter. *Schnee und Sonne (Snow and Sun).* 1911. Oil on cardboard. 50.8 × 69.8 cm (20 × 27¹/₂″). The University of Iowa Museum of Art, Iowa City, Iowa. Gift of Owen and Leone Elliott.

■ **FIGURE 23.13** A drawing in the style of Cubism.

Chapter 23 *Art of the Early Twentieth Century* **523**

CHAPTER 23
LESSON ONE

Cross Curriculum

MUSIC. Ask a group of volunteers to research and report on twentieth-century composer Arnold Schoenberg and the twelve-tone (or "serial") method of composition he developed in the 1920s. In their presentation, researchers should define the principles of twelve-tone music and the goals of the composer. If possible, obtain and play a recording of one of Schoenberg's pieces. Conclude by having the class as a whole discuss ways in which this approach to music mirrors that of Kandinsky and his followers to the visual arts.

Aesthetics

Share with students the anecdote that Kandinsky stumbled upon nonobjectivism when he entered his studio one evening and beheld one of his own works in progress that he had inadvertently turned upside down. Then have students turn their texts upside down and glance at *Improvisation 28,* Figure 23.11. Can students find tangible, recognizable shapes and forms in the work? What does this activity reveal to students about the act of perceiving "implied" images?

Art History

Ask a group of interested volunteers to assemble a series of reproductions of Münter's work, showing the development of her style and the influences of the Impressionists, the Fauves, and Kandinsky. Let these students share and discuss these works with the rest of the class.

More About... **Cubists.** Fernand Léger (1881–1955) was another artist who experimented with the Cubist style of painting. Léger pieced together fragments of everyday life to create another reality. He always painted from visual experience—that is, some artifact was always the basis of his art—though he often attained such extreme abstraction that it is not always easy to determine the original motif. In addition, Léger used color in a purely decorative way, a tendency neither Picasso nor Braque approved of, but which influenced later uses of color in art. This color aspect of Cubism that Léger pioneered was called *Orphism,* and other artists such as Robert Delaunay would go so far as to assert that color alone was both the subject and the form of art.

Art History

Have several small committees of students each locate a noteworthy work by Picasso not included in the text. (Possibilities include his remarkable *Bull's Head,* his *The Blind Man's Meal,* or one of the several paintings in his *Three Musicians* series). Have students compare the work they have selected with those illustrated in the text. Ask: Which, if any, of these works exhibit traces of Cubism? Which work, if any, would students suppose Picasso created during his Blue period? During his Rose period?

Art Criticism

Point out the date in the credit line of Figure 23.14. Then remind students that Paul Cézanne, to whom the Cubists were admittedly indebted, died four years earlier. Ask students to imagine that the Post-Impressionist had lived long enough to view this work. Have two volunteers plan and then act out a dialogue between Cézanne and Picasso, in which the former expresses his opinion of the latter's work. For background material, students should draw both on information about Cézanne covered in the text and facts gleaned from art print resources.

Studio Skills

Have students create a variety of geometric forms (e.g., a cube, a cone, a cylinder) using stiff white paper and transparent tape. Have students, as a group, agree on a still-life arrangement of these objects. Then, working individually, students are to make drawings of the arrangement as seen simultaneously from various perspectives.

process a Cubist artist used when painting a picture like *The Glass of Absinthe* (Figure 23.14).

In this Cubist painting, recognition is hampered because shapes have been broken up and reassembled. This produces a complex arrangement of new shapes that can be confusing to the viewer. It is difficult to identify when one shape is ahead of another, because part of it seems to be in front and part of it behind. This confusion is heightened by the use of lines that end suddenly when you expect them to continue, or continue when you expect them to end. Colors associated with the objects were not used. Instead, the artist chose grays, browns, and other drab colors, which painters before this time had avoided.

Cubist Collage

Cubists were also interested in making the surfaces of their paintings richer and more exciting by adding a variety of actual textures. Around 1911, Picasso, Braque, and others began to add materials such as newspaper clippings, pieces of wallpaper, and labels to the picture surface. This technique, known as **collage,** *involves adding other materials to*

■ **FIGURE 23.14** In this painting, Picasso broke up—and then reassembled—the shapes he chose as his subject. **How are the colors in this work typical of early Cubist paintings? How are harmony and variety demonstrated?**

Pablo Picasso. *The Glass of Absinthe.* 1911. Oil on canvas. 38.4 × 46.4 cm (15¹⁄₈ × 18¹⁄₄″). Allen Memorial Art Museum, Oberlin College, Oberlin, Ohio. Mrs. F. F. Prentiss Fund, 47.36.

the picture surface. It further blurred the recognizable connection between the painting and any represented object (Figure 23.15).

Cubism can be thought of as an intellectual approach to art, rather than a descriptive or an emotional one. Cubist artists *thought* their way through their paintings, trying to show what they knew was there, not what they saw or felt.

Pablo Picasso (1881–1973)

Pablo Picasso led a long and productive life during which he passed through many different stages. After working in the Cubist style, he returned to paintings of the human figure in which he used a greater range of colors. In 1937, he painted his famous antiwar picture, *Guernica.*

■ **FIGURE 23.15** Collage appealed to Cubists as a means of adding variety to the actual textures of their works. **Both this Cubist collage and the earlier Cubist painting in Figure 23.14 are Picasso's works. How do they differ?**

Pablo Picasso. *Guitar. Céret (after March 31,* 1913). Cut and pasted paper, ink, charcoal, and white chalk on blue paper, mounted on board. 66.4 × 49.6 cm (26¹⁄₈ × 19¹⁄₂″). The Museum of Modern Art, New York, New York. Nelson A. Rockefeller Bequest.

More About... **Picasso's Influence.** A year before Picasso created the mixed media image of a guitar shown in Figure 23.15, the artist assembled a sculpture of a guitar from metal and wire. The sculpture had a profound effect on other artists. For many, the new method of assembling replaced more traditional methods of sculpting. In particular, a group of Russian artists called the Constructivists found this form of sculpture very appealing and concentrated on creating assemblages. Assembling was a particular passion of Russian-born sculptor Naum Gabo (1899–1977), who worked in wood, glass, plastic, and paper, restricting the use of color to that which was inherent in the media. Gabo's subjects included heads and busts, as well as less easily identifiable objects.

Guernica

Guernica (Figure 23.16) is a large mural (11.5 × 25.7 feet) made for the Pavilion of the Spanish Republic at the Paris International Exposition. The work was inspired by the bombing of the ancient Spanish city of Guernica by German planes during the Spanish Civil War. Because the city had no military importance, the destruction served no other purpose than to test the effectiveness of large-scale bombing. As a result of this "test," the city and most of its inhabitants were destroyed.

Identifying Styles in *Art*

*P*icasso combines Expressionism and Cubism here. Like the Expressionists, he exaggerates and distorts forms. At the same time, he overlaps flat shapes in an abstract design, as did the Cubists. Picasso uses bold blacks, whites, and grays instead of color to give the impression of newsprint or newspaper photographs. Adding to the look of newsprint is the stippled effect on the horse.

■ **FIGURE 23.16** Pablo Picasso. *Guernica.* 1937. Oil on canvas. Approx. 3.5 × 7.8 m (11′6″ × 25′8″). Museo Nacional Centro de Arte Reina Sofia, Madrid, Spain.

1 The large central triangle, a reminder of the organizational technique used by such Renaissance artists as Botticelli and Raphael, links a series of tragic images.

2 At the far right, a woman crashes through the floor of a burning building.

3 In front of her, another woman dashes forward blindly in panic.

4 A horse with a spear in its back screams in terror.

5 A severed head with staring eyes rests on an outstretched arm, its hand reaching for nothing.

6 Another hand clutches a broken sword.

7 A woman holds a dead child and raises her head skyward to scream out her horror at the planes overhead.

Aesthetics

Divide the class into two groups. Ask one group to brainstorm ways in which Cubism might be considered an "intellectual" approach to art; ask the other to brainstorm ways in which the movement might be thought of as having an "emotional" basis. Then direct both groups to Picasso's *Guernica* (Figure 23.16), and have them attempt to isolate details and other aspects of the work that support their positions.

Studio Skills

Provide students with an assortment of everyday found objects with a multiplicity of textures (e.g., discarded scraps of paper, paper clips, bits of ribbon), and invite them to make a collage. Instruct them to begin by sketching a plan for arranging the objects. Have students use white glue to secure the objects to sheets of white paper. If they wish, students may use acrylic paint to fill in areas on their collages.

Did You Know?

Following the tragic and senseless bombing of the Spanish city of Guernica, a correspondent for *The London Times* wrote, "Reflections of the flames could be seen in the smoke above the mountains from ten miles away. Throughout the night houses were falling until the streets became long heaps of red impenetrable debris."

Identifying Styles in *Art*

Guide students in examining and discussing Picasso's *Guernica,* Figure 23.16. Then help students use the diagram and the numbered explanations to explore the work further. Encourage them to turn to Chapter 16 and find specific Renaissance works that might have influenced Picasso's organization of *Guernica.* Then, refer students back to Kollwitz's *Woman Greeting Death* (Figure 23.8, page 520) and ahead to Braque's *Still Life with Fruit* (Figure 23.17, page 526). Ask: With which artwork is Picasso's painting more allied in theme? With which is it more allied in terms of technique?

Study Guide

Distribute *Study Guide* 53 in the TCR. Assist students in reviewing key concepts. 📁

Art and Humanities

Have students complete *Appreciating Cultural Diversity* 33, "The Latinization of the United States," in the TCR. In this activity, students learn about the writings and television productions of Mexico's preeminent novelists and their influence on the United States. Students then research and prepare a report on Latin-American artists. 📁

ASSESS
Checking Comprehension

Have students respond to the lesson review questions. Answers are given in the box below.

Reteaching

➤ Assign *Reteaching* 53, found in the TCR. Have students complete the activity and review their responses. 📁

➤ Have students find examples of Expressionist and/or nonobjective art in magazines and newspapers. Ask: In what context did you find these works (i.e., in advertising sections, editorial sections, as an accompaniment to fiction)? How easy was it to find examples of these types of art?

Did You Know❓

At the same time Aristide Maillol was at work on *The Mediterranean*, Pablo Picasso was creating works that typify his Blue period.

The painting's powerful images convey the full impact of the event far more effectively than could the words in a newspaper account, or even photographs. The artist makes no effort to show the event itself. Instead, he combines a number of vivid images to form a forceful and moving statement about the horror, the agony, and the waste of modern warfare.

Picasso lived a long and full life; he was 91 years old when he died in 1973. He left behind a tremendous number of paintings, prints, and sculptures—and a profound influence on twentieth-century art.

Georges Braque (1882–1963)

Unlike Picasso, Georges Braque did not go through a series of dramatic style changes during his career. The changes in his painting style were more subtle and evolved gradually over time. Braque always maintained that a painting is a flat surface and should remain a flat surface. Throughout his life, he focused on ways to make that surface more interesting by using colors, lines, shapes, and textures.

From 1907 to 1914, Braque worked closely with Picasso to develop Cubism. When World War I broke out, Braque was called into the army and, in 1915, was seriously wounded. In 1917, following months in recovery, he returned to his painting. From that point on, Braque's work shows a renewed respect for subject matter, more playful curves, and brighter colors. Always interested in texture, he applied his paint, often mixed with sand, in layers to build a rich, heavy surface. In this way, he said, he made his pictures more "touchable."

Still Life with Fruit
■ FIGURE 23.17

Braque preferred to paint still lifes (Figure 23.17), but instead of concentrating only on fruits and flowers, he painted more permanent, manufactured objects, such as tables, bottles, mandolins, books, and pipes. He selected objects that people use when relaxing and enjoying pleasant thoughts. These quiet, elegant still lifes did exactly what Braque intended them to do—they put viewers in a gentle, comfortable mood.

Aristide Maillol (1861–1944)

Viewers experience the same kind of gentle, comfortable feeling when they observe the sculptures of Aristide Maillol (ah-ree-**steed** my-**yohl**). Unlike Rodin, Maillol was not interested in dramatic gestures and expressions, or

■ **FIGURE 23.17** Braque worked closely with Picasso to develop the Cubist style. In his later works, however, Braque's style showed an increased interest in texture and in presenting subject matter. **During which part of his career did Braque paint this still life? How can you tell?**

Georges Braque. *Still Life with Fruit.* 1920–23. Oil with sand on canvas. 34.9 × 64.8 cm (13³/₄ × 25¹/₂"). The University of Iowa Museum of Art, Iowa City, Iowa. Gift of Owen and Leone Elliott, 1968.

| *More About...* | **Art Nouveau.** Another art style that flourished at the same time as those mentioned in the lesson was Art Nouveau. The style, which was a reaction |

against both the technological revolution of the early modern period—the machine age—and the imitations of past styles, is characterized by the use of colored materials, molded stonework, floral motifs, curvilinear forms, wrought iron, and other unusual ornamentation. Although distortion of objects is a trait, the style is basically representational. The Art Nouveau style can be seen in both the applied and the fine arts, in everything from jewelry to furniture and architecture. A German version of this style, called *Jugendstil*, was practiced by Kandinsky early in his career.

in a sculptured surface made up of bumps and hollows. He did not seek to shock or surprise the viewer. He admired the balance, simplicity, and peacefulness of ancient Greek sculptures, and tried to capture these same qualities in his own work.

Maillol began his career as a painter, but, because he did not enjoy great success in that medium, he later turned to tapestry making. Then, when he was 40 years old, an eye ailment prevented him from weaving. Although he must have been discouraged, he refused to abandon his career in art. Instead, he became a sculptor. To his amazement, he discovered that sculpture was his true medium.

The Mediterranean
■ FIGURE 23.18

Maillol had been a sculptor for only a few months when he created a seated woman entitled *The Mediterranean* (Figure 23.18). This work contained all of the main features of his style. The figure is posed in a quiet, restful position without a hint of movement. There is no sign of nervousness or tension, or that she is even aware of what might be going on around her. There is nothing about this woman to suggest that she is a specific individual. Maillol was not attempting a portrait. He was using the woman's figure to represent a particular mood—thoughtful, gentle, and calm.

LOOKING **Closely**

USE OF THE ELEMENTS AND PRINCIPLES

- **Shape.** From the side, the figure forms a large triangular shape, which gives it a balanced, stable look. Smaller triangles are created by the raised leg and the arm supporting the head.
- **Unity.** The repetition of these triangular shapes is important here because it helps to unify the work in the same way that a certain color used over and over again can unify a painting.

■ **FIGURE 23.18**

Aristide Maillol. *The Mediterranean.* 1902-5. Cast c. 1951-53. Bronze. 104.1 × 114.3 × 75.6 cm (41 × 45 × 29³/₄"). The Museum of Modern Art, New York, New York. Gift of Stephen C. Clark.

LESSON ONE REVIEW

Reviewing Art Facts

1. Who was the leader of the Fauves, and what did he feel was the purpose of his art?
2. What did the German Expressionists wish to represent in their works? Name a famous woman artist who was associated with the German Expressionists.
3. What is nonobjective art? Who is usually regarded as its founder?
4. What impact did the discovery of nonobjective art have on future artists?

Activity... *Sketching Geometric Shapes*

Cubism is one of the cornerstone movements of early twentieth-century art. Picasso, regarded as the father of this style, revolutionized the way the world looked at art. Along with Georges Braque, he worked on the theory that all objects are based on geometric form.

Create a series of sketches that emphasize the geometric shapes of still-life objects. Work from an arrangement of simple shapes such as bottles and boxes. Move all around the still life, combining different views in your sketches. Choose one of your sketches and use it as the basis for a Cubist painting. Display your finished work.

LESSON ONE REVIEW

Answers to Reviewing Art Facts

1. Henri Matisse; his purpose was to give pleasure.
2. Strong emotional feelings; Modersohn-Becker or Kollwitz.
3. Art that makes no use of realistic subject matter; Kandinsky.
4. Painters were free from relying on nature for subject matter.

Activity... *Sketching Geometric Shapes*

Let students work in small groups to select and arrange objects to sketch. Remind group members to place their arrangement on a freestanding desk or table, so they can easily view it from all sides. Have students compare and discuss their sketches and to help one another choose appropriate sketches for their Cubist paintings in the Studio Lesson.

LOOKING **Closely**

Have students examine the sculpture by Maillol in Figure 23.18. Encourage them to discuss their understanding of the elements and principles of art exhibited in the work before they read and discuss the explanation in this feature. Then have students identify the mood or message conveyed by the work. Ask: Which of the three main aesthetic schools you have studied would deem the sculpture the greatest success? Which would consider the work the least successful?

Enrichment

Have students work in small groups to complete *Cooperative Learning* 33, "The Power of Art," in the TCR. Groups report on ways in which artists expressed power at the beginning of the twentieth century.

Extension

Have students compare Matisse's *The Red Studio* (Figure 23.2) and *The Knife Thrower* (Figure 23.3) on page 517 with Kandinsky's *Improvisation 28* (Figure 23.11) on page 522. Ask: In what important ways do Matisse's works differ from Kandinsky's? Have students identify the artistic styles of Matisse and Kandinsky.

CLOSE

Ask students to identify the art movements covered in this lesson, naming the key figures, characteristics of the movements, and ways in which the movements differed from those that had occurred before this time period.

Contributions from Mexico and the United States

Focus

Lesson Objectives

After studying this lesson, students will be able to:

- Name the Mexican muralists and tell what they chose as subject matter for their art.
- Identify and describe the American art movement responsible for challenging traditional painting techniques and subject matter.
- Discuss the importance of the Armory show of 1913.

Building Vocabulary

Write the two Vocabulary terms—*Ashcan School* and *Armory Show*—on the board, and ask students to jot down at least three words or phrases each term brings to mind. Let students share their ideas, and then compare their associations with the definitions presented in the Glossary.

Motivator

Have students select a topic of global concern (e.g., the environment, the plight of inner cities, drug abuse). Guide students in discussing the problem and their feelings in response to it. Then ask students to scour magazines for visual works that express similar feelings. Ask: What aspects of the works communicate such emotions? Are the works invariably realistic or do they also exhibit abstraction? If students were unable to read the accompanying text, would they nevertheless understand the message the work conveys?

Contributions from Mexico and the United States

Vocabulary
- Ashcan School
- Armory Show

Artists to Meet
- Diego Rivera
- José Clemente Orozco
- David Alfaro Siqueiros
- Frida Kahlo
- John Sloan
- George Bellows

Discover
After completing this lesson, you will be able to:
- Name the Mexican muralists and tell what they chose as subject matter for their art.
- Identify and describe the American art movement responsible for challenging traditional painting techniques and subject matter.
- Discuss the importance of the Armory Show of 1913.

*M*uch of the early twentieth-century art in Mexico and the United States was created in response to a bewildering assortment of events and circumstances. In Mexico, political and social turmoil motivated many artists to create bold and powerful images expressing their reactions.

At the same time, changes in all aspects of life were taking place in the United States at a pace more rapid than in any earlier period. These changes shook artists out of the conservatism that had marked their work at the beginning of the century and helped push them in new directions.

In the early twentieth century, the poor and landless in Mexico tried to free themselves from corrupt landowners. In 1911, this struggle reached a bloody climax with the fall of the dictator, Porfirio Diaz, and the start of the Mexican Revolution. The revolt ended in 1921.

The Muralists in Mexico

The years following this conflict saw the emergence and rise of Mexican mural painting. As their subject matter, muralists chose the political and social problems of the Mexican people; they adorned both the inside and outside walls of buildings with their powerful murals. Buildings in the United States also benefited from their art. (See Figure 23.1, page 514.)

The muralists revived an old tradition of creating art on building walls. The mosaics in Byzantine churches, such as those in Italy's San Vitale, were meant to teach the Christian message. Later Giotto, Masaccio, and others used a fresco technique to illustrate stories from the Bible on the interior walls of Italian churches.

Mexican artists used murals to tell a different kind of story. They told of revolutions, native traditions, festivals, and legends.

Painting their huge pictures on the walls of public buildings allowed these artists to take their work directly to the people. They did not want their paintings placed in museums, galleries, or private homes, where only a few people would see and respond to them. Instead, their works were intended to be public property.

Diego Rivera (1886–1957)

One of the most famous of these Mexican mural painters was Diego Rivera (dee-**ay**-goh ree-**vay**-rah). He created the first modern mural painting in Mexico. As a young man, Rivera studied the art of the great Italian fresco artists. This study helped him to realize his own artistic goal: to record in art the gallant struggle of the Mexican peasant.

528

LESSON TWO RESOURCES

Teacher's Classroom Resources

- Art and Humanities 39
- Cooperative Learning 34, 35
- Enrichment Activity 44
- Reproducible Lesson Plan 54
- Reteaching Activity 54
- Study Guide 54

Liberation of the Peon

■ **FIGURE 23.19**

In *Liberation of the Peon* (Figure 23.19), Rivera draws equally on his skills as a painter and as a master storyteller to create one of his finest works. It shows a group of somber revolutionary soldiers cutting the ropes that bind a dead peon, or peasant. A blanket is held ready to cover the peon's naked, whip-scarred body. In the distance, a hacienda burns; this indicates that the landowner responsible for the peon's death has already been punished. Silently and sorrowfully, the soldiers do what they can for their dead comrade. Rivera's story is not difficult to read or to understand—the peon has been "liberated" from a life of oppression and suffering. Like scores of other poor peasants, he has found his liberation in the form of death.

José Clemente Orozco (1883–1949)

Another Mexican muralist, José Clemente Orozco (hoh-**zay** kleh-**men**-tay oh-**rose**-koh), developed a style of painting that earned him the title of the Mexican Goya. It is a style stripped of everything but emotions. Orozco used it to paint pictures that expressed his anger for all forms of tyranny. Even in pictures that at first seem calm and quiet, there is an undeniable undercurrent of power and fury. *Zapatistas* (Figure 1.18, page 21) is such a painting. Here the followers of the revolutionary leader Emiliano Zapata are shown marching to battle. The determined plodding of the grim peons and the rhythm created by their forward-pressing bodies produce a steady undeniable movement across the work.

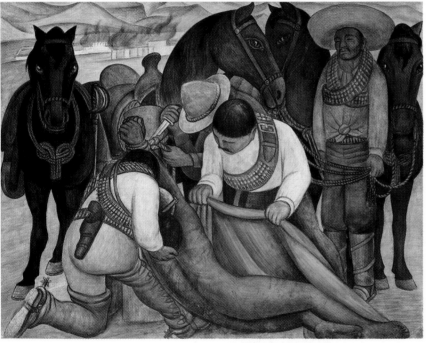

■ **FIGURE 23.19** Compare Rivera's painting to Giotto's *Lamentation* (Figure 15.21, page 345). Notice that the figures in both works have bulk and weight and seem to move in space. In both, the figures act out their story with easily understood gestures and expressions. **Compare the feelings evoked by the two works.**

Diego Rivera. *Liberation of the Peon.* 1931. Fresco. 185.4 × 239.4 cm (73 × 94¼″). Philadelphia Museum of Art, Philadelphia, Pennsylvania. Given by Mr. and Mrs. Herbert Cameron Morris.

TEACH
Introducing the Lesson

Remind students that during the Middle Ages, teachings of the Church were often communicated to the largely illiterate masses through art. Explain that in this next lesson students will read about another era, more recent and closer to home, in which art was used as a tool of enlightenment.

Art History

Point out that Rivera's *Liberation of the Peon* (Figure 23.19) bears resemblances not only to Giotto's *Lamentation Pietà* (Figure 15.21, page 345) but to other works from earlier periods of art. To underscore the point, have students turn to Rubens's *The Raising of the Cross* (Figure 19.9, page 427) and note the similarities in the use of axis line to achieve an asymmetrical balance. Ask: How does the mood of the two works compare? In what other ways are the paintings similar? How are they dissimilar?

Studio Skills

Remind students that the murals discussed in this lesson are part of a long tradition of narrative art. Then divide the class into cooperative learning groups. Have the members of each group decide on a particular story or event they wish to narrate visually, using newsprint, pencils, and pastels. When groups have completed their projects, have them use spray fixative to keep the work looking fresh. Then display the different stories. Ask students to try to identify the story without being informed beforehand what it is.

 Technology ■■■

National Gallery of Art Videodisc Use the following images as examples of more works by artists introduced in this lesson.

George Bellows
Both Members of This Club

Search Frame 2064

George Bellows
Both Members of This Club

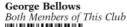

Search Frame 2068

George Bellows
My Family

Search Frame 2074

Use Glencoe's *Correlation Bar Code Guide to the National Gallery of Art* to locate more artworks.

529

Art Criticism

Have students examine *Barricade,* Figure 23.20. Reinforce the observation that the artist, José Clemente Orozco, uses movement, rhythm, and repetition to make this work powerful and frightening. Ask students to identify other paintings they have seen in the text that use movement, rhythm, and repetition as key elements of design. Ask students if the results are always the same. Have them identify the variety of emotions that these elements can be used to convey.

Critical Thinking

Ask students to brainstorm a list of other artists who, like the Mexican muralists, were preoccupied with war and the suffering that goes along with it. Encourage students to find examples of such works, both within the text and in other resources. Then have individual students compose short essays in which they note common threads running through works that make antiwar statements.

■ **FIGURE 23.20** Notice the central shape formed by the combined figures here. Use your imagination to "listen" to this painting. What sounds do you hear? What emotions do those sounds evoke?

José Clemente Orozco. *Barricade.* 1931. Oil on canvas. 139.7 × 114.3 cm (55 × 45"). The Museum of Modern Art, New York, New York. Given anonymously. © Estate of José Clemente Orozco/Licensed by VAGA, New York, New York.

Barricade
■ **FIGURE 23.20**

In his painting called *Barricade* (Figure 23.20), Orozco uses slashing diagonal lines and dramatic contrasts of hue and value to show Zapata's soldiers pulling and pushing to erect a makeshift barricade. Lacking materials, they must use their own bodies to complete the barricade. The structure is a powerful symbol of the sacrifices a proud people are willing to make to gain their freedom.

David Alfaro Siqueiros (1896–1974)

Orozco painted his first mural for the National Preparatory School of Mexico City in 1922. Working next to him was another, younger painter who was also doing his first mural: David Alfaro Siqueiros (dah-**veed** al-**far**-oh see-**kayr**-ohs). Along with Rivera and Orozco, he was to become known as a founder of Mexican mural painting.

Siqueiros was just as involved in politics as he was in art. Several times he was sentenced to prison or exiled for his political beliefs. *Echo of a Scream* (Figure 23.21) is his nightmarish

Time & Place
CONNECTIONS

Early Twentieth Century
c. 1900–1950

AUTOMOBILES. The Model T built by Henry Ford was priced so the average person could afford one. The assembly-line process cut costs, and more than 15 million autos were purchased between 1908 and 1927.

FLAPPER DRESS. Makeup, short, trimmed hair, and shorter skirts were the fashion in 1920s America. To some, it was a sign of the increased freedoms women were experiencing.

*A*ctivity **Interview.** Work with a partner and create an "on the spot" interview with a person from the 1920s. Ask about the styles of the day. Get opinions about the usefulness of the new Model T Ford.

Time & Place
CONNECTIONS

Early Twentieth Century

Guide students in discussing the images in this feature. Let students work in groups to find out more about these topics, including answers to questions such as these: What was the price of a Model T? At that time, what was the average income of an American family? What were the prices of other common household needs? How did access to automobiles change the lives of families? How did it change American society? What freedoms did American women enjoy in the 1920s? How did their daily lives compare to those of American women today?

protest against war. It was done in the year in which Picasso finished his masterpiece on the same theme—*Guernica.* If you compare these two works, you will see how two artists expressed the same antiwar theme in completely different ways.

In his painting, Picasso used overlapping flat shapes, a variety of contrasting light and dark values, and an abstract design. Siqueiros used gradations of value to model three-dimensional forms that look as if they are projecting forward in space. This three-dimensional quality makes his work more vivid, like a horrible dream brought into sharp focus.

Siqueiros centers his attention on one of the most innocent and helpless victims of war—a baby. The infant is shown sitting amid the rubble of a shattered city. The second, larger head may be a symbol for all children killed, crippled, orphaned, or made homeless by war. Its magnified scream of terror pierces an unnatural stillness, but this scream is destined to fade without having reached a single ear.

Impact of the Muralists

Clearly, the art of Rivera, Orozco, and Siqueiros reveals a strong preoccupation with suffering and war. These artists, with their strong social and political views, were products of their time. Much of their art was concerned with telling the story of the peons' bitter struggle to overthrow the corrupt landowners. They told this story in bold murals that brought about a revolution in painting. The changes in art were just as intense as the political upheaval that altered the course of events in their country.

All three of these Mexican artists visited and painted murals in the United States, where they had a great impact on many young artists. Some of these American artists even went on to show the same concern for social and political problems in their own works. In the late 1940s and 1950s, the idea of huge wall paintings was so appealing to a number of artists that they abandoned their easels and small canvases to paint on a monumental scale. One of the first of these was Jackson Pollock, whom you will meet later.

■ **FIGURE 23.21** This work communicates Siqueiros's protest against war, focusing on the most innocent victims. **How does his use of color help identify the painting's center of interest?**

David Alfaro Siqueiros. *Echo of a Scream.* 1937. Enamel on wood. 121.9 × 91.4 cm (48 × 36″). The Museum of Modern Art, New York, New York. Gift of Edward M. M. Warburg. © Estate of David Alfaro Siqueiros/Licensed by VAGA, New York, New York.

Chapter 23 *Art of the Early Twentieth Century* **531**

Aesthetics

Have students compare Siqueiros's *Echo of a Scream* (Figure 23.21) with Munch's *The Scream* (Figure 23.10, page 521). Ask: Do the works convey a similar message? Do they stir the same emotions? Challenge students to seek answers to these questions by dividing the class into two groups, assigning one Figure 23.21, the other Figure 23.10. Both groups are to create word webs with the title of their assigned painting as the hub and free-associated words and phrases at the ends of each spoke. When groups are finished, have them compare their webs, noting parallels.

Cross Curriculum

LITERATURE. Remind students that the brutality of war has been an ongoing theme in all areas of the arts, particularly literature. Have several volunteers individually investigate antiwar statements across literary genres and throughout history. Among works they might read in order to gain a sense of this theme's treatment are Stephen Crane's *Red Badge of Courage,* Kurt Vonnegut's *Slaughterhouse Five,* and poet Randall Jarrell's *The Death of the Ball Turret Gunner.* Volunteers should report to the class on the work they have read, noting ways in which the works parallel the paintings of the Mexican muralists in their antiwar sentiment.

MEETING INDIVIDUAL NEEDS

Visual/Spatial Learners. To help students remember the many art styles introduced in this chapter, have them chart the styles and periods with color cues or graphic symbols. Suggest that students use colored pneated pencils, markers, or colored paper to code the various art styles with distinctive colors and/or symbols. Reinforce the use of these codes in overhead transparencies or study aids.

Verbal/Linguistic Learners. Have students with strong linguistic abilities create crossword puzzles using the art terms, art movements, and names of artists covered in this chapter. Suggest that they use graph paper to arrange the words, and have them number the words and use the same numbers for appropriate clues.

Aesthetics

Direct students' attention to the painting by Frida Kahlo in Figure 23.22. Point out that much of the work's emotion derives from its subject matter (i.e., a wedding self-portrait of the artist and her husband). To illustrate the point, have students each select five individuals not in their class (e.g., a relative, a friend, a neighbor). Students are to show each person the reproduction of the painting in Figure 23.22 without permitting him or her to read the credit line or any of the accompanying text and then ask: *How does this painting make you feel?* Students are to repeat the question after summarizing the information presented in the text. Ask students to share their findings.

Studio Skills

Have students use oil pastels to create self-portraits that, like Frida Kahlo's, express a particular mood or feeling. Have students begin by executing pencil sketches. Emphasize that these self-portraits should be more expressive than representational, although students can strive for a likeness of themselves if they choose. Allow time for students to display their efforts.

Frida Kahlo (1907–1954)

As some Mexican artists became involved in political struggle, creating art that protested against social injustices, others used art to express their own personal feelings. One of these was Frida Kahlo (**free**-dah **kah**-loh), Diego Rivera's wife.

Born in Mexico City in 1907, Kahlo rose to prominence as a painter at a time when few women artists were taken seriously. Polio as a child and a bus accident when she was 18 sentenced her to a lifelong struggle with pain. While recovering from her accident, Kahlo turned to painting, even though she was only able to work lying down.

■ **FIGURE 23.22** Kahlo painted this wedding portrait of herself and her new husband, Diego Rivera. Notice that a symbol of their shared profession is included in the work— but Rivera is holding it. **What clues help you identify the work as a wedding portrait? What makes it unusual as a wedding portrait?**

Frida Kahlo. *Frida and Diego Rivera.* 1931. Oil on canvas. 100 × 78.7 cm (39³⁄₈ × 31″). San Francisco Museum of Modern Art, San Francisco, California. Albert M. Bender Collection. Gift of Albert M. Bender.

From the beginning, her paintings provided the opportunity to express her feelings about herself. Sometimes Kahlo showed herself as beautiful and content, but at other times she revealed the physical anguish with which she began and ended each day.

Frida and Diego Rivera
■ **FIGURE 23.22**

In 1931, Kahlo painted a wedding portrait (Figure 23.22) in which she and her husband stand stiffly, hand in hand, looking out at the viewer rather than at each other. The joy that one expects to find in a wedding portrait is lacking here, and the artist's solemn expression may hint at her uncertainty about her future with her new husband. Although often rewarding, their marriage was marked by bitter quarrels.

American Art

At the beginning of the twentieth century, the United States was a growing industrial nation. It was a land of assembly lines, locomotives, airships, steam shovels, telephones, and buildings that rose ten or more stories above sidewalks jammed with shoppers.

American art at the start of the twentieth century was conservative. Though artists like Homer, Eakins, and Ryder were still working, art as a whole did not reveal much progress or excitement. Many American artists still felt that success required study in Europe. Once there, however, they adopted traditional painting techniques and subject matter rather than seek out new approaches and images.

The Ashcan School

This conservative trend was challenged early in the century by a group of young realistic painters. These artists rebelled against the idealism of the academic approach. Instead, they chose to paint the life they saw around them. Most of these painters had been newspaper cartoonists or magazine illustrators, and that work had opened their eyes to the contemporary world.

These artists had much in common with the Dutch artists of the seventeenth century.

More About... **The Ashcan School.** The Ashcan School was a group of eight artists who, in fact, called themselves "The Eight." Early critics of their work laughed and said the group should really be called the "Ashcan School," a reference both to the subject matter of the works and to where critics felt the paintings belonged. The members of the group, which was founded by Robert Henri, all shared in common a journalistic background, which required them to identify and extract the essence of a scene and to communicate it in an easily understandable form. These artists were accustomed to taking a basic approach to art and to isolating the subject. It took some time for this approach to be appreciated by critics.

The Americans had the same feeling for the sprawling, bustling city of the twentieth century as the Dutch had for the countryside of their time. For subject matter, the Americans turned to the city's nightlife and its cafés, streets, alleys, and theaters.

Their goal was to record all the city's color, excitement, and glamour. When this group held its first show in New York in 1908, however, they were laughingly called the **Ashcan School,** *a popular name identifying the group* *of artists who made realistic pictures of the most ordinary features of the contemporary scene.*

John Sloan (1871–1951)

An example of the kind of painting produced by members of this group is John Sloan's *Backyards, Greenwich Village* (Figure 23.23). If you examine this picture carefully, you will be impressed by Sloan's skill as he guides you from one important item to the next.

Discovering Movement in Art

 ollow numbers 1 through 5 to discover how your eye is guided throughout this work of art.

 4 To prevent your eye from roaming off the right side of the picture, Sloan used the lines of the window, shutter, and bricks to take you farther back into the work. Here you discover more buildings, fences, and clothes hanging out to dry.

3 One child uses a small shovel to pat a snowman into shape. The diagonal formed by his arm and the shovel directs your attention to the fence at the right.

2 From there, your gaze moves to the second cat gingerly picking its way through the snow toward the two children.

5 The fence leads you across the painting to the face of a smiling girl peering out of a tenement window. You might have missed this child if Sloan had not carefully organized his picture to lead you to this spot.

 FIGURE 23.23 John Sloan. *Backyards, Greenwich Village.* 1914. Oil on canvas. 66 × 81.3 cm (26 × 32"). Collection of Whitney Museum of American Art, New York, New York. Purchase.

1 As your eye sweeps over this picture, it eventually comes to rest on the cat sitting contentedly on the fence at the bottom center.

Art History

Have students find and display examples of works either by other members of The Eight or by one of the American Regionalists. Ask: In what ways is the subject matter of these works similar to that of Figures 23.23 and 23.24? Do these works exhibit a similar sense of discovery? Allow time for students to share and compare their reactions to these and other questions?

Did You Know?

Around the time the Ashcan School was getting its start, the International Ladies Garment Workers' Union was founded in New York City. One of the union's key goals was to shorten a 70-hour work week. Another was to change a system in which women working at home were able to earn no more than 30 cents a day.

Discovering Movement in Art

Have students begin by examining *Backyards, Greenwich Village* without reading the numbered captions in the feature. Discuss whether—and how—this painting meets the goals of the Ashcan School as explained on the previous page. Then let students describe how they feel their eye is drawn into and through the painting. Finally, have students read the numbered captions in the *Discovering Movement in Art* feature and discuss the information presented. Encourage students to follow the explanation by moving their fingers across the work.

Art History

Guide students in discussing the representation of movement in *Stag at Sharkey's,* Figure 23.24. Help them recognize that Bellows depicts figures as if they are frozen in a position that is part of a familiar sequence of movements. Ask students to compare this technique with that used in other works, including Myron's *Discobolus* (Figure 8.16, page 179) and Raphael's *The School of Athens,* (Figure 16.23, page 352).

Study Guide

Distribute *Study Guide* 54 in the TCR. Assist students in reviewing key concepts. 📁

Art and Humanities

To provide students with another slant on the WPA and the Depression-era art consortium the agency funded, assign pairs of students to work on *Cooperative Learning* 34, "Artists and the WPA," in the TCR. In this worksheet, students will avail themselves of the theories and approaches underlying the WPA to devise methods for applying art to improving their community. 📁

Studio Activities

Assign *Studio* 29, "Drawing in the Spirit of the Ashcan School," in the TCR. Students will create drawings in the manner of the artists of this movement. 📁

Art and Humanities

Have students complete *Art and Humanities* 39, "Out of the Depression," in the TCR. In this worksheet, students discover the remarkable output in the arts through the government sponsorship of the WPA and create a poster promoting these projects. 📁

534

Sloan's work is not a sad picture. It does not dwell on the unhappy aspects of tenement living. Instead, it is a happy scene painted with sensitivity and affection. It illustrates the gift that children everywhere seem to have—the gift of finding joy and pleasure in almost any situation.

George Bellows (1882–1925)

George Bellows, although not a member of the Ashcan School, created paintings that were similar in many ways to those of Sloan and his companions. Realizing that anything could be used as subject matter for art, Bellows concentrated on the subject he loved most: sports.

Bellows left his native Ohio when he was still a young man and spent the rest of his short life in New York. He had a studio across the street from an athletic club, where he could see the boxing matches he loved to paint.

Stag at Sharkey's
■ **FIGURE 23.24**

Applying his paint to the canvas with slashing brushstrokes, Bellows was able to reproduce the violent action of the ring in

■ **FIGURE 23.24** Notice the techniques Bellows used to make the two boxers stand out in this painting. **How do the blurred contours add to the feeling of violent action? Do you think this picture is more successful in capturing the appearance or the excitement of a prizefight?**

George Bellows. *Stag at Sharkey's.* 1909. Oil on canvas. 92 × 122.5 cm (36¹/₄ × 48¹/₄"). The Cleveland Museum of Art, Cleveland, Ohio. Hinman B. Hurlbut Collection.

534   Unit Seven *Art of the Modern Era*

COOPERATIVE LEARNING

Classroom Art Show. Remind students that the Armory Show of 1913 played a significant part in the introduction of European art to Americans. Tell students that the class will work together to plan and produce a similar show for teachers, parents, and interested students. To begin, have students create a piece of art or select samples of original works with which they are pleased. When each student has a piece of art to contribute, have them arrange the artworks in the classroom, giving some thought to the arrangement that best showcases their efforts. Tell students that they should be prepared to answer any questions viewers might have about their particular artworks.

works such as *Stag at Sharkey's* (Figure 23.24). From the vantage point of a ringside seat, you share the wild excitement of the fight crowd. Illuminated by the lights overhead and silhouetted against the dark background, the two boxers flail away at each other, both willing to accept brutal punishment rather than give ground. Bellows captures this powerful determination and swift action with strong diagonal lines and blurred contours.

The Armory Show of 1913

The Ashcan School played a major role in American art from about 1908 until about 1913. This marked the opening of the famous **Armory Show,** *the first large exhibition of modern art in America.* This exhibit was organized by a group of artists who were aware of the exciting new art being done in Europe. They wanted to introduce the American public to the works of such artists as Cézanne, van Gogh, Gauguin, Matisse, Munch, and Picasso.

The show presented some 1,300 works by 300 artists. Most were Americans, but about 100 were Europeans. The European works caused the greatest excitement and the greatest controversy. For most visitors, it was their first contact with modern European art. Unlike the French public, who had seen modern art evolve slowly, most Americans were caught by surprise. Some tried to understand the new works; others tried to explain them; most either laughed or were enraged. The room where the Cubist paintings were hung was called the "Chamber of Horrors." Furthermore, it was said of Matisse, "It is a long step from Ingres to Matisse, but it is only a short one from Matisse to anger."

The End of an Era

The Armory Show marked the end of one era and the start of another. Many American artists, after seeing the new styles of the Fauves, Expressionists, and Cubists, turned away from traditional academic art to initiate their own daring experiments. Thus, the Armory Show set the stage for the development of modern art in America. In the years that followed, New York replaced Paris as the art capital of the world.

LESSON TWO REVIEW

Reviewing Art Facts
1. What event in Mexican history had an effect on the subject of artworks produced after 1911?
2. Who were the Mexican muralists? What did these artists choose as the subject matter for their art?
3. Describe the story told in Diego Rivera's *Liberation of the Peon* (Figure 23.19, page 529).
4. What early twentieth-century American art movement challenged traditional painting techniques and subject matter?

Activity... *Creating a Plan for a Mural*
Mexican muralists painted public murals concerned with social and political problems. They left a legacy for the artists of Mexico and have influenced artists everywhere. The mural tradition was taken up by American artists who created huge works of art both on walls and canvas.

Imagine that you and fellow classmates have been commissioned to paint a large mural. The work will be for your school or a public building in your community. Working in groups, plan a mural project and create a scale model of your mural plan. Investigate with your teacher the possibility of carrying out your mural plan.

LESSON TWO REVIEW

Answers to Reviewing Art Facts
1. The Mexican Revolution.
2. Rivera, Orozco, Siquieros; political and social problems of the Mexican people.
3. The painting depicts solemn expressions as soldiers retrieve the body of a peon.
4. The Ashcan School.

Activity...*Creating a Plan for a Mural*
Let students select a specific building for their mural, and have them brainstorm a list of possible mural subjects. Then divide the class into cooperative learning groups, and have the members of each group plan a mural and draw a detailed plan for it.

ASSESS
Checking Comprehension
Have students respond to the lesson review questions. Answers are given in the box below.

Reteaching
➤ Assign *Reteaching* 54, found in the TCR. Have students complete the activity and review their responses. 📁
➤ Ask pairs of students to select and describe briefly an artwork they encountered in this lesson. Pairs are to identify and describe the school of art their chosen work is from.

Enrichment
Assign *Enrichment* 44, "The Armory Show," in the TCR. Students are asked to find influences of the Armory Show of 1913 on early twentieth-century American artists and explore art critics' reactions to today's art. 📁

Extension
Have groups of students complete *Cooperative Learning* 35, "Creating a Group Mural," in the TCR. In this worksheet, students study the murals of Thomas Hart Benton. 📁

CLOSE
If possible, arrange for a group tour of a local building that contains a mural, or arrange a visit by a local artist known for political or social statements. Have students report on new insights they have gained from the experience.

European and American Architecture

Focus

Lesson Objectives

After studying this lesson, students will be able to:
- Describe the architectural contributions of Alexandre Gustave Eiffel and Antonio Gaudi.
- Identify reasons for the eclectic style of architecture practiced in the United States by Julia Morgan and others.
- Understand how architect Louis Sullivan broke with the past to create a new architectural style.

Building Vocabulary

Ask volunteers to provide informal definitions of the word *eclectic;* let students look the word up in a dictionary if necessary. Then ask students to describe what they think a building designed in the eclectic style might look like.

Motivator

Ask students whether they can identify the famous structure in Figure 23.25. Then have students collaborate on a critique of the work as they imagine it to have been received by early French critics. After allowing time for several group appraisals, proceed with the reading.

European and American Architecture

Vocabulary
- eclectic style

Artists to Meet
- Alexandre Gustave Eiffel
- Antonio Gaudi
- Julia Morgan
- Louis Sullivan

Discover
After completing this lesson, you will be able to:
- Describe the architectural contributions of Alexandre Gustave Eiffel and Antonio Gaudi.
- Discuss the reasons for the eclectic style of architecture practiced in the United States by architects such as Julia Morgan.
- Explain how American architect Louis Sullivan broke with the past to create a new architectural style.

*D*uring the nineteenth century, architects were content to rely on ideas from the past. This practice became widespread, and buildings in Europe and American showed a variety of styles: Greek, Roman, Romanesque, Gothic, and Renaissance. Some architects in the late nineteenth and early twentieth centuries, however, saw the exciting potentials for using new industrial methods and materials. They developed a new style of architecture featuring designs that reflected these new methods and materials.

Alexandre Gustave Eiffel (1832–1923)

Late in the nineteenth century, a French builder and engineer named Alexandre Gustave Eiffel (ahl-ex-**ahn**-der **goo**-stav **eye**-fel) saw the value of iron and steel, which he used to build bridges and industrial plants. He is best known for the 984-foot tower that he built for the Paris Industrial Exposition of 1889.

The Eiffel Tower
- **FIGURE 23.25**

The Eiffel Tower (Figure 23.25) is a spire boldly made of exposed ironwork. To build it, Eiffel used open beams made of small angle irons and flat irons. The entire structure was prefabricated. It was riveted together without accident by only 150 workers in just 17 months, an amazing feat at that time. It was made even more amazing by Eiffel's confident claim that his tower was strong enough to stand forever.

At first it appeared unlikely that the tower would stand until the end of the Exposition because it produced such howls of protest from artists, architects, and leading citizens. They felt the tower was a disgrace to their beautiful city and should be removed. Within two decades, though, it became one of the most popular landmarks in Europe. Despite the fact that it had been planned as a temporary monument for the Exposition, the tower still stands—and Eiffel's boast no longer seems quite so absurd.

- **FIGURE 23.25**
This tower was built as a temporary monument for the Paris Industrial Exposition of 1889. Today it is considered one of the central symbols of the French capital. What new materials and techniques did Eiffel use in constructing this tower?

Gustave Eiffel. Eiffel Tower. Paris, France. 1887–89.

536

Teacher's Classroom Resources
- Reproducible Lesson Plan 55
- Reteaching Activity 55
- Study Guide 55

Innovations in Construction

Eiffel's tower was one of a series of engineering feats that demonstrated how new materials and construction techniques could be used in major building projects. The use of cast iron and steel made it possible to erect buildings more quickly and more economically. These building materials also seemed to offer added protection against fire, but a series of disastrous fires in the United States near the end of the century showed that this was not the case. These experiences led to the practice of adding an outer shell of masonry to iron and steel buildings, making them both strong and fire-resistant.

Antonio Gaudi (1852–1926)

The work of the Spanish architect Antonio Gaudi (ahn-**toh**-nee-oh **gow**-dee) reflects his belief that an entirely new kind of architecture was possible. Gaudi turned away from current practices. Inspired by nature and his own vivid imagination, Gaudi turned away from accepted practices. Thus, the roof of a building could resemble a mountain with its ridges and slopes (Figure 23.26). Ceilings could look like the wind- and water-worn walls of caves, and columns could suggest the stout, sturdy legs of elephants.

Church of the Sacred Family
■ **FIGURE 23.27**

Gaudi's partially completed Church of the Sacred Family (Figure 23.27) rises over Barcelona, as famous a symbol for this city as the Eiffel Tower is for Paris or the Golden Gate Bridge is for San Francisco. Gaudi started work on the huge structure more than 100 years ago, and left it less than half finished at the time of his death. Today the church is an astounding combination of spiraling forms, colorful ceramic decorations, and sculptures of religious figures.

As envisioned by Gaudi, the huge structure was to have façades showing the birth, death, and resurrection of Christ. Towering over them, tall spires were planned to represent the Twelve Apostles, the Four Evangelists, and Mary, the mother of Christ. A final central

■ **FIGURE 23.26** Today, Gaudi's works are being rediscovered and showered with praise. **To what do you attribute this new interest?**

Antonio Gaudi. Casa Mila. Barcelona, Spain. 1905–07.

■ **FIGURE 23.27** An effort to complete this structure continues but Gaudi left no plans to indicate his intentions. **Do you agree with the assertion that Gaudi's architecture is similar to Expressionist painting and sculpture?**

Antonio Gaudi. Church of the Sacred Family. Barcelona, Spain. 1883–1926.

tower, representing Christ, was to project upward to a height of 500 feet.

In his later years, Gaudi turned his complete attention to work on the church. Unfortunately, no plans were prepared to indicate how he wanted construction to continue if something were to happen to him. Then, on a morning in 1926, Gaudi stepped in front of a speeding trolley. Three days later he died, taking with him the only vision of the completed Church of the Sacred Family.

Chapter 23 *Art of the Early Twentieth Century* **537**

Technology

National Gallery of Art Videodisc Use the following images as examples of more works by artists introduced in this lesson.

Wassily Kandinsky
Improvisation 31 (Sea Battle)

Search Frame 2249

Use Glencoe's *Correlation Bar Code Guide to the National Gallery of Art* to locate more artworks.

TEACH
Introducing the Lesson

Remind students that in order for a work of architecture to succeed it must be functional as well as aesthetically pleasing. The architect need not be constrained by any other aesthetic guidelines and, indeed, some architecture of the early twentieth century reveals free thinking on the part of its creator. Ask students to examine the works in this lesson and decide on which they find most original. After reading the lesson, have students review these initial opinions and see whether any of them feel differently.

Aesthetics

Direct students' attention to the buildings shown in Figures 23.26 and 23.27. Remind them of Sullivan's famous remark that "form follows function." Ask students to explain how Gaudi has used function to suggest an appropriate form.

Art Criticism

Divide the class into cooperative learning groups. Have each group select one of the works of architecture illustrated in the lesson and apply the art criticism operations to that work. Ask the groups to share their evaluations with the rest of the class.

Cross Curriculum

LANGUAGE ARTS. Have interested students investigate the etymology of the word *cityscape*. In particular, students should determine when the term became part of the English language, who coined it, and what relationship, if any, it bears to the term *landscape*. Ask students to share their findings with the class in the form of a brief oral report.

LOOKING Closely

Let students describe Hearst Castle at San Simeon, as shown in Figure 23.28, and share their reactions to the estate. Then have them read and discuss the feature information, identifying the sources of various parts of the main structure. Ask: What special challenges are involved in designing a structure in this eclectic style? How did Julia Morgan meet those challenges?

Studio Skills

Have students examine Julia Morgan's Hearst estate (Figure 23.28) and discuss how the eclectic features of the structure come together to form a unified whole. Tell students that they will work as a group to design a town that includes at least six buildings in six different but complementary architectural styles. Have students begin by planning the types of buildings they will create and the styles they will use. Instruct students to sketch their ideas and select those sketches that are aesthetically pleasing by themselves and in relation to the whole. Have the group transfer the work onto a single large sheet of white paper.

Did You Know?

San Simeon is now a California state monument visited by nearly a million tourists each year. Its attendance makes it the state's most popular historic monument.

Since Gaudi's death, the church has undergone a checkered history of starts and stops. Critics claim that Gaudi's vision has been distorted over the years, but they cannot suggest any solutions to the problem.

Julia Morgan (1872–1957)

In the United States, a widespread fondness for the architectural styles of the past continued from the late nineteenth into the early twentieth centuries. Many architects planned structures with the public's fondness for the past in mind. Both architects and patrons considered certain styles appropriate for certain types of buildings.

Gothic was considered the appropriate style for churches, Roman for banks, and Classical for museums and libraries. Tudor was the style in which many houses were built. Eighteenth-century French was the style for mansions. A fine example of this **eclectic style,** or *one composed of elements drawn from various sources,* is the estate designed for William Randolph Hearst by Julia Morgan at San Simeon, California (Figure 23.28).

Morgan was the first woman to graduate as an architect from the famous Ecole des Beaux Arts in Paris. She ranks as one of America's top architects. Between 1902 and 1952, Morgan designed more than 700 structures. Yet, she is barely known today. She chose not to publicize her work, but preferred instead to have it speak for her.

By 1919, this shy but successful architect was chosen to plan the estate of the flamboyant journalist and congressman William Randolph Hearst. The main structure on this huge estate is the 100-room house, which was started three years later.

■ **FIGURE 23.28** Julia Morgan. Hearst Castle. San Simeon, California. Begun 1919.

LOOKING Closely

USE OF STYLES IN ARCHITECTURE

The critics had a name for the free use of many styles in the main house of the Hearst estate. They called it the "Spanish, Moorish, Romanesque, Gothic, Renaissance, Hang-the-Expense" style of architecture. Examine the various styles used for the building features below:

- **Façade.** The façade includes two towers that rise to a height of 137 feet. They are replicas of a tower found on a sixteenth-century Moorish cathedral in Ronda, Spain.
- **Towers.** Each tower is topped by a prominent weather vane. These vanes were brought from Venice and date from the seventeenth century.
- **Roof.** The two towers are joined by a teakwood gable roof that came from a Peruvian palace.
- **Doors.** The main doors were taken from a Spanish convent of the sixteenth century. The doors are flanked by Spanish Gothic relief sculptures.

538 **Unit Seven** *Art of the Modern Era*

More About... **Modern Architecture.** The Museum of Modern Art in New York City "collects" modern architecture. This museum, through its Department of Architecture and Design, is one of the principal institutions in the world concerned with the collection of modern architectural, industrial, commercial, and graphic design. The first show was in 1932, and it explored the revolution that had occurred in architecture during the previous decades. There is, of course, no way to "collect" the buildings themselves, so the museum established a photographic file, one of the most comprehensive collections of documentation of modern architecture. This file now includes color slides. Scale models enhance the museum's collection.

Morgan was known for doing her best to satisfy the needs and desires of her clients. This is certainly evident at San Simeon. Hearst approved Morgan's plans for the towers, but once they were up they did not please him. At great expense, he had them torn down and replaced by the more decorative versions that now stand. When he did not like the placement of a large French Renaissance fireplace in one of the guest houses, it was moved. Later, when he decided that he liked it better in its original position, it was moved back.

Louis Sullivan (1856–1924)

America's pioneering architect of the late nineteenth and early twentieth centuries was Louis Sullivan. Other architects at this time were inspired by the past. Unlike them, Sullivan was busy exploring new approaches. In the early 1890s, he designed the Wainwright Building in St. Louis (Figure 23.29), a structure that owes little, if anything, to earlier styles.

■ **FIGURE 23.29**
Vertical steel beams support the walls of this building. **What made this building startling when it was constructed? How does it compare to familiar buildings in your community?**

Louis Sullivan. Wainwright Building. St. Louis, Missouri. 1890–91.

CHAPTER 23
LESSON THREE

Critical Thinking

Direct students' attention to the pioneering work in Figure 23.29. Have them find evidence in the work or its description that supports this statement: *Louis Sullivan is the father of the modern skyscraper.*

Study Guide

Distribute *Study Guide* 55 in the TCR. Assist students in reviewing key concepts. 📂

Art and Humanities

Have a group of volunteers locate a photograph of Antonio Gaudi's *Church of the Sagrada Familia*, located in Barcelona, Spain. Ask the group to explain in a brief report to the class how the structure simultaneously conforms to Gaudi's unique vision as an architect and meets the functional criterion of a house of worship.

Studio Activities

Emphasize that the architects covered in this lesson exhibit very different approaches to design. Divide the class into groups, assign each group to one of the four architects, and instruct them to plan a building based on the style of that architect. When the groups are finished, have them share and compare their efforts.

Time & Place
CONNECTIONS

Early Twentieth Century
c. 1900–1950

RADIO. A series of inventions in the late 1800s led finally to the first wireless voice transmission in 1920. By 1930, regular commercial broadcasting was established worldwide. President Franklin D. Roosevelt used the new medium to address the nation in weekly fireside chats.

MOTION PICTURES. In 1896, Edison gave the first motion picture presentation in New York City using the vitascope. By 1902, the first motion picture theater was opened in Los Angeles, which later became a center of motion picture production.

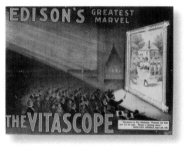

Activity Movie Poster Analysis.

What are the strengths and weaknesses of film, video, and radio as modern day tools of communication? How does the movie poster communicate its message? Is the message more visual or verbal?

Time & Place
CONNECTIONS

Early Twentieth Century

Have students work together to examine, read about, and discuss the images in this Time & Place feature. Then divide the class into several cooperative learning groups, and assign each group one of the feature topics—radio or motion pictures. Ask group members to research the assigned topic and to share their findings with the rest of the class in a brief oral and/or visual presentation. Assign the Activity, and guide students in discussing their responses to the Activity questions. Following the discussion, have students write short essays explaining and supporting their own ideas.

ASSESS

Checking Comprehension

➤ Have students respond to the lesson review questions. Answers are given in the box below.

➤ Assign students *Application 23*, "Playing with Matches," in the TCR. In this activity, students are asked to identify artists and note his or her place in art history. 📁

Reteaching

➤ Assign *Reteaching* 55, found in the TCR. Have students complete the activity and review their responses. 📁

➤ On index cards, write a word or phrase unambiguously associated with one of the architects from the lesson (e.g., *Barcelona, Paris Industrial Exposition, Eclectic, Skyscraper*). As you hold up a card, students should make the connection between the phrase and the architect it references.

Extension

Arrange for students to visit the site of an office building or other large structure that has been constructed recently. Have students identify and list its architectural features. During class, lead a discussion on the similarities and differences between the structure and buildings covered in this lesson. Ask students if they can see the influence of early twentieth-century architecture in the buildings of today.

CLOSE

Have students each decide which architect from the lesson they would most have liked to meet and write brief explanations of their choices.

For its basic support, Sullivan used a large frame, or cage, made of steel beams. This frame was then covered with vertical strips of brick. Windows and decorative panels filled the spaces in between. The cagelike frame can be seen clearly from the outside of the structure. It is evident that this steel frame, and not the brick walls, supports the building.

The simplicity and logic of buildings like Sullivan's were evident to architects who followed. During the twentieth century, buildings made with steel frames covered with glass and concrete were built everywhere, resulting in an International style of architecture. The Lever House in New York City (Figure 23.20) is an excellent example of this style as it matured into the architecture of mid-twentieth century corporate offices.

■ **FIGURE 23.30** Notice the steel framework, walls of glass, and absence of ornamental features. **How is this building different from the Wainwright Building (Figure 23.29)?**

Skidmore, Owings, and Merrill. Lever House. New York City, New York. 1952.

LESSON THREE REVIEW

Reviewing Art Facts

1. Why is the Eiffel Tower regarded as an important engineering feat?
2. What two sources provided Spanish architect Antonio Gaudi with the inspiration for his architecture?
3. Why is Julia Morgan's work on San Simeon described as eclectic?
4. What set Louis Sullivan apart from other architects of the same period?

▶ Activity . . . *Investigating Architecture*

Some of the most dramatic changes in architecture have been seen during the late nineteenth and early twentieth centuries. For centuries, architects combined the ancient elements developed by the Greeks and Romans. The column, the arch, the dome, the vault, and the atrium are elements that have been used by each age in different ways. Modern architects sought to create new and different solutions.

Investigate the work of modern architects. Research the work of Louis Sullivan, Frank Lloyd Wright, and Julia Morgan. Study examples of their works to determine how they made changes in the area of architecture. Make a class presentation or an Internet tutorial on modern architecture.

LESSON TWO REVIEW

Answers to Reviewing Art Facts

1. It successfully made use of new materials and building techniques.
2. Nature and his own imagination.
3. It draws from many styles.
4. He did not look to the past, but explored new approaches.

Activity...*Investigating Architecture*

Divide the class into four groups, and assign each group one of the four architects named in this Activity. Have group members gather and organize information about that architects work. If groups prepare Internet tutorials, be sure other class members have an opportunity to view and use the tutorials.

Complete a paper cutout featuring two large, abstract figures, one in *action* and the other *motionless*. These will be large silhouettes cut from brightly colored fadeless art paper or construction paper. Glue the figures to a white background so that they appear to relate to one another in some way. Cut out other abstract shapes in various sizes and glue them in place to increase the decorative effect and add harmony to your composition. Make no effort to suggest space or depth.

Inspiration

Look again at Henri Matisse's colorful cutout of *The Knife Thrower* (Figure 23.3, page 517). Can you locate the two figures? Which one is the knife thrower? How do you know? What is the other figure doing? How do the smaller shapes add harmony to this work? Do you think space is an important element in this composition?

Process

1. Make several pencil sketches in which two large, abstract figures dominate. One of these figures must be engaged in some kind of spirited activity. The other should appear quiet and motionless. There should be a clear relationship between these two figures, just as the knife thrower and his assistant are related in Matisse's cutout artwork.

2. Enlarge and lightly redraw your figures on the pieces of brightly colored paper. Cut these out as two abstract silhouettes, concentrating on the outlines and eliminating all unnecessary details.

3. Design and cut out several smaller, decorative shapes in a variety of sizes. These should be similar in appearance, since they will be used to add harmony to your composition.

4. Arrange your figures and shapes on the large sheet of white drawing paper and, when you are satisfied with the design, glue them in place.

Materials

- Pencil and sketch paper
- Large and small pieces of fadeless art paper or brightly colored construction paper
- Sheet of white drawing paper, 18 × 24 inches
- Scissors and glue

■ FIGURE 23.31 Student Work

Examining Your Work

Describe. Are the two figures in your work easily identified? Can others distinguish between the active figure and the motionless figure even though both are highly abstracted?

Analyze. Are repetitious, decorative shapes used to add harmony to your composition? Is variety realized by making these shapes in different sizes? Does your composition avoid the suggestion of depth?

Interpret. Are other students able to identify the relationship between the two figures? Can they determine what each is doing?

Judge. What aesthetic quality, or qualities, would you use when judging your work? Using these, would you say your work is successful? If you were to do it again, what would you do differently?

541

ASSESSMENT

Extension Activity. As a follow-up to this individual project, have students work in groups to plan and create other cutout compositions. Explain that *The Knife Thrower* is an illustration from a book, entitled *Jazz*, that Matisse created in 1947. Challenge each group to follow this example by choosing a style of music as the theme for an abstract or nonobjective paper cutout composition. The musical selection should guide group members as they design the shapes and determine the actions these shapes will exhibit in their compositions. Have the members of each group work together on a single composition. Display the completed works and ask the rest of the class to identify the style of music represented.

Studio LESSON

Cubist-Style Painting

Objectives

■ Create a painting including views of a cup and saucer seen from different angles.

■ Avoid showing a complete cup or saucer anywhere in the painting.

■ Use at least six different light and dark values mixed from a single hue.

Motivator

Write *cupsaucerspace* on the board and inform students that this could be the title for the art-work they are about to pro-duce in this lesson. Ask if they have any idea what this title refers to. Explain that their paintings will be composed of various views of cups and saucers combined with inter-esting negative shapes repre-senting the spaces between them.

Aesthetics

Ask students to focus their attention on Picasso's painting *The Glass of Absinthe* (Figure 23.14, page 524). Tell them to silently identify for themselves a single shape in this painting and draw it as accurately as possible on a sheet of paper. Call on students to reproduce their shapes on the board.

Critiquing

Have students apply the steps of art criticism to their own artwork, using the "Examin-ing Your Work" questions on this page.

Studio LESSON Cubist-Style Painting

Materials

● Pencil and sketch paper
● Sheet of white drawing paper, 12 × 18 inches
● Tempera or acrylic paint
● Brushes, mixing tray, and paint cloth
● Water container

■ **FIGURE 23.32** Student Work

Create a painting in the Cubist style based on a series of realistic draw-ings of a cup and saucer. This painting will show all sides of the two three-dimensional objects on a two-dimensional surface. To do this, make certain to include different parts of the cup and saucer as seen from the top, sides, and bottom. Do not show a complete cup or saucer anywhere. Use a vari-ety of light and dark values mixed from a single hue to paint your composi-tion. Use no fewer than six different values.

Inspiration

Look at the Cubist painting in Figure 23.14, page 524. Can you identify any of the objects in this painting? How many hues are used? Of the objects in Picasso's collage (Figure 23.15, page 524) and in Braque's painting (Figure 23.17, page 526), which are eas-ier to identify? Can you find any complete objects in these works? Which of these works do you find most appealing? Why?

Process

1. Complete several realistic pencil sketches of a cup and saucer. Draw these objects together and separately from different points of view. Examine your finished drawing carefully and identify the most interesting parts of each.

2. On the sheet of white drawing paper, create a composition that combines these parts into a visually interesting whole. Make certain to use parts selected from each of your drawings so that the top, sides, and bottom of the cup and saucer are represented.

3. Paint your composition using no fewer than six values of a single hue. Mix these values by adding white or black to the hue that you have selected. Paint shapes as flat areas of color, or use gradation of value to suggest three-dimensional forms. The contours of your shapes or forms should be crisp and smooth.

Examining Your Work

Describe. Does your painting include sections of a cup and saucer seen from different points of view? Point out and name these sections. Did you show a complete cup or saucer anywhere in your composition?

Analyze. Did you use six or more light and dark values mixed from a single hue when painting your picture?

Interpret. Can other students identify the cup and saucer elements in your picture? Do they recognize

that your painting is an attempt to show all sides of these three-dimensional objects on a two-dimensional surface?

Judge. What aesthetic quality would you want others to rely on when judging your painting? Using that aes-thetic quality, do you think your painting is successful? Which of the Cubist works in this chapter most closely resembles your own efforts in this style?

542

ASSESSMENT

Class Discussion. After students have examined and assessed their own Cubist-style paintings, explain that there are two different styles of Cubism. The first was known as *Analytic Cubism*, developed by Picasso and Braque around 1907. Later, these artists modi-fied the style by using textured surfaces, flat shapes, and rich colors. This new version of the style later became known as *Synthetic Cubism.* Point out exam-ples of Synthetic Cubism in Figures 23.15 (page 524), 23.16 (page 525), and 23.17 (page 526). Have students compare and contrast these works with the example of Analytic Cubism in Figure 23.14 (page 524). Ask students to describe the differences they see in the two styles.

Reviewing the Facts

Lesson One

1. Was Matisse more interested in literal qualities or design qualities in his paintings?
2. Name the artist associated with the Fauves whose works were a condemnation of the world's suffering.
3. The artists of what German movement were interested in representing deep emotional feelings in their work?

Lesson Two

4. What kinds of stories did the Mexican artists tell with their murals?
5. What subjects did the artists from the Ashcan School paint?
6. What event in what year introduced the American public to the works of the modern European artists?

Lesson Three

7. Name the famous American architect who designed the main structure of the Hearst estate at San Simeon in California.
8. Describe the construction of the Wainwright Building by American architect Louis Sullivan and tell what style of architecture it inspired.

Thinking Critically

1. **ANALYZE.** Look again at Georges Rouault's painting *The Old King* (Figure 23.4, page 518). Write a description of the quality of the lines in the painting. Then look through your textbook and identify an artist whose lines are very different from Rouault's lines. Write a description of the quality of that artist's lines also.
2. **COMPARE AND CONTRAST.** Refer to Maillol's sculpture *The Mediterranean* (Figure 23.18, page 527) and the Greek sculpture *Seated Boxer* (Figure 8.23, page 185). What comparisons can you make between the two sculptures? In what ways do you see that they are different or similar? Consider the literal, design, and expressive qualities of both sculptures.

 MUSIC. Use the *Performing Arts Handbook,* page 592 to learn about the music of the American Repertory Dance Company.

CAREERS IN Read about a career as a cinematographer in the *Careers in Art Handbook,* page 608.

inter NET **CONNECTION** Visit Glencoe Art Online at *www.glencoe.com/sec/art*. Explore exhibits by early twentieth-century artists and do an activity.

Technology Project

Twentieth-Century Changes in Art

The early twentieth century ushered in a virtual explosion of artists creating new styles of artistic expression. For the first time, American art exerted an international influence, with New York City replacing Paris as the art capital of the Western world. Artists began to feel the impact of rapid industrial and technological development, and the positive and negative effects this had on the lives of human beings. Never before had the world experienced such change in such a compressed time period. Artists responded to this and mirrored in their artwork the rapid pace of transformation in the culture as a whole.

1. The trends in style, themes, and content seen in modern art diverged to move in one of two directions—either toward order or toward chaos. Examine works by artists such as Kandinsky or Picasso. Choose one work that you think exemplifies order and one that depicts chaos. Share your findings with the class.
2. Combine all the images collected by the class and place them into a multimedia format or a tutorial Web page. Create a resource for use by other classes. In the multimedia format, be sure to list reasons defending your judgment.
3. As an alternate: choose one work of art that is an example of order or chaos. Place the image in a computer manipulation program. Using available tools, alter the literal and design qualities of the image. Achieve a transformation in its expressive impact by changing it from order to chaos or vice versa. Print your creation and display it.

Teaching the Technology Project

Begin by helping students discuss the two directions in which Modern art moved. Ask: Why do you think artworks exhibited these specific trends? Which trend do you think is the more significant? Why? After this introductory discussion, let students choose one of the two Project options and work independently.

 Assign the feature in the *Performing Arts Handbook,* page 590.

CAREERS IN ART If time permits, have interested students investigate the career information in the *Careers in Art Handbook,* page 608.

inter NET **CONNECTION** Have students go online and learn more about artists on preselected Web sites with the Internet activity for this chapter.

Reviewing the Facts

1. Matisse was interested in design qualities.
2. Georges Rouault, who was associated with the Fauves, created works that condemned injustice and suffering.
3. Expressionists were interested in representing emotions.
4. Mexican muralists told stories of revolution, native traditions, festivals, and legends.
5. The Ashcan School artists painted realistic features of the contemporary scene.
6. The Armory Show of 1913 introduced Americans to modern European artists.
7. Julia Morgan designed the Hearst estate.
8. Steel-framed buildings; the International style of glass and steel high-rise buildings.

Thinking Critically

1. Student descriptions of Rouault's painting should mention that the lines are bold and black, reminiscent of stained glass. Responses to the second part of the question will vary.
2. Both figures have been created in a representational fashion, and both exhibit a geometric composition. Yet, while *Seated Boxer* appears battered and emotionally beaten, *The Mediterranean* appears in a quiet, restful pose.

Modern Art Movements to the Present

ADDITIONAL CHAPTER RESOURCES

Activities

 Advanced Studio Activity 24

Application 24

Chapter 24 Internet Activity

Studio Activities 30, 31

Fine Art Resources

 Transparencies

Art in Focus Transparency 31

Charles Sheeler. *American Landscape.*

Art in Focus Transparency 32

Red Grooms. *City of Chicago.*

Fine Art Print

Focus on World Art Print 24

Stuart Davis. *Report from Rockport.*

Assessment

 Chapter 24 Test

Performance Assessment

Multimedia Resources

Artsource® Performing Arts Package

National Gallery Laser Disc

National Museum of Women in the Arts CD-ROM

Arts & Entertainment Videos

NATIONAL STANDARDS FOR ARTS EDUCATION

The National Standards for Arts Education provide guidelines for grade-appropriate competency in the visual arts. The Content Standards for grades 9–12 are:

1. Understanding and applying media, techniques, and processes.
2. Using knowledge of structures and functions.
3. Choosing and evaluating a range of subject matter, symbols, and ideas.
4. Understanding the visual arts in relation to history and cultures.
5. Reflecting upon and assessing the characteristics and merits of their work and the work of others.
6. Making connections between visual arts and other disciplines.

Listed below are the National Standards for the Visual Arts addressed in this chapter. For a breakdown of the categories listed under each content standard, refer to the *Reproducible Lesson Plans* booklet in the TCR.

1. (a, b)   **2.** (a, b)   **3.** (a)   **4.** (a, b, c)   **5.** (a, c)   **6.** (a, b)

Out of Time?   If time does not permit teaching this chapter in its entirety, you may wish to preview the artwork and captions with students. Scan the heads in each lesson with students. Discuss the Looking Closely feature and examine Environmental Art on page 566.

HANDBOOK MATERIAL

ART SOURCE Bang on a Can All-Stars *(page 593)*

CAREERS IN Art

Cinematographer *(page 608)*

Beyond the Classroom

City tours focusing on architecture can help students understand the specialties and styles of regions and cultures. Local guided tours of your community can be one way to introduce students to architecture around them. Online tours available on the Internet can broaden their horizons. Find virtual tours by visiting our Web site at *www.glencoe.com/sec/art.*

Modern Art Movements to the Present

Modern Art Movements to the Present

INTRODUCE

Chapter Overview

CHAPTER 24 introduces major developments in North American and European art after World War I.

Lesson One treats the artists of Surrealism, Regionalism, and Abstract Expressionism.

Lesson Two discusses new forms of visual expression in the realms of sculpture, architecture, and painting.

Studio Lesson guides students to create a three-dimensional relief portrait.

Art & Language Arts

Ask students to write down their reactions to Elizabeth Murray's work. Then read the following statement that Murray makes about her work: "I want the panels to look as if they had been thrown against the wall, and that's how they stuck there." How do students react to the work after hearing Murray's explanation?

Art & Language Arts
■ **FIGURE 24.1** It has been stated that twentieth-century art is an attempt to redefine the nature of art. In the second half of the century, artists increasingly relied upon verbal (or written) descriptions to explain their visual works. Elizabeth Murray tells observers to view her art as pieces of a puzzle that come together to make a whole concept. Consider how a verbal explanation of an artwork might impact the viewer's reaction to the work.

Elizabeth Murray. *Painter's Progress.* 1981. Oil on canvas, in 19 parts. Overall 294.5 × 236.2 cm (9'8" × 7'9"). The Museum of Modern Art, New York, New York. Acquired through the Bernhill Fund and gift of Agnes Gund.

544

National Standards

This chapter meets the following National Standards for the Arts.

1. (a,b)	**4.** (a,b,c)
2. (a,b)	**5.** (a,c)
3. (a)	**6.** (a,b)

CHAPTER 24 RESOURCES

Teacher's Classroom Resources
- 📁 Advanced Studio Activity 24
- 📁 Application 24
- 🖱 Chapter 24 Internet Activity
- 📁 Studio Activities 30, 31

Assessment
- 📁 Chapter 24 Test
- 📁 Performance Assessment

Fine Art Resources
- 🖐 *Art in Focus* Transparency 31
  Charles Sheeler. *American Landscape.*
  Art in Focus Transparency 32
  Red Grooms. *City of Chicago.*
- *Focus on World Art* Print 24
  Stuart Davis. *Report from Rockport.*

𝒫erhaps the word that best describes the art of the modern era is diversity. Today's artists make even greater use of new materials and techniques to express their ideas, beliefs and feelings. Many of these artists are moving away from traditional styles of art. Art movements of the past have given way to an astonishing array of individual art styles. Some of these styles reveal the influence of earlier artists while others reject entirely any reference to historical models.

Introducing the Chapter

Have students browse through the chapter, noting the multiplicity of styles that characterize twentieth-century art. Ask what this wide array of styles reveals about the goals of modern art. Proceed with the reading of the chapter.

 Music While studying this chapter, use *Performing Arts Handbook*, 593. Tell students the Bang on a Can All-Stars keeps the creation of music fresh and evolving with the times.

YOUR Portfolio

Select a realistic artwork from the text that you like. Make a thumbnail sketch of the work's subject. Consider how you would alter the realistic qualities of the subject to make them surreal. Remember that the Surrealist artist rejects control, composition, and logic in favor of the world of dreams and the subconscious. Look at one specific object or area of your sketch and consider how realistic shapes can be transformed into surreal ones. Make several sketches of the object or area to show an evolution from realism to surrealism. Which objects will be symbols and how will the viewer understand that symbolism? What media would you use? Save your sketches in your portfolio.

Focus ON THE ARTS

DANCE
Choreographer Alvin Ailey used themes from the African-American experience in his world renowned modern dance theatre. Jerome Robbins, Bob Fosse, and Agnes de Mille created dance for the new American musical art form, combining drama and song.

THEATRE
The American musical reached maturity in 1943 with *Oklahoma!* by composer Richard Rogers and lyricist Oscar Hammerstein. This musical not only incorporated a strong, clear story line and well-developed characters, but a ballet dream sequence.

MUSIC
The musical styles of many cultures, as well as the use of experimental instruments and computer technology produced exciting new combinations of sound. American avant-garde composer Philip Glass combined classical, modern, and multicultural music elements in his operas of the 1970s and 1980s *Einstein on the Beach* and *Akhnaten.*

Focus ON THE ARTS

William Butler Yeats's poem *Among School Children* ends with this famous line: "How can we know the dancer from the dance?" The line refers to all art forms, not just to dance. It implies that an artist is intricately involved in the work of art that he or she has created. Discuss the following argument in favor of Yeats's point of view: An artist's personality and intelligence appear most intensely, most vividly, in a work of art. Ask students whether they agree or disagree with this statement, and why.

545

DEVELOPING A PORTFOLIO

Assessment. A successful portfolio requires attention to organization. If a portfolio is carelessly put together, it reflects poorly on the student. Encourage students to stay focused on their goals and objectives. Assessment will include an evaluation across time, materials, and artistic content, and it will demonstrate that a student takes his or her work seriously. Remind students to give deliberate consideration to each piece of art they include, as well as the relative merit of each piece in context with the entire portfolio. With ample assignments and opportunities to undertake projects on their own, students may select portfolio pieces from a larger pool of works, allowing for greater variety.

Revolutions in European and American Art

Focus

Lesson Objectives

After studying this lesson, students will be able to:

■ Understand the roots of Dada and Surrealist art.

■ Describe the Realist styles in which American artists worked in the first half of the twentieth century.

■ Explain the goals of Abstract Expressionism.

Motivator

Have students share particularly vivid or recurrent dreams they have had. After several volunteers have spoken, ask students to identify common characteristics of dreams (i.e., they often involve distortions of reality). Inform students they are about to learn about several artists who attempted in their works to depict dreamlike landscapes and scenes.

Introducing the Lesson

Share with students the Dadaist sentiment that "art should be given a sound thrashing." Point out that sentiments like this were partly shaped by the events following World War I. Explain that students will learn about ways in which the events of our century have shaped art.

Revolutions in European and American Art

Vocabulary
- Dada
- Surrealism
- Regionalism
- Abstract Expressionism
- Pop art
- Op art
- Hard-Edge
- Photo-Realism

Artists to Meet
- Marcel Duchamp
- Joan Miró
- Salvador Dalí
- Paul Klee
- Grant Wood
- Edward Hopper
- Stuart Davis
- Georgia O'Keeffe
- Jacob Lawrence
- Willem de Kooning
- Jackson Pollock
- Helen Frankenthaler
- Robert Motherwell
- Frank Stella
- Alfred Leslie
- Audrey Flack
- Andrew Wyeth
- Emily Carr
- David Hockney
- Elizabeth Murray
- Judy Pfaff

Discover
After completing this lesson, you will be able to:
- Explain what is meant by Dada, Surrealism, and fantasy in art.
- Define Regionalism and point out the features that made it a uniquely American art style.
- Identify the most important characteristics of Pop art, Op art, Hard-Edge painting, and Photo-Realism.

*T*he years following World War I in Europe were marked by revolution and inflation, anxiety and unrest. Many people realized that the "war to end all wars" was not going to bring about peace and prosperity for long. It was a time of disillusionment, and this was apparent in much of the art that was produced.

Painting in Europe: Dada, Surrealism, and Fantasy

One group of artists expressed their disillusionment through their art. Known as **Dada,** *the movement ridiculed contemporary culture and traditional art forms.* The movement is said to have received its name when one of its members opened a dictionary at random and stuck a pin into the word *dada.* The word, which sounded like baby talk, made no sense at all. Because the members of the movement believed that European culture had lost all meaning and purpose, this word seemed appropriate.

■ **FIGURE 24.2** Duchamp's work is the first kinetic, or moving, sculpture in the history of Western art. **What makes this a work of art? Confronted by this work, what would you say?**

Marcel Duchamp. *Bicycle Wheel. New York* (1951. Third version, after lost original of 1913). Assemblage, metal wheel, 63.8 cm (25¹/₂″) diameter, painted wood stool, 60.2 cm (23³/₄″) high; overall 128.3 cm (50¹/₂″) high. Collection, The Museum of Modern Art, New York, New York. The Sidney and Harriet Janis Collection.

Marcel Duchamp
(1887–1968)

Dada artists such as Marcel Duchamp (mahr-**sell** doo-**shahn**) exhibited the most ordinary and absurd objects as works of art. These objects included a bottle rack and a bicycle wheel mounted on a stool (Figure 24.2). Perhaps no work sums up the Dada point of view as well as Duchamp's photograph of Leonardo da Vinci's *Mona Lisa*—with a carefully drawn mustache. With works like this, the Dada artists sought to ridicule the art of the past.

The Dada movement ended in 1922. It set the stage, however, for later artists who were attracted to the idea of creating art that was whimsical, humorous, and fantastic.

Teacher's Classroom Resources

📁 Appreciating Cultural Diversity 34

📁 Art and Humanities 40

📁 Cooperative Learning 36, 37

📁 Enrichment Activity 45

📁 Reproducible Lesson Plan 56

📁 Reteaching Activity 56

📁 Study Guide 56

Joan Miró (1893–1983)

Joan Miró (zhoo-**an** mee-**roh**) was a forgetful, modest little man who looked as if he should be working in a bank rather than in a painting studio. In 1925, Miró startled the Paris art world with a painting called *Carnival of Harlequin* (Figure 24.3). This work helped make the Spanish artist a major figure in twentieth-century art. The painting was among the first to introduce a new style of art called **Surrealism,** *in which dreams, fantasy, and the subconscious served as inspiration for artists.*

The Surrealists were a group of artists who rejected control, composition, and logic. They chose to paint the world of dreams and the subconscious. The world of dreams had been explored before by Hieronymus Bosch, Francisco Goya, and others. In even the most fantastic of their works, however, the subjects could be recognized. This is not true of Miró's paintings.

Miró experienced many hardships in his life, and these led to the visions that inspired paintings like *Carnival of Harlequin.* When he arrived in Paris in 1919, poverty forced him to live on one meal a week, chewing gum to deaden his appetite and eating dried figs for energy. Then, when he began painting, forms came to him as if seen in a vision. Sometimes an accidental brush mark suggested the beginnings of a picture. This period of unconscious experiment was carefully limited. Then Miró worked on each detail in the painting. The result of this effort was a carefully controlled design.

Salvador Dalí (1904–1989)

Miró's countryman Salvador Dalí (**dah**-lee) joined the Surrealist movement late and used his skills as a master showman to become its most famous member. In *The Persistence of Memory* (Figure 24.4), he created an eerie world in which death and decay are symbolized by a dead tree and a strange sea monster decomposing on a deserted beach. Ants swarm over a watch in an unsuccessful attempt to eat it.

■ **FIGURE 24.3** This was among the first works to be called Surrealist. **Identify specific Surrealistic characteristics in the painting.**

Joan Miró. *Carnival of Harlequin.* 1924–25. Oil on canvas. Approx. 66 × 92.7 cm (26 × 36⅝"). Albright-Knox Art Gallery, Buffalo, New York. Room of Contemporary Art Fund, 1940.

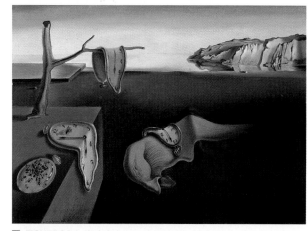

■ **FIGURE 24.4** Slightly larger than a standard sheet of typing paper, Dali's painting manages to look larger than life. **Can you find the artist's self-portrait in this picture?**

Salvador Dalí. *The Persistence of Memory. (Persistance de la memoire).* 1931. Oil on canvas. Approx. 24 × 33 cm (9½ × 13"). The Museum of Modern Art, New York, New York. Given anonymously.

Dalí's Use of Symbolism

The meaning of this unusual picture seems clear: In time, everything will die and decay except time itself. Time alone is indestructible. The limp watches indicate that someone

Chapter 24 *Modern Art Movements to the Present* **547**

TEACH
Studio Skills

Have students create their own Dada sculptures that combine two ordinary objects in an absurd way. Announce this exercise in advance so that students will have time to collect any necessary objects from outside the classroom. If possible, show students reproductions of Man Ray's tack-covered iron and Meret Oppenheim's fur-covered teacup, saucer, and spoon.

Art Criticism

Have students examine Figure 24.3 and use the four steps of art criticism to assess it. Do the students arrive at the same conclusions presented in the text? Make sure that students consider the painting's title. What does it add to their interpretations?

Studio Skills

Provide students with colored felt-tip markers and sheets of sketch paper. Challenge them to experiment with drawing playful little shapes in the manner of Miró. Instruct students to continue drawing until they have filled an entire page. If they wish, students may use fine-point black markers to add details to their shapes. Have individual students display their work and discuss whether they created shapes purely from their imagination or whether it was easier to start with a known object and develop it into an unusual shape. Examine Figure 24.3 and discuss the way in which Miró created his shapes and forms.

 ## Technology

National Gallery of Art Videodisc Use the following images as examples of more works by artists introduced in this lesson.

Joan Miró
The Flight of the Dragonfly before the Sun

Search Frame 2265

Helen Frankenthaler
Wales

Search Frame 2327

Paul Klee
The White House

Search Frame 2165

Use Glencoe's *Correlation Bar Code Guide to the National Gallery of Art* to locate more artworks.

Aesthetics

Explain to students that the modern idea that art should be original began with the Dadaists and Surrealists. Then divide the class into debating teams. One side should defend the proposition: originality in art is important. The other group should argue: great art need not be entirely new nor a unique act of self-expression. Encourage teams to refer to specific artworks that have been discussed in class in defense of their positions.

Art History

Explain to students that many twentieth-century artists have been very interested in so-called "outsider art" (i.e., art produced by people outside the mainstream, which includes isolated folk artists and visionary recluses). Have a volunteer group research outsider art and make a presentation that explains how Klee, Dali, and many other Surrealists drew inspiration from outsider art.

Critical Thinking

Have students choose partners to develop their perspective on the boundary between artistic imagination and eccentricity. One student in each pair is to play the role of an individual given to offbeat self-expression, such as painting all the walls and furniture in his or her home black with white stripes. The other student will play Dali or Miró. Have the student pairs work together to write a dialogue that expresses their ideas about art and what makes a person an artist.

has the power to twist time as he or she sees fit. That person is the artist who painted them in this way. Dalí tells you that the artist alone, through his or her works, is able to conquer time and achieve immortality.

The meanings in Dalí's other works are not always as clear. In some, the symbolism is lost to everyone but the artist. Furthermore, his images are frequently so bizarre and grotesque that some people have called them the products of a madman. Dalí, enjoying the controversy caused by his works and his unusual behavior, responded by saying, "The difference between a madman and myself is that I am not mad."

Paul Klee (1879–1940)

Although the Swiss painter Paul Klee **(clay)** was never a Surrealist, fantasy was an important part of his painting. Working on scraps of burlap, paper, glass, and linen, he produced almost 9,000 paintings and drawings based on his own imagination and wit.

Klee was fascinated by a world that he said was filled with wonders; he spent

■ **FIGURE 24.5** The son of a music teacher, Klee became so skilled with the violin that it was difficult for him to choose between a career in music or painting. What procedure did Klee follow when painting a picture like this?

Paul Klee. *Fish Magic.* 1925. Oil on canvas, mounted on board. 77.5 × 97.8 cm (30³/₈ × 38¹/₂"). Philadelphia Museum of Art, Philadelphia, Pennsylvania. The Louise and Walter Arensberg Collection.

hours studying shells, coral, butterfly wings, stained glass, and mosaics. His reactions to the world resulted in pictures that freed viewers from traditional ways of looking at things or caused them to smile with delight and amusement.

Fish Magic
■ **FIGURE 24.5**

In 1902, while in Italy, Klee visited the aquarium in Naples. For hours he stood with his nose almost pressed against the glass, watching the fish in the huge tanks dart, turn, and glide gracefully by. He was bewitched by the colorful fish, the flora that swayed gently in the current, and the bubbles that drifted lazily upward. Later, inspired by what he saw in the aquarium, Klee took his brush and slowly began to make lines and shapes on a canvas. He had no definite idea in mind, but as he worked, forms slowly began to take shape. He painted many pictures this way, each showing a marvelous dream world suggested by what he had seen in the aquarium. One of those pictures was named *Fish Magic* (Figure 24.5).

Regionalism and the American Scene

American art, from the time of the Armory Show in 1913 until the start of World War II in 1939, owed much to the modern art movements that developed in Europe at the beginning of the century. Some artists were influenced by the bright, decorative style of the Fauves or explored their own personal approaches to Cubism. Others adapted the approach of the Expressionists or the Surrealists.

Some American artists chose not to follow the art movements of Europe, because they felt those doctrines were too complicated. They wanted to paint the American scene in a clear, simple way so that it could be understood and enjoyed by all. During the 1930s, **Regionalism** became a popular art style in which *artists painted the scenes and events that were typical of their sections of America.*

More About... **Dada.** The Dada movement was rooted in disgust at the horrors of World War I. Proponents of Dada could not account for the irrational and vicious behavior exhibited during that war that seemed to confirm the bankruptcy of nineteenth-century rationalism and bourgeois values. Dada was, in essence, an attempt to subvert middle-class culture. The Dadaists rejected Cubism and traditional forms of painting as escapist and ineffective. The main Dada pioneer, Marcel Duchamp, exhibited "Readymades," ordinary objects that were intended to be devoid of aesthetic interest. In so doing, the Dadaists reduced creation to the act of selection.

LOOKING Closely

USE OF THE ELEMENTS AND PRINCIPLES

When you go beyond description to conduct a thorough analysis of this painting, you will recognize how skillfully the artist organized the work.

- **Harmony.** A curved contour line is repeated over and over again throughout the work, adding harmony. Use your finger to trace the contour line at the curve representing the top of the woman's apron. Then see how many similar curves you can find in the rest of the picture.
- **Pattern.** Notice that the pattern of the pitchfork is repeated in the seam of the man's overalls.
- **Emphasis.** The heads of the figures are given emphasis by being linked to the horizontal lines of the porch roof and the diagonals forming the peak of the house.

■ **FIGURE 24.6** Grant Wood. *American Gothic*. 1930. Oil on beaver board. Approx. 74.3 × 62.4 cm (29¼ × 24½"). The Art Institute of Chicago, Chicago, Illinois. Friends of American Art Collection. All rights reserved by The Art Institute of Chicago and VAGA, New York, New York, 1930.934.

Thomas Hart Benton painted his native Missouri; John Steuart Curry, Kansas; and Grant Wood, Iowa.

Grant Wood (1892–1942)

Like the other Regionalists, Grant Wood studied in Europe. In Paris, he was exposed to the modern art styles, but the fifteenth- and sixteenth-century Flemish and German paintings he saw on a trip to Munich, Germany, made a deep impression on him. When Wood returned to his native Iowa, he painted rural scenes using a style of Realism modeled after that of the Flemish and German works. His well-known painting *American Gothic* (Figure 24.6) captures some of the simple faith and determination of the European Gothic period.

Edward Hopper (1882–1967)

Edward Hopper was not a Regionalist in the true sense of the word, although he did paint the American scene in a realistic manner. Hopper had early ties with the Ashcan School. Unlike the Ashcan artists who used the city as a setting for their pictures, Hopper concentrated on the moods and feelings aroused by the city itself. Ignoring the congestion and excitement of city life, he set out to capture the emptiness and loneliness that are also a part of the urban scene.

Many of Hopper's works do not include people. He communicated a feeling of loneliness, isolation, and monotony through his pictures of deserted streets and vacant buildings. When he did show people, they were often seen through the windows of all-night diners, nearly empty houses, and drab apartment buildings.

Chapter 24 *Modern Art Movements to the Present* **549**

Examine the feature and the artwork by Grant Wood. Remind students that Wood was heavily influenced by the fifteenth- and sixteenth-century Flemish and German paintings he saw during his European travels. To underscore the point, have students compare Figure 24.6 with Figure 17.4 (page 383), Jan van Eyck's *The Arnolfini Wedding*. Ask: Despite the European influences, how are the time and place in which Wood painted evident in *American Gothic*? Would laborers have had their portrait painted in the fifteenth century? Identify a Gothic-style architectural detail in Figure 24.6. Would this detail confuse an art historian trying to date this work? Why or why not?

Critical Thinking

Have students imagine that the couple illustrated in Figure 24.6 has decided to seek the advice of a marriage counselor or minister. Ask three volunteers to role-play a first session between the couple and the help professional they have chosen. In preparing for their activity, the trio of students should make a list of probable quirks, worries, and problems based on Wood's acutely psychological portrait. To enhance the drama of the exercise, supply a few simple props that appear in Wood's painting such as a cameo pin, an apron, wire-rimmed glasses, and a dark jacket.

More About... **Art Movements.** The Regionalist movement was, in large part, an attempt by artists to define themselves as truly and distinctively American artists. Critics in the first decades of the twentieth century urged American artists to shake off their tendency to look to Europe for aesthetic guidance. There was a sense of freedom in this search for true self-expression, a search that was thought to inevitably produce the most truly American art as a consequence. World War I made it clear that the various nationalities in the United States had not become a melting pot, and intellectuals in many fields tried to recover a sense of national consciousness.

Art Criticism

Explain that art critics do not always agree on the message or feeling embodied in a particular artwork. For example, some critics have noted that Hopper's *Drug Store* (Figure 24.7) suggests loneliness and vulnerability, while others see the work as peaceful and serene. Have students write a paragraph in which they offer their interpretations of this painting. Invite them to share their opinions with the class.

Art History

Have students find other reproductions of paintings by Edward Hopper. Ask what themes emerge when this collection of the artist's works is taken as a whole. Point out that familiarity with an artist's entire output often influences how art historians interpret any single artwork by that artist. Ask students how seeing other paintings by Hopper extends or even changes their assessment of *Drug Store.*

Aesthetics

Have students identify as many objects as possible in Figure 24.8. Write the list on the board. Ask: How does this list help viewers interpret the work?

Cross Curriculum

MUSIC. Play some recordings of swing music by musicians such as Count Basie, Duke Ellington, Benny Goodman, and Glenn Miller. Discuss how the rhythm and instrumentation of swing music relates to Davis's use of rhythm and color in *Swing Landscape.*

Drug Store
■ **FIGURE 24.7**

Typical of Hopper's paintings is *Drug Store* (Figure 24.7). He shows the shop at night—its warm lights threatened by the darkness, the emptiness, and the silence that crowd in on all sides. The picture captures the mystery and the loneliness that, for many people, are as much a part of a great city as its wide boulevards, towering skyscrapers, and endless traffic.

■ **FIGURE 24.7** Like many of Hopper's paintings, this work communicates a sense of loneliness and isolation. **If you could use only one aesthetic theory when judging this work, would it be imitationalism, formalism, or emotionalism? Why?**

Edward Hopper. *Drug Store.* 1927. Oil on canvas. 73.6 × 101.6 cm (29 × 40″). Museum of Fine Arts, Boston, Massachusetts. Bequest of John T. Spaulding.

■ **FIGURE 24.8** Davis's mature paintings drew inspiration from the lively sights and sounds of modern American life. **In what way is this painting like the musical rhythms played by a jazz band?**

Stuart Davis. *Swing Landscape.* 1938. Oil on canvas. 2.2 × 4.4 m (7′2³/₄″ × 14′5¹/₈″). Indiana University Art Museum, Bloomington, Indiana. © Estate of Stuart Davis/Licensed by VAGA, New York, New York.

550 **Unit Seven** *Art of the Modern Era*

American Artists Take a New Direction

Painters such as Grant Wood and Edward Hopper remained convinced that art should make use of subject matter. Other artists, however, did not share this commitment to subject matter. Included among them was Stuart Davis.

Stuart Davis (1894–1964)

Although Stuart Davis's early works were influenced by the Ashcan School, the Armory Show introduced him to new models. Almost at once, he set out to find a new visual language with which to express himself. In 1927, he nailed an electric fan, a pair of rubber gloves, and an egg beater to a table; for an entire year, he painted only these objects. It was a turning point for the young artist, because it drew him away from a reliance on subject matter and opened his eyes to the possibilities of abstraction.

Swing Landscape
■ **FIGURE 24.8**

Davis's best works reveal his affection for urban America. Sometimes, as in his *Swing Landscape* (Figure 24.8), he used parts of recognizable objects in his works. At other times, he used only the colors, shapes, and textures suggested by the world around him. He painted the American scene as he saw it, felt it, and heard it.

Teacher Notes

Providing Resources. One way of adding immediacy to the art experience for students is to arrange for them to meet and speak with local artists and craftspeople. To find out who lives and works in your area, begin by getting in touch with local art gallery dealers and curators in the education departments of local museums. It is also helpful to read reviews of art shows in your area. Even though a given artist may not live in your city, he or she will very likely be in town for the opening of the show and might be willing to visit your class. Finally, art supply stores are another source of information on local artists.

Georgia O'Keeffe (1887–1986)

Georgia O'Keeffe drew her inspiration from nature. O'Keeffe studied art in Chicago, New York, and Virginia before taking a position as a high school art teacher in Amarillo, Texas. She was immediately fascinated by the beauty of the dry, open Western landscape. While in Texas, she began to paint watercolors based on her response to the flat, stark surroundings.

Without her knowledge, a friend took a group of O'Keeffe's paintings to the gallery of Alfred Stieglitz in New York. Stieglitz was a talented and well-known photographer. He was impressed by O'Keeffe's paintings and exhibited them in his gallery. Stieglitz became her most enthusiastic supporter and, eventually, her husband.

During her long career, O'Keeffe painted pictures of New York skyscrapers; the clean white bones, desert shadows, and mountains of her beloved Southwest; and flowers (Figure 24.9). Because a flower is so small, so easy to overlook, she was determined to paint it in such a way that it could not be ignored. The result was a startling close-up view, painted in sharp focus.

Jacob Lawrence (1917–)

Jacob Lawrence came out of a tradition of social protest. The flat, brightly colored shapes that marked his mature style can be traced back to the work with poster paints and cut paper Lawrence did as a boy in a New York settlement house.

Tombstones
■ FIGURE 24.10

In *Tombstones* (Figure 24.10), Lawrence simplified these flat, colorful shapes to tell a story of hopelessness. Notice how the postures and gestures of the figures in this painting provide clues to their despair. None of these people seems inclined to go anywhere or do anything. They even ignore the crying infant in the baby carriage who has dropped her doll.

In the basement apartment of the building in which they live is a tombstone dealer. Every day the people pass the tombstones on display or peer down at them from their apartment windows. This sight is a constant reminder that the only change in their dreary lives will come when their own names are carved on one of those tombstones.

■ FIGURE 24.9 Note the sharp focus in this large, close-up view of a flower. **Describe the colors and shapes used in this painting.**

Georgia O'Keeffe. *White Trumpet Flower.* 1932. Oil on canvas. 75.6 × 100.9 cm (29³/₄ × 39³/₄"). San Diego Museum of Art, San Diego, California. Gift of Mrs. Inez Grant Parker in memory of Earle W. Grant.

■ FIGURE 24.10 Lawrence's paintings portray the lives and struggles of African Americans. **To what aesthetic qualities would you refer when judging this work? What is your judgment?**

Jacob Lawrence. *Tombstones.* 1942. Gouache on paper. 73 × 52 cm (28³/₄ × 20¹/₂"). Collection of the Whitney Museum of American Art, New York, New York.

Art History

Have a volunteer research Georgia O'Keeffe's life and make a presentation that includes slides or pictures of her artwork. Discuss why O'Keeffe attracted such an enormous number of fans, especially in her later years.

Studio Skills

Have students study Figure 24.9. Then provide them with colored chalk and encourage them to draw on the board their own outsized versions of plants or other natural objects. Students should refer to detailed photographs of their subject as they work. When the students have finished, discuss the effects of working in a large scale.

Art Criticism

Have students compare Stuart Davis's use of the elements and principles of art in Figure 24.8 with that of Jacob Lawrence in Figure 24.10, paying particular attention to the elements of color, shape, and space, and the principles of balance, variety, and movement.

Did You Know?

The son of the art director of a Philadelphia newspaper, Davis knew several of the Ashcan artists who were employed there and admired their work.

Technology

Videodiscs. Videodisc technology represents an exciting new direction in the study of art history. Where once a person might dream about the day when he or she could travel to distant museums and historic locations, the technology of today changes the way we think of travel. As students of art history, they might be pioneers in videodisc technology. What developments do they predict in this field? Ask students if they can speculate about other forms of technology that is yet to come. What do they know about the concept of virtual reality? Do they feel that the value of art will be enhanced or diminished by such progress?

Critical Thinking

Have students work in small groups to give a voice to each of the people in Lawrence's *Tombstones* (Figure 24.10, page 551). Have one group write what the man on the staircase might be saying to the woman leaning out of the window, have another group write what the woman might be saying to the baby that she cradles. Have groups also write what the silent characters might be thinking. After each group has read its script aloud, develop an interpretation of this painting's mood or message based on the character's thoughts and conversation.

Aesthetics

Point out that the Abstract Expressionist movement brought with it an expanded definition of art. There was a sense that art is as much the act of creation as the object resulting from that act. Have students form small groups to discuss this idea. One member of each group should present its opinion of this interpretation of art as an act of decision-making, which had its roots in Dada.

Abstract Expressionism

After World War II, a new art movement took hold in America. Probably no other movement ever gained such instant recognition or caused so much confusion and controversy. The roots of this new movement can be traced back to the works of Wassily Kandinsky, Pablo Picasso, and especially the Surrealists.

The movement was called **Abstract Expressionism,** because *artists applied paint freely to their huge canvases in an effort to show feelings and emotions rather than realistic subject matter.* They did not try to create the illusion of space filled with figures, buildings, or landscapes. They thought of the picture surface as a flat wall and emphasized the physical action it took to paint it. Instead of carefully planned brush strokes, artists dribbled, spilled, spattered, and slashed paints onto their canvases. As they applied colors this way, they looked for and emphasized areas of interest that added structure to their work.

Willem de Kooning (1904–1997)

Willem de Kooning (**vill**-em duh **koh**-ning) was born in Holland but moved to the United States in 1926. Among his most powerful and shocking paintings are those showing the female figure, which he began to paint in the late 1940s.

Of course, many artists had painted women before. It was de Kooning's way of showing women that aroused so much controversy (Figure 24.11). Some observers said that his women were grotesque, insulting, and ugly. In fact, they express de Kooning's feeling that a woman is a great deal more than just a pretty face. She is revealed as a complex human being with unique interests, skills, and responsibilities. Her emotions range from hate to pity, anger to love, and sorrow to joy.

De Kooning knew that it would be impossible to show all this by painting a traditional picture of a woman limited to outward appearances. As he painted, de Kooning stripped away the façade to show the person within.

De Kooning's Technique

De Kooning's new vision of women grew out of the creative act of painting. Using sweeping, violent strokes, he applied an assortment of rich colors to his canvas. Giving full reign to impulse and accident, he worked until the image slowly began to come into focus. He never allowed the images to come completely into focus, however; a great deal is left to the viewer's imagination.

■ **FIGURE 24.11** His swirls and slashes of color helped define the Abstract Expressionist style. What do you feel is the artist's main concern here? Is it outward appearances, or has the exterior been stripped away to allow the viewer to see within the subject?

Willem de Kooning. *Woman VI.* 1953. Oil on canvas. 1.74 × 1.49 m (68¹/₂ × 58¹/₂"). Carnegie Museum of Art, Pittsburgh, Pennsylvania. Gift of G. David Thompson, 1955.

More About... **WPA.** WPA government art projects, which began in 1935, during the Great Depression, provided a much-needed source of income for thousands of artists in the United States, including Alice Neel and Jacob Lawrence. WPA painters were required to send in one painting every four to six weeks in exchange for a salary. These artists were free to create other works and did not necessarily give their best work to the government, which owned all of the submitted artworks. The government had no say in what an artist made, but if the work in question was a mural for a public building, the building's administrators did exercise a degree of control over what an artist painted.

Jackson Pollock (1912–1956)

De Kooning's style was unique, yet his method of painting was more traditional than that of Jackson Pollock. Pollock placed his huge canvases on the floor while he worked. He walked onto and around them, using brushes, sticks, and knives to drip and spatter his paints on the canvas. This technique enabled him to become physically involved with the creative act.

Pollock abandoned the idea that the artist should know beforehand how the painting will look when it is finished. He began each new work by randomly dripping paint over the entire canvas (Figure 24.12). He created works of line, color, and movement layered to produce complex textures.

The purpose of Pollock's art was to *express* his feelings, not just illustrate them. Other artists chose to picture feelings by painting figures crying, laughing, or suffering. Pollock's pictures were created while *he* was experiencing those feelings, and they influenced his choice of colors and how those colors were applied.

Helen Frankenthaler
(1928–)

Helen Frankenthaler (**frank**-en-tahl-er) developed her own unique painting technique as an extension of Pollock's method of applying swirls and drips of paint onto a canvas spread out on the floor. Her painting technique inspired a new art style known as Color Field painting: Nonobjective paintings that feature large areas of luminous color. Unlike Abstract Expressionists who emphasized the spontaneous, physical actions of painting, Color Field painters deliberately manipulated paint to create compositions noted for their quiet balance and harmony. Frankenthaler moved away from a heavy application of paint, and instead used paint thinned with turpentine. She poured this thinned paint onto an unprimed, or uncoated, canvas; the paint sank into the canvas and stained it. The paints produce flowing, graceful, free-form shapes of intense color. These shapes, some

with soft edges, others with hard edges, overlap, contrast, or blend with other shapes. Frankenthaler's concern centered on the way these shapes work in relation to each other.

■ **FIGURE 24.12** Jackson Pollock was known as an action painter. Can you see from this painting why he was called that?

Jackson Pollock. *Cathedral.* 1947. Enamel and aluminum paint on canvas. 181.6 × 89.1 cm (71$^1/_2$ × 35$^1/_{16}$"). Dallas Museum of Art, Dallas, Texas. Gift of Mr. and Mrs. Bernard J. Reis.

Critical Thinking

Organize a class debate on Willem de Kooning's *Woman* series of paintings, of which Figure 24.11 was the sixth. Display reproductions of as many of the other paintings in this series as possible. One team should defend the proposition that the pictures are portraits of women, however anonymous or unusually rendered they may be. The other team should argue that the paintings reveal more about de Kooning's own personality and attitudes toward women than they do about the subjects of the works. After the debate, discuss whether an artist can ever make an artwork that does not reveal something of his or her own personality.

Art Criticism

Have students compare the painting in Figure 24.12 with Figure 21.10 (page 475), J.M.W. Turner's *Snow Storm.* Review the characteristics of Romantic art and discuss whether Pollock's painting could be called *romantic.*

Chapter 24 *Modern Art Movements to the Present* **553**

More About...	**Helen Frankenthaler**. Helen Frankenthaler grew up in an apartment in Manhattan. Frankenthaler was always entranced by the spectacle of the

sky and its changing light, and her family always gave her the room with the best view of the sky when they traveled. She recalls, "I would spend time looking out my window in the early morning, and what I saw was connected in my mind with moods or states of feeling. There is an early-morning light, for example, that can remind me of the time of my worst school days. . . [a] tight time schedule, and I am failing. . . Or else it is a feeling of marvelous energy. There is nothing like the beginning of day!"

Aesthetics

Have pairs of students show Figure 24.12 to at least three people who are unfamiliar with Abstract Expressionist art and ask their interpretation. Students should compare the various responses and categorize them according to the three main aesthetic theories. Conclude with a discussion of whether people's opinions varied depending on their age, gender, or personality.

Aesthetics

Have students examine Figure 24.14 and discuss Robert Motherwell's use of black as an emblem of mourning. Ask a volunteer to research the cross-cultural meanings of color to find out whether black is a universal symbol of death and mourning. For example, how might a Japanese person who was unfamiliar with Western color symbolism interpret *Elegy to the Spanish Republic 108?*

Did You Know?

Despite their random appearance, Jackson Pollock's paintings are said to be extremely difficult to forge.

FIGURE 24.13 Unlike traditional oil painting where the paint rests on the surface of the canvas, the paint in this work has soaked into the canvas. **Do you think this painting makes use of accidental effects? Where do you see signs of a deliberate manipulation of the elements of art?**

Helen Frankenthaler. *Interior Landscape.* 1964. Acrylic on canvas. 2.66 × 2.35 m (8'8⅞" × 7'8⅝"). San Francisco Museum of Modern Art, San Francisco, California. Gift of the Women's Board.

By concentrating on shapes and colors, Frankenthaler permitted a fantasy to take shape on the canvas (Figure 24.13). Like all of Frankenthaler's works, this painting is nonobjective. Its meaning is for you to discover for yourself.

Robert Motherwell
(1915–1991)

Another leader in the Abstract Expressionist movement was Robert Motherwell. Beginning in 1948, Motherwell created a series of large paintings reflecting the horror and destruction of the civil war in Spain. Like Picasso before him (Figure 23.16, page 525), he revealed the war's impact on the defenseless in paintings such as *Elegy to the Spanish Republic* (Figure 24.14). Huge, ominous black shapes nearly obscure a background of delicate, warm hues, suggesting an overpowering sense of doom. Intent on communicating the helplessness and anguish of an entire nation on the brink of an inevitable war, Motherwell chose to use a completely nonobjective style.

FIGURE 24.14 An elegy is a speech or song of sorrow. **How is sorrow expressed in this work? How is this work similar to Picasso's painting of Guernica (Figure 23.16, page 525)? How does it differ?**

Robert Motherwell. *Elegy to the Spanish Republic 108.* 1966. Oil and acrylic on canvas. 213.4 × 373.4 cm (84 × 147"). Dallas Museum of Art, Dallas, Texas. The Art Museum League Fund. © Dedalus Foundation/ Licensed by VAGA, New York, New York.

554 **Unit Seven** *Art of the Modern Era*

More About... **Harold Rosenberg.** Not all critics championed Abstract Expressionism. Harold Rosenberg, for example, felt that Abstract Expressionist painters were incredibly narcissistic, and his writings reflect his bitterly sarcastic attitude. In the article, "The American Action Painters," Rosenberg states: "[The artist] gesticulated upon the canvas and watched for what each novelty would declare him and his art to be." Rosenberg accused Abstract Expressionist painters of releasing themselves from any obligation to promote political, moral, or aesthetic values. He said that such artworks had no real audience—they were just objects used by the powerful and "accepted" by the public as "phenomena of The Age of Queer Things."

Diversity in Contemporary American Painting

Throughout history, each new generation of artists has included some who were unwilling to follow in the footsteps of their predecessors. Abstract Expressionist artists were not immune to such challenges. Since 1960, their ideas have been challenged by a series of new art movements worldwide. The loose painting technique and the emphasis placed on personal expression, as seen in the work of de Kooning, Pollock, Motherwell, and other Abstract Expressionists, were replaced by new styles. These new art movements included Pop Art, Op Art, Hard-Edge painting, and Photo-Realism.

Pop Art

A new art form emerged during the 1950s in England. There a group of young artists broke new ground with collages made of pictures clipped from popular magazines. Collages, of course, were not new. Cubist, Dada, and other artists had used this technique earlier, but for different reasons. These British artists combined pictures of familiar household objects, such as television sets, vacuum cleaners, and canned hams, to suggest that people were letting the mass media, especially advertising, shape their lives. Their art included all media and was called **Pop art,** because it *portrayed images from the popular culture.*

Pop art made its way to the United States during the 1960s. American Pop artists such as Andy Warhol examined the contemporary scene and reported what they found without satire or criticism. Warhol and other pop artists did, however, present images of Coke bottles and Campbell's soup cans in new ways or in greatly enlarged sizes. They wanted to shake viewers out of accustomed ways of looking at the most trivial trappings of modern life.

Pop artists such as Claes Oldenburg treated ordinary objects found in the manufactured environment—for example, a three-way electrical plug (Figure 24.15)—in much the same way that Georgia O'Keeffe treated objects found in nature. Both enlarged their subjects to increase their impact on viewers. O'Keeffe did this to call attention to the beauty in nature, which is too often taken for granted (Figure 24.9, page 551). Oldenburg wanted viewers to stop and think about the products of the industrial and commercial culture in which they lived. He felt that people had come to rely too readily on these products and hoped to make viewers more conscious of that fact.

Op Art

A new nonobjective art movement developed in the United States after 1960. At about the same time, similar movements were evident in several European countries, including Germany and Italy. **Op art** was *a style that tried to create an impression of movement on the picture surface by means of optical illusion.* In traditional paintings, the aim was to

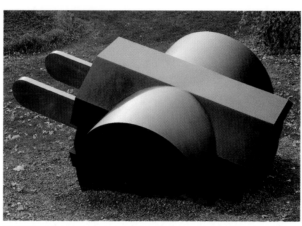

■ **FIGURE 24.15** Included in Oldenburg's list of monumental projects is a 45-foot clothespin in a city square in Philadelphia and a nearly 100-foot tall baseball bat in Chicago. **What did Pop artists hope to accomplish with their works?**

Claes Oldenburg. *Giant Three-Way Plug.* 1970. Cor-Ten steel and polished bronze. Overall 154.6 × 198.1 × 306.4 cm (60⁷/₈ × 78 × 120⁵/₈"). Allen Memorial Art Museum, Oberlin College, Oberlin, Ohio. Gift of the artist and Fund for Contemporary Art, 1970.

Chapter 24 *Modern Art Movements to the Present* **555**

CHAPTER 24
LESSON ONE

Art History
Have students research the professional background of prominent American Pop artists such as Andy Warhol, Jasper Johns, Robert Indiana, Roy Lichtenstein, and Claes Oldenburg to find out which artists had early careers in advertising. After students have presented their findings, discuss how early experiences in advertising affected their choice of commercial subject matter and their critical attitude toward the media and its influence.

Aesthetics
Display a reproduction of Pop artist Roy Lichtenstein's *Little Big Painting* (1965). Explain that this gigantic, comic-book-style image of a brushstroke was Lichtenstein's humorous jab at what he saw as the pretentiousness and self-importance of Abstract Expressionist artists, who spoke of the weight of existential decision behind each brushstroke. Have a volunteer review the tenets of Abstract Expressionism covered in Lesson One and learn more about Lichtenstein's career. In a brief report to the class, the student should reveal what happened after *Little Big Painting* was exhibited at the Leo Castelli Gallery in New York.

Did You Know ?
The name Pop Art derives from a shortened form of the word *popular*—an adjective that describes the objects most favored as subject matter by artists of the movement.

> ### *More About...*
> **Color Field Painting.** Reveal to students that the rise of a new art movement often changes the way in which an earlier style or set of artworks is viewed. Explain that, until the advent of Color Field painting (a movement closely related to Abstract Expressionism), Monet's water lily paintings were regarded as evidence of his decline. These paintings were done late in Monet's life, and their blurriness reflects the fact that his eyesight was very poor. As Color Field paintings such as those by Helen Frankenthaler gained favor, critics began to appreciate anew Monet's paintings of water lilies. People viewed them not as messy illustrations of lilies, but as extraordinary fields of color.

Art History

Have groups of students investigate the work of artists other than Frank Stella who focused on stripes for at least part of their career. These artists include Gene Davis, Sean Scully, Barnett Newman, and Kenneth Noland. Have groups prepare presentations on one of these artists. Then discuss how the various stripe painters differ.

Aesthetics

Ask students to write an essay on what, if anything, distinguishes Stella's paintings from crafts that involve two-dimensional design, such as printed textiles. The essays should address the question: If Stella's painting were printed on cotton and sewn into a shirt, would it still be art? Why or why not?

Critical Thinking

Point out that one of the most unusual aspects of Frank Stella's early paintings is the irregularly shaped canvas, which is difficult to appreciate in a reproduced photograph. Remind students that Stella is not the first to use a nonrectangular canvas, direct them to Raphael's *Alba Madonna* (Figure 16.24, page 373). Have students list on the board all the reasons for using a traditional, rectangular canvas and all the reasons why they believe Stella chose not to. Then have students identify paintings in the text that might benefit from being painted on an odd-shaped canvas.

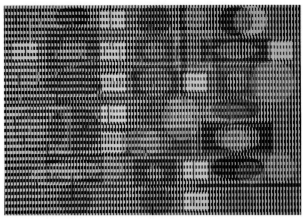

■ **FIGURE 24.16** Op artists used optical illusion to create an impression of movement. **How does this artist achieve that effect?**

Agam (Yaacov Agam). *Double Metamorphosis II.* 1964. Oil on corrugated aluminum, in eleven parts. 2.69 × 4.02 m (8'10" × 13'2¼"). The Museum of Modern Art, New York, New York. Gift of Mr. and Mrs. George M. Jaffin.

■ **FIGURE 24.17** Stella altered the shapes of his paintings because he did not want to be confined to a strict, familiar rectangular frame. **How have repetition and contrast been used to unify this painting?**

Frank Stella. *Agbatana III.* 1968. Fluorescent acrylic on canvas. 3.05 × 4.57 m (10 × 15'). Allen Memorial Art Museum, Oberlin College, Oberlin, Ohio. Fund for Contemporary Art and National Foundation for the Arts and Humanities Grant, 1968.

draw the viewer into the work. In contrast, Op pictures seem to vibrate and reach out to the viewer.

One Op artist, Bridget Riley (Figure 2.5, page 30) used gradual changes of color and wavy lines to add a sense of movement to her paintings. The effect is a surface that seems to swell out in some places and fade back in others.

Israeli-born artist Yaacov Agam, known as Agam (ah-**gahm**), went even further, creating multiple images within the same work. He used rows of thin, fixed strips that project from the surface of his painting in vertical rows (Figure 24.16). Agam painted the sides of these strips differently from their tops and from the spaces in between. In this way the artist combined several designs in a single work. The one you see depends on your position when viewing the work. When you change your position, the design changes.

Hard-Edge Painters

Another group of artists who gained prominence are known as **Hard-Edge** painters, because they *placed importance on the crisp, precise edges of the shapes in their paintings.* Their works contain smooth surfaces, hard edges, pure colors, and simple geometric shapes, and are done with great precision. Typical of Hard-Edge painters is Frank Stella.

Frank Stella (1936–)

Taking the new Hard-Edge style a step further than other artists, Stella eventually began to use different canvas shapes for his works (Figure 24.17). Many of his paintings are not rectangular or square. Working on a huge scale, Stella painted designs that complement the unique shapes of his canvases. He used a wide range of precise shapes painted with intense colors to create a vivid visual movement. Thin white lines, actually the unpainted white of the canvas, help define shapes and set off the colors. These white lines, along with large, repeated, protractorlike shapes, act as unifying elements. They hold the brightly colored work together in a unified whole.

CULTURAL DIVERSITY

Design. After examining the work by Frank Stella in Figure 24.17, groups of students may wish to investigate the use of boldly colored, two-dimensional design by cultures outside the United States. Some possibilities are the beadwork of the Pacific Northwest Coast Athapaskans, patchwork textiles by the Maroons in the Suriname rain forest of South America, Guatemalan woven textiles, woven telephone-wire baskets made by the Zulus in South Africa, and the traditional mud wall paintings that are repainted every year in Ghana after the rainy season. Groups should gather information and reproductions of the works of their culture for a round-table discussion.

Photo-Realism

One of the leading art styles of the 1970s was **Photo-Realism,** *a style so realistic it looked photographic.* Its near-instant success may have been due to the exaggerated homage it paid to the literal qualities—the same literal qualities that abstract and nonobjective artists had rejected earlier.

Alfred Leslie (1927–)

Photo-Realists such as Alfred Leslie turned away from abstract art and looked to the past for models. For Leslie, the model was Caravaggio. He emulated that artist's style to paint huge genre works with a modern flavor. In 7 *A.M. News* (Figure 24.18), Leslie shows a lone woman holding a newspaper that appears to contain only photographs. On a table next to her, another picture flickers on a television set.

As in Caravaggio's painting of *The Conversion of St. Paul* (Figure 19.7, page 425), light plays an important symbolic role in Leslie's picture. A heavenly light flashes across the fallen figure of St. Paul in the earlier painting, while the harsh, artificial light of the television illuminates the woman's face in the modern work.

In Caravaggio's work, the central figure hears a message shouted from the heavens. In Leslie's painting, the mass media deliver news and information to the woman seated at the table. She appears to be ignoring both the newspaper and the television. Her eyes are raised heavenward. Aware, perhaps, that something important is lacking in the bland and repetitive messages she has been receiving from the mass media, she turns tentatively to a new source of information. Perhaps, like St. Paul, she hears a voice from above. In this case, the voice appears to come as a whisper rather than a shout.

■ **FIGURE 24.18** This artist turned to seventeenth-century works to find inspiration for his large paintings that gloried in realism. **Notice that there are no words written on the newspaper. What meaning do you attach to this?**

Alfred Leslie. 7 *A.M. News.* 1976–78. Oil on canvas. 2.13 × 1.52 m (7 × 5'). Private Collection, Philadelphia, Pennsylvania.

Art History

Have students select an artist from a chapter that dealt with art in a past century and write a dialogue between that artist and either Alfred Leslie or Andrew Wyeth. The conversation should reveal what is different about life as an artist in the twentieth century and life as an artist in past times. The dialogues can touch on such issues as patronage, lifestyle, society's attitude toward artists, the kinds of materials and techniques available to artists (being mindful that Wyeth often works with tempera), and the kinds of goals artists bring to their work.

Did You Know?

In 1985, Frank Stella was found guilty of exceeding the speed limit on a highway in upstate New York. His somewhat unorthodox "sentence" was to give six lectures on art history in the small township of Hudson.

Chapter 24 *Modern Art Movements to the Present* **557**

More About... **Alfred Leslie.** Before he turned to Photo-Realism, Alfred Leslie was a filmmaker and Abstract Expressionist painter. By 1960, however, Abstract Expressionism no longer satisfied him, and Leslie began to paint self-portraits as a way to explore the possibilities of figurative art. A disastrous fire in his studio in 1966 solidified his new direction: "I had to start all over. . . . I decided I had to consolidate my energies into painting. I wanted to restore the practice of painting, which I felt was slipping away." Leslie took the philosophical preoccupations he had as an Abstract Expressionist and concentrated on the craft of painting and the importance of narrative in art.

Art History

Explain that although Audrey Flack was raised in a Jewish family, her art reflects her appreciation of many different religious traditions. She is concerned with mortality, healing, moral strength and the trancendence of suffering. Point out that she uses imagery from a wide range of religious cultures to express these themes. Her art is as likely to portray the Virgin Mary, a Greek goddess, or a shaman. Tell students that *Marilyn*, Figure 24.19, is a contemporary version of Protestant northern Baroque *vanitas* paintings, which used material objects to symbolize the shortness of life and the relative unimportance of earthly treasures. Have students identify the symbols present in the painting.

Critical Thinking

Tell students that Audrey Flack has said she wants to create artworks that appeal to both the art world elite and ordinary people. Ask them to consider why an artist would have such a goal. Is such a goal difficult? Is it necessary to distinguish between these two groups? Why or why not? What art forms have they learned about that are created specifically for the art world elite? Likewise, what art forms were created specifically for ordinary people? Which art forms bridge the two groups?

■ **FIGURE 24.19** Many items shown in this work remind the viewer of the fragility and brevity of life. **Compare this painting with Salvador Dali's *The Persistence of Memory* (Figure 24.4, page 547). What do these two works have in common?**

Audrey Flack. *Marilyn*. 1977. Oil over acrylic on canvas. 243.8 × 243.8 cm (96 × 96"). Collection of the University of Arizona Museum of Art, Tucson, Arizona. Museum purchase with funds provided by Edward J. Gallagher Jr. Memorial Fund.

■ **FIGURE 24.20** Although his father had him work for a time with oil paints, Wyeth was never comfortable with them, preferring instead to work with egg tempera. **Describe the colors used here. Do these colors suggest warmth or coldness?**

Andrew Newell Wyeth. *Winter, 1946*. 1946. Tempera on board. 80 × 122 cm (31³⁄₈ × 48"). North Carolina Museum of Art, Raleigh, North Carolina. Purchased with funds from the State of North Carolina.

Audrey Flack (1931–)

Audrey Flack's complex, highly detailed still-life paintings often surpass the level of reality found in photographs. In her painting *Marilyn* (Figure 24.19), she offers a crisply defined, richly complex still-life arrangement that testifies to the fleeting nature of fame and glamour. Included in the array of objects that clutter the top of a dressing table are a calendar, a watch, an egg timer, and a burning candle—reminders that time runs out for everyone. Beauty, both natural (the rose) and artificial (the makeup), is no match for the persistent assault of time.

Andrew Wyeth (1917–)

Although he is not regarded as a Photo-Realist, Andrew Wyeth (**wye**-uth) is noted for paintings in which careful attention is directed to the literal qualities. It would be a mistake, however, to think of his works as merely photographic. They are much more. In his paintings, Wyeth tries to go beyond showing what people or places look like. Instead, he tries to capture their essence.

Like his father, the well-known illustrator N. C. Wyeth, he feels that artists can paint well only those things they know thoroughly. To acquire this knowledge, an artist must live with a subject, study it, and become a part of it.

In 1945, Andrew Wyeth's father was killed in an automobile-train accident. No doubt he thought of his father constantly in the months following his death, particularly when hiking across the Pennsylvania countryside they once roamed together. His paintings of that countryside seem to reflect his grief and loss. Typical of those works is *Winter, 1946* (Figure 24.20), painted a year after his father's death. In this painting, a solitary boy runs down a hill. This particular hill appears in many of Wyeth's best-known works. The place where his father died is on the other side of this hill, in the direction from which the boy in the painting is running.

More About... **Audrey Flack (b. 1931).** Painter and sculptor Audrey Flack has always felt an affinity for the passionate, emotionally charged work of both southern and northern Baroque artists. As a child growing up in New York City, Flack enjoyed visiting the Metropolitan Museum of Art and the Hispanic Society, where she was fascinated by the polychromed sculptures by Baroque Spanish artists. Flack has stated, "I am deeply involved with seventeenth- and eighteenth-century Spanish passion. . . . I feel these artists have not received the recognition they deserve probably because they displayed openly their passion and feeling." Flack was also inspired to create art in the manner of still lifes painted by Dutch Baroque artists such as Maria van Oosterwyck.

Painting in Canada: A Passion for Nature

Modern Canadian art can trace its origins to 1920 and a small group of landscape painters working in Toronto. These painters eventually came to be known as the *Group of Seven.*

The paintings of this group did much to direct public attention away from a cautious acceptance of European styles by exposing viewers to a unique Canadian art style.

The work of the Group of Seven played an important role in the career of Emily Carr, who became Canada's best-known early modern artist. Carr studied in San Francisco before traveling abroad to perfect her painting skills in London and Paris. She saw the works of Matisse and the other Fauves while she was in Paris in 1910 and 1911. Like the painters in the Group of Seven, she was greatly impressed by the expressive qualities of those works and adapted those qualities to her own painting style. In works such as *Forest, British Columbia* (Figure 24.21), however, one senses something more. The trees in this forest join together to create a place of great spirituality. Like stout pillars in a medieval church, they define and protect a quiet sanctuary awaiting anyone in need of security and consolation. Painted with spiraling forms and intense colors, the work presents a personal and powerful vision of nature.

The paintings created by Emily Carr heralded a period of artistic activity in Canada that continues to grow in diversity and quality. Today her paintings rank among the most admired in Canadian art.

Painting Today

Artists today work in an ever-increasing variety of styles, from realistic to nonobjective, employing media and techniques that were unheard of only a few years ago. In their search for new means of expression, some artists have created works that blur the line between painting and sculpture. Although it would be impossible to examine all these artists, a sampling is offered as a means of

■ **FIGURE 24.21** Much of Carr's paintings are done outdoors and exhibit a strong affection for nature. **How are variety and harmony realized in this work? Is the subject here treated in a realistic manner?**

Emily Carr. *Forest, British Columbia.* VAG 42.3.9. c. 1931–32. Oil on canvas. 130 × 86.8 cm (51³/₁₆ × 34³/₁₆"). Vancouver Art Gallery, Vancouver, B.C. Canada.

demonstrating the amazing diversity that characterizes the contemporary art world.

David Hockney (1937–)

Regarded as the best-known British artist of his generation, David Hockney combines drawing, collage, and painting to create works based on his own experiences and opinions. Around 1963, Hockney made the first of several trips to Los Angeles, where he began interpreting the California landscape using the colors of van Gogh and Matisse, the spontaneity of Picasso, and the shallow space of Chinese landscape paintings.

Chapter 24 *Modern Art Movements to the Present* **559**

Art History

Have students select an artist from this chapter and one from either Chapter 19 or 20, and write a dialogue between the two artists that reveals what is different about life as an artist in the twentieth century and life as an artist in past times. The dialogues can touch on issues such as patronage, lifestyle, society's attitude toward artists, materials, and techniques, and whether beauty and religious truth are among the artists' goals.

Art Criticism

Direct students' attention to the work by Emily Carr in Figure 24.21. Have them apply the art criticism operations to the work, with special attention to description and the use of the elements and principles to achieve the effect of strong, expressive forms in her work.

Then have interested students identify earlier artists who achieve the same spiritual feeling in their artworks. (Suggest artists featured in Chapter 18.) Have them compare Carr's painting to these earlier works.

More About... **Op Art.** This nonobjective art movement had parallels in several European countries including Germany and Italy. Among the many artists who adopted this style after 1960, Victor Vasarely is generally regarded as the founder of this movement. He used dazzling colors and precise geometric shapes to create surfaces that appear to move. They seem to project forward in some places and to recede in others. Op art extended illusionism into the realm of non-representational art.

Study Guide

Distribute *Study Guide* 56 in the TCR. Assist students in reviewing key concepts. 👉

Art and Humanities

Have students complete *Art and Humanities* 39, "Enjoying Twentieth-Century Poetry," in the TCR. In this activity, students begin by reading poetry from American poets. They then isolate poetic images in paintings found in their art text. 👉

Studio Activities

Assign *Studio* 30, "Creating a Surrealist Collage," in the TCR in which students have an opportunity to experiment with the media and technique of collage. 👉

Art and Humanities

Assign *Cooperative Learning* 40, "Making an Ecology Statement," in the TCR. Students are called upon to think about today's ecological and social problems. They then work in teams to create a social statement. 👉

Art and Humanities

Assign groups of students *Cooperative Learning* 37 "Tracing the Status of the Artist," in the TCR. In this worksheet, student groups learn about the role of the artist in many cultures and times. 👉

Large Interior—Los Angeles
■ FIGURE 24.22

Typical of Hockney's later works is *Large Interior—Los Angeles* (Figure 24.22), which hints at his considerable success as a stage designer. Furniture, patterns, and details are arranged in a brightly illuminated, spacious interior that suggests a relaxed, unhurried way of life. Chairs of every kind conveniently await anyone who might want to read a book, listen to music, or discuss the affairs of the day. Clues to these kind of activities abound, like props on a stage. Nothing disturbs the quiet serenity of this setting, viewed as if the stage curtains have just parted. One almost expects a performer to enter at any moment, heralding the opening of the first act.

Elizabeth Murray (1940–)

Since the 1970s, Chicago-born Elizabeth Murray has been creating works consisting of several sections grouped together to form shattered images that bring to mind the Cubist paintings of Braque and Picasso. Painted on shaped canvases, Murray's large, abstract works sometimes consist of as many as 20 separate pieces, making them part painting and part sculpture. Indeed, the artist acts as a sculptor when she shapes, overlaps, and joins three-dimensional canvases. She assumes the role of painter when she adds color to these forms. Although her finished works may look accidental and haphazard at first glance, Murray spends months designing, arranging, and painting the pieces used in a single work.

Typical of Murray's mature work is the brilliantly colored *Painter's Progress* (Figure 24.1, page 544), composed of 19 pieces. Although the work is abstract, most viewers can easily identify the simplified images that show the tools of the painter: a large palette with brushes and, of course, the hand needed to manipulate them in the creation of art.

Judy Pfaff (1946–)

If works by Murray challenge the long-standing line separating painting and sculpture, the creations of Judy Pfaff erase it completely.

Born in London, Judy Pfaff received her art training in the United States and was an abstract painter until 1971. At that time, she began to question the notion of confining her images to a flat canvas or forming them in some three-dimensional medium that one walks around to examine.

■ **FIGURE 24.22**
Hockney achieved international acclaim as an artist when he was still in his 20s. Compare this painting with Matisse's *Red Studio* (Figure 23.2, page 517). How are these two works alike? How do they differ?

David Hockney. *Large Interior—Los Angeles.* 1988. Oil, ink on cut and pasted paper, on canvas. 183.5 × 305.4 cm (72¼ × 120¼"). The Metropolitan Museum of Art, New York, New York. Purchase, Natasha Gelman Gift, in honor of William S. Lieberman, 1989. (1989.279)

$\mathcal{T}$*eacher* $\mathcal{N}$*otes* _____

_____

_____

_____

_____

Installation Art

Abandoning the time-honored method of easel painting, Pfaff began to use the walls, floor, and ceiling of an entire room from which to suspend colorful shapes created with a variety of media and found objects of every kind. Known as installations, these mixed-media environments are like a three-dimensional Abstract Expressionist painting that viewers can actually walk through (Figure 24.23). Implied movement is provided by brightly colored objects that seem to spring out at viewers from every angle. Real movement is supplied by the viewers themselves, as they slowly advance and observe these objects from constantly changing points of view. As viewers move into the installation, their gaze sweeps in every direction—above, below, behind, and in front—and they begin to experience a sense of uneasiness associated with not knowing exactly where they are or what they are seeing. Divorced from reality, the imagination comes fully into play, making the experience unique and intensely personal for each viewer.

Unfortunately, Pfaff's large installations at galleries and museums are not permanent. Once they are dismantled, they endure only in the memories of those fortunate enough to have experienced them.

■ **FIGURE 24.23** In an effort that often requires weeks of hard work, Pfaff fills an entire gallery with her magical installations. **Explain how it is possible to compare the way this installation was constructed with the way Jackson Pollock created his paintings (Figure 24.12, page 553). What must one do to completely experience an installation like this?**

Judy Pfaff. *Dragons.* 1981. Mixed media. Installation view at the 1981 Biennial at the Whitney Museum of American Art, New York, New York.

LESSON ONE REVIEW

Reviewing Art Facts

1. Name the art movement that came out of a sense of disillusionment and a belief that European culture made no sense.
2. What did the Surrealists use as a source of subject matter for their art?
3. Define Abstract Expressionism.
4. What is Pop art? What did Pop artists hope to achieve with their style of art?

Activity... *Creating Abstract Expressionist Art*

Works created by Abstract Expressionists may be difficult to readily understand. They do not attempt to create the illusion of space filled with recognizable objects. These works instead exist as expressions of feeling and emotion. Instead of asking the question "what is it?" when viewing these works, they can be viewed just as they exist.

Recall a very strong emotion you have experienced and re-create it as an artwork. Choose colors that would best describe this emotion and determine lines, shapes, forms, and textures that best re-create the feelings. Consider how to express the emotion without using recognizable images. Using oil pastels or watercolors, create your own Abstract Expressionist work.

LESSON ONE REVIEW

Answers to Reviewing Art Facts

1. The Dada movement.
2. Dreams and the subconscious.
3. An art movement in which artists applied paint freely in an effort to show feelings and emotions rather than realistic subject matter.
4. Portrays images from the popular culture; to make viewers look at things differently.

Activity...*Creating Abstract Expressionist Art*

Before students begin this activity, have them work together in groups to discuss the emotions depicted in the works in this lesson. Ask them to describe how the artist achieved the effects shown in these examples.

ASSESS

Checking Comprehension

Have students complete the lesson review questions. Answers appear in the box below.

Reteaching

➤ Assign *Reteaching* 56, found in the TCR. Have students complete the activity and review their responses. 📁

➤ Ask each student to select the two artists presented in this lesson who they feel have the least in common with each other or who would be the least likely to get along easily. Have students write down their reasons. Invite students to share their ideas with the class.

Enrichment

Assign students *Enrichment* 45, "Portraiture Through the Ages" in the TCR. Students compare artists' styles and approaches to portraiture and explore how people have portrayed themselves throughout history. 📁

Extension

Have students complete *Appreciating Cultural Diversity* 34, "Marc Chagall—A Cultural Treasure." In this activity, students learn about the tapestry designed by the renowned twentieth-century artist for the Rehabilitation Institute in Chicago. 📁

CLOSE

Ask each student to state whether he or she would have preferred to paint in a Realist style or in an Abstract Expressionist style during the first half of the twentieth century.

Innovations in Sculpture and Architecture

Focus

Lesson Objectives

After studying this lesson, students will be able to:
■ Identify twentieth-century sculptors who worked with abstract forms.
■ Describe styles of architecture that developed after the International Style.

Building Vocabulary

Write the Vocabulary terms on the chalkboard and ask students to tell what they think each term means and what type of artwork each describes. Then have them look up the definitions and identify artworks in this lesson that fit the definition of each term.

Motivator

On the board, write: *Variety is the spice of life.* Ask students what relevance this adage might have to the art represented in this lesson.

Introducing the Lesson

Compare reproductions of some of the more radical works of art produced in the second half of the twentieth century (e.g., by Lucas Samaras, Dan Flavin, Christo) with works in this lesson.

Innovations in Sculpture and Architecture

Vocabulary
■ assemblage
■ mobile
■ environmental art

Artists to Meet
■ Jacques Lipchitz
■ Henry Moore
■ Barbara Hepworth
■ Louise Nevelson
■ Alexander Calder
■ Allan Houser
■ Robert Smithson
■ Christo
■ Duane Hanson
■ Le Corbusier
■ Frank Lloyd Wright
■ Maya Lin
■ Michael Graves
■ Charles Moore

Discover
After completing this lesson, you will be able to:
■ Describe the abstract and nonobjective works created by twentieth-century sculptors.
■ Identify trends in architecture since the middle of the twentieth century.
■ Describe Postmodern architecture and identify important Postmodern architects.

■ **FIGURE 24.24** Soon after arriving in Paris from his native Russia in 1909, Lipchitz became involved with the ideas of Cubism. Identify features that show the influence of Cubist paintings on this sculpture.

Jacques Lipchitz. *Sailor with Guitar.* 1914. Bronze. 78.7 × 29.5 × 21.6 cm (31 × 11⅝ × 8½"). Philadelphia Museum of Art, Philadelphia, Pennsylvania. Given by Mrs. Morris Wenger in memory of her husband. © Estate of Jacques Lipchitz/Licensed by VAGA, New York, New York.

562

The twentieth-century search for new forms was not limited to painters. Sculptors in Europe and North America were engaged in the same quest. Some of these artists felt that they had to break away from their dependence on subject matter if they were to succeed in expressing themselves in fresh ways. Others remained faithful to Realism, pushing the boundaries of that style into new territory. Although many continued to use traditional materials and techniques, an adventurous few reasoned that their creative efforts could be aided by the new materials and techniques being developed by modern technology.

Sculpture and the Search for New Forms

Many sculptors moved away from realism to create abstract and nonobjective sculptures. The focus of their work was now on the formal elements and principles of art. Sculptors such as Jacques Lipchitz, Henry Moore, and Barbara Hepworth were among the leaders of the new style.

Jacques Lipchitz
(1891–1973)

Some sculptors, including Jacques Lipchitz (zhahk **lip**-sheets), were influenced by the new movements in painting. Lipchitz arrived in Paris from his native Lithuania in 1909. Soon after, he was attracted to the ideas of Cubism. His *Sailor with Guitar* (Figure 24.24) was done in the Cubist style. It is a three-dimensional form with the same kinds of geometric shapes found in paintings by Pablo Picasso and Georges Braque. Flat surfaces of different shapes were placed at various angles to one another to suggest a jaunty sailor strumming his guitar.

LESSON TWO RESOURCES

Teacher's Classroom Resources
📁 Appreciating Cultural Diversity 35
📁 Art and Humanities 41
📁 Cooperative Learning 38
📁 Enrichment Activity 46

📁 Reproducible Lesson Plan 57
📁 Reteaching Activity 57
📁 Study Guide 57

Henry Moore (1898–1986)

Henry Moore sought to create sculptures that were completely unique and original—images in stone, wood, and bronze that had never been seen before (Figure 24.25). Because he had no desire to make copies of things, he avoided using a model and kept an open mind each time he started a new work. If Moore chose to do a sculpture in stone, he first studied the block carefully from every angle, hoping that it would suggest something to him. Then, prompted by something he saw or felt, he would take his hammer and chisel and begin cutting into the stone.

Styles Influencing *Styles*

HENRY MOORE AND BARBARA HEPWORTH Henry Moore's search for new and unusual forms led him to cut holes, or openings, into his highly abstract sculptures. This was something that had never been done before. In his wood carving of a reclining figure (Figure 24.25), rounded abstract forms combine with openings to suggest a human image worn smooth by the forces of nature. Works such as this are Moore's tribute to nature, which provided him with raw material and showed him how to transform that material into art.

Like Moore, Barbara Hepworth was a student of nature. The two sculptors followed a similar path, opening up their sculptural forms by piercing them with holes and hollowing them out. A bronze figure completed in 1959 (Figure 24.26) illustrates how Hepworth used holes as a focus in her sculptures. Even though this work is abstract, it succeeds in suggesting an image and capturing a definite movement. With arms stretched upward, a dancer leans gracefully to one side; the dancer's head is suggested by one of two holes.

■ **FIGURE 24.25**

Henry Moore. *Reclining Figure.* 1939. Elmwood. 94 × 200 × 76.2 cm (37 × 79 × 30″). The Detroit Institute of Arts, Detroit, Michigan. Founders Society Purchase with funds from the Dexter M. Ferry, Jr. Trustee Corporation.

■ **FIGURE 24.26**

Barbara Hepworth. *Figure (Archaean).* 1959. Bronze. 215.9 × 129.5 × 30.4 cm (85 × 51 × 12″). Endowment Association Art Collection. Edwin A. Ulrich Museum of Art. Wichita State University, Wichita, Kansas.

Chapter 24 *Modern Art Movements to the Present* **563**

Styles Influencing *Styles*

Read the feature on this page with the class. Have students examine Figure 24.24. Then have students browse through the text for examples of both sculptures in which a person is reclining and sculptures that depict a person standing upright. List the different effects and qualities of each posture. If possible, display reproductions of other Moore sculptures to demonstrate how often Moore used a reclining pose. Ask: What mood do you associate with Moore's art?

Art History

Have students examine Figures 24.24 (page 562), 24.25, and 24.26. Then ask students to imagine that Renaissance artist Michelangelo was visiting an art show of sculptures by Hepworth, Moore, and Lipchitz. Have students discuss Michelangelo's probable reaction to these works. Ask: Would he even regard the pieces as sculpture? Could he tell that Figure 24.26 represented a human figure?

Aesthetics

Have students bring to class an array of objects that have been eroded or weathered by nature (e.g., driftwood, beach glass, rounded stones). Ask students to think about the forces that shaped these items. Then have them write a short essay on what Moore might have meant by suggesting through his sculptures that people are "weathered" by time and nature.

Technology

National Gallery of Art Videodisc Use the following images as examples of more works by artists introduced in this lesson.

Jacques Lipchitz
Bas-Relief I

Search Frame 2545

Alexander Calder
Untitled

Search Frame 2607

Ellsworth Kelly
Colored Paper Image XI

Search Frame 3330

Use Glencoe's *Correlation Bar Code Guide to the National Gallery of Art* to locate more artworks.

Studio Skills

Invite to class a skilled stone sculptor to demonstrate the craft of chiseling stone. Allow students to experiment with using a hammer and chisel to shape stone by themselves.

Art History

Have students refer to library resources to learn which artists were working in Paris around 1909, and the kinds of works they created. Using this information, students can discuss which artists Jacques Lipchitz might have met or seen exhibited shortly after he arrived in Paris in that year and which ones most influenced his work.

Studio Skills

Provide students with a variety of found objects, such as wood scraps, old toys, and cardboard tubes. Challenge students to make their own assemblages out of these found objects. If they wish, students can mount their scraps in boxes and stack them to make Nevelson-style assemblages. After students have glued their objects together, have them apply a single color of poster paint to the exterior after making sure the surfaces are as clean as possible, so that the paint adheres well.

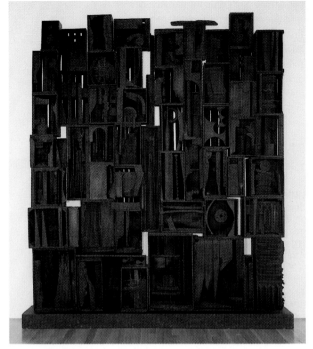

■ **FIGURE 24.27** This assemblage presents a rich variety of contrasting angles and curves. **How did Nevelson unify this composition? What makes this work so unique?**

Louise Nevelson. *Sky Cathedral.* 1958. Assemblage: wood construction, painted black. 3.4 × 3 × .4 m (135½ × 120¼ × 18″). The Museum of Modern Art, New York, New York. Gift of Mr. and Mrs. Ben Mildwoff.

Louise Nevelson (1899–1988)

The nonobjective sculptures of Louise Nevelson offer an interesting contrast to the works of minimalists like Tony Smith. Using a technique known as **assemblage,** *a number of three-dimensional objects brought together to form a work of art,* Nevelson created sculptures that confront the viewer with a rich variety of contrasting angles and curves.

In *Sky Cathedral* (Figure 24.27), she carefully assembled found objects and wood scraps into shallow boxes of different sizes and then stacked the boxes to make a large composition. To unify the composition, she spray-painted it entirely in black. The completed work represents a mixture of the familiar and the unfamiliar. Many parts are recognizable as odd pieces taken from furniture, whereas others appear to be scraps from old Victorian houses. What these parts once were is no longer important. Each now takes its place in a wall-size work of art that mysteriously brings to mind the façade of a medieval church with its sculptures tucked into their assigned niches.

Alexander Calder (1898–1976)

Viewers are required to walk around the works created by most sculptors; however, the creations of Alexander Calder can be observed from a single vantage point. Because his sculptures move through space, viewers can remain stationary and still take in every detail.

Marcel Duchamp invented a name for Calder's unique creations; he called them mobiles. A **mobile** is *a construction made of shapes that are balanced and arranged on wire arms and suspended from a ceiling or a base so as to move freely in the air currents.* This moving arrangement of sheet-metal shapes treats the viewer to constantly changing patterns of colors and shapes. Unlike traditional sculpture, these works appeal almost entirely to the sense of sight. The works are most effective when the wire arms and attached shapes begin to quiver, swing, and rotate in space.

Although they are abstract and even nonobjective, many of Calder's mobiles are based on natural forms—mammals, birds, fish, or plants—and their movements are carefully planned to imitate natural action. In *Pomegranate* (Figure 24.28), shapes representing leaves and fruit turn and bob as if stirred by a gentle breeze. Imaginative and whimsical, Calder's works breathe life into the same kind of fantasy world created by Joan Miró and Paul Klee.

Allan Houser (1914–1994)

Whereas many contemporary sculptors choose to work with abstract or nonobjective forms, others continue to work in a more realistic style. One of these was Allan Houser.

564 **Unit Seven** *Art of the Modern Era*

More About... **Louise Nevelson.** As a child, Louise Nevelson spent many long hours playing in her father's lumberyard in Maine. She loved to carve and build using the scraps of wood she found. At the age of 20, Louise married and had a child. In time, she felt the need to pursue her art further. In 1931 she left her son with her parents and headed to Europe to study art. Nevelson's first showing came in 1941. The reviews, which were favorable, spurred her on. She began more and more to experiment with "found" media. It was not uncommon to find her studio littered with wood scraps very much like the ones she had played with in her father's lumberyard. Most of Nevelson's works from the 1960s on are three-dimensional collages. They invite viewers to use their imaginations as well as their eyes.

Houser's father was the grandson of the Apache chief, Mangus Colorado, and a relative of Geronimo. Throughout his career, he directed his talent to interpreting the heritage of his people, capturing in each of his sculptures the enduring spirit of Native Americans.

Watching for Dancing Partners (Figure 24.29) is a pink Tennessee marble carving of two Native American women standing side by side at a dance. Their smooth, polished faces contrast with the strands of long hair that encircle them. Over their shoulders they wear heavily textured shawls with fringes. These shawls add further textural contrast to the faces and long, smooth skirts. The textural similarities of the two women tie them together as effectively as do their positions next to each other. This carving is meant to be explored slowly with the eyes, so the viewer can appreciate the rich surface effects.

■ **FIGURE 24.28** Calder was one of the early pioneers in creating artworks that actually moved. **In what ways do Calder's works resemble the paintings of Joan Miró and Paul Klee?**

Alexander Calder. *Pomegranate.* 1949. Painted sheet aluminum, steel rods, and wire. 181 × 183.5 × 107.3 cm (71¼ × 72¼ × 42¼"). Collection of the Whitney Museum of American Art, New York, New York. Purchase.

■ **FIGURE 24.29** Houser's most moving subjects are women and children. **Identify the importance of texture in this sculpture. How has it been used?**

Allan Houser. *Watching for Dancing Partners.* 1978. Pink Tennessee marble. 76.2 × 53.3 cm (30 × 21"). Museum of the Southwest, Midland, Texas. Gift of Mr. and Mrs. Lynn D. Durham.

Chapter 24 *Modern Art Movements to the Present* **565**

Aesthetics

Point out that some of the bronze sculptures pictured in this chapter are parts of a series of castings with between five and seven "editions." Arrange a debate in which students argue the relative value of sculptures that have been reproduced in multiples. Ask: Is it important to destroy a mold after a certain number of reproductions have been made? Is the aesthetic value of a work diminished if that piece is reproduced? Can a sculpture still be considered an original work of art if there are identical copies?

Art Criticism

Have students use colored felt-tip markers to make a drawing of Figure 24.28, using any hues they wish to color the metal shapes. Display the drawings and discuss how different colors affect the mood of the piece.

Did You Know?

Allan Houser's finished sculpture at Haskell Institute titled *Comrade in Mourning* is a depiction of a Plains Indian. It stands 8 feet tall and is carved from a 3- to 4-ton block of white Carrara marble.

About the *Artwork*

Pomegranate. Abstract mobiles like the one shown here grew out of more than the artist's having a degree in engineering and a knack for tinkering with odd scraps to make toys and jewelry. Calder's penchant for abstract and floating shapes is said to have begun in 1922, when he worked in the boiler room of a passenger ship sailing off the coast of Guatemala. Reportedly, while working on the ship, Calder saw a fiery red sunrise as the moon set like a silver coin dropping, and during that moment he felt he wanted to create art that would reflect these "mechanics" of the universe.

Art Criticism

Display photographs of interior views of the *Chapel of Notre Dame du Haut*, without identifying the building. Can students tell that it is the same structure shown in Figure 24.33? Discuss whether the structure evinces the same mood or sensibility when viewed from the outside and inside.

Cross Curriculum

HISTORY. Explain that shortly after the completion of *Chapel of Notre Dame du Haut*, a number of events changed the political world scene. These included the assassination, in 1963, of President John F. Kennedy and the commencement of U.S. troops offensive action in Vietnam two years later. Have teams of students investigate these events and how they affected artists of the times. Have them give a presentation to the class on their findings.

Did You Know?

Works by realist sculptor Duane Hanson look remarkably lifelike not only in the pages of a book but also in person. Hanson's sculptures are so realistic that people have walked up to them in museums and galleries and spoken to them!

Environmental *Art*

*A few contemporary sculptors have begun creating **environmental art**, outdoor artworks that are designed to become part of the natural landscape.*

■ **FIGURE 24.30** Robert Smithson. *Spiral Jetty.* 1970. Great Salt Lake, Utah.

1 One form of environmental art is an earthwork, in which the land itself is shaped into a gigantic sculpture.

2 Why do artists choose to create modern earthworks? Perhaps, as some suggest, they simply want to return to nature and use the earth itself as their medium. They also may be motivated by nothing more than a desire to work on a grand scale.

3 Robert Smithson (1938–1973), an American sculptor and experimental artist, created one of the best known earthworks, *Spiral Jetty* (Figure 24.30). This work consists of a huge ramp of earth and rock, 1,500 feet long, that curls out into a secluded section of Utah's Great Salt Lake. It calls to mind the spirals found in nature.

4 Because actual construction can be difficult, earthworks often fail to progress beyond the planning stage. If they are carried out, they are exposed to the destructive forces of nature, as in the case of *Spiral Jetty*. Intended as a permanent construction, Smithson's work today is barely visible beneath the rising waters of the lake.

5 A Bulgarian-born artist and a French-born artist known simply as Christo (1935–) and Jeanne-Claude (1935–) create another form of environmental art. They are the originators of wrapping art, which consists of covering familiar objects in canvas or plastic and rope.

6 One of Christo and Jeanne-Claude's best known works is *Running Fence* (Figure 24.31). The work was an 18-foot-high white nylon fence that stretched across the hills and fields of northern California for 24.5 miles. It was erected by an army of paid workers using 165,000 yards of nylon and 2,050 steel posts in September 1976. Billowing in and out with the wind, its white surface reflecting the changing light of the sun at different times of the day, the completed fence appeared to stretch without end across the rolling countryside.

■ **FIGURE 24.31** Christo and Jeanne-Claude. *Running Fence, Sonoma and Marin Counties, California, 1972–76.* H: 5.5 m, L: 40 km (H: 18', L: 24¹/₂ miles).

7 *Running Fence* remained standing for two weeks; then, as planned, it was dismantled. Today the fence exists only on film, photographs, and the artist's preliminary drawings.

Environmental *Art*

Explain to students that, while it could be argued that all works of art affect the environment to some degree, some most certainly affect it more than others. Artists such as Smithson turned to creating earthworks in which the land itself is shaped into a gigantic sculpture. Although greeted with surprise by many, remind students that earthworks are by no means a modern art form. Have them review the Great Serpent Mound created by the Adena (Figure 11.12, page 252). Ask students to collect photographs of environmental sculptures or environmental designs to share.

Duane Hanson (1925–)

Duane Hanson's lifelike portraits of people, from camera-laden tourists to weary janitors, have sometimes surprised viewers who have mistaken them for actual people. Hanson uses fiberglass, vinyl, hair, and clothes to re-create the people we pass daily in the shopping mall, at a fast-food restaurant, or on the sidelines of a football game (Figure 24.32). We might smile at their bizarre costumes or their peculiar behavior—until we realize that other people may be similarly amused at the way *we* dress and act.

Architecture Since the 1950s

As the twentieth century passed the halfway mark, the International style of architecture, exemplified by such buildings as the Lever House (Figure 23.30, page 540), began to lose its momentum. Uninspired and endless repetitions of the style in Europe and America prompted critics to charge that the urban landscape was becoming monotonous and boring. Architects, well aware of the criticism, began to search for new forms and new approaches.

■ **FIGURE 24.32** Viewers often avoid staring too long at one of Hanson's sculptures—thinking that it may indeed be real. What emotions or feelings do you associate with this work? How would you answer someone who criticized it as looking "too realistic"?

Duane Hanson. *Football Player.* 1981. Oil on polyvinyl. Life-size. 109.8 × 76.2 × 80 cm (43¹/₄ × 30 × 31¹/₂"). Collection, Lowe Art Museum, University of Miami, Coral Gables, Florida. Museum purchase through funds from Friends of Art and public subscriptions. 82.0024.

Art Criticism

Have students flip through the text and identify people in paintings and sculptures from earlier periods who Duane Hanson might have chosen as subjects for his realist sculptures. Then have students identify several examples of figures or poses that the sculptor would not have used. Ask: How does Hanson determine what is an ordinary, characteristic pose and what is an exaggerated or symbolic pose?

Studio Skills

Ask students to imagine they are furniture designers and have been given the task of designing a relief carving for a piece of furniture in their classroom. They may choose to work individually or in pairs, and they may select any wooden piece of furniture in the room (e.g., student desk, teacher's desk, chair, or bookshelf). Have them begin by focusing on one part of the piece such as the leg, back, or top. In their sketchbooks, have them first list possible images to include in the design, then make stylized sketches of those images. Have them complete their entire design on large pieces of paper. Ask them to observe how their designs conform to the shape of the furniture part.

Teacher Notes _____

_____

_____

_____

_____

Studio Skills

Discuss with students the idea that art mirrors the time in which it is created. This holds true especially for architecture. Have students make a pencil drawing of a dream dwelling of the future. Provide solutions to such growing problems as pollution and thinning of the ozone layer. After designs have been completed, have students develop their plans into a three-dimensional model. Suggest using cardboard, shoeboxes, or plastic foam as modeling media.

Art History

Divide the class into six groups. Assign each group to research one of the following types of buildings that Frank Lloyd Wright was commissioned to design: private homes, apartment buildings, office buildings, factories, churches, and hotels. Have each group present its findings along with pictures of the buildings they read about.

Le Corbusier (1887–1965)

One of the most exciting of the new forms is the Chapel of Notre Dame du Haut (Figure 24.33) in southeastern France. It was designed in the early 1950s by a Swiss-born architect named Le Corbusier (luh core-**boo**-see-**ay**). (His real name was Charles-Édouard Jeanneret.) Gone are the boxlike forms of the International style; they have been replaced by massive walls that bend and curve like slabs of soft clay. The addition of a rounded, billowing roof results in a building that is both architecture and sculpture. It reminds viewers of the curving architectural forms of Antonio Gaudi (Figure 23.26, page 537) and the abstract figures of Henry Moore (Figure 24.25, page 563).

At the same time, the building suggests the strength and durability of a medieval fortress.

Doors are difficult to locate and, when finally found, lead to an interior mysteriously illuminated by randomly placed, recessed windows. The sunlight passing through the stained glass of these windows provides a pattern of colored light on the walls, the only decoration inside this unusual church.

Frank Lloyd Wright
(1867–1959)

Frank Lloyd Wright began his architectural career in Louis Sullivan's firm. After five years, he left the firm to strike out on his own, but he never forgot his debt to his mentor. From Sullivan, Wright learned about new building materials, such as concrete and steel. Wright's innovative structural designs and

■ **FIGURE 24.33** This building represents a clear departure from the boxlike forms of the International style. In what ways does this structure resemble a sculpture? What qualities do you associate with this building—delicacy and charm or solidity and strength?

Le Corbusier. Chapel of Notre-Dame-du-Haut. Ronchamp, France. 1950–54.

COOPERATIVE LEARNING

Architecture Investigation. Point out that new materials and technologies, including the development of reinforced concrete in the late nineteenth century, have greatly expanded the possibilities for architects. Have pairs of students research modern structures built from reinforced concrete, such as the Opera House in Sydney, Australia. Work should be guided by the following questions: When and where was the building constructed? What purpose is it intended to serve? How has it been accepted by the public and by critics? Why was reinforced concrete chosen for this building? What materials were used to reinforce the concrete? Then ask pairs to make brief oral presentations to the class.

■ **FIGURE 24.34** Wright died six months after the Guggenheim Museum opened; he was 90 years old. **How does this museum differ from more traditional museums? What would you identify as its most unusual feature? Do you consider it to be a successful design? Why or why not?**

Frank Lloyd Wright. Solomon R. Guggenheim Museum. New York, New York. 1956–59.

Aesthetics

Display additional pictures of the Guggenheim Museum, including the exterior. Then ask students to consider whether Wright's circular design for the Guggenheim would be useful for any other building type. In small groups, have students write a description and make quick sketches of the Guggenheim's design as it might be adapted for a school, supermarket, or home. Ask: How would a curving ramp facilitate or impede the activities that take place in each of these settings? Have each group present its ideas and sketches to the class.

Cross Curriculum

SCIENCE. Ask a volunteer to investigate the current theories about the causes of earthquakes and then prepare a presentation on the fate of Frank Lloyd Wright's Imperial Hotel in Tokyo, during the earthquake of 1923. The student should also present information on how new buildings are designed to be seismically sound and what can be done to strengthen older buildings where earthquakes are likely to occur.

unique use of building materials would shape his entire career.

Wright designed more than 600 buildings during his long career. Among them were private homes, office buildings, factories, churches, and hotels. The Imperial Hotel he built in Tokyo met a special test; it withstood the great earthquake of 1923. That triumph helped cement Wright's reputation as one of the greatest architects of the century.

Solomon R. Guggenheim Museum
■ **FIGURE 24.34**

Wright's most controversial building is the Guggenheim Museum in New York City (Figure 24.34), a gallery for modern art. Some viewers have claimed that the outside of the building looks like a giant corkscrew or a cupcake.

Wright wanted to create a museum in which a single continuous ramp spiraled upward. He did not care for the mazelike collections of square or rectangular rooms found in traditional museums. Instead, he designed a single, round, windowless room almost 100 feet in diameter. Around this room he placed a continuous ramp. Visitors can either walk up the slight grade or take an elevator to the top and stroll down to the ground level. In either case, the gently curving ramp allows visitors to walk slowly and thoughtfully past the artworks that hang on the walls.

Chapter 24 *Modern Art Movements to the Present* **569**

MEETING INDIVIDUAL NEEDS

Kinesthetic Learners. Have students design a set of illustrated cards for each of the artists and styles described in this chapter. Then have them gather information and create a card for each artist depicting style, medium, geographical location, and cultural influences.

Verbal/Linguistic Learners. Have students research the life of a contemporary American artist. Have them prepare interview questions they would like to ask this artist about his or her artworks, lifestyle, and cultural ties and traditions.

Art History

Photocopy pictures of several war monuments from the past, such as Karl Frederich Schinkel's *Kreuzberg Monument* (1822, West Berlin), François Rude's *La Marseillaise* (1833–36, Arc de Triomphe, Paris), Giuseppe Grandi's *Monument to the Five Days* (1881–1895, Milan), and any of Augustus Saint-Gauden's Civil War memorials created in the late nineteenth century. (All of the above are reproduced in Robert Rosenblum and H. W. Janson's *Nineteenth-Century Art*, New York: Harry N. Abrams, 1984).

Then appoint six students to role-play members of a jury that will select one of these designs or the one by Maya Lin to commemorate a recent war. (If you wish, pick a specific war.) The panel should include artists, a politician, a soldier, a general, and an arts administrator. The rest of the class can take the role of the general public and the families of soldiers who died in the war. Have the panel hold an open meeting during which it decides which of the designs it will fund.

■ **FIGURE 24.35** The mirrorlike surface of the black granite reflects trees, lawns, and other monuments. **How does this monument help viewers understand the terrible cost of war?**

Maya Lin. Vietnam Veterans Memorial, Washington, D.C., 1982.

Maya Lin (1960–)

Although it is difficult to identify as either a building or a sculpture, the Vietnam Memorial has the emotional impact and the originality of expressive form that make it an important work of art. The story of this monument begins in 1980, when Congress authorized a two-acre site for a memorial honoring Americans who had died in the Vietnam War. When Maya Lin, then an architecture student at Yale University, first visited the site, she wanted to cut open the earth as a way of suggesting the violence of war.

Lin's design for the monument—one of 1,400 submitted—was selected by a jury of international artists and designers. On November 13, 1982, the Vietnam Veterans Memorial was dedicated.

Design of the Vietnam Veterans Memorial

Maya Lin's design is a V-shaped black granite wall (Figure 24.35). The tapering segments of this wall point to the Washington Monument in one direction and the Lincoln Memorial in the other.

Time & Place
CONNECTIONS
Modern Era
c. 1950–2000

SPACE WALK. Astronauts, protected with special suits and life support systems, travel outside spacecraft to perform experiments and study the earth from a distance to monitor changes and learn about our planet.

EARLY COMPUTERS. As early as 1946, researchers at the University of Pennsylvania built the first programmable computer, known as the ENIAC. Each transistor was placed inside a vacuum tube.

Activity **Speculation.** You are walking in space, looking back down to earth. What are your reactions to where you are and where you have been. Consider the changes in the past 20 years. Describe what you imagine life will be like at the end of the next 20 years.

Time & Place
CONNECTIONS
Modern Era

Have students examine the images in the Time & Place feature and write an analysis/speculation paper. Discuss the technological changes of the last 20 years. Based on the current rate of change, have students write about their predictions in one of the following areas: communications, science, technology, medicine, life span, or the arts. Students should give historically convincing reasons for the predicted change.

The wall consists of 1,560 highly polished panels, each 3 inches thick and 40 inches wide. The panels vary in height. The names of nearly 60,000 dead or missing American servicemen and servicewomen are listed on these panels. They are listed chronologically in the order of their deaths or disappearances. In order to read the names, visitors must descend gradually into the earth and then, just as gradually, work their way upward.

The monument neither preaches nor assigns blame. Instead, through its extraordinary understatement, it succeeds in touching the emotions of viewers—more than 10,000 each day.

Postmodernism

By the early 1980s, increasing disenchantment with architecture's glass-box look made it apparent that a change in direction was needed. This change was soon realized in a new style known as Postmodernism.

Architects who embraced this new style rejected the formal simplicity and clean lines of the International style in favor of designs that were dramatic, daring, and unique. While continuing to use the same steel-cage construction methods popularized by the International style, they began to incorporate decorative features borrowed from other, earlier styles of architecture as well.

Michael Graves (1934–)

One of the first and most impressive examples of Postmodern architecture in the United States is the Public Service Building in Portland, Oregon, designed by Michael Graves (Figure 24.36). Here color, decoration, and symbolism are all displayed on a grand scale. Colored in green, beige, and brown, the building is decorated along the sides with a frieze of stylized fiberglass garlands. A gigantic painted Egyptian keystone adorns the facade. Drawing freely from the vast vocabulary of historical styles in architecture, Graves constructed a building that stands out boldly from the impersonal concrete and steel boxes that are crowded around it.

Like most Postmodern structures, the Public Service Building evokes varying reactions from

■ **FIGURE 24.36**
Graves was the first to design buildings that combine art, ornamentation, and symbolism. In what ways does this building differ from the Lever House (Figure 23.30, page 540)? How is it similar?

Michael Graves. Public Service Building. Portland, Oregon. 1980–82. City of Portland Archives.

critics and from the public. Some claim that Postmodern buildings are bold and imaginative, while others regard them as unattractive architectural misfits. No one can deny, however, that they are pleasant—even fun—to look at. That is not a claim that could be made for most buildings designed in the International style.

Charles Moore (1925–1993)

One of the most striking examples of Postmodern architecture is Charles W. Moore's Piazza d'Italia (Figure 24.37, page 572), designed to breathe new life into a struggling neighborhood in New Orleans. Intended as a center for community social activities, it is constructed on a circular site that has long served as the location for an annual neighborhood festival.

Because most of the inhabitants of this part of the city are of Italian decent, Moore designed a colorful American version of a typical Italian piazza. Classical Greek and Roman architectural features and symbols blend with others that owe their inspiration to Mannerism and the Baroque. Geographical references to

Chapter 24 *Modern Art Movements to the Present* **571**

CHAPTER 24
LESSON TWO

Art Criticism
Direct students' attention to the photograph of the *Vietnam Veterans Memorial* in Figure 24.27. Then have students research the other, more traditional sculpture on the Washington Mall that commemorates those who died in the Vietnam War—Frederick Hart's sculpture of three servicemen. Ask: How does the message of the traditional monument differ from Lin's artwork? To whom would each work appeal? Which of the works do you prefer and why?

Study Guide
Distribute *Study Guide* 57 in the TCR. Assist students in reviewing key concepts. ▱

Art and Humanities
Have students complete *Art and Humanities* 41, "Modern Dance as Sculpture in Motion," in the TCR. In this activity, students explore new forms of modern dance as a means of recognizing the emphasis on coordinating body shapes and movements in sculptural compositions. They then perform a dance sculpture. ▱

Studio Activities
Divide the class into groups of three or four students. Assign groups to work on *Cooperative Learning* 38, "Finding the Fourth Dimension," in the TCR. In this worksheet, students trace the development of kinetic art. Groups then collaborate on making a design for a sculpture in motion. ▱

About the *Artwork*

Vietnam Veterans Memorial. Maya Lin's heroic monument is not the only Vietnam memorial in Washington, D.C. The committee that chose Lin's proposal was fully satisfied that it met their requirements, but later, a group of Vietnam veterans protested that the streamlined wall did not represent or honor them. Other veterans groups, which had provided much of the funding for the memorial, joined the opposition to Lin's design. A second jury was set up to choose an additional monument. They selected a design by Frederick Hart that includes three servicemen in war gear, to also be displayed.

ASSESS

Checking Comprehension

➤ Have students complete the lesson review questions. Answers appear in the box below.

➤ Assign *Application* 24, "News of the Revolution," in the TCR, to evaluate students' comprehension. 📁

Reteaching

➤ Assign *Reteaching* 57, found in the TCR. Have students complete the activity and review their responses. 📁

➤ Point out that many of the artists whose works are illustrated in this chapter have been described as working in a "childlike" or "primitive" style. Have students discuss the meaning of these terms and explain how they apply to the works of Moore, Pollock, and Calder.

Enrichment

Assign *Enrichment* 46 "Art History: Linear or Cyclical?" in the TCR. In this worksheet, students review the history of art in an effort to see how it can be viewed as a linear continuum and also as a repeating cycle. 📁

Extension

➤ Have students complete *Appreciating Cultural Diversity* 35 "Postmodern Architecture and Past Cultures," in the TCR. In this activity, students learn how contemporary architecture draws upon the styles of the past. 📁

➤ Assign *Studio* 31, "Torn Paper Collage," in the TCR. 📁

CLOSE

Have each student state which artist's work illustrated in this chapter seems the most "modern" and explain his or her choice.

572

■ **FIGURE 24.37**
Moore has praised Disneyland as one of America's most impressive public areas. In what ways does this piazza reflect the architect's appreciation for Disneyland?

Charles Moore. Piazza d'Italia. New Orleans, Louisiana. 1976–79.

Italy and Sicily are found at every turn. Even the pavement is inlaid with a map of Italy, with Sicily prominently identified. Twentieth-century innovations are represented in the form of stainless-steel columns and capitals and multicolored neon lights that accent the most important architectural details.

In addition to an elaborate fountain, the central portion of the structure features steps in concentric circles and rows of columns that direct the eye to a raised, semicircular walled space. This resembles the kind of apse found in medieval churches; it functions as a speaker's platform during the annual festivals. Come nightfall, the colored lights illuminate metal, marble, and colored stone, and are reflected in a pool of water calling to mind the Mediterranean Sea. Colorful, imaginative, exciting, gaudy, and excessive—these and many more adjectives have been applied to Moore's piazza.

It is impossible to bring this story of art to a close. Art has its roots at the dawn of civilization, and it has continued to thrive from age to age up until the present day. Every nation has produced its art in one form or another. Flourishing during periods of prosperity and grandeur, art somehow managed to survive wars and catastrophes of every kind. Whether admired, ignored, ridiculed, or condemned, it has managed to endure. Even now, at this very minute, artists all over the world are continuing to dream, to experiment, and to create. The efforts of many of these artists are destined to be recorded in future chapters of art's impressive story—a story that may have started centuries ago when someone picked up a piece of soft stone and, with a few awkward strokes, discovered that it was possible to create an image on the rough wall of a cave.

LESSON TWO REVIEW

Reviewing Art Facts

1. Why did Henry Moore avoid using models for his sculptures? What did he do that had never been done before?
2. Describe the sculptural technique of Louise Nevelson. How does her art style compare to that of Calder?
3. Who designed the Guggenheim Museum in New York? Why was the building so controversial?
4. What distinguishes Postmodern buildings from those designed and constructed earlier?

➤ Activity ...*Theories of Art*

Prepare a number of small cards and, on each, write the name of one of the theories of art discussed in Chapter 4: imitationalism, formalism, or emotionalism. Place these cards in a box and pass it around your group so that each person can select one.

Reexamine the paintings and sculptures illustrated in Chapter 24. Select one that possesses the aesthetic qualities stressed by the theory written on your card. Create a presentation in which you identify the theory of art selected and describe the aesthetic qualities favored by that theory. Identify one work of art that possesses those aesthetic qualities and point them out.

LESSON TWO REVIEW

Answers to Reviewing Art Facts

1. He had no desire to copy subjects.
2. A kind of three-dimensional collage; nonobjective yet stationary forms.
3. Frank Lloyd Wright; it was a departure from traditional styles.
4. Designs were dramatic, daring, and unique.

Activity...*Theories of Art*

Review with students the theories of imitationalism, formalism, and emotionalism from Chapter 4 in the texts. Ask students to explain each of the theories in their own words before beginning the activity.

Complete a full-face portrait in which features and expressions are exaggerated and distorted to illustrate a particular emotion. Then cut this portrait into six or more shapes and assemble those shapes to make a three-dimensional relief. Each shape will have a different simulated texture obtained with a crayon-etching technique. Select colors and color combinations that will emphasize the emotion you are trying to show.

Inspiration

Look at the face in Willem de Kooning's painting of *Woman VI* (Figure 24.11, page 552). Does it look lifelike? Can you identify the expression on this face? What feelings or emotions do you associate with that expression? Look for other portraits in this book that express emotions. What emotions do you observe? How are those emotions shown?

Process

1. Select an emotion to use as a theme for your portrait. Examples are *lonely, angry, excited,* and *joyful.*
2. Working with another student, take turns acting as artist and model. One will model an emotion by frowning, snarling, or smiling, for example, while the other draws. For this drawing, use *one continuous pencil line* and show the face from the front. Exaggerate and distort the features and expression to emphasize the emotion. Several practice sketches may be necessary before you are able to draw the portrait in one continuous line. Doing it this way enables you to break up the portrait into a number of different shapes that will provide more flexibility later, when you are adding color. When a satisfactory drawing has been completed, reverse the roles of artist and model for your partner.
3. Reproduce your portrait on the smaller sheet of illustration board. Use the same continuous-line technique as before. The face should fill the board and may even go off the edges.

(Continued on next page)

Materials

- Pencil and sketch paper
- One sheet of white illustration or mat board, 12 × 18 inches
- One sheet of white illustration or mat board, 18 × 24 inches
- Crayons, india ink, brush
- Ruler, scissors, paper cutter
- Nail or other pointed instrument for etching
- Small pieces of cardboard
- White glue

■ **FIGURE 24.38** Student Work

573

Objectives

Complete a relief portrait with exaggerated and distorted features.

■ Use six or more shapes to create a three-dimensional relief showing the face viewed from the front.

■ Use a crayon-etching technique to create simulated texture.

■ Select color combinations to emphasize emotions.

Motivator

After examining and discussing de Kooning's *Woman VI,* write the emotions listed below on the board. Instruct students to find paintings of people in the book that express each of these emotions.

Have them write the titles of these paintings after each emotion: *amusement,* (Hals, *Portrait of a Member of the Haarlem Civic Guard,* Figure 19.11, page 429); *fear,* (Munch, *The Scream,* Figure 23.10, page 521); *sorrow,* (van der Weyden, *Descent from the Cross,* Figure 17.7, page 387); *anxiety,* (St. Matthew, from the Gospel Book of Archbishop Ebbo of Reims, Figure 14.9, page 316); *sadness,* (Rouault, *The Old King,* Figure 23.4, page 518); *reserved,* (Wood, *American Gothic,* Figure 24.6, page 549).

Discuss the way the artists depicted these different emotions. Ask students to identify the artists who relied most heavily on distortion and exaggeration.

COOPERATIVE LEARNING

Expressing Emotion. In order to avoid a situation in which several students select the same emotion, prepare index cards with a single emotion written on each. Have each student select a card. The emotion indicated on a student's card is the one he or she must attempt to exhibit when acting as a model. Encourage partners to practice effective expressions before beginning their sketches. Before students begin work, demonstrate on the board the different ways to create texture with the crayon-etching technique. Show students how wavy lines, cross-hatching, and various checkerboard effects can be realized.

LESSON

Aesthetics

Tell students to act as imitationalists and examine the artworks listed on the board. Ask them to identify those works that they consider to be successful in terms of the literal qualities. When they have reached agreement, have them mark those works by placing an I after each. Then, acting as formalists concerned with the design qualities, instruct them to place an F after the paintings they regard as successful.

Be certain to indicate that it is possible for different aestheticians to respond favorably to the same artworks—but for different reasons. Finally, ask students to repeat the process by acting as emotionalists. Have them place an E after the works they feel effectively stress the expressive qualities. Were there any paintings with all three letters listed after them?

Extension

While involved in this studio lesson, students will become aware of a variety of different approaches to incorporate into a second version of the work. Rather than cutting the portrait into angular shapes, they might wish to cut a mat into a variety of angular and curvilinear shapes. Interesting effects can be realized by cutting out the various lessons of the face in this manner and assembling them to approximate the way some features project outward while others recede. They might wish to include the hands and upper arms in their portraits, cutting them to project outward in front of the face.

Critiquing

Have students apply the steps of art criticism to their own artwork using the Examining Your Work questions on this page.

574

 **LESSON**   Three-Dimensional Relief Portrait

■ **FIGURE 24.39** Student Work

(Continued from page 573)

4. Use a *heavy* application of crayon to color the shapes in your portrait. Select colors and combinations of colors that you associate with the emotion you are trying to show. Avoid dark hues, and cover the entire sheet of illustration board with crayon.

5. Divide the illustration board into six shapes by drawing straight or curved lines on the back with a pencil and ruler. Cut out these shapes with scissors or with a paper cutter.

6. Cover the crayoned surface of each shape using a brush and india ink. Several coats may be necessary to cover the crayon completely. Ink the edges of each shape as well.

7. While the ink is drying, use pencil and sketch paper to design six different textural patterns made up of closely spaced lines.

8. Use a nail or other pointed tool to etch your patterns into the inked shapes. By carefully scratching through the ink, you will bring out the crayon color beneath.

9. Assemble the six shapes of your portrait on the larger sheet of illustration board. Use small pieces of cardboard stacked to different heights to position the shapes at different levels. Glue the shapes in place to create your relief portrait.

Examining Your Work

Describe. Does your relief show a face viewed from the front? Can you point out the different features on this face? Are these features exaggerated and distorted?

Analyze. Is your relief made up of six different shapes? Does each shape have a different simulated texture? Are the shapes assembled to make a three-dimensional relief?

Interpret. What feeling or emotion does your portrait express? How does your choice of colors and combinations of colors help show this emotion? What other colors could you have used to express the same emotion? What else did you do to emphasize the feeling or emotion? Were other students able to recognize this feeling or emotion?

Judge. Using the expressive qualities as your basis for judgment, do you think your relief portrait is a success? What is its most successful feature?

574

ASSESSMENT

Examining Your Work. After students have had a chance to answer the questions to examine their own relief portraits, provide some time for each student to present his or her portrait to the class. Have them describe the work and explain how they distorted the features. Have the student allow classmates to try to identify the emotion shown in the work, and then indicate whether or not that was the emotion the student was trying to express. Then have each student make notes about whether they judge their own artworks as successful and how they would improve or make changes to their work. Have them keep their notes and their artwork in their portfolios.

Reviewing the Facts

Lesson One

1. How did Paul Klee incorporate fantasy into his paintings?
2. How does Abstract Expressionism differ from representational art? Name four artists identified with the development of this movement.
3. Describe Jackson Pollock's technique of painting.
4. What characteristics are typical of the works of Hard-Edge painters?

Lesson Two

5. What building combines the features found in the abstract figures of Henry Moore and the curving architectural forms of Antonio Gaudi? Who was the architect for this building?
6. What is environmental art and how does it differ from traditional sculptural forms? Name two artists working in this art form.
7. What did Postmodern architects accept and reject from earlier styles of architecture?
8. What memorial did Maya Lin design? Describe the symbolism of the design.

Thinking Critically

1. **ANALYZE.** Analyze the color scheme of Edward Hopper's painting *Drug Store* (Figure 24.7, page 550). What colors are used? How do they relate to each other on the color wheel? How do these colors contribute to the mood expressed by the painting?
2. **COMPARE AND CONTRAST.** Refer to Henry Moore's sculpture *Reclining Figure* (Figure 24.25, page 563) and to Alexander Calder's sculpture *Pomegranate* (Figure 24.28, page 565). Compare and contrast how each artist used natural shapes to achieve harmony.

 MUSIC. Use the *Performing Arts Handbook*, page 593 to learn about the musical innovations of the Bang on a Can All-Stars.

CAREERS IN **Art** If you enjoy studying or creating art, read about a fascinating art-related career opportunity in the *Careers in Art Handbook*, page 594.

*inter*NET
CONNECTION Visit Glencoe Art Online at *www.glencoe.com/sec/art*. Explore online museums and galleries. Visit artist's sites to view computer-generated artworks and learn about advances in art and technology.

Technology Project

Time Capsule

Artists of today encounter new developments in technology that challenge and empower them. Using a computer, artists can view thousands of works of art in museums through the Internet, laser disc, and CD-ROM technology. It is possible to teleconference with museum staff or with other artists worldwide. Art students can see and hear information about art and artists all over the globe using new technologies. Using digital technology, artists can create works of art to be viewed by others with access to the Internet all over the world. How do you think future art historians will treat these contemporary forms of electronic art?

Do you think digital images will endure as works of art that can be viewed by others in the distant future? Will archaeologists in the year 5000 unearth laser discs and CD-ROMs and have the ability to view and hear them? What problems will they face?

1. Choose a digitally created image, print a copy, and study the work. The image may be your own or a work by another computer artist you admire.
2. Write a critique of the work explaining the artist's choice of subject, use of art elements and principles, the expressive qualities of the work, and whether you judge it to be a valid work of art.
3. Create a digital time capsule by placing your notes and the image on a Web page and sending it into cyberspace for future viewing.

Teaching the Technology Project

Give students an opportunity to review several different types of Web pages on the Internet before they plan their time capsule. If students have never worked in HTML, several instructional sites are available on the World Wide Web to help them get started. If your school has a home page, students may be able to post their work on the school's Web site.

 Assign the feature in the *Performing Arts Handbook*, page 593.

CAREERS IN ART If time permits, have interested students investigate the career information in the *Careers in Art Handbook*, page 594.

*inter*NET
CONNECTION Have students go online and learn more about artists on preselected Web sites with the Internet activity for this chapter.

Reviewing the Facts

1. He paints lines and shapes based on imagination and wit.
2. Artists of this movement use paint freely to show feelings and emotions rather than realistic subject matter. De Kooning, Pollock, Frankenthaler, Motherwell.
3. He walked on and around canvases placed on the floor, applying paint with brushes, sticks, and knives.
4. Hard-edge painters create works with crisp edges, pure colors, and simple geometric shapes.
5. The *Chapel of Notre Dame du Haut,* by Le Corbusier.
6. Outdoor artworks designed as part of the landscape; Smithson, Christo
7. They used steel-cage construction methods, but rejected the formal International style.
8. *Vietnam Veterans Memorial.* The architect cut open the earth with this work to suggest the violence of war.

Thinking Critically

1. The work makes use of values and intensities of green and blue, both cool colors; analogous; shows loneliness.
2. Moore uses a continuum of smooth, vaguely human shapes punctuated by holes to lend the work an overall harmony. Calder similarly uses stylized natural shapes, but their spatial arrangement, dictated in part by the wind, is less carefully planned.

Introducing the Performing Arts

The features in the *Performing Arts Handbook* are designed to enrich students' learning by correlating what they learn about the visual arts to the performing arts—dance, music, and theatre. The featured performers and groups in this handbook were specifically chosen to supplement the chapters in the student text.

Using the Handbook

The following categories suggest ways to use the *Performing Arts Handbook*.

Mini-lessons

Use the features as stand-alone lessons about dance, music, and theatre.

Motivator

Use the features to introduce related chapters. Listed on each chapter opening page of your Teacher's Wraparound Edition is a segment that correlates each chapter to this section. As you plan lessons, consider how you might use the *Performing Arts Handbook* as a way of introducing the chapter's contents.

Extension

Refer to the recommended Artsource® feature found on the chapter opening page of the Teacher's Wraparound Edition, and use the appropriate feature to expand the study of that chapter. Students may volunteer for this Extension activity, or you might assign groups of students to read the feature and then complete the questions and activities on their own.

PERFORMING ARTS HANDBOOK

Performing Arts Handbook

$\mathcal{T}$he following pages were excerpted from *Artsource®: The Music Center Study Guide to the Performing Arts*, developed by the Music Center Education Division, an award-winning arts education program of the Music Center of Los Angeles County. The following artists and groups are featured in the Performing Arts Handbook.

More About... **Artsource®.** The materials provided in this *Performing Arts Handbook* are excerpted from *Artsource®: The Music Center Guide to the Performing Arts*, a project of the Music Center Education Division. The Music Center of Los Angeles County, the largest performing arts center in the western United States, established the Music Center Education Division in 1979 to provide opportunities for lifelong learning in the arts, and especially to bring the performing and visual arts into the classroom. The Education Division believes the arts enhance the quality of life for all people, but are crucial to the development of every child.

Chuck Davis

*C*huck Davis, a towering African-American dancer and choreographer, came from a background that was poor financially, but was rich in love. His first dance break came when he substituted for an injured member of the Richardson Dancers in Washington, D.C. He gained professional status in 1959. He studied and performed with a number of modern, jazz, Afro-Cuban, and African dance companies which led to the formation of his New York company. With a disdain for the way black people were being portrayed in the media, he set out to present the truth about black culture through dance. "I have gone to Africa and I have sat at the feet of elders and I have listened as their words poured like raindrops onto and into my being. I have danced on the dusty earth and the sound of my feet pounding against the earth brought the rhythms of life into my blood," states Davis. After two decades, he returned to North Carolina to start a second company, the African American Dance Ensemble, which he currently directs. Through dance, he works energetically to bring *all* people his message of "peace, love and respect for everybody."

The African American Dance Ensemble. Chuck Davis, artistic director and choreographer. "African Roots in American Soil." Photo: Courtesy of the African American Dance Ensemble.

PERFORMING ARTS HANDBOOK

DISCUSSION QUESTIONS

1. Look carefully at the photo on this page and describe the mood, costumes, and actions you observe. What clues do these give you about the style of dance and what is being communicated?
2. Study the clothing that the dancers are wearing. Discuss how it is similar to or different from American outfits.
3. What popular dance styles do you think have their roots in traditional African cultures?

CREATIVE EXPRESSION ACTIVITIES

Language Arts In many African ethnic groups, it is believed that wise people deliver proverbs. Read the following proverbs, then think of English equivalents: "Rain beats a leopard's skin, but it does not wash out the spots" (Ashanti); "When spider webs unite, they can tie up a lion" (Ethiopia); "Cross the river in a crowd and the crocodile won't eat you" (Kenya).

History Find your own family's heritage. Discover the cultural influences that have impacted your ancestral culture. Identify one or two traditions such as food, religion, or clothing, and describe how they have been altered from your original ancestral culture.

APPRECIATING THE PERFORMING ARTS

In the traditional societies of Africa, dance is an important medium of education. It helps African communities perpetuate themselves by assisting its members though rites of passage, teaching accepted behavior, identifying roles and rules, and assimilating its members into the prevailing attitudes, beliefs, and rituals of the group.

In African cultures, dance is not considered an art form, but is an integral part of the economic, political, social, and religious aspects of life. For example, the Ibo of Nigeria teach about leadership through dance. A popular teenage dance among the Ubakala Clan is *Zik Meme Ka Odi Uma*. The dance emphasizes cooperation with a worthy leader.

Optional
Viewing Selection:
■ Artsource® VHS tape, video segment 1 (playing time 21:57)

Setting the Stage
Direct students to read the paragraph about Chuck Davis and the African American Dance Ensemble, and view the Artsource® video, if available.

Connecting the Arts
Using the Discussion Questions on this page, help students recognize the importance of dance and music in traditional African cultures. Possible responses:
1. Mood, costumes, and actions suggest traditional African culture; they suggest that the dance echoes traditional African styles and that pride in African roots is being communicated.
2. Their outfits are traditional African rather than modern American.
3. Students may mention many current popular dances.

Extension
■ After students have responded to the Discussion Questions and, if possible, viewed the Artsource® selection, have them complete the Creative Expression Activities.
■ Have students use various research sources to trace the impact of the African Diaspora on the cultures affected, especially those of North and South America.

Use the Artsource® Performing Arts package, Lesson 1, for more information about Chuck Davis and the African American Dance Ensemble.

Lewitzky Dance Company

Optional Viewing Selection:
■ Artsource® VHS tape, video segment 2 (playing time 5:28)

Setting the Stage
Direct students to read the paragraph about dancer and choreographer Bella Lewitzky and her dance company. Have them watch the Artsource® video, if available.

Connecting the Arts
Using the Discussion Questions on this page, help students recognize how modern dance developed a new movement vocabulary that could express ideas and emotions, rather than simply tell stories. Possible responses:
1. Short brush strokes are on different colored leotards; curved lines, straight lines and angular lines are combined.
2. An explosion of color and spirals and circles in the painting is felt in the dancers' positions; also, the two dancers in front suggest the cypress tree and the two in the background could represent the hills or a portion of the sky.

Extension
■ After students have responded to the Discussion Questions and, if possible, viewed the Artsource® selection, have them complete the Creative Expression Activities.

Use the Artsource® Performing Arts package, Lesson 2, for more information about Bella Lewitzky and her piece, "Impressions #2."

578

Lewitzky Dance Company

PERFORMING ARTS HANDBOOK

Lewitzky Dance Company. Bella Lewitzky, director. "Impressions #2." Featured dancers: Kimo Kimura, Kenneth Bowman, Kenneth B. Talley, John Pennington. Photo by Vic Luke.

*D*ancer and choreographer Bella Lewitzky was born to Russian immigrants in a utopian community in the Mojave Desert in California. The vast open space, stillness, and beauty of her surroundings would later influence her dance. Although she loved to move as a child, it was not until high school that she received formal dance training. After a full career as a professional dancer, Bella formed the Lewitzky Dance Company in 1966, when she was 50 years old. Her choreography has also been inspired by the work of visual artists. "Impressions #2 (Vincent van Gogh)" is part of a trilogy of dances, each one based on Ms. Lewitzky's responses to the artworks of three different artists—Henry Moore, Vincent van Gogh, and Paul Klee. For this piece, Lewitzky brought images of artwork created by Vincent van Gogh into the studio for her dancers to view and explore through movement improvisation before the final choreography was set.

DISCUSSION QUESTIONS
1. Study the photo on this page and describe the lines that you see, both on the dancers' costumes and in the shape of their bodies.
2. Look at a replica of the painting *The Starry Night* by Vincent van Gogh (Figure 22.1, page 492) and see the possible relationships between what you see in the painting and what you see expressed in the dancers' bodies.

CREATIVE EXPRESSION ACTIVITIES
Language Arts In creating the dance "Impressions #2 (Vincent van Gogh)," Ms. Lewitzky gave her dancers the following words to stimulate movement ideas: *sharp, jagged, wavy, pulsing, shimmering, exploding, falling,* and *spiraling.* Select three or four of these words and use them to create a short poem or story.

Math/Art Using the idea of circles, see how many different combinations and variations you can create by using techniques of overlapping, intersecting, circles inside of circles, or fractions of circles. When your design is complete, add color and vary the thickness and texture of the lines.

APPRECIATING THE PERFORMING ARTS

Modern dance was born in the early part of the twentieth century. Most people credit Isadora Duncan with breaking the traditional boundaries of ballet by kicking off her ballet shoes and dancing barefoot. She rebelled against the strictly structured steps and positions of ballet and turned to a more natural way of moving to express herself. Ballet dancers strive to defy gravity and bring the art of movement to the level of ultimate grace and beauty. Most of the traditional ballet themes are based on European or Russian fairy tales and placed in romantic settings. Modern dancers, in contrast, strive to be earthy, weighty, and socially conscious. Today, however, there is an increasing crossover between these two dance styles.

Lewitzky Dance Company

Lewitzky Dance Company. Bella Lewitzky, director. "Impressions #1." Featured dancers: Jennifer Handel, Nancy Lanier, Laurie McWilliams, Theodora Fredericks, Deborah Collodel, Claudia Schneiderman. Photo: Vic Luke.

*B*ella Lewitzky has been a modern dance performer, choreographer, and dance educator for over 60 years. During her career, Bella realized that sculpture and other works of art could be used as a source of inspiration for dance movements. In particular, she focused on the work of sculptor Henry Moore. Since it was impossible to bring his sculptures into her studio, she and her dancers worked from photos found in books. They observed that his sculptures have massive physical weight and bulk and they also have two or three balance points, or places where the sculpture touches the ground. There are also holes, or negative spaces, that encourage the viewer to look through the sculptures, which alters the perspective. These observations and movement explorations evolved into a dance work called "Impressions #1 (Henry Moore)."

PERFORMING ARTS HANDBOOK

DISCUSSION QUESTIONS

1. Look at the photo of the dancers on this page. Use the elements of line, shape, form, and texture to describe what you see.
2. Can you think of other artists who were inspired by an existing work of art and used it as a point of departure for a new work?
3. Use art books to locate a sculpture by Henry Moore. (See Figure 24.25, page 563.) Observe it in terms of size, negative and positive space, form, and the number of balance points. Discuss how these concepts might be communicated through movement.

CREATIVE EXPRESSION ACTIVITIES

Theatre/Movement Working with partners, sketch out a few human *sculptures* of your own. Join with other pairs of students and position yourselves in relationship to each other to make more complex forms. Present your forms to the class.

Dance Dancers use the movements of their bodies to express action as it relates to weight, flow, space, and time. Explore ways to show the following eight actions using dance movements: press, flick, punch, float, slash, glide, wring, and dab.

Science Select an object of your choice and answer the following questions: Is it light or heavy? How does it move or balance? How many points are touching the ground? What is the object's shape? Observe it from different perspectives (for example, upside down, above your head, far away, tilted, and so on).

PERFORMING ARTS
DANCE

Lewitzky Dance Company

Optional Viewing Selection:
■ Artsource® VHS tape, video segment 3 (playing time 5:22)

Setting the Stage
Direct students to read about Bella Lewitzky, and guide them in examining the photograph on this page. Have students view the Artsource® video, if available.

Connecting the Arts
Using the Discussion Questions on this page, help students recognize the inspiration Lewitzky found in works of visual art. Possible responses:
1. The dancers' bodies are aligned and parallel in groups of two vertically and three horizontally; shapes are repeated from one group to another; textures are smooth.
2. Students might mention Mussorgsky's *Pictures at an Exhibition*, inspired by an exhibit of paintings, or Leonard Bernstein's *West Side Story*, inspired by Shakespeare's *Romeo and Juliet*.
3. Students might suggest large, sweeping movements, unusual balancing points, and formations as shown.

Extension
■ After students have responded to the Discussion Questions and, if possible, viewed the Artsource® selection, have them complete the Creative Expression Activities.

Use the Artsource® Performing Arts package, Lesson 3, for more information about Bella Lewitzky and "Impressions #1."

APPRECIATING THE PERFORMING ARTS

The art form of dance uses both sculptural designs and selected motion to achieve aesthetic expression.

Lewitzky has been a "visual collector" of Henry Moore's sculptures for many years. In her studio, she guided her company in experiencing the different aspects of his work. They explored how his pieces rested on the ground and "took off" from their resting places, how the feet, hands, and arms were carried, and how they moved with upright positions of the back. The dancers worked with interlocking shapes and have developed a "Moore movement vocabulary."

Alfredo Rolando Ortiz

Optional Listening Selection:

■ Artsource® audiotape, audio segment 1 (playing time 4:07)

Setting the Stage

Direct students to read the paragraphs about Alfredo Rolando Ortiz, a composer and performer on the Paraguayan harp, and listen to the Artsource® audiotape, if available.

Connecting the Arts

Using the Discussion Questions on this page, help students recognize some of the folk and classical traditions of Latin American music. Possible responses:

1. Students may mention specific musical works they find soothing or inspiring.
2. Students may name visual artists discussed in this text, musicians, dancers, actors, other specific artists.
3. Students may mention, for example, the balalaika, the shako hachi, or other instruments.

Extension

■ After students have responded to the Discussion Questions and, if possible, listened to an Artsource® selection, have them complete the Creative Expression Activities.

Use the Artsource® Performing Arts package, Lesson 4, for more information about the harp and for related activities.

ARTSOURCE

Alfredo Rolando Ortiz

Alfredo Rolando Ortiz with his Paraguayan harp.
Photo: Craig Schwartz.

PERFORMING ARTS HANDBOOK

A lfredo Rolando Ortiz was born in Cuba, where the harp is not a traditional instrument. His fascination for the harp began when he was 11 years old, when his family was relocating to Venezuela. Alfredo recalls that as the ship neared land, he saw green forms rising up through the clouds, and soon the mountains of Venezuela loomed in front of him. As his family drove up the mountain, he heard this beautiful music playing on the radio. "I didn't know what it was, but I fell in love with it," he recalls.

An interest in the harp soon grew into a passion after he heard a friend, 13-year-old Fernando, perform at their school. He immediately approached him and asked if he would teach him all he knew. Fernando agreed and became Alfredo's first teacher. A year later he attended a local concert performed by Alberto Romero, a renowned harpist from Paraguay. He waited to speak with him after the concert and was delighted and grateful when Mr. Romero offered to teach him.

Ortiz went on to study medicine. However, he eventually, gave up medicine to devote his life to the harp. His music is rooted in the folk and classical traditions of Latin America, and his original improvisations and compositions have received international acclaim with audiences of all ages and backgrounds. Today he lives in Southern California where he teaches, performs, and composes.

DISCUSSION QUESTIONS

1. Describe a piece of music that has inspired you. What was it about the music that moved you? Try to recall what the music made you think of, and how it made you feel.
2. An artist changed the life of Alfredo Rolando Ortiz forever. If you could meet a famous artist, who would it be? What would you like that artist to teach you?
3. Name some instruments that are not considered traditional in the United States. Have you ever heard some of these instruments being played? Describe the sounds that these instruments make.

CREATIVE EXPRESSION ACTIVITIES

Visual Arts Think of an instrument you particularly like. Find a recording of the instrument, and listen to it. Then sketch any images that come to mind that convey how the music from that instrument makes you feel. Using your sketches, design an album cover that captures the essence of the instrument.

Science The harp may have been inspired by the sound of the hunter's bow. Later a hollow sound box was added to amplify the sound. Examine a musical instrument closely. How does it make sound? How is it proportioned? What gives it a unique tone color? Name some other everyday items that might inspire a musical instrument.

APPRECIATING THE PERFORMING ARTS

It is believed that the harp began with the sounds of the hunting bow many thousands of years ago. At some point, entertainers discovered that they could attach several strings to a bent wooden structure; harps eventually were played throughout Europe, Africa, and the Middle East. Harps are mentioned in literature and images that date back 5,000 years.

The Spanish harp consisted of a wooden soundbox and multiple strings of varying lengths. These instruments were played for entertainment, dancing, singing, and religious celebrations. The harp is the ancestor of our most popular instruments, including the guitar and the piano.

Eugene Loring

Eugene Loring

*B*orn in Milwaukee, Wisconsin, as LeRoy Kerperstein, Eugene Loring was part of a large family. As a teen he became interested in the theatre and began his career in vaudeville. He trained as an actor and studied dance to gain more skills and to supplement his income. He enrolled at the School of American Ballet, where he worked under George Balanchine and Lincoln Kirstein. These two men were instrumental in creating a distinctive American ballet style which shocked traditionalists. In 1937, Kirstein invited Loring to choreograph a ballet based on the notorious outlaw, Billy the Kid. Loring accepted and also danced the lead. It was the first work to combine ballet and modern dance and to adapt old cowboy tunes from a folk to classical style. After the ballet was conceived, Loring created a storyboard and sent it to Aaron Copland who then wrote the score.

The Joffrey Ballet. Tom Mossbrucker dancing *Billy the Kid.* Choreographed by Eugene Loring, music composed by Aaron Copland. Photo: Herbert Migdoll.

PERFORMING ARTS HANDBOOK

Optional Viewing Selection:

■ Artsource® VHS tape, video segment 4 (playing time 9:25)

Setting the Stage

Direct students to read the paragraph about choreographer Eugene Loring and his American ballet, *Billy the Kid.* Then have them watch the Artsource® video, if available.

Connecting the Arts

Using the Discussion Questions on this page, help students recognize how Eugene Loring pioneered a new style of ballet based on American themes and movement. Possible responses:

1. Boots with flowers, striped pants with a belt, shirt with stars and lines; basic cowboy garments have been altered in design and fabric to be more decorative than practical.
2. Students might mention driving covered wagons, hauling wood or water, spinning, cooking, chopping and sawing wood.

Extension

■ After students have responded to the Discussion Questions and, if possible, viewed the Artsource® video, have them complete the Creative Expression Activities.

Use the Artsource® Performing Arts package, Lesson 5, for more information about the music and dance choreographed by Eugene Loring and for related activities.

DISCUSSION QUESTIONS

1. Study the photograph on this page and describe the costume. Discuss how it has been stylized to represent a cowboy of the old West. What ideas does it capture?
2. The ballet, *Billy the Kid,* begins with the opening march of pioneers traveling westward and is composed of various actions (motifs) inspired by the activities performed in their daily life. Discuss what activities these would be and show or describe some of the basic movements involved with each.

CREATIVE EXPRESSION ACTIVITIES

Theatre Choose characters from the Old West and show three different poses for each. Move from one position to the next, making each transition in four counts. Combine characters to form group portraits, called tableaux.

Mime List activities of pioneer life, such as chopping, sawing, baking, sewing, and pulling a cart. Mime each of these ideas separately. Then develop a sequence of movements that includes four or five of these activities.

APPRECIATING THE PERFORMING ARTS

Eugene Loring felt there was no true movement unless there was an emotional reason behind it. His dancers were directed to feel the emotion before performing the movement. At rehearsals, Loring asked the dancers to get inside themselves and analyze their own likes and dislikes. When dancing any role, they explored all aspects of the characters to understand their motivations. Patrice Whiteside, a student of Loring and formerly a principal dancer with the Oakland Ballet Company, safeguards the integrity of Loring's work as she reconstructs and teaches the ballets. Today it takes Whiteside 100 hours to stage, teach, and rehearse the ballet *Billy the Kid.* First, she teaches the movement; then she "fleshes it in with emotional intent."

Faustwork Mask Theater

Optional Viewing Selection:
■ Artsource® VHS tape, video segment 5 (playing time 5:13)

Setting the Stage
Direct students to read the paragraph about Faustwork Mask Theater and its creator, Robert Faust. Then have them view the Artsource® video, if available.

Connecting the Arts
Using the Discussion Questions on this page, help students recognize how masks have been used throughout history. Possible responses:
1. Although masks at first look "blank," they show characters of various ages and outlooks— young and optimistic, old and worried, etc.
2. A mask might be used to create a visual effect or to allow one actor to play many roles.
3. Athena, warrior goddess, who carries a spear and shield; Zeus, father of the gods, who carries a thunderbolt and scepter; or Hermes, who wears winged sandals.
4. Students may mention Halloween, Mardi Gras, Chinese New Year.

Extension
■ After students have responded to the Discussion Questions and, if possible, viewed the Artsource® selection, have them complete the Creative Expression Activities.

Use the Artsource® Performing Arts package, Lesson 6, for more information about masks and Robert Faust's performance.

582

ART SOURCE
ARTSOURCE

PERFORMING ARTS HANDBOOK

T H E A T R E

Faustwork Mask Theater

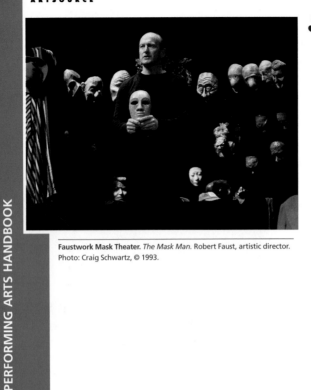

Faustwork Mask Theater. *The Mask Man.* Robert Faust, artistic director. Photo: Craig Schwartz, © 1993.

*R*obert Faust is an actor, athlete, dancer, choreographer, mask-maker and the artistic director of his company, Faustwork Mask Theater. Born and raised in New Orleans, he experienced the color and pageantry of the Mardi Gras celebration throughout his youth and college years. Through his studies he came to realize that the carnival characters that annually paraded the streets of his hometown were actually works of art rooted in theatrical traditions. His one-man show, *The Mask Man,* provides insights into the artistic, psychological, and historical aspects of masks. In his performance, Faust transforms himself into more than 20 different characters. Some characters speak, wearing *commedia dell'arte* style half-masks. Other characters are created with full masks worn on top of the head or on the back of the head. These masks can transform the performer into creatures on all fours, or create distortions that baffle or surprise. Masks, found in many cultures throughout the world, are worn at festivals, celebrations, and rituals. In whatever ways they are used, masks have the power to transform an ordinary person into someone or something else.

DISCUSSION QUESTIONS
1. The photo on this page shows Robert Faust with masks from *The Mask Man.* Study the expression of the masks. What kinds of personalities are being shown? What can you tell about the character's age, culture, and personality traits from the mask alone?
2. How might a mask be used in the theatre?
3. The first Greek masks were used in plays to impersonate gods. What Greek gods and goddesses can you name? What were their attributes or symbols?
4. Masks are often part of festivals, celebrations, and rituals. Describe activities you have participated in that used masks.

CREATIVE EXPRESSION ACTIVITIES
Language Arts Read Greek myths or Greek stories such as "Theseus and the Minotaur" or "The Golden Fleece." How might masks be used in these works?

Art Create a two-sided mask showing contrasting feelings on each side. You might choose happy and sad, or good and evil. Think of movements to go with your mask to express each emotion.

APPRECIATING THE PERFORMING ARTS

As a device for theatre, masks evolved from religious practices of ancient Greece. The traditional masks depicting Tragedy and Comedy are derived from Greek theatrical traditions. One advantage of using masks in a performance is that they can be seen from a distance; they are often larger than the human head. The mask holds enchantment and fascination, and still retains a deep and complex meaning in many cultures. Masks are worn to evoke magic; to hide and deceive; to project humor, beauty, ugliness, and mystery; as protection; and as replicas of people who have died.

Ranganiketan Manipuri Cultural Arts Troupe

*M*anipur, called the "Jewel of India," is a secluded state situated at India's northeastern frontier. Located in an oval-shaped valley, it is tucked within nine ranges of the Himalayan mountains. The ancient culture there has been preserved intact for thousands of years, meticulously passed on from one generation to the next by master artists and teachers. Ranganiketan, a cultural group, travels throughout the world sharing the culture through its music and dance. The dance, "Vasanta Rasa Lila," featured in the photo is a classical dance believed to have been created by the Hindu god Krishna. It was communicated to King Jai Singh in 1750 through a vision. The dance was re-created to exact specifications, including style and costumes. "Rasa Lila" is performed in the spring and celebrated along with Holi, the Festival of Colors, in which the dancers spray each other with colored powder or water. It begins in the early evening and continues for eighteen hours.

Ranganiketan dancer performing "Vasanta Rasa Lila."
Photo: Craig Schwartz.

DISCUSSION QUESTIONS

1. Study the costumed dancer in the photo on this page. Describe the details of her dress.
2. The people of Manipur believe that everything is divinely inspired, including all of their artistic expressions. What do you think this means?
3. From an early age, young children commit to an honored and respected relationship with a specific master teacher. If you were a master teacher to a young child, what important ideas would you want to teach him or her?

CREATIVE EXPRESSION ACTIVITIES

Dance The dances of India incorporate gestures that symbolize an idea or image. Create gestures to show the concept of the following words: tree, mountain, stream, rain, boat, friend, fish. Select three words and accompany each with an original gesture. Share and combine words and gestures with classmates.

Geography Locate India in an atlas or on a globe, and then identify Manipur (it is in the northeast corner). Read about this region to discover the topography and climate. How might the environment influence the culture (such as food, clothing, ways of doing things). Can you see any of these influences in the costume of the dancer?

Ranganiketan Manipuri Cultural Arts Troupe

Optional Viewing Selection:
■ Artsource® VHS tape, video segment 6 (playing time 9:09)

Setting the Stage
Have students read the paragraph about Ranganiketan and East Indian dance, and show the Artsource® video, if available.

Connecting the Arts
Using the Discussion Questions on this page, help students recognize that, throughout history, dance and music have been an intricate part of most traditional cultures. Possible responses:
1. The colors are bright and shiny. The dancer is wearing a veil; the top portion of her skirt is full and ruffled; the bottom portion disguises her legs.
2. Spiritual forces, or gods, create everything; they are responsible for human ideas and emotions.
3. Students may suggest truth, discipline, hard work, importance of study, respect for self and others.

Extension
■ After students have responded to the Discussion Questions and, if possible, viewed the Artsource® selection, have them complete the Creative Expression Activities.

Use the Artsource® Performing Arts package, Lesson 7, for more information about the music and dance of Manipur and for additional activities.

APPRECIATING THE PERFORMING ARTS

Dance and music are deeply rooted in Hindu life. The people of Manipur believe that everything is divinely inspired. As a symbol of their humility, the performers always touch the floor and then their forehead before they begin. From an early age, young children commit to an honored and respected relationship with a specific master teacher. Their dances are centuries old; it is believed that many dances were performed in the spiritual world before they were performed on earth.

Chuna McIntyre

Optional Viewing Selection:
■ Artsource® VHS tape, video segment 7 (playing time 7:43)

Setting the Stage
Direct students to read the paragraph about Chuna McIntyre and view the Artsource® video, if available.

Connecting the Arts
Using the Discussion Questions on this page, help students understand the ancient tradition of Yup'ik dance, song, and story. Possible responses:

1. Students may recognize some or all of these materials: seal skin; arctic squirrel fur; caribou hair; wolverine fur; rabbit hair; wolf fur; ivory; land otter fur; trade beads; earth pigments.
2. Both have a frame, and both have a skin stretched over the frame; both are struck with a kind of stick.
3. Students may suggest folk dances, folk songs, games, religious practices, holiday customs, and birthday celebrations.

Extension
■ After students have responded to the Discussion Questions and, if possible, viewed the Artsource® selection, have them complete the Creative Expression Activities.

Use the Artsource® Performing Arts package, Lesson 8, for more information about Chuna McIntyre and Yup'ik culture.

ART SOURCE
ARTSOURCE

Chuna McIntyre

PERFORMING ARTS HANDBOOK

Chuna McIntyre with a traditional Yup'ik Eskimo mask.
Photo: Craig Schwartz.

Chuna McIntyre, a Yup'ik Eskimo, was born and raised in the tiny village of Eek, Alaska, on the shores of the Bering Sea. It was there that Chuna learned the ancient traditions—the dances, songs, and stories of his Eskimo ancestors who were an integral part of village life when he was growing up. He first became aware of this culture from the stories his grandmother told him as a child. In these stories the animals sang and danced. When Chuna was a young boy, she taught him his first dance, the "Arctic Squirrel Dance." In a society with no written history, cultural traditions are passed down from generation to generation. The songs, dances, rituals, and costumes provide the narratives that keep history alive. Yup'ik dance encompasses many elements: movement, music, storytelling, folklore, masks and other art objects such as dance fans, dance sticks, headdresses, and jewelry. They are all woven together into one creative, unified work within Yup'ik ceremonies.

DISCUSSION QUESTIONS

1. Describe Chuna's ceremonial costume. Can you identify specific components or materials used in making his parka, headdress, and boots?
2. The Yup'ik drum is a large hoop covered with a membrane of seal or walrus. Look closely at the drum lying on the ground in the picture. How does this ancient drum compare to a modern drum?
3. Yup'ik dance, songs, and stories are part of an oral tradition passed down from elders through the centuries. Do you know of, or participate in, any rituals or customs that have been passed down through the ages? If so, describe them.

CREATIVE EXPRESSION ACTIVITIES

Art Chuna McIntyre's costume is designed to incorporate elements native to Alaska and ceremonial colors symbolic to the Yup'ik. The red connotes Yup'ik ancestorial blood, white represents snow or caribou fat, and black symbolizes the spirit world. Design your own costumes including the following components: garments, footwear, head coverings, accessories, use of color, symbolic or cultural elements, and a description of the dance or ceremony in which it will be worn.

Language Arts The words of Yup'ik songs are often written in the form of a poem. Write a poem or song about some aspect of man's relationship to the earth, sea, or sky. Use a specific rhyme scheme and meter for the structure.

APPRECIATING THE PERFORMING ARTS

In Yup'ik culture, people danced for pleasure, as well as to communicate with the spirits that shared their world and affected their lives. They danced to break up the monotony of long, cold winters, to nurture a sense of community, to relieve stress, and to welcome visitors. Recreational dancing was part of social gatherings, and ceremonial dances were performed during religious festivals.

There was no formal training or dance school in traditional Yup'ik culture. People learned dances by watching others perform. Yup'ik dance was pure folk dance; it could be done by everyone and was not restricted to professionals or specialists.

Anna Djanbazian

Members of the Djanbazian Dance Company performing "Sarve Kashmir." Photo: Craig Schwartz.

*C*horeographer, dancer, and teacher Anna Djanbazian began dancing at the age of three in her father's ballet school in Tehran, Iran. Her father, an extraordinary dance artist, was recognized as a National Treasure by the Shah of Iran. The daughter of a Persian mother and Armenian father, Anna grew up with a rich personal heritage. Her love of classical and cultural dance and art was encouraged in the artistic community that surrounded her family. After earning a degree in classical ballet and Armenian folk dance in Russia, she returned to Tehran, took over her father's school and began her own career as a teacher and choreographer. For twelve years, she produced and staged over forty-three dances and eight ballets. Following in her father's footsteps, she opened the Djanbazian Ballet Studio in Glendale, California, in 1988. Anna continued to explore modern dance at the University of California at Los Angeles (UCLA), earning a master's degree. While at UCLA, she was able to expand its potential for enriching her work. In 1991, she achieved her dream and formed a troupe of dynamic performers, trained in her school, who perform her cultural dances throughout southern California.

PERFORMING ARTS HANDBOOK

DISCUSSION QUESTIONS

1. Study the photo on this page. Discuss the emotions that the dancers express.
2. Examine the costumes that the dancers are wearing. What do the costumes suggest about the people, the geography, and the dance style performed in Armenia?
3. Anna Djanbazian states, "I want to keep the dances of my culture alive—to stay connected to their roots. But time is always going forward and I feel this need to grow and look at them with a new vision that is a contemporary art but still remains cultural." Discuss what you think she means.

CREATIVE EXPRESSION ACTIVITIES

Geography Armenia's geographic location is in the southern Caucasus mountainous area that covers part of Iran, Turkey, and the former U.S.S.R. A rocky terrain made access to stone, a primary building material easy to procure. Discuss how geography and natural resources can influence the architecture, crafts, and art of the culture.

Language Arts *Arabian Nights* is a collection of classic fairy tales set in the Middle East. This famous book has inspired many popular films. Compare and contrast traditional and contemporary re-tellings of this classic fairy tale.

APPRECIATING THE PERFORMING ARTS

Interlace, choreographed by Djanbazian in 1992, is a traditional Armenian dance based on the structural elements in Armenian churches built between the fourth and the seventeenth centuries. Traditional Armenian music supports the elegant sense of flow and the communal formations that are seen as the dance takes place. Graceful arm and hand movements and interlocking arms echo the lines and motifs seen on the buildings. Circular floor pathways that spiral in and out, linear formations with intricate connections between the dancers, and weaving patterns of bodies and arms visually highlight the graceful movements and quiet strength of the dance. Stunning costumes complete the performance and highlight the cultural traditions of Armenia.

Anna Djanbazian

Optional Viewing Selection:

■ Artsource® VHS tape, video segment 8 (playing time 9:52)

Setting the Stage

Direct students to read the paragraph about choreographer, dancer, and teacher Anna Djanbazian, and have them examine the photograph. Then show the Artsource® video, if available.

Connecting the Arts

Using the Discussion Questions on this page, help students recognize the cultural dances and heritage that Djanbazian shares with others in her work. Possible responses:

1. Dancers appear to feel serene and involved in their movement.
2. The dancers' costumes appear to be based on traditional Armenian and Persian outfits.
3. Djanbazian is interested in preserving historical and cultural traditions and in expressing new ideas and staying in touch with modern audiences.

Extension

■ After students have responded to the Discussion Questions and viewed the Artsource® video, have them complete the Creative Expression Activities.

Use the Artsource® Performing Arts package, Lesson 9, for more information about the dance traditions of Armenia and for additional related activities.

Paul Salamunovich

Optional Listening Selection:
■ Artsource® audiotape, audio segment 2 (playing time 1:15)

Setting the Stage
Direct students to read about Paul Salamunovich and Gregorian chants. Then have them listen to the Artsource® audiotape, if available.

Connecting the Arts
Using the Discussion Questions on this page, help students recognize that Gregorian chant, an ancient music style, has connections with modern music and musicians. Possible responses:

1. The simplicity, the smooth melodic lines, and the purity of tone often soothe the listener.
2. Students may mention game songs and chants, sports chants, cheers.
3. Students may name blues, spirituals, ballads, and opera.

Extension
■ After students have responded to the Discussion Questions and, if possible, viewed the Artsource® selection, have them complete the Creative Expression Activities.
■ Have students research the use—past and present—of Gregorian chant in religious services.

Use the Artsource® Performing Arts package, Lesson 10, for more information about Paul Salamunovich and for additional related activities.

A R T
S O U
R C
ARTSOURCE

PERFORMING ARTS HANDBOOK

Paul Salamunovich

The Los Angeles Master Chorale. Paul Salamunovich, director.
Photo: Robert Millard, Courtesy of the Los Angeles Master Chorale.

*P*aul Salamunovich first heard Gregorian chants as a young boy when he became a member of the Boys Choir at St. James Catholic Church in California. This early experience with music of the Middle Ages became a life-long pursuit. The young singer was inspired by famed choral director Roger Wagner when Wagner served at St. James Church as guest conductor. It began a close lifetime association. Paul recalls the thrill of being selected to sing in Wagner's Los Angeles Youth Honor Choir, which later became the Roger Wagner Chorale. The Chorale eventually became the Los Angeles Master Chorale with Paul Salamunovich as its director. Paul has gained recognition as an authority in the teaching and performance of Gregorian chant during his impressive career as a conductor, choral clinician, and music professor. Gregorian chant, or plainsong, was generally set to the words of the Psalms, which is poetry from the Old Testament of the Bible. Thus, even though the prose affected the structure of the melodic line, there emerged different styles for chanting each syllable.

DISCUSSION QUESTIONS

1. Gregorian chant is known for its pure, unaccompanied, nonrhythmic melodic lines. This is in direct contrast to most contemporary music. Why do you suppose Gregorian chant has recently become popular again?
2. Early Gregorian chants were performed solo or by groups of voices singing in unison. Name some chants or songs, usually performed in unison, that you might hear today.
3. One style of Gregorian chant—called melismatic —is when the singer(s) sing several notes on one syllable of a word. Identify some modern music styles that also use this style.

CREATIVE EXPRESSION ACTIVITIES

History It is believed that Gregorian chant was named for Pope Gregory I, who organized existing chant into a unified form. Identify another historical figure who has influenced an event, philosophy, or concept that was then named for that person.

Music Trained singers are able to ornament, or add extra notes, to a simple Gregorian chant, adding interest to the performance. Compare this practice with performances by contemporary popular singers.

Art Discuss the contributions of music and art to the Catholic church during the Middle Ages.

APPRECIATING THE PERFORMING ARTS

Gregorian chant evolved during the early Middle Ages. With the growth of the Catholic Church during that period, Pope Gregory elevated the chant of plainsong to prominence. The foundation of Gregorian chant, however, developed from a beautiful cultural mix. Middle Eastern and early Jewish music influenced its development. From Greece came the Byzantine chant and from Italy the Ambrosian chant. The Gallican chant, which had been in use in France and Spain and was influenced by the Moors, developed into the Mozarabic chant. The Los Angeles Master Chorale, directed by Paul Salamunovich, is known worldwide today for its purity of tone, treatment of high notes and flawless shape of phrase—all greatly influenced by the basic sounds of Gregorian chant.

Diana Zaslove

*S*inger Diana Zaslove performs popular songs of the sixteenth and seventeenth centuries. The mood of this dynamic time following the Renaissance was one of optimism and discovery. During this period composers began to emphasize the expressiveness of the human voice as a solo instrument. Poetry and music were combined to express a variety of emotions, especially aspects of love. Before the Renaissance, most music was written for the Church to express religious, or sacred, themes. Now, for the first time, music was written to express the human spirit and worldly, or secular, themes. The lute, similar to the guitar, was the most popular instrument of this period and was often used to accompany singers.

Diana Zaslove, lyric soprano. Photo: Craig Schwartz.

PERFORMING ARTS HANDBOOK

DISCUSSION QUESTIONS

1. Look carefully at the photograph of Zaslove in performance. Discuss how the type of music she sings is reflected in her dress and manner.

2. Composers of this period wrote music for more than one solo voice, sometimes for up to four or five voices in harmony. Before this time, the instruments usually played the same part that was being sung. Now the vocalist would sing the melody while the lute player carried the parts of all the other voices. This allowed the beauty of all the harmony parts to be heard. Discuss how Renaissance ideas allowed for the development of harmony.

CREATIVE EXPRESSION ACTIVITIES

Language Arts Write a rhythmical poem that expresses an aspect of love, such as friendship, loss, devotion, or romance. You may also want to set your poem to music.

Music/Dance Instrumental music and dance of this period were intimately connected. Many of the patrons who supported musicians were people of wealth and power. They commissioned works for special occasions that often included dancing. Research some dance forms such as the galliard, pavane, ronde, or bergerette.

APPRECIATING THE PERFORMING ARTS

One of the most interesting aspects of sixteenth- and seventeenth-century music was the collaboration between exceptional lyric poets and composers. During this time, words took on new importance and were carefully selected to express different emotions, especially love. Much of the music was written for theatre, to be performed in plays. This musical Renaissance started in the Netherlands, but the composers and poets were so popular, they were enticed to perform their music in Spain, Bohemia, Austria, Germany, and the cities of northern Italy. Each country had a specific Renaissance style; however, as composers moved among these countries, the character of each style was influenced by the others.

Diana Zaslove

Optional Listening Selection:
■ Artsource® audiotape, audio segment 3 (playing time 4:27)

Setting the Stage
Direct students to read the paragraph about Diana Zaslove and her performance of sixteenth- and seventeenth-century music. Then have students listen to the Artsource® audiotape, if available.

Connecting the Arts
Using the Discussion Questions on this page, help students recognize how Renaissance music and songs were reflections of the historical time period and culture. Possible responses:

1. Her dress echoes the style of Renaissance clothing, and her manner appears relaxed and optimistic, reflecting the music she sings.

2. People felt that established rules could be bent or broken and new ways were not seen as wrong, but instead as interesting and inventive.

Extension
■ After students have responded to the Discussion Questions and, if possible, listened to the Artsource® audiotape, have them complete the Creative Expression Activities.

Use the Artsource® Performing Arts package, Lessons 11, 12, for more information about Diana Zaslove and music of the Renaissance period.

Jennifer Tipton

Optional Listening Selection:

- Artsource® audiotape, audio segment 5 (playing time 9:40)

Setting the Stage

Direct students to read the paragraph about Jennifer Tipton and Shakespeare's play, *The Tempest*. Then have students listen to the Artsource® audiotape, if available.

Connecting the Arts

Using the Discussion Questions on this page, help students recognize the power of plays to show aspects of the human experience. Possible responses:

1. A director is like the conductor of an orchestra. He or she brings a vision to the words and concepts in the play and directs and coordinates the efforts of the team.
2. Tipton had experience in many aspects of performing; she was a dancer, a rehearsal director, and a lighting designer.
3. Students may mention the immediacy of a live performance and the possibilities of interaction between performers and audience members.

Extension

- After students have responded to the Discussion Questions and, if possible, listened to the Artsource® audiotape, have them complete the Creative Expression Activities.

Use the Artsource® Performing Arts package, Lesson 13, for more information about the responsibilities of a director and for additional related activities.

Jennifer Tipton

The Guthrie Theatre Ensemble and Cityscape. Jennifer Tipton, director. *The Tempest,* by William Shakespeare, 1991 Production. Photo: Michal Daniel.

Jennifer Tipton's artistry and vision have established her as one of the world's premier lighting designers for theatre, dance, and opera. She planned to major in astrophysics at Cornell University, but before long, a love of dance superseded her other interests. After graduation, she studied with Martha Graham and joined the Merry-Go-Rounder, a dance troupe that performed for children. When Tipton became rehearsal director for the troupe, she had to design their lighting as well. Soon she gave up dancing to concentrate solely on lighting. In 1991, she directed her first play, *The Tempest,* by William Shakespeare, at The Guthrie Theater in Minneapolis, Minnesota. It is a story of love, revenge, justice, despair, hope, and wisdom, all interwoven in a delicate web of poetry, imagination, and magic.

DISCUSSION QUESTIONS

1. What do you think the director of a play is responsible for?
2. How do you think Tipton's experience helped her to direct a play?
3. How do you think viewing a theatre production of *The Tempest* would be different from seeing a performance video?

CREATIVE EXPRESSION ACTIVITIES

Language Arts Work with a group to select a Shakespearean sonnet and perform it as a choral reading. Highlight the poetry and rhythm of the verse. You may have all voices reading in unison, two groups of voices, solos, or use various combinations. Try to vary the dynamics and texture of the vocal sound.

Dance The Guthrie Theater production of *The Tempest* incorporates the movement technique of mirroring in the staging of the play. With a partner, practice creating mirror images and movements. Take turns leading and following.

Language Arts Explore some of Shakespeare's most well-known quotations and discuss their meanings. For example, consider Jaques' statement in a scene from *As You Like It,* "All the world's a stage, and all the men and women merely players," (Act 2, Scene 7).

APPRECIATING THE PERFORMING ARTS

The great poet-dramatist William Shakespeare was born in 1564, and was a popular and successful playwright and actor in London. During his 20 years in London, Shakespeare wrote 37 plays, 5 long poems, and 154 sonnets. He retired in 1613, and died in 1616, on his 52nd birthday.

The actors who performed in Elizabethan times were all men. Women were not permitted on the English stage, so female roles were allocated to boys. The acting troupes, which had eight to fifteen in a company, by law had to secure a legal position and obtain a license from a powerful nobleman. He allowed the troupe to be called his servants and thus perform in his group. These actors had extensive training in acting; they also developed their skills as dancers, jugglers, singers, acrobats, and fencers.

Los Angeles Baroque Orchestra

Los Angeles Baroque Orchestra

Gregory Maldonado received his first violin when he was 12 years old. He was in his hometown of Merced, California, when he saw the instrument in a pawn shop window. "If you buy me that violin," he told his mother, "I'll make you proud one day." She went into the shop and bought the instrument. Gregory immediately began teaching himself to play with a "how-to" book. He went on to take lessons, play in orchestras, major in music at a university, study in Europe, and form his own musical company, the Los Angeles Baroque Orchestra. While completing his degree in violin performance at the University of California, Los Angeles, he heard a concert of Baroque music played by a period-instrument orchestra. The beautiful sound overwhelmed him. It was sweeter than any music he had ever heard. Baroque music was a style played during the seventeenth and eighteenth centuries by composers such as Johann Sebastian Bach. He soon packed away his modern, steel-stringed instrument and dedicated himself to the Baroque violin, a smaller, more reverberant instrument, with a shorter neck, and strings made of natural material.

Los Angeles Baroque Orchestra. Photo: Gene Partyka.

DISCUSSION QUESTIONS

1. Study the photo on this page and describe the instruments that you see. Why do you think different styles of the same instrument produce different sounds?

2. Why do you think Mr. Maldonado thought it was important to play music from the Baroque period on an authentic period instrument, rather than a modern one?

3. The Baroque period of music occurred between the seventeenth and eighteenth centuries, during the time that the first permanent English settlement was founded in America, and during the time when Shakespeare died. Can you think of other important events that took place during this period?

CREATIVE EXPRESSION ACTIVITIES

Music/History Johann Sebastian Bach's six *Brandenburg Concertos* are among the most popular of the Baroque style of music. Find out what other musical works Bach composed in his lifetime. Share what characterized Bach's musical style with your classmates.

Art The Baroque period in history was a time of enormous creativity, exploration, and inventiveness, not only in music but also in nearly all the arts and sciences. Create your own artwork that captures the essence of this exciting period in history. Do some research to find out what other inventions were introduced during this time to help you generate ideas for your artwork.

Setting the Stage

Direct students to read about Gregory Maldonado and the Los Angeles Baroque Orchestra. Have them listen to the Artsource® audiotape.

Connecting the Arts

Using the Discussion Questions on this page, help students recognize the importance of Baroque music. Possible responses:

1. Performers are holding various kinds of stringed instruments. Differences in size, materials, and age can make instruments produce different sounds.

2. He probably felt that music would sound more authentically Baroque when played on a period instrument.

3. Students may mention, for example, the French Revolution, the first use of smallpox inoculations, and the construction of St. Paul's Cathedral.

Extension

■ After students have responded to the Discussion Questions and, if possible, listened to the Artsource® audiotape, have them complete the Creative Expression Activities.

Use the Artsource® Performing Arts package, Lesson 14, for more information about the music of the Baroque period.

Optional Listening Selection:

■ Artsource® audiotape, audio segment 6 (playing time 13:17)

APPRECIATING THE PERFORMING ARTS

The *Brandenburg Concertos*, composed by Johann Sebastian Bach, are among the most celebrated, most played, and most recorded works in the entire Baroque repertoire. The pieces were not written in Brandenburg at all, but in Cöthen, Belgium, where Bach was employed by Prince Leopold. On a visit to Berlin, while negotiating the purchase of a new harpsichord for the Prince's castle, Bach met the Margrave (or hereditary ruler) of Brandenburg, Christian Ludwig, and played for him. The Margrave was so impressed with Bach that he invited the composer to submit some scores. Bach compiled the collection of six concertos and dedicated them to the Margrave of Brandenburg. Ironically, the Margrave apparently never used the score, never thanked Bach, and never paid him. Luckily, Bach composed to please himself; his work is intensely personal.

Natividad (Nati) Cano

Optional Listening Selection:
■ Artsource® audiotape, audio segment 7 (playing time 4:33)

Setting the Stage
Direct students to read the paragraph about Nati Cano and mariachi music. Then have them listen to the Artsource® audiotape, if available.

Connecting the Arts
Using the Discussion Questions on this page, help students recognize and appreciate mariachi as a distinctly Mexican style of music. Possible responses:

1. Guitar and violins are shown. Other instruments include vihuelas, trumpets, harp, and guitarron.
2. They need to pay attention to one another, so their sounds are balanced and work together, without any one instrument overwhelming the others.
3. Students may mention familiar foods such as tacos and burritos, and specific local names.

Extension
■ After students have responded to the Discussion Questions and, if possible, listened to the Artsource® selection, have them complete the Creative Expression Activities.

Use the Artsource® Performing Arts package, Lesson 15, for more information about Nati Cano and mariachi music.

590

Natividad (Nati) Cano

PERFORMING ARTS HANDBOOK

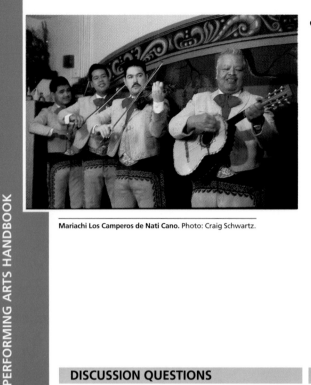

Mariachi Los Camperos de Nati Cano. Photo: Craig Schwartz.

*I*t is no surprise that Natividad (Nati) Cano chose music as a career. Born in Mexico, he grew up in a family of *jornaleros* (day workers). His family saw music as a way to earn additional money, as well as a joyous outlet from working the soil. His grandfather played the *guitarron,* the bass instrument of mariachi ensembles. A mariachi ensemble also includes violins, guitars, *vihuelas,* trumpets, and a harp. His father, a versatile musician, played all of the instruments of the mariachi, except the trumpet. Natividad began to play the *vihuela,* a five-stringed, rounded-back guitarlike instrument at the age of six. At the age of eight, he began violin lessons at the Academia de Musica in Guadalajara, Mexico. Gradually, his musical experiences, technical skills, and knowledge broadened until he became the musical director of his own group, Los Camperos de Nati Cano. Although his group performs compositions from different regions in Mexico, his arrangements adhere to the mariachi instrument ensemble and style.

DISCUSSION QUESTIONS

1. Look at the photo on this page and identify the mariachi instruments shown. Which other instruments are usually included in a mariachi ensemble?
2. What qualities or traits might be important for musicians to have if they play in an ensemble?
3. Mexico's proximity to the United States has had a cultural impact on the southwestern states. Give examples of how the Mexican culture has impacted American culture (for example, food, clothing, sports, celebrations, architecture, and names of cities and streets).

CREATIVE EXPRESSION ACTIVITIES

Geography Find an atlas or globe and look up the Mexican states of Jalisco, Colima, Michoacan, Nayarit, and Sinaloa, where mariachi music originated and continues to flourish. What else can you learn about these regions?

Math/Science Shape and size have great importance in music, just as they do in mathematics. The shape and size of instruments affect the sound that is created. For example, a trumpet needs a certain length and width of tubing to produce its pitch. Music is the manipulation of vibrations to produce different pitches, lengths of sound, rhythm, and tone color. Gather some hollow objects of different shapes and sizes. Discover how shape and size can affect sound by tapping on the objects or blowing through or across an opening.

APPRECIATING THE PERFORMING ARTS

The word *mariachi* can be used to identify the individual musician, the ensemble, or the musical genre itself. The mariachi originated in the rural areas of western Mexico, particularly from the states of Jalisco, Colima, Michoacan, Nayarit, and Sinaloa. The first groups were string-based, consisting primarily of violins, which provided the melodies, and the diatonic harp, which provided the bass line. The guitarron, a large rounded-back instrument, eventually replaced the harp in most ensembles. The five-string vihuela, a rounded-back instrument, and the guitar were also added. In the early 1930s the ensembles added a trumpet, and now most have two or three. Mariachi continues to evolve, but it never loses its ability to express the spirit of the Mexican culture.

AMAN International Folk Ensemble

AMAN International Folk Ensemble

The AMAN International Folk Ensemble was founded in 1964 to research, preserve and present the traditional dance, music, and folklore of the many ethnic groups residing in America. It depicts a wide variety of international cultural traditions, particularly those representing North American immigrants. A repertory company, AMAN takes its name from the word *Amen*, meaning "So be it!" It is an affirmative word used to add emphasis to a sentence or a thought. AMAN maintains regular education and community service activities, in addition to researching new work and fulfilling a full concert and touring schedule. They seek out experts in different forms of traditional dance to choreograph work for their company. For this suite of dances and music, they sought the expertise of choreographer Jerry Duke, who has staged Appalachian folklore and dance throughout the United States and seven European countries.

AMAN International Folk Ensemble. Photo: Craig Schwartz.

Optional Viewing Selection:
■ Artsource® VHS tape, video segment 9 (playing time 12:15)

Setting the Stage
Direct students to read the paragraph about AMAN International Folk Ensemble, a group of musicians and dancers, and view the Artsource® video, if available.

Connecting the Arts
Using the Discussion Questions on this page, help students recognize that folk dance is an expression of a culture. Possible responses:
1. The long, simple dresses and the plain shirts and vests suggest America during the time of the western movement.
2. People who know and love the same songs, music, and dances share an important bond. They feel connected to each other because of shared experiences, beliefs, values, and culture.
3. People wrote simple songs about the events of ordinary life, special characters, familiar feelings, and humor.

Extension
■ After students have responded to the Discussion Questions and, if possible, viewed the Artsource® selection, have them complete the Creative Expression Activities.

Use the Artsource® Performing Arts package, Lesson 16, for more information about AMAN and for additional activities.

DISCUSSION QUESTIONS

1. Study the photo of the AMAN International Folk Ensemble. What do the costumes tell you about the historical time period of the dance?
2. Discuss how dance and music allow a community to express common traditions and preserve the values of a culture.
3. Find a book of Appalachian folk songs and study the lyrics. Discuss the lyrics and how they often tell a story.

CREATIVE EXPRESSION ACTIVITIES

Language Arts Look at the photo on this page and discuss what you think is happening, as well as the mood portrayed. Write a paragraph describing what you think preceded the moment captured in the photo. Be very specific and descriptive.

Social Studies Select a member of your family, a neighbor, or an acquaintance who emigrated from another country. Interview the person to discover one or two of the most important events in history that happened at the time of his or her emigration. Find out if this historical event or climate influenced his or her decision to come to the United States.

Performing Arts Handbook 591

APPRECIATING THE PERFORMING ARTS

Almost every culture throughout history has a legacy of folk dance and music. It is a direct expression of the values, rhythms, and style of the cultural community. Folk dances reflect the history at the time in which they were created; they often give clues about work, social order, attitudes, climate, and geography. People who ride horses might include galloping, prancing, or leaping movements in their dances, while those who work in coal mines might include the work movements of miners. Those living in cold climates often use vigorous movement in their folk dances, while those in warmer climates may use slower, less energetic movement. Gestures usually represent universal emotions or aspects of the environment. Folk dances include everyone in the community and reinforce unity and traditions.

American Repertory Dance Company

Optional Viewing Selection:

■ Artsource® VHS tape, video segment 10 (playing time 7:24)

Setting the Stage

Direct students to read about the American Repertory Dance Company and their performance of Isadora Duncan's *Dance of the Furies*. Have students view the Artsource® video, if available.

Connecting the Arts

Using the Discussion Questions on this page, help students explore how artists derive inspiration for their creativity. Possible responses:

1. Students may point out that "dance" can be defined to include movement and expression.
2. The costume represents a Greek toga, and the plain wall suggests Greek architecture.
3. Students may mention, for example, myths about Narcissus, Psyche, and Arachne. Myths help people understand and accept the world and the place of humans in it.

Extension

■ After students have responded to the Discussion Questions and, if possible, viewed the Artsource® video, have them complete the Creative Expression Activities.

Use the Artsource® Performing Arts package, Lesson 17, for more information about the American Repertory Dance Company and for activities.

American Repertory Dance Company

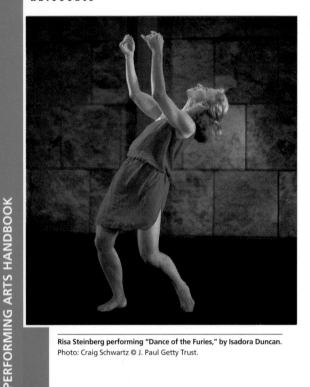

Risa Steinberg performing "Dance of the Furies," by Isadora Duncan.
Photo: Craig Schwartz © J. Paul Getty Trust.

*O*ne of the originators of twentieth-century modern dance was an American woman, Isadora Duncan, (1877-1927). This new style of dance that she created embodied a great zest for life and freedom of expression. Duncan was inspired by the splendors of the ancient Greeks and drew from this tradition to create a foundation for what she called the "Dance of the Future." Today, her work is preserved by such groups as the American Repertory Dance Company. The Company's mission is to sustain Duncan's formidable modern dance legacy through research, reconstruction, and performance of timeless choreography, such as seen in Isadora Duncan's "Dance of the Furies." Risa Steinberg, the dancer pictured here says, "I will never look like Isadora Duncan, but my goal is to strip away anything that wasn't her original intention." The Company's ultimate goal is to allow the audience to see the true intent behind American modern dance. This form of dance no longer tells a fairytale, but instead celebrates a dancer's body in ways never seen before.

DISCUSSION QUESTIONS

1. Isadora Duncan's starting point was a simple belief that dance is in all of us. Discuss the validity of her belief. Can we all dance?
2. Look at the photo on this page. What representations of ancient Greek influences do you see?
3. The "Dance of the Furies" are part of Greek myths. Describe any Greek myths with which you are familiar. What was the purpose of such mythology?

CREATIVE EXPRESSION ACTIVITIES

Language Arts Many Greek myths concern a descent into the dark, the labyrinth of the underworld. Orpheus is probably the best known of these myths. Read the myth of Orpheus, paying particular attention to the role the Furies play. Write a play or design a pantomime based on the Orpheus myth.

History As a dancer, Duncan was considered a rebel. During her lifetime, the women's suffrage movement had begun and women were calling for equal rights. How did Duncan's "new" ideal for dance fit in with the philosophies that produced such women's rights activists as Susan B. Anthony and Elizabeth Cady Stanton?

APPRECIATING THE PERFORMING ARTS

Theatre or concert dance is distinct from social dance or folk dance. Ballet is concert dance in which the artists are trained in a technique of specific dance aesthetics. Ballet is internationally recognized as having a clear structure that evolved from Renaissance court entertainments.

Modern dance developed in the twentieth century. It derived its form from the need to express the human spirit and emotion. In general, modern dance is intended to express personal emotions rather than pageantry or narrative.

Bang on a Can All-Stars

*B*ang on a Can is an exciting hybrid of many musical styles: rock, classical, folk, world, and electronic music collide in their vibrant, new sound. American composers Michael Gordon, David Lang, and Julia Wolfe founded the Bang on a Can festival in 1987. The festival is a one-week marathon of new and innovative music with no stylistic restrictions. The Bang on a Can All-Stars bring this challenging music to life with a combination of instruments resembling a rock band: drums, bass, electric guitar, keyboards, and cello. The All-stars are funky, daring, and highly energetic. Feelings of joy, fear, excitement, anxiety, and aggression are expressed in raw fashion. There is no experience required to listen to Bang on a Can. It is the perfect combination of a rock show and a classical concert. Powered by a cutting-edge attitude, Bang on a Can is clearly an undeniable force in the search and creation of new music.

Bang on a Can All-Stars. Counter-clockwise from top right: cellist Maya Beiser; clarinetist Evan Ziporyn; bassist Robert Black; guitarist Mark Stewart; pianist Lisa Moore; with a back-row stand-in for percussionist Steven Schick.

PERFORMING ARTS HANDBOOK

DISCUSSION QUESTIONS

1. Look at the photo. What kind of attitude do you think the Bang on a Can All-Stars have toward making music, and what might their music sound like?
2. How does the appearance of these musicians differ from that of a traditional musician in an orchestra? Can your attitude toward art impact your appreciation of art?

CREATIVE EXPRESSION ACTIVITIES

Language Arts Write a short concert review of your own imaginary musical ensemble that has a new and interesting combination of instruments. Include the musical styles that influenced your choice of instruments, the name of your group, and the sound of your music. Describe the message or emotion that your music will communicate to your audience.

Social Studies In small groups, discuss the following questions. What current social issues are important to you? What style of music would best describe these issues? What are the musical roots of your favorite band?

Performing Arts Handbook **593**

APPRECIATING THE PERFORMING ARTS

Modern American composers contribute greatly to an expanding definition of music. Charles Ives (1874–1954) combined American patriotic songs with interesting scales and harmonies in his *Variations on "America."* John Cage (1912–1992) used noises and strange sounds. In his piece *4'33"* (4 minutes, 33 seconds), Cage used only silence.

In the search for new sounds and methods musicians are challenged to find new techniques on their instruments. The artists of the Bang on a Can All-Stars strive to meet that challenge. In addition, they soak up the energy of their surroundings (New York City) and incorporate it into their unique and powerful music. The Bang on a Can All-Stars stretch the audience's imaginations.

PERFORMING ARTS
MUSIC

The Bang on a Can All-Stars

Optional Viewing Selection:
■ Artsource® audio tape, audio segment 8 (playing time 10:30)

Setting the Stage
Direct students to read the paragraph about the Bang on a Can All-Stars, a unique musical ensemble with many influences. Then have students listen to the Artsource® audiotape, if available.

Connecting the Arts
Using the Discussion Questions on this page, help students recognize that music is a living art form that evolves and changes. Possible responses:
1. The musicians appear to have a playful attitude toward music; their musical sounds are probably varied and not too "serious."
2. Though they are dressed formally, their attitude seems informal. Attitude plays an important role for creators of art and for viewers or audience members.

Extension
■ After students have responded to the Discussion Questions and, if possible, viewed the Artsource® selection, have them complete the Creative Expression Activities.

Use the Artsource® Performing Arts package, Lesson 18, for more information about the Bang on a Can All-Stars and the evolution of modern music in America.

Introducing Careers

This handbook introduces students to 12 careers within the art-related fields. Students are presented with an overview of the type of work and personal qualifications required of a person working in the featured occupation. In the bottom boxes under each career, addresses are provided so that students can research and obtain further information about the careers that interest them.

Using the Handbook

Try the teaching strategies that appear next to each of the career interviews to introduce students to the many art-related job opportunities and careers. Encourage students to write to the addresses provided for more information, and suggest that students keep a file in their portfolios with any responses they receive about art careers for future reference.

M any challenging and rewarding occupations exist in the visual arts. Schools, museums, galleries, small businesses, and large corporations look for creative and knowledgeable persons for art and art-related positions. An awareness of some of these opportunities may help you as you begin thinking about your own career plans. The experiences offered in your art classes may spark your interest and enthusiasm for a career in art. For more detailed information concerning the careers outlined in this handbook as well as other areas of art, consult your art teacher, guidance counselor, and librarian. You may be surprised to find that art and art-related career opportunities are plentiful and quite varied.

Table of Contents

Teacher Notes _____

_____

_____

_____

_____

Art Director

To become an artist, you must gain an understanding of the elements and principles of art. You must see things in a visual way as compared to the written word. Whatever your medium, you will most likely want to achieve a unified effect. Like artists, art directors use their creative vision. They use it to develop materials for magazines or advertising agencies. Whether he or she uses striking photographs, clever illustrations, or elegant typefaces, it is the art director's ability to present a unified artistic concept that makes an ad campaign or magazine layout successful.

■ An art director explains the main design ideas for a new advertising campaign to a team of artists and copywriters.

"As an art director, I get great satisfaction from meeting the challenge of producing artistic work that entertains and informs people."

When he was offered the position of art director for a prominent advertising agency, Joe Meola knew he would be using his artistic talent as well as his communication and management skills to do the job he had always dreamed of doing. Art directors are the creative sources of advertising agencies and magazines. They create ideas and develop strategies for advertising campaigns and page layouts. They work with graphic artists, photographers, writers, marketing staff, and clients to oversee the entire creative process of the business.

To be a successful art director, you need to be creative and be able to work well with people. You also need an inventive mind to develop new themes that enhance the presentation of your publication or advertisement and you need to make connections to current events and trends. It is important to be able to communicate your ideas to a wide variety of other artists. Finally, you need to have a passion for excellence, and the ability to analyze and criticize each completed issue or campaign. To develop these skills, you need an interest in a variety of artistic media and some experience working on visually oriented publications.

Q: Does your job encourage creativity?

A: My job requires a strong artistic sense, as well as the creative ability to visualize a finished product. I have to make my creative vision known to others so that they can accomplish their role in the process.

Q: What art education or training is required for a career as an art director?

A: An art director needs a strong background in graphic art. Most art directors hold a bachelor's or master's degree in the field. You need to take classes in drawing, painting, graphic design, printmaking, and art history. But you must also study literature, English, and history, as these are essential to an understanding of concept development, writing, and publication. It is helpful to gain some experience in publishing while you study. For example, you can work on a yearbook, school newspaper, in a print shop, or in graphic design studio.

Q: Are there specific skills one needs?

A: Art directors need to be good at combining their own ideas and visions with the talents of many artists and writers. Therefore, the one skill you need, in addition to being artistic, is the ability to supervise others effectively.

Careers in Art Handbook 595

Art Director

Discussing the Career

Begin by encouraging students to share what they know about the work of art directors. Then have students read the feature introduction. Refer students to Chapter 2 for a review of the elements and principles of art. Ask: Why is it so important for an art director to understand these elements and principles?

Then have students meet in cooperative groups to read and discuss the feature interview. Ask group members to describe their own interest in this career. Which aspects of the work seem most appealing? Why?

Investigating the Career

Ask interested students to gather more information about the specific training and experience needed to become an art director. Students may find good career sources in the school library or in a counselor's collection of manuals and catalogs. Have these students share their findings with the rest of the class.

More About... **Art Directors.** If possible, arrange to have an art director visit the class. If you are not acquainted with a local art director, send letters of inquiry home with students, and ask other members of the faculty for their suggestions.

Help students prepare for the visit by planning questions they would like to ask. Encourage the visitor to prepare a very brief talk about his or her career and, if possible, to bring work samples. Then provide time for a question-and-answer session.

After the visit, have at least one student write a thank-you note on behalf of the entire class.

Graphic Designer

Discussing the Career

Ask students to describe some of the Web sites they have seen on the Internet that they find most interesting or attractive. Then ask: Who do you think designs those Web sites? What special skills do you imagine those people need? How do you imagine they feel about their work?

Have students read and discuss the feature introduction. Refer them to Chapter 3 for a brief review and discussion of various art media. Then have students work with partners to read and discuss the feature interview.

Investigating the Career

Ask a group of interested students to gather information about local colleges that offer degrees in graphic design. Have these students list their findings and evaluations, and share the list with the rest of the class. In addition, students may want to invite a representative of a graphic design department to visit the class.

Graphic Designer

The diverse media and methods available to artists make possible a kind of visual communication. The ability to communicate visually is also important to graphic designers. By knowing how to see with an artist's eye, the graphic designer is able to select and arrange type, art, photos, and borders for layouts to create attractive materials for businesses and organizations.

"I have always loved to draw and create images on computers. Becoming a graphic designer opened up a whole new world of creative possibilities for me. The best part is that I get paid to do what I most enjoy!"

■ This graphic designer works on a computer to create an appealing graphic design.

After taking a college course in computers, Phi Nguyen discovered that she could combine her technical skills with her artistic ability by becoming a graphic designer. Now, she works for a variety of companies designing everything from record labels to web sites. Graphic designers use a variety of print, electronic, and film media to create art that meets a client's needs. Most graphic designers use computer software to create promotional displays and marketing brochures for new products, visual designs for corporate literature, distinctive logos for products or businesses, and cover designs for music CDs or video cassettes. It doesn't stop there. Film credits and TV commercials are also often designed by graphic artists.

To be successful in this field, you need to be able to solve graphics problems conceptually and communicate your ideas clearly. Good graphic designers are resourceful and original thinkers. If you love to draw and to express yourself in a variety of media, you, too, can become a graphic designer.

Q: In what ways does your job encourage creativity?

A: When I was a kid, I remember someone telling me to stay "within the lines" as I drew in my coloring book. Most young artists probably do the opposite. I always enjoyed being both artistic and disciplined. For graphic designers, creativity and problem-solving go together. I am often asked to create original designs while, at the same time, I must meet a list of requirements, restrictions, and deadlines.

Q: What art education or training is required for a career as a graphic designer?

A: Nine out of ten graphic designers have a college degree, and most major in graphic design. College programs in graphic design provide training in art as well as in computer techniques and programs. Most designers specialize in a particular area such as illustration, typography, or packaging. You also need to take basic studio courses in drawing, painting, principles of design, and in art history.

Q: Are there any specific skills needed to be a graphic designer?

A: Yes. Graphic design requires artistic and technical skills. It is important to have a mechanical aptitude and a strong background in computers.

More About...

Schools of Art and Design. Students interested in a list of accredited schools of art and design should contact:

National Association of Schools of Art and Design
11250 Roger Bacon Drive, Suite 21
Reston, Virginia 22090

Art Critic

To gain a better understanding of a work of art, an art critic uses the four-step process of description, analysis, interpretation, and judgment. To help others find enjoyment and understanding, the critic weaves this process into a well-planned, carefully executed piece of writing. Art criticism can be informative, thought-provoking, and expressive.

"Writing about art gives me a great outlet for creative expression."

■ A group of students listens as the art critic points out different elements in a painting to explain its meaning and significance.

Harold Wiggins uses his talent for writing as a free-lance art critic for an art magazine. Art critics have the special ability to write about works of art in an informed and interesting way. They review exhibits at galleries and museums. They may also write about particular works, or recent books on art. Whatever the subject, the goal of the art critic is to teach the reader.

To succeed as an art critic, you need to get as much experience as you can working with or speaking to artists. In addition to excellent writing skills, you need a background in art and art history. An ability to conceptualize critically is also important. To develop these skills, you need to enjoy the writing and thinking process. Try your hand at a short piece of criticism on a local art exhibit. You may be well on your way to becoming an art critic.

Q: Does your job encourage creativity?

A: Writing to hold the interest of readers requires creativity and a sense of one's style. I try to write in such a way that my readers enjoy the subject and the whole experience of reading. I put something of myself into every piece I write.

Q: What art education or training is required for a career as an art critic?

A: Some art critics have no formal training in art criticism, but most have a background in art history or the fine arts. In college, I majored in art, and I also took courses in journalism and literature to develop strong writing skills.

Q: Are there any additional skills needed to critique art?

A: Yes. You need know the current issues and debates in the areas of art history or criticism you write about. You also need to be persistent and resourceful to produce the kind of written work publishers want.

Careers in Art Handbook **597**

Art Critic

Discussing the Career

Have students look at the photograph on this page and ask: What do you imagine is going on here? What do you think the adult might be saying to the students? How would you feel if you were in that person's situation?

Then have students read the feature introduction. You may want to refer them to the discussion of art criticism in Chapter 4. Finally, have students read the feature interview and share their responses in a class discussion.

Investigating the Career

Suggest that students work in groups to collect and discuss reviews written by two or more different art critics. Ask students to note both similarities and differences between the work of different critics. Then suggest that each group member write a review of an artwork or exhibit to be read by the rest of the group. This exercise will help students evaluate their own interest in the career. Those who find the activity especially stimulating should conduct further research in education, training, and work opportunities for art critics.

More About... **Art Critics.** Art critics now have a relatively new career option: they can become corporate art advisers. Increasingly, major corporations are interested in developing their art collections. Art advisers help corporations make appropriate additions to their collections of paintings, sculpture, and other artworks.

The duties of corporate advisers include purchasing artworks, developing a unified collection, and advising the corporation on laws and taxation as they apply to art. Advisers also speak to various groups about the corporation's collection and may organize traveling exhibitions.

Architect

Discussing the Career

Suggest that students review the photographs of Egyptian pyramids and temples in Chapter 7. Ask: What makes these structures so powerful and inspiring? What do you imagine about the ancient Egyptians who designed these structures?

Then have students read the feature introduction and interview. Discuss with them the background and the special skills and interests a person needs to succeed as an architect.

Investigating the Career

Suggest that interested students gather more information about educational opportunities for aspiring architects. If possible, have them interview students who are preparing to be architects or young architects just starting to work in the field. Have these volunteers discuss their findings with the rest of the class.

CAREERS IN ART HANDBOOK

Architect

The designers of the Egyptian pyramids and temples had an astonishing sense of space and proportion. Their ability to visualize and execute the construction of such massive stone and brick buildings was nothing short of genius. This is especially true when you consider that such feats were accomplished without the use of modern machinery or technology. Many of today's architects continue to be inspired by the impressive structures of the past. At the same time, they bring innovation to their designs. Chinese-American architect, I. M. Pei, brought the past into the present by designing and building a contemporary pyramid based on the ancient Egyptian model. Pei's high-tech glass pyramid serves as the new entrance to the Louvre museum in Paris, France.

■ The architect is working with a computer design program.

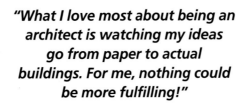

"What I love most about being an architect is watching my ideas go from paper to actual buildings. For me, nothing could be more fulfilling!"

After high school, Nancy Moretti wanted a career that would combine her love for drawing with her desire to create something practical and long lasting. She found the perfect job in the field of architecture. Responsible for the complete design of a building, an architect must take into consideration not only its appearance but also its function, cost, and accessibility. The architect often works closely with engineers, contractors, and urban planners. It is often the architect's job to make sure the design and the building codes and safety regulations are being followed.

To succeed in architecture, you need to be able to conceptualize, understand spatial relationships, and communicate your ideas visually. Good communications skills, the ability to work either independently or as part of a team, and creativity are also important.

Q: Does your job encourage creativity?

A: Yes, it does. Before I design a building or structure, I have to visualize all of its possible features. There are so many details that have to be integrated into a single, workable design. To me, planning a building that is both functional and beautiful is the ultimate creative act.

Q: What education or training is required for a career as an architect?

A: All states require that architects be licensed. To get your license, you need to hold a professional degree in architecture, usually from a 5-year bachelor of architecture program intended for students entering from high school. You need to take courses in architectural history and theory, building design, math, science, and liberal arts. However, central to most architecture programs is the design studio. Here students create three-dimensional models that put into practice the skills and concepts they learn in classes.

Q: Are there any specific skills needed to design buildings?

A: Yes. Designing a building involves bringing into harmony many varied factors. In order to visualize the finished project, you need to be detail-oriented.

More About...

Architecture. Suggest that students with a particular interest in architecture contact the American Institute of Architecture at:

American Institute of Architecture Students
1735 New York Avenue NW
Washington, D.C. 20006

Scenic Designer

The ancient Greeks are famous not only for their contribution to architecture but also for their development of the theater. Students of drama continue to read, act in, and imitate the enduring plays of Euripides and Sophocles. People interested in theatrical production are still inspired by the Greek amphitheater and its evolution. Today's scenic designers draw from classic styles as well as contemporary innovations to set the stages on which the dramas of our time unfold.

"The theater is like a second home to me. In fact, I may be more at home when I am working on the set of a play than I am in my own apartment!"

■ A scenic designer shows a model of a set he designed for a play to a theater visitor.

Frank Conrad discovered he could unite his talent for interior design and his passion for the theater by working as a scenic designer. Scenic designers are responsible for creating the look of the show by designing the sets. Working closely with the director and lighting designer, the scenic designer makes sure that the set, props, and backdrops produce the desired effects.

A successful scenic designer is creative and skilled at drawing, painting, and analyzing color. Strong communication skills and the ability to work well with others are valuable characteristics for this career, since this job demands good working relationships with producers, directors, lighting designers, carpenters, electricians, and crew members. Scenic designers should also be reliable and able to work efficiently under pressure. If you are interested in theater and design, then you can develop the skills needed to become a scenic designer.

Q: Does your job encourage creativity?

A: Yes. Creativity is essential to this job. I have to be able to take an idea from its inception and turn it into a reality on stage. I use my skills as a painter, as well as my knowledge of architecture and design, to create everything from turn-of-the-century street scenes to fantastic settings on other planets.

Q: What art education or training is required for a career as a scenic designer?

A: Most scenic designers have at least a bachelor's degree in theater arts, design, or a related field. Many colleges offer degrees in theater arts. To be a scenic designer, you should take courses in scenic design, art, lighting, and architecture. Courses in art history, drawing, and painting are also beneficial. Getting involved in school plays or volunteering at a community theater are great ways to get additional experience.

Q: Are there any specific skills needed to design sets?

A: In addition to creativity, scenic designers need the ability to conceptualize—picture an idea in their mind. A strong background in the theater and an understanding of staging techniques are also important.

Careers in Art Handbook **599**

Scenic Designer

Discussing the Career

In a brief introductory discussion, have students share their own experiences in viewing—and perhaps in helping to build or even design—sets for plays, musicals, and other productions. Then have students read the feature introduction. As they discuss the information in this section, you may want to have students review the photographs in Chapter 8; you might also ask volunteers to share information on Euripides and Sophocles.

Then have students meet in cooperative learning groups to read and discuss the feature interview. Ask group members to discuss the special background and skills an artist might need to succeed as a set designer, and encourage them to share their own responses to this career possibility.

Investigating the Career

Encourage interested students to research the theatre arts programs offered at local colleges. Students may also want to use online resources to learn about theatre arts programs in other parts of the country.

More About... **Set Design.** You may want to arrange a field trip—or have a small group of students arrange a field trip—to see a set designer at work. If you live in a major urban area, a commercial theater may welcome a visit from interested students. Many smaller cities, towns, and even neighborhoods have community theaters. These theaters use sets in their productions and are likely to enjoy a visit from high school students. Even closer to the classroom, you may find the school's theater or music department is designing and building sets for an upcoming production.

Urban Planner

Discussing the Career

Guide students in discussing their town or community. Ask: What evidence of planning do you see? What are the effects of the planning? What problems might be the result of a lack of planning?

Then have students read the feature introduction and briefly review Chapter 9. Ask: What do you think the urban planners of ancient Rome had in common with modern planners? What are the most significant differences?

Have students read the feature interview and, as a class, discuss their reactions. Help students explore the skills, interests, education, and training that a successful urban planner needs.

Investigating the Career

Have interested students use resources from the school library, counselor's office, career center, or online resources to gather information about schools that educate and train urban planners. Ask these students to share and discuss their findings with the rest of the class.

Urban Planner

We know a great deal about the art and architecture of ancient Rome because much of it has withstood the test of time. A visitor to today's Rome will marvel at the layout of a city whose ancient buildings, aqueducts, and roads are still a vital part of people's lives. Rome is an early example of urban planning at its best. Today's urban planners use computers and advanced research methods to design urban areas, but in many ways the work the Romans pioneered has not changed.

"I find my job as an urban planner deeply rewarding. I use all of my abilities to create designs aimed at improving people's daily lives."

■ An urban planner can use a computer to check on zoning laws in a neighborhood before issuing a building permit.

Maria Espinosa loves working to develop strategies for the best use of a community's land and resources. Urban planners work with local officials on plans to encourage growth or to revitalize areas. They may by involved in activities such as designing plans for alternative transportation systems or protecting the natural environment. Planners address issues such as traffic, air pollution, and the effects of growth and change on a community. They may also work on important social issues, such as plans for homeless shelters, parks, and correctional facilities.

Like artists, planners must be able to think in terms of spatial relationships. They must visualize the effects of their plans and designs. Planners should also be flexible and able to bridge the gap among different viewpoints. To be successful in this career, you need to be able to communicate well, both orally and in writing. You can develop these skills as you study art and other disciplines. If you are visually oriented and like to work with communities, you can become an urban planner, too.

Q: Does your job encourage creativity?

A: Yes, it does, but probably not in the usual ways. I must creatively visualize an area that I am planning. I imagine what it would be like to live or work there. I map the area in my mind, first. Then I factor in all of the variables and problems as I work on the design.

Q: What special education or training is required for a career as an urban planner?

A: Most employers prefer planners with advanced training. A bachelor's degree from an accredited planning program and a master's degree in architecture, landscape architecture, or civil engineering is good preparation. Many planners hold master's degrees in urban design or geography. It is also helpful to take college courses in related fields such as law, earth sciences, demography, finance, health administration, and geographic information systems. You will need to be familiar with computers and statistics, as well.

Q: Are there any specific skills needed to be an urban planner?

A: Often, the urban planner must work with various agencies, each of which has its own needs and interests. I think it helps if you are skilled at problem-solving. You need to be able to understand the needs and limitations of the city or community you are trying to help.

600 Careers in Art Handbook

More About...

Urban Planning. For additional information on careers in urban and regional planning, have students contact:

American Planning Association
1776 Massachusetts Ave. NW
Washington, D.C. 20036-1904

Landscape Architect

The designer of a Japanese Zen garden uses nature—trees, plants, rocks, and water—as a medium for art. Like a painting, the garden is both beautiful and symbolic. Its man-made elements are designed to work in harmony with the environment. The careful arrangement of paths, pools, and plants, as well as the use of sculpture, create a unique, peaceful experience for the visitor. Similarly, today's landscape architects design parks, residential areas, and shopping centers so they are functional, beautiful, and compatible with nature.

"I love working with living things. Being a landscape architect is a great job, because I am working to conserve nature and using my artistic ability at the same time."

Pat Jokela unites his knowledge of the environment with his artistic talents to design college campuses and industrial parks for a successful landscape architecture firm. As designers of the location of buildings, roads, walkways, and the arrangement of trees and flower gardens, landscape architects must find the best ways to conserve natural resources. They are responsible for analyzing the natural elements of a site, preparing a design, and complying with local and federal regulations, such as those that protect wetlands or endangered species.

Successful landscape designers enjoy working with their hands and have a good sense of spatial relationships. Creative vision and an ability to draw and draft are also desirable skills. Good oral communication skills, strong writing skills, and some knowledge of computers are necessary for conveying ideas to others. To develop these skills, you need an appreciation of nature and a willingness to study the technical subjects this job requires.

■ A landscape architect checks the placement of plants and trees in a shopping center's park he designed.

Q: Does your job encourage creativity?

A: It certainly does. Every site, every project is unique. Each time I start to work on a design, I feel as if I am creating a place I would want to visit. I try to imagine what it feels like to be there, not only for a person, but for all of the site's living inhabitants.

Q: What education or training is required for a career as a landscape architect?

A: A bachelor's or master's degree in landscape architecture is usually necessary to enter this profession. College courses required include surveying, landscape design and construction, landscape geology, site design, and urban planning. Students also study plant and soil science, geology, and environmental issues. The design studio is also important. Here students get hands-on experience designing real projects.

Q: Are there any specific skills needed?

A: Yes. An important element of landscape design is research. You need to be able to investigate the climate and circumstances of the site you are going to transform. You need to be able to gather information directly and from other experts. Then you must use what you have learned to create the design that is most compatible with the setting.

Careers in Art Handbook 601

CAREERS IN Art

Landscape Architect

Discussing the Career

Have students describe the scene in the photograph. Ask: What kind of artist works outdoors with plants? What do you think the advantages of this kind of work might be? What disadvantages would you expect?

After a brief discussion, have students read the feature introduction and review some of the photographs in Chapter 10. Then have students work with partners to read and discuss the feature interview. Encourage them to discuss why communication skills are important for a landscape architect.

Investigating the Career

Have students with a special interest in landscape architecture work together to learn more about this career. Ask them to gather information about opportunities for education and training in the field. Also suggest that they interview a local landscape architect. Let these students discuss their findings with the rest of the class.

More About...

Landscape Architects. Students who are interested in more information about careers for landscape architects and a list of colleges and universities that offer accredited programs in landscape architecture can write to:

American Society of Landscape Architects
Career Information
636 I St. NW
Washington, DC 20001-3736

Advertising Artist

Discussing the Career

Ask students to describe some of the advertisements they have seen frequently. Ask: Which ads attract your attention? Why?

Have students read the feature introduction. Help students review some of the symbols used in early Christian art, referring to Chapter 13, if necessary. Then ask: What are some symbols used in modern advertising? How are those symbols like the symbols used by the early Christians? How are they different?

Let students work with partners to read and discuss the feature interview. Suggest that partners share their thoughts and feelings about the possibility of a career as an advertising artist.

Investigating the Career

Have students with a particular interest in advertising art meet to share and discuss their ideas. Encourage them to learn about local opportunities for education and employment internships. Also encourage them to practice using their skills now, (for example, for a school paper or public affairs promotions).

CAREERS IN ART HANDBOOK

Advertising Artist

The symbols used by early Christian artists helped to tell the scripture stories in a visual way. A simple depiction of a dog, symbolizing faithfulness, or the portrayal of praying hands, suggesting the struggle for salvation, are common images in the artworks of this time. Today, symbols can still be found in art and in the images we see daily. Although they are not necessarily religious, the symbols of our society function in much the same way that early Christian symbols did. They bring messages to the public. They tell us cultural stories we already know. Where can you find such symbolic images? They are all around us in the art and images of advertisements.

■ An advertising artist uses a computer to create and record the images and symbols she is creating for an advertising campaign.

"I wanted a high-energy career as an artist. I like to be creative under a little pressure. Working as an artist for an advertising agency is perfect for me."

After graduating from college with a major in illustration, Janice McKiernan got a job as a layout and paste-up artist for a large advertising firm. Because of her strong artistic ability and enthusiasm for the fast pace of advertising work, she was promoted to assistant art director after one year. Beginning artists who work in the advertising industry may get jobs creating storyboards (drawings roughly depicting the ideas for an advertisement that are presented to clients). Another area for artists is in the production of layouts and paste-ups (dummy and drawings), which involves pasting type in position and sizing photographs.

To succeed as an advertising artist, you need a strong ability to draw, an eye for color and realistic representations, and speed, because you are usually asked to create your assignments quickly. It helps to have a love for drawing and an interest in the business of advertising.

602 Careers in Art Handbook

Q: Does your job encourage creativity?

A: Absolutely. I am expected to be creative both artistically and conceptually. I have to think about the meaning and impact of every aspect of an image.

Q: What art education or training is required for a career as an advertising artist?

A: Most advertising artists hold a bachelor of fine arts (BFA) degree in illustration and drawing. Many people working in this industry have an extensive background in fine arts, too. In addition to taking basic studio courses in art, you should study art history, film, and photography. Classes in English and literature are also useful, since you will need to match images and text, follow themes, and represent symbols in your work. Finally, some experience with new digital technologies will help you keep up with ongoing changes in the ways ads are produced and presented.

Q: Are there any specific skills needed to create art for ads?

A: Ad artists need strong artistic and communication skills. An understanding of human nature and an awareness of trends in popular culture are also very helpful.

More About...

Advertising Careers. Suggest that students who are interested in information about careers in advertising management write to:

American Advertising Federation
1101 Vermont Ave., NW
Washington, D.C. 20005-3521

Illustrator

The term *illustrate,* derived from the Latin *illustrare,* means "to make bright" or "illuminate." Artists began illuminating manuscripts as early as the fifth century. By the thirteenth century, artwork was being used to illustrate the Book of Psalms and religious history. Today, children's books provide some of the finest examples of book illustration. American artist Maxfield Parrish created brilliantly colorful and finely detailed illustrations for many publications. Illustrations can be imaginative works of art in themselves, but their main purpose is to illuminate the text they accompany.

■ An illustrator puts the finishing touches to an illustration.

"Illustrating children's books lets me live a part of my life in the realm of fantasy and make-believe. My imagination soars when I am drawing and painting!"

While studying fine art, Ellen Schmidt fell in love with the artwork she found in twentieth-century children's books. She decided to apply her skills as an artist to a career in book illustration. The job of an illustrator is to paint or draw pictures for books, magazines, and other products. Since pictures often draw readers into a text, a well-conceived illustration must be artistic, thought-provoking, and meaningful. In children's books especially, the illustrations are often used as the primary means of telling the story.

To be a successful illustrator, you need to have a strong ability in the areas of drawing and painting. You need a vivid imagination and a flexible style and approach. Good communication skills are also helpful since you need to work closely with writers and art directors. To gain these skills, you need to develop both your abilities as an artist and your background in art.

Q: Does your job encourage creativity?

A: Yes, indeed. The illustrator is the creative visual force behind the project. To me, giving a visual form to words or concepts is what being an artist is all about.

Q: What art education or training is required for a career as an illustrator?

A: Most illustrators obtain a bachelor of fine arts (BFA) degree and majored in painting and drawing. In addition to studying basic art techniques and working extensively in the art studio, you should also study art history, especially twentieth-century American art. If you are interested in a particular area of illustration, such as children's books, then you should study the literature and history of that area as well.

Q: Are there any specific skills needed to be an illustrator?

A: Yes. Many illustrators work as freelance artists, meaning they do not always keep regular hours or get regular paychecks. Many work at home or in studios. To succeed under these conditions, you need to be a self-motivated individual with a disciplined attitude toward drawing and painting.

Careers in Art Handbook **603**

Illustrator

Discussing the Career

Have students begin by reviewing the illuminated manuscripts shown in Chapter 15. Ask students to compare these works with illustrations in modern books. Ask: What are the most important similarities? How are the two kinds of art different? What is the particular appeal of each?

After this discussion have students read the feature introduction and interview. Guide them in discussing the interests, skills, and education a successful illustrator should have.

Investigating the Career

Have interested students learn more about opportunities for illustrators and about the colleges and institutes that offer appropriate training. In addition, suggest that these students collect examples of illustrations they find the most interesting or attractive. Encourage them to keep an illustrations journal of their own sketches and drawings.

More About...

Illustrators. For information on careers in illustration, have students contact:

The Society of Illustrators
128 East 63rd Street
New York, 10021-7303

Video Game Designer

Discussing the Career

Have students read the introduction to the feature. Review with them the liner perspective section in Chapter 16. Have them look at the artworks in the chapter and recognize how artists of the Renaissance used perspective in their works.

Ask students to read the interview and questions on this page. Discuss with them the background that an artist working in video game design might need in order to succeed in this career. Ask volunteers to describe some video game art they might have seen that makes use of perspective for a realistic 3-D effect.

Investigating the Career

Find out if any students in your class have experience in working with 3-D computer programs and ask them to share their expertise with the class in a demonstration or presentation. Interested students might wish to look up schools that specialize in computer training. Have them check with the career center or counseling office of the school to begin a search of art schools. Information may be shared with classmates for future reference or as part of their art portfolios.

Video Game Designer

With the invention of linear perspective in the early Renaissance, artists were suddenly able to give the illusion of distance in their paintings. Renaissance painters used perspective to give a three-dimensional reality to figures and objects depicted in their two-dimensional canvases or frescoes. In a similar fashion, today's video game designers create 3-D figures and landscapes on their 2-D computer screens.

"Every day I use my imagination in a new way."

■ Video game designers work together to create the images for a new video game they have written and designed.

Anita Chen transformed her artistic abilities, technical skills and passion for video games into a successful career as a video game designer. Responsible for conceptualizing all the elements of a game, the video game designer must make the game an exciting experience for the user. As the driving force behind the vision of the game, the designer often leads the game design and guides the production teams.

To succeed in 3-D animation, you need a strong sense of visual style, an excellent understanding of game theory and play, and familiarity with technical developments in the field. Good communication skills are also important. To develop these skills, you need an interest in interactive media and the desire to get started.

Q: Does your job encourage your creativity?

A: My job is very inspiring because my imagination is the only limit to what I create. When creating characters and the worlds they inhabit, I'm allowed to let my creativity run wild.

Q: What art education or training is required for a career as a video designer?

A: Most companies require a two- or four-year degree from a college or university. You need a solid foundation in drawing, color theory, composition, perspective, design, and other fine art skills. Of course, computer graphics skills are mandatory.

Q: Are there any specific skills needed to design games?

A: Yes. The most important element of video games is interactivity. In an interactive piece there can be no assumptions as to what path the user will take. You have to be able to use problem-solving skills to figure out all the pieces of the puzzle.

More About...

Computer Graphics Careers. Students may wish to write for more information on education and career resources in the field of computer graphics, art, and design. Have them contact the Special Interest Group on Computer Graphics (SIGGRAPH) at:

ACM SIGGRAPH
1515 Broadway, 17th Floor
New York, New York 10012

Fashion Designer

The artists of the sixteenth century in Europe focused their attention on brilliant colors and intricate designs. This interest is especially evident in the detailed representation of clothing that we find in some of the portraiture of this period. Today, fashion designers often look to the artists of the past for inspiration when it comes to designs, colors, and textures.

"To me, clothing is an art form. What you wear, and how you wear it make a statement. I love designing fashions that allow people to express themselves."

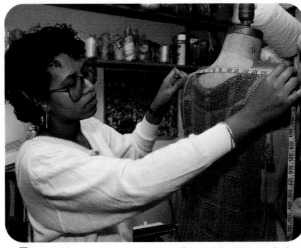

■ This fashion designer pins a piece of material to a gown she is designing.

Lakesha Dixon designs apparel for a large clothing manufacturer. She knows that contemporary consumers come from a wide variety of backgrounds and lifestyles. Fashion designers must reflect this diversity in the designs they create. They must constantly ask: Who are my customers? What do they want their clothes to say? What materials do they want and how much do they want to spend? An ability to draw, along with a background in textiles and fabrics, are important skills for this career.

Clothing designers are responsible for creating everything from high fashion to functional sportswear. To be a successful designer of garments, you must be creative and innovative, as well as practical. You should be familiar with past designs and be an interested observer of current trends, fads, and cultural influences. To develop these skills, you need to have a flair for design and the desire to get started.

Q: Does your job encourage creativity?

A: Yes. As a fashion designer, I need to have a creative imagination that can produce fresh, exciting fashions. I also get to draw constantly, which is something I love to do. However, I think what is most satisfying for me are the sessions I have with models. Here I get to see my design become a reality as a person wears what I have created.

Q: What art education or training is required for a career as a fashion designer?

A: Although a college degree is not necessary to work in this field, it is recommended. Many art schools offer programs in fashion design. In college you should take art courses in drawing, painting, sculpture, design, printmaking, and art history. Classes in home economics, English, and American history are also helpful. To gain experience with fabrics and designs, you could design costumes for your school or community theatre. Working part time in a retail store would also give you experience with fashion.

Q: Are there any specific skills needed to design clothing?

A: Some designers find it helpful to study the human body in order to create the best fitting clothing possible. It is also important to know that the fashion industry is very competitive. You should be good at working under pressure and meeting demanding deadlines.

CAREERS IN ART HANDBOOK

Discussing the Career

Ask a volunteer to read aloud the quote in this feature, and encourage other students to share their responses. Ask: What is the difference between choosing interesting clothing and designing interesting clothing as a profession?

Then have students read and discuss the feature introduction. Ask students to review the clothing styles shown in the artworks in Chapter 18. How are those styles different from current clothing styles? How do you imagine the work of clothing designers has changed since the sixteenth century? In what ways has it probably remained the same?

Have students meet in cooperative learning groups to read and discuss the remainder of the feature.

Investigating the Career

Encourage students interested in fashion design to gather information about colleges and art schools that might help them prepare for a career in this field. Suggest that they also keep a notebook with copies of designs they especially like and with sketches of their original ideas.

More About... **Fashion Design.** Give students an opportunity to learn more about the work of fashion designers by having them sketch their own wardrobe ideas. Each student should select a specific audience, such as toddler girls, teen boys, adult male athletes, dancers, aerobic exercisers, and so on. Have students sketch a variety of outfits for their chosen audience, and ask them to include color and fabric ideas. Then have students meet in groups to show and discuss their sketches.

Photographer

Discussing the Career

Encourage students to describe the scene in the photograph and to share their own experiences in taking pictures—and in having their pictures taken. Have students read and discuss the feature introduction. Ask them to review some of the realistic paintings in Chapter 21. Ask: How is a photograph like a realistic painting? What are the most important differences?

Have students meet in cooperative groups to read and discuss the feature interview. Group members should share their ideas about the advantages of a career in photography; they should also discuss the skills, interests, education, and training photographers need.

Investigating the Career

Have interested students gather information about local schools and colleges that offer programs in photojournalism, technical photography, and commercial photography. Ask these students to make their findings available to the rest of the class.

Also ask students to share information about camera clubs and other opportunities for photographers, either at school or in the community.

Photographer

Like the Realist painters of the mid-nineteenth-century, early photographers captured images of the real lives and conditions of ordinary people. As the technology of photography developed, however, so did its artistic possibilities. Although many of today's photographers might consider themselves realists, others use the photographic process to create fantastic images and artistic effects.

"I have loved taking pictures since I was a little girl. The best part, to me, is the accidental shot—the photo that unexpectedly captures something special that might have gone unnoticed."

■ A commercial photographer rearranges a model during a photographic session.

Melinda Hopkins' job as a commercial photographer requires both technical expertise and creativity. Using lenses, film, filters, and light, photographers create pictures that record events, capture moods, or tell stories. They also know a great deal about mixing chemicals, developing film, and printing photos to create particular effects.

To succeed as a commercial photographer, you need good eyesight and the ability to work with your hands. You should be imaginative and original. Whatever the subject may be, a good photographer needs to be accurate, patient, and detail-oriented. To develop the skills of a photographer, you should start taking pictures now. Practice and experiment with effects, join a camera club, and read photo magazines to learn more about this career. If you have a camera, you may already be on your way to a career as a photographer.

Q: Does your job encourage creativity?

A: Creativity is essential to what I do. Taking a successful picture begins with choosing and presenting a subject. Then I consider how to go about achieving a particular effect with light, backgrounds, filters, and angles. There is room for creativity in the developing process as well. Sometimes I use computer technology to scan my images into digital form.

Q: What art education or training is required for a career as a photographer?

A: Jobs in photojournalism or technical photography require a college degree. You should take courses in photography as well as in journalism, publishing, or design. Commercial photographers should take a course of study in the field at a university or community college. Part-time work for a photographer, newspaper, or magazine is also an excellent way to gain experience.

Q: What additional skills are needed to be a professional photographer?

A: Photography is a very competitive field, so you need to be highly skilled. It is important to have a strong business ability, and to develop a reputation in the industry. To do this, you should learn about marketing and promotion, and submit your best photos to contests.

More About...

Photography. Suggest that students who are interested in photography contact one of these organizations.

Professional Photographers of America, Inc
229 Peachtree Street NE #2200
Atlanta, Georgia 30303

American Society of Media Photographers
14 Washington Road, Suite 502
Princeton Junction, New Jersey 08550

Medical Illustrator

The development of Post-Impressionism and Realism in the art of the later nineteenth century coincided with astonishing advancements in science. In the 1850s, French chemist, Louis Pasteur discovered bacteria, which revolutionized the field of medicine. Artists such as Thomas Eakins became fascinated with the realistic portrayal of human anatomy in painting. Today, artists with similar interests can become medical illustrators.

"Being a medical illustrator is very rewarding. I get to do what I love—draw and paint—and, at the same time, make an important contribution to medical science."

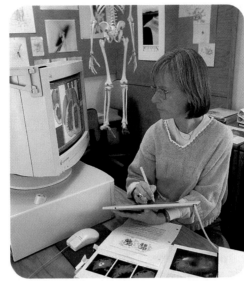

This medical illustrator creates lifelike illustrations of human and animal bodies and organs using a variety of models.

Bernadette Antrim found a way to combine her artistic skills with her interest in biology and medicine as a medical illustrator. Medical schools, medical publishers, pharmaceutical companies, and lawyers all rely on the talents of medical illustrators. As a creator of vivid and detailed illustrations of human anatomy and surgical procedures, the medical illustrator is essential to the teaching of medicine.

An ability to learn from research is important to this profession. Successful artists in this field will have the desire to learn the many different techniques used to communicate scientific information. The medical illustrator must also have knowledge and comprehension of the subject in order to portray it with precision. To develop these skills, you need to be interested in science.

Q: Does your job involve artistic expression?

A: When you look at a medical illustration, you might not think of it as a creative work of art at first. Drawings like this have to be perfectly accurate. And yet, to achieve the effect I must use all of my skills as an artist. I employ all of the elements of art—color, value, line, texture, shape, form, and space—just as a fine artist does. My illustrations are therefore both realistic and artistic.

Q: What art education or training is required for a career as a medical illustrator?

A: In addition to a talent for drawing, medical illustrators must demonstrate a detailed knowledge of living organisms, human anatomy, and medical procedures. A four-year bachelor's degree combining art and pre-medical courses is usually required. In addition, most illustrators go on to get a master's degree in medical illustration.

Q: Are there any specific skills needed to be a medical illustrator?

A: Yes, for this career, you need to have an artistic ability combined with a strong background in medical science. You need to have an eye for observation and detail, and a commitment to accuracy.

Careers in Art Handbook **607**

Medical Illustrator

Discussing the Career

Have students read the introduction to the feature and briefly review the works of Eakins and others in Chapter 22. Then ask students to read and comment on the quotation. What sense of a medical illustrator's work does this quote give you? Who do you think might be interested in a career in this field?

Let students form small groups in which to read and discuss the rest of this feature. If possible, make medical illustrations available for group members to examine. Have group members identify and discuss the interests, skills, and education a medical illustrator might need to succeed in this career.

Investigating the Career

Have interested students explore colleges and universities that offer appropriate undergraduate education and master's degrees in medical illustration. Suggest that students identify the science ·courses required in both high school and in college as preparation for a master's program. Ask these students to share their findings with the rest of the class.

More About... **Medical Illustration.** Have students use library and online resources to learn more about the work of medical illustrators. Students might work in groups to collect, examine, and discuss various medical illustrations. They might also find interviews with medical illustrators and those who teach medical illustration. If possible, arrange for these students to work with a life-sciences teacher to undertake some independent projects in medical illustration.

Cinematographer

Discussing the Career

Let students recall and discuss movies they have seen recently. Ask: What aspects of each movie did you find most interesting? How aware of the photography were you as you watched the movie? What can you recall about the photography? Then have students examine and discuss the feature photograph and read the feature introduction.

Have students form cooperative groups to read and discuss the feature interview. Direct group members to focus on the skills, experience, education, and training a cinematographer should have. Also encourage group members to discuss whether they feel interested in this career and to explain their reasons.

Investigating the Career

Encourage interested students to explore the opportunities for education in cinematography, using resources in the career center, counselor's office, or library. Suggest that they also look for books about the art of cinematography and read interviews with successful cinematographers. Let these students share their findings with the rest of the class.

Cinematographer

The invention of the first handheld camera—the cinematographe—by Louis Lumiere in 1895, opened up a world of possibilities for early twentieth-century film makers. The first films took the form of documentaries. But very quickly film making became a medium for drama and entertainment. One hundred years later, technology and innovation have raised cinematography to a captivating art form in its own right.

"Being a cinematographer is hard work but its also a lot of fun. I enjoy my role in the creative and technical process of a film."

■ The cinematographer is responsible for lighting and filming for a production.

The cinematographer, or director of photography, helps create the look of a movie. This involves directing the lighting for each scene, framing shots, choosing lenses, selecting film stock, and communicating with camera operators. Above all, the cinematographer ensures that the visual look of the film conforms to the director's vision.

Successful cinematographers are visually oriented individuals who enjoy working as part of a team. To be a cinematographer, you must be interested in all facets of the film-making process. Strong verbal communications skills are also essential, since the cinematographer must listen carefully to the director and instruct the camera operators and lighting technicians accordingly. To develop the skills of a professional cinematographer, you will need to get expert training. But you can begin by learning about cameras and photographic techniques. If you have access to a video camera, you can practice by taping friends or family.

Q: Does your job encourage creativity?

A: Yes. Often the director of the film I am working on conveys an idea about a scene. It is my job to interpret that idea visually. If the director wants to create a certain mood, it is up to me to visualize and create that atmosphere on film.

Q: What art education or training is required for a career as a cinematographer?

A: Most cinematographers study film-making and video production before or during their training in cinematographic techniques. But a background in fine art can be very helpful, as well. The cinematographer uses light and shadow, value and intensity, and space much as a painter does.

Q: Are there any specific skills needed to be a cinematographer?

A: Yes. Cinematographers need extensive training with different cameras and techniques.

608   Careers in Art Handbook

More About...

Cinematography. Students with a particular interest in cinematography may want to contact the American Society of Cinematographers.

American Society of Cinematographers
P.O. Box 2230
Hollywood, California 90078

Glossary

Abstract art   Artworks that stress the importance of the elements and principles of design rather than subject matter. Abstract artists select and then exaggerate or simplify the forms suggested by the world around them. (22-1), (24-1)

Abstract Expressionism   A twentieth-century painting style in which artists applied paint freely to huge canvases in an effort to show feelings and emotions rather than realistic subject matter. (24-1)

Academies   Art schools. (21-1)

Adobe   Sun-dried clay. (11-1)

Adze   An axlike tool with an arched blade at right angles to the handle. (12-2)

Aerial perspective   Aerial, or atmospheric, perspective is achieved by using hue, value, and intensity to show distance in a painting. (16-1)

Aesthetic qualities   The qualities that can increase our understanding of artworks and serve as the criteria on which judgments are based. (4-1)

Aesthetics   A branch of philosophy concerned with identifying the clues within works of art that can be used to understand, judge, and defend judgments about those works. (1-2), (4-2)

Aesthetician   A scholar who specializes in the study of the nature of beauty and art. (1-2)

Alcazar   A fortified Moorish palace. (13-2)

Ambulatory   A semi-circular aisle curving around the apse of a church behind the main altar. (14-2)

Analogous colors   Colors that are next to each other on the color wheel and are closely related, such as blue, blue-green, and green. (2-1)

Applied arts   The design or decoration of functional objects to make them pleasing to the eye. (1-1)

Apse   The semicircular area at the end of the nave of a church. (9-2)

Aqueduct   A channel system that carried water from mountain streams into cities by using gravitational flow. (9-1)

Architecture   The art and science of designing and constructing structures that enclose space to meet a variety of human needs. (3-4)

Aristocracy   Persons of high rank and privilege. (20-1)

Armory Show   The first large exhibition of modern art in America, held in 1913. (23-2)

Ashcan School   A popular name identifying the group of artists who made realistic pictures of the most ordinary features of the contemporary scene. (23-2)

Assemblage   A number of three-dimensional objects brought together to form a work of art. (24-2)

Assembly   A process in which the artist gathers and joins together a variety of different materials to construct a three-dimensional work of art. (3-3)

Asymmetrical balance   A way of organizing the parts of a design so that one side differs from the other without destroying the overall harmony. It is also known as informal balance. (2-2)

Atmospheric perspective   Perspective that uses hue, value, and intensity to show distance in a painting. Also called aerial perspective. (16-1)

Axis line   An imaginary line that is traced through an object or several objects in a picture. (2-1)

Balance   A principle of art, it refers to a way of combining art elements to create a feeling of equilibrium or stability in a work. (2-2)

Baroque art   An art style characterized by movement, vivid contrast, and emotional intensity. (19-1)

Barrel vault   A half-round stone ceiling made by placing a series of round arches from front to back. Also known as a tunnel vault. (3-4), (9-2)

Bas relief   Sculpture in which the forms project only slightly from the background. (3-3)

Basilica   A type of public building erected to hold large numbers of people. (9-2)

Baths   Large enclosed Roman structures that contained libraries, lecture rooms, gymnasiums, pools, shops, restaurants, and pleasant walkways. (9-2)

Binder   A liquid that holds together the grains of pigment in paint. (3-1)

Bodhisattva   A Buddha-to-be. (10-2)

Brayer   A roller used to ink a surface by hand. (14-5)

Buddhism   A religious belief based on the teachings of Gautama Buddha, who held that suffering is a part of life but that mental and moral self-purification can bring about a state of illumination, carrying the believer beyond suffering and material existence. (10-1)

Burin   A steel engraving tool. (3-2)

Buttress   A support or brace that counteracts the outward thrust of an arch or vault. (15-1)

Byzantine art   The art of the Eastern Roman Empire. Byzantine paintings and mosaics are characterized by a rich use of color and figures that seem flat and stiff. (13-1)

Campanile   A bell tower near, or attached to, a church. (13-1)

Candid   Unposed views of people. (21-3)

Capital   The top element of a pillar or column. (8-1)

Carving   The process of cutting or chipping a form from a given mass of material to create a sculpture. (3-3)

Casting   The process of pouring melted-down metal or other liquid substance into a mold to harden. (3-3)

Catacombs   Underground tunnels in which early Christians met and buried their dead. Some catacombs also contained chapels and meeting rooms. (13-1)

Chiaroscuro   The arrangement of dramatic contrasts of light and shadow. (19-1)

Cloister   An open court or garden and the covered walkway surrounding it. (14-1)

Coffer An indented panel. (9-2)

Collage A technique that involves adding materials such as newspaper clippings, wallpaper pieces, or photographs to the surface of a picture. (23-1)

Colonnade A line of columns supporting lintels or arches. (8-1)

Color An element of art made up of three distinct qualities: *hue,* the color name, e.g., red, yellow, blue; *intensity,* the purity and brightness of a color, e.g., bright red or dull red; and *value,* the lightness or darkness of a color. (2-1)

Column An upright post used to bear weight. Columns usually consist of a base at the bottom, a shaft, and a capital. (8-1)

Complementary colors Colors that are directly opposite each other on the color wheel, such as red and green, blue and orange, and violet and yellow. When complements are mixed together in the right proportions, they form a neutral gray. (2-1)

Concave Inwardly curved.

Content The subject matter in a work of art. (3-1)

Contour drawing A drawing in which contour lines alone are used to represent subject matter.

Contour line A line or lines that surround and define the edges of an object or figures. (2-1)

Contrapposto A way of sculpting a human figure in a natural pose with the weight of the body balanced on one leg while the other is free and relaxed. (8-2) (16-2)

Contrast Closely related to emphasis, a principle of art, this term refers to a way of combining art elements to stress the differences between those elements. (2-2)

Convex Outwardly rounded.

Cool colors Colors often associated with water, sky, spring, and foliage and suggest coolness. These are the colors that contain blue and green and appear on one side of the color wheel, opposite the warm colors. (2-1)

Corinthian order Columns with elongated capitals decorated with leaves. (8-1)

Cornice A horizontal element positioned across the top of the frieze. (8-1)

Counter-Reformation An effort by the Catholic Church to lure people back and to regain its former power. (19-1)

Criteria Standards for judgment; rules or principles used for evaluation. (1-2)

Cubism A twentieth-century art movement in which artists tried to show all sides of three-dimensional objects on a flat canvas. (23-1)

Cuneiform Writing with wedge-shaped characters. (6-2)

Curator The museum employee responsible for securing and exhibiting artworks for the general public and scholars to view.

Dada An early twentieth-century art movement that ridiculed contemporary culture and traditional art forms. (24-1)

Design A skillful blend of the elements and principles of art. (2-2)

Design qualities How well the work is organized, or put together. This aesthetic quality is favored by formalism. (4-1)

Diagonal Having a slanted direction. A diagonal line is one that suggests movement and tension. (2-1)

Dome A hemispheric vault or ceiling placed on walls that enclose a circular or square space. (3-4)

Doric order Simple, heavy columns without a base, topped by a broad, plain capital. (8-1)

Dry media Those media that are applied dry and include pencil, charcoal, crayon, and chalk or pastel. (3-1)

Dynasty A period during which a single family provided a succession of rulers. (7-1)

Early Medieval A period that dates from c. A.D. 476 to 1050. (14-1)

Eclectic style A style composed of elements drawn from various sources. (23-3)

Elements of art The basic components, or building blocks, used by the artist when producing works of art. The elements consist of color, value, line, shape, form, texture, and space. (2-1)

Emotionalism A theory of art that places emphasis on the expressive qualities. According to this theory, the most important thing about a work of art is the vivid communication of moods, feelings, and ideas. (4-1)

Emphasis A principle of art, it refers to a way of combining elements to stress the differences between those elements. (2-2)

Engraving A method of cutting or incising a design into a material, usually metal, with a sharp tool. A print can be made by inking such an engraved surface. (3-2)

Entablature The upper portion of a classical building that rests on the columns and consists of the lintel, frieze, and cornice. (8-1)

Environmental art Outdoor artworks that are designed to become part of the natural landscape. (24-2)

Etching To engrave a metal plate with acid. A copper or zinc plate is first covered with a coating made of a mixture of beeswax, asphalt, and resin known as a ground. The ground is incised with a sharp tool to produce a drawing. A print can be made by inking such an etched surface. (3-2)

Expressionism A twentieth-century art movement in which artists tried to communicate their strong emotional feelings through artworks. (23-1)

Expressive qualities Those qualities having to do with the meaning, mood, or idea communicated to the viewer through a work of art. Art exhibiting this aesthetic quality is favored by the emotionalists. (4-1)

Façade The front of a building that accents the entrance and usually prepares the visitor for the architectural style found inside. (19-1)

Fauves Artists whose paintings were so simple in design, so brightly colored, and so loose in brushwork that an enraged critic called the artists *Fauves,* or Wild Beasts. (23-1)

Fauvism   An early twentieth-century style of painting in France. The leader of the Fauves was Henri Matisse. (23-1)

Feudalism   A system in which weak noblemen gave up their lands and much of their freedom to more powerful lords in return for protection. (14-1)

Fine arts   Refers to painting, sculpture, and architecture, arts which generally have no practical function (architecture is the exception), and are valued by their success in communicating ideas or feelings. (1-1)

Flying buttress   *See* Buttress.

Foreshortening   A way of drawing figures or objects according to the rules of perspective so that they appear to recede or protrude into three-dimensional space. (16-2)

Form   An element of art, it describes an object with three-dimensions. (2-1)

Formalism   A theory of art that emphasizes design qualities. According to this theory, the most important thing about a work of art is the effective organization of the elements of art through the use of the principles. (4-1)

Fresco   A method of painting in which pigments are applied to a thin layer of wet plaster so that they will be absorbed and the painting becomes part of the wall. (15-3)

Frieze   A decorative horizontal band running across the upper part of a wall. (8-1)

Function   Refers to the intended use or purpose of an object. The term is usually applied to manufactured products, particularly crafts. It is also used when discussing designs for architecture. (1-1)

Gargoyle   The grotesque carved monsters that project out from the upper portions of huge churches. (15-2)

Genre   A representation of people, subjects, and scenes from everyday life. (19-2)

Geometric Period   The name given to the years 900–700 B.C. when geometric shapes were used on Greek pottery. (8-1)

Gesso   A mixture of glue and a white pigment such as plaster, chalk, or white clay. (17-1)

Gothic   A period that began around the middle of the twelfth century and lasted to the end of the fifteenth or sixteenth centuries. (15-1)

Gradation   A principle of art, it refers to a way of combining art elements by using a series of gradual changes in those elements. (2-2)

Griots   Oral historians who are also musicians and performers. (12-1)

Groin vault   A vault formed when two barrel vaults meet at right angles. (3-4), (9-2)

Hard-edge   A twentieth-century movement in painting in which the edges of shapes are crisp and precise rather than blurred. (24-2)

Harmony   A principle of art, it refers to a way of combining similar elements in an artwork to accent their similarities. (2-2)

Hellenistic   A period of Mediterranean culture influenced by Greece following the conquests of Alexander the Great. The expression of inner emotions

was more important than beauty to the artists of this period. (8-2)

Hieroglyphics   The characters and picture-writing used by the ancient Egyptians. (7-2)

High relief   Sculptured forms extend boldly out into space from the flat surface of the relief sculpture. (3-2)

Hue   A color's name. *See* Color. (2-1)

Humanism   An interest in the art and literature of ancient Greece and Rome. (16-1)

Illuminated manuscript   A manuscript, popular during the Medieval period, in which the pages are decorated with silver, gold, and rich colors. Often these manuscripts contain small pictures known as illuminations or miniatures. (14-1)

Illuminations   Manuscript paintings, particularly those done during the Medieval period. (14-1)

Imitationalism   A theory of art that places emphasis on the literal qualities. According to this theory, the most important thing about a work of art is the realistic representation of subject matter. (4-1)

Impressionism   A style of painting in which artists captured an impression of what the eye sees at a given moment and the effect of sunlight on the subject. (21-3)

Intaglio   A process in which ink is forced to fill lines cut into a metal surface. (3-2)

Intensity   The quality of brightness and purity of a color. *See* Color. (2-1)

Intermediate (or tertiary) colors   Colors produced by mixing unequal amounts of two primary colors. (2-1)

Inuit   The Eskimos inhabiting the area from Greenland to western arctic Canada. (11-1)

Ionic order   Columns with an elaborate base and a capital carved into double scrolls that look like the horns of a ram. (8-1)

Kente cloth   A brilliantly colored and patterned fabric. (12-1)

Keystone   The central and highest top stone in an arch. (9-2)

Kinetic art   A sculptural form that actually moves in space. (3-3)

Kiva   Circular underground structure that serves as a spiritual and social center in Pueblo cultures. (11-1)

Koran   The holy scripture of Islam. (13-2)

Kore   A Greek statue of a clothed maiden. (8-2)

Kouros   A Greek statue of a male youth who may have been a god or an athlete. (8-2)

Landscape   A painting, photograph, or other work of art that shows natural scenery such as mountains, valleys, trees, rivers, and lakes. (3-1)

Line   An element of art that refers to the continuous mark made on some surface by a moving point (pen, pencil, etc.). (2-1)

Linear   A painting technique in which importance is placed on contours or outlines. (2-2)

Linear perspective A graphic system that showed artists how to create the illusion of depth and volume on a flat surface. (16-1)

Lintel A horizontal beam spanning an opening between two walls or posts. (3-4)

Literal The word *literal* means true to fact. It refers, here, to the realistic presentation of subject matter. (4-1)

Literal quality The realistic presentation of subject matter in a work of art. This aesthetic quality is favored by imitationalism. (4-1)

Lithography A printmaking method in which the image to be printed is drawn on a limestone, zinc, or aluminum surface with a special greasy crayon. (3-2)

Logo A graphic representation of a company name or trademark. People who design such identifying symbols are known as graphic designers. (1-1)

Lost wax A wax model is coated to form a mold, heated in a kiln, and the wax melts and is allowed to run out. The process is called *cire-perdue,* or lost wax. (3-3)

Low relief The sculptured forms project only slightly from the surface of the background. Also called bas relief. (3-3)

Mannerism A European art style that rejected the calm balance of the High Renaissance in favor of emotion and distortion. (18-2)

Mastaba A low, rectangular Egyptian tomb made of mud brick with sloping sides and a flat top, covering a burial chamber. (7-1)

Meditation The act of focusing thoughts on a single object or idea. An important element in the Buddhist religion. (10-1)

Medium A material used by an artist to produce a work of art. (3-1)

Megalith A large monument created from huge stone slabs. (6-1)

Mihrab A niche in the wall of a mosque that indicates the direction of Mecca and is large enough to accommodate a single standing figure. (13-2)

Minaret A spiral tower attached to a mosque. (13-2)

Mixed media The use of several different materials in one work of art. (3-3)

Mobile A construction made of shapes that are balanced and arranged on wire arms and suspended from a ceiling or base so as to move freely in the air currents. (24-2)

Modeling A sculpture technique in which a soft, pliable material is built up and shaped into a sculptural form. (3-3)

Modeling tools Tools for working with, or modeling, clay. (3-3)

Monasticism A way of life in which individuals joined together in isolated communities called monasteries spend their days in prayer and self-denial. (14-1)

Monochromatic Consisting of only a single color. (2-1)

Mosaic A decoration made with small pieces of glass and stone set in cement. (13-1)

Mosque Muslim place of worship. (13-2)

Movement A principle of art used to create the look and feeling of action and to guide the viewer's eye throughout the work of art. (2-2)

Muezzin A prayer caller. (13-2)

Mural A large design or picture, painted directly on the wall of a public building. (9-2)

Nave A long, wide, center aisle. (9-2)

Neoclassicism A nineteenth-century French art style that sought to revive the ideals of ancient Greek and Roman art and was characterized by balanced compositions, flowing contour lines, and noble gestures and expressions. (21-1)

Niche A recess in a wall. (9-2)

Nonobjective art Any artwork that contains no apparent reference to reality. (4-2), (23-1)

Oba An African ruler, or king. (12-2)

Obelisk A tall, four-sided shaft of stone, usually tapering, that rises to a pyramidal point. (7-1)

Oil paints A mixture of dry pigments with oils, turpentine, and sometimes varnish. (17-1)

Old Stone Age The historical period believed to have lasted from 30,000 B.C. until about 10,000 B.C. Also known as the Paleolithic period. (6-1)

Op art A twentieth-century art style in which artists sought to create an impression of movement on the picture surface by means of optical illusion. (24-2)

Pagoda A tower several stories high with roofs slightly curved upward at the edges. (10-3)

Painterly A painting technique in which forms are created with patches of color rather than with hard, precise edges. (18-1)

Paleolithic period *See* Old Stone Age. (6-1)

Parable A story that contains a symbolic message. (18-3)

Pastel Pigments mixed with gum and pressed into a stick form for use as chalky crayons. Works of art done with such pigments are referred to as pastels. (3-1)

Patina A surface film, produced naturally by oxidation, on bronze or copper. It can also be produced artificially by the application of acid or paint to a surface. (3-3)

Pediment A triangular section of the top of a building framed by a cornice, along with a sloping member called a raking cornice. (3-4)

Perspective A method for representing three-dimensional objects on a two-dimensional surface. *See also* Aerial perspective and Linear perspective. (16-1)

Pharaoh An Egyptian king or ruler, also considered to be a god in the eyes of the people. (7-1)

Philanthropy An active effort to promote human welfare. (22-2)

Photo-Realism An art movement of the late twentieth century in which the style is so realistic it looks photographic. (24-2)

Photography A technique of capturing optical images on light-sensitive surfaces. (3-2)

Pier   A massive vertical pillar that is used to support an arch or vault made of cut stone. (13-1)

Pietà   A sculpture or painting of the Virgin Mary mourning over the body of Christ. The term comes from the Italian word for pity. (16-3)

Pigment   Finely ground powder that gives every paint its color. (3-1)

Pilasters   Flat, rectangular columns attached to a wall. They may be decorative or used to buttress the wall. (3-4)

Pilgrimage   A journey to a holy place. (14-2)

Plane   A surface. Cézanne applied patches of color placed side by side so that each one represented a separate plane. (22-1)

Pop art   An art style that portrayed images of the popular culture such as comic strips and commercial products. (24-1)

Porcelain   A fine-grained, high-quality form of china made primarily from a white clay known as kaolin. (10-2)

Portal   A door or gate, usually of importance or large in size. In most Gothic cathedrals there were three portals in the main façade. (15-2)

Portrait   The image of a person, especially of the face. It can be made of any sculptural material or any two-dimensional medium. (3-1)

Post and lintel   The simplest and oldest way of constructing an opening. Two vertical posts were used to support a horizontal beam, or lintel, creating a covered space. (3-4) (6-1)

Post-Impressionism   A French art movement that immediately followed Impressionism. The artists involved showed a greater concern for structure and form than did the Impressionist artists. (22-1)

Potlatch   An elaborate ceremonial feast that enabled members of one Kwakuitl clan to honor those of another while adding to their own prestige. (11-1)

Pre-Columbian   The term that is used when referring to the various cultures and civilizations found throughout the Americas before the arrival of Christopher Columbus in 1492. (11-2)

Primary colors   The basic colors of red, yellow, and blue, from which it is possible to mix all the other colors of the spectrum. (2-1)

Principles of art   Refers to the different ways that the elements of art can be used in a work of art. The principles of art consist of balance, emphasis, harmony, variety, gradation, movement, rhythm, and proportion. (2-2)

Prodigal   Referring to the recklessly wasteful son in the painting by Bartolomé Murillo. (19-3)

Propaganda   Information or ideas purposely spread to influence public opinion. (21-1)

Proportion   The principle of art concerned with the relationship of certain elements to the whole and to each other. (2-2)

Protestant Reformation   A movement in which a group of Christians led by Martin Luther left the Catholic Church in revolt to form their own religion in 1517. (18-2)

Raking cornice   A sloping element that slants above the horizontal cornice. (8-1)

Realism   A mid-nineteenth-century style of art representing everyday scenes and events as they actually looked. (21-2)

Regionalism   A popular style of art in which artists painted the American scenes and events that were typical of their regions of America. (24-1)

Relief   A type of sculpture in which forms project from a background. In high relief the forms stand far out from the background. In low relief (also known as bas relief), the sculpture is shallow. (3-3)

Relief printing   The image to be printed is raised from the background. (3-2)

Renaissance   A period of great awakening. The word *renaissance* means rebirth. (16-1)

Repetition   A principle of art, this term refers to a way of combining art elements so that the same elements are used over and over. (2-2)

Rhythm   A principle of art, it refers to the careful placement of repeated elements in a work of art to cause a visual tempo or beat. (2-2)

Rococo art   An eighteenth-century art style that placed emphasis on portraying the carefree life of the aristocracy rather than on grand heroes or pious martyrs. (20-1)

Romanesque   An artistic style that, in most areas, took place during the eleventh and twelfth centuries. The style was most apparent in architecture and was characterized by the round arch, a large size, and solid appearance. (14-2)

Romanticism   A style of art that portrayed dramatic and exotic subjects perceived with strong feelings. (21-2)

Salon   An annual exhibition of art held by the academies in Paris and London. (21-1)

Sarcophagus   A coffin, usually of stone, although sometimes made of wood, metal, or clay. In ancient times they were often decorated with carvings of the deceased or with some religious or mythological subject. (7-1)

Satire   The use of sarcasm or ridicule to expose and denounce vice or folly. (20-2)

Screen printing   Paint is forced through a screen onto paper or fabric. (3-2)

Scroll   A long roll of illustrated parchment or silk. (10-2)

Sculpture   A three-dimensional work of art. Such a work may be carved, modeled, constructed, or cast. (3-3)

Sculpture in the round   Freestanding sculpture surrounded on all sides by space. (3-3)

Secondary colors   The colors obtained by mixing equal amounts of two primary colors. The secondary colors are orange, green, and violet. (2-1)

Serfs   Poor peasants who did not have land. (14-1)

Serigraph   A screen print that has been handmade by an artist. (3-2)

Shaft   The main weight-bearing portion of a column. (8-1)

Shaman   A leader believed to have healing powers. (11-1)

Shape   An element of art referring to a two-dimensional area clearly set off by one or more of the other visual elements such as color, value, line, texture, and space. (2-1)

Sipapu   A hole in the floor of a kiva that symbolized the place through which the Pueblo people originally emerged into this world. (11-1)

Sketch   A quick drawing that captures the appearance or action of a place or situation. Sketches are often done in preparation for larger, more detailed works of art. (3-1)

Slip   A mixture of clay and water used in the making of pottery to cement together parts that have been formed separately. (3-3)

Solvent   The material used to thin the binder in paint. (3-1)

Space   An element of art that refers to the distance or area between, around, above, below, or within things. (2-1)

Stained glass   The art of cutting colored glass into different shapes and joining them together with lead strips to create a pictorial window design. (15-1)

Stele   An inscribed stone pillar. (6-2)

Still life   A drawing or painting of an arrangement of inanimate objects, such as food, plants, pots, and other inanimate objects. (3-1)

Stupa   A small, round burial shrine erected over a grave site to hold relics of the Buddha. (10-1)

Style   The artist's personal way of using the elements and principles of art to reproduce what is seen and to express ideas and feelings. (5-1)

Stylobate   The top step of a three-step platform used to support a row of columns. (3-4)

Stylus   A pointed, needle-like tool. (6-2)

Surrealism   A twentieth-century art style in which dreams, fantasy, and the subconscious served as the inspiration for artists. (24-1)

Symbol   A form, image, or subject representing a meaning other than the one with which it is usually associated. (1-1)

Symmetrical balance   A way of organizing the parts of a design so that one side duplicates, or mirrors, the other. Also known as formal balance. (2-2)

Tactile   Of, or relating to, the sense of touch. (2-2)

Tapestry   Textile wall hanging that is woven, painted, or embroidered with decorative designs or colorful scenes. (14-2)

Technique   Any method of working with art materials to create an art object. The manner in which an artist uses the technical skills of a particular art form. (1-1)

Tempera   A paint made of dry pigments, or colors, which are mixed with a binding material. (17-1)

Tensile strength   The capacity of a material to withstand bending. (3-4)

Tertiary colors   *See* Intermediate colors. (2-1)

Texture   The element of art that refers to the way things feel, or look as if they might feel if touched. (2-1)

Thrust   The outward force produced by the weight of an arch or vault. It is counterbalanced by buttressing. (3-4)

Totem poles   Tall wood posts carved and painted with a series of animal symbols associated with a particular family or clan. (11-1)

Transept   An aisle that cuts directly across the nave and the side aisles in a basilica and forms a cross-shaped floor plan. (14-1)

Triptych   A painting on three hinged panels that can be folded together. (17-2)

Triumphal arch   A heavily decorated arch often consisting of a large central opening and two smaller openings, one on each side. (9-2)

Trompe l'oiel   A painting technique designed to fool the viewer's eye by creating a very realistic illusion of three-dimensional qualities on a flat surface.

Tympanum   The half-round panel that fills the space between the lintel and the arch over a doorway of a church. (14-2)

Ukiyo-e   A Japanese painting style, which means pictures of the passing world. (10-3)

Unity   The look and feel of wholeness or oneness in a work of art. (2-2)

Value   An element of art that describes the lightness or darkness of a hue. *See* Color. (2-1)

Vanishing point   In perspective drawing, the point at which receding parallel lines seem to converge. (10-2)

Variety   A principle of art that refers to a way of combining art elements in involved ways to create intricate and complex relationships. (2-2)

Vault   An arched roof or covering made of brick, stone, or concrete. A dome is a hemispherical vault. (3-4)

Visual arts   Unique expressions of ideas, beliefs, experiences, and feelings presented in well-designed visual forms. (1-1)

Volume   Refers to the space within a form. Thus, in architecture, volume refers to the space within a building. (2-2)

Warm colors   Colors suggesting warmth. These are colors that contain red and yellow. (2-1)

Watercolor   Transparent pigments mixed with water. Paintings done with this medium are known as watercolors. (3-1)

Wet media   Media in which the coloring agent is suspended in a liquid, such as ink and paints. (3-1)

Woodblock printing   A process that involves transferring and cutting pictures into wood blocks, inking the raised surface of these blocks, and printing. (10-3)

Yamato-e   Painting in the Japanese manner. (10-3)

Zen   A Chinese and Japanese school of Buddhism that believes that enlightenment can be attained through meditation, self-contemplation, and intuition. (10-3)

Ziggurat   A stepped mountain made of brick-covered earth. (6-2)

Artists and Their Works

Index

—*A*—

Abstract Expressionism, 552–554
Academies, 466
Acropolis, The, 171, *Fig. 8.6*
Adam and Eve Banished from the Garden of Eden, 317, *Fig. 14.11*
Adam and Eve Eating the Forbidden Fruit, 317, *Fig. 14.10*
Adams, Ansel, *Clearing Winter Storm, Yosemite Valley,* 63, *Fig. 3.20*
Adena culture
    Serpent Mound State Memorial, 252, *Fig. 11.12*
    stone pipe, 253, *Fig. 11.13*
Adobe, 250, 269
Adoration of the Lamb, from The Ghent Altarpiece, 384, *Fig. 17.5*
The Adoration of the Magi, 34, 366, *Fig. 2.10, Fig. 16.16*
The Adoration of the Shepherds, 38, 389–390, *Fig. 2.14, Fig. 17.9–17.10*
Advertising Artist, 602
Adze, 274
Aerial perspective, 357
Aeschylus, 167
Aestheticians, 18, 91–94
Aesthetic qualities, 86
    art criticism and, 96
    design qualities, 87–89
    expressive qualities, 90
    literal qualities, 86–87
    theories of art and, 93, *Fig. 4.9*
Aesthetics, 91
    as a reason for art creation, 10
    understanding, 18
Aesthetic theories
    emotionalism, 92, 95, 386–390
    formalism, 91, 95
    imitationalism, 91, 95
    use of several, 92–93
Africa
    ancestors and cultural heroes, 274–276, 275, *Fig. 12.14–12.15*
    map of African cultural groups, 266, *Fig. 12.2*
    role of art in culture, 266
    Yoruba religion and philosophy, 267
African-American, Virginia. Iron figure, *Fig. 12.8,* 269
African-American artists, 506–510
African kingdoms art, 266–272
    ancient Ife, 266–268
    Asante, 271
    Benin, 270
    Ethiopia, 272
    Mali, 268–270
African sculpture, 273–281
    artists, 280–281
    carved figures, 274–275, 274, *Fig. 12.14*
    guardian figures, 276, *Fig. 12.16*
    helmet masks, 279, *Fig. 12.22*
    Luba neckrest, 280–281, 281, *Fig. 12.24*
    masks, 278–279, 278, *Fig. 12.19, Fig. 12.20,* 279, *Fig. 12.21*
    primordial couples, 277, *Fig. 12.17*
    spirit spouse figures, 277, *Fig. 12.18*
    wood carvings, 273
Agam, Yaacov, *Double Metamorphosis II,* 556, *Fig. 24.16*
Agbatana III, 556, *Fig. 24.17*
Ailey, Alvin, 545

Aisles, 299
Aix-la-Chapelle, 311–312
    Palatine Chapel of Charlemagne, 312, *Fig. 14.4*
Akan people, Asante kingdom, Ghana. Necklace, 271, *Fig. 12.10*
Akbar Hunting with Trained Cheetahs (Akbar Nama), 212, *Fig. 10.1*
Akhenaton, 149–150
    Portrait of Akhenaton, 158, *Fig. 7.10. See also* Queen Nefertiti
Akkadian Period, 137
    King Naram-Sin of Akkad in Horned Tiara Near Mountain Summit, 138, *Fig. 6.13*
The Alba Madonna, 373, *Fig. 16.24*
Alcazar, 300
Alexander the Great, 141, 142, 150, 183
Alhambra, 301–303, *Fig. 13.22–13.24*
Allies Day, May 1917, 107, *Fig. 5.2,* 111, *Fig. 5.8*
Altamira Caves, Spain, 128, 130–132, *Fig. 6.2, Fig. 6.4–6.5*
AMAN International Folk Ensemble, 591
Ambience, 118
Ambulatory, 320
Amenhotep III, 149
Amenhotep IV. *See* Akhenaton
American art, 532–535
    late nineteenth-century, 501–510
    regionalism, 548–550
    revolutions in, 548–561
American Gothic, 549, *Fig. 24.6*
American Repertory Dance Theatre, 592
Amiens Cathedral, 341, *Fig. 15.16*
Analysis, 97
    art history and work, 108, 110–111, 116–118, 425
Ancient Egypt
    development of the civilization, 148–150
    history, 149–150
    map, 148, *Fig. 7.2*
    temples, 153–154
Ancient Egyptian Art
    Egyptian tombs and, 160
    painting, 160–161
    relief sculpture, 158–159
    rules, 160
    sculpture, 155–158
Ancient Greece
    history, 168–169
    map, 168, *Fig. 8.2*
    spread of culture, 183–184
Ancient Greek art
    architecture, 169–173
    orders of decorative style, 172–173, *Fig. 8.7*
    Parthenon, 166, *Fig. 8.1,* 169, *Fig. 8.3*
    sculpture. *See* Greek sculpture
    vase decoration, 174–176, 174, *Fig. 8.11,* 175, *Fig. 8.13*
Ancient Roman architecture
    aqueducts, 199, *Fig. 9.11*
    basilicas, 206
    baths, 200–201
    buildings for sports events, 201–204
    innovation in structure and materials, 197, *Fig. 9.8*
    Pantheon, The, 76, 204–205, 204, *Fig. 9.16, 205, Fig. 9.17*
    public buildings and structures, 204–206
    spread of, 197–198, 198, *Fig. 9.9, Fig. 9.10*
    temple complex in Palestrina, 196
    temples, 195–196, 196, *Fig. 9.6, Fig. 9.7*
    triumphal arches, 206

Ancient Roman art
    architecture. *See* Ancient Roman architecture
    mural painting, 194, *Fig. 9.5*
    portrait sculpture, 193, *Fig. 9.3*
Ancient Rome
    declining power, 206–207
    Greek influence in, 193
    map, 192, *Fig. 9.2*
    music in, 191
    Roman Republic, 192
Angel with the Superscription, 68, *Fig. 3.28*
Anguissola, Sofonisba, 374–375
    Double Portrait of a Boy and Girl of the Attavanti Family, 375, *Fig. 16.25*
Anne of Cleves, 413–414, 414, *Fig. 18.16*
The Annunciation, 358, *Fig. 16.6*
Annunciation, leaf from a Psalter, 327, *Fig. 14.28*
Anonymous (formerly attributed to Dong Yuan), *Clear Weather in the Valley,* 108, *Fig. 5.3*
The Apotheosis of Homer, 470
Applied arts, 9
Apse, 206
Aqueduct, 199
    Roman aqueduct (Segovia, Spain), 199, *Fig. 9.11*
Arch/arches, 75–76, 299
    round arch, 75, *Fig. 3.41*
Architect, 598
Architecture, 73–79. *See also* Castles; Churches; St. Paul's Cathedral, London
    ancient Egypt, 153–154
    ancient Greek, 169–173
    ancient Rome, 194–199
    art criticism operations and, 101
    Baroque church, 420–421
    basilicas, 290–291
    Buddhist, 216–218
    Byzantine, 292–296, 292, *Fig. 13.7–13.9*
    early twentieth-century American, 538–540
    early twentieth-century European, 536–538
    empire of Mali, 269–270, 270, *Fig. 12.9*
    functions, 74
    Gothic cathedral, 333–337
    Hindu, 220, *Fig. 10.10*
    Inca, 260
    Islamic. *See* Mosque
    Japanese Buddhist, 233–234
    materials and processes, 73
    Maya, 256, *Fig. 11.16*
    Persian, 141–142
    post-1950, 567–572
    Postmodern, 571–572
    Renaissance, 363. *See also* Brunelleschi, Filippo
Arch of Constantine, 206, 207, 323, *Fig. 9.19, Fig. 14.21a*
Aristocracy, 446
Aristotle, 184
Arman, *Long-Term Parking,* 18, *Fig. 1.15*
Armory Show of 1913, 535
The Arnolfini Wedding, 382–383, 383, *Fig. 17.4*
Art
    careers in, 22
    in the community, 15–16
    definition, 6–8
    forms of, 8–9
    reasons for creation of, 9–12
    self-expression, 13–15

INDEX

T

Back Cover Images

From top to bottom: *Two Bisons.* Cave painting. Altamira Caves, Spain. Scala/Art Resource, New York; *Flutist.* Etruscan wall painting. Tomb of the Leopards, Tarquinia, Italy. Early 5th century B.C. Scala/Art Resource, New York; *Statue of Tutankhamun as royal "Ka" of the sun god Harakhte.* From the tomb of Tutankhamun. Egypt, 18th Dynasty. Wood and gilded bronze. Egyptian Museum, Cairo, Egypt. Scala/Art Resource, New York; *Figure of a warrior with facial tattooing.* Mayan, Classic to late Classic, A.D. 600-900. Terra-cotta. Excavated on the Island of Jonuta. Private Collection, New York. Werner Forman/Art Resource, New York; Vincent van Gogh. *Self-Portrait with Bandaged Ear.* Courtauld Institute Galleries, London, Great Britain. Giraudon/Art Resource, New York.

Artists Rights Society

Photo Credits